A New Star-Rating System & Other Exciting News from Frommer's!

In our continuing effort to publish the savviest, most up-to-date, and most appealing travel guides available, we've added some great new features.

Frommer's guides now include a new **star-rating system.** Every hotel, restaurant, and attraction is rated from 0 to 3 stars to help you set priorities and organize your time.

We've also added **seven brand-new features** that point you to the great deals, in-the-know advice, and unique experiences that separate travelers from tourists. Throughout the guide, look for:

Finds	Special finds—those places only insiders know about
Fun Fact	Fun facts—details that make travelers more informed and their trips more fun
Kids	Best bets for kids—advice for the whole family
Moments	Special moments—those experiences that memories are made of
Overrated	Places or experiences not worth your time or money
Tips	Insider tips—some great ways to save time and money
Value	Great values—where to get the best deals

We've also added a **"What's New"** section in every guide—a timely crash course in what's hot and what's not in every destination we cover.

COPENHAGEN — HOTEL OPERA
GET ROOM 305
NEVER ROOM 321

Here's what the critics say about Frommer's:

"Amazingly easy to use. Very portable, very complete."
— *Booklist*

"Detailed, accurate, and easy-to-read information for all price ranges."
— *Glamour Magazine*

"Hotel information is close to encyclopedic."
— *Des Moines Sunday Register*

"Frommer's Guides have a way of giving you a real feel for a place."
— *Knight Ridder Newspapers*

Other Great Guides for Your Trip:

Frommer's Denmark
Frommer's Norway
Frommer's Sweden
Frommer's Europe

Frommer's®

Scandinavia
20th Edition

by Darwin Porter & Danforth Prince

WILEY

Wiley Publishing, Inc.

About the Authors

Coauthors **Darwin Porter** and **Danforth Prince** have written numerous best-selling Frommer's guides, notably to England, France, the Caribbean, Italy, and Germany. Porter was a bureau chief for the *Miami Herald* when he was 21, and Prince was formerly with the Paris bureau of *The New York Times*. They are also the authors of Frommer's guides to Sweden, Denmark, and, soon-to-be-published, Norway.

Published by:

Wiley Publishing, Inc.

909 Third Ave.
New York, NY 10022

ISBN 0-7645-2466-6
ISSN 0278-1069

Editors: Lisa Torrance Duffy, William Fox
Production Editor: Donna Wright
Cartographer: Elizabeth Puhl
Photo Editor: Richard Fox
Production by Wiley Indianapolis Composition Services

For information on our other products and services or to obtain technical support, please contact our Customer Care Department within the U.S. at 800-762-2974, outside the U.S. at 317-572-3993 or fax 317-572-4002.

Wiley also publishes its books in a variety of electronic formats. Some content that appears in print may not be available in electronic formats.

Manufactured in the United States of America

5 4 3 2

Contents

5 Exploring the Danish Countryside   126

6 The Best of Norway   166

7 Planning Your Trip to Norway   172

⑬ Introducing Stockholm   335

⑭ Exploring Stockholm   365

⑮ Gothenburg   403

Appendix A: Denmark in Depth   570

Appendix B: Norway in Depth   579

Appendix C: Sweden in Depth   587

Appendix D: Finland in Depth   597

Index   605

List of Maps

An Invitation to the Reader

In researching this book, we discovered many wonderful places — hotels, restaurants, shops, and more. We're sure you'll find others. Please tell us about them, so we can share the information with your fellow travelers in upcoming editions. If you were disappointed with a recommendation, we'd love to know that, too. Please write to:

Frommer's Scandinavia, 20th Edition
Wiley Publishing, Inc. • 909 Third Ave. • New York, NY 10022

An Additional Note

Please be advised that travel information is subject to change at any time—and this is especially true of prices. We therefore suggest that you write or call ahead for confirmation when making your travel plans. The authors, editors, and publisher cannot be held responsible for the experiences of readers while traveling. Your safety is important to us, however, so we encourage you to stay alert and be aware of your surroundings. Keep a close eye on cameras, purses, and wallets, all favorite targets of thieves and pickpockets.

New! Frommer's Star Ratings & Icons

Every hotel, restaurant, and attraction listing in this guide has been ranked for quality, value, service, amenities, and special features using a star-rating scale. In country, state, and regional guides, we also rate towns and regions to help you narrow down your choices and budget your time accordingly. Hotels and restaurants in the Very Expensive and Expensive categories are rated on a scale of one (highly recommended) to three stars (exceptional). Those in the Moderate and Inexpensive categories rate from zero (recommended) to two stars (very highly recommended). Attractions, towns, and regions are rated according to the following scale: zero stars (recommended), one star (highly recommended), two stars (very highly recommended), and three stars (must-see).

In addition to the rating system, we also use seven icons to highlight insider information, useful tips, special bargains, hidden gems, memorable experiences, kid-friendly venues, places to avoid, and other useful information:

(*Finds*   (*Fun Fact*   (*Kids*   (*Moments*   (*Overrated*   (*Tips*   (*Value*

The following abbreviations are used for credit cards:

AE	American Express	DISC	Discover	V	Visa
DC	Diners Club	MC	MasterCard		

FROMMERS.COM

Now that you have the guidebook to a great trip, visit our website at **www.frommers.com** for travel information on nearly 2,500 destinations. With features updated regularly, we give you instant access to the most current trip-planning information available. At Frommers.com, you'll also find the best prices on airfares, accommodations, and car rentals—and you can even book travel online through our travel booking partners. At Frommers.com, you'll also find the following:

- Online updates to our most popular guidebooks
- Vacation sweepstakes and contest giveaways
- Newsletter highlighting the hottest travel trends
- Online travel message boards with featured travel discussions

What's New in Scandinavia

Many of the old towns and villages remain relatively the same year after year. But in the four capitals of Scandinavia, where the pulse beats faster, changes are also emerging as these great cities in the far north of Europe remain forever cutting edge.

COPENHAGEN Getting Around More and more passengers to the Danish capital are riding the Metro, which was expanded in 2001 and 2002 and now provides an alternative to the long role played by the traditional tram. See chapter 3 for details.

COPENHAGEN Where to Dine Based on the ancient Danish custom of drinking *snaps* (or *akvavit*) with your meal, **Akvavit** (℗ 33-32-88-44) is unique in the Danish capital. The bar is the best-stocked *akvavit* watering hole in town, and the delectable Danish menu provides helpful tips about what drinks go best with what order. Try the chilled dill *snaps,* for example, with a fjord shrimp salad.

Another culinary breakthrough is provided by **Passagens Spiesehus** (℗ 33-22-47-57), which is being celebrated for its wide range of Scandinavian dishes, including some that haven't been on menus since before World War I. The restaurant could be a setting for *Northern Exposure,* with such delights as fried game-bird liver or else a good moose steak. See chapter 3 for details.

SILKEBORG Where to Stay In the Jutland city of Silkeborg, in the midst of some of the most beautiful scenery in Denmark, **Radisson SAS Hotel** (℗ 88-82-22-22) has recycled

a 150-year-old paper factory into the newest and best hotel in the area. A short walk from the harbor, it coddles first-class guests in comfort. See chapter 5 for more details.

OSLO Where to Stay Getting a lot of well-deserved press attention is a boutique hotel, **First Hotel Nobel House** (℗ 23-10-72-01), which is small and personal with a seven-story glassed-in atrium. A recycled industrial building, it's a bit of an oddity but features total comfort. See chapter 8 for more details.

OSLO Where to Dine The hot restaurant ticket is **Magma** (℗ 23-08-58-10), whose chic Mediterranean and Continental cuisine draws hip Norwegians to its precincts. Norway's "chef of the moment" is Ms. Sonja Lee, born of Korean and Norwegian parents. She'll dazzle your palate.

In a neck-and-neck race with Magma, **Oro** (℗ 23-01-02-40) achieves near-perfection with its Continental cuisine, a showcase for the viands of Norwegian-born chef Terje Ness. It's a three-in-one operation with a gourmet restaurant, a glamorous tapas bar, and a boutique-style deli. The seven-course fish and shellfish menu is Oslo's best, and the competition is keen in that category. See chapter 8 for more details.

BERGEN Where to Stay Two of Bergen's most traditional moderately priced hotels were recently "wed" to form the new **Hotel Ambassadeur** (℗ 55-90-08-90). Together the old Anker and the old Ambassadeur make a better hotel now since the buildings were combined and the guest rooms renewed. The best accommodations are on the fourth floor, opening onto dramatic views of this ancient Hanseatic port city. See chapter 9 for more details.

BERGEN   Where to Dine   Serious Bergen diners are flocking to **Enhjørningen** (The Unicorn; ⓒ 55-32-79-19) for the best fish dishes and Continental specialties in town. Set within an antique building adjacent to the harbor, the restaurant features a bountiful lunchtime buffet and dazzles you with a savory dinner of specialties prepared with market-fresh ingredients. See chapter 9 for more details.

BODØ   Where to Stay   In a Norwegian city north of the Arctic circle, the **Golden Tulip Rainbow Nordlys Hotel** (ⓒ 75-53-19-00) rises six floors overlooking the city harbor. It's not the best hotel in town, but it's the newest and one of the most affordable, with fresh, airy guest rooms, and a management that likes to collect modern art. See chapter 10 for more details.

STOCKHOLM   Where to Stay   The Swedish capital's newest hotel is one of its most daring. Nothing evokes life in the far north more than the **Nordic Hotel** (ⓒ 800/337-4685, or 08/21-71-77), a hotel, restaurant, and resort complex whose decor was inspired by both the watery calm of the Nordic Sea and by the "post-minimalist luminescence" of the northern lights. See chapter 13.

STOCKHOLM   Where to Dine   Stockholm flocks to a new temple of gastronomy, **Bon Lloc** (ⓒ 08/660-60-60), featuring a refined Mediterranean cuisine. Chef Mathias Dahlgren has justifiably become the darling of Stockholm food critics, some of whom have labeled his food "nouveau Euro-Latino." Whatever it's called, it is inspired and prepared with only the freshest and best ingredients. See chapter 13.

STOCKHOLM   After Dark   The "coolest" bar in Stockholm is the **Icebar** at the newly opened Nordic Hotel (ⓒ 08/21-71-77). Temperatures are kept at 27°F (–5°C) all year, and even the cocktail glasses are made of pure, clear ice shipped down from the Torne River in Sweden's Arctic wasteland to the north. If you own a fur coat, wear it here. See chapter 14.

GOTHENBURG   Where to Stay   In Sweden's second city, dominating the western coast, the deluxe **Elite Plaza** (ⓒ 031/720-40-00) is setting the standards by which other city hotels are judged. A palatial 1889 building was recycled into this 144-unit citadel of comfort and convenience, in the center of town near the rail station. See chapter 15.

HELSINGBORG   Where to Dine   This western-coast Swedish city has a new entry on the gourmet dining scene, **Gastro** (ⓒ 042/24-34-70), which now serves some of the finest Continental cuisine in the area. Overlooking the city's historic core, the restaurant allows local diners to enjoy many dishes that became favorites on their journeys to the seashores of the Mediterranean. See chapter 16.

MALMÖ   Where to Dine   Now within an easy commute of the city of Copenhagen because of the opening of the Øresund Bridge, Sweden's third city is host to the hippest restaurant in town. Appropriately named **Hipp** (ⓒ 040/94-70-30), it serves the best of both French and Swedish cuisines. An 1897 cabaret theater has been converted into this super-chic rendezvous for gourmets. Equally hip and equally hot is **Centiliter & Gram** (ⓒ 040/12-18-12), which is becoming increasingly known for its refined Continental cuisine. Popular with media and PR types, it offers a menu that changes with the seasons. Its chefs keep up with whatever food fad is the rage in European capitals such as Paris and London. See chapter 16 for more details.

LUND Where to Dine This ancient university city is home to a charmingly new but still traditional restaurant, **Barntorget 9** (© **046/32-02-00**), offering the best Swedish and Continental cuisine to professors and students alike. The restaurant has taken over a wood-sided 1860s building and transformed it into this much-gentrified rendezvous, attracting a sophisticated crowd of diners, both young and old, who feast off such dishes as duck breast in orange sauce. See chapter 16.

HELSINKI Where to Dine The Finnish capital is now graced with two new Michelin-starred restaurants, a rarity in this part of the world. **Chez Dominique** (© **09/612-73-93**) is located near Esplanadi Park in the center. This citadel of Scandinavian cuisine is a showcase for the culinary talents of Hans Välimäki, one of Finland's grandest chefs, who prepares a first-rate cuisine based on the use of market-fresh ingredients. Equally exciting is **G. W. Sundmans** (© **09/622-64-10**), celebrated locally for its refined Scandinavian and French food. This gourmet bastion, opening onto panoramic vistas at Market Square, is installed in the mansion of a former sea captain. You get both an antique atmosphere and superb food at the same time. See chapter 20 for more details.

The Best of Denmark

Denmark presents visitors with an embarrassment of riches—everything from exciting Copenhagen to historic castles, unusual offshore islands to quaint villages, and more. To help you decide how best to spend your time, we've compiled a list of our favorite experiences and discoveries. In the following pages, you'll find the kind of candid advice we'd give our close friends.

1 The Best Travel Experiences

- **A Week Down on the Farm:** The best way to see the heart of Denmark and meet the Danes is to spend a week on one of their farms. Nearly 400 farms, all over the country, take in paying guests. Stick a pin anywhere on a map of Denmark away from the cities and seacoast, and you'll find a thatched and timbered farm, or perhaps a more modern homestead. Almost anyplace makes a good base from which to explore the rest of the country on day trips. You join the host family and other guests for meals. You can learn about what's going on at the farm, and pitch in and help with the chores if you like. Activities range from bonfires and folk dancing to riding lessons or even horse-and-buggy rides. Although the official agency that used to arrange such holidays is no longer in existence, many visitors seeking this kind of offbeat accommodation often surf the Internet for farms that advertise their willingness to receive guests. Or, decide which part of Denmark you'd like to be located in, then contact the nearest tourist office to see which farms are willing to accept paying guests.

- **On the Road on a Bike:** Denmark is relatively flat, making it one of the best countries in Europe for touring on two wheels. You pass green hills, half-timbered villages, castles, manor houses, beech forests, and lakes as you roll along. Cyclists are given high priority in traffic. You can set out on your own, but a company that's loosely affiliated with the Danish tourist office is **Bike Denmark,** Olaf Poulsens Allé 1A, DK-3480 Fredensborg (© **48-48-58-00;** www.bikedenmark.com). It offers eight different self-guided bike tours of Denmark. Some depart from Copenhagen; others cover parts of Funen and, in some cases, southern Sweden. Tours last for 5 to 10 days, and cover 20km to 60km (13–37 miles) per day. Detailed maps and directions are given to each cyclist, who proceeds at his or her own pace along itineraries especially selected for their exposure to areas of historic interest or natural beauty. Luggage is transported ahead of time and awaits participants in their hotel rooms at the end of a long day of cycling.

- **A Day (& Night) at the Tivoli:** These 150-year-old pleasure gardens are worth the airfare to

Copenhagen all by themselves. They're a little bit of everything: open-air dancing, restaurants, theaters, concert halls, an amusement park . . . and, oh yes, gardens. From the first bloom of spring until the autumn leaves start to fall, they're devoted to light-hearted fun. The gardens are worth a visit anytime, but are especially nice at twilight, when the lights begin to glint off the trees. See chapter 4.

- **On the Trail of the Vikings:** Renowned for 3 centuries of fantastic exploits, the Vikings explored Greenland, North America, and the Caspian Sea from roughly A.D. 750 to 1050. Their legacy endures in Denmark. Relive the age at the Nationalmuseet in Copenhagen, which displays burial grounds of the Viking period, along with the largest and richest hoards of treasure, including relics from the "Silver Age." Even Viking costumes are on exhibit. At Roskilde, explore the Viking Ship Museum. It contains five vessels found in a fjord nearby, the largest of which was built in Ireland around 1060 and manned by 60

to 100 warriors. And if you're in Ribe, check out the Museum of the Viking Age, where a multimedia room, "Odin's Eye," introduces the visitor to the world of the Vikings through an all-around sound and vision experience. See chapters 4 and 5.

- **In the Footsteps of Hans Christian Andersen:** To some visitors, this storyteller is *the* symbol of Denmark. The fairy tale lives on in Odense, on the island of Funen, where the shoemaker's son was born in 1805. His childhood home, a small half-timbered house on Munkemøllestræde where he lived from 1807 to 1817, has been turned into a museum. You can also visit the H. C. Andersens Hus, see the large store of memorabilia (including his walking stick and top hat), and take a few moments to listen to his tales on tape. But mostly you can wander the cobblestone streets that he knew so well, and marvel at his life and works. In the words of his obituary, they struck "chords that reverberated in every human heart," as they still do today. See chapter 5.

2 The Best Scenic Towns & Villages

- **Dragør:** At the doorstep of Copenhagen, this old seafaring town once flourished as a bustling herring-fishing port. Time passed it by, however, and for that we can be grateful. It looks much as it used to, with half-timbered ocher-and-pink 18th-century cottages— all with thatched or red-tiled roofs. The entire village is under the protection of the National Trust. A 35-minute ride from the Danish capital will take you back 2 centuries. See chapter 4.
- **Ærøskøbing:** This is storybook Denmark. The little village on the country's most charming island,

Ærø, lies 29km (18 miles) across the water south of Svendborg. A 13th-century market town, it is a Lilliputian souvenir of the past, complete with little gingerbread houses. You expect Hansel and Gretel to arrive at any moment. See chapter 5.

- **Ribe:** On the peninsula of Jutland, this is the best-preserved medieval town in Denmark. It's famous for its narrow cobblestone lanes and crooked, half-timbered houses. An important trading center during the Viking era, it's known today as the town where the endangered stork—often the subject of European myth and legend—flies back in April to nest. The medieval center of Ribe is protected by the National Trust. From April until mid-September, a night watchman circles the town, spinning tales of its legendary days and singing traditional songs. See chapter 5.

- **Odense:** Thousands of Hans Christian Andersen's fans visit the storyteller's birthplace every year. Denmark's third-largest city has a medieval core, and you can walk its cobblestone streets and admire its half-timbered houses, including the H. C. Andersens Hus. Odense is also a worthwhile destination in its own right, with many attractions (including St. Canute's Cathedral) in the city and nearby. On the outskirts you can explore everything from the 1554 Renaissance castle Egeskov to a 22m (72-ft.) long 10th-century Viking ship (at Ladby, 19km/12 miles northeast of Odense). See chapter 5.

- **Ebeltoft:** On Jutland, this well-preserved town of half-timbered buildings is the capital of the Mols hill country. It's a town of sloping row houses, crooked streets, and local handicraft shops. The Town Hall looks as though it were erected for kindergartners to play in. In Ebeltoft you can also visit the 1860 frigate *Jylland,* the oldest man-of-war in Denmark. See chapter 5.

3 The Best Active Vacations

- **Biking:** A nation of bikers, Denmark has organized the roads to suit the national sport. A network of bike routes and paths is protected from heavy traffic, and much of the terrain is flat. Bicycling vacations are available as inclusive tours that cover bike rental, ferry tickets, and accommodations en route. Some deluxe tours transport your luggage from one hotel to the next. For more information, contact the **Danish Cycling Federation,** Rømersgade 7, DK-1362 Copenhagen (© **33-32-31-21;** www.dcf.dk).

- **Camping:** There are a number of pleasant, well-equipped campgrounds near Copenhagen and elsewhere, and a total of 516 throughout the country. For information about campsites and facilities, contact the tourist information office in the town or region that appeals to you. You can also write to a nationwide organization devoted to marketing Danish campgrounds to the rest of the world, the **Campingraadet,** Mosedalvei 15, DK-2500 Copenhagen (© **39-27-88-44**).

- **Fishing:** For centuries, Danes relied on what fishers could pull out of the sea for their diet. Since then, no smørrebrød buffet has been complete without a selection of shrimp, herring, and salmon. The preparation of plaice, cod, eel, perch, and trout are culinary art forms. The seas off Funen's 1,095km (680-mile) coastline, especially within the Great Belt, have yielded countless tons of seafood, and that tradition has encouraged anglers and sport enthusiasts to test their luck in the rich waters of the Baltic. Many outfitters can introduce you to the mysteries of fresh- and saltwater fishing. One of the most consistently reliable is **Ole Dehn,** Søndergard 22, Lohals, DK-5953 Tranekær (© **62-55-17-00;** www.oledehn.dk). Its most popular offering involves half-day deep-sea fishing tours on the Great Sound, which cost 220DKK ($29) per person. The 6-hour

Scandinavia

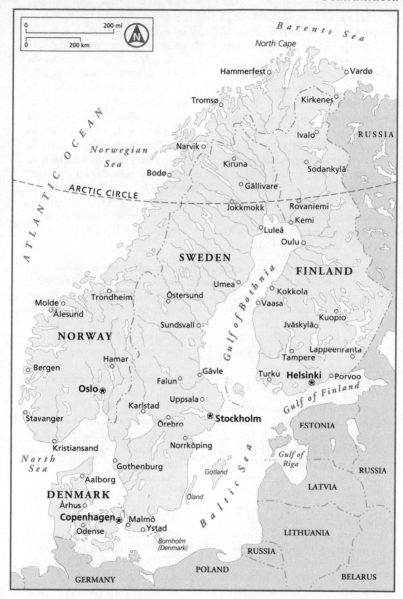

fishing experience, from 8am to 2pm, is conducted whenever business warrants it. Their headquarters are not on the island of Funen but on a long and skinny barrier island, Langeland, directly fronting the Great Belt's rich schools of fish.

- **Golfing:** In recent years, golf has become quite popular in Denmark. There are more than

100 clubs throughout the country, most of which welcome visitors— all you need is a membership card from your club at home. Several clubs have a pro trainer, golf shop, clubroom, and restaurant. Contact local tourist offices for a list of the golf courses in the regions you plan to visit.

- **Horseback Riding:** Riding schools throughout Denmark rent horses; local tourist offices can offer advice. Our favorite place for riding is the Isle of Læsø (off the northern coast of Jutland), which you can explore on the back of an Icelandic pony; a 1-hour riding tour costs 130DKK ($17) for adults or 110DKK ($14) for children ages 4 to 15. The stable is large, with 140 Icelandic ponies, the sturdy, cold-resistant breed which, although small, are very sturdy with a comfortable "seat." As opposed to most other breeds, Icelandic ponies have five gaits—not only walk, trot, and canter, but a tilt and a "pass." After you gallop past salt marshes and birds, you can stop from time to time to relax on the beach. For more information, contact **Krogbækgaard,** Byrum, DK-9940 Læsø (© **98-49-15-05;** www.rideferie.dk). Boats sail to Læsø from the port of Frederikshavn in North Jutland.

4 The Best Festivals & Special Events

- **July 4 Festival** (Rebild, near Aalborg): This is one of the few places outside the United States that celebrates U.S. independence. Each year Danes and Danish-Americans gather for picnic lunches, outdoor entertainment, and speeches. See chapter 2.
- **Fire Festival Regatta** (Silkeborg): This is the country's oldest and biggest festival, with nightly cruises on the lakes and illumination provided by thousands of candles onshore. The fireworks display on the final night is without equal in Europe, and Danish artists provide the entertainment at a large fun fair. Usually held the first week in August. See chapter 2.
- **Aalborg Carnival:** Celebrated on May 21, this is one of the country's great spring events. Happy folk in colorful costumes fill the streets. Almost 10,000 people take part in the celebration, honoring the victory of spring over winter. The whole city bursts with joy. See chapter 2.
- **Copenhagen Jazz Festival:** One of the finest jazz festivals in Europe takes place in July. Some of the best musicians in the world show up to jam in the Danish capital. Indoor and outdoor concerts—many of them free—are presented. See chapter 2.
- **Viking Festival** (Frederikssund): During this annual festival (June 19–July 15), bearded Vikings revive Nordic sagas in an open-air theater. After each performance, there's a traditional Viking banquet. See chapter 4.

5 The Best Castles & Palaces

- **Kronborg Slot** (Helsingør): Shakespeare never saw this castle, and Hamlet (if he existed) lived centuries before it was built. But Shakespeare set his immortal play here—the Bard has spoken, and that's that. Its cannon-studded bastions are full of intriguing secret passages and openings for guns, and it often serves as the backdrop for modern productions of *Hamlet*. The brooding mythical hero Holger Danske is said to be asleep in the dungeon and, according to the legend, the Viking chief will rise again to defend Denmark if it is endangered. See chapter 4.

- **Christiansborg Palace** (Copenhagen): The queen receives official guests in the Royal Reception Chamber, where you must don slippers to protect the floors. The complex also holds the Parliament House and the Supreme Court. From 1441 until the fire of 1795, this was the official residence of Denmark's monarchs. You can tour the richly decorated rooms, including the Throne Room and banquet hall. Below you can see the well-preserved ruins of the 1167 castle of Bishop Absalon, founder of Copenhagen. See chapter 4.

- **Rosenborg Castle** (Copenhagen): Founded by Christian IV in the 17th century, this redbrick Renaissance castle remained a royal residence until the early 19th century, when it was converted into a museum. It still houses the crown jewels, and its collection of costumes and royal memorabilia is unequaled in Denmark. See chapter 4.

- **Frederiksborg Castle** (Hillerød): Known as the Danish Versailles, this *slot* (castle) with a moat is the most elaborate in Scandinavia. Built in the Dutch Renaissance style of red brick with a copper roof, the castle's oldest parts date from 1560. Much of the castle was constructed under the direction of the "master builder," Christian IV, from 1600 to 1620. Now a major national history museum, the castle was ravaged by fire in 1859 and had to be completely restored. See chapter 4.

- **Egeskov Castle** (Kværndrup): On the island of Funen, this 1554 "water castle" is set amid splendid gardens. It's the most romantic example of Denmark's fortified manors. Built in the middle of a moat, it's surrounded by a 74-hectare (30-acre) park. The best-preserved Renaissance castle of its type in Europe, it has many attractions on its grounds, including an airplane museum and a vintage automobile museum. See chapter 5.

6 The Best Offbeat Experiences

- **Calling on Artists & Craftspeople:** West Jutland has many open workshops where you can see craftspeople in action; you can meet the potter, the glassblower, the painter, the textile designer, and even the candlestick maker. Local tourist offices can tell you which studios are open to guests in such centers as Tønder, Ribe, Esbjerg, Varde, Billund, Herning, Struer, and Skive. One of our favorite crafts studios lies in Jutland, 26km (16 miles) west of Esbjerg, near the town of Blåvand, on a farmstead in the tiny agrarian hamlet of Ho. Here, the husband-and-wife team of Asger Kristensen and Inga Sørensen directs the **Havlit Stentøj studios,** at Vesterballevej 1, Ho, DK 6857 Blåvand (© **75-27-95-93**). Jointly, the couple produces charming ceramics, including hand-painted replicas of birds—some rustic, some more detailed and refined. The artists take their inspiration from the rugged landscapes of West Jutland in their fabrication of such additional objects as urns, pots, and bas-reliefs. Hours are from April to October, Monday through Friday from 10am to 5:30pm; from November to

March, Monday through Friday from noon to 4pm.

- **Making People-to-People Contacts:** If you'd like to meet Scandinavians with interests and backgrounds like yours, the best "bridge" is **Friends Overseas,** 68-04 Dartmouth St., Forest Hills, NY 11375 (© **718/544-5660**). There's a $25 fee for your "hookup" in Scandinavia, but for many it's worth the money to have this close encounter with these bright, articulate people, who are among the most educated in the world. Know in advance that there isn't any background investigation of the people you're going to be matched with, and everything is very casual and free-form—basically the Scandinavians listed in the company's handbook are whoever happens to fill out the proper forms. But based on the instincts of company founder Larry Eisner, and the natural friendliness of the Scandinavians, social encounters usually work out happily, without unpleasant incidents. Contact information is grouped into subcategories that include families with children, couples, and singles. For more information, see "People to People," in chapter 2.

- **Journeying Back to the 1960s:** If you're nostalgic for the counterculture, it lives on in Christiania, a Copenhagen community at the corner of Prinsessegade and Badsmandsstræde on the island of Christianshavn. Founded in 1972, this is an anarchists' commune that occupies former army barracks; its current residents preach the gospel of drugs and peace. Christiania's residents have even organized their own government and passed laws, for example, to legalize drugs. They're not complete anarchists, however—they do venture into the city at least once a month to pick up their social welfare checks. Today you can wander about the community, which has a theater, cafes, grocery stores, and even a local radio station. See chapter 4.

- **Exploring Erotica:** Denmark was the first country to "liberate" pornography, in 1968, and today there's a museum in Copenhagen devoted to the subject. In the Erotica Museum (at Købmagergade 24), you can learn about the sex lives of such famous figures as Nietzsche, Freud, and Duke Ellington. Founded by a photographer of nudes, the exhibits range from the tame to the tempestuous—everything from Etruscan drawings to pictures of venereal skin disease and sadomasochism videos. See chapter 4.

7 The Best Buys

- **Danish Design:** The simple but elegant lines that became fashionable in the 1950s have made a comeback. Danish modern chairs, glassware, and even buildings have returned. "Old masters" such as Arne Jacobsen, Hans Wegner, and Poul Kjærhom are celebrated; their designs from the 1940s and 1950s are sold in antiques stores. Wegner, noted for his sculptured teak chairs, is now viewed as the grand old man of Danish design. Younger designers have followed in the footsteps of the "old masters," producing carefully crafted items for the home—everything from chairs, desks, and furnishings to table settings and silverware. For the best display of Danish design today, walk along the pedestrians-only Strøget,

Copenhagen's major shopping street. The best single showcase for modern Danish design may be **Illums Bolighus,** Amagertorv 10 (© 33-14-19-41).

- **Crystal & Porcelain:** Holmegaard crystal and Royal Copenhagen porcelain are household names, known for their beauty and craftsmanship. The items cost less in Denmark than in the States, although signed art glass is always extremely costly. To cut costs, you can shop for seconds, which are discounted by 20% to 50%—sometimes the imperfection can be detected only by an expert. Copenhagen's best centers

for these collectors' items are **Royal Copenhagen Porcelain,** Amagertorv 6 (© 33-13-71-81), and **Holmegaards Glasværker,** Amagertorv 6 (© 33-12-44-77).

- **Silver:** Danish designers have made a name for themselves in this field. Even with taxes and shipping charges, buying silver in Denmark is about half as costly as doing so in the States. If you're willing to consider "used" silver, you can get some remarkable discounts. The big name in international silver is **Georg Jensen,** Amagertorv 6, Copenhagen (© 33-11-40-80)— and you can buy it at the source.

8 The Best Hotels

- **Phoenix Copenhagen** (Copenhagen; © 33-95-95-00): The Danish Communist Party used to have its headquarters here, but the "Reds" of the Cold War era wouldn't recognize this pocket of posh today. It reeks of capitalistic excess and splendor, from its dazzling public rooms with French antiques to its bedrooms with dainty Louis XVI styling. See p. 60.
- **Hotel d'Angleterre** (Copenhagen; © 800/44-UTELL in the U.S., or 33-12-00-95): Some critics rate this the finest hotel in Denmark. It drifted toward mediocrity a few years back, before a massive investment saved it. Now the hotel is better than ever, and houses a swimming pool and a nightclub. The service is among the finest in Copenhagen. See p. 60.
- **Falsled Kro** (Falsled; © 62-68-11-11): Funen Island's finest accommodation is this quintessential Danish inn, with origins going back to the 1400s. A Relais & Châteaux property, it has been elegantly furnished and converted

into a stellar inn with a top-quality restaurant that rivals the very best in Copenhagen. See p. 137.
- **Hotel Dagmar** (Ribe; © 75-42-00-33): Jutland's most glamorous hotel was converted from a private home in 1850, and the building dates to 1581. This half-timbered hotel encapsulates the charm of the 16th century, with carved chairs, sloping wooden floors, and stained-glass windows. Many of the rooms have antique canopy beds. A fine restaurant that serves Danish and international dishes completes the picture. See p. 151.
- **Hotel Hesselet** (Nyborg; © 65-31-30-29): This stylish, modern hotel on Funen is set in a beech forest. The spacious guest rooms are artfully decorated, often with traditional furnishings. A library, Oriental carpets, and an open fireplace add graceful touches to the public areas. Many Copenhagen residents head here for a retreat, patronizing the hotel's gourmet restaurant at night. See p. 129.

9 The Best Restaurants

- **Era Ora** (Copenhagen; ✆ 32-54-06-93): The Golden Age (its English name) is the grandest Italian restaurant in Denmark, and one of the best of its kind in northern Europe, even attracting members of the royal family. The cuisine is based on the best recipes of Tuscany and Umbria, using the freshest of Danish produce when available. See p. 69.

- **Kommandanten** (Copenhagen; ✆ 33-12-09-90): A house built by a Danish commander for his family in 1698 accommodates this restaurant. The menu reflects the finest Continental and Mediterranean influences in such dishes as foie gras with lobster and truffle sauce, and pigeon sautéed with bacon, cabbage, and cherries. Fresh seafood is served in every conceivable way. The wooden floors and beams date to the 17th century, but the Warhol art makes the restaurant look trendy. See p. 70.

- **Divan II** (Copenhagen; ✆ 33-12-51-51): This early-19th-century slate house was constructed when the lush Tivoli Gardens were being laid out. In this romantic setting, you can enjoy both a meal and a view over the lake across from the Hans Christian Andersen Castle. The chefs prepare the gardens' most refined cuisine, ranging from rack of Danish lamb roasted with garlic and sage to mousseline of lobster baked with turbot and served with asparagus spears. See p. 68.

- **Marie Louise** (Odense; ✆ 66-17-92-95): Glittering with crystal and silver, this dining room, located on a pedestrian street, is one of the finest on the island of Funen. In an antique house, this Danish-French alliance offers excellent cuisine, preparation, and service. Seafood and fish are the favored dishes. See p. 133.

- **Falsled Kro** (Falsled; ✆ 62-68-11-11): Even if you don't stay here, consider enjoying a meal. A favorite among well-heeled Europeans, the restaurant produces stellar French-inspired cuisine, often using seasonal produce from its own gardens. The succulent salmon is smoked on the premises in one of the outbuildings, and the owners breed quail locally. Such care and attention to detail make this one of Denmark's top restaurants. See p. 137.

2

Planning Your Trip to Denmark

In the following pages we've compiled the practical advice you'll need—airline information, what things cost, a calendar of events—so that you may plan your trip to Denmark with ease.

1 The Regions in Brief

ZEALAND Home to Denmark's capital, **Copenhagen,** Zealand draws more visitors than any other region. It's the largest island, and the wealthiest, most densely populated section. Other cities include **Roskilde,** 32km (20 miles) west of Copenhagen, which is home to a landmark cathedral (burial place of many kings) and a collection of Viking vessels discovered in a fjord. In the medieval town of **Køge,** witches were burned in the Middle Ages. One of the most popular attractions on the island is **Helsingør** ("Elsinore," in English), about 40km (25 miles) north of Copenhagen, where visitors flock to see "Hamlet's castle." Off the southeast corner of the island lies the island of **Møn,** home to Møns Klint, an expanse of white cliffs that rises sharply out of the Baltic.

JUTLAND The peninsula of Jutland links the island nation of Denmark with Germany. Jutland has miles of coastline, with some of northern Europe's finest sandy beaches. Giant dunes and moors abound on the west coast, whereas the interior has rolling pastures and beech forests. Jutland's more interesting towns and villages include **Jelling,** heralded as the birthplace of Denmark and the ancient seat of the Danish kings; here you can see an extensive collection of Viking artifacts excavated from ancient burial mounds. The Viking port of **Ribe** is

the oldest town in Denmark. It's known throughout the world as the preferred nesting ground of numerous endangered storks. The resort of **Fanø,** with its giant dunes, heather-covered moors, and forests, is an excellent place to bird-watch or view Denmark's varied wildlife. The university city of **Århus** is Jutland's capital and second only to Copenhagen in size. **Aalborg,** founded by Vikings more than 1,000 years ago, is a thriving commercial center in northern Jutland. It lies close to Rebild National Park and the Rold Forest.

FUNEN With an area of 1,850 sq. km (1,150 sq. miles), Funen is Denmark's second-largest island. Called the "garden of Denmark," Funen is known to the world as the birthplace of Hans Christian Andersen. Its rolling countryside is dotted with orchards, stately manors, and castles. **Odense,** Andersen's birthplace, is a mecca for fairy-tale writers and fans from around the world. Nearby stands Egeskov Castle, Europe's best-preserved Renaissance castle, resting on oak columns in the middle of a small lake. Funen has a number of bustling ports, including **Nyborg** in the east and **Svendborg** at the southern end of the island. **Ærøskøbing,** nearby on the island of Ærø and accessible by ferry, is a medieval market town that's a showplace of Scandinavian heritage.

BORNHOLM In the Baltic Sea, southeast of Zealand and close to Sweden, lies the island of Bornholm. The countryside is peppered with prehistoric monuments and runic stones, and numerous fishing villages dot the shoreline. Some of Europe's largest castle-ruins are in this region. The town of **Rønne** is the site of Denmark's oldest regional theater; it stages numerous concerts and shows year-round. The island of **Christiansø,** off the coast of Bornholm, was the site of Denmark's penal colony. Criminals sentenced to life imprisonment were deported to the island, where they spent their lives in slavery.

2 Visitor Information

In the **United States,** contact the **Scandinavian Tourist Board,** 655 Third Ave., 18th Floor, New York, NY 10017 (© **212/885-9700;** www.go scandinavia.com), at least 3 months in advance for maps, sightseeing information, ferry schedules, and advice. Call or write for information; walk-in clients are no longer accepted.

If you contact a **travel agent,** make sure the agent is a member of the American Society of Travel Agents (ASTA). If a problem arises, you can complain to the society's Consumer Affairs Department, 1101 King St., Alexandria, VA 22314 (© **703/706-0387;** www.astanet.com).

In the **United Kingdom,** contact the **Danish Tourist Board,** 55 Sloane St., London SW1X 9SY (© **020/ 7259-5959**).

3 Entry Requirements

American, Canadian, Irish, Australian, and New Zealand citizens, and British subjects, need only a passport to enter Denmark. You must apply for a visa only if you want to stay more than 3 months. A British Visitor's Passport is also valid, for holidays and some business trips of less than 3 months. The passport can include your spouse, and it's valid for 1 year. Apply in person at a main post office in the British Isles, and the passport will be issued that day.

Your current domestic **driver's license** is acceptable in Denmark—an international driver's license is not required.

4 Money

CURRENCY Although a member of the European Union, a majority of Danes rejected the euro as their form of currency in September 2000. They continue to use the **krone** (crown), which breaks down into 100 **øre.** The plural is **kroner.** The international monetary designation for the Danish kroner is "DKK." (The Swedish currency is the kronor, but note the different spelling.) At press time, 1 krone equals about 13 US¢, or 8 DKK to the U.S. dollar. One krone equals 9 British pence, or approximately 11 kroner to the British pound. These rates are subject to change, so check the current rates shortly before you go.

Bank notes in circulation include 50, 100, 200, 500, and 1,000 kroner. Coins are in denominations of 25 øre; 50 øre; 1 krone; and 2, 5, 10, and 20 kroner. Still in circulation, but being phased out, are 5- and 10-øre coins.

When converting your currency into Danish kroner, be aware of varying exchange rates. In general, banks offer better rates than currency-exchange bureaus, but they do charge

Denmark

The Danish Krone

For American Readers   At this writing, $1 = approximately 7.64 kroner (or 1 krone = approximately 13 US¢); this was the rate of exchange used to calculate the dollar values given throughout this edition. Bear in mind that throughout this book, dollar amounts less than $10 are rounded to the nearest nickel, and dollar amounts greater than $10 are rounded to the nearest dollar.

For British Readers   At this writing, £1 = approximately 11 kroner (or 1 krone = approximately 9 pence). This was the rate of exchange used to calculate the pound values in the table below.

Regarding the Euro   At the time of this writing, the U.S. dollar and the euro traded almost on par (i.e., $1 approximately equals 1€). But that relationship can and probably will change during the lifetime of this edition. For more exact ratios between these and other currencies, check an up-to-date source at the time of your arrival in Denmark

DKK	US$	UK£	Euro	DKK	US$	UK£	Euro
1	0.13	0.09	0.13	75	9.83	6.75	9.83
2	0.26	0.18	0.26	100	13.10	9.00	13.10
3	0.39	0.27	0.39	125	16.38	11.25	16.38
4	0.52	0.36	0.52	150	19.65	13.50	19.65
5	0.66	0.45	0.66	175	22.93	15.75	22.93
6	0.79	0.54	0.79	200	26.20	18.00	26.20
7	0.92	0.63	0.92	225	29.48	20.25	29.48
8	1.05	0.72	1.05	250	32.75	22.50	32.75
9	1.18	0.81	1.18	275	36.03	24.75	36.03
10	1.31	0.90	1.31	300	39.30	27.00	39.30
15	1.97	1.35	1.97	350	45.85	31.50	45.85
20	2.62	1.80	2.62	400	52.40	36.00	52.40
25	3.28	2.25	3.28	500	65.50	45.00	65.50
50	6.55	4.50	6.55	1,000	131.00	90.00	131.00

a commission. Hotels generally offer the worst rates. If you are cashing American Express traveler's checks, you will get the best rate at American Express.

ATMS   PLUS, Cirrus, and other networks connecting automated teller machines operate throughout Scandinavia. If your credit card has a PIN (personal identification number), you can probably use your card at Scandinavian ATMs to withdraw money as a cash advance. Always determine the frequency limits for withdrawals, and

check to see if your PIN must be reprogrammed for use abroad. Discover cards are accepted in the United States only. For **Cirrus** locations abroad, call © **800/424-7787.** For **PLUS** usage abroad, check www.visa.com or call © **800/843-7587.**

CREDIT CARDS   These can be used throughout Scandinavia. American Express, Diners Club, and Visa are widely recognized. If you see a Eurocard or Access sign, it means the establishment accepts MasterCard. With an American Express, MasterCard, or

Visa card, you can also withdraw currency from cash machines (ATMs). Always check with your credit- or charge-card company about this before leaving home.

CURRENCY EXCHANGE Many hotels in Scandinavia simply do not accept a dollar- or pound-denominated check; those that do will certainly charge for the conversion. In some cases a hotel may accept countersigned traveler's checks or a credit or charge card.

If you're making a deposit on a hotel reservation, it's cheaper and easier to pay with a check drawn on a Scandinavian bank. This can be arranged by a large commercial bank or by a specialist like **Ruesch International,** 700 11th St. NW, 4th Floor, Washington, DC 20001 (© **800/ 424-2923** or 202/408-1200; www. ruesch.com). It performs a wide variety of conversion-related tasks, usually for about $15 per transaction.

If you need a check payable in a Scandinavian currency, call Ruesch's toll-free number, describe what you need, and write down the transaction number. Mail your dollar-denominated personal check (payable to Ruesch International) to the Washington, D.C., office. When it's received, the company will mail you a check denominated in the requested currency

for the specified amount, minus the $15 charge. The company can also help you with wire transfers, as well as the conversion of VAT (value-added tax) refund checks. Information is mailed upon request.

In England, contact Ruesch International Ltd., Marble Arch Tower, 14th Floor, 55 Bryanston St., London W1H 7AA (© **0207/563-3300;** fax 0207/563-3390).

TRAVELER'S CHECKS Traveler's checks are a bit outdated due to ATMs sprouting up around the world, but some visitors still prefer this old-fashioned means of carrying money. Most banks give you a better exchange rate for traveler's checks than for cash. Checks denominated in U.S. dollars or British pounds are accepted virtually anywhere; sometimes you can also get checks in a local currency.

The agencies listed below will replace checks if they're lost or stolen, provided you produce documentation. When purchasing checks, ask about refund hot lines. American Express has the most offices around the world.

Issuers sometimes have agreements with groups to sell traveler's checks without a commission. For example, American Automobile Association (AAA) clubs sell commission-free

 Emergency Cash—the Fastest Way

If you need emergency cash over the weekend when all banks and American Express offices are closed, you can have money wired to you from **Western Union** (© **800/325-6000;** www.westernunion.com). You must present valid ID to pick up the cash at the Western Union office. However, in most countries, you can pick up a money transfer even if you don't have valid identification, as long as you can answer a test question provided by the sender. Be sure to let the sender know in advance that you don't have ID. If you need to use a test question instead of ID, the sender must take cash to his or her local Western Union office, rather than transfer the money over the phone or online.

What Things Cost in Copenhagen	US$
Taxi from the airport to the city center	17.00
Subway from Central Station to outlying suburbs	1.85
Local telephone call	.13
Double room at the Hotel d'Angleterre (very expensive)	324.00
Double room, with bathroom, at the Hotel Kong Arthur (moderate)	183.00
Double room, without bathroom, at the Hotel Valberg (inexpensive)	118.00
Lunch for one at Restaurant Els (moderate)	26.00
Lunch for one at Ida Davidsen (inexpensive)	12.00
Dinner for one, without wine, at Kommandanten (very expensive)	50.00
Dinner for one, without wine, at Copenhagen Corner (moderate)	39.00
Dinner for one, without wine, at Nyhavns Færgekro (inexpensive)	22.00
Pint of beer (draft Pilsner)	5.25
Coca-Cola	3.30
Cup of coffee	2.60
Admission to the Tivoli	7.20
Movie ticket	7.85
Roll of ASA 100 color film, 36 exposures	11.00
Ticket to the Royal Theater	7.85–81.00

American Express traveler's checks in several currencies.

American Express (© 800/721-9768 in the U.S. and Canada; www.americanexpress.com) is one of the largest and most recognizable issuers of traveler's checks. Holders of certain types of American Express cards pay no commission. For questions or problems arising outside the United States or Canada, contact any of the company's many regional representatives. We'll list locations throughout this guide.

Citicorp (© 800/645-6556 from all over the world; www.citibank.com)

issues traveler's checks in several currencies.

Thomas Cook (© 800/223-7373; www.thomascook.com all over the world) issues MasterCard traveler's checks denominated in several currencies; not all currencies are available at every outlet.

Visa Travelers Checks (© 800/732-1322 in the U.S. and Canada, or 212/858-8500, collect, from most other parts of the world; www.visa.com) sells Visa traveler's checks denominated in several major currencies.

5 When to Go

CLIMATE

Denmark's climate is mild for Scandinavia—New England farmers experience harsher winters. Summer temperatures average 61°F to 77°F

(16°C–25°C). Winter temperatures seldom go below 30°F (–1°C), thanks to the warming waters of the Gulf Stream. From a weather perspective, mid-April to November is a good time to visit.

Denmark's Average Daytime Temperatures

	Jan	Feb	Mar	Apr	May	June	July	Aug	Sept	Oct	Nov	Dec
°F	32	32	35	44	53	60	64	63	57	49	42	37
°C	0	0	2	7	12	16	18	17	14	9	6	3

HOLIDAYS

Some of these dates may vary slightly, so check with a local tourist office. Danish public holidays (and dates of those that do not vary) are New Year's Day (Jan 1), Maundy Thursday, Good Friday, Easter Sunday, Easter Monday, Labor Day (May 1), Common Prayers Day (4th Fri after Easter), Ascension Day (mid-May), Whitsunday (late May), Whitmonday, Constitution Day (June 5), Christmas Day (Dec 25), and Boxing Day (Dec 26).

DENMARK CALENDAR OF EVENTS

Note: Exact dates below apply for 2003. Should you be using this guide in 2004, check with local tourist boards for exact dates.

May

Ballet and Opera Festival (Copenhagen). Classical and modern dance and two operatic masterpieces are presented at the Old Stage of the Royal Theater in Copenhagen. For tickets, contact the Royal Theater, Box 2185, DK-1017 København (℃ **33-69-69-69;** www.kgl-teater. dk). Mid-May to June.

Aalborg Carnival. This is one of the country's great spring events. The streets fill with people in colorful costumes. Thousands take part in the celebration, which honors the victory of spring over winter. For information, call ℃ **98-13-72-11.** May 18 to 24.

June

Carnival in Copenhagen. This is a great citywide event. There's also a children's carnival. For information, call ℃ **33-38-85-04;** or check www.karneval.dk. June 7 to 9.

Viking Festival (Frederikssund, 13km/8 miles southwest of Hillerød). For almost a month every summer, bearded "Vikings" present old Nordic sagas in an open-air setting. After each performance, a traditional Viking meal is held. Call ℃ **47-31-06-85** for more information. Mid-June to July 6.

Midsummer's Night. This age-old event, on the longest day of the year, is celebrated throughout the country. Festivities throughout the tiny nation begin at around 10pm with bonfires and celebrations along the myriad coasts. June 21.

Roskilde Festival. Europe's biggest rock festival has been going strong for more than 30 years, now bringing about 90,000 revelers each year to the central Zealand town. Beside major rock concerts, which often draw "big names," scheduled activities include theater and film presentations. For more information, call ℃ **46-36-66-13;** or check www.roskilde-festivaldk. June 26 to June 29.

July

Funen Festival. This annual musical extravaganza frequently draws big, international headliners. The festival's music is often hard-core rock, but gentler, classical melodies are presented as well. It takes place in the city of Odense, on the island of Funen. For more information, call the Odense tourist bureau ((℃ **66-12-75-20).** July 16 to August 10.

July 4 (Rebild). Rebild, near Aalborg, is one of the few places outside the United States to honor American Independence Day. For more information, contact the Aalborg Tourist Office, Østerågade 8, DK-9000 Aalborg (© **98-12-60-22**). July 4.

Copenhagen Jazz Festival. International jazz musicians play in the streets, squares, and theaters. Pick up a copy of *Copenhagen This Week* to find the venues. For information, call © **33-93-20-13;** or check www.festival.jazz.dk. July 4 to July 13.

Sønderborg Tilting Festival. Dating to the Middle Ages, the "tilting at the ring" tradition has survived only in the old town of Sønderborg on the island of Als in southern Jutland. While riding at a gallop, the horseman uses his lance to see how many times (in 24 attempts) he can take the ring. Parades, music, and entertainment are included. For more information, contact the Turistbureau, Rådhustorvet 7, DK-6400 Sønderborg (© **74-42-35-55**). Early July.

August

Fire Festival Regatta (Silkeborg). Denmark's oldest and biggest festival features nightly cruises on the lakes, with thousands of candles illuminating the shores. The fireworks display on the last night is the largest and most spectacular in northern Europe. Popular Danish artists provide entertainment at a large fun fair. For more information, contact the Turistbureau, 4, DK-8600 Silkeborg (© **86-82-19-11**). Early August.

Fall Ballet Festival (København). The internationally acclaimed Royal Danish Ballet returns home to perform at the Old Stage of the Royal Theater just before the tourist season ends. For tickets, contact the Royal Theater, Box 2185, DK-1017 København (© **33-69-69-69;** www.kgl-teater.dk). Mid-August to September 1.

September

Århus Festival Week. A wide range of cultural activities—including opera, jazz, classical, and folk music; ballet; and theater—is presented. This is the largest cultural festival in Scandinavia. Sporting activities and street parties abound as well. For more information, contact Århus Tourist Office, Rådhuset, Århus C, DK-8000 Århus (© **89-31-82-70**). September 6 to September 14.

6 The Active Vacation Planner

BEACHES With some 8,000km (5,000 miles) of coastline, Denmark has several long strips of sandy beach. In many cases, dunes protect the beaches from sea winds. Most beaches are relatively unspoiled, and the Danes like to keep them that way—any polluted beaches are clearly marked. Many Danes like to go nude at the beach. Nudist beaches aren't clearly identified; often you'll see bathers with and without clothing using the same beach. The best beach resorts are those on the north coast of Zealand and the southern tip of the island of Bornholm. Beaches on the east coast of Jutland are also good, and often attract Germans from the south. Funen has a number of good beaches, too, especially in the south.

BIKING The Danes have organized their roads to suit their national sport. Bikers can pedal along a network of biking routes and paths protected from heavy traffic. The Danish landscape is made for this type of vacation. Most tourist offices publish biking tour suggestions for their districts, a great way to see the sights and get in shape at the same time. The **Danish Cycling Federation (Dansk Cyklist Forbund),** Rømersgade 7, Copenhagen (© **33-32-31-21;** www.dcf.dk), publishes excellent tour suggestions covering the whole country. The federation can also provide data about package vacations.

FISHING No place in Denmark is more than 56km (35 miles) from the sea, so fishing is a major pastime. The country also has well-stocked rivers and lakes, including fjord waters around the Limfjord. Anglers between the ages of 18 and 67 must get a Ministry of Fisheries permit for 120DKK ($16); it's available at any post office. Jutland is known for its good trout fishing (salmon is available, but found more readily in Norway). Anglers who fish from the beach can catch eel, mackerel, turbot, sea trout, plaice, and flounder. For more information, contact **Sportfiskerforbund,** Worsåesgade 1 DK-7100 Vejle (𝄐 **75-82-06-99**).

GOLFING In recent years, golf has become very popular in Denmark. The undulating landscape is ideal for the construction of courses. For the most favorable treatment, prospective golfers should bring a valid golf club membership card from home. For information on the best courses near where you're staying, contact local tourist offices.

SAILING Denmark has about 600 large and small harbors. Sailing enthusiasts will have many opportunities, especially in the open waters of the Baltic or the more sheltered waters of the South Funen Sea between Lolland and Falster, and Zealand. The Limfjord in northern Jutland is also ideal for sailing. Many sailboats are available for rent, as are cruisers. For information, contact local tourist offices.

WALKING Local tourist offices distribute folders that describe short and long walks in Danish forests. Twenty are printed in English; check at tourist offices.

7 Health & Insurance

TRAVEL INSURANCE AT A GLANCE

Since Scandinavia for most of us is far from home, and a number of things could go wrong—lost luggage, trip cancellation, a medical emergency—consider the following types of insurance.

Check your existing insurance policies before you buy travel insurance to cover trip cancellation, lost luggage, medical expenses, or car rental insurance. You're likely to have partial or complete coverage. But if you need additional coverage, ask your travel agent about a comprehensive package. The cost of travel insurance varies widely, depending on the cost and length of your trip, your age and overall health, and the type of trip you're taking. Insurance for extreme sports or adventure travel, for example, will cost more than coverage for a European cruise. Some insurers provide packages for specialty vacations, such as skiing or backpacking. More dangerous activities may be excluded from basic policies.

For information, contact one of the following popular insurers:

- **Access America** (𝄐 **800/284-8300;** www.accessamerica.com)
- **Travel Assistance International** (𝄐 **800/821-2828;** www.travelassistance.com)
- **Travel Guard International** (𝄐 **800/826-1300;** www.travelguard.com)
- **Travel Insured International** (𝄐 **800/243-3174;** www.travelinsured.com)
- **Travelex Insurance Services** (𝄐 **800/228-9792;** www.travel-insurance.com)

TRIP-CANCELLATION INSURANCE (TCI)

There are three major types of trip-cancellation insurance—one, in the event that you pre-pay a cruise or tour that gets cancelled, and you can't get your money back; a second when you or someone in your family gets sick or dies, and you can't travel (but beware that you may not be covered for a pre-existing condition); and a third, when bad weather makes travel impossible. Some insurers provide coverage for events like jury duty; natural disasters close to home, like floods or fire; even the loss of a job. A few have added provisions for cancellations because of terrorist activities. Always check the fine print before signing on, and don't buy trip-cancellation insurance from the tour operator that may be responsible for the cancellation; buy it only from a reputable travel insurance agency. Don't overbuy. You won't be reimbursed for more than the cost of your trip.

MEDICAL INSURANCE

Most health insurance policies cover you if you get sick away from home—but check, particularly if you're insured by an HMO. With the exception of certain HMOs and Medicare/Medicaid, your medical insurance should cover emergency medical treatment—even hospital care—overseas. However, most out-of-country hospitals make you pay your bills upfront, and send you a refund after you've returned home and filed the necessary paperwork. Members of **Blue Cross/Blue Shield** can now use your cards at select hospitals in most major cities worldwide (© **800/810-BLUE** or www.bluecares.com for a list of hospitals).

Some credit cards (American Express and certain gold and platinum Visas and MasterCards, for example) offer automatic flight insurance against death or dismemberment in case of an airplane crash if you charged the cost of your ticket.

If you require additional insurance, try one of the following companies:

• **MEDEX International,** 8501 LaSalle Rd., Suite 200, Towson, MD 21286 (© **888/MEDEX-00** or 410/453-6300; fax 410/453-6301; www.medexassist.com).

• **Travel Assistance International** (© **800/821-2828;** www.travelassistance.com), 9200 Keystone Crossing, Suite 300, Indianapolis, IN 46240 (for general information on services, call the company's Worldwide Assistance Services, Inc., at © 800/777-8710).

The cost of travel medical insurance varies widely. Check your existing policies before you buy additional coverage. Also, check to see if your medical insurance covers you for emergency medical evacuation. If you have to buy a one-way same-day ticket home and forfeit your nonrefundable round-trip ticket, you may be out big money.

LOST-LUGGAGE INSURANCE

On international flights (including U.S. portions of international trips), baggage is limited to approximately $9.07 per pound, up to approximately $635 per checked bag. If you plan to check items more valuable than the standard liability, you may purchase "excess valuation" coverage from the airline, up to $5,000. Be sure to take any valuables or irreplaceable items with you in your carry-on luggage. If you file a lost luggage claim, be prepared to answer detailed questions about the contents of your baggage, and be sure to file a claim immediately, as most airlines enforce a 21-day deadline. Before you leave home, compile an inventory of all packed items and a rough estimate of the total value to ensure you're properly compensated if your luggage is lost. You will not be reimbursed for more than the actual amount lost. Once you've filed a complaint, persist in securing your reimbursement; there are no laws governing the length of time it takes for a carrier to reimburse you. If you arrive at a destination without your bags, ask the airline to forward them to your hotel or

> **Tips   Quick ID**
>
> Tie a colorful ribbon or piece of yarn around your luggage handle, or slap a distinctive sticker on the side of your bag. This makes it less likely that someone will mistakenly appropriate it. And if your luggage gets lost, it will be easier to find.

to your next destination; they will usually comply. If your bag is delayed or lost, the airline may reimburse you for reasonable expenses, such as a toothbrush or a set of clothes, but the airline is under no legal obligation to do so.

Lost luggage may also be covered by your homeowner's or renter's policy. Many platinum and gold credit cards cover you as well. If you choose to purchase additional lost-luggage insurance, be sure not to buy more than you need. Buy in advance from the insurer or a trusted agent (prices will be much higher at the airport).

CAR-RENTAL INSURANCE (LOSS/DAMAGE WAIVER OR COLLISION DAMAGE WAIVER)

If you hold a private auto insurance policy, you probably are covered in the U.S., but not abroad, for loss or damage to the car, and liability in case a passenger is injured. The credit card you used to rent the car also may provide some coverage.

Car rental insurance probably does not cover liability if you caused the accident. Check your own auto insurance policy, the rental company policy, and your credit card coverage for the extent of coverage. Is your destination covered? Are other drivers covered? How much liability is covered if a passenger is injured? (If you rely on your credit card for coverage, you may want to bring a second credit card with you, as damages may be charged to your card and you may find yourself stranded with no money.)

Car rental insurance costs about $20 a day.

THE HEALTHY TRAVELER

All of Scandinavia is viewed as a "safe" destination, although problems, of course, can and do occur anywhere. You don't need to get shots; most foodstuff is safe, and the water in cities and towns potable. If you're concerned, order bottled water. It is easy to get a prescription filled in towns and cities, and nearly all places throughout Scandinavia contain hospitals with English-speaking doctors and well-trained medical staffs.

WHAT TO DO IF YOU GET SICK AWAY FROM HOME

If you worry about getting sick away from home, consider purchasing **medical travel insurance** and carry your ID card in your purse or wallet. In most cases, your existing health plan will provide the coverage you need. See the section on insurance earlier in this chapter for more information.

If you suffer from a chronic illness, consult your doctor before your departure. For conditions like epilepsy, diabetes, or heart problems, wear a **Medic Alert Identification Tag** (© 800/825-3785; www.medicalert.org), which will immediately alert doctors to your condition and give them access to your records through Medic Alert's 24-hour hot line.

Pack **prescription medications** in your carry-on luggage, and carry prescription medications in their original containers. Also bring along copies of your prescriptions in case you lose or run out of your pills. Carry the generic name of prescription medicines, in case a local pharmacist is unfamiliar with the brand name.

And don't forget sunglasses and an extra pair of contact lenses or prescription glasses.

Contact the **International Association for Medical Assistance to Travelers (IAMAT)** (℗ 716/754-4883; www.iamat.org) for tips on travel, health concerns, and lists of English-speaking doctors in Denmark; in Canada, call ℗ 519/836-0102. The United States **Centers for Disease Control and Prevention** (℗ 800/311-3435; www.cdc.gov) provides up-to-date information on necessary vaccines and health hazards by region or country. (Their booklet, *Health*

Information for International Travel, is $25 by mail; on the Internet, it's free.) Any foreign consulate can provide a list of area doctors who speak English. If you get sick, consider asking your hotel concierge to recommend a local doctor—even his or her own. You can also try the emergency room at a local hospital; many have walk-in clinics for emergency cases that are not life-threatening. You may not get immediate attention, but you won't pay the high price of an emergency room visit (usually a minimum of $300 just for signing your name).

8 Tips for Travelers with Special Needs

FOR TRAVELERS WITH DISABILITIES

If you're flying around Europe, the airline and ground staff can help you on and off planes and reserve seats with enough legroom, but you must arrange for this assistance *in advance* through the airline.

AGENCIES/OPERATORS

• **Flying Wheels Travel** (℗ 507/451-5005; www.flyingwheels travel.com) offers escorted tours and cruises that emphasize sports and private tours in minivans with lifts.

• **Access Adventures** (℗ 716/889-9096), a Rochester, New York–based agency, offers customized itineraries for travelers with disabilities.

• **Accessible Journeys** (℗ 800/TINGLES or 610/521-0339; www.disabilitytravel.com) caters specifically to slow walkers and wheelchair travelers and their families and friends.

ORGANIZATIONS

• **The Moss Rehab Hospital** (℗ 215/456-5882; www.moss resourcenet.org) provides helpful phone assistance through its **Travel Information Service.**

• **The Society for Accessible Travel and Hospitality** (℗ 212/447-7284; fax 212/725-8253; www. sath.org) offers a wealth of travel resources for all types of disabilities, and informed recommendations on destinations, access guides, travel agents, tour operators, vehicle rentals, and companion services. Annual membership costs $45 for adults, $30 for seniors and students.

• **The American Foundation for the Blind** (℗ 800/232-5463; www.afb.org) provides information on traveling with Seeing Eye dogs.

PUBLICATIONS

• **Mobility International USA** (℗ 541/343-1284; www.miusa. org) publishes *A World of Options,* a 658-page book of resources covering everything from biking trips to scuba outfitters, and a biannual newsletter, *Over the Rainbow.* Annual membership is $35.

• **Twin Peaks Press** (℗ 360/694-2462) publishes travel-related books for travelers with special needs.

• *Open World for Disability and Mature Travel* magazine,

published by the Society for Accessible Travel and Hospitality (see above), is full of good resources and information. A year's subscription is $14 ($21 outside the U.S.).

FOR BRITISH TRAVELERS

The **Royal Association for Disability and Rehabilitation (RADAR),** Unit 12, City Forum, 250 City Rd., London EC1V 8AF (© **020/7250-3222;** www.radar.org.uk), publishes three holiday "fact packs" for £2 each or £5 for all three. The first provides general information, including tips for planning and booking a holiday, obtaining insurance, and handling finances; the second outlines transportation available when going abroad and equipment for rent; the third deals with specialized accommodations. Another good resource is **Holiday Care,** Imperial Building, 2nd Floor, Victoria Road, Horley, Surrey RH6 7PZ (© **01293/774-535;** www.holiday care.org.uk), a national charity advising on accessible accommodations for the elderly and persons with disabilities. Annual membership is £35.

IN DENMARK In general, trains, airlines, ferries, and department stores and malls are accessible. For information about wheelchair access, ferry and air travel, parking, and other matters, contact the **Danish Tourist Board** (see "Visitor Information" above).

Useful information for people with disabilities is provided by *De Samvirkende Invalideorganisationer* (Danish Disability Council, abbreviated in Denmark as DSI), Kløverprisvej 10 B, DK-2650 Hvidovre, Denmark (© **36-75-17-77**). Established in 1934, it organizes 29 smaller groups, each involved with issues of concern to people with disabilities, into one coherent organization that represents the estimated 300,000 persons with disabilities living in Denmark today. For the best overview of what this organization does, click on their website at www.handicap.dk.

FOR GAY & LESBIAN TRAVELERS

In general, Denmark is one of the most gay-friendly countries in Europe, and was one of the first to embrace same-sex marriages. Anti-discrimination laws have been in effect since 1987. Most Danes are exceptionally friendly and tolerant of lifestyles of either sexual preference. Obviously, an urban center such as Copenhagen will have a more openly gay life than rural areas. In many ways, the Erotic Museum in Copenhagen illustrates the city's attitudes toward sex—both heterosexual and homosexual. The history of both forms of sexual pleasure is presented in an unprejudiced manner.

IN DENMARK The Danish National Association for Gays and Lesbians (*Landesforeningen for Bøsser og Lesbiske,* abbreviated LBL) maintains its headquarters at Teglgaardstræde 13, 1007 København (© **33-3-19-48;** www.lbl.dk), with branches in at least four of the larger cities of Denmark. You might find it hard to reach a live body on their telephone line (their hours of operation are very limited), but they maintain one of the most informative and user-friendly websites of any gay organization in Europe, complete with maps on how to reach whichever of the gay and lesbian venues they describe on their site.

The **International Gay & Lesbian Travel Association (IGLTA)** (© **800/448-8550** or 954/776-2626; fax 954/776-3303; www.iglta.org) links travelers with gay-friendly hoteliers, tour operators, and airline and cruise-line representatives. It offers monthly newsletters, marketing mailings, and a membership directory that's updated once a year. Membership is $200 yearly, plus a $100 administration fee for new members.

AGENCIES/OPERATORS

- **Above and Beyond Tours** (© 800/397-2681; www.above beyondtours.com) offers gay and lesbian tours worldwide and is the exclusive gay and lesbian tour operator for United Airlines.
- **Now, Voyager** (© 800/255-6951; www.nowvoyager.com) is a San Francisco–based gay-owned and -operated travel service.
- **Olivia Cruises & Resorts** (© 800/631-6277 or 510/655-0364; http://olivia.com) charters entire resorts and ships for exclusive lesbian vacations all over the world.

PUBLICATIONS

- *Frommer's Gay & Lesbian Europe* is an excellent travel resource.
- *Out and About* (© 800/929-2268 or 415/644-8044; www.out andabout.com) offers guidebooks and a newsletter 10 times a year. A subscription to the newsletter is $49, and each issue is packed with solid information on the global gay and lesbian scene.
- *Spartacus International Gay Guide* and *Odysseus* are good, annual English-language guidebooks which focus on gay men, with some information for lesbians. You can get them from most gay and lesbian bookstores, or order them from **Giovanni's Room** bookstore, 1145 Pine St., Philadelphia, PA 19107 (© 215/923-2960; www.giovannisroom. com).
- *Gay Travel A to Z: The World of Gay & Lesbian Travel Options at Your Fingertips,* by Marianne Ferrari (Ferrari Publications), is a very good gay and lesbian guidebook series.

SENIOR TRAVEL

Mention the fact that you're a senior when you first make your travel reservations. All major airlines and many Scandinavian hotels offer discounts for seniors.

Members of **AARP** (formerly known as the American Association of Retired Persons), 601 E St. NW, Washington, DC 20049 (© 800/424-3410 or 202/434-2277; www. aarp.org), gets discounts on hotels, airfares, and car rentals. AARP offers members a wide range of benefits, including *AARP: The Magazine* and a monthly newsletter. Anyone over 50 can join.

Alliance for Retired Americans, 888 16th St. NW, Washington, DC 20006 (© **888/373-64** or 202/974-8256; www.retiredamericans.org), offers a newsletter six times a year and discounts on hotel and auto rentals; annual dues are $10 per person or couple. *Note:* Members of the former National Council of Senior Citizens receive automatic membership in the Alliance.

AGENCIES/OPERATORS

- **Grand Circle Travel** (© 800/221-2610 or 617/350-7500; www.gct.com) offers package deals for the 50-plus market, mostly of the tour-bus variety, with free trips thrown in for those who organize groups of 10 or more.
- **SAGA Holidays** (© 800/343-0273; www.sagaholidays.com) offers inclusive tours and cruises for those 50 and older. SAGA also offers a number of single-traveler tours. Order a free brochure from the website.
- **Elderhostel** (© 877/426-8056; www.elderhostel.org) arranges study programs for those ages 55 and over (and a spouse or companion of any age) in the U.S. and in more than 80 countries around the world, including Scandinavia. Most courses last 5 to 7 days in the U.S. (2–4 weeks abroad), and

many include airfare, accommodations in university dormitories or modest inns, meals, and tuition.

- **Interhostel** (© 800/733-9753; www.learn.unh.edu), organized by the University of New Hampshire, also offers educational travel for seniors. On these escorted tours, the days are packed with seminars, lectures, and field trips, with sightseeing led by academic experts. **Interhostel** takes travelers 50 and over (with companions over 40) on 1- and 2-week trips, mostly international.
- **Elder Travelers,** 1615 Smelter Ave., Black Eagle, MT 59414, aids people over 50 who like travel and meeting others. Their stated purpose is to provide members with "zero cost lodging" anywhere in the world, including Scandinavia, as seniors are matched with their counterpart hosts in the lands in which they travel. For $40 annually, subscriptions are given to their informative newsletter, which provides links to the best travel data sites worldwide. For more information on this unique group, seek them out at www.eldertravelers.com.
- **Vantage Deluxe World Travel,** 90 Canal St., Boston, MA 02114 (© 800/322-6677 or 617/878-6000), for some 2 decades has taken thousands of mature travelers on out-of-the-ordinary travel experiences in various European countries. Travel is on luxurious river cruises and fully escorted land tours. Groups are deliberately kept small. For more details, contact www.vantagetravel.com.

PUBLICATIONS
- *The Book of Deals* is a collection of more than 1,000 senior discounts on airlines, lodging, tours, and attractions around the country; it's available for $9.95 by calling © 800/460-6676.
- *101 Tips for the Mature Traveler* is available from Grand Circle Travel (© 800/221-2610 or 617/350-7500; fax 617/346-6700).
- *The 50+ Traveler's Guidebook* (St. Martin's Press).
- *Unbelievably Good Deals and Great Adventures That You Absolutely Can't Get Unless You're Over 50* (Contemporary Publishing Co.).

IN DENMARK Seniors with valid age identification (such as a passport) are entitled to discounts on rail travel and ferries to Sweden, plus certain attractions and performances, including those at the Royal Theater. However, you may have to belong to a seniors' organization to qualify (an AARP card will suffice) for certain discounts.

STUDENT TRAVEL
If you're planning to travel outside the U.S., you'd be wise to arm yourself with an **international student ID card,** which offers substantial savings on rail passes, plane tickets, and entrance fees. It also provides you with basic health and life insurance and a 24-hour help line. The card is available for $22 from the **Council on International Educational Exchange,** or CIEE (www.ciee.org). CIEE's travel branch, **Council Travel Service** (© 800/226-8624; www.counciltravel.com), is the biggest student travel agency in the world. If you're no longer a student but are still under 26, you can get a **GO 25 card** from the same people, which entitles you to insurance and some discounts (but not on museum admissions). **STA Travel** (© 800/781-4040; www.statravel.com) is another travel agency catering especially to young travelers, although their bargain-basement prices are available to people of all ages.

In Canada, **Travel Cuts** (© **800/ 667-2887** or 905/361-2022; www. travelcuts.com) offers similar services. In London, **Usit Campus** (© **0870/ 240-1010;** www.usitworld.com), opposite Victoria Station, is Britain's leading specialist in student and youth travel.

PUBLICATIONS

The Hanging Out Guides (www. frommers.com), published by Frommer's, is the top student travel series for today's students, covering everything from adrenaline sports to the hottest club and music scenes.

FAMILY TRAVEL

The family vacation is a rite of passage for many households, one that in a split second can devolve into a *National Lampoon* farce. But as any veteran family vacationer will assure you, a family trip can be among the most pleasurable and rewarding times of your life.

Most Scandinavian hoteliers will let children 12 and under stay in a room with their parents for free; others do not. Sometimes this requires a little negotiation at the reception desk.

At attractions, and even if it isn't specifically posted, inquire if a kids' discount is available. European Community citizens under 18 are admitted free to all state-run museums.

Throughout the guide, look for our kid-friendly icons.

AGENCIES/OPERATORS
• **Familyhostel** (© **800/733-9753;** www.learn.unh.edu) takes the whole family on moderately priced domestic and international learning vacations. All trip details are handled by the program staff, and lectures, field trips, and sightseeing are guided by a team of academics. The trips are for kids ages 8 to 15 accompanied by their parents and/or grandparents.

PUBLICATIONS
• *How to Take Great Trips with Your Kids* (The Harvard Common Press) is full of good general advice that can apply to travel anywhere, including Denmark.

WEBSITES
• **Family Travel Network** (www. familytravelnetwork.com) offers travel tips and reviews of family-friendly destinations, vacation deals, and thoughtful features such as "What to Do When Your Kids Are Afraid to Travel" and "Kid-Style Camping."
• **Travel with Your Children** (www.travelwithyourkids.com) is a comprehensive site offering sound advice for traveling with children.
• **The Busy Person's Guide to Travel with Children** (http:// wz.com/travel/TravelingWith Children.html) offers a "45-second newsletter" where experts weigh in on the best websites and resources for travel with children.

9 Getting There

BY PLANE

Summer (generally June–Sept) is the peak season and the most expensive. Scandinavia's off season is winter (from about Nov 1–Mar 21). Shoulder season (spring and fall) is in between. In any season, midweek fares (Mon–Thurs) are the lowest.

REGULAR AIRFARES & APEX FARES

Regular airfares include, in order of increasing price, economy, business class, and first class. These tickets carry no restrictions. In economy you pay for drinks, and the seats are not spacious; in business, the drinks are free, and the seats are wider; in first class, amenities and services are the best.

Currently the most popular discount fare is the **APEX** (advance-purchase excursion), which usually carries restrictions—advance-purchase requirements, minimum or maximum stays—and cancellation or change-of-date penalties.

In addition, airlines often offer **promotional discount fares.** Always check the travel sections of your local newspapers for such advertisements.

THE MAJOR AIRLINES
FROM NORTH AMERICA SAS (Scandinavian Airlines Systems; ✆ **800/221-2350** in the U.S. or 020/8990-7159 in the U.K.; www.Scandinavia.net) has more nonstop flights to Scandinavia from more North American cities than any other airline, and more flights to and from Denmark and within Scandinavia than any other airline in the world. From Seattle and Chicago, SAS offers nonstop flights to Copenhagen daily in midsummer and almost every day in winter; from Newark, New Jersey, there are daily flights year-round to Copenhagen. SAS's agreement with United Airlines, the "Star Alliance," connects other U.S. cities (such as Dallas/Fort Worth, Denver, Houston, Los Angeles, Minneapolis/St. Paul, New York, San Francisco, and Washington, D.C.) to the three U.S. gateway cities.

SAS offers one of the lowest fares to Copenhagen from New York. With restrictions, and flying during specific off-peak seasons, round-trip tickets can cost as little as $425 for those who pay for their tickets within 2 days after booking and stay abroad between 7 and 30 days. No refunds or changes in flight dates are permitted. A similar round-trip ticket from Chicago to Copenhagen costs $565. Both tickets cost $60 more for travel on Friday,

Saturday, or Sunday. These prices can—and almost certainly will—change during the lifetime of this edition. Always confirm prices before booking your ticket.

Nonstop flights to Copenhagen from the greater New York area take about 7½ hours; from Chicago, around 8½ hours; from Seattle, 9½ hours.

FROM THE U.K.   British Airways (✆ **800/AIRWAYS,** or 08457/733-377 in the U.K.; www.ba.com) offers convenient connections through Heathrow and Gatwick to Copenhagen. The price structure (and discounted prices on hotel packages) sometimes makes a stopover in Britain less expensive than you might think. **SAS** offers five daily nonstop flights to Copenhagen from Heathrow (1¾ hr.), two daily nonstops from Glasgow (2 hr.), and three daily nonstops from Manchester (2 hr., 20 min.). Other European airlines with connections through their home countries to Copenhagen include **Icelandair** (✆ **800/223-5500** in the U.S., or 020/7874-1000 in the U.K.; www.icelandair.com), **KLM** (✆ **800/374-7747** in the U.S., or 0870/507-4074 in the U.K.; www.klm.com), and **Lufthansa** (✆ **800/645-3880** in the U.S., or 0845/773-7747 in the U.K.; www.lufthansa-usa.com). Be aware, however, that unless you make all your flight arrangements in North America before you go, you might find some of these flights prohibitively expensive.

NEW AIR TRAVEL SECURITY MEASURES
In the wake of the September 11, 2001, terrorist attacks, the airline industry began implementing sweeping security measures in airports. Expect a lengthy check-in process and extensive delays. Although regulations vary from airline to airline, you can expedite the process by taking the following steps:

- **Arrive early.** Arrive at the airport at least 2 hours before your scheduled flight.
- **Try not to drive your car to the airport.** Parking and curbside access to the terminal may be limited. Call ahead and check.
- **Don't count on curbside check-in.** Some airlines and airports have stopped curbside check-in altogether, whereas others offer it on a limited basis. For up-to-date information on specific regulations and implementations, check with the individual airline.
- **Be sure to carry plenty of documentation.** A government-issued photo ID (federal, state, or local) is now required. You may need to show this at various checkpoints. With an E-ticket, you may be required to have with you printed confirmation of purchase, and perhaps even the credit card with which you bought your ticket (see "All about E-Ticketing," below). This varies from airline to airline, so call ahead to make sure you have the proper documentation. And be sure that your ID is **up-to-date;** an expired driver's license, for example, may keep you from boarding the plane altogether.
- **Know what you can carry on— and what you can't.** Travelers in the United States are now limited to one carry-on bag, plus one personal bag (such as a purse or a briefcase). The FAA has also issued a list of newly restricted carry-on items; see the box "What You Can Carry On—and What You Can't."
- **Prepare to be searched.** Expect spot-checks. Electronic items, such as laptops or cellphones, should be readied for additional screening. Limit the metal items you wear on your person.
- **It's no joke.** When a check-in agent asks if someone other than you packed your bag, don't decide that this is the time to be funny. The agents will not hesitate to call an alarm.

Tips   What You Can Carry On—and What You Can't

The Federal Aviation Administration (FAA) has devised new restrictions on carry-on baggage, not only to expedite the screening process, but to prevent potential weapons from passing through airport security. Passengers are now limited to bringing just one carry-on bag and one personal item onto the aircraft (previous regulations allowed two carry-on bags and one personal item, like a briefcase or a purse). For more information, go to the FAA's website, www.faa.gov. The agency has released a new list of items passengers are not allowed to carry onto an aircraft.

Not permitted: knives, box cutters, corkscrews, straight razors, metal scissors, metal nail files, golf clubs, baseball bats, pool cues, hockey sticks, ski poles, ice picks.

Permitted: nail clippers, tweezers, eyelash curlers, safety razors (including disposable razors), syringes (with documented proof of medical need), walking canes, and umbrellas (must be inspected first).

The airline you fly may have additional policies on items you can and cannot carry on board. Call ahead to avoid problems.

Tips All About E-Ticketing

Only yesterday **electronic tickets (E-tickets)** were the fast and easy ticket-free alternative to paper tickets. E-tickets allowed passengers to avoid long lines at airport check-in, all the while saving the airlines money on postage and labor. With the increased security measures in airports, however, an E-ticket no longer guarantees an accelerated check-in. You often can't go straight to the boarding gate, even if you have no bags to check. You'll probably need to show your printed E-ticket receipt or confirmation of purchase, as well as a photo ID, and sometimes even the credit card with which you purchased your E-ticket. That said, buying an E-ticket is still a fast, convenient way to book a flight; instead of having to wait for a paper ticket to come through the mail, you can book your fare by phone or on the computer, and the airline will immediately confirm by fax or e-mail. In addition, airlines often offer frequent flier miles as incentive for electronic bookings.

- **No ticket, no gate access.** Only ticketed passengers will be allowed beyond the screener checkpoints, except for those people with specific medical or parental needs.

FLYING FOR LESS: TIPS ON GETTING THE BEST AIRFARE

Passengers within the same airplane cabin rarely pay the same fare. Business travelers who need to purchase tickets at the last minute, change their itinerary at a moment's notice, or get home for the weekend, pay the premium rate. Passengers who can book their ticket long in advance, who can stay over Saturday night, or who are willing to travel on a Tuesday, Wednesday, or Thursday after 7pm, will pay a fraction of the full fare. Here are a few other easy ways to save.

- **Take advantage of APEX fares.** Advance-purchase booking, or APEX, fares are often the key to getting the lowest fare. You generally must be willing to make your plans and buy your tickets as far ahead as possible: The **21-day APEX** is seconded only by the **14-day APEX**, with a stay in Denmark of 7 to 30 days. Because the number of seats allocated to APEX fares is sometimes less than 25% of plane capacity, the early bird gets the low-cost seat. There's often a surcharge for flying on a weekend, and cancellation and refund policies can be strict.

- **Watch for sales.** You'll almost never see sales during July and August or the Thanksgiving or Christmas seasons, but at other times you can get great deals. If you already hold a ticket when a sale breaks, it might pay to exchange it, even if you incur a $50 to $75 penalty charge. Note, however, that the lowest-priced fares are often nonrefundable, require advance purchase of 1 to 3 weeks and a certain length of stay, and carry penalties for changing dates of travel. Make sure you know exactly what the restrictions are before you commit.

- If your schedule is flexible, ask if you can secure a cheaper fare by **staying an extra day** or by **flying midweek.** (Many airlines won't volunteer this information.)

- **Consolidators,** also known as bucket shops, are a good place to find low fares, often below even the airlines' discounted rates. Basically, they're just big travel agents who get discounts for buying in bulk and pass some of the savings on to you. Before you pay, however, be aware that consolidator tickets are usually nonrefundable or come with stiff cancellation penalties.

- We've gotten great deals on many occasions from **Cheap Tickets** (© 800/377-1000; www.cheaptickets.com). **Council Travel** (© 800/2COUNCIL; www.counciltravel.com) and **STA Travel** (© 800/781-4040; www.sta.travel.com) cater especially to young travelers, but their bargain-basement prices are available to people of all ages. Other reliable consolidators include **Cheap Seats** (© 800/451-7200; www.cheapseatstravel.com); and **1-800/FLY-CHEAP** (www.flycheap.com).
- Join a travel club such as **Moment's Notice** (© 718/234-6295; www.moments-notice.com) or **Sears Discount Travel Club** (© 800/433-9383 or 800/255-1487; www.travelersadvantage.com), which supply unsold tickets at discounted prices. You pay an annual membership fee to get the club's hot-line number. Of course, you're limited to what's available, so you have to be flexible.
- Join **frequent-flier clubs.** It's best to accrue miles on one program, so you can rack up free flights and achieve elite status faster. But it makes sense to open as many accounts as possible, no matter how seldom you fly a particular

airline. It's free, and you'll get the best choice of seats, faster response to phone inquiries, and prompter service if your luggage is stolen, if your flight is canceled or delayed, or if you want to change your seat.
- Search the **Internet** for cheap fares—though it's still best to compare your findings with the research of a dedicated travel agent, if you're lucky enough to have one, especially when you're booking more than just a flight. Among the better-respected virtual travel agents are **Travelocity** (www.travelocity.com), **Expedia** (www.expedia.com), and **Yahoo! Travel** (http://travel.yahoo.com).

A NOTE FOR BRITISH TRAVELERS

Because regular airfares from the U.K. to Scandinavia tend to be high, savvy Brits usually call a travel agent for a "deal"—a charter flight or special promotion. These so-called deals are often available because of Scandinavia's popularity as a tourist destination. If you can't get a deal, the next-best choice is an APEX ticket. Although these tickets must be reserved in advance, they offer a discount without the usual booking restrictions. You could also inquire about a "Eurobudget ticket," which carries restrictions or length-of-stay requirements.

British newspapers typically carry lots of classified advertisements touting "slashed" fares from London to other parts of the world. One good source is *Time Out,* a magazine published in London. London's *Evening*

Tips Cancelled Plans

If your flight is cancelled, don't book a new fare at the ticket counter. Find the nearest phone and call the airline directly to reschedule. You'll be relaxing while other passengers are still standing in line.

Standard has a daily travel section, and the Sunday editions of almost all British newspapers run ads. Although competition is fierce, one recommended company that consolidates bulk ticket purchases and passes the savings on to its customers is **Trailfinders** (✆ **020/7937-5400** in London; www.trailfinder.com). It offers tickets on such carriers as SAS, British Airways, and KLM. You can fly from London's Heathrow or Gatwick airport to Copenhagen, Oslo, Stockholm, and Helsinki.

In London, many bucket shops around Victoria Station and Earl's Court offer low fares. Make sure the company you deal with is a member of the IATA, ABTA, or ATOL. These umbrella organizations will help you if anything goes wrong.

CEEFAX, a television information service carried on many home and hotel TVs, runs details of package holidays and flights to Europe and beyond. On your CEEFAX channel, you'll find a menu of listings that includes travel information.

Make sure you understand the bottom line on any special deal you purchase—ask if all surcharges, including airport taxes and other hidden costs, are indicated before you commit. Upon investigation, people often find that some of these "deals" are not as attractive as advertised. Also, make sure you understand what the penalties are if you're forced to cancel at the last minute.

BY CAR

You can easily drive to Denmark from Germany. Many people drive to Jutland from Hamburg, Bremerhaven, and Lübeck. A bridge links Jutland and the central island of Funen. In 1998 a bridge opened that goes across the Great Belt from Funen to the island of Zealand, site of the city of Copenhagen. The bridge lies near Nyborg, Denmark. Once in West Zealand, you'll still have to drive east across the island to Copenhagen.

Car-ferry service to Denmark from the United Kingdom generally leaves passengers at Esbjerg, where they must cross from Jutland to Copenhagen. From Germany, it's possible to take a car ferry from Travemünde, northeast of Lübeck, which will deposit you at Gedser, Denmark. From here, connect with E55, an express highway north to Copenhagen.

BY TRAIN

If you're in Europe, it's easy to get to Denmark by train. Copenhagen is the main rail hub between Scandinavia and the rest of Europe. For example, the London–Copenhagen train—through Ostende, Belgium, or Hook, Holland—leaves four times daily and takes 22 hours. About 10 daily express trains run from Hamburg to Copenhagen (5½ hr.). There are also intercity trains on the Merkur route from Karlsruhe, Germany, to Cologne to Hamburg to Copenhagen. The Berlin–Ostbahnhof–Copenhagen train (8½ hr.) connects with Eastern European trains. Two daily express trains make this run.

Thousands of trains run from Britain to the Continent, and at least some of them go directly across or under the Channel, through France or Belgium and Germany into Denmark. For example, a train leaves London's Victoria Station daily at 9am and arrives in Copenhagen the next day at 8:25am. Another train leaves London's Victoria Station at 8:45pm and arrives in Copenhagen the next day at 8:20pm. Both go through Dover–Ostende, or with a connection at Brussels. Once you're in Copenhagen, you can make rail connections to Norway, Finland, and Sweden. Because of the time and distances involved, many passengers rent a couchette (sleeping berth), which costs around £18 per person. Designed like padded benches stacked bunk-style, they're usually clustered six to a compartment.

RAIL PASSES FOR NORTH AMERICAN TRAVELERS

If you plan to travel extensively on European railroads, get a copy of the latest edition of the *Thomas Cook European Timetable of Railroads.* It's available exclusively in North America from **Forsyth Travel Library,** 44 S. Broadway, White Plains, NY 10604 (© **800/FORSYTH;** www.forsyth. com), at a cost of $28, plus $4.95 priority shipping in the U.S. or $6.95 airmail shipping to Canada.

EURAILPASS If you plan to travel extensively in Europe, the **Eurailpass** may be a good bet. It's valid for first-class rail travel in 17 European countries. With one ticket, you travel whenever and wherever you please; more than 160,000 rail kilometers (100,000 miles) are at your disposal. The pass is sold only in North America. A Eurailpass good for 15 days costs $588, a pass for 21 days is $762, a 1-month pass costs $946, a 2-month pass is $1,338, and a 3-month pass goes for $1,654. Children under 4 travel free if they don't occupy a seat; all children under 12 who take up a seat are charged half price. If you're under 26, you can buy a **Eurail Youthpass,** which entitles you to unlimited second-class travel for 15 days ($414), 21 days ($534), 1 month ($664), 2 months ($938), or 3 months ($1,160). Travelers considering a 15-day or 1-month pass should estimate rail distance before deciding whether a pass is worthwhile. To take full advantage of the tickets for 15 days or a month, you'd have to spend a great deal of time on the train. Eurailpass holders are entitled to substantial discounts on certain buses and ferries as well. Travel agents in all towns and railway agents in such major cities as New York, Montréal, and Los Angeles sell all of these tickets.

For information on Eurailpasses, and other European train info, call RailEurope at © **800/438-7245,** or visit them on the Web at **www.raileurope. com.**

Eurail Saverpass offers 15% discounts to groups of three or more people traveling together between April and September, or two people traveling together between October and March. The price of a Saverpass, valid all over Europe for first class only, is $498 for 15 days, $648 for 21 days, $804 for 1 month, $1,138 for 2 months, and $1,408 for 3 months. Even more freedom is offered by the **Saver Flexipass,** which is similar to the Eurail Saverpass, except that you are not confined to consecutive-day travel. For travel over any 10 days within 2 months, the fare is $592; for any 15 days over 2 months, $778.

Eurail Flexipass allows even greater flexibility. It's valid in first class and offers the same privileges as the Eurailpass. However, it provides a number of individual travel days over a much longer period of consecutive days. Using this pass makes it possible to stay longer in one city and not lose a single day of travel. There are two Flexipasses: 10 days of travel within 2 months for $694, and 15 days of travel within 2 months for $914.

With many of the same qualifications and restrictions as the Eurail Flexipass, the **Eurail Youth Flexipass** is sold only to travelers under age 25. It allows 10 days of travel within 2 months for $488 and 15 days of travel within 2 months for $642.

SCANRAIL PASS If your visit to Europe will be primarily in Scandinavia, the Scanrail pass may be better and cheaper than the Eurailpass. This pass allows its owner a designated number of days of free rail travel within a larger time block. (Presumably, this allows for days devoted to sightseeing scattered among days of rail transfers between cities or sights of interest.) You can choose a total of any 5 days of unlimited rail travel during a 15-day period, 10 days of rail travel within a 1-month period, or 1 month of unlimited rail travel. The pass, which is valid on all lines of the state railways of Denmark, Finland, Norway, and Sweden, offers discounts or free travel on some (but not all) of the region's ferry lines as well. The pass can be purchased only in North America. It's available from any office of **RailEurope** (*C* **800/848-7245** in the U.S., 800/361-RAIL in Canada) or from **ScanAm World Tours,** 108 N. Main St., Cranbury, NJ 08512 (*C* **800/545-2204;** www.scandinavian travel.com).

Depending on whether you choose first- or second-class rail transport, 5 days out of 2 months ranges from $214 to $290, 10 days out of 2 months ranges from $288 to $388, and 21 consecutive days of unlimited travel ranges from $332 to $448. Seniors get an 11% discount; students a 25% discount.

RAIL PASSES FOR BRITISH TRAVELERS
If you plan to do a lot of exploring, you may prefer one of the three rail passes designed for unlimited train travel within a designated region during a predetermined number of days. These passes are sold in Britain and several other European countries.

An **InterRail Pass** is available to passengers of any nationality, with some restrictions—they must be under age 26 and able to prove residency in a European or North African country (Morocco, Algeria, and Tunisia) for at least 6 months before buying the pass. It allows unlimited travel through Europe, except Albania and the republics of the former Soviet Union. Prices are complicated and vary depending on the countries you want to include. For pricing purposes, Europe is divided into eight zones; the

cost depends on the number of zones you include. The most expensive option (£249) allows 1 month of unlimited travel in all eight zones and is known to BritRail staff as a "global." The least expensive option (£119) allows 12 days of travel within only one zone.

Passengers age 25 and older can buy an **InterRail 26-Plus Pass** which, unfortunately, is severely limited geographically. Many countries—including France, Belgium, Switzerland, Spain, Portugal, and Italy—do not honor this pass. It is, however, accepted for travel throughout Denmark, Finland, Norway, and Sweden. Second-class travel with the pass costs £169 for 12 days or £209 for 22 days. Passengers must meet the same residency requirements that apply to the InterRail Pass (described above).

For information on buying individual rail tickets or any of the just-mentioned passes, contact **National Rail Inquiries,** Victoria Station, London (*C* **08705/848-848** or 0845/748-4950). Tickets and passes also are available at any of the larger railway stations as well as selected travel agencies throughout Britain and the rest of Europe.

BY SHIP & FERRY
It's easy to travel by water from several ports to Denmark. Liners carrying cars and passengers operate from England, Germany, Poland, Norway, and Sweden. Check with your travel agent about these cruises.

FROM BRITAIN DFDS Seaways (*C* **800/533-3755** in the U.S., or 019/129-362-62) runs vessels year-round between Harwich, England, and Esbjerg in West Jutland. The crossing takes 16 to 20 hours. The same line also sails from Newcastle-upon-Tyne to Esbjerg, but only in the summer, as part of a 22-hour passage. Overnight cabins and space for cars are available on both routes.

FROM NORWAY & SWEDEN
The **Norwegian Coastal Boyage/ Bergen Line Services** (© **800/323-7436** in the U.S., or 212/319-1300; www.coastalvoyage.com) operates vessels from Oslo to Hirtshals in northern Jutland.

Stena Line runs popular sea links from Oslo to Frederikshavn in northern Jutland (11½ hr.), and from Gothenburg, Sweden, to Frederikshavn (3 hr.). For information, schedules, and fares, contact **Stena Line**

UK, Ltd., Charter House Park St., Ashford, Kent TN24 8EX (© **08705/ 707-070;** www.stenaline.co.uk). For 24-hour updates on sailing, call © **08705/755755.**

FROM GERMANY From the Baltic coast, ferries operate between Kiel and Bagenkop on the Danish island of Langeland. Reserve tickets at **Langeland–Kiel Touristik,** Oslokai 3, Kiel (© **0431/97415-0**).

10 Package Deals & Special-Interest Vacations

PACKAGE TOURS

For travelers who feel more comfortable if everything is prearranged—hotels, transportation, sightseeing excursions, luggage handling, tips, taxes, and even meals—a package tour is the obvious choice, and it may even help you save money.

One of the best tour operators to Denmark, Sweden, and Norway is **Bennett Tours,** 342 Madison Ave., New York, NY 10073 (© **800/221-2420** in the U.S., or 212/697-1092). It offers land packages with experienced guides and a wide range of prices.

Other reliable tour operators include **Olson Travelworld,** 1145 Clark St., Stevens Point, WI 54481 (© **800/826-4026**), and **Scantours, Inc.,** 3439 Wade St., Los Angeles, CA 90006 (© **800/223-7226** or 310/ 636-4656; www.scantours.com).

BUS TOURS Scanam World Tours (© **800/545-2204** or 609/ 655-1600; www.scandinaviantravel. com) offers a tour through the "Heart of Fairy Tale Denmark." You can choose a 3- or 6-day trip through Hans Christian Andersen country, including a visit to Odense (his birthplace) and an excursion to Legoland. Tours begin at $410 per person.

SELF-DRIVE TOURS Several companies offer self-drive tours, which usually include accommodations, rental cars, and customized itineraries. **Scantours, Inc.** (© **800/223-7226;** www.scantours.com) features the 5-day "A Taste of Danish Castles," which is available year-round. Prices begin at $950 per person. The company also sponsors a tour of Danish inns. The 4-day self-drive tour includes accommodations, breakfast, car rental, and an itinerary. Prices start at $290 per person.

BICYCLE TOURS An excellent way to explore the flat, rolling Danish countryside is on a bicycle. Numerous organizations (including Scantours, Inc., and Scanam Tours) sponsor bike tours through various regions of the country. You can choose one that covers the castles, beaches, and fjords of northern Denmark; the southern Funen islands; the beaches and marshland of western Jutland; or the lake country in eastern Jutland. **Blue Marble Travel** (© **800/258-8689;** www. bluemarble.org) offers 7-day excursions to Hans Christian Andersen country and several small islands in the Baltic for $1,595 per person. **Dansk Cyklist Forbund,** Rømersgade 7, DK-1362 København K (© **33-32-31-21**), can provide the latest information on cycling tours in Denmark.

ADVENTURE TRAVEL OPERATORS

In North America, a few companies offer adventure trips to Scandinavia (see chapter 7, "Planning Your Trip to Norway," chapter 12, "Planning Your Trip to Sweden," and chapter 19, "Planning Your Trip to Finland," for specific country information). **Crossing Latitudes,** 420 W. Koch St., Bozeman, MT 59715 (© **800/572-8747** or 406/585-5356; www.crossinglatitudes. com), offers sea kayaking and backpacking expeditions throughout the region; and **Blue Marble Travel,** 222A Race St., Philadelphia, PA 19106 (© **800/258-8689** or 215/923-3788; www.bluemarble.org), features reasonably priced biking and hiking trips in Denmark and Norway.

IN THE U.K.

The oldest travel agency in Britain, **Cox & Kings,** Gordon House 10, Greencoat Place, London SW1P 1PH (© **020/7873-5000;** www.coxand kings.co.uk), was established in 1758. Today the company specializes in unusual, if pricey, holidays. Its offerings in Scandinavia include cruises through the spectacular fjords and waterways, bus and rail tours through sites of historic and aesthetic interest, and visits to the region's best-known handicraft centers, Viking burial sites, and historic churches. The company's staff is noted for its focus on tours of ecological and environmental interest.

To cycle through the splendors of Scandinavia, you can join Britain's oldest and largest association of bicycle riders, the **Cyclists' Touring Club,** Cotterell House, 69 Meadrow, Godalming, Surrey GU7 3HS (© **01483/417-217;** www.ctc.org. uk). Founded in 1878, it charges £10 a year for membership, which includes information, maps, a subscription to a newsletter packed with practical information and morale boosters, plus recommended cycling routes through virtually every country in Europe. The organization's information bank on scenic routes through Scandinavia is especially comprehensive. Membership can be arranged over the phone with a credit card (such as Master-Card, Visa, Access, or Barclaycard).

LEARNING VACATIONS

Danish Cultural Institute (Det Danske Kultur Institutu), Kultorvet 2, DK-1175 København (© **33-13-54-48;** fax 33-15-10-91; www.dan kultur.dk), offers summer seminars in English, including a course in Danish culture. Credit programs are available, but many courses are geared toward professional groups from abroad. An especially interesting course for those with some knowledge of Danish is "Danmark, Danskerne, Dansk," which includes language instruction.

An international series of programs for persons over 50 who are interested in combining travel and learning is offered by **Interhostel,** developed by the University of New Hampshire. Each program lasts 2 weeks, is led by a university faculty or staff member, and is arranged in conjunction with a host college, university, or cultural institution. Participants may stay longer if they want. Interhostel offers programs consisting of cultural and intellectual activities, with field trips to museums and other centers of interest. For information, contact the University of New Hampshire, Division of Continuing Education, 6 Garrison Ave., Durham, NH 03824 (© **800/733-9753** or 603/862-1147; www.learn. unh.edu).

Another good source of information about courses in Denmark is the **American Institute for Foreign Study (AIFS),** River Plaza, 9 W. Broad St., Stamford, CT 06902 (© **800/727-2437** or 203/399-5000; www.aifs.org). This organization can set up transportation and arrange for summer courses, with bed and board included.

The biggest organization dealing with higher education in Europe is the **Institute of International Education (IIE),** 809 United Nations Plaza, New York, NY 10017 (© **800/445-0443** or 212/883-8200; www.iie.org). A few of its booklets are free; for $47, plus $6 for postage, you can buy the more definitive *Vacation Study Abroad.* The Information Center in New York is open to the public Tuesday through Thursday from 11am to 4pm. The institute is closed on major holidays.

One recommended clearinghouse for academic programs throughout the world is the **National Registration Center for Study Abroad (NRCSA),** 823 N. 2nd St., P.O. Box 1393, Milwaukee, WI 53203 (© **414/278-0631;** www.nrcsa.com). The organization maintains language study programs throughout Europe.

PEOPLE TO PEOPLE

Established in 1971, **Friends Overseas** matches American visitors and Scandinavians with similar interests and backgrounds. Names and addresses are given to each applicant, and letters must be written before the visitors depart; Scandinavians may not meet visitors unless they have ample time to plan. For more information, write to Friends Overseas, 68-04 Dartmouth St., Forest Hills, NY 11375 (© **718/544-5660** after 5pm; www.nordbalt.com). Send a self-addressed, stamped business-size envelope, and include your age, occupation or occupational goals, approximate dates of your visit, and names of your traveling companions. The fee is $25.

11 Getting Around

BY PLANE

The best way to get around Scandinavia is to take advantage of air passes that apply to the whole region. If you're traveling extensively in Europe, special European passes are available.

SAS'S VISIT SCANDINAVIA FARE

The vast distances encourage air travel between Scandinavia's far-flung points. One of the most worthwhile promotions is SAS's **Visit Scandinavia Pass.** Available only to travelers who fly SAS across the Atlantic, it includes up to six coupons, each of which is valid for any SAS flight within or between Denmark, Norway, and Sweden. Each coupon costs $75, a price that's especially appealing when you consider that an economy-class ticket between Stockholm and Copenhagen can cost as much as $250 each way. The pass is especially valuable if you plan to travel to the far northern frontiers of Sweden or Norway; in that case, the savings over the price of a regular economy-class ticket can be

substantial. For information on buying the pass, call **SAS** (© **800/221-2350**).

WITHIN DENMARK   For those in a hurry, **SAS** (© **70-10-20-00** in Copenhagen) operates daily service between Copenhagen and points on Jutland's mainland. From Copenhagen it takes about 40 minutes to fly to Aalborg, 35 minutes to Århus, and 30 minutes to Odense's Beldringe Airport.

Fares to other Danish cities are sometimes included in a transatlantic ticket at no extra charge, as long as the additional cities are specified when the ticket is written.

BY TRAIN

Flat, low-lying Denmark, with its hundreds of bridges and absence of mountains, has a large network of railway lines that connect virtually every hamlet with the largest city, Copenhagen. For **information, schedules, and fares** anywhere in Denmark, call © **70-13-14-15.** Waiting times for a live person on this telephone line range from long to very long.

An alternative way to gather schedules and prices, even reserving space on specific trains, involves clicking onto the website maintained by the Danish National Railways (www.dsb. dk). A word you're likely to see and hear frequently is *Lyntog* ("Express Trains"), which are the fastest trains presently operational in Denmark. Be warned in advance that the most crowded times on Danish trains are Fridays, Sundays, and national holidays, so plan your reservations accordingly.

On any train within Denmark, children between the ages of 12 and 15 are charged half price if they're accompanied by an adult, and up to two children under 12 can travel for free with any adult on any train in Denmark. Seniors (age 65 or older) receive a discount of 25% for travel on Fridays, Sundays, and holidays, and 50% every other day of the week. No identification is needed when you buy your ticket, but the conductor who checks your ticket might ask for proof of age.

The Danish government offers dozens of discounts on the country's rail networks—depending on the type of traveler, days or hours traveled, and destination. Because discounts change often, it's always best to ask for a discount based on your age and the number of days (or hours) you intend to travel.

BY BUS

By far the best way to visit rural Denmark is by car, but if you want or need to travel by bus, be aware that you'll probably get your bus at the railway station. (In much of Scandinavia, buses take passengers to destinations not served by the train; therefore, the bus route often originates at the railway station.) The arrival of trains and departure of buses are usually closely timed.

For seniors (age 65 and over), round-trip bus tickets are sometimes offered at one-way prices (excluding Sat, Sun, and peak travel periods around Christmas and Easter). Most discounts are granted only to seniors who are traveling beyond the city limits of their point of origin.

BY CAR

RENTALS Avis, Budget, and Hertz offer well-serviced, well-maintained fleets of cars. You may have to reserve and pay for your rental car in advance (usually 2 weeks, but occasionally as little as 48 hr.) to get the lowest rates. Unfortunately, if your trip is canceled or your arrival date changes, you might have to fill out a lot of forms to arrange a refund. All three companies may charge slightly higher rates to clients who reserve less than 48 hours in advance and pay at pickup. The highest rates are charged to walk-in customers who arrange their rentals after they arrive in Denmark.

Before you rent, you should know that the Danish government imposes a whopping 25% tax on all car rentals. Agencies that encourage prepaid rates almost never collect this tax in advance—instead, it's imposed as part of a separate transaction when you pick up the car. Furthermore, any car retrieved at a Danish airport is subject to a one-time supplemental tax of 190DKK ($25); you might prefer to pick up your car at a downtown location. Membership in certain travel clubs or organizations (such as AAA or AARP) might qualify you for a modest discount.

Note: The following rates are for a 1-week rental of a Volkswagen Polo (the smallest car available). They include unlimited mileage and are subject to change.

Avis (© **800/331-1084** in the U.S.; www.avis.com) maintains two offices in Copenhagen, one at the arrivals hall of the airport and another at Kampmannsgade 1 (© **33-15-22-99**). The rate is $312—if you pay 2 weeks before your departure. "Walk-in" customers who don't reserve from North America pay double that rate.

Budget (© **800/472-3325** in the U.S.; www.budget.com) has about 14 rental locations in Denmark. That's fewer than Avis or Hertz, but they tend to be in cities and regions most frequented by foreign visitors. Budget's rate is $317 if you pay in North America. The price is considerably higher for walk-in customers. Budget has a large branch at the Copenhagen airport (© **32-52-39-00**).

Hertz (© **800/654-3001** in the U.S.; www.hertz.com) charges a prepaid rate of $302 and about $306 for those who have not prepaid. Hertz's office in central Copenhagen is at Ved Vesterport 3 (© **33-17-90-20**); another office is at the airport (© **32-50-93-00**).

Also consider using a small company. **Kemwel** (© **800/678-0678** in the U.S.; www.kemwel.com) is the North American representative for two Denmark-based car companies, Van Wijk and Hertz. It may be able to offer attractive rental prices to North Americans who pay in full at least 10 days before their departure. Seniors and members of AAA get a 5% discount.

12 Planning Your Trip Online

Researching and booking your trip online can save time and money. Then again, it may not. It is simply not true that you always get the best deal online. Most booking engines do not include schedules and prices for budget airlines, and from time to time you'll get a better last-minute price by calling the airline directly, so it's best to call the airline to see if you can do better before booking online.

On the plus side, Internet users today can tap into the same travel-planning databases that were once accessible only to travel agents—and do it at the same speed. Sites such as **Frommers.com, Travelocity.com, Expedia.com,** and **Orbitz.com** allow consumers to comparison shop for airfares, search for special bargains, book flights, and reserve hotel rooms and rental cars.

But don't fire your travel agent just yet. Though online booking sites offer tips and hard data to help you bargain-shop, they cannot endow you with the hard-earned experience that makes a seasoned, reliable travel agent an invaluable resource, even in the Internet age. And for consumers with a complex itinerary, a trusty travel agent is still the best way to arrange the most direct flights to and from the best airports.

Some sites, such as Expedia.com, will send you **e-mail notification** when a cheap fare becomes available to your favorite destination. Some will also tell you when fares to a particular destination are lowest.

TRAVEL-PLANNING & BOOKING SITES

Keep in mind that because several airlines are no longer willing to pay commissions on tickets sold by online travel agencies, these agencies may either add a $10 surcharge to your bill if you book on that carrier—or neglect to offer those carriers' schedules.

The list of sites below is selective, not comprehensive. Some sites will have evolved or disappeared by the time you read this.

Travelocity (www.travelocity.com or www.frommers.travelocity.com) and **Expedia** (www.expedia.com) are among the most popular, offering an excellent range of options. Travelers search by destination, dates, and cost.

Qixo (www.qixo.com) is another search engine that allows you to search for flights and accommodations from some 20 airline and travel-planning sites (such as Travelocity) at once. Qixo sorts results by price.

SMART E-SHOPPING

Savvy travelers arm themselves with good information. Here are a few tips to help you navigate the Internet successfully and safely.

- **Know when sales start.** Last-minute deals may vanish in minutes. If you have a favorite booking site or airline, find out when last-minute deals are released to the public. (For example, Southwest's specials are posted every Tues at 12:01am Central Standard Time).
- **Shop around.** Compare results from different sites and airlines—and against a travel agent's best fare. If possible, try range of times and alternate airports before making a purchase.
- **Follow the rules of the trade.** Book in advance, and choose an off-peak time and date if possible. Some sites will tell you when fares to a particular destination tend to be cheapest.
- **Stay secure.** Book only through secure sites (some airline sites are not secure). Look for a key icon (Netscape) or a padlock (Internet Explorer) at the bottom of your Web browser before you enter credit-card information or other personal data.
- **Avoid online auctions.** Sites that auction airline tickets and frequent-flier miles are the number-one perpetrators of Internet fraud, according to the National Consumers League.
- **Maintain a paper trail.** If you book an E-ticket, print out a confirmation or write down your confirmation number, and keep it safe

and accessible—or your trip could be a virtual one!

ONLINE TRAVELER'S TOOLBOX

Veteran travelers usually carry some essential items to make their trips easier. Following is a selection of online tools to bookmark and use.

- **Visa ATM Locator** (www.visa.com) or **MasterCard ATM Locator** (www.mastercard.com). Find ATMs in hundreds of cities in the U.S. and around the world.
- **Foreign Languages for Travelers** (www.travlang.com). Learn basic terms in more than 70 languages and click on any underlined phrase to hear what it sounds like. *Note:* Free audio software and speakers are required.
- **Intellicast** (www.intellicast.com). Weather forecasts for all 50 states and cities around the world. *Note:* Temperatures are in Celsius for many international destinations.
- **Mapquest** (www.mapquest.com). The best of the mapping sites, Mapquest lets you choose a specific address or destination, and in seconds, it returns a map and detailed directions.
- **Cybercafes.com** (www.cybercafes.com) or **Net Café Guide** (www.netcafeguide.com). Locate Internet cafe locations around the globe. Catch up on your e-mail and log onto the Web for a few dollars per hour.
- **Universal Currency Converter** (www.xe.com). See what your dollar or pound is worth in more than 100 countries.
- **U.S. State Department Travel Warnings** (www.travel.state.gov). Reports on places where health concerns or unrest may threaten U.S. travelers and lists the locations of U.S. embassies around the world.

13 Recommended Books

HISTORY & PHILOSOPHY *A Kierkegaard Anthology,* edited by Robert Bretall (Princeton University Press), explores the work of the Copenhagen-born philosopher who developed an almost-pathological sense of involvement in theology. A representative selection of some of his more significant works is included.

Copenhagen, A Historical Guide, by Torben Ejlersen (published by Høst & Søn in Denmark, and available at most bookstores there), an 88-page guide, takes you on a brief tour of the city that began as a ferry-landing and became one of the most important capitals of Europe.

Of Danish Ways, written by two Danish-Americans, Ingeborg S. MacHiffic and Margaret A. Nielsen (Harper & Row, 1984), is a delightful account of a land and its people, and has a little bit of everything: history, social consciousness, customs, food, handicrafts, art, music, and theater.

BIOGRAPHY & LITERATURE *Andersen's Fairy Tales,* by H. C. Andersen (New American Library), and *The Complete Hans Christian Andersen Fairy Tales* (Crown), include all his most important works, such as *The Little Mermaid, The Tinderbox,* and *The Princess and the Pea.*

Danish Literature: A Short Critical Guide, by Paul Borum (Nordic Books), is a well-written review that explores Danish literature from the Middle Ages to the 1970s.

Out of Africa (Modern Library), *Letters from Africa* (University of Chicago Press), *Winter's Tales* (Penguin), and *Seven Gothic Tales* (Random House) are all by Karen Blixen (Isak Dinesen), who gained renewed fame with the release of the 1985 film *Out of Africa,* with Meryl Streep and Robert Redford. One of the major authors of the 20th century, twice nominated for the Nobel Prize, Blixen describes her world in these almost-flawless stories. *Seven Gothic Tales* is her masterpiece.

Isak Dinesen, by Judith Thurman (St. Martin's Press), is the definitive biography of the Danish writer who has been called "witch, sybil, lion hunter, coffee planter, aristocrat, and despot, a paradox in herself and a creator of paradoxes." The story chronicles an amazing life from an unhappy childhood in Denmark to marriage to Baron Blixen to immigration to Kenya to her passionate love affair with Denys Finch Hatton.

SUGGESTED ITINERARIES

If You Have 1 Week

Days 1–3 Spend your first 3 days in Copenhagen. After a day recovering from the flight, have dinner at the Tivoli Gardens (in the summer) or Nyhavn (in the winter). If you're arriving from nearby and will not have jet-lag on your first day, explore Copenhagen by walking along Stroget—the world's largest pedestrian street—then visiting Kongens Nytorv (King's New Square). Spend the morning of the second day taking one of our walking tours (see chapter 4, "Exploring Copenhagen"); then (in the summer) spend the afternoon wandering through the Tivoli and listening to the free music. Devote Day 3 to more serious sightseeing, including visits to Christiansborg Palace and the Ny Carlsberg Glyptotek.

Day 4 Leave Copenhagen and head north, stopping over at the modern art museum, Louisiana, before heading to Helsingør, site of Kronborg Castle of *Hamlet* fame. Spend the night in Helsingør, or return to Copenhagen.

Day 5 Journey to Odense on the island of Funen, birthplace of Hans

Christian Andersen. Spend the rest of the day and evening exploring its many attractions.

Day 6   Stop in Roskilde to see its cathedral and the Viking Ship Museum. Return to Copenhagen and spend the night.

Day 7   Try another walking tour, and schedule interior visits to Rosenborg Castle and, if you have time, the National Museum. Return to the Tivoli for a farewell drink.

If You Have 2 Weeks

Day 1   Recover from jet lag and have dinner at the Tivoli (in the summer) or at Scala, a restaurant complex across from the Tivoli (in the off season).

Day 2   In the morning, take our first walking tour (see chapter 4). Spend the afternoon wandering around the Tivoli Gardens (in the summer).

Day 3   Take another walking tour and visit Christiansborg Palace and the Ny Carlsberg Glyptotek.

Day 4   Head north from Copenhagen. Visit the modern art museum, Louisiana, and have lunch at Helsingør, site of Kronborg Castle of *Hamlet* fame. Spend the night in Helsingør.

Day 5   Explore North Zealand, with visits to the royal palace at Fredensborg and the 17th-century Frederiksborg Castle at Hillerød. Spend the night in Helsingør.

Day 6   Return to Copenhagen and visit Rosenborg Castle and the National Museum.

Day 7   In Copenhagen, explore the other attractions of Zealand, journeying outside the capital to the open-air museum, Frilandsmuseet. Head to Roskilde for lunch, and visit the cathedral, the Viking Ship Museum, and the Iron Age Village at Lejre.

Day 8   Head south from Copenhagen to explore South Zealand. Visit the old market town of Køge, Vallø Castle, and Selso Slot. Spend the night in a typical inn on Zealand.

Day 9   Go west, crossing mid-Zealand. At Korsør, cross the bridge to Nyborg. Visit Nyborg Castle before driving to Odense to explore the city of Hans Christian Andersen. Stop overnight in Odense.

Day 10   Spend time exploring more of Odense, and then visit the Viking ship at Ladby and Egeskov Castle, outside Odense.

Day 11   Drive south from Odense to Svendborg. Explore the nearby islands of Thurø and Tåsinge.

Day 12   From Svendborg, board a ferry (make a reservation) and head for the island of Ærø. Spend the night in the capital, Ærøskøbing, or at an island inn.

Day 13   Leave Ærø and return to Svendborg by ferry. Drive north toward Odense along Route 9 until you connect with E20 west, the highway into Jutland. In Jutland, take Route 32 at the junction with E20 to Ribe. Spend the night in Ribe.

Day 14   Leave Ribe in the morning and drive to Silkeborg to view Sky Mountain. Ride on a paddlewheel steamer on the Silkeborg Lakes. Visit the Silkeborg Museum. From Silkeborg, drive to Århus, where you can explore the Old Town. Have fun at Århus's Tivoli amusement park. Spend the night.

FAST FACTS: Denmark

Area Code The country code for Denmark is **45.** It precedes any call made to Denmark from another country. There are no city area codes. Every telephone number has 8 digits.

Business Hours Most **banks** are open Monday through Friday from 9:30am to 4pm (Thurs to 6pm), but outside Copenhagen, banking hours vary. **Stores** are generally open Monday through Thursday from 9am to 5:30pm, Friday from 9am to 7 or 8pm, and Saturday from noon to 2pm; most are closed Sunday.

Cameras & Film Film is so expensive that we suggest you bring what you'll need. Processing is also expensive, so wait until you're home. There are no special restrictions on taking photographs, except in certain museums (signs are generally posted). When in doubt, and in the Christiania area of Copenhagen, ask first.

Customs Nearly all items that can reasonably be viewed as "personal" are allowed in duty-free. Tobacco is limited. You can bring in 250 cigarettes or 250 grams of tobacco. You can also bring in 1 liter (a standard bottle) of spirits or 2 liters of strong wine, depending on whether you're coming into Denmark from an EU or non-EU country. There are no restrictions on the importation of currency. However, nonresidents cannot take out more Danish kroner than they brought in, unless they can prove they obtained it by converting foreign currency.

Upon leaving Denmark, U.S. citizens who have been outside their home country for 48 hours or more are allowed to take home $800 worth of merchandise duty -free—if they have claimed no similar exemption within the past 30 days. If you make purchases in Denmark, keep your receipts.

Doctors Most areas have doctors on duty 24 hours a day on Saturdays, Sundays, and holidays; weekday emergency hours are from 4pm to 7:30am. Every doctor speaks English.

Drug Laws Penalties for the possession, use, purchase, sale, or manufacturing of drugs are severe. The quantity of the controlled substance is more important than the type of substance. Danish police are particularly strict with cases involving the sale of drugs to children.

Drugstores They're known as *apoteker* in Danish and are open Monday through Thursday from 9am to 5:30pm, Friday from 9am to 7pm, and Saturday from 9am to 1pm.

Electricity Voltage is generally 220 volts AC, 50 to 60 cycles. In many camping sites, 110-volt power plugs are also available. Adapters and transformers may be purchased in Denmark. It's always best to check at your hotel desk before using an electrical outlet.

Embassies All embassies are in Copenhagen. The embassy of the **United States** is at Dag Hammärskjölds Allé 24, DK-2100 København (© 35-55-31-44). Other embassies are the **United Kingdom,** Kastelsvej 40, DK-2100 København (© 35-44-52-00); **Canada,** Kristen Berniskows Gade 1, DK-1105 København (© 33-48-32-00); **Australia,** Dampfaergeveg 26, DK-2100

København (𝄢 70-26-36-76); and **Ireland,** Østbanegade 21 (𝄢 35-42-32-33).

Emergencies Dial 𝄢 **112** for the fire department, the police, or an ambulance, or to report a sea or an air accident. Emergency calls from public telephone kiosks are free (no coins needed).

Holidays See "When to Go," earlier in this chapter.

Language Danish is the national tongue. English is commonly spoken, especially among young people. You should have few, if any, language barriers. The best phrase book is *Danish for Travellers* (Berlitz).

Liquor Laws To consume alcohol in Danish bars, restaurants, or cafes, customers must be 18 or older. There are no restrictions on children under 18 who drink at home or, for example, from a bottle in a public park. Danish police tend to be lenient unless drinkers become raucous or uncontrollable. There is no leniency, however, in the matter of driving while intoxicated. It's illegal to drive with a blood-alcohol level of 0.8 or more, which can be produced by two drinks. If the level is 1.5, motorists pay a serious fine. If it's more than 1.5, drivers can lose their license. If the level is 2.0 or more (usually produced by six or seven drinks), a prison term of at least 14 days might follow. Package stores in Denmark are closed on Sunday.

Mail Most post offices are open Monday through Friday from 9 or 10am to 5 or 6pm and Saturday from 9am to noon; they're closed Sunday. All mail to North America is sent airmail without extra charge. The cost for mail weighing 20 grams (.175 oz.) is 5.50DKK (70¢). Mailboxes are painted red and display the embossed crown and trumpet of the Danish Postal Society.

Maps The best map for touring Denmark is part of the series published by Hallwag. It's for sale at all major bookstores in Copenhagen, including the most centrally located one, **Boghallen,** Rådhuspladsen 37 (𝄢 **33-11-85-11**), in the Town Hall Square.

Newspapers & Magazines English-language newspapers are sold at all major news kiosks in Copenhagen, but are much harder to find in the provinces. London papers are flown in for early-morning delivery, but you may find the *International Herald Tribune* or *USA Today* more interesting. Pick up a copy of *Copenhagen This Week,* printed in English, which contains useful information.

Pharmacies See "Drugstores," above.

Photographic Needs See "Cameras & Film," above.

Police Dial 𝄢 **112** for police assistance.

Radio & TV No English-language radio or TV stations broadcast from Denmark. Only radios and TVs with satellite reception can receive signals from countries such as Britain. News programs in English are broadcast Monday through Saturday at 8:30am on Radio Denmark, 93.85 MHz. Radio 1 (90.8 MHz VHF) features news and classical music. Channels 2 and 3 (96.5/93.9 MHz) include some entertainment, broadcast light news items, and offer light music. Most TV stations transmit from 7:30 to

11:30pm. Most films (many of which are American) are shown in their original languages, with Danish subtitles.

Restrooms All big plazas, such as Town Hall Square in Copenhagen, have public lavatories. In small towns and villages, head for the marketplace. Hygienic standards are usually adequate. Sometimes men and women patronize the same restrooms (signs read TOILETTER or WC). Otherwise, men's rooms are marked HERRER or H, and women's rooms are marked DAMER or D.

Safety Denmark is one of the safest European countries for travelers. Copenhagen, the major population center, naturally experiences the most crime. Muggings have been reported in the vicinity of the railway station, especially late at night, but crimes of extreme violence are exceedingly rare. Exercise the usual precautions you would when traveling anywhere.

Taxes The 25% VAT (value-added tax) on goods and services is known in Denmark as *moms* (pronounced "mumps"). Special tax-free exports are possible, and many stores will mail goods home to you, circumventing *moms*. If you want to take your purchases with you, look for shops displaying Danish tax-free shopping notices. Such shops offer tourists' tax refunds for personal export. This refund applies to purchases of at least 300DKK ($39) for U.S. and Canadian visitors. Your tax-free invoice must be stamped by Danish Customs when you leave the country. You can receive your refund at Copenhagen's Kastrup International Airport when you depart. If you go by land or sea, you can receive your refund by mail. Mail requests for refunds to Danish Tax-Free Shopping A/S, H. J. Holstvej 5A, DK-2605 Brøndby, Denmark. You'll be reimbursed by check, cash, or credit- or charge-card credit in the currency you want.

For the refund to apply, the 300DKK must be spent in one store, but not necessarily at the same time. Some major department stores allow purchases to be made over several days or even weeks, at the end of which receipts will be tallied. Service and handling fees are deducted from the total, so actual refunds come to about 18%. Information on this program is available from the Danish Tourist Board (see "Visitor Information," above).

A 25% *moms* is included in hotel and restaurant bills, service charges, entrance fees, and repair bills for foreign-registered cars. No refunds are possible on these items.

Telephone The country code for Denmark is **45.** It should precede any call made to Denmark from another country.

Danish phones are fully automatic. Dial the 8-digit number; there are no city area codes. Don't insert any coins until your party answers. At public telephone booths, use two 50-øre coins or a 1-krone or 5-krone coin only. You can make more than one call on the same payment if your time hasn't run out. Remember that it can be expensive to telephone from your hotel room. Emergency calls are free.

Time Denmark operates on Central European Time—1 hour ahead of Greenwich Mean Time and 6 hours ahead of Eastern Standard Time.

Daylight savings time is observed from the end of March to the end of September.

Tipping Tips are seldom expected, but when they are, you should give only 1 or 2DKK. Porters charge fixed prices, and tipping is not customary for hairdressers or barbers. Service is built into the system, and hotels, restaurants, and even taxis include a 15% service charge in their rates. Because of the service charge, plus the 25% *moms,* you'll probably have to pay an additional 40% for some services!

Consider tipping only for special services—some Danes would feel insulted if you offered them a tip.

Water Tap water is safe to drink throughout Denmark.

3

Introducing Copenhagen

Copenhagen, the capital of Denmark, got its name from the word *køben-havn,* or "merchants' harbor." It grew in size and importance because of its position on the Øresund (the Sound), the body of water between Denmark and Sweden that guards the entrance to the Baltic.

In the summer of 2000 the Øresund Bridge was officially opened, linking Sweden and Denmark physically for the first time ever. Today there's a 16km (10-mile) motor and railway link between Zealand (the eastern part of Denmark) and Skån, the southern part of Sweden. If you'd like to tie in a visit to Copenhagen with the châteaux country of Sweden, it is as easy as driving across the bridge.

From its humble beginnings, Copenhagen has become the largest city in Scandinavia, home to 1.5 million people. It's the seat of the oldest kingdom in the world.

Over the centuries Copenhagen has suffered more than its share of disasters. In the 17th century the Swedes repeatedly besieged it, and in the 18th century it endured the plague and two devastating fires. The British attacked twice during the Napoleonic wars in the early 1800s. The last major disaster occurred in 1940, when the Nazis invaded Denmark. They held it until 1945, when British soldiers moved in again, this time as liberators.

Copenhagen's canals, narrow streets, and old houses reflect its considerable charm. Its most famous resident was Hans Christian Andersen, whose memory lives on. Another world-renowned inhabitant was Søren Kierkegaard, who planned his works as he took long morning strolls in the city; his completed essays eventually earned him the title "the father of existentialism."

Copenhagen retains some of the characteristics of a village. If you forget the suburbs, you can cover most of the central belt on foot, which makes it a great tourist spot. It's almost as though the city were designed for strolling, as reflected by its Strøget, the longest and oldest pedestrians-only street in Europe.

1 Orientation

ARRIVING

BY PLANE You arrive at **Kastrup Airport** (© **70-10-30-30**), 12km (7¼ miles) from the center of Copenhagen. Since 1998, air rail trains have linked the airport with Copenhagen's Central Railway Station, in the center of the hotel zone, and the whole affair now takes a mere 11 minutes and costs 23DKK ($2.95). The Air Rail Terminal is underneath the airport's arrivals and departure halls, just a short escalator ride from the gates. It has more than 30 check-in counters, ticketing offices, information desks, restaurants, and fast-food chains. You can also take an SAS bus to the city terminal; the fare is 23DKK ($2.95). A taxi to the city center costs around 128DKK ($17). Yet another option is a local bus, no. 250S, which leaves from the international arrivals terminal every 15 or

20 minutes for Town Hall Square in central Copenhagen and costs 23DKK ($2.95).

BY TRAIN   Trains arrive at the **Hoved Banegaård (Central Railway Station)**, in the center of Copenhagen, near the Tivoli Gardens and the Rådhuspladsen. Call ℂ **70-13-14-15** for rail information. The station operates a luggage-checking service, but room bookings are available only at the tourist office (see "Visitor Information," below). You can exchange money at Den Danske Bank (ℂ **33-12-04-11**), open daily from 7am to 8pm.

From the Central Railroad Station, you can connect with the **S-tog,** the local subway system. Trains depart from platforms in the terminal. Ask the staff at the information desk near Tracks 5 and 6 which train you should board.

BY BUS   Buses from Zealand and elsewhere in Denmark also pull into the Central Railroad Station. For bus information call ℂ **70-10-00-10** (daily 7am–9:30pm).

BY CAR   If you're driving from Germany, a car ferry will take you from Travemünde to Gedser in southern Denmark. From Gedser, express highway E55 north runs to the southern outskirts of Copenhagen. If you're coming from Sweden and crossing at Helsingborg, you'll land on the Danish side of Helsingør. Take express highway E55 south to the northern outskirts of Copenhagen.

BY FERRY   Most ferries land at Havnegade, at the end of the south side of Nyhavn, a short walk from the center of Copenhagen. Taxis wait here for ferry arrivals. Most come from Malmö, Sweden; ferries from continental Europe usually land in South Zealand.

VISITOR INFORMATION
The **Copenhagen Tourist Information Center,** Bernstorffsgade 1 (ℂ **33-25-38-44**), is across from the Tivoli's main entrance. In July and August, it's open daily from 8am to 11pm; in May, June, and early September, daily from 9am to 8pm; from September 16 to April, Monday through Friday from 9am to 4:30pm, Saturday from 9am to 1:30pm. Pick up a copy of *Copenhagen This Week* at the tourist center; its "Events Calendar" has good listings for entertainment and sightseeing events.

CITY LAYOUT
MAIN ARTERIES & STREETS   The heart of Old Copenhagen is a maze of pedestrian streets, formed by Nørreport Station to the north, Rådhuspladsen (Town Hall Square) to the west, and Kongens Nytorv to the east. **Strøget,** the longest pedestrians-only street in Europe at 1.2km (¾ mile) long, goes east from Town Hall Square to Kongens Nytorv, and consists of five streets: Frederiksberggade, Nygade, Vimmelskaftet, Amagertorv, and Østergade. Strøget is lined with shops, bars, restaurants and, in summer, sidewalk cafes. **Pistolstræde** is a maze of galleries, restaurants, and boutiques, all housed in restored 18th-century buildings.

Fiolstræde (Violet St.), a dignified street with antiques shops and bookshops, cuts through the university (in the Latin Quarter). If you turn into Rosengaarden at the top of Fiolstræde, you'll come to **Kultorvet (Coal Square)** just before you reach Nørreport Station. Here you join the third main pedestrian street, **Købmagergade (Butcher St.),** which winds around and finally meets Strøget and Amagertorv.

At the end of Strøget, you approach **Kongens Nytorv (King's Square),** the site of the Royal Theater and of Magasin, the largest department store in Copenhagen. It's the beginning of **Nyhavn,** the former seamen's quarter that has been gentrified into an upscale area of expensive restaurants, apartments, cafes, and boutiques.

The national government is centered on the small island of **Slotsholmen,** which is connected to the center by eight bridges. Several museums, notably Christiansborg Castle, are here.

The center of Copenhagen is **Rådhuspladsen (Town Hall Square).** From here it's a short walk to Copenhagen's biggest attraction, the Tivoli Gardens, and to the Central Railroad Station, the main railroad, subway, and bus terminus. The wide boulevard, **Vesterbrogade,** passes by the Tivoli until it reaches the Central Railroad Station. Another major boulevard is named after Denmark's most famous writer. **H. C. Andersens Boulevard** runs along Rådhuspladsen and the Tivoli Gardens.

FINDING AN ADDRESS   Even numbers are on one side of the street, odd numbers on the other. Buildings are in numerical order, with A, B, or C often inserted after the street number.

NEIGHBORHOODS IN BRIEF

Tivoli Gardens In the heart of Copenhagen, on the south side of Rådhuspladsen (Town Hall), these amusement gardens were built on the site of fortifications. A total of 160,000 flowers and 110,000 electric light bulbs set the scene. Built in 1843, the Tivoli is made up of a collection of restaurants, dance halls, theaters, beer gardens, and lakes. If you're in Copenhagen in summer, there is no more fun place to dine, and restaurants range from the pricey deluxe dining room with formal service to a beer hall with typically Danish food. The downside? Prices at the restaurants in Tivoli are about 30% higher than elsewhere in the city.

Nyhavn & Kongens Nytorv This is the harbor area, for years the haunt of sailors looking for tattoos and other diversions. Nowadays, it's one of the most elegant sections of the city, site of the deluxe Hotel d'Angleterre and many other stellar hotels and prestigious restaurants. The central canal, filled with yachts and boats, and the 18th-century facades of the buildings along the water contribute to the area's ambience and elegance. Kongens Nytorv (King's Square) is the entryway to Nyhavn and the home of the Royal Theater. For years, this was the section of Copenhagen where nobility erected their town houses. The centerpiece of the square is an elaborate equestrian statue of King Christian V, depicting a quad of classical figures seated submissively under His Majesty's horse. In and around the square, and along Nyhavn, you'll find a selection of the grandest and most romantic hotels in Copenhagen.

Near Rådhuspladsen (Town Hall) This is the very core of Copenhagen—nothing could be more central, or more convenient. This location puts you right near Tivoli Gardens, the pedestrians-only shopping street, Strøget, and the Central Railway Station. Hotels east of the station tend to be more upscale than those west of the station at Vesterbro (see below). Some of the most expensive hotels in Copenhagen, including the Palace and Kong Frederik, are here, but

NEIGHBORHOODS IN BRIEF · 51

you'll find moderate and inexpensive ones as well. The same holds true for restaurants.

Strøget This is the longest pedestrians-only street in Europe, beginning at Rådhuspladsen. The most interesting parts are Gammeltorv and Nytorv ("old" and "new" squares), on either side of Strøget. They're the sites of fruit and vegetable markets, as well as stalls selling bric-a-brac and handmade jewelry. The word Strøget doesn't appear on most city maps (though we've marked it on ours). Instead, Strøget encompasses five streets: Frederiksbrerggade, Nygade, Villelskaftet, Amagertorv, and Østergade. In addition to shopping, this area has a lot of cafes, fast-food places, and some minor restaurants. The better restaurants of Copenhagen lie off the Strøget along adjoining streets, and in other parts of the city.

Indre By This is the Old Town, in the heart of Copenhagen. Once filled with monasteries, it's a maze of old streets, alleyways, and squares. If you cross Gammeltorv and Nørregade, you'll be in the university area, nicknamed the Latin Quarter, as in Paris. Although not a district for hotels, this is one of the best places for dining in Copenhagen, especially for those on a budget or traveling moderately. Most of the restaurants are clustered on or near Gråbrødretorv or "Greyfriars Square" in the heart of Copenhagen's medieval core. Today it's a charming and hip area, especially after dark, when the clubs and cafes are buzzing. Don't expect the architectural grandeur of Kongens Nytorv. What you get instead is a setting that is low-key and unpretentious, representative of the brown-brick buildings that fill most of Copenhagen. The Vor Frue Kirke (cathedral of Copenhagen) is here, as is the Rundetårn (Round Tower).

Slotsholmen On this island, site of Christiansborg Palace, Bishop Absalon built the first fortress in the city in 1167. Today it's the seat of parliament and the site of Thorvaldsen's Museum, among others. Bridges link Slotsholmen to Indre By. You can also visit the Royal Library, the Theater Museum, and the Royal Stables. The 17th-century Børsen (Stock Exchange) is also here. This is an area to visit for sightseeing attractions, not a hotel and restaurant district.

Christianshavn This was the "new town" ordered by master builder Christian IV in the early 1500s, originally constructed to house shipbuilding workers. Visitors come here today mainly to see the Danish Film Museum at Gothersgade 55, and Vors Frelsers Kirke, on the corner of Prinsessegade and Skt. Annægade, where sightseers climb the old church's spire for a panoramic view. Again, this is a section to visit for its attractions rather than hotels and restaurants.

Christiania Within walking distance of Vor Frelsers Kirke at Christianshavn is this offbeat district, once a barracks for soldiers. Entrances are on Prinsessegade. In 1971 many young and homeless people moved in without the city's permission, proclaiming that Christiania was a "free city." It has been a controversial place ever since. Regrettably, the area, founded on idealism, also became a shelter for criminals, especially drug pushers. There are crafts shops and restaurants here; merchandise and food are fairly cheap because the residents refuse to pay Denmark's crippling 25% tax. Don't photograph anyone without permission. As some out-of-towners say about New York, "It's a great place to visit but I wouldn't want to live there."

Vesterbro (the rail station area)
This district lies to the immediate west of the Central Railway Station. Its main street, Istedgade, runs west from the main rail depot. This area is filled with some of the least expensive hotels in Copenhagen. It is seedy in some parts, gentrified in others. In the early 1970s when Denmark legalized pornography, visitors from all over the world flocked here, and the place took on somewhat of a red-light district aura. Although pornography is still hawked here, the district is also the site of respectable budget and moderately priced family hotels, especially along Helgolandsgade and Colbjørnsensgade. Today, with many of its original 19th-century facades restored, the district has been considerably cleaned up. Refugees from Turkey and Pakistan, followed by citizens of other countries, have settled heavily in the area, and you'll find many ethnic restaurants and crafts shops.

Nørrebro Even in the middle of the 19th century, this section—adjacent to Vesterbro—was a blue-collar neighborhood. The original Danish settlers departed long ago, and the neighborhood has increasingly filled with immigrants (the overflow from Vesterbro) who don't always get a friendly reception in Copenhagen. The area also abounds with artists, students, and musicians who can't afford the high rents elsewhere. Nørrebro is rich in artisan shops and ethnic (especially Turkish and Pakistani) restaurants. There are so many secondhand clothing stores—especially in the district around Sankt Hans Torv—that Nørrebro is taking on overtones of a Middle Eastern bazaar. Alleged antiques shops also fill the area along Ravnsborgade, but believe us: Many of the furnishings and objets

d'art aren't authentic. On Saturday morning a flea market is in full swing along the wall of Assistens Kirkegård, to the west of Nørrebrogade. Although not a hotel or restaurant district, Nørrebro attracts those seeking a look at off-the-beaten-path Copenhagen.

Near Nørreport Station This district lies to the north of Vesterbro and though it may seem inconvenient, you can arrive at it in just 15 minutes from the central station. Its chief landmark is Assistens Kirkegard, the largest cemetery in Copenhagen—containing the tombs of Hans Christian Andersen and Sören Kierkegaard—which is now a public park. The area is visited chiefly because it's the setting of one of Copenhagen's best-known budget hotels, Ibsens, and a leading gay hotel, Jørgensen.

Frederiksberg Vesterbrogade runs west from the inner city to the residential and business district of Frederiksberg. It grew around Frederiksberg Palace, constructed in the Italianate style with an ocher facade. A park, Frederiksberg Have, surrounds the palace. To the west of the palace is the Zoologisk Have, one of the largest zoos in Europe.

Dragør This seems to be everybody's favorite spot, after the Tivoli. It's especially recommended if you have time to see only the Copenhagen area and not the countryside. Dragør is a fishing village south of Copenhagen that dates from the 16th century. Walk its cobblestone streets and admire its 65 red-roofed houses, which have been designated national landmarks. Chances are, you'll patronize one of the restaurants here at lunch, returning to a city hotel at night. However, there are hotels and inns here should you decide to stay.

Impressions

What strikes me now most as regards Denmark is the charm, beauty, and independence of the women.

—Arnold Bennett, *Journal*, 1913

The Danes that drench their cares in wine.

—Ben Jonson, "Ode Allegorical," 1603

2 Getting Around

Copenhagen is a walker's paradise, neat and compact, with many of its major sightseeing attractions in close proximity to one another.

BY PUBLIC TRANSPORTATION

A joint zone fare system includes Copenhagen Transport buses and State Railway and S-tog trains in Copenhagen and North Zealand, plus some private railway routes within a 40km (25-mile) radius of the capital. You can transfer from train to bus and vice versa with the same ticket.

FARES   A *grundbillet* (basic ticket) for both buses and trains costs 15DKK ($1.95). You can buy 10 tickets for 90DKK ($12). Children under 12 pay half price; those under 5 ride free on local trains, and those under 7 go free on buses. For 70DKK ($9.15), you can purchase a ticket good for 24 hours of bus and train travel through nearly half of Zealand—it's worth it for a heavy day of sightseeing. It's half price for children 7 to 11, free for children under 7.

DISCOUNT PASSES   The **Copenhagen Card** entitles you to free and unlimited travel by bus and rail throughout the metropolitan area (including North Zealand), 25% to 50% discounts on crossings to and from Sweden, and free admission to many sights and museums. The card is available for 1, 2, or 3 days and costs 215DKK ($28), 375DKK ($49), or 495DKK ($65), respectively. Children under 12 pay half price. For more information, contact the Copenhagen Tourist Information Center (see "Visitor Information," above).

Students who have an **International Student Identity Card (ISIC)** are entitled to discounts. You can buy a card in the United States at any Council Travel office; for the office nearest you, call ✆ **800/GET-AN-ID.**

For information about low-cost train, ferry, and plane trips, go to **Wasteels,** Skoubogade 6 (✆ **33-14-46-33**), in Copenhagen. It's a travel agency specializing in discount train and plane tickets for travelers age 26 and under, and it's open Monday through Friday from 9am to 6pm and Saturday from 10am to 2pm.

Eurailpasses can be purchased at any train station in Scandinavia and are good on local trains in Copenhagen.

BY BUS   Copenhagen's well-maintained buses are the least expensive method of getting around. Most buses leave from Rådhuspladsen. Buses run along the major routes every 10 to 15 minutes, and a basic ticket allows 1 hour of travel and unlimited transfers within the zone where you started your trip. For information, call ✆ **70-10-00-10.**

BY S-TOG (SUBWAY)   The S-tog connects central Copenhagen with its suburbs. Use of the tickets is the same as on buses (see above). You can transfer from a bus line to an S-tog train on the same ticket. Eurailpass holders generally ride free. For more information, call ✆ **33-14-17-01** at any time.

BY METRO   In 2001 Copenhagen launched its first Metro line, taking passengers from east to west across the city or vice versa. Operating around the clock, the Metro runs as far west as Vanløse and as far south as Vestamager. Nørreport is the transfer station to the S-tog system, the commuter rail link to the suburbs. Metro trains run every 2 minutes during rush hours and every 15 minutes at night. Fares are integrated into the existing zonal system (see "By Bus," above).

BY CAR

Because of the prevalence of traffic-free walkways, and because of its many parks, gardens, and canal-side promenades, Copenhagen is well suited to pedestrians. It's best to park your car in any of the dozens of city parking lots, and then retrieve it when you're ready to explore the suburbs. Many parking lots are open 24 hours a day, but a few close between 1 and 7am; some close on Saturday afternoon and on Sunday when traffic is generally lighter. The cost ranges from 23DKK to 25DKK ($2.95–$3.30) per hour or 240DKK ($31) for 24 hours. Two centrally located parking lots are **Industriens Hus,** H. C. Andersens Blvd. 18 (© **33-91-21-75**), open Monday through Friday from 7am to 1:30am, Saturday and Sunday from 9am to 12:45am; and **Statoil,** Israels Plads (© **33-14-37-76**), open 24 hours.

BY TAXI

Watch for the FRI (free) sign or green light to hail a taxi. Be sure the taxi has a meter. **Københavns Taxa** (© **35-35-35-35**) operates the largest fleet. **Tips are included in the meter price:** 23DKK ($2.95) when the flag drops, then 11DKK ($1.45) per kilometer (approximately ½ mile), Monday through Friday from 6am to 6pm. From 6pm to 6am, and all day on Saturday and Sunday, the cost is 15DKK ($1.95) per kilometer. Many drivers speak English.

BY BICYCLE

Many Copenhageners ride bicycles. For 75DKK ($9.85) per day, you can rent a bike at **Københavns Cykler,** Reventlowsgade 11 (© **33-33-86-13**). Hours are Monday through Friday from 8:30am to 5:30pm, Saturday from 9am to 1pm, and Sunday from 10am to 1pm.

 FAST FACTS: **Copenhagen**

American Express   American Express is represented throughout Denmark by **Neiman & Schultz,** Nørregade 7A (© **33-13-11-81**), with a branch in Terminal 3 of the Copenhagen Airport. Fulfilling all the functions of American Express except for foreign-exchange services, the main office is open Monday through Thursday from 8:30am to 4:30pm, and Friday from 8:30am to 4pm. The airport office remains open till 8:30pm Monday through Friday. On weekends, and overnight on weekdays, a recorded message, in English, will deliver the phone number of a 24-hour Amex service in Stockholm. This is useful for anyone who has lost a card or traveler's checks. As for foreign exchange, you'll find Neiman & Schultz offices scattered throughout Copenhagen, including a branch that's open 24 hours a day at the railway station.

Area Code The country code for Denmark is **45**. There are no city area codes. Every Danish telephone number has 8 digits.

Bookstores One of the best and most centrally located is **Boghallen,** Rådhuspladsen 37 (✆ **33-47-27-60**). The shop carries books in Danish and English. Hours are Monday through Friday from 10am to 7pm, and Saturday from 10am to 4pm.

Business Hours Most **banks** are open Monday through Friday from 10am to 4pm (Thurs to 6pm). **Stores** are generally open Monday through Thursday from 9am to 6pm, Friday from 9am to 7 or 8pm, Saturday from 9am to 2pm; most are closed Sunday. **Offices** are open Monday through Friday from 9 or l0am to 4 or 5pm.

Camera Repair The biggest photography shop and camera supply center in Denmark is **Kontant Foto,** Købmagergade 44 (✆ **33-12-00-29**). It's open Monday through Thursday from 9am to 5:30pm, Friday from 9am to 7pm, Saturday from l0am to 2pm.

Car Rentals See "Getting Around" in Chapter 2, "Planning Your Trip to Denmark."

Currency Exchange Banks are generally your best bet. The main branch of **Den Danske Bank (The Danish Bank),** Amagertorv 24 (✆ **33-63-72-70**), is open Monday through Friday from 10am to 4pm (till 6pm on Thurs). When banks are closed, you can exchange money at **Forex** (✆ **33-11-29-05**) in the Central Railroad Station, daily from 8am to 9pm, or at the **Change Group,** Østergade 16 (✆ **33-93-04-55**), Monday through Saturday from 9am to 10pm, Sunday from 9am to 8pm.

Dentists During regular business hours, ask your hotel to call the nearest English-speaking dentist. For emergency dental treatment, go to **Tandlægevagten,** Oslo Plads 14 (✆ **35-38-02-51**), near Østerport Station and the U.S. Embassy. It's open Monday through Friday from 8am to 9:30pm; Saturday, Sunday, and holidays from 10am to noon. Be prepared to pay cash.

Doctors To reach a doctor, dial ✆ **33-93-63-00** from 9am to 4pm or ✆ **38-88-60-41** after hours. The doctor's fee is payable in cash, although some have started accepting credit cards. Virtually every doctor speaks English.

Drugstores See "Pharmacies," below.

Emergencies Dial ✆ **112** to report a **fire** or to call the **police** or an **ambulance.** State your phone number and address. Emergency calls from public telephones are free (no coins needed).

Eyeglass Repair The largest and oldest optical chain in Denmark is **Synoptik,** Købmagergade 22 (✆ **33-15-05-38**), with branches throughout Denmark. Most glasses can be replaced in 2 or 3 hours. Bifocals can take 10 to 14 days. Synoptik also specializes in contact lenses, with hundreds of types in stock. Hours are Monday through Thursday from 9:30am to 6pm, Friday from 9:30am to 7pm, Saturday from 10am to 4pm.

Hospitals In case of a sudden illness or accident, even foreigners are entitled to free medical treatment in Denmark. One centrally located hospital is **Rigshospitalet,** Blegdamsvej 9 (✆ **35-45-35-45**).

Internet Access To check your e-mail or to send messages, go to **Copenhagen Hovebibliotek,** Krystalgade 15 (© **33-73-60-60**), open Monday through Friday from 10am to 7pm, Saturday from 10am to 2pm.

Laundry & Dry Cleaning There are coin-op laundries in all neighborhoods. Some are independent, others part of the Vascomat and Møntvask chains that seem to dominate the business. Some of the most convenient are at Borgergade 2, Nansensgade 39, and Istedgade 45. They are open daily from 8am to 10pm. **Dry Cleaning,** Vester Farimagsgade 3 (© **33-12-45-45**), is a block from the Central Railroad Station. It's open Monday through Friday from 8am to 6pm, Saturday from 9:30am to 2pm.

Libraries Try the **Københavns Bibliotek (Copenhagen Library),** Krystalgade 15 (© **33-73-60-60**). Open Monday through Friday from 10am to 7pm, Saturday from 10am to 2pm, it has a large collection of English-language publications.

Lost Property The **Lost and Found Property office** at Slotsherrensvej 113, 2720 Vanløse (© **38-74-88-22**), is open Monday through Thursday from 9am to 5:30pm, Friday from 9am to 2pm. For property lost on **buses,** phone © **36-45-45-45**; on **trains,** © **33-16-21-10**. These numbers operate only Monday through Saturday from 10am to 3pm (to 6pm on Thurs).

Luggage Storage & Lockers Luggage can be stored in rental lockers at **Central Railroad Station.** Lockers are available daily from 4:30am to midnight. The cost is 35DKK ($4.60) for 24 hours. For information, call © **33-14-04-08.**

Newspapers Foreign newspapers, notably the *International Herald Tribune* and *USA Today,* are available at the Central Railroad Station in front of the Palladium movie theater on Vesterbrogade, on Strøget, and at the newsstands of big hotels.

Pharmacies An *apotek* (pharmacy) open 24 hours a day in central Copenhagen is **Steno Apotek,** Vesterbrogade 6C (© **33-14-82-66**).

Photographic Needs See "Camera Repair," above.

Police In an emergency, dial © **112.** For other matters, go to the police station at Halmtorvet 20 (© **33-25-14-48**).

Post Office For information about the Copenhagen post office, phone © **33-41-56-00.** The main post office, where your *poste restante* (general delivery) letters can be picked up, is at Tietgensgade 35–39, DK-1704 København (© **33-41-56-00**). It's open Monday through Friday from 8am to 6pm, Saturday from 10am to 1pm. The post office at the Central Railroad Station is open Monday through Friday from 8am to 10pm, Saturday from 9am to 4pm, Sunday from 10am to 4pm.

Religious Services **St. Ansgar's Roman Catholic Church** is at Bredgade 64 (© 33-13-37-62); **the English Church of St. Alban's (Anglo-Episcopalian) on Langelinie** (© 39-62-77-36); **the American Church (Protestant and interdenominational)** at the U.S. Embassy, Dag Hammarskjølds Allé 24 (© 35-55-31-44); and **the synagogue at Krystalgade 12** (© 33-12-88-68). **The International Church of Copenhagen (affiliated with the American Lutheran church)** holds services at the Vartov Church, Farvergade 27 (© 39-62-47-85), across from the Town Hall.

Restrooms Some free public toilets can be found at Rådhuspladsen (Town Hall Square), at the Central Railroad Station, and at all terminals. Look for the markings TOILETTER, WC, *damer* or D (women), or *herrer* or H (men).

Safety Compared with other European capital cities, Copenhagen is relatively safe. However, since the early 1990s, with the influx of homeless refugees from around the world—many of whom have become pickpockets—crime has risen. Guard your wallet, purse, and other valuables as you would when traveling in any big city.

Shoe Repair The department store **Magasin,** Kongens Nytorv 13 (© **33-11-44-33**), has a great shoe-repair franchise, **Mister Minit,** in its basement. Service is available Monday through Friday from 10am to 7pm, Saturday from 10am to 5pm.

Taxes Denmark imposes a value-added tax of 25%, known as *moms* (and pronounced "mumps"). It's included in hotel and restaurant bills, service charges, entrance fees, and repair bills for foreign-registered cars. No refunds are given on these items. For more information, see "The Shopping Scene" in chapter 4, "Exploring Copenhagen."

Transit Information Phone © **36-45-45-45** for bus information or © **33-14-17-01** for S-tog (subway) information.

3 Where to Stay

Peak season in Denmark is summer, from May to September, which pretty much coincides with the schedule at the Tivoli Gardens. Once the Tivoli closes for the winter, lots of rooms become available. Make sure to ask about winter discounts.

Nearly all doubles come with a private bathroom. Find out, though, whether this means a shower or a bathtub. You can undercut these prices by requesting a room without a bathroom at moderate and inexpensive hotels. Ask if breakfast is included (usually it isn't).

A word of warning: In most moderate and nearly all inexpensive hotels in Copenhagen, the bathrooms are cramped, and there's never enough room for all your stuff. Many of the bathrooms were added to older buildings that weren't designed for bathrooms. Also, get used to towels that are much thinner than you might like.

RESERVATIONS SERVICE At Bernstorffsgade 1, across from the Tivoli's main entrance, the Tourist Information Center maintains a useful hotel-booking service, **Værelsænvisningen** (© **70-22-24-42**). The charge for this service, whether you book a private home, a hostel, or a B&B, is 60DKK ($8) per person. Actual hotel rooms are booked free. A deposit, about 8.6% of the room cost, must be paid, but it's deducted from your bill later. You'll also be given a city map and bus directions. This office doesn't accept advance reservations; it can arrange private accommodations if the hotels in your price range are full. The office is open from April 19 to September 30, daily from 9am to 9pm; from October to April 18, Monday through Friday from 9am to 5pm, Saturday from 9am to 2pm.

In the same building, the **Hotel Booking Service** (© **33-25-38-44**) will reserve hotel rooms in advance.

Copenhagen Accommodations

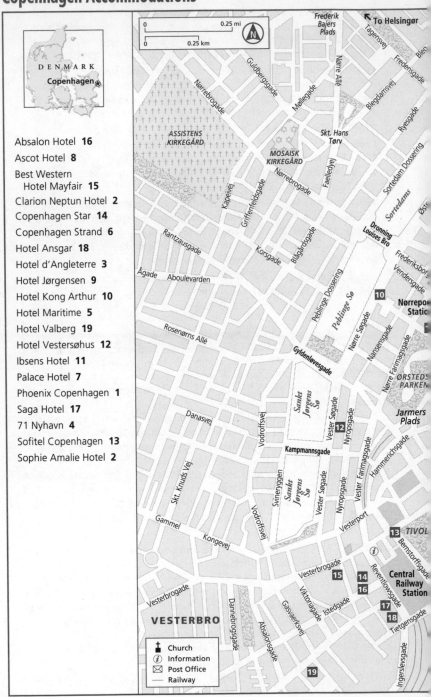

Absalon Hotel **16**

Ascot Hotel **8**

Best Western
  Hotel Mayfair **15**

Clarion Neptun Hotel **2**

Copenhagen Star **14**

Copenhagen Strand **6**

Hotel Ansgar **18**

Hotel d'Angleterre **3**

Hotel Jørgensen **9**

Hotel Kong Arthur **10**

Hotel Maritime **5**

Hotel Valberg **19**

Hotel Vestersøhus **12**

Ibsens Hotel **11**

Palace Hotel **7**

Phoenix Copenhagen **1**

Saga Hotel **17**

71 Nyhavn **4**

Sofitel Copenhagen **13**

Sophie Amalie Hotel **2**

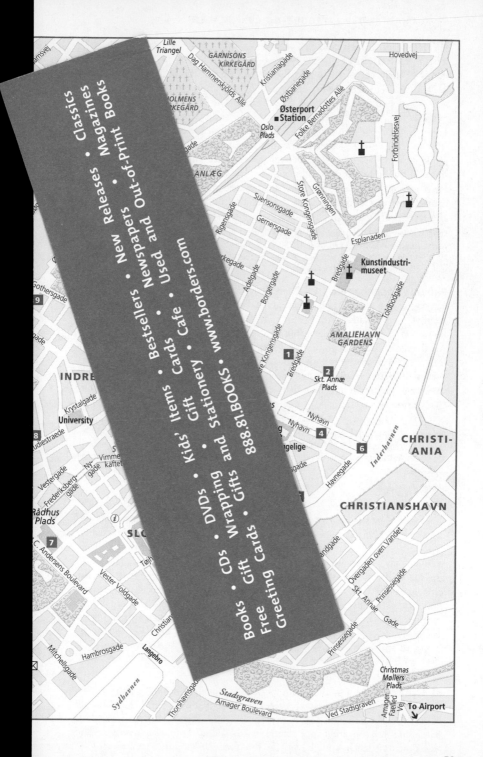

Lille
Triangel

GARNISONS
KIRKEGÅRD

Dag Hammerskjölds Allé

Kristianiagade

Østbanegade

Hovedvej

Østerport
■ Station

HOLMENS
RKEGÅRD

Oslo
Plads

Folke Bernadottes Allé

Forbindelsesvej

ANLÆG

Store Kongensgade

Grønningen

Suensonsgade

Rigensgade

Gernersgade

Esplanaden

rkegade

Adelgade

Borgergade

Bredgade

Kunstindustri-
museet

Toldbodgade

AMALIEHAVN
GARDENS

le Kongensgade

Bredgade

1

2
Skt. Annæ
Plads

Nyhavn

Nyhavn

4

ngelige

Inderhavnen

CHRISTI-
ANIA

6

Havnegade

CHRISTIANSHAVN

INDRE

Krystalgade

University

udiestraede

8

andgade

Overgaden oven Vandet

Prinsessegade

Vestergade
Frederiksberg-
gade

Ny-
gade

Vimme
kaftet

Skt Annæ

Gade

Rådhus
Plads

i

SLC

Tøjh

Prinsessegade

C. Andersens Boulevard

Vester Voldgade

Christian

Gothersgade

9

ade

Mitchellsgade

Hambrosgade

Langebro

Christmas
Møllers
Plads

Sydhavnen

Thorshavnsga

Stadsgraven
Amager Boulevard

Ved Stadsgraven

Amager
Fælled
Vej

To Airport

Books • Classics
Free Gift • Magazines
Greeting Cards • New Releases • Books
CDs • DVDs • Kids' Items • Bestsellers • Newspapers • Out-of-Print
Gift Wrapping and Stationery • Cards • Cafe • Used and
Gifts • 888.81.BOOKS • www.borders.com

NYHAVN & KONGENS NYTORV
VERY EXPENSIVE

Hotel d'Angleterre ☆☆☆   At the top of Nyhavn, this is the premier choice in Denmark. Though it's a bit staid and stodgy, it's impeccably bourgeois and correct—there's no better address in Copenhagen. The seven-story hotel, a *Leading Hotels of the World* member, was built in 1755 and extensively renovated in the 1980s. Guests have included Hans Christian Andersen and almost every celebrity who has ever visited Denmark. It's a medley of styles: Empire, Louis XVI, and modern. The guest rooms are beautifully furnished with art objects and occasional antiques. Room sizes and views vary, but each has a high ceiling and marble bathroom, complete with robes, phone, and shower-tub combination. The deluxe rooms are in front, but those facing the courtyard are more tranquil and also receive a fair amount of sunlight—when the sun is shining, that is.

Kongens Nytorv 34, DK-1050 København. ℂ 800/44-UTELL in the U.S., or 33-12-00-95. Fax 33-12-11-18. www.remmen.dk. 123 units. 2,470DKK–3,470DKK ($324–$455) double; from 4,470DKK ($586) suite. AE, DC, MC, V. Parking 180DKK ($24). Bus: 1, 6, or 9. **Amenities:** Restaurant; bar; pool; fitness center; sauna; room service; babysitting; laundry/dry cleaning. *In room:* A/C, TV, minibar, hair dryer, safe.

Phoenix Copenhagen ☆☆   More than any other hotel in Copenhagen, this top-of-the-line lodging poses a serious challenge to the discreet grandeur of the nearby Hotel d'Angleterre. Opened in 1991, the Phoenix was a royal guesthouse, originally built in the 1700s to accommodate the aristocratic courtiers of Amalienborg Palace. Beginning in 1988, tons of white and colored marble were imported to create the elegant Louis XVI–style decor that has impressed guests ever since. Beds are large, and wool carpeting and chandeliers add graceful notes to the guest rooms. The Italian marble bathrooms are sufficiently large and contain shower-tub combinations and robes. The best accommodations also have faxes, trouser presses, and phones in the bathrooms.

Bredgade 37, DK-1260 København. ℂ 33-95-95-00. Fax 33-33-98-33. 213 units. 1,990DKK–2,890DKK ($261–$379) double; from 3,500DKK ($459) suite. AE, DC, MC, V. Parking 113DKK ($15). Bus: 1, 6, 9, or 10. **Amenities:** Restaurant; bar; room service; babysitting; laundry/dry cleaning. *In room:* A/C, TV, minibar, hair dryer, safe.

EXPENSIVE

Clarion Neptun Hotel ☆   Modernized in 1990, the interior of this 1854 hotel resembles an upper-crust living room, with English-style furniture and even a chess table. Some rooms overlook two quiet, covered interior courtyards. On the hotel's outdoor terrace on the sixth floor, you can order drinks in the summer. The rooms are tastefully furnished in modern style. Closets are small, and the tiled bathrooms with shower-tub combinations are only modest in size. Only some units are air-conditioned. Ask for a room that opens onto the courtyard—they are the brightest during the day and the most tranquil in the evening. Suites, most often booked by businesspeople, have dataports and faxes.

Skt. Annæ Plads 18–20, DK-1250 København. ℂ 800/654-6200 in the U.S., or 33-96-20-00. Fax 33-96-20-66. www.choicehotels.dk. 133 units. 1,695DKK ($222) double; 2,495DKK ($327) suite. Rates include buffet breakfast. AE, DC, MC, V. Free parking. Bus: 1, 6, 9, or 19. **Amenities:** Restaurant; bar; room service; babysitting; laundry/dry cleaning. *In room:* A/C, TV, minibar, hair dryer, safe.

71 Nyhavn ☆☆   On the corner between Copenhagen harbor and Nyhavn Canal, this redbrick hotel is a restored warehouse that dates from 1804—one of the few buildings in the area spared by an 1807 British bombardment. The warehouse was converted into a hotel in 1971, and thoroughly renovated and redecorated in 1997, while leaving the fine Pomeranian pine beams intact.

Most rooms have a view of the harbor and canal. Nice touches in the rooms include trouser presses and double-glazed windows. The best units also have ironing boards, faxes, and robes, and computer plugs are available at the reception desk. Nonsmoking accommodations are available. Bathrooms are rather small but are tiled, and most contain shower-tub combinations.

Nyhavn 71, DK-1051 København. ℂ 33-43-62-00. Fax 33-43-62-01. www.71nyhavnhotelcopenhagen.dk. 150 units. Mon–Thurs 1,650DKK–1,710DKK ($216–$224) double, 3,000DKK–5,000DKK ($393–$655) suite. Fri–Sun 1,290DKK–1,790DKK ($169–$234) double, 2,190DKK–3,800DKK ($287–$498) suite. Rates include breakfast. AE, DC, MC, V. Free parking. Bus: 550-S. **Amenities:** Restaurant; bar; room service; babysitting; laundry/dry cleaning. *In room:* A/C, TV, minibar, hair dryer, safe.

MODERATE

Copenhagen Strand 𝑅 *Value*   One of the city's newest hotels opened in July 2000 within what had been built in the 1800s as a pair of brick-and-timber factories. The savvy architects retained as many of the old-fashioned details as they could, adding a nautical gloss to the lobby—lots of varnished wood, brass hardware, and paintings of sailing ships and the nearby piers that used to service them. There's a bar within the lobby, and a reception staff that works double time mixing drinks and pulling pints. The medium-sized guest rooms are less richly decorated than the lobby, but filled with comfortable, contemporary furnishings. All units contain well-kept bathrooms with shower-tub combinations. The hotel is rated three stars by the Danish government, but frankly, all that it lacks for elevation into a four-star status is a full-fledged restaurant.

Havnegade 37, DK-1058 København K. ℂ 33-48-99-00. Fax 33-48-99-01. www.copenhagenstrand.dk. 174 units. 1,613DKK ($211) double; 2,858DKK–3,270DKK ($374–$428) suite. AE, DC, MC, V. Parking 113DKK ($15). Tram: 1 or 6. **Amenities:** Bar; business center; room service; babysitting; laundry/dry cleaning. *In room:* TV, minibar, hair dryer.

Sophie Amalie Hotel   The Sophie Amalie is a first-class hotel on the harbor front, close to Amalienborg Castle. From the rooms facing north, you can see the castle, where Queen Margrethe II lives. Within walking distance of Nyhavn, it's convenient for exploring the business and shopping districts. Dating from 1948, the hotel has been vastly improved and upgraded over the years. Its guest rooms are furnished with the best of Scandinavian modern design. Double-glazing on the windows cuts down on street noise. Closets are large, but bathrooms are small, with mosaic tiles and shower-tub combinations. In the sixth-floor suites, curved staircases connect the two levels. The hotel is named for Sophie Amalie (1628–85), a German duke's daughter who married King Frederik III at the age of 15.

Skt. Annæ Plads 21, DK-1021 København. ℂ 33-13-34-00. Fax 33-11-77-07. www.remmen.dk. 134 units. 1,208DKK–1,313DKK ($158–$172) double; 1,830DKK–2,138DKK ($240–$280) suite. Winter discounts available. AE, DC, MC, V. Free parking. Bus: 550-S. **Amenities:** Restaurant; bar; sauna; room service; babysitting; laundry/dry cleaning. *In room:* TV, minibar, hair dryer.

INEXPENSIVE

Hotel Maritime   Although the guest rooms here are comfortable and tastefully conservative in style, you might be put off by the pretentious and somewhat rigid staff. Ignore them, and relish your hotel's enviable location near hotels that cost a lot more. The neighborhood lies between high glamour (Kongens Nytorv, site of the Hotel d'Angleterre) and the Nyhavn Canal, a reminder of seafaring Copenhagen. Built more than a century ago, the building was converted into a hotel in 1953, and the guest rooms were completely renovated in 1996. Each unit is well kept with a bathroom containing a shower unit.

Peder Skrams Gade 19, DK-1054 København. 🕻 **33-13-48-82.** Fax 33-15-03-45. www.hotel-maritime.dk. 64 units. 1,100DKK–1,325DKK ($144–$174) double; 1,600DKK ($210) triple. AE, DC, DISC, MC, V. Bus: 1, 6, or 9. **Amenities:** Restaurant; bar; lounge; laundry/dry cleaning. *In room:* TV.

NEAR RÅDHUSPLADSEN (TOWN HALL)
VERY EXPENSIVE
Palace Hotel 🕏 Opened in 1910 and declared a historic landmark in 1985, the Palace Hotel has been a respite for countless camera-shy celebrities. Although the hotel has tried to keep abreast of the times, it's no longer the front-runner it once was (that distinction now belongs to some other recommended hotels, including the Kong Frederik). The modern rooms are attractively furnished in an English country style—conservative furniture, floral chintz curtains. Most bathrooms are cramped, but they do have shower-tub combinations. The best rooms are on the top floor, away from street noises. If you're assigned a room on floors two or three, you are still in luck—they have high ceilings and tasteful furnishings and appointments. The reception desk staff is especially helpful in arranging for theater tickets, tours, and transportation. There's also a roof terrace.

Rådhuspladsen 57, DK-1550 København. 🕻 **800/448-8355** or 33-14-40-50. Fax 33-12-75-86. www.palace-hotel.dk. 162 units. 2,175DKK ($285) double; 3,525DKK ($462) suite. 25% discount may be available on weekends and midwinter, depending on occupancy. AE, DC, MC, V. Parking 225DKK ($29). Bus: 2, 30, 32, 33, 34, or 35. **Amenities:** Restaurant; bar; room service; babysitting; laundry/dry cleaning. *In room:* TV, minibar, hair dryer, safe.

EXPENSIVE
Sofitel Copenhagen 🕏 Rich with turn-of-the-20th-century atmosphere, this successful overhaul of an older hotel combines first-class comfort and antique furnishings. Opposite the Tivoli Gardens, the hotel was commissioned by King Frederik VIII in 1913, and has entertained its share of celebrities and royalty. Guest rooms of varying dimensions resemble what you might find in an English country house—but with all the modern amenities. Antiques, double-glazed windows, and views from many units make this a good choice; rooms on the top floor have dormer windows. Bathrooms are generous in size, completely tiled, and contain shower-tub combinations and make-up mirrors. There are some smoke-free accommodations.

Bernstorffsgade 4, DK-1577 København. 🕻 **800/223-5652** or 33-14-92-62. Fax 33-93-93-62. www.accorhotel.dk. 93 units. 1,943DKK ($255) double; 2,220DKK–6,450DKK ($291–$845) suite. AE, DC, MC, V. Parking 142DKK ($19). Bus: 1 or 6. **Amenities:** Restaurant; bar; fitness center; room service; babysitting; laundry/dry cleaning. *In room:* A/C, TV, minibar, hair dryer, safe.

MODERATE
Ascot Hotel 🕏 *Value* This is one of the best small hotels in Copenhagen. On a side street about a 2-minute walk from Rådhuspladsen, it was built in 1902 (on 492 wooden pilings rescued from a medieval fortification that had previously stood on the site). In 1994 the hotel annexed an adjacent building designed in the 19th century as a boathouse; its black-marble columns and interior bas-reliefs are historically important. The guest rooms have been renovated and modernized, and although the furniture is rather standard, the atmosphere is inviting. The finest units open onto the street, but the rooms in the rear get better air circulation and more light. The tiled bathrooms are generous in size and equipped with shower-tub combinations.

Studiestræde 61, DK-1554 København. 🕻 **33-12-60-00.** Fax 33-14-60-40. www.ascothotel.dk. 163 units. 1,280DKK ($168) double; 2,190DKK–2,560DKK ($287–$335) suite. Rates include buffet breakfast. Winter discounts available. AE, DC, MC, V. Free parking. Bus: 14 or 16. **Amenities:** Restaurant; bar; fitness center; room service; laundry/dry cleaning. *In room:* TV, hair dryer.

Hotel Kong Arthur ☆ *Value*   Built as an orphanage in 1882, this hotel sits behind a private courtyard next to tree-lined Peblinge Lake in a residential part of town. It's a terrific value. It has been completely renovated into a contemporary hostelry, and a recent expansion offers more spacious rooms, including 20 nonsmoking units. Each of the comfortably furnished and carpeted guest rooms has a VCR. The spacious bathrooms are tiled and contain shower-tub combinations. Breakfast is served in a large greenhouse-like room that's filled with light on sunny days.

Nørre Søgade 11, DK-1370 København. ☎ **33-11-12-12**. Fax 33-32-61-30. www.kongarthur.dk. 107 units. 1,400DKK–1,600DKK ($183–$210) double; from 3,113DKK ($408) suite. Rates include buffet breakfast. AE, DC, MC, V. Free parking. Bus: 5, 7, or 16. **Amenities:** 3 restaurants; bar; sauna; room service; babysitting; laundry/dry cleaning. *In room:* TV, minibar, hair dryer, safe.

INEXPENSIVE

Hotel Valberg   Simple but well kept, this five-story hotel is about a 10-minute walk from the Central Railroad Station. Renovated in the late 1980s, it's unpretentious and unassuming, with bright, acceptably decorated guest rooms. Each has a sink with hot and cold running water, but aside from six of the rooms, toilets and showers are in the central corridors. Breakfast is the only meal served.

Sønder Blvd. 53, DK-1720 København. ☎ **33-25-25-19**. Fax 33-25-25-83. www.valberg.dk. 20 units, 6 with bathroom. 900DKK ($118) double. Rates include breakfast. DC, DISC, MC, V. Bus: 10. **Amenities:** Lounge. *In room:* TV, hair dryer (in some).

Hotel Vestersøhus   One of the best features of this simple hotel is the view from about half the guest rooms (top two floors). They overlook a canal-shaped body of water, Skt. Jørgens Lake, which the Danes refer to as "the lakes." (The remainder of the rooms sit above the quiet, more prosaic backyard.) Set in the heart of town, behind a redbrick facade, the Vestersøhus was originally built around 1900 as an apartment house. Its simple rooms are small and comfortably—but not particularly imaginatively—furnished. Most units come with well-maintained bathrooms with shower-tub combinations. If you want to do your own cooking, know in advance that the 12 rooms with kitchenettes are usually booked far in advance by business travelers setting up long-term lodgings. Only breakfast is served, but it's included in the room price.

Vester Søgade 58, DK-1601 København. ☎ **33-11-38-70**. Fax 33-11-00-90. www.vestersoehus.dk. 44 units, 36 with bathroom. 715DKK ($94) double without bathroom; 1,240DKK ($162) double with bathroom; 1,525DKK ($200) double with bathroom and kitchenette. AE, DC, MC, V. Bus: 29. **Amenities:** Bar; lounge; laundry/dry cleaning. *In room:* TV.

INDRE BY
MODERATE
Best Western Hotel Mayfair   This older, highly respected hotel retained some of its original architectural detailing after a radical overhaul that brought it up to modern-day standards about a decade ago. Two blocks west of the main railroad station, it boasts a conservative decor that might remind you of the furnishings in a well-heeled private home in England. Guest rooms are comfortable, representing better-than-expected value for a hotel that's rated three stars by the Danish government. Guest accommodations have full marble bathrooms which contain shower-tub combinations. Some recently upgraded accommodations have sitting areas.

Helgolandsgade 3, DK-1653 København V. (C) 800/528-1234 in the U.S., or 33-31-48-01. Fax 33-23-96-86. www.themayfairhotel.dk. 105 units. 1,325DKK–1,525DKK ($174–$200) double; 1,900DKK–2,175DKK ($249–$285) suite. Rates include breakfast. AE, DC, MC, V. Bus: 6, 16, 28, 29, or 41. **Amenities:** Bar; lounge; laundry/dry cleaning. *In room:* TV, minibar, hair dryer, safe.

Copenhagen Star   Located a short walk from the railroad station, this hotel was created in 1990 when a simple older lodging was connected to a neighboring building and upgraded. Its neoclassical facade was originally built around 1880. The outside is lit with neon, and the interior is definitely postmodern, with leather chairs, teakwood tables, and granite columns. Guest rooms are traditionally furnished and well maintained, with neatly kept bathrooms with shower-tub combinations. The suites have Jacuzzis.

Colbjørnsengade 13, DK-1652 København. (C) 33-22-11-00. Fax 33-21-21-86. www.ibishotel.com. 134 units. 970DKK ($127) double; 1,395DKK–1,995DKK ($183–$261) suite. Rates include breakfast. AE, DC, MC, V. Bus: 6, 16, 28, 29, or 41. **Amenities:** Breakfast room, bar; lounge; laundry/dry cleaning. *In room:* A/C, TV, safe.

INEXPENSIVE
Absalon Hotel ⚐ *Value*   This family-run lodging, one of the best-managed hotels in the neighborhood, consists of four town houses that were joined into one building and became a hotel in 1938. It has a spacious blue-and-white breakfast room, and an attentive staff directed by Eric and Mogens Nedergaard. The guest rooms are simple and modern, but cramped. Those with private bathrooms are equipped with shower-tub combinations.

The Absalon traces its origins to a love story that unfolded at the nearby railroad station. Shortly after the yet-to-be father of the present owners began his first job as a porter at a neighboring hotel, he was asked to go to the station to pick up a new babysitter who had just arrived from Jutland. They fell in love, married, and bought the first of the buildings that became the hotel. Two of their children were born in Room no. 108, including one of the brothers you'll probably meet behind the reception desk.

A short walk from the Absalon, and under the same management, is the roughly equivalent **Selandia Hotel,** Helgolandsgade 12 ((C) **33-31-46-10**), where the 80 rooms go for the same prices as the Absalon's. If one of these two hotels is full, management will direct you toward the other.

Helgolandsgade 15, DK-1653 København. (C) 33-24-22-11. Fax 33-24-34-11. www.absalon-hotel.dk. Summer 830DKK ($109) double, 1,030DKK ($135) triple, 1,300DKK–1,500DKK ($170–$197) suite. Winter 1,050DKK–1,300DKK ($138–$170) double, 1,250DKK ($164) triple, 1,400DKK–1,600DKK ($183–$210) suite. Rates include all-you-can-eat buffet breakfast. AE, DC, MC, V. Closed Dec 14–Jan 2. Bus: 6, 10, 16, 27, or 28. **Amenities:** Lounge; laundry/dry cleaning. *In room:* TV, hair dryer (in some).

Hotel Ansgar *Kids*   Although this five-story hotel was built in 1885, its comfortable, cozy rooms have modern Danish furniture. A dozen large rooms that

can accommodate up to six are perfect for families, and are available at nego-
tiable rates. All units contain well-kept bathrooms with shower units. There is
often free parking outside the hotel after 6pm. Guests arriving at Kastrup Airport can take the SAS bus to the Air Terminal at the Central Railroad Station,
walk through the station, and be inside the hotel in less than 4 minutes.

Colbjørnsensgade 29, DK-1652 København. ℂ **33-21-21-96.** Fax 33-21-61-91. www.ansgar-hotel.dk. 81
units. 875DKK–1,095DKK ($115–$143) double. Extra bed 200DKK ($26). Rates include buffet breakfast. AE,
DC, MC, V. Bus: 6, 10, 28, or 41. **Amenities:** Lounge; room service; laundry/dry cleaning. *In room:* TV.

Saga Hotel   This is a reasonably priced, acceptable choice on a sometimes-
troublesome street. About half of its accommodations tend to be booked by
groups of foreign visitors in the summer, and by Danish student and convention
groups in the winter. The hotel was created in 1947 from two late-19th-century
apartment buildings. Each of the guest rooms, renovated in 1989, is unique—
each has its own layout. All units have well-maintained bathrooms with shower-
tub combinations. The five-story building has no elevator, so hauling luggage
upstairs might present a problem. The reception and breakfast areas are one
floor above street level.

Colbjørnsensgade 18–20, DK-1652 København. ℂ **33-24-49-44.** Fax 33-24-60-33. www.sagahotel.dk. 79
units, 31 with bathroom. 470DKK–720DKK ($62–$94) double without bathroom; 550DKK–920DKK
($72–$121) double with bathroom. Extra bed 200DKK ($26). Modest winter discounts. Rates include break-
fast. AE, DC, MC, V. Bus: 6, 10, 16, 28, or 41. **Amenities:** Lounge. *In room:* TV.

NEAR NØRREPORT STATION
MODERATE

Ibsens Hotel *(Kids*   A favorite with budget-conscious travelers and families,
Ibsens Hotel, built in 1906 and completely renovated in 1998, offers comfortable, well-maintained guest rooms. Most of the traditionally furnished rooms
are doubles or triples. They now have private bathrooms, which are cramped but
contain shower-tub combinations.

Vendersgade 23, DK-1363 København. ℂ **33-13-19-13.** Fax 33-13-19-16. www.ibsenshotel.dk. 118 units.
1,113DKK–1,330DKK ($146–$174) double; 2,100DKK ($275) suite. Rates include buffet breakfast. AE, DC,
MC, V. Bus: 5, 14, or 16. **Amenities:** Restaurant; bar; babysitting; laundry/dry cleaning. *In room:* TV.

INEXPENSIVE

Hotel Jørgensen   This white stucco 1906 building, a former textbook publishing house, became Denmark's first gay hotel in 1984. On a busy boulevard
in central Copenhagen, it obviously appeals to gay men and lesbians, but also
welcomes straight guests. The staff is most helpful. Prices are reasonable, and the
rooms are conventional and well organized. Those units with bathrooms are well
kept and contain shower-tub combinations. The 13 dormitory rooms, which
accommodate 6 to 14 people each, are segregated by gender.

Rømersgade 11, DK-1362 København. ℂ **33-13-81-86.** Fax 33-15-51-05. www.hoteljorgensen.dk. 24 units;
13 dormitory rooms (72 beds). 700DKK ($92) double; 120DKK ($16) per person in dormitory. Rates include
breakfast. MC, V. Free parking. Bus: 14 or 16. **Amenities:** Lounge. *In room:* TV.

4 Where to Dine

Copenhagen has more than 2,000 cafes, snack bars, and restaurants. Most of the
restaurants are in the Tivoli, where you'll pay extra for the privilege of dining,
around Rådhuspladsen (Town Hall Square) or the Central Railroad Station, or
in Nyhavn. Others are in the shopping district, on streets that branch off from
Strøget.

Copenhagen Dining

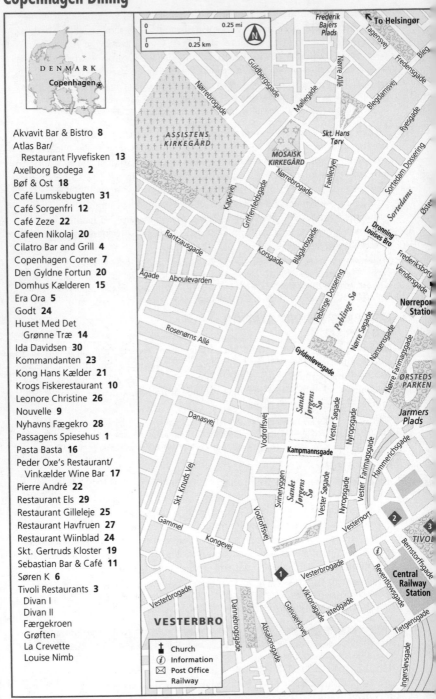

DENMARK

Copenhagen

Akvavit Bar & Bistro **8**
Atlas Bar/
  Restaurant Flyvefisken **13**
Axelborg Bodega **2**
Bøf & Ost **18**
Café Lumskebugten **31**
Café Sorgenfri **12**
Café Zeze **22**
Cafeen Nikolaj **20**
Cilatro Bar and Grill **4**
Copenhagen Corner **7**
Den Gyldne Fortun **20**
Domhus Kælderen **15**
Era Ora **5**
Godt **24**
Huset Med Det
  Grønne Træ **14**
Ida Davidsen **30**
Kommandanten **23**
Kong Hans Kælder **21**
Krogs Fiskerestaurant **10**
Leonore Christine **26**
Nouvelle **9**
Nyhavns Fægekro **28**
Passagens Spiesehus **1**
Pasta Basta **16**
Peder Oxe's Restaurant/
  Vinkælder Wine Bar **17**
Pierre André **22**
Restaurant Els **29**
Restaurant Gilleleje **25**
Restaurant Havfruen **27**
Restaurant Wiinblad **24**
Skt. Gertruds Kloster **19**
Sebastian Bar & Café **11**
Søren K **6**
Tivoli Restaurants **3**
  Divan I
  Divan II
  Færgekroen
  Grøften
  La Crevette
  Louise Nimb

0   0.25 mi
0   0.25 km

Frederik
Bajers
Plads

↖ To Helsingør

ASSISTENS
KIRKEGÅRD

MOSAISK
KIRKEGÅRD

Skt. Hans
Torv

Nørrebrogade

Guldbergsgade

Møllegade

Nørre Allé

Tagensvej

Fredensgade

Blegdamsvej

Ryesgade

Bleg

Sortedam Dossering

Øste

Fælledvej

Kapelvej

Griffenfeldtsgade

Blågårdsgade

Rantzausgade

Korsgade

Ågade   Aboulevarden

Dronning
Louises Bro

Sortedams Sø

Peblinge Dossering

Frederiksborg

Vendersgade

Nørrepo
Statio

Rosenørns Allé

Peblinge Sø

Nørre Søgade

Nansensgade

Nørre Farimagsgade

Gyldenløvesgade

ØRSTEDS
PARKEN

Danasvej

Sankt
Jørgens
Sø

Vester Søgade

Nyropsgade

Vester Farimagsgade

Hammerichsgade

Jarmers
Plads

Kampmannsgade

Vodroffsvej

Svineryggen

Sankt
Jørgens
Sø

Vester Søgade

Nyropsgade

Vester Farimagsgade

Vesterport

2

3

TIVOLI

Skt. Knuds Vej

Vodroffsvej

Gammel   Kongevej

1

Vesterbrogade

Reventlovsgade

Central
Railway
Station

Bernstorffsgade

Vesterbrogade

Viktoriagade

Istedgade

Gasværksvej

Vesterbrogade

Dannebrogsgade

VESTERBRO

Absalonsgade

Tietgensgade

Ingerslevgade

✝ Church
ⓘ Information
✉ Post Office
— Railway

Reservations are not usually required (except in the most exclusive restaurants), but it's a good bet to phone ahead where reservations are recommended in the following guide. (Nearly everyone who answers the phones at restaurants speaks English.)

TIVOLI GARDENS

Prices at the restaurants in the Tivoli are about 30% higher than elsewhere. To compensate, skip dessert and buy something less expensive (perhaps ice cream or pastry) later at one of the many stands in the park. Take bus no. 1, 6, 8, 16, 29, 30, 32, or 33 to reach the park and any of the following restaurants.

Note: These restaurants are open only from May to mid-September.

VERY EXPENSIVE

Divan II 𝒜𝒜 DANISH/FRENCH   In a garden setting, this is the finest restaurant in the Tivoli, and certainly the most expensive. It was established in 1843, the same year as the gardens, and despite its name, it's older than its nearby competitor, the less formal Divan I. The service is impeccable, and the cuisine is among the most sophisticated in Copenhagen. The chefs create excellent meals using the best ingredients, but without audacious inventions. The carpaccio of Norwegian wild salmon marinated with lemon grass and virgin olive oil is a success, as is the terrine of goose foie gras baked with fresh truffles. Everything is elegant and well prepared, whether it be the redfish braised with saffron and garlic (served with sautéed fennel) or medallions of free-range poultry from Bresse, France, stuffed with squash and served with goose foie gras. Many ingredients are home grown, and those dishes are the most likely to achieve taste-perfection—try the rack and leg of Danish spring lamb (in truffle cream sauce) or the lightly salted breast of Danish free-range duck with an unusual horseradish beurre blanc sauce. You may think you'll never be hungry again, but then the waiter mentions strawberries Romanoff (marinated in Smirnoff vodka, Grand Marnier, and orange juice), chocolate mousse, walnut nougat, a crepe filled with custard cream and fresh berries, or a spicy cake with raspberry sorbet—all on the same platter. No wonder it's called the chef's "grand dessert."

Vesterbrogade 3, Tivoli. © **33-12-51-51.** Reservations recommended. Main courses 125DKK–365DKK ($16–$48); fixed-price lunch 395DKK ($52). AE, DC, MC, V. Daily noon–midnight.

EXPENSIVE

La Crevette 𝒜 SEAFOOD   This restaurant offers a wider variety of seafood dishes than any of its Tivoli competitors. Housed in a 1909 pavilion, it has an outdoor terrace, a tastefully modern dining room, and a well-trained staff. The seafood is fresh, flavorful, and prepared in innovative ways—for example, pickled slices of salmon with oyster flan and egg cream with chives, or bisque of turbot with veal bacon and quail's eggs. The imaginative main dishes might include grilled sea bass and scampi on crispy spinach and sautéed eggplant, or fried filet of red mullet with chive sauce and a delightful "pyramid" of shellfish. Meat and poultry courses are scarce, but you don't come here for that. Finish with a selection of cheeses from France, Denmark, and Italy (served with marinated prunes, a nice touch), or the freshly made pastries of the day. The restaurant has its own confectionery.

Vesterbrogade 3, Tivoli. © **33-14-68-47.** Reservations recommended. Main courses 225DKK–285DKK ($29–$37); 3-course fixed-price lunch 345DKK ($45); 4-course fixed-price dinner 445DKK ($58). AE, DC, MC, V. Daily noon–11pm.

Louise Nimb ℛ DANISH/FRENCH   Next door to its companion restaurant, La Crevette, this is the most formal restaurant in the Tivoli. It's styled like a Moorish pavilion, decorated with antique accessories. Louise Nimb was a chef who prepared soup in what was then a smaller kitchen. Those modest days are long gone, and the present menu is one of the most elaborate in the city; the chef uses only the freshest produce. Your first course might be smoked Baltic salmon, freshly peeled fjord shrimp, or oysters gratinée in lemon sabayon. The chef is rightfully proud of his shellfish medley, which includes Norwegian lobster, mussels, oysters, crab claws, and North Sea shrimp. Other fish choices include grilled red mullet with chive sauce. Meat eaters might prefer tournedos of beef with marrow and red-wine sauce. Live piano music is featured at dinner.

Bernstorffsgade 5, Tivoli. ℂ 33-14-60-03. Reservations required. Main courses 210DKK–295DKK ($28–$39); fixed-price lunch 295DKK ($39); fixed-price dinner 335DKK ($44). AE, DC, MC, V. Daily noon–4pm and 5–11pm.

MODERATE

Færgekroen DANISH   In a cluster of trees at the edge of the lake, this restaurant resembles a pink half-timbered Danish cottage. In warm weather, try to sit on the outside terrace. The menu offers drinks, snacks, and full meals. Meals might include omelets, beef with horseradish, fried plaice with melted butter, pork chops with red cabbage, curried chicken, and fried meatballs. If you like honest and straightforward fare, without fancy trimmings, and don't like to spend a lot of money, this might be the place for you. A pianist provides sing-along music every evening starting at 8pm.

Vesterbrogade 3, Tivoli. ℂ 33-12-94-12. Main courses 85DKK–185DKK ($11–$24); fixed-price lunch 115DKK ($15). AE, DC, MC, V. Daily 11am–midnight (hot food until 9:45pm).

Grøften ℛ *(Kids)* DANISH   Partly because of its low prices, partly because it recalls the rustic restaurants many Danes fondly remember from their childhood vacations, this is the most popular spot in the Tivoli. The outdoor terrace and indoor dining room hold about 750 diners. We always start here with freshly peeled shrimp, though smoked salmon with cream of morels is equally tempting. Cold potato soup with bacon and chives is the Danish version of vichyssoise. Ask the waiter for the day's fish offering. The chef's specialty is grilled beef tenderloin with bitter greens, tomatoes, olive oil, and black truffle essence. Old-time Danes have come here for years for the skipper's *lobscouse* (Danish hash). Glasses of beer sell for 35DKK to 50DKK ($5–$7).

Vesterbrogade 3, Tivoli. ℂ 33-12-11-25. Main courses 90DKK–185DKK ($12–$24). AE, DC, MC, V. Daily noon–10pm.

NYHAVN & KONGENS NYTORV
VERY EXPENSIVE

Era Ora ℛℛℛ ITALIAN   Meaning "Golden Age," Era Ora is on virtually everyone's list as the best Italian restaurant in Denmark, and is one of the consistently best restaurants of any kind within Copenhagen. Established in 1982 by Tuscan-born partners Alessandro and Elvio, it offers an antique dining room painted in tones of soft green and gold. Parties of up to 12 may be seated in the wine cellar. You're likely to find some remarkably chic people dining here, including members of Denmark's royal family, lots of politicians, and writers and artists who are household names throughout the country. The cuisine is based on Tuscan and Umbrian models, with sophisticated variations that are inspired by Denmark's superb array of fresh seafood and produce. Traditional favorites include a platter of 10 types of antipasti. Among them is a variation of

Valletta (tender roast beef with olive oil, Parmesan, and herbs) that's one of the prides of the restaurant. All pastas are made fresh every day. Depending on the season and the inspiration of the chef, main courses may include succulent veal dishes, rack of venison with balsamic vinegar and chanterelles, or ultra-fresh fish.

Overgaden Neden Vandet 33B. © **32-54-06-93**. Reservations required. Fixed-price menus 540DKK–650DKK ($71–$85). AE, DC, MC, V. Mon–Sat 6pm–midnight. Bus: 2 or 8.

Godt 🐸🐸🐸 INTERNATIONAL   A consistent favorite that's known to everyone in the neighborhood, including the queen of Denmark, this restaurant offers two floors of minimalist and very modern decor (all in tones of gray) that never exceed more than 20 diners at a time. Despite its fame, there's an appealing lack of pretentiousness here and the willingness to welcome all clients in the most democratic and egalitarian of ways. Food is prepared fresh daily, based on ingredients that are the best at the market that day. The repertoire of dishes is splendid, the service is minutely choreographed, and the atmosphere is so special it is worth reserving for your final night to kiss Copenhagen good-bye until another time. The chefs have prodigious talent and imagination, and the dishes are constantly changing. The sauces are sublime, as are the herbs and seasonings. Examples include crab and *rascasse* soup with leeks, fried Norwegian redfish with a purée of celery and watercress sauce, roasted rack of hare with cranberries and roasted chanterelles, and fresh figs marinated with black currant liqueur, wrapped in phyllo pastry and served with a *coulis* of pears and chocolate mousse.

Gothersgade 38. © **33-15-21-22**. Reservations required. Fixed-price menus 445DKK–565DKK ($58–$74). Tues–Sat 6–10pm. Closed July and Dec 23–Jan 3. Bus: 6, 10, or 14.

Kommandanten 🐸🐸 INTERNATIONAL   Built in 1698 as the residence of the city's military commander, Kommandanten is the epitome of Danish chic and charm. The menu offers a mouthwatering array of classic dishes as well as innovative selections. Each dish of flawless seasonal foods reflects a pleasing personal touch. The finest ingredients are used, and the menu changes every 2 weeks. You might be offered the grilled catch of the day, breast of duck with port-wine sauce, braised turbot with olive sauce, or gratinée of shellfish. The service is the best in Copenhagen. Make sure you see the three Warhols of Margrethe II in the downstairs dining room.

Ny Adelgade 7. © **33-12-09-90**. Reservations required. Main courses 270DKK–320DKK ($35–$42); fixed-price menu 380DKK ($50). AE, DC, MC, V. Mon–Fri noon–2pm; Mon–Sat 6–10pm. Bus: 1 or 6.

Kong Hans Kælder 🐸🐸🐸 INTERNATIONAL   This vaulted Gothic cellar, once owned by King Hans (1455–1513), may be the best restaurant in Denmark. Its most serious competition is the Kommandanten, which many discriminating critics claim is the best. It's one of the few restaurants in Copenhagen where you're likely to see clients as diverse as Roger Moore, Lars Ulrich (drummer from Metallica), Renée Russo, and various heads of state, all enjoying the candlelit ambience and the medieval setting. The chef creates dishes that one critic credited to "Matisse or Picasso." You may experience the artistry a la carte or by selecting a fixed-price menu (one offered at lunch, five at dinner). A typical three-course dinner would include smoked salmon from the restaurant's smokehouse, breast of duck with *bigarade* (sour orange) sauce, and plum ice cream with Armagnac. The a la carte menu is divided into "country cooking," including such items as *coq au vin* (chicken with wine) from Alsace and daube of beef; and *les spécialités*, featuring tournedos with foie gras sauce or fresh fish from the daily market, perhaps beginning with an essence and ballotine of quails with truffles. Other stellar examples include cutlets of Danish veal with peanut oil, cèpe mushrooms, and truffle-flavored butter; North Sea turbot prepared at table, cooked in a salt crust and served in puff pastry in a mousse-line of wasabi mustard; lemon sole wrapped in a crust of seasonal mushrooms and Serrano ham; and fresh Canadian lobster removed from its shell and braised with butter, spices, and herbs. Located on "the oldest corner of Copenhagen," the building has been carefully restored and is now a Relais Gourmands. Hans Christian Andersen once lived upstairs.

Vingårdsstræde 6. ℂ **33-11-68-68.** Reservations required. Main courses 195DKK–345DKK ($26–$45); fixed-price menus 605DKK–790DKK ($79–$103). AE, DC, DISC, MC, V. Mon–Sat 6pm–1am. Closed July 20–Aug 4, Dec 24–26. Bus: 1, 6, or 9.

Pierre André ★★ FRENCH/ITALIAN Everything we've sampled here has been a sheer delight—vivid flavors, masterful technique—ranking with the top restaurants of Paris or London. The chefs have considerable talent and create imaginative, elegant, but never overpowering dishes packed with robust flavors.

Choosing what to eat at this thriving Nyhavn eatery is a delicious dilemma: You might begin with a house specialty of carpaccio of foie gras "Emilia-Romagna," served with shaved Parmesan and truffles, or a salad of curried lobster with broccoli. Entrees include braised filet of turbot with mushrooms, leeks, and mango sauce, and wild venison with a bitter chocolate sauce, corn, and cranberries. For a sweet ending, consider the special chocolate cake wherein a partially liquefied filling runs onto your plate in a gooey, glorious mess.

Ny Østergade 21. ℂ **33-16-17-19.** Reservations required. Main courses 245DKK–355DKK ($32–$47); fixed-price menus 375DKK–695DKK ($49–$91). AE, DC, MC, V. Mon–Sat noon–2:30pm and 6–10pm. Closed 3 weeks July–Aug. Bus: 6, 10, or 14.

EXPENSIVE

Leonore Christine ★ DANISH This restaurant, on the sunny (south) side of the canal, is the best in Nyhavn. It's open year-round, but seems at its best in summer, when the terrace is open and you can dine overlooking the canal and the throngs of passersby. The menu changes weekly, and reflects whatever is seasonal at the time of your arrival. Stellar examples include oven-baked halibut with mussels and saffron; grilled butterfish with squash marmalade and tomatoes; North Sea turbot with fjord shrimp and asparagus; grilled salmon with couscous, fried eggplant, and balsamic vinegar; roasted red snapper with bay leaves, balsamic vinegar, and basil; and sliced breast of wild duck with polenta and wild mushrooms. For dessert, expect dishes such as white chocolate cake with mango sherbet. The restaurant is named for the sister-in-law and bitter enemy of Sophie Amalie, the 17th-century queen of Denmark and wife of Frederik III. As the king's sister, Leonore was "the lady of the land"—until Sophie Amalie arrived.

Nyhavn 9. ℂ **33-13-50-40.** Reservations required. Main courses 205DKK–255DKK ($27–$33); 4-course fixed-price menu 425DKK ($56). AE, DC, MC, V. Mon–Fri noon–3pm; Sat–Sun noon–4pm; daily 6–10pm. Bus: 1, 6, 9, or 650.

MODERATE

Café Lumskebugten ★ *Finds* DANISH This restaurant is a well-managed bastion of Danish charm, with an unpretentious elegance that's admired throughout the capital. It was established in 1854 as a rowdy tavern for sailors. As the tavern's reputation grew, aristocrats, artists, and members of the Danish royal family came to dine and see what the fun was all about. A gentrified version of the original beef hash is still served.

Two glistening-white dining rooms are decorated with antique model ships. (Two smaller rooms are usually reserved for private functions.) The food and service are excellent. Specialties include tartar of salmon with herbs, Danish fish cakes with mustard sauce and minced beet root, sugar-marinated salmon with mustard-cream sauce, and a symphony of fish with saffron sauce and new potatoes. A filling lunch platter of assorted house specialties is offered for 190DKK ($25).

Esplanaden 21. (℃ **33-15-60-29.** Reservations recommended. Main courses 178DKK–225DKK ($23–$29); 3-course fixed-price lunch 275DKK ($36); 4-course fixed-price dinner 540DKK ($71). AE, DC, MC, V. Mon–Fri 11am–10:30pm; Sat 5–10:30pm. Bus: 1, 6, or 9.

Restaurant Els DANISH/FRENCH   Restaurant Els preserves its original 1854 decor. Several murals are believed to be the work of Christian Hitsch, the 19th-century muralist who adorned parts of the interior of the Danish Royal Theater. Hans Christian Andersen was a regular here.

Each day there's a different fixed-price menu, and a selection of Danish open-faced sandwiches at lunch for those who want a lighter meal. The cuisine at night is French, accompanied by excellent wines. The menu is based on what's fresh at the market.

Menu items are creative and unusual, and change at least every month. Examples include ragout of whitefish with cabbage and wild rice; breast of wild duck with blackberry sauce; and tournedos of beef with beans, shallots, and tomatoes. Starters that are likely to be on the menu, regardless of the season, include a selection of five "Els" appetizers, or a saffron-laced version of mussel soup.

Store Strandstræde 3 (off Kongens Nytorv). (℃ **33-14-13-41.** Reservations recommended. Main courses 45DKK–115DKK ($6–$15) lunch, 178DKK–225DKK ($23–$29) dinner. AE, DC, MC, V. Mon–Sat noon–3pm; daily 5:30–10pm. Closed July. Bus: 1, 6, or 10.

Restaurant Gilleleje DANISH/INTERNATIONAL   The nautical decor here is appealing, but diners come mainly for the endless procession of dishes deftly prepared by the skilled kitchen staff. You get tasty fare and plenty of it. You might start with the specialty, a velvet-smooth lobster soup that will make you want to order a second helping (but that would fill you up too quickly). Other special dishes include the Danish herring platter, a popular first course. The fish soup is always savory, as is the whiskey steak flambé with grilled tomatoes. For dessert (if you have room), try the Danish crepes with vanilla ice cream.

Nyhavn 10. (℃ **33-12-58-58.** Reservations recommended. Main courses 178DKK–218DKK ($23–$29). AE, DC, MC, V. Mon–Sat 11:30am-10pm. Closed Sat Apr–Sept. Bus: 1, 6, 9, 10, 19, or 31.

Restaurant Havfruen 🎯 *Finds* SEAFOOD   Small and usually full, this restaurant is a cozy, nautically outfitted hideaway with a reputation for serving good fish. A carved wooden mermaid hangs from the heavy ceiling beams. The lunch menu emphasizes salmon, different preparations of herring, and such shellfish as clams and oysters. Dinner is fancier, with platters of whatever was fresh in the fish market. Especially flavorful is Greenland turbot in beurre blanc (white butter) sauce, which tastes wonderful when served with a fruity white wine from the Loire valley. The staff can get rather hysterical when the place fills up.

Nyhavn 39. (℃ **33-11-11-38.** Reservations recommended. Main courses 175DKK–250DKK ($23–$33). DC, MC, V. Daily 11:30am–11pm. Bus: 1, 6, or 9.

Restaurant Wiinblad DANISH/INTERNATIONAL   This is the less formal of the two restaurants in the upscale Hotel d'Angleterre, which is known for selecting some of the city's finest chefs. Many diners prefer Restaurant Wiinblad to its more restrictive and expensive sibling, Restaurant d'Angleterre. Bjørn Wiinblad, a beloved illustrator of children's fables, helped design his namesake's decor. Lunch might consist of *smørrebrød* (open-faced sandwiches), salads, and Danish platters that combine three oft-changing ingredients into a satisfying meal. Dinners are more elaborate, and might include grilled salmon with lobster-flavored saffron sauce; shrimp served with Thai-style lemon grass; and tenderloin of Charolais beef with lobster tail and drawn butter.

In the Hotel d'Angleterre, Kongens Nytorv 14. © **33-12-00-95.** Reservations recommended. Main courses 168DKK–295DKK ($22–$39). AE, DC, MC, V. Daily 11:30am–5pm; Sun–Thurs 5–10pm; Fri–Sat 5–11pm. Bus: 1, 6, or 9.

INEXPENSIVE

Café Zeze CONTINENTAL   This is a hip bistro and cafe with a reputation for good food and brisk service. Late night tends to be more about drinking than eating (which accounts for the increased noise level), but overall, the place can be a lot of fun. You'll find a cheerful setup with a high ceiling, mirrors, and a sunny yellow interior. Menu items change frequently, but expect a well-prepared medley of dishes that includes sautéed breast of turkey with coconut and chile sauce; roasted guinea fowl with shrimp and braised arugula; and filets of lamb with shiitake mushrooms.

20 Ny Ostergade 20. © **33-14-23-90.** Reservations recommended. Main courses 42DKK–75DKK ($6–$10) lunch; 92DKK–135DKK ($12–$18) dinner. Fixed-price lunch 58DKK ($8); fixed-price dinner 94DKK ($12). AE, DC, MC, V. Mon–Sat 11:30am–4:30pm and 5:30–10pm (last order). Bar and cafe, Mon–Thurs 8am–midnight; Fri 8am–2am; Sat 9am–2am. Bus: 1, 6, 9, or 10.

Ida Davidsen ⊛ *(Kids)* SANDWICHES   This restaurant has flourished since 1888, when the forebears of its present owner, Ida Davidsen, established a sandwich shop. Today, five generations later, the matriarch and namesake is known as the "smørrebrød queen of Copenhagen." Her restaurant sells a greater variety of open-faced sandwiches (250 kinds) than any other in Denmark. The fare has even been featured at royal buffets at Amalienborg Castle. You select by pointing to your choice in a glass-front display case; a staff member carries it to your table. The vast selection includes salmon, lobster, smoked duck with braised cabbage and horseradish, liver paté, ham, and boiled egg. Two of them, perhaps with a slice of cheese, make a worthy lunch. If in doubt, a member of the service team, or perhaps Ida's charming husband, Adam Siesbye, will offer suggestions.

Store Kongensgade 70. © **33-91-36-55.** Reservations recommended. Sandwiches 45DKK–250DKK ($6–$33). DC, MC, V. Mon–Fri 9am–4pm. Bus: 1, 6, or 9.

Nyhavns Færgekro ⊛ *(Finds)* DANISH/FRENCH   The "Nyhavn Ferry Inn" has a long tradition and many loyal fans. The house is old, dating from the final years of the 18th century. The popular summer terrace offers a view of other

---

(Kids) **Family-Friendly Restaurants**

Copenhagen Corner (p. 75)   A special children's menu features such dishes as shrimp cocktail and grilled rump steak.

Ida Davidsen (see above)   When has your kid ever faced a choice of 250 sandwiches? At the "smørrebrød queen's" cozy eatery, that's what you get. Even the queen of Denmark has praised these sandwiches and ordered them for royal buffets at Amalienborg Castle.

18th-century houses and boats in the canal. Inside, the decor is unusual, with a spiral stairway from an antique tram. Lights serve as call buttons to summon the staff when you want service.

The daily homemade buffet consists of 10 types of herring, including fried fresh herring, rollmops, and smoked herring. Some people make a full meal of it. You can also order smørrebrød—everything from smoked eel with scrambled eggs to chicken salad with bacon. A true Dane orders schnapps or aquavit at lunch. (Denmark has a tradition of making spicy aquavit from herbs and plants.) For dinner you can enjoy one of Copenhagen's most succulent entrecôtes.

Nyhavn 5. 🕿 **33-15-15-88.** Reservations required. Fixed-price dinner 165DKK ($22). DC, MC, V. Daily 11:30am–4pm and 5–11:30pm. Closed Jan 1, Dec 24–25. Bus: 1, 6, or 9.

NEAR RÅDHUSPLADSEN
MODERATE
Akvavit Bar & Bistro 🏆 *Finds* DANISH   The trick is to come here and have a unique experience without staggering out drunk. On Gammel Strand, close to Strøget, the restaurant is based on the ancient Danish custom of drinking snaps (schnapps, or *akvavit* in Danish) with each dish. The bar is stocked with the best and most varied collection of snaps in the capital, and each glass costs 18DKK ($2). The menu gives several helpful tips about what type of snaps goes with what particular course: a chilled dill snaps with a fjord shrimp salad, for example, or fresh oysters with Brøndum aquavit. A selection of open-faced sandwiches is always featured, including a delectable liver paté with mushrooms and crisp bacon. You might enjoy, as we did, the warm goat cheese salad with fresh tomatoes and olives, followed by one of the chef's specialties, tender filet of pork with a zesty lemon sauce. The steamed mussels were especially savory.

Gammel Strand 44. 🕿 **33-32-88-44.** Reservations required. Main courses 49DKK–119DKK ($6–$16). AE, DC, DISC, MC, V. Daily 10am–6pm. Bus: 29.

Atlas Bar/Restaurant Flyvefisken DANISH/THAI/INTERNATIONAL   The food served at these two restaurants derives from the same kitchen, and adheres to the same culinary philosophy. They include lots of vegetarian food inspired by the cuisines of Thailand, Mexico, and India, always with a Danish view toward tidiness and coziness. On the street level, the cramped and cozy Atlas Bar, whose walls are painted terra cotta, gets busy serving a lunchtime crowd, but slackens off a bit at night, when the wood-sheathed *Flyvefisken* (Flying Fish) opens for dinner. Upstairs, expect a greater emphasis on Thai cuisine and its fiery flavors, including lemon grass, curries, and several of the hot and spicy fish soups native to Bangkok. Although the authenticity of the Thai cuisine has lost just a bit of its zest in the long jump from Thailand, it's still a marvelous change of pace from typical Danish fare.

Lars Bjørnstræde 18. 🕿 **33-14-95-15.** Reservations recommended. Main courses 75DKK–140DKK ($10–$18) lunch; 105DKK–175DKK ($14–$23) dinner. DC, MC, V. Atlas Bar, Mon–Sat noon–10pm; Restaurant Flyvefisken, Mon–Sat 5–10pm. Bus: 5, 6, or 16.

Cilatro Bar and Grill 🏆 *Finds* INTERNATIONAL   Established in 1910 as the Café Sonderberg, and named after Prags (Prague) Boulevard, which runs nearby, this restaurant was revitalized under the direction of the Michelsen family, and today does a thriving business from a position near the Radisson SAS Scandinavia Hotel, east of Tivoli. It resembles a warm Danish *kro* (inn), with dark-wood trim, white stucco walls, and impeccable service. As much attention

Quick Bites

Copenhagen has many hot dog stands, chicken and fish grills, and smørrebrød counters that serve good, fast, inexpensive meals.

Hot dog stands, especially those around Rådhuspladsen, offer *polser* (steamed or grilled hot dogs) with shredded onions on top and *pommes frites* (french fries) on the side.

The *bageri* or *konditori* (bakery), found on almost every block, sells fresh bread, rolls, and Danish pastries.

Viktualiehandler (small food shops), found throughout the city, are the closest thing to a New York deli. You can buy roast beef with free *log* (fried onions). The best buy is smoked fish. Ask for a Bornholmer—a large, boneless sardine from the Danish island of Bornholm—or for *røgost,* a popular and inexpensive smoked cheese. Yogurt fans will be delighted to know that the Danish variety is cheap and tasty. It's available in small containers—just peel off the cover and drink it right out of the cup as the Danes do. *Hytte ret* (cottage cheese) is also good and cheap.

The favorite lunch of Scandinavians, particularly Danes, is smørrebrød. The purest form is made with dark rye bread, called *rugbrød.* Most taverns and cafes offer smørrebrød, and many places serve it as takeout food.

You can picnic in any of the city parks in the town center. Try Kongsgarten near Kongens Nytorv, the Kastellet area near *The Little Mermaid* statue, Botanisk Have (site of the Botanical Gardens), the lakeside promenades in southeastern Copenhagen, and the old moat at Christianshavn. Remember not to litter.

is paid to the way a dish looks as to the way it tastes. Menu items include lobster bisque with cognac; risotto with shellfish; roasted mackerel with tomatoes and garlic; carpaccio of duck; goose liver with apples and Calvados; and any of several fresh fish of the day, sometimes served with seasonal mushrooms.

Amagerbrogade 37. ℂ **32-54-44-44.** Reservations recommended. Main courses 45DKK–85DKK ($6–$11) lunch; 188DKK–265DKK ($25-$35) dinner. Fixed-price lunches 200DKK–240DKK ($26–$31); fixed-price dinners 250DKK–365DKK ($33–$48). AE, DC, MC, V. Mon–Fri noon–3pm and 5–10pm; Sat 5–10pm. Closed July. Bus: 2 or 9.

Copenhagen Corner *Kids* SCANDINAVIAN Surrounded by some of the heaviest pedestrian traffic in Copenhagen, this restaurant opens onto Rådhuspladsen, around the corner from the Tivoli Gardens. It offers well-prepared, unpretentious meals. The menu features the Danes' favorite dishes, beginning with three kinds of herring or freshly peeled shrimp with dill and lemon. There's even carpaccio of filet of deer for the most adventurous. Soups are excellent—try consommé of white asparagus flavored with chicken and fresh herbs. The fish is fresh and beautifully prepared, especially the steamed Norwegian salmon with a "lasagne" of potatoes, and baked halibut with artichokes. Meat and poultry courses, although not always as inspired as the fish, are tasty and tender, especially the veal liver Provençal.

H. C. Andersens Blvd. 1A. ☏ **33-91-45-45.** Reservations recommended. Main courses 98DKK–225DKK ($13–$29); 3-course fixed-price menu 295DKK ($39). AE, DC, MC, V. Daily 11:30am–11pm. Bus: 1, 6, or 8.

Sebastian Bar & Café INTERNATIONAL   Long recognized for its role as a gay bar and cafe, this institution opened a restaurant on its premises in 2000. Today, it functions as a catch-all rendezvous where many of the Danish capital's gay men and women meet, cruise, and kibitz. Expect a cafe ambience at lunch, when sandwiches, salads, and light platters are served in an old-fashioned tavern with yellow walls and lots of wood trim. During the dinner hour, when food service expands onto an upper floor, the venue and menu are both a bit more grand. Thanks to a former chef of Maxim's in Paris, the food here can be more eclectic and urbane than you might have imagined, sometimes with an emphasis on dishes from Mexico, Thailand, India, and France. Still, plenty of people just come for the bar. Expect temporary art exhibitions, often semi-erotic photographs that change frequently. On Friday and Saturday nights the bar is especially busy, a meeting place before a night of clubbing.

Hyskenstræde 10. ☏ **33-32-22-79.** Reservations recommended. Lunch platters 42DKK–85DKK ($6–$11); dinner main courses 100DKK–185DKK ($13–$24). DC, MC, V. Bar and cafe, daily noon–2am; restaurant, daily 5–11pm. Bus: 6 or 29.

Søren K ✦ INTERNATIONAL   Named after Denmark's most celebrated philosopher, this is an artfully minimalist dining room on the ground floor of the newest addition to the Royal Library. Opened in 1999, it has the kind of monochromatic gray-and-flesh-toned decor you might expect in Milan, and big window views of the sea. Menu items change frequently, but might include carpaccio of veal, foie gras, oyster soup, and main courses such as veal chops served with lobster sauce and a half-lobster, or venison roasted with nuts and seasonal berries and a marinade of green tomatoes. The restaurant virtually never cooks with butter, cream, or high-cholesterol cheeses, making a meal here a health-conscious and savory experience. To reach this place, you'll have to enter the main entrance of the library and pass through its lobby.

On the ground floor of the Royal Library's Black Diamond Wing, 1 Søren Kierkegaards Plads. ☏ **33-47-49-49.** Reservations recommended. Main courses 65DKK–125DKK ($9–$16) lunch; 195DKK–225DKK ($26–$29) dinner. 3-course fixed-price dinner 330DKK ($43). DC, MC, V. Mon–Sat noon–midnight. Bus: 8.

INEXPENSIVE

Axelborg Bodega DANISH   Across from the Benneweis Circus and near Scala and the Tivoli, this 1912 cafe has outdoor tables where you can enjoy a brisk Scandinavian evening. Order the *dagens ret* (daily special). Typical Danish dishes are featured, including *frikadeller* (meatballs) and pork chops. A wide selection of club sandwiches is also available for 48DKK to 76DKK ($6–$10) each. Although the atmosphere is somewhat impersonal, this is a local favorite; diners enjoy recipes that seem drawn from grandma's kitchen.

Axeltorv 1. ☏ **33-11-06-38.** Reservations recommended. Main courses 74DKK–135DKK ($10–$18). AE, DC, MC, V. Daily 11:30am–8:45pm; bar daily 10am–2am. Bus: 1 or 6.

Café Sorgenfri SANDWICHES   Don't come here expecting grand cuisine, or even a menu with much variety. Café Sorgenfri, in the pedestrian shopping zone in the commercial heart of town, has thrived for 150 years selling beer, schnapps, and a medley of smørrebrød. Two to four sandwiches might form a reasonable lunch, depending on your appetite. Partly because it holds only about 50 seats, it's likely to be crowded around the lunch hour, with somewhat more space at mid-afternoon. Consider having an early dinner here, if it suits you.

Everything reeks of old-time Denmark, from the potted shrubs that adorn the facade to the well-oiled paneling.

Brolæggerstræde 8. ℂ **33-11-58-80.** Reservations recommended for groups of 4 or more. Smørrebrød 38DKK–68DKK ($5–$9). DC, MC, V. Daily 11am–8:30pm. Bus: 5 or 6.

Domhus Kælderen DANISH/INTERNATIONAL   The good food at this bustling, old-fashioned emporium of Danish cuisine draws a mixed crowd from City Hall's courtrooms across the square as well as visiting foreigners. The half-cellar room holds memorabilia from its 50 years as a restaurant (before that, it was a butcher shop). Lunch tends to be more conservative and more Danish than dinner. It might include *frikadeller* (meatballs) and heaping platters of herring, cheeses, smoked meats and fish, and salads. Dinner could be pickled salmon; prime rib of beef with horseradish; and fine cuts of beef, served with béarnaise or pepper sauce. Also look for the catch of the day, prepared just about any way you like. You get no culinary surprises here, but you are rarely disappointed.

Nytorv 5. ℂ **33-14-84-55.** Reservations recommended. Main courses 42DKK–128DKK ($6–$17) lunch; 98DKK–168DKK ($13–$22) dinner. Fixed-price menus 190DKK–225DKK ($25–$29). AE, DC, MC, V. Daily 11am–4pm and 5:30–10:30pm. Bus: 5.

Huset Med Det Grønne Træ DANISH   The only drawback here is that the hours are shorter than those of virtually any other restaurant in the neighborhood. Nevertheless, the place quickly fills with shoppers and longtime patrons. Specialties include artfully crafted sandwiches in the open-faced Danish style. Among the least pretentious is herring, sliced and arranged on rough-textured bread with butter. Other versions include hot smørrebrød (more like full-fledged platters, really) garnished with chopped beef, horseradish, chopped onions, and pickles. The *pièce de la résistance* is a "sampler platter" composed of the most-loved culinary specialties of Denmark, including herring, chopped beef, liver paté, potato salad, horseradish, cheese, and a scattering of radishes, scallions, lettuces, and pickles. Beer tastes wonderful with sandwiches like this, but if you really want to pretend you're Danish, opt for one of 12 kinds of aquavit (schnapps). They're 30DKK ($4) a glass. The staff will suggest one that you might find appealing.

Gammel Torv 20. ℂ **33-12-87-86.** Reservations recommended. Sandwiches and platters 37DKK–120DKK ($5–$16). MC, V. Mon–Sat noon–2:45pm. Closed Sat May–Aug. Bus: 5.

INDRE BY
VERY EXPENSIVE
Skt. Gertruds Kloster ⚜ INTERNATIONAL   Near Nørreport Station and south of Rosenborg Castle, this is the most romantic restaurant in Copenhagen. There's no electricity in the labyrinth of 14th-century underground vaults, and the 1,500 flickering candles, open grill, iron sconces, and rough-hewn furniture create an elegant medieval ambience. The food is equally impressive, each dish balanced to perfection. Try the fresh homemade foie gras with black truffles, lobster served in turbot bouillon, scallops sautéed with herbs in sauterne, venison with green asparagus and truffle sauce, or fish and shellfish terrine studded with chunks of lobster and salmon.

Hauser Plads 32. ℂ **33-14-66-30.** Reservations required. Main courses 248DKK–295DKK ($32–$39); fixed-price menus 425DKK–690DKK ($56–$90); children's menu 95DKK ($12). AE, DC, MC, V. Daily 5–11pm. Closed Dec 25–Jan 1. Bus: 4E, 7E, 14, or 16.

MODERATE
Bøf & Ost DANISH/FRENCH   "Beef & Cheese" is in a 1728 building, and its cellars come from a medieval monastery. In the summer there's a pleasant

outdoor terrace overlooking Greyfriars Square. Specialties include lobster soup, fresh Danish bay shrimp, a cheese plate with six different selections, and some of the best grilled tenderloin in town. One local diner confided: "The food is not worthy of God's own table, but it's so good for me I come here once a week."

Gråbrødretorv 13. ☎ **33-11-99-11**. Reservations required. Main courses 149DKK–189DKK ($20–$25); fixed-price lunch 118DKK ($15). DC, MC, V. Mon–Sat 11:30am–10:30pm. Closed Jan 1, Dec 24–25. Bus: 5.

Peder Oxe's Restaurant/Vinkælder Wine Bar DANISH The building dates from the 1700s, but this restaurant and wine bar attracts a young crowd. The salad bar is 20DKK ($3) when accompanied by a main course. It's so tempting that many prefer to enjoy it alone for 56DKK ($7) per person. Dishes include lobster soup, Danish bay shrimp, fresh asparagus, open-faced sandwiches, hamburgers, and fresh fish. The bill of fare, although standard, is well prepared.

Gråbrødretorv 11. ☎ **33-11-00-77**. Reservations recommended. Main courses 79DKK–189DKK ($10–$25); fixed-price lunches 108DKK–118DKK ($14–$15). DC, MC, V. Daily 11:30am–midnight. Bus: 5.

INEXPENSIVE

Pasta Basta *Value* ITALIAN This restaurant's main attraction is an enormous buffet (sometimes called the "Pasta Basta Table") loaded with cold antipasti and salads. With more than nine selections, it's one of the best deals in town at 69DKK ($9). The restaurant is divided into half a dozen cozy dining rooms decorated in the style of ancient Pompeii, with faded frescoes patterned after originals from Italy. It's on a historic cobblestone street off the main shopping street, Strøget.

Menu choices include at least 15 kinds of pasta (all made fresh on the premises), carpaccio (raw marinated filet of beef) with olive oil and basil, a platter with three kinds of Danish caviar (whitefish, speckled trout, and vendace, served with chopped onions, lemon, toast, and butter), mozzarella with a sauce of pine nuts and fresh basil, fresh mussels cooked in dry white wine with pasta and creamy saffron sauce, thinly sliced salmon with a cream-based sauce of salmon roe, and sliced Danish suckling lamb with fried spring onions and tarragon. Dessert offerings include an assortment of Danish, French, and Italian cheeses; crème brûlée; and tartufo.

Valkendorfsgade 22. ☎ **33-11-21-31**. Reservations recommended. Main courses 64DKK–150DKK ($8–$20). DC, MC, V. Sun–Thurs 11:30am–3am; Fri–Sat 11:30am–5:30am. Bus: 5.

SLOTSHOLMEN
EXPENSIVE

Krogs Fiskerestaurant *✦* SEAFOOD A short walk from Christiansborg Castle, the most famous restaurant in the district was built in 1789 as a fish shop. The canal-side plaza where fishers once moored their boats is now the site of the restaurant's outdoor dining terrace. The restaurant serves fresh seafood in a single large room decorated in antique style, with old oil paintings. The well-chosen menu includes lobster soup, bouillabaisse, oysters, mussels steamed in white wine, and poached salmon-trout with saffron sauce. Each dish is impeccably prepared and flavorful. A selection of meat dishes is available, but the fish is better.

Gammel Strand 38. ☎ **33-15-89-15**. Reservations required. Main courses 328DKK–585DKK ($43–$77); 4-course fixed-price menu 685DKK ($90); 5-course fixed-price menu 895DKK ($117). AE, DC, MC, V. Mon–Sat 11:30am–4pm and 5:30–10:30pm. Bus: 1, 2, 10, 16, or 29.

Nouvelle *✦✦* DANISH Nouvelle has been one of the capital's special restaurants since 1950. It's on the first floor of an 1870 house beside a canal. If you've won the lottery, the restaurant has a special caviar menu, with Sevruga and Beluga. Otherwise, you can explore the a la carte menu, which changes frequently but is likely to include goose-liver terrine with three kinds of glazed onions, or

warm oysters and mussels gratinée. The superb fish dishes include North Sea turbot grilled or poached and served on a tomato, rosemary, and artichoke parfait.
Lobster is served as a fricassee with green apples and curry hollandaise. Meat
selections are likely to include grilled goose liver with glazed spring cabbage and
curry, or lamb medallions with white truffles and new onions.

Gammel Strand 34. ℂ **33-13-50-18.** Reservations required. Main courses 272DKK–330DKK ($36–$43); 3-course fixed-price lunch 475DKK ($62); 4-course fixed-price dinner 610DKK ($80). AE, DC, MC, V. Mon–Fri 11:30am–3pm and 6–10pm; Sat 7:30–9pm. Closed Dec 22–Jan 6. Bus: 28, 29, or 41.

MODERATE
Den Gyldne Fortun ⭐ DANISH/SEAFOOD   Popular at lunchtime, this
restaurant opposite Christiansborg Castle lives up to its name, "golden fortune."
Dating from 1796, it has been visited by Hans Christian Andersen, Jenny Lind,
and Henry Wadsworth Longfellow. You climb green marble stairs to enter the
formal restaurant, which resembles an English club. Amid crystal chandeliers,
modern lithographs, and bubbling aquariums, you can order the kinds of dishes
requested by members of Denmark's royal family after shopping expeditions on
the nearby Strøget. Choices include a Scandinavian version of bouillabaisse
(served only in winter); fried filet of plaice in butter sauce; fried Danish lamb
with red wine and tarragon sauce; oven-baked salmon with Noilly Prat (a vermouth) sauce; and halibut with red wine sauce and herbs. Dessert offerings
include the restaurant's well-known sweet plate, with the day's freshest mousses
and pastries, or a range of exotic sherbets that changes almost every week.

Ved Stranden 18. ℂ **33-12-20-11.** Reservations recommended. Main courses 178DKK–200DKK ($23–$26); 4-course fixed-price menu 398DKK ($52). AE, DC, MC, V. Mon–Sat 10am–11pm. Bus: 1, 6, or 10.

INEXPENSIVE
Cafeen Nikolaj DANISH   This cafe, which to some evokes Greenwich Village in the 1950s, is on the site where Hans Tausen, a father of the Danish
Reformation, delivered thundering sermons in the 16th century. Today no one
is thundering—they're ordering an array of typical Danish lunches, including a
tasty variety of open-faced sandwiches and homemade soups. You can always
count on various types of herring. Danish sliced ham on good homemade bread
is a perennial favorite, and there is also a selection of Danish cheeses. The place
makes no pretensions of being more than it is: a simple cafe that prepares good
tasting food with fresh ingredients at fair prices.

Nikolaj Plads 12. ℂ **70-26-64-64.** Main courses 75DKK–225DKK ($10–$29). AE, DC, DISC, MC, V. Mon–Sat 11:30am–5pm. Bus: 2, 6, 10, 27, 28, or 29.

VESTERBRO
MODERATE
Passagens Spiesehus ⭐ (Finds) SCANDINAVIAN   For "Nuances of the
North," head to this rare treat (called "The Eatery" in English) for a broad range
of Scandinavian dishes, many of which have not been seen around town since
grandmother's time. Where else can you get a good moose steak these days?
Many items will be a culinary first for you, including "electric" orange roe from
a trout-like fish called *sellak,* dubbed the beluga of the Arctic Circle. The *caper-
caillie* is a dark, meaty bird caught in northern Sweden. And wait until you sample the smoked reindeer heart. Marc Davidsen is a chef with a unique vision. As
every other chef in Copenhagen switches to a Franco-Italian fare, he is on a zeal-
ous mission to revive forgotten Nordic cuisine.

Vesterbrogade 42. ℂ **33-22-47-57.** Reservations required. Main courses 119DKK–149DKK ($16–$20). MC, V. Bus: 1, 6, or 8.

4

Exploring Copenhagen

In sights and nightlife, perennially youthful Copenhagen offers the charm of the past, the magic of the present, and the promise of the future.

For all the tourist-propaganda emphasis on "life-seeing," amusement parks, shopping expeditions, beer gardens, and bustling nightspots, Copenhagen is also proud of its vast storehouse of antiquities. It holds its own with the other capitals of Europe.

The "fun, fun" slogans and the "wonderful, wonderful" Copenhagen melodies tend to detract from an important fact. The Danish capital is an excellent center not only for pleasure seekers, but also for serious visitors who want to inspect art galleries, museums, and castles.

In the morning, museum-goers can wander back to classical or Renaissance days in such showcases of art as Thorvaldsen's Museum. You can stroll down corridors, inspecting diverse sculptured creatures, such as Cupid driving two wild boars, a she-wolf, even Apollo Belvedere.

In the afternoon, head south to the little town of Dragør on the island of Amager, long connected to the mainland and now almost a suburb of Copenhagen. Here you'll see the legacy of the Dutch inhabitants who lived and farmed on the island for some 300 years, displayed in museums and evident in the architecture.

On a summer evening, visitors can stroll through the Tivoli pleasure gardens, which seem to have emerged intact from the days when the world was young . . . and so were we. The Danes apparently love childhood too much to abandon it forever, no matter how old they get—so the Tivoli keeps alive the magic of fairy lights and the wonder of yesteryear.

Amusement parks, shopping, beer gardens, and bustling nightspots vie with galleries, museums, and castles for your time in Copenhagen. So many hidden nooks wait to be explored that it's hard to decide what to do first. Here are a few ideas.

SUGGESTED ITINERARIES

If You Have 1 Day

Take our walking tour through the old city (see "Walking Tour 1: The Old City," later in this chapter), which isn't too taxing if you're still recovering from jet lag. Spend the late afternoon at Christiansborg Palace, on Slotsholmen, where the queen receives guests. Early in the evening, head to the Tivoli. However, if it's winter, explore Kongens Nytorv (King's New Square) and the now-charming old sailors' quarter called Nyhavn. At some point in the day, climb the Rundetårn (Round Tower) for a glorious panorama of Copenhagen.

If You Have 2 Days

On the first day, follow the suggestions above. On Day 2, visit Amalienborg Palace, the queen's residence. Try to time your visit so that you can see the changing of the guard. It doesn't have the precision or pomp of the changing of the guard at Buckingham Palace, but nonetheless it remains a "Kodak moment." Continue beyond the palace to the city's beloved statue, *The Little Mermaid,* perched upon a rock in the harbor. In the afternoon, see the art treasures of Ny Carlsberg Glyptotek. At night, visit Scala, the restaurant and shopping complex.

If You Have 3 Days
Follow the suggestions above for the first 2 days. On the morning of Day 3, visit 17th-century Rosenborg Castle, summer palace of Christian IV, and wander through its park and gardens. Have lunch at one of the restaurants that line the canal at Nyhavn, the old seamen's quarter. Visit the National Museum in the afternoon.

If You Have 4 or 5 Days
For the first 3 days, see the suggestions above. On Day 4, head north from Copenhagen to Louisiana, the modern-art museum located in a 19th-century mansion on the Danish Riviera. Continue to Helsingør to visit Kronborg Castle, made famous by Shakespeare's *Hamlet.* Return by train to Copenhagen in time for a stroll along Strøget, the longest pedestrians-only street in Europe. Have dinner at a restaurant in Dragør. On the fifth day, visit Frilandsmuseet, a re-created village of farmsteads and rural cottages at Lyngby, a half-hour train ride from Copenhagen. Have lunch at the park. Return to Copenhagen and take our second walking tour, which covers Kongens Nytorv to Langelinie (see "Walking Tour 2," later in this chapter). If time remains, tour the Carlsberg Brewery. Pay a final visit to the Tivoli to cap your adventure.

1 In & Around the Tivoli Gardens

Tivoli Gardens ★★★   Since it opened in 1843, this 8-hectare (20-acre) garden and amusement park in the center of Copenhagen has been a resounding success. It boasts thousands of flowers, a merry-go-round of tiny Viking ships, games of chance and skill (pinball arcades, slot machines, shooting galleries), and a Ferris wheel of hot-air balloons and cabin seats. There's even a playground.

An Arabian-style fantasy palace complete with towers and arches houses more than two dozen restaurants in all price ranges, from a lakeside inn to a beer garden. Finer, pricier meals are to be had at Divan II, La Crevette, and Louise Nimb. Walk around the edge of the tiny lake, with its ducks, swans, and boats.

Tivoli's newest attraction, The Golden Tower, rises 19 stories high over the city's skyline, and is crowned with a golden cupola. Patrons are taken 57m (190 ft.) straight up to enjoy a panoramic view over Copenhagen before being dropped back to earth at a blazing speed that's even faster than a natural free fall. The tower is set in elaborate Asian-themed surroundings, with exotic plants and colored tiles.

A parade of the red-uniformed Tivoli Boys Guard takes place on weekends at 6:30 and 8:30pm, and their regimental band gives concerts on Saturday at 3pm on the open-air stage. The oldest building at the Tivoli, the Chinese-style Pantomime Theater, stages performances in the evening.

For more specifics on nighttime happenings—fireworks, brass bands, orchestras, dance parties, and variety acts—see "Copenhagen After Dark," later in this chapter.

Copenhagen Attractions

Amalienborg Palace **6**
Børsen **21**
Botanisk Have **14**
Christiansborg Palace **22**
Copenhagen University **17**
Davids Samling **10**
Erotica Museum **15**
Frederikskirche
  (Marble Church) **5**
Frihedsmuseet **3**
Grundtvigs Kirke **32**
Hirschsprung Collection **13**
Holmens Kirke **19**
Kastellet **2**
Københavns Bymuseum **31**
Kongelige Bibliotek **23**
Kongelige Teater **9**
Kunstindustrimuseet **4**
The Little Mermaid **1**
Louis Tussaud
  Wax Museum **29**
Nationalmuseet **25**
Ny Carlsberg Glyptotek **27**
Orlogsmuseet **7**
Rådhus (Town Hall) **26**
Rosenborg Castle **11**
Rundetårn
  (Round Tower) **16**
Statens Museum
  for Kunst **12**
Thorvaldsens Museum **20**
Tivoli Gardens **28**
Tøjhusmuseet **24**
Tycho Brahe
  Planetarium **30**
Vor Frelsers Kirken **8**
Vor Frue Kirke **18**

Church
Information
Post Office
Railway

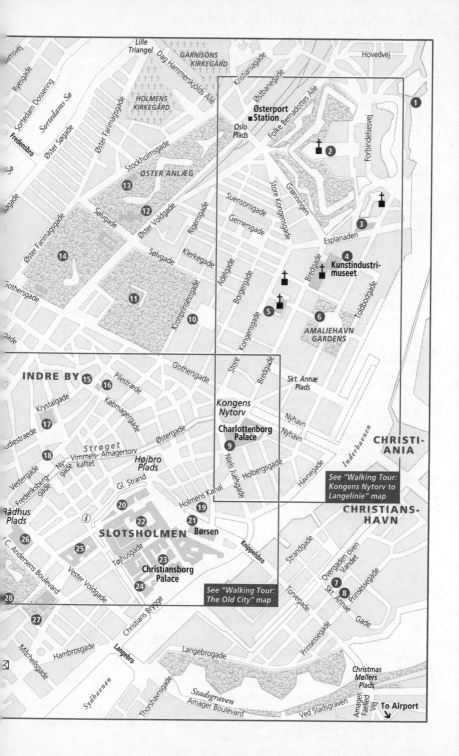

Lille Triangel

Dag Hammerskjolds Allé

GARNISONS KIRKEGÅRD

Hovedvej

Ryesgade

Kristianiagade

Østbanegade

Sortedam Dossering

HOLMENS KIRKEGÅRD

Østerport Station

Oslo Plads

Folke Bernadottes Allé

1

Forbindelsesvej

Fredensbro

Øster Søgade

Sortedams Sø

Øster Farimagsgade

Stockholmsgade

† **2**

ØSTER ANLÆG

Suensonsgade

Store Kongensgade

Grønningen

13

Rigensgade

Gernersgade

Esplanaden

† **3**

12

Sølvgade

Øster Voldgade

Klerkegade

Sølvgade

Adelgade

Borgergade

Bredgade

Toldbodgade

4 Kunstindustri-museet

Øster Farimagsgade

14

Gothersgade

11

Kronprinsessegade

10

Store Kongensgade

† **5**

6

AMALIEHAVN GARDENS

Gothersgade

Store

Bredgade

Skt. Annæ Plads

INDRE BY **15**

Pilestræde

16

Kongens Nytorv

Nyhavn

CHRISTI-ANIA

Krystalgade

Købmagergade

Charlottenborg Palace

Nyhavn

Inderhavnen

17

Østergade

9

Niels Juelsgade

Holbergsgade

Havnegade

Vestergade

Studiestraede

18

Strøget

Vimmels- Amagertorv gade kaftet

Højbro Plads

Nw.

Gl. Strand

Holmens Kanal

See "Walking Tour: Kongens Nytorv to Langelinie" map

CHRISTIANS-HAVN

Frederiksberg gade

Rådhus Plads

i

20

22

19

21

Børsen

Knippelsbro

Strandgade

Overgaden oven Vandet

26

25

SLOTSHOLMEN

Tøjhusgade

Vester Voldgade

23

Christiansborg Palace

24

See "Walking Tour: The Old City" map

Torvegade

Skt. Annæ

Prinsessegade

7

8

Gade

H.C. Andersens Boulevard

28

27

Christians Brygge

Langebro

Hambrosgade

Mitchellsgade

Langebrogade

Prinsessegade

Christmas Møllers Plads

Sydhavnen

Stadsgraven

Thorshavnsgade

Amager Boulevard

Ved Stadsgraven

Amager Fælled Vej

To Airport

83

Vesterbrogade 3. 🅒 **33-15-10-01.** Admission 55DKK ($7.20) adults, 30DKK ($3.95) children under 14; combination ticket including admission and all rides 100DKK ($13). May to mid-Sept daily 11am–midnight. Partial Christmastime opening from mid-Nov until Christmas Eve (reduced admission). Closed mid-Sept to Apr. Bus: 1, 16, or 29.

Ny Carlsberg Glyptotek 🅐🅐🅐   The Glyptotek, behind the Tivoli, is one of the most important art museums in Scandinavia. Founded by the 19th-century art collector Carl Jacobsen ("Mr. Carlsberg Beer" himself), the museum devotes two floors each to its modern (mainly 19th-c.) and antiquities collections; in 1996, the excellent French masters' wing was added. The modern section has both French and Danish art, including works by Rodin and Impressionist paintings including van Gogh's *Landscape from St. Rémy.* The antiquities department is separated from the modern section by a conservatory and houses Egyptian, Greek, and Roman art on the main floor; Etruscan, Greek, and Cypriot art on the lower floor. The Egyptian collection is outstanding; the most notable prize is a prehistoric rendering of a hippopotamus. Fine Greek originals (headless Apollo, Niobe's tragic children) and Roman copies of original Greek bronzes (4th-c. Hercules) are also on display, as are busts of Roman nobles—Pompey, Virgil, Augustus, and Trajan. A favorite of ours is the Etruscan art display, with sarcophagi, a winged lion, bronzes, and pottery.

Constructed of white marble and granite, the French masters' wing is in the inner courtyard and can be reached only through the conservatory. There are works by Manet, Monet, Degas, and Renoir, as well as an impressive collection of French sculpture, such as Rodin's *Burghers of Calais,* and one of only three complete sets of Degas bronzes. The display features Cézanne's famous *Portrait of the Artist,* as well as about 35 paintings by former Copenhagen resident Gauguin.

Dantes Plads 7. 🅒 **33-41-81-41.** Admission 30DKK ($3.95) adults, free for children; free for all Wed and Sun. Tues–Sun 10am–4pm. Bus: 1, 2, 5, 6, 8, or 10.

Rådhus (Town Hall) and World Clock   Built in 1905, the Town Hall has impressive statues of Hans Christian Andersen and of Niels Bohr, the Nobel Prize–winning physicist. Jens Olsen's famous World Clock is on the ground floor and is open for viewing weekdays from 10am to 4pm and Saturday from 10am to 1pm. Frederik IX set the clock on December 15, 1955. The clockwork is so exact that it's calibrated to lose just .4 seconds in 300 years.

Climb the tower for an impressive view. To the east of the Rådhus is one of Copenhagen's most famous landmarks, the Lurblæserne (Lur Blower Column), the column topped by two Vikings blowing an ancient trumpet called a *lur.* It involves a bit of artistic license—the lur dates from the Bronze Age (around 1500 B.C.), and the Vikings lived some 1,000 years ago. But it's a fascinating sight just the same. City tours often begin here.

Rådhuspladsen. 🅒 **33-66-25-82.** Rådhus, 30DKK ($3.95); clock, 10DKK ($1.30) adults, 5 DKK (65¢) children. Guided tour: Rådhus, Mon–Fri 3pm, Sat 10am; tower, Mon–Sat noon. Bus: 1, 6, or 8.

Louis Tussaud Wax Museum   A visit to the Louis Tussaud Wax Museum, so the publicity goes, is the closest some of us will ever get to meeting our heroes. It *is* a major Copenhagen attraction and it features more than 200 wax figures— everybody from Danish kings and queens to Leonardo da Vinci to the Fab Four. Children can visit the Snow Queen's Castle, or watch Frankenstein and Dracula guard the monsters and vampires.

H. C. Andersens Blvd. 22. 🅒 **33-11-89-00.** Admission 65DKK ($8.50) adults, 54DKK ($7.05) seniors, 29DKK ($3.80) children. Apr 29–Sept 13 daily 10am–10pm; Sept 14–Apr 28 daily 10am–6pm. Bus: 1, 2, 16, 28, 29, or 41.

2 Amalienborg Palace & Environs

Amalienborg Palace ✿✿ These four 18th-century French-style rococo mansions have been the home of the Danish royal family since 1794, when Christiansborg burned. They open onto one of the most attractive squares in Europe, Amalienborg. When the royal family is in residence, visitors flock to witness the changing of the guard at noon. A swallowtail flag signifies that the queen is in Copenhagen, not at her North Zealand summer home, Fredensborg Palace. The Royal Life Guard, in black bearskin busbies, leaves Rosenborg Castle at 11:30am and marches along Gothersgade, Nørre Voldgade, Frederiksborggade, Købmagergade, Østergade, Kongens Nytorv, Bredgade, Sankt Annæ Plads, and Amaliegade to Amalienborg. After the event, the guard, accompanied by a band, returns to Rosenborg Castle via Frederiksgade, Store Kongensgade, and Gothersgade. In 1994 some official and private rooms in Amalienborg opened to the public for the first time. The rooms, reconstructed to reflect the period from 1863 to 1947, belonged to members of the reigning royal family, the Glücksborgs, who ascended the throne in 1863. The highlight is the period devoted to the long reign (1863–1906) of Christian IX (1818–1906) and Queen Louise (1817–98). The items in his study and her drawing room—gifts from their far-flung children—reflect their unofficial status as "parents-in-law to Europe." Both came from distant sides of the then–heir-less royal family to create a true "love match." The author of the verses for their wedding song (a Danish tradition), in 1842, was none other than Hans Christian Andersen.

Christian and Louise gave their six children a simple but internationally oriented upbringing. One daughter, Alexandra, married Edward VII of England; another, Dagmar, wed Tsar Alexander III of Russia. The crown prince, who became Frederik VIII, married Louise of Sweden-Norway; another son became king of Greece, and yet another declined the throne of Bulgaria. In 1905 a grandson became king of Norway.

In the 1880s, members of the Danish royal family, numbering more than 50, got together each summer at Fredensborg Palace, north of Copenhagen. The children, now monarchs, brought Christian IX and Louise presents—works of art from the imperial workshops and from jewelers such as Fabergé—as well as souvenirs, embroideries, and handicrafts made by the grandchildren. All became treasures for the aging king and queen, and many are exhibited today.

Also open to the public are the studies of Frederik VIII and Christian X. Thanks to his marriage to Louise of Sweden-Norway, the liberal-minded Frederik VIII (1843–1912), who reigned from 1906 to 1912, had considerable wealth, and he furnished Amalienborg Palace sumptuously. The king's large study is decorated in lavish neo-Renaissance style.

The final period room in the museum is the study of Christian X (1870–1947), king from 1912 to 1947 and grandfather of Queen Margrethe II. He became a symbol of national resistance during the German occupation of Denmark during World War II. Along with the period rooms, a costume gallery and jewelry room are open to the public. The Amalienborg Museum rooms are one of two divisions of the Royal Danish Collections; the other is at Rosenborg Palace.

Christian VIII's Palace. ℂ **33-12-21-86.** Admission 40DKK ($5.25) adults, 25DKK ($3.30) students and seniors, 5DKK (65¢) children 5–12, free for children under 5. Jan–Apr and Oct–Dec 13 Tues–Sun 11am–4pm; May, Sept–Oct, Dec 26–30 daily 11am–4pm; June–Aug daily 10am–4pm. Closed Dec 14–25. Bus: 1, 6, 9, or 10.

Den Lille Havfrue (The Little Mermaid) ✿ This is the one statue in Copenhagen *everybody* wants to see. The life-size bronze of *Den Lille Havfrue*

Frommer's Favorite Copenhagen Experiences

Sitting at an Outdoor Cafe. Because of Copenhagen's long gray winters, sitting outdoors and drinking beer or eating is a favorite, savored summer pastime. The best spot is at Nyhavn (New Harbor), beginning at Kongens Nytorv. Enjoy ice cream while admiring the tall ships moored in the canal.

Going to the Tivoli. This is the quintessential summer adventure, a tradition since 1843. It's an amusement park with a difference—even the merry-go-rounds are special, using a fleet of Viking ships instead of the usual horses.

Strolling Strøget. The Danish word strøget means "to stroll"—and that's exactly what shopping addicts do along this nearly 1.2km (¾-mile) stretch, from Rådhuspladsen to Kongens Nytorv.

Exploring Alternative Lifestyles. Not for everybody, but worth a look, is a trip to the Free City of Christiania, on the island of Christianshavn (take bus no. 8 from Rådhuspladsen). Since 1971 some 1,000 squatters have taken over 130 former army barracks (spread across 8 hectares/20 acres) and declared themselves a free city. You can shop, dine, and talk to the natives about the experimental community, which has its own doctors, clubs, and stores. It even flies its own flag. Exercise caution here, however.

was inspired by Hans Christian Andersen's *The Little Mermaid*, one of the world's most famous fairy tales. Edvard Eriksen's sculpture, unveiled in 1913, rests on rocks right off the shore. In spite of its small size, the statue is as important a symbol to Copenhageners as the Statue of Liberty is to New Yorkers.

The mermaid has fallen prey to vandals over the years. In the early 1900s, her arm was cut off and later recovered. She was decapitated on April 25, 1964, and the head was never returned. (The original mold exists, so missing body parts can be recast.) In January 1998, she lost her head again, and most of the city responded with sadness. "She is part of our heritage, like the Tivoli, the queen, and stuff like that," said local sculptor Christian Moerk.

Although not taking blame for the attack, the Radical Feminist Faction sent flyers to newspapers to protest "the woman-hating, sexually fixated male dreams" allegedly conjured by the statue's nudity. The head mysteriously turned up at a TV station, delivered by a masked figure. Welders restored it, making the seam invisible.

Nearby is the **Gefion Fountain (Gefion Springvandet),** sculpted by Anders Bundgaard. Gefion is is a character from Scandinavian myth who plowed Zealand away from Sweden by turning her sons into oxen. Also in the area is **Kastellet** at Langelinie (© **33-11-22-33**), a citadel constructed by King Frederik III in the 1660s. Some of Copenhagen's original ramparts surround the structure. The citadel was the capital's main fortress until the 18th century, when it fell into disuse. During the Nazi occupation of Copenhagen in World War II, the Germans made it their headquarters. Today the Danish military uses the buildings, and the beautiful grounds of Churchillparken that surround Kastellet are open to visitors. At the entrance to the park stands St. Alban's, the English church of Copenhagen. You can still see the double moats built as part of Copenhagen's

defense in the wake of the Swedish siege of the capital on February 10, 1659. This ruined citadel can be explored daily from 6am to sunset. Admission is free.
Langelinie, on the harbor. Bus: 1, 6, or 9.

Frihedsmuseet (Museum of Danish Resistance, 1940–45) This museum displays the tools of espionage and sabotage that the Danes used to throw off the Nazi yoke in World War II. Beginning with peace marches in the early days of the war, the resistance movement grew into a skilled underground that eventually electrified and excited the Allied world. "Danes Fighting Germans!" blared the headlines.

A moment in history is graphically and dramatically preserved. The museum highlights the workings of the outlaw press, the equipment used in the wireless and illegal films, relics of torture and concentration camps, British propaganda leaflets dropped in the country, satirical caricatures of Hitler, information about Danish Jews and Danish Nazis, and the paralyzing nationwide strikes. An armed car, used against Danish Nazi informers and collaborators, is displayed on the grounds.
Churchillparken. ℂ 33-13-77-14. Admission 30DKK ($3.95) adults, free for children under 16. May–Sept 15 Tues–Sat 10am–4pm, Sun 10am–5pm; Sept 16–Apr Tues–Sat 11am–3pm, Sun 11am–4pm. Bus: 1, 6, or 9.

Kunstindustrimuseet (Museum of Decorative and Applied Art) 𝄢 This rococo building consists of four wings surrounding a garden, and was part of the Royal Frederik Hospital built from 1752 to 1757 under King Frederik V. It was restored in the early 1920s and adapted to house the museum's collections, which consist mostly of European decorative and applied art from the Middle Ages to the present, arranged in chronological order. Important collections include furniture, tapestries and other textiles, pottery, porcelain, glass, and silver. There are also collections of Chinese and Japanese art and handicrafts. The library contains some 65,000 books and periodicals that deal with arts and crafts, architecture, costumes, advertising, photography, and industrial design.
Bredgade 68. ℂ 33-18-56-56. Museum, 40DKK ($5.25) adults, free for children under 16; library, free. Museum, Tues–Sun 1–4pm; library, Tues–Sat 10am–4pm. S-tog: Østerport. Bus: 1, 6, or 9.

Davids Samling 𝄢 Finds Danish attorney C. L. David (1878–1960) established this museum shortly after World War II on the premises of his private house across from the park surrounding Rosenborg Castle. This privately funded museum is visited mainly because it has Scandinavia's largest collection of Islamic art. However, Samling didn't stop there in his collecting, as he had rather global tastes: He also accumulated an exquisite collection of French china from the 18th century, along with centuries-old antiques and paintings, and an especially strong collection of English furniture. He was also an inveterate collector of Scandinavian ceramics and silver.

David's other major bequest to Denmark was his summer villa in the northern suburbs of Copenhagen at Marienborg, which is for the prime minister's use.
Kronprinsessegade 30. ℂ 33-73-49-49. Free admission. Tues–Sun 1–4pm. Bus: 1, 6, 9, 10, 19, 29, 31, 42, or 43.

Impressions

There is nothing of Hamlet in their character.

—R. H. Bruce Lockhart,
My Europe, 1952

Copenhagen is the best-built city of the north.

—William Coxe, *Travels,* 1792

---

3 Rosenborg Castle, Botanical Gardens & Environs

Rosenborg Castle ★★   Founded by Christian IV in the 17th century, this redbrick Renaissance-style castle houses everything from narwhal-tusk and ivory coronation chairs to Frederik VII's baby shoes. Most impressive are the dazzling crown jewels and regalia housed in the basement Treasury, where there's also a lavishly decorated coronation saddle from 1596. The Knights Hall (Room no. 21) boasts a coronation seat, three silver lions, and relics from the 1700s. Another important attraction is Room no. 3, a bedroom decorated with Asian lacquer art and a stucco ceiling in which founding father Christian IV died. The king's *Have* (garden) surrounds the castle, and the Botanical Gardens are across the street.

Øster Voldgade 4A. ✆ **33-15-32-86.** Admission 60DKK ($7.85) adults, 40DKK ($5.25) students and seniors, 10DKK ($1.30) children 5–12, free for children 4 and under. Palace and treasury (royal jewels), June–Aug daily 10am–4pm; May and Sept to mid-Oct daily 11am–3pm; mid-Oct to Apr Tues-Sun 11am–2pm. S-tog: Nørreport. Bus: 5, 10, 14, 16, 31, 42, 43, 184, or 185.

Botanisk Have (Botanical Gardens)   Planted from 1871 to 1874, the Botanical Gardens are at a lake that was once part of the city's defensive moat. Across from Rosenborg Castle, they contain hothouses with tropical and subtropical plants. Special features include a cactus house and a palm house, all of which appear even more exotic so far north. An alpine garden contains mountain plants from all over the world.

Gothersgade 128. ✆ **35-32-22-40.** Free admission. May–Sept daily 8:30am–6pm; Oct–Apr Tues–Sun 8:30am–4pm. S-tog: Nørreport. Bus: 5, 7, 14, 16, 24, 40, or 43.

Statens Museum for Kunst (Royal Museum of Fine Arts) ★★   The largest art museum in Denmark, the Royal Museum is well stocked with painting and sculpture from the 13th century to the present. There are Dutch golden age landscapes and marine paintings by Rubens and his school, plus portraits by Frans Hals and Rembrandt. Eckersberg, Købke, and Hansen represent the Danish golden age. French 20th-century art includes 20 works by Matisse. In the Royal Print Room are 300,000 drawings, prints, lithographs, and other works by such artists as Dürer, Rembrandt, Matisse, and Picasso. The museum is especially strong in artifacts unearthed from the Viking era. A sculpture garden is filled with classical and contemporary works.

A major expansion in 1998 added a concert hall, a Children's Art Museum, and a glass wing designed for temporary exhibits.

Sølvgade 48–50. ✆ **33-74-84-94.** Admission 50DKK–60DKK ($6.55–$7.85) adults, 35DKK ($4.60) students, free for children under 16. Higher admission for special exhibitions only. Tues and Thurs–Sun 10am–5pm; Wed 10am–8pm. Bus: 10, 14, 43, or 184.

Den Hirschsprungske Samling (Hirschsprung Collection) ★ *Finds*   This collection of Danish art from the 19th and early 20th centuries lies in Ostre Anlaeg, a park in the city center. Heinrich Hirschsprung (1836–1908), a tobacco merchant, created the collection and it has grown ever since. The emphasis is on the Danish golden age, with such artists as Eckersberg, Købke, and Lundbye, and on the Skagen painters—P. S. Krøyer and Anna and Michael Ancher. Some furnishings from the artists' homes are exhibited.

Stockholmsgade 20. ✆ **35-42-03-36.** Admission 35DKK ($4.60) adults, free for children under 16. Wed–Mon 11am–4pm. Bus: 10, 14, 40, 42, or 43.

4 Christiansborg Palace & Environs

Christiansborg Palace ✿✿✿   This granite-and-copper palace on Slotshol-men—a small island that has been the center of political power in Denmark for more than 800 years—houses the parliament, Supreme Court, prime minister's offices, and Royal Reception Rooms. A guide leads you through richly decorated rooms, including the Throne Room, Banqueting Hall, and Queen's Library. Before entering, you'll be asked to put on soft overshoes to protect the wood floors. Under the palace, visit the well-preserved ruins of the 1167 castle of Bishop Absalon, founder of Copenhagen. At **Kongelige Stalde & Kareter,** Christianborg Ridebane 12 (✆ 33-40-10-10), you can see the royal stables and coaches. Elegantly clad in riding breeches and jackets, riders exercise the horses. Vehicles include regal coaches and "fairy-tale" carriages, along with a display of harnesses in use by the royal family since 1778. Admission is 10DKK ($1.30) for adults, 5DKK (65¢) for children. The site can be visited from May to September, Friday through Sunday from 2 to 4pm. During other months, hours are Saturday and Sunday from 2 to 4pm.

Christiansborg Slotsplads. ✆ **33-92-64-92.** Royal Reception Rooms, 45DKK ($5.90) adults, 10DKK ($1.30) children; parliament, free; castle ruins, 20DKK ($2.60) adults, 5DKK (65¢) children. Reception rooms, guided tours May–Sept daily at 11am, 1pm, and 3pm; Oct–Apr Tues–Thurs and Sat–Sun at 3pm. Parliament, English-language tours daily 11am, 1pm, and 3pm year-round. Ruins, May–Sept daily 9:30am–3:30pm; Oct–Apr Tues-Thurs and Sat–Sun 9:30am–3:30pm.

Nationalmuseet (National Museum) ✿   This gigantic repository of anthropological artifacts ambitiously surveys 10,000 years of history. The first of five areas represented focuses on prehistory, the Middle Ages, and the Renaissance in Denmark. Collections date from the Stone Age and include Viking stones, helmets, and fragments of battle gear. Especially interesting are the *lur* (horn), a Bronze Age piece that's among the oldest musical instruments in Europe, and the world-famous "Sun Chariot," an elegant Bronze Age piece of pagan art. The next area is a study of the 18th-century royal palace in which the museum is housed. There's also the Royal Collection of Coins and Medals and the Collection of Egyptian and Classical Antiquities, which offers outstanding fragments of ancient civilizations such as Roman chalices depicting Homeric legends. Finally, in the ethnographic section, relics of Inuit culture and the peo ple of Greenland and Denmark are represented.

Ny Vestergade 10. ✆ **33-13-44-11.** Admission 40DKK ($5.25) adults, 30DKK ($3.95) students, free for children under 16. Tues–Sun 10am–4pm. Closed Dec 24, 25, and 31. Bus: 1, 2, 5, 6, 8, 10, or 41.

Erotica Museum *(Finds*   This is perhaps the only museum in the world where you can learn about the sex lives of such famous people as Freud, Nietzsche, and Duke Ellington—assuming that you were interested in the first place. Founded by Ole Ege, a well-known Danish photographer of nudes, it's within walking distance of the Tivoli and the Central Railway Station. In addition to providing a glimpse into the sex lives of the famous, it presents a survey of erotica from around the world and through the ages. The exhibits range from tame to torrid—everything from Etruscan drawings and Chinese paintings to Greek vases depicting a lot of sexual activity. On display are remarkably lifelike naughty tableaux created by craftspeople from Tussaud's Wax Museum, as well as a collection of those dirty little postcards Americans tried to sneak through Customs in the 1920s and 1930s.

As you ascend the floors of the museum, the exhibits get steamier and seamier. By the time you reach the fourth (top) floor, a dozen video monitors are showing erotic films, featuring everything from black-and-white underground films from the 1920s to today's XXX-rated releases in full-bodied color, with the emphasis on "bodied."

Købmagergade 24. ⓒ **33-12-03-11.** Admission 89DKK ($12). May–Sept daily 10am–11pm; Oct–Apr Mon–Fri 11am–8pm, Sat 10am–9pm, Sun 10am–8pm. S-tog: Nørreport. Those ages 16–18 must be accompanied by an adult. No one under 16 admitted.

Tøjhusmuseet (Royal Arsenal Museum) This museum, housed in the former arsenal (erected 1598–1604), features a fantastic display of weaponry and hunting devices. On the ground floor—the longest vaulted Renaissance hall in Europe—is the Cannon Hall, stocked with artillery from 1500 to the present. Above the Cannon Hall is the impressive Armory Hall, with one of the world's finest collections of small arms, colors, and armor.

Tøjhusgade 3. ⓒ **33-11-60-37.** Admission 40DKK ($5.25) adults, 20DKK ($2.60) students and seniors, free for children under 15. Tues–Sun noon–4pm. Closed Jan 1, Dec 24, 25, and 31. Bus: 1, 2, 5, 6, 8, 10, 28, 29, 30, 32, 33, 34, or 35.

Thorvaldsen's Museum *(Finds)* On Slotsholmen next to Christiansborg, this museum houses the greatest collection of the works of Bertel Thorvaldsen (1770–1844), the most significant name in neoclassical sculpture. Thorvaldsen's life personified the romanticism of the 18th and 19th centuries—he rose from semi-poverty to the pinnacle of success. The sculptor is famous for his classical works taken from mythology: Cupid and Psyche, Adonis, Jason, Hercules, Ganymede, and Mercury, all of which are on display here. The museum also contains Thorvaldsen's extensive, private collection, which includes everything from Egyptian relics of Ptolemy to contemporary paintings such as *Apollo Among the Thessalian Shepherds.* After many years of exile in Italy, Thorvaldsen returned in triumph to his native Copenhagen, where he died a national figure and was buried in the courtyard of his museum.

Bertel Thorvaldsens 2. ⓒ **33-32-15-32.** Admission 20DKK ($2.60) adults, free for children under 15; free to all Wed. Tues–Sun 10am–5pm. Bus: 1, 2, 5, 6, 8, 10, 28, 29, or 550S.

5 In the Old Town (Indre By)

Rundetårn (Round Tower) This 17th-century public observatory, attached to a church, is visited by thousands who climb the spiral ramp (there are no steps) for a panoramic view of Copenhagen. The tower is one of the crowning architectural achievements of the Christian IV era. Peter the Great, in Denmark for a state visit, galloped up the ramp on horseback, preceded by his carriage-drawn tsarina. On the premises is a Bibliotekssalen (Library Hall), which holds changing exhibits on art, culture, history, and science.

Købmagergade 52A. ⓒ **33-73-03-73.** Admission 20DKK ($2.60) adults, 5DKK (65¢) children. Tower, June–Aug Mon–Sat 10am–8pm, Sun noon–8pm; Sept–May Mon–Sat 10am–5pm, Sun noon–5pm. Observatory, Oct 15–Mar 20 Tues–Wed 7–10pm. Closed Mar 21–Sept 25. Bus: 5, 7E, 14, 16, or 42.

Vor Frue Kirke (Copenhagen Cathedral) This Greek Renaissance–style church, built in the early 19th century near Copenhagen University, features Bertel Thorvaldsen's white marble neoclassical works, including *Christ and the Apostles.* Hans Christian Andersen's funeral took place here (in 1875), as did Søren Kierkegaard's (in 1855).

Nørregade. ⓒ **33-14-41-28.** Free admission. Mon–Fri 9am–5pm. Bus: 5.

6 More Museums

Kongelige Bibliotek (Royal Library) ⚘ The Royal Library, which dates from the 1600s, is the largest library in Scandinavia. As a national library, Kongelige Bibliotek owns the world's most complete collection of works printed in Danish; some volumes go back as far as 1482. It reopened in the late fall of 1998 following a restoration. In a classic building with high-ceilinged reading rooms and column-filled hallways, it is a grand and impressive place for storing some two million volumes—everything from sagas of Viking journeys to America (yes, before Columbus "discovered" the already inhabited continent), to enough prints, maps, and manuscripts to keep the most intense scholar busy for several lifetimes. The library owns original manuscripts by such fabled Danish writers as Hans Christian Andersen and Karen Blixen (who wrote as Isak Dinesen).

While it was closed, a gargantuan granite annex, The Black Diamond, expanded the library all the way to the waterfront. The growth was necessary because of the vast output of Danish works since World War II. Likened to the Taj Mahal or Sydney's Opera House for its evocative and enigmatic appearance, the Black Diamond's progressive design suits its central location on Christians Brygge—by the harbor between the bridges Langebro and Knippelsbro. The origin of the building's name is easy to surmise: Its facade is covered with a myriad of dazzling, reflective black granite tiles from Zimbabwe (the granite itself was cut in Portugal and polished in Italy), and its exterior walls slant sharply toward the water. Apart from space for 200,000 books, the Black Diamond features a bookshop, a restaurant with a spectacular view of the harbor, six reading rooms, a courtyard for exhibitions, and a concert hall. After viewing the interior of the library, you can wander through its formal gardens, past the fishpond and statue of philosopher Søren Kierkegaard (1813–55).

Sørenkierkegaards Plads 1. © 33-47-47-47. Free admission. Mon–Fri 9am–4pm. Bus: 1, 2, 5, 6, 8, or 9.

Orlogsmuseet (Royal Naval Museum) In Søkvasthuset, the former naval hospital, this museum opens onto Christianshavn canal. It traces the history of the navy, and because Denmark is a maritime nation, it almost becomes a saga of the country. More than 300 model ships, many from as early as the 1500s, are on display. The models served as prototypes for the ships, which were launched into the North Sea. Some models are fully "dressed," with working sails; others are merely cross-sections, with their frames outlined. You can see a vast array of other naval artifacts here, especially an intriguing collection of figureheads. Also look for navigational instruments, and even the propeller from the German U-boat that sank the *Lusitania* in 1915. Finally, there is a display of uniforms worn by Danish officers and sailors over the decades.

Overgaden Oven Vandet 58. © **32-54-63-63**. Admission 40DKK ($5.25) adults, 20DKK ($2.60) children. Tues–Sun noon–4pm. Bus: 2, 8, 9, 28, 31, or 350S.

7 The Churches of Copenhagen

For information on the Copenhagen Cathedral, refer to "In the Old Town (Indre By)," above.

Holmens Kirke This royal chapel and naval church lies across the canal from Slotsholmen, next to the National Bank of Denmark. The structure was converted into a church for the royal navy in 1619, but its nave was originally built in 1562, when it was first used as an anchor forge. By 1641 the ever-changing church had become predominantly Dutch Renaissance, an architectural style maintained to this day. The "royal doorway" was brought here from Roskilde Cathedral in the 19th century. Inside, look for a baroque altar of unpainted oak and a carved pulpit by Abel Schrøder the Younger. Both artifacts date from the middle of the 17th century. In the burial chamber are the tombs of some of Denmark's most important naval figures, including Adm. Niels Juel, who successfully fought off an attack by Swedes in 1677 in the epic Battle of Køge Bay. Peder Tordenskjold, who defeated Charles XII of Sweden during the Great Northern War in the early 1700s, is also entombed here. On a happier note, this is the church where Queen Margrethe II took her wedding vows in 1967.

Holmens Kanal. ℭ **33-13-61-78.** Free admission. Mon–Fri 9am–2pm; Sat 9am–noon. Bus: 1, 2, 6, 8, 9, 10, 31, 37, or 43.

Frederikskirke   This 200-year-old church, with its massive green copper dome—one of the largest in the world—is a short walk from Amalienborg Palace. Lined with valuable Norwegian marble, it's often called the Marmorkirken (marble church). After an unsuccessful start during the neoclassical revival of the 1750s, the church was finally completed in Roman baroque style in 1894. In many ways it's even more impressive than the Copenhagen Cathedral, not just for its dome, but for its rich, lush decorations and its facade decorated with statues of great figures in ecclesiastical history.

Frederiksgade 4. ℭ **33-15-01-44.** Free admission to church; dome, 20DKK ($2.60) adults, 10DKK ($1.30) children. Church, Mon–Thurs 10am–5pm; Fri–Sun noon–5pm. Dome, June 15–Sept 1 daily 1–3pm; Oct–May Sat–Sun 1–3pm. Bus: 1, 6, or 9.

Vor Frelsers Kirken (Our Savior's Church)   This baroque church with an external tower staircase dates from 1696. Local legend maintains that when the encircling staircase was constructed going the wrong way, the architect climbed to the top, realized what he'd done, and then jumped to his death. The Gothic structure's green and gold tower is a Copenhagen landmark, dominating the Christianshavn area. Inside, view the splendid baroque altar, richly adorned with cherubs and other figures. There are also a lovely font and richly carved organ case. Climb 400 steps to the top, where you'll find a gilded figure of Christ standing on a globe, and a panoramic view of the city.

Skt. Annægade 29. ℭ **32-57-27-98.** Admission to tower, 20DKK ($2.60) adults, 10DKK ($1.30) children; church, free. Apr–Aug Mon–Sat 11am–4:30pm and Sun noon–4:30pm; Sept–Oct Mon–Sat 11am–3:30pm and Sun noon–3:30pm; Nov–Mar daily 11:30am–3:30pm. Bus: 1, 2, 5, 8, or 9.

8 A Glimpse into the Past Outside Copenhagen

Frilandsmuseet (Open-Air Museum) 𝓡𝓡   This reconstructed village in Lyngby, on the edge of Copenhagen, recaptures Denmark's rural character. The "museum" covers nearly 36 hectares (90 acres), a 3.2km (2-mile) walk around the compound, and includes a dozen re-created buildings—farmsteads, windmills, fishers' cottages. Exhibits include a half-timbered 18th-century farmstead from a tiny, windswept Danish island; a primitive longhouse from the remote Faeroe Islands; thatched fishermen's huts from Jutland; tower windmills, and a mid-19th-century potter's workshop.

On summer afternoons, organized activities are staged. On a recent visit, folk dancers in native costume performed, and there were demonstrations of lace making and loom weaving.

The park is about 15km (9 miles) from the Central Railroad Station. At the entry to the museum is an old-style restaurant.

Kongevejen 100. ✆ **33-13-44-11.** Admission 40DKK ($5.25) adults, free for children under 16. Easter–Sept Tues–Sun 10am–5pm; Oct 1–20 Tues–Sun 10am–4pm. Closed Oct 21–Easter. S-tog: Copenhagen Central Station to Sorgenfri (trains leave every 20 min.). Bus: 184 or 194.

9 Literary Landmarks

Admirers of **Hans Christian Andersen** may want to seek out the addresses where he lived in Copenhagen, including Nyhavn 18 and Nyhavn 20 (where he lived only briefly) and Nyhavn 67 (where he lived during the 1860s). He also lived for a time at Vingårdsstræde 6.

Assistens Kirkegård (Assistens Cemetery) The largest cemetery in Copenhagen, dating from 1711, holds the tombs of Søren Kierkegaard, Hans Christian Andersen, and Martin Andersen Nexø, a famous novelist of the working class. The cemetery is now a public park.

Nørrebrogade/Kapelvej. Free admission. Mar–Apr and Sept–Oct daily 8am–6pm; May–Aug daily 8am–8pm; Nov–Feb daily 8am–4pm. Bus: 5, 7E, or 16.

Kobenhavns Bymuseet (Copenhagen City Museum) The permanent exhibition here presents the history of Copenhagen in artifacts and pictures. A smaller, separate department is devoted to Søren Kierkegaard (1813–55), the father of existentialism; you'll find exhibits of his drawings, letters, books, photographs, and personal belongings.

Vesterbrogade 59. ✆ **33-21-07-72.** Admission 30DKK ($3.95) adults, 15DKK ($1.95) children under 12. Wed–Mon 10am–4pm. Bus: 6, 16, 27, or 28.

10 Architectural Highlights

Børsen (Stock Exchange) One of the most unusual buildings in Copenhagen, on Slotsholmen, must be viewed from the outside because it's not open to the public. Architects Hans and Lorenz Steenwinkel built the long, low Renaissance structure for Christian IV. The spire, 53m (177 ft.) high, resembles a quartet of intertwined dragon tails. The Stock Exchange is no longer housed here; the building is now the headquarters of the Copenhagen Chamber of Commerce.

Børsgade. Bus: 1, 2, 5, 6, 8, or 9.

Grundtvigs Kirke (Grundtvig Church) This church, built from 1921 to 1940, was designed by Jensen Klint, who died before it was completed. About six million yellow bricks were used in its construction. The interior is 75m (250 ft.) wide and 35m (115 ft.) tall; the exterior resembles a huge organ. The church is a popular venue for concerts.

På Bjerget, Bispebjerg. ✆ **35-81-54-42.** Free admission. Apr–Oct daily 9am–4:45pm; Nov–Mar daily 9am–4pm. Bus: 10, 16, 43, or 69.

11 Of Artistic Interest

Arken Museum of Modern Art 🎭 Adjacent to a popular public beach in Ishøj, a suburb south of Copenhagen, this museum houses an extensive collection of modern art. The impressive structure was designed by the Danish architect Søren Robert Lund, while he was a student at the Royal Academy of Fine Arts. Constructed of stark white concrete and steel, it opened in 1996. The lines evoke the hull of a beached ship. Lund designed both the structure and the interiors, including display space and furniture. In addition to gallery space, the museum contains a concert hall, sculpture courtyards, and a restaurant. Recent exhibitions have included an Emil Nolde retrospective.

Ishøj Strandpark, Skovvej 100. ✆ 43-54-02-22. Admission 65DKK ($8.50) adults, 35DKK ($4.60) seniors, 25DKK ($3.30) children. Tues and Thurs–Sun 10am–5pm; Wed 10am–9pm. Train: E or A to Ishøj Station, then bus no. 128.

12 Especially for Kids

Copenhagen is a wonderful place for children, and many adult attractions also appeal to youngsters. See the listings above for details on the following diversions.

If you're traveling with kids, the **Tivoli** is the obvious choice, as is *The Little Mermaid* at Langelinie. Try to see the changing of the queen's Royal Life Guard at **Amalienborg Palace,** including the entire parade to and from the royal residence. Kids also enjoy **Frilandsmuseet,** the open-air museum. Other attractions great for kids include the following.

Bakken Amusement Park   On the northern edge of Copenhagen, about 12km (7½ miles) from the city center, this amusement park was created 35 years before the Pilgrims landed at Plymouth Rock. It's a local favorite, featuring roller coasters, dancing, the tunnel of love, and a merry-go-round. Open-air restaurants are plentiful, as are snack bars and ice cream booths. Proceeds from the amusements support this unspoiled natural preserve. There are no cars—only bicycles and horse-drawn carriages.

Dyrehavevej 62, Klampenborg. ✆ 39-63-73-00. Free admission. Daily noon–midnight. Closed late Aug to late Mar. S-tog: Klampenborg train from Central Railroad Station to Klampenborg (about 20 min.); then walk through the Deer Park or take a horse-drawn cab.

Denmark's Aquarium   North of Copenhagen along the Øresund coast, this is one of the most extensive aquariums in Europe; it boasts all four of the major marine groups in the world. This is also the oldest aquarium in Scandinavia, established in 1939. Hundreds of saltwater and freshwater species are on exhibit. Of special interest is the collection of piranhas, whose codfish feeding occurs every Wednesday and Saturday at 2pm—watch the schoolchildren squeal.

Strandvejen, in Charlottenlund Fort Park, Charlottenlund. ✆ 39-62-32-83. Admission 65DKK ($8.50) adults, 35DKK ($4.60) children. Mar–Oct daily 10am–6pm; Nov–Feb Mon–Fri 10am–4pm, Sat–Sun 10am–5pm. S-tog: Line C to Charlottenlund. Bus: 6.

Experimentarium (Hands-On Science Center)   Here's one museum where your children won't be scolded for touching the exhibits. Housed in the old mineral-water bottling hall of the Tuborg breweries, this museum encourages visitors to use all their senses as they participate in some 300 exhibitions and demonstrations on three themes: "Man," "Nature," and "The Interaction Between Man and Nature." Visitors hear what all the world's languages sound like, make a wind machine blow up to hurricane force, dance in an "inverted" disco, or visit a slimming machine. Families can work as a team to examine enzymes, make a camera from paper, or test perfume. Exhibitions change frequently.

Tuborg Havnevej 7, Hellerup. ✆ 39-27-33-33. Admission 89DKK ($12) adults, 62DKK ($8.10) children 4–14, free for children under 4. Mon, Wed, Fri 10am–5pm; Tues 9am–9pm; Sat–Sun 11am–5pm. S-tog: Hellerup or Svanemøllen. Bus: 6 or 21.

Tycho Brahe Planetarium   A star projector re-creates the marvel of the night sky, with its planets, galaxies, star clusters, and comets, using the planetarium dome as a screen. Named after the famed Danish astronomer Tycho Brahe (1546–1601), the planetarium also stages OMNIMAX film productions. There's an information center and a restaurant.

Gammel Kongevej 10. ℂ **33-12-12-24**. Admission 25DKK ($3.30) adults, 15DKK ($1.95) children; OMNI-MAX films 85DKK ($11) adults, 65DKK ($8.50) children. Daily 10am–9pm. Bus: 1 or 14.

Zoologisk Have (Copenhagen Zoo) With more than 2,000 animals from Greenland to Africa, this zoo boasts spacious new habitats for reindeer and musk oxen as well as an open roaming area for lions. Take a ride up the small wooden Eiffel Tower, or walk across the street to the petting zoo. The zoo is mobbed on Sunday.

Roskildevej 32, Frederiksberg. ℂ **36-30-25-55**. Admission 80DKK ($10) adults, 40DKK ($5.25) children. Daily 9am–6pm. S-tog: Valby. Bus: 6, 18, 28, 39, or 550S.

13 Copenhagen on Foot: Walking Tours

WALKING TOUR 1 | THE OLD CITY

Start:	Rådhuspladsen.
Finish:	Tivoli Gardens.
Time:	1½ hours.
Best Time:	Any sunny day.
Worst Times:	Rush hours (weekdays 7:30–9am and 5–6:30pm).

Start at:
❶ Rådhuspladsen (Town Hall Square)

You can stop in at the Town Hall, in the center of Copenhagen, but even more appealing is a bronze statue of Hans Christian Andersen. The spinner of fairy tales stands near a boulevard bearing his name. Also on this square is a statue of two *lur* (horn) players that has stood here since 1914.

Bypassing the horn players, walk southeast along Vester Voldgade onto a narrow street on your left. This is:
❷ Lavendelstræde

Many houses along here date from the late 18th century. At Lavendelstræde 1, Mozart's widow, Constanze, lived with her second husband, Georg Nikolaus Nissen, a Danish diplomat, from 1812 to 1820.

The little street quickly becomes Slutterigade.
❸ Courthouses

This short street, joined by elevated walkways, is flanked on both sides by courthouses. Built between 1805 and 1815, this was Copenhagen's fourth town hall. It now holds the city's major law courts. The main courthouse entrance is on Nytorv.

Slutterigade leads to:
❹ Nytorv

You can admire fine 19th-century houses at this famous square. Søren Kierkegaard, the noted philosopher (1813–55), lived in a house adjacent to the courthouse at the corner of Nytorv and Frederiksberggade. It's a private residence, however, and not open to visitors.

Cross Nytorv, and veer slightly to your left until you reach Nygade, part of the famed:
❺ Strøget

This traffic-free shopping street begins at Rådhuspladsen, where it's called Frederiksberggade. The major shopping street of Scandinavia, Strøget is a stroller's and shopper's delight, stretching 1.2km (¾ mile) through the heart of Copenhagen.

Nygade is one of the five streets that make up Strøget. Turn right and head northeast along the street. It quickly becomes winding and narrow Vimmelskaftet, and then turns into Amagertorv. Along Amagertorv on your left, you'll come across the:

⑥ Helligåndskirken (Church of the Holy Ghost)

This abbey, founded at the beginning of the 15th century, is the oldest church in Copenhagen. Partially destroyed in 1728, it was reconstructed in 1880 in a neoclassical style. Some of the buildings on this street date from 1616. The sales rooms of the Royal Porcelain Factory are at Amagertorv 6.

Next you'll come to Østergade, the last portion of Strøget. You'll see Illum's department store on your left.

Østergade leads to:

⑦ Kongens Nytorv

Many interesting buildings surround Copenhagen's largest square, and there's an equestrian statue of Christian IV in the center. The statue is a bronze replica of a 1688 sculpture. (For more about this square, see "Walking Tour 2," below.)

From Kongens Nytorv, follow Niels Juels Gade until you come to Laksegade.

Turn right and follow this street until you reach the intersection with Nikolajgade. Turn right. This street leads to the:

⑧ Nikolaj Church

This church dates from 1530. It was the scene of the thundering sermons of Hans Tausen, a father of the Danish Reformation.

> **TAKE A BREAK**
> A mellow spot for a pick-me-up—a cool drink or an open-faced sandwich—is the **Cafeen Nikolaj**, Nikolaj Plads 12 (© 33-11-63-13). It attracts older shoppers and young people. You can linger over a cup of coffee, and no one is likely to hurry you. Visit any time in the afternoon, perhaps making it your lunch stop.

After viewing the church, head left down Fortunstræde to:

⑨ Højbro Plads

This plaza is situated off Gammel Strand. You'll have a good view of Christiansborg Palace and Thorvaldsen's Museum on Slotsholmen. On Højbro Plads is an equestrian statue honoring Bishop Absalon, who founded Copenhagen in 1167. Several handsome buildings line the square.

Continue west along:

⑩ Gammel Strand

Gammel Strand means "old shore." A number of interesting old buildings line this waterfront promenade, the former edge of Copenhagen. Christiansborg Palace is across the way. Continue west along this street, which becomes Nybrogade, also bordering the water.

At the intersection with Naboløs, cut north and take an immediate right onto:

⑪ Snaregade

This old-fashioned provincial street is typical of the old city. Walk west on this street to Knabrostræde. Both streets boast structures built just after the great fire of 1795. Where the streets intersect at Knabrostræde, you'll see the Church of Our Lady.

From here, continue straight (or west) along:

⑫ Magstræde

This is one of Copenhagen's best-preserved streets. Proceed along to Rådhusstræde. Just before you reach Rådhusstræde, notice the two buildings facing that street. These private residences are the oldest structures in the city, dating from the 16th century.

Walk across Vandkunsten, a square at the western end of Magstræde. Turn right down Gasegade, then quickly left or west along Farvergade. At this street's intersection with Vester Voldgade, you'll see the Vartov Church. Continue west until you reach Rådhuspladsen. Across the square, you'll see the:

⑬ Tivoli Gardens (entrance at Vesterbrogade 3)

This amusement park draws some 4.5 million visitors every summer. It has 25 attractions, and numerous restaurants and beer gardens.

COPENHAGEN

Area of detail

1 Rådhuspladsen
2 Lavendelstraede
3 Courthouses (Slutterigade)
4 Nytorv
5 Stroget
6 Helligåndskirken
7 Kongens Nytorv
8 Nikolaj Church
9 Hojbro Plads
10 Gammel Strand
11 Snaregade
12 Magstraede
13 Tivoli Gardens

✝ Church
⊠ Post Office

KONGENS NYTORV TO LANGELINIE

Start:	Kongens Nytorv.
Finish:	*The Little Mermaid.*
Time:	1½ hours.
Best Time:	Any sunny day.
Worst Times:	Rush hours (weekdays 7:30–9am and 5–6:30pm).

Although the Nyhavn quarter, once a boisterous sailors' town, has quieted down, it's still a charming part of old Copenhagen, with its 1673 canal and 18th-century houses.

Begin at:

❶ Kongens Nytorv

The "King's New Market" dates from 1680. It contains Magasin, the biggest department store in the capital, plus an equestrian statue of Christian IV.

On the northeast side of the square is:

❷ Thott's Mansion

This mansion was completed in 1685 for a Danish naval hero and restored in 1760. It now houses the French Embassy. Between Bredgade and Store Strandstræde, a little street angling to the right near Nyhavn, is Kanneworff House, a beautifully preserved private home that dates from 1782. On the west side of the square, at no. 34, is the Hotel d'Angleterre, the best in Copenhagen. Also here is an old anchor memorializing the Danish seamen who died in World War II.

On the southeast side of the square stands the:

❸ Royal Theater

Founded in 1748, this theater presents ballets, operas, and plays. Statues of famous Danish dramatists are out front. The present theater, constructed in 1874, is in neo-Renaissance style.

With your back to the Hotel d'Angleterre, walk toward the water along:

❹ Nyhavn

This section was once filled with maritime businesses and seamen's bars and lodgings. Nowadays, it's restaurant row. First, walk along the north (left) side of Nyhavn. In the summer, cafe tables border the canal, giving it a festive atmosphere. At the port end of the canal you can see the Naval Dockyards, and Christianshavn across the harbor. High-speed craft come and go all day here, connecting Copenhagen with Malmö, Sweden.

On the quieter (south) side of the canal, you can see:

❺ Charlottenborg Palace

The Danish Academy of Fine Arts now occupies this former palace. A pure baroque work, it takes its name from Queen Charlotte Amalie, who moved there in 1700. Beautiful old homes, antiques shops, and more restaurants line the southern bank. Nyhavn was the home of Hans Christian Andersen at various times. He lived at no. 20, where he wrote his first fairy tales, in 1835, and at no. 67 from 1845 to 1864. He spent the last 2 years of his life at no. 18, where he died in 1875.

Walk back to the harbor end of Nyhavn and turn left onto Kvæsthusgade, which will take you to:

❻ Skt. Annæ Plads

Ferries depart for Oslo from this location. Many consulates, two hotels, and fine old buildings open onto this square. Walking inland along the plads, turn right onto Amaliegade. It leads under a colonnade into the cobblestone Amalienborg Plads.

Walking Tour: Kongens Nytorv to Langelinie

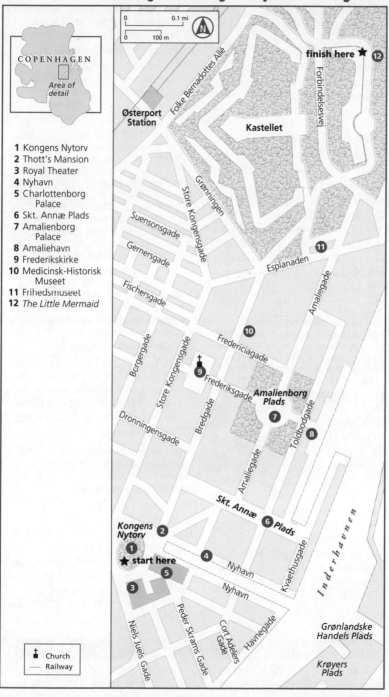

COPENHAGEN

Area of detail

0   0.1 mi
0   100 m

1 Kongens Nytorv
2 Thott's Mansion
3 Royal Theater
4 Nyhavn
5 Charlottenborg Palace
6 Skt. Annæ Plads
7 Amalienborg Palace
8 Amaliehavn
9 Frederikskirke
10 Medicinsk-Historisk Museet
11 Frihedsmuseet
12 *The Little Mermaid*

finish here ★ 12

Østerport Station

Kastellet

Forbindelsesvej

Folke Bernadottes Alle

Grønningen

Store Kongensgade

Suensonsgade

Gernersgade

Fischersgade

Borgergade

Store Kongensgade

Esplanaden

Amaliegade

11

Fredericiagade

10

† 9 Frederiksgade

Bredgade

Amalienborg Plads

7

Dronningensgade

Toldbodgade

8

Amaliegade

Skt. Annæ Plads

6

Kongens Nytorv 2

1

★ start here

5

3

Niels Juels Gade

Peder Skrams Gade

Cort Adelers Gade

Nyhavn

Nyhavn

Havnegade

Kvaethusgade

Inderhavnen

Grønlandske Handels Plads

Krøyers Plads

† Church
— Railway

99

❼ Amalienborg Palace

Amalienborg Plads is the site of this palace. A statue of Frederik V sits at the core of this palace. When the queen is in residence, the changing of the guard takes place here daily at noon. The palace is the official residence of the queen and her French prince, but sections of it are open to visitors. Four identical mansion-like palaces flank the square. The queen lives in the right wing, next to the colonnade.

Between the square and the harbor are the gardens of:

❽ Amaliehavn

Among the most beautiful in Copenhagen, these gardens were laid out by Jean Delogne, who made lavish use of Danish granite and French limestone. The bronze pillars around the fountain were the work of Arnaldo Pomodoro, an Italian sculptor.

After viewing the waterfront gardens, walk away from the water, crossing Amalienborg Plads and emerging onto Frederiksgade. Continue along this short street until you reach:

❾ Frederikskirke (no. 1)

This is often called the *Marmorkirken* or "marble church." Construction began in 1740, but had to stop in 1770 because of the staggering costs. The church wasn't completed until 1894—using Danish marble instead of more expensive Norwegian marble. The church was modeled on and intended to rival St. Peter's in Rome; indeed, it ended up with one of the largest church domes in Europe. Supported on a dozen towering piers, the dome has a diameter of 32m (108 ft.).

Facing the church, turn right and head north along Bredgade, passing at no. 22 the:

❿ Medicinsk-Historisk Museet (Medical History Museum)

The collection here is gruesome, with aborted fetuses, dissected heads, and the like.

TAKE A BREAK
Before you approach *The Little Mermaid*, consider tea and a snack at **Café Lumskebugten**, Esplanaden 21 (☎ **33-15-60-29**; see chapter 3, "Introducing Copenhagen"). Dating from 1854, this cafe serves a cold plate throughout the afternoon. There are five specialties: beef tartare, fish cakes with mustard sauce, marinated salmon, baked cod, and shrimp.

Bredgade ends at Esplanaden, which opens onto Churchillparken, a green belt bordering the water. Turn right and walk along Esplanaden until you come to the:

⓫ Frihedsmuseet, Churchillparken

The Danish Resistance museum commemorates the struggle against the Nazis from 1940 to 1945 (see listing earlier in this chapter in "Amalienborg Palace & Environs").

After leaving the museum, walk toward the water along Langelinie where signs point the way to:

12 *The Little Mermaid*

Perched on rocks just off the harbor bank, *Den Lille Havfrue*, the most photographed statue in Scandinavia, dates from 1913. The bronze figure, by Edvard Eriksen, was modeled after the figure of prima ballerina Ellen Price. In time, this much-attacked and abused statue became the symbol of Copenhagen.

14 Organized Tours

BUS & BOAT TOURS The boat and bus sightseeing tours in Copenhagen range from get-acquainted jaunts to in-depth excursions. Either of the following tours can be arranged through **Copenhagen Excursions** (☎ **32-54-06-06**) or **Vikingbus** (☎ **31-57-26-00**). Inexpensive bus tours depart from the *lur* (horn) blowers' statue at Town Hall Square, and boat trips leave from Gammel Strand (the fish market) or Nyhavn.

For orientation, hop on a bus for the 1½-**hour City Tour,** which covers major scenic highlights like *The Little Mermaid,* Rosenborg Castle, and Amalienborg Palace. Monday through Friday, tours also visit the Carlsberg Brewery, which adds 1 hour to the time if you choose to continue.

Tours depart from Rådhuspladsen daily at 1pm from May 30 to September 13. They cost 130DKK ($17) for adults, 90DKK ($12) for children.

We heartily recommend the **City and Harbor Tour,** a 2½-hour trip by launch and bus that departs from Town Hall Square. The tour gives you a wonderful overview of the cityscape in relation to the sea. The boat tours the city's main canals, passing *The Little Mermaid* and the Old Fish Market. It operates from May 30 to September 13, daily at 1pm. It costs 175DKK ($23) for adults, 90DKK ($12) for children.

Shakespeare buffs may be interested in an afternoon excursion to the castles of North Zealand. The 7-hour tour explores the area north of Copenhagen, including Kronborg (Hamlet's castle), a brief visit to Fredensborg, the queen's residence, and a stopover at Frederiksborg Castle and the National Historical Museum. Tours depart from Town Hall Square. They run from May 2 to October 16, Wednesday, Saturday, and Sunday at 10:15am. The cost is 335DKK ($44) for adults, half price for children.

For more information about these tours and the most convenient place to buy tickets in advance, call **Vikingbus** or **Copenhagen Excursions.**

GUIDED WALKS THROUGH COPENHAGEN   Staff members of the Copenhagen Tourist Information Office conduct 2-hour guided walking tours of the city Monday through Saturday at 10:30am, between May and September. The price is 80DKK ($10) for adults, 25DKK ($3.30) for children. For information, contact the **Copenhagen Tourist Information Center,** Bernstorffsgade 1 (✆ **33-25-38-44** or 32-97-14-40; www.woco.dk).

A VISIT TO COPENHAGEN'S MOST FAMOUS BREWERY *Finds*   Carlsberg is the most famous beer in Denmark, and will likely be associated with many of the good times you'll have within that country. You can take a self-guided tour of the factory that turns out three million bottles of beer a day, walking around an observation gallery whose English-language signs explain the brewing process and why Carlsberg does it so well. The factory is open for visits Tuesday through Sunday from 10am to 4pm. Entrance is free, and each visitor is given a quota of one free beer at the end of the tour, with the option of buying more at the on-site pub. The entrance to the factory is prefaced with a pair of sculpted elephants, each with armored regalia that includes a swastika. That doesn't mean the company was a Nazi sympathizer—Carlsberg used the symbol as part of its image long before Hitler. Take bus no. 6 from Rådhuspladsen to **Carlsberg Brewery,** Di Carlsberg Vej 11 (✆ **33-27-13-14**).

15 Active Sports

BICYCLING   The absence of hills and the abundance of parks and wide avenues with bicycle lanes make cycling the best way to explore Copenhagen. Bike-rental shops and stands are scattered throughout the city. Two suggestions are **Københavns Cyker,** Reventlowsgade 11 (✆ **33-33-86-13**), and **Dan Wheel,** Colbjørnsensgade 3 (✆ **33-21-22-27**).

FITNESS   Form & Fitness, Øster Allé 42E (© **35-55-00-78**), offers a day pass for 75DKK ($9.85). Aerobics, weights, and fitness machines are available Monday through Thursday from 6:30am to midnight, Friday from 6:30am to 9pm, and Saturday and Sunday from 8am to 6pm.

GOLF   Denmark's best-known golf course, and one of its most challenging, is at the **Rungsted Golf Klub,** Vestre Stationsvej 16 (© **45-86-34-14**). It's in the heart of Denmark's "Whiskey Trail," a string of upper-crust homes and mansions known for their allure to retirees, about 21km (13 miles) north of Copenhagen. Golfers visit from around the world. Some degree of competence is required, so beginners and intermediate golfers might want to hold off. If you're an advanced golfer, call for information and to arrange a tee time. Greens fees run 375DKK and 425DKK ($49 and $56) for a full day's use of the club's 18 holes. To play, you must present evidence of a 20 handicap on Saturday and Sunday, or 25 on weekdays. With advance notice, you can rent clubs for 250DKK ($33). The course is closed between November and March. No carts are allowed on the ecologically fragile course.

JOGGING   The many parks (known to locals as "green lungs") of Copenhagen provide endless routes for joggers. Our favorite, just west of the city center, circles Lakes Sortedams, St. Jorgens, and Peblinge. The paths that wind through the Frederiksborg gardens are also well suited for joggers.

SWIMMING   Swimming is a favorite Danish pastime. The **Frederiksborg Svømmehal,** Helgesvej 29 (© **38-14-04-04**), is open to the public Monday through Friday from 8am to 8pm, Saturday from 8am to 2pm, and Sunday from 9:30am to 2:15pm. Tickets cost 30DKK ($3.95). You can also try **Sundby Swimming-pool,** Sundbyvestervej 50 (© **32-58-55-68**); or **Kildeskovshallen,** Adolphsvej 25 (© **39-68-28-22**).

TENNIS   Visitors usually pay a large supplement to play tennis at hotels and clubs in Copenhagen. There's a high hourly rate, and courts must be reserved in advance. Indoor courts may be rented at the **Hotel Mercur,** Vester Farimagsgade 17 (© **33-12-57-11**); visitors pay 130DKK ($17) for the first hour, 100DKK ($13) for each additional hour. Another club is **Københavns Boldklub,** Peter Nagsvej 147 (© **38-71-41-80**).

16 The Shopping Scene

Copenhagen is in the vanguard of shopping in Europe, and much of the action takes place on **Strøget,** the pedestrian street in the heart of the capital. Strøget begins as Frederiksberggade, north of Rådhuspladsen, and winds to Østergade, which opens onto Kongens Nytorv. The jam-packed street is lined with stores selling everything from porcelain statues of *Youthful Boldness* to Greenland shrimp to Kay Bojesen's teak monkeys.

Between stops, relax with a drink at an outdoor cafe, or just sit on a bench and watch the crowds.

In two nearby walking areas—**Gråbødretorv** and **Fiolstræde**—you can browse through antiques shops and bookstores.

Bredgade, beginning at Kongens Nytorv, is the antiques district. Prices tend to be very high. **Læderstræde** is another shopping street that competes with Bredgade in antiques.

BEST BUYS   In a country famed for its designers and craftspeople, the best buys are in stainless steel, porcelain, china, glassware, toys—especially Kay

Bojesen's wooden animals—functionally designed furniture, textiles, and jewelry (decorative, silver, and semiprecious stones).

STORE HOURS In general, shopping hours are from 9:30 or 10am to 5:30pm Monday through Thursday, until 7 or 8pm on Friday, and until 2pm on Saturday. Most shops are closed Sunday, except the kiosks and supermarket at the Central Railroad Station. Here you can purchase food until 10pm or midnight. The Central Railroad Station's bakery is open until 9pm, and one of the kiosks at Rådhuspladsen, which sells papers, film, and souvenirs, is open 24 hours.

SHIPPING IT HOME & RECOVERING VAT Denmark imposes a 25% tax on goods and services, a "value-added tax" known in Denmark as *moms* (pronounced "mumps"). Tax-free exports are possible. Many stores will mail goods to your home so you can avoid paying the tax. If you want to take your purchases, look for shops displaying Danish tax-free shopping notices. Such shops offer tourists tax refunds for personal export. This refund applies to purchases of over 300DKK ($39) for visitors from the United States and Canada—spent at the same store, but not necessarily all at once. For more information, see "Taxes" in "Fast Facts: Denmark," in chapter 2, "Planning Your Trip to Denmark." For answers to tax-refund questions, call **Global Refund** (© **32-52-55-66**).

SHOPPING A TO Z
AMBER
The Amber Specialist The owners, known to customers as the "Amber Twins," deal in "the gold of the north." This petrified resin originated in the large coniferous forests that covered Denmark some 35 million years ago. The forests disappeared, but the amber remained, and is now used to create handsome jewelry. Frederiksberggade 28. © **33-11-88-03**. Bus: 28, 29, or 41.

ART GALLERIES & AUCTION HOUSES
Bruun Rasmussen Auctioneers of Fine Arts Established shortly after World War II, this is Denmark's leading auction house. July is usually quiet, although the premises remain open for appraisals and purchases. The season begins in August, with an auction of paintings and fine art. Viewing time is allowed before auctions, which take place about once a month. There are also auctions of modern art, wine, coins, books, manuscripts, and antique weapons. Bredgade 23. © **33-13-69-11**. Bus: 1, 6, 9, or 10.

Galerie Asbaek This modern-art gallery has a permanent exhibit of the best local artists, along with changing shows by Scandinavian and foreign artists. There's a bookshop and a cafe that serves French-inspired Danish food. Graphics and posters are for sale. Bredgade 20. © **33-15-40-04**. Bus: 1, 6, 9, 10, 28, 29, or 41.

Kunsthallens Kunstauktioner Established in 1926, this is Europe's leading dealer in the pan-European school of painting known as COBRA (an acronym for Copenhagen, Brussels, and Amsterdam, where the artists originated). These works, produced from 1948 to 1951, were important precursors of abstract expressionism. The gallery holds 12 auctions yearly, eight with modern art; the others concentrate on the 19th century. Gothersgade 9. © **33-32-52-00**. Bus: 1, 6, 9, or 10.

BOOKS
Boghallen This big store at Town Hall Square carries many books in English, as well as a wide selection of travel-related literature, including maps. It stocks

books in English on Danish themes, such as the collected works of Hans Christian Andersen. Rådhuspladsen 37. (€ **33-11-85-11.** Bus: 2, 8, or 30.

DEPARTMENT STORES

Illum   One of Denmark's top department stores, Illum is on Strøget. Take time to browse through its vast store of Danish and Scandinavian design. There's a restaurant and a special export cash desk at street level. Østergade 52. (€ **33-14-40-02.** Bus: 1, 6, 9, or 10.

Magasin   An elegant department store, Magasin is the biggest in Scandinavia. It offers a complete assortment of Danish designer fashion, a large selection of glass and porcelain, and souvenirs. Goods are shipped abroad tax-free. Kongens Nytorv 13. (€ **33-11-44-33.** Bus: 1, 6, 9, or 10.

FASHIONS

Sweater Market   Take your pick from top-grade Scandinavian and Icelandic cardigans, pullovers, hats, scarves, and mittens, hand-knit in Denmark of 100% wool. There's also a large selection of Icelandic wool jackets and coats. Frederiksberggade 15. (€ **33-15-27-73.** Bus: 2, 8, or 30.

FLEA MARKETS

Det Blå Pakhus *(Finds*   The motto of "The Blue Warehouse," Copenhagen's largest indoor marketplace with 325 booths, is that you can find "everything between heaven and earth here," and that's probably right; at the very least it includes secondhand furniture, antiques, carpets, and assorted bric-a-brac. It is open Saturday and Sunday from 10am to 5pm. The entrance fee is 10DKK ($1.25). Holmbladsgade 113. (€ **32-95-17-07.** Bus: 5 or 37.

GLASSWARE, PORCELAIN & CRYSTAL

Holmegaards Glasværker   This is Denmark's most famous and visible producer of glasswork, with a pedigree that extends back at least 200 years, and a series of elegant products that have graced the table settings of politicians and aristocrats for generations. Look for reissues of famous patterns of the past, including "Wellington," dedicated to English military hero the duke of Wellington, an 1859 pattern recently re-released to a small but select audience. In the Royal Copenhagen retail center, Amagertorv 6 (Strøget). (€ **33-12-44-77.** Bus: 1, 6, 8, 9, or 10.

Rosenthal Studio-Haus   You'll find an array of ceramic works here, especially by well-known Danish artist Bjørn Wiinblad, whose figures we find whimsical and delightful. You can also get good buys on Orrefors crystal, including some stunning bowls. The sculptural reliefs, handmade in lead crystal, range from miniatures to giant animals in limited world editions of 199 pieces. They often depict the animals of the far north. Frederiksberggade 21. (€ **33-14-21-01.** Bus: 28, 29, or 41.

Royal Copenhagen Porcelain   Royal Copenhagen's trademark, three wavy blue lines, has come to symbolize quality in porcelain throughout the world. Founded in 1775, the factory was a royal possession before passing into private hands in 1868. Royal Copenhagen's Christmas plates—an annual release since 1908—are collectors' items. Most of the motifs depict the Danish countryside in winter. On the top floor is a huge selection of seconds and, unless you're an expert, you probably can't tell the difference.

In this location are various porcelain and silver retailers, as well as the Royal Copenhagen Antiques shop. It specializes in buying and selling antique Georg Jensen silver, Royal Copenhagen and Bing & Grøndahl porcelain, and Michelson Christmas spoons.

Anyone who's interested in the laborious processes whereby Denmark's most famous porcelain is made is welcome to tour the **Royal Copenhagen factory,** Smallegade 47 (© **38-14-48-48**). A 15-minute drive east of Copenhagen's center, it's accessible by bus no. 1 or 14. You must call ahead to reserve a spot within one of the hour-long tours, priced at 40DKK ($5.25) per person. They're conducted Monday through Friday at 9am, 10am, 11am, 1pm, and 2pm. There's a sales outlet on the premises, selling basically the same inventories that are available at the organization's more glamorous main showroom at Amagertorv 6. In the Royal Scandinavia retail center, Amagertorv 6 (Strøget). © 33-13-71-81. Bus: 1, 2, 6, 8, 28, 29, or 41 for the retail outlet; 1 or 14 for the factory.

HOME FURNISHINGS
Illums Bolighus   A center for modern Scandinavian and Danish design, this is one of Europe's finest showcases for household furnishings and accessories. It stocks furniture, lamps, rugs, textiles, bedding, glassware, kitchenware, flatware, china, jewelry, and ceramics. The store also sells women's and men's clothes and accessories. There's a gift shop, too. Amagertorv 10 (Strøget). © 33-14-19-41. Bus: 28, 29, or 41.

Lysberg, Hansen & Therp   This major interior-decorating center offers fabrics, carpets, and furniture. The model apartments are furnished in impeccable taste. The company manufactures its own traditionally designed furniture and imports fabrics, usually from Germany or France. The gift shop has many hard-to-find creations. Bredgade 3. © 33-14-47-87. Bus: 1, 6, 9, or 10.

Paustian   Copenhagen's leading furniture showroom, in the somewhat distant industrial Nordhavn section, will ship anywhere in the world. The finest of Scandinavian design is on display, along with reproductions of the classics. The adjoining restaurant is highly recommended. Kalkbrænderiløbskaj 2. © 39-16-65-65. S-tog: Nordhavn.

JEWELRY
Hartmann's Selected Estate Silver & Jewelry   This shop buys second-hand silver and jewelry from old estates and sells them at reduced prices. Sometimes it's possible to purchase heirloom Georg Jensen estate silver. Ulrik Hartmann, the store's owner, launched his career as a 10-year-old trading at a local flea market. The shop is near Kongens Nytorv. While in the neighborhood, you can walk for hours, exploring the various auction rooms, jewelry shops, and nearby art galleries. Bredgade 4. © 33/33-09-63. Bus: 1, 6, 9, or 10.

Kaere Ven   One of the city's oldest diamond dealers, in business since 1901, this outlet claims to offer "prices from another century"—the 19th century, that is. That's a bit of an exaggeration but you can often find bargains here in antique jewelry, even old Georg Jensen silver. An array of rings, earrings, necklaces, and bracelets is sold, along with other items. A few items in the store are sold at 50% off the already-competitive prices, but you have to shop carefully for those and know what you're buying. Stor Kongens Gade 30. © 33-11-43-15. Bus: 1, 6, 9, or 10.

MUSIC
Axel Musik   One of the best-stocked music stores in the Danish capital, Axel also has a newer branch in the city's main railway station. In Scala Center (ground floor), Axeltorv 2. © 33-14-05-50. Bus: 1, 6, or 8.

NEEDLEWORK

Eva Rosenstand A/S—Clara Wæver   You'll find Danish-designed cross-stitch embroideries here. The material is usually linen in medium or coarser grades, but cotton is also available. The admission-free needlework museum is the only one of its kind in Europe. Østergade 42. ✆ **33-13-29-40.** Bus: 1, 6, 9, or 10.

SHOPPING CENTERS

For excellent buys in Scandinavian merchandise, as well as tax-free goods, we recommend the **shopping center at the airport.** The prices cannot be higher than those downtown, and there's a VAT-refund office nearby.

Bolten's   Near Kongens Nytorv and the Hotel d'Angleterre, the small-scale development incorporates private offices and apartments, a series of traffic-free interior courtyards filled with flowers, and a handful of shops, restaurants, and cafes. The half-dozen shops on the site usually sell private-label merchandise, including children's clothing, lacy undergarments, hats, and shoes. On the premises are two dance clubs (the Kitsch and X-Ray Underground), a theater that stages comedy acts and satire, and scattered gallery space (some of it underground) for modern art. There's also a ticket kiosk where you can arrange bookings for cultural events throughout Copenhagen. Store Kongensgade 5/Gothersgade 8. ✆ **33-32-44-44.** Bus: 1, 6, or 9.

SILVER

Georg Jensen   Legendary Georg Jensen is known for its fine silver. For the connoisseur, there's no better address—the store displays the largest and best collection of Jensen holloware in Europe. Gold and silver jewelry in traditional and modern Danish designs is also featured. In the Royal Scandinavia retail center, Amagertorv 4 (Strøget). ✆ **33-11-40-80.** Bus: 1, 6, 8, 9, or 10.

17 Copenhagen After Dark

Danes really know how to party. A good night means a late night, and on warm weekends, hundreds of rowdy revelers crowd Strøget until sunrise. Merrymaking in Copenhagen is not just for the younger crowd; jazz clubs, traditional beer houses, and wine cellars are routinely packed with people of all ages. The city has a more serious cultural side as well, exemplified by excellent theater, opera, ballet, and one of the best circuses in Europe.

To find out what's happening at the time of your visit, pick up a free copy of *Copenhagen This Week* at the tourist information center. Ignore the "Copenhagen by Night" section, which usually focuses on women advertising themselves as companions for visiting males. The "Events Calendar" has a week-by-week roundup of the most interesting entertainment and sightseeing events.

TIVOLI GARDENS

In the center of the gardens, the large **open-air stage** books vaudeville acts (tumbling clowns, acrobats, aerialists) who perform daily at 7 and 10:30pm, and also on Saturday at 5pm. Spectators must enter through the turnstiles to get seats, but there's an unobstructed view from outside if you'd rather stand. Special arrangements with jazz, rock, and folkloric groups are made during the season. Admission is free.

Near the Vesterbrogade 3 entrance, the 150-year-old outdoor **Pantomime Theater,** with a Chinese stage and peacock curtain, presents shows Tuesday through Sunday at 6:15 and 8:30pm. The repertory consists of 16 *commedia* *dell'arte* productions with the entertaining trio of Pierrot, Columbine, and Harlequin—authentic pantomimes that have been performed continuously in Copenhagen since 1844. Admission is free.

The modern **Tivolis Koncertsal (concert hall)** is a great place to hear talented artists led by equally famous conductors. Inaugurated in 1956, the concert hall can seat 2,000, and its season—which runs for more than 4 months, beginning in late April—has been called "the most extensive music festival in the world." Performances of everything from symphony to opera are presented Monday through Saturday at 7pm, and sometimes at 9pm, depending on the event. Good seats are available at prices ranging from 200DKK to 400DKK ($26–$52) when major artists perform, but most performances are free. Tickets are sold at the main booking office on Vesterbrogade 3 (© **33-15-10-12**).

Tivoli Glassalen (© **33-15-10-12**) is housed in an octagonal gazebo-like century-old building with a glass, gilt-capped canopy. Shows here are often comedic or satirical performances by Danish comedians in Danish, and they usually don't interest non-Danish audiences. But there are also musical revues. Call for the unpredictable schedule. Tickets cost 205DKK to 240DKK ($27–$31).

THE PERFORMING ARTS

For **discount seats** (sometimes as much as 50% off the regular price), go in person to a ticket kiosk across from the Nørreport train station, at the corner of Fiolstræde and Nørre Voldgade. Discount tickets are sold only on the day of the performance and may be purchased Monday through Friday from noon to 5pm, Saturday from noon to 3pm.

Det Kongelige Teater (Royal Theater)   A major winter cultural event in Copenhagen is a performance by the world-renowned **Royal Danish Ballet** or **Royal Danish Opera.** Because the arts are state-subsidized, ticket prices are comparatively low. Some seats may be available at the box office the day before a performance. The season runs from August to May. Kongens Nytorv. © **33-69-69-69.** Tickets are 60DKK–615DKK ($7.85–$81); half price for seniors (over 66) and young people (under 26). Bus: 1, 6, 9, or 10.

THE CLUB & MUSIC SCENE
JAZZ, ROCK & BLUES

Copenhagen JazzHouse   This place plays host to more non-Danish jazz artists (U.S., Britain, Germany, Africa) than just about any other jazz bar in town. Shows begin relatively early, at around 8:30pm, and usually finish reasonably early. Around midnight on Thursday, Friday, and Saturday, the venue shifts from a live concert hall into a dance club. It's closed Monday; otherwise, the ever-changing schedule depends on the bands' agendas. Niels Hemmingsensgade 10. © **33-15-26-00.** Cover 70DKK–360DKK ($9.15–$47) for live music. Bus: 10.

La Fontaine   This is the kind of place your parents might have considered a "dive," but it's the kind of dive that—if you meet the right conversational partner, or if you groove with the music—can be a lot of fun. Small, and cozy to the point of being cramped, it's a bordeaux-colored womb whose decor hasn't changed much since the 1950s. It's a bar Tuesday through Saturday from 8pm till 6 or even 8am. Sunday hours are from 9pm to 1:30am. There's live music on Friday and Saturday, when free-form jazz artists hold court beginning at around 11:30pm. Kompagnistræde 11. © **33-11-60-98.** Cover 45DKK ($5.90) Fri–Sat only. Bus: 5 or 10.

Mojo Blues Bar   Mojo is a candlelit drinking spot that offers blues music, mostly performed by Scandinavian groups. It's open daily from 8pm to 5am. Løngangsstræde 21C. ℂ **33-11-64-53.** Cover 50DKK ($6.55) Fri–Sat only. Bus: 2, 8, or 30.

DANCE CLUBS

Baron & Baroness   A short walk from the Tivoli, this is a relatively upscale nightclub with a faux-medieval decor. It attracts a crowd that's a bit more prosperous and mature than nearby competitors that cater to teenagers. It's really best for dancing, but dinner is available at about 150DKK to 250DKK ($20–$33). The bars are open nightly from 6pm till at least 3am; the restaurant, from 6 to 11pm. The dance club, which is one floor above the street-level restaurant, spins music only Thursday through Saturday, from 10pm till dawn. On nights when there's no dancing, you'll find a solo musician. Vesterbrogade 2E. ℂ **33-16-01-01.** Cover 50DKK ($6.55) for dance club. Bus: 250E or 350E.

Den Røde Pimpernel   The lively, club-like atmosphere of "The Scarlet Pimpernel" makes it a good place for dancing. If you can withstand the scrutiny, you'll be admitted after being inspected through a peephole. A live band plays dance music. It's open Tuesday through Saturday from 9pm to 8am. A beer will set you back 30DKK ($3.95), and mixed drinks cost 45DKK to 50DKK ($5.90–$6.55). H. C. Andersens Blvd. 7 (near Rådhuspladsen). ℂ **33-12-20-32.** Cover 50DKK ($6.55) Fri–Sat only. Bus: 2, 8, or 30.

Enzo   Few other nightclubs in Copenhagen offer as many bars. In this case, each has a different theme, ranging from plush intimate hideaways to more spartan stand-up affairs where patrons compete elbow-to-elbow on how fast they can throw back a shot of liquor. Come here for an all-around introduction to Copenhagen's night owls, then gravitate to either the Couch Lounge (where cozy, tucked away sites are pre-reserved); the Cigar Lounge; a dance bar; a Water Bar (where, despite its name, you can still get a drink of whiskey); and the Shot Bar, which boasts a comprehensive collection of tequilas, exotic rums, and vodkas. Enzo is open to the public only on Friday and Saturday; the rest of the week it's reserved for private parties. Nørregade 41. ℂ **33-13-67-88.** Cover 60DKK ($7.85). S-tog: Nørreport Station.

NASA   Its name has changed several times in the past decade, but even so, this is the most posh and prestigious of three nightclubs that occupy three floors of the same building. The late-night crowd of 25- to 40-year-olds includes many avid fans of whatever musical innovation has just emerged in London or Los Angeles. The decorative theme includes lots of white, lots of mirrors, and lots of artfully directed spotlights. Don't be surprised to see a room full of expensively, albeit casually, dressed Danes chattering away in a cacophony of languages. Technically, the site is a private club, but polite and presentable newcomers can usually gain access. It's open Thursday through Sunday from 10pm to 6am. Gothersgade 8F, Bolthensgaard. ℂ **33-93-74-15.** Cover 100DKK ($13) for non-members. Bus: 1, 6, or 9.

Rosie McGee's   Across the boulevard from the Tivoli, this is a funky, American-style nightclub that caters to high-energy Generation X-ers. Lots of teenyboppers come here to mingle, compare notes, and dance, dance, dance. The simple restaurant serves mostly Mexican food and frothy, foamy drinks. The bars and restaurant open nightly at 5:30pm, with dance music featured every Thursday through Saturday from 11:30pm till dawn. Vesterbrogade 2A. ℂ **33-32-19-23.** Cover 40DKK ($5.25) on dance nights only. Bus: 250E or 350E.

Rust   Rust sprawls over a one-story setting in the Nørrebro district. It combines a restaurant, several hopping bars, a dance floor, and a stage where live musicians perform every Tuesday at around 9pm. Meals are served Monday through Saturday from 5:30pm to around midnight, and things get going on the dance floor after 9:30pm. The setting is dark and shadowy. There are seats, but none so comfortable that you'll opt to remain in one place for too long. No one under 21 is admitted, and you'll spot very few people over 45. Rust is open from 5:30pm to at least 2am Monday through Saturday. Guldbergsgade 8. © 35-24-52-00. Cover 20DKK–40DKK ($2.60–$5.25) Wed–Sat only. Bus: 5 or 6.

Subsonic   Thanks to an armada of designers who developed it, this self-proclaimed "Design Disco" has an interior that's more artfully outfitted than that of any other competitor in Copenhagen. Expect lots of post-modern gloss, references to the California rave movement, an occasional emphasis on dance music of the 1980s, a small corner outfitted like a cozy beer hall, and a clientele that seems familiar with the music and ambience of some very hip clubs in Europe and the U.S. Part of its interior was copied directly from the waiting room of a 1970s Scandinavian airport, complete with the then-innovative streamlined design that's been associated with Denmark ever since. It's open Friday and Saturday from 11pm till at least 5:30am. Skindergade 45. © 33-13-26-25. Cover 50DKK–70DKK ($6.55–$9.15). Bus: 1 or 6.

THE BAR SCENE
PUBS

Det Lille Apotek *(Finds*   This is a good spot for English-speaking foreign students to meet their Danish contemporaries. The menu varies, but keep an eye out for the prawn cocktail and the tenderloin, which are highly recommended. Main courses run about 88DKK to 138DKK ($12–$18), and a beer costs 16DKK to 32DKK ($2.10–$4.20). It's open daily from 11am to midnight; closed December 24 to December 26. Stor Kannikestraede 15. © 33-12-56-06. Bus: 2, 5, 8, or 30.

Drop Inn   This is not a dance club, but it does offer live, iconoclastic bands who perform for patrons in their late teens and twenties. The room combines antique and modern oil paintings and features a long bar. It's open daily from 11pm to 5am. Beer starts at 21DKK ($2.75). Kompagnistræde 34. © 33-11-24-04. Bus: 28, 29, or 41.

Library Bar   Malcolm Forbes once rated this place one of the top five bars in the world. Surrounded by antique books and art, you can order everything from cappuccino to cocktails. The setting is the lobby level of the landmark Plaza, commissioned in 1913 by Frederik VIII. The bar, which attracts celebrities and royalty, was originally the hotel's ballroom. The oversized mural of George Washington and his men dates from 1910. It's open Monday through Saturday from 11:30am to 1am, Sunday from 11:30am to midnight. Beer costs 35DKK ($4.60); drinks are 55DKK ($7.20) and up. In the Hotel Plaza, Bernstorffsgade 4. © 33-14-15-19. Bus: 6.

Nyhavn 17   This cafe is the last of the honky-tonks that made up the former sailors' quarter. It's a short walk from the patrician Kongens Nytorv and the luxurious Hotel d'Angleterre. In the summer you can sit outside. It's open Sunday through Thursday from 10am to 2am, Friday and Saturday until 3am. Nyhavn 17. © 33-12-54-19. Bus: 1, 6, 27, or 29.

The Queen's Pub   Cozy, traditional, and rich in Baltic history, this is the kind of bar where a businessperson can feel at home after a transatlantic flight. The older members of the staff have served every politician and journalist in Denmark. On the ground floor of one of Copenhagen's most legendary (and discreet) hotels, it's open daily from noon to midnight. Beer costs 25DKK to 47DKK ($3.30–$6.15); drinks begin at 55DKK ($7.20). In the Kong Frederik Hotel, Vester Voldgade 25. © 33-12-59-02. Bus: 1, 2, 6, 8, or 28.

A WINE BAR

Hvids Vinstue   Built in 1670, this old wine cellar is a dimly lit safe haven for an eclectic crowd. Many patrons—theater-goers, actors, dancers—come from the Royal Theater across the way. It's open daily from 10am to 1am, but closed Sunday in July and August. Kongens Nytorv 19. © 33-15-10-64. Bus: 1, 6, 9, or 10.

GAY & LESBIAN CLUBS

See chapter 3 for a recommendation of the **Sebastian Bar & Café,** Copenhagen's most popular gay restaurant that has also has a "cruisy" bar.

Cosy Bar   It runs a fine line between a crowd that favors leather, and what you'd expect from a crew of manual laborers down by the harbor. A popular spot for cruising, the bar is open daily from 10pm till 8am, dispensing ample amounts of schnapps and suds during the course of a working night. Studiestraede 24. © 33-12-74-27. Bus: 6 or 29.

The Men's Bar   This is the only leather bar in town, filled with an unusual collection of uniforms, leather, and Levi's. Open daily from 3pm to 2am. Teglårdsstræde 3. © 33-12-73-03. Bus: 2, 8, or 30.

Pan Society   This nationwide organization was established in 1948 for the protection and advancement of gay and lesbian rights. Its headquarters is a 19th-century yellow building off the Strøget. A dance club occupies three floors, and a modern cafe is on the ground level. Every night is gay night, although a lot of straights come here for the music. The cafe is open daily from 8pm to 5am. The dance club is open Sunday and Wednesday from 11pm to 3am, Thursday from 10pm to 4am, Friday and Saturday from 10pm to 5am. Knabrostræde 3. © 33-11-37-84. Cover 55DKK ($7.20) for dance club. Bus: 28, 29, or 41.

SLM (Scandinavia Leather Men) Club   Set amid the densest concentration of gay bars in Denmark, just around the corner from the also-recommended Men's Bar, this is technically a private club that caters to men interested in the way other men look and act in leather. Non-members visiting from other countries—if they're dressed properly—can usually pay 100DKK ($13) for a temporary membership that will get them past the doorman. It's open Friday and Saturday nights only, from 10pm till at least 4am, and usually later. Studiestraede 14. © 33-32-06-01. Bus: 6 or 29.

GAMBLING

Casino Copenhagen   The country's first fully licensed casino has operated in this first-class hotel since 1990. It offers popular games such as roulette, baccarat, punto banco, and blackjack, as well as slot machines. It's open daily from 2pm to 4am. In the SAS Scandinavia Hotel, Amager Blvd. 70. © 33-96-59-65. Cover 80DKK ($10); free for guests at any of Copenhagen's SAS hotels. Bus: 5, 11, 30, or 34.

18 Side Trips from Copenhagen

BEACHES

The closest beach to Copenhagen is **Bellevue** (S-tog: Klampenborg), but the water is not recommended for swimming. If you want to take a dip at a sandy beach, ride the train or drive to the beaches at North Zealand—**Gilleleje, Hornbæk, Liseleje,** and **Tisvildeleje.** Although these are family beaches, minimum bathing attire is worn. To reach them, take the train to Helsingør and continue by bus. Or make connections by train to Hillerød and switch to a local train; check at the railroad station for details. If you drive, you may want to check out the dance clubs at the little beach resort towns that dot the north coast of Zealand.

DRAGØR ☆☆
4.8km (3 miles) S of Copenhagen's Kastrup Airport

This old seafaring town on the island of Amager is filled with well-preserved 18th-century cottages with steep red-tile or thatched roofs. Many are under the protection of the National Trust.

Dragør (pronounced *Drah*-wer) was a busy port on the herring-rich Baltic Sea in the early Middle Ages; when fishing fell off, it became just another sleepy little waterfront village. After 1520, Amager Island and its villages—Dragør and Store Magleby—were inhabited by the Dutch. They brought along their own customs, Low German language, and agricultural expertise, especially their love of bulb flowers. In Copenhagen you still see wooden-shoed Amager Dutch selling hyacinths, tulips, daffodils, and lilies in the streets.

GETTING THERE   Take bus no. 30, 33, or 73E from Rådhuspladsen (Town Hall Square) in Copenhagen. It's a 35-minute trip.

SEEING THE SIGHTS

Amager Museum   This museum outside Dragør holds a rich trove of historic treasures. The exhibits reveal the affluence the Amager Dutch achieved, with rich textiles, fine embroidery, and carved silver buckles and buttons. The rooms of a Dutch house are especially interesting, showing how the people decorated their homes and achieved comfort.

Hovedgaden 4–12, Store Magleby. ✆ **32-53-93-07.** Admission 20DKK ($2.60) adults, 10DKK ($1.30) children. Apr–Sept Wed–Sun noon–4pm; Oct–Mar Wed and Sun noon–4pm. Bus: 30, 33, or 350S.

Dragør Museum   The exhibits at this museum on the harbor show how the Amager Dutch lived from 1520 to the 20th century. Pictures and artifacts illustrate farming, goose breeding, seafaring, fishing, ship piloting, and ship salvage.

Havnepladsen 2–4. ✆ **32-53-41-06.** Admission 20DKK ($2.60) adults, 10DKK ($1.30) children. May–Sept Tues–Sun noon–4pm. Closed Oct–Apr. Bus: 30, 33, or 350S.

WHERE TO STAY & DINE

Restaurant Beghuset DANISH/FRENCH   This restaurant on a cobblestone street in the center of town looks like an idyllic cottage. The menu changes every 2 to 3 months. Selections might include fish soup, Swedish caviar, thinly sliced smoked lamb with balsamic dressing on a bed of seasonal greens, and fresh oysters. Main courses include perfectly cooked guinea fowl braised in red wine and served with bacon of veal (the restaurant's invention) and herbs, and Dragør plaice roasted in butter and served with parsley sauce or bacon-thyme sauce. To reach the restaurant, walk through the cafe.

Strandgade 14. ✆ **32-53-01-36**. Reservations recommended. 1-platter lunch 138DKK–189DKK ($18–$25); 2-course lunch 168DKK ($22); 3-course lunch 325DKK ($43); dinner main courses 178DKK–198DKK ($23–$26); 3-course fixed-price dinner 325DKK ($43); 4-course fixed-price dinner 375DKK ($49). AE, DC, MC, V. Tues–Sun noon–3pm and 6–9:45pm. Bus: 30, 33, or 73E.

Restaurant Dragør Kro ⍟ DANISH/FRENCH   This beautiful *kro* (inn) has one of the oldest continuously operated restaurants in Denmark. The building dates from 1650, and the inn was established in 1721, with a new wing added in 1795. There's a rose-filled courtyard for outdoor dining and drinking. Try filet of plaice with white-wine sauce, filet of beef with pepper sauce, or perhaps filet of veal in mustard sauce. "Falling star" (boiled or fried fish with caviar and shrimp) is a house specialty.

The hotel on the upper floors rents five attractively furnished and well-maintained double bedrooms, each with a private bathroom. Prices range from 1,000DKK to 1,200DKK ($131–$157) a night.

Kongvejen 23, DK-2791 Dragør. ✆ **32-53-01-87**. Fax 32-53-00-53. Reservations recommended. Main courses 175DKK–205DKK ($23–$27). AE, DC, MC, V. Winter daily noon–9:30pm; summer daily noon–10:30pm. Closed Dec 22–Jan 15. Bus: 30, 33, or 73E.

Strandhotel DANISH   One of Dragør's most visible restaurants is the Strandhotel (which has no guest rooms). It has welcomed such guests as Frederik III (who usually ordered eel soup) and the philosopher Søren Kierkegaard. At lunch an ample spread of smørrebrød is served; other offerings include filet of pork in paprika sauce, savory smoked filet of eel, fried or poached plaice, and delectable trout with almonds.

Strandlinbyn 9, Havnen. ✆ **32-53-00-75**. Reservations recommended. Lunch smørrebrød 72DKK–170DKK ($9.45–$22); "quick lunch" 75DKK ($9.85); main courses 105DKK–188DKK ($14–$25). AE, DC, MC, V. Daily 10am–10pm. Closed Oct–Mar. Bus: 30, 33, 73E, or 350S.

HUMLEBÆK (LOUISIANA MUSEUM)
32km (20 miles) N of Copenhagen

ESSENTIALS
GETTING THERE   By Train   Humlebæk is on the Copenhagen-Helsingør train line; two trains per hour leave Copenhagen's main railway station heading toward Humlebæk. The trip takes 40 minutes. Once you reach Humlebæk, the Louisiana Museum is a 10-minute walk.

By Bus   Take the S-tog, Line A or B, to Lyngby station. Then take bus no. 388 along the coast road. There's a bus stop at the museum.

By Car   Follow the Strandvej (coastal road no. 152) from Copenhagen. The scenic drive takes about 45 minutes.

SEEING THE SIGHTS
Louisiana Museum of Modern Art ⍟⍟⍟   This museum is idyllically situated in a 19th-century mansion on the Danish Riviera. It's surrounded by elegant gardens that open onto the Øresund. Exhibits include paintings and sculptures by modern masters (Giacometti and Henry Moore, to name two) as well as the best and most controversial works of modern art. Look especially for paintings by Carl-Henning Pedersen. The museum's name comes from the wives of the first owner of the estate, Alexander Brun—all three named Louise.

The museum has one of the largest exhibition spaces in Europe, and mounts major contemporary art shows. There is also a program of lectures, films, discussions with authors, and public debates. The concert series is known throughout Denmark. For children, there's the Børnehuset (children's house) and

Side Trips from Copenhagen

Søhaven (sea garden). The museum's cafe is on the famed terrace with Alexander Calder's playful sculptures.

Gl. Strandvej 13. (©) **49-19-07-19.** Admission 68DKK ($8.90) adults, 60DKK ($7.85) students, 20DKK ($2.60) children 5–16, free for children under 5. Wed 10am–10pm; Thurs–Tues 10am–5pm. Closed Dec 24, 25, and 31.

WHERE TO DINE

Gamla Humlebæk Kro DANISH This is the obvious luncheon choice for anyone visiting the Louisiana Museum, a short walk away. Built in 1722, the inn has a large dining room and three hideaway rooms. Selections include a range of open-faced sandwiches, deep-fried filet of plaice with shrimp and mayonnaise sauce, Wiener schnitzel, medallions of veal with morel sauce, and herring with sherry sauce. The food is old-fashioned and satisfying.

Ny Strandvej 2A. (©) **49-19-02-65.** Reservations recommended. Main courses 45DKK–158DKK ($5.90–$21) lunch; 178DKK–225DKK ($23–$29) dinner. AE, DC, DISC, MC, V. Daily 11:30am–9:30pm.

HILLERØD
35km (22 miles) NW of Copenhagen

Hillerød offers some very interesting sights, including one of Scandinavia's most beautiful castles. The ideal time to visit Hillerød is for its summer Viking festival (see "A Special Event," below).

But there's always something of interest here, as Hillerød lies in the heart of North Zealand, surrounded by some of the most beautiful and extensive woodlands in Denmark.

The city's history goes back 4 centuries, and it became a significant place in 1602 when Christian IV began the construction of Frederiksborg Castle (see "Exploring the Town," below).

The wide forests around Hillerød remain as vestiges of the prehistoric North Zealand wilderness. To the south sprawls the woodlands of Store Dyrehave, and to the north stretch the forests of **Gribskov,** the second largest in the country. The forests today are still rich in game, notably the pale fawn-colored roe deer with no tail. Gribskov forest contains some 800 fallow deer distinguished by their white-speckled hide. The great philosopher, Søren Kierkegaard, regularly reveled in the tranquillity of these forests.

Leaflets outlining the best walks and trails to follow in Gribskov and Store Dyrehave are available at the tourist office (see "Visitor Information," below).

ESSENTIALS
GETTING THERE By Train The S-tog from Copenhagen arrives every 10 minutes throughout the day, and the journey to Hillerød takes 40 minutes. Trains also link Hillerød with Helsingør in the east, and there are also rail links with Gilleleje and Tisvildeleje.

By Bus Hillerød has good bus connections with the major towns of North Zealand: bus no. 305 from Gilleleje; bus nos. 306, 336, and 339 from Hornbæk; and bus nos. 336 and 339 from Fredensborg.

By Car Take Route 16 north from Copenhagen.

VISITOR INFORMATION The **tourist office,** at Slotsgade 52 ((©) **48-24-26-26**), is open from June to August, Monday through Saturday from 9am to 6pm; from September to May, Monday through Saturday from 9am to 4pm.

A SPECIAL EVENT One of the most important Viking festivals in Scandinavia takes place every year near Hillerød. **Frederikssund** is a little town 13km

(8 miles) southwest of Hillerød and 48km (30 miles) northwest of Copenhagen. It stages a 2-week **Viking festival** 🐸 each summer where Nordic sagas are sometimes revived—and the record is set straight about who "discovered" America 5 centuries before Christopher Columbus. A revolving series of medieval and modern plays concerning the Vikings is what this festival is all about.

The festival begins in mid-June. The traditional play is performed nightly at 8pm, and a Viking banquet follows. Tickets for the festival are 110DKK ($14) for adults, and 25DKK ($3.30) for children 5 to 12 (it's not suitable for children under 5). The dinner costs 150DKK ($20) for adults, 75DKK ($9.85) for children 5 to 12. Trains depart at 20-minute intervals from Copenhagen's Central Railroad Station for Frederikssund. Travel time is 50 minutes, and there are enough trains back to Copenhagen after the spectacle ends to allow commutes from the capital. From Frederikssund station, it's a 20-minute walk to the site of the pageant. For details, contact the Copenhagen tourist information office or phone the Frederikssund Tourist Office (© **47-31-06-85**).

EXPLORING THE TOWN

Det Nationalhistoriske Museum på Frederiksborg 🐸🐸   This *slot* (castle)
with a moat, known as the Danish Versailles, is the major castle in Scandinavia, constructed on three islands in the castle lake. Like Kronborg, it was built in Dutch Renaissance style (red brick, copper roof, sandstone facade). The oldest parts date from 1560 and the reign of Frederik II. However, the main part of the castle was erected by his son, Christian IV, from 1600 to 1620. The castle was used by Danish monarchs for some 2 centuries. From 1671 to 1840 Danish kings were crowned in Christian IV's chapel, which is used to this day as a parish church. Since 1693 it has been a chapel for the Knights of the Order of the Elephant and of the Grand Cross of Danneborg. Standing in the gallery is an old organ built by Esaias Compenius in 1610. Every Thursday from 1:30 to 2pm, the chapel organist plays for museum guests. In 1859 the castle was ravaged by fire, but it has been restored.

Since 1878 the Museum of National History has been housed at the castle. Founded by the brewer J. C. Jacobsen as a special department of the Carlsberg Foundation, it encompasses the Great Hall and the former Audience Chamber of Danish monarchs. The museum contains the most important collection of portraits and historical paintings in the country. The collection, organized on a chronological basis, illustrates Danish history from the 16th century until today. The modern collection covering the 20th century was added on the third floor in 1993.

To reach the castle, it's a 15-minute walk or a short taxi ride from the train station.

In Frederiksborg Slot. © **48-26-04-39**. Admission 50DKK ($6.55) adults, 10DKK ($1.30) children 6–15, free for children under 6. Nov–Mar daily 11am–3pm; Apr and Oct daily 10am–5pm. Bus: 701 from Hillerød Station.

Frederiksborg Castle Garden 🐸 *Finds*   In the beginning of the 18th century,
this baroque garden, laid out north of the castle by Frederik IV, became one of the finest in the country. The royal architect and landscape designer, Johan Cornelius Krieger, was responsible for its actual look.

The garden was built around a central axis, creating continuity between building, garden, and the open land. Along the main axis, a cascade was built with water canals and fountains. Symmetrically surrounding the cascades were avenues, *bosquets* (thickets), and *parterres* (ornamental gardens arranged in patterns) sporting royal monograms. The parterres were planted with box hedges exactly as King Frederik had seen similar gardens arranged in France and Italy. The garden existed for 40 years, and enjoyed the patronage of three kings, Frederik IV, Christian VI, and Frederik V.

The last remains of the cascade were removed during the reign of Christian VII (1766–1808), presumably because the garden had grown out of style and become too expensive to maintain. In 1993, all that remained of the original baroque garden was the terraced ground, avenues in decay, and deformed box hedges.

Finally, the baroque garden was re-created when funds became available, and it was inaugurated on June 5, 1996. As many as 65,000 box plants and 166 pyramid-shaped yews have been planted in the parterres, and 375 limes and 7,000 hornbeam plants have been used to create the avenues and bosquets. The cascade floor consists of .4km (¼ mile) of dressed granite stones.

During the summer the garden offers a venue for several recurring concerts, Maypole celebrations, and other cultural events.

Rendelæggerbakken 3. 📞 42-26-02-62. Free admission. May–Aug daily 10am–9pm; Sept and Apr daily 10am–7pm; Oct–Mar daily 10am–5pm; Nov–Feb daily 10am–4pm. Bus: 701 from Hillerød Station.

Nordsjællandsk Folkemuseet (North Zealand Folk Museum)   Collections depict the rural history of North Zealand, with special emphasis on the pre-industrialization era in Hillerød.

There are supplementary displays at **Sophienborg,** Sophienborg Allé (📞 **48-24-34-48**), an estate on the western outskirts of Hillerød. Sophienborg is easily reached by bus no. 734 from Hillerød station. From there, it's an 8-minute walk. By car, take either Frederiksværksgade or Herredsvejen, turn right at Tulstrupvej, and follow the signs to the Folkemuseet Sophienborg. It keeps the same hours as the folk museum, and admission is on the same ticket.

Helsingørsgade 65. 📞 **48-24-34-48.** Admission 15DKK ($1.95) adults, free for children. Tues–Sun 10am–4pm. Closed Nov–Apr. Bus: 701.

Aebelholt Klostermuseum   You'll find the ruins of this Augustinian monastery founded in 1175, 6km (4 miles) west of Hillerød. A museum on this site—housed in the ruins—exhibits human skeletons dating from medieval times that provide clues to diseases that were commonplace at the time. Healing methods used by these early monks are also revealed. You can wander through a medicinal garden adjoining the museum.

Abelholt 4 📞 **48-21-03-51.** Admission 15DKK ($1.95) adults, free for children under 17. Mar–Apr and Oct Sat–Sun 1–4pm; May–Aug Tues–Sun 11am–4pm; Sept Tues–Sun 1–4pm.

WHERE TO DINE
Slotsherrens Kro DANISH   Since the 1970s, this well-managed tavern has flourished here in what were formerly the stables for nearby Frederiksborg Castle. It's the most sought-after dining spot in town for anyone visiting the castle, partly because of its carefully crafted array of open-faced sandwiches. The place also serves grilled meats and salads, which usually are a meal in themselves.

Frederiksborg Slot. 📞 **48-26-75-16.** Main courses 76DKK–158DKK ($9.95–$21); 2-course fixed-price menu 162DKK ($21); lunch plate 76DKK ($9.95); smørrebrød 32DKK–68DKK ($4.20–$8.90). MC, V. Tues 10am–5pm; Wed–Mon 10am–5pm. Closed Dec–Mar. Bus: 701.

FREDENSBORG
9.5km (6 miles) W of Helsingør, 40km (25 miles) N of Copenhagen

On the southeast shore of Esrum Sø, the country's second largest lake, Fredensborg is visited mainly for its royal palace. Many visitors rush through just for the

Book your air, hotel, and transportation all in one place.

Hotel or hostel? Cruise or canoe? Car? Plane? Camel? Wherever you're going, visit Yahoo! Travel and get total control over your arrangements. Even choose your seat assignment. So. One hump or two? travel.yahoo.com

powered by **COMPAQ**

YAHOO!
Travel

day, visiting the palace and then departing immediately. However, you can stay and dine in the area, and enjoy a number of other attractions as well (see below).

Naturally, the first inhabitants of the town were people who helped service the royal court. But over the years many others moved in, and today the town is a lively little place even when the queen isn't in residence. To Denmark, it occupies a position somewhat similar to Windsor in England. The town is home to some 40 specialty shops, which can be enjoyed in a pedestrian-street environment.

The palace is a major backdrop for events in the royal family's life, such as weddings and birthday parties. Here, heads-of-state from many other countries are received when they pay official visits, and foreign ambassadors present their credentials to the monarch.

ESSENTIALS

GETTING THERE   By Train & Bus   From Copenhagen's Central Railroad Station, frequent trains run to Fredensborg. Bus nos. 336 and 384 from Copenhagen's Central Railroad Station go to Fredensborg.

By Car   From Copenhagen, head north on the E55 toward Helsingør, turning west on Route 6.

VISITOR INFORMATION   The **Fredensborg Turistinformation,** Slotsgade 2 (© **48-48-21-00**), is open Monday through Friday from 10am to 4pm.

SEEING THE SIGHTS

Fredensborg Slot ⓡ   This is the summer residence of the Danish royal family. Founded in 1720, the present building dates from the end of the Great Northern War. Although the palace has been expanded many times, it still retains its baroque, rococo, and classical features.

The palace was particularly celebrated during the reign of Christian IX, who assembled the greats of European royalty here in the days of Queen Victoria. When the queen is in residence, visitors assemble at noon to watch the changing of the guard. On Thursdays, except in July, the queen often makes an appearance to acknowledge a regimental band concert in her honor.

The palace was built for King Frederik IV by the Danish architect J. D. Krieger. Originally there was only the main building with a Cupola Hall. Over the years, the palace was extended with such additions as the Chancellery House and the Cavaliers Wing.

Frederik IX and Queen Ingrid began the tradition of spending several months of the year at Fredensborg Palace. They preferred spring and autumn. That tradition is still upheld today by Queen Margrethe and Prince Henrik.

Today the palace is hardly one of the impressive royal palaces of Europe, but it has its own charm, especially in the Domed Hall and the Garden Room.

The palace opens onto a 275-year-old baroque garden. There is a public part of the palace garden open all year. However, the private royal garden is open only in July daily from 9am to 5pm. The orangery in the royal garden is also open in July daily from 1 to 4:30pm.

These are some of the largest and best-preserved gardens in Denmark. Note how strictly symmetrical and geometrical the shapes are. The palace gardens were laid out in the 1720s by Frederik IV and J. C. Krieger, drawing on Italian designs for their inspiration. In the 1760s Frederik V redesigned the garden, adding elements from French baroque horticulture.

Slottet. © **33-40-31-87**. Admission 30DKK ($3.95) adults, 10DKK ($1.30) children. Palace, July only 1–5pm.

HELSINGØR (ELSINORE): IN SEARCH OF HAMLET ✿
40km (25 miles) N of Copenhagen, 24km (15 miles) NE of Hillerød, 72km (45 miles) NE of Roskilde

Once you reach Helsingør, usually by train from Copenhagen, you'll be in the center of town and can cover all the major attractions on foot. Helsingør (Elsinore in English) is visited chiefly for "Hamlet's Castle." Aside from its literary associations, the town has a certain charm: a quiet market square, medieval lanes, and old half-timbered and brick buildings—remains of its once prosperous shipping industry.

In 1429 King Erik of Pomerania ruled that ships passing Helsingør had to pay a toll for sailing within local waters. The town quickly became a center for international shipping, bringing in a lot of revenue. King Erik also constructed the Castle of Krogen, later rebuilt by Christian IV as the Castle of Kronborg. For a while Helsingør prospered and grew so much that it was the second largest town in the country.

ESSENTIALS
GETTING THERE   By Train   There are frequent trains from Copenhagen, taking 50 minutes. Buses have been discontinued.

By Ferry   Ferries ply the waters of the narrow channel separating Helsingør (Denmark) from Helsingborg (Sweden) in less than 25 minutes per trek. They're operated by **Scandlines** (✆ **33-15-15-15**) around the clock, which charges 40DKK ($5.25) each way for a pedestrian without a car, and 245DKK ($32) each way for a car with up to five persons inside. Between 6am and 11pm, departures are every 20 minutes; between 11pm and 6am, departures are timed at intervals of between 40 and 80 minutes. The venue is simple and straightforward: You simply drive your car on board, and wait in your car in a line that might remind you of those on the Staten Island ferryboat. Border formalities during the crossing between Denmark and Sweden are perfunctory, and although you should carry a passport, it might not even be requested.

By Car   Take E-4 north from Copenhagen.

VISITOR INFORMATION   The **tourist office,** at Havnepladsen 3 (✆ **49-21-13-33**), is open Monday through Friday from 9am to 5pm, Saturday from 10am to 1pm.

SEEING THE SIGHTS
Kronborg Slot ✿✿✿   There is no evidence that Shakespeare ever saw this sandstone-and-copper Dutch Renaissance–style castle, full of intriguing secret passages and casemates (artillery compartments on ramparts), but he made it famous in *Hamlet.* If Hamlet had really lived, it would have been centuries before Kronborg was built (1574–1585). Over the years a number of famous productions of the Shakespearean play have been staged here. One great performance was Derek Jacobi's interpretation in 1979. In 1954 the parts of Hamlet and Ophelia were played by Richard Burton and Claire Bloom.

The castle, on a peninsula jutting out into Øresund, was restored in 1629 by Christian IV after it was gutted by fire. Other events in its history include looting, bombardment, occupation by Swedes, and use as a barracks (1785–1922). The facade is sandstone covered, and the entire castle is surrounded by a deep moat. You approach the castle via a wooden bridge and by going through Mørkeport, a gate dating from the 16th century. This leads you to the main courtyard of Kronborg. Instead of immediately entering the castle, you can walk around the moat to the waterfront where you can see a spectacular vista of the Swedish coast. At the platform—backed by massive bronze guns—Hamlet is said to have seen the ghost of his father, shrouded in pea-soup fog.

The starkly furnished Great Hall is the largest in northern Europe. Originally 40 tapestries portraying 111 Danish kings were hung around this room on special occasions. They were commissioned by Frederik II and woven around 1585. Only seven remain at Kronborg, seven are in the Nationalmuseet in Copenhagen, and the rest have disappeared. The church with its original oak furnishings and the royal chambers are worth seeing. The bleak and austere atmosphere adds to the drama. Lying beneath the castle is Holger Danske, the mythological hero who is believed to assist Denmark whenever the country is threatened. Also on the premises is the **Danish Maritime Museum** (© **49-21-06-85**), which explores the history of Danish shipping. Guided tours are given every half hour from October to April. In summer you can explore on your own. The castle is .8km (½ mile) from the rail station.

Kronborg. © **49-21-30-78**. Admission 40DKK ($5.25) adults, 15DKK ($1.95) children 6–14, free for children under 6. May–Sept daily 10:30am–5pm; Apr and Oct Tues–Sun 11am–4pm; Nov–Mar Tues–Sun 11am–3pm. Closed Dec 25.

Karmeliterklostret
This well-preserved 15th-century former Carmelite monastery, at the intersection of Havnegade and Kronborgvej, is the best of its kind in Scandinavia. After the Reformation it became a hospital, but by 1630 it was a poorhouse.

Skt. Annagade 38. © **49-21-17-74**. Admission 20DKK ($2.60) adults, 5DKK (65¢) children. Guided tours, mid-May to mid-Sept daily at 2pm.

Skt. Mariæ Church
An addition to the Karmeliterklostret complete with late 15th-century frescoes, St. Mary's also contains the still-in-use organ played by baroque composer Dietrich Buxtehude from 1660 to 1668.

Skt. Annagade 38. © **49-21-17-74**. Free admission. May 15–Sept 14 daily 10am–3pm; Sept 15–May 14 daily 10am–2pm.

Skt. Olai's Kirke
Built between 1480 and 1559, this christening chapel with a spire is worth a visit. The interior of the church and the baptistery in particular are one of a kind. The church, near the intersection of Havnegade and Kronborgvej, is connected to the Carmelite cloisters.

Skt. Annagade 12. © **49-21-04-43**. Free admission. May–Aug Mon–Sat 10am–4pm; Sept–Apr daily 10am–2pm.

Helsingør Bymuseet
Installed in part of the Carmelite monastery (see listing for Karmeliterklostret, above), this museum houses the town's historic archives and various exhibits. Of special interest are 15th-century items related to Helsingør's collection of duties in the sound. The exhibits present materials of the trades practiced in days gone by, including a printing house. There's also a collection of about 200 antique dolls and a fine scale model of the town in 1801. The museum is a short walk from the bus, train, and ferryboat stations.

Skt. Annagade 36. © **49-28-18-30**. Admission 10DKK ($1.30) adults, free for children. Daily noon–4pm.

Marienlyst Slot
Marienlyst was built from 1759 to 1763 in a neoclassical style by the French architect N. H. Jardin. The building was intended to be a royal summer home, but was never used as such. Up until 1953 it served as a private residence. Today it's a museum, with well-preserved interiors in the original

Louis XVI style and a permanent collection of paintings from Helsingør, along with an exhibit of silverwork. Special exhibits are arranged upstairs in summer. The castle is surrounded by a fine park, and there is a panoramic view of the sound from the top of a steep slope behind the castle.

Marienlyst Allé 32. ℭ **49-28-18-30.** Admission 20DKK ($2.60) adults, free for children. Daily noon–5pm.

Denmark's Tekniske Museet (Technical Museum of Denmark) This museum contains technical, industrial, scientific, and transportation exhibits, including the oldest Danish airplanes and trains, the world's first typewriter, and the world's first electromagnetic sound recorder (tape recorder). There's also an 1888 Danish automobile, the Hammelvognen. The museum is next door to the train station.

Nodre Strandvej 23. ℭ **49-22-26-11.** Admission 35DKK ($4.60) adults, 13DKK ($1.70) children. Tues–Sun 10am–5pm.

WHERE TO DINE

Typical Danish hot meals, such as *hakkebøf* (hamburger steak), *frikadeller* (Danish rissoles or meatballs), rib roast with red cabbage, cooked or fried flounder or herring, and *æggekage* (egg cake) with bacon, are served in the local restaurants. Helsingør has many fast-food places, too, and you won't want to miss the celebrated ice-cream wafers.

Anno 1880 DANISH   Set in a long, narrow, half-timbered building that originally functioned as a greengrocer's shop, this comfortable and traditional restaurant is owner-managed and always alert to the freshness of its ingredients. Within old-fashioned dining rooms, you'll enjoy seasonal meals that might include cream of clam soup with saffron; filets of salmon, haddock, or plaice in butter sauce with herbs; fried steak with fried onions and boiled potatoes; and such desserts as a kirsch-flavored parfait.

Kongensgade 6. ℭ **49-21-54-80.** Reservations recommended. Main courses 165DKK–190DKK ($22–$25); fixed-price menu 285DKK ($37). AE, DC, MC, V. Mon–Sat 11:30am–10pm.

Ophelia Restaurant DANISH/FRENCH/ITALIAN   The Ophelia is one of the most appealing restaurants in town. In the elegantly rustic dining room, photos of various world *Hamlet* productions line the brick walls. Specialties of the house include Hamlet veal steak and richly caloric desserts. Lunches cost only half as much as dinner. Although not overly imaginative, the cookery is very competent, with dish after tasteful dish emerging from the kitchen.

In the Hotel Hamlet, Bramstræde 5. ℭ **49-21-05-91.** Reservations recommended. Main courses 148DKK–185DKK ($19–$24). AE, DC, MC, V. Daily noon–9:30pm. Bus: 801 or 802.

Samos GREEK   Situated near Helsingør Castle and the ferryboat terminal for passengers heading back to Copenhagen, this restaurant was inspired by a Greek island *taverna*. It's part of Færgaarden, the former 1770 Customs House that's now a complex of international restaurants and the most popular choice for dining in Helsingør. Amid a color scheme of Ionian blue and white and a decor of fishnets and murals of such monuments as the Acropolis, you can order heaping portions of moussaka, roast lamb, grilled fish, meatballs, and the honey-enriched dessert, baklava. The buffet offers more than 20 delightful items. Additional seating is available on a breezy outdoor pavilion overlooking the sea.

Stengade 81 (at Færgaarden). ℭ **49-21-39-46.** Reservations recommended. Main courses 110DKK–85DKK ($14–$11); all-you-can-eat buffet dinner 110DKK ($14). MC, V. Daily 11am–11pm.

ROSKILDE 🐾🐾
32km (20 miles) W of Copenhagen

Roskilde, once a great ecclesiastical seat, was Denmark's leading city until the mid–15th century. Today the twin spires of Roskilde Cathedral stand out from the landscape like elegantly tapered beacons. These towers are the first landmark you see when approaching the city that celebrated its 1,000th anniversary in 1998.

Once the capital of Denmark, Roskilde is centuries past its peak, but it is no sleepy museum town, either. It's filled with a dynamic student community, boutique-lined walking streets, several landmarks and major sights, and a population of more than 52,000 people who call themselves *Roskildenser*.

Today Roskilde's cobble streets and towering cathedral only hint at the power and mystery of its Viking past. Toward the end of the last millennium, the Vikings settled the area, drawn no doubt by its sinuous coastline where they could launch their ships. In 1957 divers in the Roskilde Fjord came upon shards of wood. Their discovery turned out to be bigger than anyone imagined. Here, sunken and preserved by mud, were five Viking ships that presumably had been put there to block the passage of enemy ships.

Archaeologists began the painstaking job of building a watertight dam and draining that section of the fjord, while keeping the chunks and splinters of wood wet enough so as not to disintegrate. Splinter by splinter, they began reconstructing and reassembling the boats—a process that continues today. You can see their efforts on display at the **Viking Ship Museum** (see "Seeing the Sights," below), a modern museum that contains the five found ships.

Between 990 and the turn of the century, Roskilde's prominence grew, becoming the home of the royal residence. By the 11th century, a Catholic church and a Bishop's Seat resided at Roskilde, which remained Denmark's capital until the Reformation in 1536.

At that time, all the parish churches were abolished and the Catholic hierarchy disappeared. The government and the monarchy moved to Copenhagen. Nonetheless, at its peak, Roskilde's importance was expressed in its architecture. By 1150, it was surrounded by an embankment and a moat, inside of which stood 12 churches and a cathedral. In 1170 Bishop Absalon built a new church on the same site where Harald Bluetooth had erected his church 2 centuries before. Though it took 300 years in its construction, and was subsequently burned, destroyed, ravaged, and rebuilt, Absalon's cathedral laid the foundation for the existing Roskilde Cathedral, or Domkirche, which today is a UNESCO World Heritage site.

ESSENTIALS
GETTING THERE   By Train & Bus   Trains leave three times an hour from Copenhagen's Central Railroad Station for the 35-minute trip to Roskilde. Buses depart for Roskilde several times daily from Copenhagen's Central Railroad Station.

By Car   Take the E-21 express highway west from Copenhagen.

VISITOR INFORMATION   The **Roskilde-Egnens Turistbureau,** Gullandsstræde 15 (© **46-35-27-00**), provides pamphlets about the town and the surrounding area. The office is open from April to June, Monday through Friday from 9am to 5pm and Saturday from 10am to 1pm; July and August, Monday through Friday from 9am to 6pm, Saturday from 9am to 3pm, and Sunday from 10am to 2pm; and from September to March, Monday through Friday from 9am to 5pm, and Saturday from 10am to 1pm. While at the tourist office, inquire about a Roskilde card, which costs 120DKK ($16) for adults or 60DKK ($7.85) for children. The card admits you to the 10 major attractions in the area and is valid for 7 days from the date of issue. Without the card, it would cost 260DKK ($34) to visit these same attractions.

A SPECIAL EVENT The **Roskilde Festival** (© **46-35-27-00**), held out-doors from July 1 to July 4 on a large grassy field, attracts fans of rock music. To get information on the festival's dates and performances, call the above number or contact the Roskilde-Egnens Turistbureau (see "Visitor Information," above).

SEEING THE SIGHTS

Roskilde Domkirke ☆☆☆ This cathedral elevated Roskilde into the spiritual capital of Denmark and northern Europe. Today it rises out of a modest townscape like a mirage—a cathedral several times too big for the town surrounding it. Construction started in 1170 when Absalon was bishop of Roskilde. Work continued into the 13th century, and the building's original Romanesque features gave way to an early Gothic overlay. The twin towers weren't built until the 14th century.

Today the cathedral's beauty goes beyond a single architectural style, providing almost a crash course in Danish architecture. Although damaged by a fire in 1968, the cathedral, including its magnificent altarpiece, has been restored.

The Domkirke is the final abode of 38 Danish monarchs whose tombs are here, ranging from the modest to the downright eccentric. Not surprisingly, the tomb of Christian IV, the builder king who was instrumental in constructing nearly all of Copenhagen's famous towers and castles, is in a grandiose chapel with a massive painting of himself in combat and a bronze likeness by the Danish sculptor Bertel Thorvaldsen. In humble contrast is the newest addition, from 1972, of the simple brick chapel of King Frederik IX, which stands outside the church. This octagonal chapel is decorated with hand-painted tiles designed by the architects Johannes and Inger Exner and Vilhelm Wohlert.

Other notable tombs include the white marble sarcophagus of Queen Margrethe I. In King Christian I's chapel, from the 15th century, there is a column marked with the heights of several kings. The tallest monarch was Christian I at 6 feet, 9 inches. This, no doubt, was an exaggeration as his skeleton measures only 6 feet, 2 inches. The late-18th and early-19th-century chapel of King Frederik V is graced by a large, bright cupola. Note also the Gothic choir stalls, each richly and intricately carved with details from the Old and New Testaments.

The choir's gilded winged altar, made in Antwerp in the 1500s, was originally intended for Frederiksborg Castle. Pictures on the wings of the altar depict scenes from the life of Jesus, ranging from the Nativity to the Crucifixion. Following the fire, a new altar cloth was created by the renowned artisan Anna Thommesen.

The most charming aspect of the cathedral is its early-16th-century clock poised on the interior south wall above the entrance. A tiny St. George on horseback marks the hours by charging a dragon. The beast howls, the sound of which echoes through the cavernous church causing Peter Doever, "the Deafener," to sound the hour. A terrified Kirsten Kiemer, "the Chimer," shakes in fright but pulls herself together to strike the quarter hours.

Domkirkestræde 10. © **46-35-27-00**. Admission 15DKK ($1.95) adults, 10DKK ($1.30) children. Apr–Sept Tues–Fri 9am–4:45pm, Sat 9am–noon, Sun 12:30–4:45pm; Oct–Mar Tues–Fri 10am–3:45pm, Sat 11:30am–3:45pm, Sun 12:30–3:45pm. Bus: 602, 603, or 604.

Viking Ship Museum (Vikingeskibshallen) ⚓ Five vessels found in Roskilde Fjord, and painstakingly reconstructed from countless pieces of wreckage, are on display here. It's presumed that the craft (dating from 1000–1050) were deliberately sunk about 20km (13 miles) north of Roskilde at the narrowest section of the fjord to protect Roskilde from a sea attack. The discovery was relatively unprotected and unpublicized until 1962 when the Danish National Museum carried out a series of underwater excavations.

Also on display are a merchant cargo ship used by the Vikings, a small ferry or fishing boat, and a Danish Viking warship similar to the ones portrayed in the Bayeux Tapestry. Also discovered was a "longship," a Viking man-of-war that terrorized European coasts. You can buy copies of Viking jewelry in the museum gift shop, and there's a cafeteria.

To understand the attraction better, you can see a short film, *The Ships of the Vikings*, about excavating and preserving the ships and building and navigating *Roar Ege*, a Viking ship replica.

The Viking Ship Museum operates a museum harbor for its collection of Nordic vessels, including *Roar Ege*, plus another Viking ship replica, *Helge Ask*. Also moored here is the museum's restored sloop, *Ruth*. Opposite the boatyard are the workshops for old maritime crafts, such as rope- and sail-making and woodworking.

Vindeboder 12, 4000 Roskilde. ℂ 46-30-02-00. Admission 60DKK ($7.85) adults, 30DKK ($3.95) children 6–16, free for children under 6; family ticket 135DKK ($18). May–Sept daily 9am–5pm; Oct–Apr daily 10am–4pm. Bus: 605.

Roskilde Museum This museum, set in a former merchant's house 90m (300 ft.) from the Town Square, features exhibits of the celebrated Hedebo embroidery, regional costumes, and antique toys. Displays also include an aurochs (extinct wild ox) skeleton, a unique Viking tomb, and many medieval finds from the town. The museum also has a grocer's courtyard, with the shop in operation.

Sankt Ols Gade 15–18. ℂ 46-36-60-44. Admission 25DKK ($3.30) adults, free for children under 12. Daily 11am–4pm. Closed Dec 24–25 and Dec 31–Jan 1. Bus: 601, 602, 603, or 605.

Museet for Samtidskunst (Museum of Contemporary Art) Housed in a beautiful 18th-century palace, this museum of modern art has frequently changing exhibitions, along with performances, film shows, and modern dance and classical music concerts. It also houses a "videothèque" that presents programs featuring Danish and foreign artists. "The Palace Collections" (see below) are also here.

Stændertorvet 3A. ℂ 46-36-88-74. Admission 20DKK ($2.60) adults, 10DKK ($1.30) seniors, free for children. Tues–Fri 11am–5pm; Sat–Sun noon–4pm. Bus: 601, 602, 603, or 605.

Palæsamlingerne (The Palace Collections) After a visit to the Museet for Samtidskunst (see above), you can view the collections in Roskilde Palace at the same site. Most of these objets d'art and paintings date from the era of great prosperity Roskilde merchants enjoyed in the 1700s and 1800s. Here such local families as the Bruuns and the Borchs amassed a great deal of art and antiques, which you can see today.

Stændertorvet 3E. ℂ 46-35-78-80. Admission 25DKK ($3.30) adults, free for children. May 15–Sept 14 daily 11am–4pm; off season Sat–Sun 2–4pm. Bus: 601, 602, 603, or 605.

MORE ATTRACTIONS

St. Jørgensbjerg quarter was originally a small fishing village, and a number of old, half-timbered houses, some with thatched roofs, remain. These houses cluster around **Skt. Jørgensbjerg Kirke,** Kirkegade, which stands on the top of a hill with a panoramic view of Roskilde Fjord. This is one of the oldest and best-preserved stone buildings in Denmark. The nave and choir of the church date from the beginning of the 12th century, but the walled-up north door is even older, maybe from 1040. In the corners of the church and in the center of the nave are slender billets (ornamentations in Norman moldings), found only in wooden churches. A model of a medieval merchant vessel, or *kogge,* has been engraved in a wall. The church is open Monday through Friday from 10am to noon, from June 22 to August 31. From Roskilde, take bus no. 605 toward Boserup.

The same bus will deliver you to **Skt. Ibs Kirke (The Church of St. James),** Skt. Ibs Vej, also in the north of Roskilde. This ruin dates from around 1100. Abolished as a church in 1808, it was later a field hospital and a merchant's warehouse. Regrettably, the merchant destroyed the tower, the chancel, the porch, and the church vaults of this medieval relic, but spared the nave. From sunup to sundown, it is open for visits from April 4 to October 18.

NEARBY ATTRACTIONS

Lejre Research Center *(Finds)*   Eight kilometers (5 miles) west of Roskilde, this archaeological research center is the site of a reconstructed Iron Age community on 10 hectares (25 acres) of woodland. The main features are clay-walled and thatch houses built with the type of tools used some 2,000 years ago. Staffers re-create the physical working conditions as they thatch Iron Age huts, plow with "ards," weave, and make pottery by an open fire. They also sail in dugout canoes, grind corn with a stone, and bake in direct fire. Visitors can take part in these activities. Jutland black pottery is produced here, and handicrafts and books are for sale at the gift shop. There are tables where you can enjoy a picnic lunch.

Slagealléen 2, DK-4320 Lejre. (C) **46-48-08-78.** Admission 70DKK ($9.15) adults, 35DKK ($4.60) children. Daily 10am–5pm. Closed mid-Sept to Apr. Take the train from Copenhagen to Lejre, then bus no. 233 to the center. From Roskilde, there are frequent buses to Lejre; then take bus no. 233.

Ledreborg Park Og Slot   A baroque manor house and French-English–style park 7km (4½ miles) southwest of Roskilde and 44km (27 miles) west of Copenhagen, Ledreborg is one of the best-preserved monuments in Denmark. A 33-room house with a landscaped garden and 90-hectare (217-acre) park, this manor has been owned by one family, the Holstein-Ledreborgs, for eight generations. It was built by a minister to Christian IV, Johan Ludwig Holstein. Between 1741 and 1757 it was turned from a farmhouse into a baroque manor. Inside is a collection of antiques from the 17th and 18th centuries and a gallery of Danish paintings. It's approached by a 6.5km (4-mile) long *alleé* of lime trees, some 2 centuries old. A nearby passage grave dates from the late Stone Age, approximately 3000 B.C.

Allé 2, DK-4320 Lejre. (C) **46-48-00-38.** Admission 60DKK ($7.85) adults, 35DKK ($4.60) children 6–16, free for children under 6. Family ticket 150DKK ($20). Mid-June to Aug daily 11am–5pm; May 1 to mid-June and Sept Sun 11am–5pm. Closed Oct–Apr. From Copenhagen's Central Railroad Station, take the direct train to Lejre, which leaves hourly and takes 35 min.; from Lejre station, take the 3-min. bus (no. 233) ride to the castle and park. From Roskilde, there are frequent buses to Lejre, followed by the short bus ride.

The Tramway Museum   In Justrup, some 16km (10 miles) southwest of Roskilde, in a pleasant woodland area close to Glydenveshj, the summer season Tramway Museum with its collection of antique trams is situated on the highest point on Zealand, 125m (416 ft.) above sea level. Board an old tram at the entrance and travel the 300m (1,000 ft.) to the museum's main building.

Skjoldenæsholm, Skjoldenæsvej 107. ℂ 57-52-88-33. Admission 60DKK ($7.85) adults, 30DKK ($3.95) children. May 6–June 20 and Aug 3–Oct 22 Sat 1–5pm, Sun 10am–5pm. June 21–Aug 2 Sun and Tues–Thurs 10am–5pm, Sat 1–5pm. Take a train from Copenhagen to Borup, and then bus no. 249 from the station.

WHERE TO DINE

Club 42 (Restaurant Den Hvide Fugl) DANISH/INTERNATIONAL Sandwiched between two similar houses in the heart of town, this brick building originally housed a blacksmith's shop 300 years ago, where most of the town's horses were fitted with shoes. In a long narrow interior with a greenhouse-style roof that can be opened during good weather, it offers a selection of open-faced sandwiches, pork ribs prepared in barbecue sauce or in garlic-onion sauce, filet steak with red-wine sauce, a fish platter of the house served with butter sauce, and grilled pepper steak. This is one of the middle-bracket staples of Roskilde. Although the food is a bit standard, it is well prepared with tasty ingredients.

Skomagergade 42. ℂ 46-35-17-64. Reservations recommended. Main courses 100DKK–200DKK ($13–$26); 3-course fixed-price menu 229DKK ($30). DC, MC, V. Daily 11am–10pm.

Raadhuskælderen ⍟ DANISH One of the oldest restaurants in Roskilde occupies the street level of a redbrick building erected in 1430, across the street from the town's cathedral. Although it's tempting to remain in the vaulted and arcaded interior (you have to descend only about four steps to reach it), there's also an outdoor terrace that's appealing during midsummer, especially because of its view of the cathedral. Menu items are carefully prepared using very fresh ingredients. Examples include lobster soup served with homemade bread, smoked salmon with a small portion of scrambled eggs, tournedos in red-wine sauce, and pepper steak that's flambéed at your table. One particularly succulent main course is a *Raadhus teller* that's composed of paprika-dusted pork cutlets with noodles and herbs.

Stændertorvet, Fondens Bro 1. ℂ 46-36-01-00. Reservations recommended. Lunch menu 32DKK–108DKK ($4.20–$14); main courses 88DKK–208DKK ($12–$27); fixed-price dinner 245DKK ($32). AE, DC, MC, V. Mon–Sat 11am–10pm; Sun 11am–9pm.

Restaurant Toppen DANISH At the top of a 1961 water tower, 80m (275 ft.) above sea level, Restaurant Toppen offers a panoramic view of the whole town, the surrounding country, and Roskilde Fjord—all from the dining room. Begin with a shrimp cocktail served with dill and lemon, accompanied by salad, bread, and butter. Main dishes include sirloin of pork a la Toppen with mushrooms and béarnaise sauce, with a baked potato and salad. For dessert, try the chef's nut cake with fruit sauce and sour cream. The cookery has greatly improved in recent months, and there is a finesse and consistency that wasn't here before. The restaurant lies about 1.5km (1 mile) east of the town center between Vindingevej and Københavnsvej. The water tower doesn't revolve, but some clients, in the words of the management, "get the feeling that it's turning only if they drink enough." There's a free elevator to the top.

Bymarken 37. ℂ 46-36-04-12. Reservations recommended. Main courses 62DKK–117DKK ($8.10–$15). DC, MC, V. Mon–Fri 3:30–10pm; Sat–Sun noon–10pm. Bus: 601.

5

Exploring the Danish Countryside

Denmark, a relatively flat country with good roads, is easy to explore on your own in several driving tours. To reach Bornholm from Copenhagen and Zealand, you'll need to rely on ferry connections. A new bridge links Funen and Zealand. Another bridge connects Funen and Jutland, which is linked to the mainland of Europe.

If you have time for only one destination outside Copenhagen, make it **Funen.** It's the most visited island, mainly because of its capital, Odense, the birthplace of Hans Christian Andersen. Some of northern Europe's best-preserved castles are here.

Denmark's western peninsula, **Jutland** (also called Jylland), is the only part of the country that's connected to the European mainland; its southern border touches Germany.

Bornholm, "the pearl of the Baltic," can be reached only by plane or boat. Inhabited since the Iron Age, the island is quite different from the rest of Denmark. A visit is a good choice if you're looking for something offbeat.

1 Funen

Funen (*Fyn* in Danish), the country's second-largest island, separates Zealand from the mainland peninsula, Jutland. It offers unique attractions, from a Viking ship to runic stones.

Hans Christian Andersen was born on Funen in the town of Odense. A visit to the storyteller's native island is a journey into a land of hop gardens and roadside orchards, busy harbors, market towns, castles, and stately manor houses.

Funen has some 1,130km (700 miles) of coastline, with wide sandy beaches in some parts; in others, woods and grass grow all the way to the water's edge. Steep cliffs provide sweeping views of the Baltic and the Kattegat.

Although ferries have plied the waters surrounding Denmark's islands and peninsulas since ancient times, the government has always regretted the lack of bridges. In 1934 the first plans were developed for a bridge over the 13km (8-mile) span of water known as the **Great Belt (Storebaelt),** the silt-bottomed channel that separates Zealand and Copenhagen from Funen and the rest of continental Europe. War, technical embarrassments, and lack of funding caused many delays. After the submission of 144 designs by engineers from around the world, construction began in 1988 on an intricately calibrated network of bridges and tunnels. Finally, in 1998 the bridge over the Storebaelt opened to motor traffic.

This driving tour of the island of Funen begins at Nyborg. You reach it by crossing the bridge from the town of **Korsør** on the island of Zealand. To reach Korsør from Copenhagen, take E20 heading south, then west to Korsør.

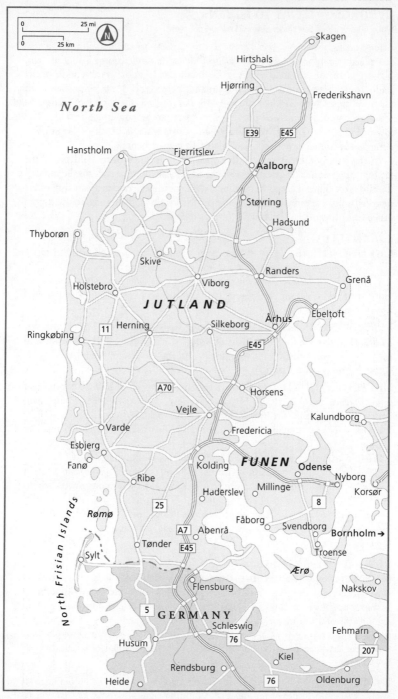

NYBORG: GATEWAY TO FUNEN
130km (81 miles) W of Copenhagen, 34km (21 miles) E of Odense

After crossing the bridge, you'll come to this old seaport and market town, a perfect place to explore before you head to Odense. Founded some 700 years ago, Nyborg is one of the oldest towns in Denmark. Its location in the middle of the trade route between Zealand and Jutland helped boost its importance. In medieval times, from about 1200 to 1413, Nyborg was the capital of Denmark. Medieval buildings and well-preserved ramparts are testaments to that era. The town square, the **Torvet,** was created in 1540, when a block of houses was demolished to make room for Christian III's tournaments.

In the summer, Denmark's oldest open-air theater, **Nyborg Voldspil,** is the setting for an annual musical or operetta under the light beeches on the old castle ramparts. Throughout the summer, classical music concerts featuring international soloists are performed in the castle's Great Hall. Inquire at the tourist office (see "Essentials," below) for further details.

ESSENTIALS
GETTING THERE   Ferry service from Zealand has been eliminated. Drive across the bridge at Korsør and follow the directions into Nyborg.

If you're not driving, you can reach Nyborg by train or bus. Trains leave Copenhagen every hour, and there's frequent bus service. Trains arrive twice an hour from Odense.

VISITOR INFORMATION   The **Nyborg Turistbureau** is at Torvet 9 (© 65-31-02-80). It's open from June 15 to August, Monday through Friday from 9am to 5pm, Saturday from 9am to 2pm; from September to June 14, Monday through Friday from 9am to 4pm, Saturday from 9am to noon.

GETTING AROUND   Buses cover the major arteries of town; a typical fare costs 11DKK ($1.45). If you plan to visit several sights in and around town, consider a 24-hour pass costing 25DKK ($3.30). Both individual tickets and the 24-hour passes are available directly from the bus driver of whichever bus you choose.

Thanks to the city administration, a network of coin-operated kiosks has been installed whereby you can deposit 20DKK ($2.60) into a machine, and a bright yellow bicycle will be released from its moorings for rides about town. Whenever you return it, the 20DKK ($2.60) will be returned to you automatically. Several of these kiosks lie at strategic intervals throughout Nyborg's core, but the most central and most visible is on the Norregade, just around the corner from the tourist office, at Torvet 9 (© **65-31-02-80**).

SEEING THE SIGHTS
Mads Lerches Gård (Nyborg Og Omegns Museet) ⊛ *Finds*   This two-story structure is the finest and best-preserved half-timbered house in Nyborg. It was constructed in 1601 by Mads Lerche, the mayor. The 30 rooms contain exhibitions on local history.

Slotsgade 11. © **65-31-02-07**. Admission 10DKK ($1.30) adults, 5DKK (65¢) children 6–14, free for children 5 and under. Mar–May and Sept–Oct Tues–Sun 10am–3pm; June–Aug daily 10am–5pm. Closed Nov–Feb. Bus: 1, 3, or 4.

Nyborg Slot   Nyborg Castle, with its ramparts still intact, is the oldest royal seat (1170) in Scandinavia. King Erik Glipping signed Denmark's first constitution in this castle in 1282, and Nyborg Castle was the seat of the Danish parliament, the Danehof, until 1413. The present furnishings date primarily from the 17th century, when Nyborg was a resplendent Renaissance palace. It's directly north of the landmark Torvet (tower) in the town center.

Slotspladsen. © **65-31-02-07.** Admission 30DKK ($3.95) adults, 15DKK ($1.95) children 6–14. Mar–May and Sept–Oct daily 10am–3pm; June–Aug daily 10am–5pm. Closed Nov–Feb. Bus: 1, 2, or 3.

Vor Frue Kirke   Dating from the late 14th and the early 15th century, the Church of Our Lady has a fine Gothic spire, three aisles, woodcarvings, old epitaphs, candelabra, and model ships. Nightly at 9:45pm, the Watchman's Bell from 1523 is rung, continuing a long-standing tradition. Opposite the church is the 12th-century **chapter house** of the Order of St. John (Korsbrødregård), with a fine vaulted cellar that's now a gift shop. The church is at the end of Kongegade in the town center.

Adelgade. © **65-31-16-08.** Free admission. June–Aug Mon–Sat 9am–6pm, Sun 9am–1pm. Sept–May Mon–Sat 9am–4pm, Sun 9am–1pm.

WHERE TO STAY

Hotel Hesselet ⭐⭐   Set among beech trees, with a view across the Great Belt, this redbrick building with a pagoda roof is one of the most stylish hotels in Denmark. Completely refurbished in 1996, it offers spacious rooms, good-sized bathrooms with shower-tub combinations, and firm beds. The Oriental carpets, leather couches, fireplace, tasteful library, and sunken living rooms create a glamorous aura. The hotel's gourmet restaurant, with a view of the Great Belt, is one of the finest on Funen.

Christianslundsvej 119, DK-5800 Nyborg. © **65-31-30-29.** Fax 65-31-29-58. www.hesselet.dk. 46 units. Mon–Thurs 1,580DKK–1,780DKK ($207–$233) double; Fri–Sun 1,480DKK–1,680DKK ($194–$220) double. All week long, 2,400DKK–2,800DKK ($314–$367) suite. Rates include breakfast. AE, DC, MC, V. Free parking. **Amenities:** Restaurant; bar; pool; 2 tennis courts; sauna; room service; babysitting; laundry/dry cleaning. *In room:* TV, minibar, hair dryer, safe.

WHERE TO DINE

The Hotel Hesselet (see "Where to Stay," above) has an excellent restaurant.

Danehofkroen DANISH/FRENCH   This restaurant was built in 1815 as a barracks for the soldiers who guarded the nearby castle. The Jensen family took over in 1993. The well-managed restaurant has two dining rooms outfitted in elegant country tavern style. Tasty menu items include fish soup with saffron, fried duck liver flavored with bacon and leeks, turbot with mushroom sauce, delectable veal fried with chanterelle mushrooms, and a dessert specialty of raspberry parfait with fresh melon.

Slotsplads. © **65-31-02-02.** Reservations recommended. Main courses 150DKK–200DKK ($20–$26). MC, V. Tues–Sun 12:30–9pm. Closed Oct–Mar.

Restaurant Østervemb DANISH/FRENCH   The heartwarming fare, served here since 1924, is the sort that might be offered to a hungry crew by a nurturing Danish aunt. You can order platters piled high with three preparations of herring, cold potato soup with bacon and chives, breast of Danish hen served with spinach and mushrooms, curried chicken salad with bacon, and slices of grilled beef tenderloin served with a fricassee of oyster mushrooms and tarragon-flavored glaze.

Mellengade 18. © **65-30-10-70.** Reservations recommended. Lunch platters 184DKK ($24); dinner main courses 192DKK–258DKK ($25–$34). DC, MC, V. Tues–Fri noon–3pm and 5–9pm.

ODENSE ☆☆: BIRTHPLACE OF HANS CHRISTIAN ANDERSEN

156km (97 miles) W of Copenhagen, 34km (21 miles) W of Nyborg, 43km (27 miles) NW of Svendborg

This ancient town, the third largest in Denmark, has changed greatly since Hans Christian Andersen walked its streets. However, it's still possible to discover a few unspoiled spots.

ESSENTIALS

GETTING THERE   From Nyborg, head west on E20 to Allerup and then follow Route 9 north to Odense. From Copenhagen, it's an easy 3-hour trip by train or bus. About 12 trains or buses a day leave Copenhagen's Central Railroad Station.

VISITOR INFORMATION   Odense Tourist Bureau is at Rådhuset Vestergade 2A (© 66-12-75-20; www.odenseturist.dk). It's open from mid-June to August, Monday through Saturday from 9am to 7pm, Sunday from 10am to 4pm; from September to mid-June, Monday through Friday from 9:30am to 4:30pm, Saturday from 10am to 1pm.

Besides helping arrange excursions, the tourist bureau sells the **Odense Adventure Pass.** It gives you access to 13 of the city's museums, the Odense Zoo, six indoor swimming pools, and unlimited free travel on the city buses and DSB trains within the municipality. It also entitles you to discounts on river cruises and admission to the summer-only presentation of the city's Hans Christian Andersen plays (see "Seeing the Sights," below). Passes are valid for 1 or 2 days. A 1-day pass is 100DKK ($13) for adults, 40DKK ($5.25) for children under 14; 2-day passes cost 140DKK ($18) and 50DKK ($6.55).

GETTING AROUND   You can hop aboard a bus at various stops and buy your ticket once you're aboard. You can also rent a bike from **City Cykler,** Vesterbro 27 (© 66-13-97-83), for prices ranging from 99DKK to 150DKK ($13–$20) per day, depending on the type of cycle.

SEEING THE SIGHTS

Odense Tourist Bureau (see above) offers **2-hour walking tours** from mid-June to August. They leave every Tuesday, Wednesday, and Thursday at 11am from a meeting place behind the tourist office, and cover the town's major sights. Tours are given in English, and advance reservations are recommended. Tours cost 40DKK ($5.25) per adult, 20DKK ($2.60) per child.

Also at the tourist office, you can get information about the **Hans Christian Andersen plays,** presented every year from mid-July to mid-August. The plays are given on an outdoor stage in the Funen Village, where members of the audience stand (if it's raining or the ground is wet) or sit on the grass (often on blankets, if it's dry).

Even if you don't understand Danish, the visuals afford lots of entertainment value. The 90-minute plays begin every day at 4pm. They cost 60DKK ($7.85) for adults, 35DKK ($4.60) for children, and are usually mobbed with Andersen fans.

Carl Nielsen Museet *Finds*   Adjoining the Odense Concert Hall, this museum documents the life and work of composer Carl Nielsen and his wife, the sculptor Anne Marie Nielsen. Visitors hear excerpts of Nielsen's music while they look at the exhibits and biographical slide show. Parking is available outside the concert hall.

Claus Bergsgade 11. © **66-14-88-14.** Admission 25DKK ($3.30) adults, 10DKK ($1.30) children 5–14, free for children under 5. Tues–Sun 10am–4pm. Bus: 2.

Danmarks Jernbanemuseum (Railway Museum)   The displays here—original locomotives and carriages that illustrate Denmark's railway history—include the first railroad in Denmark, from 1847. One of the oldest locomotives in the collection is an 1869 "B-Machine." Also on display are three royal coaches, a double-decker carriage, and a model railway. The museum is next to the train station.

Dannebrogsgade 24. ℂ **66-13-66-30.** Admission 40DKK ($5.25) adults, 16DKK ($2.10) children. Daily 10am–4pm. Bus: 2.

Funen Village/Den Fynske Landsby 🅡🅡   A big open-air regional culture museum, this is an archive of 18th- and 19th-century Funen life. It's in the Hunderup Woods, 2.4km (1½ miles) south of the town center. The old buildings—a toll house, weaver's shop, windmill, farmstead, jail, vicarage, village school, and brickworks—have been reassembled and authentically furnished. Plays and folk dances are staged at the Greek theater. You can also visit workshops and see a basket maker, spoon cutter, blacksmith, weaver, and others at work.

Sejerskovvej 20. ℂ **66-14-88-14.** Admission 55DKK ($7.20) adults, 15DKK ($1.95) children. Apr–May and Sept–Oct Tues–Sun 11am–3pm; June–Aug daily 9:30am–7pm; Nov–Mar Sun 11am–3pm. Bus: 21 or 22 from Flakhaven.

H. C. Andersens Barndomshjem (Andersen's Childhood Home)   This is Andersen's humble boyhood home, where the fairy-tale writer lived from age 2 to 14. From what is known of Andersen's childhood, his mother was a drunken, superstitious washerwoman, and he was a gawky boy, lumbering and graceless, the victim of his fellow urchins' cruel jabs. All is serene at the cottage today, however, and the "garden still blooms," as in *The Snow Queen.*

Munkemøllestraede 3. ℂ **66-14-88-14.** Admission 10DKK ($1.30) adults, 5DKK (65¢) children. July–Aug daily 10am–5pm; Sept–June daily 10am–3pm. Bus: 2.

H. C. Andersens Hus 🅡🅡   The object of most Funen pilgrimages is the house and museum of Hans Christian Andersen. It's popular with both adults and children. You'll see his famous walking stick, top hat, and battered portmanteau, plus letters to his dear friend Jenny Lind and fellow writer Charles Dickens. In addition, hundreds of documents, manuscripts, and reprints of his books in dozens of languages are on display.

Hans Jensensstraede 37–45. ℂ **66-14-88-14.** Admission 35DKK ($4.60) adults, 15DKK ($1.95) children 5–14, free for children under 5. June 16–Aug daily 9am–7pm; Sept–June 15 daily 10am–4pm. Bus: 2.

St. Canute's Cathedral   Despite its unimpressive facade, this is the most important Gothic-style building in Denmark. A popular feature of the 13th-century brick structure is the gold altar screen, an elegant triptych carved by Claus Berg in 1526 at Queen Christina's request. King Canute was killed by angry Jutland taxpayers in 1086 and canonized 15 years later. The church stands opposite the Town Hall.

Klosterbakken 2. ℂ **66-12-61-23.** Free admission. May 15–30 and Sept 1–14 Mon–Sat 10am–5pm; Apr–May 14 and Sept 15–30 Mon–Sat 10am–4pm; June–Aug Mon–Sat 10am–5pm, Sun and holidays noon–3pm; Oct–Mar Mon–Fri 10am–4pm, Sat 10am–2pm. Bus: 21 or 22.

NEARBY ATTRACTIONS

Egeskov Castle 🅡🅡   This 1554 Renaissance water castle, northeast of Fåborg at Kvaerndrup, is the most romantic and splendid of Denmark's fortified manors. The castle, which has magnificent gardens, was built on oak pillars in the middle of a moat or small lake. It's the best-preserved Renaissance castle of its type in Europe.

Every year some 200,000 visitors roam the 12-hectare (30-acre) park and cas-tle, located on the main road between Svendborg and Odense. There's a vintage automobile, horse carriage, and airplane museum on the grounds. Chamber music concerts are held in the Great Hall of the castle on 10 summer Sundays beginning in late June, starting at 5pm.

The most dramatic story in the castle's history is about an unfortunate maiden, Rigborg, who was seduced by a young nobleman and bore him a child out of wedlock. Banished to the castle, she was imprisoned by her father in a tower from 1599 to 1604.

Egeskovgade 18, Kvaerndrup. ℂ 62-27-10-16. Admission including castle, park, and maze 110DKK ($14) adults, 60DKK ($7.85) children 4–12; park, maze, museum 75DKK ($9.85) adults, 37DKK ($4.85) children 4–12. Both free for children under 4. May and Sept, park and castle daily 10am–5pm. June and Aug, park daily 10am–8pm; castle daily 10am–6pm. July, park daily 10am–8pm; castle daily 10am–6pm. Closed Oct–May. Train: From Odense or Svendborg every hour. Bus: 920 from Nyborg.

Ladbyskibet   Ladby, 20km (12 miles) northeast of Odense, is the site of a 22m (72-ft.) long 10th-century Viking ship, discovered in 1935. The ship's remains are displayed in a burial mound along with replicas from the excavation (the originals are in the National Museum in Copenhagen). A skeleton of the pagan chieftain buried in this looted ship was never found, but the bones of his horses and dogs were.

Vikingevej 123, Ladby. ℂ 65-32-16-67. Admission 25DKK ($3.30) adults, free for children under 15. Mar–May 14 and Sept 15–Oct daily 10am–4pm; May 15–Sept 14 daily 10am–5pm; Nov–Feb Wed–Sun 11am–3pm. Bus: 482 from Kerteminde, which is accessible by bus from Odense.

SHOPPING

Inspiration Zinch, Vestergade 82-84 (ℂ **66-12-96-93**), offers the widest selec-tion of Danish design and handicrafts on the island of Funen. All the big names are here, from Royal Copenhagen to Georg Jensen, but you will also come across younger, more modern designers. In the heart of the old town, opposite Hans Christian Andersen's house, you'll find a display of Danish crafts and Christmas decorations in an atmosphere typical of old Funen at **Klods Hans,** Hans Jensens Staede 34 (ℂ **66-11-09-40**). A most interesting outlet is **Smykker,** 3 Klaregade (ℂ **66-12-06-96**). It offers museum jewelry copies from the Bronze, Iron, and Viking ages—all made in gold, sterling silver, and bronze in the outlet's work-shop. **College Art,** Grandts Passage 38 (ℂ **66-11-35-45**), has assembled a unique collection of posters, lithographs, silkscreens, original art, and cards. The best gallery for contemporary art is **Galleri Torso,** Vintappersstraede 57 (ℂ **66-13-44-66**). Finally, if none of these shops has what you want, head for **Rosengårdcentret,** Munkerisvej and Ørbaekvej; it's Denmark's biggest shop-ping center, with more than 100 stores under one roof.

WHERE TO STAY

Hotel Ansgar   Built a century ago as an affiliate of a local church, this hotel dropped its religious connections many years ago. In the heart of town, behind a brick-and-stone facade, it boasts a modern interior. Double-glazed windows cut traffic noise considerably. The rooms are well furnished and vary in size from spacious to small. Likewise, bathrooms are medium-sized or cramped. All rooms have a well-kept bathroom with a shower-tub combination. The hotel's reason-ably priced restaurant serves Danish food. A particularly good value is the two-course fixed-price dinner for 100DKK ($13). The hotel is a 5-minute walk from the train depot.

Østre Stationsvej 32, DK-5000 Odense. © **66-11-96-93**. Fax 66-11-96-75. 64 units. June–Aug 650DKK ($85) double; Sept–May 795DKK ($104) double. Extra bed 150DKK ($20). AE, DC, MC, V. Free parking. Bus: 31, 33, 35, or 36. **Amenities:** Restaurant; bar; laundry/dry cleaning. *In room:* TV, minibar, hair dryer.

Odense Plaza Hotel ★★   Less than .5km (¼ mile) from the town center, Odense's classic hotel is one of its most alluring hostelries. It was built in 1915, and many guest rooms were renovated in 1997. The rooms evoke an English country home, and open onto scenic views. Some are quite spacious, and all contain well-kept bathrooms with shower-tub combinations. Units for non-smokers can be requested.

The terrace overlooks a park and garden.

Østre Stationsvej 24, DK-5000 Odense. © **800/233-1234** in the U.S., or 66-11-77-45. Fax 66-14-41-45. www.odenseplaza.dk. 68 units. July–Aug 795DKK ($104) double; 875DKK ($115) suite. Sept–June 1,250DKK ($164) double; 1,550DKK ($203) suite. Rates include breakfast. AE, DC, MC, V. Free parking. Bus: 31, 33, 35, or 36. **Amenities:** Restaurant; bar; room service; laundry/dry cleaning. *In room:* TV, minibar, hair dryer, safe.

Radisson SAS H. C. Andersen Hotel ★   This brick hotel in the heart of the old city lies next to a former residence of Hans Christian Andersen. Decorated in 1960s Nordic modern, it is one of Funen's premier hotels. Most guests are businesspeople. Rooms vary in size from large to a bit cramped; the quietest open onto the interior. Bathrooms tend to be small, but have thoughtful extras such as make-up mirrors and shower-tub combinations. Accommodations for nonsmokers can be requested, and some units are suitable for those with disabilities.

Claus Bergs Gade 7, DK-5000 Odense. © **800/333-3333** in the U.S., or 66-14-78-00. Fax 66-14-78-90. www.radisson.dk. 145 units. 1,345DKK ($176) double. Rates include breakfast. AE, DC, MC, V. Free parking. Bus: 4 or 5. **Amenities:** Restaurant; bar; sauna; room service; laundry/dry cleaning. *In room:* TV, minibar, hair dryer, safe.

WHERE TO DINE

Den Gamle Kro ★ DANISH/FRENCH   At this well-preserved 1683 inn in the town center, two cozy dining rooms are furnished with antiques. It also offers a cellar-level bar lined with antique masonry, with the main dining at street level. The inn has long been known for its accomplished chefs who use the best ingredients. Two of the best menu items are trout fried in butter and herbs, served with creamed potatoes, asparagus, and parsley; and beef tenderloin with herbs and green vegetables.

Overgade 23. © **66-12-14-33**. Reservations recommended. Main courses 169DKK–258DKK ($22–$34); fixed-price menus 158DKK–348DKK ($21–$46). AE, DC, MC, V. Mon–Sat 11am–10:30pm, Sun 11am–9:30pm. Bus: 2.

Marie Louise ★★ *Finds* FRENCH   A centrally located antique house painted yellow is the home of Odense's smallest, most exclusive restaurant. Its dining room is a white-walled re-creation of an old-fashioned country tavern, although closer inspection reveals a decidedly upscale slant. The polished staff serves well-planned dishes based on French recipes. Delectable specialties include salmon-and-dill mousse with shrimp sauce, platters of fresh fish, turbot in Riesling or champagne sauce, lobster in butter or Provençal sauce, and an array of tooth-some desserts.

Lottrups Gaard, Vestergade 70–72. © **66-17-92-95**. Reservations recommended. Main courses 318DKK–387DKK ($42–$51); fixed-price menus 395DKK–610DKK ($52–$80). AE, DC, MC, V. Mon–Sat noon–2pm and 6–9:30pm. Closed July. Bus: 2.

Under Lindetraeet DANISH/INTERNATIONAL This 2½-century-old inn is across the street from Hans Christian Andersen's house. For more than a quarter-century it has been a landmark restaurant, with a menu based on fresh, high-quality ingredients. Skillfully prepared dishes include tender Danish lamb, filet of plaice with butter sauce, escalope of veal in sherry sauce, fried herring with new potatoes, and an upscale version of *lobscouse,* the famed sailors' hash. In the summer, meals and light refreshments are served outside under linden trees. Artists often sit here to sketch Andersen's house.

Ramsherred 2. ℭ **66-12-92-86.** Reservations required. Main courses 225DKK–495DKK ($29–$65); fixed-price lunch 198DKK ($26); fixed-price dinner 355DKK ($47). DC, MC, V. Mon–Sat 11am–11pm.

SVENDBORG

43km (27 miles) S of Odense, 147km (91 miles) W of Copenhagen

This old port on Svendborg Sound has long been a popular boating center, and you can see yachts, ketches, and kayaks in the harbor. The town retains some of its medieval heritage, but many buildings have been torn down in the name of progress. Visitors find that Svendborg makes a good base for touring the Danish châteaux country and the South Funen archipelago.

Svendborg is a market town. On Sunday morning, visit the cobblestone central plaza, where flowers and fish are sold. Wander through the many winding streets where brick and half-timbered buildings still stand. On **Ragergade** you'll see the old homes of early seafarers. **Møllergade,** a pedestrian thoroughfare with about 100 shops, is one of the oldest streets in town.

The German playwright Bertolt Brecht lived at Skovsbo Strand west of Svendborg from 1933 to 1939, but he left at the outbreak of World War II. During this period he wrote *Mother Courage and Her Children.*

ESSENTIALS

GETTING THERE From Odense, head south on Route 9 for 44km (27 miles) to the port of Svendborg. If you're not driving, you can take a train from Copenhagen to Odense, where you can get a connecting train to Svendborg.

VISITOR INFORMATION **Svendborg Tourist Office** is at Centrumpladsen (ℭ **62-21-09-80**). It's open from June 14 to August, Monday through Friday from 9am to 6pm, Saturday from 9am to 3pm; from January 2 to June 13 and from September to December 22, Monday through Friday from 9am to 5pm, Saturday from 9:30am to 1pm. The office is closed from December 23 to January 1.

SEEING THE SIGHTS

Viebaeltegård The headquarters of the Svendborg County Museum's four branches, Viebaeltegård is in the town center. The building, a former poorhouse and workhouse constructed in 1872, is the only one of its kind still existing in a Danish town. These social-welfare buildings, including the garden, now make up a historical monument. Inside, see displays from ancient times and the Middle Ages, including excavation finds from old Svendborg and South Funen. Available workshops include goldsmithing, pottery-making, and printing. There's a big museum shop, and you can picnic in the garden.

Grubbemøllevej 13 (near Dronningemaen). ℭ **62-21-02-61.** Admission 40DKK ($5.25) adults, free for children accompanied by an adult. May 1–Oct 24 Mon–Fri 10am–5pm; Oct 25–Apr Mon–Fri 10am–4pm.

Anne Hvides Gård The oldest secular house in Svendborg, a branch of the County Museum, was built around 1558. It's a beautiful half-timbered structure with 18th- and 19th-century interiors and collections of Svendborg silver, glass, copper, brass, and faience. It's in the center of the Torvet.

Fruestraede 3. ✆ **62-21-76-15.** Admission 20DKK ($2.60) adults, 10DKK ($1.30) seniors, free for children accompanied by an adult. June–Aug 31 daily 10am–5pm; off season by arrangement with the main office.

St. Nicolaj Church   Svendborg's oldest church is among a cluster of old houses off Kyseborgstraede, in the vicinity of Gerrits Plads. Built before 1200 in the Romanesque style and last restored in 1892, its redbrick walls and white vaulting complement the fine altarpiece and stained-glass windows.

Skt. Nicolajgade 2B. ✆ **62-21-12-96.** Free admission. May–Aug daily 9am–4pm; Sept–Apr daily 10am–noon.

St. Jørgen's Church   The beauty of St. George's Church is exceeded only by that of the Church of St. Nicolaj (above). The core of the church is a Gothic longhouse with a three-sided chancel from the late 13th century. During restoration of the church in 1961, an archaeological dig of the floor disclosed traces of a wooden building. Note the glass mosaics.

Strandvej 97. ✆ **62-21-14-73.** Free admission. Daily 8am–4pm.

WHERE TO STAY

Hotel Svendborg ✮   This stylish hotel offers the best accommodations in Svendborg. Built in the 1950s, it rises four floors above the commercial core of town. Except for five or six rooms that missed out on an overhaul in 1994 (and are priced accordingly), the comfortable accommodations have Scandinavian modern furniture and good bathrooms with shower-tub combinations. On the premises is a restaurant that serves international food, and a cafe-bar with a glassed-in front terrace. There's also an on-site tanning facility.

Centrumpladsen 1, DK-5700 Svendborg. ✆ **62-21-17-00.** Fax 62-21-90-12. www.hotel-svendborg.dk. 132 units. June to mid-Aug 920DKK ($121) double; mid-Aug to May 1,050DKK ($138) double. Rates include breakfast. AE, DC, MC, V. Free parking. Bus: 200 or 204. **Amenities:** Restaurant; bar; room service; laundry/dry cleaning. *In room:* TV, minibar, hair dryer, safe.

Missionshotellet Stella Maris *Value*   This is an old-fashioned place, the former dormer house of a large estate, built in 1904. Rooms are comfortable, if dated, and each has a small bathroom with shower stall. Sea-view rooms opening onto Svendborg Sound are more expensive. A private park leads directly to the sound. In the southwest of the city, this lovely old seaside villa, as part of a Christian hotel chain, still maintains its smoke-free and alcohol-free atmosphere.

Kogtvedvaenget 3, DK-5700 Svendborg. ✆ **62-21-38-91.** Fax 62-22-41-74. www.stellamaris.dk. 25 units, 15 with bathroom. 530DKK ($69) double without bathroom; 585DKK–700DKK ($77–$92) double with bathroom. Rates include breakfast. DC, MC, V. Bus: 202. From Svendborg, head west along Kogtvedvej. *In room:* No phone.

WHERE TO DINE

Restaurant Gaasen ✮ DANISH/SEAFOOD   At the edge of the harbor in a former ironmonger's smithy, this is one of the most appealing and congenial restaurants in town. Its creative force derives from chef and owner Claus Holm, who invents many of the dishes that attract a steady stream of locals. This is clearly a labor of love. Three dishes of which he is most proud are grilled freshwater crabs with saffron-flavored bouillon and homemade lobster-stuffed ravioli; veal stuffed with black truffles and sweetbreads, served with Madeira sauce; and gray mullet with herbs, beurre blanc (white butter), and sautéed spinach.

The establishment's name (which means "goose") comes from its location a few steps from the site where live poultry was bought and sold in the Middle Ages.

Kullinggade 1B. © 62-22-92-11. Reservations recommended. Main courses 150DKK–280DKK ($20–$37); fixed-price menu 425DKK ($56). MC, V. Mon–Sat noon–2pm and 5:30–10pm.

Svendborgsund DANISH/FRENCH   A 5-minute walk south of the commercial center, this waterfront restaurant is the oldest in town. The stone house was built in the 1830s. From the windows or summer terrace, you can see the harbor and its ferries, trawlers, and yachts. The talented chef specializes in fresh fish and meat, including the very filling *biksemad* (meat, potatoes, and onions). The separate bar is popular with locals.

Havnpladsen 5A. © 62-21-07-19. Reservations recommended. Lunch smørrebrød 60DKK–100DKK ($7.85–$13); main courses 100DKK–170DKK ($13–$22). AE, MC, V. Daily 11am–midnight.

NEARBY ATTRACTIONS ON TÅSINGE

The largest island in the South Funen archipelago, Tåsinge has been connected to Funen by the Svendborg Sound Bridge since 1966. **Troense** 𝔸𝔸, the "skipper town" of Tåsinge, is one of the best-preserved villages in Denmark. Many half-timbered houses still stand on Badstuen and on Grønnegade, which has been declared Denmark's prettiest street.

The island was the setting for the tragic story of forbidden love depicted in the film *Elvira Madigan*. After checking out of a hotel in Svendborg, Danish tightrope walker Elvira Madigan and her lover, Sixten Sparre, a Swedish lieutenant, crossed by ferry to Tåsinge, where they committed suicide. The Romeo and Juliet of Denmark were buried in the Landet Kirkegård, Elvira Madigansvej, at Landet in the middle of Tåsinge. Even today, many brides throw their wedding bouquets on the graves. The 100th anniversary of the lovers' death was widely observed throughout Scandinavia in 1989; many ballads were written to commemorate the date. The island is best explored by car—drive over the causeway bridge (following Rte. 9). You can also take local bus no. 200. The most important attraction, **Valdemar's Slot (Castle),** can be seen by taking the **vintage steamer** MS *Helge* (© **62-22-51-06** for information), which departs several times daily from the harbor at Svendborg. The steamer operates from May 11 to September 8. A round-trip ticket costs 55DKK ($7.20). Tickets are sold on board or at the Svendborg Tourist Office (see above).

Søfartssamlingerne I Troense   The Maritime Museum (a branch of the County Museum), housed in a 1790 school, traces nautical history from the early 19th century to the present. Displays include pictures of ships, panoramas, yachting models, and memorabilia of the China and East India trade routes. You'll see Staffordshire figures, Liverpool ware, Sunderland china, rope-work art, and ships in bottles.

Strandgade 1, Troense. © 62-22-52-32. Admission 25DKK ($3.30) adults, 15DKK ($1.95) children and seniors. May–Sept daily 10am–5pm; Oct–Apr Mon–Fri 10am–5pm, Sat 9am–noon. Cross the causeway to Tåsinge, turn left and then left again, heading down Bregningevej toward the water; turn right at Troensevej and follow the signs to the old port of Troense and the old village school (now the museum) on Strandgade.

Valdemars Slot 𝔸   This castle was built between 1639 and 1644 by order of Christian IV for his son, Valdemar Christian. In 1678 it was given to the naval hero Niels Juel after his third victory over the Swedes in a Køge Bay battle. The Juel family still owns the structure, which is in considerably better condition than when the admiral arrived. The enemy Swedes had occupied the estate, sent the copper roof home to make bullets, and stabled horses in the church. The castle is now a museum.

Valdemar's Castle Church, in the south wing, was cleaned up by Admiral Juel and consecrated in 1687. Two stories high, it's overarched by three star vaults and illuminated by Gothic windows.

Slotsalléen 100, Troense. ℂ **62-22-61-06.** Admission 55DKK ($7.20) adults, 35DKK ($4.60) children. Apr–May and Oct 1–18 Sat–Sun 10am–5pm; May–Sept daily 10am–5pm. Closed Oct 19–Mar. Take the MS *Helge* from Svendborg harbor. By car, from Troense follow Slotsalléen to the castle.

Where to Stay & Dine

Hotel Troense   Since 1905 this establishment has been both a hotel and a restaurant. It was last renovated in 1993. Most rooms are in the main white-walled building, with several in comfortable but lackluster annexes nearby. Accommodations cost the same with or without bathrooms. The units with bathrooms contain shower-tub combinations. In the nautically decorated restaurant, which is also open to the public, specialties include filet of lemon sole; plaice stuffed with shrimp, asparagus, and mushrooms; and medallions of pork with cream-and-curry sauce. The restaurant is open daily for lunch and dinner.

Strandgade 5–7, Troense, DK-5700 Svendborg. ℂ **62-22-54-12.** Fax 62-22-78-12. www.hoteltroense.dk. 28 units, 24 with bathroom. 775DKK ($102) double. Rates include breakfast. AE, DC, MC, V. Free parking. Bus: 200. **Amenities:** Restaurant; bar; lounge. *In room:* TV.

Restaurant Slotskælderen *finds* DANISH/FRENCH   Inside the thick stone walls of one of the region's most foreboding castles, this restaurant is divided into a simple Danish bistro and an upscale French restaurant. The bistro serves such dishes as schnitzels, *lobscouse* (hash), and roulades of beef with Danish beer and aquavit. The views over the tidal flats and sea are better from the restaurant, but most visitors prefer the informality and lower prices of the bistro.

If you'd like to stay overnight, five luxurious guest rooms (four with private bathrooms) and one suite are in a modern outbuilding of the historic castle. Doubles without bathroom cost 775DKK ($102), doubles with bathroom are 950DKK ($124), and the suite goes for 1,450DKK ($190).

In Valdemars Slot, Slotsalléen, Troense, DK-5700 Svendborg. ℂ **62-22-59-00.** Restaurant, main courses 75DKK–195DKK ($9.85–$26); bistro, main courses 75DKK–175DKK ($9.85–$23). AE, MC, V. Apr–May and mid-Sept to Oct Tues–Sat 11am–10pm; June to mid-Sept daily 11am–9pm.

Nearby at Millinge

The epitome of Danish roadside lodging, the following 15th-century smugglers' inn has been converted into a premier hotel, the finest in Funen, just 40km (24 miles) from Odense and 42km (25 miles) from Svendborg.

Falsled Kro ☆☆☆   This Relais & Châteaux property offers tradition and quality in its colony of thatched buildings clustered around a cobblestone courtyard with a fountain. Each accommodation is elegantly furnished and comfortable. Some are in converted outbuildings, others in cottages across the road. All units have well-kept bathrooms with shower-tub combinations. A garden leads to the water and a yacht harbor. Bonuses include luggage service, translation and guide service, fishing and bathing areas, a heliport, and nearby tennis courts and horseback riding.

Dining at this *kro* (inn) may be the culinary highlight of your stay in Denmark, so be sure to make a reservation. The kitchen uses only fresh seasonal produce, much of it grown there. The preparations are inspired by French cuisine.

Some of this restaurant's most noted dishes are among the simplest, such as the succulent salmon, smoked on the premises. Other choices include scallop salad with basil sauce, fish-and-shellfish soup with sorrel, fiery lobster in the style of Tiger Lee (spiced with hot peppers), French duck liver with wild rice and sweet-corn relish, and saddle of rabbit or braised beef in red-wine sauce. The owners breed quail locally and cook and serve them with a port wine sauce. The chef's seafood platter is a gift to put before Neptune. Try salmon grilled or flamed over fennel. Game dishes predominate in autumn. The kitchen also bakes its own bread and cakes. The wine list is well chosen.

The restaurant serves lunch daily from noon to 2:30pm and dinner Tuesday through Sunday from 6 to 9:30pm (closed Mon Oct–Mar). Main courses are about 310DKK to 370DKK ($41–$48); three- to five-course fixed-price menus are 480DKK to 660DKK ($63–$86) and 790DKK ($103).

Assensvej 513, Falsled, DK-5642 Millinge. © **62-68-11-11.** Fax 62-68-11-62. www.falsledkro.dk. 19 units. 1,100DKK–2,100DKK ($144–$275) double; 2,400DKK ($314) suite. AE, DC, MC, V. Bus: 930. **Amenities:** Restaurant; bar; room service; babysitting; laundry/dry cleaning. *In room:* TV, minibar, hair dryer.

ACROSS THE WATER TO ÆRØ ✿✿✿

29km (18 miles) S of Svendborg, 74km (46 miles) S of Odense, 177km (110 miles) SW of Copenhagen

Ærø, an island 35km (22 miles) long and 9.5km (6 miles) wide, has seaside and country hamlets linked by winding, sometimes single-lane roads, with thatched-roof farmhouses in pastures and cultivated fields. The island has both sand and pebble beaches good for bathing along the north and east coasts.

There are many good places to eat and sleep—cozy inns in the country, and comfortable little hotels in town. Try some of the local rye bread, which is the best in Denmark. With your aquavit, ask for a dash of Riga balsam bitters, a tradition that started when Ærø sailors brought them back from Riga.

ESSENTIALS

GETTING THERE   The only way to reach Ærø is by ferry. Car ferries depart from Svendborg six times daily. The trip takes about an hour. It costs around 416DKK ($55) for the average car, and a one-way passenger fare costs 128DKK ($17). For a schedule, contact the tourist office or the ferry office at the harbor in Svendborg. Bookings are made through **Det Æroske Færgegrafikselskab Ærø** in Ærøskøbing (© **62-52-40-00**). Ferry service is also available on the west coast of Funen, at Fåborg (© **02-61-14-88**).

VISITOR INFORMATION   The **Ærøskøbing Turistbureau** is at Vestergade 1 (© **62-52-13-00;** www.aeroeturistbureau.dk). It's open from June 15 to August, Monday through Friday from 9am to 5pm; from September to June 14, Monday through Friday from 9am to 4pm, Saturday from 9am to noon. **Marstal Turistbureau,** Havnegade 5 (© **62-53-19-60**), is open from mid-June to August, Monday through Friday from 9am to 5pm, Saturday from 10am to 3pm. In July, the peak month to visit Ærø, it is also open Sunday from 9:30am to 12:30pm. Off-season hours are Monday through Friday from 9am to 4pm.

GETTING AROUND   It's best to take a car on the ferry because there's limited **bus service** on Ærø. Call © **62-53-10-10** in Ærøskøbing for bus information. Bus no. 990 runs every hour on the hour in the afternoon between Ærøskøbing, Marstal, and Søby. Morning service is limited. Tourist offices (see "Visitor Information," above) provide bus schedules, which change seasonally. Tickets, which cost 62DKK ($8.10) for the day, can be bought on the bus. If you'd like to take a bus tour of the island, call **Jesper "Bus" Jensen** (© **62-58-13-13**). His bus holds 12 to 14 passengers, and costs 50DKK ($6.55) per person.

Ærø is one of the best islands in Denmark for **cycling** because of its low-lying terrain and scenic paths. Local tourist offices provide maps outlining routes for 15DKK ($1.95). You can use these maps for bike rides but also for **walks.** Cycle trails around the coast are marked by the numbers 90, 91, and 92. Bike rentals cost 41DKK ($5.35) a day, and rentals in Ærøskøbing are available at the Ærøskøbing Vandrerhjem, Smedevejen 15 (© **62-52-10-44**); at Marstal at Nør-remark Cykelforretning, Møllevejen 77 (© **62-53-14-77**); and at Søby Cykelforretning, Langebro 4A (© **62-58-18-42**).

EXPLORING THE ISLAND

The neat little village of **Ærøskøbing** 🏖️🏖️ was a 13th-century market town that came to be known as a skippers' town in the 17th century. Called "a Lilliputian souvenir of the past," it has small gingerbread houses, intricately carved wooden doors, and cast-iron lamps. Few Scandinavian towns have retained their heritage as much as Ærøskøbing. In the heyday of the windjammer, nearly 100 commercial sailing ships made this their home port.

The ferry from Fåborg docks at **Søby,** in the northwest part of the island. Before you rush to Ærøskøbing, visit a mellow manorial property, **Søbygård.** Now in ruins, this manor house in the center of Søby is complete with a moat and dank dungeons. Photographers are fond of the local **church.** Its octagonal steeple dates from about 1200, and it has had many additions and alterations over the centuries. See, in particular, Claus Berg's triptych, a primitive rendition of the Crucifixion.

Marstal, a thriving little port on the east coast of Ærø, has had a reputation in sailors' circles since the days of the tall ships. The harbor, protected by a granite jetty, is still busy. It has a shipyard that produces steel and wooden vessels, an engine factory, a ferry terminal, and one of Denmark's biggest yacht basins. The street names attest to Marstal's seafaring background—Skonnertvej, Barkvej, and Galeasevej (Schooner, Bark, and Ketch roads); Danish naval heroes such as Rasmus Minor and Christen Hansen; and Seven Ferry Lanes.

Visit the **seamen's church,** with the spire and illuminated clock, in the town center. Inside are ship models and an altarpiece that depicts Christ stilling the tempest at sea.

Twice a day a mail boat takes a limited number of passengers on a 45-minute trip to tiny **Birkholm Island** for swimming and exploration. There are no cars on Birkholm. Reservations on the mail boat can be made at the Marstal Tourist Office.

SEEING THE SIGHTS

Ærøskøbling Kirke   Built between 1756 and 1758 to replace a rather dilapidated church from the Middle Ages, this reconstruction still maintains the original 13th-century font and the pulpit stem, donated by Duke Philip of Lyksborg in 1634, the year he bought Gråsten County on the island of Ærø. (The year before that, he had inherited the market town of Ærøskøbing and an estate in Voderup.) The altarpiece is a copy of Eckersberg's picture hanging in Vor Frue Kirke in Svendborg. The colors selected for the interior of the church, along with the floral motifs, were the creation of Elinar V. Jensen in connection with an extensive restoration project carried out in 1950.

Søndergade 43. © **62-52-11-72.** Free admission. Daily 8:30am–5pm.

Flaskeskibssamlingen *Finds*   The seafaring life is documented in this museum of Peter Jacobsen's ships-in-bottles, which represent his life's work. Upon his death in 1960 at the age of 84, this former cook, nicknamed "Bottle Peter," had crafted more than 1,600 bottled ships and some 150 model sailing vessels built to scale, earning him the reputation in Ærøskøbing of "the ancient mariner." The museum also has Ærøclocks, furniture, china, and carved works by sculptor H. C. Petersen.

Smedegade 22. ⓒ **62-52-29-51.** Admission 25DKK ($3.30) for adults, 10DKK ($1.30) for children. Daily 10am–5pm.

Ærø Museum   This is the best museum on Ærø. In the old days it was inhabited by the bailiff, but today you'll find a rich collection of the island's past, including antiques and paintings from the mid-1800s.

Brogade 35 (at the corner of Nørregade). ⓒ **62-52-29-50.** Admission 20DKK ($2.60). Daily 10am–4pm.

WHERE TO STAY
In Ærøskøbing
Det Lille Hotel 👍 *Value*   Lying 90m (300 ft.) from the ferry and harbor, Det Lille Hotel was built in 1844 as a private home. Today it offers simple but cozy guest rooms. All units contain well-kept bathrooms with shower-tub combinations. The hotel is also a good dining choice. It serves meals daily from 11:30am to 2pm and 6 to 9pm. Try asparagus soup, pork chops with vegetables, ham cutlets with mushrooms, beef steaks, fried chicken, or hash.

Smedegate 33, DK-5970 Ærøskøbing. ⓒ **62-52-23-00.** 6 units, none with bathroom. 565DKK ($74) double. Rates include breakfast. MC, V. Free parking on street. **Amenities:** Restaurant; lounge. *In room:* TV.

Hotel Ærøhus 👍   This typical Danish inn is charming, with many traditional features, such as copper kettles hanging from the ceiling and warm lamps glowing. The guest rooms are traditional—in vaguely French boudoir style—although they've been modernized. Most units have a well-kept bathroom with a shower-tub combination. You can also enjoy good Danish meals here. In the summer there's dining in the large garden. The hotel, a 3-minute walk from the harbor, offers live music on summer weekends.

Vestergade 38, DK-5970 Ærøskøbing. ⓒ **62-52-10-03.** Fax 62-52-21-23. 65 units, 50 with bathroom. 540DKK ($71) double without bathroom; 880DKK ($115) double with bathroom. Rates include breakfast. AE, DC, MC, V. Closed Dec 24–Feb 1. Free parking. **Amenities:** Restaurant; bar; babysitting; laundry/dry cleaning. *In room:* TV, hair dryer, safe.

In Marstal
Ærø Kongreshotel   A 5-minute walk south of the center of town and less than .5km (¼ mile) from the beach, this hotel, opened in 1989, is the largest and most up-to-date on the island. Surrounded by sea grass and sweeping vistas, the rooms are first class, decorated in pastel colors, with well-maintained bathrooms containing shower-tub combinations. The suites are twice the size of regular rooms.

Egehovedvej 4, DK-5960 Marstal. ⓒ **62-53-33-20.** Fax 62-53-31-50. www.hotelaeroestrad.dk. 100 units. 845DKK ($111) double; 1,170DKK ($153) suite. Rates include breakfast. DC, MC, V. Closed Dec 18–Jan 2. Free parking. Bus: 990 to Marstal. **Amenities:** Restaurant; bar; pool; sauna; room service; babysitting. *In room:* TV.

WHERE TO DINE
Restaurant Mumm AMERICAN/INTERNATIONAL   In a simple house whose foundation dates from 1780, this restaurant enjoys a reputation for well-prepared dishes. There are two dining rooms; the less formal offers a view into the busy kitchen. There's also a terrace in the garden in back, where umbrellas and candles usually adorn the tables. The restaurant offers an unusual combination of American- and Danish-style dishes (a former owner had been a chef at a Florida resort). There's a copious salad buffet, flavorful steaks, and an abundance of seafood, mostly from local waters. You might try filet of plaice, grilled salmon with hollandaise sauce, sole in parsley-butter sauce, or various preparations of shrimp and snails.

Søndergade 12, Ærøskøbing. © **62-52-12-12**. Main courses 240DKK–290DKK ($31–$38). AE, DC, MC, V. May and Sept Tues–Sun 11:30am–2:30pm and 6–9:30pm; June–Aug daily 11:30am–2:30pm and 6–9:30pm. Closed Oct–Apr.

2 Bornholm ★★

153km (95 miles) E of Copenhagen

Surrounded by the Baltic Sea, astride the important shipping lanes that connect St. Petersburg with Copenhagen and the Atlantic, Bornholm sits only 37km (23 miles) off the coast of Sweden. It's 153km (95 miles) from Copenhagen and the rest of Denmark. Prized as a strategic military and trading outpost since the early Middle Ages, Bornholm has been the focus of bloody territorial disputes by the Danes, Germans, and Swedes. It's home to 45,000 year-round residents, and a vacation spot for an additional 450,000 during the balmy summer months. Besides tourism, which is growing rapidly, the economy relies on trade, fishing, herring-processing, agriculture, and the manufacture of ceramics. Thanks to the island's deep veins of clay, ceramics has been an important industry since the 1700s.

A thin but rich layer of topsoil covers a terrain of granite and sandstone; the island's rock-studded surface consists of forests and moors. The unusual topography and surprisingly temperate autumn climate—a function of the Baltic waters—promotes the verdant plant growth. Figs, mulberries, and lavish conifers create the third-largest forest in Denmark.

Don't expect to enjoy a holiday on Bornholm without some inconvenience. Boats from Copenhagen take 7 hours each way, and if you plan to visit in midsummer, reservations are essential. All ferries arrive at Rønne.

ESSENTIALS

GETTING THERE   The most popular route from Copenhagen is the 7-hour ferry ride. **Bornholmstraffiken** (© **33-13-18-66**) ferries depart from the pier at Kvaesthusbroen near the center of Copenhagen every evening year-round at 11:30pm, with scheduled arrival at 6:30am. Between late June and mid-August, there's an additional departure at 8:30am every day except Wednesday. Passage costs 232DKK ($30) per person each way, plus an optional supplement of 167DKK ($22) for a private cabin. Transporting a car from Copenhagen costs about 900DKK ($118) each way. **Bornholm Ferries,** Havnen, Rønne (© **56-95-18-66**), take 2½ hours to cross from Ystad on the southern coast of Sweden. There are up to five departures daily. A car with a maximum of five passengers costs 900DKK ($118) one-way. You can also travel from Sassnitz-Mukran (Rügen) in northern Germany to Rønne; the crossing takes 3½ hours, and there's tax-free shopping on board. From Germany, one-way passage for a car with a maximum of five passengers is 1,135DKK ($149). Each ferry has a restaurant or bistro featuring a buffet with Danish and Bornholm specialties.

Cimbir Air (© **56-95-11-11**) has about five flights a day from Copenhagen to Bornholm's airport, 5.6km (3½ miles) south of Rønne. Round-trip fares are 790DKK to 1,712DKK ($103–$224).

VISITOR INFORMATION   The **Bornholm Welcome Center** is at Kystvej 3, Rønne (© **56-95-95-00;** www.bornholminfo.dk). It's open June through August daily from 9:30am to 5pm; September through May, Monday through Friday from 9am to 4pm, Saturday from 11:30am to 2:30pm, closed on Sunday.

GETTING AROUND   Eurocars (𝄐 **800/654-3001** in the U.S., or 30-54-00-15) is the island's leading car-rental agency. The cheapest cars rent for 2,640DKK ($346) for 1 week, which includes unlimited mileage, all insurance coverage, and the whopping government tax. **Avis** is at Snellamark 21, Rønne (𝄐 **800/331-2112** in the U.S., or 56-95-22-08).

During nice weather, bicycling around the island is almost as popular as driving. If you want to do as the Danes do, rent a bike; the prices are pretty much the same throughout the island—about 60DKK ($7.85) a day. Bike-rental companies in Rønne include **Bornholms Cykleudleijning,** Nordre Kystveg 5 (𝄐 **56-95-13-59**).

EXPLORING THE ISLAND

Even if you have a car, you might want to bike the tour we've outlined below. Ask at any tourist office for a map of the island's more than 190km (120 miles) of bicycle trails, and divide this tour into several days, hitting the highlights at your own speed.

This tour begins at Rønne, but you can join at almost any point; the route goes counterclockwise around the island's periphery. Be aware that Bornholm's highways do not have route numbers. Some maps show the main east-west artery as Route 38, but local residents call it "the road to Nexø," also called Neksø. Consistent with local customs, this tour suggests that you follow the directional signs pointing to towns you'll eventually reach en route.

RØNNE

This is the island's capital and largest settlement, with 15,000 permanent residents.

SEEING THE SIGHTS

Hjorth's Fabrik (Bornholm Ceramic Museum) *Finds*   The island's unusual geology includes deep veins of a clay that potters have appreciated for many generations. Since the 1700s, hundreds of island residents have produced large numbers of pots, plates, and cups, many of them whimsical, highly idiosyncratic reminders of another way of life. In 1858 a small-scale factory, Hjorth's Ceramics, began making pottery from the island's rich clay deposits. It survived until 1993. In 1995 the island's newest museum was established in the company's original factory. It's an intriguing hybrid of art gallery and industrial museum. You'll see the island's best examples of the dark brown, yellow, and gray pottery that was produced in abundance beginning in the 1700s; samples of the dishes and bowls made by the Hjorth company over the years; and some work by Bornholm's modern-day potters. Several ceramic artists maintain studios inside, casting, spinning, or glazing pots in view of visitors. Small-scale and charming, the museum is run by two descendants of the Hjorth family. The museum shop sells modern-day replicas of Hjorth ceramics, and many exhibits trace the production of ceramics from start to finish.

Krystalgade 5. 𝄐 **56-95-01-60.** Admission mid-Apr to mid-Oct 30DKK ($3.95) adults, 10DKK ($1.30) children; mid-Oct to mid-Apr 10DKK ($1.30) adults, free for children. May–Oct Tues–Sat 10am–5pm; Nov–Apr Tues–Fri 1–5pm, Sat 10am–1pm.

Bornholms Museum *𝄐*   This is the largest, most distinguished museum on Bornholm. It focuses on the island's unique position in the Baltic. Set in a former hospital, it has displays on archaeology, local traditions and costumes, ethnology, and the seafaring and agrarian traditions that made the island what it is today. Several rooms are outfitted with 19th-century antique furniture, toys, island-made silverware, and accessories. Of special interest is the collection of Bornholm-made clocks, copied from a shipment of English clocks salvaged from a Dutch shipwreck in the late 1700s.

Skt. Mortensgade 29. ✆ **56-95-07-35.** Admission 35DKK ($4.60) adults, 10DKK ($1.30) children. Mid-Apr to mid-Oct Mon–Sat 10am–5pm; mid-Oct to mid-Apr Tues, Thurs, Sat 1–5pm.

Forsvarsmuseet   Housed within a citadel built around 1650 by the Danish king, this Defense Museum is in the southern part of town. With its massive round tower, this old castle is filled with weapons, maps, and models of fortifications. There is also a collection of antique armaments and military uniforms. In our view, the most interesting displays depict the Soviet aerial bombardment of Bornholm in 1945 and the subsequent Russian occupation of the island.

Arsenal Vej 8. ✆ **56-95-65-83.** Admission 30DKK ($3.95) adults, 10DKK ($1.30) children ages 6–12, free for children 5 and under. May–Oct Tues–Sat 10am–4pm.

WHERE TO STAY

Hotel Griffen ⚓   Near the heart of Rønne, a 5-minute walk from the beach, the town center, and an upscale marina, this hotel is the largest on Bornholm. Built in the 1970s, its buildings vaguely resemble 18th-century hip-roofed manor houses. Two of the four buildings contain only lodgings, and because of their isolation from dining, drinking, and convention facilities, they tend to be quiet and peaceful. Guest room furnishings are contemporary and minimalist, but with occasional touches of elegance enhanced by floor-to-ceiling windows and glass doors that afford views of the sea. All units have well-managed bath-rooms with shower-tub combinations.

NDR Kystvej 34, DK-3700 Rønne. ℂ **56-95-51-11.** Fax 56-95-52-97. www.hotelgriffen.dk. 140 units. 795DKK–1,145DKK ($104–$150) double; 1,650DKK ($216) suite. AE, DC, MC, V. **Amenities:** Restaurant; bar; pool; sauna; room service. *In room:* TV, hair dryer.

Radisson Hotel Fredensborg   This is one of the few hotels on the island that remains open year-round. In a quiet forest, adjacent to a beach about a mile south of the Rønne harbor, it was built during the 1960s. There's Danish mod-ern furniture in the comfortable guest rooms; each contains a bathroom with a shower-tub combination. Prices vary according to season and views of the water.

Strandvejen 116, DK-3700 Rønne. ℂ **800/528-1234** in the U.S., or 56-95-44-44. Fax 56-95-03-14. www.radissonhotels.com. 72 units. 1,195DKK ($157) double; 1,495DKK–1,795DKK ($196–$235) suite. Rates include buffet breakfast. AE, DC, MC, V. **Amenities:** Restaurant; bar; tennis court; sauna; room service; babysitting; laundry/dry cleaning. *In room:* TV, minibar, hair dryer.

WHERE TO DINE
De 5 Stâuerna 😺😺 DANISH/INTERNATIONAL   This is the best and most upscale restaurant in Rønne, with a clientele that tends to select it for cel-ebratory meals of any ilk, including family gatherings during important rites of passage. Its name translates to "the five rooms," each of which is outfitted in a rustic country-Danish style, with white walls and light filtered through yellow-tinted windows. There's always a platter of the proposed fish of the day, which is invariably prepared in a simple, Danish-derived style, usually fried in butter and served with new potatoes in a way that Bornholmers have witnessed since their childhood. Other, more elaborate options include Hereford beefsteak pre-pared *cordon bleu*–style, with salted cured ham and Emmenthaler cheese; tournedos of beef flambéed in Calvados and served with apples and onions; an exotic sautéed filet of ostrich with Mexican pimentos and peppers; marinated and minced beefsteak with chili; and a dish that we personally prefer more than almost anything else on the menu, Bornholm lamb served with a sauce con-cocted from rosemary, olive oil, and tarragon.

In the Hotel Fredensborg, Strandvejen 116. ℂ **56-95-44-44.** Reservations recommended. Main courses 75DKK–210DKK ($9.85–$28); fixed-price "menu degustation" 265DKK ($35). AE, DC, MC, V. Daily 11:30am–9:30pm.

Rådhuskroen DANISH   This is the most visible and, in its own way, most charming restaurant in Rønne. Set in the dark, intimate cellar of the Town Hall, a 140-year-old building, Rådhuskroen has a long history of feeding island resi-dents in a cozy setting protected from midwinter winds. The well-trained staff serves such dishes as filet of salmon in a fresh tomato "summer sauce" and two sizes of steak ("Mr. Beef" and "Mrs. Beef").

Nørregade 2, Rønne. ℂ **56-95-00-69.** Reservations recommended on weekends. Main courses 80DKK–145DKK ($10–$19). AE, DC, MC, V. Daily noon–10pm.

FROM RØNNE TO NEXØ
From Rønne, drive east along the island's modern highway, A38, following signs for Nexø. About 5km (3 miles) later, stop in **Nylars,** a town that's known as the site of the best-preserved of Bornholm's four round churches. The **Nylarskirke** (ℂ **56-97-20-13**) was built around 1250. It rises prominently from the center of a community with no more than about 50 buildings. Frescoes inside depict Creation and the expulsion of Adam and Eve from the Garden of Eden. It's open from April to October 20, Monday through Saturday from 9am to 5pm. Admis-sion is free.

Drive another 5km (3 miles) east until you reach **Åkirkeby,** the only inland settlement of any size. Its economy is based on farming and an animal-fodder factory (the Bovaerk Company). Small and sleepy, this is Bornholm's oldest settlement—its town charter dates from 1346. It's also home to the island's oldest and largest church, the **Åkirke,** Torvet (*©* **56-97-41-03**), built around 1250. This church isn't as eccentric as some of the others; it's a sandstone-fronted monument built with defense in mind, as you'll note from the small windows. Notice the Romanesque baptismal font with runic inscriptions; it's believed they were carved by the master craftsman Sigraf on the island of Gotland. Other runic inscriptions appear on the cloverleaf-shaped arches. The church is open daily from 10am to 4pm; admission is 6DKK (80¢).

From Åkirkeby, cut southeast for 4.4km (2¾ miles), following the signs to **Pedersker,** a hamlet with three shops. (They close during the cold-weather months.) About 6km (4 miles) later you'll reach **Dueodde,** the name of both a raffish beachfront community and the entire region around the island's southern tip. The village marks the southern edge of a stretch of coastline that some people believe is Bornholm's finest beach. The best beaches on the island stretch north and east to the town of Balke, 4.8km (3 miles) beyond. The white sand grains are so fine that they were used for generations to fill hourglasses. The towns themselves are little more than backdrops for seasonal kiosks and a scattering of holiday homes. Most of the landscape is a virtual wilderness of pine and spruce trees, salt-tolerant shrubs, and sand dunes, some of which rise more than 12m (40 ft.) above the sea.

The focal point of this southeastern coastline is the **Dueodde Fyr (Lighthouse).** It's the tallest on the island, built in 1962 to warn ships away from the extreme southern tip of the island. Weather permitting, you can climb to its top during daylight hours between May and October for a fee of 5DKK (65¢), which you pay directly to the lighthouse keeper. For more information, call *©* **56-48-80-42.**

From Dueodde, continue northeast along the coast, passing through the unpretentious fishing hamlets of **Snogebæk** and **Balke,** a sleepy midsummer resort area that's even sleepier in winter.

WHERE TO DINE ALONG THE WAY

Den Lille Havfrue DANISH   Housed in a cozy modern building erected in the 1980s, this is one of the least pretentious but most reliable restaurants on the island. Its woodsy setting is accented with dozens of pottery pieces crafted by local artist Kirsten Kleman. The hardworking staff serves traditionally prepared fish and meat dishes, including salmon with lobster sauce (a perennial favorite), codfish with potatoes and onions, beefsteak and calves' liver, and broiled plaice with lemon and parsley-butter sauce. The menu includes an ample selection of soups, salads, and simple desserts.

Hovedgaden 5, Snogebæk. *©* **56-48-80-55.** Reservations recommended. Main courses 100DKK–170DKK ($13–$22). AE, DC, MC, V. Daily 11:30am–10pm. Closed Oct–Apr.

FROM NEXØ TO ALLINGE

Nexø, with a year-round population of 3,900, is the island's largest fishing port. It's home to excellent replicas of the privately owned 17th- and 18th-century buildings that were considered architectural highlights of the island before World War II. In May 1945, several days after the rest of Denmark had been liberated from the Nazis, the Russians bombed Nexø heavily for 2 days. It had been a final holdout of Nazi soldiers during the closing days of the war. (Bornholm was also the last area of Denmark to get rid of its Soviet "liberators," who didn't completely evacuate until 1946.)

The destruction of most of the town's 900 buildings and their restoration along original lines is the stuff of which legends are made. Because the region around Nexø is composed mostly of sandstone, much of the town's masonry is tawny, rather than the granite gray found elsewhere on the island.

One of the town's more eccentric monuments is the **Nexø Museum,** Havnen (*©* **56-49-25-56**). You'll see displays of the fishing-related equipment that has sustained the local economy, and memorabilia of the author Martin Andersen (1869–1954). He was better known as Martin Andersen Nexø, the name he adopted to honor his native village. His novel, *Pelle the Conqueror,* which was set in Bornholm and later made into an acclaimed film, showed how Danish landowners in the early 20th century exploited Swedish newcomers to the island. The museum is open from May to October daily from 10am to 4pm. Admission is 20DKK ($2.60).

After Nexø, the topography of the island gradually changes from sandstone to a more heavily forested area that has thin topsoil, deep veins of clay, and out-croppings of gray granite.

Continue 5.5km (3½ miles) north along the coastal road, following the signs to **Svaneke.** Denmark's easternmost settlement has fewer than 1,200 year-round residents. It bears some resemblance to eastern regions of the Baltic with which it has traded, and has many 17th- and 18th-century cottages along cobblestone streets leading to the harbor. Many writers, sculptors, and painters buy homes in Svaneke, an idyllic retreat from the urban life of Copenhagen. Svaneke is the most photogenic town on Bornholm; in 1975 it won the European Gold Medal for town preservation. Its most famous citizen was J. N. Madvig, an influential philologist who was born here in 1804.

From Svaneke, leave the Baltic coastline and head inland through the north-ern outskirts of the third largest forest in Denmark, the **Almindingen.** Dotted with creeks and ponds, and covered mostly with hardy conifers, it's known for its wildflowers—especially lilies-of-the-valley—and well-designated hiking trails. Head for **Østermarie,** a village of about 40 relatively nondescript buildings. Three kilometers (2 miles) northwest of Østermarie is the more culturally signif-icant **Østerlars,** home to the largest of the island's distinctive round churches. The **Østerlarskirke** is at Gudhjemsveg 28 (*©* **56-49-82-64**). It's open from early April to mid-October, Monday through Saturday from 9am to 5pm. The entrance fee is 6DKK (80¢) for adults, free for children. It was built around 1150 by the Vikings, who used rocks, boulders, and stone slabs. The church was dedicated to St. Laurence and later enlarged with chunky-looking buttresses; it was intended to serve in part as a fortress against raids by Baltic pirates. Inside are several wall paintings that date from around 1350, depicting scenes from the life of Jesus.

From Østerlars, drive 3.2km (2 miles) north, following the signs to **Gudhjem (God's Home),** a steeply inclined town that traded with the Hanseatic League during the Middle Ages. Most of its population died of the plague in 1653 and 1654, but the town was repopulated some years later by Danish guerrilla fight-ers and sympathizers following territorial wars with Sweden. You'll find a town with many fig and mulberry trees and steep slopes that give it a vaguely Mediter-ranean flavor.

SEEING THE SIGHTS ALONG THE WAY IN GUDHJEM

Especially charming are Gudhjem's 18th-century half-timbered houses and the 19th-century smokehouses, known for their distinctive techniques of preserving herring with alderwood smoke. Its harbor, blasted out of the rocky shoreline in the 1850s, is the focal point for the town's 1,200 permanent residents.

Landsbrugs Museum (Bornholm Agricultural Museum)   This museum is in a half-timbered, thatched-roof farmhouse built in 1796. It displays the kind of farm implements that were commonplace as recently as 1920. Also on view are a group of pigs, goats, cows, and barnyard fowl that are genetically similar to those bred on Bornholm a century ago.

Melstedvej 25 (.8km/½ mile south of Gudhjem). ℂ **56-48-55-98**. Admission 30DKK ($3.95) adults, 5DKK (65¢) children. Mid-May to mid-Oct Tues–Sun 10am–5pm. Closed mid-Oct to mid-May.

Gudhjem Museum   This museum is in Gudhjem's old train station, an early-20th-century building that closed in 1952 along with the island's railways. Its exhibits honor the now-defunct rail lines that once crisscrossed the island. There are locomotives and other train-related memorabilia.

Stationsveg 1. ℂ **56-48-54-62**. Admission 20DKK ($2.60) adults, free for children under 16. Daily 10am–5pm. Closed mid-Sept to mid-May.

CONTINUING ON TO ALLINGE

Proceed west along the coastal road. Between Gudhjem and Allinge (15km/9 miles), you'll enjoy dramatic vistas over granite cliffs and sometimes savage seascapes. The entire coastline is known as **Helligdoms Klipperne (Cliffs of Sanctuary)**, for the survivors of the many ships that foundered along this granite coastline over the centuries.

Midway along the route, you'll see **Bornholms Kunstmuseet (Art Museum of Bornholm)**, Helligdommen (ℂ **56-48-43-86**). Opened in 1993, it contains the largest collection of works by Bornholm artists, including Olaf Rude and Oluf Høst. It's open from May to September, daily from 10am to 5pm. Admission is 40DKK ($5.25), free for children under 16. From the rocky bluff where the museum sits, you can see the wind-tossed island of **Christiansø**, about 11km (7 miles) offshore. It's home to only about 120 year-round residents, most of whom make their living from the sea.

Continue driving northwest until you reach the twin communities of **Allinge** and **Sandvig**. Allinge's architecture is noticeably older than that of Sandvig. The 200- and 300-year-old half-timbered houses were built for the purveyors of the herring trade, and the smokehouses preserved the fish for later consumption or for export abroad. The newer town of Sandvig, to the northwest, flourished around the turn of the 20th century, when many ferries connected it with Sweden. Sandvig became a stylish beach resort. The woods that surround the twin communities are known as the **Trolleskoe (Forest of Trolls)**, home to wart-covered and phenomenally ugly magical creatures that delight in brewing trouble, mischief, and the endless fog that sweeps over this end of the island.

From Allinge, detour inland (southward) for about 4km (2½ miles) to reach **Olsker**, site of the **Olskirke (Round Church of Ols)**, Lindesgordsvej (ℂ **56-48-05-29**). Built in the 1100s, it's the smallest of the island's round churches, and was painstakingly restored in the early 1950s. Dedicated to St. Olav (Olav the Holy, king of Norway, who died in 1031), it looks something like a fortress—an image the original architects wanted very much to convey.

Now double back to Allinge and head north toward Sandvig, a distance of about a kilometer (less than a mile). You'll soon see **Madsebakke,** a well-signposted open-air site that contains the largest collection of Bronze Age rock carvings in Denmark. There's no building, enclosed area, or even curator. Simply follow the signs beside the main highway. The carvings include 11 depictions of high-prowed sailing ships of unknown origin. The carvings were made in a smooth, glacier-scoured piece of bedrock close to the side of the road.

From here, proceed just over a mile to the island's northernmost tip, **Hammeren,** for views that—depending on the weather—may extend all the way to Sweden. Here you'll see the island's oldest lighthouse, **Hammerfyr** (1871).

WHERE TO STAY IN SANDVIG

Strandhotellet ★★   The foundations and part of the core of this historic hotel were built as stables in 1896; a decade later it became the largest, most stylish hotel on Bornholm. Today it's a reminder of a former way of life, when Sandvig was the main point of access from abroad. Nowadays Rønne has that role, and Sandvig is less commercial and more isolated than it was a century ago. A worthy detour for diners who drive from other parts of the island, the hotel offers three floors of spartan accommodations with lots of exposed birch wood and (in most cases) sea views. Each unit has a well-maintained bathroom with a shower-tub combination. The interior was modernized in 1991, making it suitable for a secluded getaway.

Strandpromenaden 7, DK-3770 Sandvig. ✆ **56-48-03-14.** Fax 56-48-02-09. 49 units. 900DKK–950DKK ($118–$124) double; 1,000DKK–1,275DKK ($131–$167) suite. No credit cards. Closed Nov–Mar. **Amenities:** Restaurant; bar; sauna; room service. *In room:* TV.

WHERE TO DINE IN SANDVIG

Strandhotellet Restaurant (Value DANISH/SEAFOOD   This hotel dining room was designed in the 1930s as a dance hall and supper club. Big windows overlook the sea, and you'll sense the care and attention to detail that's consistent with the Strandhotellet's role as a special dining destination on Bornholm. Choices include smoked filet of wild salmon with tomato tapenade, a mixed platter of the daily catch, and medallions of beef with a ragout of fresh vegetables and fresh mushrooms. The abundance of food and flavor makes this a good value.

Strandpromenaden 7, Sandvig. ✆ **56-48-03-14.** Main courses 59DKK–69DKK ($7.75–$9.05) lunch; 93DKK–130DKK ($12–$17) dinner. Daily noon–10pm. AE, DC, MC, V. Closed Nov–Mar.

FROM ALLINGE & SANDVIG BACK TO RØNNE

Now turn south, following the signs pointing to Rønne. After about a mile you'll see the rocky crags of a semi-ruined fortress that Bornholmers cite as the most historically significant building on the island.

The **Hammershus Fortress** ✿ was begun in 1255 by the archbishop of Lund, Sweden. He planned for this massive fortress to reinforce his control of the island. Since then, Bornholm has passed from Swedish to German to Danish hands several times; it was a strategic powerhouse controlling what was then a vitally important sea lane. The decisive moment came in 1658, when the Danish national hero Jens Kofoed murdered the Swedish governor and sailed to Denmark to present the castle (and the rest of the island) to the king.

The fortress's dilapidated condition was caused by the regrettable actions of later builders, who used it as a rock quarry. It supplied the stone used in some of the buildings and streets (including Hovedvagten) of Rønne, as well as several structures on Christiansø, the tiny island 11km (7 miles) northeast of Bornholm. The systematic destruction of the fortress ended in 1822, when it was "redefined" as a Danish national treasure. Much of the work that restored the fortress to the eerily jagged condition you'll see today was completed in 1967. Interestingly, Hammershus escaped the fate of the second-most powerful fortress on the island, Lilleborg. Deep in the forest, Lilleborg was gradually stripped of its stones for other buildings after its medieval defenses became obsolete.

Some 4km (2½ miles) south of Hammershus, on the coastal road heading back to Rønne, is a geological oddity called **Jons Kapel (Jon's Chapel).** To see the rocky bluff and its marvelous panoramic view of the island's western coast, follow the signs for the mile hike from the highway. Ancient legend says this is where an agile but reclusive hermit, Brother Jon, preached to the seagulls and crashing surf below.

From here, continue driving south another 13km (8 miles) to Rønne, passing through the hamlet of **Hasle.**

3 Jutland

Dramatically different from the rest of Denmark, Jutland ("Jylland" in Danish) is a peninsula of heather-covered moors, fjords, farmland, lakes, and sand dunes. Besides its major tourist centers—Ribe in the south, Århus and Aalborg (Ålborg) in the north—it has countless old inns and undiscovered towns.

Jutland borders the North Sea, the Skagerrak, and the Kattegat. It extends 400km (250 miles) from the northern tip, Skagen, to the German border in the south. The North Sea washes up on many kilometers of sandy beaches, making this a favorite holiday place.

The meadows are filled with rich bird life and winding rivers; nature walks are a popular pastime. The heart of Jutland is mainly beech forest and lake country, sprinkled with modest-sized towns and light industry. Steep hills surround the deep fjords of the east coast. Gabled houses in the marshlands of southern Jutland add to the peninsula's charm. Two of the most popular vacation islands are Rømø and Fanø, off the southwest coast. Here, many traditional homes of fishermen and ship captains have been preserved.

Our driving tour of Jutland begins at Ribe. If you're arriving in east Jutland from Copenhagen, take Route 32 west. From mainland Europe, take Route 11 from Tønder. Esbjerg is connected to Ribe by Route 24, which joins Route 11 south.

RIBE 🏵🏵
32km (20 miles) S of Esbjerg, 300km (186 miles) W of Copenhagen

Ribe is a town of narrow cobblestone lanes and crooked half-timbered houses. It became legendary because of the graceful—and endangered—storks that build their nests on top of its red-roofed medieval houses. Every year the residents of Denmark's oldest town ponder the question: Will the storks return in April?

This port was an important trading center during the Viking era (the 9th c.) and became an episcopal seat in 948, when one of the first Christian churches in Denmark was established here. It was also the royal residence of the ruling Valdemars around 1200.

In medieval days, sea-trade routes linked Ribe to England, Germany, Friesland, the Mediterranean, and other ports, but then the waters receded. Today marshes surround Ribe. The town watchman, armed with a lantern and staff, has made his rounds since the ancient custom was revived in 1936.

ESSENTIALS
GETTING THERE   If you're not driving, Ribe is easy to reach by train; there is hourly service from Copenhagen by way of Bramming. Train and bus schedules are available at the tourist office.

VISITOR INFORMATION   The **Ribe Turistbureau** is at Torvet 3 (ⓒ **75-42-15-00;** www.ribetourist.dk). It's open from June 15 to August, Monday through Saturday from 9:30am to 5:30pm, Sunday from 10am to 2pm; from April to June 14 and September to October, Monday through Friday from 9am to 5pm, Saturday from 10am to 1pm; from November to March, Monday through Friday from 9:30am to 4:30pm, Saturday from 10am to 1pm.

SEEING THE SIGHTS

Ribe Domkirke ☆   This stone-and-brick cathedral, the little town's crowning achievement, was under construction from 1150 to 1175. Inspired by Rhineland architecture, it's a good example of Romanesque influence on Danish architecture, although it has Gothic arches. A century later a tower was added. Climb it if you want to see how the storks view Ribe. The legendary "Cat's Head Door" was once the principal entrance to the church, and the granite tympanum, *Removal from the Cross,* is the most significant piece of medieval sculpture in Denmark. Mosaics, stained glass, and frescoes in the eastern apse are by the artist Carl-Henning Pedersen.

Torvet (in the town center off Sønderportsgade). ℂ **75-42-06-19**. Admission 12DKK ($1.55) adults, 5DKK (65¢) children. May and Sept daily 10am–5pm; June–Aug daily 10am–5:30pm; Oct–Apr Mon–Sat 11am–3pm, Sun 1–3pm.

Ribe Vikinger (Museum of the Viking Age and the Middle Ages in Ribe)   Opened in 1995, this museum traces the story of Ribe. Beginning in A.D. 700, it depicts the Viking age and the medieval period. Archaeological finds are on display, along with such reconstructed scenes as a Viking-age marketplace, dating from around 800, and a church building site from around 1500.

Odins Plads. ℂ **76-88-11-22**. Admission 50DKK ($6.55) adults, 20DKK ($2.60) children. Apr–June 14 and Sept 15–Oct daily 10am–4pm; June 15–Sept 14 daily 10am–6pm; Nov–Mar Tues–Sun 10am–4pm.

Ribe Kunstmuseet   The Ribe Kunstmuseet displays an extensive collection of Danish art, including works of acclaimed artists like Eckersberg, Kobke, C. A. Jensen, Hammershøj, and Juel. Housed in a stately mid-19th-century villa in a garden on the Ribe River, many paintings are from the golden age of Danish art. Exhibits change occasionally.

Skt. Nicolai Gade 10. ℂ **75-42-03-62**. Admission 30DKK ($3.95) adults, free for children 16 and under. Feb–June 14 and Sept–Dec Tues–Sat 1–4pm, Sun 11am–4pm; June 15–Aug daily 11am–5pm. Closed Jan.

Det Gamle Rådhus (Town Hall Museum)   In the oldest existing town hall in Denmark, built in 1496, the medieval Town Hall Museum houses Ribe's artifacts and archives. Included are a 16th-century executioner's sword, ceremonial swords, the town's money chest, antique tradesmen's signs, and a depiction of the "iron hand," still a symbol of police authority.

Von Støckends Plads. ℂ **79-89-89-55**. Admission 15DKK ($1.95) adults, 5DKK (65¢) children 7–14, free for children under 7. June–Aug daily 1–3pm; May and Sept Mon–Fri 1–3pm. Closed Oct–Apr.

St. Catharine's Church and Monastery   The Black Friars, or Dominicans, came to Ribe in 1228 and began constructing a church and chapter house (the east wing of a monastery). Parts of the original edifice can still be seen, especially the southern wall. The present church, near Dagmarsgade, dates from the first half of the 15th century, and the tower is from 1617. Extensive restorations have made this one of the best-preserved abbeys in Scandinavia. Only the monks' stalls and the Romanesque font remain from the Middle Ages. The handsome pulpit dates from 1591, the altarpiece from 1650.

You can walk through the cloisters and see ship models and religious paintings hanging in the southern aisle. Tombstones of Ribe citizens from the Reformation and later are along the outer walls of the church.

Skt. Catharine's Plads. © **75-42-05-34.** Free admission to church; cloisters, 3DKK (40¢) adults, 1DKK (15¢) children under 14. May–Sept daily 10am–noon and 2–5pm; Oct–Apr daily 10am–noon and 2–4pm. Closed during church services.

A SIDE TRIP TO RØMØ ⭐

Rømø, the largest Danish island in the North Sea, is about 9km (5½ miles) long and 6.5km (4 miles) wide. It has a certain appeal because of its wild, windswept appearance. In the summer it attracts lots of tourists (especially Germans), possibly because of the nude sunbathing. In the off season it's one of the sleepiest places in Europe, making it great for rest and relaxation.

To reach Rømø, take the 9.5km (6-mile) stone causeway from mainland Jutland. Or you can take a bus south from Ribe to Skaerbaek, then bus no. 29 across the tidal flats.

WHERE TO STAY

Weis' Stue (see "Where to Dine," below) also rents rooms.

Den Gamle Arrest ⭐⭐ *Finds* One of the town's most charming hotels occupies a structure built in 1546 as the town jail. Set on the main square of Ribe, and constructed of the same russet-colored bricks that formed most of the town's important buildings, it functioned as a jail until 1989. The present owners transformed it into a cozy hotel. The guest rooms are snug, often with exposed brick and enough old-fashioned amenities to remind you of a gentrified version of the building's original function. There's a restaurant on the premises (see "Where to Dine," below).

Torvet 11, DK-6760 Ribe. © **75-42-37-00.** 11 units, 2 with bathroom. 540DKK–690DKK ($71–$90) double without bathroom; 750DKK–990DKK ($98–$130) double with bathroom. Rates include breakfast. No credit cards. **Amenities:** Restaurant; bar. *In room:* TV (in some), no phone.

Hotel Dagmar ⭐⭐⭐ A Denmark legend, this historic 1581 building is the most glamorous address in the region. Converted from a private home in 1850, it's named after a medieval Danish queen. The guest rooms are comfortable and roomy, with lovely traditional furniture and state-of-the-art bathrooms with shower-tub combinations. On Friday and Saturday nights (except in summer), there's music and dancing. The hotel has a restaurant (see "Where to Dine," below).

Torvet 1, DK-6760 Ribe. © **75-42-00-33.** Fax 75-42-36-52. www.hoteldagmar.dk. 50 units. 995DKK–1,345DKK ($130–$176) double. Rates include breakfast. AE, DC, MC, V. **Amenities:** 3 restaurants; bar; room service; laundry/dry cleaning. *In room:* TV, minibar, hair dryer, safe.

Hotel Fru Mathies Set behind a bright yellow stucco facade, a very short walk from the city's pedestrian zone, this hotel was named after its present guardian and supervisor, Fru (Mrs.) Inga Mathies. There's a shared TV/living room on the premises, and guest rooms are simple but cozy affairs, each with a bathroom equipped with a shower-tub combination and a modest number of old-fashioned accessories. Breakfast is the only meal served.

Saltgade 15, DK-67660 Ribe. © **75-42-34-20.** 6 units, 4 with bathroom. 490DKK ($64) double without bathroom; 640DKK ($84) double with bathroom. Rates include breakfast. AE, DC, MC, V. **Amenities:** Bar; lounge. *In room:* TV, minibar, no phone.

Kalvslund Kro This 1865 inn offers comfortable rooms but few frills. The furniture, according to the management, "is old but not antique." Each unit contains a neatly kept bathroom with a shower-tub combination. The restaurant serves home-style cooking that is well prepared and presented. Full meals include such dishes as asparagus soup, Danish beef with sautéed onions, and pork cutlets.

Koldingvej 105 (at Kalvslund), DK-6760 Ribe. ℂ **75-43-70-12.** 5 units, none with bathroom. 300DKK ($39) double. Rates include breakfast. No credit cards. May–Sept daily 11am–10pm; other times of year by advance reservation only. Free parking. Bus: 57 or 921 from Ribe. 9km (5½ miles) north of Ribe on Rte. 52. **Amenities:** Bar; lounge. *In room:* No phone.

WHERE TO DINE
Den Gamle Arrest DANISH   One of the newest restaurants in Ribe has one of the most unusual histories. This redbrick monument was built in the 1500s as the town's debtor's prison and jail. You can stroll in the redbrick courtyard that functioned for centuries as an exercise yard. Menu items include grilled filets of salmon with spicy herb sauce, filet of ox meat with fresh vegetables and red-wine sauce, and roasted turkey with mango-flavored chutney sauce. Nothing overtaxes the chef's imagination, but the fare is good and tasty, the portions filling, and the ingredients fresh.

Torvet 11. ℂ **75-42-37-00.** Reservations recommended. Main courses 34DKK–68DKK ($4.45–$8.90). No credit cards. June–Sept daily noon–3pm. Closed Oct–May.

Restaurant Dagmar ⚜ DANISH/INTERNATIONAL   Opposite the cathedral and near the train station, the Hotel Dagmar's four dining rooms are a 19th-century dream of ornate furnishings and accessories. The international cuisine is the best in town, and it's impeccably served and complemented by a good wine list. Two fresh North Sea fish dishes of the day are usually offered. Among meat and poultry selections, try the fried quail stuffed with mushrooms on beurre blanc (white butter), or veal tenderloin with shallot mousse in port sauce. There's also a cozy cellar restaurant.

In the Hotel Dagmar, Torvet 1. ℂ **75-42-00-33.** Reservations required. Main courses 165DKK–265DKK ($22–$35); fixed-price lunch 15DKK–165DKK ($1.95–$22); fixed-price dinner 235DKK–355DKK ($31–$47). AE, DC, MC, V. Daily noon–10pm.

Restaurant Saelhunden *Finds* DANISH/INTERNATIONAL   One of the most evocative and cheerful restaurants in Ribe occupies a venerable but cozy brick building whose history goes back to 1634. Set beside the river that flows through Ribe, within full view of the craft that kept its commerce alive during its mercantile heyday, it has flourished as a restaurant since 1969. Today, you'll find an engaging staff hailing from every corner of Europe, and an antique format whose size is doubled during mild weather thanks to an outdoor terrace. Menu items include at least three kinds of steaks that might be T-bone, French-style entrecôte, or something known as "English steak" that presumably gives British visitors access to the kinds of meat no longer legal in England. There are also fried filets of plaice cooked in white wine with leeks; platters of meatballs or smoked salmon; and a local delicacy, smoked and fried dab, a flat fish not unlike flounder that flourishes in the local estuaries. The cookery is imaginative and versatile, using fresh, quality ingredients. No one will mind if you come here just for a beer or a simple snack. In summertime, it's one of the closest approximations in town to the kind of beer garden you might expect to find in Hamburg.

Skibbroen 13, DK-6760 Ribe. ℂ **75-42-09-46.** Reservations recommended. Main courses 56DKK–186DKK ($7.35–$24). DC, MC, V. Apr–Oct 11am–9:45pm (last food order); Nov–Mar 11am–8:45pm (last food order). Beer served till 11pm.

Weis' Stue ⚜ DANISH   Small, charming, and rich with history, this brick-and-timber inn is on the market square next to the cathedral. Originally built in the 1500s, it was gradually enlarged over the centuries. The food in the ground-floor restaurant is plentiful and well prepared. You might try shrimp with mayonnaise, marinated herring with raw onions, smoked Greenland halibut with scrambled eggs, liver paste with mushrooms, sliced ham and Italian salad, filet of beef with onions, or two cheeses with bread and butter.

The inn also has four upstairs guest rooms. They're cozy, but don't have private bathrooms. A double costs 595DKK ($78), including breakfast.

Torvet 2, DK-6760 Ribe. (C) **75-42-07-00.** Reservations recommended. Main courses 105DKK–215DKK ($14–$28); 2-course fixed-price menu 165DKK ($22). DC, MC, V. Daily 11am–10pm.

FANØ ᴀᴀ
47km (29 miles) NW of Ribe, 283km (176 miles) W of Copenhagen

Nordby, where the ferry arrives, is a logical starting point for exploring the island of Fanø. Here you'll find heather-covered moors, windswept sand dunes, fir trees, wild deer, and bird sanctuaries. From Ribe, Fanø makes a great day's excursion (or a longer trip if there's time).

Fanø is a popular summer resort for the Danes, Germans, and English. **Sønderho,** on the southern tip, is our favorite spot. It's somewhat desolate, but that's its charm.

A summer highlight on Fanø is the **Fannikerdagene** festival, during the second weekend in July. It includes traditional dancing, costumes, and events connected with the days when sailing ships played a major part in community life.

If you miss the festival, try to be on Fanø on the third Sunday in July for **Sønderho Day.** The high point is a wedding procession that passes through the town to the square by the old mill. Attractions include traditional costumes and bridal dances.

ESSENTIALS
GETTING THERE   From Ribe, head north on Route 11 to Route 24. Follow Route 24 northwest to Esbjerg, where you can board a **Scandlines** ferry ((C) **70-10-17-44**). From May to October, ferries depart Esbjerg every 20 minutes during the day for the 12-minute crossing. In the winter, departures are during the day every 45 minutes. A round-trip ticket costs 30DKK ($3.95) for adults, 15DKK ($1.95) for children. One car with five passengers travels for 310DKK ($41) round-trip.

VISITOR INFORMATION   The **Fanø Turistbureau** is at Færgevej 1, Nordby ((C) **75-16-26-00;** www.fanoe.nv.). It's open Monday through Friday from 8:30am to 5:30pm, Saturday from 9am to 1pm, Sunday from 11am to 1pm. From June 6 to August 23, it's open until 6pm on weekdays, Saturday until 7pm, Sunday from 9am to 5pm.

WHERE TO STAY & DINE
Fanø Krogaard ᴀ   This old-fashioned inn has welcomed wayfarers ever since it was constructed in 1624. Located 90m (300 ft.) from the ferry dock, its rooms are simple but comfortable. The rooms come equipped with a well-kept bathroom with a shower-tub combination. The inn has the best food on the island; main dishes cost 57DKK to 135DKK ($7.45–$18). The restaurant is open daily from noon to 2pm and 5:30 to 9pm. There's also a popular bar, open daily from 8am to midnight, and an outdoor terrace that's used in the summer.

Langelinie 11, Nordby, DK-6720 Fanø. (C) **75-16-20-52.** Fax 75-16-23-00. 9 units. 795DKK ($104) double. Rates include breakfast. MC, V. Free parking. **Amenities:** Restaurant; bar. *In room:* Hair dryer.

Sønderho Kro ᴀᴀᴀ   This is an unbeatable choice. The 1722 thatched-roof, ivy-covered inn, a National Trust House, nestles behind the sand dunes. Each room has a distinctive character, yet all contribute to the inn's traditional atmosphere. Antiques add a nice touch. The first-floor lounge offers views of the tidal flats. The dining room's cuisine is superb and plentiful; meals begin at 315DKK ($41) for three courses. Sønderho Kro is 13km (8 miles) south of the Nordby ferry dock; a bus connects with ferry arrivals.

Kropladsen 11, Sønderho, DK-6720 Fanø. © **75-16-40-09.** Fax 75-16-43-85. sdrhokro@post6.tele.dk. 14 units. 960DKK–1,290DKK ($126–$169) double. Rates include full breakfast. AE, DC, MC, V. Free parking. **Amenities:** Restaurant; lounge; room service; laundry/dry cleaning. *In room:* TV, hair dryer.

ÅRHUS *✿*
160km (99 miles) NE of Fanø, 175km (109 miles) W of Copenhagen

Jutland's capital and Denmark's second-largest city, Århus is a cultural center and university town with a lively port. You can enjoy the city's many restaurants, hotels, and nighttime amusements, and then use Århus as a base for excursions to Silkeborg, Ebeltoft, and the manors and castles with moats to the north.

ESSENTIALS
GETTING THERE   When you return to the mainland from Fanø, head northeast on Route 30 to Grinsted. Here, follow Route 28 east until you connect with E45, near Vejle. Drive north on E45 to Århus. If you aren't driving, you can easily reach Århus by plane, train, or bus. **SAS** (© **70-10-20-00**) flies from Copenhagen to Århus. An airport bus from the airport to Århus's Central Station costs 60DKK ($7.85). About a half-dozen trains a day leave Copenhagen for the 5-hour trip to Århus. Two buses a day leave Copenhagen for Århus. Travel time is 4 hours.

VISITOR INFORMATION   The **Tourist Århus** office is in the Rådhuset, Park Allé (© **89-40-67-00**). It is open from mid-June to mid-September Monday through Friday from 9:30am to 6pm, Saturday from 9:30am to 5pm, Sunday from 9:30am to 1pm; off season Monday through Friday from 10am to 5pm, Saturday from 10am to 1pm.

GETTING AROUND   A regular bus ticket, valid for one ride, can be purchased on the rear platform of all city buses for 14DKK ($1.85). You can buy a **tourist ticket** for 88DKK ($12) at the tourist office or at newsstands (kiosks) throughout the city center. The 24-hour ticket covers an unlimited number of rides within the central city and includes a 2½-hour guided tour of Århus. The **Århus Pass** allows unlimited travel by public transportation and free admission to many museums and attractions. It also includes a 2½-hour guided tour. A 2-day pass costs 110DKK ($14) for adults and 55DKK ($7.20) for children; 1-week passes are 155DKK ($20) and 75DKK ($9.85). The Århus Pass is sold at the tourist office, many hotels, camping grounds, and kiosks throughout the city.

SEEING THE SIGHTS
For the best introduction to Århus, head for the town hall's tourist office, where a 2½-hour **sightseeing tour** leaves daily at 10am from June 24 to August 31. It costs 50DKK ($6.55) per person and is free with the purchase of the Århus Pass (see "Getting Around," above).

Cathedral of St. Clemens (Århus Domkirke)   This late Gothic cathedral is the longest in Denmark, practically as deep as it is tall. The redbrick, copper-roofed structure has a 95m (315-ft.) spire, begun in the early 13th century and completed in the 15th. Of chief interest are the Renaissance pulpit, 15th-century triptych, and 18th-century pipe organ.

After you see the cathedral, we suggest a visit to the nearby medieval **arcade,** Vestergade 3. It has half-timbered buildings, a rock garden, an aviary, and antique interiors.

Bispetorvet. ℂ **86-12-38-45.** Free admission. May–Sept Mon–Sat 9:30am–4pm; Oct–Apr Mon–Sat 10am–3pm. Bus: 3, 11, 54, or 56.

Den Gamle By 🏛🏛   Århus's top attraction, Den Gamle By displays more than 75 buildings representing Danish urban life from the 16th century to the 19th century, re-created in a botanical garden. The open-air museum differs from similar attractions near Copenhagen and Odense, where the emphasis is on rural life. Visitors walk through the authentic-looking workshops of bookbinders, carpenters, hatters, and other craftspeople. There's also a pharmacy, a school, and even an old-fashioned post office. A popular attraction is the Burgomaster's House, a wealthy merchant's antique-stuffed, half-timbered home, built at the end of the 16th century. Be sure to see the textile collection and the Old Elsinore Theater, erected in the early 19th century. The museum also houses a collection of china, clocks, delftware, and silverware; inquire at the ticket office. Summer music programs are staged, and there's a restaurant, tea garden, bakery, and beer cellar.

Viborgvej 2. ℂ **86-12-31-88.** Admission 60DKK ($7.85) adults, 15DKK ($1.95) children. Sept–Oct and Apr–May daily 10am–5pm; Nov–Dec and Feb–Mar daily 10am–4pm; Jan daily 11am–3pm; June–Aug daily 9am–6pm. Bus: 3, 14, or 25.

Rådhuset (Town Hall)   A crowning architectural achievement in the center of Århus, the Rådhuset was built between 1936 and 1941 to commemorate the 500th anniversary of the Århus charter. It's been the subject of controversy ever since. Arne Jacobsen was one of the designers of the modern marble-plated structure, with lots of airy space and plenty of glass. It can be seen only on a guided tour. An elevator (and 346 steps) runs to the top of the 59m (197-ft.) tower, where a carillon occasionally rings. *Note:* The guided tour at 11am includes the tower. Otherwise, the tower can be visited only at noon and again at 4pm. The elevator and stairs are open three times a day: 11am, noon, and 4pm.

Rådhuspladsen. ℂ **89-40-20-00.** Guided tour 10DKK ($1.30); admission to tower only, 5DKK (65¢). Guided tours Mon–Fri 11am. Tower only, 11am, noon, and 4pm. Closed Sept–June 23. Bus: 3, 4, 5, or 14.

THE MANOR HOUSES OF EAST JUTLAND

Clausholm 🏛🏛   Seventeenth-century Clausholm is a splendid baroque palace, one of the earliest in Denmark. It was commissioned by Frederik IV's chancellor, whose adolescent daughter, Anna Sophie, eloped with the king. When Frederik died, his son by his first marriage banished the queen to Clausholm, where she lived with her court until her death in 1743.

The rooms are basically unaltered, but few of the original furnishings remain. The salons and ballroom feature elaborate stucco ceilings and decorated panels, and an excellent collection of Danish rococo and Empire furnishings has replaced the original pieces. The Queen's Chapel, where Anna Sophie and her court worshipped, is unchanged and contains the oldest organ in Denmark. In 1976 the Italian baroque gardens were reopened, complete with a symmetrically designed fountain system.

Clausholm is about 13km (8 miles) southeast of Randers and 31km (19 miles) north of Århus.

Voldum, Hadsten. ℂ **86-49-16-55.** Admission (including guided tour) 70DKK ($9.15) adults, 20DKK ($2.60) children 13 and under. Daily 11am–5pm. Closed Sept–May 14. Bus: 221 from Randers.

The Museums at Gammel Estrup 🐾   Positioned 21km (13 miles) from Randers, and 39km (24 miles) from Århus, this compound of buildings includes the **Jutland Manor House Museum,** complete with a great hall, chapel, and richly decorated stucco ceilings; and the **Danish Agricultural Museum,** which celebrates the role of Danish farming over the past thousand years. The entire compound dates from the 14th century, but the structures you see were extensively rebuilt and remodeled in the early 1600s. Expect a glimpse into medieval fortifications, baronial furnishings, the changing nature of tools and machines used during Danish plantings and harvests, and an enormous sense of pride in Denmark and its traditions.

Jyllands Herregårdsmuseum, Randersvej 204, Auning. ℂ 86-48-30-01. Admission 65DKK ($8.50) adults, free for children under 14. Grounds: Apr–Oct daily 10am–6pm. Agricultural Museum: May–Sept Tues–Sun 10am–4pm. Manor House Museum: May–Sept Tues–Sun 11am–3pm. From Randers, take Route 16 east to Auning. Bus: 214.

Rosenholm Slot 🐾   On an islet 21km (13 miles) north of Århus and .8 km (½ mile) north of Hornslet, this Renaissance manor with a moat has been the Rosenkrantz family home for 4 centuries. The four-winged castle, encircled by about 15 hectares (35 acres) of parkland, houses a Great Hall, as well as a large collection of Flemish woven and gilded leather tapestries, old paintings, Spanish furniture, a vaulted gallery walk, and pigskin-bound folios.

Hornslet. ℂ 86-99-40-10. Admission 60DKK ($7.85) adults, 35DKK ($4.60) children 6–12, free for children under 6. May–June 19 and Sept Sat–Sun 11am–4pm; June 20–Aug daily 11am–4pm. Closed Oct–Apr. Bus: 119 or 121 from Århus.

SHOPPING
Århus is the biggest shopping venue in Jutland, with some 400 specialty stores. They're tightly clustered within an area more than .8 sq. km (½ sq. mile). The centerpiece of this district is Strøget, whose terminus is the Store Torv, dominated by the Århus Domkirke.

You might try a large-scale department store first, such as **Salling,** Søndergade 17 (ℂ **86-12-18-00**), with some 30 specialty boutiques under one roof. **Magasin du Nord,** Immervad 2–8 (ℂ **86-12-33-00**), is the largest department store in Scandinavia. The staff will assist foreign visitors with tax-free purchases.

"The greatest silversmith the world has ever seen" is a common description of **Georg Jensen,** Søndergade 1 (ℂ **86-12-01-00**). A tradition since 1866, Georg Jensen is known for style and quality. The company produces unique silver and gold jewelry, elegant clocks and watches, and stainless steel cutlery, among other items.

WHERE TO STAY
Low-cost accommodations in this lively university city are limited. Those on a modest budget should check with the tourist office in the Rådhuset (ℂ **86-12-16-00**) for bookings in **private homes.** Prices begin at 300DKK ($39) per person, single or double occupancy, but they could go higher depending on the home.

Hotel La Tour   Since its construction in 1956, and its rebuilding in 1986, this hotel has followed a conscious policy of downgrading (yes, downgrading) its accommodations and facilities from a once lofty status to a decidedly middle-brow formula. The result is a hotel that's far from the best in town—viewed, we imagine, as a great success by the management—that attracts hundreds of foreign visitors. The hotel, appropriately housed in an unimaginative two-story building, is 3.5km (2¼ miles) north of Århus center. It offers clean, simple guest rooms with small bathrooms containing shower-tub combinations. There's a patio-style restaurant serving competently prepared Danish and international food, a bar, and a children's playroom (open May–Sept only).

Randersvej 139, DK-8200 Århus. ② **86-16-78-88.** Fax 86-16-79-95. 101 units. 920DKK ($121) double; 1,250DKK ($164) suite. Rates include breakfast. AE, DC, MC, V. Bus: 2, 3, or 11. **Amenities:** Restaurant; bar; room service; laundry/dry cleaning. *In room:* TV, minibar, safe.

Hotel Royal 🏠🏠 This is the most glamorous accommodation in town. The gilt date on its neo-baroque facade commemorates the hotel's establishment in 1838. There have been numerous additions and upgrades since. The Royal stands close to the city's symbol, its cathedral. A vintage elevator takes you to the guest rooms, many of which are quite spacious. They're modernized, with good-size bathrooms containing shower-tub combinations. Beds are newly refurbished, with strong, durable mattresses, and accommodations are fitted with high-quality furniture, carpeting, and fabrics.

Stove Torv 4, DK-8000 Århus. ② **86-12-00-11.** Fax 86-76-04-04. www.hotelroyal.dk. 102 units. 1,695DKK–1,895DKK ($222–$248) double; 3,000DKK ($393) suite. Rates include breakfast. AE, DC, MC, V. Parking 150DKK ($20). Bus: 56 or 58. **Amenities:** Restaurant; bar; sauna; room service; babysitting; laundry/dry cleaning. *In room:* TV, minibar, hair dryer.

Radisson SAS Scandinavia Hotel Århus 🏠🏠🏠 This is one of the most modern and dynamic modern hotels in Denmark, and a city showplace that municipal authorities proudly show off to dignitaries visiting on trade missions from abroad. It was built in 1995 directly above the largest convention facilities in Jutland and, as such, maintains a closer contact with the dynamics of huge conventions and their planners than any other hotel in the region. Guest rooms occupy floors 4 to 11 of a glass-and-stone-sheathed tower that's visible from throughout the city. Lower floors contain check-in, dining, drinking, and convention facilities. Guest rooms are outfitted with plush upholstery with bright colors. Each has a tasteful decor that's different from its immediate neighbor, incorporating Scandinavian, English, Japanese, or Chinese themes. Each has a well-kept bathroom with a shower-tub combination, and large-windowed views over the city.

Margrethepladsen 1, DK-8000 Århus C. ② **800/333-3333** or 86-12-86-65. Fax 86-12-86-75. 234 units. 1,195DKK–1,860DKK ($157–$244) double; from 1,495DKK ($196) suite. Rates include breakfast. AE, DC, MC, V. Bus: 1, 2, 6, or 16. **Amenities:** Restaurant; bar; sauna; room service; babysitting; laundry/dry cleaning. *In room:* TV, minibar, hair dryer.

Scandi Plaza This dignified and traditional hotel is convenient to the Town Hall and city center attractions. Completely renovated and vastly improved in 1997, it is part of an original hotel that opened in 1930. The hotel is now first-class, with tastefully decorated guest rooms, good beds, and modern bathrooms with shower-tub combinations.

Banegårdsplads 14, DK-8100 Århus C. ② **87-32-01-00.** Fax 87-32-01-99. www.scandi-hotels.com. 162 units. 1,495DKK–1,595DKK ($196–$209) double; 1,995DKK ($261) suite. Rates include breakfast. DC, MC, V. Bus: 3, 17, 56, or 58. **Amenities:** Restaurant; bar; pool; fitness center; Jacuzzi; sauna; room service; laundry/dry cleaning. *In room:* TV, minibar, hair dryer, safe.

WHERE TO DINE

Kroen i Krogen DANISH   "The inn in the corner" has built a loyal clientele since it was established across from the railway station in 1934. It's got a good, conventional Danish menu and one of the most unusual interiors in town—the walls are decorated with about two dozen panels depicting local artist Michael Fisker's interpretation of the history of Århus from the 14th century to the mid–20th century. They were painted shortly after World War II on the back of canvas coffee sacks because conventional art supplies weren't available.

You can order something as straightforward and simple as grilled sausages with black bread—a worthy foil for a glass of beer—or the house specialty, *kroens Anretning,* a platter with two kinds of herring, a fish filet, a handful of shrimp, and a small steak with fried onions. Other items include a savory orange-marinated salmon, perfectly grilled rib-eye steak, and hazelnut cake. Between April and September, there are at least 50 additional seats on an outdoor terrace.

Banegårdspladsen 4. ⓒ **86-19-24-39.** All main courses 198DKK ($26); fixed-price menus 228DKK–258DKK ($30–$34). AE, DC, MC, V. Mon–Sat noon–10pm.

Le Canard ★ *Finds* FRENCH   One of Århus's most appealing French restaurants sits in the heart of the city's pedestrian shopping zones. Within a contemporary but conservative black-and-white setting that's softened with bouquets of fresh flowers, the staff will propose a series of fixed-price menus that are cosmopolitan and sophisticated. A meal might begin with beef carpaccio served with pesto and baby greens; home-smoked salmon with quail eggs; or roasted scallops on a bed of arugula and peanut sauce. Main courses include breast of duck with raspberry sauce, rack of baby lamb with a mild mustard sauce, and Danish veal chops with tomato-and-basil sauce. Dessert might be a pear strudel with pear sorbet, served in a coconut shell.

Frederiksgade 74. ⓒ **86-12-58-38.** Reservations recommended. Fixed-price menus 325DKK–575DKK ($43–$75). DC, MC, V. Mon–Sat 5pm–midnight (last order).

Prins Ferdinand ★★ DANISH/INTERNATIONAL   On the edge of Århus's historic center in a former tea salon, this is one of the city's finest restaurants. It was established in 1988 by Per Brun and his wife, Lotte Norrig, who create a version of modern Danish cuisine that has won favor with the region's business community. In two pink-toned dining rooms laden with flickering candles and flowers, you can order a platter of fresh smoked salmon served with tartare of salmon and pepper-cream sauce, turbot with Russian caviar and a drizzle of olive oil, sea devil with lobster prepared Thai-style with lemon grass, or boneless pigeon stuffed with fresh goose liver served with a raspberry sauce. A dessert specialty is pears cooked with elderberries and served with vanilla ice cream, nougat, and almonds. The restaurant's array of dessert cheeses, the most unusual array in Jutland, includes esoteric local creations produced by small farmers.

Viborgvej 2. ⓒ 86-12-52-05. Reservations recommended. Main courses 135DKK–165DKK ($18–$22) lunch, 150DKK–235DKK ($20–$31) dinner. Fixed-price lunch 170DKK–235DKK ($22–$31); fixed-price dinner 375DKK–545DKK ($49–$71). AE, DC, MC, V. Tues–Sat 11am–3pm and 6–9pm. Bus: 3.

Restaurant de 4 Arstider (Four Seasons) FRENCH   The kitchen presents a carefully crafted cuisine based on the specialties of the season and presented as fixed-price menus. In spring that means fresh asparagus (sometimes with foie gras), along with the catch of the day, perhaps red snapper in a zesty sauce. Succulent preparations of veal and lamb are always featured, and in the autumn there are game dishes. Because the menu is always changing, we can't recommend specific specialties, but over the years it's always been a heartwarming experience to arrive on the doorstep and discover the chef's surprises.

Aboulevarden 47. ⓒ **86-19-96-96.** Reservations required. Fixed-price menus 295DKK–525DKK ($39–$69). AE, DC, MC, V. Mon–Sat 11am–10pm. Closed July. Bus: 1, 2, 3, 6, 9, or 16.

Teater Bodega DANISH   Originally established at a different address in 1907, Teater Bodega in 1951 moved across the street from both the Århus Dramatic Theater and the Århus Cathedral. It tries to provide an amusing dining ambience for theater and art lovers. The walls are covered with illustrations of theatrical costumes along with other thespian memorabilia. The food is solid and flavorful in the Danish country style. Various kinds of Danish hash, including *biksemad,* are served along with regular or large portions of Danish roast beef. There's also English and French beef, fried plaice, and flounder.

Skolegade 7. (𝄞 **86-12-19-17.** Reservations recommended. Lunch smørrebrød 129DKK ($17); main courses 80DKK–170DKK ($10–$22); 3-course fixed-price menu 218DKK ($29). DC, MC, V. Mon–Sat 11am–11:30pm. Bus: 6.

SILKEBORG
44km (27 miles) W of Århus, 280km (174 miles) W of Copenhagen

Silkeborg is in the midst of some of Denmark's most beautiful scenery. It's an ideal spot to explore **Himmelbjerget (Sky Mountain),** the highest peak in low-lying Denmark. *But be warned:* The "mountain" is less than 150m (500 ft.) high.

ESSENTIALS
GETTING THERE   From Århus, follow Route 15 west to Silkeborg. If you aren't driving, there's frequent train service from Copenhagen by way of Fredericia.

VISITOR INFORMATION   The **Silkeborg Turistbureau** is at Godthåbsvej 4 ((𝄞 **86-82-19-11;** www.silkeborg.com). It's open from June 15 to August, Monday through Friday from 9am to 5pm, Saturday from 9am to 3pm, Sunday from 9:30am to 12:30pm; off season, Monday through Friday from 9am to 4pm, Saturday from 9am to noon.

GETTING AROUND   Numerous bus routes service the city; all local buses depart from the bus stop on Fredensgade. There's no number to call for information. Tickets cost 14DKK ($1.85) per individual ride, or 17DKK ($2.25) if you need a transfer.

SEEING THE SIGHTS
The most intriguing way to see Sky Mountain and the surrounding countryside is aboard the paddle steamer *Hjejlen.* It has operated since 1861, and sails frequently in the summer. For schedules and more information, call **Hjejlen Co. Ltd.,** Havnen ((𝄞 **86-82-07-66**). A round-trip ticket costs 84DKK ($11) for adults, half price for children. Departures from Silkeborg Harbor are daily at 10am and 2pm from mid-June until mid-August.

Silkeborg Museum   This 18th-century manor by the Gudenå River, directly east of Torvet, houses the 2,200-year-old **Tollund Man** 𝄐𝄐𝄐, discovered in a peat bog in 1950. His face is the least spoiled found to date. His body was so well preserved, in fact, that scientists were able to determine that his last meal was flax, barley, and oats. His head capped by fur, the Tollund Man was strangled by a plaited leather string, probably as part of a ritual sacrifice. Equally well preserved is the **Elling Woman,** who was found near the same spot. Scientists estimate that she was about 25 years old when she died in 210 B.C.

The museum also has a special exhibition of old Danish glass, a clogmaker's workshop, a collection of stone implements, antique jewelry, and artifacts from the ruins of Silkeborg Castle. In the handicraft and Iron Age markets, artisans use ancient techniques to create iron, jewelry, and various crafts.

Hovedgaardsvej 7. ℂ **86-82-14-99.** Admission 40DKK ($.25) adults, 10DKK ($1.30) children 6–14, free for children 5 and under. May to mid-Oct daily 10am–5pm; mid-Oct to Apr Wed and Sat–Sun noon–4pm. Bus: 10.

WHERE TO STAY

Silkeborg Turistbureau (see "Visitor Information," above) can book you into nearby **private homes.** Prices begin at 300DKK ($39) per person.

Hotel Dania ⓡ   On Silkeborg's main square, within a 5-minute walk of the railway station, this is the oldest hotel in town. Established in 1848, it underwent a radical upgrade and renovation in 1997. Antiques fill the corridors and reception lounge, but the guest rooms have been completely renovated in functional, modern style. Each unit contains a neatly kept bathroom with a shower-tub combination. Outdoor dining on the square is popular in the summer, and the Underhuset restaurant serves typical Danish food along with Scandinavian and French dishes. The hotel's dining room is one of the longest restaurants in Denmark.

Torvet 5, DK-8600 Silkeborg. ℂ **86-82-01-11.** Fax 86-80-20-04. www.hoteldania.dk. 47 units. 1,060DKK–1,195DKK ($139–$157) double; 1,450DKK–1,850DKK ($190–$242) suite. Rates include breakfast. AE, DC, MC, V. Free parking. Bus: 3. **Amenities:** Restaurant; bar; room service; babysitting; laundry/dry cleaning. *In room:* TV, minibar, hair dryer, safe.

Radisson SAS Hotel ⓡⓡ ⒻⒾⓃⒹⓈ   In a historical building, a 150-year-old paper factory, this is the newest and best hotel to open in the area. It lies right by the harbor, a short walk to attractions, shops, and restaurants. The hotel offers a wide range of rooms from standard to suites. Each is furnished in a traditional style, containing a state-of-the-art bathroom with tub and shower combination. The lobby bar with its fireplace is the best place to be in Silkesborg when it's snowing outside. Another favorite spot, this one for fair weather, is the restaurant with its spacious terrace offering panoramic views of the Remstrup River.

Papirfabrikken 12, DK-8600 Silkesborg. ℂ **88-82-22-22.** Fax 88-82-22-23. www.radisson.com. 86 units. 1,195DKK ($157) double; 1,745DKK ($229) suite. Rates include continental breakfast. AE, DC, MC, V. **Amenities:** Restaurant; bar; Jacuzzi in the suites; sauna; room service; laundry/dry cleaning. *In room:* A/C, TV, minibar, fridge, hair dryer, iron/ironing board.

WHERE TO DINE

Spiesehuset Christian VIII DANISH/FRENCH   The best restaurant in Silkeborg, this establishment was founded about a decade ago in what was originally a private house built in the late 1700s. It seats only 30 people in a dining room painted in what the owners describe as the color of heaven (cerulean blue), accented with dramatic modern paintings. Delectable choices include lobster ravioli, carpaccio of marinated sole and salmon with saffron sauce, filet of beef with truffle sauce, medallions of veal stuffed with a purée of wild duck and herbs, and tender rack of Danish lamb with garlic sauce. Service is attentive and professional.

Christian VIII Vej 54. ℂ **86-82-25-62.** Reservations required. Main courses 165DKK–255DKK ($22–$33). AE, DC, MC, V. Mon–Sat 5–10pm.

EBELTOFT ⓡ

97km (60 miles) E of Silkeborg, 53km (33 miles) NE of Århus, 336km (209 miles) W of Copenhagen

A well-preserved town of half-timbered buildings, Ebeltoft ("apple orchard") is the capital of the Mols hill country. This is a village of cobblestone streets, hidden-away lanes, old inns, and ruddy-faced fishermen who carry on the profession of their ancestors.

ESSENTIALS
GETTING THERE From Silkeborg, head east on Route 15 through Århus and continue around the coast; then follow Route 21 south to Ebeltoft. There's no direct train service to Ebeltoft. From Copenhagen, take the train to Århus by way of Fredericia; at Århus Central Station, board bus no. 123 for Ebeltoft.

VISITOR INFORMATION The **Ebeltoft Turistbureau** is at Strandvejen 2 (© **86-34-14-00;** www.ebeltofturist.dk). It's open from June 15 to August, Monday through Saturday from 10am to 6pm, Sunday from 10am to 4pm; from September to June 14, Monday through Friday from 9am to 4pm, Saturday from 10am to 1pm.

SEEING THE SIGHTS
Fregatten Jylland The *Jylland* is the oldest man-of-war in Denmark (1860) and the world's longest wooden ship at 71m (233 ft.); it's 13m (43 ft.) wide. The frigate is moored in the harbor.

Strandvejen 4. © **86-34-10-99**. Admission 60DKK ($7.85) adults, 20DKK ($2.60) children. Daily 10am–7pm.

Det Gamle Rådhus The 1789 Town Hall looks like something erected just for kindergarten children to play in—it has blackened half-timbering, a redbrick and timber facade, and a bell tower. Its museum houses an ethnographic collection from Thailand and artifacts from the town's history. It's in the town center north of Strandvejen.

Torvet. © **86-34-13-82**. Admission 25DKK ($3.30) adults, 5DKK (65¢) children. Apr–May Tues–Sun 11am–3pm; Sept–Oct Tues–Sun 11am–3pm; Nov–Mar Sat–Sun 11am–3pm.

WHERE TO STAY & DINE
Hotel Ebeltoft Strand This centrally located two-story hotel was constructed in 1978 and most recently renovated in 1995. Each comfortable, well-furnished guest room has a balcony or terrace that overlooks Ebeltoft Bay. All units are also equipped with well-kept bathrooms with shower-tub combinations. The hotel has a restaurant, bar, open fireplace, and playground. It's about a 5-minute drive from the ferry and a 15-minute drive from Tirstrup Airport.

Nordre Strandvej 3, DK-8400 Ebeltoft. © **86-34-33-00**. Fax 86-34-46-36. 72 units. 1,195DKK ($157) double. Rates include breakfast. AE, DC, MC, V. Free parking. Bus: 123 from Århus. **Amenities:** Restaurant; bar; room service; laundry/dry cleaning. *In room:* TV, minibar, hair dryer, safe.

Mols Kroen ⚜ This hotel was vastly upgraded in 1998, and its prices rose dramatically, too. Nevertheless, it's one of the better places to stay in the area. Many rooms have terraces overlooking Mols Hills, and a fine white sandy beach is only 100m (350 ft.) away. The *kro* (inn) is in the center of an area of summer houses mostly built in the 1920s and 1930s. The medium-sized guest rooms are now sleek, functional, and comfortable, with freshly tiled bathrooms equipped with shower-tub combinations.

Hovegaden 16, Femmøller Strand, DK-8400 Ebeltoft. © **86-36-22-00**. Fax 86-36-23-00. www.molskroen.dk. 18 units. 1,480DKK–1,680DKK ($194–$220) double; 3,200DKK ($419) suite. Rates include breakfast. AE, DC, V. Free parking. Closed Dec 24–Jan 8. Bus: 123 from Århus. **Amenities:** Restaurant; bar; room service; babysitting; laundry/dry cleaning. *In room:* TV, minibar, hair dryer, safe.

AALBORG ⚜
132km (82 miles) NW of Ebeltoft, 383km (238 miles) W of Copenhagen

The largest city in northern Jutland, Aalborg (Ålborg) is known worldwide for its aquavit. Although essentially a shipping town and commercial center,

Aalborg makes a good base for sightseers, with its many hotels and attractions, more than 300 restaurants, and diverse nightlife.

History is a living reality in Aalborg. The city was founded 1,000 years ago when the Viking fleets assembled in these parts before setting off on their predatory expeditions. The city's historic atmosphere has been preserved in its old streets and alleys. Near the Church of Our Lady are many beautifully restored and reconstructed houses, some of which date from the 16th century.

Denmark's largest forest, **Rold,** where robber bandits once roamed, is just outside town. **Rebild National Park** is the site of the annual American Fourth of July celebration.

Not far from Aalborg, on the west coast of northern Jutland, some of the finest beaches in northern Europe stretch from Slettestrand to Skagen. The beach resort towns of **Blokhus** and **Løkken** are especially popular with Danes, Germans, and Swedes.

ESSENTIALS

GETTING THERE From Ebeltoft, follow Route 21 north until you reach the junction with Route 16. Drive west on Route 16 until you come to E45, which runs north to Aalborg. You can fly from Copenhagen to Aalborg; the **airport** (© 98-17-11-44) is 6.5km (4 miles) from the city center. There is frequent train service from Copenhagen by way of Fredericia to Århus; there you can connect with a train to Aalborg, a 90-minute ride. Aalborg's bus station is the transportation center for northern Jutland, and is served from all directions. For all bus information in northern Jutland, call **Nordjyllands Trafikselskab** (© 98-11-11-11).

VISITOR INFORMATION The **Aalborg Tourist Bureau** is at Østerågade 8 (© 98-12-60-22; www.aalborg-turist.dk). It's open from June to August, Monday through Friday from 9am to 6pm, Saturday from 9am to 5pm; from September to May, Monday through Friday from 9am to 4:30pm, Saturday from 10am to 1pm.

GETTING AROUND For bus information, call © 98-11-11-11. Most buses depart from Østerågade and Nytorv in the city center. A typical fare costs 13DKK ($1.70), although you can buy a 24-hour tourist pass for 84DKK ($11) and ride on all the city buses for a day. Information about bus routes is available from the *Aalborg Guide,* which is distributed free by the tourist office.

SEEING THE SIGHTS

The finest example of Renaissance domestic architecture in northern Europe is **Jens Bang's Stenhus** *★*, Østerågade 9. The six-floor mansion was built in 1624 in glittering Renaissance style. It once belonged to a wealthy merchant, Jens Bang. The historic wine cellar, Duus Vinkjaelder, is the meeting place of the Guild of Christian IV. On the ground floor is an old apothecary shop. The mansion is privately owned and not open to the public. To get there, take bus no. 3, 5, 10, or 11.

Aalborgtårnet This tower rises 100m (325 ft.) above sea level, offering a perfect view—reachable by stair or elevator—of the city and the fjord.

Søndre Skovvej, at Skovbakken. © 98-12-04-88. Admission 25DKK ($3.30) adults, 15DKK ($1.95) children. June 17–Aug 11 daily 10am–7pm; May–June 16 and Aug 12–Sept 15 daily 10am–5pm. Closed Sept 16–Apr. Bus: 8 or 10.

Aalborg Zoologiske Have *★* Set 4km (2½ miles) south of Aalborg, this is the second largest zoo in Scandinavia, where some 800 animal specimens from all over the world wander freely in surroundings designed to mirror an open African range. Apes and beasts of prey are kept under minimal restrictions. There's a good bistro, and snack bars here and there. The zoo is in Mølleparken, a large park with a lookout where you can see most of Aalborg and the Isle of Egholm. Look for Roda Reilinger's sculpture *Noah's Ark* near the lookout.

Mølleparkvej 63. ℂ 96-31-29-29. Admission 75DKK ($9.85) adults, 40DKK ($5.25) children, free for children under 12. Jan–Mar and Nov–Dec daily 10am–3pm; Apr and Sept–Oct daily 10am–5pm; May–Aug daily 9am–7pm. Last ticket is sold 1 hr. before closing. Bus: 1.

Nordjyllands Kunstmuseet (Museum of Modern and Contemporary Art)

This building is a prime example of modern Scandinavian architecture. Built from 1968 to 1972, it was designed by Elissa and Alvar Aalto and Jean-Jacques Baruël as a showplace for 20th-century Danish and international art. It has changing exhibits, sculpture gardens, two auditoriums, a children's museum, an outdoor amphitheater, and a restaurant, the Museumscafeen.

Kong Christians Allé 50. ℂ 98-13-80-88. Admission 30DKK ($3.95) adults, free for children. Daily 10am–5pm. Bus: 1, 4, 8, 10, or 11.

WHERE TO STAY

Helnan Phønix Hotel

This is the oldest, largest, most prestigious hotel in Aalborg. The old-fashioned public rooms disguise how modern it is. It originated in 1783 on the town's main street as a private home. It became a hotel in 1853, and entered the modern age after three significant expansions, in the 1960s, 1970s, and 1980s. Today, it looks deceptively small from Aalborg's main street, and very imposing from the back, where you can see the modern wings. Guest rooms are outfitted with a combination of dark-grained furniture based on turn-of-the-20th-century English models and light-grained Danish modern pieces. Each unit has a well-kept bathroom with a shower-tub combination.

Vesterbro 77, DK-9000 Aalborg. ℂ 98-12-00-11. Fax 98-10-10-20. www.helnan.com. 210 units. 1,095DKK ($143) double; 2,500DKK ($328) suite. AE, DC, MC, V. Bus: 8, 10, or 11. **Amenities:** Restaurant; bar; fitness center; sauna; room service; laundry/dry cleaning. *In room:* TV, minibar, hair dryer, safe.

Hotel Hvide Hus ⭐ *Finds*

The first-rate "White House Hotel" is in Kilde Park, about a 12-minute walk from the heart of Aalborg. Many international businesspeople have started staying here instead of at the traditional Hotel Helnan Phønix. In cooperation with well-known galleries, the hotel is decorated with works by some of Denmark's leading painters. The guest rooms are well furnished in fresh Scandinavian modern style; all have private balconies with a view of Aalborg. Each unit is also equipped with a well-maintained bathroom with a shower-tub combination.

Vesterbro 2, DK-9000 Aalborg. ℂ 98-13-84-00. Fax 98-13-51-22. www.hotelhvidehus.dk. 200 units. 1,095DKK–1,295DKK ($143–$170) double; 2,150DKK ($282) suite. Rates include breakfast. AE, DC, MC, V. Free parking. Bus: 1, 4, 8, 10, or 11. **Amenities:** Restaurant; bar; room service; massage; babysitting; laundry/dry cleaning. *In room:* TV, minibar.

Limsfordhotellet ⭐

This the most avant-garde hotel in town—a five-story yellow brick structure with huge expanses of glass in a streamlined Danish modern layout. In the center of town, a 3-minute walk east of the cathedral, the hotel opens onto the famous Limsjorden Canal. It's near Jomfru Anegade, a street packed with bars and restaurants. The public rooms are sparsely furnished with modern, streamlined furniture. Many of the comfortable guest rooms overlook the harbor. The medium-sized rooms have good-sized tile bathrooms with shower-tub combinations. Everything is maintained in state-of-the-art condition. The suites have Jacuzzis.

Ved Stranden 14–16, DK-9000 Aalborg. © **98-16-43-33.** Fax 98-16-17-47. 188 units. 895DKK–1,250DKK ($117–$164) double; 2,430DKK ($318) suite. Rates include breakfast. AE, DC, MC, V. Parking 50DKK ($6.55). Closed Dec 24–26. Bus: 1, 4, 40, or 46. **Amenities:** Restaurant; bar; nightclub; fitness center; sauna; room service; laundry/dry cleaning. *In room:* TV, minibar.

WHERE TO DINE

Fyrtøjet DANISH/INTERNATIONAL   A cozy, small restaurant in the center of town, Fyrtøjet serves competent, filling—though not especially exciting— fare. We suggest a Danish specialty, the *almueplatte* (peasant's plate), with marinated herring, curry salad, two warm rissoles, cold potato salad and chives, and deep-fried Camembert cheese with black-currant jam. Other main dishes include stuffed plaice with shrimp, pepper steak, and breast of duck. In the summertime, enjoy your meal at outdoor tables.

Jomfru Anegade 17. © **98-13-73-77.** Reservations recommended. Main courses 100DKK–190DKK ($13–$25). AE, DC, MC, V. Mon–Sat 11:30am–11pm; Sun noon–11pm. Bus: 1, 3, 5, or 15.

Hos Boldt ✿ DANISH/FRENCH   One of Aalborg's most likable restaurants was established in 1992 in a 19th-century building that had been a simple tavern for many years. The family-run business consists of two deliberately old-fashioned dining rooms filled with antique furniture and candles. Menu items change with the availability of the ingredients, but might include such perfectly prepared dishes as steamed turbot with julienne of leeks, consommé of veal with herbs and quail eggs, lobster bisque, a platter with various preparations of salmon, snails in herb-flavored cream sauce, rack of Danish lamb in rosemary-flavored wine sauce, and sea bass cooked in salt crust.

Ved Stranden 7. © **98-16-17-77.** Reservations recommended. Main courses 140DKK–400DKK ($18–$52); fixed-price menus 200DKK–400DKK ($26–$52). AE, DC, MC, V. Mon–Sat 5pm–midnight. Bus: 1, 4, 40, or 46.

SKAGEN ✿
105km (65 miles) NE of Aalborg, 488km (303 miles) W of Copenhagen

The "Land's End" of Denmark, Skagen (pronounced "skane") is the northernmost tip of Jutland. It has been compared to a bony finger pointing into the North Sea. Skagen is the country's second-biggest fishing port and is enlivened by a thriving artists' colony.

ESSENTIALS
GETTING THERE   By Car   Take E45 northeast to Frederikshavn. From there, head north on Route 40 to Skagen.

By Train   Several trains a day run from Copenhagen to Århus, where you connect with another train to Frederikshavn. From Frederikshavn there are 12 daily trains to Skagen.

VISITOR INFORMATION   The **Skagen Turistbureau** is at Skt. Laurentiivej 22 (© **98-44-13-77;** www.skagen-tourist.dk). It's open from June 22 to August 4, daily from 9am to 7pm; from June 1 to June 21 and August 5 to August 31, Monday through Saturday from 9am to 5:30pm, Sunday from 10am to 2pm; May and September, Monday through Saturday from 9am to 5:30pm, Sunday from 10am to 2pm; from October to April, Monday through Friday from 9am to 5:30pm, Saturday from 10am to 1pm.

SEEING THE SIGHTS
If you walk to a point of land called **Grenener,** you'll be at the northernmost point of mainland Europe and can dip your toes into the Skagerrak and Kattegat

seas. Another charming oasis to seek out is **Gammel Skagen,** a little seaside resort set against a backdrop of dunes and sea grass.

The most important attraction in the town is the **Skagens Museum,** Brøndumsvej 4 ((C) **98-44-64-44**). It houses the work of many local artists. You'll see paintings by P. S. Krøyer (1851–1909), Micheal Ancher (1849–1909), and Anna Ancher (1859–1935). Admission is 50DKK ($6.55), free for children under 16. It's open from May to September, daily from 10am to 5pm; April and October, Tuesday through Sunday from 11am to 4pm; from November to March, Wednesday through Friday from 1 to 4pm, Saturday from 11am to 4pm, and Sunday from 11am to 3pm.

WHERE TO STAY

Color Hotel Skagen (R) (Finds)   Southwest of Skagen, beside the only road leading into town from the rest of Jutland, this sprawling, one-story hotel lies 2km (1¼ miles) from the sea. There, alone on sandy flatlands, it possesses an almost otherworldly sense of isolation. Unlike many of its competitors, which cater to families with children, this place appeals mostly to couples. Built in 1969, and enlarged and modernized in 1997, the hotel has an appealing formal restaurant. The spacious, attractively furnished guest rooms have hardwood floors, padded armchairs, and big windows. Each unit also contains neatly kept bathrooms with shower-tub combinations. Of the accommodations, 45 are listed as apartments and, as such, are rented only for 3 days at a time, with the exception of midsummer, when they are rented per week.

Gammel Landevej 39, DK-9990 Skagen. ((C)) **98-44-22-33**. Fax 98-44-21-34. www.skagenhotel.dk. 153 units. 880DKK–1,180DKK ($115–$155) double; 1,650DKK–2,550DKK ($216–$334) suite; 4,000DKK–8,000DKK ($524–$1048) apt per week. AE, DC, MC, V. From Skagen, drive 2km (1¼ miles) southwest of town along Rte. 40. **Amenities:** Restaurant; bar; pool; fitness center; sauna; room service. *In room:* TV, hair dryer, safe.

6

The Best of Norway

From snowcapped mountains to fjords warmed by the Gulf Stream, Norway is a land of stunning contrasts. Although the "Land of the Midnight Sun" is a modern, industrial nation, it is equally a world of remote towns and villages, with a population devoted to outdoor activities. So you won't have to exhaust yourself making difficult decisions, we've searched out the best deals and once-in-a-lifetime experiences for this section. What follows is the best of the best.

1 The Best Travel Experiences

- **Enjoying Nature:** Norway is one of the last major countries of the world where you can experience nature on an exceptional level. The country extends 1,770km (1,100 miles) from south to north (approximately the distance from New York to Miami). Spread across it are 19,964km (12,400 miles) of fjords, narrows, and straits, which gave the country its name—Norway means "the way to the North." It's a land of contrasts, with soaring mountains, panoramic fjords, ice-blue glaciers, deep-green forests, fertile valleys, and rich pastures. The glowing red midnight sun reflects off snow-covered mountains, and the northern lights have fired the imaginations of artists and crafts-people for centuries.

- **Experiencing Norway in a Nutshell:** One of Europe's great train rides, this 12-hour excursion is Norway's most exciting. The route encompasses two arms of the Sognefjord, and the section from Myrdal to Flåm—a drop of 600m (2,000 ft.)—takes you past seemingly endless waterfalls. Tours leave from the Bergen train station. If you have limited time but want to see the country's most

dramatic scenery, take this spectacular train trip. See chapter 9.

- **Visiting the North Cape:** For many, a trip to one of the northernmost inhabited areas of the world will be the journey of a lifetime. Accessible by ship, car, or air, the North Cape holds a fascination for travelers that outweighs its bleakness. Ship tours started in 1879 and, except in wartime, have gone to the Cape ever since. Hammerfest, the world's northernmost town of significant size, is an important port of call for North Cape steamers. See chapter 10.

- **Exploring the Fjord Country:** Norway's fjords are stunningly serene and majestic, some of the world's most awe-inspiring sights. The fjords are reason enough for a trip to Norway. Bergen can be your gateway; two of the country's most famous fjords, the Hardangerfjord and the Sognefjord, can easily be explored from there. You can go on your own or take an organized tour, which will probably include the dramatic Folge-fonn Glacier. Norway's longest fjord, the Sognefjord, can be crossed by express steamer to Gudvangen. See chapter 10.

- **Seeing the Midnight Sun at the Arctic Circle:** This is one of the major reasons visitors flock to Norway. The Arctic Circle marks the boundary of the midnight sun of the Arctic summer and the sunless winters of the north. The midnight sun can be seen from the middle of May until the end of July. The Arctic Circle cuts across Norway south of Bodø. Bus excursions from that city visit the circle. The adventurous few who arrive in the winter miss the midnight sun, but are treated to a spectacular display of the aurora borealis (northern lights), the flaming spectacle of the Arctic winter sky. In ancient times, when the aurora could be seen farther south, people thought it was an omen of disaster. See chapter 10.

2 The Best Scenic Towns & Villages

- **Fredrikstad:** Founded in 1567 at the mouth of the River Glomma, Fredrikstad preserved its Old Town, which had become a fortress by 1667. Today Fredrikstad (about 97km/60 miles south of Oslo) offers a glimpse of what a Norwegian town looked like several hundred years ago. The old buildings in the historic district have been converted into studios for craftspeople and artisans, while maintaining their architectural integrity. After a visit here, you can drive along Oldtidsveien (the "highway of the ancients"), the most concentrated collection of archaeological monuments in Norway. See chapter 8.

- **Tønsberg:** On the western bank of the Oslofjord, this is Norway's oldest town. It was founded in A.D. 872, a year before King Harald Fairhair united parts of Norway. This Viking town became a royal coronation site. Its hill fortress is sometimes called "the Acropolis of Norway." Its ancient district, Nordbyen, is filled with well-preserved homes, and the folk museum houses a treasure trove of Viking-era artifacts. See chapter 8.

- **Bergen:** The gateway to Norway's fjord country, this town is even more scenic than the capital, Oslo. It was the capital of Norway for 6 centuries, and a major outpost of the medieval Hanseatic merchants. The town's biggest tourist event is the Bergen International Music Festival, but there are also many year-round attractions. Many visitors come to explore Bergen's museums (including Edvard Grieg's former home) as well as its varied environs—fjords galore, mountains, and waterfalls. See chapter 9.

- **Trondheim:** Norway's third-largest city traces its history to 997, when the Vikings flourished. Norway's kings are crowned at the ancient cathedral, Nidaros Domen; Scandinavia's largest medieval building, it was erected over the grave of St. Olaf (also spelled Olav), the Viking king. Trondheim is the popular stopover for travelers from Oslo to destinations north of the Arctic Circle. See chapter 10.

- **Bodø:** Lying 1,306km (811 miles) north of Oslo, this far northern seaport, the terminus of the Nordland railway, is the gateway to the Arctic Circle, which lies just south of this breezy town. Another excellent place to observe the midnight sun from June 1 to July 13, Bodø is the capital of Nordland. From here you can also explore the environs, filled with glaciers and "bird islands." Bodø is also a gateway to the remote Lofoten Islands. See chapter 10.

3 The Best Active Vacations

- **Fishing:** The cold, clear waters of Norway's freshwater streams are renowned for their salmon and trout, and the storm-tossed seas off the coast have traditionally provided enough cod and mackerel to satisfy most of the nation's population. Serious anglers sometimes end up losing themselves in the majesty of the scenery. Tips on fishing in and around the Norwegian fjords are provided by the **Bergen Sportsfiskere (Bergen Angling Association),** Fosswinckelsgate 37, Bergen (© **55-32-11-64**), and by the tourist information offices in Oslo and Bergen. Rural hotels throughout the nation can also point you to likely spots. For a truly unusual fishing experience, **Borton Overseas** (© **800/843-0602**) can arrange treks and accommodations in old-fashioned fishermen's cottages in the isolated Lofoten Islands. The rustic-looking, fully renovated cottages are adjacent to the sea. Rentals are for 3 days, and include bed linens, maid service, boat rentals, and fishing equipment. The most popular seasons are March, when cod abounds, and June through August, when the scenery and weather are particularly appealing.
- **Hiking:** The woods (Marka) around Oslo are ideal for jogging or walking. There are thousands of kilometers of trails, hundreds of which are lit. If you don't want to leave the city, Frogner Park also has many paths. Any Norwegian regional tourist bureau can advise you about hiking and jogging. In Bergen, for example, you can take a funicular to Fløyen, and within minutes you'll be in a natural forest filled with trails. Longer, guided hikes (5–8 days) may be arranged through the **Norwegian Mountain Touring Association,** Stortingsgata 3, N-0125 Oslo 1 (© **22-82-28-05;** www.dntoa.no).
- **Skiing:** This is the undisputed top winter sport in Norway, attracting top-notch skiers and neophytes from around the world. Norway is a pioneer in promoting skiing as a sport for persons with disabilities. Modern facilities comparable to those in Europe's alpine regions dot the landscape. If you're a serious skier, consider the best winter resorts, in Voss, Geilo, and Lillehammer (site of the 1994 Winter Olympics). See chapters 8 and 10.
- **Mountain Climbing:** Local tourist offices can offer advice. What we like best are guided hikes to the archaeological digs of the 8,000-year-old Stone Age settlements near the Hardangerjøkulen (Hardanger Glacier). The digs are about an hour's drive north of the mountain resort of Geilo. For information, contact the **Geilo Tourist Office** (© **32-09-50-00**). See chapter 10.

4 The Best Festivals & Special Events

- **Bergen International Festival:** This European cultural highlight, which takes place in late May and early June, ranks in importance with the Edinburgh and Salzburg festivals. Major artists from all over the world descend on the small city to perform music, drama, opera, ballet, folkloric presentations, and more. The works of Bergen native Edvard Grieg dominate the festival, and daily concerts are held at his former home, Troldhaugen. Contemporary plays are also performed, but the major focus is on the works of Ibsen. See chapter 7.

- **Molde International Jazz Festival:** In this "city of roses," Norway's oldest jazz festival is held every summer, usually around mid-July. Some of the best jazz artists in the world wing in for this event. People stay up most of the night listening to music and drinking beer. Sometimes the best concerts are the impromptu jam sessions in smoky little clubs. See chapter 7.
- **Nobel Peace Prize Ceremony:** The most prestigious event on the Oslo cultural calendar, the ceremony takes place at Oslo City Hall on December 10. Even though it's only possible to attend by invitation, the event is broadcast around the world. See chapter 7.
- **Holmenkollen Ski Festival:** This large ski festival takes place in February at the Holmenkollen Ski Jump, on the outskirts of Oslo. The agenda is packed with everything from international ski-jumping competitions to Norway's largest cross-country race for amateurs. See chapter 7.

5 The Best Museums

- **Viking Ship Museum** (Oslo): Three stunning burial vessels from the Viking era were excavated on the shores of the Oslofjord and are now displayed in Bygdøy, Oslo's "museum island." The most spectacular is the *Oseberg,* from the 9th century, a 19m (64-ft.) long dragon ship with a wealth of ornaments. See chapter 8.
- **Edvard Munch Museum** (Oslo): Here you'll find the most significant collection of the work of Edvard Munch (1863–1944), Scandinavia's most noted artist. It was his gift to the city, and it's a staggering treasure trove: 1,100 paintings, 4,500 drawings, and about 18,000 prints. See chapter 8.
- **Norwegian Folk Museum** (Oslo): Some 140 original buildings from all over Norway were shipped here and reassembled on 14 hectares (35 acres) at Bygdøy. Although Scandinavia is known for such open-air museums, this one is the best. The buildings range from a rare, stave church constructed around 1200 to one of the oldest wooden buildings still standing in Norway. Old-time Norwegian life is captured here as nowhere else. See chapter 8.
- **Vigelandsparken** (Oslo): This stunning park in western Oslo displays the lifetime work of Gustav Vigeland, the country's greatest sculptor. In the 30-hectare (75-acre) Frogner Park, you can see more than 200 sculptures in granite, bronze, and iron. Included is the "Angry Boy," his most celebrated work, and the most recognizable. See chapter 8.
- **Det Hanseatiske Museum** (Bergen): Depicting commercial life on the wharf in the early 18th century, this museum is housed in one of the city's best-preserved wooden buildings. German Hanseatic merchants lived in similar medieval houses near the harbor. See chapter 9.

6 The Best Buys

Most of the products mentioned below are available at better shops in Oslo and Bergen; see "Shopping" in chapters 8 and 9.

- **Knitwear:** Many visitors eagerly seek Norwegian knitwear. Among the best buys are hand-knit or "half-handmade" garments. The latter, knit on electric looms, are so personalized and made in such small quantities that only an expert can tell that they aren't completely handmade. The tradition of women hand-knitting sweaters while rocking a cradle or tending a fire thrives in rural Norway, especially during the long winter.

- **Costumes:** Norway boasts more than 450 regional costumes, especially in the coastal communities. The original fishermen's sweater was knit of naturally colored wool (beige, brown, black, or off-white) in a deliberately large size, and then washed in hot water so that it shrank. The tightly woven sweater could then resist water. Modern versions of these sweaters are known for their nubby texture, sophisticated patterns, and varying shades of single colors.

- **Crystal:** In Norway you can buy flawless crystal that's as clear as a Nordic iceberg. Norwegian tastes lean toward the clean, uncluttered look, stressing line, form, and harmony.

- **Ceramics:** In the 1960s and 1970s, Norway earned a reputation among potters and stoneware enthusiasts for its chunky, utilitarian pottery. The trend today is to emulate the fragile, more decorative designs popular in France, England, and Germany, so Norwegian ceramists are producing thinner, more delicate, and more ornate forms.

7 The Best Hotels

- **Grand Hotel** (Oslo; ℂ 800/223-5652 in the U.S., or 23-21-20-00): This is Norway's premier hotel, the last of Oslo's classic old-world palaces. It opened in 1874 and is still going strong. Ibsen and Munch were regular visitors. Constant renovations keep the hotel up-to-date and in great shape. The opulent suites house the Nobel Peace Prize winner every year. See p. 201.

- **Hotel Bristol** (Oslo; ℂ 22-82-60-00): Inspired by Edwardian-era British taste, the interior design is the most lavish and ornate in Oslo. You enter a world of rich paneling, leather chairs, glittering chandeliers, and carved pillars. The most inviting area is the bar off the lobby, decorated in a library motif. The guest rooms boast painted classic furnishings and rich fabrics. See p. 204.

- **Radisson SAS Hotel Norge** (Bergen; ℂ 800/333-3333 in the U.S., or 55-57-30-00): This grand hotel on Norway's west coast is sleek, modern, and cosmopolitan. The center of Bergen's major social events, the hotel is both traditional and handsomely up-to-date. It's also equipped with all the amenities guests expect in a deluxe hotel. The service is highly professional. See p. 261.

- **Dr. Holms Hotel** (Geilo; ℂ 32-09-57-00): One of Norway's most famous resort hotels, this establishment was opened by Dr. Holms in 1909. It still stands for elegance, comfort, and tradition, all of which are especially evident during the winter ski season. Due to its face-lift in 1989, the hotel offers beautifully furnished rooms with classic styling, and two completely new wings with a swimming complex. Famed musical artists often perform here. See p. 291.

- **Clarion Grand Olav Hotel** (Trondheim; ℂ 73-80-80-80): This is the most stylish hotel in Norway's medieval capital, a tasteful enclave of comfort and good living. Next to the city's concert house, it is modern, filled with amenities, and imaginatively decorated. See p. 295.

8 The Best Restaurants

- **Oro** (Oslo; ☎ **23-01-02-40**): A hyper-stylish restaurant, Oro is as good as it gets in Norway's capital, ranking right up there with anything Norway has to offer. The Continental cuisine at this first-class dining citadel evokes the best of the restaurants of Paris. See p. 212.

- **Statholdergaarden** (Oslo; ☎ **22-41-88-00**): Gourmets from all over Norway have flocked to this citadel of refined cuisine to sample chef Bent Stiansen's interpretation of modern Norwegian cooking. Stiansen is almost fanatically attuned to what's best in each season, and he serves some of the capital's finest dishes. He uses great imagination and a wide variety of ingredients—everything from Arctic char to a rare vanilla bean imported from Thailand. See p. 216.

- **Restaurant Julius Fritzner** (Oslo; ☎ **23-21-20-00**): One of the most impressive dining establishments to make its debut in Norway in the mid-1990s, this restaurant in the Grand Hotel is still getting rave reviews. The chef

uses only the finest Scandinavian ingredients in contemporary and traditional dishes; the emphasis is on enhancing and balancing flavors rather than creating surprises. See p. 212.

- **Finnegaardstuene** (Bergen; ☎ **55-55-03-00**): In a converted Hanseatic League warehouse, this Norwegian-French restaurant is one of the finest in western Norway. The cuisine revolves around only the freshest ingredients, especially fish. The kitchen uses classical French preparation methods to create such delectable items as lime-marinated turbot in caviar sauce or breast of duck in lime and fig sauce. See p. 265.

- **Bryggen** (Trondheim; ☎ **73-52-02-30**): This restaurant's excellent cuisine is a harmonious blend of Norwegian and French dishes. Menus change seasonally so that only the best and freshest ingredients are used. Ever had reindeer filet salad with a cranberry vinaigrette? Here's your chance. Norwegian duck, when it appears on the menu, is a rare treat. See p. 297.

Planning Your Trip to Norway

This chapter contains many of the details you'll need to plan your trip to Norway. See chapter 2, "Planning Your Trip to Denmark," which includes information pertaining to Scandinavia as a whole.

1 The Regions in Brief

WESTERN NORWAY Western Norway is fabled for its fjords, saltwater arms of the sea that stretch inland. Many date from the end of the last Ice Age. Some fjords cut into mountain ranges as high as 990m (3,300 ft.). The longest fjord in western Norway is the Sognefjord, north of Bergen, which penetrates 177km (110 miles) inland. Other major fjords in the district are the Nordfjord, Geirangerfjord, and Hardangerfjord. The capital of the fjord district is **Bergen,** the largest city on the west coast. **Lofthus,** a collection of farms extending along the slopes of Sørfjorden, offers panoramic views of the fjord and the **Folgefonn Glacier.** Hiking is the primary activity in this region. The area north of the **Hardangerfjord** is a haven for hikers. Hardangervidda National Park is here, on Europe's largest high-mountain plateau, and is home to Norway's largest herd of wild reindeer. The town of **Voss,** birthplace of the American football great Knute Rockne, is surrounded by glaciers, fjords, rivers, and lakes.

CENTRAL NORWAY Fjords are also common in central Norway; the two largest are the Trondheimsfjord and Narnsfjord. It's not unusual for roads to pass waterfalls that cascade straight down into fjords. Many thick forests and snowcapped peaks fill central Norway. The town of **Geilo,** halfway between Bergen and Oslo, is one of Norway's most popular ski resorts. It boasts more than 130km (80 miles) of cross-country trails. **Trondheim,** central Norway's largest city, is home to Nidaros Domen, the 11th-century cathedral that was once the burial place for kings. **Røros** is a well-preserved 18th-century mining town. The medieval city of **Molde,** Norway's capital during World War II, plays host to one of Europe's largest jazz festivals. **Geiranger,** site of the Seven Sisters waterfall, is one of Norway's most popular resorts.

EASTERN NORWAY On the border with Sweden, eastern Norway is characterized by clear blue lakes, rolling hills, and green valleys. In some ways it's the most traditional part of the country. Because of its many fertile valleys, it was one of the earliest areas to be settled. Some of the biggest valleys are Valdres, Østerdal, Hallingdall, Numedal, and Gudbrandsdalen. Campers and hikers enjoy the great forests of the Hedmark region, site of Norway's longest river, the Glomma (Gløma), which flows about 580km (360 miles). The area has many ski resorts, notably **Lillehammer,** site of the 1994 Winter Olympics. Norway's most visited destination is the capital, **Oslo,** which rises from the shores of the Oslofjord. The city of **Frederikstad,** at the

Norway

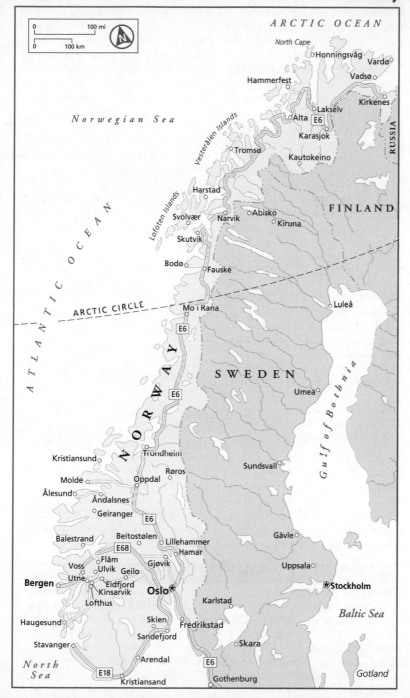

mouth of the Glomma, was once the marketplace for goods entering the country. Its 17th-century Kongsten Fort was designed to defend Norway from Sweden. **Tønsberg,** Norway's oldest town, dates to the 9th century. This area is also the site of the **Peer Gynt Road,** of Ibsen fame, and the mountainous region is home to numerous ski resorts.

SOUTHERN NORWAY Southern Norway is sometimes referred to as "the Riviera" because of its unspoiled and uncrowded—but chilly—beaches. It's also a favorite port of call for the yachting crowd. **Stavanger,** the oil capital of Norway, is the largest southern city and also quite popular. There is much to explore in this Telemark region, which is filled with lakes and canals popular for summer canoeing and boating. **Skien,** birthplace of the playwright Henrik Ibsen (1828–1906), is primarily an industrial town. In Skien, you can board a lake steamer to travel through a series of canals. The southern part of **Kristiansand** links Norway with continental Europe. Close by is 10km (6-mile) **Hamresanden Beach,** one of the longest uninterrupted beaches in Europe. Along the western half of the district are more fjords, notably the Lysefjord, Sandefjord, and Vindefjord.

NORTHERN NORWAY The "Land of the Midnight Sun" is a region of craggy cliffs that descend to the sea and of deep, fertile valleys along the deserted moors. It has islands with few, if any, inhabitants, where life has remained relatively unchanged for generations. The capital of the Nordland region is **Bodø,** which lies just north of the Arctic Circle; it's a base for Arctic fishing trips and visits to the wild Glomfjord. Norway's second-largest glacier, **Svartisen,** is also in this region, as is the city of **Narvik,** a major Arctic port and the gateway to the **Lofoten Islands.** The islands, which have many fishing villages, make up one of the most beautiful areas of Norway. Visitors come here from all over the world for sport fishing and bird-watching.

TROMS The main city in this region is **Tromsø,** from which polar explorations launch. A key attraction is the world's northernmost planetarium. Troms contains one of Norway's most impressive mountain ranges, the Lyngs Alps, which attract winter skiers and summer hikers. **Alta,** site of the Altafjord, is reputed to have the best salmon-fishing waters in the world.

FINNMARK At the top of Norway is the Finnmark region, home of the Lapps (or Samis). Settlements here include **Kautokeino** (the Lapp town) and **Hammerfest,** the world's northernmost town. Most tourists come to Finnmark to see the **North Cape,** Europe's northernmost point and an ideal midnight-sun viewing spot. **Vardø** is the only Norwegian mainland town in the Arctic climate zone. In the 17th century it was the site of more than 80 witch burnings. The town of **Kirkenes** lies 274km (170 miles) north of the Arctic Circle, close to the Russian border.

2 Visitor Information

TOURISM BOARDS

In the **United States,** contact the **Norwegian Tourist Board,** 655 Third Ave., Suite 1810, New York, NY 10017 (© **212/885-9700**), at least 3 months in advance for maps, sightseeing pointers, ferry schedules, and other information.

In the **United Kingdom,** contact the **Norwegian Tourist Board,** a division of the Scandinavian Tourist Board, Charles House, 5 Lower Regent St., London SW1Y 4LR (© **0906/302-2003**).

You might also try the tourist board's official website: **www.visit norway.com**.

TRAVEL AGENTS

If you get in touch with a travel agent, make sure the agent is a member of the American Society of Travel Agents (ASTA). If a problem arises, you can complain to the Consumer Affairs Department of the society at 1101 King St., Alexandria, VA 22314 (© 703/706-0387; www.astanet.com).

ENTRY REQUIREMENTS

Citizens of the United States, Canada, Ireland, Australia, and New Zealand, and British subjects, need a valid **passport** to enter Norway. You need to apply for a visa only if you want to stay more than 3 months. A British Visitor's Passport is also valid for holidays and some business trips of less than 3 months. The passport can include your spouse, and it's valid for 1 year. Apply in person at a main post office in the British Isles, and the passport will be issued that day.

Your current domestic **driver's license** is acceptable in Norway. An international driver's license is not required.

3 Money

For a general discussion of changing money, using credit and charge cards, and other money matters, see "Money," in chapter 2.

CURRENCY   The Norwegian currency is the **krone** (plural: **kroner**), written as "NOK." There are 100 **øre** in 1 krone. Bank notes are issued in denominations of 50, 100, 200, 500, and 1,000 kroner. Coins are issued in denominations of 50 øre, 1 krone, and 5, 10, and 20 kroner.

4 When to Go

CLIMATE

In the summer, the average temperature in Norway ranges from 57°F (14°C) to 65°F (18°C). In January, it hovers around 27°F (–3°C), ideal for winter sports. The Gulf Stream warms the west coast, where winters tend to be temperate. Rainfall, however, is heavy.

Above the Arctic Circle, the sun shines night and day from mid-May until late July. For about 2 months every winter, the North Cape is plunged into darkness.

Norway's Average Daytime Temperatures

		Jan	Feb	Mar	Apr	May	June	July	Aug	Sept	Oct	Nov	Dec
Oslo	°F	25	26	32	41	51	60	64	61	53	42	33	27
	°C	–4	–3	0	5	11	16	18	16	12	6	1	–3
Bergen/Stavanger	°F	35	35	38	41	40	55	59	58	54	47	42	38
	°C	2	2	3	5	4	13	15	14	12	8	6	3
Trondheim	°F	27	27	31	38	47	53	58	57	50	42	35	31
	°C	–3	–3	–1	3	8	12	14	14	10	6	2	–1

THE MIDNIGHT SUN   In the summer, the sun never fully sets in northern Norway, and even in the south, the sun may set around 11pm and rise at 3am.

The best vantage points and dates for seeing the spectacle of the midnight sun are the **North Cape,** from May 12 to August 1; **Hammerfest,** from May 14 to July 30; **Tromsø,** from May 19 to

The Norwegian Krone

For American Readers   At this writing, $1 = approximately 7.5 kroner
(or 1 krone = approximately 13 US¢); this was the rate of exchange used to
calculate the dollar values given throughout this edition. Bear in mind that
throughout the context of this book, dollar amounts less than $10 are
rounded to the nearest nickel, and dollar amounts greater than $10 are
rounded to the nearest dollar.

For British Readers   At this writing, £1 = approximately 11.5 kroner (or
1 krone = approximately 8.7 pence). This was the rate of exchange used to
calculate the pound values in the table below.

Regarding the Euro   At the time of this writing, the U.S. dollar and the
euro traded almost on par (i.e., $1 approximately equals 1€). But that rela-
tionship can and probably will change during the lifetime of this edition.
For more exact ratios between these and other currencies, check an up-to-
date source at the time of your arrival in Norway.

NOK	US$	UK£	Euro	NOK	US$	UK£	Euro
1	0.13	0.09	0.13	75	9.98	6.53	9.98
2	0.27	0.17	0.27	100	13.30	8.70	13.30
3	0.40	0.26	0.40	125	16.63	10.88	16.63
4	0.53	0.35	0.53	150	19.95	13.05	19.95
5	0.67	0.44	0.67	175	23.28	15.23	23.28
6	0.80	0.52	0.80	200	26.60	17.40	26.60
7	0.93	0.61	0.93	225	29.93	19.58	29.93
8	1.06	0.70	1.06	250	33.25	21.75	33.25
9	1.20	0.78	1.20	275	36.58	23.93	36.58
10	1.33	0.87	1.33	300	39.90	26.10	39.90
15	2.00	1.31	2.00	350	46.55	30.45	46.55
20	2.66	1.74	2.66	400	53.20	34.80	53.20
25	3.33	2.18	3.33	500	66.50	43.50	66.50
50	6.65	4.35	6.65	1,000	133.00	87.00	133.00

July 26; **Lofoten Islands,** from May
23 to July 17; and **Harstad,** from May
23 to July 22. All are accessible by
public transportation. Keep in mind
that although the sun shines at midnight, it's not as strong as at midday.
Bring a warm jacket or sweater.

HOLIDAYS

Norway celebrates the following pub-
lic holidays: New Year's Day (Jan 1),
Maundy Thursday, Good Friday,
Easter, Labor Day (May 1), Ascension
Day (mid-May), Independence Day
(May 17), Whitmonday (late May),

Christmas (Dec 25), and Boxing Day
(Dec 26).

NORWAY CALENDAR OF EVENTS

Specific dates are for 2003; others are
approximate. Check with the local tourist
office before making plans to attend a specific event, especially in 2004.

January

Northern Lights Festival, Tromsø.
Classical and contemporary music
are performed by musicians from
Norway and abroad. For informtion,

What Things Cost in Oslo	US$
Taxi from Gardermoen Airport to the city center	67.00
Bus from Gardermoen Airport to the city center	15.00
Local telephone call	.65
Double room at the Grand Hotel (very expensive)	257.00
Double room at the Tulip Inn Rainbow Cecil (moderate)	182.00
Double room at the Cochs Pensjonat (inexpensive)	80.00
Lunch for one at the Primo Restaurant Ciaou-Ciaou (moderate)	34.00
Lunch for one at Mamma Rosa (inexpensive)	26.00
Dinner for one, without wine, at Babette's Gjestehus (expensive)	66.00
Dinner for one, without wine, at Lipp (moderate)	40.00
Dinner for one, without wine, at Friskport Vegeta Vertshus (inexpensive)	19.00
Pint of beer (draft Pilsner)	6.00
Coca-Cola (in a restaurant)	3.20
Cup of coffee	2.95
Admission to Viking Ship Museum	5.30
Movie ticket	10.00
Theater ticket (at National Theater)	20.00–29.00

check www.nordlysfestivalen.no. Late January.

February

Kristiansund Opera Festival. The festival features Kristiansund Opera's productions of opera and ballet, plus art exhibitions, concerts, and other events. For details, see www.oik.no. Early February.

March

Holmenkollen Ski Festival, Oslo. This is one of Europe's largest ski festivals, with World Cup Nordic skiing and biathlons, international ski-jumping competitions, and Norway's largest cross-country race for amateurs. Held at Holmenkollen Ski Jump on the outskirts of Oslo. To participate, attend, or request more information, contact Skiforeningen, Kongeveien 5, Holmenkollen, N-0390 Oslo 3 (© **22-92-32-00;** www.skiforeningen.no). March 6 to March 9.

Narvik Winter Festival. Sports events, carnivals, concerts, and opera performances highlight this festival dedicated to those who built the railway across northern Norway and Sweden. For information go to www.vinterfestuka.no. Second week of March to mid-April.

Birkebeiner Race, Rena to Lillehammer. This historic international ski race, with thousands of participants, crosses the mountains between Rena and Lillehammer, site of the 1994 Olympics. It's a 53km (33-mile) cross-country trek. For details, phone © **61-27-58-00;** or go to www.birkebeiner.no. March 21.

April

Vossa Jazz Festival. Three days of jazz and folk music performances are presented by European and American artists. For details, go to www.vossajazz.no. First week of April.

May

The Grete Waitz Run, Oslo. This women's run through the streets of Oslo includes participation by the famous marathoner Grete Waitz. For details, phone ℭ **23-21-55-00;** or go to www.gwl.no. May 2.

The Viking Run, Sognefjord. An international half-marathon is staged in the Sognefjord. Some participants extend their stay to participate in other sports, such as summer skiing, glacier climbing, biking, boating, or mountain climbing. For more information, call ℭ **55-55-20-00.** Late May.

Bergen International Festival (Bergen Festspill). This world-class music event features artists from Norway and around the world. Many styles of music are presented, but classical music—especially the work of Grieg—is emphasized. This is one of the largest annual musical events in Scandinavia. It's held at various venues in Bergen. For information, contact the Bergen International Festival, Slottsgaten 1, 4055, Dregen N-5835 Bergen (ℭ **55-21-06-30**). May 21 to June 1.

June

Faerder Sailing Race. Some 1,000 sailboats participate in this race, which ends in Borre, by the Oslofjord. Call ℭ **23-11-78-80** for more information. First week of June.

North Cape March. This trek from Honningsvåg to the North Cape is one of the world's toughest. The round-trip march is 68km (42 miles). For more information, see www.visitnorthcape.com. Mid-June.

Emigration Festival, Stavanger. This commemoration of Norwegian immigration to North America features exhibitions, concerts, theater, and folklore. For more information, call ℭ **51-85-92-00.** Mid-June.

Midsummer Night, nationwide. Celebrations and bonfires are held all over Norway. June 23.

Emigration Festival, Kvinesdal. Norwegian immigration to the United States is commemorated. Call ℭ **71-58-54-54** for more information. Late June to early July.

July

Kongsberg International Jazz Festival. International artists participate in one of the most important jazz festivals in Scandinavia, with open-air concerts. Call ℭ **32-73-31-66** or check out www.kongsberg-jazzfestival.no. July 1 to July 4.

Midnight Sun Marathon, Tromsø. The marathon in northern Norway starts at midnight. Contact them at ℭ **77-69-61-24** or www.msm.no. July 4.

Exxon Mobil Bislett Games, Oslo. International athletic competitions are staged in Oslo, with professional participants from all over the world. Call ℭ **22-59-17-59;** or go to www.bislettgames.com. July 15.

Molde International Jazz Festival. The "City of Roses" is the site of Norway's oldest jazz festival. It attracts international stars from both sides of the Atlantic every year. It's held at venues in Molde for 6 days. For details, contact the Molde Jazz Festival, Box 271, N-6401 Molde (ℭ **71-21-60-00;** www.moldejazz.no). Mid-July.

Norway Cup International Youth Soccer Tournament, Oslo. The world's largest youth soccer tournament attracts 1,000 teams from around the world to Oslo. Call ℭ **22-28-90-57** or visit www.Norway-cup.no. Last week of July.

August

International Folk Music Festival, Bø. An international festival of folk music and folk dance takes place in the home of many famous fiddlers, dancers, and singers. July 30 to August 2.

Peer Gynt Festival, Vinstra. Art exhibitions, evenings of music and song, parades in national costumes, and other events honor Ibsen's fictional character. Phone © **61-29-47-70** or go to www.peergynt.no. July 31 to August 8.

Oslo Jazz Festival. This annual festival features music from the earliest years of jazz (1920–25), as well as classical concerts, opera, and ballet. Call © **22-42-91-20,** or go to www.oslojazz.no. First week of August.

Chamber Music Festival, Oslo. Norwegian and foreign musicians perform at Oslo's Akershus Castle and Fortress, which dates from A.D. 1300. Phone © **23-10-07-30;** or visit www.oslokammermusikk festival.no. Second week of August.

World Cup Summer Ski Jumping, Marikollen. Takes place in Marikollen, Raelingen, just outside

the center of Oslo. For more information, call © **23-11-78-80.** Mid-August.

September
International Salmon Fishing Festival, Suldal. Participants come from Norway and abroad to the Suldalslagen River outside Stavanger in western Norway. Check out www.vestkysten.no. Dates vary.

Oslo Marathon. This annual event draws some of Norway's best long-distance runners. Call © **23-11-78-80** for information. Mid-September.

December
Nobel Peace Prize Ceremony, Oslo. This major event on the Oslo calendar attracts world attention. It's held at Oslo City Hall on December 10. Attendance is by invitation only. For information, contact the Nobel Institute, Drammensveien 19, N-0255 Oslo 2 (© **22-44-36-80;** www.nobel.se).

5 The Active Vacation Planner

BICYCLING   Bikes can be rented in just about every town in Norway. Inquire at your hotel or the local tourist office. The Norwegian Mountain Touring Association (see "Hiking," below) provides inexpensive lodging for those who take overnight bike trips. For suggestions on tours, maps, and brochures, contact **Den Rustne Eike,** Vestbaneplassen 2, N-0458 Oslo (© **22-83-52-08**). The only large bike-rental firm in Oslo, it can arrange guided tours in the Oslo area and elsewhere in Norway. Tours last 3 hours to 14 days.

BIRD-WATCHING   Some of Europe's noteworthy bird sanctuaries are on islands off the Norwegian coast or on the mainland. Rocky and isolated, the sanctuaries offer ideal nesting places for millions of seabirds that vastly outnumber the local human

population during certain seasons. Foremost among the sanctuaries are the **Lofoten Islands**—particularly two of the outermost islands, Vaerøy and Røst—and the island of Runde. A .40km (¼-mile) bridge (one of the longest in Norway) connects **Runde** to the coastline, a 2½-hour drive from Ålesund. Runde's year-round human population is about 150, and the colonies of puffins, cormorants, razor-billed auks, guillemots, gulls, and eider ducks number in the millions. Another noteworthy bird sanctuary is at **Fokstumyra,** a national park near Dombås.

The isolated island of **Lovund** is a 2-hour ferry ride from the town of Sandnesjøen, south of Bødo. Lovund ("the island of puffins") has a human population of fewer than 270 and a bird population in the hundreds of thousands. You can visit Lovund and the other famous Norwegian bird-watching sites on your own, or sign up for one of the organized bird-watching tours sponsored by such highly recommended companies as **Borton Overseas,** 5412 Lyndale Ave., Minneapolis, MN 55419 (© **800/843-0602** or 612/882-4640; www.bortonoverseas.com).

Brochures and pamphlets are available from the tourist board **Destination Lofoten** (© **76-07-30-00**).

FISHING Norway has long been famous for its salmon and trout fishing. The best months for salmon are June and July, and the season extends into August. Sea trout fishing takes place from June to September, and is best in August. The brown trout season varies with altitude.

Fishing in the ocean is free. To fish in lakes, rivers, or streams, anyone over 16 must have a fishing license. A license to fish in a lake costs from 90NOK ($12); or in a river, 180NOK ($24). National fishing licenses can be purchased at local post offices. For more information, contact the **Bergen Angling Association,** Fosswinckelsgata 37, Bergen (© **55-32-11-64**).

One company that arranges fishing tours in Norway is **Passage Tours of Scandinavia,** 239 Commercial Blvd., Fort Lauderdale, FL 33308 (© **800/ 548-5960** in the U.S., or 954/ 776-7070; www.passagetours.com).

A U.S.-based company that can arrange fishing (as well as hunting) excursions anywhere within Norway and the rest of Scandinavia is **Five Stars of Scandinavia,** 13104 Thomas Rd., KPN, Gig Harbor, WA 98329 (© **800/722-4126;** www.5stars-of-scandinavia.com). For a truly unusual fishing experience, consider their ability to arrange rentals of old-fashioned fishermen's cottages in the isolated Lofoten Islands. The rustic-looking, fully renovated cottages each

lie adjacent to the sea, and evoke 19th-century isolation in a way that you'll find either wondrous or terrifying, depending on your point of view. Five Stars will rent you a cottage for as short a period as 1 night, although we recommend a minimum stay of 3 nights to best appreciate this offbeat adventure. Rentals include bed linens.

One of the most qualified fishing outfitters in Bergen spends part of its time delivering food, tools, and spare parts to the thousands of fishermen who make their living in boats and isolated fjords along the western coast of Norway. **Camperlan,** P.O. Box 11, Strandkaien 2, N-5083 Bergen (© **55-32-34-72;** www.camperlan.no) and its president and founder, Capt. Dag Varlo, will take between two and four passengers out for deep-sea fishing excursions in the teeming seas off the country's western coast. Although his boats go out in all seasons, midsummer is the most appealing, because of the extended daylight hours. Most avidly pursued are codfish, valued as a "good-eating" fish, and a local species known as *saet,* prized for its fighting properties as a game fish. (They range anywhere from 1.5kg–10kg/3lb.–22 lb. each.) A full-day's fishing excursion, with all equipment included, for up to six passengers, costs 6,000NOK ($798). In midsummer, full-day excursions depart from Bergen's harbor, and are usually scheduled from 9am to around 5pm.

GOLFING Many golf clubs are open to foreign guests. Greens fees tend to be moderate. Clubs include the **Oslo Golf Klubb** (18 holes), at Bogstad, Oslo (© **22-50-44-02**), and the 18-hole **Meland Golf Club,** Meland/Frekhaug, 36km (22 miles) north of Bergen (© **56-17-46-00**).

HIKING The mountains and wilderness make hiking a favorite pastime. The **Norwegian Mountain Touring Association,** Storgata 3,

N-0101 Oslo 1 (℃ **22-82-28-22;** www.dntoa.no), offers guided hikes that last 5 to 8 days. They cost $415 to $520, including meals and lodging.

HORSEBACK RIDING Many organizations offer horseback tours of Norway's wilderness, enabling visitors to see some of the more spectacular scenery. Tours can range from a few hours to a full week, and they're available all over the country. Luggage is transported by car. One tour organizer is **Borton Overseas,** 5412 Lyndale Ave., Minneapolis, MN 55419 (℃ **800/843-0602** or 612/882-4640; www.bortonoverseas.com).

SAILING Norway's long coast can be a challenge to any yachting enthusiast. The most tranquil havens are along the southern coast. To arrange rafting or boat trips, along with boat rentals and evening parasailing, call **SeaAction** at ℃ **90-58-43-00** or 33-33-69-93; www.seaaction.com.

SCUBA DIVING Excellent diving centers provide scuba-diving trips and instruction. Divers who enjoy harpooning often catch their own dinners, with many kinds of fish to choose from. The conditions for submarine photography are generally good, with underwater visibility of 9m to 30m (30ft.–100 ft.). There are a number of shipwrecks along Norway's extensive coastline and fjords. Diving information is available from **Dykkernett** at ℃ 22-54-78-02; www.dykkernett.no.

SKIING Norway's skiing terrain is world class. The optimum season is February and March (the first half of Apr also tends to be good). Two of the principal resorts, **Geilo** and **Voss,** lie on the Oslo–Bergen rail line. The most famous and easily accessible resort is **Lillehammer,** north of Oslo. In and around the Norwegian capital skiing is common; the famous ski jump, **Holmenkollen,** with its

companion ski museum, is minutes from the heart of Oslo. Its yearly ski championship attracts ace skiers from all over Europe and North America every March.

Norwegian ski resorts are known for their informality, which is evident in the schools and the atmosphere. The emphasis is on simple pleasures, not the sophistication often found at alpine resorts. (Incidentally, the word *ski* is an Old Norse word, as is *slalom.*)

Much of Norwegian skiing is cross-country—perfect for the amateur—and there are lots of opportunities for downhill skiing. Other winter sports include curling, sleigh rides, and skating. All major centers have ski lifts, and renting equipment in Norway is much cheaper than in some luxury resorts.

Norway also offers summer skiing, both downhill and cross-country, at summer ski centers near glaciers. You can get more information from the **Galdhø-piggen Sommerskisenter,** N-2687 Bøverdalen (℃ **61-21-17-50**), and the **Stryn Sommerskisenter,** N-6880 Stryn (℃ **57-87-40-40**).

WHALE-WATCHING In Norway you can catch a glimpse of 19m (65-ft.) long, 39,600-kilogram (88,000-lb.) sperm whales, the largest toothed whales in the world. You can also see killer whales, harbor porpoises, minke whales, and white-beaked dolphins. Whale researchers conduct 6-hour whale-watching tours in the Arctic Ocean.

For information and bookings, contact **Passage Tours of Scandinavia,** 239 Commercial Blvd., Fort Lauderdale, FL 33308 (℃ **800/ 548-5960** or 954/776-7070). Whale-watching in the Lofoten Islands can be arranged by **Borton Overseas,** 5412 Lyndale Ave., Minneapolis, MN 55419 (℃ **800/843-0602** or 612/ 882-4640; www.bortonoverseas.com).

Tracing Your Norwegian Roots

If you're of Norwegian ancestry, you can get information on how to trace your family from the nearest Norwegian consulate. In Norway, contact the **Norwegian Emigration Center,** Strandkaien 31, N-4005 Stavanger (✆ **51-53-88-60;** www.emigrationcenter.com), for a catalog of information about Norwegian families who emigrated to the United States.

In the United States, the **Family History Library of the Church of Jesus Christ of Latter-day Saints,** 35 N. West Temple, Salt Lake City, UT 84150 (✆ **801/240-2331**), has extensive records of Norwegian families who emigrated to the United States and Canada. The library is open to the public without charge for genealogical research. Mormon churches in other cities have listings of materials available in Salt Lake City; for a small fee you can request pertinent microfilms, which you can view at a local church.

6 Health & Insurance

For a general discussion of health and insurance, see "Health & Insurance" in chapter 2.

Put your essential medicines in your carry-on luggage and bring enough prescription medications to last through your stay. In Norway, pharmacists cannot legally honor a prescription written outside the country; if you need more of your medications, you'll have to see a doctor and have a new prescription written.

Norway's national health plan does not cover American or Canadian visitors. Medical expenses must be paid in cash. Medical costs are generally more reasonable than elsewhere in Western Europe.

7 Tips for Travelers with Special Needs

A number of resources and organizations in North America and Britain can assist travelers with special needs in trip planning. For details, see "Tips for Travelers with Special Needs" in chapter 2.

FOR TRAVELERS WITH DIS-ABILITIES Scandinavian countries have been in the vanguard of providing services for people with disabilities. In general, trains, airlines, ferries, and department stores and malls are accessible. For information about wheelchair access, ferry and air travel, parking, and other matters, contact the Norwegian Tourist Board (see "Visitor Information," above).

The **Norwegian Association of the Disabled,** Schweigaardsgt no. 12, 9217 Grænland, 0312 Oslo (✆ **22-17-02-55;** www.nhf.no), provides useful information.

FOR GAY & LESBIAN TRAVEL-ERS Call **Gay/Lesbian Visitor Information,** St. Olavs Plass 2, N-0165 Oslo (✆ **22-11-05-09**). An English-speaking representative will give you up-to-date information on gay and lesbian life in Oslo and let you know which clubs are currently in vogue. In Norway, gays and lesbians have the same legal status as heterosexuals, with the exception of adoption rights. Legislation passed in 1981

protects gays and lesbians from dis-
crimination. In 1993, a law was passed
recognizing the "partnerships" of
homosexual couples—in essence, a
recognition of same-sex marriages.

The age of consent for both men and
women in Norway is 16 years of age.

FOR SENIORS   People over 67 are
entitled to 50% off the price of first-
and second-class train tickets. Ask for
the discount at the ticket office.

8 Getting There

BY PLANE

For a more complete discussion of
plane travel options, see "Getting
There," in chapter 2.

All transatlantic flights from North
America land at Oslo's Fornebu Airport. **SAS** (© **800/221-2350** in the
U.S.; www.Scandinavia.net) flies nonstop daily from Newark to Oslo. The
trip takes about 7½ hours. Most other
SAS flights from North America go
through Copenhagen. Flying time
from Chicago is 10¾ hours; from
Seattle, 11¾ hours, not including the
layover in Copenhagen.

Prices for flights to Denmark (see
chapter 2) are similar to those for
flights to Oslo and Bergen. Transatlantic passengers on SAS are occasionally allowed to transfer to a Norwegian
domestic flight from Oslo to Bergen
for no additional charge.

If you fly to Norway on another airline, you'll be routed through a gateway
city in Europe, and sometimes continue on a different airline. **British Airways** (© **800/AIRWAYS** in the U.S.),
for example, has dozens of daily flights
from many North American cities to
London, and you can continue to Oslo.
Icelandair (© **800/223-5500** in the
U.S.; www.icelandair.com) can be an
excellent choice, with connections
through Reykjavik. **KLM** (© **800/
347-7747** in the U.S.; www.nwa.com)
serves Oslo through Amsterdam.

For passengers from the U.K.,
British Airways (© **08457/733-377**
in London) operates at least four daily
nonstops to Oslo from London. **SAS**
(© **020/8990-7159** in London) runs
four daily flights from Heathrow to

Oslo. Flying time from London to
Oslo on any airline is around 2 hours.

BY CAR

If you're driving from the Continent,
you must go through Sweden. From
Copenhagen, take the E47/55 express
highway north to Helsingør and catch
the car ferry to Helsingborg, Sweden.
From there, E6 runs to Oslo. From
Stockholm, drive across Sweden on
E18 to Oslo.

BY TRAIN

Copenhagen is the main rail hub for
service between Scandinavia and the
rest of Europe. There are three daily
trains from Copenhagen to Oslo, seven
from Copenhagen to Stockholm, and
six from Copenhagen to Gothenburg.
All connect with the Danish ferries
operating either to Norway through
Helsingør or Hirtshals, or to Sweden
via Helsingør or Frederikshavn.

Most rail traffic from Sweden into
Norway follows the main corridors
between Stockholm and Oslo and
between Gothenburg and Oslo.

For information on rail passes,
please refer to "Getting There" in
chapter 2.

BY SHIP & FERRY

FROM DENMARK   The trip from
Frederikshavn at the northern port of
Jutland in Denmark to Oslo takes 11
hours. **Stena Line** (© **08705/707-
070** for general reservations 24 hr.)
operates the service.

FROM SWEDEN   From Strømstad, Sweden, in the summer, the daily
crossing to Sandefjord, Norway, takes
2½ hours. Bookings can be made

through **Color Scandi Line,** Tollbugata 5, N-3210 Sandefjord (© **33-42-10-00**).

FROM ENGLAND The **Norwegian Coastal Voyages/Bergen Line,** 405 Fifth Ave., New York, NY 10022 (© **800/323-7436** in the U.S., or 212/319-1300; www.coastalvoyage.com), operates from Newcastle, England, to Stavanger and Bergen on the west coast of Norway.

BY CRUISE SHIP

Norway's fjords and mountain vistas are among the most spectacular panorama in the world. Many ship owners and cruise lines offer excursions along the Norwegian coast.

One of the most prominent lines is **Cunard** (© **800/528-6273** in the U.S. and Canada; www.cunard.com).

Readers using this guide in 2004 will be able to sail on 14-day cruises on the new Cunard flagship, *Queen Mary 2. Queen Mary 2* re-creates the grandeur of those old Queen liners, *Queen Mary* and *Queen Elizabeth,* but overall is more modern and larger. The 150,000-ton ship carries a total of 2,620 passengers.

Departing from Southampton, England, the ship calls at Oslo, Bergen, Trondheim, the offshore island of Spitzbergen, Stavanger, and the North Cape; en route it also stops at the most frequently visited fjords. Prices for the 5-day cruise include round-trip airfare to London on British Airways from 79 gateway cities throughout the world.

Cunard also maintains about half a dozen smaller ships; one of the most luxurious specializes in cruises through the Baltic Sea and along the coast of Norway. The 677-passenger *Caronia* offers cruises throughout the summer from Southampton, England, that travel as far north as Norway's North Cape and as far east as St. Petersburg, Russia. Cruises last 13 to 21 days and include round-trip airfare on British Airways from most cities along the eastern seaboard of North America. Transportation from the U.S. West Coast can be arranged for a reasonable supplement. Hotel or theater packages in London or side trips to almost anywhere else in Europe can be arranged through Cunard and British Airways at favorable discounts.

The Bergen Line offers much less expensive cruises aboard steamer ships that also carry mail and supplies to fjord communities. For more information, see "By Coastal Steamer" in "Getting Around," below, and in chapter 10, "Exploring the Norwegian Coast."

9 Getting Around

BY PLANE

The best way to get around Scandinavia is to take advantage of air passes that apply to the whole region. If you're traveling extensively in Europe, special European passes are available. For information on **SAS's Visit Scandinavia Fare,** see "By Plane" under "Getting Around" in chapter 2.

WITHIN NORWAY Norway has excellent air service. In addition to SAS, two independent airways, Braathens and Wideroe Flyveselskap, provide quick and convenient ways to get around this large country with many hard-to-reach areas. All three airlines offer reduced rates available when booked outside Norway, known as "minifares."

BRAATHENS In a new partnership with **SAS,** Braathens (© **67-12-20-70** in Oslo or 55-23-55-23 in Bergen; www.braathens.no) carries more passengers on domestic routes than any other airline in Norway. It has regularly scheduled flights inside Norway, linking major cities as well as more remote places not covered by other airlines. Its air routes directly link Oslo with all major Norwegian cities; it also offers frequent flights along the coast, from Oslo to Tromsø and to Longyearbyen on the island of Spitsbergen.

You might also inquire about the **Northern Light Pass,** which provides discounts and is valid for 1 month between May and September. There are two sets of fares. Flights between airports in north Norway are short journeys, and the one-way fare for pass-holders is $84. Flights from south Norway to north Norway or vice versa count as long journeys, and the one-way fare is $155. The Visit Norway Pass is sold by airlines that have agreements with Braathens airlines. To buy one, call **Passage Tours of Scandinavia** (© **800/548-5960** in the U.S.) or **SAS** (© **800/221-2350** in the U.S.).

SAS   Regularly scheduled domestic flights on SAS (© **800/221-2350** in the U.S., or 81-00-33-00 in Oslo) crisscross Norway. They connect Bergen, Oslo, Trondheim, and Bodø. SAS also flies to the Arctic gateway of Tromsø; to Alta in Finnmark, the heart of Lapland; and to Kirkenes, near the Russian border. Transatlantic SAS passengers might also consider SAS's Visit Scandinavia Fare (see "By Plane" under "Getting Around," in chapter 2).

OTHER AIRLINES   Linked to the SAS reservations network, **Wideroe** specializes in STOL (short takeoff and landing) aircraft. It services rarely visited fishing communities on offshore islands, isolated fjord communities, and destinations north of the Arctic Circle. For more information or tickets, contact SAS or local travel agents in Norway.

BY TRAIN

Norway's network of electric and diesel-electric trains runs as far as Bodø, 100km (62 miles) north of the Arctic Circle. (Beyond that, visitors must take a coastal steamer, plane, or bus to Tromsø and the North Cape.) Recently upgraded express trains (the fastest in the country) crisscross the mountainous terrain between Oslo, Stavanger, Bergen, and Trondheim.

The most popular, and the most scenic, run covers the 480km (300 miles) between Oslo and Bergen. Visitors with limited time often choose this route for its fabled mountains, gorges, white-water rivers, and fjords. The trains often stop for passengers to enjoy breathtaking views.

Second-class travel on Norwegian trains is recommended. In fact, second class in Norway is as good as or better than first-class travel anywhere else in Europe, with reclining seats and lots of unexpected comforts. The one-way second-class fare from Oslo to Bergen is 633NOK ($84), plus a mandatory seat reservation of 20NOK ($2.65). Another popular run, from Oslo to Trondheim, costs 707NOK ($94) one-way in second class.

One of the country's most scenic trips, from Bergen to Bodø, is not possible by train because of the terrain. Trains to Bodø leave from Oslo. Express trains are called *Expresstog,* and you have to read the fine print of a railway schedule to figure out whether an Expresstog is much faster than a conventional train.

On express and other major trains, you must reserve seats at the train's starting station. Sleepers are priced according to the number of berths in each compartment. Children 4 to 15 years of age and seniors pay 50% of the regular adult fare. Group and midweek tickets are also available.

There are special compartments for persons with disabilities on most medium- and long-distance trains. People in wheelchairs or with disabilities, and their companions, may use the compartments. Some long-distance trains offer special playrooms

("Kiddie-Wagons") for children, complete with toys and educational items.

NORWAY RAIL PASS   A restricted rail pass applicable only to the state railway lines, the Norway Rail Pass is available for 7 or 14 consecutive days of unlimited rail travel in 1 month, or any 3 days of travel within 1 month. It's suitable for anyone who wants to cover the long distances that separate Norwegian cities. The costs are $190 for adults in first class or $146 in second class for any 3 days in 1 month; $236 in first class or $182 in second class for any 4 days in 1 month; and $264 in first class or $202 in second class for any 5 days in 1 month. Children 4 to 15 years of age pay half the adult fare. Those under 4 ride free.

OTHER SPECIAL TICKETS & DISCOUNTS   With a **Miniprice Ticket** you can travel in second class for 360NOK ($48) one-way, but only on routes that take you more than 150km (93 miles) from your point of origin. No stopovers are allowed except for a change of trains. Tickets are valid only on selected trains, for boarding that begins during designated off-peak hours. You can buy Miniprice Tickets at any railway station in Norway.

Travelers over age 67 are entitled to a 50% discount, called an **Honnorrabatt,** on Norwegian train trips of more than 50km (31 miles). Regardless of age, the spouse of someone over 67 can also receive the 50% discount.

BY BUS

Where the train or coastal steamer stops, passengers can usually continue on a scenic bus ride. Norway's bus system is excellent, linking remote villages along the fjords. Numerous all-inclusive motor-coach tours, often combined with steamer travel, leave from Bergen and Oslo in the summer. The train ends in Bodø; from there you can get a bus to Fauske (63km/39 miles east). From Fauske, the Polar

Express bus spans the entire distance along the Arctic Highway, through Finnmark (Lapland) to Kirkenes near the Russian border and back. The segment from Alta to Kirkenes is open only from June to October, but there's year-round service from Fauske to Alta. Passengers are guaranteed hotel accommodations along the way.

Buses have air-conditioning, toilets, adjustable seats, reading lights, and a telephone. Reservations are not accepted on most buses, and payment is made to the driver on board. Fares depend on the distance traveled. Children under 4 travel free, and children 4 to 16 and seniors pay half price. For the Oslo–Sweden–Hammerfest "Express 2000," a 30-hour trip, reservations must be made in advance.

For more information about bus travel in Norway, contact **Norway Buss Ekspress AS,** Karl Johans Gate (© 81-54-44-44; www.nor-way.no) in Oslo, or **Passage Tours of Scandinavia** (© 800/548-5960 in the U.S.).

BY CAR & FERRY

Dazzling scenery awaits you at nearly every turn. Some roads are less than perfect (often dirt or gravel), but passable. Most mountain roads are open by May 1; the so-called motoring season lasts from mid-May to the end of September. In western Norway hairpin curves are common, but if you're willing to settle for doing less than 250km (155 miles) a day, you needn't worry. The easiest and most convenient touring territory is in and around Oslo and south to Stavanger. However, you can drive to the North Cape.

Bringing a car into Norway is relatively uncomplicated. If you own the car you're driving, you must present your national driver's license, car registration, and proof that the car is insured. (This proof usually takes the form of a document known as a "Green Card," which customs agents will refer to specifically.) If you've rented a car in another country and want to drive it into Norway, be sure to verify at the time of rental that the registration and insurance documents are in order—they probably will be. Regardless of whether you own or rent the car you're about to drive into Norway, don't assume that your private North American insurance policy will automatically apply. Chances are good that it will, but in the event of an accident, you may have to cope with a burdensome amount of paperwork.

If you're driving through any of Norway's coastal areas, you'll probably have to traverse one or many of the country's famous fjords. Although more and more bridges are being built, Norway's network of privately run ferries is essential for transporting cars across hundreds of fjords and estuaries. Motorists should ask the tourist bureau for the free map, "Norway by Car," and a timetable outlining the country's dozens of car ferry services. The cost for cars and passengers is low.

RENTALS Avis, Budget, and Hertz offer well-serviced, well-maintained fleets of rental cars. Prices and terms tend to be more favorable for those who reserve vehicles in North America before their departure and who present evidence of membership in such organizations as AAA or AARP. The major competitors' prices tend to be roughly equivalent, except for promotional deals scheduled from time to time.

The prices quoted here include the 23% government tax. Rates are always best when you pay for them before you leave home. At **Budget** (℃ **800/472-3325** in the U.S. and Canada), the cheapest car is a cramped but peppy Volkswagen Polo that rents for $569 a week with unlimited mileage. **Hertz** (℃ **800/654-3001** in the U.S.), charges $584 a week, with unlimited mileage, for its smallest car, a VW Polo. **Avis** (℃ **800/331-1084** in the U.S.) matches Hertz, charging

around $594 for its cheapest car, a Nissan Micra. Despite the pressure you may receive from the telephone sales representative, it pays to ask questions before you commit to a prepaid reservation. Each company maintains an office at the Oslo airport, in the center of Oslo, and at airports and city centers elsewhere around the country.

Note: Remember that prices and the relative merits of each company can and will change during the lifetime of this edition, depending on promotions and other factors.

An alternative to the big three companies is a small but reliable outfit called **Kemwel** (℃ **800/678-0678** in the U.S.). As part of a special promotion, Kemwel sometimes offers discounts to some SAS passengers.

INSURANCE Rates include nominal insurance coverage, which is probably enough for most drivers and most accidents. However, if you did not buy additional insurance and you have a mishap, your responsibility depends on the car-rental firm. At some companies, without additional insurance you might be held responsible for the car's full value. Obviously, you need to learn what your liability would be in case of an accident. To avoid this responsibility, you might want to get an additional insurance policy (a collision-damage waiver) for about $15 a day. We usually find that buying additional insurance is well worth the expense, considering the unfamiliar driving conditions.

Note that when certain credit or charge cards are used to pay for a car rental, no additional insurance purchases are necessary. Although many readers have taken advantage of this cost-saving approach, the fine print of these insurance options must be individually verified directly with the card issuer.

No matter what type of insurance you choose, remember that driving after having consumed even a small amount of alcohol is punishable by heavy fines, imprisonment, or both.

BY COASTAL STEAMER

The fjords of western Norway are among the most beautiful sights in Europe. For a view from the sea, nothing beats the indomitable steamer ships that carry mail, supplies, and passengers. If you have the time and enjoy offbeat adventures, you can book a 12-day, all-inclusive round-trip steamer trip from Bergen to Kirkenes (one of the northernmost ports). It covers some 4,000km (2,500 miles) of jagged, scenic coastline.

Because of the long distances, steamers are equipped with cabins similar to those on transatlantic liners. Depending on the accommodations and the time of year, cabins cost $981 to $1,340 per person, double occupancy, for the 12-day round-trip excursion. Because sailings in June,

July, and August are the most expensive, many visitors choose a spring or autumn trip. All meals are included in the price. Children under 12 receive a 25% discount on round-trip voyages. During special periods, travelers over age 67 may be eligible for discounts. Steamers make scheduled stops in hamlets and cities along the way, ranging from half an hour to half a day. Passengers who prefer to spend more time in selected cities usually choose port-to-port tickets, for which children under 12 receive a special rate. Be warned, however, that booking cabins on a port-to-port basis from May to August is often extremely difficult because of the popularity of these cruises. Cruises are available even in winter—the Norwegian coast is famous for remaining ice-free all year.

For reservations and information, contact the **Norwegian Coastal Voyages/Bergen Line,** 405 Park Ave., New York, NY 10022 (© **800/323-7436** or 212/319-1300 in the U.S.; www.coastalvoyage.com).

10 Organized Tours

One of the best ways to see Norway's wilderness is by organized tour. The following are a few of the wide variety that's available. Check with your travel agent for other options or a custom-designed tour. All prices in this section are per person with double occupancy.

Norway's brisk waters are known for the abundance and quality of their salmon, with a season lasting only from June 1 to August 31. The best salmon-fishing tours are arranged in central Norway, especially along the Guala River, one of the country's best-known salmon-fishing rivers. Week-

long fishing tours are offered in Trondheim by **Ursus Major** (© **99-22-49-60;** www.ursus-major.no), costing 15,730NOK to 22,750NOK ($2,092–$3,026) per person, including meals and accommodations.

In July and August, 7-day **bike trips** run through the Lofoten Islands. They offer moderately rolling terrain, dramatic scenery, traditional *rorbuer* (fishing cottage) lodging, and hearty regional cuisine. Prices begin at 15,000NOK ($2,000). Tours are offered by **Backroads** (© **800/GO-ACTIVE;** www.backroads.com).

11 Recommended Books

HISTORY & MYTHOLOGY *The Vikings,* by Johannes Brøndsted (Penguin), is one of the most enjoyable

and best-written documents of the age of the Vikings.

Quisling: A Study in Treason, by Oddvar K. Hoidal (Oxford University

Press), studies the world's most famous traitor, Quisling, who was executed by the Norwegians for running the Nazi puppet government there.

The Vinland Sagas: The Norse Discovery of America, was translated by Magnus Magnusson and Hermann Palsson (Penguin). Viking fans will not be able to put down this incredible chronicle, detailing how Norwegian Vikings sailed in their long ships to the eastern coast of "Vinland" (America) as early as the 10th century.

The Norwegians, by Arthur Spencer (David & Charles), is the best book on the market today for understanding the Norwegian people and their advanced society.

ADVENTURE   *The Kon-Tiki Expedition,* by Thor Heyerdahl (Washington Square Press), which was made into a film, details the saga of a modern Norwegian "Viking," who set out on a raft with five comrades and sailed 6,900km (4,300 miles) in 1947—all the way from Peru to Polynesia. *Kon-Tiki Man: An Illustrated Biography of Thor Heyerdahl,* by Thor Heyerdahl with Christopher Ralling (Chronicle), highlights Heyerdahl's attempt to document his idea that Polynesia was settled by people migrating west by water from South America rather than from Asia.

LITERATURE & THEATER   *The Governor's Daughter,* by Camilla Collett (several editions), published in 1854, is called the first modern Norwegian novel.

Ibsen Plays: One to Six, by Henrik Ibsen (Heinemann Educational), presents the works of Norway's greatest playwright, including *A Doll's House* and *Hedda Gabler.*

The Ferry Crossing, by Edvard Hoem (Garland), a success in 1989, depicts a tiny Norwegian coastal village in an unorthodox story form.

SUGGESTED ITINERARIES

If You Have 1 Week

Day 1   Fly to Oslo, check into your hotel, and relax. Few can fight jet lag on their first day in the Norwegian capital.

Day 2   After breakfast in Oslo, take the ferry to the Bygdøy peninsula to visit the *Kon-Tiki* Museum, the polar ship *Fram,* the Viking ships, and the Norwegian Folk Museum.

Day 3   In Oslo, visit Frogner Park to see the Vigeland sculptures and Edvard Munch paintings. You should have enough time to see the Henie–Onstad Foundation art center, 11km (7 miles) from Oslo. Return in time to go to the Lookout Tower and ski jump at Holmenkollen, where you can dine and enjoy a panoramic view of Oslo.

Day 4   Head south for a day trip to some of the major towns along the Oslofjord. In the morning, drive to Fredrikstad on the Glomma River, and visit its Old Town as well as Norway Silver Designs, its handicraft center. Drive back to Moss and take a ferry across the fjord. From Horten on the west bank, drive south to Tønsberg, Norway's oldest town, and visit the Vestfold Folk Museum. Drive back to Oslo for dinner.

Day 5   Head west to Bergen by train on a 480km (300-mile) all-day trip. You go across the "rooftop of Norway," past the ski resorts of Geilo and Voss, before reaching Bergen.

Day 6   Explore Bergen's many attractions, such as Troldhaugen (Trolls' Hill), the summer villa of composer Edvard Grieg.

Day 7   Visit Ulvik, on the Hardanger-fjord in the western fjord district, reached by public transportation from Bergen. Spend the night in the beautiful town, which typifies the fjord towns in this district.

If You Have 2 Weeks

Week 1 See "If You Have 1 Week," above.

Day 8 In Ulvik (see "Day 7," above), continue exploring the fjord district.

Day 9 Return to Bergen, and then fly to Trondheim.

Day 10 If it's summer, take a 13-hour train ride from Trondheim to Bodø on the *Midnight Sun Special.* Spend the night in Bodø, north of the Arctic Circle.

Day 11 From Bodø, fly to Tromsø, 400km (250 miles) north of the Arctic Circle (it doesn't have rail service). Stay overnight in Tromsø and see its limited, but interesting, attractions.

Day 12 Rent a car in Tromsø and head north for the last leg of the trip: a 451km (280-mile) run over the Arctic Highway. Spend the night in Alta. Travel is slow, because the road wraps around inlets and fjords.

Day 13 Continue driving north to Hammerfest, the world's northernmost town of any significant size. Stay overnight.

Day 14 From Hammerfest, take an excursion boat directly to the North Cape. Those with more time can drive to Honningsvåg, the world's northernmost village and the gateway to the North Cape. Buses leave its marketplace daily for the cape, a 35km (22-mile) run.

Return to Tromsø, where air connections can be made to Oslo and your return flight to North America or elsewhere.

 FAST FACTS: Norway

Area Code The international country code for Norway is **47**. If you're calling from outside the country, the city code is **2** for Oslo and **5** for Bergen. Inside Norway, no area or city codes are needed. Phone numbers have 8 digits.

Business Hours Most **banks** are open Monday through Friday from 8:15am to 3:30pm (Thurs to 5pm), and are closed Saturday and Sunday. The bank at Fornebu Airport is open daily from 7am to 10:30pm, and there's another bank at Gardermoen Airport, open Monday through Saturday from 6:30 am to 8pm, and Sunday from 7am to 8pm. Most **businesses** are open Monday through Friday from 9am to 4pm. **Stores** are generally open Monday through Friday from 9am to 5pm (many stay open on Thurs until 6 or 7pm) and Saturday from 9am to 1 or 2pm. Sunday closings are observed.

Customs With certain food exceptions, personal effects intended for your own use can be brought into Norway. If you take them with you when you leave, you can bring in cameras, binoculars, radios, portable TVs, and the like, as well as fishing and camping equipment. Visitors of all nationalities can bring in 400 cigarettes, or 500 grams of tobacco, and 200 sheets of cigarette paper, or 50 cigars, and 1 liter of spirits or 1 liter of wine. Upon leaving, you can take with you up to 25,000NOK ($3,325) in Norwegian currency.

Dentists For emergency dental services, ask your hotel or host for the nearest dentist. Most Norwegian dentists speak English.

Doctors If you become ill or injured while in Norway, your hotel can refer you to a local doctor; nearly all physicians speak English. If you don't stay at a hotel, call ℂ **113,** the national 24-hour emergency medical number.

Drugstores Drugstores, called *apotek,* are open during normal business hours.

Electricity Norway uses 220 volts, 30 to 50 cycles, A.C., and standard continental two-pin plugs. Transformers and adapters will be needed with Canadian and American equipment. Always inquire at your hotel before plugging in any electrical equipment.

Embassies & Consulates In case you lose your passport or have some other emergency, contact your embassy in Oslo. The Embassy of the **United States** is at Drammensveien 18, N-0244 Oslo (ℂ 22-44-85-50); **United Kingdom,** Thomas Heftyes Gate 8, N-0244 Oslo (ℂ 23-13-27-00); and **Canada,** Wergelandsveien 7, N-0244 Oslo (ℂ 22-99-53-00). The **Irish Embassy** is at Haakon VII's gate 1, N-0161 Oslo (ℂ 22-20-43-70); the **Australian Embassy** at Jernbanetorget N-0244 Oslo (ℂ 22-47-91-70); and the **New Zealand Embassy,** Drammensveien 230, N-0212 (ℂ 22-50-90-50). There is a British consulate in Bergen at Carl Konowsgate 34 (ℂ 55-94-47-05).

Emergencies Throughout Norway, call ℂ **112** for the **police,** ℂ **110** to report a **fire,** or ℂ **113** to request an **ambulance.**

Laundry & Dry Cleaning Most hotels provide these services. There are coin-operated launderettes and dry cleaners in most Norwegian cities.

Liquor Laws Most restaurants, pubs, and bars in Norway are licensed to serve liquor, wine, and beer. The drinking age is 18 for beer and wine and 20 for liquor.

Mail Airmail letters or postcards to the United States and Canada cost 7NOK (95¢) for up to 20 grams (¾ oz.). Airmail letters take 7 to 10 days to reach North America. The principal post office in Norway is Oslo Central Post Office, Dronningensgate 15, N-0101 Oslo. Mailboxes are vibrant red, embossed with the trumpet symbol of the postal service. They're found on walls, at chest level, throughout cities and towns. Stamps can be bought at the post office, at magazine kiosks, or at some stores.

Only the post office can weigh, evaluate, and inform you of the options for delivery time and regulations for sending parcels. Shipments to places outside Norway require a declaration on a printed form stating the contents and value of the package.

Maps Many tourist offices supply free maps of their district. You can also contact the Norwegian Automobile Club, Storgata 2, N-0155 Oslo 1 (ℂ **22-34-14-00**), which offers free or inexpensive road maps. Most visitors find it quicker and more convenient to buy a detailed road map; this is the best approach for anyone who plans to tour extensively outside the major cities. Some of Norway's most reliable maps are published by Cappelen.

Police Dial ℂ **112** nationwide.

Radio & TV Radio and television broadcasts are in Norwegian. However, Norwegian National Radio (NRK) has news summaries in English several times weekly.

Restrooms All terminals, big city squares, and the like have public restrooms. In small towns and villages, head for the marketplace. Hygiene standards are usually adequate. If you patronize the restrooms in a privately run establishment (such as a cafe), it's polite to buy at least a small pastry or coffee.

Taxes Norway imposes a 19.4% value-added tax (VAT) on most goods and services, which is figured into your final bill. If you buy goods in any store bearing the tax-free sign, you're entitled to a cash refund of up to 18.7% on purchases costing over 310NOK ($41). Ask the shop assistant for a tax-free shopping check, and show your passport to indicate that you're not a resident of Scandinavia. You may not use the articles purchased before leaving Norway, and they must be taken out of the country within 3 months of purchase. Complete the information requested on the back of the check you're given at the store; at your point of departure, report to an area marked by the tax-free sign, not at Customs. Your refund check will be exchanged there in *kroner* for the amount due you. Refunds are available at airports, ferry and cruise-ship terminals, borders, and train stations.

Telephone & Telegrams Direct-dial long-distance calls can be made to the United States and Canada from most phones in Norway by dialing © 00 (double zero), then the country code (1 for the U.S. and Canada), followed by the area code and phone number. Check at your hotel's front desk before you place a call. Norwegian coins of 1NOK (15¢), 5NOK (65¢), and 10NOK ($1.35) are used in pay phones.

   Telegrams can be sent from private or public phones by dialing © 0138.

Time Norway operates on Central European Time—1 hour ahead of Greenwich Mean Time and 6 hours ahead of Eastern Standard Time. (For example: at noon Eastern Standard Time—say, in New York City—it's 6pm in Norway.) Norway goes on summer time—1 hour earlier—from the end of March until around the end of September.

Tipping Hotels add a 10% to 15% service charge to your bill, which is sufficient unless someone has performed a special service. Most bellhops get at least 10NOK ($1.35) per suitcase. Nearly all restaurants add a service charge of up to 15% to your bill. Barbers and hairdressers usually aren't tipped, but restroom attendants and hat-check people expect at least 3NOK (40¢). Don't tip theater ushers. Taxi drivers don't expect tips unless they handle heavy luggage.

Water Tap water is generally safe to drink throughout Norway. Never drink from a mountain stream, fjord, or river, regardless of how clean it might appear.

Oslo

One of the oldest Scandinavian capitals, Oslo has never been on the mainstream European tourist circuit. Many have the impression that it's lean on historic and cultural sights. In fact, it offers enough sights and activities to fill at least 3 or 4 busy days. It's also the starting point for many easy excursions along the Oslofjord or to nearby towns and villages.

In the 1990s Oslo grew surprisingly—from what even the Scandinavians considered a backwater to one of the glittering cities of Europe. Restaurants, nightclubs, cafes, shopping complexes, and other places have opened. A Nordic joie de vivre permeates the city. The only problem is that Oslo is one of the most expensive cities in Europe. Proceed with caution if you're on a strict budget.

Oslo was founded in the mid–11th century by a Viking king, and became the capital around 1300 under Haakon V. In the course of its history, the city burned down several times; it was destroyed by fire in 1824. The master builder, Christian IV, king of Denmark and Norway, ordered the town rebuilt near the Akershus Castle. He named the new town Christiania (after himself), and that was its official name until 1924, when the city reverted to its former name.

In 1814 Norway separated from Denmark and united with Sweden, a union that lasted until 1905. During that period the Royal Palace, the House of Parliament, the old university, the National Theater, and the National Gallery were built.

After World War II, Oslo grew to 280 sq. km (175 sq. miles). Today it's one of the 10 largest world capitals in area. Oslo is also one of the most heavily forested cities, and has fewer than half a million inhabitants.

One final point: Oslovians love nature. They devote much time to pursuits in the forests and on the fjords. It takes only half an hour by tram to go from the Royal Palace to the 120m (390-ft.) Tryvann Observation Tower, where you can enjoy a view over Oslo Marka, the giant forest. The Krogskogen forest was the setting for many Norwegian folk tales about princesses, kings, penniless heroes, and the inevitable forest trolls. From this observation tower in the summer, you can look down on hundreds of sailboats, motorboats, and windsurfers among the numerous islands of the Oslo archipelago.

1 Orientation

ARRIVING

BY PLANE Since the recent closing of a small-scale, relatively outmoded airport named Fornebu, Oslo has learned to cope with all of its air traffic being funneled into the **Oslo International Airport** in Gardermoen (© 81-55-02-50), about 50km (31 miles) east of downtown Oslo, a 45-minute drive from the center. All domestic and international flights coming into Oslo arrive through this much-upgraded airport, including aircraft belonging to SAS, British Airways, and Icelandair.

There's frequent bus service, departing at intervals of between 15 and 30 minutes throughout the day, into downtown Oslo. It's maintained by both SAS (whose buses deliver passengers to the Central Railway station and to most of the SAS hotels within Oslo) and the **Norwegian Bus Express** (© **81-54-44-44**), whose buses head for the main railway station. Both companies charge 110NOK ($15) per person, each way. There's also a high-speed railway service between Gardermoen and Oslo's main railway station, requiring transit time of only 20 minutes, priced at 180NOK ($24) per person each way. If you want to take a taxi, be prepared for a lethally high charge of around 500NOK ($67) for up to four passengers plus their luggage. If you need a "maxi-taxi," a minivan that's suitable for between 5 and 15 passengers, plus your luggage, you'll be assessed 800NOK ($106).

BY TRAIN The first high-speed train between Oslo and Stockholm has reduced travel time to 4 hours and 50 minutes between these two once remotely linked Scandinavian capitals. Depending on the day, there are two to three trains daily in each direction. This high-speed train now competes directly with air travel. Trains from the Continent, Sweden, and Denmark arrive at **Oslo Sentralstasjon,** Jernbanetorget 1 (© **81-50-08-88** for train information). It's at the beginning of Karl Johans Gate, in the center of the city. The station is open daily from 7am to 11pm. From the Central Station, trains leave for Bergen, Stavanger, Trondheim, Bodø, and all other rail links in Norway. You can also take trams to all major parts of Oslo. Lockers and a luggage office are available at the station, where you can also exchange money.

BY CAR If you're driving from mainland Europe, the fastest way to reach Oslo is to take the car ferry from Frederikshavn, Denmark. From Frederikshavn, car ferries run to several towns near Oslo, and to Gothenburg, Sweden. You can also take a car ferry from Copenhagen to several points in western Sweden, or from Helsingør, Denmark, to Helsingborg, Sweden. Highway E6 runs the length of Sweden's western coast from Malmö through Helsingborg and Gothenburg, right up to Oslo. If you're driving from Stockholm to Oslo, take E3 west to Örebro, where it connects with E18 to Oslo. Once you near the outskirts of Oslo from any direction, follow the signs into the Sentrum.

BY FERRY Ferries from Europe arrive at the Oslo port, a 15-minute walk (or a short taxi ride) from the center. From Denmark, Scandinavia's link with the Continent, ferries depart for Oslo from Copenhagen, Hirtshals, and Frederikshavn.

From Strømstad, Sweden, in the summer, the daily crossing to Sandefjord, Norway, takes 2½ hours; from Sandefjord, it's an easy drive or train ride north to Oslo.

VISITOR INFORMATION

Assistance and information for visitors are available at the **Tourist Information Office,** Vestbaneplassen 1, N-0250 Oslo (© **22-83-00-50**). Free maps, brochures, sightseeing tickets, and guide services are available. The office is open from June to August daily from 9am to 7pm; May and September Monday through Saturday from 9am to 4pm; from October to April Monday through Friday from 9am to 4pm.

The information office at the **Oslo Sentralstasjon (Central Station),** Jernbanetorget 1, is open daily from 8am to 11pm. There's no phone.

CITY LAYOUT

MAIN ARTERIES & STREETS   Oslo is at the mouth of the 97km (60-mile) long Oslofjord. Opening onto the harbor is **Rådhusplassen (City Hall Square),** dominated by the modern City Hall, a major attraction. Guided bus tours leave from this point, and the launches that cruise the fjords depart from the pier facing the municipal building. You can catch Bygdøy-bound ferries from the quay at Rådhusplassen. On a promontory to the east is **Akershus Castle.**

Karl Johans Gate, Oslo's main street (especially for shopping and strolling), is north of City Hall Square. This boulevard begins at Oslo Sentralstasjon (Central Station) and stretches all the way to the 19th-century Royal Palace at the western end.

A short walk from the palace is the famed **Students' Grove (Studenter Lunden),** where seemingly everybody gathers on summer days to socialize. The University of Oslo is nearby. Dominating this center is the National Theater, guarded by statues of Ibsen and Bjørnson, the two greatest names in Norwegian theater. South of the theater, near the harbor, is **Stortingsgaten,** another shop-filled street.

The main city square is **Stortorvet,** although it's no longer the center of city life, which has shifted to Karl Johans Gate.

At a subway stop near the National Theater, you can catch an electric train to **Tryvannstårnet,** the loftiest lookout in Scandinavia, and to the **Holmenkollen Ski Jump.**

FINDING AN ADDRESS   Street numbers begin on the southern end of streets running north-south and on the eastern end of streets running east-west. Odd numbers are on one side of the street, and even numbers are on the other. Some large buildings hold several establishments, so different addresses are designated by A, B, and C.

STREET MAPS   Maps of Oslo are distributed free at the tourist office (see above). For extensive exploring, especially of some back streets, you may need a more detailed map. Opt for a pocket-sized map with a street index that can be opened and folded like a wallet. Such maps are sold at most newsstands in the central city. If you can't find one, go to the city's most central bookstore, **Tanum Karl Johan,** Karl Johans Gate 43 (℡ 22-41-11-00).

NEIGHBORHOODS IN BRIEF

Oslo is made for walking—in fact, you can walk from the Central Station all the way to the Royal Palace (Slottet) in a straight line. Except for excursions to the museum-loaded Bygdøy peninsula and the Holmenkollen Ski Jump, most attractions can be covered on foot.

Oslo is not neatly divided into separate neighborhoods or districts. It consists mainly of **central Oslo,** with the Central Station to the east of the city center and the Royal Palace to the west. Karl Johans Gate, the principal street, connects these two points. Central Oslo is the heart of the city—the most crowded and traffic congested, but also the most convenient place to stay. It's not a real neighborhood but the core of the city, as Piccadilly Circus is to London. Most Oslo hotels and restaurants are here, as are almost 50 museums and galleries—enough to fill many a rainy day. The most interesting include Akershus Castle, the Historical Museum, and the National Gallery.

The streets Drammensveien and Frognerveien lead northwest to Frogner Park (Frognerparken), whose main entrance is on Kirkeveien. This historical area is the site of the Vigeland Sculpture Park, which displays some masterpieces of Gustav Vigeland (1869–1943).

The **Old Town (or Gamlebyen)** lies south of the Parliament Building (the Stortinget) and Karl Johans Gate. This section contains some of the city's old-fashioned restaurants, along with the Norwegian Resistance Museum and the Old Town Hall.

Aker Brygge is Oslo's newest neighborhood, an excellent place for dining and diversions, but not for hotels. It emerged near the mouth of the Oslofjord in the old wharf area formerly used for shipbuilding yards. Fueled by oil wealth, steel-and-glass buildings now rise from what had been a relatively dilapidated section. Some of the best shops, theaters, restaurants, and cultural attractions are here, along with apartments for such well-heeled owners as Diana Ross.

The main attractions in **eastern Oslo** are the Botanisk Hage (Botanic Garden), the Zoological Museum, and the Munch Museum in Tøyen—little more is worth seeing there.

The **West End** is a chic residential area graced with some of the city's finest hotels and restaurants. It's a more tranquil setting than the center, which we prefer, and only 15 minutes away by public transportation.

Further west—6km (4 miles) by car but better reached by car ferry—is the **Bygdøy** peninsula. Here you'll find such attractions as the Norwegian Folk Museum, the Viking ships, the polar ship *Fram* Museum, and the *Kon-Tiki* Museum. Break up your sightseeing venture with a meal here but plan to stay elsewhere.

The suburb of Frogner begins .8km (½ mile) west of Oslo center and stretches for a kilometer or so. There's a good hotel and restaurant here.

Many Oslo neighborhoods lie along the **Oslofjord,** which stretches more than 95km (60 miles) north from the Skagerrak to Oslo, and is filled with basins dotted with islands. (There are 40 islands in the immediate Oslo archipelago.)

Nearly all visitors want to see **Holmenkollen,** a wooded range of hills northwest of the city rising about 520m (1,740 ft.). You can reach it in 35 minutes by electric train from the city center.

Marka, Oslo's forest, is a sprawling recreation area that offers hiking, bicycle riding, skiing, fishing, wild berry picking, jogging trails, and more. It contains 343 lakes, 500km (310 miles) of ski trails, 623km (387 miles) of trails and roads, 11 sports chalets, and 24 ski jumps and alpine slopes.

2 Getting Around

BY PUBLIC TRANSPORTATION

Oslo has an efficient citywide network of buses, trams (streetcars), and subways. Buses and electric trains take passengers to the suburbs; from mid-April to October, ferries to Bygdøy depart from the harbor in front of the Oslo Rådhuset (City Hall).

DISCOUNT PASSES The **Oslo Card (Oslo-Kortet)** can help you become acquainted with the city at a fraction of the usual price. It allows free travel on public transportation, free admission to museums and other top sights, discounts on sightseeing buses and boats, a rebate on your car rental, and special treats in restaurants. You can purchase the card at hotels, fine stores, and tourist information offices, from travel agents, and in the branches of Sparebanken Oslo Akershus. Adults pay 180NOK ($24) for a 1-day card, 270NOK ($36) for 2 days, and 410NOK ($55) for 3 days. Children's cards cost 60NOK ($8), 80NOK ($11), and 110NOK ($15).

The 24-hour **Tourist Ticket (Turistkort)** lets you travel anywhere in Oslo by bus, tram, subway, local railway, or boat, including the Bygdøy ferries in the summer. The Tourist Ticket costs 40NOK ($5.30) for adults, half price for children 4 to 15; children under 4 travel free. The ticket is stamped when it's used for the first time and is good for the next 24 hours.

BY BUS, TRAM & SUBWAY   Jernbanetorget is Oslo's major **bus and tram** terminal stop. Most buses and trams passing through the heart of town stop at Wessels Plass, next to the Parliament, or at Stortorget, the main marketplace. Many also stop at the National Theater or University Square on Karl Johans Gate, as well as Oslo's suburbs.

The **subway (T-banen)** has four branch lines to the east. The Western Suburban route (including Holmenkollen) has four lines to the residential sections and recreation grounds west and north of the city. Subways and trains leave from near the National Theater on Karl Johans Gate.

For schedule and fare information, call **Trafikanten** (© 22-05-70-37). Drivers sell single-trip tickets for 22NOK ($2.95); children travel for half fare. Automated machines cancel tickets. An eight-coupon Maxi card costs 135NOK ($18), half price for children. Maxi cards can be used for unlimited transfers for 1 hour from the time the ticket was stamped.

BY TAXI

If you need a taxi, call © **22-38-80-90,** 24 hours a day. Reserve at least an hour in advance.

The approximate fare from Oslo International Airport to the center of Oslo is 500NOK ($67). All taxis have meters, and Norwegian cab drivers are generally honest. When a cab is available, a roof light goes on. Taxis can be hailed on the street, provided they're more than 90m (300 ft.) from a taxi rank. The worst time to hail a taxi is Monday through Friday from 8:30 to 10am and 3 to 5pm, and Saturday from 8:30 to 10am.

BY CAR

Driving is not a practical way to get around Oslo because parking is limited. The efficient network of public transportation makes a private car unnecessary. You can reach even the most isolated areas by public transportation.

Among the multistory parking lots in the city center, the best is **Vestre Vika Bilpark,** Dronning Mauds Gate (© **22-83-35-35**). The cost of parking a car in a public garage is 40NOK ($5.30) per hour or 175NOK ($23) for 24 hours. Illegally parked cars are towed away. For car problems, call the **NAF Alarm Center** (© **22-34-16-00**), 24 hours a day.

BY FERRY

Beginning in mid-April, ferries depart for Bygdøy from Pier 3 in front of the Oslo Rådhuset. For schedules, call **Båtservice** (© 23-35-68-90). The ferry or bus to Bygdøy is a good choice, because parking there is limited. Other ferries leave for various parts of the Oslofjord. Inquire at the **Tourist Information Office,** Vestbaneplassen 1 (© **22-83-00-50**).

BY BICYCLE

Den Rustne Eike, Vestbaneplassen 2 (© 22-83-52-08), rents bikes at moderate rates, complete with free maps of interesting routes in Oslo and its environs. The cost is 265NOK ($35) per day or 800NOK ($106) per week, with a 1,000NOK ($133) deposit required. It's open from May to October daily from 10am to 6:30pm; in the off season, Monday through Friday from 10am to 6pm.

 FAST FACTS: Oslo

American Express American Express Reisebyrå, Karl Johans Gate 33 (© 22-98-37-00), is open Monday through Friday from 9am to 6pm, Saturday from 10am to 3pm.

Area Code The country code for Norway is **47.** If you're calling from outside the country, the city code for Oslo is **2.** Inside Norway, no area or city codes are needed. Telephone numbers have 8 digits.

Babysitters Hotels can often enlist the help of a housekeeper for "childminding." Give at least a day's notice, two if you can. You can also contact the tourist office (see "Visitor Information," above), which keeps a list of available sitters on file.

Bookstores Oslo has many bookstores. The most central and one of the best stocked is **Tanum Karl Johan,** Karl Johans Gate 43 (© 22-41-11-00).

Currency Exchange **Banks** will exchange most foreign currencies or cash traveler's checks. Bring your passport for identification. If banks are closed, try automated machines at the Oslo Sentralstasjon to exchange currency. You can also exchange currency at the **Bureau de Change** at the main Oslo post office, Dronningensgatan 15 (© 22-97-60-00).

Dentists In an emergency, contact the **Tøyen Senter,** Kolstadgate 16 (© 22-67-78-00), which is open daily from 11am to 2pm and 7 to 10pm. If you can wait, volume 1B of the telephone directory lists private dentists under *Tannleger,* (literally "tooth doctors"). There's rarely a language barrier.

Doctors Some larger hotels have arrangements with doctors in case a guest becomes ill. You can also try the 24-hour **Oslo Kommunale Legevakten,** Storgata 40 (© 22-93-22-93). A privately funded alternative is **Oslo Akutten,** Nedre Vollgate 8 (© 22-00-81-60). For more routine medical assistance, you can contact the biggest hospital in Oslo, **Ullaval,** Kirkeveien 166 (© 22-11-80-80). To consult a private doctor (nearly all of whom speak English), check the telephone directory or ask at your hotel for a recommendation.

Drugstores A 24-hour pharmacy is **Jernbanetorvets Apotek,** Jernbanetorget 4A (© 22-41-24-82).

Embassies & Consulates See "Fast Facts: Norway," in chapter 7, "Planning Your Trip to Norway."

Emergencies Dial the Oslo **police** at © **112;** report a **fire** to © **110;** call an **ambulance** at © **113.**

Eyeglass Repair **Ulf Jacobsen Optiker,** Karl Johans Gate 20 (© 22-42-85-14), is a big supplier. Most contact lenses are in stock, too. Unusual prescriptions take about 2 days. Hours are Monday and Wednesday through Friday from 9am to 5pm, Tuesday from 9am to 6pm, Saturday from10am to 2pm.

Internet Access You can log on free at the Rådhuset, the City Hall on Råd-husplassen (© **22-46-16-00**). For hours, refer to "Seeing the Sights," later in this chapter. There is also free service at the library (see below) where you must sign up for a slot.

Laundry & Dry Cleaning Washing and drying can usually be completed in an hour. You must have your coins ready to put in the machines. Dry cleaning is extremely expensive in Oslo, and many establishments take more than a week to return clothing. Try **Oslo American Rens,** Griniveien 1 (© **22-50-57-41**), which promises 24-hour service.

Libraries The Oslo municipal library, **Diechmann Library,** Henrik Ibsens Gate 1 (© **22-43-29-00**), is the largest in Norway. It has many English-language volumes, a children's department, and a music department. It's open Monday through Friday from 10am to 8pm (to 6pm in summer), Saturday from 9am to 2pm.

Lost Property The **Lost and Found Office,** Hittegodskontoret, Grøland-sleiret 44 (© **22-66-98-65**), is open from May 15 to September 15, Monday through Friday from 8:15am to 4:30pm; from September 16 to May 14, Monday through Friday from 8:15am to 3pm.

Luggage Storage & Lockers Facilities for luggage storage are available at the **Oslo Sentralstasjon,** Jernbanetorget 1 (© **81-50-08-88**). It's open daily from 7am to 11pm. Lockers cost 25NOK to 45NOK ($3.35–$6) per day, depending on size.

Newspapers & Magazines English-language newspapers and magazines are sold—at least in the summer months—at newsstands (kiosks) through-out Oslo. International editions, including the *International Herald Tri-bune* and *USA Today,* are always available, as are the European editions of *Time* and *Newsweek.*

Photographic Needs Try **Preeus Photo,** Karl Johans Gate 33 (© **22-42-98-04**), for supplies, including black-and-white and color film. Film can be developed in 1 hour. It's open Monday through Friday from 9am to 5pm, Saturday from 10am to 3pm.

Police Dial © **112.**

Post Office The **Oslo General Post Office** is at Dronningensgatan 15 (© **23-14-90-00** for information). Enter at the corner of Prinsensgate. It's open Monday through Friday from 8am to 5pm, Saturday from 9am to 2pm; closed Sunday and public holidays. You can arrange for mail to be sent to the main post office c/o General Delivery. The address is Poste Restante, P.O. Box 1181-Sentrum, Dronningensgatan 15, N-0101 Oslo, Nor-way. You must show your passport to collect it.

Radio & TV The most important broadcaster is the Norwegian govern-ment, which owns and controls programming on the NRK station. Oslo receives many broadcasts from other countries, including BBC programs from London. Radio Norway International broadcasts on MHz frequency.

Restrooms Clean public toilets can be found throughout the city center, in parks, and at all bus, rail, and air terminals. For a detailed list, contact the Tourist Information Office.

Safety Of the four Scandinavian capitals, Oslo is widely considered the safest. However, don't be lulled into a false sense of security. Oslovians no longer leave their doors unlocked. Be careful, and don't carry your wallet visibly exposed or sling your purse over your shoulder.

Taxes Oslo has no special city taxes. You pay the same value-added tax throughout the country (see "Fast Facts: Norway," in chapter 7).

Taxis See "Getting Around," above.

Transit Information For information about tram and bus travel, call **Trafikanten** (℃ **22-05-70-37**), located in front of the Central Station. For information about train travel, go to the Central Station or call ℃ **23-15-00-00**.

Weather See the temperature chart in "When to Go," in chapter 7.

3 Where to Stay

By the standards of many U.S. and Canadian cities, hotels in Oslo are very expensive. If the prices make you want to cancel your trip, read on. Oslovian hotels lose most of their business travelers, and their main revenue source, during the peak tourist months in midsummer. Even though the city is filled with visitors, many hotels slash their prices. July is always a month for discounts. Some hotels' discounts begin June 21. Regular pricing usually resumes in mid-August. For exact dates of discounts, which often change from year to year, check with the hotel.

Hotels also slash prices on weekends—usually Friday and Saturday, and sometimes Sunday. Again, hotels often change their policies, so it's best to check when you make your reservations. Don't always expect a discount—a quickly arranged conference could lead hotels to increase their prices.

The most economy-minded tourists can cut costs by staying at one of the old-fashioned hotels that offer a number of rooms without private bathrooms. Sometimes a room has a shower but no toilet. In most cases, corridor toilets and bathrooms are plentiful. Even the rooms without bathrooms usually have a sink with hot and cold running water.

HOTEL RESERVATIONS   The worst months for finding a place to stay in Oslo are May, June, September, and October, when many business conferences are held. July and August are better, even though that's the peak time of the summer tourist invasion.

If you happen to arrive in Oslo without a reservation, head for the Oslo Tourist Information Office (see above), which will book you into a room in your price category. The minimum stay is 2 days. Don't try to phone—the service is strictly for walk-ins who need a room on the night of their arrival.

Note: Rates quoted below include the service charge and tax. Breakfast—usually a generous Norwegian buffet—is almost always included. Unless otherwise indicated, all our recommended accommodations come with bathrooms.

CENTRAL OSLO
VERY EXPENSIVE

Grand Hotel ★★★ *Kids*   Norway's leading hostelry is on the wide boulevard that leads to the Royal Palace. The stone-walled hotel with its mansard gables and copper tower has been an integral part of Oslo life since 1874. Famous guests have included Arctic explorer Roald Amundsen, Edvard Munch, Gen. Dwight Eisenhower, Charlie Chaplin, Henry Ford, and Henrik Ibsen, who was especially fond of the place. More recent guests have included Elton John and Michael Jackson.

Renovated in 1996, the guest rooms are in the 19th-century core or one of the tasteful modern additions. Newer rooms contain plush facilities and electronic extras, and the older ones have been completely modernized. Most of the old-fashioned bathrooms are done in marble or tile and have shower-tub combinations. An eight-story extension contains larger, brighter doubles, but many guests prefer the old-fashioned accommodations in the older section.

The hotel has several restaurants that serve international and Scandinavian food. The Palmen, the Julius Fritzner, and the Grand Café offer live entertainment. The Grand Café is the most famous in Oslo. Frankly, although still the grande dame of Norway hotels, we feel the Grand has lost its cutting edge. Both the Bristol and Continental aren't as stuffy.

Karl Johans Gate 31, N-0101 Oslo. © 800/223-5652 in the U.S., or 23-21-20-00. Fax 23-21-21-00. www.grand-hotel.no. 289 units. Summer 1,200NOK ($160) double; 2,160NOK–22,000NOK ($287–$2,926) suite. Fall, winter, spring 1,935NOK ($257) double; 2,740NOK–22,000NOK ($364–$2,926) suite. Rates include buffet breakfast. AE, DC, MC, V. Parking 240NOK ($32). T-banen: Stortinget. **Amenities:** 3 restaurants; 2 bars; nightclub; pool; health club; sauna; boutiques; massage; room service; laundry/dry cleaning. *In room:* A/C, TV, minibar, hair dryer.

Hotel Continental ★★★   This is a major, immensely prestigious hotel with a serious allure for members of Norway's business community. Founded in 1898 by owners of a local brewery, it opened as a rival to the also-recommended Grand Hotel in 1900. Since then, at least two (Annen Etage and Theatercafeen) of its five dining and drinking outlets have become enduring and successful staples on the city's restaurant scene. The only Norwegian member of Leading Hotels of the World, and the only major hotel in Oslo that's still mostly owned by an individual family (as headed by Elizabeth Brockmann), it's cozy, a bit inbred, and thoroughly conservative in its approach to virtually everything. Expect lots of personalized touches, such as a masterful collection of framed original lithographs and woodcuts by Edvard Munch in a salon near the reception area, and service that's based on "Continental" models as defined by aristocratic precedents in Paris and Vienna. Bedrooms are plush and intensely well-decorated, often with wallpaper and an unerring upper-crust touch, sometimes evoking extremely comfortable bedrooms in private homes. Bathrooms are tiled or clad in marble, each with a shower and tub combination.

Stortingsgaten 24–26, Oslo N-0117. © 22-82-40-00. Fax 22-42-96-89. www.hotel-continental.no. 154 units. Sun–Thurs 2,330NOK ($310) double; 3,500NOK ($466) suite. Fri–Sat 1,320NOK ($176) double; 2,650NOK ($352) suite. Rates include breakfast. AE, DC, MC, V. Parking 180NOK ($24). T-banen: Nationaltheatret. **Amenities:** 3 restaurants; 2 bars; 2 cafes; room service; babysitting; laundry/dry cleaning. *In room:* A/C (in some), TV, minibar, hair dryer, safe.

EXPENSIVE

Clarion Hotel Royal Christiania ★★   This is the second-largest hotel in Norway, a soaring 14-story tower built to house athletes and administrators

Oslo Accommodations

Clarion Royal Christiania **18**
Cochs Pensjonat **5**
First Hotel Millennium **15**
First Hotel Nobel House **16**
Frogner House **2**
Gabelshus **1**
Golden Tulip Rainbow
  Hotel Stefan **8**

Grand Hotel **12**
Gyldenløve **4**
Hotel Ambassadeur **3**
Hotel Bondeheimen **10**
Hotel Bristol **9**
Hotel Continental **13**
Norlandia Karl Johan **11**

Nrrøna **19**
Radisson SAS Scandinavia Hotel **6**
Rainbow Hotel Opera **17**
Tulip Inn Rainbow Cecil **14**
Tulip Inn Rainbow Munch **7**

† Church
ⓘ Information
✉ Post Office
--Ⓜ-- Metro
—— Railway

during the 1952 Winter Olympics. It was radically upgraded in 1990, with the addition of two nine-story wings, and in 1999 it was enlarged again. Today it's a luxury hotel that is often favorably compared to the nearby Oslo Plaza. This modern hotel and the high-traffic neighborhood around it don't in any way evoke old-fashioned Norway, but you will find comfort, efficiency, good design, and a hardworking staff. Guest rooms are quiet, conservatively decorated, and blandly tasteful. The well-maintained bathrooms have shower-tub combinations and heated towel racks.

Biskop Gunnerus Gate 3, N-0106 Oslo. ⓒ **23-10-80-00.** Fax 23-10-80-80. www.royalchristiania.no. 503 units. Sun–Thurs 1,995NOK ($265) double, 2,295NOK ($305) suite. Fri–Sat and June 15–Aug 1 1,095NOK ($146) double, 1,395NOK ($186) suite. Rates include breakfast. AE, DC, MC, V. Parking 195NOK ($26). Bus: 30, 31, or 41. **Amenities:** Restaurant; 2 bars; pool; fitness center; sauna; room service; massage; babysitting; laundry/dry cleaning. *In room:* TV, minibar, hair dryer.

Hotel Bristol ⭐⭐⭐ *(Kids)*   Loaded with character, and the source of many entertaining anecdotes, this 1920s-era hotel competes aggressively and gracefully with two other historic hotel "dragons" of Oslo, the Grand and the Continental. Of the three, the Bristol consistently emerges as the most liberal, the hippest, and the most accessible. Set in the commercial core of Oslo, 1 block north of Karl Johans Gate, it's warm, inviting, rich with tradition, and comfortable. It also isn't as stuffy, as formal, or as oppressive as either the Grand or the Continental. To an increasing degree, it's becoming the preferred hotel of the media, arts, and show-biz communities, with a sense of playfulness and fun that's unmatched by either of its more chillingly formal rivals.

In 2001, the hotel almost doubled its room count, thanks to the annexation and conversion of an office building next door. Guest rooms are comfortable and dignified, but not as plush or as intensely decorated as the rooms in either of its grander competitors. Each accommodation comes with a tiled or marble bathroom with a tub and shower combination. Lavish public areas still evoke the Moorish-inspired Art Deco style in which they were built. There's enormous life and energy in this hotel, which is an undeniably fine address in Oslo and which—thanks to active restaurants, piano bars, and a sense of elegant yet unpretentious conviviality, continues to exert an enormous appeal.

Kristian IV's Gate 7, N-0164 Oslo 1. ⓒ **22-82-60-00.** Fax 22-82-60-01. www.bristol.no. 252 units. Mon–Thurs 1,350NOK–1,960NOK ($180–$261) double. Fri-Sun year-round and late June to early Aug 1,195NOK ($159) double. Suite 4,000NOK–8,000NOK ($532–$1,064) year-round. AE, DC, MC, V. Tram: 10, 11, 17, or 18. **Amenities:** 3 restaurants; 3 bars; live pianist in the lobby; nightclub/dance bar; small-scale

(Kids) **Family-Friendly Hotels**

Hotel Bristol (see above)   One of the most elegant and comfortable hotels in Oslo welcomes children and lets those under 15 stay free in their parent's room. The chef will even put a "junior steak" on the grill.

Grand Hotel (p. 201)   The Grand's indoor pool provides an outlet for your child's energy. The "solve-everything" concierge can recommend babysitting services and diversions for children.

Norrøna (p. 208)   This reliable choice attracts economy-minded families. There's a moderately priced cafe on the premises.

exercise room and health club; room service; babysitting; laundry/dry cleaning. *In room:* A/C, TV, minibar, hair dryer, trouser press.

Radisson SAS Scandinavia Hotel 🐦
This hotel was built in 1975 as the Norwegian flagship of the group now known as Radisson SAS. Black, angular, and reminiscent of the international modern style made famous by the Seagram building in Manhattan, it's the best of the 1970s internationalism that eventually swept across Scandinavia. With 22 floors, it's the third-biggest (after the Radisson SAS Plaza and the Royal Christiana) hotel in Oslo, the second-tallest building, and the first hotel that most Oslovians think of when they hear the name "SAS Hotel."

It also has a wider range of amenities than many of the newer palaces with which it competes. Guest rooms are relatively large and very comfortable, and come in about a dozen different styles, including Scandinavian, Japanese, Chinese, ersatz "rococo," Art Deco, "Continental" (vaguely based on a combination of French "Louis" styles), and—newest of all—a nautical style inspired by the maritime traditions of Norway. Each guest room comes with a well-maintained bathroom with tub and shower. Thanks to aggressive price adjustments that vary according to the season, and a very appealing hotel product, this "grandfather" of Oslo modern palaces boasts an average occupancy rate of 73%, as opposed to the Norwegian national average of only 54%. The lobby, far more stylish and efficiently laid out than it was after the hotel's initial opening in 1975, was radically renovated in 2002.

Holbergsgate 30, N-0166 Oslo. © **23-29-30-00.** Fax 23 29 30 01. www.radissonsas.com. 488 units. Mon–Thurs 1,800NOK–2,100NOK ($239–$279) double; Fri–Sun and mid-June to Aug 980NOK–1,280NOK ($130–$170) double. 3,500NOK–5,000NOK ($466–$665) suite all week and all year. AE, DC, MC, V. Parking 195NOK ($26). T-banen: Nationaltheatret. **Amenities:** 3 restaurants; 2 bars (1 with a panoramic view from the 21st floor), indoor pool; health club/fitness center; sauna; concierge; underground shopping arcade; babysitting; laundry/dry cleaning. *In room:* A/C, TV, minibar.

Rainbow Hotel Opera 🐦🐦 (Finds)
In April 2002, it took a lot of imagination and a lot of courage for its developers to plunk this avant-garde hotel directly atop the barren-looking industrial wasteland that stretches between Oslo's railway station and its harbor front. But don't expect the "no-man's land" where it's sited to look that way forever. The municipal government and its Port Authority have announced firm plans to build a new opera house nearby, to bury a roaring stretch of coastal highway, and to encourage the construction of upscale condominiums overlooking the fjord. The result will be a complete re-definition of the surrounding neighborhood into something much more plush and gilt-edged than it is now.

Even if these changes never occurred, Rainbow Hotel Opera is one of the most exciting hotels to rise in Oslo in many years. There's an opera-related theme that permeates this place, one that anticipates the construction, about 90m (300 ft.) away, of the new opera house. You'll enter a lobby whose theatrical staircases, piped-in classical music, and soaring ceilings evoke the entrance to a concert hall. Guest rooms are compact but plush, each with copies of French Empire furniture, framed artwork based on operatic themes (the costume changes, for example, for *Lucia di Lammermoor*), and depictions of librettos running maniacally across the sheets and pillowcases. Each has carpeted or hardwood floors (you can express your preference when you check in) and a tiled bathroom, usually, but not always, with a shower-tub combination. It's positioned just a few steps from the railway station, allowing rail arrivals to walk through a labyrinth of inner and outdoor passageways to reach it.

Christian Frederiks Plass 5. N-0154 Oslo. © **24-10-30-00.** Fax 24-10-30-10. www.rainbow-hotels.no/opera. 434 units. Sun–Thurs 1,820NOK–2,120NOK ($242–$282) double; Fri–Sat and June 21–Aug 18, for people who buy a 90NOK ($12) Scan Hotel Pass, 990NOK ($132) double. Suite 6,250NOK ($831) all week and all year long. Rates include breakfast. AE, DC, MC, V. Parking 105NOK ($14). T-banen: Central Stasjon. **Amenities:** Restaurant; 2 bars, indoor pool; fitness center; jogging track; sauna; laundry/dry cleaning. *In room:* A/C, TV, minibar, coffeemaker.

MODERATE
First Hotel Millennium ⭐ *Finds*   One of Oslo's newest large-scale hotels opened late in 1998 within what was originally a 1930s Art Deco office building. It's within walking distance of virtually everything in central Oslo, including the Akershus fortress and the shops of the Karl Johans Gate. Rising nine floors behind a pale pink facade, it's noted for a stylish kind of minimalism, which in the guest rooms translates into ocher-colored walls with dark wood trim, streamlined wooden furniture, and lots of comfort. This is one of the "personality" hotels of Oslo, known for its atmosphere and character. The accommodations are among the most spacious in town, with many Art Deco touches in the furnishings and designs. Each unit has a large bathroom equipped with a tub-shower combination. Some of the accommodations are suitable for persons with disabilities. This is the most inflexibly nonsmoking hotel in Oslo; no cigarettes are allowed anywhere inside.

Tollbugate 25, N-0157 Oslo. © **21-02-28-00.** Fax 21-02-28-30. www.firsthotels.com. 112 units. Mon–Thurs 1,103NOK–1,510NOK ($147–$201) double; Fri–Sun 703NOK–853NOK ($94–$113) double. AE, DC, MC, V. Tram: 30 or 42. **Amenities:** Restaurant; bar; room service; babysitting; laundry/dry cleaning. *In room:* TV, minibar, hair dryer.

First Hotel Nobel House ⭐ *Finds*   There's something that's distinctly personal and thoughtful about this consciously elegant boutique hotel, whose lobby has a seven-story glassed-in atrium flooded with sunlight, Oriental carpets, Ionic-style columns, and a fireplace. It's a member of a Sweden-based hotel chain, an adaptation of an industrial building, with a polite staff and a lot of idiosyncratic style. Oddly, this is one of the few hotels anywhere where we prefer the regular rooms more than the oddly laid-out, curiously spartan-looking suites, where lots of room might be devoted, say, to an interior hallway or a bedroom without windows looking over the building's exterior. Each of the suites is theme-based on the life of a famous Scandinavian, usually with photographic tributes to, among others, opera giant Kirsten Flagsted. Rooms and suites are accessible via a labyrinthine path of stairs and many, angled hallways, and are sometimes a bit hard to find unless you're being escorted by a staff member. Each unit has a mini-kitchen, some kind of original art and, in many cases, exposed brick. Each unit comes with a neatly tiled bathroom with tub and shower.

Kongensgaten 5, N-0153 Oslo. © **23-10-72-01.** Fax 23-10-72-10. 69 units. Mon–Thurs 1,602NOK ($213) double; 2,149NOK–2,999NOK ($286–$399) suite. Fri–Sun 1,420NOK ($189) double; 1,789NOK–2,499NOK ($238–$332) suite. Rates include breakfast. AE, DC, MC, V. Parking 150NOK ($20) per night. T-banen: Stortinget. **Amenities:** Restaurant; bar; laundry/dry cleaning. *In room:* A/C, TV, minibar, iron/ironing board.

Golden Tulip Rainbow Hotel Stefan   In an excellent location in the center of the city, this hotel is comfortable and unpretentious. Built in 1952, it has been modernized and much improved, with a partial renovation in 1996. The color-coordinated guest rooms are traditional in style and well furnished and maintained, with small but adequate bathrooms containing shower-tub combinations. Two guest rooms offer facilities for people with disabilities. From May until September 1, weekend rates are granted only to those who make reservations less than 48 hours before arrival.

Rosenkrantzgate 1, N-0159 Oslo 1. © **23-31-55-00.** Fax 23-31-55-55. www.rainbow-hotels.no. 139 units. Mon–Thurs 1,015NOK ($135) double; Fri–Sat 735NOK ($98) double. Rates include breakfast. AE, DC, MC, V. Parking 180NOK ($24). Tram: 10, 11, 17, or 18. **Amenities:** Restaurant; bar; room service; babysitting; laundry/dry cleaning. *In room:* TV, minibar, hair dryer, safe.

Hotell Bondeheimen

In the city center, a short block from the Students' Grove at Karl Johans Gate, the Bondeheimen was built in 1913. A cooperative of farmers and students established it to provide inexpensive accommodations when they visited Oslo from the countryside. Although small, the compact rooms are comfortably furnished, often with Norwegian pine pieces; accommodations for nonsmokers are offered. The hotel was renovated in 1995. The beds are good, and the bathrooms, although small and mostly without tubs, contain shower units and heated floors.

Rosenkrantzgate 8 (entrance on Kristian IV's Gate), N-0159 Oslo 1. © **800/528-1234** in the U.S., or 23-21-41-00. Fax 22-41-94-37. www.bondeheimen.com. 81 units. Mon–Thurs 2,105NOK ($280) double; Fri–Sun 834NOK ($111) double. Rates include breakfast. AE, DC, MC, V. Parking 180NOK ($24). Tram: 7 or 11. **Amenities:** Restaurant; bar; room service; laundry/dry cleaning. *In room:* TV, minibar, hair dryer.

Norlandia Karl Johan

For the past century or so, an old-fashioned aura hung above this gray stone hotel, the former Karl Johan. Now, a recent renovation has made it brighter, more inviting, and a lot less dim compared to its neighbor across the street, the more prestigious and still far better Grand Hotel. Filled with Norwegian folk art, it welcomes you to a reception area filled with mirrors and marble, along with rugs from Asia and antiques (or reproductions at least). The medium-sized guest rooms have a classic decor with excellent fabrics, good beds, double glazing on the windows to cut down on the noise outside, and tiny marble-clad bathrooms with shower-tub combinations. The best units open onto the front, and contain French windows with panoramic views of the central city. About 50% of the accommodations are reserved for nonsmokers.

Karl Johans Gate 33, N-0162 Oslo. © **23-16-17-00.** Fax 22-42-05-19. www.norlandia.no. 111 units. Mon–Thurs 1,570NOK ($209) double; 1,890NOK ($251) suite. Fri–Sun 990NOK ($132) double; 2,300NOK ($306) suite. Rates include breakfast. AE, DC, MC, V. Parking 187NOK ($25) in nearby public garage. T-banen: Stortinget. **Amenities:** Restaurant; bar; room service; laundry/dry cleaning. *In room:* TV, minibar, hair dryer.

Tulip Inn Rainbow Cecil

This contemporary hotel was built following a fire in the mid-1980s, when an older building on this centrally located site was destroyed. Thanks to the eccentrically shaped site, only four rooms on each of the eight floors overlook the street (the sometimes rowdy, at least late at night, Rosenkrantzgate). The others look out over a quiet inner courtyard. Expect relatively simple styling with none of the trappings of more expensive nearby competitors—there's no health club, sauna, or full-fledged room service. The well-maintained rooms are cozy and contain neatly kept bathrooms with shower-tub combinations.

Stortingsgate 8 (entrance on Rosenkrantzgate); N-0130 Oslo. © **23-31-48-00.** Fax 23-31-48-50. www.rainbow-hotels.no. 112 units. Mon–Thurs 1,370NOK ($182) double; Fri–Sat 830NOK ($110) double. AE, DC, MC, V. Parking 165NOK ($22). T-banen: Stortinget. **Amenities:** Lounge; laundry/dry cleaning. *In room:* A/C, TV, minibar, hair dryer.

INEXPENSIVE

Cochs Pensjonat *Value* Built more than a century ago, with an ornate facade that curves around a bend in a boulevard that flanks the northern edge of the Royal Palace, this is a clean, well-conceived, inexpensive hotel that represents excellent value. In 2002, major renovations added a postmodern gloss to many of the guest rooms, with the remainder scheduled for overhauls sometime between 2003 and

2004. The result is a comfortable but simple lodging whose newer rooms have high ceilings and birch furniture, and a spartan but pleasant appearance. Older rooms evoke touches of the slightly dowdy, slightly battered 1970s, but are still very comfortable. You'll climb a flight of antique steps from the ground floor to reach the second-floor lobby. The hotel has four stories, and there is a communal TV lounge that's sometimes packed with residents. Expect very few, if any, amenities and services at this hotel—none of the rooms have TV or telephone, and no meals are served, but because of the in-room kitchens and a nearby restaurant that offers hotel guests a 25% discount on meals, no one really seems to mind.

Parkveien 25, N-0350 Oslo. ℂ **23-33-24-00.** Fax 23-33-24-10. booking@cochs.no. 88 units, 78 with bathroom and kitchenette. Rooms with bathroom and kitchenette 600NOK–660NOK ($80–$88) double; 735NOK–795NOK ($98–$106) triple; 860NOK ($114) quad. Rooms without kitchenette and without private bathroom 500NOK ($67) double; 615NOK ($82) triple; 740NOK ($98) quad. AE, DC, MC, V. Tram: 11 or 12. *In room:* Kitchenette in some, no phone.

Norrøna *(Kids* In the heart of Oslo's old section, occupying the upper floors of a modernized building, this hotel is ideal for families. Convenient to both sightseeing and shopping, it offers well-equipped rooms that have Scandinavian modern furnishings and good beds. A few have private balconies. Many rooms are large enough for families of three or four, although bathrooms have only minimal space, but do contain shower-tub combinations.

Grensen 19, N-0159 Oslo 1. ℂ **23-31-80-00.** Fax 23-31-80-01. www.rainbow-hotels.no. 93 units. 850NOK–1,310NOK ($113–$174) double. Rates include breakfast. AE, DC, MC, V. Parking 140NOK ($19). T-banen: Stortinget. Tram: 1 or 7. Bus: 17. **Amenities:** Restaurant; lounge; laundry/dry cleaning. *In room:* A/C, TV.

Tulip Inn Rainbow Munch This hotel is somewhat like a bed-and-breakfast, and it's just 5 minutes north of Karl Johans Gate. Built in 1983, the solid, nine-floor hotel offers comfortably furnished, well-maintained guest rooms, decorated with reproductions of Edvard Munch's paintings. Although not overly large, the rooms are cozy and comfortable. The bathrooms are tiny but come equipped with shower-tub combinations. If you don't plan to spend a lot of time in your room, this is an adequate choice, charging a fair price for what it offers.

Munchsgaten 5, N-0130 Oslo 1. ℂ **23-21-96-00.** Fax 23-21-96-01. www.rainbow-hotels.no. 180 units. Mon–Thurs 1,145NOK ($152) double; Fri–Sun 720NOK ($96) double. Rates include breakfast. AE, DC, MC, V. Parking 140NOK ($19). T-banen: Stortinget. Tram: 7 or 11. Bus: 37. **Amenities:** Lounge; laundry/dry cleaning. *In room:* TV, minibar, hair dryer, safe.

WEST END
EXPENSIVE
Hotel Ambassadeur One of the most consistently reliable hotels in Oslo, the Ambassadeur was built around 1890 as an apartment house. Near the Royal Palace, in an upscale residential neighborhood, it boasts a well-upholstered salon with tapestries and antiques. The theme-decorated guest rooms were renovated between 1994 and 1998. They have double-glazed windows, good beds, and trouser presses. The small, tiled bathrooms have shower-tub combinations and heated towel racks. Suites are more elaborate.

Camilla Colletts Vei 15, N-0258 Oslo. ℂ **23-27-23-00.** Fax 22-44-47-91. www.bestwestern.com/no/ambassadeur. 41 units. Mon–Thurs 1,375NOK ($183) double; 1,750NOK ($233) suite. Fri–Sun 910NOK ($121) double; 1,350NOK ($180) suite. Rates include breakfast. AE, DC, MC, V. Free parking. Bus: 21. **Amenities:** Restaurant; bar; fitness room; sauna; laundry/dry cleaning. *In room:* TV, minibar, hair dryer.

MODERATE
Gabelshus On a quiet, tree-lined street, this 1912 building has been a small hotel since 1945. Discreet and conservative, it looks like an English manor

house, laced with climbing ivy. The public rooms are filled with antiques, art, burnished copper, and working fireplaces. Guest rooms are decorated with tasteful colors and textiles, and some have terraces. You have a choice of Scandinavian modern furniture or traditional styling. The accommodations are well maintained and equipped with double-glazed windows and good beds. Bathrooms are small but immaculate, with shower-tub combinations. It's a brisk 15-minute walk from the city center.

Gabels Gate 16, N-0272 Oslo 2. © **23-27-65-00.** Fax 23-27-65-60. www.gabelshus.no. 43 units. July and Fri–Sun year-round 950NOK ($126) double; rest of year 1,495NOK ($199) double, 1,790NOK ($238) suite. Rates include breakfast. AE, DC, MC, V. Free parking. Tram: 10. **Amenities:** Lounge; laundry/dry cleaning. *In room:* TV, hair dryer.

Gyldenløve (Golden Lion) This once-dowdy *hospits* (an inexpensive hotel, but better than a youth hostel), built in 1937, was radically upgraded in 1992 and incorporated into the well-recommended Rainbow chain of Norwegian hotels. It's 10 minutes on foot from the Royal Palace, on a tree-lined street known for its exclusive boutiques. The guest rooms have Scandinavian modern styling and firm beds, but small bathrooms with shower units.

Bogstadveien 20, N-0355 Oslo 3. © **22-60-10-90.** Fax 22-60-33-90. www.rainbow-hotels.no. 168 units. 1,220NOK ($162) double. Rates include breakfast. AE, DC, MC, V. Parking 90NOK ($10). Tram: 11, 13, or 19. **Amenities:** Restaurant; bar; laundry/dry cleaning. *In room:* A/C, TV, minibar, hair dryer.

AT FROGNER
Frogner House ⋆ *Finds* In 1992, a turn-of-the-20th-century redbrick apartment house was transformed into this stylish, upscale hotel. In the affluent Oslo suburb of Frogner, about .8km (½ mile) west of the city's commercial core, it's outfitted in conservative but cozy English style, with lots of lace curtains, a scattering of antiques, and soft cheerful colors. This hotel has built its reputation by catering to international business travelers, many involved in shipping and real estate. This is an upscale bed-and-breakfast, loaded with attentive service and comforts, but most luxuries must be arranged through outside suppliers by the reception staff. Each room is well maintained and equipped with a well-kept bathroom with shower-tub combination.

Skovveien 8, Frogner, N-0257 Oslo. © **22-56-00-56.** Fax 22-56-05-00. www.frognerhouse.com. 60 units. Sun–Thurs 1,515NOK ($202) double; Fri–Sat 1,025NOK ($136) double. AE, DC, MC, V. Tram: 12. **Amenities:** Lounge; room service. *In room:* TV, minibar, hair dryer.

4 Where to Dine

You can now "dine around the world" without leaving the city of Oslo. The biggest concentration of restaurants is at Aker Brygge. The former shipbuilding yard on the harbor is now the smartest dining and shopping complex in Norway.

Not all restaurants in Oslo are new. Some have long been associated with artists and writers—the Grand Café, for example, was the stomping ground of Henrik Ibsen and Edvard Munch. Blom is also a traditional favorite.

The influx of foreigners in recent years has led to the growth of Mexican, Turkish, Moroccan, Chinese, Greek, and other international restaurants. Among European cuisines, French and Italian are the most popular. Many restaurants offer American-style food.

At nearly all restaurants recommended below, a 15% service charge and the 20% value-added tax are included in the bill. No further tipping is required, although it's customary to leave some small change if the service has been satisfactory.

Wine and beer can be lethal to your final bill, so be careful.

Oslo Dining

Albertine Café & Bar **11**
A Touch of France **22**
Babette's Gjestehus **13**
Bagatelle **3**
Brasserie 45 **17**
Bristol Grill **18**
Det Gamle Rådhus **26**
Dionysos **29**

Engebret Café **28**
Feinschmecker **5**
Friskport Vegeta
 Vertshus **12**
Frognerseteren
 Hoved-Restaurant **1**
Golden Tulip Rainbow
 Stefan Hotel **19**

Grand Café **21**
Hos Thea **9**
Kastanjen **4**
Lanternen **8**
Lipp **15**
Lofoten
 Fiskerestaurant **10**
Louise Restaurant **11**

Magma **6**
Mamma Rosa **24**
Najaden **7**
Oro **14**
Primo Restaurant
  Ciaou-Ciaou **25**
Restaurant Julius Fritzner **21**
Restaurant Le Canard **2**

Statholderens Krostue **27**
Statholdergaarden **27**
Stortorvets Gjæstgiveri **20**
Theatercafeen **15**
3 Brødre **23**
Von Angels Delikatesse **16**

✝ Church
ⓘ Information
✉ Post Office
Ⓜ Metro
Railway

CENTRAL OSLO
VERY EXPENSIVE
Oro ✸✸✸ CONTINENTAL Gallons of ink have already been used in the Norwegian press to describe this new, hyper-stylish restaurant, winner of the American Express service award 2 years in a row. Norwegian-born chef Terje Ness directs the kitchen of a three-faceted establishment that includes an intensely European gourmet restaurant, a separate but still very glamorous tapas bar, and a boutique-style deli (open Mon–Sat 9am–5pm) for fans of the place who want to haul some of its raw ingredients back home. The restaurant and the tapas bar are curvaceous, slick-looking testimonials to the appeal of stainless steel and warm-toned hardwoods. The best way to handle the esoteric choice of foods here involves ordering one of the set-price menus, although be warned in advance that each of them will be prepared only for every member of the table at the same time. The one priced at 925NOK ($123) includes 10 different courses, each of them composed differently every day, according to the availability of the ingredients and the whim of the chef. Other set menus include a seven-course fish and shellfish menu, priced at 825NOK ($110); and a three-course vegetarian menu at 425NOK ($57). Representative dishes, each one delectable, include lobster ravioli; glazed scallops with Serrano ham; a platter that combines three different versions of foie gras (grilled, *en terrine,* and *en brioche*); and spit-roasted pigeon stuffed with foie gras.

Tordenskioldsgate 6A (entrance on Kjeld Stubs Gate). ℂ **23-01-02-40.** Reservations required. Main courses 315NOK–345NOK ($42–$46). Set-price menus 425NOK–925NOK ($57–$123). AE, DC, M C, V. Dinner Mon–Sat 6–10pm. Closed 2 weeks in Nov. T-banen: Stortinget.

Restaurant Julius Fritzner ✸✸✸ NORWEGIAN/CONTINENTAL This is one of the best and most impressive restaurants in Oslo. It opened in 1995 to rave reviews and the accolades keep coming. It's one floor above street level in Norway's most prestigious hotel. The venue is appropriately conservative, with a battalion of impeccably trained waiters who maintain their humor and personal touch despite the sophisticated setting. The dishes, all made with the finest Scandinavian ingredients, change with the season and the chef's inspiration. Examples include pan-fried turbot, lobster and caviar sauce, crispy fried cod with sautéed vegetables, poached halibut with vermouth sauce, filet of veal with crispy fried sweetbreads, and roast saddle of lamb with rosemary. Desserts, which are delicious and occasionally theatrical, include a terrine of chocolate with a compote of peaches and sorbet flavored with basil and cinnamon. The restaurant, incidentally, is named after the controversial entrepreneur who established the Grand Hotel in 1874.

In the Grand Hotel, Karl Johans Gate 31. Tel. **23-21-20-00.** Reservations recommended. Main courses 220NOK–300NOK ($29–$40); 3-course fixed-price menu 470NOK ($63); 4-course fixed-price menu 550NOK ($73); 6-course fixed-price menu 640NOK ($85). AE, DC, MC, V. Mon–Sat 5–10:30pm. Closed July–Aug 5. T-banen: Stortinget.

EXPENSIVE
Babette's Gjestehus ✸ SCANDINAVIAN Named for the heroine of the film *Babette's Feast*—which almost every Scandinavian has seen at least once—this restaurant is decorated in the style of a turn-of-the-20th-century Norwegian home. Walls are blue, antiques are genuine, curtains are lace, and there's a scattering of old paintings. Menu items are authentic as well, with such time-tested favorites as filet of reindeer with lingonberries, steamed brill with mustard sauce and stewed tomatoes, breast of pheasant with mushroom sauce, and pan-fried

breast of duck with creamed cabbage. The masterful chefs use seasonal products to produce reliable, good-tasting food all year.

Rådhuspassasjen, Roald Amundsensgate 6. ℭ **22-41-64-64.** Reservations recommended. Main courses 249NOK–265NOK ($33–$35). AE, DC, MC, V. Mon–Sat 5–11pm. T-banen: Centrum.

MODERATE

Bristol Grill ✹✹ CONTINENTAL   This is the premier dining room of one of Oslo's most prestigious hotels. You'll find old-world courtliness, formal service without a lot of flash or frenzy, and elegant decor that evokes a 1920s baronial hunting lodge (the restaurant was founded in 1924). At the time, it was an all-male smoking, drinking, and dining club. A few years later, it evolved into the dining venue you'll see today, with an allure that eventually attracted such entertainers as Sonja Henie, Josephine Baker, Eartha Kitt, Frank Sinatra, and Sophia Loren. There's a cozy, woodsy-looking piano bar (the Winterhavn Bar) that you'll pass through to reach the restaurant. In 2002, the menus and culinary focus of this restaurant were radically upgraded, and are now among the finest in the Norwegian capital. There's a spectacular version of bouillabaisse, prepared with Nordic (not Mediterranean) fish and seasoned with saffron, that can be configured as either a starter or a main course. We followed this with one of the chef's most successful specialties: medallions of venison sautéed with vanilla and bacon, served on a bed of mushrooms with a terrine of potatoes.

In the Hotel Bristol, Kristian IV's Gate 7. ℭ **22-82-60-00.** Reservations recommended. Main courses 210NOK–285NOK ($28–$38). AE, DC, MC, V. Daily 5–11pm. Tram: 10, 11, 17, or 18.

Golden Tulip Rainbow Stefan Hotel *(Value* NORWEGIAN   This bustling, unpretentious restaurant is better known than the hotel it's in. Local businesspeople come for the city's best smörgåsbord, laden with traditional Norwegian foods that include cucumber salad, fish and meat salads, sausages, meatballs, potato salad, smoked fish, assorted cheeses, and breads. During the evening, you can order from a rich a la carte menu if you don't feel like waiting in line, plate in hand. Selections from the a la carte menu include "Stefan's special platter"—an old-fashioned but flavorful dish that incorporates slices of reindeer, moose meat, and ox tongue, with lingonberries and potatoes, on the same heaping plate.

Rosenkrantzgate 1. ℭ **23-31-55-00.** Reservations recommended. Main courses 180NOK–200NOK ($24–$27); lunch smörgåsbord 195NOK ($26). AE, DC, MC, V. Smörgåsbord, Mon–Fri 11:30am–2:30pm; Sat noon–2:30pm; Thurs–Fri 4:30–10:30pm. A la carte, Mon–Sat 4:30–10:30pm. Tram: 7 or 11.

Grand Café ✹✹ NORWEGIAN   This traditional cafe is an Oslo legend. A large mural on one wall depicts Ibsen (a fan of whale steaks), Edvard Munch, and many other patrons. A postcard sold at the reception desk identifies the mural's subjects.

You can order everything from a napoleon with coffee to a full meal with fried stingray or reindeer steaks. Sandwiches are available for 80NOK ($11) and up. The atmosphere and tradition here are sometimes more compelling than the cuisine. The menu, nonetheless, relies on Norwegian country traditions (after all, how many places still serve elk stew?). If you like solid, honest flavors, this is the place go.

In the Grand Hotel, Karl Johans Gate 31. ℭ **24-14-53-00.** Reservations recommended. Main courses 145NOK–280NOK ($19–$37). AE, DC, MC, V. Mon–Sat 11am–11pm; Sun noon–11pm. T-banen: Stortinget.

Lipp INTERNATIONAL   Stylish and lighthearted, this restored brasserie is the Oslovian version of Paris in the 1920s. Painted a canary yellow, it employs a traditionally dressed, bistro-style, black-vested staff. Each day a special dish is

Dining Secrets of Oslo

One of the Oslovians' favorite pastimes is visiting **Aker Brygge**. Formerly a dilapidated shipbuilding yard, the futuristic complex now combines more shopping, entertainment, and dining diversions in one area than anywhere else in Norway. Many people, some with children, come here to check out the restaurants and cafes, watch the people, and listen to the music playing in the bars. Part of the fun is strolling through the complex and picking a restaurant. Norwegian food is served along with a representative selection of foreign food offerings, including American. An especially good choice is the Louise Restaurant (see below). In the summer, visitors and locals fill the outdoor tables overlooking the harbor. There are also many nightlife options (see "Oslo After Dark," later in this chapter). To reach Aker Brygge, take bus no. 27 or walk down from the center west of the Rådhus.

Not as formal as Louise, but a local favorite, is the **Albertine Café & Bar,** Stranden 3, Aker Brygge (© **22-83-00-60**), an informal place on the wharf's edge, offering a panoramic view over the harbor and Akershus fortress. Consistently, this place serves some of the freshest and tastiest oysters in Oslo. You can drop in for just a hamburger or for a full Norwegian seafood dinner. It's an easy place for singles to meet.

A good choice for the makings of a picnic is **Von Angels Delikatesse,** Karl Johans Gate 41B (© **23-13-95-02**). It's open Monday through Friday from 10am to 8pm, Saturday from 10am to 5pm.

In front of the Rådhuset, you can join Oslovians for a special picnic treat. From 7 to 8am, **shrimp fishermen** pull their boats into the harbor after having caught and cooked fresh batches of shrimp during their night at sea. You can order shrimp in a bag (it comes in two sizes). Seafood fanciers take their shrimp to the dock's edge, remove the shells, and feast. The fishermen usually stick around until they've sold the last batch, saving just enough for their families.

offered of which the chef is justly proud. On our last visit it was roasted grouse served with a wild mushroom pie with crisp bacon. The menu changes about every 5 weeks, and it is seasonally adjusted, using the finest of produce from the field, not to mention river and lake. You might face a delectable salmon in a white-wine sauce, or reindeer in a mushroom sauce. Lighter fare is offered as well for those watching their weight—perhaps an array of freshly made salads or grilled fish dishes. Succulent pastas are also regularly featured.

In the Hotel Continental, Stortingsgaten 24. © 22-82-40-60. Reservations recommended. Main courses 172NOK–255NOK ($23–$34). AE, DC, MC, V. Daily 4–11:30pm. T-banen: Nationaltheatret.

Primo Restaurant Ciaou-Ciaou MEDITERRANEAN/NORWEGIAN
The food here is a cut above what you'd expect in the average hotel dining room. Norwegian ingredients get inspiration from the Italian and Spanish chefs who use them, resulting in dishes with a bit more verve than you might have expected in this Nordic clime. Try baked swordfish with a piquant tomato sauce, homemade paté of venison served with marinated olives, filet of beef braised with broccoli and mushrooms with a spicy *salsa de pepperoni,* and succulent

preparations of Norwegian lamb. There's also a bar here, with a staff that mixes a medley of American libations.

In the First Hotel Millennium, Tollbugate 25. ⓒ **21-02-28-00.** Reservations recommended. Main courses 200NOK–245NOK ($27–$33); pastas 130NOK–145NOK ($17–$19). AE, DC, MC, V. Mon–Sat 11:30am–10:30pm. Tram: 30 or 42.

Theatercafeen ⓚ INTERNATIONAL   The last of the grand Viennese cafes in the north of Europe, this long-standing favorite was founded a century ago to rival the Grand Café. Each has its devotees, although we like this one better because of its Viennese *schmaltz.* The serenading pianist and violinists would have pleased the Habsburg emperor Franz-Josef, had he ever ventured this far north. It attracts present-day *boulevardiers* and businesspeople. With soft lighting, antique bronzes, cut-glass lighting fixtures, and Art Nouveau mirrors, it is the type of place that encourages lingering. Menu items are well prepared and traditional, and are adjusted accordingly to get the best flavors out of each new season. That might mean fresh asparagus and spring lamb, or in the autumn, breast of wild goose and other game dishes. The fish dishes are particularly well prepared, including a recently sampled casserole of mussels. You can also enjoy such traditional Norwegian fare as reindeer with wild mushrooms or Norwegian fjord salmon.

In the Hotel Continental, Stortingsgaten 24. ⓒ **22-82-40-50.** Reservations recommended. Main courses 195NOK–365NOK ($26–$49); 3-course menu 635NOK ($84); open-faced sandwiches 85NOK–95NOK ($11–$13) at lunch. AE, DC, MC, V. Mon–Sat 11am–midnight; Sun 3–10pm. T-banen: Stortinget.

A Touch of France ⓚ FRENCH   This aptly named place is one of Oslo's best French bistros. In summer tables spill out onto the sidewalk. The decor is that of a typical French brasserie, the kind you find alongside the road in Alsace. A Touch of France is known for serving the freshest oysters in town. On our most recent visit, we opted for the traditional salt-baked leg of duck that was served in a beautifully made garlic sauce. On other occasions we've enjoyed classic calves' liver with mushrooms, spinach, and bacon. Bouillabaisse is a specialty but that grand dish loses something in translation this far north. After your main course, a dessert trolley is wheeled around, loaded with such temptations as crème brûlée or a delectable chocolate and almond cake.

Øvre Slottsgate 16. ⓒ **23-10-01-60.** Reservations recommended. Main courses 185NOK–285NOK ($25–$38). AE, DC, MC, V. Mon–Sat noon–11:30pm. Bus: 27, 29, 30, 41, or 61.

INEXPENSIVE
Brasserie 45 CONTINENTAL   Airy and stylish, this second-story bistro overlooks the biggest fountain along downtown Oslo's showplace promenade. The uniformed staff bears steaming platters of ambitious, imaginative cuisine, including especially flavorful versions of fried catfish with lemon-garlic sauce; fried chicken in spicy, tomato-based sweet-and-sour sauce; pork schnitzels with béarnaise sauce and shrimp; and tartare of salmon with dill-enriched boiled potatoes. For dessert, try chocolate terrine with cloudberry sorbet.

Karl Johans Gate 45. ⓒ **22-41-34-00.** Reservations recommended. Main courses 89NOK–189NOK ($12–$25). AE, DC, MC, V. Mon–Thurs noon–midnight; Fri–Sat noon–1am; Sun 2:30–11pm. T-banen: Centrum.

OLD TOWN (GAMLEBYEN/KVADRATUREN)
VERY EXPENSIVE
Statholderens Krostue ⓚ SWEDISH/DANISH   This relatively uncomplicated cellar-level bistro is associated with Statholdergaarden, one of Oslo's most prestigious restaurants (see above). Unlike its more sophisticated sibling, it's open

for lunch as well as dinner, and features relatively uncomplicated food that's mostly based on traditional Swedish and Danish recipes. The cuisine provides many original and, most of the time, happy combinations of ingredients. Beneath the vaulted Renaissance-era ceiling, you can order *frikadeller* (meatballs), minced veal patties in creamy dill sauce, steak with fried onions, fried eel with potato and herb dumplings, and grilled salmon with saffron-flavored noodles. Lunch specialties include platters piled high with Danish or Norwegian ham, herring, boiled eggs, and vegetables, and a selection of smørrebrød (Danish open-faced sandwiches).

Rådhusgata 11. © 22-41-88-00. Main courses 245NOK–330NOK ($33–$44); fixed-price menu 400NOK ($53). AE, DC, MC, V. Tues–Sat 11:30am–10pm. Tram: 11, 15, or 18.

Statholdergaarden ✿✿✿ NOUVELLE NORWEGIAN One of Oslo's most historic restaurant settings (the building dates to 1640) has one of its most successful chefs, Bent Stiansen, whose unique interpretation of Norwegian nouvelle cuisine has attracted the admiration of gastronomes throughout the country. At this restaurant (which dates from 1901), menu items change frequently, according to what's in season. Examples include grilled crayfish served with scallop and salmon tartare, and thyme-infused codfish with crabmeat mousse and two sauces (a simple white-wine sauce and another based on a rare vanilla bean imported from Thailand). One of our all-time favorite dishes is lightly fried Arctic char with sautéed savoy cabbage and lime beurre blanc (white butter). Also appealing are roasted rack of lamb with sage sauce, platters of French cheeses, and cloudberry crepes. Don't confuse this upscale and prestigious site with the less expensive bistro Statholderens Krostue (see below), which occupies the building's vaulted cellar.

Rådhusgata 11. © 22-41-88-00. Reservations recommended. Main courses 290NOK–350NOK ($39–$47); 4-course fixed-price menu 725NOK ($96); 6-course fixed-price menu 875NOK ($116). AE, DC, MC, V. Mon–Sat 6pm–midnight. Tram: 11, 15, or 18.

EXPENSIVE

Det Gamle Rådhus (Old Town Hall) ✿ NORWEGIAN The oldest restaurant in Oslo, Det Gamle Rådhus is in Oslo's former Town Hall (1641). This is strictly for nostalgia buffs, as the restaurant is not at all hip or cutting edge. It's still there for those wanting to see Oslo the way it used to be, but the innovative fires died a long time ago. You'll dine within a network of baronial or manorial-inspired rooms linked with dark wooden panels and Flemish, 16th-century-styled wooden chairs. In the spacious dining room, a full array of open-faced sandwiches is served on weekdays only. A la carte dinner selections can be made from a varied menu that includes fresh fish, game, and Norwegian specialties. Although it sounds like a culinary turn-off, the house specialty is quite delectable. It's lutefisk, a Scandinavian specialty made from dried fish that has been soaked

---

Kids **Family-Friendly Restaurants**

Mamma Rosa (p. 218) The best place to fill up on one of the 15 kinds of pizzas or a pasta dish, each a meal in itself.

Najaden (p. 221) As if being in the Norwegian Maritime Museum weren't enough for kids, they can also enjoy an elaborate summer lunch buffet for half price—they must be under 12.

in lye, and then poached in broth. If you want to sample a dish that Ibsen might have enjoyed, check this one out. More to your liking might be smoked salmon (it's smoked right on the premises), a parfait of chicken livers, freshwater pike-perch from nearby streams sautéed in a lime sauce, or filet of reindeer with lin-gonberry sauce. Norwegian lamb is coated with herbs and baked with a glaze.

Nedre Slottsgate 1. ℃ **22-42-01-07.** Reservations recommended. Main courses 200NOK–275NOK ($27–$37); open-faced sandwiches 85NOK–115NOK ($11–$15); 3-course set dinner 398NOK ($53). AE, DC, MC, V. Mon–Fri 11am–3pm; Mon–Sat 4–11pm. Kroen Bar, Mon–Sat 4pm–midnight. Closed last 3 weeks of July. Bus: 27, 29, 30, 41, or 61.

MODERATE

Stortorvets Gjæstgiveri ✿ NORWEGIAN   This is the oldest restaurant in Oslo, and one of only three buildings to have escaped complete destruction dur-ing the many fires that roared through the city during the late 19th century. The present restaurant is composed of a trio of wood-framed buildings, the oldest dating from the 1700s. An inn originally stood on this spot with stables out back reserved for horses. The inn's bedchambers upstairs are virtually unchanged since their original construction. But these antique rooms with their wood-burning stoves are now used as private dining rooms. Today, the restaurant is revered as a genuine vestige of Oslo the way it used to be. It's also one of the principal per-formance sites during Oslo's midsummer jazz festival every year.

Its venue changes radically throughout the course of the day: Expect a cafe near the entrance; an old-fashioned, charming, and usually packed restaurant in back; and a hard-drinking, highly convivial nightclub venue every Thursday through Saturday from 8 to 11pm, where there's a 60NOK ($8) cover charge imposed on anyone who isn't dining. Menu items are traditional, well prepared, and flavorful, and include grilled halibut with beurre blanc sauce; veal with smoked ham and sausage; chicken breast stuffed with spinach and creamed porcini mushrooms; filet of reindeer with a compote of onions and apples; and freshwater trout with arugula and balsamic vinegar. *Lutefisk,* an elaborate and ultra-traditional preparation of aged, air-dried cod, is one of the trademark dishes here, a dish so complicated (with such a high possibility of spoilage) that many lesser restaurants don't even try to prepare it. Here, thanks to automated high-tech kitchen equipment, they sell thousands of portions of it a year, mostly in autumn, when it's at its best and most aromatic.

Grensen 1. ℃ **23-35-63-60.** Small platters and snacks 92NOK–160NOK ($12–$21). Main courses 170NOK–260NOK ($23–$35). AE, DC, MC, V. Cafe daily 11am–8pm; restaurant daily 3–11pm. Tram: 12, 17, or 21.

3 Brødre ✿ NORWEGIAN   "Three Brothers" is named after the glove man-ufacturers who once occupied this building. This is a longtime favorite drawing more locals than visitors. Habitués know of its fresh food, which is well prepared with hearty portions and reasonable prices. You might begin with Norwegian salmon tartare or snails, followed by an almond-and-garlic gratinée. The most popular appetizer is a selection of fresh mussels poached with leeks, parsley, garlic, and cream. For a main course, try the fried catfish with prawns, mussels, red pep-pers, and capers, or beefsteak with béarnaise sauce. The entire street level houses the bustling bar. Upstairs is a piano bar. A large beer costs 56NOK ($7.45). Lighter meals, such as snacks and sandwiches ranging in price from 75NOK to 98NOK ($10–$13), are available on the outside dining terrace in the summer.

Øvre Slottsgate 14. ℃ **23-10-06-70.** Main courses 138NOK–222NOK ($18–$30). AE, DC, MC, V. Kaelleren, Mon–Sat 4pm–1am; street-level bar, Mon–Sat 11pm–2:30am; piano bar, Mon–Sat 5pm–2:30am. Bus: 27, 29, or 30.

INEXPENSIVE

Engebret Café NORWEGIAN   A favorite since 1857, this restaurant is directly north of Akershus Castle in two landmark buildings. It has an old-fashioned atmosphere—it was formerly a bohemian literati haunt—and good food. During lunch, a tempting selection of open-faced sandwiches is available. The evening menu is more elaborate; you might begin with a terrine of game with blackberry port-wine sauce, or Engebret's fish soup. Main dishes include red wild boar with whortleberry sauce, Norwegian reindeer, salmon Christiania, or Engebret's big fish pot. For dessert, try the cloudberry parfait.

Bankplassen 1. © **22-33-66-94.** Reservations recommended. Main courses 265NOK–590NOK ($35–$78). AE, DC, MC, V. Mon–Sat 11am–11pm. Bus: 27, 29, or 30.

Friskport Vegeta Vertshus VEGETARIAN   Since 1938 this basement cafeteria near the Rådhus has been Oslo's major vegetarian restaurant. It's a stronghold of social activism and a spot to share news of countercultural activities. At street level is a cafe with a buffet of 25 salad dishes and many hot dishes, along with bread, butter, cheese, and coffee. A new smoke-free bar downstairs serves a special student buffet for 112NOK ($15) Tuesday through Saturday. The kitchen is also proud of its pizza. You can order juices, mineral water, soft drinks, or nonalcoholic wine. To go to the buffet once, a small plate costs 85NOK ($11), a large plate, 95NOK ($13).

Munkedamsveien 3B. © **22-83-42-32.** Soups and salads 60NOK ($8); buffet 140NOK ($19). AE, DC, MC, V. Daily noon–10pm. Bus: 27.

Mamma Rosa *(Kids)* ITALIAN   Established by two Tuscan brothers, this trattoria enjoys popularity that's a good indication of Norwegians' changing tastes. The second-floor dining room is decorated in "reproduction rococo." You can order 15 kinds of pizza, fried scampi and squid, rigatoni, pasta Mamma Rosa (three kinds of pasta with three sauces), grilled steaks, and gelato. Frankly, some of the dishes have lost a bit of flavor on the trip this far north, but Mamma Rosa is nonetheless a marvelous change of taste and texture.

Øvre Slottsgate 12. © **22-42-01-30.** Main courses 91NOK–210NOK ($12–$28); pizzas from 97NOK ($13). DC, MC, V. Mon–Sat noon–11:30pm; Sun 3–10:30pm. T-banen: Stortinget.

AKER BRYGGE

EXPENSIVE

Lofoten Fiskerestaurant ✿ SEAFOOD   Near one of the most distant corners of the Aker Brygge dining complex, on the ground floor with views over the harbor, this is one of the city's most appealing seafood restaurants. The interior sports nautical accessories that might remind you of an upscale yacht. In good weather, tables are set up on an outdoor terrace lined with flowering plants. Menu items change according to the available catch, with few choices for meat-eaters. The fish is plentiful, served in generous portions, and very fresh. Examples include filet of trout poached in white wine and served with tomato-enriched beurre blanc (white butter) sauce; grilled halibut with assorted shellfish and coconut-flavored risotto; and grilled filet of tuna with garlicky potato cakes, Parmesan cheese, and red-pepper cream sauce. Look for culinary inspirations from Italy and France, and ample use of such Mediterranean preparations as pesto.

Stranden 75, Aker Brygge. © **22-83-08-08.** Reservations recommended. Main courses 138NOK–258NOK ($18–$34) lunch; 138NOK–258NOK ($18–$34) dinner. AE, DC, MC, V. Mon–Sat 11am–11pm; Sun noon–11pm. Bus: 27.

Louise Restaurant NORWEGIAN   Named for a 19th-century Norwegian steamboat, Louise Restaurant is considered the best restaurant in the Aker Brygge complex. The chef prepares such tasty specialties as braised hare with Brussels sprouts and stewed mushrooms and cranberries, and a "cold symphony" of shrimp, salmon, hare, roast beef, potato salad, and cheese. A house specialty, also a complete meal, is the Brygge Tallerken—fried horse meat with stewed mushrooms.

Stranden 3, Aker Brygge. © **22-83-00-60.** Reservations recommended. Main courses 260NOK–275NOK ($35–$37). AE, DC, MC, V. Mon–Sat 11am–11pm; Sun 11am–10pm. Bus: 27.

EASTERN OSLO
MODERATE
Dionysos GREEK   This restaurant, which resembles a family-oriented *taverna* in Greece, serves specialties that include dishes from Cyprus, Crete, Thessalonika, and the Peloponnese. The exuberant Greek waiters serve up *gastra manis* (a northern Greek dish made with ox meat, eggplant, pepperoni, vegetables, and potatoes), moussaka, souvlaki, and a wide selection of kabobs. Recorded bouzouki music is played from 7pm to midnight.

Calmeyersgate 11. © **22-60-78-64.** Reservations recommended. Main courses 110NOK–198NOK ($15–$26). AE, MC, V. Daily 3–11pm. Tram: 1, 2, or 11.

WEST END
VERY EXPENSIVE
Bagatelle FRENCH   This contemporary, informal restaurant is widely regarded as one of Oslo's premier dining choices. Owner-chef Eyvind Hellstrøm serves light, modern cuisine, using market-fresh ingredients. Seafood is the star here, and the menu changes daily. You can begin with a selection of warm or cold appetizers that include carpaccio of scallops in oyster sauce. Fish entrees include smoked catch of the day, steamed halibut with caviar cream sauce, and sole steamed in seaweed. Other main dishes are saddle of reindeer with pears and pepper sauce, loin of veal with sage, and herb-roasted Norwegian rack of lamb for two.

Bygdøy Allé 3. © **22-44-63-97.** Reservations required. Main courses 280NOK–380NOK ($37–$51); 3-course fixed-price menu 650NOK ($86); 5-course fish menu 950NOK ($126); 7-course fixed-price menu 1,150NOK ($153). AE, DC, MC, V. Mon–Sat 6–10:30pm. Bus: 30, 31, 45, 72, or 73.

Magma MEDITERRANEAN/CONTINENTAL   This is one of the genuinely hot restaurants of Oslo, with strong links to some of Europe's most stratospherically chic chefs. Established in 2000 on a busy boulevard within the city's quietly prosperous West End, on the street level of the Rica Hotel Bygdøy (with which it is not directly associated), it's outfitted in a postmodern, punk-conscious style that might have been inspired by a hip-hop club in London or the stage of a fashion *défilé* in Milan. Expect lots of space, a post-industrial decor of vinyl/leatherette sofas and banquettes, pillbox-shaped stools, splashy pop art reminiscent of Andy Warhol—and, most important, the absolutely superb cuisine of Norway's chef-of-the-minute, Ms. Sonja Lee. Born of Korean and Norwegian parents, and one of the most successful culinary entrepreneurs in Norway, she studied at places in Paris, Monaco, and southern France that read like a Who's Who of culinary chic. Even better, she has assembled a team of hip young assistants (including the brilliant Philip Womersley) who seem to work beautifully together in the hyper-modern kitchens, which, incidentally, are available for visits from any diner who's interested in a tour. Ingredients that go into these dishes are pure and perfect, and usually based on flavors of the faraway Mediterranean. Try the braised rabbit with tomatoes and olives, homemade ravioli studded with ricotta and Norwegian wild mushrooms, and (direct from the Ducasse kitchens) spit-roasted veal with a gratin of macaroni and veal jus—a real masterpiece!

Bygdøy Allé 53. ℂ **23-08-58-10**. Reservations recommended. Main courses 180NOK–230NOK ($24–$31); 9-course set menu 650NOK ($86). AE, DC, MC, V. Daily 11am–2pm and 5:30–10:30pm. Tram: 10, 12, or 15.

EXPENSIVE
Feinschmecker ⊛ SCANDINAVIAN　One of the most prestigious restaurants in Oslo will entertain you with the same style and verve it produced for King Harald and his queen, Sonya, during their recent visit. The dining room's antique furniture and small-paned windows evoke old-time style despite the building's modernity. Menu items change frequently; the roster of staples includes grilled scallops with crispy potatoes and celeriac purée; sautéed ocean crayfish tails with apple cider, wild rice, and sun-dried tomatoes; and grilled monkfish with sautéed mushrooms and morel-enriched cream sauce. A particularly sought-after main course is rack of Norwegian lamb, and a dessert that has been preeminent here since the place was established in the late 1980s is a gratin of raspberries. One of our local friends, a savvy food critic, has proclaimed this the best restaurant in Oslo. We're not prepared to go that far, but it ranks at the top.

Balchensgate 5. ℂ **22-44-17-77**. Reservations recommended. Main courses 265NOK–345NOK ($35–$46); fixed-price menu 625NOK ($83). AE, DC, MC, V. Mon–Sat 4:30–10:30pm. Closed 3 weeks in July. Tram: 12 or 19 to Ilesberg.

MODERATE
Hos Thea SCANDINAVIAN　This stylish, well-managed restaurant attracts a loyal crowd of people active in the media and the arts. The waitstaff and chefs share duties, so the person who prepares your meal is likely to carry it to your table as well. Depending on the staff's mood and the season, the superbly prepared menu items might include medallions of veal served with beurre blanc (white butter) and carrots, breast of duck with red-wine sauce, whitefish filets with saffron sauce, and venison with a sauce of mixed Nordic berries. The century-old building, once a private home, is in a West End neighborhood about 3km (2 miles) south of Oslo's commercial center.

Gabelsgate 11 (entrance on Drammensveien). ℂ **22-44-68-74**. Reservations recommended. Main courses 100NOK–250NOK ($13–$33). AE, DC, MC, V. Daily 4:30–10:30pm. Tram: 10 or 13.

Kastanjen NORWEGIAN　Named for the chestnut trees that line the street, this restaurant is in a residential area, near several embassies. The decor, illuminated by candlelight, is modern and unpretentious. The menu changes monthly, and fixed-price menus change daily. Six or seven dishes every night may be ordered as appetizers or main courses; a good choice is salmon with crayfish. There are one or two luxurious main-dish selections, but most are moderately priced. Monkfish is sautéed and served with a crayfish sauce, or you might order reindeer, which is sautéed, baked, and served with reindeer gravy and red currants.

Bygdøy Allé 18. ℂ **22-43-44-67**. Reservations required. Main courses 178NOK–195NOK ($24–$26). AE, DC, MC, V. Mon–Sat 6–11pm. Closed July. Tram: 30.

BYGDØY
Lanternen ⊛ CONTINENTAL　Set close to the arrivals point for the Bygdøy ferry from the quays near Town Hall, within a low-slung white-painted clapboard-covered house from the 19th century, this restaurant is charming, welcoming, and sophisticated. From the windows of its woodsy, hypermodern

interior, you'll see about a thousand privately owned sailboats and motorboats bobbing in the nearby marina, giving the entire venue a distinct nautical appeal.

Both appetizers and main courses are wisely limited but very well chosen, well prepared, and intriguing to the taste buds. On our most recent visit, we launched our repast with a homemade fish soup, while our companions delighted in the chile-flavored steamed mussels flavored with fresh garlic and white wine, as well as the stuffed salmon roll with a pepper-laced cream sauce. Fresh, seasonal, and high quality ingredients characterize the main courses, which range from poached sole with lobster sauce and shrimps to an herb-marinated filet of lamb. The baked chicken breast is enlivened with the additions of cured ham and mozzarella with a Madeira-laced sauce.

Huk Aveny 2. ✆ **22-43-78-38.** Reservations recommended. Main courses 245NOK–275NOK ($33–$37). AE, DC, MC, V. Daily 11am–10pm. Closed Nov. Bus: 30 or the Bygdøy ferry from the quays near Town Hall.

Najaden *(Kids)* NORWEGIAN   In the Norwegian Maritime Museum, this restaurant (the name translates as "mermaid") overlooks a room of sculptures removed from 19th-century clipper ships. The popular summer lunch buffet offers an elaborate array of freshly prepared fish and meat dishes; the rest of the year, lunch is a la carte. You don't get a lot of culinary excitement, but the food is fresh and served in generous portions—and the location is unbeatable when you're sightseeing on Bygdøy.

Bygdøynesveien 37. ✆ **22-43-81-80.** Reservations recommended. Main courses 193NOK–225NOK ($26–$30); lunch buffet (summer only, 11am–3pm) 185NOK ($25), half price for children under 12. AE, DC, MC, V. May 16–Oct 14, daily 11am–7pm; Oct 15–May 15, Mon–Wed and Sat 11am–4pm, Thurs–Fri 11am–7pm. Bus: 30. Ferry: Bygdøy.

HOLMENKOLLEN

Frognerseteren Hoved-Restaurant NORWEGIAN   On a mountain ledge, this lodge offers a panoramic view of Oslo and the fjord. The restaurant is a historic monument, built by entrepreneur Thomas Heftey in 1896. Prices in the cafe are about 15% lower than those in the dining room, and there's a breezy outdoor terrace for snacks and beer. The chef specializes in delectable game dishes, including pheasant paté with Cumberland sauce, medallions of reindeer, and filet of elk sautéed in honey and nuts. You can also order poached, marinated, or smoked Norwegian salmon. The chef's specialty is a scrumptious apple cake.

The restaurant is a 40-minute ride on the T-banen to the Frognerseteren stop some 480m (1,600 ft.) above sea level, or it's 300m (1,000 ft.) downhill from the Holmenkollen railway stop.

Holmenkollveien 200. ✆ **22-92-40-40.** Reservations recommended. Cafe: platters 75NOK–110NOK ($10–$15). Restaurant: main courses 265NOK–275NOK ($35–$37), set-price menus 455NOK–625NOK ($61–$83). DC, MC, V. Restaurant, Tues–Fri noon–3pm, Mon–Sat 5–10pm, Sun 1–8pm; cafe, daily 11am–10pm. T-banen: 15 to Frognerseteren.

FROGNER

Restaurant Le Canard *(Finds)* FRENCH/CONTINENTAL   The mansion that contains this prestigious restaurant is almost as interesting as the cuisine. Designed in the 1880s by a noted Jewish architect named Lowzow, it contains many religious symbols. Look for the Star of David in some of the stained-glass windows, and representations of the Lion of Judah here and there throughout. Everyone from the queen of Norway to British comedian John Cleese has dined on the first-class cuisine. A meal might include grilled lobster with sautéed chanterelles and watercress sauce, carpaccio of smoked scallops, or baked artichokes with creamy mussel and lobster sauce. One enduringly popular meat dish is roasted duck with fig and foie gras sauce. Guinea fowl is stuffed with foie gras and served with a sauce of Banyuls (a sweet French red wine). The food here is always impeccable. The restaurant is in the suburb of Frogner, about a kilometer west of the center of Oslo.

President Harbitzgate 4. (✆ 22-54-34-00. Reservations recommended. Main courses 270NOK–380NOK ($36–$51); 3-course fixed-price menu 545NOK ($72); 5-course fixed-price menu 765NOK ($102); 7-course fixed-price menu 925NOK ($123). AE, DC, DISC, MC, V. Mon–Thurs 5–10:30pm; Fri–Sat 6–10pm.

5 Seeing the Sights

Some would be happy to come to Oslo just for the views of the harbor and the Oslofjord. Panoramas are a major attraction, especially the one from Tryvannstårnet, a 120m (390-ft.) observation-tower atop 570m (1,900-ft.) high Tryvann Hill in the outlying area. Many other attractions are worthy of your time and exploration, too. The beautiful surroundings make these sights even more appealing.

SUGGESTED ITINERARIES

If You Have 1 Day

Arm yourself with a bag of freshly cooked shrimp (see the sidebar "Dining Secrets of Oslo," earlier in this chapter) and take a ferry to the Bygdøy peninsula. Explore the Viking ships, the polar ship *Fram* Museum, the *Kon-Tiki* Museum, the Norwegian Maritime Museum, and the Norwegian Folk Museum. In the late afternoon, go to Frogner Park to admire the Vigeland sculptures.

If You Have 2 Days

On your first day, follow the itinerary above. On your second day, take a walking tour (see later in this chapter), have lunch in a Norwegian restaurant, and explore the Edvard Munch Museum in the afternoon. In the summer, visit the Students' Grove, near the National Theater, for some beer and fresh air.

If You Have 3 Days

For your first 2 days, follow the suggestions above. On Day 3, take another walking tour (see later in this chapter), eating lunch along the way. Explore Akershus Castle and the adjoining Norwegian Resistance Museum in the afternoon. By late afternoon, visit the lofty lookout tower at Tryvannstårnet and see the Skimuseet at Holmenkollen, taking in a panoramic view of the area. Have dinner at Holmenkollen.

If You Have 4 or 5 Days

For the first 3 days, follow the itinerary above. On Day 4, head south on an excursion to the Oslofjord country, with stopovers at the Old Town at Fredrikstad; Tønsberg, Norway's oldest town; and Sandefjord, an old whaling town. Head back to Oslo for the night.

On Day 5, see the rest of Oslo's major sights, such as the National Gallery, the Historical Museum, and the Henie-Onstad Art Center (11km/7 miles from Oslo), a major museum of modern art.

IN CENTRAL OSLO

Oslo Domkirke (Oslo Cathedral)   Oslo's 17th-century cathedral at Stortorvet (the marketplace) was restored in 1950, when Hugo Louis Mohr completed its modern tempera ceiling decorations.

The cathedral contains works by 20th-century Norwegian artists, including bronze doors by Dagfin Werenskiold. Try to view the pulpit and altar, which date from the cathedral's earliest days. There are stained-glass windows by

Emanuel Vigeland (not to be confused with the sculptor, Gustav) in the choir and by Borgar Hauglid in the transepts. The organ is five stories tall. A bilingual service (in Norwegian and English) is conducted on Wednesday at noon, and an organ recital is presented on summer Saturdays at noon.

Stortorvet 1. ℂ **23-31-46-10.** Free admission. Daily 10am–4pm. T-banen: Stortinget. Bus: 17.

Rådhuset (City Hall)
The modern City Hall, inaugurated in 1950, must be seen to be judged. It has been called everything from "aggressively ugly" to "the pride of Norway." Its simple brick exterior with double towers houses, among other things, the stunning 25m-by-13m (85 ft.-by-43-ft.) wall painted by Henrik Sørensen, and the mural *Life* by Edvard Munch. Tapestries, frescoes, sculpture, and woodcarvings by Dagfin Werenskiold are also on display. Guided tours in English are available. In the courtyard you can see the astronomical clock and Dyre Vaa's swan fountain.

Rådhusplassen. ℂ **23-46-16-00.** 40NOK ($5.30) adults, free for children. May–Sept Mon–Sat 9am–5pm, Sun noon–5pm; Oct–Apr Mon–Sat 9am–4pm, Sun noon–4pm. Guided tours, Mon–Fri at 10am, noon, and 2pm. Bus: 30, 31, 32, 45, or 81.

Akershus Castle
One of the oldest historical monuments in Oslo, Akershus Castle was built in 1300 by Haakon V Magnusson. It was a fortress and a royal residence for several centuries. A fire in 1527 devastated the northern wing, and the castle was rebuilt and transformed into a royal Renaissance palace under the Danish-Norwegian king, Christian IV. Now the government uses it for state occasions. English-speaking guided tours are offered Monday through Saturday at 11am, 1pm, and 3pm, and on Sunday at 1 and 3pm.

Festnings-Plassen. ℂ **22-41-25-21.** Admission 30NOK ($4) adults, 10NOK ($1.35) children, family ticket 70NOK ($9.30). May–Sept 15 Mon–Sat 10am–4pm, Sun 12:30–4pm. Closed Sept 16–Apr 14. Tram: 10 or 12. Bus: 60.

Astrup Fearnley Museum of Modern Art
A 5- to 10-minute walk from the Oslo City Hall, this museum was created by some of Norway's leading architects and designers and showcases postwar art. The changing exhibits are often drawn from the museum's permanent collection. Here, you might see works by Francis Bacon, Lucian Freud, Gerhard Richter, or less familiar Norwegians, including Arne Ekeland, Knut Rose, or Bjørn Carlsen.

Dronningensgatan 4. ℂ **22-93-60-60.** Admission 50NOK ($6.65) adults; 25NOK ($3.35) children, students, and seniors. Tues–Wed and Fri 11am–5pm; Thurs noon–7pm; Sat–Sun noon–5pm. T-banen: Stortinget. Tram: 10, 12, 13, 15, or 19. Bus: 60.

Forsvarsmuseet (Armed Forces Museum)
This museum documents Norwegian military history from the dawn of the Viking Age to the 1950s. Guns, tanks, bombs, and planes are all here, from fighter planes to German tanks left over from World War II. The weapons and modern artillery are housed in a 19th-century military arsenal. The museum has a cafeteria.

Akershus Fortress, Bygning 62. ℂ **23-09-35-82.** Free admission. June–Aug Mon–Fri 10am–6pm, Sat–Sun 11am–4pm; Sept–May Mon–Fri 10am–3pm, Sat–Sun 11am–4pm. Tram: 1, 2, or 10.

Historisk Museum (University Museum of Cultural Heritage)
Devoted to ethnography, antiquities, and numismatics, this museum, operated by the University of Oslo, houses an interesting collection of prehistoric objects on the ground floor. Viking artifacts and a display of gold and silver from the 2nd century to the 13th century are in the Treasure House. In the medieval hall, look for the reddish Ringerike Alstad Stone, which was carved in relief, and the Dynna Stone, an

Oslo Attractions

NORWAY
Oslo

Akershus Castle **15**
Astrup Fearnley Museum
  of Modern Art **17**
Botanisk Hage og Museum **1**
Christiania Bymodell **13**
Den Norske Opera **4**
Edvard Munch Museum **1**

Forsvarsmuseet **19**
Frogner Park **22**
Gamler Aker Kirche **3**
Historisk Museum **6**
Ibsen Museum **29**
Kunstindustrimuseet **2**
Museet for Samtidskunst **18**

Scale:
0 — 0.25 mi
0 — 0.25 km

VÅR FRELSERS GRAVLUND

Sofies-gate
Stensberggata
Pilestredet
Nordahl Brunsgate
Thor Olsens Gate
St. Olavs plass
St Olavs Gate
Universitetsgata
Frederiks Gate
Kristian IV's Gate
Oslo Universitet
National Theater
Stortingsgaten
Karl Johans Gate
Fridtjof-Nansens-plass
Haakon VII's Gate
Rosenkrantzgate
Wessels plass
Rådhus-plassen
Rådhusgata
Vestbane-stasjonen
Dokkveien
Akersgata
Pier 4
Pier 3
Pier 2
Pier 1
Akershusstranda
Pipervika
Oslo-tunnelen
Skippergata

Fredensborgveien
Gate
Osterhaus gate
Hausmannsgate
Møllergata
Bernt Ankers Gate
Torggata
Storgata
Henrik Ibsens Gate
Youngs gate
Ploensgate
Akersgata
Torggata
Storgata
Grensen
CENTRAL OSLO
Biskop
Gunnerus Gate
Stor-torvet
Sentralstasjon
Jernbane-torget
Havnegata
Prinsensgate
Øvre
Slottsgate
Kongensgate
Kirkegata
Dronningensgate
Tollbugata
Tollbugata
GAMLEBYEN (Old Town)
Rådhusgata
Bank plassen
Myntgata
Bjørvika
Nylandsveien
Bispe Brua

Norbygata
Lakkegata
Grønland
Brugata
EASTERN OSLO
Schwei-gaards Brua

Arne-Garborgs-plass

Legend:
† Church
ⓘ Information
✉ Post Office
– Ⓜ Metro
— Railway

Nasjonalgalleriet 5
Nationaltheatret 8
Norsk Arkitekturmuseum 16
Norges Hjemmefront-museum 14
Oslo Bymuseum 23
Oslo Domkirke 9

Oslo Konserthus 12
Oslo Universitet 7
Rådhuset 11
Royal Palace (Slottet) 20
Stortinget (Parliament) 10
Slottsparken 21
Vigelandsparken 22

BYGDØY PENINSULA
Kon-Tiki Museum 26
Norsk Sjøfartsmuseum 28
Norwegian Folk Museum 24
Polar Ship *Fram* 27
Vikingskiphuset 25

11th-century runic stone honoring the handiest maiden in Hadeland. There's also a rich collection of ecclesiastical art in a series of portals from stave churches.

Frederiksgate 2 (near Karl Johans Gate). ☎ **22-85-99-12.** Free admission. May 15–Sept 14 Tues–Sun 10am–4pm; Sept 15–May 14 Tues–Sun 11am–4pm. Tram: 7, 8, 11, or 17.

Kunstindustrimuseet (Museum of Applied Art)   Founded in 1876, this is one of the oldest museums in Norway and among the oldest applied-arts museums in Europe. Extensive collections embrace Norwegian and international applied art, design, and fashion. Highlights include the 13th-century Baldishol tapestry and the fashion collection in the Royal Norwegian gallery. The museum displays pieces of 18th-century silver and glass, as well as an impressive selection of contemporary Scandinavian furniture and crafts. The ground floor houses temporary craft and design exhibits.

The museum schedules lectures, guided tours, and concerts. Café Solliløkken and the museum shop on the ground floor are in rooms from the 1830s that originally were in a small country house.

St. Olavs Gate 1. ☎ **22-03-65-40.** Admission 65NOK ($8.65) adults, free for children under 12. Tues–Fri 11am–3pm; Sat–Sun noon–4pm. T-banen: Stortinget. Bus: 37.

Museet for Samtidskunst (Museum of Contemporary Art)   Opened in 1990, this collection of works acquired by the state after World War II presents an array of international and Norwegian contemporary art. Once grouped together in the National Gallery, it has more room to "breathe" in its new home. Exhibits change frequently.

Bankplassen 4. ☎ **22-86-22-10.** 40NOK ($5.30) adults, free for children. Tues–Wed and Fri 10am–5pm; Thurs 10am–8pm; Sat–Sun 11am–4pm. Tram: 10, 12, 13, 15, or 19. Bus: 60.

Nasjonalgalleriet (National Gallery) ✸✸   This state museum, a short walk from the Students' Grove, is recommended chiefly for its paintings by Norwegians but also has an intriguing collection of works by world-famous artists,

Frommer's Favorite Oslo Experiences

Enjoying Fresh Shrimp off the Boats. Head for the harbor in front of the Rådhuset and buy a bag of freshly caught and cooked shrimp from a fisherman. Buy a beer at an Aker Brygge cafe, and shell and eat your shrimp along the harbor.

Experiencing Life on the Fjords. In the summer, head for the harbor, where boats wait to take you sightseeing, fishing, or to the beach.

Hanging Out in the Students' Grove. Summer is short in Oslo, and it's savored. Late-night drinkers sit in open-air beer gardens, enjoying the endless nights.

Listening to Street Musicians. Hundreds of musicians flock to Oslo in the summer. You can enjoy their music along Karl Johans Gate and at the marketplace Stortorget.

Taking the Ferry to Bygdøy. The Bygdøy peninsula is a treasure trove of Viking ships, Thor Heyerdahl's *Kon-Tiki*, seafood buffets, a sailboat harbor, and bathing beaches. At the folk museum are old farmsteads, houses, and often folk dancing.

including Cézanne and Matisse. The leading Norwegian Romantic landscape painter Johan Christian Dahl (1788–1857) is well represented here, as are three outstanding Norwegian Realists. Harriet Backer, a leading painter in the 1880s, was famous for interior portraits of Norwegian life; Christian Krohg painted subjects from seafarers to prostitutes; and Erik Werenskiold is noted for *Peasant Funeral*. On the main staircase is a display of Norwegian sculpture from 1910 to 1945. Note especially the works of Gustav Vigeland and the two rooms devoted to Edvard Munch. His much-reproduced work *The Scream* was painted in 1893. It was stolen in 1994 and subsequently recovered.

Universitetsgata 13. ℭ **22-20-04-04.** Free admission. Mon, Wed, Fri 10am–6pm; Thurs 10am–8pm; Sat 10am–4pm; Sun 11am–4pm. Tram: 7 or 11.

Norges Hjemmefrontmuseum (Norwegian Resistance Museum)

From underground printing presses to radio transmitters, from the German attack in 1940 to the liberation in 1945, this museum documents Norway's resistance activities during World War II. Outside is a monument dedicated to Norwegian patriots, many of whom were executed by the Nazis at this spot.

Akershus Fortress. ℭ **23-09-31-38.** Admission 25NOK ($3.35) adults, 10NOK ($1.35) children. Apr 15–June 14 and Sept Mon–Sat 10am–4pm, Sun 11am–4pm; June 15–Aug Mon–Sat 10am–5pm, Sun 11am–5pm; Oct–Apr 14 Mon–Sat 10am–3pm, Sun 11am–4pm. Tram: 10, 12, 15, or 19.

Stortinget (Parliament)

Constructed from 1861 to 1866, the Parliament, in the center of the city, was richly decorated by contemporary Norwegian artists. The style is neo-Romanesque. The public is admitted only on guided tours.

Karl Johans Gate 22. ℭ **23-31-35-96.** Free admission. Guided tours in English, July 1–Aug 15 Mon–Fri 10am, 11:30am, and 1pm; Sept 15–June 15 Sat 10am, 11:30am, and 1pm. T-banen: Stortinget. Tram: 13, 15, or 19.

IN FROGNER PARK

Vigelandsparken 𝕽𝕽   The lifetime work of Gustav Vigeland, Norway's greatest sculptor, is on display in the 30-hectare (75-acre) Frogner Park. More than 200 sculptures in granite, bronze, and iron are here. Notice his four granite columns, symbolizing the fight between humanity and evil (a dragon, the embodiment of evil, embraces a woman). The "Angry Boy" is the most photographed statue in the park. The most celebrated work is the 16m (52-ft.) monolith composed of 121 colossal figures, all carved into one piece of stone.

Nearby, the **Vigeland Museum,** Nobelsgate 32 (ℭ **22-54-25-30**), is the sculptor's former studio. It contains more of his works, sketches, and woodcuts. It is open Tuesday through Saturday from 10am to 6pm, Sunday from noon to 7pm. Admission is 40NOK ($5.30) for adults, 20NOK ($2.65) for children.

Frogner Park, Nobelsgate 32. ℭ **22-54-25-30.** Free admission to park; museum, 40NOK ($5.30) adults, 30NOK ($4) children. Park, daily 24 hr. Museum, May–Sept Tues–Sat 10am–6pm, Sun noon–7pm; Oct–Apr Tues–Sat noon–4pm, Sun noon–4pm. Tram: 12 or 15. Bus: 20, 45, or 81.

ON BYGDØY

Located south of the city, the peninsula is reached by commuter ferry (summer only) leaving from Pier 3, facing the Rådhuset (Town Hall). Departures during the day are every 40 minutes, and a one-way fare costs 22NOK ($2.95). The no. 30 bus from the National Theater also runs to Bygdøy. The museums lie only a short walk from the bus stops on Bygdøy.

Kon-Tiki Museum   *Kon-Tiki* is a world-famous balsa-log raft. In 1947, the young Norwegian scientist Thor Heyerdahl and five comrades sailed it from Callao, Peru, to Raroia, Polynesia (6,920km/4,300 miles). Besides the raft, there are other exhibits from Heyerdahl's subsequent visits to Easter Island. They include casts of stone giants and small originals, a facsimile of the whale shark, and an Easter Island family cave, with a collection of sacred lava figurines hoarded in secret underground passages by the island's inhabitants. The museum also houses the original papyrus *Ra II,* in which Heyerdahl crossed the Atlantic in 1970.

Bygdøynesveien 36. Ⓒ **23-08-67-67.** Admission 35NOK ($4.65) adults, 20NOK ($2.65) children, family ticket 90NOK ($12). Apr–May and Sept daily 10:30am–5pm; June–Aug daily 9:30am–5:45pm; Oct–Mar daily 10:30am–4pm. Ferry: From Pier 3 facing the Rådhuset (summer only). Bus: 30 from the National Theater.

Norsk Sjøfartsmuseum (Norwegian Maritime Museum)   This museum chronicles the maritime history and culture of Norway, complete with a ship's deck with helm and chart house. There's also a three-deck section of the passenger steamer *Sandnaes.*

The Boat Hall features a fine collection of original small craft. The fully restored polar vessel *Gjoa,* used by Roald Amundsen in his search for the Northwest Passage, is also on display. The three-masted schooner *Svanen (Swan)* is moored at the museum. Built in Svendborg, Denmark, in 1916, it sailed under the Norwegian and Swedish flags. The ship now belongs to the museum and is used as a training vessel and school ship for young people.

Bygdøynesveien 37. Ⓒ **22-43-82-40.** Admission to museum and boat hall 40NOK ($5.30) adults, 20NOK ($2.65) children. May–Sept daily 10am–6pm; Oct–Apr Mon and Fri–Sat 10:30am–4pm, Tues–Thurs 10:30am–6pm. Ferry: From Pier 3 facing the Rådhuset (summer only). Bus: 30 from the National Theater.

Norwegian Folk Museum 𝆕𝆕   From all over Norway, 140 original buildings have been transported and reassembled on 14 hectares (35 acres) of the Bygdøy peninsula. This open-air folk museum, one of the oldest of its kind, includes a number of medieval buildings. The Raulandstua is one of the oldest wooden dwellings still standing in Norway, and a stave church dates from about 1200. The rural buildings are grouped together by region of origin, and the urban houses are laid out in the form of an old town.

Inside, the museum's 225,000 exhibits capture every imaginable facet of Norwegian life, past and present. Furniture, household utensils, clothing, woven fabrics, and tapestries are on display, along with fine examples of rose painting and woodcarving. Farming implements and logging gear pay tribute to the development of agriculture and forestry. Also look for the outstanding exhibit on Norway's Lapp population.

Museumsveien 10. Ⓒ **22-12-37-00.** Admission 70NOK ($9.30) adults, 20NOK ($2.65) children under 17. Jan 1–May 14 and Sept 15–Dec 31 Fri–Sat 11am–3pm, Sun 11am–4pm; May 15–June 14 and Sept 1–Sept 14 daily 10am–5pm; June 15–Aug 31 daily 10am–6pm. Ferry: From Pier 3 facing the Rådhuset (summer only). Bus: 30 from the National Theater.

Polar Ship Fram (Frammuseet)   This museum contains the sturdy polar exploration ship *Fram,* which Fridtjof Nansen sailed across the Arctic (1893–96). The vessel was later used by the famed Norwegian explorer Roald Amundsen, the first man to reach the South Pole (1911).

Bygdøynesveien. Ⓒ **23-28-29-50.** Admission 30NOK ($4) adults, 15NOK ($2) children. Mar–Apr Mon–Fri 11am–3:45pm, Sat–Sun 11am–3:45pm; May 1–15 and Sept daily 10am–4:45pm; May 16–Aug daily 9am–5:45pm; Oct–Nov Mon–Fri 11am–2:45pm, Sat–Sun 11am–3:45pm; Dec–Feb Sat–Sun 11am–3:45pm. Ferry: From Pier 3 facing the Rådhuset (summer only). Bus: 30 from the National Theater.

Vikingskiphuset (Viking Ship Museum, University Museum of Cultural Heritage) 𝆕𝆕𝆕   Displayed here are three Viking burial vessels that were excavated on the shores of the Oslofjord and preserved in clay. The most spectacular find is the 9th-century *Oseberg,* discovered near Norway's oldest town.

The richly ornamented 20m (64-ft.) dragon ship is the burial chamber of a Viking queen and her slave.

The *Gokstad* find is an outstanding example of Viking vessels because it's so well preserved. The smaller *Tune* ship was never restored. Look for the *Oseberg's* animal-head post and four-wheeled cart, and the elegantly carved sleigh used by Viking royalty.

Huk Aveny 35, Bygdøy. © 22-43-83-79. Admission 40NOK ($5.30) adults, 20NOK ($2.65) children. Apr daily 11am–4pm; May–Aug daily 9am–6pm; Sept daily 11am–5pm; Oct daily 11am–6pm; Nov–Mar daily 11am–3pm. Ferry: From Pier 3 facing the Rådhuset (summer only). Bus: 30 from the National Theater.

NEAR OSLO

Henie-Onstad Kunstsenter (Henie-Onstad Art Center) ᏩᏩ   Former skating champion and movie star Sonja Henie and her husband, shipping tycoon Niels Onstad, opened this museum to display their art collection. On a handsome site beside the Oslofjord, 11km (7 miles) west of Oslo, it's an especially good 20th-century collection. There are some 1,800 works by Munch, Picasso, Matisse, Léger, Bonnard, and Miró. Henie's contributions can be seen in her Trophy Room. She won three Olympic gold medals—she was the star at the 1936 competition—and 10 world championships. In all, she garnered 600 trophies and medals.

Besides the permanent collection, there are plays, concerts, films, and special exhibits. An open-air theater-in-the-round is used in the summer for folklore programs, jazz concerts, and song recitals. On the premises is a top-notch, partly self-service, grill restaurant, the Piruetten.

Høkvikodden, Baerum. © 67-80-48-80. Admission 75NOK ($10) adults, 45NOK ($6) ages 15–25, free for children 14 and under. June–Aug Mon 11am–6pm, Tues–Fri 10am–9pm, Sat–Sun 11am–6pm; Sept–May Tues 10am–9pm, Sat–Mon 11am–5pm. Bus: 151, 152, 251, or 261.

Skimuseet (Ski Museum)   At Holmenkollen, an elevator takes visitors up the jump tower for a view of Oslo and the fjord. At the base of the ski jump, the Ski Museum (Skimuseet) displays a wide range of exhibits. They include a 4,000-year-old pictograph from Rødøy in Nordland, which documents skiing's thousand-year history. The oldest ski in the museum dates from around A.D. 600. The museum has exhibits on Nansen's and Amundsen's polar expeditions, plus skis and historical items from various parts of Norway, including the first "modern" skis, from about 1870.

Kongeveien 5, Holmenkollen. © 22-92-32-00. Admission (museum and ski jump) 60NOK ($8) adults, 30NOK ($4) children. May and Sept daily 10am–5pm; June daily 9am–8pm; July–Aug daily 9am–10pm; Oct–Apr daily 10am–4pm. T-banen: Holmenkollen SST Line 15 from near the National Theater to Voksenkollen (30-min. ride), then an uphill 15-min. walk.

Tryvannstårnet (Lookout Tower)   The loftiest lookout tower in Scandinavia offers a view of the Oslofjord with Sweden to the east. The gallery is approximately 570m (1,900 ft.) above sea level.

A walk down the hill returns you to Frognerseteren (see "Where to Dine," earlier in this chapter). Another 20-minute walk down the hill takes you to the Holmenkollen Ski Jump, where the 1952 Olympic competitions took place. It's also the site of Norway's winter sports highlight, the Holmenkollen Ski Festival.

Voksenkollen. © 22-14-67-11. Admission 40NOK ($5.30) adults, 20NOK ($2.65) children. May and Sept daily 10am–5pm; June daily 10am–7pm; July daily 9am–8pm; Aug daily 9am–8pm; Oct–Apr Mon–Sun 10am–4pm. T-banen: Frognerseteren SST Line 1 from near the National Theater to Voksenkollen (30-min. ride), then an uphill 15-min. walk.

PARKS & GARDENS

Marka, the thick forest that surrounds Oslo, is a giant pleasure park, and there are others. You can take a tram marked "Holmenkollen" from the city center to Oslomarka, a forested pleasure and recreational area. Locals go here for summer hikes in the forest and for skiing in winter. The area is dotted with about two dozen *hytter* (mountain huts) where you can seek refuge from the weather if needed. **Norske Turistforening,** Storgate 3 (© **22-82-28-22**), sells maps with the hiking paths and roads of the Oslomarka clearly delineated. It's open Monday through Friday from 10am to 4pm, Saturday from 10am to 2pm.

Botanisk Hage og Museum (Botanical Gardens) *Finds*   At Tøyen, near the Munch Museum, this is an oasis in the heart of Oslo. It's home to many exotic plants, including cacti, orchids, and palms. More than 1,000 mountain plants can be viewed in the rock garden, which has waterfalls. There's also a museum in the park, with a botanical art exhibit.

Sars Gate 1. © **22-85-17-00**. Free admission. Apr–Sept Mon–Fri 7am–8pm, Sat–Sun 10am–8pm; Oct–Mar Mon–Fri 7am–5pm, Wed until 8pm, Sat–Sun 10am–5pm. Bus: 20.

Slottsparken   The park surrounding the Royal Palace (Slottet) is open to the public year-round. The changing of the guard takes place daily at 1:30pm. When the king is in residence, the Royal Guard band plays Monday through Friday during the changing of the guard.

The palace was constructed from 1825 to 1848. Some first-time visitors are surprised at how open and relatively unguarded it is, without walls or rails. You can walk through the grounds, but can't go inside unless you have an invitation from the king. The statue at the front of the castle (at the end of Karl Johans Gate) is of Karl XIV Johan himself, who ruled Norway and Sweden. He ordered the palace constructed, but died before it was finished.

Drammensveien 1. Free admission. Daily dawn–dusk. T-banen: Nationaltheatret.

OF ARTISTIC INTEREST

Aula (Great Hall)   Admirers of the work of Edvard Munch will want to see the Great Hall of the university, where Scandinavia's greatest artist painted murals. Until it moved to larger headquarters at the City Hall, this used to be the site of the Nobel Prize award ceremony.

University of Oslo, Karl Johans Gate 47. © **22-85-95-55**. Free admission. June 20–Aug 20 daily 24 hr. T-banen: Stortinget.

Edvard Munch Museum   Devoted exclusively to the works of Edvard Munch (1863–1944), Scandinavia's leading painter, this collection was his gift to the city. It traces his work from early realism to latter-day expressionism. The collection comprises 1,100 paintings, some 4,500 drawings, around 18,000 prints, numerous graphic plates, six sculptures, and important documentary material. The exhibits change periodically.

Tøyengate 53. © **23-24-14-00**. Admission 60NOK ($8) adults, 30NOK ($4) children. June to mid-Sept daily 10am–6pm; mid-Sept to May Tues–Wed and Fri–Sat 10am–4pm, Thurs and Sun 10am–6pm. T-banen: Tøyen. Bus: 20.

LITERARY LANDMARKS

"Walking Tour 2," below, follows in the footsteps of Ibsen.

Ibsen Museum   In 1994 Oslo opened a museum to honor its most famous writer. Ibsen lived in an apartment within walking distance of the National

The Man Behind *The Scream*

Scandinavia's greatest artist, Edvard Munch (1863–1944), was a pioneer in the expressionist movement. *The Scream,* painted in 1893, is his best-known painting. He grew up in Oslo (then called Christiania) and was often ill. Early memories of illness, death, and grief in his family had a tremendous impact on his later works. His father's death may have contributed to the loneliness and melancholy of one of his most famous works, *Night* (1890).

By the early 1890s, Munch had achieved fame (though slight in comparison with his renown today). He was at the center of a *succès de scandale* in Munich in 1892, when his art was interpreted as "anarchistic provocation." A major exhibit was closed in protest.

Munch went to Berlin, entering a world of literati, artists, and intellectuals. He met August Strindberg, and they discussed the philosophy of Nietzsche, symbolism, psychology, and occultism. The discussions clearly influenced his work. His growing outlook was revealed to the world in an 1893 show in Berlin, where several paintings had death as their theme. *Death in a Sickroom* created quite a stir.

In 1896 Munch moved to Paris, where he made exquisite color lithographs and his first woodcuts. By the turn of the century he was painting in a larger format and incorporating some of the Art Nouveau aesthetics of the time. *Red Virginia Creeper* and *Melancholy* reflect the new influences.

A nervous disorder sent him to a sanitarium, and he had a turbulent love affair with a wealthy bohemian nicknamed "Tulla." The affair ended in 1902 when a revolver permanently injured a finger on Munch's left hand. He became obsessed with the shooting incident, and poured out his contempt for "Tulla" in such works as *Death of Murat* (1907).

Prominent people asked Munch to paint their portraits, and he obliged. The group portrait of Dr. Linde's sons (1904) is a masterpiece of modern portraiture. Munch became increasingly alcoholic, and in 1906 painted *Self-Portrait with a Bottle of Wine.*

From 1909 until his death, Munch lived in Norway. In his later years he retreated into isolation, surrounded only by his paintings, which he called "my children." The older Munch placed more emphasis on the monumental and the picturesque, as in landscapes or people in harmony with nature.

In 1940 he decided to leave his huge collection of paintings to the city of Oslo upon his death. Today the Munch Museum provides the best introduction to this strange and enigmatic artist.

Theater from 1895 until his death in 1906. Here he wrote two of his most famous plays, *John Gabriel Borkman* and *When We Dead Awaken.* The museum curators have tried to re-create the apartment (a longtime exhibit at the Norwegian Folk Museum) as authentically as possible. The study, for example, has Ibsen's original furniture, and the entire apartment is decorated as though Ibsen still lived in it. The attraction has been called "a living museum," and regularly scheduled talks on play-writing and the theater, recitations, and theatrical performances are planned.

Arbinsgate 1. ✆ 22-55-20-09. Admission 50NOK ($6.65) adults, 20NOK ($2.65) children. Tues–Sun noon–3pm; guided tour in English at noon, 1pm, and 2pm. T-banen: Nationaltheatret.

Oslo Bymuseum (City Museum)   Housed in the 1790 Frogner Manor at Frogner Park, site of the Vigeland sculptures, this museum surveys the history of Oslo. It also contains mementos of Henrik Ibsen, such as the chair and marble-topped table where he sat at the Grand Café. Four glasses from which he drank are engraved with his name.

Frognerveien 67. ✆ 23-28-41-70. Admission 40NOK ($5.30) adults, 20NOK ($2.65) children. June–Aug Tues–Fri 10am–6pm, Sat–Sun 11am–5pm; Sept–May Tues–Fri 10am–4pm, Sat–Sun 11am–4pm. Bus: 20, 45, or 81. Tram: 12 or 15.

ARCHITECTURAL HIGHLIGHTS

Those interested in modern architecture should head to **Vaterland,** in East Oslo. One of Oslo's major development sites, launched in the 1980s, this "city within a city" includes a 9,000-seat hall for musical and sporting events, an art gallery, a train station, and large conference facilities.

Those interested in old districts that have been revived will want to explore **Aker Brygge,** along the harbor. The "Fisherman's Wharf of Oslo" opened in 1986 in what had been shipbuilding yards. It's a modern complex of shops, nightspots, restaurants, delis, wine bars, and ice-cream parlors. Take bus no. 27 or walk west from the Rådhus.

Christiania Bymodell   Norway's capital was called Oslo, then Christiania, and then Oslo again. This architectural model of the city of Christiania in 1838 is part of a multimedia program that traces the city's history from its foundation in 1624 until 1840.

Høymagasinet, Akershus Festning. ✆ 22-33-31-47. Free admission. Tues–Sun noon–5pm. Closed Sept–May. Tram: 10 or 12.

Gamle Aker Kirke (Old Aker Church)   Constructed in 1100, this is the oldest stone church in Scandinavia that's still in use by a parish. Guided tours in English are conducted year-round. There are occasional church concerts, and Masses on Sunday at 9 and 11am.

Akersbakken 26. ✆ 22-69-35-82. Free admission. Mon–Sat noon–4pm. Bus: 37. T-banen: Bjerregårdsgaten.

Norsk Arkitekturmuseum (Norwegian Museum of Architecture)   Near Akershus Castle and the Oslo City Hall, right in the center of the city, this museum presents changing exhibits. Most are examples of Norwegian architecture from this century. In 1996 it gained a new permanent exhibit that delineates Norway's architectural history. Temporary exhibits change frequently.

Kongensgate 4. ✆ 22-42-40-80. Free admission. Mon–Fri 11am–4pm; Sat–Sun noon–4pm. Tram: 10, 12, or 13. Bus: 60.

6 Especially for Kids

Oslo rivals Copenhagen when it comes to attractions suitable for both children and grown-ups. Some of the top thrills are the excavated **Viking burial ships** on the Bygdøy peninsula and the **Norwegian Maritime Museum** and Boat Hall.

Other sights already discussed will be of special interest to children. They include the polar exploration ship *Fram,* which took Nansen and Amundsen on their ventures to the North and South Poles; the balsa-log raft *Kon-Tiki*, in which Thor Heyerdahl and his comrades made their historic journey across the Pacific; the lookout tower, ski jump, and Ski Museum at **Holmenkollen;** the **folk museum,** depicting life in Norway since the Middle Ages; and the ancient fortress on the Oslofjord, **Akershus Castle.**

Barnekunst Museum (International Children's Art Museum) The collection in this unique museum consists of children's drawings, paintings, ceramics, sculpture, tapestries, and handicrafts from more than 30 countries, some of which would have pleased Picasso. There's also a children's workshop devoted to painting, drawing, music, and dance.

Lille Frøens vei 4. ✆ **22-46-85-73.** Admission 50NOK ($6.65) adults, 30NOK ($4) children. Jan 20–June 25 and Sept 10–Dec 15 Tues–Thurs 9:30am–2pm, Sun 11am–4pm; June 26–Aug 15 Tues–Thurs and Sun 11am–4pm. Closed Dec 16–Jan 19 and Aug 16–Sept 9. T-banen: Frøen.

Norgesparken Tusenfryd This is the largest amusement park in Norway, conceived as a smaller version of Copenhagen's Tivoli. It includes a number of simple restaurants, a roller coaster with a loop and corkscrew, an amphitheater with all-day entertainment by performers such as musicians and clowns, and many games of skill or chance. The park is 19km (12 miles) south of the Central Station.

Vinterbro by E6/E18/Mossevelen. ✆ **64-97-66-99.** All-day ticket 210NOK ($28) adults, 110NOK ($15) children. June–Sept 19 daily 10:30am–7pm. Closed Sept 20–May. Bus: Shuttle service from Oslo's Central Station daily 10am–1pm (every 30 min.) and 3, 4, and 5pm; final return shortly after park closes. Fare: 30NOK ($4) adults, 20NOK ($2.65) children.

7 Oslo on Foot: Walking Tours

WALKING TOUR 1   HISTORIC OSLO

Start:	Aker Brygge.
Finish:	Royal Palace.
Time:	2½ hours.
Best Time:	Any day when it's not raining.
Worst Times:	Rush hours (weekdays 7–9am and 5–7pm).

Start at:

❶ Aker Brygge
On the harbor to the west of the Rådhuset, this steel-and-glass complex is a rebuilt district of shops and restaurants that was developed from Oslo's old shipbuilding grounds. It has a fine view of Akershus Castle.

Head east along Rådhusplassen, looking at the:

❷ Rådhuset
The Oslo City Hall, built in 1950, is decorated with artwork by Norwegian artists.

Climb the steps at the east end of the square and a small hill to see the:

❸ Statue of Franklin D. Roosevelt
Eleanor Roosevelt flew to Oslo to dedicate this statue.

This area is the heart of the 17th-century Renaissance city. Take Rådhusgata east to:

❹ Christiania Torv
A feature of this traffic hub is the yellow house on your left, the Young Artists Association, which was once the home of a dreaded executioner. His fee depended on the type of execution performed.

TAKE A BREAK
To the right of the Young Artists Association is **Kafé Celsius,** Rådhusgata 19 (℗ **22-42-45-39**), Oslo's oldest residential house. Today it's a charming arts-oriented cafe that serves tasty food. Sandwich prices start at 79NOK ($11). You can also order pasta salads and such dishes as ratatouille or tortellini. On cold days there's a fire in the fireplace. It's open Sunday, Tuesday, and Wednesday from 11:30am to 12:30am, Thursday through Saturday from 11:30am to 1:30am.

Continue along Rådhusgata, turning right onto Nedre Slottsgate. Walk to the end of the street. At Myntgata, turn right and pass through a gate. You are now on the greater grounds of Akershus Castle. The first building on the right is the:

❺ Norwegian Resistance Museum

Here you'll find displays on events related to the Nazi occupation of Norway from 1940 to 1945. Also at the site is:

❻ Akershus Castle and Fortress

The castle dates from 1300 but was rebuilt in the 17th century. Take a guided tour of the fortress and walk its ramparts. Pause on the grounds to look at the:

❼ Execution Site

The Norwegian Resistance Museum stands at the spot where the Nazis shot prisoners, including Norwegian freedom fighters. There's a memorial to the resistance movement, and you'll have a good view of the harbor in the distance.

Cross the drawbridge to the east, right before Kongens Gate, and continue through the castle grounds to the:

❽ National Monument to the German Occupation

This monument commemorates Norway's suffering at the hands of the Nazis.

After seeing the monument, turn left (north) into:

❾ Grev Wedels Plass

In 1850 Ibsen wrote poems at the site of Den Gamle Logen (Freemason's Lodge). At no. 9 and Dronningensgatan 4 is the Astrup Fearnley Museum of Modern Art, with changing exhibits of Norwegian and foreign art from the postwar period.

Head north along Kirkegata until you reach:

❿ Bankplassen

At the site of the old Bank of Norway you'll find the Museum of Contemporary Art (Bankplassen 4), with the state collection of international and Norwegian modern art acquired since World War II. This square was once Oslo's social center. Ibsen staged his first play here in 1851 (at a theater that burned down in 1877).

From Bankplassen, turn right onto Revierstredet and left onto Dronningensgatan. (At one time the waterfront came up to this point.) Go right at the Central Post Office onto Tollbugata. At the intersection with Fred Olsens Gate, turn left and walk to the:

⓫ Oslo Sentralstasjon

Trains arrive at this rail hub from the Continent and depart for all points linked by train in Norway.

Turn left onto:

⓬ Karl Johans Gate

The main pedestrian-only street stretches from the Central Station in the east to the Royal Palace in the west end.

On your right you'll pass the:

⓭ Basarhallene

This huge complex is filled with boutiques and shops.

Turn right at Kirkegata, heading for the:

⓮ Oslo Domkirke

Stortorvet is the 17th-century cathedral at Oslo's old marketplace. Like the City Hall, the cathedral is decorated with outstanding works by Norwegian artists.

Walking Tour: Historic Oslo

finish here ★

16 SLOTTS-PARKEN

Kristian Augusts Gate
Kristian IV's Gate
Fredriks Gate
Pilestredet
Munchs gate
Keysers Gate
Arbeidersamfundets Plass
Henrik Ibsens Gate
Hospitalsgata
C.J. Hambros Plass
Arne Garborgs Plass
Johanne Dybwads Plass
Apotekergata
7 Juni Plassen
Karl Johans Gate
Universitetsgata
Aschehougs Plass
Arbins gate
Kron prinsens Gate
Ruseløkkveien
Dramsveien
Haakon VII's Gate
Amund-sens Gate
Klingenberggata
Stortingsgata
Akersgata
Grensen
Grubbegata
Møller Gata
Torggata
Ploensgate
Storgata
Munke-Gate
Dronning Mauds Gate
Kronpr. Märthas Plass
Fridtjof Nansens Plass
Tordenskjolds Gate
Rosenkrantz Gate
Karl Johans Gate
Dokkveien
Rådhus-plassen
Rådhus-brygge
Rådhusgata
Øvre Vollgate
Nedre Vollgate
Akersgata
Øvre Slottsgate
Nedre Slottsgate
Prinsens Gate
Kongens Gate
Tollbugata
Dronningens Gate
Skippergata
Fred. Olsens Gate
Strandgata
Rådhusgata
Akershusstranda
Kirkegata
Myntgata
Glacisgata
Kongens Gate
Skippergata

start here ★

Pipervika

Festningsplassen

Bjørvika

OSLO
Area of detail

0 — 0.2 mi
0 — 0.2 km

– – – Tunnel

1 Harbor of Aker Brygge
2 Rådhuset
3 Statue of Franklin D. Roosevelt
4 Christiania Torv
5 Norwegian Resistance Museum
6 Akershus Castle and Fortress
7 Execution Site
8 National Monument to the German Occupation
9 Grev Wedels Plass
10 Bankplassen
11 Oslo Sentralstasjon
12 Karl Johans Gate
13 Basarhallene
14 Oslo Domkirke
15 Norwegian Parliament (Stortinget)
16 Royal Palace (Slottet)

From Stortorvet, walk west along Grensen. You're probably ready to:

TAKE A BREAK
Old Oslo atmosphere lives on at the **Stortorvets Gjaest-giveri**, Grensen 1 (© **23-35-63-60**), on a busy commercial street. This drinking and dining emporium, dating from the 1600s, is often filled with spirited beer drinkers. A beer costs 49NOK ($6.50). It's open Monday through Saturday from 11am to 9pm, Sunday (Nov–Apr only) from 3 to 9pm.

Continue west on Grensen until you reach Lille Grensen. Cut left onto this street,

returning to Karl Johans Gate. On your left will be the:

⓯ Norwegian Parliament (Stortinget)
Karl Johans Gate 22 was constructed from 1861 to 1866, and it is richly decorated with works by contemporary Norwegian artists.

Continue west along Karl Johans Gate, passing many of the monuments covered on "Walking Tour 2" (see below). Eventually you'll reach the:

⓰ Royal Palace (Slottet)
Located at Drammensveien 1, this is the residence of the king of Norway and his family. The public is permitted access only to the park.

WALKING TOUR 2

IN THE FOOTSTEPS OF IBSEN & MUNCH

Start:	National Theater.
Finish:	National Gallery.
Time:	2 hours.
Best Time:	Any day when it's not raining.
Worst Times:	Rush hours (weekdays 7–9am and 5–7pm).

The tour begins at the:

❶ Nationaltheatret
Stortingsgaten 15 is off Karl Johans Gate near the Students' Grove in Oslo's center. Study your map in front of the Henrik Ibsen statue at the theater, where many of his plays were first performed and are still presented. The Norwegian National Theater, inaugurated in 1899, is one of the most beautiful in Europe. Phone (© **22-00-14-00**) for information.

Facing the statue of Ibsen, continue up Stortingsgaten toward the Royal Palace (Slottet). Cut left at the next intersection and walk along Ruselokkveien. The Vika Shopping Terraces, an unattractive row of modern storefronts tacked onto an elegant 1880 Victorian terrace, used to be among Oslo's grandest apartments. During World War II it was the Nazi headquarters.

Continue along this complex to the end, turning right onto Dronnings Mauds Gate, which quickly becomes Lokkeveien. At the first building on the right, you come to:

❷ Ibsen's Private Apartment
Look for the blue plaque marking the building. The playwright lived here from 1891 to 1895. When his wife complained that she didn't like the address, even though it was one of Oslo's most elegant, they moved. Ibsen wrote two plays while living here.

Turn right onto Arbinsgate and walk to the end of the street until you reach Drammensveien and the:

❸ Ibsen Museum
Arbinsgate 1, the first building on the left, is at the corner of Arbinsgate and Drammensveien. You'll see an Omega store, but look for the blue plaque on the building. Ibsen lived here from 1895 until his death in 1906. He

Walking Tour: In the Footsteps of Ibsen & Munch

1 Nationaltheatret
2 Ibsen's private
    apartment
3 Ibsen Museum
4 University of Oslo
5 Akersgata
6 Birthplace of Ibsen's son
7 Trefoldighetskirken
8 Damplassen
9 Damstredet
10 Telthusbakken
11 Gamle Aker Kirke
12 Vår Frelsers Gravlund
13 Tomb of Ibsen
14 Tomb of Bjørnson
15 Tomb of Edvard Munch
16 Kunstindustrimuseet
17 Pilestredet
18 National Gallery

= = = Tunnel

0   0.25 mi
0   0.25 km

often sat in the window, with a light casting a glow over his white hair. People lined up in the street below to look at him. The great Italian actress Eleanora Duse came here to bid him a final *adieu,* but he was too ill to see her. She stood outside in the snow and blew him kisses.

The king of Norway used to give Ibsen a key to enter the private gardens surrounding the Royal Palace. Everybody has that privilege today.

Turn right on Drammensveien and continue back to the National Theater. Take Karl Johans Gate, on the left side of the theater, and walk east. On your left, you'll pass the:

❹ University of Oslo

At Karl Johans Gate 47 (℃ **22-85-98-55**) you'll find Aula, the Great Hall of the university. The hall is decorated with murals by Edvard Munch. It's open to the public only from June 15 to August 15, daily from noon to 2pm.

Twice a day Ibsen followed this route to the Grand Café. Admirers often threw rose petals in his path, but he pretended not to see. He was called "the Sphinx," because he wouldn't talk to anybody.

TAKE A BREAK
The **Grand Café,** Karl Johans Gate 31 (℃ **23-21-20-00**), was the center of social life for the literati and the artistic elite, including Munch. It was and is the most fashionable cafe in Oslo (see "Where to Dine," earlier in this chapter). On the far wall of the cafe you can see Per Krogh's famous mural, painted in 1928. Ibsen, with a top hat and gray beard, is at the far left, and Munch—called the handsomest man in Norway—is seated at the second window from the right at the far right of the window. The poet and playwright Bjørnstjerne Bjørnson can be spotted on the street outside (2nd window from the left, wearing a top hat), because he wouldn't deign to come into the cafe. You can order food and drink, a big meal, or a snack.

Returning to the street, note the Norwegian Parliament building (Stortinget) on your left. Proceed left and turn left onto Lille Grensen. Cross the major boulevard, Grensen, and walk straight to:

❺ Akersgata

This is the street of Ibsen's funeral procession. Services were conducted at the Holy Trinity Church on June 1, 1906.

Veer left to see the:

❻ Birthplace of Ibsen's Son

On your left, at the corner of Teatergata and Akersgata, is the site of the famous Strømberg Theater, which burned down in 1835. It was also a residence, and Ibsen's son was born here in 1859.

Also on Akersgata is:

❼ Trefoldighetskirken (Holy Trinity Church)

This is the site of Ibsen's funeral. A little farther along Akersgata is St. Olav's Church.

Turn on the right side of this imposing house of worship onto Akersveien and go to:

❽ Damplassen

This small square—one of the most charming in Oslo—doesn't appear on most maps. Norway's greatest poet, Henrik Wergeland, lived in the pink house on this square from 1839 to 1841.

Take a right at the square and head down:

❾ Damstredet

This is a typical old Oslo street, with antique wooden houses mainly occupied by artists.

Damstredet winds downhill to Fredensborgveien. Here a left turn and a short walk will take you to Maridalsveien, a busy but dull thoroughfare. As you walk north along this street, on the west side look for a large unmarked gateway with wide stone steps inside. Climb to the top, follow a little pathway, and go past gardens and flower beds.

Pass a set of brick apartment buildings on the left, and proceed to:

⑩ Telthusbakken

On this little street you'll see a whole row of early Oslo wooden houses. Look right in the far distance at the green building where Munch used to live. Telthusbakken leads to Akersveien.

On your left you can see the:

⑪ Gamle Aker Kirke (Old Aker Church)

Enter at Akersbakken, where Akersveien and Akersbakken intersect. Built in 1100, this is the oldest stone parish church in Scandinavia that's still in use. It stands on a green hill with an old graveyard around it, inside a stone wall.

A short block from the church along Akersbakken (veer left outside the front of the church and go around a corner), you'll come to the north entrance of:

⑫ Vår Frelsers Gravlund (Our Savior's Cemetery)

This is the city's expansive burial ground. In a section designated as the "Ground of Honor" are the graves of famous Norwegians, including Munch, Ibsen, and Bjørnson. Signs don't point the way, but it's easy to see a tall obelisk.

This is the:

⑬ Tomb of Ibsen

Ibsen's wife, Susanna, whom he called "the cat," is buried to the playwright's left. She died in 1914. The hammer on the obelisk symbolizes his work *The Miner,* indicating how he "dug deep" into the soul of Norway.

To the right of Ibsen's tomb is the:

⑭ Tomb of Bjørnson

The literary figure Bjørnstjerne Bjørnson (1832–1910) once raised money to send Ibsen to Italy. Before the birth of their children, Ibsen and Bjørnson agreed that one would have a son and the other a daughter, and that they would marry each other. Miraculously,

Ibsen had a son, Bjørnson a daughter, and they did just that. Bjørnson wrote the national anthem, and his tomb is draped in a stone representation of a Norwegian flag.

To the far right of Bjørnson's tomb is the:

⑮ Tomb of Edvard Munch

Scandinavia's greatest painter has an unadorned tomb. If you're visiting on a snowy day, it will be buried, because the marker lies close to the ground. Munch died during the darkest days of the Nazi occupation. His sister turned down a request from the German command to give Munch a state funeral, feeling that it would be inappropriate.

On the west side of the cemetery you'll come to Ullevålsveien. Turn left on this busy street and head south toward the center of Oslo. You'll soon see St. Olav's Church, this time on your left. Stay on the right (west) side of the street. Ullevålsveien intersects with St. Olavs Gate at the:

⑯ Kunstindustrimuseet (Museum of Applied Art)

Even if you don't have time to visit the museum at St. Olavs Gate 1, you may want to go inside to the cafe.

After visiting the museum, continue along St. Olavs Gate to:

⑰ Pilestredet

Look to the immediate right at no. 30. A wall plaque on the decaying building commemorates the fact that Munch lived here from 1868 to 1875. In this building he painted, among other masterpieces, *The Sick Child.* He moved here when he was 5, and many of his "memory paintings" were of the interior. When demolition teams started to raze the building in the early 1990s, a counterculture group of activists known as "The Blitz Group" illegally took over the premises to prevent its destruction. On its brick wall side, his masterpiece *The Scream* was re-created in spray paint. The protesters are still in control of the city-owned building, and they are viewed as squatters on very valuable land. It's suspected that if a more conservative government comes into power, officials will toss out the case, throw out the activists, and demolish the building. For the moment, however, they remain in control.

At Pilestredet, turn left. One block later, turn right onto Universitetsgata, heading south

toward Karl Johans Gate. You'll pass a number of architecturally interesting buildings, and will eventually arrive at the:

⑱ National Gallery
The state museum, at Universitetsgata 13, has a large collection of Norwegian and foreign art. Two rooms are devoted to masterpieces by Munch.

8 Organized Tours

CRUISES AROUND THE FJORD   Båtservice Sightseeing, Rådhusbrygge 3, Rådhusplassen (✆ **23-35-68-90**), offers a 50-minute boat tour. You'll see the harbor and the city, including the ancient fortress of Akershus and the islands in the inner part of the Oslofjord. Cruises depart from Pier 3 in front of the Oslo Rådhuset (City Hall). They run from mid-May to late August, daily on the hour from 11am to 8pm during the high season, less frequently at the beginning and end of the season. Tickets are 90NOK ($12) for adults, 40NOK ($5.30) for children.

If you have more time, take a 2-hour cruise through the maze of islands and narrow sounds in the Oslofjord. From May to September, boats leave daily at 10:30am, 1pm, 3:30pm, and 5:45pm; the cost is 165NOK ($22) for adults, 80NOK ($11) for children. Refreshments are available on board. The 2-hour fjord cruise with lunch runs from May to mid-September. It leaves daily at 10:30am and costs 295NOK ($39) for adults, 155NOK ($21) for children. Lunch is served at Lanternen Restaurant after the cruise.

The 2-hour evening fjord cruise includes a seafood buffet, also at the Lanternen. It's offered from late June to August, daily at 3:30 and 5:45pm. Prices are 295NOK ($39) for adults, 155NOK ($21) for children.

CITY TOURS   H. M. Kristiansens Automobilbyrå, Hegdehaugsveien 4 (✆ **22-20-82-06**), has been showing visitors around Oslo for more than a century. Both of their bus tours are offered daily year-round. The 3-hour "Oslo Highlights" tour is offered at 10am and 1:30pm. It costs 250NOK ($33) for adults, 130NOK ($17) for children. The 2-hour "Oslo Panorama" tour costs 170NOK ($23) for adults, 90NOK ($12) for children. It departs at 10am and 5:30pm. The starting point is the Norway information center, Vestbaneplassen 1; arrive 15 minutes before departure. Tours are conducted in English by trained guides.

9 Active Sports

From spring to fall, the Oslofjord is a center of swimming, sailing, windsurfing, and angling. Daily excursions are arranged by motor launch at the harbor. Suburban forest areas await hikers, bicyclists, and anglers in the summer. In the winter, the area is ideal for cross-country skiing (on marked trails that are illuminated at night), downhill or slalom skiing, tobogganing, skating, and more. Safaris by Land Rover are arranged year-round.

BATHS   The most central municipal bath is **Vestkantbadet,** Sommerrogate 1 (✆ **22-56-05-66**), which offers a Finnish sauna and Roman baths. Admission is 100NOK ($13). The baths are reserved for men on Monday, Wednesday, and Friday from noon to 4pm, and for women on Tuesday and Thursday from noon to 9pm and Saturday from 9:30am to 3pm. Prices for massages start at 300NOK ($40) for 30 minutes. If you book a massage, you can use the baths free. This municipal bath is near the American Embassy, about a kilometer north of Oslo's center. It's primarily a winter destination, and closed in July.

Frognerbadet, Middelthunsgate 28 (℃ **22-44-74-29**), in Frogner Park, is an open-air pool near the Vigeland sculptures. The entrance fee is 44NOK ($5.85) for adults, 22NOK ($2.95) for children. It's open from mid-May to mid-August, Monday through Friday from 7am to 7pm, Saturday and Sunday from 11am to 5pm. Take tram no. 2 from the National Theater.

BEACHES   Avoid the polluted inner-harbor area. The nearest and most popular beach is at **Hovedøya,** which is also the site of a 12th-century Cistercian monastery erected by English monks. Swimming is from a rocky shore. From Oslo's central station, local trains run frequently throughout the day to Sandvika. Also try **Drøbak,** 39km (24 miles) south of Oslo (take bus no. 541).

Oslovian beach devotees say **Gressholmen** and **Langøyene,** a 15-minute ride from Vippetangen, have the finest beaches in the vicinity. Nudism is practiced at beaches on the south side of Langøyene.

The closest clean beaches are those west of the Bygdøy peninsula, including **Huk** (where there's nude bathing) and **Paradisbukta.** Bygdøy can be reached by bus no. 30 from the National Theater. There are also beaches at **Langåra,** 16km (10 miles) west of Oslo. Take the local train to Sandvika and make ferry connections from there.

You can reach a number of beaches on the east side of the fjord by taking bus no. 75B from Jernbanetorget in East Oslo. Buses leave about every hour on weekends. It's a 12-minute ride to **Ulvøya,** the closest beach and one of the best and safest for children. Nudists prefer **Standskogen.**

GYMS   Male and female weight lifters call **Harald's Gym,** Hausmannsgate 6 (℃ **22-20-34-96**), the most professional gym in Oslo. Many champion bodybuilders have trained here, and its facilities are the most comprehensive in Norway. Nonmembers pay 70NOK ($9.30) for a day pass. It's open Monday through Friday from 10am to 9pm, Saturday and Sunday from noon to 6pm.

JOGGING   Marka, the forest that surrounds Oslo, has hundreds of trails. The easiest and most accessible are at Frogner Park. You can also jog or hike the trails along the Aker River, a scenic route. A great adventure is to take the Sognasvann train to the end of the line, where you can jog along the fast-flowing Sognasvann stream. **Norske Turistforening,** Storgata 28 (℃ **22-82-28-00**), sells maps outlining jogging trails around the capital, and the staff can give you advice about routes.

SKATING   Oslo is home to numerous skating rinks. **Grünerhallen,** Seilduksgate 30 (℃ **22-35-55-52**), admits the public for pleasure skating. For a 2-hour session, the price is 20NOK ($2.65) for adults, 5NOK (65¢) for children. Skate rentals cost 10NOK to 20NOK ($1.35–$2.65). Grünerhallen is open from October to March; days and hours are erratic because it's used primarily for hockey, so call in advance. Other skating rinks include **Narvisen,** Spikersuppa, near Karl Johans Gate (℃ **22-33-30-33**), open from October to March.

SKIING   A 15-minute tram or bus ride from central Oslo to Holmenkollen will take you to Oslo's winter wonderland, **Marka,** a 2,595km (1,612-mile) ski-track network. Many ski schools and instructors are available in the winter. You can even take a sleigh ride. Other activities include dog-sled rides, snowshoe trekking, and Marka forest safaris. There are 14 slalom slopes to choose from, along with ski jumps in all shapes and sizes, including the famous one at Holmenkollen. For information and updates on ski conditions, you can call Skiforeningen, Kongeveien 5 (© **22-92-32-00**). The tourist office can give you details about the venues for many of these activities.

TENNIS   The municipal courts at **Frogner Park** are usually fully booked for the season by the locals, but ask at the kiosk about cancellations.

Njårdhallen, Sørkedalsceien 106 (© **22-14-67-74**), offers indoor tennis Monday through Thursday from 7am to 10pm, Friday through Sunday from 7am to 8pm. Book your court well in advance. During nice weather, you might prefer outdoor tennis at **Njårds Tennis,** Jenns Messveien 1 (© **22-14-67-74**), a cluster of courts that are generally open whenever weather and daylight permit.

10 Shopping

THE SHOPPING SCENE

Oslo has many **traffic-free streets** for strollers and shoppers. The heart of this district is the **Stortorvet,** where more than two dozen shops sell everything from handicrafts to enameled silver jewelry. At the marketplace on Strøget, you can stop for a glass of beer at an open-air restaurant in fair weather. Many stores are clustered along **Karl Johans Gate** and the streets branching off it.

BEST BUYS   Look for bargains on sportswear, silver and enamelware, traditional handicrafts, pewter, glass by Hadeland Glassverk (founded in 1762), teak furniture, and stainless steel.

SHIPPING GOODS & RECOVERING VAT   Norway imposes a 20% value-added tax (VAT), but there are ways to avoid paying it. See "Taxes" in "Fast Facts: Norway," in chapter 7. Special tax-free exports are possible; many stores will mail goods home to you, which makes paying and recovering tax unnecessary.

SHOPPING HOURS   Most stores are open Monday through Friday from 9am to 5pm, Saturday from 9am to 3pm. Department stores and shopping malls keep different hours—in general, Monday through Friday from 9am to 8pm, Saturday from 9am to 6pm. Many shops stay open late on Thursday and on the first Saturday of the month. Shoppers call this *super lørdag* ("super Saturday"). During the holiday season, stores are open on Sunday.

SHOPPING A TO Z
ARTS & CRAFTS

Baerum Verk   For a unique adventure you can head outside of town to a restored ironworks site dating from 1610. There are more than 65 different shops selling handicrafts and other items, including jewelry and woolens, plus there are exhibitions and six restaurants to choose from. If time remains, visit the ironworks museum on-site and see a smelting production dating back to the 17th century. Verksgata 15, Baerum Verk. © **67-13-00-18.** Bus: 143 or 153.

Den Norske Husfliden   Near the marketplace and the cathedral, Husfliden is the display and retail center for the Norwegian Association of Home Arts and Crafts, founded in 1891. Today it's almost eight times larger than any of its competitors, offering an unparalleled opportunity to see the finest Norwegian designs in ceramics, glassware, clothing, furniture, and woodworking. It also carries souvenirs, gifts, textiles, rugs, knotted Rya rugs, embroidery, and wrought iron. Goods are shipped all over the world. Møllergata 4. © **22-42-10-75.** T-banen: Stortinget.

Norway Designs   This is the only store in Norway that came into being as the result of a crafts exhibit. Shortly before it was established in 1957, an exposition of Norwegian crafts went to Chicago and New York, and it attracted a lot of attention. The upscale merchandise here—crystal, pewter, jewelry, and knitwear—emerged from the innovative designs of that exposition. The store's distinguished owner, Mr. Westlund, refuses to display or sell what he refers to as "touristic junk." Stortingsgaten 28. © 23-11-45-10. Tram: 2, 8, or 9.

The Troll Shop *Finds*   There's a wide and classy-looking array of Norway-inspired souvenirs, art objects, jewelry, and kitchen items for sale in this shop, but the really charming merchandise is its collection of trolls—probably the largest in Norway. They're made of wood, porcelain (breakable), or plastic (unbreakable) in virtually any format. They include trolls carrying passports, royal trolls, Viking trolls, trolls playing golf, trolls on skateboards, trolls drinking beer, trolls going fishing, and more. Your favorite trolls will cost between 100NOK and 900NOK ($13–$120) each, depending on their size and material. There are also well-made T-shirts, and sweaters, hats, scarves, and gloves in traditional Norwegian patterns. Shopping Arcade, SAS Hotel Scandinavia. Holbergsgate 30. © 22-11-17-12. T-banen: Nationaltheatret.

BOOKS
Damms Antikvariat   This shop, established in 1843, specializes in old and rare books, atlases, maps, and nautical prints. Tollbugata 25. © 22-41-04-02. T-banen: Stortinget.

Tanum Karl Johan   A fine bookstore in the center of town, this is the largest and most comprehensive in Oslo. It offers a vast selection, including many English titles. Karl Johans Gate 37-41. © 22-41-11-00. T-banen: Stortinget.

DEPARTMENT STORES
Glasmagasinet   Claiming that smaller boutiques tend to charge more, locals usually head for this big department store, which specializes in unusual home and kitchen accessories. It's the largest outlet in Norway for the Hadelands Glassverk (Glassworks); there's also a coffee shop and a restaurant. Stortorvet 9. © 22-42-53-05. T-banen: Stortinget. Bus: 7, 8, 11, 37, or 92.

Steen & Strøm   The largest department store in Norway, Steen & Strøm specializes in Nordic items. Look for hand-knit sweaters and caps, hand-painted wooden dishes reflecting traditional Norwegian art, and pewter dinner plates made from old molds. There's a souvenir shop on the ground floor. Kongensgate 23. © 22-00-40-00. T-banen: Stortinget.

FOLK COSTUMES
Heimen Husflid   This leading purveyor of modern and traditional Norwegian handicrafts and apparel carries antique and reproduction folk costumes. More than three dozen different *bunads* (styles) include different regions of Norway, both north and south. Hand-knit sweaters in traditional Norwegian patterns are a special item, as are pewter and brass goods. The store is about a block from Karl Johans Gate. Rosenkrantzgate 8. © 22-41-40-50. T-banen: Stortinget. Tram: 7, 8, or 11.

GLASS
Hadeland Glassverk   The most famous name in Norwegian glass dates from 1762. You can see glass being blown and shaped, and visit a glass museum and gallery with changing exhibits. You can also buy Hadeland's complete collection

and discounted "seconds." There's a restaurant on the premises. From June 15 to August 15, the museum is open daily from 9am to 7pm, shops daily from 10am to 8pm. The rest of the year, the museum is open daily from 9am to 3pm, shops daily from 10am to 7pm. The complex can easily be reached by public transportation; it's a 90-minute ride east of Oslo. Jevnaker. ℂ **61-31-64-00.** Museum admission 30NOK ($4) adults, 15NOK ($2) children 7–15, free for children under 7. Bus: Hønefoss/Jevnaker bus from Jernbanetorget, leaving on the hour.

JEWELRY, ENAMELWARE & SILVER

David-Andersen   This outstanding jeweler, established more than a century ago, sells enameled demitasse spoons and sterling silver bracelets with enamel. They're available in many stunning colors, such as turquoise and dark blue. Multicolored butterfly pins are also popular in gold-plated sterling silver with enamel. David-Andersen's collection of Saga silver was inspired by Norwegian folklore and Viking designs, combined with the pristine beauty of today's design. The store also offers an exquisite collection of pewter items. Karl Johans Gate 20. ℂ **22-41-69-55.** T-banen: Stortinget.

MUSIC

Norsk Musikforlag   This centrally located store's selection of CDs, records, and tapes is the best in Oslo. Karl Johans Gate 39A. ℂ **22-17-34-70.** T-banen: Stortinget.

PEWTER

Heyerdahl   Between the City Hall and Karl Johans Gate, this store offers an intriguing selection of silver and gold Viking jewelry. There are also articles in pewter and other materials, including Viking vessels, drinking horns, and cheese slicers. It has an array of trolls, as well as one of Oslo's largest collections of gold and silver jewelry. Roald Amundsens Gate. ℂ **22-41-59-18.** T-banen: Nationaltheatret.

SHOPPING MALLS

Oslo has three large shopping arcades: Oslo City and Galleri Oslo, both near the Central Station, and Aker Brygge, at the west side of the harbor, a short walk from the Rådhuset.

Oslo City, Stenersgate 1, opposite the Central Station, is the biggest shopping center in Norway; it's loaded with shops and restaurants.

Also near the Central Station, **Galleri Oslo,** at Vaterland, has been called Europe's longest indoor shopping street. Businesses are open daily until midnight, including Sunday. A walkway connects Galleri Oslo to the Central Station.

Aker Brygge is a unique shopping venue by the Oslofjord. It carries a wide variety of merchandise, and the complex also includes restaurants, theaters, cinemas, and cafes.

SOUVENIRS & GIFTS

William Schmidt   Established in 1853, William Schmidt is a leading purveyor of unique souvenirs. It carries pewter items (from Viking ships to beer goblets), Norwegian dolls in national costumes, woodcarvings—the troll collection is of the best quality in Oslo—and sealskin items, such as moccasins and handbags. The shop specializes in hand-knit cardigans, pullovers, gloves, and caps. Sweaters are made from mothproofed 100% Norwegian wool. Karl Johans Gate 41. ℂ **22-42-02-88.** T-banen: Stortinget.

SWEATERS

Oslo Sweater Shop   Some 5,000 handicrafted sweaters are in stock here, close to the Royal Palace. Try them on before you buy. The store has branches

OSLO AFTER DARK   245

at the Oslo Cruise Terminal, Skur 35 (© 22-41-87-71), and the Royal Christiania Hotel, Biskop Gunnerus Gate 3 (© 22-42-42-25). In the Radisson SAS Scandinavia Hotel, Tullins Gate 5. © 22-11-29-22. T-banen: Stortinget.

11 Oslo After Dark

Oslo has a bustling nightlife. Midnight is no longer the curfew hour. The city boasts more than 100 night cafes, clubs, and restaurants, 35 of which stay open until 4am.

Autumn and winter are the seasons for cabaret, theater, and concerts. There are four cabarets and nine theater stages. Oslo is also a favorite destination of international performing artists in classical, pop, rock, and jazz music.

For movie lovers, Oslo has a lot to offer. The city has one of the most extensive selections in Europe, with 30 screens and five large film complexes. Films are shown in their original languages, with subtitles.

THE ENTERTAINMENT SCENE

The best way to find out what's happening is to pick up a copy of *What's On in Oslo,* detailing concerts and theaters and other useful information.

Oslo doesn't have agents who specialize in discount tickets, but it does have an exceptional number of free events. *What's On in Oslo* lists free happenings as well as the latest exhibits at art galleries, which can be a delightful place to spend the early part of an evening.

Tickets to the theater, ballet, and opera are sold at box offices and at **Billettsentralen,** Karl Johans Gate 35 (© **81-53-31-33**). Tickets to most sporting and cultural events in Oslo can be purchased by computer at any post office in the city. The same postal clerk who sells you stamps can also sell you a voucher for a ticket to the ballet, the theater, or a hockey game.

The world-famous **Oslo Philharmonic** performs regularly under the leadership of Mariss Janson. There are no Oslo performances between June 20 and the middle of August.

If you visit Oslo in the winter season, you might be able to see its thriving opera and ballet company, **Den Norske Opera.** Plays given at the **Nationaltheatret** (where Ibsen is regularly featured) are in Norwegian. Those who know Ibsen in their own language sometimes enjoy hearing the original version of his plays.

THE PERFORMING ARTS
CLASSICAL MUSIC

Oslo Konserthus Two blocks from the National Theater, this is the home of the widely acclaimed Oslo Philharmonic. Performances are given from autumn to spring, on Thursday and Friday. Guest companies from around the world often appear on other nights. The hall is closed from June 20 until mid-August, except for occasional performances by folkloric groups. Munkedamsveien 14. © 23-11-31-11. Tickets 200NOK–700NOK ($27–$93). Box office Mon–Fri 10am–5pm, Sat 11am–2pm. T-banen: Stortinget.

THEATER

Nationaltheatret (National Theater) This theater at the upper end of the Students' Grove opens in August, so it may be of interest to off-season drama lovers who want to hear Ibsen and Bjørnson in the original. Avant-garde productions go up at the **Amfiscenen,** in the same building. There are no performances in July and August. Guest companies often perform plays in English.

Johanne Dybwads Plass 1. ℂ 81-50-08-11. Tickets 150NOK–220NOK ($20–$29) adults, 85NOK–170NOK ($11–$23) for students and seniors. Box office Mon–Fri 8:30am–7:30pm, Sat 11am–6pm. T-banen: Nationaltheatret. Tram: 12, 13, or 19.

OPERA & DANCE

Den Norske Opera (Norwegian National Opera)   The Norwegian opera and ballet troupes make up Den Norske Opera. The 1931 building, originally a movie theater, was dedicated to the Norwegian National Opera in 1959. It's also the leading venue for ballet—the companies alternate performances. About 20 different operas and operettas are staged every year. There are no performances from mid-June to August. Unlike those for some European opera companies, tickets are generally available to nonsubscribers; seats can be reserved in advance and paid for with a credit card. Storgaten 23. ℂ 23-31-50-00. Tickets 170NOK–320NOK ($23–$43), except for galas. Box office Mon–Sat 10am–6pm, to 7:30pm on performance nights. Bus: 56, 62, or 66.

SUMMER CULTURAL ENTERTAINMENT

Det Norske Folkloreshowet (Norwegian Folklore Show) performs from July to early September at the Oslo Konserthus, Munkedamsveien 15 (ℂ 23-11-31-11 for reservations). The 1-hour performances are on Monday and Thursday at 8:30pm. Tickets cost 160NOK ($21) for adults, 90NOK to 110NOK ($12–$15) for children (T-banen: Stortinget).

The ensemble at the **Norwegian Folk Museum,** on Bygdøy, often presents folk-dance performances at the open-air theater in the summer. See *What's On in Oslo* for details. Most shows are given on Sunday afternoon. Admission to the museum includes admission to the dance performance. Take the ferry from Pier 3 near the Rådhuset.

SPECIAL & FREE EVENTS

Oslo has many free events, including summer jazz concerts at the National Theater. In front of the theater, along the Students' Grove, you'll see street entertainers, including singers, musicians, clowns, and jugglers.

Concerts are presented in the chapel of **Akershus Castle & Fortress,** Akershus Command, on Sunday at 2pm. During the summer, promenade music, parades, drill marches, exhibits, and theatrical performances are also presented on the castle grounds.

In August the **Chamber Music Festival** at Akershus Castle & Fortress presents concerts by Norwegian and foreign musicians.

The **Oslo Jazz Festival,** also in August, includes not only old-time jazz, but also classical concerts, opera, and ballet performances.

FILMS

American and British films are shown in English, with Norwegian subtitles. Tickets are sold for specific performances only. Many theaters have showings nightly at 5pm, 7pm, and 9pm, but really big films are usually shown only once in an evening, generally at 7:30pm.

Two of the city's biggest theaters are the **Colosseum,** on Freitjoj Nansens vei 6 (T-banen: Majorstua), and **Filmteatret,** Stortingsgaten 16 (T-banen: Nationaltheatret). Most tickets cost 90NOK ($12) for adults, half price for children; at Monday and Thursday matinees the cost is 65NOK ($8.65) for adults, 45NOK ($6) for children. For information about all films presented in Oslo, call ℂ 82-03-00-01.

THE CLUB & MUSIC SCENE
DANCE CLUBS
Smuget   This is the most talked-about nightlife emporium in Oslo, with long lines, especially on weekends. It's behind the Grand Hotel in a 19th-century building that was a district post office. There's an active dance floor with disco and retro 1970s music, and a stage where live bands (sometimes two a night on weekends) perform. The clientele includes artists, writers, rock stars, and a cross section of the capital's night owls. The complex is open every night except Sunday. A restaurant serves Thai, Chinese, Norwegian, Italian, and American food from 8pm to 3am; live music plays from 11pm to 3am; and there's disco music from 10pm till very late. Half-liters of beer cost 39NOK ($5.20); main courses run 80NOK to 175NOK ($11–$23). Rosenkrantzgate 22. © 22-42-52-62. Cover 60NOK–70NOK ($8–$9.30). T-banen: Stortinget.

A SUPPER CLUB
Bristol Night Spot   The entrance to this cellar nightclub is visible from the sidewalk near the hotel's main entrance. A popular dance bar with an intimately lit restaurant, a dance floor, and a cellar tavern, this has become one of the most popular places in Oslo. Conservative dress is suggested. A dance band starts playing at 8pm. Main dishes include poached salmon with butter-cream sauce, chateaubriand with béarnaise sauce, filet of veal Oscar with asparagus, and mixed grill. Cocktails include a Norwegian bomb called *Fjellbekk* (mountain stream), made with aquavit, vodka, lime juice, and Sprite. Meals begin at 250NOK ($33), drinks at 65NOK ($8.65). It's open Monday through Saturday from 9pm to 3am. Reservations are recommended. In the Hotel Bristol, Kristian IV's Gate 7. © 22-82-60-30. Cover 100NOK ($13). T-banen: Stortinget.

JAZZ & ROCK
Herr Nilsen   This is a conventional pub on most evenings, with recorded jazz. On Wednesday at 9pm and Saturday at 4pm and 11pm, live jazz is played to an appreciative audience. Expect everything from progressive jazz to Dixieland or blues. The rest of the time, entrance is free. Beer, depending on the time of evening, costs 36NOK to 49NOK ($4.80–$6.50). It's open Monday through Saturday from 10am to 3am, Sunday from noon to 3am. C.J. Hambros Plass 5. © 22-33-54-05. Cover 75NOK–100NOK ($10–$13) Wed and Sat. T-banen: Stortinget.

Rockefeller Music Hall   With a capacity of 1,200 patrons, this concert hall and club is one of the largest establishments of its kind in Oslo. It's one floor above street level in a 1910 building, formerly a public bath. Live concerts feature everything from reggae to rock to jazz. When no concert is scheduled, films are shown on a wide screen. Simple foods, such as pasta and sandwiches, are available in the cafe. Most of the crowd is in the 18-to-37 age bracket. It's usually open Sunday through Thursday from 8pm to 2:30am, Friday and Saturday from 9pm to 3:30am. Show time is about an hour after the doors open. Torggata 16. © 22-20-32-32. Tickets cost 100NOK–700NOK ($13–$93), depending on act. T-banen: Stortinget.

THE BAR SCENE
PUBS & BARS
Buddha Bar *(Finds*   This is the bar and nightclub in Oslo that everyone clamors to get into, with a reputation that's akin to the way Studio 54 used to affect die-hard night owls in New York City during the 1970s. Often, even on weeknights, long lines form outside this place, composed of hipsters whose occasional aggression seems to fade once they reach the incense-scented interior of a suite

of rooms dotted with iconic statues of Lord Buddha. They include fat-bellied Chinese versions, and ascetic-looking versions from Burma and Thailand, all staring benignly over a pan-European crowd that's very familiar with the rituals of the late-night playing and mating games. Bruce Springsteen was spotted here, along with various members of the Rolling Stones. There's a dining area (Restaurant Fogo) shoved off into a side room, where set menus cost from 400NOK to 650NOK ($53–$86). But most people come here just to drink, meet other like-minded extroverts, and perhaps to dance. The crowd graciously combines gay and straight people. The minimum age for entrance, unless you're very, very cool and irresistibly attractive, is 28. There might be a cover charge of 70NOK ($9.30), but often it's waived, depending on business and the mood of the security staff. The bar is open Tuesday through Sunday from 7pm till 3am, but the heat doesn't really begin to rise till around 10:30pm. Klingenberggata 4. ℂ 22-82-86-50. Bus: 30, 31, 32, 45, or 8.

Café Onkel Donalds   Of the many bars and pubs that flourish after dark in Oslo, this is the most artfully designed (in this case, in 2001 by well-known Norwegian architect Petter Abrahamsen). Its soaring interior spaces evoke the entranceway to a postmodern opera house, and a network of short staircases will take you from the surging energy of the glossy-looking main bar to a series of tucked away, more intimate mezzanines. The house special cocktail is an Onkel Donald, a head spinner combining vodka, peach liqueur, cranberry juice, and sour mash. This bar is a great catalyst for conversation—and sometimes romance. It's open daily from 11am to 3am. Universitetsgata 26. ℂ 22-42-44-20. Tram: 5, 6, or 7.

John's Bar   This pub isn't flashy or glamorous, but it does enjoy a powerful cachet among the hip nightlife denizens of Oslo, as well as a growing underground role as a cultural icon. In the case of its decor, less is more. At John's, you'll never be entirely sure who or what to expect: frost-bitten fishermen exhausted from hauling in herring from the North Sea, or perhaps a group of scary-looking bikers in town for some binge drinking. It's open Wednesday through Sunday from 10pm to 3am. Universitetsgata 26. ℂ 22-42-44-20. Tram: 5, 6, or 7.

Library Bar   In a lobby that evokes the Edwardian era, this is a perfect spot for people-watching. You'll be sheltered behind racks of leather-bound books, which you can remove and read. It's like being in a well-furnished private club. There's live piano music at lunchtime, when you can order from a selection of open-faced sandwiches for 40NOK to 80NOK ($5.30–$11). Specialty cocktails have such coy names as "Take Me Home" and "Norwegian Kiss." It's open daily from 10am to 11:30pm; alcohol service starts at 1pm. A beer will cost you 52NOK ($6.90); mixed drinks begin at 80NOK ($11). In the Hotel Bristol, Kristian IV's Gate 7. ℂ 22-82-60-22. T-banen: Stortinget.

Limelight   Steeped in the atmosphere of the theater, this fashionable bar next door to the Oslo Nye Theater is a favorite rendezvous for drinks before or after a show. It's open daily from 6pm to midnight. Beer and mixed drinks cost 65NOK ($8.65) and up. In the Grand Hotel, Karl Johans Gate 31. ℂ 23-21-20-36. T-banen: Stortinget.

NIGHT CAFES

Lorry *Finds*   The most remarkable thing about this busy, suds-drenched cafe and restaurant is its contrast with the neighborhood it occupies. It was established 120 years ago as a working-class bar. Since then, the neighborhood that surrounds it (virtually across the street from the park that flanks the Royal Palace) has zoomed upward in both prestige and price. Despite that, from a low-slung wood-sided house tucked in among much grander villas, it continues its rip-roaring business. There's an outdoor terrace for warm weather dining, but the earthy heart and soul of the place is found in its all-Victorian, black-stained interior. Here, you can order any of up to 130 kinds of beer, 11 of which are on tap. From 5 to 10:30pm, the menu focuses only on a short list of platters of the day, priced at 100NOK to 150NOK ($13–$20) each, and from around 10:30pm to closing, all everybody seems to do here is drink. It's open Monday through Saturday from 11am to 3am, and Sunday from noon to 1am. Parkveien 12. (℃ **22-69-69-04**. Tram: 11, 12.

GAY & LESBIAN BARS

Gay and lesbian nightlife is more limited than in Copenhagen or Stockholm, but there is some—two gay bars in a city of 500,000. Pick up a copy of *Blick* for 30NOK ($4), available at most newsstands within the central city. Otherwise call Gay/Lesbian Visitor Information (℃ **22-11-05-09**), Monday through Friday from 9am to 4pm.

London Pub   This is the most consistent and reliable gay pub in Oslo, with a relatively mature crowd of unpretentious gay men, and—to a much lesser extent—women. Set within the cellar of a building a few steps from the prestigious Hotel Bristol, it sports a battered-looking, beer-hall–style trio of underground rooms that include two bar areas and a pool table. At its best—whenever it's busy, usually late in the week—this place can be fun, convivial, and genuinely welcoming to newcomers from faraway places. At its worst, it can be glum, low-energy, and depressing. Whether you like it or not, this is one of the mainstays of gay life in Oslo. It's open Monday through Friday from 6pm to 4am, Saturday and Sunday from 3pm to 4am. 5 C. J. Hambros Plass (entrance on Rosenkrantzgate). (℃ **22-70-87-00**. T-banen: Stortinget.

Soho   This place rivals the London, which tends to attract a more mature clientele, as the pre-eminent gay (both male and female) venue in Oslo. It's accessible via a covered passageway that leads in from the street. Your experience here will vary hugely depending on when you arrive. The venue can either be animated or morbidly comatose, but if more than one room here is open, be sure to check out the upper or lower floors (there's a total of four bars on four floors), which open or close according to the number of clients on that particular night. Entrance is 70NOK ($9.30), collected only Friday and Saturday nights. An additional entrance fee of 200NOK ($27) is collected for drag shows, which are usually presented Friday and Saturday at 10pm and midnight. Open Wednesday and Thursday from 5pm to 3am, Friday and Sunday from 3pm to 3am, Saturday from noon to 3am. Kirkegaten 34. (℃ **22-42-19-00**. Bus: 8, 30, 31, 32, or 45.

12 Side Trips from Oslo

The Oslo area offers a variety of 1-day excursions that are manageable by boat, car, or bus. Except for boat tours of the Oslofjord (see "Organized Tours," earlier in this chapter), getting around is a do-it-yourself activity.

Fredrikstad is in Østfold on the east bank of the Oslofjord. A day trip can be combined with a visit to the port of **Tønsberg** on the west bank by crossing on the ferry from Moss to Horten, then heading south.

The summer resort and ski center of **Lillehammer,** to the north, was the site of the 1994 Olympics.

FREDRIKSTAD ✿
97km (60 miles) S of Oslo

In recent years Fredrikstad has become a major tourist center, thanks to its Old Town and 17th-century fortress. Across the river on the west is a modern industrial section; although a bridge links the areas, the best way to reach the Old Town is by ferry, which costs 6NOK (80¢). The departure point is about 4 blocks from the Fredrikstad railroad station. Follow the crowd out the main door of the station, make an obvious left turn, and continue down to the bank of the river. You can also travel between the two areas by bus (no. 360 or 362), although most pedestrians prefer the ferry.

ESSENTIALS
GETTING THERE   By Train   Trains from Oslo's Central Station depart for Fredrikstad about every 2 hours. The trip takes about 30 minutes from central Oslo.

By Bus   There is frequent bus service daily from Oslo to Fredrikstad.

By Car   Take Highway E6 south from Oslo heading toward Moss. Continue past Moss until you reach the junction at Route 110, and follow the signs south to Fredrikstad.

VISITOR INFORMATION   The **Fredrikstad Turistkontor** is on Turistsenteret, Østre Brohode, Gamle Fredrikstad (✆ **69-30-46-00**). It's open from June to September, Monday through Friday from 9am to 6pm, Saturday from 10am to 4pm, and Sunday from noon to 4pm; from October to May, Monday through Friday from 9am to 4pm.

SEEING THE SIGHTS
Fredrikstad was founded in 1567 as a marketplace at the mouth of the River Glomma. **Gamlebyen** (the Old Town) became a fortress in 1663 and continued in that role until 1903, boasting some 200 guns in its heyday. It still serves as a military camp. The main guardroom and the old prison contain the headquarters and most of the exhibition space of the **Fredrikstad Museum,** Gamleslaveri (✆ **69-30-68-75**). It's open from May to September, Tuesday through Friday from noon to 5pm, Saturday from 11am to 5pm, and Sunday from noon to 5pm; closed from October to April. Admission is 30NOK ($4) for adults, 10NOK ($1.35) for children.

Outside the gates of the Old Town is **Kongsten Fort,** on what was first called Gallows Hill, an execution site. When Fredrikstad Fortress was built, it was provisionally fortified in 1677, and became known as Svenskeskremme (Swede Scarer). Today's Kongsten Fort was built there, with 20 cannons, underground chambers, passages, and countermines.

Since Fredrikstad's heyday as a trading port and merchant base, the Old Town has attracted craftspeople and artisans, many of whom create their wares in historic houses and barns. Many of these glassblowers, ceramic artists, and silversmiths don't display or sell their products at their studios, but leave that to local shops. One of the best emporiums is **Plus,** Kirkegatan 28 (✆ **69-32-06-78**). It's open Monday through Friday from 10am to 4:30pm, Saturday from 10am to 2pm, Sunday from 1 to 3pm.

After leaving Fredrikstad, drive along the **Oldtidsveien** ("highway of the ancients"), Norway's most concentrated collection of archaeological monuments. It lies along Route 110 between Fredrikstad and Skjeberg. The ancient monuments include 3,000-year-old rock carvings at Begby, Hornes, and Solberg, and 2,000-year-old burial grounds with stone circles at Hunn.

WHERE TO DINE

Balaklava Guestgiveri *(Finds* NORWEGIAN   For tradition and atmosphere, this restaurant has no competition in the Old Town. It was built in 1803 as the home of the village priest in a style known in North America as "carpenter Gothic." Today, simple but flavorful meals are served in the cellar, near a massive fireplace. There's access to an outdoor courtyard. The well-prepared fare includes baked salmon with dill sauce, filet of sole with lemon-butter sauce, fish-and-clam casserole with herbs, and an assortment of fresh game dishes.

Faergeportgate 78. (C) **69-32-30-40.** Reservations recommended. Main courses 225NOK–275NOK ($30–$37). AE, DC, MC, V. Daily noon–10:30pm. Bus: Gamlebyen from the center.

Majorstuen INTERNATIONAL   In an 18th-century house at the edge of the Old Town, this restaurant has a large dining room, a pub, and a warm-weather outdoor terrace. The food is unpretentious but plentiful. Among the most popular dishes are pizzas, filet of beef served with vegetables and salad, Wiener schnitzel, fish platters, and marinated whale steak in black peppercorn sauce. Majorstuen is the only restaurant in the region that offers whale steak year-round.

Vollportgatan 73. (C) **69-32-15-55.** Main courses 110NOK–245NOK ($15–$33); pizzas (for 1–4 people) 149NOK–189NOK ($20–$25). AE, DC, MC, V. Sun–Thurs noon–10pm; Fri–Sat 11am–10pm.

TØNSBERG ⭑
103km (64 miles) S of Oslo

Bordering the western bank of the Oslofjord, Tønsberg is Norway's oldest town. It consists of a historic area, filled with old clapboard-sided houses, and the commercial center, where the marketplace is. The 64-sq.-km (40-sq.-mile) town has some 32,000 residents.

Tønsberg was founded a year before King Harald Fairhair united parts of the country in 872, and the Viking town became a royal coronation site. Svend Foyn, who invented modern whaling and seal hunting, was born here.

ESSENTIALS
GETTING THERE   By Train   Trains depart for Tønsberg from Oslo's main railway station at intervals of between 60 and 90 minutes around 6am to 11:30pm every day, requiring a travel time of about 90 minutes and a fare of 160NOK ($21) each way. The railway station is in the town center, thanks to the fact that the island on which Tønsberg sits is connected to the mainland with a bridge. For information and schedules, call (C) **33-35-02-00** or visit www.nsb.no.

There is no NOR bus service from Oslo.

By Car   Take Route 18 south from Oslo via Drammen.

VISITOR INFORMATION   Tønsberg **Tourist Information** is at Nedre Langgate 36B, N-3100 Tønsberg ((C) **33-35-02-00**). It's open in July daily from 10am to 5:30pm; from August to June, Monday through Friday from 8:30am to 4pm. A little tourist kiosk on the island of Tjøme provides information in July, daily from 11am to 5pm.

SEEING THE SIGHTS
Slottsfjellet, a huge hill fortress near the train station, is touted as "the Acropolis of Norway." It has only some meager ruins, and people mostly visit for the view from the 1888 lookout tower, **Slottsfjelltårnet** ((C) **33-31-18-72**). It's open

from May 18 to June 23, Monday through Friday from 10am to 3pm; from June 24 to August 18, daily from 11am to 6pm; from August 19 to September 15, Saturday and Sunday from noon to 5pm; September 16 to September 29, Saturday and Sunday from noon to 3pm. Admission is 20NOK ($2.65) for adults, 10NOK ($1.35) for children.

Nordbyen is the old, scenic part of town, with well-preserved houses. **Haugar** cemetery, at Møllebakken, is in the center of town. It contains the Viking graves of King Harald's sons, Olav and Sigrød.

Sem Church, Hageveien 32 (© **33-36-93-99**), the oldest church in Vestfold, was built of stone in the Romanesque style around 1100. It's open Tuesday through Friday from 9am to 2pm; inquire at the vestry. Admission is free.

Another attraction is **Fjerdingen,** a street of charming restored houses near the mountain farmstead. Tønsberg was also a Hanseatic town during the Middle Ages, and some houses have been redone in typical Hanseatic style—wooden buildings constructed along the wharfs as warehouses to receive shipments of goods among fellow Hanseatic League members.

Vestfold Folk Museum, Frammannsveien 30 (© **33-31-29-19**), contains many Viking and whaling treasures. One of the chief sights is the skeleton of a blue whale, the largest mammal the world has ever known—they sometimes weigh 150 tons. There's also a real Viking ship, the *Klastad* from Tjolling, built about A.D. 800.

In the rural section of the museum, visit the **Vestfold Farm,** which includes a 1600 house from Hynne, a timbered barn from Bøen, and a storehouse from Fadum (with the characteristic apron, or platform). The Heierstadloft (ca. 1350) is the oldest preserved timbered building in Vestfold, and there's a smithy with a charcoal shed, a grain-drying house, and a mountain farmstead.

At the museum, you can have lunch at a real mountain farmstead. A typical meal includes *rømmergrøt* (porridge made with sour cream) and other farm foods. The area is perfect for a picnic.

Admission is 30NOK ($4) for adults, 20NOK ($2.65) for children. It's open from mid-May to mid-September, Monday through Saturday from 10am to 5pm, Sunday and holidays from noon to 5pm; closed from mid-September to mid-May.

WHERE TO DINE
Fregatten INTERNATIONAL   In the Hotel Maritim building (in the town center), Fregatten is one of the best restaurants in Tønsberg. Main courses include filet of reindeer with mushroom sauce and filet of tenderloin with paprika sauce and fresh vegetables. Fresh fish is often prepared with shrimp-and-lobster sauce. The restaurant is a 10-minute walk east of the train station.
Storgaten 17. © **33-31-47-76.** Main courses 205NOK–225NOK ($27–$30). AE, DC, MC, V. Mon–Sat 5–10pm.

LILLEHAMMER ☆☆
170km (105 miles) N of Oslo, 364km (226 miles) S of Trondheim

Surrounded by mountains, Lillehammer is a favorite resort for Europeans. The town, at the head of Lake Mjøsa, became internationally famous when it hosted the 1994 Winter Olympics.

ESSENTIALS
GETTING THERE   By Train   From Oslo, express trains take about 2 hours, 20 minutes, and local trains about 3 hours. Depending on the time of year, there are five to eight trains per day. Call © **81-50-08-88** for information.

By Bus   Bus trips between Oslo and Lillehammer take about 2½ hours, and depart two or three times a day.

By Car   Head north from Oslo along E6.

VISITOR INFORMATION   The **Lillehammer Tourist Office** is at Lilletorget 1 (© **61-25-92-99**). From mid-June to mid-August it is open Monday through Saturday from 9am to 7pm. Off-season hours are Monday through Friday from 9am to 4pm.

SEEING THE SIGHTS

During the peak summer season, usually from June 20 to August 20, the tourist bureau schedules several excursions. They include a trip to the **Maihaugen Open-Air Museum (Sandvig Collections)** and one on **Lake Mjøsa** aboard the *White Swan of Lake Mjøsa,* an 1850s paddle steamer. Ask the tourist bureau (see "Visitor Information," above) for a list of activities.

Hunderfossen Family Park *(Kids*   Here you'll find an interesting presentation of the most popular Norwegian fairy tales, more than 50 activities for children and adults, and lots of space just to roam around. There are a merry-go-round and Ferris wheel, as well as carnival booths, a cafeteria, and a swimming pool. A 12m (40-ft.) troll at the gate welcomes visitors. The park is 12km (7½ miles) north of Lillehammer on E6.

Fåberg. © **61-27-72-22.** Admission 210NOK ($28) adults, 120NOK ($16) seniors, 175NOK ($23) children 3–14, free for children under 3. May–Sept daily 10am–8pm. Closed Oct–Apr. Bus: Hunderfossen from Lillehammer.

Lillehammer Art Museum   This museum, in the center of town, displays one of Norway's largest collections of national art. The pieces date from the 1830s to the present. Opened in the winter of 1992, it was one of the major cultural venues during the 1994 Olympics.

Stortorget. © **61-05-44-60.** Admission 60NOK ($8) adults, 50NOK ($6.65) students and seniors, free for children under 16. June 17–Sept 2 Mon–Wed 11am–4pm, Thurs–Sun 11am–5pm; Sept 3–June 16 Tues–Sun 11am–4pm.

Maihaugen Open-Air Museum (Sandvig Collections) *☆☆*   This museum consists of 150 buildings, from manor farms to the cottage of the poorest yeoman worker. There are more than 40,000 exhibits. The houses reassembled here and furnished in 17th- to 18th-century style came from all over the Gudbrandsdal (Gudbrands Valley). Of particular interest is the Garmo Stave Church, built in 1200. The 37 old workshops range from gunsmithing to wood engraving. A large exhibit covers Norwegian history from 10,000 B.C. to the present. The city's concert hall is also at the museum. The two cafeterias serve Norwegian food. The museum is about .8km (½ mile)—10 minutes on foot—from the town center.

Maihaugveien 1. © **61-28-89-00.** Admission 90NOK ($12) adults, 40NOK ($5.30) children 7–15, free for children under 7. June–Aug daily 9am–6pm; May and Sept daily 10am–5pm; Oct–Apr (indoor museum only) Tues–Sun 11am–4pm. Bus: Rte. 007.

Museum of Norwegian Vehicle History   Norway's only vehicle museum shows the development of transportation from the first sledges and wagons to the car of today. It's east of the town center; from the bus stop, head out on Elvegata.

Lilletorget 7. © **61-25-61-65.** Admission 40NOK ($5.30) adults, 20NOK ($2.65) children 7–14, free for children under 7. June 15–Aug 20 daily 10am–6pm; Aug 21–June 14 Mon–Fri 11am–3pm, Sat–Sun 11am–4pm.

OUTDOOR ACTIVITIES

The **Hafjell Alpine Center,** the main venue for Olympic alpine competitions in 1994, is about 15km (9 miles) from the center of Lillehammer. It has seven lifts and 19km (12 miles) of alpine slopes. Lillehammer is also the starting point for 400km (250 miles) of prepared tracks, 5km (3 miles) of which are illuminated. The ski center has three lifts and 3.2km (2 miles) of alpine slopes.

Lillehammer gears up in December for its winter sports season. In addition to the ski center, there's an admission-free **skating rink.** It's open in the winter Monday through Friday from 11am to 9pm, Sunday from 11am to 5pm. In the winter there are also festivals, folklore nights, and ski races.

SKIING Lillehammer has a 92m (307-ft.) slope for professionals and a smaller jump for the less experienced. The lifts take skiers 450m (1,500 ft.) above sea level up the slalom slope, and more than 400km (250 miles) of marked skiing trails are packed by machines. The Lillehammer Ski School offers daily classes, and several cross-country tours are held weekly. Ask at the tourist office (see "Visitor Information," above) for details.

SPORTS FACILITIES The **Olympiaparken** or Olympic Park (© **61-05-42-00**) is a legacy of the 1994 Winter Games. Many sports, including gymnastics, can be performed here. For example, **Håkons Hall** (© **61-25-21-00**), the main venue for Olympic ice hockey, is a multipurpose arena for indoor sports. It has squash courts and an indoor mountaineering wall. A guide shows visitors around the hall. Admission is 60NOK ($8), free for children under 10. The hall is open from May 19 to September 15, daily from 10am to 6pm; off season, daily from 11am to 4pm.

In the upper part of the park, the **Birkebeineren Nordic Center** has areas for cross-country skiing, a ski lodge, and a cafeteria. The **Kanthaugen Freestyle Facility** is one of the most compact facilities of its type in the world, with hills for aerials, moguls, and "ballet." Skiing instruction is offered on the ballet hill. The **Lysgårdsbakkene** ski-jumping facilities, centrally located in the park, have a jumping hill tower and a chairlift. The lift operates from mid-June to mid-August, daily from 10am to 7pm, depending on the weather. Admission is 20NOK ($2.65) for adults, 15NOK ($2) for children under 12. Ask at the tourist office (see "Visitor Information," above) for information about these facilities.

The most recent addition to the park is the **Norwegian Olympic Museum** (© **61-25-21-00**). It's intended to capture the experience of the Lillehammer Games, and to explore the history of the Olympic spirit. Exhibitions are presented with captions in English. Admission to the museum is 60NOK ($8). A double ticket, for 80NOK ($11), also allows admission to the Maihaugen Open-Air Museum.

Bergen

In western Norway the landscape takes on an awesome beauty, with iridescent glaciers, deep fjords that slash into rugged, snowcapped mountains, roaring waterfalls, and secluded valleys that lie at the end of twisting roads. From Bergen the most beautiful fjords to visit are the Hardanger (best at blossom time, May and early June), to the south; the Sogne, Norway's longest fjord, immediately to the north; and the Nordfjord, north of that. A popular excursion on the Nordfjord takes visitors from Loen to Olden along rivers and lakes to the Brixdal Glacier.

On the Hardangerfjord you can stop over at a resort such as Ulvik or Lofthus. From many vantage points, it's possible to see the Folgefonn Glacier, Norway's second-largest ice field. It spans more than 161 sq. km (100 sq. miles). Other stopover suggestions include the summer resorts (and winter ski centers) of Voss and Geilo. For resorts in the fjord district, see chapter 10, "Exploring the Norwegian Coast."

Bergen, with its many attractions, its good hotels, boardinghouses, and restaurants, and its excellent boat, rail, and coach connections, makes the best center in the fjord district. It's an ancient city that looms large in Viking sagas. Until the 14th century, it was the seat of the medieval kingdom of Norway. The Hanseatic merchants established a major trading post that lasted until the 18th century.

Bergen has survived many disasters, including several fires and the explosion of a Nazi ship during World War II. It's a town with important traditions in shipping, banking, insurance, and the oil service industry, and its modern industries are expanding rapidly.

1 Orientation

ARRIVING

BY PLANE Planes to and from larger cities such as Copenhagen and London land at the **Bergen Airport** in Flesland, 19km (12 miles) south of the city. Dozens of direct or nonstop flights go to just about every medium-sized city in Norway on such airlines as **SAS** (© 67-59-60-50) and **Braathens SAFE** (© 55-99-82-50).

Frequent **airport bus** service connects the airport to the Radisson SAS Royal Hotel, Braathens SAFE's office at the Hotel Norge, and the city bus station. Departures are every 20 minutes Monday through Friday and every 30 minutes Saturday and Sunday. The one-way fare is 60NOK ($8).

BY TRAIN Day and night trains arrive from Oslo and stations en route. For information, call © **55-96-60-00.** Travel time from Oslo to Bergen is 6 to 8½ hours.

BY BUS Express buses travel to Bergen from Oslo, Trondheim, Ålesund, and the Nordfjord area. The trip from Oslo takes 11 hours. Contact © 55-55-90-70 for more information.

BY CAR   A toll is charged on all vehicles driven into the city center Monday through Friday from 6am to 10pm. A single ticket costs 10NOK ($1.35); a book of 20 tickets, 90NOK ($12).

The trip from Oslo to Bergen is a mountainous drive filled with dramatic scenery. Because mountains split the country, there's no direct road. The southern route, E76, takes you through mountain passes until the junction with Route 47; then you head north to Kinsarvik and make the ferry crossing to E16 leading to Bergen. It's quickest to take the northern route following E16 west. For the first time it's possible to make a ferry-free road connection to Bergen. In 2001 the world's longest tunnel opened, going as deep as 1,470m (4,900 ft.) beneath one of Norway's most scenic mountain areas beginning 300km (185 miles) northwest of Oslo. The 40km (25-mile) Laerdal Tunnel surpasses the 17km (11-mile) St. Gothard Tunnel in the Swiss Alps. It takes 20 minutes to go through the tunnel.

Visitors with a lot of time may spend 2 or 3 days driving from Oslo to Bergen. Fjords and snowcapped peaks line the way, and you can photograph waterfalls, fjord villages, and perhaps ancient stave churches.

To reduce driving time, motorists can use a tunnel—almost 11km (7 miles), the longest in northern Europe—that goes between Flåm (see chapter 10) and Gudvangen. From Gudvangen, follow E16 southwest to Bergen.

VISITOR INFORMATION

The **Bergen Tourist Office,** Bryggen 7 (© **55-32-14-80**), provides information, maps, and brochures about Bergen and the rest of the region. It's open from June to August daily from 8:30am to 10pm; May and September daily from 9am to 8pm; from October to April Monday through Saturday from 9am to 4pm. The Bergen Tourist Office can also help you find a place to stay (see "Where to Stay," below), exchange foreign currency, and cash traveler's checks when banks are closed. You can also buy tickets for city sightseeing or for tours of the fjords.

CITY LAYOUT

Bergen is squeezed between mountain ranges and bounded by water. The center of the city lies between the harbor, **Bryggen** (see "The Top Attractions," below), the railway station, and the main square, **Torgalmenningen.**

Like Rome, Bergen is said to have grown up around seven hills. For the best overall view, take the funicular to **Fløien** (see "Seeing the Sights," below). The northern section of the city, **Sandviken,** is filled with old warehouses. The area south of central Bergen has recently been developed at an incredible rate.

In the center of Bergen, walk on cobblestone streets as you explore the quayside with its medieval houses and the open-air fish market. The center has colonnaded shops and cafes, and in **Gamle Bergen,** you can step back to the early 19th century.

2 Getting Around

The **Bergen Card** entitles you to free bus transportation and (usually) free museum entrance throughout Bergen, plus discounts on car rentals, parking, and some cultural and leisure activities. It's a good value. Ask for it at the tourist office (see "Visitor Information," above). A 24-hour card costs 165NOK ($22) for adults, 80NOK ($11) for children 3 to 15. A 48-hour card is 245NOK ($33) or 120NOK ($16). Children under 3 generally travel or enter free.

BY BUS

The **Central Bus Station (Bystasjonen),** Strømgaten 8 (© **55-55-90-70**), is the terminal for all buses serving the Bergen and Hardanger areas, as well as the airport bus. The station has luggage storage, shops, and a restaurant. City buses are marked with their destination and route number. For **bus information** in the Bergen area, call © **177.** A network of yellow-sided city buses serves the city center only. For information, call © **55-59-32-00.**

BY TAXI

Taxis are readily available at the airport. To request one, call © **55-99-70-00.** A ride from the Bergen Airport to the city center costs 262NOK ($35). Sightseeing by taxi costs about 390NOK ($52) for the first hour and 300NOK ($40) for each additional hour.

BY CAR

PARKING   Visitors can park on most streets in the city center after 5pm. For convenient indoor parking, try the **Bygarasjen Busstation** (© **55-56-88-70**), a large garage near the bus and train stations, about a 5-minute walk from the city center. It's open 24 hours a day and charges 15NOK ($2) per hour from 7am to 5pm, 11NOK ($1.45) per hour from 5pm to 7am. You can park for 24 hours for 75NOK ($10).

RENTAL CARS   You might want to rent a car to explore the area for a day or two. **Budget** (© **800/472-3325** in the U.S.) maintains offices at the airport (© 55-22-75-27) and downtown at Lodin Leppsgate 1 (© 55-90-26-15). Its least expensive car is 1,190NOK ($158) per day, which includes the 23% government tax, collision-damage waiver, and unlimited mileage. Rates per day are lower for rentals of a week or more.

Hertz (© **800/654-3001** in the U.S.) has locations at the airport (© 55-22-60-75) and downtown at Nygårdsgate 89 (© 55-96-40-70). For a 2-day rental, its smallest car, a Renault Clio, costs 1,290NOK ($172) per day, including tax, collision-damage waiver, and 300km worth of mileage.

Avis (© **800/331-2112** in the U.S.) has branches at the airport (© 55-22-76-18) and downtown at Lars Hillesgate 20 (© 55-32-01-30). For a 2-day rental, its smallest car, a Ford Fiesta, costs 2,800NOK ($372) per day with unlimited mileage. The price includes the 23% tax and the optional collision-damage waiver.

Of course, rates are subject to change. The lowest rates are almost always offered to those who reserve their cars from their home country before they leave.

Remember that Norway imposes severe penalties—including stiff fines and, in some cases, imprisonment—on anyone who drinks and drives.

BY FERRY

You can take a ferry across the harbor Monday through Friday from 7am to 4:15pm; they don't run on Saturday or Sunday. One-way fares are 12NOK ($1.60) for adults, 6NOK (80¢) for children. Ferries arrive and depart from either side of the harbor at Dreggekaien and MunkeBryggen. For information, call © **55-32-14-80.**

BY COASTAL STEAMER

Bergen is the cruise capital of Norway, home to a flotilla of well-engineered ships *(Hurtigruten)* that carry passengers, cars, and vast amounts of freight up and down the coast. At least 10 of the boats begin and end their itineraries in Bergen and make about 30 stops en route before landing 5 to 6 days later at Kirkenes, far north of the Arctic Circle, near the Russian border. You can book a berth on any of one of these ships for short- or long-haul transits, and do a quick bit of sightseeing while the ship docks in various ports.

Depending on the season and the category of berth you select, a full 11-day round-trip excursion from Bergen to Kirkenes and back costs $895 to $4,000 per person, double occupancy. It's best to book these cruises through the New York City office of the **Bergen Line** (© 800/323-7436 or 212/319-1300). The line owns some of the ships and acts as a sales agent for the others. If you're already in Norway, talk to any travel agent. You can make arrangements through Bergen-based **Cruise Spesialisten,** Veiten 2B, N-5020 Bergen (© 55-23-07-90). It has brochures and lots of information concerning the crop of newly built Norwegian coastal steamers. They include *Nord Norge* (launched in 1997); *Polarys* (1996); *Nordkapp* (1996); *Nordlys* (1994); *Richard With* (1993); *Kong Harald* (1993); and the older but stalwart *Narvik* (1982), *Midnatt Sol* (1982), and *Lofoten* (1964).

Other routes head south from Bergen to Stavanger and other ports, and tours go to some of the fjords to the south. For information and reservations, contact the Bergen Line, Cruise Spesialisten (see above), or a local operator. They include **Flaggruten** (© 55-23-87-00) and **H.S.D.** (© 55-23-87-90). The firms share offices at P.O. Box 2005, Nordnes, N-5024 Bergen. Faster than many hydrofoils, they go to the inner reaches of the world's longest fjord, the Sogne-fjord. They stop frequently en route to pick up cargo and passengers, and are worthy vehicles for sightseeing expeditions. Many of them dock at Bergen's inner harbor, near the Stradkaiterminalen.

FAST FACTS: Bergen

Area Code The country code for Norway is **47.** If you're calling from out-side the country, the city code for Bergen is **5.** Inside Norway, no area or city codes are needed. Phone numbers have 8 digits.

Banking Bergen has dozens of banks. The most visible is **Den Norske Bank,** Torg Almenning 2 (© 55-21-10-00). Branches of many of its competitors can be found near the Radisson SAS Hotel Norge, on Rådstuplass.

Bookstores One of the best, with a wide range of books in English, is **Melvaer Libris,** in the Galleriet, Torgalmenningen 8 (© 55-96-28-10). It's open Monday through Friday from 9am to 8pm, Saturday from 9am to 6pm.

Business Hours Most **banks** are open Monday through Friday from 8:15am to 3:30pm, and Thursday until 6pm. Most **businesses** are open Monday through Friday from 9am to 4pm. **Shops** are generally open Monday through Wednesday and Friday from 9am to 4:30pm, Thursday from 9am to 7pm (sometimes also on Fri until 7pm), Saturday from 9am to 2pm.

Currency Exchange There's a currency exchange at the Bergen Airport. In town, you can exchange money at several banks. When the banks are closed, you can exchange money at the tourist office (see "Visitor Information," above).

Dentists Emergency care only is available at **Bergen Legevakt,** Lars Hilles-gate 30 (© 55-32-11-20), 24 hours a day.

Doctors For medical assistance, call **Bergen Legevakt,** Lars Hillesgate 30 (© **55-32-11-20**), daily from 4 to 9pm. If it's not an emergency, your hotel can make an appointment with an English-speaking doctor.

Drugstores One convenient pharmacy is **Apoteket Nordstjernen,** at the Central Bus Station (© **55-31-68-84**). It's open Monday through Saturday from 8am to midnight, Sunday from 8am to 10pm.

Embassies & Consulates Most foreign nationals will have to contact their embassies in Oslo if they have a problem; only the **United Kingdom** maintains a consulate in Bergen, at Carl Konowsgate 34–35 (© **55-94-47-05**).

Emergencies For the **police,** dial © **112;** to report a **fire,** call © **110;** for an **ambulance,** dial © **113.**

Eyeglass Repair A good optician is **Optiker Svabø,** Strandgaten 18 (© **55-31-69-51**).

Hairdressers & Barbers One of the best in town is **Prikken Frisørsalong,** Strandkaien 2B (© **55-32-31-51**). It's open Monday through Friday from 9am to 5pm, Saturday from 9am to 6pm.

Hospitals A medical center, **Accident Clinic,** is open around the clock. It's at Lars Hillesgate 30 (© **55-32-11-20**). There is a general hospital, but you can't go directly there; you must go through the Accident Clinic or call **Syke-besøksformidling (Sick Call Help)** at © **55-32-40-60.**

Laundry Try **Jarlens Vaskoteque,** Lilleøvregate 17 (© **55-32-55-04**). It's near the Hotel Victoria in a little alley about 45m (150 ft.) northeast of the 17th-century Korskirken church, off Kong Oscars Gate. It's open Monday through Friday from 10am to 8pm, Saturday from 9am to 3pm.

Libraries The **Bergen Public Library,** Strømgaten (© **55-56-85-60**), is open in July and August on Tuesday, Wednesday, and Friday from 10am to 3pm, Monday and Thursday from 9am to 7pm, Saturday from 9am to 1pm; the rest of the year, Monday through Friday from 10am to 8pm, Saturday from 10am to 4:30pm.

Lost Property Various agencies recover lost objects. For assistance, contact the local police station or **Tourist Information** (© **55-32-14-80**).

Luggage Storage & Lockers Rental lockers and luggage storage are available at the **Jernbanestasjonen (railway station),** Strømgaten 1, which is open daily from 7am to 11:50pm. The cost is 20NOK ($2.20) per day.

Photographic Needs Go to **Foto Knutsen,** in the Galleriet, Torgalmenningen 8 (© **55-31-16-78**). It's open Monday through Friday from 8:30am to 8pm, Saturday from 9am to 6pm.

Police Call © **112.**

Post Office The main post office is on Småstrandgaten (© **55-54-15-00**), 1 block from Torget. It's open Monday through Friday from 8am to 6pm, Saturday from 9am to 3pm. If you want to receive your mail c/o General Delivery, the address is Poste Restante, N-5002 Bergen. You'll need your passport to pick it up.

Taxes Bergen adds no city taxes to the national value-added tax.

Telephone Public telephones take 1NOK (15¢) coins. Local calls cost 2NOK to 3NOK (25¢–40¢). To call abroad, dial © **00;** to call collect, dial © **115.**

3 Where to Stay

Easily found at Bryggen 7, the **Bergen Tourist Office** (see "Visitor Information," above) books guests into hotels and secures accommodations in private homes. More than 30 families take in guests during the summer. The booking service costs 15NOK to 30NOK ($2–$4), and prospective guests also pay a deposit that's deducted from the final bill. Double rooms in **private homes** usually cost 360NOK to 400NOK ($48–$53), with no service charge. Breakfast is not served.

The rates quoted for the hotels below include service and tax. Many expensive accommodations lower their rates considerably on weekends and in midsummer. We've mentioned it when these reductions are available, but the situation is fluid, and it's best to check on the spot. All our recommended accommodations come with private bathrooms unless otherwise indicated.

EXPENSIVE

Clarion Admiral Hotel ⚐ When it was built in 1906, this building was one of the largest warehouses in Bergen, with six sprawling floors peppered with massive trusses and beams. In 1987, it became a comfortable, tastefully appointed hotel, and in 1998, it was enlarged and renovated into the bustling establishment you'll see today. Rooms are a bit smaller than you might hope (with small bathrooms equipped with shower-tub combinations) but they are comfortable and have excellent beds. Many rooms lack water views, but the ones that open onto flower-bedecked balconies have the best harbor views in town.

Christian Sundts Gate 9, N-5004 Bergen. ⓒ **55-23-64-00.** Fax 55-23-64-64. www.admiral.no. 211 units. Mon–Thurs 1,695NOK ($225) double; 1,895NOK–4,000NOK ($252–$532) suite. Fri–Sun 950NOK ($126) double; 1,150NOK–2,550NOK ($153–$339) suite. AE, DC, MC, V. Bus: 2, 4, or 11. **Amenities:** 2 restaurants; bar; room service; laundry/dry cleaning. *In room:* TV, minibar, hair dryer, safe.

First Hotel Marin ⚐⚐ In the heart of Bergen, this first-class hotel is one of Bergen's most modern and streamlined. The brown brick building is set on a steep hillside. The bedrooms are moderate to spacious in size, and each is handsomely furnished in functional, stylish Nordic modern, with immaculately-kept tile bathrooms equipped with shower-tub combinations. For Bergen, the hotel offers a large number of suites—34 deluxe ones in all—the best of which are a trio of penthouse units with views so panoramic they encompass all seven mountains surrounding Bergen. Many accommodations are reserved for nonsmokers, and the finest units are in front, overlooking the harbor.

Rosenkrantzgaten 8, N-5003 Bergen. ⓒ **53-05-15-00.** Fax 53-05-15-01. 131 units. 1,450NOK–1,670NOK ($193–$222) double; 2,210NOK ($294) suite. AE, DC, MC, V. Bus: 1, 5, or 9. **Amenities:** Restaurant; bar; fitness center; sauna; room service; laundry/dry cleaning. *In room:* TV, minibar, hair dryer, safe.

Radisson SAS Hotel Norge ⚐⚐ In the city center, near Torgalmenningen, the Norge has been a Bergen tradition since 1885; it continues to be a favorite of visiting celebrities. The current building opened in 1962 and in 1997 the lobby was upgraded. Rooms are better than ever after a refurbishment, with double-glazed windows, bedside television controls, and ample bathrooms with showers and in some cases with bathtubs big enough for two. Ninth-floor units open onto private balconies overlooking the flower-ringed borders of a nearby park. Nonsmoking and wheelchair-accessible rooms are available.

The best service and the best cuisine, both Norwegian and international, are in the Grillen. The American Bar is a piano bar, and Bull's Eye is an English pub. The Night Spot, in the cellar, is a leading nightlife venue.

Nedre Ole Bulls Plass 4, N-5807 Bergen. © **800/333-3333** in the U.S., or 55-57-30-00. Fax 55-57-30-01. www.radissonsas.com. 345 units. 1,845NOK–1,945NOK ($245–$259) double; 2,500NOK–4,000NOK ($333–$532) suite. Rates include breakfast. Children under 18 stay free in parent's room. DC, MC, V. Parking 160NOK ($21); reserve with room. Bus: 2, 3, or 4. **Amenities:** 2 restaurants; bar; pool; fitness center; sauna; room service; babysitting; laundry/dry cleaning. *In room:* TV, minibar, hair dryer.

Radisson SAS Royal Hotel ℛ   Opened in 1982, this hotel was built on the fire-ravaged site of old warehouses that stood here since 1170. It's contemporary, with the finest services and amenities in Bergen. The guest rooms are beautifully maintained, with lithographs and comfortable, upholstered furniture. Newly renovated guest rooms are exceedingly comfortable. Although the bathrooms are small, they have shower-tub combinations and phones. Some rooms are reserved for nonsmokers; some are designed for guests with disabilities.

The hotel has a nightclub, Engelen, and a pub, Madame Felle, named after a lusty matron who ran a sailors' tavern on these premises during the 19th century. The pub's outdoor terrace (Madame Felle's Promenade) does a thriving business in the summer.

Bryggen, N-5835 Bergen. © **800/333-3333** in the U.S., or 55-54-30-00. Fax 55-32-48-08. www.radissonsas. com. 273 units. May–Sept 1,895 NOK ($210) double; Oct–Apr 1,795 NOK ($199) double. Year-round 2,200NOK–3,500NOK ($244–$389) suite. Rates include breakfast. AE, DC, MC, V. Parking 100NOK ($11). Bus: 1, 5, or 9. **Amenities:** 2 restaurants; 2 bars; pool; fitness center; sauna; room service; babysitting; laundry/dry cleaning. *In room:* TV, minibar, hair dryer, safe.

MODERATE

Augustin Hotel ℛ *(Finds*   The Augustin has one of the best locations in Bergen—right in the harbor's shopping district—with front rooms that have terrific harbor views. Constructed in 1909 in the Jugend or Art Nouveau style, Augustin has been in the same family for four generations. In 1995 it more than doubled in size by adding a new wing, with new modern rooms (equipped with all the modern trimmings) designed by award-winning Bergen architect Aud Hunskår. The old section retains more traditional rooms. Bathrooms in both sections have both showers and tubs. The hotel is decorated with lots of art, many pieces from well-known contemporary Norwegian artists. Special accommodations are available for nonsmokers, wheelchair users, and allergy sufferers.

One of the city's oldest taverns, the Altona (dating back to 1600), used to stand on the site of the hotel, and the tavern became known as the gathering spot for artists and musicians in west Norway. That nostalgic memory is evoked in the hotel's wine cellar, which is open to the public.

Carl Sundts Gate 24, N-5004 Bergen. © **55-30-40-40.** Fax 55-30-40-10. www.augustin.no. 109 units. Mon–Thurs 1,550NOK ($206) double; 1,890NOK ($251) suite. Fri–Sun 800NOK ($106) double; 1,290NOK ($172) suite. AE, DC, MC, V. Bus: 2 or 4. **Amenities:** Restaurant; bar; babysitting; laundry/dry cleaning. *In room:* A/C, TV, minibar, hair dryer.

Best Western Hotell Hordaheimen   This hotel near the harbor has long been a base for young people from nearby districts. It's operated by the Bonde-ungdomslaget i Bergen, an association that sponsors cultural and folkloric programs. School and civic groups sometimes reserve nearly all the rooms. The hotel was built at the beginning of the 20th century and renovated in stages between 1989 and 1995. Lars Kinsarvik, an internationally known designer, created the furniture in the late 19th century. Although Laura Ashley designs are widely featured in the hotel's literature, they are few in number. Some accommodations for nonsmokers are available, and some units are suitable for those with disabilities. The small, simple guest rooms are immaculate, with good beds and tiny bathrooms equipped with shower-tub combinations.

Christian Sundts Gate 18, N-5004 Bergen. ✆ **55-33-50-00.** Fax 55-23-49-50. 64 units. May 15–Sept 15 Mon–Thurs 1,450NOK ($193) double; Fri–Sun 850NOK ($113) double. Sept 16–May 14 Mon–Thurs 1,230NOK ($164) double; Fri–Sun 850NOK ($113) double. Year-round 1,430NOK–1,550NOK ($190–$206) suite. Rates include breakfast. AE, DC, MC, V. Bus: 1, 5, or 9. **Amenities:** Restaurant; lounge; laundry/dry cleaning. *In room:* TV, minibar, hair dryer.

Grand Hotel Terminus   A Bergen landmark since 1928, this hotel, located between the bus and railroad stations, offers quality and tradition. If explorer Roald Amundsen checked in today, as he once did, he would find the downstairs familiar. Once a Lutheran temperance hotel, it was most recently updated in 1994. The guest rooms have been modernized and furnished attractively in light Nordic pastels; all are equipped with average-size tiled bathrooms with shower-tub combinations.

Zander Kaaesgate 6, N-5001 Bergen. ✆ **55-31-16-55.** Fax 55-21-25-01. dhh@atm.no. 131 units. 1,460NOK ($194) double; 1,660NOK ($221) suite. Rates include breakfast. AE, DC, MC, V. Parking 100NOK ($13). Bus: 2 or 4. **Amenities:** Restaurant; bar; fitness center; sauna; laundry/dry cleaning. *In room:* TV, minibar, hair dryer.

Quality Edvard Grieg Hotel and Suites ✦ *Finds*   Opened in 1987, this modern, all-suite hotel—Norway's first—lies 19km (12 miles) south of Bergen and 5km (3 miles) from the airport. Luxuriously appointed suites are amply sized, with good beds in the rather small sleeping quarters, and a separate lounge. The bathrooms are excellent, with shower-tub combinations and lots of shelf space. Some accommodations for nonsmokers are available, as are units for persons with disabilities. Three suites are wheelchair accessible. Monday through Friday, guests can dine in the intimate and expensive Mozart Restaurant, or can enjoy Norwegian and international food in the H. C. Andersen Restaurant. The lobby bar is cozy, and patrons can also dance at the Amitra nightclub. Free airport transfers are arranged for arriving and departing guests Monday through Friday from 7am to 10pm.

Sandsliåsen 50, N-5049 Sandsli. ✆ **55-98-00-00.** Fax 55-98-01-50. 153 units. Mon–Fri 1,550NOK ($206) suite for 2; Sat–Sun 1,090NOK ($145) suite for 2. Rates include breakfast. AE, DC, MC, V. Free parking. Bus: 30 from the Bergen bus station. **Amenities:** Restaurant; bar; pool; fitness center; sauna; room service; laundry/dry cleaning. *In room:* TV, minibar, hair dryer.

Rosenkrantz   This 1921 hotel, near Bryggen in the city center, is a simple, unpretentious choice. The lobby leads to a comfortable dining room and bar. The rooms are pleasantly furnished; the small bathrooms come equipped with shower-tub combinations. Half the rooms are reserved for nonsmokers. Facilities include a TV lounge, a piano bar, a restaurant (Harmoni), and a nightclub (Rubinen) with live music.

Rosenkrantzgate 7, N-5003 Bergen. ✆ **55-30-30-14-00.** Fax 55-31-14-76. rosenkrantz@rainbow-hotels.no. 129 units. 1,520NOK ($202) double. Rates include breakfast. AE, DC, MC, V. Parking 70NOK ($9.30) in adjacent covered garage. Bus: 1, 5, or 9. **Amenities:** Restaurant; 2 bars; laundry/dry cleaning. *In room:* TV, minibar, hair dryer.

Victoria Hotel ✦ *Value*   Set behind a graceful, bay-fronted facade, this hotel—one of the oldest in town— was renovated in 1987, and today operates as one of only two members of the Best Western chain in Bergen. Smaller and more personalized than many equivalently priced hotels in Bergen, and noted for relatively reasonable rates, it's cozy, staffed with concerned employees, and loaded with worthwhile, sometimes rather valuable, art—a result of almost 50 years of collecting on the part of the well-traveled owners. Guest rooms are clean and bright, outfitted with contemporary birch-veneer furniture and lots of contemporary art. Bathrooms are tiled and modern, each with shower but without bathtub.

Kong Oscarsgt 29, N-5017 Bergen. © **800/528-1234** or 55-21-23-00. Fax 55-21-23-50. www.victoriahotel.no. 43 units. Mid-May to mid-Sept 1,490NOK ($198) double; mid-Sept to mid-May Mon–Thurs 1,030NOK ($137) double, Fri–Sun 1,490NOK ($198) double. Rates include breakfast. AE, DC, MC, V. Parking 130NOK ($17). Bus: 2 or 4. **Amenities:** Greek restaurant Sokrates (under separate ownership); bar; babysitting; laundry/dry cleaning. *In room:* A/C, TV, minibar, hair dryer.

INEXPENSIVE

Comfort Hotel Holberg Set near the Nykirk, a 15-minute walk from Bergen's Fish Market, this hotel (ca. 1995) commemorates the life of a late 18th-century writer and dramatist. Holberg—"The Molière of the North"—was one of the most famous writers in Danish and Norwegian letters. He was born in a since-demolished house on the site of this hotel's parking garage. In honor of that fact, the hotel's lobby looks like a testimonial to the author's life, with an informative biography, memorabilia, and photographs of stage productions based on his works. Guest rooms are based on a modernized and cozy-looking re-interpretation of the Norwegian "farmhouse" style, thanks to wooden floors, rough-textured half paneling stained in tones of forest green, and big windows—some of them floor-to-ceiling—that swing open directly onto a view of the quiet residential street below. Bathrooms are tiled, with acute angles that make them seem bigger than they actually are; half of them have shower-bath combinations.

Strandgaten 190, Postboks 1949 Nordnes, N-5817 Bergen. © **55-30-42-00**. Fax 55-23-18-20. www.choice hotels.no. 140 units. Mon–Thurs 790NOK–1,560NOK ($105–$207) double; Fri–Sun 890NOK ($118) double. Rates include breakfast. AE, DC, MC, V. Parking 90NOK ($12). **Amenities:** Restaurant; bar; babysitting; laundry/dry cleaning. *In room:* A/C, TV, minibar.

Hotel Ambassadeur *Value* This unpretentious, cost-conscious hotel was formed from the union in 2002 of two middle-bracket 1920s hotels, the Ambassadeur and the Anker, which for at least a century had been side-by-side competitors. The hotel is sheathed on the outside with a layer of sienna-colored stucco. More than any other hotel in town, it resembles the sometimes raucous drinking facilities of Bergen's biggest and most popular sports bar, the separately recommended Football Pub; as such, it's likely to get clients who are either soccer players in town for matches, or locals who have a passionate interest in the game. Each guest room comes with a bathroom with shower (separated from the rest of the bathroom with a plastic curtain pulled around a spot above a floor drain). We prefer rooms on the uppermost floor, because of their better views of Bergen and their sometimes inclined ceilings beneath the mansard-style roof. Access to these upper-floor rooms requires climbing an additional flight of stairs beyond the point where elevator access ends. Everything here is adequate and comfortable, but far from plush.

Vestre Torvgate 9, 5015 Bergen. © **55-90-08-90**. Fax 55-90-05-84. 83 units. Year-round Sun-Thurs and May 21-Aug 31 daily 980NOK ($130) double; Sept 1-May 20 Fri–Sat 860NOK ($115).Rates include breakfast. AE, DC, MC, V. Bus: 1 or 9. **Amenities:** 2 pubs (in lobby and on ground floor); babysitting; laundry/dry cleaning. *In room:* TV.

Hotel Dreggen *Kids* Reasonable prices and an accommodating staff make this a family favorite. Located in the heart of Bergen, this hotel is walking distance from the embarkation point for the fjords. Rather dull architecturally from the outside, it improves considerably once you enter the seven-story structure. Guest rooms are medium in size and have been recently renewed. About one-third of the rooms have private bathrooms with shower-tub combinations.

Sandbrugaten 3, N-5835 Bergen. © **55-31-61-55**. Fax 55-31-54-23. www.hotel-dreggen.no. 31 units, 9 with bathrooms. 690NOK ($92) double without bathroom; 790NOK ($105) double with bathroom. Rates include breakfast. AE, DC, MC, V. Bus: 2 or 5. **Amenities:** Bar; lounge; room service; laundry/dry cleaning. *In room:* TV.

Hotel Park (⚜ This converted 1890 town house is in an attractive university area near Grieghall and Nygård Park. The rooms are traditionally furnished, often with antiques. Accommodations vary in size but all have good beds and adequate bathrooms equipped with shower-tub combinations. In the summer, a neighboring building (furnished in the same style) accommodates overflow guests. A delicious Norwegian breakfast is served in the dining room; later in the day, sandwiches, small hot dishes, and wine and beer are available there. In the summer, reserve well in advance. The Park is a 10-minute walk from the train and bus stations.

Harald Hårfagresgaten 35 and Allegaten 20, N-5007 Bergen. ℰ **55-54-44-00.** Fax 55-54-44-44. www.park hotel.no. 33 units. 980NOK ($130) double. Rates include breakfast. AE, DC, MC, V. Parking 50NOK ($6.65). Bus: 11. **Amenities:** Lounge. *In room:* TV, hair dryer.

Steens Hotel (*Value* This is a stylish 1890 house that was successfully converted to receive guests. Owned and operated by the same family since 1950, Steens offers great accommodations at most-reasonable prices. The modern guest rooms are moderate in size and comfortable, and the bathrooms, though small, are beautifully maintained. The public rooms have plenty of atmosphere. The best rooms are in front and open onto a park. Within a short walk are the bus and railway stations, and shops and attractions in the center of town. All doubles have a private bathroom with a shower unit; a few singles are rented without bathroom for 620NOK ($82) per night. Throughout the day coffee and light meals are served.

22 Parkveien, N-5007 Bergen. ℰ/fax **55-31-40-50.** 20 units, 16 with bathroom. 600NOK–920NOK ($80–$122) double. Extra bed 150NOK ($20). Rates include Norwegian breakfast. AE, MC, V. Bus: 1 or 5. **Amenities:** Lounge. *In room:* TV.

4 Where to Dine

EXPENSIVE

Enhjørningen (the Unicorn) (⚜⚜ FISH/CONTINENTAL Part of the charm of this restaurant derives from the crooked floors, low doorways, and inconvenient access to the second-floor dining room via narrow staircases. Set within one of the very old wooden buildings of the Bryggen complex, adjacent to the harbor, it boasts a history and a name that was recorded as early as 1304, when "the Unicorn" was mentioned in a court trial as the home of a German-born Hanseatic merchant, Herman Skult. After several fires and the removal of lots of rotted timbers, the inn was restored to the condition it might have enjoyed during the 1700s.

You'll sit in one of several old-fashioned dining rooms set railway-style (end-to-end) and outfitted like an early-19th-century parlor with framed oil paintings (primarily landscapes). It's usually mobbed, and the staff struggles to maintain order and a sense of gentility amid swarms of diners, especially in midsummer. The lunchtime buffet focuses on salads and fish; evening meals are more substantial, with choices that include a local and good version of fish soup; savory fresh mussels steamed in white wine with cream, curry, and saffron; cognac-marinated salmon; herb-fried medallions of angler fish with a cream-based pepper sauce; steamed halibut served with shellfish sauce; and catfish with bacon and mushroom sauce. The star offering of the restaurant's limited supply of meat dishes is a "no fish Olsen," an amusing way to describe grilled filet of beef with a pepper-flavored cream sauce.

Bryggen. ✆ **55-32-79-19.** Reservations recommended. Main courses 240NOK–275NOK ($32–$37); set-price buffet (lunch only) 175NOK ($23). Set-price menus 395NOK–520NOK ($53–$69). AE, DC, MC, V. Lunch June–Sept daily noon–11pm. Closed 2 weeks at Christmas. Bus: 5 or 21.

Finnegaardstuene ✮✮ *Finds* NORWEGIAN/FRENCH The foundations of this popular restaurant were laid around 1400, when Hanseatic League merchants used it as a warehouse. Today, some of the woodwork dates from the 1700s, and four small-scale dining rooms create a cozy atmosphere. The chefs have created magic in sleepy Bergen. The menu is well thought out, with carefully prepared dishes. It revolves around Norwegian ingredients, especially fresh fish, and classical French methods of preparation. The menu changes with the season and the inspiration of the chef. It might include platters of crayfish served with filets of French foie gras in a cider and foie gras sauce; lime-marinated turbot with caviar sauce; gratin of monkfish with sea scallops; filets of venison with juniper berry sauce; and breast of duck with lime and fig sauce. An appropriate and satisfying dessert is berries from the Norwegian tundra, especially lingonberries and cloudberries.

Rosenkrantzgate 6. ✆ **55-55-03-00.** Reservations recommended. Main courses 285NOK–295NOK ($38–$39); fixed-price menu 635NOK ($84). AE, DC, MC, V. Mon–Sat 4:30–11pm. Closed 1 week at Easter, Dec 22–Jan 8. Bus: 5 or 21.

Fiskekroen ✮ FISH/GAME One of the smallest (36 seats) and most exclusive restaurants in Bergen, this dining room occupies rustically elegant premises in the historic Zacchariasbrygge harbor complex. There's a panoramic view of the harbor and a menagerie of stuffed animals. Menu specialties, which change with the seasons, might include a delectable combination of salmon, wolf fish, and anglerfish in lobster sauce; fried filet of reindeer with green-pepper gravy; halibut poached in white sauce; and several preparations of venison.

Zacchariasbrygge 50. ✆ **55-55-96-46.** Reservations required. Main courses 285NOK–325NOK ($38–$43). AE, DC, MC, V. May–Aug Mon–Sat noon–11pm, Sun 11am–10pm; Sept–Apr Mon–Sat 4–11pm. Bus: 1, 5, or 9.

Restaurant Potetkjeller ✮ *Finds* SEAFOOD Set within a few steps of Bergen's Fish Market, in an antique wood-fronted building, this is one of the oldest restaurants in Bergen. Its most ancient feature is an antique flagstone floor at the base of a cellar, and a vaulted ceiling dates from the mid-1400s. After most of the city's clapboard-sided houses burned to the ground in 1702, the stone cellar was used as a dump for the ashes and debris that remained behind. In 2000, new owners cleaned away the refuse, giving the cellar a new role as additional seating for the upstairs restaurant. Watch your footing on the floors here, as they're deceptively uneven. There's even reputed to be a coffin buried beneath the flagstones of the ground floor. If you ask a staff member, they'll either point out the location, or deny the allegation completely. ("It tends to put people off their food, knowing there's a burial site in here.") Menu items emerge from a kitchen that's open to view. They're likely to include gazpacho with a shellfish crostini; oven-roasted halibut with saffron and blue mussels; saltwater perch with lentils cooked in red wine; breast of guinea fowl with a foie gras sauce; and a dessert special of baked nectarines with syrup and semifreddo (gelato with whipped cream folded into it). If you opt for wine to accompany your meal, there will be a different wine for each course, each selected and approved by management and the evening's chef.

Kong Oscargate 1A. ✆ **55-32-00-70.** Reservations recommended. Set menus 405NOK–595NOK ($54–$79) without wine, 695NOK–1,150NOK ($92–$153) with wine. AE, DC, MC, V. Mon–Sat 4–10pm. Bar Mon–Sat till 1am. Bus: 1, 5, or 9.

To Kokker *ℱ* FRENCH/NORWEGIAN   To Kokker ("Two Cooks") is a favorite with celebrities, including Britain's Prince Andrew and a bevy of French starlets. Savvy local diners increasingly gravitate here for the chef's well-considered juxtaposition of flavors and textures. Menu items include such time-tested favorites as lobster soup; whitebait roe with chopped onions, sour cream, and fresh-baked bread; reindeer with lingonberry sauce; and filet of lamb with mustard sauce and pommes Provençal. The 1703 building is adjacent to the oldest piers and wharves in Bergen. The dining room, one floor above street level, has scarlet walls, old paintings, and a solid staff that works competently under pressure, albeit without a lot of flair.

Enhjørninggården. ℭ 55-32-28-16. Reservations required. Main courses 495NOK–695NOK ($66–$92). AE, DC, MC, V. Mon–Sat 5–10pm. Bus: 1, 5, or 9.

MODERATE

Holberg-Stuen NORWEGIAN   One floor above street level, this restaurant was established in 1927 midway between the harbor and Ole Bulls Plass. It was named in honor of the 18th-century writer Ludvig Holberg. He divided his time between Bergen and Copenhagen, and both cities ferociously claim him as part of their cultural heritage. The setting is much like a tavern, with beamed ceilings, an open log fire, and lots of exposed wood. The well-prepared dishes include fish filets in white-wine sauce with prawns, mushrooms, and asparagus; and a variety of meats, some of them grilled. This is a longtime favorite; you come here for old-fashioned flavors, not trendy experiments.

Torgalmenningen 6. ℭ **55-31-80-15**. Reservations recommended. Main courses 188NOK–200NOK ($25–$27). AE, DC, MC, V. Mon–Sat 11am–11pm; Sun 1–10pm. Bus: 1, 5, or 9.

Wessel-Stuen NORWEGIAN   This restaurant (named for the 18th-century humorist Johan Herman Wessel) has all the trappings of an 18th-century wine cellar. It's decorated in old tavern style with beamed ceilings, and its adjoining pub is a famous meeting place for locals. Meals are likely to include such dishes as grilled filet of catfish with coriander and lime, grilled tournedos with forest mushroom sauce, and breast of duck with honey-blackberry sauce. The daily steak special is one of the most popular dishes in town. The chefs can be experimental at times, but they are also soundly grounded in the classics.

Engen 14. ℭ **55-55-49-49**. Reservations recommended. Main courses 139NOK–290NOK ($18–$39); fixed-price menu 85NOK–120NOK ($11–$16). AE, DC, MC, V. Mon–Sat 3–11pm; Sun 11:30am–10pm. Bus: 2, 3, or 4.

INEXPENSIVE

Bryggeloftet and Stuene *ℱ* NORWEGIAN   The Bryggeloftet and Stuene is the best established restaurant along the harbor. At street level, the Stuene has low-beamed ceilings, carved banquettes, and 19th-century murals of old Bergen, along with dozens of clipper-ship models. For a more formal meal, head upstairs to the Bryggeloftet, with its high ceilings and wood paneling. Dinner in either section might include fried porbeagle (a form of whitefish) served with shrimp, mussels, and white-wine sauce; roast reindeer with cream sauce; or pepper steak with a salad. Several different preparations of salmon and herring are featured, along with roast pork with Norwegian sour cabbage. This is a quintessential Norwegian place—come here if you're seeking authentic flavors.

Bryggen 11. ℭ **55-31-06-30**. Reservations recommended. Main courses 159NOK–275NOK ($21–$37); lunch smørbrød 85NOK–149NOK ($11–$20). AE, DC, MC, V. Mon–Sat 11am–11:30pm; Sun 1–11:30pm. Bus: 1, 5, or 9.

5 Seeing the Sights

SUGGESTED ITINERARIES

If You Have 1 Day See the top attractions of Bergen, including the old Hanseatic Bryggen, with its nearby museums. Explore the shops and artisans' workshops along the harbor and, to end the day, take the funicular to Fløien for a panoramic view.

If You Have 2 Days On your first day, follow the suggestions for Day 1. On your second day, head for the Bergen area, which you can reach by public transportation. Visit Troldhaugen, Edvard Grieg's former home. In the afternoon, journey to Ole Bull's Villa, 26km (16 miles) south of Bergen.

If You Have 3 Days For your first 2 days, follow the suggestions above. On the third day, take the 12-hour "Norway in a Nutshell" tour (see "Side Trips from Bergen," below).

If You Have 4 or 5 Days On the first 3 days, follow the itinerary above. On Day 4, explore the Hardangerfjord and the Folgefonn Glacier by round-trip bus from Bergen (see "Side Trips from Bergen," below). On the fifth day, explore the Sognefjord by express steamer, going by bus through Voss and returning by train to Bergen (see "Side Trips from Bergen," below).

THE TOP ATTRACTIONS

In addition to the sights below, take a stroll around **Bryggen** ✦✦✦. This row of Hanseatic timbered houses, rebuilt along the waterfront after a disastrous fire in 1702, is what remains of medieval Bergen. The northern half burned to the ground in 1955. Bryggen has been incorporated into UNESCO's World Heritage List as one of the most significant cultural and historical re-creations of a medieval settlement, and it skillfully blends with the surroundings of modern Bergen. It's a center for arts and crafts, where painters, weavers, and craftspeople have their workshops. Some workshops are open to the public.

Bergen Aquarium ✦   A 15-minute walk from the city center, this aquarium is one of the largest and finest in Scandinavia. The exceptional marine life includes seals, penguins, lobsters, and piranhas. In the outer hall you can get the feel of the fish—dip your hand into the shallow pool of unpolluted water pumped up from a depth of 120m (400 ft.) in the fjord outside. Nine glass tanks, each containing about 62,500 gallons of water, ring the hall. Downstairs, a wide range of marine life in 42 small aquariums demonstrates many colorful forms of sea life and illustrates evolutionary development. A popular attraction is seal and penguin feeding time. In the summer, they eat daily at 11am, 2pm, and 6pm; in the winter, daily at noon and 4pm.

Nordnesbakken 4. ☎ **55-55-71-71.** Admission 80NOK ($11) adults, 50NOK ($6.65) children. May–Sept daily 9am–8pm; Oct–Apr daily 10am–6pm. Bus: 11 from the fish market.

Bergen Art Museum   In the center of the city, this museum displays works by Norwegian and international artists. It has three galleries: the Bergen Billedgalleri, the Stenersen Collection, and the Rasmus Meyers Collection. Picasso, Braque, Miró, and Kandinsky are represented here, and the Stenersen Collection has one of Europe's finest assemblages of the works of Paul Klee. In the Rasmus Meyers Collection, you can see some of Edvard Munch's most important works. In the Bergen Billedgalleri are excellent examples of paintings from some of Norway's leading "old masters," including Munch, I. C. Dahl, Lars Hertervig, Christian Krohg, and Harriet Backer.

Rasmus Meyers Allé 3–7 and Lars Hillesgate 10. ⓒ **55-56-80-00.** Admission 35NOK–50NOK ($4.65–$6.65) adults, free for children. May 15–Sept 15 daily 11am–5pm; Sept 16–May 14 Tues–Sun 11am–5pm. Bus: 1, 5, or 9.

Bryggens Museum   This museum illustrates the daily and cultural life of Bergen in the Middle Ages, and displays artifacts unearthed during extensive archaeological excavations of Bryggen from 1955 to 1972. Exhibits include remains of the oldest buildings in Bergen (from the 12th c.) in their original settings. You can also see runic inscriptions and changing exhibits.

Bryggen. ⓒ **55-58-80-10.** Admission 30NOK ($4) adults, free for children. May–Aug daily 10am–5pm; Sept–Apr Mon–Fri 11am–3pm, Sat noon–3pm, Sun noon–4pm. Bus: 20, 21, 22, 23, 50, 70, 71, 80, or 90.

Det Hanseatiske Museum ⓡ   In one of the best-preserved wooden buildings at Bryggen, this museum illustrates Bergen's commercial life on the wharf centuries ago. German merchants, representatives of the Hanseatic League centered in Lübeck, lived in these medieval houses built in long rows up from the harbor. With dried cod, grain, and salt as articles of exchange, fishers from northern Norway met German merchants during the busy summer season. The museum is furnished with authentic articles dating from 1704.

Finnegårdsgaten 1A, Bryggen. ⓒ **55-31-41-89.** May–Sept admission 40NOK ($5.30) adults; Oct–Apr admission 25NOK ($3.35) adults; free for children. June–Aug daily 9am–5pm; Sept–May daily 11am–2pm. Bus: 1, 5, or 9.

Fløibanen   A short walk from the fish market is the station where the funicular heads up to Fløien, the most famous of Bergen's seven hills. The view of the city, the neighboring hills, and the harbor from 315m (1,050 ft.) is worth every øre.

Vetrlidsalm 23A. ⓒ **55-33-68-00.** Round-trip 60NOK ($8) adults, 25NOK ($3.35) children. May 25–Aug Mon–Fri 7:30am–midnight, Sat 8am–midnight, Sun 9am–midnight; Sept–May 24 Mon–Thurs 8am–11pm, Fri–Sat 8am–11:30pm, Sun 9am–11pm. Bus: 6.

Gamle Bergen ⓡ   This collection of houses from the 18th and 19th centuries is set in a park. The Old Town is complete with streets, an open square, and narrow alleyways. Some of the interiors are exceptional, including a merchant's living room in the typical style of the 1870s, with padded sofas, heavy curtains, and potted plants. It might call to mind Ibsen's *A Doll's House.*

Elsesro and Sandviken. ⓒ **55-39-43-00.** Admission 50NOK ($6.65) adults, 25NOK ($3.35) children and students. Houses, mid-May to Aug only, guided tours daily on the hour 10am–5pm. Park and restaurant, daily noon–6pm. Bus: 1 or 9 from the city center (every 10 min.).

Gamlehaugen   The king's official Bergen residence was originally occupied in the 19th century by Christian Michelsen, one of the first prime ministers of Norway after it separated from Denmark in 1814. It's open for just a short time each summer. The rambling wood-sided villa lies about 9.5km (6 miles) south

---

Impressions

Reaching Bergen we fail to find it particularly attractive. Everything is fishy. You eat fish and drink fish and smell fish and breathe fish.
                                        —Lilian Leland, *Traveling Alone: A Woman's Journey Round the World,* 1890

Bergen Attractions

Bergen Aquarium **13**
Bergen Art Museum **10**
Bryggen **6**
Bryggens Museum **5**
Den National Scene **12**
Det Hanseatiske Museum **7**
Fløibanen **8**
Gamle Bergen **1**
Grieghallen **9**
Håkonshallen **2**
Mariakirke **4**
Rosenkrantz Tower **3**
West Norway Museum
of Applied Art **11**

of the city, overlooking the Nordåsvannet estuary. Its gardens are open to the public all year. Don't expect the hoopla you might see at Buckingham Palace— the venue is understated, discreet, and (probably for security reasons) aggressively mysterious.

Fjøsanger. (C) **55-92-51-20.** Admission 10NOK ($1.35) adults, 5NOK (65¢) children. June–Sept 1 Mon–Fri 10am–1pm. Closed Sept 2–May. Bus: Fjøsanger-bound bus from the Central Bus Station.

Håkonshallen (Håkon's Hall)   If you walk along the water from Bryggen, you come upon the Håkonshallen, built between 1247 and 1261. It was damaged in a 1944 fire caused by the explosion of an overloaded Nazi munitions ship, and later restored. The explosion damaged nearly every building in Bergen, and sent the ship's anchor flying almost to the top of a nearby mountain. Håkonshallen is the largest and most imposing building remaining on the site of the royal residence of Bergen, which was the political center of the 13th-century kingdom of Norway. Guided tours are conducted hourly.

Bergenhus, Bradbenken. (C) **55-31-60-67.** Admission 20NOK ($2.65) adults, 10NOK ($1.35) children. Mid-May to Aug daily 10am–4pm; Sept to mid-May daily noon–3pm, Thurs until 6pm. Closed various days in May.

Mariakirke (St. Mary's Church)   The oldest building in Bergen (the exact date is unknown, but it could have been built in the mid–12th c.) is this Romanesque church, one of the most beautiful in Norway. Its altar is the oldest ornament in the church. The baroque pulpit, donated by Hanseatic merchants, bears carved figures depicting everything from Chastity to Naked Truth. Church music concerts are given May through August several nights a week.

Dreggen. (C) **55-31-59-60.** Admission 10NOK ($1.35) adults, free for children; free to all Sept 10–May 17. May 18–Sept 9 Mon–Fri 11am–4pm; Sept 10–May 17 Tues–Fri noon–1:30pm. Bus: 5, 9, 20, 21, or 22.

Rosenkrantz Tower   This defensive and residential tower was constructed in the 13th century by the governor of Bergenhus (Bergen Castle), Erik Rosenkrantz. Two older structures were incorporated into the tower: King Magnus the Lawmender's keep, from about 1260, and Jørgen Hanssøn's keep, from about 1520. It was rebuilt and enlarged in the 1560s. There are guided tours of the tower and Håkonshallen (see above) about every hour.

Bergenhus, Bradbenken. (C) **55-31-43-80.** Admission 20NOK ($2.65) adults, 10NOK ($1.35) children. May 15–Aug 31 daily 10am–4pm; Sept 1–May 14 Sun noon–3pm. Bus: 1, 5, or 9.

Troldhaugen (Trolls' Hill) ⊛   This Victorian house, in beautiful rural surroundings, was the summer villa of composer Edvard Grieg. The house still contains his furniture, paintings, and other mementos. His Steinway grand piano is frequently used at concerts given in the house during the annual Bergen festival, and at Troldhaugen's summer concerts. Grieg and his wife, Nina, are buried in a cliff grotto on the estate. He composed many of his famous works at his cottage by the sea.

Troldhaugveien 65, Hop. (C) **55-91-17-91.** Admission 50NOK ($6.65) adults, free for children. Jan–Apr 20 Mon–Fri 10am–2pm; Apr 21–Sept daily 9am–6pm; Oct–Nov Mon–Fri 10am–2pm, Sat–Sun 10am–4pm. Closed Dec. Bus: To Hop from the Bergen bus station (Platforms 18–20); exit, turn right, walk about 180m (600 ft.), turn left at Hopsvegen, and follow signs (15-min. walk). Hop is about 5km (3 miles) from Bergen.

Vestlandske Kunstindustrimuseum (West Norway Museum of Applied Art) *Finds*   In the center of Bergen, this unique (for Norway) museum has one of the largest collections of Chinese applied art outside China. Its main attraction is a series of huge marble Buddhist temple sculptures created over a range of centuries. The collection also includes applied art from 1500 to the present

OUTDOOR ACTIVITIES 271

day, with special attention paid to the Bergen silversmiths of the 17th and 18th
centuries, who were celebrated for their heavy but elaborate baroque designs.
Their collection of tankards, for example, is stunning. Most of them are
embossed with floral motifs and others are inlaid with silver coins.

Permanenten, Nordahl Bruns Gt. 9. (C) **55-33-66-33**. Admission 40NOK ($5.30). May 15–Sept 14 Tues–Sun
11am–4pm; Sept 15–May 14 Tues–Sun noon–4pm. Bus 1, 5, or 9.

IN NEARBY LYSØEN

To reach the island of Lysøen, 26km (16 miles) south of Bergen, drive or take a
bus (from Platform 20 at the Bergen bus station, marked FANA-OS-MILDE) to
Sørestraumen on Road 553. Take the Ole Bull ferry across the channel from
Sørestraumen, Buena Kai. The round-trip fare is 40NOK ($5.30) for adults,
20NOK ($2.65) for children. When the museum and villa are open, ferry
schedules coincide with the site's hours, and boats depart for the mainland at
hourly intervals. The last boat leaves a few minutes after the museum closes.

Museet Lysøen/Ole Bull's Villa   This villa and concert hall were built in
1872 and 1873 for the world-famous violin virtuoso and Norwegian national
hero, Ole Bull. The building, now a national monument, is preserved as it was
when the musician died in 1880. Thirteen kilometers (8 miles) of trails built by
Bull meander around the island.

Lysøen. (C) **56-30-90-77**. Admission 25NOK ($3.35) adults, 10NOK ($1.35) children. Guided tours, early
May–Sept Mon–Sat noon–4pm, Sun 11am–5pm. Closed Oct to early May. Transportation: See "Organized
Tours," below.

ORGANIZED TOURS

For information about and tickets to tours, contact **Tourist Information,**
Bryggen 7 ((C) **55-32-14-80**).

The most popular and most highly recommended tour of Bergen is the 3-
hour city bus tour. It departs daily at 10am and covers the major attractions,
including Troldhaugen and "Old Bergen." It operates from May to September
and costs 250NOK ($33) for adults, 160NOK ($21) for children.

6 Outdoor Activities

FISHING   In the region around Bergen, anyone can fish in the sea without
restrictions. If you plan to fish in fresh water (ponds, streams, and most of the
best salmon and trout rivers), you'll need a permit. These are sold at any post
office. You'll also need the permission of the owner of the land on either side of
the stream. Information and fishing permits, which cost 95NOK to 150NOK
($13–$20), are available from **Bergen Sportsfiskere (Bergen Angling Association),** Fosswinckelsgate 37 ((C) **55-32-11-64**). It's open Monday through Friday
from 9am to 2pm.

GOLFING   The **Åstvelt Golf Course** ((C) **55-18-20-77**) has nine holes and is
open to nonmembers; call in advance. It's a 15-minute drive north of Bergen on
E16. You can also take the Åsane bus from the central station in Bergen. Greens
fees range from 200NOK to 250NOK ($27–$33).

SWIMMING   The **Sentralbadet,** Theatersgaten 37 ((C) **55-56-95-70**) has a
heated saltwater indoor pool. An open-air pool whose season is limited to the fleet-
ing Nordic summer is at **Nordnes Sjøbad,** Nordnes. For hours, check with the
tourist office. At either pool, adults pay 20NOK ($2.65), children 15NOK ($2).

TENNIS   Paradis Sports Senter, Highway R1, Paradis (✆ **55-91-26-00**), lies 6.5km (4 miles) south of Bergen. The club has five indoor courts, four squash courts, four badminton courts, a health club and gym, and a solarium. It's open Monday through Friday from 9am to 10pm, Saturday from 10am to 6pm, Sunday from noon to 6pm.

WALKING   Only 10 minutes away from town by the funicular, several roads and footpaths lead to **Mount Fløien,** an unspoiled wood and mountain plateau with lakes and rivers.

The **Bergen Touring Club,** Tverrgaten 4–6 (✆ **55-32-22-30**), arranges walking tours farther afield and supplies information on huts and mountain routes all over Norway. It also provides maps and advice on where to hike. The office is open Monday through Friday from 10am to 4pm (until 6pm on Thurs).

7 Shopping

Shoppers who live outside Scandinavia and spend more than 300 NOK ($33) in a tax-free tourist shop can receive a refund of 10% to 15% of the purchase price when they leave Norway. See "Taxes" in "Fast Facts: Norway," in chapter 7, "Planning Your Trip to Norway."

THE SHOPPING SCENE
Bargain hunters head to the **Marketplace (Torget).** Many local handicrafts from the western fjord district, including rugs and handmade tablecloths, are displayed. This is one of the few places in Norway where bargaining is welcomed. The market keeps no set hours, but is best visited between 8am and noon. Take bus no. 1, 5, or 9.

HOURS   Stores are generally open Monday through Friday from 9am to 6pm (until 8pm Thurs and sometimes Fri), Saturday from 9am to 4pm. Shopping centers outside the city are open Monday through Friday from 10am to 8pm, Saturday from 9am to 6pm. Some food stores stay open until 8pm Monday through Friday and 6pm on Saturday.

SHOPPING A TO Z
DEPARTMENT STORE
Sundt & Co.   Many Bergeners remember this leading department store from childhood shopping expeditions with their parents. The store now faces stiff competition from such newer emporiums as Galleriet (see "Shopping Mall," below). Torgalmenningen. ✆ **55-32-31-00.**

FASHION
Berle Bryggen   Set directly on the quays, near the innermost edge of Bergen's historic harbor, this is a large, well-stocked gift and clothing store with an upscale and well-chosen collection of men's and women's sweaters, pewter, troll dolls, and gift items. It's also a repository for the diverse articles of clothing that, when worn collectively, are referred to by the Norwegians as Bunad or Norwegian national costume. Bryggen 5. ✆ **55-31-73-00.**

Kløverhuset   Next to the fish market on the harbor, this four-story shopping center has been Bergen's largest fashion store since 1923. Besides the latest in modern design, it also offers bargains such as moderately priced and attractively designed knit sweaters, gloves, and Lapp jackets. The special gift shop is open only in the summer. Strandgaten 13–15. ✆ **55-31-37-90.**

Shopping Tour

Norway has a centuries-old tradition of crafts, which undoubtedly developed to help people pass the time during the cold, dark winters when farm families were more or less housebound for many months. Some of the major crafts were woodcarving, weaving, and embroidery, and these skills live on today at many local arts and crafts centers. Some of the best areas include Hardanger (around the Hardangerfjord, near Bergen); Song (just north of the Sognefjord, also near Bergen); and Telemark (the district around Skien, within a day's drive from Oslo). For a true, behind-the scenes look at Norway, **Five Stars of Scandinavia,** 13104 Thomas Rd., KPN, Gig Harbor, WA 98329 (✆ **800/722-4126**), will set up a self-drive, self-guided tour, factoring in everything they know about local artisans who you can then visit on your own wheels.

Viking Design   Opposite the Flower Market, this shop has the most unusual knitwear in Bergen—many of its designs have even won prizes. In addition to fashion, there is also a selection of quality pewter produced in Bergen, along with a selection of intriguing Norwegian gifts and souvenirs. Items purchased can be shipped abroad. Strandkaien 2A. ✆ **55-31-05-20.**

HANDICRAFTS

In and around **Bryggen Brukskunst,** the restored Old Town near the wharf, many craftspeople have taken over old houses and ply ancient Norwegian trades. Crafts boutiques often display Bergen souvenirs, many based on designs 300 to 1,500 years old. For example, we purchased a reproduction of a Romanesque-style cruciform pilgrim's badge. Other attractive items are likely to include sheepskin-lined booties and exquisitely styled hand-woven wool dresses.

Prydkunst-Hjertholm   The leading outlet for glassware and ceramics purchases much of its merchandise directly from the artisans' studios. The quality goods include glass, ceramics, pewter, wood, and textiles. Gift articles and souvenirs are also available. Olav Kyrres Gate 7. ✆ **55-31-70-27.**

JEWELRY

Juhls' Silver Gallery   Next to the SAS Royal Hotel, along the harbor, Juhls' displays the town's most unusual selection of quality jewelry. The designers take for their inspiration the constantly changing weather of the far north and, in their words, provide "a cultural oasis in a desert of snow." Bryggen. ✆ **55-32-47-40.**

SHOPPING MALL

Galleriet   This is the most important shopping complex in the Bergen area, with 70 stores offering tax-free shopping. Close to the fish market, it displays a wide array of merchandise and features summer sales and special exhibitions. It has several fast-food establishments, too. Torgalmenningen 8. ✆ **55-30-05-00.**

8 Bergen After Dark

THE PERFORMING ARTS

Grieghallen   The modern Grieg Hall, which opened in 1978, is Bergen's monumental showcase for music, drama, and a host of other cultural events. The stage is large enough for an entire grand opera production, and the main foyer comfortably seats 1,500 guests for lunch or dinner. Snack bars provide drinks and light snacks throughout the performances. The upper floors house the offices of the Philharmonic Orchestra.

The Bergen Symphony Orchestra, founded in 1765, performs here from August to May, often on Thursday at 7:30pm and Saturday at 12:30pm (closed in July). Its repertoire consists of classical and contemporary music, as well as visiting opera productions. International conductors and soloists perform. Lars Hillesgate 3A. ℭ 55-21-61-50. Tickets 100NOK–350NOK ($13–$47). Bus: 2, 3, or 4.

Den National Scene   September through June is the season for Norway's oldest theater, founded in the mid–19th century. It stages classical Norwegian and international drama, contemporary plays, and musical drama, as well as visiting productions of opera and ballet. Engen 1. ℭ 55-54-97-10. Tickets 180NOK–280NOK ($24–$37). Bus: 2, 3, or 4.

SUMMER CULTURAL ENTERTAINMENT

Bergen Folklore   The Bergen Folklore dancing troupe performs from June to August on Tuesday and Thursday at 9pm. The program, which lasts about an hour, consists of traditional folk dances and music from rural Norway. Tickets are on sale at the Bergen Tourist Office (see "Visitor Information," above) and at the door. Bryggens Museum, Bryggen. ℭ 97-52-86-30. Tickets 100NOK ($13) adults, free for children. Bus: 1, 5, or 9.

FILMS

Bergen has two large movie theaters, **Konsertpaleet,** Neumannsgate 3 (ℭ 55-56-90-83), and **Forum,** in Danmarkplass (ℭ 55-20-62-48), that show films in their original versions. The earliest performance is at 11am, the latest at 11pm. Tickets usually cost 85NOK ($11).

THE CLUB & MUSIC SCENE

Engelen   This is one of Bergen's more elegant dance clubs. Wednesday through Friday night, an older, sedate crowd gathers to enjoy the music and ambience. On Saturday, beware—the atmosphere changes drastically with the arrival of noisy, fun-seeking 20-somethings. Light meals are available. Drink prices begin at 74NOK ($9.85), 55NOK ($7.30) for a beer. It's open Wednesday through Saturday from 9pm to 3am. In the Radisson SAS Royal Hotel, Bryggen. ℭ 55-54-30-00. Cover 60NOK–80NOK ($8–$11), free to hotel guests. Bus: 1, 5, or 9.

Maxime   One of Bergen's most reliable drinking venues caters to unattached men and women. In a prominent location near the Hotel Norge, it boasts three bar areas. Sandwiches and platters of food are served every day from noon to around 9:30pm, making it a well-known lunchtime spot. The bars are open Monday through Saturday from 7pm to 1am, Sunday from 3pm to 1am. Less popular, but a viable alternative on Saturday night, is the cellar-level dance club. It's open Thursday through Saturday from 11pm to 2:30am. Regardless of where you drink it, a large beer costs 50NOK ($6.65). Ole Bulls Plass. ℭ 55-30-71-35. Cover 55NOK ($7.30) for the dance club. Bus: 2, 3, or 4.

Rick's Café   This is something of a labyrinth, with rooms devoted to the after-dark pursuit of cabaret and comedy (there's a small stage for small-scale acts); some serious drinking (on cold winter nights, things can get rather sudsy); or a friendly pick-up (no doubt encouraged by the bar's potent cocktails). It's open Wednesday through Saturday from 5pm till around 2am, depending on business. Veiten 3. ℭ 55-55-31-31. No cover. Bus: 1, 5, or 9. No one under 24 permitted.

Rubinen Rubinen is one of Bergen's most popular nightclubs, attracting an over-35 crowd of mostly married couples. It plays all kinds of music, including country-western and rock. Drinks cost about 75NOK ($10). It's open Wednesday through Saturday from 10pm to 3am, with live music nightly. Rosenkrantzgate 7. ☎ 55-31-74-70. Cover 80NOK ($11). Bus: 2, 3, or 4.

THE BAR SCENE

The English Pub This is one of the most authentic imitations of a merrie Olde English pub in Norway, with battered paneling, a pool table, much-used dartboards, foaming mugs of beer, and a clientele composed of equal parts local office workers and nearby residents. It's open Monday through Thursday from 7pm to 1am, Friday through Sunday from 3pm till 2am. Ole Bulls Plass. ☎ 55-30-71-39. Bus: 2, 3, or 4.

Football Pub This is the biggest sports pub in Bergen, a rocking and rolling beer-soaked place whose theme revolves around an undeniable affection for football (soccer) and, to a lesser degree, rugby. Feel free to wander through this crowded establishment's labyrinth of inner chambers, whose corners and edges are sometimes upholstered with vinyl padding (installed out of a fear of falls by inebriated sports fans?). Giant TV screens show live and pre-recorded sports events—especially any intensely contested matches. The staff here prides itself on serving the cheapest beer in Bergen, priced at from 32NOK to 39NOK ($4.25–$5.20) per mug, depending on the time of day. It's open Monday through Thursday from 9am to 1am, Friday and Saturday from 9am to 2am, Sunday from noon to 1am. Vestre Torggate 9. ☎ 55-36-66-61. Bus: 1 or 9.

Kontoret Pub The most-frequented pub in the city center, the Kontoret is next to the Dickens restaurant and pub. Drinkers can wander freely between the two places, which are connected. In the Kontoret Pub you can order the same food served at Dickens, although most people seem to come here to drink. The local brew is called Hansa; a half-liter of draft beer is 53NOK ($7.05). It's open Sunday through Thursday from 4pm to 1am, Friday and Saturday from noon to 3am. In the Hotel Norge, Ole Bulls Plass 8–10. ☎ 55-36-31-33. Bus: 2, 3, or 4.

Zacchariasbrygge Pub On the harbor of Old Bergen, in the same oxblood-colored former warehouse as the restaurant Fiskekroen (see "Where to Dine," above), this is one of Bergen's most popular, and sometimes noisiest, pubs. Piano music and a live singer accompany copious quantities of flowing suds. A half-pint of lager goes for 72NOK ($9.60), and French and Italian wines by the glass cost about the same. There's additional, quieter seating upstairs. Open Monday through Friday from 11am to 12:30am, Saturday from noon to 12:30am, Sunday from 1 to 10pm. Zacchariasbrygge 50. ☎ 55-55-96-40. Bus: 2, 3, or 4.

A GAY CAFE

Café Fincken This cafe and bar serves refreshments, wine, and beer. It's open Monday through Saturday from noon to 2am, Sunday from 3pm to 2am. The clientele is mostly gay and lesbian. There's a new art exhibition every month. Nygårdsgaten 2A. ☎ 55-32-13-16. Bus: 2, 3, or 4.

9 Side Trips from Bergen

Norway's longest and deepest fjord, the **Sognefjord** ✷✷✷, is a geologic and panoramic marvel. The terrain soars upward from the watery depths of the North Atlantic, and many waterfalls punctuate its edges with spray. The best way to view it involves a full-day jaunt that's possible only between May 18 and

September 15. It combines self-guided travel by boat, bus, and rail. Begin by heading to the Bergen harbor (the Strandkaien), where you'll board a ferry for the 4½-hour ride to the fjord-side hamlet of Gudvangen. A bus carries participants on to the town of Voss (see chapter 10, "Exploring the Norwegian Coast"). In Voss, after exploring the town, you can board a train to carry you back to Bergen. Many schedule permutations are possible, but one that's particularly convenient involves leaving Bergen at 8:30am and returning at 5:15pm. The combined round-trip fare is 630NOK ($84). Details on this and on several other explorations by public transport are available from the Bergen Tourist Office (see "Visitor Information," above).

NORWAY IN A NUTSHELL   This 12-hour tour ✶✶✶ has been cited as the most scenically captivating 1-day tour of Norway. Its breadth and diversity of landscapes encapsulates the majesty of the country's fjords and mountains.

Several different transit options operate throughout the day. The one most aggressively recommended by Bergen's Tourist Office runs from June to August only. It starts at 8:30am at Bergen's railway station. After a 2-hour train ride, you disembark in the mountaintop hamlet of **Myrdal,** where you sightsee for about 20 minutes. In Myrdal, you board a cog railway for one of the world's most dramatically inclined train rides. The trip down to the village of **Flåm,** a drop of 870m (2,900 ft.), takes an hour and passes roaring streams and seemingly endless waterfalls.

After a 1-hour stopover in Flåm, where you can have lunch or take a brief hike, you board a fjord steamer for a ride along the Sognefjord. You reach the fjord-side town of Gudvangen after a 2-hour ride. After 30 minutes in Gudvangen, you board a bus for the 75-minute ride to Voss. There you spend 30 minutes before boarding a train for the 75-minute ride back to Bergen. Arrival is scheduled for 8:18pm.

Expect only a rushed overview of each town, for there is more scenery than you can digest in a 12-hour day. The round-trip fare, excluding meals, is 630NOK ($84) for adults, 315NOK ($42) for children under 12. There are discounts for holders of Eurail or Scanrail passes. For more information, contact Bergen's **Tourist Office** (© **55-32-14-80**).

Exploring the Norwegian Coast

The west coast of Norway is the heart of the fjord country (see map, p. 173). Fjords are narrow arms of the sea that snake inland. It took 3 million years to form the furrows and fissures that give the Norwegian coast its distinctive look. At some points the fjords become so narrow that a boat can hardly wedge between the mountainsides.

Bergen is the best departure point for trips to the fjords. To the south lies the famous Hardangerfjord, and to the north, the Sognefjord, cutting 179km (111 miles) inland. We'll begin our journey in Bergen, heading north by coastal steamer.

1 By Coastal Steamer

Coastal steamers 𝒜𝒜 are elegantly appointed ships that travel along the Norwegian coast from Bergen to Kirkenes, carrying passengers and cargo to 34 ports. A total of 11 ships make the journey year-round. Along the route, the ships sail through Norway's more obscure fjords, revealing breathtaking scenery and numerous opportunities for adventure. At points along the way, passengers have the opportunity to take sightseeing trips to the surrounding mountains and glaciers, and excursions on smaller vessels.

The chief cruise operator is the **Norwegian Coastal Voyage/Bergen Line,** 405 Park Ave., New York, NY 10022 (℃ **800/323-7436** or 212/319-1300). Various packages are available. Tours may be booked heading north from Bergen, south from Kirkenes, or round-trip. The 7-day one-way northbound journey costs $551 to $4,113 per person, including meals and taxes. The 12-day round-trip voyage from Bergen to Kirkenes and back to Bergen is $818 to $6,134 per person. For information on these and other trips, including air-cruise packages from the United States, contact the Bergen Line.

We'll focus on two of the most popular and interesting ports of call along the coastal steamer route.

HAMMERFEST
2,315km (1,438 miles) N of Bergen, 145km (90 miles) N of Alta, 2,196km (1,364 miles) N of Oslo

The Hammerfest area stretches from Måsøy, near the North Cape, to Loppa in the south. The wide region includes the rugged coasts along the Arctic Sea. The regional capital, Hammerfest, often serves as a base for exploring the North Cape.

Hammerfest is a major traffic hub, and in the summer there's a wide choice of boat and bus excursions. The tourist office can tell you what's available.

ESSENTIALS
GETTING THERE If you don't take the coastal steamer, you can drive, although it's a long trek. From Oslo, take E6 north until you reach the junction with Route 94 west. Hammerfest is at the end of Route 94. During the summer, there are three buses a week from Oslo. Travel time is 29 hours. SAS has daily

flights from Oslo and Bergen to Alta, where you can catch a bus to Hammerfest (Apr–Sept only). For bus information, call **Finnmark Fylkesrederi** (© 78-40-70-00).

VISITOR INFORMATION   The **Hammerfest Tourist Office,** Strandgate (© 78-41-21-85), in the town center, is open daily from 9am to 5pm.

SEEING THE SIGHTS

This is the world's northernmost town of significant size, and a port of call for North Cape coastal steamers. Destroyed during World War II by the retreating Nazis, it has long since been rebuilt. Lapps from nearby camps often come into town to shop. Count yourself lucky if they bring their reindeer.

The port is ice-free year-round, and shipping and exporting fish is a major industry. The sun doesn't set from May 12 to August 1—and doesn't rise from November 21 to January 23.

For a panoramic view over the town, take a zigzag walk up the 72m (240-ft.) **Salen** "mountain." Atop Salen is a 6m (20-ft.) tall square tower, with walls built of gray and blue stones. The old tower was torn down during the war, but restored in 1984.

Why not take time to do as 150,000 others have and join the **Royal and Ancient Polar Bear Society** (© 78-41-31-00) here? Apply in person while you're in Hammerfest. Membership costs 150NOK ($20) annually, and the money is used to protect endangered Arctic animals through conservation programs. The society's building is filled with stuffed specimens of Arctic animals. There's a small museum devoted to the hunting heyday of Hammerfest, which lasted from 1910 to 1950, when eagles, Arctic foxes, and polar bears were trapped by the English, and then by German officers during the war. It's in the basement of the Town Hall, on Rådhusplassen. The center is open only from June to August, Monday through Friday from 6am to 6pm.

Gjenreisningsmuseet, Söröygatan (© 78-42-26-40), opened adjacent to the Rica Hotel in 1998. This small museum commemorates the cold bleak years after World War II, when local residents, deprived of most of their buildings, livelihoods, and creature comforts, heroically rebuilt Finnmark and northern Norway in the wake of Nazi devastation. Entrance is 40NOK ($5.30) per person, and it's open from June to September, daily from 10am to 6pm; off season, daily from 11am to 2 pm.

WHERE TO STAY

Rica Hotel Hammerfest   This is the largest hotel in town and the preferred place to stay in the area. It's in the town center, opening directly onto the waterfront. Built in the mid-1970s on steeply sloping land, the hotel was completely redecorated in 1989 and has been regularly spruced up since then. The small, modern guest rooms are decorated with Nordic-inspired pastels, but the look is strictly functional. The plumbing has been upgraded, but bathrooms tend to be small. Each unit contains a shower-tub combination.

Sørøygata 15, N-9600 Hammerfest. © **78-41-13-33.** Fax 78-41-13-11. 80 units. 960NOK–1,325NOK ($128–$176) double; 1,385NOK ($184) suite. AE, DC, MC, V. Bus: 1 or 2. **Amenities:** Restaurant; bar; fitness center; sauna; babysitting; laundry/dry cleaning. *In room:* TV, minibar, hair dryer.

WHERE TO DINE

Odd's Mat og Vinhus 𝕬𝕬 NORTHERN NORWEGIAN   Since it opened in 1992, this rustic restaurant has become famous, thanks to a survey by a Trondheim radio station that voted it the best restaurant in Norway. It's adjacent to the town's largest pier, overlooking the harbor. Inside, every effort has been made to simulate the wild splendor of Finnmark (northern Norway), with the use of roughly textured wood, stone, and many yards of natural hemp knotted into ropes that form curtains. A kitchen opens to the dining room.

The recipes and ingredients are almost completely derived from northern Norway, with an emphasis on fish and game. You might try filet of carp, partially sun-dried, then boiled and served with mustard sauce and bacon fat; or freshly killed grouse prepared "like beef," with a game-laced cream sauce. To start, filet of reindeer is served, raw and chopped, like a tartare, or smoked and thinly sliced, like a carpaccio.

Strandgata 24. 🕐 **78-41-37-66.** Reservations recommended. Main courses 210NOK–290NOK ($28–$39). AE, DC, MC, V. Mon–Thurs 1–11pm; Fri 1pm–1am; Sat 6–11pm. Bus: 1, 5, or 9.

Rica Hotel Restaurant NORWEGIAN/INTERNATIONAL   This dining room in the cellar of the Rica Hotel Hammerfest opens onto the harbor. Specialties include pepper steak and filet of reindeer. It also serves delicious dishes based on the day's catch from the fjord, as well as some international selections, including Mexican and Chinese cuisine. The Rica Bar and Disco, also in the cellar of the hotel, is open Monday through Thursday from 5pm to 1am, Friday and Saturday from 5pm to 3:30am. Admission is 70NOK ($9.30) on Friday and Saturday nights; other nights, it's free. The minimum age is 20, and beer costs 45NOK ($6) per half liter.

In the Rica Hotel Hammerfest, Sørøygata 15. 🕐 **78-41-13-33.** Main courses 179NOK–259NOK ($24–$34). AE, DC, MC, V. Daily 11am–11pm. Bus: 1 or 2.

HONNINGSVÅG

130km (81 miles) NE of Hammerfest, 2,446km (1,519 miles) NE of Bergen

The world's northernmost village, the gateway to the North Cape, is a completely modern fishing harbor. Only the chapel withstood the German destruction of 1944. It's some 80km (50 miles) closer to the North Pole than Hammerfest, on the Alta–Hammerfest bus route.

Honningsvåg is on the southern side of the island of Magerøy, connected to the North Cape by a 36km (22-mile) road.

ESSENTIALS

GETTING THERE   If you don't take the coastal steamer, you can reach Honningsvåg by car. From Oslo (a very long trip—about 30 hr. June–Sept), take E6 north to the junction with Route 95 north. That route leads to Honningsvåg, with one ferry crossing. SAS flies from Oslo or Bergen to Alta; there you can catch a bus to Hammerfest (Apr–Sept only), where you change to another bus to Honningsvåg. For bus information, call **Finnmark Fylkesrederi** (🕐 **78-40-70-00**).

VISITOR INFORMATION   The **Honningsvåg Tourist Office,** in the Nordkapphuset (🕐 **78-47-25-99**), can give you information on sightseeing boat trips, museums, walks, and deep-sea fishing. The office is open from June to August, Monday through Friday from 8:30am to 8pm, Saturday and Sunday from noon to 8pm; from September to May, Monday through Friday from 8:30am to 4pm.

A SPECIAL EVENT   The **North Cape Festival,** held for 1 week in mid-June each year, presents a diverse display of local culture. During the festival, participants in the **North Cape March** trek from Honningsvåg to the North Cape and back, a total of around 71km (44 miles).

Frommer's Favorite Offbeat Adventures

- **Dog Sledding:** Traveling over the frozen tundra or through snow-laced forests at the speed of a dog can be one of the great experiences of the Nordic world. You can be a passenger, bundled aboard a sled, or a driver urging on a team of huskies. A Norway-based outfitter who specializes in the experience, usually as part of midwinter camping trips under a canopy of stars, is **Canyon Huskies,** Stengelsen, N-9518lta, Norway (✆ **78-43-33-06;** www.canyonhuskies.no). Tours last 1 to 10 days and are conducted by owner Roger Dahl. They run between December and May, and involve overnight stays in mountain cabins, which usually contain five to six bunk beds each. Negotiate with these folks directly, or contact U.S.-based outfitter **Borton Overseas** (✆ **800/843-0602;** www.bortonoverseas.com).

- **Observing Musk Oxen:** A remnant of the last Ice Age, the musk ox had become nearly extinct by the 1930s. Between 1932 and 1953, musk oxen were shipped from Greenland to the Dovrefjell (a national park that's about an hour's train ride south of Trondheim), where about 60 still roam. On a safari, you can observe this thriving herd—take along some binoculars. The mountainous park, another remnant of the last Ice Age, is Europe's most bountiful spot for wildflowers. As part of your treks throughout the region, you can also observe the purest herd of original mountain reindeer in Norway. Accommodations in or near the park can be arranged through **Borton Overseas** (✆ **800/843-0602;** www.bortonoverseas.com). Hotel staff members are adept at indicating the locations where the animal herds were last sighted, and where they're most likely to be.

- **Rafting:** Norway's abundant snow and rainfall and its steep topography feed dozens of roaring white-water streams. Experience these torrents firsthand as part of white-water treks downriver. One of Norway's most respected river outfitters is **Norwegian Wildlife and Rafting AS,** Randswerk, N-2680 Vågå (✆ **61-23-87-27;** www.nwr.no). Based in central Norway, about a 90-minute drive north of Lillehammer, it

SEEING THE SIGHTS

Nordkapphallen   This visitor center has a video presentation and museum exhibits. Downstairs you'll find a cinema and a cave with a panoramic window facing the Arctic Ocean. On the way to the cave, you'll see several scenes from the history of the North Cape. A monument commemorates the visit of King Oscar (king of Norway and Sweden) to the Cape in 1873, and another exhibit commemorates the arrival of King Chulalongkorn of Siam (now Thailand) who came for a look at the Cape in 1907; Chulalongkorn was the son of the king in the musical *The King and I.* There's also a monument marking the terminus of the "Midnight Sun Road." Although the admission price is steep, the views from inside are incredible and unforgettable. Call before you visit because opening hours and days are subject to change without notice.

employs a part-time staff of 30 and a flotilla of devices suitable for helping you float, meander, or shoot down the white-water streams of Norway. Whatever conveyance you can imagine (paddle boards, kayaks, canoes, or inflatable rafts), this company can provide. Trips last 1 to 8 days.

- **Trekking the Fjords:** Two respected U.S.-based outfitters, **Borton Overseas** (℃ 800/843-0602; www.bortonoverseas.com) and **Five Stars of Scandinavia** (℃ 800/722-4126; http://5stars-of-scandinavia.com), offer 7- and 8-day treks through Norway designed to acquaint you with the country's heritage and its thousands of scenic wonders. Amid the cliffs and waterfalls of the fjords, you can participate in point-to-point guided treks that average around 24km (15 miles) per day. En route, you'll visit wooden churches, mountain hamlets and, in some cases, snow fields and slow-moving glaciers. Depending on your budget and your tastes, overnight accommodations range from first-class hotels to simple mountain huts favored by rock climbers and many trekkers.

- **Bicycling in the Lofoten Islands:** Some of the weirdest and most isolated tundra and lichen-covered rock formations in Norway lie within the Lofoten archipelago, north of the Arctic Circle. Ecologists insist that one of the best and least invasive ways to experience the wildlife here is on a bicycle.

    Berkeley, California-based **Backroads Travel** (℃ 800/GO-ACTIVE; www.backroads.com) conducts 6-day hiking and biking (they refer to them as "multi-sport") tours of the isolated archipelago at least twice a year, during July and August, with an emphasis on ecology and natural beauty. Washington state-based **Five Stars of Scandinavia** (℃ 800/722-4126; http://5stars-of-scandinavia.com) offers comparable tours and tends to be cheaper than Backroads. Both operators house their participants in simple mountain huts and lodges, and make frequent trips across bodies of water by bridge, tunnel, and ferryboat.

Nordkapp. ℃ **78-47-22-33.** Admission 185NOK ($25) adults, 50NOK ($6.65) children, 350NOK ($47) family. Apr 1–May 17 daily 2–5pm; May 18–June 5 daily noon–1am; June 6–10 daily 9am–2am; June 11–Aug 11 daily 9am–2am; Aug 12–20 daily 9am–1am; Aug 21–Sept 9 daily noon–5pm; Sept 10–30 daily noon–5pm. Closed Oct–Mar.

Nordkappmuseet   This museum has displays about the cultural history of the North Cape, fishery artifacts, and an exhibit that details the effects of World War II on the North Cape. The museum lies at the harbor and town center, a 3-minute walk from the coastal steamer and the North Cape Hotel.

In the Nordkapphuset, Fergeveien 4. ℃ **78-47-28-33.** Admission 25NOK ($3.35) adults, 5NOK (65¢) children, free for children under 6. June 15–Aug 15 Mon–Sat 11am–8pm, Sun noon–8pm; Aug 16–June 14 Mon–Fri 12:30–4pm.

WHERE TO STAY

Rica Hotel   The world's northernmost hotel, 34km (21 miles) from the North Cape, is in the central zone, near the quay. Early reservations are strongly advised. This five-story, yellow-fronted 1956 building was enlarged and considerably upgraded in the 1990s. The guest rooms, which have views of the harbor, are functionally furnished with modern but plain pieces. The guest rooms and bathrooms are a bit small (each bathroom equipped with a shower-tub combination), but the beds are good. In this part of the world, you'll happily settle for a roof over your head. Restaurant Carolina is one of the best in town. The hotel also runs an unpretentious grill and offers dance club action on Friday and Saturday nights.

Nordkappgata 2–4, N-9750 Honningsvåg. ℂ **78-47-23-33.** Fax 78-47-33-79. 163 units. 960NOK–1,260NOK ($128–$168) double; 1,400NOK–1,800NOK ($186–$239) suite. AE, DC, MC, V. **Amenities:** Restaurant; lounge. *In room:* TV.

WHERE TO DINE

Restaurant Carolina *(finds)* NORWEGIAN   In the cellar of the North Cape Hotel, this place is at its most elegant in the winter, when the tour groups are gone. During the summer, the smörgåsbord is in the dining room and a la carte dinners are served in the less formal Bistro. The cuisine is competently prepared but never exciting; most of the ingredients are shipped in. In the evening music begins at 8pm, and the place is very popular with locals. It's decorated with old-fashioned photographs of Honningsvåg.

In the Rica Hotel, Nordkappgata 2–4. ℂ **78-47-23-33.** Reservations recommended. Main courses 160NOK–225NOK ($21–$30). AE, DC, MC, V. Summer daily 5–11pm.

A TRIP TO THE NORTH CAPE ✮✮✮

The **Nordkapp (North Cape)** symbolizes the "top of Europe." (Knivskjellodden actually extends about 1,350m/4,500 ft. farther north, but it is inaccessible.) In prehistoric times the North Cape Horn was a Sami place of sacrifice. The North Cape's name used to be Knyskanes, but in 1553 it was named "North Cape" by the Lord Richard Chancellor of England, who was searching for a sea passage to China. The road to the North Cape is open to traffic from May 1 to October 20.

The first tour ships arrived in 1879. They anchored in Hornvika Bay, and the visitors had to climb 276m (921 ft.) up to the plateau. After the road from Honningsvåg opened in 1956, the flow of tourists turned into a flood. In summer, buses to the North Cape leave daily from outside the tourist office at Fergeveien 4 at Honningsvåg, stop briefly at the ferry terminal across from the Sifi Sommerhotell, and then continue to the visitor center at the North Cape. The one-way passage from any point along the route is 60NOK ($8) adults, 30NOK ($4) children. For more information, call **FFR** (ℂ **78-47-58-50**).

On the road to the Cape is a Lapp encampment. It's a bit contrived, but visitors do have an opportunity to go inside one of the tents, and you come away with an idea of how nomadic Lapps used to live.

2 The Fjords

For visitors who'd like to explore the fjords by driving, we begin our tour in Bergen. From Bergen, head east on Route 7 to Ulvik.

ULVIK

150km (93 miles) E of Bergen

Ulvik is a rarity—an unspoiled resort. It lies like a fist at the end of an arm of the Hardangerfjord, and is surrounded in the summer by misty peaks and fruit farms. The village's 1858 church is attractively decorated in the style of the region. It's open from June to August, daily from 9am to 5pm. Concerts are presented here.

ESSENTIALS
GETTING THERE   If you're not driving, you can reach Ulvik by train or bus from Bergen or Oslo. From either city, take a train to Voss, where you can catch a bus for the 40km (25-mile), 45-minute ride to Ulvik. Buses run from Voss daily, five times in the summer, three in the winter. In Ulvik the bus stops in front of the Ulvik church in the town center. There's no formal bus station.

VISITOR INFORMATION   Contact the **Ulvik Tourist Office,** in the town center (© **56-52-63-60**). It's open from May 15 to September 15, Monday through Saturday from 8:30am to 5pm, Sunday from 1 to 5pm; from September 16 to May 14, Monday through Friday from 8:30am to 5pm. It can arrange excursions, from trips on fjord steamers to bus tours of the Osa mountains.

SEEING THE SIGHTS
A number of do-it-yourself excursions begin at Ulvik; they change seasonally and depend on the weather—see the tourist office for details. You can explore the Eidfjord district, which is the northern tip of the Hardangerfjord and a paradise for hikers. It's home to some 1,000 people and the Continent's largest herd of wild reindeer. Mountain trout attract anglers to the area.

The district contains nearly one-quarter of **Hardangervidda National Park** ★★, on the largest high-mountain plateau in Europe. Some 20,000 wild reindeer live there. Well-marked hiking trails connect a series of 15 tourist huts.

Several canyons, including the renowned **Måbø Valley,** lead down from the plateau to the fjords. Here you'll see the famous 165m (550-ft.) Voringfoss waterfall. The Valurefoss in Hjømo Valley has a free fall of almost 240m (800 ft.). Part of the 1,000-year-old road across Norway, traversing the Måbø Valley, has been restored for hardy hikers. The Måbø Valley, like the neighboring Hjømo Valley, is part of the previously mentioned Hardangervidda National Park.

After exploring the area around Eidfjord, you can drive south along the fjord banks to Kinsarvik, another major region of tourist interest. The main village of **Kinsarvik** stands on a glacier-formed ridge at the mouth of the Kinso River, which flows into four magnificent waterfalls as it drops from the plateau to Husedalen on its way to the sea. Since early times, Kinsarvik has been the marketplace for the region.

Kinsarvik was Hardanger's principal timber port in the 17th and early 18th centuries. When the export of timber was transferred to Bergen in 1750, Kinsarvik developed a shipbuilding industry that continued until 1870, when the village became a center for woodcarving. Today one of its principal industries is a pewter factory.

Borstova, the building on the fjord side of the green facing the church, was constructed partly from the timbers of St. Olav's Guildhall, the meeting place of the local guild until 1680. It's now a council chamber and social center.

Kinsarvik Church, said to have been constructed by Scottish master builders at the end of the 12th century, is one of the oldest stone churches in Norway. The interior was restored in 1961 to its pre-Reformation condition. It has a 17th-century pulpit painted by Peter Reimers, a painted and carved altarpiece, and medieval frescoes.

The stone **column** *(minnestein)* on the green commemorates the local men who fought in the wars that led to the end of Norway's union with Denmark in 1814.

The **Tillegg i Tekst (Hardanger Recreation Park),** in the middle of Kinsarvik, is open on weekends from May to mid-June and in September, and daily from mid-June to August.

About 14km (9 miles) from Kinsarvik en route to Eidfjord, off Highway 7, is the **Bu Museum,** Ringøy (© **53-66-69-00**). It has three old houses containing furniture and domestic and craft equipment. The basement of an old farmhouse is filled with artifacts dating from the Stone Age to modern times. The museum also has a collection of national costumes from the Hardanger area. It's open from June 1 to August 10, daily from 11am to 4pm, and by request the rest of the year. Admission is 50NOK ($6.65) for adults, 30NOK ($4) for seniors and students, and free for children.

WHERE TO STAY & DINE
Moderate
Rica Brakanes Hotel ✣   There's a famous view of the Hardangerfjord and the surrounding forest from this well-recommended hotel. It's near the town center, at the edge of the fjord. The original building, from the 1860s, burned during a World War II bombing raid and was reconstructed in 1952. Today all that remains of the original building is one small dining room. The rest of the hotel is airy, sunny, and comfortable. The guest rooms are small but well maintained, with good beds and sparkling-clean bathrooms with shower-tub combinations. In the summer, plane rides over the fjords can be arranged, and windsurfing and boat rentals are available.

N-5730 Ulvik. © **56-52-61-05.** Fax 56-52-64-10. brakanes.hotel@hl.telia.no. 144 units. 1,470NOK ($196) double; 3,000NOK ($399) suite. Rates include breakfast. AE, DC, MC, V. Free parking. **Amenities:** Restaurant; bar; pool; 2 tennis courts; fitness center; sauna. *In room:* TV, minibar.

Inexpensive
Ulvik Fjord Pensjonat *Value*   Ulvik Fjord Pensjonat, constructed in two stages in 1946 and 1977, is one of the finest guesthouses along the Hardangerfjord. The rooms are spacious and pleasantly furnished in regional Norwegian style. Most units contain well-kept bathrooms with shower-tub combinations. You'll be welcomed by the Hammer family, who won the Norwegian Hospitality Prize in 1989. A sauna and solarium are available for guests' use.

N-5730 Ulvik. © **56-52-61-70.** Fax 56-52-61-60. www.ulvikfjordpensjonat.no. 19 units, 17 with bathroom. 620NOK ($82) double without bathroom; 780NOK ($104) double with bathroom. Rates include breakfast. V. Closed Oct–Apr. Free parking. **Amenities:** Restaurant; bar; lounge. *In room:* Hair dryer.

Ulvik Hotel   Updated in 1996, the guest rooms are modern and comfortable, with good beds and well-maintained bathrooms equipped with shower-tub combinations. More than half the units overlook the fjord. A dining room serves excellent Norwegian food; the shrimp and salmon are the most popular items on the menu. The hotel is on the fjord in the town center.

N-5730 Ulvik. © **56-52-62-00.** Fax 56-52-66-41. 57 units. 860NOK–1,150NOK ($114–$153) double. Rates include breakfast. AE, DC, MC, V. Free parking. **Amenities:** Restaurant; bar; lounge. *In room:* TV.

VOSS ✣
40km (25 miles) W of Ulvik, 101km (63 miles) E of Bergen

Between two fjords, Voss is a famous year-round resort, also known for its folklore. It was the birthplace of the American football hero Knute Rockne. Maybe the trolls don't strike fear in the hearts of farm children anymore, but revelers dressed as trolls do appear in costumed folklore programs to give visitors a little fun.

Voss is a natural base for exploring the two largest fjords in Norway, the **Sognefjord** to the north and the **Hardangerfjord** to the south. In and around Voss are glaciers, mountains, fjords, waterfalls, orchards, rivers, and lakes.

ESSENTIALS

GETTING THERE   From Ulvik, take Highway 20 to Route 13; then follow Route 13 northwest to Voss. If you're not driving, there's frequent train service from Bergen (trip time 1¼ hr.) and Oslo (5½ hr.). There are six daily buses from Bergen (1¾ hr.) and one bus a day from Oslo (9 hr.).

VISITOR INFORMATION CENTER   The **Voss Information Center** is at Hestavangen 10 (℃ **56-52-08-00**). It's open from June to August, Monday through Saturday from 9am to 7pm, Sunday from 2 to 7pm; from September to May, Monday through Friday from 9am to 4pm.

SEEING THE SIGHTS

St. Olav's Cross, Skulegata, is near the Voss Cinema. It's the oldest historic relic in Voss, believed to have been raised when the townspeople adopted Christianity in 1023.

A ride on the **Hangursbanen cable car** (℃ **56-51-12-12**) will be a memorable part of your visit. It offers panoramic views of Voss and its environs. The mountaintop restaurant serves refreshments and meals. The hardy take the cable car up, and then spend the rest of the afternoon strolling down the mountain. A round-trip ride costs 60NOK ($8) for adults, 40NOK ($5.30) for children 8 to 16, free for children under 8. Entrance to the cable car is on a hillside, a 10-minute walk north of the town center. It's open in summer and winter, but closes during the often gray and rainy months of May and September to December.

Finnesloftet *(Finds*   This is one of the oldest timbered houses in Norway, dating from the mid–13th century. It's located about 1.5km (1 mile) west of Voss and is a 15-minute walk west from the train station.

Finne. ℃ **56-51-16-75**. Admission 20NOK ($2.65) adults, 10NOK ($1.35) children. Tues–Sun 11am–4pm. Closed Aug 16–June 14.

Vangskyrkje   This 1277 church with a timbered tower contains a striking Renaissance pulpit, a stone altar and triptych, fine woodcarvings, and a painted ceiling. It's in the center of Voss, a 5-minute walk east from the train station. Call in advance if you would like to reserve an English-speaking guide.

Vangsgata 3. ℃ **56-51-22-78**. Admission 15NOK ($2) adults, free for children under 17. Daily 10am–4pm. Closed Sept–May.

Voss Folkemuseum   About 1km (½ mile) north of Voss on a hillside overlooking the town, this museum consists of more than a dozen farmhouses and other buildings dating from the 1500s to around 1870. They were built on this site by two farm families.

Mølster. ℃ **56-51-15-11**. Admission 35NOK ($4.65) adults, free for children. May and Sept daily 10am–5pm; June–Aug daily 10am–5pm; Oct–Apr Mon–Sat 10am–3pm, Sun noon–3pm.

SKIING

Voss continually adds to its facilities, and is definitely in the race to overtake Geilo and Lillehammer as Norway's most popular winter playground. Its chairlifts, ski lifts, and aerial cable car carry passengers up 788m (2,625 ft.).

The town offers what it calls a "ski circus." Beginners take the Hangursbanen cable car; one ski lift (900m/3,000 ft. long) goes from Traastolen to the top of Slettafjell (with a wide choice of downhill runs); the Bavallen lift is for the slalom slopes; and the downhill runs are at Lonehorgi.

Lessons at the **Ski School** (© **56-51-00-32** in winter or 56-51-34-36 in summer), at the end of the cable car run, are moderately priced. The tourist office and hotels can arrange bookings. All equipment is available for rent.

Children over 7 are allowed on the slopes. A special branch of the Ski School handles these youngsters. Babysitting is available for children under 7.

WHERE TO STAY
Moderate

Fleischers Hotel ®   On the lakefront beside the Voss train station, Fleischers Hotel couldn't be more convenient. The gracious 1889 frame hotel has a modern wing with 30 units, all with private showers, toilets, and terraces overlooking the lake. In the older part of the hotel, the rooms are old-fashioned and more spacious. The restaurant serves an a la carte menu; main courses cost 145NOK to 235NOK ($19–$31). In the summer, a buffet is served for 325NOK ($43).

Evangerveiten 13, N-5700 Voss. © **56-52-05-00.** Fax 56-52-05-01. www.fleischers.no. 90 units. 1,350NOK ($180) double; 1,600NOK ($213) suite. Rates include breakfast. AE, DC, MC, V. Free parking. **Amenities:** Restaurant; bar; lounge; pool; sauna; room service; babysitting; laundry/dry cleaning. *In room:* TV, minibar.

Hotel Jarl   This centrally located hotel offers comfortably modern singles, doubles, and suites. Guest rooms and bathrooms are a bit small, but the beds are firm. The bathrooms are also a bit cramped but are neatly kept and equipped with shower-tub combinations. Built in 1972, the hotel was enlarged and renovated in 1996. You can take your meals in the pleasant dining room or in the intimate bistro and bar.

Voss Sentrum, N-5700 Voss. © **56-51-19-33.** Fax 56-51-37-69. 78 units. 995NOK ($132) double. Rates include breakfast. AE, DC, MC, V. Free parking. **Amenities:** Restaurant; bar; nightclub; pool; sauna. *In room:* TV, minibar, safe.

Park Hotel Vossevangen   The product of a 1990 merger, this hotel consists of two sections (originally the Park Hotel and the Vossevangen Hotel), joined by a covered passageway. The guest rooms are attractively furnished and contain well-kept bathrooms with shower-tub combinations. The hotel is family-owned and houses the best restaurant in town, the Elysée (see "Where to Dine," below). Facilities include the Café Stationen, the Pentagon Dance Bar, the Stallen Pub, and the Pianissimo Bar. It's in the town center, about 90m (300 ft.) from the train station.

Uttrågate, N-5701 Voss. © **56-51-13-22.** Fax 56-51-00-39. 131 units. 1,150NOK–1,590NOK ($153–$211) double. Rates include breakfast. AE, DC, MC, V. Free parking. **Amenities:** Restaurant; bar; lounge; babysitting. *In room:* TV, minibar.

Inexpensive

Kringsjå Pension   This pleasant three-story guesthouse is in the center of Voss; some parts were built in the 1930s, others much more recently. The public rooms are spacious and airy, and the guest rooms are simply, comfortably furnished, with good beds but small bathrooms with shower-tub combinations. Breakfast is served daily, and other meals are sometimes available. The hall bathrooms are well maintained and are also equipped with shower-tub combinations.

Strengjarhaujen 6, N-5700 Voss. © **56-51-16-27.** Fax 56-51-63-30. www.kringsja.no. 18 units, 14 with bathroom. 600NOK ($80) double without bathroom; 750NOK ($100) double with bathroom. Rates include breakfast. AE, DC, MC, V. Free parking. **Amenities:** Lounge. *In room:* No phone.

Nøring Pensjonat   The Nøring is a first-class pension built in 1949 near the river, about a 10-minute walk from the town center. It provides clean, functional accommodations, which are small but comfortable, with well-kept bathrooms with shower units. Half of the rooms face the mountains. The boardinghouse serves good, hearty breakfasts, plus light meals (with beer or wine) at lunch and dinner. The lounge opens onto a terrace.

Uttrågate 41, N-5700 Voss. ℂ **56-51-12-11.** Fax 56-51-12-23. 20 units, 9 with bathroom. 600NOK ($80) double without bathroom; 790NOK ($105) double with bathroom. Rates include breakfast. AE, DC, MC, V. Free parking. **Amenities:** Restaurant; bar; lounge. *In room:* No phone.

WHERE TO DINE
Moderate

Elysée *(Finds* FRENCH/NORWEGIAN   The decor of this prestigious restaurant includes trompe l'oeil murals based on a modern interpretation of the Parthenon. It features such dishes as baked sea scorpion, filet of lamb marinated in honey, and a daily game dish. Homemade ice cream with berries and vanilla sauce makes a smooth dessert. The food here, based on fresh ingredients, is satisfying. You leave feeling you've had an adequate, substantial, and hearty meal. There's an extensive wine list.

In the Park Hotel Vossevangen, Uttrågate. ℂ **56-51-13-22.** Reservations recommended. Main courses 185NOK–255NOK ($25–$34); lunch smörgåsbord 275NOK ($37); fixed-price dinner 350NOK ($47). AE, DC, MC, V. Sun–Thurs 1–10:30pm; Fri–Sat 1–11pm.

Fleischers Restaurant ⊛ NORWEGIAN   The dining room of this landmark hotel, a few steps from the Voss train station, hasn't been altered since the hotel opened over a century ago. Long the leading restaurant in the Voss area, the Victorian-style Fleischers remains the traditionalists' favorite. Its lunchtime smörgåsbord is a lavish array of all-you-can-eat Norwegian delicacies. Specialties include smoked salmon and filet of beef, lamb, pork, and veal. This is authentic cuisine that would have pleased Ibsen—a real "taste of Norway." What you don't get is dash and culinary sophistication.

Evangerveiten 13. ℂ **56-52-05-00.** Reservations recommended. Lunch smörgåsbord 195NOK ($26); main courses 160NOK–255NOK ($21–$34); summer buffet 325NOK ($43). AE, DC, MC, V. Mon–Sat 1–10:30pm; Sun 1–9:45pm.

Inexpensive

Vangen Café NORWEGIAN   The least expensive cafeteria-style spot in Voss is one floor above street level over a small souvenir shop and food market. It's in the center of town, a 5-minute walk south of the train station. Soft drinks and fruit juices are sold, but no alcohol. The *dagens menu* (daily specials) is the best food value in town.

Vangen Super-Market, Vangsgata. ℂ **56-51-12-05.** Smørbrød 35NOK–42NOK ($4.65–$5.60); *dagens menu* 85NOK–125NOK ($11–$17). No credit cards. Mon–Fri 10:30am–6pm; Sat 10:30am–4pm; Sun noon–6pm.

VOSS AFTER DARK
Fleischers Top Spot Nightclub   In the cellar of Fleischers Hotel (see "Where to Stay," above), you'll find this well-established nightspot. Dance bands play nightly for an older crowd that's a bit dressed up. Many people come here just to drink—beer costs 53NOK ($7.05). The club is open Monday through Thursday from 9:30pm to 1am, Friday and Saturday until 3am. In Fleischers Hotel, Evangerveiten 13. ℂ **56-52-05-00.** Cover 60NOK ($8) Fri–Sat only (no cover for hotel guests).

A SIDE TRIP TO THE SOGNEFJORD

If you have a car and time to spare, you may want to visit the Sognefjord district, around the largest of the Norwegian fjords. From Voss, the northern route leads to **Vik.** The scenery is beautiful, and the road runs for kilometers across a desolate tableland at 900m (3,000 ft.) above sea level. On summer days the lakes appear green, and there's snow on the distant slopes.

In Vik, try to see the **stave church,** one of the most attractive in Norway. Then take the road to Vangsnes, where you can make ferry connections across the Sognefjord to Balestrand or Dragsvik. On the other side, take Route 5 north. The steep highway runs through rolling countryside with waterfalls to Viksdalen, about 64km (40 miles) from Dragsvik.

BALESTRAND

90km (56 miles) N of Voss, 209km (130 miles) NE of Bergen

Long known for its arts and crafts, Balestrand lies on the northern rim of the Sognefjord, at the junction of the Vetlefjord, the Esefjord, and the Fjaerlandsfjord.

ESSENTIALS

GETTING THERE   From Voss, continue driving north on Route 13 to Vangsnes and board a car ferry for the short crossing northwest to Balestrand. You can also take a train from Bergen or Oslo to Voss or Flåm, and then make bus and ferry connections north to Balestrand. Bus and ferry schedules are available at the Voss tourist office (© **56-52-08-00**) and the Flåm tourist office (© **57-63-21-06**). From Bergen there are daily express boats to Balestrand; the trip takes 3½ hours.

VISITOR INFORMATION   The **Tourist Office** (© **57-69-16-17** in winter or 57-69-12-55 in summer) is in the town center. From June to August, it's open daily from 8:30am to 10pm; May and September, daily from 9am to 8pm; from October to April, Monday through Saturday from 9am to 4pm.

SEEING THE SIGHTS

The staff at the tourist office can help you plan a tour of the area and put you in touch with local craftspeople. Pick up a list of excursions and buy tickets for one of the scheduled 1½-day tours—for example, a taxi plane across the **Jostedal Glacier.**

Kaiser Wilhelm II, a frequent visitor to Balestrand, presented the district with two **statues of old Norse heroes,** King Bele and Fridtjof the Bold. They stand in the center of town. Another sight is the English church of **St. Olav,** a tiny wooden building that dates from 1897.

You can explore the area by setting out in nearly any direction on scenic country lanes with little traffic or a wide choice of marked trails and upland farm tracks. The tourist office sells a touring map. There's good sea fishing, as well as lake and river trout fishing. Fishing tackle, rowboats, and bicycles can all be rented in the area.

WHERE TO STAY
Moderate

Kviknes Hotel ⚱   Built in 1913 as a summer retreat for Europeans, this hotel was much enlarged in 1970. At its core it's an elaborately detailed building with balconies opening onto the edge of the fjord. All but a few of the guest rooms have fjord views. They vary widely in size and style. The most popular units are those in the original structure, with old-fashioned Norwegian style, flowery fabrics, good beds, and spacious bathrooms with shower-tub combinations. Some of these accommodations are furnished with antiques. The less personal rooms are in the annex, where bland Nordic style prevails. Bathrooms tend to be very small. Many of the accommodations are set aside for nonsmokers, and others are wheelchair accessible. The hotel has a large dining room, several lounges, and a dance club. An extensive buffet is served every night; lunches are less elaborate, with brasserie-style meals. Sports such as water-skiing, windsurfing, and fjord fishing can be arranged, as can helicopter flights to the Jostedal Glacier.

Balholm, N-6898 Balestrand. (C) **57-69-42-00.** Fax 57-69-42-01. www.kviknes.no. 210 units. 1,360NOK ($181) double; 1,560NOK ($207) suite. Rates include breakfast. AE, DC, MC, V. Closed Oct–Apr. Free parking. **Amenities:** Restaurant; bar; fitness center; Jacuzzi; sauna; room service; babysitting; laundry/dry cleaning. *In room:* TV, hair dryer.

Inexpensive

Dragsvik Fjord Hotel   About 1km (½ mile) from Balestrand and 270m (900 ft.) from the ferry quay at Dragsvik, this hotel is a bargain. Doubles in the new wing have the most up-to-date plumbing. The units are comfortable, though small. They're well maintained, but bathrooms equipped with shower-tub combinations are tiny. The large dining room offers a panoramic view of the Fjaerlandsfjord. You can rent bicycles, rowboats, and motorboats.

Dragsvik, N-6899 Balestrand. (C) **57-69-12-93.** Fax 57-69-13-83. www.dragsvik.no. 19 units. Feb–May and Sept–Oct 730NOK ($97) double; June–Aug 785NOK ($104) double. Rates include breakfast. AE, MC, V. Closed Nov–Jan. Free parking. **Amenities:** Restaurant; bar; room service. *In room:* Hair dryer.

Midtnes Pensjonat   This well-run, reasonably priced boardinghouse, in the center of Balestrand next to the English church, is family-owned and -managed. The rooms are pleasantly furnished, and most open onto the Sognefjord. The rooms aren't terribly spacious, but housekeeping is good and the bathrooms are well maintained with shower-tub combinations. There's a private pier with rowboats. The boardinghouse offers good food and the dining room has a view of the fjord.

N-6899 Balestrand. (C) **57-69-11-33.** Fax 57-69-15-84. www.midtnes.no. 34 units. 625NOK–790NOK ($83–$105) double. Rates include breakfast. No credit cards. Free parking. **Amenities:** Restaurant; lounge. *In room:* Hair dryer.

FROM BALESTRAND TO FLÅM

From Balestrand, take Route 55 east along the Sognefjord, crossing the fjord by ferry at Dragsvik and by bridge at Sogndal. At Sogndal, drive east to Kaupanger, where you'll cross the Ardalsfjord by ferry, and head south to Revsnes. In Revsnes, pick up Route 11 heading southeast. Drive east until you connect with a secondary road that heads southwest through Kvigno and Aurland. From Aurland, take Route 601 southwest to Flåm. The whole trip takes 2 to 3 hours, depending on weather and road conditions.

FLÅM 🕄

97km (60 miles) SE of Balestrand, 166km (103 miles) E of Bergen

Flåm (pronounced "Flawm") lies on the Aurlandsfjord, a tip of the more famous Sognefjord. In the village you can visit the old church (1667), with walls painted in typical Norwegian country style.

ESSENTIALS

GETTING THERE   If you're not driving, the best and most exciting approach to Flåm is aboard the **electric train from Myrdal** 🕄🕄🕄, which connects with trains from Bergen and Oslo. The electric train follows a 19km (12-mile) route overlooking a 870m (2,900-ft.) drop, stopping occasionally for passengers to photograph spectacular waterfalls. The trip takes 50 minutes. In winter about four or five trains a day make the run to Flåm. In summer, depending on business, service begins at 7:40am and runs throughout the day. Tickets must be purchased in advance. The one-way fare from Myrdal to Flåm is 125NOK ($17).

Bus travel is less convenient. One **bus** a day Monday through Saturday runs between Aurland and Flåm. The trip takes 30 minutes.

From May to September, two **ferries** per day cross the fjord between Aurland and Flåm. The trip takes 30 minutes.

Flåm can also be reached by high-speed **express boats** from Bergen, Balestrand (see above), and Leikanger. The boats carry passengers only. In Bergen, call **Fylkesbaatana** (© **55-32-40-15**); the one-way trip costs 550NOK ($73).

VISITOR INFORMATION The **tourist office** (© **57-63-21-06**) is near the railroad station. It's open from May to September, daily from 8:30am to 8:30pm.

SEEING THE SIGHTS
Flåm is an excellent starting point for car or boat excursions to other well-known centers on the Sognefjord, Europe's longest and deepest fjord. Worth exploring are two of the wildest and most beautiful fingers of the Sognefjord: the Nærøyfjord and the Aurlandfjord. Ask at the tourist office about a summer-only cruise from Flåm to both fjords. From Flåm by boat, you can disembark in Gudvangen or Aurland and continue by bus. Alternatively, you can return to Flåm by train.

There are also a number of easy walks in the Flåm district. A map with detailed information is available from the tourist office.

WHERE TO STAY
Heimly Pension *finds* At the edge of the fjord, this simple lodge was built in the 1950s as a family-run pension. It later housed the clients of a nearby ski school. Designed in the style of an A-frame chalet, it offers a ground-floor lounge, guest rooms with bathrooms equipped with shower units and views over the fjord on the two upper floors, and a separate pub and restaurant in an annex across the road.

N-5743 Flåm. © 57-63-23-00. Fax 57-63-23-40. www.heimly.no. 26 units. 690NOK–880NOK ($92–$117) double. Rates include breakfast. AE, DC, MC, V. Free parking. Closed Dec 24–Jan 2. **Amenities:** Restaurant; bar; room service. *In room:* No phone.

GEILO *☆*
109km (68 miles) SE of Flåm, 240km (149 miles) E of Bergen, 240km (149 miles) W of Oslo

One of Norway's best-known ski resorts is also an attractive summer resort. Geilo lies some 780m (2,600 ft.) above sea level in the Hol mountain district. Although it's not strictly in the fjord country, it's included here because it's a "gateway" there en route from Oslo to Bergen.

The Geilo area boasts 130km (81 miles) of marked cross-country skiing tracks.

ESSENTIALS
GETTING THERE From Flåm, return to Aurland to connect with Route 50. It runs southeast through the towns of Steine, Storestølen, Hovet, and Hagafoss. In Hagafoss, connect with Route 7 going southwest into Geilo.

VISITOR INFORMATION   The **Turistinformasjonen** office is at Vesleslåt-teveien 13 in the town center (✆ **32-09-59-00**). It's open from June to August, daily from 9am to 9pm; from September to May, Monday through Friday from 8:30am to 5pm, Saturday from 8:30am to 3pm. The town doesn't use street addresses, but everything is easy to find.

SEEING THE SIGHTS

The main ski season is from January to March. The **Ski School** has more than two dozen instructors, known for their patience with amateurs. Other fun activities include sleigh rides, curling, and skating at the **Geilo Stadium.**

From Geilo you can visit the historical museum in **Hol,** 9.7km (6 miles) northeast, to see 16th-century woodcarvings and a 12th-century stave church. Another destination is the ancient Viking burial ground at **Fekjo.** The tourist office can supply maps and help you plan day-long excursions.

The chairlift ride is great for dramatic scenery of the mountain plateau and fjords. The lift terminal is a short walk from the railway station.

WHERE TO STAY
Very Expensive
Dr. Holms Hotel ⭐⭐⭐   One of the most famous resort hotels in Norway, this is the finest place to stay in the area. Here, near the railroad station, you get elegance, comfort, and traditional styling. Dr. J. C. Holms opened the hotel in 1909, and there have been many changes since, including the addition of two wings and a swimming complex. The most recent face-lift took place in 1999. Original works of art decorate the hotel. Guest rooms are beautifully furnished in traditional style and offer many luxuries including good beds and well-kept bathrooms with shower-tub combinations.

N-3580 Geilo. ✆ **32-09-57-00.** Fax 32-09-16-20. www.drholms.com. 127 units. May–Aug 1,015NOK ($135) double; Sept–Apr 1,520NOK ($202) double. Year-round 1,790NOK–2,270NOK ($238–$302) suite. Rates include breakfast. Rates may be higher during Christmas and New Year's. AE, DC, MC, V. Free parking. **Amenities:** Restaurant; bar; pool; fitness center; sauna; library; room service; babysitting; laundry/dry cleaning. *In room:* TV, minibar.

Moderate
Bardøla Hoyfjellshotel   This well-run hotel lies in tranquil surroundings, about 1.5km (1 mile) east of the train station. Built in the 1930s, it's been expanded and renovated many times. It attracts many guests in summer and winter, partly because it has a higher proportion of suites than any other hotel in the region. Each year the hotel renovates five rooms and five suites. Many of the traditionally styled guest rooms are generous in size. All have ample bathrooms with shower-tub combinations.

N-3580 Geilo. ✆ **32-09-04-00.** Fax 32-09-45-01. www.bardoela.no. 128 units. May–Aug 920NOK ($122) double. Rates include breakfast. Sept–Apr 1,280NOK–1,350NOK ($170–$180) double. Rates include half board. Year-round 500NOK ($67) supplement for suite. Rates higher during Christmas and New Year's. AE, DC, MC, V. Free parking. **Amenities:** Restaurant; bar; pool; 2 tennis courts; fitness center; sauna; room service. *In room:* TV, minibar, hair dryer.

Norlandia Geilo Hotell   In the center of the resort, a short walk from the train station, the Geilo was the town's first hotel. The oldest part dates from 1880. The guest rooms are attractive and warmly furnished. Most of the medium-sized rooms have a sitting area. Bathrooms are a bit small but ample for your stuff, with shower-tub combinations. The nearest ski lift is only 180m (600 ft.) away. In 1994 the cozy restaurant was upgraded in charming 19th-century Nordic style.

Gamleveien 2, Box 113, N-3580 Geilo. ℂ **32-09-05-11.** Fax 32-09-17-30. www.norlandia.no. 72 units. 1,700NOK–2,220NOK ($226–$295) double. Rates include full board. AE, DC, MC, V. Free parking. **Amenities:** Restaurant; bar; fitness center; sauna; babysitting. *In room:* TV, minibar, hair dryer.

Quality Hotel Vestlia *(Finds)*   This isn't a fancy hotel, but it keeps guests coming back. It's about 1km (½ mile) east of the train station, 180m (600 ft.) from the ski lifts and cross-country slopes. Built in the 1960s, the hotel was completely renovated in the early 1990s, with all the bathrooms equipped with shower-tub combinations that were renewed in 1999. The regular guest rooms are furnished in an attractive ski-chalet style with lots of wood; some large family rooms with four beds cost the same as regular rooms. About half the accommodations are in comfortable annexes scattered about the grounds. In addition to its obvious allure to skiers, the hotel is a good summer choice—guests can go hiking, boating, or horseback riding. Live dance music is provided almost every evening year-round except Sunday.

N-3580 Geilo. ℂ **32-09-06-11.** Fax 32-08-72-01. 75 units. May–Aug 1,500NOK ($200) double; Sept–Apr 1,800NOK–2,400NOK ($239–$319) double. Rates include half board. AE, DC, MC, V. Free parking. **Amenities:** 3 restaurants; bar; pool; fitness center; sauna; babysitting; laundry/dry cleaning. *In room:* TV, minibar.

WHERE TO DINE
Most visitors to Geilo eat at their hotels.

Café Alpin NORWEGIAN   On the second floor above the bank, this cafe is the best low-cost dining choice in town. It's good for coffee, sandwiches, or hot meals. The cafeteria serves hot but rather standard fare starting at noon. Be sure to try the creamed fish soup if it's on the menu. For main dishes, you might like such Norwegian specialties as chopped reindeer meat cakes with mixed vegetables, or cured herring with sliced beets, raw onions, and boiled potatoes. For dessert, a tempting selection of Norwegian pastries is offered.

Geiloveien. ℂ **32-09-03-84.** Main courses 90NOK–125NOK ($12–$17). MC, V. Mon–Sat 10am–6pm; Sun noon–6pm.

3 Trondheim to Narvik

To explore the northern Norwegian coast by car, begin your tour in Trondheim.

TRONDHEIM 🌟🌟🌟
684km (425 miles) N of Bergen, 552km (343 miles) NW of Oslo

Founded by the Viking king Olaf I Tryggvason in the 10th century, Trondheim is Norway's third-largest city. Scenic and pleasant, it's an active university center. The city lies on the south bay of the Trondheim Fjord, at the mouth of the Nidelven River.

Noted for its timbered architecture, Trondheim retains much of its medieval past, notably the Gothic-style Nidaros Cathedral. Until the early 1200s Trondheim was the capital of Norway. Pilgrims came from all over Europe to worship at the shrine of Olav, who was canonized in 1031. With the Reformation, however, the city's fortunes declined.

ESSENTIALS
GETTING THERE   Flights to Trondheim land at **Vaernes Airport** (ℂ **74-84-30-00**), 32km (20 miles) from town. Service is available from **SAS** (ℂ **74-88-41-00**). Buses to the city center take about 30 minutes. There are two trains a day from Stockholm (trip time 12 hr.) and three trains a day from Oslo (7 hr.). One bus a day arrives from Bergen; the trip takes 15 hours. Contact **Norway**

Buss Ekspress (℃ **81-54-44-44**) for information. The coastal steamer (see "By Coastal Steamer," earlier in this chapter) from Bergen to Kirkenes calls at Trondheim.

VISITOR INFORMATION   Contact the **Trondheim Tourist Office,** Munkegaten 19 (℃ **73-80-76-60;** www.trondheim.com), near the marketplace. The staff can make hotel reservations or arrange for rooms in a private home. Double rooms in private homes cost from 350NOK ($47); the service fee is 20NOK ($2.65), which is deducted at checkout time. The tourist office is open from September 4 to May 14, Monday through Friday from 8:30am to 4pm; from May 15 to June 4 and from August 21 to September 3, Monday through Friday from 8:30am to 6pm, Saturday and Sunday from 10am to 4pm; from June 5 to June 25 and from August 7 to 20, Monday through Friday from 8:30am to 8pm, and Saturday and Sunday from 10am to 6pm; and from June 26 to August 6, Monday through Saturday from 8:30am to 10pm and Saturday and Sunday from 10am to 8pm.

GETTING AROUND   You can travel all over Trondheim and to outlying areas on city buses operated by **Trondheim Trafikkselskap (TT),** Dronningens Gate (℃ **73-50-28-70**). Tickets for **single rides** are sold on buses for 22NOK ($2.95) for adults, 11NOK ($1.45) for children 4 to 16; children under 4 travel free. If you don't have exact change, you'll get a credit slip from the driver, which can be redeemed at the TT office or on a later trip. A **day card** for 24 hours of unlimited rides costs 55NOK ($7.30) per person.

SEEING THE SIGHTS
Museum of Natural History and Archaeology   The collections and exhibits at this university museum cover natural history, archaeology, and the social history of central Norway from prehistoric times to the Middle Ages. Special features include a diorama of birds, archaeological displays, collections of church art, and a small ethnographic exhibit. One exhibit shows the most important habitats of central Norway and central Scandinavia. The exhibit also reveals how people have used and exploited nature through history.

At the Norwegian University of Science and Technology, Erling Skakkes Gate 47. ℃ **73-59-21-45.** Admission 25NOK ($3.35) adults, 10NOK ($1.35) children. May–Aug Mon–Fri 9am–4pm, Sat–Sun 11am–4pm; Sept–Apr Tues–Fri 9am–2pm, Sat–Sun noon–4pm. Bus: 63.

Nidaros Cathedral ★★★   Dating from the 11th century, this cathedral is one of the major ecclesiastical buildings in Scandinavia. It's in the town center, near the Rådhus. The burial place of the medieval Norwegian kings, it was also the site of the coronation of Haakon VII in 1905, an event that marked the beginning of modern Norway.

A classical European cathedral representing different architectural styles, including Gothic and Romanesque, it features an intricate rose window on the west front. Gustav Vigeland carved the gargoyles and grotesques for the head tower and northern transept. The 12th-century Archbishop's Palace, Erkebispegården, is behind the cathedral.

A small museum inside the cathedral displays the crown jewels of Norway.

Bispegaten 5. ℃ **73-53-91-60.** Admission (cathedral and museum) 35NOK ($4.65) adults, 20NOK ($2.65) children. Cathedral, May–June 19 and Aug 20–Sept 14 Mon–Sat 9am–3pm, Sun 1–4pm; June 20–Aug 19 Mon–Sat 9am–6pm, Sun 1–4pm; Sept 15–Apr Mon–Sat noon–4pm, Sun 1–3pm. Bus: 2, 5, 6, 7, or 9.

Ringve Museum ★★ (Finds   This museum can be viewed only on guided tours. At specified times, concerts are given on carefully preserved antique

instruments, including an impressive collection of spinets, harpsichords, clavichords, pianofortes, and string and wind instruments. Also on the premises is an old *kro* (inn) that serves waffles, light refreshments, and coffee. The mansion was the birthplace of Admiral Tordenskiold, the Norwegian sea hero.

Lade Allé 60 (3.2km/2 miles from the center of town at Ringve Manor). ℂ **73-92-24-11.** Admission 70NOK ($9.30) adults, 25NOK ($3.35) children, 40NOK ($5.30) students, 140NOK ($19) family. Guided tours, May 20–June daily at 11am, noon, 12:30pm, and 2:30pm; July–Aug 10 daily at 11am, 12:30pm, and 4:30pm; Aug 11–31 daily at 11am and 2:30pm; Sept daily at 11am and 3pm; Oct–May 19 Sun at 11am and 4pm. Bus: 3 or 4.

Stiftsgården   This buttercup-yellow royal palace near the marketplace was built as a private home by a rich merchant's widow in the 1770s, when Trondheim began to regain its prosperity. It's the largest wooden building in northern Europe, with 144 rooms encompassing approximately 3,600 sq. m (12,000 sq. ft.). The exterior walls were notched together, log cabin style, then sheathed with wooden exterior panels. The unpretentious furnishings represent an amalgam of design styles.

Munkegaten 23. ℂ **73-84-28-80.** Admission 50NOK ($6.65) adults, 25NOK ($3.35) children, 100NOK ($13) family. Guided tours every hour on the hour. Mon–Sat 10am–5pm; Sun noon–5pm. Closed Sept to late June. Bus: 2, 5, 6, 7, or 9.

Trøndelag Folk Museum   One of Norway's major folk-culture museums, this complex is filled with farmhouses and cottages. With churches and town buildings, they represent aspects of everyday life in the region over the past 3 centuries. The proudest possession is Norway's northernmost stave church. The museum is surrounded by a nature park with animals. It also has a ski museum, with a lively introduction to the region's long skiing tradition, and demonstrations of old handicrafts. A restaurant (see "Where to Dine," below) in a 1739 building serves traditional Norwegian dishes.

Sverresborg Allé. ℂ **73-89-01-00.** Admission 75NOK ($10) adults, 25NOK ($3.35) children. June–Aug daily 11am–6pm; off season, Tues–Sat 11am–3pm, Sun noon–4pm. Bus: 8 or 9.

Tyholttårnet   This 120m (400-ft.) concrete tower, built in 1985 to relay radio signals along the coast, is the tallest structure in central Norway. The tower, 5km (3 miles) east of Trondheim, offers a sweeping view over the entire area. There's a revolving restaurant near the top (see "Where to Dine," below). You can go to the viewing gallery even if you don't patronize the restaurant; admission to the tower is free for diners.

Otto Nielsens Vei 4, Blussuvoll. ℂ **73-87-35-00.** Free admission. Mon–Sat 11am–11:30pm; Sun and holidays noon–10pm. Bus: 20 or 60 (ask the driver to tell you when to get off).

ORGANIZED TOURS

From June to August, a 2-hour **bus tour** departs from the marketplace daily at noon. It costs 160NOK ($21) for adults, 75NOK ($10) for children. The highlight is a guided tour of the cathedral, but the price does not include admission.

There are also daily boat trips from May 22 to August 31. They leave Ravnkloa for **Munkholmen Island (Monks Island)** every hour on the hour from 10am to 5pm. In ancient times the island was an execution site. In the 11th century Benedictine monks constructed a monastery, one of the first two in Scandinavia. In 1658 it was turned into a prison fort. You can take a guided tour of the island's historic fortress. Lunch is not included in the fare but is available at Munkholmen. The boat fare is 45NOK ($6) for adults, 25NOK ($3.35) for children. A guided tour of the fortress costs 25NOK ($3.35) for adults, 15NOK

($2) for children. Bookings can be made at the Lilletorget Hotel, Ciccgnons Plass, Lilletorget (© **73-52-05-24**).

EXPLORING NEARBY ISLANDS

You can reach the islands of **Hitra (Ansnes)** and **Frøya (Sistranda)** by fast steamer from Trondheim Monday through Saturday. For more information, ask at the tourist information office in Trondheim.

Hitra is one of Norway's largest islands, with an array of forests, wooded hills, well-stocked lakes, weathered rocks, and small fjords. The island is also known for its large herds of red deer. Other attractions include the **Dolm Church** and **Dolmen town,** a miniature community designed and built by a Dolmoy crofter and fisherman. After you reach Hitra, you might want to visit neighboring Frøya by ferry.

WHERE TO STAY

Many hotels offer special summer prices from mid-June to the end of August. The rest of the year, hotels offer weekend discounts if you stay 2 nights.

Expensive

Clarion Grand Olav Hotel ★★ This six-story hotel is the most stylish in Trondheim. It was designed in 1989 by the architect of the nearby Radisson SAS Royal Garden Hotel, a close competitor. The hotel (which became the Clarion Grand in 1998) is adjacent to a building complex that includes elegant boutiques and Trondheim's largest concert hall. Its modern interior is plush and imaginative; guest rooms are decorated in one of 27 different styles. They have good beds and ample bathrooms, with shower-tub combinations and state-of-the-art plumbing.

Kjøpmannsgaten 48, N-7010 Trondheim. © **73-80-80-80.** Fax 73-80-80-81. www.grandolav.no. 106 units. 1,130NOK–1,900NOK ($150–$253) double; 3,000NOK–6,000NOK ($399–$798) suite. Rates include breakfast. AE, DC, MC, V. Parking 150NOK ($20). Bus: 54. **Amenities:** Restaurant; bar; room service; laundry/dry cleaning. *In room:* A/C, TV, minibar, hair dryer.

Radisson SAS Royal Garden Hotel ★★ This architecturally innovative hotel lies at the northwestern edge of the Old Town, southwest of the train station. Opened in 1984, it has a soaring atrium in the lobby and public rooms that are lavishly furnished and filled with plants. The comfortable guest rooms, all designed as doubles, attract an international business trade and many tour groups in the summer. Mirrored walls and classic appointments characterize the ample rooms, which have double-glazed windows. The marble bathrooms are medium-sized with shower-tub combinations.

Kjøpmannsgaten 73, N-7010 Trondheim. © **800/333-3333** in the U.S., or 73-80-30-00. Fax 73-80-30-50. www.radissonsas.com. 298 units. Mon–Thurs 1,640NOK ($218) double, from 2,500 NOK ($333) suite. Fri–Sun and daily mid-June to Aug 995NOK ($132) double, 995NOK ($132) suite. Children under 15 stay free in parent's room. Rates include buffet breakfast. AE, DC, MC, V. Parking 165NOK ($22). Bus: 54. **Amenities:** 2 restaurants; bar; pool; fitness center; sauna; room service; laundry/dry cleaning. *In room:* TV, minibar, hair dryer.

Moderate

Britannia Hotel ★ This turn-of-the-20th-century lodging is Trondheim's most traditional hotel, with many of its original details intact. The ornate Palm Garden (Palmehave), with its Art Nouveau winter garden, fountain, and piano, captures the grand spirit. The renovated guest rooms have wooden floors. The most tranquil rooms, which front the courtyard, are also the smallest. Most accommodations are medium-sized with excellent beds and tiled bathrooms with shower-tub combinations.

Dronningens Gate 5, N-7001 Trondheim. ℂ **73-53-53-53.** Fax 73-51-29-00. www.britannia.no. 247 units. Mon–Thurs 1,500NOK–1,850NOK ($200–$246) double; Fri–Sun 950NOK ($126) double. Year-round from 3,200NOK ($426) suite. Rates include breakfast. AE, DC, MC, V. Parking 186NOK ($25). Bus: 2, 5, 6, 7, or 9. **Amenities:** 3 restaurants; 3 bars; fitness center; sauna; room service; babysitting; laundry/dry cleaning. *In room:* TV, minibar, hair dryer.

Scandic Hotel Residence
On the market square opposite the Royal Palace, the Hotel Residence, built in 1915 in Jugend (Art Nouveau) style, has recently been renovated. Accommodations are tastefully decorated, and the units in front open onto the marketplace. The generously sized guest rooms have triple-glazed windows and good beds. The big marble bathrooms offer great shelf space, shower-tub combinations, and, in some cases, bidets. Much of the hotel's ground floor is given over to the Café Amsterdam, a trio of rustically decorated rooms reminiscent of a Dutch tavern, with an area for drinking and separate areas for well-prepared platters and snacks.

Munkegaten 26, N-7011 Trondheim. ℂ **800/528-1234** in the U.S., or 73-52-83-80. Fax 73-52-64-60. residence@scandic-hotels.com. 66 units. Sun–Thurs 1,450NOK ($193) double; Fri–Sat 996NOK ($132) double. Rates include breakfast. AE, DC, MC, V. Parking 50NOK ($6.65). Bus: 2, 5, 6, 7, or 9. **Amenities:** Restaurant; bar; laundry/dry cleaning. *In room:* TV, minibar, hair dryer.

Inexpensive
Gildevagen Hotell *Value*
Locals often cite this hotel as offering good value. Built in the late 19th century, it has been renovated many times, most recently in 1994. It's a short walk uphill from the harbor, near the Old Town's famous bridge and the train station. The guest rooms are generally quite large; 33 are reserved for nonsmokers. Beds are good, and rooms come in a variety of sizes, from snug to spacious. Bathrooms are small but come equipped with shower-tub combinations. A big Norwegian "cold table" breakfast is served in an old-fashioned dining room; no other meals are offered.

Søndre Gate 22B, N-7010 Trondheim. ℂ **73-87-01-30.** Fax 73-52-38-98. www.rainbow.hotels.no. 110 units. 1,245NOK ($166) double. AE, DC, MC, V. Parking 60NOK ($8). **Amenities:** Bar; lounge; laundry/dry cleaning. *In room:* TV, minibar, hair dryer.

Singsaker Sommerhotell
This student residence hall is also a choice bargain hotel in summer. It's about a 10-minute walk from the center of Trondheim. The small rooms are cozy, and all have wash basins. A few units have neatly kept private bathrooms. The least expensive rooms are no-frills dormitory-style. The dining room serves good, wholesome breakfasts. In the evening, young people gather around the open fireplace or play billiards or other games.

Rogertsgate 1, N-7016 Trondheim. ℂ **73-89-31-00.** Fax 73-89-32-00. http://sommerhotell.singsaker.no. 106 units, 16 with bathroom. 560NOK ($74) double without bathroom; 670NOK ($89) double with bathroom; 765NOK ($102) triple without bathroom; 870NOK ($116) triple with bathroom; 165NOK ($22) per person in dormitory room. Rates include breakfast. AE, DC, MC, V. Closed Aug 20–May 15. Bus: 63. **Amenities:** Lounge.

Trondheim Hotell
This hotel, near the market square, offers medium-size guest rooms with upholstered classic bentwood furniture. Many have an extra foldaway bed. Some rooms are suitable for persons with disabilities, and others are reserved for nonsmokers. The beds are good, and the bathrooms, though small, are equipped with shower-tub combinations. Constructed in 1913, it was renovated and expanded in 1990. The nearby Monte Cristo Disco admits hotel guests free.

Kongensgate 15, N-7013 Trondheim. ℂ **73-50-50-50.** Fax 73-51-60-58. www.rainbow-hotels.no. 131 units. 1,245NOK ($166) double. Rates include breakfast. AE, DC, MC, V. Parking 113NOK ($15). Bus from airport stops here. **Amenities:** Restaurant; bar; lounge; laundry. *In room:* TV, minibar, hair dryer.

WHERE TO DINE

Try a local specialty, *vafler med øst* (**waffle and cheese**), sold at most cafeterias and restaurants.

Expensive

Bryggen 🅚 NORWEGIAN/FRENCH   One of the most atmospheric restaurants in Trondheim is in a 1749 warehouse with a heavily trussed brick interior. It's on the verdant banks of the Nidelven River, a few steps from the town's oldest bridge, the Gamle Bybro. The restaurant is a 10-minute walk from the town center. The menu varies with the season. It might include fish-and-shellfish soup, suprême of Norwegian duck, medallions of reindeer in juniper-berry cream sauce, or poached fresh fish of the day. You'll find the staff devoted and professional, and justifiably proud of the interesting cuisine. There's an extensive wine list and an impressive selection of cognac and cigars.

Øvre Bakklandet 66. (℃ **73-52-02-30.** Reservations recommended. Main courses 240NOK–290NOK ($32–$39); 3-course fixed-price menu 475NOK ($63); 5-course fixed-price dinner 650NOK ($86). AE, DC, MC, V. Mon–Sat 6–11pm. Bus: 1, 5, or 9.

Jonathan's 🅚 NORWEGIAN/FRENCH   One of the best hotel restaurants in town, Jonathan's is designed like a Mediterranean wine cellar, with antiques, a big open fireplace, and waiters colorfully dressed as troubadours. The beautifully prepared food relies on high-quality ingredients. Dinner might include canapés of shrimp, smoked salmon, and local caviar, followed by grilled salmon garnished with shellfish and fresh vegetables, or a grilled steak—perhaps a veal schnitzel.

In the Brittania Hotel, Dronningens Gate 5. (℃ **73-53-53-53.** Reservations required. Main courses 210NOK–245NOK ($28–$33). AE, DC, MC, V. Daily 5–11pm. Bus: 2, 5, 6, 7, or 9.

Monte Cristo 🅚 NORWEGIAN/INTERNATIONAL   The region's busiest and most popular supper club, the Monte Cristo lies within the thick walls of an 1832 private house. The club serves simple but delightfully flavorful, expertly prepared food, not the usual dull nightclub fare. It also books the leading traditional dance bands of Norway and Sweden. Menu choices include filet of monkfish in sour-cream sauce, barbecued spareribs in spicy Cajun sauce, and filet of Norwegian lamb. The dance club upstairs attracts a younger group for live music Tuesday through Saturday from 7pm to 3am. Entrance is free for diners, 50NOK ($6.65) for others.

Prinsensgaten 38. (℃ **73-52-18-80.** Reservations recommended on weekends. Main courses 175NOK–250NOK ($23–$33). AE, DC, MC, V. Tues–Sat 7–11:30pm. Bus: 2, 5, 6, 7, or 9.

Moderate

Egon Tårnet AMERICAN   In the early 1980s, the skyline about 3km (2 miles) east of Trondheim was altered with the addition of a soaring television transmittal tower, at the top of which an elegant and exclusive restaurant served glamorous, high-ticket meals. About a decade later, the owners downsized the gourmet aspects of the restaurant, refocusing the high-altitude dining venue into a family-friendly burger, pizza, and steak joint with a menu that's equivalent to what you might find in a Denny's or IHOP restaurant in America's heartland. The result incorporates all the engineering marvels of the original upscale restaurant (a revolving deck that takes about an hour for a full circle, and big-windowed views that sweep out in miles in all directions) with a burger and fries menu that's much more affordable than the setting and the circumstances would suggest. Expect a menu that features club sandwiches and BLTs, about a dozen kinds of pizza, stuffed baked potatoes, meal-sized salads, Tex-Mex tacos and faji-tas, blackened chicken, ribs, and grilled steaks. An elevator will carry you, with-out charge, from the parking lot to the restaurant's upper levels.

Otto Nielsensveien 4. Tel. **73-87-35-00.** Reservations recommended on Fri–Sat nights. Pizzas, burgers, salads, and platters 85NOK–209NOK ($11–$28). AE, DC, MC, V. Mon–Thurs 11am–11pm; Fri–Sat 11am–11:30pm; Sun noon–10pm. Bus: 20 or 60.

Havfruen ⊕ SEAFOOD   The better of the two fish restaurants in Trond-heim, Havfruen Fiskerestaurant is in a memorable setting. The 1680 warehouse is near the Nidelven River and the town's most famous bridge, so naturally it's decorated in a nautical style. The staff seems to enjoy evaluating and offering advice about the daily harvest of fish. The menu changes each season, based on local fish migration patterns. Staples include fried and peppered sea wolf served with ragout of mushrooms, poached halibut (a summer favorite) in crabmeat sauce, and grilled filet of salmon in dill-flavored cream sauce.

Kjøpmannsgaten 7. ⓒ **73-87-40-70.** Reservations required. Main courses 235NOK–285NOK ($31–$38). AE, DC, MC, V. Mon–Fri 5pm–midnight; Sat 6pm–midnight; Sun 2–9pm. Bus: 2, 5, 6, 7, or 9.

Inexpensive
Tavern På Sverresborg ⊕ *Finds* NORWEGIAN   No restaurant in town offers more authentic Norwegian cuisine than this historic eatery, 5km (3 miles) south of Trondheim's commercial center. Built as a private merchant's house in 1739, and later transformed into a clapboard-sided tavern, it's one of the few wooden buildings of its age in this area. Cramped and cozy, it's the town's most vivid reminder of the past, with wide-plank flooring and antique rustic acces-sories. There's an emphasis on 18th- and 19th-century recipes. Try *blandet speke-mat,* served with *flatbrød;* it consists of thinly sliced smoked ham, diced meat, slices of salami, smoked mutton, and garnishes of lettuce and tomato. Other comparably priced items include *rømmergrøt* (sour-cream porridge), *finnbiff* (reindeer meat), omelets, herring, and meatballs.

Sverresborg Allé, at Trøndelag Folk Museum. ⓒ **78-87-80-70.** Reservations recommended. Snack-style main dishes 80NOK ($11); main courses 60NOK–130NOK ($8–$17). MC, V. Mon–Fri 4–10pm; Sat 2–10pm; Sun 2–9pm. Bus: 8 or 9.

TRONDHEIM AFTER DARK
Monte Cristo (see "Where to Dine," above) has a dance club.

Frekken   Set in the heart of Trondheim, and catering to a crowd of drinkers and dancers ages 20 to 40, this is one of the more visible dance clubs in town. Separate areas are devoted to a pub, a dance floor, and a piano bar. It's open daily from 9:30pm to around 3am, charging an entrance of 40NOK ($5.30) on Fri-day and Saturday nights only. Dronningensgaten 12. ⓒ **73-52-24-42.**

FROM TRONDHEIM TO BODØ
On the long trek north on E6, the first town of any size is **Steinkjer.** It's a mil-itary base for "boot campers." Another 351km (218 miles) along is **Mo i Rana,** whose poetic name ("Mo on the Ranafjord") sounds more romantic than it in fact is. It's a center for iron and steel production. Thirty kilometers (19 miles) north of the town lies **Svartisen (Black Ice),** a glacier.

Eighty kilometers (50 miles) north of Mo i Rana, at the Arctic Circle, you'll come to the **Polarsirkelsenteret,** on E6. It offers a multi-screen show depicting the highlights of Norway. Many people send cards and letters from here with a special postmark from the Arctic Circle. There's also a cafeteria and gift shop on the grounds. The center is at N-8242 Polarsirkelen (ⓒ **75-12-96-96**). It's open in May and June, daily from 9am to 6pm; from July to September, daily from 8am to 10pm. Admission is 50NOK ($6.65).

Continue north to Fauske, and then follow Route 80 west along the Skjerstadfjord. Depending on weather conditions, you should reach Bodø in under an hour.

BODØ ⟨★⟩
750km (466 miles) N of Trondheim, 1,431km (889 miles) N of Bergen, 1,306km (811 miles) N of Oslo

This seaport, the terminus of the Nordland railway, lies just north of the Arctic Circle. Visitors flock to Bodø, the capital of Nordland, for a glimpse of the midnight sun, which shines brightly from June 1 to July 13. But don't expect a clear view of it—many nights are rainy or hazy. From December 19 to January 9, Bodø gets no sunlight at all.

From Bodø you can take excursions in many directions to glaciers and bird islands; perhaps the most important are to the Lofoten Islands (see below).

ESSENTIALS
GETTING THERE   If you're not driving or traveling by coastal steamer, you can reach Bodø from major cities throughout Norway, usually with connections through either Trondheim or Oslo, on **SAS** (✆ 75-54-47-00). The airport lies less than 1km (1 mile) southwest of the city center, and is accessed by a bus (it's marked CENTRUMS BUSSEN) that departs at 20-minute intervals every Monday through Friday. Passengers arriving on a Saturday or Sunday must hire one of the many taxis waiting at the arrivals gate. Bodø is at the end of the Nordland rail line.

Two **trains** a day leave Trondheim for Bodø. The trip takes 10 hours, 20 minutes.

For **bus** information, contact **Saltens Bilruter** in Bodø (✆ 75-54-80-20). Fauske is a transportation hub along the E6 highway to the north and Route 80 west to Bodø. From Fauske there are two buses a day to Bodø. The trip takes an hour and 10 minutes. If you take the train from Stockholm to Narvik (north of Bodø), you can make bus connections to Fauske and Bodø, a total trip of 5 hours.

VISITOR INFORMATION   The **tourist office,** called **Destination Bodø,** is at Sjøgaten 3, N-8000 Bodø (✆ 75-54-80-00), in the town center. It's open from mid-June to mid-August, daily from 9am to 8:30pm; from mid-August to mid-June, Monday through Friday from 9am to 4pm.

SEEING THE SIGHTS
Bodin Kirke   Dating from 1240, this church is 3.2km (2 miles) east of the town center. It has a baroque altarpiece. This is the most famous church in the district, and one of the few in the north from the Middle Ages. Local residents are proud of it, despite its simplicity.

Gamle Riksvei 68. ✆ 75-54-80-00. Free admission. June–Aug Mon–Fri 10am–2:30pm. Closed Sept–May. Bus: 23 from the station.

Bodø Domkirke   Completed in 1956, this is the most notable building constructed since German bombers leveled Bodø on May 27, 1940. It features tufted rugs depicting ecclesiastical themes, wall hangings, and a stained-glass window that captures the northern lights. A memorial outside honors those killed in the war with the inscription NO ONE MENTIONED, NO ONE FORGOTTEN. There's also an outstanding spire that stands separate from the main building.

Torv Gate 12. ✆ 75-52-17-50. Free admission. May–Sept daily 9am–2:30pm. Closed Oct–Apr.

Nordlandmuseet (Nordland Museum)   In the town center, the main building of this museum is one of the oldest structures in Bodø. Here you'll find, among other exhibits, artifacts recalling the saga of local fishermen and artifacts from the Lapp culture. There's also a "dry" aquarium, along with silver treasure dating from the Viking era.

Prinsengate 116. ⓒ 75-52-16-40. Admission 30NOK ($4), 15NOK ($2) for children under 15. Mon–Fri 9am–3pm; Sat 10am–3pm; Sun noon–3pm.

ACTIVE SPORTS

If you'd like to go horseback riding under the midnight sun, **Bodø Hestecenter,** Soloya Gård (ⓒ 75-51-41-48), about 15km (9 miles) southwest of Bodø, rents horses. Buses go there Monday through Friday morning and evening and Saturday morning. For more information, ask at the Bodø Tourist Office. The cost is 100NOK ($13) for a 45-minute ride.

Svømmehallen, Sivert Nielsens Gate 63 (ⓒ 75-55-75-20), is Bodø's largest and busiest indoor swimming pool. It's open from September to May, Tuesday through Friday from 10am to 8pm, Saturday and Sunday from 10am to 3pm; from June to August, Monday, Wednesday, and Friday from 10am to 2pm, Tuesday and Thursday from 3 to 8pm (closed Sat and Sun). Admission is 40NOK ($5.30) for adults, 20NOK ($2.65) for children under 18.

EXPLORING A SPECTACULAR LANDSCAPE

THE MAELSTROM   From Bodø, you can take a bus to the mighty maelstrom, the **Saltstraumen Eddy** ☆, 32km (20 miles) south of the city. The variation between high- and low-tide levels pushes immense volumes of water through narrow fjords, creating huge whirlpools known as "kettles." When the eddies and the surrounding land vibrate, they produce an odd yelling sound. Saltstraumen is nearly 3.2km (2 miles) long and only about 150m (500 ft.) wide, with billions of gallons of water pressing through at speeds of about 10 knots. It's best to go in the morning when it's most dramatic. Buses from Bodø run five times a day Monday through Saturday, twice on Sunday. The cost is 56NOK ($7.45) for adults round-trip, half price for children. A round-trip taxi excursion costs 500NOK ($67) for two passengers.

VISITING A GLACIER   One of Norway's major tourist attractions, **Svartisen** ☆☆ is second in size in the country only to the Jostedal Glacier. This ice plateau 99m (330 ft.) above sea level covers 240 sq. km (150 sq. miles) of high mountains and narrow fjords. About 160km (100 miles) from Bodø, the glacier can be reached by car, although a boat crossing over the Svartisenfjord is more exciting. Tours to the glacier on the Helgeland Express, a combination bus-and-ferry excursion, are offered from Bodø several times in the summer (usually every 2nd Sat in July and Aug). The cost is 390NOK ($52) for adults, 200NOK ($27) for children under 16. The tours leave Bodø at 1pm and return around 8pm. You can go ashore to examine the Engaglacier and see the nearby visitor center (ⓒ 75-75-00-11). The local tourist office, or the local tour operator **Nordtrafikk** (ⓒ 75-72-12-00), can provide more information and make reservations. Depending on ice conditions, the visitor center may be able to arrange boat transportation across a narrow but icy channel so you can have a closer look at the ice floe.

WHERE TO STAY

The Bodø Tourist Office (see above) can help you book a room in a hotel.

Expensive

Radisson SAS Royal Hotel 🐱🐱   By far the finest hotel in the area, this glistening structure is an inviting oasis. A complete renovation of the exterior, the public rooms, and all guest rooms was completed in 2000. The guest rooms are furnished in sleek contemporary style. They're good-sized and decorated in a number of motifs, including Japanese, Nordic, Chinese, and British. Rooms have medium-size bathrooms equipped with shower-tub combinations. The Royal is on the main street at the harbor.

Storgaten 2, N-8000 Bodø. 🕿 **800/333-3333** in the U.S., or 75-52-41-00. Fax 75-52-74-93. 190 units. June–Aug 855NOK ($114) double, 1,440NOK ($192) suite; Sept–May 1,500NOK ($200) double, 2,250NOK ($299) suite. Rates include breakfast. AE, DC, MC, V. Free parking. **Amenities:** 2 restaurants; 2 bars; lounge; fitness center; sauna; babysitting; laundry/dry cleaning. *In room:* TV, minibar, hair dryer.

Rica Hotel 🐱   Located at the harbor and offering a view of Vestfjorden, this is one of Bodø's best hotels, built in 1986 and enlarged in 1990. Most of the somberly furnished rooms have large writing desks. Only moderate in size, rooms are comfortable and well maintained, with good beds and rather small bathrooms equipped with shower-tub combinations. The hotel has two popular restaurants (see "Where to Dine," below).

Sjøgata 23, N-8001 Bodø. 🕿 75-54-70-00. Fax 75-54-70-55. hotel@diplomat-hotel.no. 103 units. Mid-June to Aug 5 790NOK ($105) double; Aug 6 to mid-June 1,440NOK ($192) double. Year-round 1,440NOK ($192) suite. Rates include breakfast. AE, DC, MC, V. Free parking. **Amenities:** 2 restaurants; bar; fitness center; sauna; room service; laundry/dry cleaning. *In room:* TV, minibar, hair dryer.

Moderate

Bodø Hotell *Value*   Opened in 1987, this hotel quickly became known for its good value. In the town center 2½ blocks from the harbor, it has a helpful staff and modern rooms. Bathrooms are small, but they are kept sparkling clean and equipped with shower units. The hotel also offers rooms for nonsmokers and persons with disabilities.

Professor Schyttesgate 5, N-8001 Bodø. 🕿 75-52-69-00. Fax 75-52-57-78. www.bodohotell.no. 31 units. June 20–Aug 15 and Fri–Sat year-round 600NOK ($80) double; rest of year Sun–Thurs 850NOK ($113) double. Year-round 750NOK–1,000NOK ($100–$133) suite. Rates include breakfast. AE, DC, MC, V. Closed Dec 20–Jan 3. Free parking. **Amenities:** Bar; lounge; laundry/dry cleaning. *In room:* TV, hair dryer.

Golden Tulip Rainbow Nordlys Hotel   The newest hotel in town rises six floors, behind a pale brick exterior, with big windows overlooking Bodø's harbor. Inside, there's a polite and hardworking staff, and a collection of valuable contemporary art, both in the lobby and within the bedrooms, some of which is for sale through the frequent art exhibitions. Guest rooms have color schemes of yellow with wooden floors, original artwork on the walls, and contemporary styling, plus tiled bathrooms with tub-shower combinations.

Moloveien 14, N8001 Bodø. 🕿 75-53-19-00. Fax 75-53-19-99. www.rainbow-hotels.no. 150 units. Mon–Thurs 850NOK–1,415NOK ($113–$188) double; Fri–Sun 850NOK ($113) double. AE, DC, MC, V. **Amenities:** Restaurant Egon, specializing in robust American and Norwegian fare; small gym; babysitting. *In room:* TV, minibar.

Inexpensive

Norrøna   The Norrøna is run by the nearby Radisson SAS Royal Hotel, which uses it primarily as a bed-and-breakfast. Its prime location is one of its chief advantages. The functional modern building stands in the center of Bodø. The simply furnished guest rooms, though small and plain, are comfortable. Each unit contains a well-kept bathroom with shower-tub combinations. Guests enjoy the same privileges—a sauna, solarium, and fitness center—as patrons of the more expensive Radisson SAS Royal Hotel. The hotel operates a British-style pub, Piccadilly.

Storgaten 4, N-8000 Bodø. © **75-52-41-18.** Fax 75-52-33-88. 99 units. 600NOK–750NOK ($80–$100) double. Rates include breakfast. AE, DC, MC, V. No parking. **Amenities:** Bar; lounge; sauna; laundry/dry cleaning. *In room:* TV.

WHERE TO DINE

China Garden CANTONESE   This well-managed restaurant, run by emigrants from Hong Kong, is one of the only Asian restaurants in town. It serves sophisticated, flavorful Chinese food. The red-and-gold restaurant, behind large signs with Chinese calligraphic symbols, is quite popular. Three favorite dishes are sweet-and-sour prawns, sweet-and-sour pork, and sweet-and-sour pork served with black beans and garlic. Although it doesn't rank with Oslo's better Chinese restaurants, China Garden is a welcome change of pace this far north.

Storgata 60. © **75-52-71-25.** Reservations recommended. Main courses 92NOK–139NOK ($12–$18). AE, MC, V. Sun–Thurs 2–10:45pm; Fri–Sat 2pm–midnight.

Holmer ⭐ *(Finds* NORTH NORDIC/CONTINENTAL   When Bodø's newest and best-recommended restaurant opened in December 2001, it was named after the town's first mayor, a 19th-century patriarch who did much to establish Bodø as an important settlement. Its outside is a conventional-looking red brick structure; inside, the coziness factor is radically elevated, thanks to the paneling and architectural remnants that were salvaged, then reinstalled, from a century-old farmhouse that, before it was demolished, lay about 8km (5 miles) away. Within this cozy venue with a color scheme of burnt lemon and brown, you can enjoy the most thoughtfully prepared and sophisticated cuisine in town. The best examples include grilled scallops served with coconut cream sauce and baked tomatoes; a cream-based version of soup made completely with local fish and shellfish; duck breast with an herb-based creamy risotto and a purée of celery; and filet of venison with a "wilderness" sauce made by boiling the venison bones into a thick reduction flavored with wild herbs and berries. Crème brûlée, or perhaps a parfait made from fresh Arctic berries, make worthy desserts.

Dronningensgate 26. © **75-52-50-50.** Reservations recommended. Main courses 190NOK–245NOK ($25–$33). AE, DC, MC, V. Mon–Fri 6–11pm; Sat 5–11pm.

Rica Hotel Restaurants NORWEGIAN/INTERNATIONAL   Although the Rica is best known for its well-maintained accommodations, it also runs two restaurants (the Spisestuen and Blix) that serve some of the best food in town. Usually the Spisestuen serves lunch and the Blix dinner, but the arrangement changes depending on the number of bus tours and cruise ships expected. Wherever the meal is served, you're likely to be joined by local residents, especially at lunch. Choices include lasagna, steak, filets of reindeer, fish soup, and fresh local fish. You don't get palate-tantalizing excitement here, but the solid, reliable fare uses some of the freshest ingredients that reach the far north.

Sjøgata 23. © **75-54-70-00.** Main courses 209NOK–230NOK ($28–$31); daily lunch plates 130NOK ($17); lunch buffet 200NOK ($27). AE, DC, MC, V. Daily 7–11pm.

LOFOTEN ISLANDS ⭐⭐⭐
280km (174 miles) N of Bodø, 1,426km (886 miles) NE of Bergen, 1,250km (777 miles) N of Oslo

The island kingdom of Lofoten, one of the most beautiful regions of Norway, lies 198km (123 miles) north of the Arctic Circle. Its population of 35,000 spreads over large and small islands. Many visitors come just to fish, but the area offers abundant bird life and flora. The midnight sun shines from mid-May to the end of July.

The Lofoten Islands stretch from Vågan in the east to Røst and Skomvær in the southwest. The steep Lofoten mountain peaks—often called the Lofot-wall—shelter farmland and deep fjords from the elements.

The Gulf Stream contributes to the seasonal Lofoten fishing, *Lofotfisket.* Beyond Lofoten, and especially in the Vestfjord, Arctic Sea codfish spawn; huge harvesting operations are carried out between January and April.

The first inhabitants of the Lofoten Islands were nomads who hunted and fished, but excavations show that agriculture existed here at least 4,000 years ago. The Vikings pursued farming, fishing, and trading; examples of Viking housing sites can be seen on Vestbågøya, where more than 1,000 burial mounds have been found.

Harsh treatment of local residents by the Nazis during World War II played a major part in the creation of the famous Norwegian resistance movement. Allied forces that landed here to harass the German iron-ore boats sailing from Narvik withdrew in June 1940. They evacuated as many Lofoten residents as they could to Scotland for the duration of the war.

Today the Lofotens have modern towns with shops, hotels, restaurants, and public transportation.

ESSENTIALS
Svolvær is the largest town on the archipelago's largest island.

GETTING THERE   From Bodø, drive east on Route 80 to Fauske. Take E6 north to Ulvsvåg, and head southwest on Route 81 toward the town of Skutvik. From Skutvik, take the 2-hour ferry to Svolvær. For ferry information and reservations, contact **Ofotens og Vesterålens Dampskibsselskab A/S,** Box 375, N-8451 Stokmarknes (📞 **76-96-76-00**).

You can fly to Svolvær on **Widerøe Airline,** which has seven flights a day from Bodø. For information, call 📞 **75-51-35-00** in Bodø or **81-00-12-00** for reservations.

You can also reach the Lofotens by using a combination of rail, bus, and ferry. Many visitors take a train to Bodø, and then transfer to a bus that crosses from Bodø to Svolvær on a ferry. Most bus departures from Bodø are timed to coincide with the arrival of trains from Oslo, Bergen, and other points. Buses also take passengers from elsewhere in Norway to Ulvsvåg, then on to Skutvik, where you can board a ferry to Svolvær. For information on train-bus-ferry connections, contact **Destination Bodø Office** (📞 **75-54-80-00**).

The coastal steamer (see "By Coastal Steamer," earlier in this chapter) calls at Stamsund and Svolvær. The steamer departs from Bodø at 3pm daily.

VISITOR INFORMATION   Contact **Destination Lofoten,** Box 210, N-8301 Svolvær (📞 **76-07-30-00**), near the ferry docks in a big red building. It's open from July to mid-August, daily from 9am to 9:30pm; from mid-June to June 30 and from mid-August to August 31, daily from 9am to 8pm; from September to mid-June, Monday through Friday from 8am to 4pm.

GETTING AROUND   At the tourist office at Svolvær you can pick up a free pamphlet, "Lofoten Info-Guide," with information about all ferries and buses throughout the archipelago. All inhabited islands are linked by ferry, and buses service the four major islands, including Svolvær.

SEEING THE SIGHTS
Outdoor activities include mountain climbing, diving, canoeing, rambling through the countryside, bird-watching (see "Røst & Vaerøy: World-Class Bird-Watching," below), whale-watching, sailing, riding, downhill and cross-country skiing, and ice fishing.

There are handicraft shops at Svolvær, Leknes, Sørvågen, and Vaerøy.

You can also find examples of a special old-fashioned method of knitting—needle binding, which dates to Viking times. The **Glass Cabin** at Vikten, near Napp, is northern Norway's only such studio. It's open to the public and offers products of top quality and original design.

Many artists visit the islands, and there are galleries at Svolvær, Oersnes, Stamsund, and Leknes. Local and international artists are represented. The North Norway Artists' Center is in Svolvær.

The fishing village of **Nusfjord** has been cited by UNESCO for its well-preserved historic buildings, especially traditional *rorbuer* (fishing cottages).

Lofoten Museum   The regional museum depicts past life in the islands. Excavations are under way at the site of an old trading post, Vagar, Europe's northernmost town in the Middle Ages. The museum is on the outskirts of Kabelvåg, 5km (3 miles) from Svolvær.

Kabelvåg. (℃ **76-06-97-90.** Admission 45NOK ($6) adults, 15NOK ($2) children. June 1–14 and Aug 16–31 daily 9am–6pm; June 15–Aug 15 daily 10am–10pm; Sept–May Mon–Fri 9am–3pm.

Skaftnes Section   Skaftnes is a small fishing community where visitors can explore the main house and a boathouse that date from the 1860s. Other buildings, including a blacksmith shop, re-create an earlier period when local people relied almost entirely on the sea for their livelihood. This village is at Sennesvik, on the main road (Rte. 837) 8km (5 miles) from Leknes and 16km (10 miles) from Stamsund. Skaftnes is now operated by the Vestvågøy Museum (see below).

Sennesvik. (℃ **76-08-00-43.** Admission 35NOK ($4.65) adults, 20NOK ($2.65) children. June–Aug Tues–Fri 11am–6pm; Sept–May by appointment only.

Vestvågøy Museum   This museum has exhibits depicting the lifestyle of the typical Lofoten fisherman-farmer. It's on the main road at Fygle, 1.5km (1 mile) from Leknes and 15km (9 miles) from Stamsund.

Fygleveien 109. (℃ **76-08-00-43.** Admission 35NOK ($4.65) adults, 20NOK ($2.65) children. Mon–Fri 10am–4pm. Closed Sept–May.

RØST & VAERØY: WORLD-CLASS BIRD-WATCHING
Mountains speckled with birds range from Andøy in the north all the way to the southern tip of Lofoten. Many different types of seabird can be seen during nesting season. The most famous nesting cliffs are at Røst and Vaerøy, remote islands that can be reached by steamer, plane, or helicopter.

On the flat island of **Røstlandet,** the main attraction is the bird sanctuary, made up of approximately 1,000 little offshore islands. The highly prized eider duck is found here. Locals provide small nesting shelters for the ducks and collect eiderdown after the ducklings hatch. Cormorants and sea gulls nest on the steep cliffs. Puffins nest at the end of narrow tunnels in the grassy hills, and auks and sea eagles nest high up on ledges.

Vaerøy's **Mount Mostadfjell** is the nesting place for more than 1.5 million seabirds, including sea eagles, auks, puffins, guillemots, kittiwakes, cormorants, and others that breed from May to August.

North Vaerøy Church, with its onion-shaped dome, was brought here from Vagån in 1799. The altarpiece, from around 1400, is a late medieval English alabaster relief. It depicts the Annunciation, the Three Magi, the Resurrection, and the Ascension.

For information about these islands, contact Destination Lofoten or the ferry company, **Ofotens og Verterålens Dampskibsselskab A/S,** Box 375, N-8451 Stokmarknes (€ **76-96-76-00**).

WHERE TO STAY & DINE

Destination Lofoten (see "Visitor Information," above) publishes an accommodations guide to the islands.

In addition to hotels, guesthouses, and campsites, the Lofoten Islands offer lodging in old traditional fishing cottages known as *rorbuer.* The larger (often two stories), usually more modern version is a *sjøhus* (sea house). The traditional *rorbu* was built on the edge of the water, often on piles, with room for 10 bunks, a kitchen, and an entrance hall used as a work and storage room. Many *rorbuer* today are still simple and unpretentious, but some have electricity, a woodstove, a kitchenette with a sink, and running water. Others have been outfitted with separate bedrooms, private showers, and toilets. **Backroads** (€ **800/462-2848**) is the best and most convenient outfitter; or try Destination Lofoten.

In Stamsund
Stamsund Lofoten   This hotel in the heart of town offers a view of the harbor. The small guest rooms are simply furnished but have good beds, and many have well-kept bathrooms equipped with shower-tub combinations. On the premises are a bar and a restaurant that serves standard Norwegian fare.

N-8340 Stamsund. € **76-08-93-00.** Fax 76-08-97-26. www.stamsund.no. 28 units. 760NOK–994NOK ($101–$132) double. Rates include breakfast. AE, DC, MC, V. Free parking. **Amenities:** Bar; lounge. *In room:* TV, minibar, hair dryer.

In Svolvær
Royal Hotel Lofoten   About half of the well-furnished rooms at this 1975 hotel overlook the sea. It's in the town center, near the express steamer quay. The look is rather functional, but maintenance is good. The bathrooms, though cramped, are sparkling clean and equipped with shower-tub combinations. On the premises are a bar and a lively dance club. Restaurant Lofoten specializes in fish and steak.

Sivert Nelsen Gate, N-8300 Svolvær. € **76-07-12-00.** Fax 76-07-08-50. 48 units. 1,095NOK ($146) double; 1,400NOK ($186) suite. Rates include breakfast. AE, DC, MC, V. Free parking. **Amenities:** Restaurant; bar; lounge. *In room:* TV, minibar.

Vestfjord Hotel   This building was a former warehouse that stored marine supplies and fish. After extensive remodeling in the late 1980s, it reopened as this well-managed hotel. The guest rooms are functional but comfortable, many of them overlooking the sea. The bathrooms are tiny, with shower-tub combinations. Facilities include a lobby bar and a pleasant restaurant that specializes in fish and steaks. It serves sustaining fare—nothing remarkable.

Box 386, N-8301 Svolvær. € **76-07-08-70.** Fax 76-07-08-54. 63 units. June–Aug 1 and Sun–Thurs year-round 1,295NOK ($172) double; Aug 2–May Fri–Sat 700NOK ($93) double. Year-round 1,495NOK ($199) suite. Rates include breakfast. AE, DC, MC, V. Free parking. **Amenities:** Restaurant; bar; room service; laundry/dry cleaning. *In room:* TV, minibar, hair dryer.

NARVIK

301km (187 miles) NE of Bodø, 1,635km (1,022 miles) NE of Bergen, 1,480km (919 miles) N of Oslo

This ice-free seaport on the Ofotfjord is in Nordland *fylke* (country), 400km (250 miles) north of the Arctic Circle. Narvik, founded in 1903 when the Ofoten (not to be confused with "Lofoten") railway line was completed, boasts Europe's most modern shipping harbor for iron ore. It's the northernmost electrified railway line in the world. It covers a magnificent scenic route, through precipitous mountain terrain and tunnels, over ridges, and across tall stone embankments.

Only 11km (6½ miles) from Narvik, Straumsnes station is the last permanent habitation as you go east. The last Norwegian station, Bjørnfjell, is well above the timberline and about 3 hours from Kiruna, Sweden, some 140km (87 miles) north of the Arctic Circle. You can catch a train at Kiruna to Stockholm. A road connects Kiruna and Narvik.

ESSENTIALS

GETTING THERE   From the Lofoten Islands, take the ferry to Skutvik. Take Route 81 northeast to the junction with E6, and then take E6 north to Bognes. Cross the Tysfjord by ferry. Continue north on E6 to Narvik.

The **train** from Stockholm to Narvik takes 21 to 24 hours. There are also two buses a day from Fauske/Bodø (5 hr.).

VISITOR INFORMATION   The **Narvik Tourist Office** is at Konensgate 66 (© 76-94-33-09). It's open daily from 9am to 4pm.

SEEING THE SIGHTS

To get a good look at Narvik, take the **Gondolbanen cable car** (© 76-96-04-94), whose departure point is directly behind the Norlandia Narvik Hotel, a 10-minute walk from the town center. The car operates from March to October, and the round-trip fare is 85NOK ($11) for adults, 50NOK ($6.65) for children 6 to 15 (free for 5 and under). In just 13 minutes it takes you to an altitude of 630m (2,100 ft.), at the top of Fagernesfjell. You can see the impressive panorama of the town and its surroundings. From mid-February to mid-June, and in August and September, the cable operates Monday through Friday from 1 to 9pm and every Saturday and Sunday from 10am to 5pm. From mid-June to the end of July it operates daily from noon to 1am. It is closed otherwise.

The **midnight sun** shines from May 27 to July 19.

Nordland Røde Kors Krigsminnemuseum (War Museum)   Near
Torghallen in the town center, this is one of the most important sights in town. Most of Narvik was destroyed by the Germans, who occupied it until the end of the World War II. Following Hitler's attack on Denmark and Norway, a bitter battle for Narvik and its iron ore raged for 2 months. German forces fought troops from France, Poland, and Norway, and a considerable British flotilla at sea. Events of that era are depicted, as well as experiences of the civilian population and foreign POWs.

© 76-94-44-26. Admission 40NOK ($5.30) adults, 10NOK ($1.35) children. Mar–June 7 daily 11am–3pm; June 8–Aug 20 Mon–Sat 10am–10pm, Sun 11am–5pm; Aug 21–Sept daily 11am–3pm. Closed Oct–Feb.

Ofoten Museum   In the town center, this museum preserves the cultural history of the area. The Ofoten Museum has artifacts tracing the oldest human settlements in the area. They go back to the Stone Age, which is revealed in rock carvings. Other exhibits (including a scraper for animal skins and a

flint-and-tinder box) show how the people lived and worked in the area. Most of the display is from the 20th century, beginning when the rail line was under construction.

Administrasjonsveien 3. (℃ **76-96-00-50.** Admission 30NOK ($4) adults, 5NOK (65¢) children. July Mon–Fri 11am–3:30pm, Sat–Sun noon–3pm; Aug–June Mon–Fri 10am–4pm.

WHERE TO STAY

These hotels are among the few buildings in Narvik that survived World War II.

Moderate

Grand Royal 🐾 This hotel is the largest and best equipped in Narvik. It opens onto the main street in the town center, between the train station and the harbor. Built in the 1920s, it has seen many enlargements since. It's called the Grand Royal because the late King Olav was a frequent visitor. Portraits of him adorn some of the public rooms. The comfortable, good-sized rooms are traditionally furnished and among the most tasteful in the area. Beds are good, and the well-equipped, medium-sized bathrooms with shower-tub combinations are the best in town. The finest restaurant in town is also here (see "Where to Dine," below). The recently redecorated lobby bar is one of the best cocktail bars in northern Norway.

Kongensgate 64, N-8501 Narvik. (℃ **76-97-70-00.** Fax 76-97-70-07. 119 units. Sun–Thurs 1,000NOK–1,390NOK ($133–$185) double. Year-round 1,600NOK ($213) suite. Rates include breakfast. AF, DC, MC, V. Free parking. Bus: 14, 15, 16, or 17. **Amenities:** 2 restaurants; 2 bars; sauna; babysitting; laundry/dry cleaning. *In room:* TV, minibar, hair dryer, safe.

Inexpensive

Nordst Jernen Hotel In the town center, south of the bus station, the Nordst Jernen has long been known as one of the best hotel values in the area. Guest rooms are decorated in pastels to offset the winter gloom. Rooms vary in size, but all are comfortable and well maintained. Bathrooms are small but equipped with shower-tub combinations.

Kongensgate 26, N-8500 Narvik. (℃ **76-94-41-20.** Fax 76-94-75-06. 24 units. 750NOK ($100) double. Rates include breakfast. DC, MC, V. Free parking. Bus: 14 or 16. **Amenities:** Lounge. *In room:* TV, hair dryer, safe.

WHERE TO DINE

Royal Blue 🐾 NORWEGIAN The best restaurant in the region is decorated appropriately in strong royal blues. It's the preferred choice of visiting dignitaries, including the king. Service is polite and the food delectable. Specialties include thinly sliced, sauna-smoked ham with asparagus, cured salmon with crème fraîche, reindeer curry with Brussels sprouts and apricots, and large beefsteaks. It's on the lobby level of the Grand Royal (see "Where to Stay," above). The menu changes seasonally.

In the Grand Royal hotel, Kongensgate 64. (℃ **76-97-70-00.** Reservations recommended. Main courses 200NOK–350NOK ($27–$47). AE, DC, MC, V. Daily 11am–11pm. Bus: 14, 15, 16, or 17.

11

The Best of Sweden

In the towns and cities of Scandinavia's largest country, you can let yourself be dazzled by the contemporary or wander back to a bygone era—the choice is yours. From the castles and palaces in the south to the barren tundra of Lapland, we have combed this vast land of forests, lakes, and glacier-ringed mountains to bring you the best.

1 The Best Travel Experiences

- **Soaking Up Local Culture:** Home to a great cultural tradition, Sweden is acclaimed for its symphony orchestras, theater, ballet (including the renowned Swedish Cullberg Ballet), and opera companies. During the long days of summer, open-air concerts are staged all over the country (local tourist offices can provide details). Many concerts, especially those featuring folk dancing and regional music, are free.
- **Touring the Stockholm Archipelago:** The capital lies in a bucolic setting with more than 24,000 islands (if you count big rocks jutting out of the water). Boats leave frequently in summer from Stockholm's harbor, taking you to Vaxholm and other scenic islands, where you'll typically find interesting shops and restaurants. See chapter 14.
- **Seeing the Country from the Water:** Passengers glide through

Sweden's scenic heartland, between Stockholm and Gothenburg, on a Göta Canal Cruise. The route takes you along three of the country's largest lakes and through 58 carefully calibrated locks. The cruise, available between mid-May and mid-September, offers a glimpse of the best of Sweden in a nutshell. See chapter 17.
- **Exploring the Land of the Midnight Sun:** Above the Arctic Circle, the summer sun never dips below the horizon. You have endless hours to enjoy the beauty of the region and the activities that go with it, from hiking to whitewater rafting. After shopping for distinctive wooden and silver handicrafts, you can dine on filet of reindeer served with cloudberries. You can climb rocks and glaciers in Sarek National Park. See "Swedish Lapland" in chapter 17.

2 The Best Scenic Towns & Villages

- **Sigtuna:** Sweden's oldest town, founded at the beginning of the 11th century, stands on the shores of Lake Mälaren northwest of Stockholm. Walk its High Street, believed to be the oldest street in

Sweden. Traces of Sigtuna's Viking and early Christian heritage can be seen throughout the town. See chapter 14.
- **Uppsala:** Sweden's major university city lies northwest of Stockholm.

Gamla (Old) Uppsala, nearby, is especially intriguing. It's built on the site of Viking burial grounds where humans and animals were sacrificed. See chapter 14.

- **Lund:** This town, 18km (11 miles) northeast of Malmö, rivals Uppsala as a university town. It, too, is ancient—Canute the Great founded it in 1020. Centuries-old buildings, winding passages, and cobblestone streets fill Lund; a major attraction is its ancient cathedral, one of the finest expressions of Romanesque architecture in northern Europe. See chapter 16.
- **Jokkmokk:** Just north of the Arctic Circle, this is the best center for absorbing Lapp (or Sami) culture. In early February, the Lapps hold their famous "Great Winter Market" here, a tradition that goes back 4 centuries. You can visit a museum devoted to Sami culture,

and then go salmon fishing in the town's central lake. See chapter 17.
- **Rättvik:** This great resort borders Lake Siljan in the heart of Dalarna, a province known for its regional painting, handicrafts, and folk dancing. Timbered houses characterize Dalarna's old-style architecture, and on a summer night you can listen to fiddlers, whose music evokes the past. See chapter 17.
- **Visby:** On the island of Gotland, this was once a great medieval European city and Viking stronghold. For 8 days in August, during Medieval Week, the sleepy Hanseatic town awakens. The annual festival features fire-eaters, belly dancers, and jousting tournaments. Filled with the ruins of 13th- and 14th-century churches and memories of a more prosperous period, Visby is intriguing in any season. See chapter 17.

3 The Best Active Vacations

- **Fishing:** Sweden offers some of the world's best fishing in pristine lakes and streams. You can even fish in downtown Stockholm! Many varieties of fresh- and saltwater fish are available in Sweden's waters.
- **Golfing:** Many Swedes are obsessed with golf. Most courses are open to the public, from the periphery of Stockholm to Björkliden (above the Arctic Circle), where enthusiasts play under the midnight sun. One unusual course is the "Green Zone," on the Swedish-Finnish border. You tee off in Sweden and sink your putt in Finland! Players cross the border four times during one round. See chapter 17.
- **Hiking:** The Kungsleden ("King's Trail") might provide the hike of a lifetime. It takes you through the mountains of Lapland, including Kebnekaise, at 2,090m (6,965 ft.) the highest mountain in Sweden.

This 500km (310-mile) trail cuts through the mountains of Abisko National Park to Riksgränsen on the Norwegian frontier. For more information about this adventure, contact the **Svenska Turistförening (Swedish Touristing Club)**, P.O. Box 25, Amiralitetshuset 1, Flagmansvägen 8, S101 20 Stockholm (© **08/463-21-00**; www.stfurist.se). The club will also provide information about hiking and outdoor venues in any season in each of the 25 provinces of Sweden. See chapter 17.
- **Skiing:** In Lapland you can enjoy downhill and cross-country skiing year-round. One of Sweden's main downhill skiing areas is in Åre in Jämtland. Serious skiers head for the Kebnekaise mountain station, where skiing can be combined with dog sledding and other sports. See chapter 17.

- **White-Water Rafting:** Sweden has some of Europe's best white-water rafting. Trips run the gamut from short, comfortable rides along lazy rivers to fast descents down white-water rapids. In Dalarna the best white-water rafting is on the moderately difficult Västerdalälven River rapids. An experienced organization in southwestern Dalarna will rent, with or without a guide, watercraft suitable for between 1 and 23 occupants, including inflatable rafts, kayaks, and fiberglass canoes. Most excursions last a half day and include access to a foaming stretch of river, plus a barbecue picnic, some local sightseeing and, if it appeals to you, a soak in a communal hot tub. Other options available at this year-round outfitter include moose-watching safaris, mountain-biking excursions and, in winter, cross-country and downhill ski expeditions. For more information, contact **Dalarnas & Värmlands Äventyrscentrum AB,** Ulfshittan 6, 78196 Börlange, Sweden (© **0243/25-11-07;** www.dalarnasaventyr.se).

4 The Best Festivals & Special Events

- **Walpurgis Eve:** One of Europe's great celebrations to welcome spring takes place in Sweden on April 30. Bonfires, songs, lively festivals, and all sorts of antics herald the demise of winter. The best—and rowdiest—celebrations are at the university cities of Umeå, Lund, Uppsala, Stockholm, and Gothenburg.
- **Stockholm Waterfestival:** In August, much of the city turns out for a weeklong festival along the waterfront. It's entertainment galore—everything from concerts to fireworks. Stockholm goes wild before the chilly months arrive. Theoretically, the concept behind the festival is water preservation, but it offers a great opportunity to have a good time. See chapter 12.
- **Drottningholm Court Theater** (Drottningholm): In May, Sweden's cultural highlight is a series of 30 opera and ballet performances presented at this theater, which dates from 1766. The theater's original stage machinery and settings are still used. Drottningholm Palace (the "Versailles of Sweden") is on an island in Lake Mälaren, about 11km (7 miles) from Stockholm. See chapter 14.
- **Falun Folkmusik Festival:** This annual gathering of folk musicians from around the world at the town of Falun is one of Scandinavia's major musical events. Folkloric groups—many of them internationally famous—perform. Concerts, films, lectures, and seminars round out the events, which usually last for 4 days in July. See chapter 17.
- **Medieval Week** (Gotland): On the island of Gotland, Swedes celebrate the Middle Ages for about a week every August. Visby, especially, swarms with people in medieval garb. Many of them—from the blacksmith to the cobbler—tend market stalls as in olden days. Musicians play the hurdy-gurdy or the fiddle, and jesters play the fool. A program of some 100 medieval events, from tournaments to a nightly king's procession, is scheduled in Visby. See chapter 17.

5 The Best Museums

- **Royal Warship *Vasa*** (Stockholm): In the Djurgården, this 17th-century man-of-war—now a museum—is a popular tourist attraction, and deservedly so. The *Vasa* is the world's oldest known complete ship. It capsized and sank on its maiden voyage in 1628 before horrified onlookers. The ship was salvaged in 1961 and has been carefully restored; 97% of its 700 original decorative sculptures were retrieved. See chapter 14.
- **National Museum** (Stockholm): One of the oldest museums in the world (it celebrated its 200th birthday in 1992) houses Sweden's treasure trove of rare paintings and sculpture. From Rembrandt to Rubens, from Bellini to van Gogh, a panoply of European art unfolds before your eyes. Artifacts include everything from porcelain to antiques. See chapter 14.
- **Millesgården** (Lidingö, outside Stockholm): Sweden's foremost sculptor, Carl Milles (1875–1955), lived here and created a sculpture garden by the sea. Milles relied heavily on mythological themes in his work, and many of his best-known pieces are displayed in what's now a museum. See chapter 14.
- **Göteborgs Konstmuseum** (Gothenburg): This is the city's leading art museum, a repository of modern painting that's strong on French Impressionism. Modern artists such as Picasso and Edvard Munch are also represented, as are sculptures by Milles. See chapter 15.
- **Ájtte** (Jokkmokk): In Lapp country, this is the best repository of artifacts of the Sami people. Integrating nature with culture, the museum is the largest of its kind in the world. It depicts how the Lapps lived and struggled for survival in a harsh terrain, and shows the houses they lived in and the animals and weapons needed for their livelihood. See chapter 17.

6 The Best Offbeat Experiences

- **Log-Rafting on the Klarälven River:** You can enjoy a lazy trip down the river, winding through beautiful, unspoiled valleys among high mountains, with sandy beaches where you can occasionally swim. There's excellent fishing for pike and grayling. You travel through northern Värmland at a speed of 2kmph (1¼ mph) from the mouth of the Vingängssjön Lake in the north to Edebäck in the south. It takes 6 days to cover the 110km (68 miles). Overnight accommodations are on the moored raft or ashore. Each raft can accommodate two to five people, and the trips are available from May to August. Participants in the rafting expeditions down the Klarälven River will make their own rafts on the first day of the experience (it can last 1, 2, 3 or 6 days, and incorporate some or all of the river's length). Pine logs are lashed together with rope. Other offerings include beaver and elk-watching safaris, whitewater rafting expeditions, and canoeing. Contact **Vildmark i Farmland,** P.O. Box 209, 68525 Torsby (© **0560/140-40;** www.vildmark.se).
- **Exploring the Orsa "Outback" by Horse & Covered Wagon:** In the province of Dalarna (central Sweden), you can rent a horse and

covered wagon (with space for up to five) for a 3- or 5-day trek across the forest and tundra of the Orsa "outback," an almost unpopulated area of wild beauty. For more information, contact Häst och Vagn Svante Inemyr, Torsmo 1646, S-794 91 Orsa (© 0250/55-30-14; http://itadventure.se/hast.vagn/). See the "Happy Trails" box in chapter 17. On-site, they have 18 horses and 60 huskies. The huskies are used in dog-sledding tours of the outback, as part of 6-day tours priced at 10,000SEK ($1,060) per person. The fee is all-inclusive, and that means picking up participants at the airport. See chapter 17.

- **Playing Golf by the Light of the Midnight Sun:** In a land where the Lapps and reindeer still lead a nomadic life, you can play at the Björkliden Arctic Golf Course, some 240km (150 miles) north of the Arctic Circle (near the hamlet of Björkliden, 97km/60 miles west of Kiruna). The 18-hole course is open between late June and late August only. For information, contact the Björkliden Arctic Golf Club at © 0980/64100. The rest of the year, contact its affiliate, the Stockholm-based Bromma Golf Course, Kvarnbacksvägen 28, 16874 Bromma, Stockholm (© 08/26-29-55). See chapter 17.

- **Seeing Lapland on a Safari:** On this tour you can explore the last wilderness of Europe and record your impressions on film. You can see Swedish Lapland up close, and become acquainted with the Sami people's rich culture. Highlights include visits to old churches and village settlements (usually along a lake), and seeing reindeer. The outdoors outfitter **Borton**

Overseas (© 800/843-0602) offers summer tours of the tundra between May and early September, and winter tours of the snow-covered tundra from January to April. The winter is arguably the most beautiful time to see the tundra. See chapter 17.

- **Riding the Rails of the Longest Stretch of Abandoned Railway Track in Europe:** Around 1900, a consortium of logging companies, with the help of the Swedish government, built a railway track running across a 180km (112-mile) stretch of forested wilderness between Dalarna and Värmland, beginning and ending in the hamlets of Perfberg and Venfbro. Trains stopped running along the track in 1967, and today, the stretch of rails is part of Sweden's national patrimony. You can ride along these tracks in specially designed foot-pedalled trolleys, in tandem with up to four passengers. Since there's only one track, travel can become inconvenient if you meet up with another trolley headed in the opposite direction. Rules of the road, as laid out by camping associations across Sweden, say that passengers in the less heavily loaded of the trolleys must dismount, unpack your camping gear, lift your trolley off the railway track, let the more heavily loaded trolley by, then reposition your trolley back onto the railway tracks. An outfit that's highly experienced in this and many other forms of outdoor activities in the Swedish wilderness, during both summer and winter, is Dalarnas & Värmlands Äentyrscentrum AB, Ulfshittan 6, 78196 Börlange, Sweden (© 0243/25-11-07; www.dalarnasaventyr.se).

7 The Best Buys

- **Glass:** In the deep woods of Småland, Swedish glasswork has helped set the world standard. Glass has been a local tradition since King Gustav Vasa invited Venetian glass blowers to come to Sweden in the 16th century. The first glass was melted here in 1556. The oldest name in Swedish glass, Kosta, was founded in 1742 and is now part of the Orrefors group, the best-known manufacturer. Fifteen major glassworks in Småland, which encompasses Växjö and Kalmar, are open to visitors. Glass is sold at department stores and specialty outlets throughout Sweden.

- **Handicrafts:** Designers create a wide variety of objects, often in wood, but also in pewter, enamel, tapestry, brass, and even reindeer skins and antlers. Many handicrafts are based on Viking designs, and most objects are in the traditional Lapp (or Sami) style. Shoppers eagerly seek wall textiles, leatherwork, hand-woven carpets, and embroidered items. Swedish cutlery and china are valued for their quality and craftsmanship. Stockholm has the widest selection of shops, and Gothenburg and other towns have specialty outlets.

- **Swedish Design:** Good design and craftsmanship are the hallmarks of Swedish housewares—swinging metal CD racks, wooden chickens on rockers, tea wagons, and more. One of the best places to find products of Swedish design is in the constantly changing display at **DesignTorget,** in the Kulturhuset in the center of Stockholm. It's open daily year-round. See chapter 14.

8 The Best Hotels

- **Grand Hotel** (Stockholm; ✆ **800/223-5652** in the U.S., or 08/679-35-00): Opposite the Royal Palace, this is the most prestigious hotel in Sweden. Well-known guests have included actress Sarah Bernhardt and many Nobel Prize winners. It dates from 1874 and is continuously renovated to keep it in excellent condition. The rooms are luxuriously decorated, and the bathrooms are Italian marble with heated floors. See p. 343.

- **Lady Hamilton Hotel** (Stockholm; ✆ **08/506-401-00**): This is one of Old Town's stellar properties. It's made up of three buildings that have been artfully connected and provide sumptuously furnished accommodations for those who prefer an old-fashioned atmosphere. Even the sauna is luxurious! See p. 350.

- **Victory Hotel** (Stockholm; ✆ **08/506-400-00**): In the Old Town, this small but stylish hotel was built in 1642. It's famous for the treasure once buried here, part of which can be seen at the Stockholm City Museum. The well-furnished guest rooms typically have exposed beams and pine floors. On a small rooftop terrace, tables are arranged around a fountain. See p. 350.

- **Radisson SAS Park Avenue Hotel** (Gothenburg; ✆ **800/333-3333** in the U.S., or 031/758-40-00): Since it opened in 1950, Gothenburg's premier hotel has played host to everybody from the Beatles to David Rockefeller. On the attractive main boulevard, near the cultural center, it's a cosmopolitan hotel with a fresh and contemporary aura. The best double rooms are quite spacious and sleek; about a quarter of the guest rooms have balconies. See p. 408.

- **Radisson SAS Scandinavia Hotel** (Gothenburg; ✆ **800/333-3333** in the U.S., or 031/80-60-00): Fashioned in marble and glass with bay windows, this hotel, with

innovative styling and beautiful architecture, is more than just a typical chain hotel. Balconies overlook a vast atrium with eye-catching elevators and trees. Amenities include everything from a gym and sauna to a well-equipped health club; the gourmet dining room has a bar. See p. 408.

9 The Best Restaurants

- **Bon Lloc** (Stockholm; ✆ **08/660-60-60**): The capital of Sweden has a new temple of gastronomy, the showcase for the town's hottest chef, Mathias Dahlgren. From his kitchen emerges a so-called nouveau Euro-Latin cuisine—we prefer to call it Mediterranean—which is sublime enough to earn him the position of number one when it comes to rattling those pots and pans. See p. 352.
- **Operakällaren** (Stockholm; ✆ **08/676-58-00**): This historic monument, part of the Royal Opera Complex, dates from 1787. The chef is a culinary adviser to the king and queen. This is the best place to sample Sweden's legendary smörgåsbord—a groaning table of delectable dishes with an emphasis on fresh fish. All the northern delicacies, from smoked eel or reindeer to Swedish red caviar and grouse, appear on the menu. See p. 352.
- **Paul & Norbert** (Stockholm; ✆ **08/663-81-83**): With only eight tables, this exclusive restaurant on the fashionable Strandvägen is in a patrician residence that dates from 1873. The most innovative restaurant in Stockholm, it's the culinary domain of German owners Paul Beck and Norbert Lang. The Swedish game served here in the winter (such as pigeon with Calvados sauce) is without equal in the country. Always count on something tempting and

unusual—perhaps sautéed sweetbreads in nettle sauce. See p. 353.
- **Wedholms Fisk** (Stockholm; ✆ **08/611-78-74**): This classic Swedish restaurant serves some of the capital's finest local food, skillfully prepared with a French touch. Traditional and haute cuisine dishes have been modernized. Each dish seems guaranteed to ignite your enthusiasm, although nothing is showy or ostentatious. The fresh ingredients retain their natural flavor. See p. 356.
- **Gripsholms Värdshus Restaurant** (Mariefred; ✆ **0159/347-50**): If you're seeking traditional Swedish food with French overtones, this is the best dining choice on the periphery of the capital. Local game dishes, including wild grouse, are featured in autumn, and marinated salmon with mild mustard sauce is a year-round favorite. Tastings in the wine cellar can be arranged. See p. 399.
- **Sjömagasinet** (Klippan, outside Gothenburg; ✆ **031/773-59-20**). By far the most interesting restaurant in town, this is one of the finest seafood places on the west coast of Sweden. In a converted warehouse, it serves an array of fresh fish in wonderful concoctions, and the sauces and preparations never diminish the flavor of the seafood. Pot-au-feu of fish and shellfish with chive-flavored crème fraîche is worth the trek out of town. See p. 412.

Planning Your Trip to Sweden

This chapter gives you many of the details you need to plan your trip to Sweden. Also see chapter 2, "Planning Your Trip to Denmark," which discusses travel to Scandinavia as a whole.

1 The Regions in Brief

GÖTALAND The southern part of Sweden takes its name from the ancient Goths. Some historians believe they settled in this region, which is similar in climate and architecture to parts of northern Europe, especially Germany. This is the most populated part of Sweden, comprising eight provinces—Östergötland, Småland (the "kingdom of glass"), Västergötland, Skåne, Dalsland, Bohuslån, Halland, and Blckinge—plus the islands of Öland and Gotland. The Göta Canal cuts through this district. **Gothenburg** is the most important port in the west, and **Stockholm,** the capital, the chief port in the east. Aside from Stockholm, **Skåne,** the châteaux district, is the most heavily visited area. It's often compared to the Danish countryside. Many seaside resorts are on both the west and east coasts.

SVEALAND The central region encompasses the folkloric province of **Dalarna** (Dalecarlia in English) and **Värmland** (immortalized in the novels of Selma Lagerlöf). These districts are the ones most frequented by visitors. Other provinces include Våstmanland, Uppland, Södermanland, and Nårke. Ancient Svealand is often called the cultural heart of Sweden. Some 20,000 islands lie along its eastern coast.

NORRLAND Northern Sweden makes up Norrland, which lies above the 61st parallel and includes about 50% of the landmass. It's inhabited by only about 15% of the population, including Lapps and Finns. Norrland consists of 24 provinces, of which **Lapland** is the most popular with tourists. It's a land of thick forests, fast-flowing (and cold) rivers, and towering mountain peaks. Lapland, the home of the Lapp reindeer herds, consists of tundra. **Kiruna** is one of Norrland's most important cities because of its iron-ore deposits. Many bodies of water in Norrland freeze for months every year.

2 Visitor Information

In the **United States,** contact the **Scandinavian Tourist Board,** 655 Third Ave., 18th Floor, New York, NY 10017 (© **212/885-9700;** www.goscandinavia.com), at least 3 months in advance for maps, sightseeing information, ferry schedules, and other advice.

In the **United Kingdom,** contact the **Swedish Travel & Tourism Council,** 11 Montague Place, London W1H 2AL (© **020/7870-5609**).

You also can try the website **www.visit-sweden.com.**

If you get in touch with a travel agent, make sure the agent is a member of the **American Society of Travel Agents (ASTA)**. If a problem arises, you can complain to the society's Consumer Affairs Department at 1101 King St., Suite 200, Alexandria, VA 22314 (© 703/739-8739; www.astanet.com).

3 Entry Requirements

ENTRY REQUIREMENTS
U.S., Canadian, U.K., Irish, Australian, and New Zealand citizens with a **valid passport** don't need a visa to enter Sweden if they don't expect to stay more than 90 days and don't expect to work there. If after entering Sweden you want to stay more than 90 days, you can apply for a permit for an extra 90 days, which as a rule is granted immediately. Go to the nearest police headquarters or to your home country's consulate. If your passport is lost or stolen, head to your consulate as soon as possible for a replacement.

4 Money

For a general discussion of changing money, using credit and charge cards, and other matters, see "Money," in chapter 2.

CURRENCY   Sweden's basic unit of currency is the **krona** (plural: **kronor**), written **SEK**. (Denmark and Norway also use kroner, but note the different spelling.) There are 100 **öre** in 1 krona. Bank notes are issued in denominations of 20, 50, 100, 500, 1,000, and 10,000 SEK. Silver coins are issued in denominations of 50 öre and 1 and 5 SEK.

What Things Cost in Stockholm	US$
Taxi from the airport to the city center	42.00
Basic bus or subway fare	2.10
Local telephone call	.30
Double room at the Grand Hotel (very expensive)	349.00
Double room at the Kung Carl Hotel (moderate)	196.00
Double room at the Hotell City (inexpensive)	125.00
Lunch for one at Eriks Bakfica (moderate)	30.00
Lunch for one at Cattelin Restaurant (inexpensive)	7.65
Dinner for one, without wine, at Operakällaren (very expensive)	55.00
Dinner for one, without wine, at Prinsens (moderate)	35.00
Dinner for one, without wine, at Tennstopet (inexpensive)	20.00
Pint of beer (draft Pilsner) in a bar	4.30
Coca-Cola in a cafe	3.50
Cup of coffee in a cafe	3.10
Admission to Drottningholm Palace	6.35
Movie ticket	11.00
Budget theater ticket	13.00

Sweden

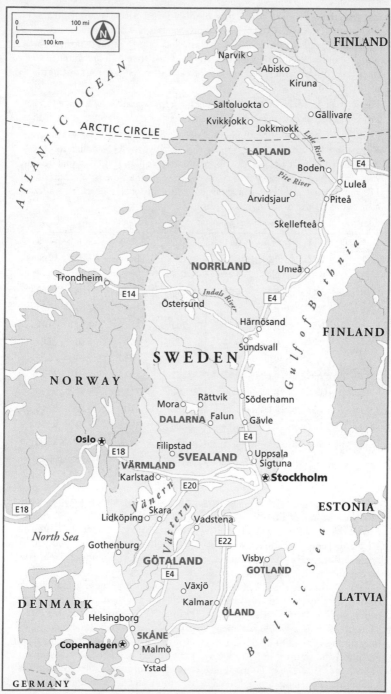

The Swedish Krona

For American Readers At the time of this writing, $1 US = approximately 9 kronor (or 1 krona = 10.6 US¢). This was the rate of exchange used to calculate the dollar values given in this edition. Bear in mind that throughout the context of this book, dollar amounts less than $10 are rounded to the nearest nickel, and dollar amounts greater than $10 are rounded to the nearest dollar.

For British Readers At this writing, £1 = approximately 14 kronor (or 1 krona = approximately 7.2 pence). This was the rate of exchange used to calculate the pound values in the table below.

Regarding the Euro At the time of this writing, the U.S. dollar and the euro traded almost on par ($1 approximately equals 1€). But that relationship can and probably will change during the lifetime of this edition. For more exact ratios between these and other currencies, check an up-to-date source at the time of your arrival in Sweden.

SEK	US$	UK£	Euro	SEK	US$	UK£	Euro
1	0.11	0.07	0.11	75	7.95	5.40	7.95
2	0.21	0.14	0.21	100	10.60	7.20	10.60
3	0.32	0.22	0.32	125	13.25	9.00	13.25
4	0.42	0.29	0.42	150	15.90	10.80	15.90
5	0.53	0.36	0.53	175	18.55	12.60	18.55
6	0.64	0.43	0.64	200	21.20	14.40	21.20
7	0.74	0.50	0.74	225	23.85	16.20	23.85
8	0.85	0.58	0.85	250	26.50	18.00	26.50
9	0.95	0.65	0.95	275	29.15	19.80	29.15
10	1.06	0.72	1.06	300	31.80	21.60	31.80
15	1.59	1.08	1.59	350	37.10	25.20	37.10
20	2.12	1.44	2.12	400	42.40	28.80	42.40
25	2.65	1.80	2.65	500	53.00	36.00	53.00
50	5.30	3.60	5.30	1,000	106.00	72.00	106.00

5 When to Go

CLIMATE

It's hard to generalize about Sweden's climate. Influenced by the Gulf Stream, temperatures vary considerably from the fields of Skåne to the wilderness of Lapland. The upper 10th of Sweden lies north of the Arctic Circle.

The country as a whole has many sunny summer days, but it's not super-hot. July is the warmest month, with temperatures in Stockholm and Gothenburg averaging around 64°F (18°C). February is the coldest month, when the temperature in Stockholm averages around 26°F (–3°C), and Gothenburg is a few degrees warmer.

It's not always true that the farther north you go, the cooler it becomes. During the summer, the northern parts of the country (Halsingland to northern Lapland) may suddenly have the warmest weather and bluest skies. Swedes claim the weather forecasts on television and in the newspapers are 99% reliable.

Sweden's Average Daytime Temperatures

		Jan	Feb	Mar	Apr	May	June	July	Aug	Sept	Oct	Nov	Dec
Stockholm	°F	27	26	31	40	50	59	64	62	54	45	37	32
	°C	–3	–3	–1	4	10	15	18	17	12	7	3	0
Karesuando	°F	6	5	12	23	39	54	59	51	44	31	9	5
	°C	–14	–15	–11	–5	3	12	15	11	7	–1	–13	–15
Karlstad	°F	33	30	28	37	53	63	62	59	54	41	29	26
	°C	–1	–1	–2	3	12	17	17	15	12	5	–2	–3
Lund	°F	38	36	34	43	57	63	64	61	57	47	37	37
	°C	3	2	1	6	14	17	18	16	14	8	3	3

THE MIDNIGHT SUN In the summer, the sun never fully sets in northern Sweden; even in the south, daylight may last until 11pm—and then the sun rises around 3am.

The best vantage points and dates for seeing the thrilling spectacle of the midnight sun are **Björkliden,** from May 26 to July 19; **Abisko,** from June 12 to July 4; **Kiruna,** from May 31 to July 14; and **Gällivare,** from June 2 to July 12. All are accessible by public transportation.

Remember that although the sun shines brightly late at night, it's not as strong as at midday. Bring a warm jacket or sweater.

HOLIDAYS

Sweden celebrates the following public holidays: New Year's Day (Jan 1); Epiphany (Jan 6); Good Friday; Easter Sunday; Easter Monday; Labor Day (May 1); Ascension Day (mid-May); Whitsunday and Whitmonday (late May); Midsummer Day (June 21); All Saints' Day (Nov 1); and Christmas Eve, Christmas Day, and Boxing Day (Dec 24, 25, and 26). Inquire at a tourist bureau for the dates of the holidays that vary.

SWEDEN CALENDAR OF EVENTS

The dates given here may in some cases be only approximations. Be sure to check with the tourist office before you make plans to attend a specific event. For information on Walpurgis Night and midsummer celebrations, call the local tourist offices in the town where you plan to stay. (See individual chapters for the phone numbers.)

April

Walpurgis Night, nationwide. Celebrations with bonfires, songs, and speeches welcoming the advent of spring. There are especially lively celebrations among university students at Uppsala, Lund, Stockholm, Gothenburg, and Umeå. April 30.

May

Drottningholm Court Theater. Some 30 opera and ballet performances, from baroque to early romantic, are presented in the unique 1766 Drottningholm Court Theater, Drottningholm, with original decorative paintings and stage mechanisms. Call © **08/660-82-25** for tickets. Take the T-bana to Brommaplan, then bus no. 301 or 323. A steamboat runs in the summer; call © **08/411-70-23** for information. Late May to late September.

June

Midsummer, nationwide. Swedes celebrate Midsummer Eve all over the country. Maypole dances to the sound of the fiddle and accordion are the typical festive events of the day. Dalarna observes the most traditional celebrations. Mid-June.

July

Falun Folk Musical Festival. International folk musicians gather to participate in and attend concerts, seminars, lectures, exhibitions, and films on folk music. Events are conducted at various venues; contact the **Falun Folk Music Festival,** S-791 13 Falun (📞 **023/830-90;** www.falunfolk.com), for more information. Mid-July.

Around Gotland Race, Sandhamn. The biggest and most exciting open-water Scandinavian sailing race starts and finishes at Sandhamn in the Stockholm archipelago. About 450 boats, mainly from Nordic countries, take part. Call the Stockholm tourist office for information. Two days in mid-July.

Rättviksdansen (International Festival of Folk Dance and Music), Rättvik. Every other year for some 20 years, around 1,000 folk dancers and musicians from all over the world have gathered to participate in this folkloric tradition. Last week in July.

August

Medieval Week, Gotland. Numerous events are held throughout the island of Gotland—tours, concerts, medieval plays, festivities, and shows. For more information, contact the Tourist Office, Hamngatan 4, S-621 25 Visby (📞 **0498/20-17-00**). Early August.

Stockholm Waterfestival. A tradition since 1989, this weeklong festival around the city's shores offers entertainment such as fireworks, competitions, and concerts, as well as information about the care and preservation of water. An award of $150,000 is given to an individual or organization that has made an outstanding contribution to water preservation. Call the Stockholm tourist office for information. Begins second week in August.

Minnesota Day, Utvandra Hus, Växjö (Småland). Swedish-American relations are celebrated at the House of Emigrants with speeches, music, singing, and dancing; climaxing in the election of the Swedish-American of the year. Call 📞 **0470/201-20** for information. Second Sunday in August.

December

Nobel Day, Stockholm. The king, members of the royal family, and invited guests attend the Nobel Prize ceremony for literature, physics, chemistry, medicine, physiology, and economics. Attendance is by invitation only. The ceremony is held at the concert hall and followed by a banquet at City Hall. December 10.

Lucia, the Festival of Lights, nationwide. To celebrate the shortest day and longest night of the year, young girls called "Lucias" appear in restaurants, offices, schools, and factories, wearing floor-length white gowns and special headdresses, each holding a lighted candle. They are accompanied by "star boys"—young men in white with wizard hats covered with gold stars, each holding a wand with a large golden star at the top. One of these "Lucias" eventually is crowned queen. In olden days, Lucia was known as "Little Christmas." December 13.

This celebration is observed nationwide. Actual planned events change from year to year and vary from community to community. The best place for tourists to observe this event is at the open-air museum at Skansen in Stockholm.

6 Health & Insurance

For a general discussion of health and insurance concerns, see "Health & Insurance" in chapter 2.

Put your essential medicines in your carry-on luggage and bring enough prescription medications to last through your stay. In Sweden, pharmacists cannot legally honor a prescription written outside the country; if you need more of your medications, you have to see a doctor and have a new prescription written.

Sweden's national health-care program does not cover American or Canadian visitors. Medical expenses must be paid in cash. Medical costs in Sweden are generally more reasonable than elsewhere in western Europe.

7 Tips for Travelers with Special Needs

A number of resources and organizations in North America and Britain can assist travelers with special needs in trip planning. For details, see "Tips for Travelers with Special Needs," in chapter 2.

FOR TRAVELERS WITH DISABILITIES Scandinavian countries have been in the vanguard of providing services for people with disabilities. In general, trains, airlines, ferries, and department stores and malls are accessible. For information about wheelchair access, ferry and air travel, parking, and other matters, contact the Scandinavian Tourist Board (see "Visitor Information," above).

About two million people in Sweden have a disability, and the country is especially conscious of special needs. Contact **Svenska Turistförening** or STF (Swedish Touring Club), P.O. Box 25, S-101 20 Stockholm (✆ 08/463-21-00; www.stfturist.se), for information, including data about youth hostels with special rooms for those with disabilities.

FOR GAY & LESBIAN TRAVELERS Stockholm is the gay capital of Scandinavia, and Sweden ranks along with Norway, Denmark, and The Netherlands as among the most tolerant and gay-friendly nations on earth. Even gay marriage is now legal in this enlightened and relatively sophisticated country. The age of consent is almost uniformly the same as for heterosexuals, usually 15 or 16. However, outside Stockholm and Gothenburg you'll find very few gay bars.

Many gay and lesbian organizations in Stockholm welcome visitors from abroad. Foremost among these is the **Federation for Gay and Lesbian Rights (RFSL),** Sveavägen 57 (Box 45090), S-104 30 Stockholm (✆ 08/736-02-12), open Monday through Friday from 9am to 5pm. Established in 1950, the group's headquarters are located on the upper floors of the biggest gay nightlife center in Stockholm. Meetings are held weekly—a Wednesday 3pm meeting for gay men over 60 and a twice-monthly meeting of "Golden Ladies" (yes, they use the English expression) for lesbians over 50, plus a Monday-night youth session for those 18 to 21. They also operate a **Gay Switchboard** (✆ 08/736-02-12), staffed with volunteers; call daily from 8am to 11pm for information. The biggest event of the year is **Gay Pride Week,** usually held the first week in August. Call or write the RFSL for information.

FOR SENIORS Visitors over age 65 can obtain 30% off first- and second-class train travel (except Fri and Sun) on the Swedish State Railways. There also are discounts on the ferries crossing from Denmark to Sweden, and on certain attractions and performances. However, you may have to belong to a seniors organization to qualify for certain discounts. **In Stockholm,** there are discounts on transportation, concert, theater, and opera tickets.

8 Getting There

BY PLANE

See "Getting There," in chapter 2.

THE MAJOR AIRLINES

Travelers from the U.S. East Coast usually choose **SAS** (℗ **800/221-2350** in the U.S.; www.Scandinavia.net). Another major competitor is **American Airlines** (℗ **800/443-7300** in the U.S.; www.aa.com), which offers daily flights to Stockholm from Chicago, and excellent connections through Chicago from American's vast North American network. Between November and March (excluding the Christmas holidays), American offers round-trip fares as low as $509 for weekday departures from Chicago. There's a supplemental charge of $50 for travel on a Friday, Saturday, or Sunday. This fare, matched for the most part by SAS, requires a stay abroad of between 7 and 60 days, as well as several other restrictions. Although these fares probably will have changed by the time you make your vacation plans, the new prices are likely to be somewhat similar. Travelers from Seattle usually fly SAS to Copenhagen, then connect to one of the airline's frequent shuttle flights into Stockholm.

Other airlines fly to gateway European cities and then connect to flights into Stockholm. **British Airways** (℗ **800/247-9297** in the U.S.; www.britishairways.com), for example, flies from almost 20 North American cities to London/Heathrow, and then connects with onward flights to Stockholm. **Northwest** (℗ **800/225-2525** in the U.S.; www.nwa.com) also flies at frequent intervals to London, from which ongoing flights to Stockholm are available on either SAS or British Airways. Finally, **Icelandair** (℗ **800/223-5500** in the U.S.; www.icelandair.com) has proved to be an excellent choice for travel to Stockholm, thanks to connections through its home-port of Reykjavik. It often offers great deals.

People traveling **from Britain** can fly **SAS** (℗ **020/8990-7159** in London) from London's Heathrow to Stockholm on any of five daily nonstop flights. Flying time is about 2½ hours each way. Likewise, SAS flies daily to Stockholm from Manchester, making a brief stop in Copenhagen en route. Flight time from Manchester to Stockholm is about 3½ hours each way.

BY CAR

The ferry routes from England to Denmark and from Denmark to Sweden are the most traveled (see "Getting There," in chapter 2), but there are better choices from the Continent.

FROM GERMANY You can drive to the northern German port of Travemünde and catch the 7½-hour ferry to the Swedish port of Trelleborg, a short drive south of Malmö. This route saves many hours by avoiding transit through Denmark. If you want to visit Denmark before Sweden, you can take the 3-hour car ferry from Travemünde to Gedser in southern Denmark. From Gedser, the E64 and the E4 express highways head north to Copenhagen. After a visit here, you can take the Øresund Bridge from Copenhagen to Malmö.

FROM NORWAY From Oslo, E18 goes east through Karlstad all the way to Stockholm. This is a long but scenic drive.

FROM DENMARK The most popular way of reaching Sweden from Denmark is to drive across the new $3 billion Øresund Fixed Link, a bridge and a tunnel, plus an artificial island spanning the icy Øresund Sound between Copenhagen and Malmö. The bridge provides road and rail connections between the Scandinavian peninsula and the rest of Europe and is the final link in the centuries-old dream of connecting the Continent from its northern tip to its southern toe. In other words, you can now drive all the way in either direction without taking a boat, ferry, or hydrofoil. Car ferries run frequently from Copenhagen to Malmö, and from Helsingør in North Zealand to Helsingborg on Sweden's west coast. To reach Stockholm from Malmö, take E6 north along the coast toward Helsingborg. In the Helsingborg area, turn northeast at the junction with E4 and continue across southern Sweden. Part of this highway is a four-lane express motorway, and part is a smaller national highway.

BY TRAIN

Copenhagen is the main rail hub between Scandinavia and the rest of Europe. There are seven daily trains from Copenhagen to Stockholm and six from Copenhagen to Gothenburg. All connect with the Danish ferries that operate to Sweden via Helsingør or Frederikshavn (see "Getting There," in chapter 2).

There are at least three trains a day from Oslo to Stockholm. Travel time is about 6½ hours. There are three trains a day from Oslo to Gothenburg. Travel time is about 4 hours.

RAIL PASSES FOR NORTH AMERICAN TRAVELERS

For information on rail passes, please refer to "Getting There" in chapter 2.

BY SHIP & FERRY

FROM DENMARK   Ferries ply the waters for the brief run from Helsingör,

a short drive north of Copenhagen, and Helsingborg, Sweden, just across the narrow channel that separates the countries. The 25-minute trip on a conventional ferry (not a catamaran) begins at 20- to 40-minute intervals, 24 hours a day. Operated by **Scandlines** (© **33-15-15-15** in Copenhagen), it's one of the most popular ferry routes in Europe. Round-trip passage costs 460DKK ($60) for a car with up to nine passengers; the ticket is valid for up to 2 months. If you return to Denmark the same day, round-trip passage for a car and up to five passengers costs 245DKK ($32). Pedestrians pay 34DKK ($4.45) round-trip, regardless of when they return.

FROM ENGLAND   Two English ports, Harwich (year-round) and Newcastle-upon-Tyne (summer only), offer ferry service to Sweden. Harwich to Gothenburg takes 23 to 25 hours; Newcastle to Gothenburg, 27 hours. Boats on both routes offer overnight accommodations and the option of transporting cars. Prices are lower for passengers who book in advance through the company's U.S. agent. For details, call **Sea Europe Holidays,** 6801 Lake Worth Rd., Suite 103, Lake Worth, FL 33463 (© **800/533-3755,** fax 561/649-8124 in the U.S.; or 019/129-362-62 in the U.K.; www.seaeurope.com).

FROM GERMANY   Stena Line Ferries (© **031/704-00-00**) sails daily from Kiel to Gothenburg. The trip takes 14 hours and costs 900SEK ($95) one-way.

9 Escorted Tours

Sweden's various regions, especially Dalarna and Lapland, offer such a variety of sights and activities that you may want to take an escorted tour. The following tours are just a small sample of what's available. Contact

your travel agent to learn about tours of interest to you or to design a special one for you.

ScanAm World Tours (© **800/545-2204**) offers a tour of the Dalarna folklore region by rail. "Mora and the Folklore District" includes round-trip train fare from Stockholm to Mora and 2 nights at the First Resort Mora. The 3-day tour is available May through September; prices start at $430 per person. The company also offers a "Kalmar and the Swedish Glass District" rail tour. The 3-day excursion includes round-trip train fare from Stockholm to Kalmar and 2 nights at the Kalmar Stadshotell. Prices start at $595 per person. The tour is available May through September.

"Gotland Island and the City of Roses" is a cruise on the Gotland Line from Stockholm to Nynäshamn or from Oskarshamn to Visby, including 2 nights at the Visby Hotel or Hotel Solhem. The 3-day tour is available May through September.

Scantours (© 800/223-7226; www.scantours.com) offers the most widely diverse tours of Sweden ranging from a 2-day "Taste of Sweden" tour by steamboat and vintage train to a 2-day canal cruise. One of the best of the tours is a 3-day journey through the folkloric province of Dalarna and along the shores of Lake Siljan.

For the more adventurous, Sweden's rugged north offers endless opportunities to achieve an adrenaline rush. On the "Midnight Sun Skiing" package offered by **Passage Tours** (© 800/ 548-5960), you can ski in shorts. Offered from May to June, the tour has additional options, including a reindeer sleigh safari and Stockholm

lodging packages. This company also offers hiking tours that include a trip through the mountains; the views are panoramic. Prices vary according to the season.

The archipelago that fronts Stockholm's harbor is one of the most frequently visited wilderness areas in northern Europe, thanks to its convenience to the Swedish capital. An outfitter that can help you appreciate the archipelago's resources in any season is 30,000 Öar (30,000 Islands), Fågelbrouhus, S-139 60 Vårmdö (© 08/ 571-419-30). There, owner Bengt Kull will propose a range of activities. For example, how about midwinter ice-skating in the environs of Stockholm? During mild winters, the venue will be the frozen surface of Lake Malaren; during very cold winters, you might join the dozen of skaters who fly in regularly from Holland for Hans Brinker–style skating excursions on the frozen sea between some of the islands of the archipelago. (*Note:* we emphatically urge you not to try this yourself, without a guide, since pockets of warm water from undersea springs can make the ice treacherously thin in some spots.) Warm-weather hiking and boating, and midwinter cross-country skiing, are all part of this outfit's expertise. Trips are organized individually, and for some upscale gatherings can even include a string quartet to greet you with a concert of Beethoven sonatas in a lakeside chalet after your hiking or waterborne excursions.

10 The Active Vacation Planner

BIKING   Much of Sweden is flat, which makes it ideal for cycling tours. Bicycles can be rented all over the country, and country hotels sometimes make them available free of charge. A typical rental is 200SEK ($21) per day. For more detailed information, contact the **Svenska Turistförening (Swedish Touring Club)**,

P.O. Box 25, Amiralitetshuset 1, Flagmansvägen 8, S101 20 Stockholm (© 08/463-21-00).

FISHING   In Stockholm, within view of the king's palace, you can cast a line for what are some of the finest salmon in the world. Ever since Queen Christina issued a decree in 1636, Swedes have had the right to fish in waters adjoining the palace. Throughout the country, fishing is an everyday affair; it has been estimated that one of every three Swedes is an angler.

But if you'd like to fish elsewhere in Sweden, you'll need a license; the cost varies from region to region. Local tourist offices in any district can give you information about this. Pike, pike-perch, eel, and perch are found in the heartland and the southern parts of the country.

GOLFING   After Scotland, Sweden may have more golf enthusiasts than any other country in Europe. There are about 400 courses, and they're rarely crowded. Visitors often are granted local membership cards, and greens fees vary, depending on the club. Many golfers fly from Stockholm to Boden in the far north in the summer months to play by the light of the midnight sun at the **Björkliden Arctic Golf Course,** which opened in 1989 some 240km (150 miles) north of the Arctic Circle. It's not only the world's northernmost golf course, it's one of the most panoramic anywhere, set against a backdrop of snowcapped peaks, green valleys, and crystal lakes. The narrow fairways and small greens of this nine-hole, par-36 course offer multiple challenges. For details, contact the **Björkliden Arctic Golf Club,** Kvarnbacksvägen 28, Bromma S-168 74 (© **09/804-00-40**). For general information on courses in Sweden, contact the **Svenska Golfförbundet,** P.O. Box 84, Daneered S-182 11 (© **08/622-15-00;** www.golf.se).

HIKING   Sarek, in the far north, is one of Europe's last real wilderness areas; Swedes come here to hike in the mountains, pick mushrooms, gather berries, and fish. The **Svenska Turistförening (Swedish Touring Club),** P.O. Box 25, Amiralitetshuset 1, Flagmansvägen 8, S101 20 Stockholm (© **08/463-21-00**), provides accommodations in the area in mountain

huts with 10 to 30 beds. The staff knows the northern part of Sweden very well, and can advise you about marked tracks, rowboats, the best excursions, the problems you're likely to encounter, communications, and transportation. The company also sells trail and mountain maps.

HORSEBACK RIDING   There are numerous opportunities for overnight horseback pack trips in such wilderness areas as the forests of Värmland or Norrbotten, where reindeer, musk oxen, and other creatures roam. The most popular overnight horseback trips start just north of the city of Karlstad in Värmland. There also are covered-wagon trips with overnight stopovers. A typical horseback trip begins in the lakeside village of Torsby and follows a forested trail up a mountain. An average of 4 hours a day is spent on the horse, with meals cooked over an open fire.

In northern Sweden, two popular starting points are Funäsdalen, close to the Norwegian border, and Ammarnäs, not far from the Arctic Circle and the midnight sun. These trips begin in June. Local tourist offices can provide further information.

Sweden also has many riding stables and riding schools. Ask about them at local tourist offices. One of the most popular excursions is a pony trek through the region of Sweden's highest mountain, Knebnekaise.

In sites convenient to Stockholm, you might try a ride or two around the rinks at **Djurgårdens ridskola,** Kaknäs, Djurgårend (© **08/660-21-11**), or a bit farther afield at **Bögs Gård AB,** in Sollentuna (© **08/96-79-71**), which maintains a complement of Icelandic ponies which seem to thrive throughout the region's frigid winters. Both sites can help arrange overnight treks through the surrounding fields and forests, even though most of their business derives from rink riding and improvement of equestrian forms.

One more unusual choice is exploring the Orsa (outback) by horse and covered wagon. In the province of Dalarna, you can rent a horse and wagon with space for up to five people. The outback is an almost unpopulated area of wild beauty, and the route goes past beautiful summer pastures, small forest lakes, and panoramic views. Rides are available June through August. Clients cover about 15km (9 miles) a day, following a pre-selected itinerary, sleeping in or beside the covered wagon, usually beside lakes or rivers. For more information, contact **Häst och Vagn,** Torsmo 1646, S-794 91 Orsa (© **2505/530-14**).

If you prefer to make your horse-back riding arrangements before your departure from the United States, perhaps as part of an organized bus, rail, or self-drive tour, **Passage Tours of Scandinavia,** 239 Commercial Blvd., Fort Lauderdale, FL 33308 (© **800/ 548-5960** or 954/776-7070; www. passagetours.com), can custom design a suitable tour for you, usually configured with visits to Sweden's cultural, architectural, or historical highlights en route.

RAFTING   White-water rafting and river rafting are the two major forms of this sport. For white-water rafting, you go in a fast river boat; the trip is made all the more exciting by a series of rapids. Throughout the country there are both short trips and those lasting a week or so. In Värmland, contact **Branäs Sport AB,** Branäs Fritidsanläggnin, P.O. Box 28, S-680 60 Sysslebäck (© **564/475-50;** www. branas.se).

River rafting is much tamer, because you go gently down a slow-moving river in Sweden's heartland. For information about the best river rafting in Sweden, contact **Kukkolaforsen-Turist & Konferens,** P.O. Box 184, S-593 91 Haparanda (© **922/310-00**). If you want to try log-rafting, we recommend

a lazy trip down the Klarälven River, winding through beautiful and unspoiled valleys between high mountains, with sandy beaches where you can swim if temperatures and river conditions allow. There also is excellent fishing for pike and grayling. You will travel through northern Värmland at a speed of 2km (1¼ miles) per hour from the mouth of the Vingümngssjön Lake in the north to Ekshärad in the south, a distance of 110km (68 miles) in 6 days. Overnight accommodations are arranged either on the moored raft or ashore. Each raft can accommodate between two and five people, and the trips are available from May to August. For a 6-day tour, adults pay 2,100SEK ($223); for a 3-day tour, 1,750SEK ($186). Rental of a tent and kitchen equipment costs an additional 300SEK to 400SEK ($32–$42) per person. Participants supply their own food and fishing equipment. Contact **Sverige-flotten,** Transtrand 20, S-680 63 Likenäs (© **564/402-27;** www.sverige flotten.se).

SAILING & CANOEING   Canoes and sailing boats can be rented all over the country; you can obtain information about this from the local tourist office. Often hotels situated near watersports areas have canoes for rent.

SWIMMING   If you don't mind swimming in rather cool water, Sweden has one of the world's longest coast-lines—plus some 100,000 lakes—in which you can take the plunge. The best bathing beaches are on the west coast. Both the islands of Öland and Gotland have popular summer seaside resorts. Beaches in Sweden generally are open to the public, and nude bathing is allowed on certain designated beaches. Topless bathing for women is prevalent everywhere. If a Swedish lake is suitable for swimming, it's always signposted.

WALKING & JOGGING   Sweden is ideal for either activity. Local tourist

Tips Planning Your Trip Online

More and more "webbies" are planning their trip online. For a full discussion of this technique, refer to "Planning Your Trip Online" in chapter 2.

offices can provide details and sometimes even supply you with free maps of the best trails or jogging paths. In Stockholm, hotel reception desks often can tell you the best places to go jogging nearby.

11 Getting Around

BY PLANE

The best way to get around Scandinavia is to take advantage of air passes that apply to the whole region. If you're traveling extensively in Europe, special European passes are available. For information on **SAS's Visit Scandinavia Pass,** see "By Plane" under "Getting Around," in chapter 2.

WITHIN SWEDEN   For transatlantic flights coming from North America, Stockholm is Sweden's major gateway for Scandinavia's best-known airline, **SAS (Scandinavian Airlines System).** For flights arriving from other parts of Europe, the airport at Gothenburg supplements Stockholm's airport by funneling traffic into the Swedish heartland. In the mid-1990's, SAS acquired **LIN Airlines (Linjeflyg);** thus it now has access to small and medium-size airports throughout Sweden, including such remote but scenic outposts as Kiruna in Swedish Lapland. Among the larger Swedish cities serviced by SAS are Malmö, capital of Sweden's châteaux country; Karlstad, center of the verdant and folklore-rich district of Värmland; and Kalmar, a good base for exploring the glassworks district.

During the summer, SAS offers a number of promotional "minifares," which enable you to travel round-trip between two destinations for just slightly more than the price of a conventional one-way ticket on the same route. Children 11 and under travel free during the summer, and up to two children 12 to 17 can travel with a parent at significantly reduced rates. Airfares tend to be most reduced during July, with promotions almost as attractive during most of June and August. A minimum 3-night stopover at the destination is required for these minifares, and it must include a Friday or a Saturday night. When buying your tickets, always ask the airline or travel agency about special promotions and corresponding restrictions.

Those under 26 can take advantage of SAS's special **standby fares,** and seniors over 65 can apply for additional discounts, depending on the destination.

BY TRAIN

The Swedish word for train is *tåg,* and the national system is the Statens Järnvägar, the Swedish State Railways.

Swedish trains follow tight schedules. Trains leave Malmö, Helsingborg, and Gothenburg for Stockholm every hour throughout the day, Monday through Friday. There are trains every hour, or every other hour, to and from most big Swedish towns. On *expresståg* runs, seats must be reserved.

Children under 12 travel free when accompanied by an adult, and those up to age 18 are eligible for discounts.

BY BUS

Rail lines cover only some of Sweden's vast distances. Where the train tracks end, a bus usually serves as the link with remote villages. Buses usually are equipped with toilets, adjustable seats, reading lights, and a telephone. Fares depend on the distance traveled; for example, the one-way fare for the 525km (326-mile) trip from Stockholm to Gothenburg is 245SEK ($26). **Swebus** (℡ **08/503-094-00**), the country's largest bus company, provides information at the bus or railway stations in most cities. For travelers who don't buy a special rail pass (such as Eurail or ScanRail), bus travel between cities sometimes can be cheaper than traveling the same distances by rail. It's a lot less convenient and frequent, however—except in the far north, where there isn't any alternative.

BY CAR FERRY

Considering that Sweden has some 100,000 lakes and one of the world's longest coastlines, ferries play a surprisingly small part in the transportation network.

After the car ferry crossings from northern Germany and Denmark, the most popular route is from the mainland to the island of Gotland, in the Baltic. Service is available from Oskarshamn and Nynäshamn (call ℡ **08/20-10-20,** Destination Gotland, for more information). The famous "white boats" of the Waxholm Steamship Company (℡ **08/679-58-30**) also travel to many destinations in the Stockholm archipelago.

BY CAR

As one of the best-developed industrialized nations in Europe, Sweden maintains an excellent network of roads and highways, particularly in the southern provinces and in the central lake district. Major highways in the far north are kept clear of snow by heavy equipment that's in place virtually year-round. If you rent a car at any bona-fide rental agency, you'll be given the appropriate legal documents, including proof of adequate insurance (in the form of a "Green

Card") as specified by your car rental agreement. Current driver's licenses from Canada, the United Kingdom, New Zealand, Australia, and the United States are acceptable in Sweden.

RENTALS   The major U.S.-based car rental firms are represented throughout Sweden, both at airports and in urban centers. The companies' rates are aggressively competitive, although periodic sales promotions will favor one company over the others from time to time. Prior to your departure from North America, it would be advantageous to phone around to find out about the lowest available rates. Membership in AAA or another auto club may enable you to get a moderate discount. Be aware that you may avoid a supplemental airport tax by picking your car up at a central location rather than at the airport.

Avis (℡ **800/331-1084** in the U.S. and Canada; www.avis.com) offers a wide variety of cars. If you pay before you leave North America, the least expensive car, a VW Polo, rents for around $193 a week. Avis's most expensive car, a Swedish-made Saab 905, goes for around $450 a week.

If you pay before your departure from the United States, **Hertz** (℡ **800/654-3001** in the U.S. and Canada) offers a Ford Fiesta for $210 a week.

The popular **Budget Rent-a-Car** no longer operates in Sweden.

INSURANCE   All of these U.S. car rental companies include a basic amount of automatic liability insurance in their rates. Nevertheless, most renters feel more comfortable arranging for additional insurance to protect them from financial liability in the event of theft or damage to the car. A collision-damage waiver (CDW) is an optional insurance policy that can be purchased when you sign a rental agreement. For a fee of around $10 a day or more, depending on the value of the car, the rental agency will eliminate all but a token amount of your financial responsibility for collision damage in case of an accident. If you don't have a CDW and you have an accident, you'll usually have to pay the full cost of repairing the vehicle. Exact figures, penalties, and deductibles vary from company to company.

Some credit and charge card companies (including American Express, MasterCard, Visa, and Diners Club) will reimburse card users for the deductible in the event of an accident. Because of that, many renters waive the cost of the extra CDW. However, although the card issuer usually will reimburse the renter for the cost of damages (several weeks after the accident), sometimes payments have been delayed with such coverage until after the filing of certain legal and insurance-related documents. Unless there's a large line of credit associated with a particular card, some car renters involved in an accident could have to pay a large amount of cash on the spot. Considering that you're in a foreign country, if you have any doubt whatsoever—even at the risk of "double coverage"—it's usually best to purchase the CDW, if only for your peace of mind.

SUGGESTED ITINERARIES
If You Have 1 Week
Day 1 Settle into Stockholm and relieve your jet lag. If you're feeling up to it, take a walking tour of Gamla Stan (the old town). Select a favorite restaurant to return to for dinner, but only after a pre-dinner stroll along the harbor.

Days 2–3 Explore Stockholm's attractions, including the raised royal flagship *Vasa*. Reserve one morning or afternoon for a boat trip through the archipelago and another for exploring Drottningholm Palace, on an island in Lake Mälaren.

Day 4 Take a day trip north. Visit Sweden's oldest town, Sigtuna, on the shores of Lake Mälaren, and nearby Skokloster Castle, which houses one of the most interesting baroque museums in Europe. Then it's on to the university city of Uppsala and to the neighboring Gamla (Old) Uppsala to see Viking burial mounds.

Day 5 Begin a fast 3-day excursion through the most interesting folkloric provinces, Dalarna and Värmland. In the mining town of Falun, visit the Falun Copper Mine and the home of Carl Larsson, the famous Swedish painter. Spend the night here or in one of the smaller Lake Siljan resort towns, such as Tällberg, Rättvik, Mora, or Leksand.

Day 6 Visit the Lake Siljan towns just mentioned. Glacial Lake Siljan, ringed by lush forests, is one of the most beautiful in Europe. Take a boat tour from Rättvik. On its outskirts, you can visit Gammelgården, an old farmstead, for a glimpse into the past. Stay overnight in one of the lakeside villages or towns.

Tips Drop-Off Charges

Some travelers prefer to begin and end their trip to Sweden at different points, perhaps landing in Stockholm but departing by ferryboat elsewhere. For an additional fee, often car rental companies will allow you to drop off your rented car elsewhere, but only if you tell them of your plans when you first pick up the car. Otherwise, you may be in for an unpleasant surprise at the end of your trip.

Day 7 From Falun, Route 60 heads south to Karlstad. You'll pass through the heart of Selma Lagerlöf (Sweden's most famous novelist) country. Have lunch at Filipstad, the birthplace of John Ericsson, who designed the U.S. Civil War ironclad ship *Monitor.* Spend the night in Karlstad.

If You Have 2 Weeks

Days 1–7 Spend the first week as described above.

Day 8 Spend another night in Karlstad, exploring its attractions and branching out into the area, including Rottneros Manor.

Day 9 In the morning, head south along the eastern shore of Lake Vänern. After lunch in charming lakeside Lidköping, head for Gothenburg, Sweden's second-largest city.

Day 10 Explore Gothenburg and make a side trip to Kungälv or Marstrand, a former royal resort.

Days 11–13 From Gothenburg, take the Göta Canal excursion, which covers the 560km (350 miles) to Stockholm. As you pass through 58 locks, you'll have a chance to see the essence of Sweden.

Day 14 Arrive in Stockholm and prepare for your return flight.

12 Recommended Books

ART & ARCHITECTURE The most comprehensive survey of Swedish art is found in *A History of Swedish Art,* by Mereth Lindgren (Signum i Lung), published in 1987. In architecture, *Sweden: 20th Century,* edited by Claes Caldenby (Prestel Publishing), was published in 1998, so it's current almost to the dawn of the 21st century. You can see the emergence of Swedish modern in this opus.

HISTORY & MYTHOLOGY *The Early Vasas: A History of Sweden, 1523-1611,* by Michael Roberts (Cambridge), covers one of the most dramatic and action-filled eras in Sweden's long history.

Scandinavian Folk & Fairy Tales, edited by Claire Booss (Avenel), is an extraordinary collection filled with elves, dwarfs, trolls, goblins, and other spirits of the house and barnyard.

BIOGRAPHY *Sweden in North America (1638-1988),* by Sten Carlsson (Streiffert & Co.), follows the lives of some of the 2% of the North American population of Swedish background—from Greta Garbo to Charles Lindbergh.

Alfred Nobel and the Nobel Prizes, by Nils K. Ståhle (Swedish Institute), traces the life of the 19th-century Swedish industrialist and creator of the coveted awards that bear his name.

Garbo: Her Story, by Antoni Gronowicz (Simon & Schuster), is a controversial, unauthorized memoir based on a long and intimate friendship; it goes beyond the fabulous face, with many candid details of this most reluctant of movie legends.

LITERATURE & THEATER *A History of Swedish Literature,* by Ingemar Algulin (Swedish Institute), is the best overview on the subject—from the runic inscriptions of the Viking age up to modern fiction.

The Story of Gösta Berling, by Selma Lagerlöf (in various international editions), is the acclaimed work—originally published in 1891—that Garbo filmed.

Three Plays: Father, Miss Julie, Easter, by August Strindberg (Penguin), provides an insight into the world of this strange Swedish genius who wrote a number of highly arresting dramas, of which these are some of the best known.

FILM *Ingmar Bergman: The Cinema as Mistress,* by Philip Mosley (Marion Boyards), is a critical study of Bergman's *oeuvre* dating from his earliest work as a writer/director in the late 1940s up to *Autumn Sonata.*

Swedish Cinema, from Ingeborg Holm to Fanny and Alexander, by Peter Cowie (Swedish Institute), covers the complete history of Swedish films, from the emergence of the silent era, to the rise of Ingmar Bergman, up to the most recent wave.

PIPPI LONGSTOCKING TALES The world was saddened to learn of the death in 2002 of Astrid Lindgren, the Swedish writer of the Pippi Longstocking tales, who died at the age of 94 at her home in Stockholm. One of the world's most widely translated authors, Lindgren horrified parents but captivated millions of children around the globe with her whimsical, rollicking stories about a carrot-haired *enfant terrible.* In 1999 Lindgren was voted the most popular Swede of the century, having produced more than 70 books for young people. The best known is *Pippi Longstocking,* first published in 1945.

FAST FACTS: Sweden

Area Code The international country code for Sweden is **46**. The local city (area) codes are given for all phone numbers in the Sweden chapters.

Business Hours Generally, **banks** are open Monday through Friday from 9:30am to 3pm. In some larger cities banks extend their hours, usually on Thursday or Friday, until 5:30 or 6pm. Most **offices** are open Monday through Friday from 8:30 or 9am to 5pm (sometimes to 3 or 4pm in the summer); on Saturday, offices and factories are closed, or open for only a half day. Most **stores and shops** are open Monday through Friday between 9:30am and 6pm, and Saturday from 9:30am to somewhere between 1 and 4pm. Once a week, usually on Monday or Friday, some of the larger stores are open from 9:30am to 7pm (during July and Aug, to 6pm).

Camera & Film Cameras (especially the famed Hasselblad), film, projectors, and enlarging equipment are good values in Sweden. Practically all the world's brands are found here. Photographic shops give excellent service, often developing and printing in 1 day.

Dentists For emergency dental services, ask your hotel or host for the location of the nearest dentist. Nearly all dentists in Sweden speak English.

Doctors Hotel desks usually can refer you to a local doctor, nearly all of whom speak English. If you need emergency treatment, your hotel also should be able to direct you to the nearest facility. In case of an accident or injury away from the hotel, call the nearest police station.

Drug Laws Sweden imposes severe penalties for the possession, use, purchase, sale, or manufacture of illegal drugs ("illegal" is defined much like in the U.S.). Penalties often (but not always) are based on quantity. Possession of a small amount of drugs, either hard or soft, can lead to a heavy fine and deportation. Possession of a large amount of drugs can entail imprisonment from 3 months to 15 years, depending on the circumstances and the presiding judge.

Drugstores Called *apotek* in Swedish, drugstores generally are open Monday through Friday from 9am to 6pm and on Saturday from 9am to

1pm. In larger cities, one drugstore in every neighborhood stays open until 7pm. All drugstores post a list of the names and addresses of these stores (called *nattapotek*) in their windows.

Electricity In Sweden, the electricity is 220 volts AC (50 cycles). To operate North American hair dryers and other electrical appliances, you'll need an electrical transformer (sometimes erroneously called a converter) and plugs that fit the two-pin round continental electrical outlets that are standard in Sweden. Transformers can be bought at hardware stores. Before using any American-made appliance, always ask about it at your hotel desk.

Embassies & Consulates All embassies are in Stockholm. The Embassy of the **United States** is at Strandvägen 101, S-115 89 Stockholm (© 08/783-53-00); **United Kingdom,** Skarpögatan 6-8, S-115 27 Stockholm (© 08/671-30-00); **Canada,** Tegelbacken 4, S-101 23 Stockholm (© 08/453-30-00);and **Australia,** Sergels Torg 12, S-103 27 Stockholm (© 08/613-29-00). **New Zealand** does not maintain an embassy in Sweden.

Emergencies Call © **90-000** from anywhere in Sweden if you need an ambulance, the police, or the fire department *(brandlarm).*

Language The national language is Swedish, a Germanic tongue, and there are many regional dialects. Some minority groups speak Norwegian and Finnish. English is a required course of study in school and is commonly spoken, even in the hinterlands, and especially among young people.

Liquor Laws Most restaurants, pubs, and bars in Sweden are licensed to serve liquor, wine, and beer. Some places are licensed only for wine and beer. Purchases of wine, liquor, and export beer are available only through the government-controlled monopoly, *Systembolaget.* Branch stores, spread throughout the country, usually are open Monday through Friday from 9am to 6pm. The minimum age for buying alcoholic beverages in Sweden is 21.

Mail Post offices in Sweden usually are open Monday through Friday from 9am to 6pm and Saturday from 9am to noon. To send a postcard to North America costs 6.50SEK (70¢) by surface mail, 8SEK (85¢) by airmail. Letters weighing not more than 20 grams (¾ oz.) cost the same. Mailboxes can easily be recognized—they carry a yellow post horn on a blue background. You also can buy stamps in most tobacco shops and stationers.

Maps Many tourist offices supply routine maps of their districts free of charge, and you also can contact one of the Swedish automobile clubs. Bookstores throughout Sweden also sell detailed maps of the country and of such major cities as Gothenburg and Stockholm. The most reliable country maps are published by Hallweg. The best and most detailed city maps are those issued by Falk, which have a particularly good and properly indexed map to Stockholm.

Newspapers & Magazines In big cities such as Stockholm and Gothenburg, English-language newspapers, including the latest editions of the *International Herald Tribune* and *USA Today,* usually are available. American newspapers are not commonly available, but in Stockholm and Gothenburg you can purchase such London newspapers as *The Times.* At kiosks or newsstands in major cities, you also can purchase the European editions of *Time* and *Newsweek*.

Police   In an emergency, dial ℂ **90-000** anywhere in the country.

Radio & TV   In summer, Radio Stockholm broadcasts a special program for English-speaking tourists, "T-T-T-Tourist Time," on 103.3 MHz (FM) from 6 to 7pm daily. Swedish radio transmits P1 on 92.4 MHz (FM) and P2 on 96.2 MHz (FM) in the Stockholm area. P3 is transmitted on 103.3 MHz (102.9 MHz in southern Stockholm), a wavelength shared by Radio Stockholm and local programs.

The two most important TV channels, STV1 and STV2, are nonprofit. There are three major privately operated stations—Channel 4, TV3, and TV5, as well as several minor stations.

Restrooms   The word for toilet in Swedish is *toalett,* and public facilities are found in department stores, rail and air terminals, and subway (T-bana) stations. They're also located along some of the major streets, parks, and squares. DAMER means women and HERRAR means men. Sometimes the sign is abbreviated to D or H, and often the toilet is marked WC. Most toilets are free, although a few have attendants to offer towels and soap. In an emergency you also can use the toilets in most hotels and restaurants, although in principle they're reserved for guests.

Shoe Repairs   Shoe-repair shops rarely accommodate you while you wait. In summer, especially in July, many shops close, but the larger stores in the center of Stockholm have their own repair departments. If all you need is a new heel, look for something called *klackbar* in the stores or shoe departments of department stores. They'll make repairs while you wait.

Taxes   Sweden imposes a "value-added tax," called *moms,* on most goods and services. Visitors from North America can beat the tax, however, by shopping in stores with the yellow-and-blue tax-free shopping sign. There are more than 15,000 of these stores in Sweden. To get a refund, your total purchase must cost a minimum of 200SEK ($21). Tax refunds range from 14% to 18%, depending on the amount purchased. *Moms* begins at 19% on food items, but is 25% for most goods and services. The tax is part of the purchase price, but you can get a tax-refund voucher before you leave the store. When you leave Sweden, take the voucher to a tax-free customs desk at the airport or train station you're leaving from. They will give you your *moms* refund (minus a small service charge) before you wing off to your next non-Swedish destination. Two requirements: You cannot use your purchase in Sweden (it should be sealed in its original packaging), and it must be taken out of the country within 1 month after purchase. For more information, call **Global Refunds** at ℂ **0410/486-06.**

Telephone, Telex & Fax   Instructions in English are posted in public phone boxes, found on street corners. Very few phones are coin operated; most require a phone card, sold at most newspaper stands and tobacco shops. You can send a telegram by phoning ℂ **00-21** anytime. Avoid placing long-distance calls from your hotel, where the charge may be doubled or tripled when you get your final bill.

Time Sweden is on Central European Time—Greenwich Mean Time plus 1 hour, or Eastern Standard Time plus 6 hours. The clocks are advanced 1 hour in summer.

Tipping Hotels include a 15% service charge in your bill. Restaurants, depending on their class, add 13% to 15% to your tab. Taxi drivers are entitled to 8% of the fare, and cloakroom attendants usually get 6SEK (65¢).

Water The water is safe to drink all over Sweden. However, don't drink water from lakes, rivers, or streams, regardless of how clear and pure it appears.

Introducing Stockholm

Stockholm, a city of 1.5 million people, stands on 14 islands in Lake Mälaren. It marks the beginning of an archipelago of 24,000 islands, skerries, and islets stretching all the way to the Baltic Sea. Stockholm is a city of bridges and islands, towers and steeples, cobblestone squares and broad boulevards, Renaissance splendor, and steel-and-glass skyscrapers. Access to nature is just a short distance away. You can even go fishing in the downtown waterways, thanks to a 17th-century decree signed by Queen Christina.

Although the city was founded more than 7 centuries ago, it did not become the official capital of Sweden until the middle of the 17th century. While today it reigns over a modern welfare state, and the medieval walls of the Old Town (Gamla Stan) no longer remain, the old winding streets have been preserved.

1 Orientation

ARRIVING

BY PLANE You'll arrive at **Stockholm Arlanda Airport** (✆ **08/797-61-00** for flight information), about 46km (28 miles) north of the city on the E4 highway. A long covered walkway connects the international and domestic terminals.

A bus outside the terminal building takes you to the City Terminal, on Klarabergsviadukten in Stockholm, for 80SEK ($8.50). The trip takes about 40 minutes.

A taxi to or from the airport is expensive, costing 400SEK to 500SEK ($42–$53) or more. *Travelers beware:* Smaller taxi companies may charge up to 650SEK ($69) for the same ride. Be sure to ask in advance what the price is to your destination. For the name of a reputable company, see "Getting Around," below.

BY TRAIN The first high-speed train between Stockholm and Oslo has reduced travel time to 4 hours and 50 minutes between these two once remotely linked Scandinavian capitals. Depending on the day, there are two to three trains daily in each direction. This high-speed train now competes directly with air travel. Trains arrive at Stockholm's **Centralstationen (Central Station)** on Vasagatan, in the city center (✆ **07/717-575-75** in Sweden, or 08/696-75-09 from abroad). There you can make connections to Stockholm's subway, the T-bana. Follow the TUNNELBANA sign.

BY BUS Buses also arrive at the Centralstationen city terminal, where you can catch the T-bana (subway). For bus information or reservations, check with the **ticket offices** at the station (✆ **08/440-85-70**).

BY CAR Getting into Stockholm by car is relatively easy. The major national expressway from the south, E4, joins the national expressway E3, from the west, and leads into the heart of the city. Stay on the highway until you see the turnoff for central Stockholm (or Centrum).

Parking in Stockholm is extremely difficult unless your hotel has a garage, which is unlikely. Call in advance and find out what the parking situation is. If you're driving into the city, you can often park long enough to unload your luggage and ask a member of the hotel staff to direct you to the nearest garage.

BY FERRY   Large ships, including those of the **Silja Line,** Kungsgatan 2 (© **08/22-21-40**), and the **Viking Line,** Centralstationen (© **08/452-40-00**), arrive at berths near the junction of Södermalm and the entrance to Gamla Stan. This neighborhood is Stadsgården, and the avenue that runs along the adjacent waterfront is Stadsgårdshamnen. The Slussen T-bana stop, right at the berths, is a 3-minute walk from the Old Town. Holders of a valid Eurailpass receive discounts on Silja ferries to Helsinki and Turku.

Ferries from Gotland (whose capital is Visby) dock at Nynäshamn, south of Stockholm. Take a Nynäshamn-bound bus from the Central Station in Stockholm or the SL commuter train to reach the ferry terminal at Nynäshamn.

VISITOR INFORMATION

The **Tourist Center** is at Sweden House, Hamngatan 27, off Kungsträdgården (Box 7542), S-103 93 Stockholm (© **08/789-24-00** or 08/789-24-90). It's open from June to August, Monday through Friday from 9am to 7pm, Saturday and Sunday from 9am to 5pm; from September to May, Monday through Friday from 9am to 6pm, Saturday and Sunday from 10am to 3pm. Maps and other free materials are available.

Kulturhuset, Sergels Torg 3 (© **08/508-314-00**), distributes information about cultural activities and organizations throughout Sweden and Europe. The largest organization of its kind in Sweden, it was built in 1974 by the city of Stockholm as a showcase for Swedish and international art and theater. There are no permanent exhibits; display spaces hold a changing array of paintings, sculpture, photographs, and live performance groups. Inside are a snack bar, a library (which has newspapers in several languages), a reading room, and a collection of recordings. Admission is 40SEK ($4.25) for adults, 20SEK ($2.10) children 12 to 18, free for children under 12. It's open Tuesday through Thursday from 11am to 7pm, Friday from 11am to 6pm, Saturday from 11am to 4pm, and Sunday from noon to 4pm.

CITY LAYOUT

MAIN STREETS & ARTERIES   Stockholm's major streets are in the neighborhood of Norrmalm, north of Gamla Stan or Old Town. They are **Kungsgatan** (the main shopping street), **Birger Jarlsgatan,** and **Strandvägen** (which leads to Djurgården). **Stureplan,** which lies at the junction of Kungsgatan and Birger Jarlsgatan, is the commercial hub of the city.

About 4 blocks east of Stureplan is **Hötorget City,** a landmark of modern urban planning, which includes five 18-story skyscrapers. Its main, traffic-free artery is **Sergelgatan,** a 3-block shoppers' promenade that leads to the modern sculptures in the center of Sergels Torg.

About 9 blocks south of Stureplan, at **Gustav Adolfs Torg,** are the Royal Dramatic Theater and the Royal Opera House.

A block east of the flaming torches of the opera house is the verdant north-to-south stretch of **Kungsträdgården.** Part avenue, part public park, it serves as a popular gathering place for students and a resting perch for shoppers.

Three blocks to the southeast, on a famous promontory, are the landmark Grand Hotel and the National Museum.

Most visitors to Stockholm arrive at the SAS Airport Bus Terminal, the Central Station, or Stockholm's Central (Public) Bus Station. They're in the heart of the city, on the harbor, about 7 blocks due west of the opera house. **Kungsholmen** (King's Island) lies across a narrow canal from the rest of the city, a short walk west from the Central Station. It's visited chiefly by those who want to tour Stockholm's elegant Stadshuset (City Hall).

South of **Gamla Stan (Old Town),** and separated from it by a narrow but much-navigated stretch of water, is **Södermalm,** the city's southern district. Quieter than its northern counterpart, it's an important residential area.

To the east of Gamla Stan, on a large, forested island surrounded by complicated waterways, is **Djurgården (Deer Park).** The summer pleasure ground of Stockholm is the site of many of its most popular attractions (see "Neighborhoods in Brief," below).

FINDING AN ADDRESS   Even numbers are on one side of the street, odd numbers on the other. Buildings are in numerical order, often with A, B, or C after the number.

MAPS   Free maps of Stockholm are available at the tourist office. If you want to explore the narrow old streets of Gamla Stan, you'll need a more detailed map. The best, published by **Falk,** is a pocket-size map with a street index that can be opened and folded like a wallet. It's sold at most newsstands in central Stockholm and at major bookstores, including **Akademibokhandeln,** Mäster Samuelsgatan 32 (© **08/613-61-00**).

NEIGHBORHOODS IN BRIEF

On 14 major islands in an archipelago, the city naturally has many neighborhoods. Those of interest to the average visitor lie in central Stockholm.

Gamla Stan (Old Town) The "cradle" of Stockholm lies at the entrance to Lake Mälaren on the Baltic. Its oldest city wall dates from the 13th century. The Old Town and the Vasa are the city's most popular attractions. Gamla Stan has only a few hotels, but dozens of restaurants. Its major shopping street is Västerlånggatan, and many little artisans' galleries and antiques stores abound on its small lanes. The main square, and the heart of the ancient city, is Stortorget.

Långholmen Queen Christina donated Långholmen, meaning "long island," to the city of Stockholm in 1647, and for many years it was a bleak prison site on a rocky terrain. Female prisoners planted thousands of trees and today the island is a "green lung," a virtual park perfect for a fine leafy stroll

that's linked by bridge to the center of Stockholm. Even the prison has been transformed to a most unusual hotel with a fine restaurant.

Norrmalm North of Gamla Stan, this is the cultural and commercial heart of modern Stockholm, with a good concentration of moderately priced hotels. Once a city suburb, now it virtually *is* the city. If you come by train, you arrive at Central Station on Vasagatan in Norrmalm. The major pedestrian shopping street is Drottninggatan, which starts at the bridge to the Old Town.

The most famous park in Stockholm, Kungsträdgården (King's Garden), is in Norrmalm. In the summer this park is a major rendezvous point. Norrmalm also embraces the important squares of Sergels Torg and Hötorget (a modern shopping complex).

Vasastaden As Norrmalm pushed north, this new district was created. It's split by the main arteries St. Eriksgatan, Sveavägen, and Odengatan. The area around St. Eriksplan is called "the Off-Broadway of Stockholm" because it has so many theaters. Increasingly, this district has attracted fashionable restaurants and bars and become a popular residential area for young Stockholmers in such fields as journalism, television, and advertising.

Kungsholmen Once known as "Grey Friars Farm," today Kungsholmen (King's Island), to the west of Gamla Stan, is the site of City Hall. Established by Charles XI in the 17th century as a zone for industry and artisans, the island has been gentrified. One of its major arteries is Fleminggatan. Along Norrmälarstand, old Baltic cutters tie up to the banks. The headquarters of Stockholm's newspapers are at Marieberg on the southwestern tip of the island.

Södermalm South of Gamla Stan, Södermalm (where Greta Garbo was born) is the largest and most populated district of Stockholm. Once synonymous with poverty, today the working-class area is becoming more fashionable, especially with artists, writers, and young people. If you don't come here to stay in one of the moderately priced hotels or to dine in one of its restaurants, you may want to take the Katarina elevator, at Södermalmstorg, Slussen, for a good view of Stockholm and its harbor. Admission is 10SEK ($1.05), free for ages 6 and under.

Östermalm In central Stockholm, east of Birger Jarlsgatan, the main artery, lies Östermalm. In the Middle Ages the royal family kept horses, and even armies, here. Today it's the site of the Army Museum. It has wide, straight streets and one of the city's biggest parks, Humlegården, dating from the 17th century.

Djurgården To the east of Gamla Stan (Old Town) is Djurgården (Deer Park), forested island in a lake that's the city's summer recreation area. Here you can visit the open-air folk museums of Skansen, the *Vasa* man-of-war, Gröna Lunds Tivoli (Stockholm's version of Copenhagen's pleasure garden), the Waldemarsudde estate and gardens of the "painting prince" Eugen, and the Nordic Museum. The fastest way to get here is over the bridge at Strandvägen and Narvavägen.

2 Getting Around

BY PUBLIC TRANSPORTATION

You can travel throughout Stockholm county by bus, local train, subway (T-bana), and tram, going from Singö in the north to Nynäshamn in the south. The routes are divided into zones, and one ticket is valid for all types of public transportation in the same zone within 1 hour of being stamped.

REGULAR FARES The basic fare for public transportation (subway, tram, streetcar, or bus) is 20SEK ($2.10). Purchase a ticket for a tram or streetcar at the tollbooth on the subway platform. On buses you pay the driver. To travel in most of Stockholm, all the way to the borders of the inner city, requires two tickets. The maximum ride, to the outermost suburbs, requires five tickets. You can transfer free (or double back and return to your starting point) within 1 hour of your departure. Day passes can be purchased at the SL Center (see "Transit Information" under "Fast Facts," below).

SPECIAL DISCOUNT TICKETS   Your best transportation bet is a **tourist season ticket.** A 1-day card costs 80SEK ($8.50) and is valid for 24 hours of unlimited travel by T-bana, bus, and commuter train within Stockholm. It also includes passage on the ferry to Djurgården. Most visitors will probably prefer the 3-day card for 150SEK ($16), valid for 72 hours in Stockholm and the adjacent county. The 3-day card is also valid for admission to the Skansen museum, the Kaknäs tower, and Gröna Lunds Tivoli. A card for a child 8 to 17 costs 50SEK to 90SEK ($5.30–$9.55), and kids under 8 travel free with an adult. Tickets are available at tourist information offices, in subway stations, and from most news vendors. Call ℭ **08/689-10-00** for more information.

   Stockholmskortet (Stockholm Card) is a discount card that allows unlimited travel by bus (except airport buses), subway, and local trains throughout the city and county of Stockholm. Admission to 70 attractions is included in the package. You can also take a sightseeing tour with City Sightseeing, getting on and off as often as you please. Tours are available daily from mid-June to mid-August. The card is good for a 50% discount on a boat trip to the Royal Palace of Drottningholm.

   You can buy the card at several places in the city, including the Tourist Center in Sweden House, HotellCentralen, the Central Station, the tourist information desk in City Hall (summer only), the Kaknäs TV tower, SL-Center Sergels Torg (subway entrance level), and Pressbyrån newsstands. The cards are stamped with the date and time at the first use. A 24-hour card costs 220SEK ($23) for adults, 60SEK ($6.35) for children 7 to 17.

BY T-BANA (SUBWAY)   Subway entrances are marked with a blue T on a white background. Tickets are bought on the platform. For information about schedules, routes, and fares, phone ℭ **08/600-10-00.**

BY BUS   Where the subway line ends, the bus begins. If the subway doesn't reach an area, a bus will. Many visitors ride the bus to Djurgården (although you can walk), where the T-bana doesn't go. If you're staying long enough to warrant it, you can buy the *SL Stockholmskartan* booklet (80SEK/$8.50) at the Tourist Center at Sweden House, Hamngatan 27, off Kungsträdgården (ℭ **08/789-24-95**), for a list of bus routes.

BY CAR

In general, you can park in marked spaces Monday through Friday from 8am to 6pm, but these spaces are hard to come by. Consider leaving your car in a parking garage—there are several in the city center and on the outskirts—and using public transportation. Parking exceptions or rules for specific areas are indicated on signs in the area. At Djurgården, parking is always prohibited, and from April to mid-September, it's closed to traffic Friday through Sunday.

BY TAXI

Taxis in Stockholm are the most expensive in the world. The meter starts at 32SEK ($3.40), and a short ride can easily cost 80SEK ($8.50). You can hail those that display the sign LEDIG, or you can order one by phone. **Taxi Stockholm** (ℭ **08/15-00-00** or 08/15-04-00) is a large, reputable company.

BY FERRY

Ferries from Skeppsbron on Gamla Stan (near the bridge to Södermalm) can take you to Djurgården if you don't want to walk or go by bus. They leave every 20 minutes Monday through Saturday, and about every 15 minutes on Sunday,

Impressions

It [Stockholm] is not a city at all. It is ridiculous of it to think of itself as a city. It is simply a rather large village, set in the middle of some forests and some lakes. You wonder what it thinks it is doing there, looking so important.

—Ingmar Bergman, in an interview with James Baldwin, 1960

from 9am to 6pm. They cost 20SEK ($2.10) for adults, 15SEK ($1.60) for seniors and children 7 to 12; passage is free for children under 7.

BY BICYCLE

The best place to go cycling is on Djurgården. You can rent bicycles from **Skepp o Hoj,** Djurgårdsbron (℃ **08/660-57-57**), for about 150SEK ($16) per day. It's open from May to August, daily from 9am to 9pm.

FAST FACTS: Stockholm

American Express For local 24-hour customer service call ℃ **08/429-56-00**.

Area Code The international country code for Sweden is **46**; the city code for Stockholm is **08**. If you're calling Stockholm from abroad, drop the zero.

Babysitters Stockholm hotels maintain lists of competent women who babysit. Nearly all of them speak English. There is no official agency. Your hotel reception desk can assist you.

Bookstores For a good selection of English-language books, including maps and touring guides, try **Akademibokhandeln,** Mäster Samuelsgatan 32 (℃ **08/613-61-00**). It's open Monday through Friday from 10am to 7pm, Saturday from 10am to 4pm, and Sunday from noon to 4pm.

Car Rentals See "Getting Around," in chapter 12, "Planning Your Trip to Sweden." In Stockholm, some of the big companies include **Avis,** Ringvägen 90 (℃ **08/644-99-80**), and **Hertz,** Vasagatan 24 (℃ **08/24-07-20**).

Currency Exchange The currency-exchange office at the Central Station, **Forex** (℃ **08/411-67-34**), is open daily from 7am to 9pm. It's approved by the Bank of Sweden and the Swedish tourist authorities, offers some of the best exchange rates in town, and takes some of the lowest commissions for cashing traveler's checks. Several other offices are scattered throughout the city.

Dentists In an emergency, go to **Sct. Eriks Hospital,** Fleminggatan 22 (℃ **08/545-51-20**), open daily from 8am to 5pm.

Doctors For 24-hour emergency medical care, check with **Medical Care Information** (℃ **08/672-10-00**). There's also a private clinic, **City Akuten,** Apelberg Sq. 481, 4th Floor (℃ **08/412-29-61**).

Drugstores C. W. Scheele, Klarabergsgatan 64 (℃ **08/454-81-00**), is open 24 hours a day.

Embassies & Consulates See "Fast Facts: Sweden," in chapter 12.

Emergencies Call ℃ **112** for the police, ambulance service, or the fire department.

Eyeglasses **Nordiska Kompaniet (NK),** Hamngatan 18–20 (© **08/762-80-00**), a leading department store, has a registered optician on duty at its ground-floor Service Center. The optician performs vision tests, stocks a large selection of frames, and makes emergency repairs.

Hospitals Call **Medical Care Information** (© **08/32-01-00**), 24 hours a day, and an English-speaking operator can direct you to the nearest hospital.

Internet Access One of the most central places for receiving e-mail or checking messages is **Café Nine,** Odengatan 44 (© **08/673-67-97;** info@ninestudios.com). It charges only 1SEK (10¢) per minute, and is open Monday through Friday from 10am to 1am and Saturday and Sunday from 11am to 1am.

Laundry & Dry Cleaning The system of coin-operated launderettes is pretty much outmoded in Sweden. **City Kemtvatt,** Drottningsholmsvägen 9 (© **08/654-95-34**), offers same-day delivery of dry cleaning and laundry (by the kilo, or 2.2 lb.) brought in before 10am. It's open Monday through Friday from 7am to 6pm, Saturday from 10am to 2pm. The cost for doing laundry is 55SEK ($5.85) per kilo.

Libraries The **Stockholms Stadsbibliotek,** Sveavägen 73 (© **08/508-311-00**), is the biggest municipal library in Sweden, with 2.5 million books (many in English) and audiovisual materials. It also subscribes to 1,500 newspapers and periodicals (many in English). It's open Monday through Friday from 9am to 7pm and Saturday from noon to 4pm.

Lost Property If you've lost something on the train, go to the Lost and Found office in the Central Station, lower concourse (© **08/762-25-50**). There's another office at the police station at Bergsgatan 39 (© **08/401-07-88**). The Stockholm Transit Company (SL) keeps its recovered articles at the Rådmansgatan T-bana station (© **08/736-07-80**).

Luggage Storage & Lockers Facilities are available at the Central Station on Vasagatan, lower concourse (© **08/762-25-50**). You can also rent lockers at the ferry stations at Värtan and Tegelvikshamnen, at the Viking Line terminal, and at the Central Station.

Photographic Needs Stockholm has many photo shops. One of the most centrally located is the **Kodak Image Center,** Hamngatan 16 (© **08/21-40-42**). It's open Monday through Friday from 10am to 6pm, Saturday from 10am to 2pm.

Police Call © **112** in an emergency.

Post Office The main post office, at Vasagatan 28–34 (© **08/781-20-00**), is open Monday through Friday from 8am to 6pm, Saturday from 9am to 1pm. General-delivery mail can be sent to Poste Restante, c/o Postens Huyudkontor (Main Post Office), Vasagatan 28–34, S-104 30 Stockholm, Sweden.

Radio & TV Sweden has two TV channels and three national radio stations, plus a local station for Stockholm, broadcasting on 103.3 MHz (FM). Many hotels get English-language TV programs broadcast from England, and many of the more expensive hotels have 24-hour CNN news broadcasts in English.

Restrooms Public facilities are in the Central Station, all subway stations, and department stores, and along some major streets, parks, and squares. In an emergency, you can also use the toilets in most hotels and restaurants, although in principle they're reserved for patrons.

Shoe Repair The shoe-repair place in the basement of **Nordiska Kompaniet (NK),** Hamngatan 18–20 (*©* **08/762-80-00**), a leading department store, may also be able to repair broken luggage.

Taxis See "Getting Around," above.

Telephone, Telex & Fax Instructions in English are posted in public phone boxes, which can be found on street corners. Very few phones in Sweden are coin operated; most require a phone card, which you can buy at most newspaper stands and tobacco shops. You can send a telegram by phoning *©* **00-21** anytime.

Post offices throughout Stockholm offer phone, fax, and telegram services. All but the smallest boardinghouses in Stockholm have fax services.

Transit Information For information on all services, including buses, subways (T–bana), and suburban trains *(pendeltåg),* call *©* **08/600-10-00.** The SL Center, on the lower level of Sergels Torg, provides transportation information. It also sells a map of the city's system, including suburban trains, and day and discount passes for public transportation. It's open in summer, Monday through Thursday from 9am to 6pm, Friday from 9am to 5:30pm, Saturday from 9am to 4pm, Sunday from 10am to 3pm; the rest of the year, Monday through Friday from 9am to 5pm.

3 Where to Stay

By the standards of many U.S. and Canadian cities, hotels in Stockholm are very expensive. If the prices make you want to cancel your trip, read on. Dozens of hotels offer reduced rates on weekends all year and daily from around mid-June to mid-August. For further information, inquire at a travel agency or the Tourist Center (see "Visitor Information," above). In the summer, it's best to make reservations in advance just to be on the safe side.

Most medium-priced hotels are in Norrmalm, north of the Old Town, and many of the least expensive lodgings are near the Central Station. There are comparably priced inexpensive accommodations within 10 to 20 minutes of the city, easily reached by subway, streetcar, or bus. We'll suggest a few hotels in the Old Town, but they're limited and more expensive.

Note: In most cases a service charge ranging from 10% to 15% is added to the bill, plus the inevitable 21% *moms* (value-added tax). Unless otherwise indicated, all our recommended accommodations come with a private bathroom.

BOOKING SERVICES   HotellCentralen, Vasagatan (*©* **08/789-24-56**), on the lower level of the Central Station, is the city's official housing bureau. It can arrange accommodations in hotels, pensions (boardinghouses), and youth hostels, but not in private homes. There's a 50SEK ($5.30) service fee. It's open from June to August, daily from 7am to 9pm; May and September, daily from 8am to 7pm; from October to April, daily from 9am to 6pm. Credit and charge cards are accepted.

The least expensive accommodations in Stockholm are rooms in private homes. The best way to book one is to go to the **Hotell Tjänst AB,** Vasagatan 15–17 (© **08/10-44-37** or 08/10-44-57; fax 08/21-37-16); it's open Monday through Friday from 9am to noon and 1 to 5pm. As you leave the Central Station, turn left on Vasagatan and walk to this address, which is on the fourth floor of an older building. Mr. Gustavsson and his staff will book you into a private room, without breakfast, for around 500SEK ($53) in a double, including the reservation fee. From June 15 to August 15, the agency can also book you into Stockholm's major hotels at a big discount.

This service is usually available only in person. The agency maintains a long "secret" list of private addresses, and Mr. Gustavsson doesn't answer letters requesting reservations. The hours listed above are firm and advanced booking is rarely accepted, but if you're going to arrive in Stockholm on a weekend, call or fax the office and Mr. Gustavsson might bend the rules.

NORRMALM (CENTER OF STOCKHOLM)
VERY EXPENSIVE
Grand Hotel ⚜⚜⚜   Opposite the Royal Palace, this hotel—a bastion of elite hospitality since 1874—is the finest in Sweden. The most recent restoration was in 1996, but its old-world style has always been maintained. Guest rooms come in all shapes and sizes, all elegantly appointed with traditional styling. Some feature an air-cooling system. The bathrooms are decorated with Italian marble and tiles and have heated floors and shower-tub combinations. The priciest rooms overlook the water. The hotel's ballroom is an exact copy of Louis XIV's Hall of Mirrors at Versailles.

Södra Blasieholmshamnen 8, S-103 27 Stockholm. © **800/223-5652** in the U.S. and Canada, or 08/679-35-00. Fax 08/611-86-86. www.grandhotel.se. 320 units. 3,295SEK–4,095SEK ($349–$434) double; from 7,995SEK ($847) suite. Rates include breakfast. AE, DC, MC, V. Parking 350SEK ($37). T-bana: Kungsträdgården. Bus: 46, 55, 62, or 76. **Amenities:** 2 restaurants; bar; fitness center; sauna; room service; laundry/dry cleaning. *In room:* TV, minibar, hair dryer, safe.

EXPENSIVE
Berns' Hotel ⚜⚜   During its 19th-century heyday, this was the most elegant hotel in Sweden, with an ornate Gilded Age interior that was the setting for many a legendary rendezvous. In 1989, following years of neglect, it was rebuilt in the original style, and the restaurant facilities were upgraded. Although the dining and drinking areas are usually crowded with club kids and bar patrons, the guest rooms are soundproof and comfortably isolated from the activities downstairs. Each room has a bathroom sheathed in Italian marble. Bathrooms are small but have neatly maintained shower units. Some units are reserved for nonsmokers, and others are accessible to those in wheelchairs. The Red Room is the setting and namesake of Strindberg's novel *Röda Rummet.*

Näckströmsgatan 8, S-111 47 Stockholm. © **08/566-322-00.** Fax 08/566-322-01. www.berns.se. 65 units. 2,750SEK–3,900SEK ($292–$413) double; 4,600SEK–6,300SEK ($488–$668) suite. Rates include breakfast. AE, DC, MC, V. Parking 300SEK ($32). T-bana: Östermalmstorg. **Amenities:** Restaurant; bar; sauna; room service; babysitting; laundry/dry cleaning. *In room:* TV, minibar, hair dryer.

Hotell Diplomat ⚜   Well-managed, discreet, and solid, this hotel is a dignified and conservative operation that knows how to handle business clients and corporate conventions. Built in 1911, it retains hints of its original Art Nouveau styling. Public areas are more streamlined. The guest rooms are decorated with well-crafted furniture. Many rooms contain bay windows overlooking the

Stockholm Accommodations

Adlon Hotel & Kontor **8**
AF *Chapman* **23**
Berns' Hotel **22**
Elite Hotel
  Stockholm Plaza **14**
Esplanade Hotel **19**

First Hotel Reisen **24**
Grand Hotel **20**
Hotel City **10**
Hotel Tegnérlunden **11**
Hotell Diplomat **21**
Hotell Kom **12**

Hotell Örnsköld **18**
Kung Carl Hotel **13**
Lady Hamilton Hotel **3**
Långholmen Hotel **1**
Lydmar Hotel **15**
Mälardrottningen **4**

Mornington Hotel **16**
Nordic Hotel **9**
Radisson SAS
  Royal Viking Hotel **7**
Scandic Hotel
  Sergel Plaza **6**

Sheraton Stockholm
  & Towers **5**
Victory Hotel **2**
Wellington **17**

† Church
ⓘ Information
✉ Post Office
⊣Ⓣⱼ Subway
— Railway

345

harbor; most of the less expensive accommodations face a quiet inner courtyard. Rooms range in size from cramped singles to spacious doubles with sitting areas. All have good beds and average-size bathrooms, with tiled vanities, bidets, and both tubs and hand-held showers. At least once, take the circular stairs for views of the hotel's antique stained-glass windows.

Strandvagen 7C, Östermalm, S-104 40 Stockholm. ✆ **08/459-68-00.** Fax 08/459-68-20. 128 units. Mon–Thurs 2,195SEK–2,995SEK ($233–$317) double; Fri–Sun 1,095SEK–1,995SEK ($116–$211) double. All week long from 3,695SEK ($392) suite. AE, DC, MC, V. Rates include breakfast. Parking 350SEK ($37). T-bana: Storeplan. **Amenities:** Restaurant; 2 bars; room service; babysitting; laundry/dry cleaning. *In room:* TV, minibar, hair dryer.

Lydmar Hotel ✪   Opposite the garden of the King's Library, in what looks like an office building, the Lydmar opened in 1930 (as the Eden Terrace). The guest rooms are cozy and traditionally furnished, and come in many shapes and sizes. Although the rooms aren't large, they are exceptionally well maintained. The bathrooms are well appointed and contain shower-tub combinations. The hotel has a large dining room and a rooftop terrace where guests can enjoy drinks in the summer. In recent years, the Matsalen restaurant has become ever-so-chic.

Sturegatan 10, S-114 36 Stockholm. ✆ **08/566-113-00.** Fax 08/566-113-01. www.lydmar.se. 62 units. 2,250SEK–4,950SEK ($239–$525) double; 7,500SEK ($795) junior suite. Rates include buffet breakfast. AE, DC, MC, V. Parking 300SEK ($32). T-bana: Östermalmstorg. Bus: 41, 46, 56, or 91. **Amenities:** 2 restaurants; bar; room service; babysitting; laundry/dry cleaning. *In room:* TV, minibar, hair dryer.

Nordic Hotel ✪✪ *Finds*   There's nothing quite like this hotel in Scandinavia. Stockholm's newest major hotel is like a split personality— its astrological sign is definitely Gemini. You're given a choice of a room of "watery calm" in the 367-room Nordic Sea or "post-minimalist luminescence" in the 175-room Nordic Light. Lying on either side of a new square, Vasaplan, the hotel stands adjacent to the express rail link with the airport, or the central rail station.

Each hotel has its own individual design. Nordic Sea, of course, turns to the ocean for its inspiration and features a 530-liter (2,400-gal.) aquarium and steel walls constructed from ship hulls. Approached by an underground walkway, Nordic Light is filled with sun-shaped projections that guarantee a bright light even in the darkest winter days of February. Surprisingly for a hotel, the lobby emits sounds and lighting effects when it senses the presence of a guest. The suggestive light patterns projecting from the walls re-create the ever-changing patterns of the lights of the north. This hotel is not just about gimmicks but offers real comfort.

Nordic Light guest rooms have the best sound insulation in town, and rooms come in a variety of sizes, but all have grand comfort and bathrooms with tub and shower. Wood, steel, and glass create both club-like and maritime auras in Nordic Sea rooms. Rooms have a certain elegant simplicity with excellent comfort and beautiful bathrooms with tub and shower. These accommodations range in size from extra small to extra large.

4-7 Vasaplan. ✆ **800/337-4685** in the U.S., or 08/50-56-30-00, Fax: 08/50-56-30-60. www.nordichotels.se. 367 units in Nordic Sea, 175 units in Nordic Light. 2,400–3,600SEK ($254–$382) double in Nordic Sea; 2,900–3,600SEK ($307–$382) double in Nordic Light. June 20–Aug 17, and during selected Fri-Sun nights throughout the winter, rates are reduced to 1,190–1,990SEK ($126–$211) double in Nordic Sea, and 1,390–1,990SEK ($147–$211) double in Nordic Light. AE, DC, MC, V. T-bana: Centralen. **Amenities:** Restaurant; bar; mini-gym; spa treatments; sauna; steam bath; room service; laundry/dry cleaning. *In room:* TV, minibar, coffeemaker, iron/ironing board, safe.

Scandic Hotel Sergel Plaza ✪✪   This hotel opened in 1984 at the entrance to Drottninggatan, the main shopping street. Designed as living quarters for

---

Kids Family-Friendly Hotels

AF Chapman (p. 351)   Although there are no family rooms, kids delight in staying in a stateroom (with two to eight beds) aboard an authentic three-masted schooner.

Hotel Tegnérlunden (p. 349)   Twenty big, airy rooms are ideal for families on a budget.

Sheraton Stockholm & Towers (p. 348)   This well-run chain has always pampered children. The spacious rooms can be comfortably shared with parents.

---

parliament members, improvements have made it one of the city's leading hotels. The elegant decor includes 18th-century artwork and antiques. The beautifully decorated guest rooms are done in modern but traditional style. The average-size tiled bathrooms have shower-tub combinations. Maintenance is first rate, and there are some accommodations for nonsmokers and wheelchair users. A special executive floor offers enhanced luxuries and several electronic extras, such as dataports.

Brunkebergstorg 9, S-103 27 Stockholm. $\mathcal{C}$ **800/THE-OMNI** in the U.S., or 08/517-263-00. Fax 08/ 517-263-11. www.scandic-hotels.se. 418 units. 1,250SEK–2,280SEK ($133–$242) double; from 7,000SEK ($742) suite. Rates include breakfast. AE, DC, MC, V. Parking 210SEK ($22). T-bana: Centralen. Bus: 47, 52, or 69. **Amenities:** Restaurant; bar; room service; laundry/dry cleaning. *In room:* TV, minibar, hair dryer.

MODERATE
Adlon Hotell & Kontor   This 1890s building was redesigned by brothers Axel and Hjalmar Jumlin in the 1920s. Upgraded and improved many times since, it lies near the Central Station (and the subway) and is convenient to buses to and from Arlanda Airport. All the rather small rooms have been renovated and are comfortably furnished; 70% of them are designated for nonsmokers. The small bathrooms have shower-tub combinations.

Vasagatan 42, S-111 20 Stockholm. $\mathcal{C}$ **08/402-65-00.** Fax 08/20-86-10. www.adlon.se. 78 units. 1,155SEK–2,800SEK ($122–$297) double. Rates include breakfast. AE, DC, MC, V. Parking 300SEK ($32) in garage 1 block away. T-bana: Centralen. **Amenities:** Bar; lounge; laundry/dry cleaning. *In room:* TV, minibar, hair dryer.

Elite Hotel Stockholm Plaza ⋆   Built on a triangular lot that might remind some visitors of New York's Flatiron Building, this first-class hotel is a well-run and inviting choice in the city center. From the time of its construction in 1903 until its renovation in 1984, the building had many uses—a run-down rooming house, private apartments, and offices. The light, fresh guest rooms have firm beds and tiled bathrooms with shower-tub combinations.

Birger Jarlsgatan 29, S-103 95 Stockholm. $\mathcal{C}$ **08/566-220-00.** Fax 08/566-220-20. www.elite.se. 151 units. 1,290SEK–2,190SEK ($137–$232) double; 2,690SEK–4,045SEK ($285–$429) suite. Rates include breakfast. AE, DC, MC, V. Parking 260SEK ($28). T-bana: Hötorget or Östermalmstorg. **Amenities:** Restaurant; bar; dance club; sauna; room service; laundry/dry cleaning. *In room:* TV, minibar, hair dryer.

Esplanade Hotel ⋆   This informal hotel, next to the more expensive Diplomat, attracts representatives from the nearby embassies and others who like its comfortable charm and traditional atmosphere. Constructed in 1910, it became a family-style hotel in 1954. Many of the rooms, furnished in old-fashioned style, have minibars. Single rooms are minuscule. Most doubles have double-glazed windows, extra-long beds, and well-kept, decent-size tile bathrooms with shower-tub combinations. Four rooms have a water view, and the English lounge features a balcony with a view of Djurgården. Only breakfast is served.

Strandvägen 7A, S-114 56 Stockholm. © **08/663-07-40.** Fax 08/662-59-92. www.hotelesplanade.se. 34 units. Mon–Thurs 2,295SEK ($243) double; Fri–Sun 1,795SEK ($190) double. Rates include breakfast. AE, DC, MC, V. Parking 250SEK ($27). T-bana: Östermalmstorg. Bus: 47 or 69. **Amenities:** Lounge; sauna; laundry/dry cleaning. *In room:* TV, minibar.

Kung Carl Hotel ⭐   Discreet, tasteful, and quietly glamorous, this hotel in the heart of Stockholm was built in the mid-1800s by a religious group that offered lodgings to women newly arrived in Stockholm from the country. It's one of the longest-operating hotels in the city. Transformed into a hotel in the 1870s, and elevated to four-star status thanks to many improvements, it retains an old-fashioned charm. The conservatively furnished guest rooms were expanded and renovated in 1998. The bathrooms, although small, are well maintained and equipped with shower-tub combinations. There's no restaurant on the premises, but the lobby bar sells pizza and sandwiches.

Birger Jarlsgatan 21, S-111 45 Stockholm. © **08/463-50-00.** Fax 08/463-50-50. www.hkchotels.se. 112 units. 1,850SEK–2,450SEK ($196–$260) double; 5,500SEK ($583) suite. Rates include breakfast. AE, DC, MC, V. Parking 300SEK ($32). T-bana: Östermalmstorg. **Amenities:** Bar; lounge; pool; fitness center; sauna; room service; laundry/dry cleaning. *In room:* TV, minibar, hair dryer, safe.

Radisson SAS Royal Viking Hotel ⭐   This airline-affiliated hotel in a nine-story tower is in a commercial neighborhood near the railway station and the Stockholm World Trade Center. It has a soaring, plant-filled atrium. Especially popular in summer with organized tours and conventioneers, it offers rooms with stylized modern furniture and good, firm beds. Bathrooms are on the small side, but big enough for shower-tub combinations and phones. Some rooms are set aside for nonsmokers, and others are wheelchair accessible. Many units are mini-suites, well accessorized with electronic extras.

Vasagatan 1, S-101 23 Stockholm. © **800/333-3333** in the U.S., or 08/506-540-00. Fax 08/506-540-01. www.radissonsas.com. 429 units. 1,499SEK–2,650SEK ($159–$281) double; 6,900SEK ($731) suite. Rates include breakfast. AE, DC, MC, V. Parking 310SEK ($33). T-bana: Centralen. **Amenities:** Restaurant; bar; pool; fitness center; sauna; room service; laundry/dry cleaning. *In room:* TV, minibar, hair dryer.

Sheraton Stockholm & Towers ⭐ *Kids*   Sheathed with Swedish granite, this eight-story hostelry is within view of Stockholm's City Hall (Rådhuset). Short on Swedish charm, it's excellent by chain hotel standards, attracting many business travelers and families, both foreign and domestic. The guest rooms are the largest in the city with one king or two double beds with bedside TV controls and closets with mirrored doors. A family of three or four can fit comfortably into most of them. Medium-sized tile bathrooms have shower-tub combinations and heated towel racks, and some units have bidets. Most units offer sweeping views of the city, many over Gamla Stan.

Tegelbacken 6, S-101 23 Stockholm. © **800/325-3535** in the U.S. and Canada, or 08/412-34-00. Fax 08/412-34-09. www.sheratonstockholm.com. 461 units. 3,380SEK ($358) double; from 4,300SEK ($456) suite. Rates include breakfast. AE, DC, MC, V. Parking 240SEK ($25). T-bana: Centralen. **Amenities:** 2 restaurants; bar; fitness center; sauna; room service; babysitting; laundry/dry cleaning. *In room:* TV, minibar, hair dryer.

INEXPENSIVE

Hotel City   Set in a desirable location between two of Stockholm's biggest department stores (PUB and Åhléns City), Hotel City has small but clean, comfortable guest rooms. They have been elegantly refurbished using mirrors, hardwood trim, carpeting, and tile. All units have neatly kept bathrooms with shower-tub combinations. Although the hotel doesn't serve alcohol, it maintains a simple restaurant that's open Monday through Friday from 11am to 3pm.

Slöjdgatan 7 (at Hötorget), S-111 81 Stockholm. (C) **08/723-72-00.** Fax 08/723-72-09. www.rica.cityhotel.se. 283 units. 1,180SEK–1,800SEK ($125–$191) double. Rates include breakfast. AE, DC, MC, V. Parking 250SEK ($27). T-bana: Hötorget. **Amenities:** Restaurant; lounge; sauna; laundry/dry cleaning. *In room:* TV, minibar, hair dryer, safe.

Hotell Kom   Don't expect too much at this former youth hostel—people stay here mainly for the price. But Hotell Kom was upgraded to a hotel over 20 years ago and is certainly appropriate for extended stays. Each unit has a small kitchenette, creating an apartment-like ambience. It's in a residential neighborhood scattered with stores and private apartments. The rooms are clean and decent, with reasonably comfortable beds, and rather small but immaculate bathrooms with shower units. Only breakfast is served.

17 Döbelnsgatan, S-111 40 Stockholm. (C) **08/412-23-00.** Fax 08/412-23-10. www.komhotel.se. 99 units. Mon–Thurs 1,650SEK–1,860SEK ($175–$197) double; Fri–Sun 1,160SEK ($123) double. Rates include breakfast. AE, DC, MC, V. Parking 160SEK ($17). T-bana: Rådmansgatan. **Amenities:** Bar; lounge; fitness center; sauna; laundry/dry cleaning. *In room:* TV, minibar, hair dryer, safe.

Hotell Örnsköld   The five-story building that contains this hotel was built in 1910, and today the nearby Royal Dramatic Theater uses most of it for prop storage and staff housing. The hotel is situated on the second floor. High-ceilinged rooms have simple, contemporary furnishings, and more expensive units are big enough to hold extra beds if necessary. All units contain well-kept bathrooms with shower units.

Nybrogatan 6, S-114 34 Stockholm. (C) **08/667-02-85.** Fax 08/667-69-91. 27 units. 1,275SEK–1,975SEK ($135–$209) double. Rates include breakfast. AE, MC, V. Parking 250SEK ($27) in nearby public garage. T-bana: Östermalmstorg. **Amenities:** Lounge; laundry/dry cleaning. *In room:* TV, minibar, hair dryer.

Hotel Tegnérlunden *(Kids)*   In a 19th-century building at the edge of a city park, this hotel has a few public rooms, a lobby, and a bar. The best feature is the tasteful, functionally furnished rooms, many suitable for families. They're blissfully quiet, especially those opening onto the rear. The rooms vary in size and shape, and those we inspected were well maintained. The hotel offers comfort but not a lot of style. The bathrooms equipped with shower units are small but beautifully kept.

Tegnérlunden 8, S-113 59 Stockholm. (C) **08/545-455-50.** Fax 08/545-455-51. www.hoteltegnerlunden.se. 103 units. 990SEK–1,560SEK ($105–$165) double; 1,895SEK ($201) junior suite. Rates include breakfast. AE, DC, MC, V. Parking 150SEK ($16) in nearby garage. Bus: 47, 53, or 69. **Amenities:** Bar; sauna; laundry/dry cleaning. *In room:* TV, hair dryer.

Mornington Hotel   Proud of its image as an English-inspired hotel, this efficient modern establishment has a concrete exterior brightened with rows of flower boxes. It was built in 1956 and has been renovated several times, most recently in 1997. Most rooms have standard decor, and many are quite small. Each unit contains a well-kept bathroom with shower-tub combination. The lobby contains a small rock garden. The hotel offers rooms for nonsmokers and guests with disabilities.

Nybrogatan 53, S-102 44 Stockholm. (C) **800/528-1234** in the U.S. and Canada, or 08/663-12-40. Fax 08/507-330-00. www.morningtonhotel.com. 141 units. June 26–Aug 9 1,295SEK ($137) double; Aug 10–June 25 2,020SEK ($214) double. Year-round from 2,500SEK ($265) suite. Rates include breakfast. AE, DC, MC, V. Parking 220SEK ($23). Closed Dec 23–26. T-bana: Östermalmstorg. Bus: 49, 54, or 62. **Amenities:** Restaurant; bar; sauna; room service; laundry/dry cleaning. *In room:* TV, minibar, hair dryer.

Wellington 🏨   A longtime favorite with frugal travelers, the Wellington sounds like something you'd find in London. Built in the late 1950s, it maintains some English decorative touches and lies in a quiet but convenient neighborhood less than 1km (½ mile) east of Stockholm's commercial core. The public rooms are filled with leather-covered chairs and engravings of English hunting scenes. Some of the small but stylish guest rooms overlook a flower-filled courtyard. Some rooms on higher floors have panoramic views. Beds are firm, and the small bathrooms are well equipped and include shower-tub combinations. Two floors are reserved for nonsmokers.

Storgatan 6, S-114 51 Stockholm. ℂ 08/667-09-10. Fax 08/667-12-54. www.wellington.se. 60 units. Summer and Fri–Sat year-round 1,295SEK ($137) double; rest of year 2,095SEK ($222) double. Rates include breakfast. AE, DC, MC, V. Parking 325SEK ($34). T-bana: Östermalmstorg. **Amenities:** Bar; sauna; laundry/dry cleaning. *In room:* TV, hair dryer.

IN GAMLA STAN (OLD TOWN)
EXPENSIVE
First Hotel Reisen 🏨🏨   Just three alleyways from the Royal Palace, this hotel faces the water. Dating from the 17th century, the three-building structure attractively combines the old and the new. The rooms are comfortably furnished in a stylish modern fashion inspired by traditional designs. Beds are frequently renewed, and the bathrooms are excellent, with deep tubs, massaging shower-heads, scales, marble floors, heated towel racks, and phones. Some suites have Jacuzzis. Some units for nonsmokers are available, and the top-floor accommodations open onto small balconies.

Skeppsbron 12–14, S-111 30 Stockholm. ℂ 08/22-32-60. Fax 08/20-15-59. www.firsthotels.com. 144 units. Mon–Thurs 2,543SEK–2,743SEK ($270–$291) double, from 2,943SEK ($312) suite; Fri–Sun 1,403SEK–1,503SEK ($149–$159) double, from 1,693SEK ($179) suite. Rates include breakfast. AE, DC, MC, V. Parking 315SEK ($33). Bus: 43, 46, 55, 59, or 76. **Amenities:** Restaurant; bar; pool; sauna; room service; laundry/dry cleaning. *In room:* TV, minibar, hair dryer.

Lady Hamilton Hotel 🏨 *(Finds)*   This hotel, consisting of three connected buildings, stands on a quiet street surrounded by antiques shops and restaurants—a very desirable location indeed. Dozens of antiques are scattered among the well-furnished guest rooms. Most rooms have beamed ceilings. The beds (queen or double) are of high quality. Bathrooms are tiled but vary in size from spacious to cramped. All have heated towel racks, heated floors, and shower-tub combinations. Top-floor rooms have skylights and memorable views over the Old Town. Some rooms for nonsmokers are available. You'll get a sense of the 1470 origins of this hotel when you use the luxurious sauna, which encompasses the stone-rimmed well that formerly supplied the building's water. The ornate staircase wraps around a large model of a clipper ship suspended from the ceiling.

Storkyrkobrinken 5, S-111 28 Stockholm. ℂ 08/506-401-00. Fax 08/506-401-10. www.lady-hamilton.se. 34 units, some with shower only. 1,690SEK–2,390SEK ($179–$253) double. Rates include breakfast. AE, DC, MC, V. Parking: 295SEK ($31). T-bana: Gamla Stan. Bus: 48. **Amenities:** Restaurant; bar; sauna; room service; babysitting; laundry/dry cleaning. *In room:* TV, minibar, hair dryer.

Victory Hotel 🏨🏨   A small but stylish hotel, the Victory offers warm, inviting rooms, each named after a prominent sea captain. They sport a pleasing combination of exposed wood, antiques, and 19th-century memorabilia. Many rooms are smoke-free, and the beds are comfortable, with firm mattresses. The average-size bathrooms are tiled and have heated floors and shower units. Only the suites have tubs. The hotel rests on the foundations of a 1382 fortified tower. In the 1700s the building's owners buried a massive silver treasure under the basement floor—you can see it in the Stockholm City Museum. There's a shiny brass elevator, but from the stairs you'll see one of Sweden's largest collections of 18th-century nautical needlepoint, much of it created by the sailors during their long voyages.

Lilla Nygatan 3–5, S-111 28 Stockholm. ℂ 08/506-400-00. Fax 08/506-400-10. www.victory-hotel.se. 48 units, some with shower only. 1,790SEK–2,490SEK ($190–$264) double; 2,690SEK–3,890SEK ($285–$412) suite. Rates include breakfast. AE, DC, MC, V. T-bana: Gamla Stan. Bus: 48. **Amenities:** Restaurant; bar; pool; sauna; room service; babysitting; laundry/dry cleaning. *In room:* TV, minibar, hair dryer, safe.

MODERATE

Mälardrottningen ⭐ *Finds*   During its heyday, this was the most famous motor yacht in the world, the subject of gossip columns everywhere, thanks to the complicated friendships that developed among the passengers and, in some cases, the crew. Built in 1924 by millionaire C. K. G. Billings, it was the largest (72m/240 ft.) motor yacht in the world, and was later acquired by the Woolworth heiress, Barbara Hutton. The below-deck space originally contained only seven suites. The yacht was converted into a hotel in the early 1980s, and was permanently moored beside a satellite island of Stockholm's Old Town. The cabins are now cramped and somewhat claustrophobic. Most have bunk-style twin beds. All units have neatly kept bathrooms with shower-tub combinations. Considering the hotel's conversation-piece status, and its location close to everything in the Old Town, it might be worth an overnight stay.

Riddarholmen, S-111 28 Stockholm. ℂ **08/545-187-80.** Fax 08/24-36-76. www.malardrottningen.se. 60 units. Mon–Thurs 1,100SEK–2,100SEK ($117–$223) double; Fri–Sun 980SEK–1,300SEK ($104–$138) double. Rates include breakfast. AE, DC, MC, V. Parking 17SEK ($1.80) per hour. T-bana: Gamla Stan. **Amenities:** Restaurant; bar; sauna; laundry/dry cleaning. *In room:* TV, hair dryer.

ON LÅNGHOLMEN

Långholmen Hotel   Beginning in 1724, on the little island of Långholmen, this structure was a state penitentiary for women charged with "loose living." The last prisoner was released in 1972 and today it's a newly restored and reasonably priced accommodation which, in addition to comfortable but small rooms, also houses a museum of Sweden's prison-history and one of the best restaurants in the country. Instead of a prison induction area, you get the hotel's reception area and a 24-hour snack bar. Accommodations were carved from some 200 cells, creating cramped but serviceable rooms equipped with small showers and toilets.

Ten of the bedrooms are suitable for persons with disabilities, and 91 are reserved for nonsmokers. This is one of the best hotels in Stockholm for the single visitor on a budget, as 89 rooms are rented only to solo travelers. Just 13 rooms are large enough to accommodate two persons.

Kronohåktet, S-102 72 Stockholm. ℂ **08/668-05-00.** Fax 08/720-85-75. www.langholmen.com. 102 units. Sun–Thurs 1,395SEK ($148) double; Fri–Sat 1,095SEK ($116) double. Extra bed 210SEK ($22) per person. Rates include breakfast. AE, MC, V. T-bana: Hornstul. Bus: 4, 40, or 66. **Amenities:** Restaurant; bar; laundry/dry cleaning. *In room:* TV, hair dryer.

ON SKEPPSHOLMEN

AF Chapman *Kids*   Moored off Skeppsholmen, this authentic three-masted schooner has been converted into a youth hostel ideal for families. Staterooms have two, four, six, or eight beds; there are no single cabins. Each section—one for men, one for women—has showers and washrooms. Personal lockers are available. The gangplank goes up at 2am, with no exceptions, and there's a 5-day maximum stay. The rooms are closed from 11am to 3pm. No cigarette smoking is allowed. A summer cafe operates on the ship's deck. Breakfast, at an extra charge, is available in the self-service coffee bar and dining room. International Youth Hostel Association cards can be obtained at the AF *Chapman*.

Västra Brobänken, Skeppsholmen, S-111 49 Stockholm. © **08/463-22-66.** Fax 08/611-98-75. www.stfchap man.com. 136 beds in 36 cabins, none with bathroom. Members 150SEK ($16) per adult, 70SEK ($7.40) per child; nonmembers 195SEK ($21) per adult, 95SEK ($10) per child. MC, V. Closed Dec 16–Apr 1. Bus: 65. **Amenities:** Lounge. *In room:* No phone.

4 Where to Dine

Food is expensive in Stockholm, especially with the 21% "value-added tax" included in the bill. Those on a budget can stick to self-service cafeterias. At all restaurants other than cafeterias, a 12% to 15% service charge is added to the bill to cover the tip. Wine and beer can be lethal to your final bill, so proceed carefully. For good value, try ordering the *dagens ratt* (daily special), if available.

One tip to save you a little inconvenience: Don't rush into a bar for a martini. "Bars" are self-service cafeterias, and the strongest drink many of them offer is apple cider.

NORRMALM (CENTER OF STOCKHOLM)
VERY EXPENSIVE

Bon Lloc ✦✦✦ MEDITERRANEAN   This is a Swedish temple of gastronomy. Chef Mathias Dahlgren is a darling of food critics, and is hailed by some of his admirers as the finest chef in Sweden. *Bon Lloc* in Catalan means "good luck," and you'll need it to get a table here. The interior looks like a sophisticated blend of the best of contemporary Swedish and post-Movida Spanish decors. There's a bar at the entrance, and an intensely contemporary-looking dining room on two tiers (something like a stage set at an opera). The room is sheathed in massive amounts of oak (on the floor and in the wood trim), with occasional touches of reddish stone, gray walls, and minimalist furniture.

Some members of the press call Dahlgren's cuisine "nouveau Euro-Latino." His actual cuisine is hard to define. Even though Mediterranean in inspiration, dishes are prepared with such skill and imagination that they seem to merit a category of their own. His style balances delicacy and richness. This is not overly fussy cookery, but it makes a tremendous impact.

An oven-roasted cod comes with a lobster *brandade* and a gazpacho salsa, and it's as good as this dish gets. Out of the same oven popped the most delicious roasted ham with apple cider glaze we've ever had. Who would have thought that Dahlgren could take such a lowly ingredient as a pig's foot and turn it into a platter of such flavorful, crispy joy? The free-range pork glazed with white pepper and served with plum vinegar gravy was exciting and original at the same time. We could make a meal of the creamy Roquefort served here. Its secret: The cheese is made only from nursing cows.

Regeringsgatan 111. © **08/660-60-60.** Reservations required. Main courses 275SEK–335SEK ($29–$36). Mon–Sat 5–11pm. T-bana: Rådmansgatan.

Operakällaren ✦✦✦ FRENCH/SWEDISH   Opposite the Royal Palace, this is the most famous and unashamedly luxurious restaurant in Sweden. Its elegant decor and style are reminiscent of a royal court banquet. The service and house specialties are impeccable. Many come here for the elaborate fixed-price menus; others prefer the classic Swedish dishes or the modern French ones. A house specialty that's worth the trip is the platter of northern delicacies, with everything from smoked eel to smoked reindeer, along with Swedish red caviar. Salmon and game, including grouse from the northern forests, are prepared in various ways. There's a cigar room, too.

Operahuset, Kungsträdgården. (C) **08/676-58-00**. Reservations required. Main courses 370SEK–420SEK ($39–$45); 3-course fixed-price menu 520SEK ($55); 4-course fixed-price menu 880SEK ($93); 7-course *menu dégustation* 1,450SEK ($154). AE, DC, MC, V. Daily 5–10pm. Closed July. T-bana: Kungsträdgården.

Paul & Norbert ★★★ CONTINENTAL   In a patrician residence dating from 1873, adjacent to the Hotell Diplomat, this is the finest and most innovative restaurant in Stockholm. Seating only 30 people, it has vaguely Art Deco decor, beamed ceilings, and dark paneling. Owners Paul Beck and Norbert Lang worked in many top European restaurants before opening this establishment. To start, they prepare a tantalizing terrine of scallops in saffron sauce. The foie gras is the finest in town. Perfectly prepared main dishes include sautéed medallion of fjord salmon, scallops, and scampi in lobster sauce; crisp breast of duck with caramelized orange sauce; and juniper-stuffed noisettes of reindeer immersed in caraway sauce with portobello mushrooms.

Strandvägen 9. (C) **08/663-81-83**. Reservations required. Main courses 250SEK–310SEK ($27–$33); 9-course *grand menu de frivolité* 1,300SEK ($138). AE, DC, MC, V. Mid-Aug to June Tues–Fri noon–3pm, Mon–Sat 6–10pm. July to mid-Aug Mon–Sat 6–10pm. Closed Dec 24–Jan 6. T-bana: Östermalmstorg.

EXPENSIVE

Franska Matsalen (French Dining Room) ★★ FRENCH   Widely acclaimed as one of the greatest restaurants in Stockholm, this elegant establishment is on the street level of the city's finest hotel. The dining room is appointed with polished mahogany, ormolu, and gilt accents under an ornate plaster ceiling. Tables on the enclosed veranda overlook the Royal Palace and the Old Town. Begin with a cannelloni of foie gras with cèpes, or perhaps mousseline of scallops with Sevruga caviar. Main dishes include seared sweetbreads served with artichokes, *langoustines* (prawns) and frogs' legs with broad beans, and veal tartare with caviar. Fresh Swedish salmon is also featured. The chefs—highly trained professionals working with the finest ingredients—have pleased some of Europe's more demanding palates.

In the Grand Hotel, Södra Blasieholmshamnen 8. (C) **08/679-35-84**. Reservations required. Main courses 225SEK–465SEK ($24–$49); 7-course fixed-price menu 925SEK–1,300SEK ($98–$138). AE, DC, MC, V. Mon–Fri 6–11pm. T-bana: Kungsträdgården. Bus: 46, 55, 62, or 76.

Fredsgatan 12 ★★★ SWEDISH/CONTINENTAL   In the Royal Academy of Arts Building, this is one of the premier restaurants of Stockholm. The decor is ultra-sophisticated and hip, almost nightclubbish in aura in its use of mauve walls and gold chairs, with long shimmering curtains. Since it's near the Parliament and various government ministries, it draws officials at lunch but a far trendier and classier crowd in the evening. Danyel Couet and Melker Andersson combine their talents to create dishes with clear, robust flavors. For our latest meal here, we dined with a Swedish food critic. In translation, his verdict was "confident, generous, and brilliantly handled," and we concur. For an appetizer, you're faced with such imaginative choices as *bleak* (a freshwater fish) roe in a Mexican-style taco with cream laced with lemon zest. One member of our party found the anise-flavored black bread and the salty butter so enticing he was unable to tackle his main course. A pity, really, since the main courses here are even more delectable than the starters, including, for example, a perfectly cooked turbot with an amusing salmon "pastrami" and a very good rendering of

Stockholm Dining

Akvarium **9**
Bakfickan **11**
Ben Lloc **5**
Berns **26**
Cattelin Restaurant **15**
Clas på Hornet **4**
Den Gyldene Freden **20**
Edsbacka Krog **3**

Eriks Bakfica **29**
Fem Små Hus **21**
Franska Matsalen
(French Dining Room) **24**
Fredsgatan 12 **12**
Garlic & Shots **18**
Grand Veranda **23**
Hannas Krog **19**

KB Restaurant **8**
Långholmen
Restaurant **17**
Leijontornet **4**
Lisa Elmquist **10**
Mälardrottningen **14**
Operakällaren **11**
Paul & Norbet **28**

Pontus in the
  Green House **22**
Prinsens **27**
Restaurangen **6**
Stadshuskällaren **13**
Stortorgskällaren **16**
Sturehof **7**

Tennstopet
  (Pewter Tankard) **1**
Tranan **2**
Ulla Winbladh **30**
Ulriksdals Wärdshus **4**
Wedholms Fisk **25**

† Church
ⓘ Information
✉ Post Office
Ⓣ Subway
⎯⎯ Railway

sweet-and-sour venison (not always available). Among the more successful desserts is a blood-orange sorbet with a citrus salad.

Fredsgatan 12. © **08/24-80-52.** Reservations required. Main courses 265SEK–325SEK ($28–$34). AE, DC, MC, V. Mon–Fri 11:30am–2pm; Mon–Sat 5–10:30pm. T-bana: Kungsträdgården.

Restaurangen ☆☆ INTERNATIONAL   Come here for a high-ceilinged decor whose angularity might remind you of an SAS airport lounge, and for combinations of cuisine that many cosmopolitan Swedes have found absolutely fascinating. Owner and chef Malker Andersson divides his menu into "fields of flavor" as defined by unexpected categories. These include, among others, lemon-flavored themes or coriander-flavored themes, which can be consumed in any order you prefer. If you want a "taste of the lemon," for example, it might appear to flavor fresh asparagus and new potatoes. Freshly chopped coriander is used to flavor a delectable shellfish ceviche. The chef roams the world and doesn't try to duplicate classical international dishes but to take the flavor of one country and combine its traditional dish with the time-honored dish of another country. An amazing and very tasty example of this is tacos from Mexico combined with foie gras of France and caviar from Russia. Since none of the portions are overly large, some diners interpret a meal here as something akin to tapas, each permeated with flavors that linger on your palate after you consume them.

Oxtorgsgatan 14. © **08/22-09-52.** Reservations recommended. 3-course fixed-price menu 250SEK ($27); 5-course fixed-price menu 350SEK ($37); 7-course fixed-price menu 450SEK ($48). AE, DC, MC, V. Mon–Fri 11:30am–2pm; Mon–Sat 5–11pm. T-banen: Hörtorget.

Wedholms Fisk ☆☆☆ SWEDISH/FRENCH   This is one of the classic—and one of the best—restaurants in Stockholm. It has no curtains in the windows and no carpets, but the display of modern paintings by Swedish artists is riveting. You might begin with marinated herring with garlic and bleak roe, or tartare of salmon with salmon roe. The chef has reason to be proud of such dishes as perch poached with clams and saffron sauce, prawns marinated in herbs and served with Dijon hollandaise, and grilled filet of sole with Beaujolais sauce. For dessert, try the homemade vanilla ice cream with cloudberries. The cuisine is both innovative and traditional—for example, chevre mousse accompanies simple tomato salad. On the other hand, the menu features grandmother's favorite: cream-stewed potatoes.

Nybrokajen 17. © **08/611-78-74.** Reservations required. Main courses 110SEK–225SEK ($12–$24) lunch, 265SEK–525SEK ($28–$56) dinner. AE, DC, MC, V. Mon–Sat 5–11pm. Closed July. T-bana: Östermalmstorg.

MODERATE

Bakfickan ☆ *Finds* SWEDISH   Tucked away behind the Operakällaren, the "Back Pocket" is a chic place to eat for a moderate price. It shares a kitchen with its glamorous neighbor Operakällaren (see above), but its prices are more bearable. Main dishes are likely to include salmon in several varieties, including boiled with hollandaise and salmon roe. You might also try beef Rydberg (thin-sliced tenderloin). In season you can order reindeer and elk. In the summer, nothing's finer than the rich ice cream with a sauce of Arctic cloudberries. Many patrons prefer to eat at the horseshoe-shaped bar.

Jakobs Torg 12. © **08/676-58-09.** Reservations not accepted. Main courses 92SEK–189SEK ($9.75–$20). AE, DC, MC, V. Aug–June Mon–Sat noon–11:30pm. T-bana: Kungsträdgården.

Berns ☆ SWEDISH/INTERNATIONAL   Built in 1860, this "pleasure palace" was one of Stockholm's most famous restaurants and nighttime venues. It was dramatically renovated in 1999 and is now one of the most attractive restaurants in the capital. Three monumental chandeliers light the main hall. August Strindberg frequented the *Röda Rummet* ("Red Room"), and described it in his novel of the same name. It's still there—plush furniture and all—and is used by guests at Berns' Hotel. Each day a different Swedish specialty is featured, including fried filet of suckling pig with fresh asparagus. You might also try calves' liver with garlic and bacon, or grilled tournedos. More-innovative main dishes include cuttlefish with black pasta and tomato sauce, and filet of ostrich with mushroom cannelloni and Marsala sauce. More and more exotic dishes are appearing on the menu—tandoori-marinated lamb with mango, curry sauce, and couscous, for example.

Näckströmsgatan 8. © 08/566-322-22. Reservations recommended. Main courses 165SEK–350SEK ($17-$37). AE, DC, MC, V. Mon 11:30am–5pm; Tues–Fri 11:30am–11pm; Sat 11:30am–2:30pm and 5–11pm; Sun 11:30am–2:30pm. T-bana: Östermalmstorg.

Clas på Hornet ⚡ SWEDISH/CONTINENTAL   Decorative touches evocative of the late 1700s adorn these five cream-colored dining rooms. This restaurant is owned by the entrepreneur who made Nils Emil (also recommended) into one of the capital's most-acclaimed restaurants. Homage to the place has even appeared in the poetic verse of one of Sweden's most-valued poets, Carl Michael Bellman. There's a sometimes crowded bar area that many clients visit regularly, in some cases even those who have no interest in dining. No one will mind if you come just for a drink, but the true value of the place only emerges at the table. Here, menu items change with the seasons, but are likely to include an "Archipelago Platter," named after the islands near Stockholm that provide many of its ingredients. It contains assorted preparations of herring, a medley of Swedish cheeses, and homemade bread. Other delectable choices include blinis stuffed with bleak roe, trout roe, and onions; cream of wild-mushroom soup with strips of reindeer; grilled char that's served with a hollandaise sauce enriched with fish roe; baked turbot in horseradish sauce; and roasted venison with a timbale of chanterelles.

Surbrunnsgatan 20. © 08/16-51-30. Reservations recommended. Main courses 230SEK–265SEK ($24–$28). AE, DC, MC, V. Mon–Fri 11:30am–10pm; Sat–Sun 5–10pm. Bus: 46 or 53.

Eriks Bakfica ⟨Value⟩ SWEDISH   Although other restaurants in Stockholm bear the name Eriks, this one is relatively inexpensive and offers particularly good value. Established in 1979, it features a handful of Swedish dishes from the tradition of *husmanskost* (wholesome home cooking). A favorite opener is toast Skagen, with shrimp, dill-flavored mayonnaise, spices, and bleak roe. There's also a daily choice of herring appetizers. Try the tantalizing "archipelago stew," a ragout of fish prepared with tomatoes and served with garlic mayonnaise. Marinated salmon is served with hollandaise sauce. You might also try Eriks cheeseburger with the special secret sauce, but you have to ask for it—the secret specialty is not on the menu.

Fredrikshovsgatan 4. © 08/660-15-99. Reservations recommended. Main courses 145SEK–298SEK ($15–$32). AE, DC, MC, V. Mon–Fri 11:30am–11pm; Sat 5–11pm; Sun 5–10pm. Bus: 47.

Grand Veranda ⚡ ⟨Kids⟩ SWEDISH   On the ground floor of Stockholm's most prestigious hotel, and fronted with enormous sheets of glass, this restaurant opens onto a stunning view of the harbor and the Royal Palace. The Veranda is famous for its daily buffets, which occasionally feature a medley of shellfish, including all the shrimp and lobster you can eat. Many foreign families like to patronize this place because of the lavishness of its buffets. Try such a la carte dishes as filet of reindeer marinated in red wine or braised wild duck and deep-fried root vegetables served with an apple-cider sauce. Here is your chance to sample the offerings of the most famous hotel in Sweden, to enjoy wonderful food, and to have one of the best views in town—all for a reasonable price.

In the Grand Hotel, Södra Blasieholmshamnen 8. © **08/679-35-86.** Reservations required. Main courses 125SEK–295SEK ($13–$31); Swedish buffet 315SEK ($33). AE, DC, MC, V. Daily 11am–11pm. T-bana: Kungsträdgården. Bus: 46, 55, 62, or 76.

KB Restaurant SWEDISH/CONTINENTAL A traditional artists' rendezvous in the center of town, KB Restaurant features good Swedish food as well as Continental dishes. Fish dishes are especially recommended. You might begin with salmon trout roe and Russian caviar, followed by boiled turbot or lamb roast with stuffed zucchini in thyme-flavored bouillon. Dishes usually come with aromatic, freshly baked sourdough bread. Desserts include sorbets with fresh fruits and berries, and a heavenly lime soufflé with orange-blossom honey. There's also a relaxed and informal bar.

Smålandsgatan 7. © **08/679-60-32.** Reservations recommended. Main courses 210SEK–300SEK ($22–$32); fixed-price lunch 270SEK–335SEK ($29–$36); fixed-price dinner 375SEK–470SEK ($40–$50). AE, DC, MC, V. Mon–Fri 11:30am–11:30pm; Sat 5–11:30pm. Closed June 23–Aug 7. T-bana: Östermalmstorg.

Lisa Elmquist ⚓ *(Kids)* SEAFOOD Under the soaring roof, amid the food stalls of Stockholm's produce market (the Östermalms Saluhall), you'll find this likable cafe and oyster bar. Because of its good, affordable food, this is the most popular choice for Stockholm families visiting the market. It's owned by one of the city's largest fish distributors, so its menu varies with the catch. Some patrons come here for shrimp with bread and butter for 90SEK to 115SEK ($9.55–$12). Typical dishes include fish soup, salmon cutlets, and sautéed filet of lemon sole. It's not the most refined cuisine in town—it's an authentic "taste of Sweden," done exceedingly well. The establishment looks like a pleasant bistro under the tent at a country fair.

Östermalms Saluhall, Nybrogatan 31. © **08/553-404-10.** Reservations recommended. Main courses 86SEK–336SEK ($9.10–$36). AE, DC, MC, V. Mon–Thurs 10am–6pm; Fri 10am–6:30pm; Sat 10am–4pm. T-bana: Östermalmstorg.

Prinsens SWEDISH A 2-minute walk from Stureplan, this artists' haunt has become increasingly popular with foreign visitors. It has been serving people since 1897. Seating is on two levels, and in summer some tables are outside. The fresh, flavorful cuisine is basically Swedish food prepared in a conservative French style. It includes such traditional Swedish dishes as veal patty with homemade lingonberry preserves, sautéed fjord salmon, and roulades of beef. For dessert, try the homemade vanilla ice cream. Later in the evening, the restaurant becomes something of a drinking club.

Mäster Samuelsgatan 4. © **08/611-13-31.** Reservations recommended. Main courses 124SEK–269SEK ($13–$29). AE, DC, MC, V. Mon–Fri 11:30am–10:30pm; Sat 1–10:30pm; Sun 5–9:30pm. T-bana: Östermalmstorg.

Sturehof SWEDISH This seafood restaurant in the center of town was founded in 1897. Tasty and carefully prepared specialties include Swedish or Canadian lobsters and oysters, fried plaice, boiled salmon with hollandaise, and fresh shrimp. A daily changing menu of genuine Swedish *husmanskost* (home cooking) is a bargain. Sample, for example, boiled salted veal tongue or potato and beet soup with sour cream. Try the famous *sotare* (grilled small Baltic herring served with boiled potatoes) if you want to sample a local favorite. Many locals come here to make an entire meal from the various types of herring—everything from tomato herring to curry herring.

Stureplan 2. © **08/440-57-30.** Main courses 100SEK–350SEK ($11–$37). AE, DC, MC, V. Mon–Fri 11am–2am; Sat noon–2am; Sun 1pm–2am. T-bana: Östermalmstorg.

Tranan *(Value* SWEDISH A real local restaurant, this 1915 tavern serves very good food and draws a friendly crowd attracted by affordable prices and the kitchen's deft handling of fresh ingredients. Its decor gives clues to the place's former role as a blue-collar beer tavern. The menu is only in Swedish, but the waiters speak English and will help guide you through an array of traditional Swedish dishes that often have French overtones. Nothing is more typical than the filet of beef served with fried potatoes, egg yolk, and horseradish. One Swede told us he comes here at least twice a week to order the Swedish meatballs and mashed potatoes. Other menu items are conservative and flavorful, in many cases virtually unchanged since the day the restaurant was founded. Examples include Swedish pork and lard sausage served with mashed potatoes and picked beet-root, herring platters, "Toast Skagen" piled high with shrimp, and "Beef Rydberg" : cubes of sautéed filet steak served with braised onions, sautéed potatoes, egg yolk, cream, and horseradish. Later you can go downstairs to enjoy an authentic local bar, where DJs spin the latest hits on Friday and Saturday nights. Patrons must be 23 or older to enter the bar.

Karlbergvagen 14. © **08/527-281-02.** Main courses 95SEK–265SEK ($10–$28). AE, DC, MC, V. Mon–Fri 11:30am–11:45pm; Sat–Sun 5–11:45pm. Cellar bar until 1am. T-bana: Odenplan.

IN GAMLA STAN (OLD TOWN)
VERY EXPENSIVE
Leijontornet SWEDISH/INTERNATIONAL This is one of the Old Town's most stylish restaurants, noted for its fine food and the quality of its service. From the small street-level bar, patrons descend into the intimately lit cellar (the hotel was built around a medieval defense tower). To reach the restaurant, you have to negotiate a labyrinth of brick passageways through the Victory Hotel.

You might begin with grilled marinated calamari with eggplant and paprika cream, salad with roast deer and curry dressing, or perhaps a potato crepe with bleak roe vinaigrette and fried herring. Main courses include roast lamb with moussaka and basil; grilled salmon with tomato, spinach, and lime *taglierini* (a

---

Kids Family-Friendly Restaurants

Grand Veranda (p. 357) If you'd like to introduce your kid to one of the most affordable—and one of the best—buffets in Stockholm, head here. Kids especially like it because they get to see what's going on their plate without having to order a la carte.

Lisa Elmquist (p. 358) Because this restaurant is in the produce market, Östermalms Saluhall, having lunch here with the family is a colorful adventure. One particular favorite is shrimp with bread and butter. Families can dine under a tent, which evokes a country fair setting.

Solliden Near the top of the Skansen compound, a Williamsburg-type park dating from 1891, Solliden (© **08/662-93-03**) is a cluster of restaurants in a sprawling building. The array of dining facilities makes the dining emporium attractive to families. Solliden offers a lunch smörgåsbord.

pasta similar to tagliatelle); and risotto with pumpkin and *cèpes* (flap mushrooms). Dishes often arrive looking like works of art, and they incorporate some of the country's finest produce.

In the Victory Hotel, Lilla Nygatan 5. € 08/14-23-55. Reservations required. Main courses 210SEK–335SEK ($22–$36). AE, DC, MC, V. Mon–Sat 6pm–midnight. Closed July, bank holidays. T-bana: Gamla Stan.

Pontus in the Green House 🌟🌟 FRENCH/SWEDISH/ASIAN   Set within a building whose foundations date back to the 16th century, this is a well-orchestrated and elegant restaurant that attracts some of the most powerful figures in Stockholm. Your dining experience will begin with a drink or aperitif in the ground-floor bar and cocktail lounge, where a staff member will explain the menu and record your choices. You'll then be ushered upstairs to a gold-and-green dining room with high arched windows and an undeniable sense of respect for the presentation of food. Chef Pontus Frithiof was inspired by two of the grand Francophile chefs of England, Marco Pierre White and Gordon Ramsay. Their influence is seen in dishes that include garlic-sautéed turbot with sweetbreads; tender veal tongue with Jerusalem artichokes; steamed turbot with horseradish, prawns, and brown butter; and citrus-glazed *Challonais* duck breast served with foie gras, shiitake mushrooms, spring onions, and teriyaki sauce. In our view, the herring with vinegar-and-onion marmalade is the Old Town's tastiest. It's worth the trek across town to sample the creamy Roquefort made from the first milk nursing cows produce. After tasting this cheese, you'll never go back—except with regret—to that store-bought stuff again.

Österlånggatan 17. € 08/23-85-00. Reservations recommended. Main courses 350SEK–450SEK ($37–$48); 8-course fixed-price menu 985SEK ($104). AE, DC, MC, V. Mon–Fri 11:30am–3pm and 6–11pm; Sat noon–4pm and 5:30–11pm. T-bana: Gamla Stan.

EXPENSIVE

Den Gyldene Freden 🌟 SWEDISH   "Golden Peace" is said to be Stockholm's oldest tavern. The restaurant opened in 1722 in a structure built the year before. The Swedish Academy owns the building, and members frequent the place every Thursday night. The cozy dining rooms are named for Swedish historical figures who were patrons. Today it's popular with artists, lawyers, and poets. You get good traditional Swedish cooking, especially fresh Baltic fish and game from the forests. Herring is a favorite appetizer. More imaginative appetizers include a creamy artichoke soup, Jerusalem artichokes with a dollop of caviar, and an especially intriguing consommé of oxtail with tiny ravioli stuffed with quail breast. Notable main courses are fried breast of wild duck in Calvados sauce, and roast of reindeer in juniper-berry sauce. A particular delight is homemade duck sausage with three kinds of mushrooms in black pepper sauce. Want something different for dessert? How about warm rose hip soup with vanilla ice cream? Of course, if you order that, you'd be denying yourself the "symphony" of lingonberries or the longtime favorite, Stockholm's best chocolate cake.

Österlånggatan 51. € 08/24-97-60. Reservations recommended. Main courses 98SEK–395SEK ($10–$42). AE, DC, MC, V. Mon–Fri 6–11pm; Sat 1–11pm. T-bana: Gamla Stan.

Fem Små Hus 🌟 SWEDISH/FRENCH   This historic restaurant, with cellars that date from the 17th century, is furnished like a private castle, with European antiques and oil paintings. The nine rooms in the labyrinthine interior hold candlelit tables. You can order assorted herring, slices of fresh salmon in Chablis, braised scallops with saffron sauce, terrine of duckling with goose liver and truffles, filet of beef with herb sauce, and sorbets with seasonal fruits and berries.

The best ingredients from Sweden's forests and shores appear on the menu. The cuisine and staff are worthy of the restaurant's hallowed reputation.

Nygränd 10. ℂ 08/10-87-75. Reservations required. Main courses 225SEK–350SEK ($24–$37). AE, DC, MC, V. Sun–Mon 5–11pm; Tues–Sat 5pm–midnight. T-bana: Gamla Stan.

MODERATE

Mälardrottningen ℛ Finds INTERNATIONAL This upscale floating restaurant occupies the showplace deck of a motor yacht, built by industrialist C. K. G. Billings in 1924, that's now a hotel (see "Where to Stay," earlier in this chapter). Admittedly, a lot of its allure derives from its novelty, but the food is well prepared, with some of the flair associated with the ship's heyday. Menu items change with the seasons, but might include imaginative offerings such as salmon-filet spring roll with pepper-garlic vinaigrette; pear-and-goat-cheese salad with thyme-flavored honey; and skewered scampi served with Parmesan cheese and chutney made from pesto and bananas. One of the least-expensive main courses—appropriate for foggy days beside the harbor—is a heaping portion of marinated mussels in white wine and butter sauce, served with french fries. More formal dishes include a parfait of chicken livers with an apricot and oregano brioche; cream of chanterelle soup with a pumpkin- and sage-flavored gnocchi; prosciutto-wrapped tiger prawns; grilled Dublin Bay prawns with a fennel-flavored butter sauce; and fried filets of pike-perch with crisp-fried paella, red peppers, and lobster sauce.

Riddarholmen. ℂ 08/545-187-80. Reservations recommended. Main courses 150SEK–255SEK ($16–$27). AE, DC, MC, V. Mon–Fri 11am–2pm and 3–10pm; Sat 5–10pm. T-bana: Gamla Stan.

Stortorgskällaren SWEDISH In the winter, this restaurant occupies medieval wine cellars whose vaulted ceilings date from the 15th century. Old walls and chandeliers complement plush carpeting and subtle lighting. In summer, seating is on the outdoor terrace, beside a charming square opposite the Stock Exchange or, in bad weather, in the street-level dining room.

The menu changes often. You might begin with paté of wild game with blackberry chutney and pickled carrots, or cured salmon and white bleak roe served with crème fraîche and onions. There's also fried salmon with mushroom sauce. Another specialty is a casserole of Baltic fish seasoned with saffron. After you've sampled some of these dishes, you'll know why Stockholmers have long cited this restaurant as one of their most reliable. You don't get fireworks, but you do get a cheerful atmosphere, lots of flavor, and a hearty menu.

Stortorget 7. ℂ 08/10-55-33. Reservations required. Main courses 150SEK–295SEK ($16–$31); 3-course fixed-price dinner 316SEK ($34). AE, DC, MC, V. Mon–Fri 11am–11pm; Sat noon–11pm; Sun noon–10pm. T-bana: Gamla Stan.

INEXPENSIVE

Cattelin Restaurant Value SWEDISH This restaurant on a historic street opened in 1897 and continues to serve fish and meat in a boisterous, convivial setting. Don't expect genteel service—the clattering of china can sometimes be almost deafening, but few of the regular patrons seem to mind. First-rate menu choices include various preparations of beef, salmon, trout, veal, and chicken, which frequently make up the daily specials often preferred by lunch patrons. This restaurant has survived wars, disasters, and changing food tastes, so it must be doing something right. It remains a sentimental favorite—and not just for the memories. In a city where people have been known to faint when presented with their dining tabs, it has always been a good, reasonably priced choice. The fixed-price lunch is served only Monday through Friday from 11am to 2pm.

Storkyrkobrinken 9. ℂ 08/20-18-18. Reservations recommended. Main courses 95SEK–200SEK ($10–$21); dagens (daily) menu 72SEK ($7.65). AE, DC, MC, V. Mon–Fri 11am–10pm; Sat–Sun noon–10pm. T-bana: Gamla Stan.

ON KUNGSHOLMEN

Stadshuskällaren SWEDISH/INTERNATIONAL   Near the harbor, in the basement of the City Hall, you'll find two dignified restaurants. After passing through a beautiful carved wooden doorway, you'll enter an interior that is divided into two sections: the Skänken, which serves lunch only, and the Stora Matsalen, where chefs prepare the annual banquet for the Nobel Prize winners; you can actually sample a Nobel menu. Dining here is like taking a culinary trip through Sweden. To go truly local, you'll want to try the elk or reindeer dishes (in season). Swedish salmon is our all-time favorite, and here it's prepared with consummate skill. Lately the chefs have become more imaginative, preparing such dishes as marinated filet of chicken breasts with avocado pesto (yes, avocado pesto), or perhaps almond-fried catfish with olives and mushrooms. Our vote for the finest dish offered on recent Nobel menus goes to roast pigeon breast with cèpe and pigeon meat ragout, flavored with tart raspberry vinegar and accompanied by onion and potato compote.

Stadshuset. ℂ 08/650-54-54. Main courses 140SEK–255SEK ($15–$27); 2-course fixed-price lunch 235SEK ($25); 3-course fixed-price dinner 475SEK ($50). AE, DC, MC, V. Skänken, Mon–Fri 11am–2pm. Stora Matsalen, Mon–Fri 11:30am–11pm, Sat 2–11pm. T-bana: Rådhuset. Bus: 48 or 62.

ON DJURGÅRDEN

Ulla Winbladh ✿ SWEDISH   Since it opened in 1994, this restaurant has enjoyed an explosion of publicity, which has impressed even the most jaded of Stockholm's restaurant aficionados. It's in a white stone structure, built as part of Stockholm's International Exposition of 1897. There's a large dining room decorated with works by Swedish artists, and a summer-only outdoor terrace laced with flowering plants. The menu focuses on conservative Swedish cuisine, all impeccably prepared. (Patrons who agree with this assessment include members of the Swedish royal family and a bevy of well-known TV, theater, and art-world personalities.) In 1996 the king presented a medal to chef Emel Ahalen for his proficiency in preparing Swedish cuisine. Menu choices include tender steak with artichokes and a perfectly prepared rack of Swedish lamb flavored with bacon. Fish selections might be platters of herring (marinated and fried), whitefish or pike-perch in white-wine sauce, divine turbot with saffron sauce, the inevitable salmon with dill sauce, and others that vary with the season.

Rosendalsvägen 8. ℂ 08/663-05-71. Reservations required. Main courses 95SEK–270SEK ($10–$29). AE, DC, MC, V. Mon 11:30am–10pm; Tues–Fri 11:30am–11pm; Sat 1–11pm; Sun 1–10pm. Bus: 47.

NEAR VASAPARKEN

Tennstopet (Pewter Tankard) SWEDISH   A well-known pub and restaurant, Tennstopet is in the northern part of town, near the Hotel Oden. It's the oldest pub in Sweden, adjacent to a classic dining room. Main dishes might include a ragout of fish and shellfish, salmon schnitzel, and plank steak. At lunch, you can dine on pork chops, vegetables, bread, butter, and coffee. Or just order a draft beer, toss some darts, and admire the setting. This is the type of

Perfect Picnics

Fast-food eateries and fresh-food markets abound in Stockholm, especially in the center of the city, around Hötorget. **Hötorgs Hallen** is a fresh food market where you can buy the makings of an elegant picnic. Recently arrived immigrants sell many Turkish food products, including stuffed pita bread.

For the most elegant fare of all, go to **Östermalms Hallen,** at the corner of Humlegårdsgatan and Nybrogatan, east of the center. Stall after stall sells picnic fare, including fresh shrimp and precooked items that will be wrapped carefully to go.

With your picnic fixings in hand, head for **Skansen** or the wooded peninsula of **Djurgården.** If you like to picnic with lots of people around, go to **Kungsträdgården,** "the summer living room of Stockholm," in the center of town.

food that accompanies heavy drinking—it's good, hearty, and filling, but nothing more. The place prides itself on serving genuine English pints.

Dalagatan 50. ✆ **08/32-25-18.** Reservations recommended. Main courses 95SEK–220SEK ($10–$23). AE, DC, MC, V. Mon–Fri 4pm–1am; Sat–Sun 1pm–1am. T-bana: Odenplan. Bus: 54.

AT SÖDERMALM

Garlic & Shots   This theme restaurant follows two strong, overriding ideas: Everyone needs a shot of garlic every day, and everything tastes better if it's doctored with a dose of the Mediterranean's most potent ingredient. The no-frills setting is artfully spartan, with bare wooden tables that have hosted an unexpectedly large number of rock stars. Expect garlic in just about everything, from soup (try garlic-ginger with clam) to such main courses as beefsteak covered with fried minced garlic, and Transylvania-style vampire steak drenched in horseradish-tomato-and-garlic sauce. Dessert might be a slice of garlic-laced cheese or garlic-honey ice cream garnished with honey-marinated cloves of garlic. An appropriate foil for all these flavors? Garlic ale or garlic beer, if you're up to it.

Folkungagatan 84. ✆ **08/640-84-46.** Reservations recommended. Main courses 85SEK–190SEK ($9–$20). MC, V. Daily 5pm–1am. T-bana: Medborgarplatsen.

Hannas Krog INTERNATIONAL   This bustling bistro is one of the most appealing neighborhood restaurants in Södermalm. In its own way, it's fashionable. The decor, with such artfully rustic touches as a collection of cuckoo clocks, might remind you of a Swedish version of a British pub. Hannas Krog serves a medley of food with inspirations from around the world. You might begin with a slice of pie made with Swedish cheddar cheese, then move on to marinated and baked salmon wrapped in Italian pancetta ham, Provençal-style lamb, or grilled butterfish with tiger prawns wrapped in wontons and served with crayfish consommé. Trendy Stockholmers, who used to avoid Södermalm like the plague, are increasingly showing up for the good fare, excellent service, and inviting ambience.

Skånegatan 80. ✆ **08/643-82-25.** Reservations recommended. Main courses 128SEK–208SEK ($14–$22). AE, DC, MC, V. Mon–Fri 11:30am–3pm; daily 5pm–midnight. T-bana: Medborgarplatsen.

ON LÅNGHOLMEN

Långholmen Restaurant INTERNATIONAL   This premier dining venue is housed within the Långholmen Hotel, the former state penitentiary turned hotel. From the windows of the old-fashioned dining room, you can still see the high brick walls and the paraphernalia of what caused a lot of inmates a great deal of mental distress—small doors with heavy bolts, and bars on the windows. Ironically, within the establishment's new venue, these mementos are showcased, rather than concealed—even the paintings, many in gentle pastels, reflect the workhouse drudgery that used to prevail here. Come here for an unusual insight into the hardships of the 19th century, and menu items that change with the seasons. Examples include a carpaccio of shellfish, smoked breast of duck with a walnut-cranberry vinaigrette, a combination of lobster and turbot stewed with vegetables in a shellfish bouillon, and tournedos of venison with juniper berries, smoked ham, pepper sauce, and Swedish potatoes. This is hardly prison food—in fact, the most dedicated devotees of the restaurant hail it as one of the finest in Stockholm. Only market-fresh ingredients are used, and the staff here is clearly dedicated to pleasing your palate.

Kronohäktet. ☎ **08/720-85-50.** Reservations recommended. Main courses 158SEK–256SEK ($17–$27). AE, DC, MC, V. Daily noon–9pm. T-bana: Hornstul. Bus: 4, 40, or 66.

AT SOLNA

Ulriksdals Wärdshus ☆ *Finds* SWEDISH   This out-of-town establishment serves the best smörgåsbord in Sweden. On the grounds of Ulriksdal's Royal Palace on Edviken Bay, you can dine in the all-glass Queen Silvia Pavilion, which opens onto gardens owned by the king and queen. The smörgåsbord, featuring 86 delicacies (both shellfish and meat), and is accompanied by beer or aquavit. Most people eat the smörgåsbord in five courses, beginning with herring that comes in 20 varieties. They follow with salmon and then meat dishes, including *frikadeller* (meatballs) or perhaps reindeer, then a choice of cheese, and finally dessert. Some dishes are based on old farm-style recipes, including "Lansson's Temptation," which blends anchovies, heavy-cream potatoes, and onions. Over the Christmas season, the almost-doubled buffet is lavishly decorated in a seasonal theme, and costs 450SEK ($48) per person.

Ulriksdals Royal Park, S-170 79 Solna. ☎ **08/85-08-15.** Reservations required. Main courses 275SEK–295SEK ($29–$31); fixed-price menus 380SEK–500SEK ($40–$53). AE, DC, MC, V. Mon–Fri noon–10pm; Sat 12:30–10pm; Sun 12:30–6:30pm. Closed Dec 24–26. Take Sveavägen toward Arlanda Airport (Exit E18), 5km (3 miles) north of Stockholm.

AT SOLLENTUNA

Edsbacka Krog ☆ *Finds* SWEDISH/FRENCH   In a historic, thick-walled building from 1626, this was the first licensed inn in Stockholm. Ten minutes by taxi from the town center, you'll find dining rooms with an upscale country atmosphere. Menu items include combinations you're not likely to find in many other restaurants. Examples include whitebait roe with marinated halibut and avocado; boiled lobster in vegetable terrine; scallops with smoked cod in duck liver sauce; terrine of duck liver served with fried sweetbreads; and a platter that combines oxtail and beef tongue with duck liver and duck liver sauce. Chef Christer Lindström's dishes attract visitors from around the district. He is dedicated to sturdy Continental cooking served with immaculate taste.

Sollentunavägen 220, Sollentuna. ☎ **08/96-33-00.** Reservations recommended. Main courses 270SEK–425SEK ($29–$45); fixed-price menus 585SEK–1,300SEK ($62–$138). AE, DC, MC, V. Tues–Fri noon–2:30pm and 5:30pm–midnight; Sat 2pm–midnight. T-bana: Sollentuna.

Exploring Stockholm

In every season, Stockholm is loaded with interesting sights and activities for people of all ages—from the *Vasa* Ship Museum to the changing of the guard at the Royal Palace to the Gröna Lunds Tivoli amusement park. Even just window-shopping for beautifully designed crafts can be an enjoyable way to spend an afternoon. After dark, Stockholm is one of the livelier cities in northern Europe.

SUGGESTED ITINERARIES

If You Have 1 Day

Take a ferry to Djurgården and visit the *Vasa* Ship Museum, Stockholm's most famous attraction, and explore the open-air Skansen folk museum. In the afternoon, take our walking tour (see later in this chapter) of Gamla Stan (Old Town) and have dinner there.

If You Have 2 Days

On your first day, follow the suggestions above. On Day 2, get up early and visit the Kaknästornet television tower for a panoramic view of the city and its archipelago. Go to the Museum of Nordic History for a review of 5 centuries of life in Sweden. After lunch, visit the Millesgården of Lidingö, the sculpture garden and former home of Carl Milles, Sweden's most famous sculptor.

If You Have 3 Days

For the first 2 days follow the itinerary above. On the third morning, take our second walking tour (see later in this chapter). At noon (1pm on Sun), return to Gamla Stan to see the changing of the guard at the Royal Palace. The French-inspired building has been the residence of Swedish kings for more than 700 years. In winter, if your visit doesn't coincide with the changing of the guard, you can visit Kungsträdgården Park in the center of the city and enjoy the ice-skating (the Swedes are superb at this). Schedule a visit to Stockholm's renowned city hall. In the afternoon, visit the National Museum.

If You Have 4 or 5 Days

For Days 1 to 3, follow the suggestions above. On Day 4, take one of the many available tours of the Stockholm archipelago. Return to Stockholm and spend the evening at the Gröna Lunds Tivoli amusement park on Djurgården. For your last day, visit Drottningholm Palace and its 18th-century theater. In the afternoon go to Uppsala, which is easily reached by public transportation (see "Side Trips from Stockholm," later in this chapter).

1 On Gamla Stan & Neighboring Islands

Kungliga Slottet (Royal Palace) & Museums ★★ Kungliga Slottet is one of the few official residences of a European monarch that's open to the public. Although the king and queen prefer to live at Drottningholm, this massive

Stockholm Attractions

Arkitektur Museet **6**

Drottningholm Palace
and Theater **21**

Gröna Lunds Tivoli **7**

Hallwylska Museet **12**

Historiska Museet **2**

Kaknästornet **1**

Kungliga Slottet **15**

Moderna Museet **9**

Nationalmuseum **11**

Nordiska Museet **3**

Operahauset (Royal
Opera House) **13**

Östasiatiskamuseet **10**

Prins Eugens
Waldemarsudde **5**

Rådhuset **22**

Riddarholm Church **17**

Royal Warship Vasa **8**

Skansen **4**

Stadshuset **20**

0.25 mi
0
0
0.25 km
N

Floragatan
Östermalmsgatan
Artillerigatan
Valhallavägen

GÅRDEN
Sturegatan
Brahegatan
Turegatan
Nybrogatan
Karlavägen
Skeppargatan
Banérgatan
Valhallavägen

Linnégatan
Grev
Kommendörsgatan
Karlaplan

Humlegårdsgatan
ÖSTERMALM
Linnégatan
Narvavägen
GUSTAV-ADOLFS-
PARKEN
Karlavägen

Birger Jarls-
gatan
Nybrogatan
Sibyllegatan
Artillerigatan
Storgatan
Greygatan
Linnégatan
Banérgatan
❷
✝ ◼
Storgatan
❶→

Riddargatan
Skeppargatan
Styrmansgatan
Riddargatan
NOBEL-
PARKEN

Hamngatan
❿ BERZELIIPARKEN
Nybroviken
Strandvägen
Djurgårdsbron

Arsenalsgatan
Nybrokajen
❸
Lusthus porten

Stallgatan
BLASIEHOLMEN
Rosendalsvägen

Strömbron
Södra Blasieholms-
hamnen
⑪
Skepps-
holmsbron
❽
❹

Strömmen
❿
Skeppsbron
⑨
✝ ◼
SKEPPSHOLMEN
Svensksundsvägen
Djurgårdsvägen
DJURGÅRDEN
❼
❻
❺→

Saltsjön
KASTELL-
HOLMEN

ⓘ

See "Walking Tour:
Along the Harbor" map

Stadsmuseet **16**
Stadsteatern **18**
Stockholms Medeltidsmuseum **14**
Strindbergsmuseet **19**
Thielska Galleriet **5**

✝ Church
ⓘ Information
⊠ Post Office
-T- Subway
Railway

608-room showcase remains their official address. Severe, dignified, even cold-looking on the outside, it has a lavish interior designed in the Italian baroque style and built between 1691 and 1754.

Visitors may walk through the Council Chamber, where the king and his ministers meet several times a year. The **State Apartments,** with magnificent baroque ceilings and fine tapestries, the **Bernadotte Apartment,** and the **Guest Apartment** are on view. They're beautifully furnished in Swedish rococo, Louis XVI, and Empire style.

The **Skattkammaren,** or Treasury, in the cellar, is worth a visit. It exhibits one of the most celebrated collections of crown jewels in Europe. You'll see a dozen crowns, scepters, and orbs, along with antique jewelry. Be sure to see the **Royal Armory,** Slottsbacken 3, also in the cellar. Kings used to ride in these elegant gilded coaches. You'll also see coronation costumes from the 16th century, weapons, and armor.

Gustav III's collection of sculpture from the days of the Roman Empire can be viewed in the **Antikmuseum (Museum of Antiquities).**

Changing of the Royal Guard: In summer you can watch the parade of the military guard daily. In winter it takes place on Wednesday and Sunday; on the other days there's no parade, but you can see the changing of the guard. The parade route Monday through Saturday begins at Sergels Torg and proceeds along Hamngatan, Kungsträdgårdsgatan, Strömgatan, Gustav Adolfs Torg, Norrbro, Skeppsbron, and Slottsbacken. On Sunday the guard departs from the Army Museum, going along Riddargatan, Artillerigatan, Strandvägen, Hamngatan, Kungsträdgårdsgatan, Strömgatan, Gustav Adolfs Torg, Norrbro, Skeppsbron, and Slottsbacken. For information on the time of the march, ask at the Tourist Center in Sweden House. The changing of the guard takes place at noon Monday through Saturday and at 1pm on Sunday in front of the Royal Palace.

Kungliga Husgerådskammaren. (✆ **08/402-61-30** for Royal Apartments & Treasury, 08/402-61-34 for the Skattkammaren, 08/10-24-88 for Royal Armory, 08/402-61-30 for Museum of Antiquities. Royal Apartments, 70SEK ($7.40) adults, 50SEK ($5.30) students, free for children under 7; Royal Armory, 65SEK ($6.90) adults, 50SEK ($5.30) seniors and students, 20SEK ($2.10) children, free for children under 7; Museum of Antiquities, 70SEK ($7.40) adults, 35SEK ($3.70) seniors and students, free for children under 7; Treasury, 70SEK ($7.40) adults, 60SEK ($6.35) seniors and students, free for children under 7. Combination ticket to all parts of palace 120SEK ($13) adults, 60SEK ($6.35) students and children. Apartments and Treasury, Sept–June Tues–Sun noon–3pm; July–Aug daily 10am–4pm; closed during government receptions. Royal Armory, Sept–Apr Tues–Sun 11am–4pm; May–Aug daily 11am–4pm. Museum of Antiquities, May–Aug daily 10am–4pm. T-bana: Gamla Stan. Bus: 43, 46, 59, or 76.

Riddarholm Church (✿) The second-oldest church in Stockholm is on the tiny island of Riddarholmen, next to Gamla Stan. It was founded in the 13th century as a Franciscan monastery. Almost all the royal heads of state are entombed here (except Christina, who is buried in Rome).

There are three principal royal chapels, including one—the Bernadotte wing—that belongs to the present ruling family. Karl XIV Johan, the first king of the Bernadotte dynasty, is buried here in a large marble sarcophagus.

Riddarholmen. (✆ **08/402-61-30.** Admission 20SEK ($2.10) adults, 10SEK ($1.05) students and children. May–Aug daily 10am–4pm; Sept Sat–Sun noon–3pm. Closed Oct–Apr. T-bana: Gamla Stan.

Stockholms Medeltidsmuseum (Museum of Medieval Stockholm)
Built around archaeological excavations, this museum traces the city's founding and development during the Middle Ages. Exhibits include parts of the old city wall that date to 1530, which were discovered from 1978 to 1980. In essence, the museum opens a window on the Middle Ages. Objects tell you about

Frommer's Favorite Stockholm Experiences

Exploring Skansen From butter churning or folk dancing, there's always something to intrigue people of all ages here. Wander at leisure through the world's oldest open-air museum (which covers about 30 hectares/75 acres of parkland), getting a glimpse of Swedish life in the long-ago countryside.

Strolling Through Gamla Stan at Night To walk the narrow cobblestone alleys of the Old Town after dark, with special lighting, is like going back in time. It takes little imagination to envision what everyday life must have been like in this "city between the bridges."

Taking the Baths Both men and women are fond of roasting themselves on wooden platforms like chickens on a grill, and then plunging into a shower of Arctic-chilled water. After this experience, bathers emerge lighthearted and lightheaded into the fresh air, fortified for an evening of revelry.

Watching the Summer Dawn In midsummer at 3am, you can get out of bed, as many Swedes do, sit on a balcony, and watch the eerie blue sky—pure, crystal, exquisite. Gradually it's bathed in peach, as the early dawn of a "too-short" summer day approaches. Swedes don't like to miss a minute of summer, even if they have to get up early to enjoy it.

children's games, women's work, monastic life, and other activities. The museum also houses the *Riddarsholm* ship (ca. 1520), which was excavated in 1930, with some of its leather goods, ceramics, and nautical artifacts well preserved.

Strömparterren, Norrbro. © 08/508-317-90. Admission 40SEK ($4.25) adults, 5SEK (55¢) children. July–Aug Tues–Thurs 11am–6pm, Fri–Mon 11am–4pm; Sept–June Tues and Thurs–Sun 11am–4pm, Wed 11am–6pm. Bus: 43.

Östasiatiskamuseet (Museum of Far Eastern Antiquities) *Finds* The permanent collection at this small, intimate museum consists of archaeological objects, fine arts, and handicrafts from China, Japan, Korea, and India. The collection is one of the finest and most important of its kind outside Asia. Among the outstanding displays are Chinese Neolithic painted pottery, bronze ritual vessels, archaic jades, woodcarvings, ivory, lacquerwork, and enamelware. You might see Chinese glass, Buddhist sculpture, Chinese painting and calligraphy, T'ang tomb pottery figurines, Sung classical stoneware (such as celadon and *temmoku*), Ming blue-and-white wares, and Ch'ing porcelain made for the Chinese and European markets. The building was erected around 1700 as stables for Charles (Karl) XII's bodyguard.

Skeppsholmen. © 08/519-557-50. Admission 50SEK ($5.30) adults, free for children under 16. Tues noon–8pm; Wed–Sun noon–5pm. T-bana: Kungsträdgården. Bus: 65 to Karl XII Torg; 7-min. walk.

2 On Norrmalm

Hallwylska Museet (Hallwyl Museum) *Finds* Sweden has never seen a collector to compare with Countess Wilhelmina von Hallwyl. She spent nearly three-quarters of a century collecting "things," most of them rare and valuable. She carefully cataloged them and left them to the state upon her death. Today the most eccentric of Stockholm's museums is in a turn-of-the-20th-century residence of great splendor. The house is a fine example of the skilled craftsmanship of its day.

The catalog of this passionate collector came to 78 volumes, so you can imagine the amount of decorative art on display. Open to the public since 1938, the collection includes priceless paintings, rare tapestries, silver, armor, weapons, antique musical instruments, glassware, even umbrellas and buttons (but only the finest ones). The aristocratic Hallwyl family occupied this town house from 1898 to 1930. One of the three daughters became a sculptor and studied with the great Carl Milles. On the tour, you learn historical tidbits. This house had a modern bathroom even before the royal palace. Ask about summer evening concerts presented in the central courtyard. Visits are by guided tour only.

Hamngatan 4. (© 08/519-555-99. Guided tours 65SEK ($6.90) adults, 30SEK ($3.20) students, free for children under 7. Mar–Sept English-language tours daily at 1pm, 2pm, and 3pm, with an additional tour Wed at 6pm. Oct–Feb guided tour in English only Sun at 1pm. Tues–Sun 1–3pm. T-bana: Kungsträdgården.

Kaknästornet (Kaknäs Television Tower) *Moments*   In the northern district of Djurgården stands the tallest man-made structure in Scandinavia—a 152m (508-ft.) radio and television tower. Two elevators run to an observation platform, where you can see everything from the cobblestone streets of Gamla Stan (Old Town) to the city's modern concrete-and-glass structures and the archipelago beyond. A moderately priced restaurant that serves classic Swedish cuisine is at the top of the tower.

Mörkakroken. (© 08/789-24-35. Admission 25SEK ($2.65) adults, 15SEK ($1.60) children 7–15, free for children under 7. May–Aug daily 9am–10pm; Sept–Apr daily 10am–9pm. Closed Dec 24–25. Bus: 69.

Nationalmuseum (National Museum of Art) *★★*   At the tip of a peninsula, a short walk from the Royal Opera House and the Grand Hotel, is Sweden's state treasure house of paintings and sculpture. Founded in 1792, it's one of the oldest museums in the world. Its collections include a wide assortment of masterpieces by such artists as Rembrandt and Rubens *(Sacrifices to Venus).*

The first floor focuses on applied arts (silverware, handicrafts, porcelain, Empire furnishings, and the like). First-time visitors, if pressed for time, may want to head directly to the second floor. Here, among the paintings from northern Europe, is Lucas Cranach's amusing *Venus and Cupid.* Also displayed is a rare collection of Russian icons, most of them—such as *St. George and the Dragon*—from the Moscow School of the mid–16th century.

The museum shows an exceptional number of excellent paintings by such masters as Perugino *(St. Sebastian),* Ribera (his oft-rendered *Martyrdom of Bartolomé*), El Greco *(Peter and Paul),* Giovanni Bellini *(Portrait of Christ),* Lotto *(Portrait of a Man),* and Poussin *(Bacchus).* The gallery contains some outstanding Flemish works, notably Rubens's *Bacchanal at Andros* and *Worship of Venus,* and Jan Brueghel's *Jesus Preaching from the Boat.*

Perhaps the most important room in the museum has one whole wall featuring the works of Rembrandt—*Portrait of an Old Man, Portrait of an Old Woman,* and *Kitchen Maid* (one of the most famous works in Stockholm). Here also is *The Oath of the Batavians.*

In yet another room is Watteau's *Lesson in Love,* and another room is noted for its Venetian works by Guardi and Canaletto, as well as English portraits by Gainsborough and Reynolds.

Modern works include Manet's *Parisienne;* Degas's dancers; Rodin's nude male *(Copper Age)* and his bust of Victor Hugo; van Gogh's *Light Movements in*

Green; landscapes by Cézanne, Gauguin, and Pissarro; and paintings by Renoir, notably *La Grenouillère.*

Södra Blasieholmshamnen. ℭ **08/519-543-00.** Admission 75SEK ($7.95) adults, 60SEK ($6.35) seniors and students, free for children under 16. Tues and Thurs 11am–8pm; Wed and Fri–Sun 11am–5pm. T-bana: Kungsträdgården. Bus: 46, 62, 65, or 76.

Moderna Museet (Museum of Modern Art) 𝕲

The museum focuses on contemporary works, including kinetic sculpture, by Swedish and international artists. Highlights include a small but good collection of cubist art by Picasso, Braque, and Léger; Matisse's *Apollo* découpage; the famous *Enigma of William Tell* by Salvador Dalí; and works by Brancusi, Max Ernst, Giacometti, and Arp, among others. There's also a collection of pop art—Robert Rauschenberg *(Monogram),* Claes Oldenburg, and Andy Warhol. Among 1960s works by prominent New York artists are Oldenburg's 3.6m (12-ft.) high *Geometric Mouse; Fox Trot,* an early Warhol; and *Total Totality All,* a large sculpture by Louise Nevelson.

Museum activities include a children's workshop, concerts, films, discussions, and theater. There's also a cafe and pub.

Klaravergsviadukten 61. ℭ **08/519-552-00.** Free admission. Tues–Thurs 10am–8pm; Fri–Sun 10am–6pm. T-bana: Kungsträdgården. Bus: 65.

Historiska Museet (Museum of National Antiquities) 𝕲𝕲

This is the nation's finest repository of Swedish—especially Viking-era—relics; many were unearthed from ancient burial sites. The collection of artifacts dates from prehistoric to medieval times, and includes Viking stone inscriptions and coins minted in the 10th century. In 1994, in the presence of King Carl XVI Gustaf and Queen Silvia, a Gold Room was inaugurated. It features Viking silver and gold jewelry, large ornate charms, elaborate bracelet designs found nowhere else in the world, and a unique neck collar from Färjestaden. The valuable treasury is underground, along long corridors and behind solid security doors.

Narvavägen 13–17. ℭ **08/519-556-00.** Admission 60SEK ($6.35) adults, 50SEK ($5.30) seniors and students, 35SEK ($3.70) children 7–15, free for children under 7, 140SEK ($15) family. Apr–Sept Tues–Sun 11am–5pm; Oct–Mar Tues–Wed and Fri–Sun 11am–5pm, Thurs 11am–8pm. T-bana: Karlaplan or Östermalmstorg. Bus: 44, 47, or 54.

3 On Djurgården

The forested island of Djurgården (Deer Park) lies about 3km (2 miles) to the east of Gamla Stan (Old Town).

Vasamuseet (Royal Warship Vasa) 𝕲𝕲𝕲

This 17th-century man-of-war is the top attraction in Scandinavia—and for good reason. Housed near Skansen in a museum specially constructed for it, the *Vasa* is the world's oldest identified and complete ship.

On its maiden voyage in 1628, in front of thousands of onlookers, the Royal Warship *Vasa* capsized and sank almost instantly to the bottom of Stockholm harbor. Its salvage in 1961 was an engineering triumph. On board were more than 4,000 coins, carpenters' tools, sailors' pants (in a color known as Lübeck gray), fish bones, and other items of archaeological interest. Best of all, 97% of the ship's 700 original decorative sculptures were found. Carefully restored and impregnated with preservatives, they are now back aboard the stunning ship. It once again carries grotesque faces, lion masks, fish-shaped bodies, and other carvings, some still covered with the original paint and gilt.

A full-scale model of half of the *Vasa*'s upper gun deck has been built, together with the admiral's cabin and the steering compartment. Several carved wooden figures represent the crew. By walking through the "gun deck" and the exhibit of original objects (including medical equipment, preserved clothes, and a backgammon board), you can get an idea of life aboard the ship.

Another exhibit tells the story of naval warfare in the *Vasa*'s brief heyday. A diorama shows a battle fought by the Swedish and Polish navies in 1627. The ships, sculpted in copper, are positioned on a large cupola. Inside the cupola a film illustrates the horrors of war at sea.

Galärvarvsvägen, Djurgården. ✆ **08/519-548-00.** Admission 70SEK ($7.40) adults, 40SEK ($4.25) seniors and students, 10SEK ($1.05) children 7–15, free for children under 7. June 10–Aug 20 daily 9:30am–7pm; Aug 21–June 9 Wed 10am–8pm, Thurs–Tues 10am–5pm. Closed Jan 1, May 1, Dec 23–25. Bus: 44, 47, or 69. Ferry from Slussen year-round, from Nybroplan in summer only.

Skansen ✮✮✮   Often called "Old Sweden in a Nutshell," this open-air museum contains more than 150 dwellings on some 30 hectares (75 acres) of parkland. They originally stood all over the country, from Lapland to Skåne, and most are from the 18th and 19th centuries.

The exhibits range from a windmill to a manor house to a complete town quarter. Browsers can explore the old workshops and see where book publishers, silversmiths, and druggists plied their trades. Many handicrafts for which Swedes later became noted (glass blowing, for example) are demonstrated, along with traditional peasant crafts, such as weaving and churning. For a tour of the buildings, arrive no later than 4pm. Folk dancing and open-air concerts are also featured. In summer, international stars perform at Skansen. Check at the Tourist Center for information on special events. There's much to do on summer nights (see "Stockholm After Dark," later in this chapter), and many places to eat.

Djurgården 49–51. ✆ **08/442-80-00.** Admission 30SEK–60SEK ($3.20–$6.35) adults, depending on time of day, day of the week, and season; 20SEK–30SEK ($2.10–$3.20) children 6–15; free for children 5 and under. Historic buildings, May–Aug daily 10am–8pm; Sept–Apr daily 10am–5pm. Bus: 47 from central Stockholm. Ferry from Slussen.

Nordiska Museet ✮✮   This museum houses an impressive collection of Swedish implements, costumes, and furnishings from the 1500s to the present. The most outstanding museum of national life in Scandinavia contains more than a million objects. Highlights include dining tables and period costumes ranging from matching garters and ties for men to purple flowerpot hats from the 1890s. In the basement is an extensive exhibit of the tools of the Swedish fishing trade, plus relics from nomadic Lapps.

Djurgårdsvägen 6–16, Djurgården. ✆ **08/519-560-00.** Admission 60SEK ($6.35) adults, 50SEK ($5.30) seniors, 30SEK ($3.20) students, 20SEK ($2.10) children 7–12, free for children under 7. Daily 10am–5pm. Bus: 44, 47, or 69.

Prins Eugens Waldemarsudde ✮✮   This one-time residence of the "painting prince" functions as an art gallery and a memorial to one of the most famous royal artists in recent history, Prince Eugen (1865–1947). The youngest of Oscar II's four children, he was credited with making innovative contributions to the techniques of Swedish landscape painting. He specialized in depictions of his favorite regions in central Sweden. Among his most publicly visible works are the murals on the inner walls of the City Hall.

Built between 1903 and 1904, and set directly on the water, the house is surrounded by a flower and sculpture garden. Eugen's private collection of paintings, which includes works by Edvard Munch, Carl Larsson, and Anders Zorn, is one of the most rewarding aspects of the residence. The house and its contents were willed to the Swedish government after the prince's death, and opened to the public in 1948.

The house and art gallery are furnished as the prince left them. While at Waldemarsudde, see the **Old Mill,** built in the 1780s.

Prins Eugens Väg 6. © **08/545-837-00.** Admission 70SEK ($7.40) adults, 50SEK ($5.30) seniors and students, free for children under 17. June–Aug Tues and Thurs 11am–8pm, Wed and Fri–Sun 11am–5pm; Sept–May Tues–Sun 11am–4pm. Bus: 47 to the end of the line.

Thielska Galleriet (Thiel Gallery) ⟨⟨ *Finds*   At the tip of Djurgården, this gallery houses one of Sweden's major art collections. Many feel it surpasses the Prins Eugens Waldemarsudde collection. The sculptures and canvases here were acquired by Ernst Thiel, a financier and banker who eventually went bankrupt. The Swedish government acquired the collection in 1924.

Some big names in Scandinavian art are here, including Norway's Edvard Munch and Sweden's Anders Zorn (see his nude *In Dreams*). Gustav Fjaestad's furniture is also displayed. You'll also see a portrait of Nietzsche, whom Thiel greatly admired. Works by Manet, Rodin, and Toulouse-Lautrec, among others, round out the collection. Thiel is buried on the grounds beneath Rodin's statue *Shadow.*

Sjötullsbacken 6–8, Djurgården. © **08/662-58-84.** Admission 50SEK ($5.30) adults, 30SEK ($3.20) seniors and students, free for children under 12. Mon–Sat noon–4pm; Sun 1–4pm. Bus: 69.

4 On Kungsholmen

Stadshuset (Stockholm City Hall) ⟨⟨⟨   Built in the "National Romantic Style," the Stockholm City Hall (Stadshuset), on the island of Kungsholmen, is one of the finest examples of modern architecture in Europe. Designed by Ragnar Ostberg, it was completed in 1923. A lofty square tower 105m (348 ft.) high dominates the redbrick structure. It bears three gilt crowns, the symbol of Sweden, and the national coat-of-arms. There are two courts: the open civic court and the interior covered court. The Blue Hall is used for banquets and other festive occasions, including the Nobel Prize banquet. About 18 million pieces of gold and colored-glass mosaics cover the walls, and the southern gallery contains murals by Prince Eugen, the painter prince. The 101 City Council members meet in the council chamber.

Hantverksgatan 1. © **08/508-290-59.** Admission 50SEK ($5.30) adults, free for children under 12. Tower additional 15SEK ($1.60). May–Sept daily 10am–4pm. City Hall tours (subject to change), June–Sept daily at 10am, 11am, noon, and 2pm; Oct–Apr daily at 10am and noon. T-bana: Centralen or Rådhuset. Bus: 3 or 62.

5 On Södermalm

Stadsmuseet (Stockholm City Museum)   Housed in a building dating from 1684, the Stadsmuseet depicts the history of Stockholm and its citizens. Exhibits portray life in the industrial city throughout the past few centuries. Daily at 1pm, a 30-minute slide show in English describes Stockholm from the 16th century to the present.

Ryssgården, Slussen. © **08/508-316-00.** Admission 50SEK ($5.30) adults, free for children under 6. June–Aug Tues–Wed and Fri–Sun 11am–5pm, Thurs 11am–7pm; Sept–May Tues–Wed and Fri–Sun 11am–5pm, Thurs 11am–9pm. T-bana: Slussen. Bus: 43 or 46.

6 Near Stockholm

Drottningholm Palace and Theater ⭐⭐⭐   Conceived as the centerpiece of Sweden's royal court, this regal complex of stately buildings sits on an island in Lake Mälaren. Dubbed the "Versailles of Sweden," Drottningholm (Queen's Island) lies about 11km (7 miles) west of Stockholm. The palace, loaded with courtly art and furnishings, sits amid fountains and parks, and still functions as one of the royal family's official residences.

On the grounds is one of the most perfectly preserved 18th-century theaters in the world, **Drottningholm Court Theater** (📞 **08/759-04-06**). Between June and August, 30 performances are staged. Devoted almost exclusively to 18th-century opera, it seats only 450 for one of the most unusual entertainment experiences in Sweden. Many performances sell out far in advance to season-ticket holders. The theater can be visited only as part of a guided tour, which focuses on the original sets and stage mechanisms.

For tickets to the evening performances, which cost 165SEK to 600SEK ($17–$64), call 📞 **08/660-82-25.**

Ekerö, Drottningholm. 📞 **08/402-62-80.** Palace, 60SEK ($6.35) adults, 30SEK ($3.20) students and persons under 26; theater, guided tour 60SEK ($6.35) adults, 30SEK ($3.20) students and persons under 26; Chinese Pavilion, 50SEK ($5.30) adults, 25SEK ($2.65) students. All free for children under 7. Palace, Oct–Apr Sat–Sun noon–3:30pm; May–Aug daily 10am–4:30pm; Sept daily noon–3:30pm. Theater, guided tours in English, May daily 12:30pm, 1:30pm, 2:30pm, 3:30pm, and 4:15pm; June–Aug daily 11:30am, 12:30pm, 1:30pm, 2:30pm, 3:30pm, and 4:15pm; Sept daily 1:30pm, 2:30pm, 3:30pm. Chinese Pavilion, Apr and Oct daily 1–3:30pm; May–Aug daily 11am–4:30pm; Sept daily noon–3:30pm. T-bana: Brommaplan, then bus no. 301 or 323 to Drottningholm. Ferry from the dock near City Hall.

Millesgården ⭐⭐   On the island of Lidingö, northeast of Stockholm, is Carl Milles's former villa and sculpture garden beside the sea, now a museum. Many of his best-known works, including *Hand of God,* are displayed here (some are copies), as are works of other artists. Milles (1875–1955), who relied heavily on mythological themes, was Sweden's most famous sculptor.

Carl Milles Väg 2, Lidingö. 📞 **08/446-75-90.** Admission 75SEK ($7.95) adults, 60SEK ($6.35) seniors and students, 20SEK ($2.10) children 7–16, free for children under 7. May–Sept daily 10am–5pm; Oct–Apr Tues–Sun noon–4pm. T-bana: Ropsten, then bus to Torsviks Torg or train to Norsvik.

7 A Literary Landmark

Strindbergsmuseet (Strindberg Museum)   This building, popularly known as "The Blue Tower," is where August Strindberg, the dramatist and novelist, spent his last 4 years (1908–12). It contains a library; three furnished rooms; and books, articles, and letters representing the last 20 years of his life. Of special interest to those familiar with Strindberg's work is the fact that he furnished his rooms like stage sets from his plays, with color schemes as he visualized them. The dining room contains sculptures, casts of busts, and masks representing people and events that were important to him.

Drottninggatan 85. 📞 **08/411-53-54.** Admission 40SEK ($4.25) adults, 25SEK ($2.65) students, free for children. Tues noon–7pm (June–Aug noon–4pm); Wed–Sun noon–4pm. T-bana: Rådmansgatan.

8 Architectural Highlights

Arkitektur Museet (Museum of Architecture)   Founded in 1962 in a building designed by the Spanish architect Rafael Moneo, this museum illustrates the art of architecture combined with social planning. It displays copies of rooms, buildings, places, and cities from different eras, covering 1,000 years of Swedish architecture. The history of the buildings is presented in chronological sections. The collection consists of some two million sketches, drawings, and documents, plus a half million photographs and about 1,000 architectural models. The library alone has some 25,000 volumes, most donated by Swedish architects. The library is dedicated to the memory of the Swedish diplomat Raoul Wallenberg, known for his humanitarian efforts in Hungary in 1944 and 1945. Less well known is that Wallenberg was a trained architect. His few existing drawings, mainly from his student days in the United States, are in the museum's archives.

Skeppsholmen. $\textcircled{C}$ 08/587-270-00. Call for admission costs and hours. Bus: 65.

9 Especially for Kids

The open-air park, Skansen, on Djurgården, contains **Lill-Skansen,** "Little Skansen." There's a petting zoo with lots of child-friendly animals, including pigs, goats, and horses. Lill-Skansen offers a break from the dizzying (and often tantrum-inducing) excitement frequently generated by commercial amusement parks. A miniature train ride through the park (see above) is about as wild as it gets. Lill-Skansen is open daily in summer from 10:30am to 4pm.

Kids can spend a day or several at Skansen and not get bored. Before going to Skansen, stop off at the *Vasa* **Museum,** which many youngsters find an epic adventure. The evening can be capped by a visit to **Gröna Lunds Tivoli** (see "Stockholm After Dark," later in this chapter), also on Djurgården.

10 Stockholm on Foot: Walking Tours

WALKING TOUR 1   GAMLA STAN (OLD TOWN)

Start:	Gustav Adolfs Torg.
Finish:	Slussplan.
Time:	3 hours.
Best Time:	Any day when it's not raining.
Worst Times:	Rush hours (weekdays 8–9:30am and 5:30–7pm).

Begin at:
❶ Gustav Adolfs Torg
Facing the Royal Palace, with the Royal Opera on your left, here is where Gustavus III, patron of the arts, was assassinated at a masked ball in 1792.

Walk across Norrbro (North Bridge), heading toward the Royal Palace. On your right you'll pass the:
❷ Swedish Parliament (Riksplan)
The Parliament building at Helgeandsholmen dates from 1897, when its foundation stone was laid. It can be visited only on guided tours.

Along the bridge on your left are stairs leading to the:

❸ Medeltidsmuseet (Museum of Medieval Stockholm)
This museum on Strömparterren contains objects and settings from medieval Stockholm, including the Riddarholmship and parts of the old city wall.

 TAKE A BREAK
One of the hidden cafes of Stockholm, **Café Strömparterren,** Helgeandsholmen ($(\textcircled{C}$ 08/ 21-95-45), also is one of the most centrally located—just next door to the Medel-tids-museet. Many Stockholmers come here for a morning cup of coffee and a stunning view of the waterfront. In summer, tables are placed outside; the interior of the cafe is built into the walls under Norrbro.

After leaving the museum, turn to the right and walk back to the bridge until you come to Slottskajen. Here, directly in front of the Royal Palace, make a right turn and head to Mynttorget, site of the Kanslihuset, a government office building erected in the 1930s. The neoclassical, columned facade remains from the Royal Mint of 1790.

Continue straight along Myntgatan until you reach Riddarhustorget. On your right is the:

❹ Riddarhuset

The Swedish aristocracy met in this 17th-century House of Nobles during the Parliament of the Four Estates (1665–68).

Continue straight across Riddarholmsbron (bridge) until you come to the little island of:

❺ Riddarholmen

Called "the island of the knights," Riddarholmen is closely linked to the Old Town. You'll immediately see its chief landmark, the **Riddarholm-skyrkan (church)** with its cast-iron spire. Founded as an abbey in the 13th century, it has been the burial place of Swedish kings for 4 centuries.

Walk along the right side of the church until you reach Birger Jarls Torg. From there, take the 1-block-long Wrangelska Backen to the water. Then go left and walk along Södra Riddarholmshamnen.

Veer left by the railroad tracks, climb some steps, and go along Hebbes Trappor until you return to Riddarholmskyrkan. From here, cross over Riddarholmsbron and return to Riddarhustorget.

Cross Stora Nygatan and take the next right onto Storkyrkobrinken, passing the landmark Cattelin Restaurant on your right. Continue along this street, past the Lady Hamilton Hotel, turning right onto Trångsund, which leads to:

❻ Stortorget (Great Square)

Take a seat on one of the park benches—you've earned the rest. This plaza was the site of the Stockholm Blood Bath of 1520 when Christian II of Denmark beheaded 80 Swedish noblemen and displayed a "pyramid" of their heads in the square. The Börsen on this square is the Swedish Stock Exchange, a building dating

from 1776. This is where the Swedish Academy meets every year to choose the Nobel Prize winners in literature.

At the northeast corner of the square, take Källargränd north to view the entrance, opening onto Slottsbacken, of the:

❼ Royal Palace

The present palace dates mainly from 1760 after a previous one was destroyed by fire. The changing of the guard takes place here on this square.

On your right is the site of the:

❽ Storkyrkan

This church was founded in the mid-1200s but has been rebuilt many times since. It's the site of coronations and royal weddings; kings are also christened here. The most celebrated sculpture here is *St. George and the Dragon*, a huge work dating from 1489. The royal pews have been used for 3 centuries, and the altar, mainly in ebony and silver, dates from 1652. This is still a functioning church, so it's best to visit when services are not in progress. It's open Monday through Saturday from 9am to 7pm and on Sunday from 9am to 5:30pm; admission is free.

Continue right along Slottsbacken, either visiting the palace now or saving it for later. Go right as you reach Bollhusgränd, a cobblestone street of old houses leading to:

❾ Köpmantorget

One of the most charming squares of the Old Town, Köpmantorget contains a famous copy of the *St. George and the Dragon* statue.

From the square, take Köpmanbrinken, which runs for 1 block before turning into:

❿ Österlånggatan

Now the site of many restaurants and antiques shops, Österlånggatan was once Old Town's harbor street.

Continue along Österlånggatan, but take the first left under an arch, leading into:

⓫ Stora Hoparegränd

This is one of the darkest and narrowest streets in Gamla Stan. Some buildings along this dank thoroughfare date from the mid-1600s.

Walking Tour: Gamla Stan (Old Town)

1 Gustav Adolfs Torg
2 Swedish Parliament
3 Medeltidsmuseet
☕ Café Strömparterren
4 Riddarhuset
5 Riddarholmen
6 Stortorget
7 Royal Palace
8 Storkyrkan
9 Köpmantorget
10 Österlånggatan
11 Stora Hoparegränd
12 Mårten Trotzigs Gränd
13 Tyska Kyrkan
14 Västerlånggatan
15 Järntorget
16 Slussplan

Walk down the alley toward the water, emerging at Skeppsbron (bridge). Turn right and walk 2 blocks to Ferkens Gränd. Go right again up Ferkens Gränd for a block until you return to Österlånggatan. Go left on Österlånggatan and follow it to Tullgränd. Take the street on your right, Prästgatan.

As you climb this street, note on your left:

⑫ Mårten Trotzigs Gränd

This street of steps is the narrowest in Gamla Stan.

Continue along Prästgatan, passing a playground on your right. Turn right onto Tyska Brinken and walk to the church:

⑬ Tyska Kyrkan

Since the beginning of the 17th century, this has been the German church of Stockholm. The church has a baroque interior and is exquisitely decorated.

After you leave the church, the street in front of you will be Skomakargatan. Head up this street until you come to Stortorget once again. From Stortorget, take Kåkbrinken, at the southwest corner of the square. Follow this little street until turning left at:

⑭ Västerlånggatan

This pedestrian street is the main shopping artery of Gamla Stan, and the best place to purchase gifts and souvenirs of Sweden.

Follow Västerlånggatan to:

⑮ Järntorget

This street used to be known as Korntorget when it was the center of the copper and iron trade in the 16th and 17th centuries. At times in its long history, Järntorget has been the place of punishment for "wrongdoers." The most unusual statue in Stockholm stands here—a **statue of Evert Taube,** the troubadour and Swedish national poet of the early 1900s. He's carrying a newspaper under his arm, his coat draped nonchalantly, his sunglasses pushed up high on his forehead.

From the square, take Järntorgsgatan to:

⑯ Slussplan

Here you can catch a bus to return to the central city or you can board a ferry to Djurgården and its many museums.

WALKING TOUR 2   ALONG THE HARBOR

Start:	Stadshuset.
Finish:	Museum of Architecture.
Time:	3 hours.
Best Time:	Any day when it's not raining.
Worst Times:	Rush hours (weekdays 8–9:30am and 5:30–7pm).

Start at Hantverkargatan 1, on Kungsholmen:

❶ Stadshuset (Stockholm City Hall)

This island has some of the loveliest and most varied waterfront walks in the city. It took 12 years, eight million bricks, and 19 million gilded mosaic tiles to erect this city hall, which can be visited on a guided tour. Go inside the courtyard on your own and admire the architecture.

When exiting the building, turn right and walk across Stadshusbron (City Hall Bridge) to Norrmalm. You'll see the Sheraton Hotel

on your left, and on your right the Stadshus-cafeet, where sightseeing boats depart on canal cruises in summer. Walk past the boats and go under an underpass (watch out for fast-riding bicyclists).

Continue along the canal until you reach Tegelbacken, a waterfront square. At the entrance to the Vasabron (bridge), cross the street and continue along Fredsgatan. Veer right at the intersection, hugging the canal. This will take you to Rosenbad, a little triangular park.

At the canal bordering Strömgatan, look at the building on your right:

1 Stadshuset
2 Swedish Parliament
3 Gustav Adolfs Torg

4 Kungsträdgården
5 Grand Hotel
6 National Museum

7 Skeppsholmen
8 AF Chapman
9 Kastellholmen

10 Museum of Architecture

② Swedish Parliament
You can visit this building on a guided tour.

Continue on to:

③ Gustav Adolfs Torg
From here you have a panoramic view of the Royal Palace across the canal and of the Royal Opera straight ahead. This is one of the most famous landmark squares of Stockholm, and the most scenically located.

Strömgatan resumes at the corner of the Opera House, site of the Operakällaren, for many years the finest restaurant in Stockholm. Continue along until you reach the southern tier of the:

④ Kungsträdgården
These royal gardens, the summer living room of Stockholm, reach from Hamngatan on the north side down to the water. Established in the 1500s as a pleasure garden for the court, they are now open to all, with cafes, open-air restaurants, and refreshment kiosks.

TAKE A BREAK
Since the late 1800s, the **Café Victoria**, Kungsträdgården (© 08/10-10-85), in the center of Stockholm, has attracted crowds. It's an ideal spot for a refreshing drink or snack at any time during the day or evening. It's open Monday through Saturday from 11:30am to 10pm and Sunday from noon to 7pm. (See "Stockholm After Dark," later in this chapter, for more information.)

Continue along the waterfront, past Strömbron, a bridge leading to Gamla Stan, and emerge onto Södra Blasieholmshamnen. At no. 8 is the:

⑤ Grand Hotel
For decades this has been the prestige address of Stockholm, attracting Nobel Prize winners as well as most visiting dignitaries and movie stars. On your right, any number of sightseeing boats depart in summer for tours of the Stockholm archipelago.

From this vantage point, you'll have a good view of the Royal Palace and Gamla Stan.

Continue along Södra Blasieholmshamnen until you reach (on your right) the:

⑥ National Museum
Here you find a repository of the state's art treasures—everything from Renoir to Rembrandt.

Cross the Skeppsholmsbron (bridge) leading to the little island of:

⑦ Skeppsholmen
The island holds a number of attractions (see "On Gamla Stan & Neighboring Islands," earlier in this chapter).

After crossing the bridge, turn right along Västra Brobänken. On your right you'll pass the:

⑧ AF *Chapman*
This "tall ship" with fully rigged masts once sailed the seas under three different flags before being permanently anchored in 1949 as a youth hostel.

Turn left onto Flaggmansvägen. Continue along Holmamiralens Torg, passing the Nordiska Institute on your right. Cut right toward the water at Södra Brobänken. Take a right turn and cross the bridge leading to:

⑨ Kastellholmen
This is one of the most charming, but least-visited, islands in Stockholm. Head right along the water, going around Kastellholmskajen. Circle around and turn left at the end of Kastelleton. Walk back along Örlogsvägen, which runs through the center of the small island.

Cross the Kastellholmsbron (bridge) and return to the larger island of Skeppsholmen. This time go straight along Amiralsvägen, turning left onto Långa Raden. Cut right and continue to walk along Långa Raden. The first building on your left is the:

⑩ Museum of Architecture
The collection contains slides and thousands of architectural drawings and sketches from the last 100 years.

From this point at the end of the walking tour, you can catch bus no. 65 to take you back to the heart of Stockholm.

11 Organized Tours

CITY TOURS   The quickest and most convenient way to see the highlights of Stockholm is to take one of the bus tours that leave from Karl XII Torg, near the Kungsträdgården.

Stockholm Sightseeing, Skeppsbron 22 (© **08/587-140-20**), offers a variety of tours, mostly in the summer. The 3-hour "Royal Stockholm" tour visits the Royal Palace or the Treasury and the *Vasa* Museum, with daily departures from mid-April to mid-October from Gustav Adolfs Torg, by the Royal Opera House. They cost 280SEK ($30). The quickest, cheapest tour—but also the most superficial—is the 1-hour "City Tour," for 170SEK ($18). It leaves daily year-round from Gustav Adolfs Torg. "Under the Bridges" takes 2 hours and goes through two locks and two bodies of water. Departures are from Stromkajen (near the Grand Hotel), daily from mid-April to mid-September. The cost is 190SEK ($20). The 1-hour "Sightseeing Anno 1935" explores the Stockholm harbor in an open-topped wooden boat, with a captain in period uniform. The tour costs 110SEK ($12). Daily departures, from early July to mid-August, are from the statue of Gustavus III by the Royal Palace.

OLD TOWN STROLLS   Authorized guides lead 1½-hour walking tours of the medieval lanes of Gamla Stan (Old Town). Walks depart from the Royal Opera House at Gustav Adolfs Torg, daily from June to mid-August. They cost 80SEK ($8.50). Tickets and departure times are available from **Stockholm Sightseeing,** Skeppsbron 22 (© **08/587-140-20**).

CANAL CRUISES   **Stockholm Sightseeing** (© **08/587-140-20**) offers the "Royal Canal Tour" daily from May to September, every 30 minutes. Tours cost 90SEK ($9.55) for adults, 45SEK ($4.75) for children. The tour goes around the canals of Djurgården.

12 Spectator Sports

Soccer and **ice hockey** are the most popular spectator sports in Sweden, and Stockholm is the home of world-class teams. The most important sports venue in the capital, the **Stockholm Globe Arena (Globen),** is less than 6.5km (4 miles) south of central Stockholm. Built in 1989, it's believed to be the biggest round building in the world, with a seating capacity of 16,000. It stages political rallies, motorcycle competitions, sales conventions, basketball and ice hockey games, tennis matches, and rock concerts. The ticket office (© **08/600-34-00**) also sells tickets for most of Stockholm's soccer games, which are played in an open-air stadium nearby. It's open Monday through Friday from 9am to 4pm. The Globen complex lies in the suburb of Johnneshov (T-bana: Globen).

Another popular sport is **trotting races,** with the associated gambling. They usually take place on Wednesday at 6:30pm and occasionally on Saturday at 12:30pm, summer and winter. (Slippery snow and ice on the racecourse sometimes lead to unpredictable results.) Admission to **Solvalla Stadium** (© **08/635-90-00**), about 6.5km (4 miles) north of the city center, is 40SEK ($4.25). From Stockholm, take the bus marked SOLVALLA.

For schedules and ticket information, inquire at your hotel or the tourist office, or buy a copy of *Stockholm This Week* from a newspaper kiosk.

13 Outdoor Activities

GOLFING   For those who want to play golf at the "top of Europe," there is the **Bromma Golf Course,** Kvarnbacksvägen 28, 16874 Bromma (© **08/ 564-888-30**), lying about 5km (3 miles) west of the center of Stockholm. It's a nine-hole golf course with well-maintained greens. Greens fees are 140SEK ($15); rental clubs are available.

HORSEBACK RIDING (VIKING STYLE)   You can ride small, gentle Icelandic horses at the **Haninge Iceland Horse Center** in Hemfosa, 37km (23 miles) south of Stockholm (© **08/500-481-81**). For 400SEK ($42) you can ride for 2½ hours; the price includes a picnic lunch. Besides walking, galloping, trotting, and cantering, the horses have another gait, the *tölt,* which is a kind of equine speed walk that has no English translation.

SAUNA & SWIMMING   Vilda Vanadis (© **08/30-12-11**) is a combination sauna, outdoor heated pool, and children's paddling pool. It's at Vanadislunden, near the northern terminus of Sveavägen, within easy walking distance of the Oden Hotel and the city center. This is really an adventure park, with a variety of attractions. There's also a sauna and a restaurant. The entrance fee is 50SEK ($5.30), and once you're inside, the attractions are free. It's open from early May to the end of August, daily from 10am to 6pm.

TENNIS, SQUASH & WEIGHT LIFTING   At the **Royal Tennis Hall,** Lidingövägen 75 (© **08/459-15-00** for reservations), you can play racquet sports, lift weights, and enjoy a sauna and solarium. The center has 16 indoor courts, five outdoor clay courts, and eight squash courts. Tennis courts cost 255SEK ($27) per hour; squash courts, 80SEK to 205SEK ($8.50–$22) for a 30-minute session. Use of the weight room costs 40SEK ($4.25). The center is open Monday through Thursday from 7am to 11pm, Friday from 7am to 9pm, Saturday and Sunday from 8am to 9pm.

14 Shopping
THE SHOPPING SCENE
Stockholm is filled with shop after shop displaying dazzling merchandise—often at dazzlingly steep prices. Sweden's craftspeople are well paid for their considerable skills, which translates into high costs to the consumer.

Bargain shoppers should proceed with caution. There are some good buys, but they take a lot of searching. If you're a casual shopper, you might want to confine your purchases to handsome souvenirs and gifts.

Swedish glass is world famous. The wooden items are outstanding, and many people love the functional furniture in blond pine or birch. Other items to look for include children's playsuits, silver necklaces, reindeer gloves, hand-woven neckties and skirts, sweaters and mittens in Nordic patterns, clogs, and colorful handicrafts from the provinces. The most famous souvenir is the Dala horse from Dalarna.

TAXES & REFUNDS   Sweden imposes the value-added tax, *moms,* on all products and services. When buying larger and more expensive items, you can avoid *moms* if you spend more than 200SEK ($21). Give the store your name, address, and passport number, and ask for a "Tax-Free Check." Don't unwrap your purchase until after you've left Sweden. The Customs official will want to see both the Tax-Free Check and your purchase. You'll be given a cash refund, minus a small commission, on the spot. If you're departing by plane, hold onto your luggage until after you've received your refund, and then you can pack your purchase in your bag and check it (or carry the purchase with you, if it's not too big). At the **Tourist Center,** Hamngatan 27 (℃ **08/789-24-95**), you can pick up a pamphlet about tax-free shopping in Sweden. Additional information is available by phone; call ℃ **0410/613-01.** (For more information, see "Taxes" in "Fast Facts: Sweden," in chapter 12.)

SHOPPING STREETS & DISTRICTS   Everybody's favorite shopping area in Stockholm is **Gamla Stan (Old Town).** It's near the Royal Palace—even the queen has been seen shopping there. The main street for browsing is **Västerlånggatan.** Many antiques stores are there, but don't expect low prices.

In the summer, **Skansen** is an interesting area to explore. Many craftspeople display their goods there. There are gift shops (some sell "Skansen glass"), as well as individuals who offer their handmade goods on temporary stands.

In the **Sergels Torg** area, the main shopping street is **Hamngatan.** There you'll find the famous shopping center Gallerian, at the corner of Hamngatan and Sergels Torg, and bordering Kungsträdgården at Sweden House. Big department stores, such as NK and Åhléns City, are nearby.

Other major shopping districts include the **Kungsgatan** area, which stretches from Hötorget to the intersection of Kungsgatan and Vasagatan, and **Hötorget,** home to the PUB department store. **Drottninggatan** is one long pedestrian mall, flanked with shops. Many side streets off this mall are also filled with shops.

SHOPPING HOURS   Shops are open Monday through Friday from 10am to 6pm, Saturday from 10am to somewhere between 1 and 4pm. Once a week, usually on Monday or Friday, some larger stores are open from 9:30am to 7pm (during July and Aug, to 6pm).

SHOPPING A TO Z
AUCTIONS
Stockholms Auktionsverket (Stockholm Auction Chambers)   The oldest auction company in the world—it dates from 1674—holds auctions 3 days a week from noon to "whenever." You can view the merchandise on Friday from 11am to 5pm and Saturday from 10am to 4pm. An estimated 150,000 lots are auctioned each year—everything from ceramics to Picassos. In Gallerian, Hamngatan 37. ℃ 08/453-67-00. T-bana: Kungsträdgården.

BOOKS & MAPS
Akademibokhandeln   The biggest bookstore in Sweden carries more than 100,000 titles. A wide range of fiction and nonfiction is available in English. Many travel-related materials, such as maps, are also sold. Mäster Samuelsgatan 32. ℃ 08/613-61-00. T-bana: Hötorget.

Sverige Bokhandeln (Sweden Bookshop)   Whatever's available in English about Sweden can be found at this bookstore above the Tourist Center. The store sells many rare items, including recordings of Swedish music. Sweden House (Sverigehuset), 2nd Floor. Kungsträdgården. ℃ 08/789-21-31. T-bana: Kungsträdgården.

CERAMICS
Blås & Knåda   This store sells the best products made by members of a cooperative of 50 Swedish ceramic artists and glassmakers. Prices begin at 120SEK ($13) for a single teacup, and rise to as much as 35,000SEK ($3,710) for museum-quality pieces. Hornsgatan 26. ℃ 08/642-77-67. T-bana: Slussen.

Keramiskt Centrum Gustavsberg   Bone china, stoneware dinner services, and other fine table and decorative ware are made at the Gustavsberg Ceramics Center. A museum at the center displays historic pieces such as *parian* (a type of unglazed porcelain) statues based on the work of the famous Danish sculptor Torvaldsen and other artists. You'll also see hand-painted vases, Toby jugs, majolica, willowware, examples of Pyro (the first ovenware), royal dinner services, and sculptures by modern artists.

Visitors can watch potters at work and see artists hand-painting designs. You can even decorate a mug or plate yourself. A shop at the center sells Gustavsberg-ware, including seconds. Värmdö Island (21km/13 miles east of Stockholm). ℂ 08/570-356-58. Bus: 422 or 440.

DEPARTMENT STORES
Åhléns City   In the center of Stockholm, the largest department store in Sweden has a gift shop, a restaurant, and a famous food department. Also seek out the fine collection of home textiles, and Orrefors and Kosta Boda crystalware. The pewter with genuine Swedish ornaments makes a fine gift item. Klarabergsgatan 50. ℂ 08/676-60-00. T-bana: Centralen.

Nordiska Kompanient (NK)   A high-quality department store since 1902, NK displays most of the big names in Swedish glass, including Orrefors (see the Nordic Light collection) and Kosta. Thousands of handcrafted Swedish items can be found in the basement. Stainless steel, also a good buy in Sweden, is profusely displayed. It's open Monday through Friday from 10am to 7pm, Saturday from 10am to 5pm, Sunday from noon to 5pm. Hamngatan 18–20. ℂ 08/762-80-00. T-bana: Kungsträdgården.

PUB   Greta Garbo worked in the millinery department here from 1920 to 1922. It's one of the most popular department stores in Stockholm; the boutiques and departments generally sell mid-range clothing and good-quality housewares, but not the international designer names of the more prestigious (and more expensive) NK. Massive and bustling, with an emphasis on traditional and conservative Swedish clothing, it offers just about anything you'd need to stock a Scandinavian home. There's also a restaurant. Hötorget 13. ℂ 08/402-16-11. T-bana: Hötorget.

FLEA MARKET
Loppmarknaden i Skärholmen (Skärholmen Shopping Center)   At the biggest flea market in northern Europe, you might find a pleasing item from an attic in Värmland. You might indeed find *anything*. Try to go on Saturday or Sunday (the earlier the better), when the market is at its peak. Admission is 10SEK ($1.05) for adults, free for children. Skärholmen. ℂ 08/710-00-60. Bus: 13 or 23 to Skärholmen (20 min.).

GEMS & MINERALS
Geocity *(finds)*   Geocity offers exotic mineral crystals, jewelry, Scandinavian gems, Baltic amber, and lapidary equipment. The staff includes two certified gemologists who will cut and set any gem you select and do appraisals. The inventory holds stones from Scandinavia and around the world, including Greenland, Madagascar, Siberia, and South America. Tysta Marigången 5, Tegelbacken. ℂ 08/411-11-40. T-bana: Centralen.

GIFTS & SOUVENIRS
Slottsbodarna (Royal Gift Shop)   This unusual outlet sells products related to or copied from the collections in the Royal Palace. Items are re-created in

silver, gold, brass, pewter, textiles, and glass. Every item is made in Sweden. Royal Palace south wing, Slottsbacken. ☎ 08/402-61-48. T-bana: Gamla Stan.

GLASS & CRYSTAL

Rosenthal Studio-Haus This is the largest outlet in Sweden for delicate German-made Rosenthal porcelain. You'll find mostly modern patterns of crystal, porcelain, glass, and upscale stainless steel. Birger Jarlsgatan 6. ☎ 08/611-66-01. T-bana: Östermalmstorg.

Svenskt Glas Royal families patronize this establishment, which features Swedish-made glass at every price level. You'll see Orrefors and Kosta Boda stemware, candlesticks, flower-shaped bowls in full lead crystal, bar sets, vases, wineglasses, pitchers, and perfume bottles. Worldwide shipping is available. Karlavägen 61. ☎ 08/679-79-09. T-bana: Östermalmstorg.

HANDICRAFTS & GIFTS

Brinken Konsthantverk On the lower floor of a building near the Royal Palace in the Old Town, this elegant purveyor of gift items will ship handcrafted brass, pewter, wrought iron, or crystal anywhere in the world. About 95% of the articles are made in Scandinavia. Storkyrkobrinken 1. ☎ 08/411-59-54. T-bana: Gamla Stan.

DesignTorget In 1994, the government-owned Kulturhuset (Swedish Culture House) reacted to declining attendance by inviting one of Stockholm's most influential designers and decorators, Jerry Hellström, to organize an avant-garde art gallery. Swedes modestly refer to it as a "shop." In a large room in the cellar, you'll find a display of handicrafts created by 150 to 200 mostly Swedish craftspeople. The work must be approved by a jury of connoisseurs before being offered for sale. The merchandise includes some of the best pottery, furniture, textiles, clothing, pewter, and crystal in Sweden, for 25SEK to 20,000SEK ($2.65–$2,120) per object. The most expensive object in the gallery, at the time of this writing, was a magnificently proportioned bathtub assembled from glued and laminated strips of wood. Almost as impressive were a series of ergonomically designed computer workstations. The organization maintains a branch in southern Stockholm, **DesignTorget Mode,** Götgatan 31 (☎ **08/462-35-20**). It stocks clothing for men, women, and children, and furniture, with less emphasis on ceramics and handicrafts. In the Kulturhuset, Sergels Torg 3. ☎ **08/508-315-20**. T-bana: Centralen.

Duka A large selection of crystal, porcelain, and gifts is available in this shop near the Konserthuset (Concert Hall). It offers tax-free shopping and shipping. Kungsgatan 41. ☎ 08/20-60-41. T-bana: Hötorget.

Gunnarssons Träfigurer *(Finds* This is one of the city's most interesting collections of Swedish carved wooden figures. All are by Urban Gunnarsson, a second-generation master carver. They include World War II figures, such as Winston Churchill, and U.S. presidents from Franklin D. Roosevelt to Bill Clinton. There's also a host of mythical and historical European personalities. Prices range from 300SEK to 800SEK ($32–$85); larger pieces cost up to 2,000SEK ($212). The carvings are usually made from linden or basswood. Drottninggatan 77. ☎ 08/21-67-17. T-bana: Rådmansgatan.

Konsthantverkarna This store has an unusual selection of some of the best Swedish handicrafts, created by a group of artisans. All pieces must pass scrutiny by a strict jury before they're offered for sale. Choose from glass, sculpture, ceramics, wall textiles, clothes, jewelry, silver, brass, and wood and leather work. Each item is handmade and original. Ask about the tax-free service. Mäster Samuelsgatan 2. ☎ 08/611-96-60. T-bana: Östermalmstorg.

Svensk Hemslojd (Society for Swedish Handicrafts) Svensk Hemslojd offers a wide selection of glass, pottery, gifts, and wooden and metal handicrafts by some of Sweden's best artisans. There's a display of hand-woven carpets, upholstery fabrics, hand-painted materials, tapestries, lace, and embroidered items. You'll also find beautiful yarns for weaving and embroidery. Sveavägen 44. ℂ 08/23-21-15. T-bana: Hötorget.

HOME FURNISHINGS
Nordiska Galleriet This store features the finest in European furniture design, including the best from Scandinavia. Two floors hold the latest contemporary furniture. The store can arrange shipment. Nybrogatan 11. ℂ 08/442-83-60. T-bana: Östermalmstorg.

Svenskt Tenn Along "embassy row," Swedish Pewter (its English name) has been Sweden's most prominent store for home furnishings since 1924. Pewter is no longer king, and the shop now sells Scandinavia's best selection of furniture, printed textiles, lamps, glassware, china, and gifts. The inventory is stylish, and although there aren't a lot of bargains, it's an excellent place to see the newest trends in Scandinavian design. It carries an exclusive collection of Josef Frank's hand-printed designs on linen and cotton. It will pack, insure, and ship your purchases anywhere in the world. Strandvägen 5. ℂ 08/670-16-00. T-bana: Östermalmstorg.

LINENS
Solgården For the dwindling few who really care about luxury linens and elegant housewares, such as lace and embroidery, this shop is the finest of its kind in Scandinavia. It was conceived by owner Marianne von Kantzow Ridderstad as a tribute to Gustav III, the king who is said to have launched the neoclassical style in Sweden. Ridderstad designed her shop like a country house, with rough-hewn wood and whimsical furnishings. Each of her linens is virtually a work of art. The tablecloths are heirloom pieces. You'll cherish the work for its originality and loveliness. Karlavägen 58. ℂ 08/663-93-60. T-bana: Rådmansgatan.

MARKETS
Östermalms Saluhall One of the most colorful indoor markets in Scandinavia features cheese, meat, vegetable, and fish merchants who supply food for much of the area. You may want to have a snack or a meal at one of the restaurants. Nybrogatan 31. No central phone. T-bana: Östermalmstorg.

SHOPPING MALLS
Gallerian Arcade A short walk from Sweden House at Kunådgården, this modern two-story shopping complex is, to many, the best shopping destination in Sweden. Merchandise in most of the individually managed stores is designed to appeal to local shoppers, not the tourist market—although in summer that changes a bit as more souvenir and gift items appear. Hamngatan 37. No phone. T-bana: Kungsträdgården.

Sturegallerian In the center of Stockholm, this mall has a dazzling array of foreign and domestic merchandise, in some 50 specialty shops. Summer brings out more displays of Swedish souvenirs and gift items. There are also restaurants and cafes. Sturegallerian opened in 1989 and a year later was named "Shopping Center of the Year in Europe" by the International Council of Shopping Centers. Stureplan. ℂ 08/611-46-06. T-bana: Östermalmstorg.

TEXTILES
Handarbetets Vänner   This is one of the oldest and most prestigious textile houses in Stockholm. It also sells art-weaving and embroidery items. Djurgårdsslatten 82–84. ✆ 08/667-10-26. Bus: 47.

JOBS   Hand-painted fabrics from the JOBS family workshops in Dalarna are prized for their quality and the beauty of their design. Patterns are inspired by the all-too-short Swedish summer and by rural traditions. If you plan to be in Dalarna, you might enjoy visiting the **JOBS factory,** Västanvik 201, Leksand (✆ **0247/122-22**). Other items include tablecloths, handbags, and children's clothing. Stora Nygatan 19. ✆ **08/20-98-16**. T-bana: Gamla Stan.

TOYS
Bulleribock (Toys)   Since it opened in the 1960s, this store has carried only traditional, non-computerized toys made of wood, metal, or paper. You won't find any plastic toys here. There are no war games that many parents find objectionable. Many of these charming playthings are suitable for children up to age 10. As many as possible are made in Sweden, with wood from Swedish forests. Sveavägen 104. ✆ 08/673-61-21. T-bana: Rådmansgatan.

15 Stockholm After Dark

Djurgården is the favorite spot for indoor and outdoor events on a summer evening. Although the more sophisticated might find it corny, Djurgården is the best bet in the early evening. Afterward, you can make the rounds of jazz venues and dance clubs, some of which stay open until 3 or 4 in the morning.

Pick up a copy of *Stockholm This Week,* distributed at the Tourist Center at Sweden House (see chapter 13) to see what's going on.

THE PERFORMING ARTS
The major opera, theater, and concert seasons begin in the fall, except for special summer festival performances. Most major opera and theatrical performances are funded by the state, which keeps ticket prices reasonable.

CONCERT HALLS
Berwaldhallen (Berwald Concert Hall)   This hexagonal concert hall is Swedish Radio's big music studio. The Radio Symphonic Orchestra performs here, and other musical programs include lieder and chamber music recitals. The hall has excellent acoustics. The box office is open Monday through Friday from 11am to 6pm and 2 hours before every concert. Strandvägen 69. ✆ 08/784-18-00. Tickets 50SEK–400SEK ($5.30–$42). T-bana: Karaplan.

Filharmonikerna i Konserthuset (Concert Hall)   Home of the Stockholm Philharmonic Orchestra, this is the principal place to hear classical music in Sweden. The Nobel Prizes are awarded here. Constructed in 1920, the building houses two concert halls. One seats 1,600 and is better suited to major orchestras; the other, seating 450, is suitable for chamber music groups. Besides local orchestras, the hall features visiting ensembles, such as the Chicago Symphony Orchestra. Some series sell out in advance to subscription-ticket holders; for others, visitors can readily get tickets. Sales begin 2 weeks before a concert and continue until the performance begins. Concerts usually start at 7:30pm, with occasional lunchtime (noon) or "happy hour" (5:30pm) concerts. Most performances are broadcast on Stockholm's main classical music station, 107.5 FM. The box office is open Monday through Friday from 10am to 6pm, Saturday from 10am to 1pm. The concert hall is closed in July and early August. Hötorget 8. ℂ 08/10-21-10. Tickets 120SEK–400SEK ($13–$42). T-bana: Hötorget.

OPERA & BALLET

Drottningholm Court Theater   Founded by Gustavus III in 1766, this unique theater is on an island in Lake Mälaren, 11km (7 miles) from Stockholm. It stages operas and ballets with full 18th-century regalia, period costumes, and wigs. Its machinery and 30 or more complete theater sets are intact and in use. The theater, a short walk from the royal residence, seats only 450, which makes it difficult to get tickets. Eighteenth-century music performed on antique instruments is a perennial favorite. The season is from May to September. Most performances begin at 7:30pm and last 2½ to 4 hours. You can order tickets in advance by phone with an American Express card. Drottningholm. ℂ 08/660-82-25. Tickets 150SEK–550SEK ($16–$58). T-bana: Brommaplan, then bus no. 301 or 323. Boat from the City Hall in Stockholm.

Operahauset (Royal Opera House)   Founded in 1773 by Gustavus III (who was later assassinated here at a masked ball), the Opera House is the home of the Royal Swedish Opera and the Royal Swedish Ballet. The building dates from 1898. Performances are usually Monday through Saturday at 7:30pm (closed mid-June to Aug). The box office is open Monday through Friday from noon to 6pm (until 7:30pm on performance nights), Saturday from noon to 3pm. Gustav Adolfs Torg. ℂ 08/24-82-40. Tickets 100SEK–400SEK ($11–$42); 10%–30% senior and student discounts. T-bana: Kungsträdgården.

THEATER

The theater season begins in mid-August and lasts until mid-June.

Kungliga Dramatiska Teatern (Royal Dramatic Theater)   Greta Garbo got her start in acting here, and Ingmar Bergman stages two productions a year at this theater. It presents the latest experimental plays and the classics—in Swedish only. The theater is open all year (with a slight slowdown in July), and performances are scheduled Tuesday through Saturday at 7pm and Sunday at 4pm. The box office is open Monday through Saturday from 10am to 6pm. Nybroplan. ℂ 08/667-06-80. Tickets 100SEK–300SEK ($11–$32); student discount available. T-bana: Östermalmstorg.

Oscars Teatern   Oscars is the flagship of Stockholm's musical entertainment world. It's been the home of classic operetta and musical theater since the turn of the 20th century. Known for its extravagant staging of traditional operettas, it was also one of the first theaters in Europe to produce such hits as *Cats* in Swedish. The box office is open Monday through Saturday from 11am to 6pm. Kungsgatan 63. ℂ 08/20-50-00. Tickets 240SEK–375SEK ($25–$40). T-bana: Hötorget.

LOCAL CULTURE & ENTERTAINMENT

Skansen   Skansen arranges traditional seasonal festivities, special events, autumn market days, and a Christmas Fair. In summer there are concerts, sing-alongs, and guest performances. Folk dancing performances are staged from June to August, Monday through Saturday at 7pm and Sunday at 2:30 and 4pm. From June to August, outdoor dancing is presented with live music Monday through Friday from 8:30 to 11:30pm. Djurgården 49–51. ℂ 08/442-80-00. Admission 30SEK–60SEK ($3.20–$6.35) adults, 20SEK–30SEK ($2.10–$3.20) children 6–15, free for children 5 and under. Bus: 44 or 47. Ferry from Nybroplan.

AN AMUSEMENT PARK

Gröna Lunds Tivoli   Unlike its Copenhagen namesake, this is an amusement park, not a fantasyland. For those who like Coney Island–type amusements, it can be a nighttime adventure. One of the big thrills is to go up to the revolving tower for an after-dark view. The park is open daily from the end of April to August, usually from noon to 11pm or midnight. Call for exact hours. Djurgården. ⓒ 08/587-501-00. Admission 60SEK ($6.35), free for children under 17. Bus: 44 or 47. Ferry from Nybroplan.

THE CLUB & MUSIC SCENE
A HISTORIC NIGHTCLUB

Café Opera   This is one of the most crowded nightclubs in Stockholm. A stairway near the entrance leads to one of the Opera House's most beautiful corners, the club-like Operabaren (Opera Bar). It's likely to be as crowded as the cafe. The bar is a monumental but historically charming place to have a drink; beer costs 57SEK ($6.05). After 10pm, there is less emphasis on food and more on disco activities. Open daily from 5pm to 3am. At night, long lines form outside. Don't confuse this establishment with the opera's main (and far more expensive) dining room, the Operakällaren. Operahauset, Kungsträdgården. ⓒ 08/676-58-07. Cover 100SEK ($11) after 11pm. T-bana: Kungsträdgården.

DANCE CLUBS & DISCOS

The Daily News   One of the capital's most enduring entertainment emporiums, this place has flourished through dozens of changes over the years. Currently there's a dance club and a pub in the cellar, a somewhat smaller dance floor and a bar on the street level, and a street-level restaurant that serves platters of Swedish and international food. On weekends, there's sometimes a line. Platters of food begin at around 75SEK ($7.95), full dinners at around 220SEK ($23). Beer costs about 50SEK ($5.30). The place is open every night from 11pm to between 4 and 5am. In Sweden House (Sverigehuset), at Kungsträdgården. ⓒ 08/21-56-55. Cover 60SEK–90SEK ($6.35–$9.55). T-bana: Kungsträdgården.

Göta Källare   Stockholm's largest and most successful supper-club–style dance hall has a reputation for successful matchmaking. Large, echoing, and paneled with lots of wood in *faux-Español* style, it has a terrace that surrounds an enormous tree. The restaurant serves platters of food priced at 90SEK to 200SEK ($9.55–$21). Menu items include tournedos, fish, chicken, and veal. Expect a middle-aged crowd. The live orchestra (which performs *Strangers in the Night* a bit too frequently) plays every night. The hall opens nightly at 8:30pm. In the Medborgplatsen subway station, Södermalm. ⓒ 08/642-08-28. Cover 80SEK ($8.50) after 11pm only. T-bana: Medborgplatsen.

ROCK & JAZZ CLUBS

Hard Rock Cafe   The Swedish branch of this chain is fun and gregarious. Sometimes an American, British, or Scandinavian rock band presents a live concert; otherwise, rock blasts from the sound system. Club sandwiches, hamburgers, T-bone steaks, and barbecued spareribs are available. Burgers cost 119SEK ($13), steaks are 209SEK to 249SEK ($22–$26), and a beer goes for 45SEK ($4.75). It's open Sunday through Thursday from 11am to midnight, Friday and Saturday from 11am to 1am. Sveavägen 75. ⓒ 08/545-494-00. T-bana: Rådmansgaten.

Pub Engelen/Nightclub Kolingen   The Engelen Pub, the Restaurant Engelen, and the Nightclub Kolingen (in the 15th-century cellar) share a single address. The restaurant, which serves some of the best steaks in town, is open

The Capital of Gay Scandinavia

Today, thanks partly to the huge influence of London's gay subcultures, no other city in Scandinavia offers gay-friendly nightlife options as broad and diverse as Stockholm's. Some of the new gay bars and clubs maintain fixed hours and addresses. Others, configured as roving parties, constantly change addresses. The acknowledged king of the gay underground is Swedish-born entrepreneur Ulrik Bermsio, who has been compared to the legendary Steve Rubell of Studio 54 fame. Listings for his entertainment venues—and those promoted by his less visible competitors—appear regularly in *QX,* a gay magazine published in Swedish and English. It's available at news kiosks throughout Stockholm. You can also check out the magazine's website (www.qx.se). And don't overlook the comprehensive website (www.rfsl.se) maintained by RSFL, a Swedish organization devoted to equal rights for gays.

Permanent bars & clubs: The Disco, Torsgatan 1 (© **08/22-51-70;** T-bana: Centralen), is open every Wednesday, Friday, and Saturday at 8pm. The music shuts down at 3am. If you opt to dine here before dancing, it's free; otherwise you'll pay 60SEK ($6.35) to enter after 11pm. The high-energy venue is styled after clubs in New York and Los Angeles. Fridays are the most fun.

Looking for a non-confrontational bar peopled with regular guys who happen to be gay? Consider a round or two at **Sidetrack,** Wollmar Yxkullsgatan 7 (© **08/641-16-88;** T-bana: Mariatorget). Small, and committed to shunning trendiness, it's named after the founder's favorite gay bar in Chicago. It's open every night from 6pm to 1am. Tuesday seems to be something of a gay Stockholm institution. Other nights are fine, too—something like a Swedish version of a bar and lounge at the local bowling alley, where everyone happens to be into same-sex encounters.

To find a Viking, or Viking wannabe, in leather, head for **SLM** (Scandinavian Leather Men), Wollmar Yxkullsgatan 18 (© **08/643-31-00;** T-bana: Mariatorget). Technically, this is a private club. If you look hot, wear just a hint (or even a lot) of cowhide or rawhide, or happen to have spent the past 6 months felling timber in Montana, you stand a good chance of

Sunday through Thursday from 5 to 11:30pm, Friday and Saturday from 5pm to 1:30am. Prices for platters of bar food run 80SEK to 200SEK ($8.50–$21). Live performances, usually soul, funk, and rock by Swedish groups, take over the pub daily from 8:30pm to midnight. The pub is open Tuesday through Thursday from 4pm to 1am, Friday and Saturday from 4pm to 3am, Sunday from 5pm to 3am. Beer begins at 34SEK ($3.60), and items on the bar menu cost 30SEK to 70SEK ($3.20–$7.40). The Nightclub Kolingen is a dance club nightly from 10pm to about 3am. It charges the same food and drink prices as the pub, and you must be at least 23 to enter. Kornhamnstorg 59B. © **08/20-10-92.** Cover 40SEK–60SEK ($4.25–$6.35) after 8pm. T-bana: Gamla Stan.

Stampen   This pub attracts jazz lovers in their 30s and 40s. Guests crowd in to enjoy live Dixieland, New Orleans, mainstream, and swing music from the 1920s, 1930s, and 1940s. On Tuesday, it's rock 'n' roll from the 1950s and getting in. Wednesday and Friday from 10pm to 2am, the place functions as Stockholm's premier leather bar. You'll find lots of masculine-looking men on the street level and a handful of toys and restrictive accouterments in the cellar-level dungeon. On Saturday from 10pm to 2am, a DJ spins highly danceable music. It's closed on other nights.

If you need a caffeine fix and a slice of chocolate cake before all that leather and latex, you might want to drop into Stockholm's most appealing, best-managed gay cafe, **Chokladkoppen,** Stortorget (© **08/ 20-31-70;** T-bana: Gamla Stan). Open daily from 11am to 11pm, it specializes in sandwiches, "gorgeous" pastries, and all manner of chocolate confections that appeal even to straight people. The staff is charming, and the clientele more gay than not.

Our remaining selections involve venues that cater to a gay crowd only on specific nights of the week. They're subject to change according to the outrageous whims of fashion and scheduling concerns. Examples include **Häcktet ("The Jail"),** Hornsgatan 82 (no phone; T-bana: Mariatorget). Most of the week, its clientele is supposedly straight. Every Wednesday and Friday from 7pm till around 1am, the place promotes itself to a gay clientele, with a high percentage of lesbians. Disco music energizes a too-small dance floor; otherwise, people just drink. There's no cover charge. In the summer, a barbecue pit in the courtyard does an active business.

Then there's **Patricia,** Stadsgårdskajen 152 (© **08/743-05-70;** T-bana: Slussen). It's straight most of the week, and avowedly gay every Sunday between 7pm and 5am. Sprawling and labyrinthine, with three bars and a good sound system, it attracts gay folk from all walks of life and income levels. It's most crowded on Sundays during the summer, much less so in the winter. There's a restaurant on the premises.

Lesbians appreciate the freedom afforded by a roving party held at a series of rented catering halls throughout Stockholm. **The Bitch Girl Club** takes place on the second Saturday of every month. The usual admission price is 75SEK ($7.95). For information, consult *QX* magazine or either of the websites mentioned above.

1960s. A menagerie of stuffed animals and lots of old, whimsical antiques are suspended from the high ceiling. It's open Monday through Wednesday from 8pm to 1am, Thursday through Saturday from 8pm to 2am. In summer, an outdoor veranda is open when the weather permits. The club has two stages, and there's dancing downstairs almost every night. Stora Nygatan 5. © **08/20-57-93.** Cover 100SEK ($11). T-bana: Gamla Stan.

THE BAR SCENE

Cadier Bar   From the bar of this deluxe hotel—one of the most famous in Europe—you'll have a view of the harbor and the Royal Palace. It's one of the most sophisticated places in Stockholm. Light meals—open-faced sandwiches and smoked salmon—are served all day in the extension overlooking the waterfront. Drinks run 96SEK to 120SEK ($10–$13); imported beer is 45SEK ($4.75). The bar is named for the hotel's builder. It's open Monday through

Saturday from noon to 2am, Sunday from noon to 12:30am; a piano player performs Wednesday through Saturday from 9:30pm to 1:30am. In the Grand Hotel, Södra Blasieholmshamnen 8. © 08/679-35-00. T-bana: Kungsträdgården.

Café Victoria   The most central cafe in Stockholm fills up after 9pm in winter and after 7pm in summer. It attracts a varied crowd. Many patrons come just to drink, but you can have lunch or dinner in an interior section beyond the lively bar area. Light snacks cost 80SEK to 130SEK ($8.50–$14); main dishes are 120SEK to 230SEK ($13–$24). A bottle of beer will set you back 46SEK ($4.90). It's open Monday through Saturday from noon to 3am, Sunday from 1 to 7pm. Kungsträdgården. © 08/10-10-85. T-bana: Kungsträdgården.

Gondolen   You might find Gondolen's architecture as impressive as the view. Part of the structure is suspended beneath a pedestrian footbridge that soars above the narrow channel separating the island of Gamla Stan from the island of Södermalm. The engineering triumph was executed in 1935. The elevator hauls customers (without charge) up the equivalent of 11 stories to the '40s-style restaurant. The view encompasses Lake Malar, the open sea, and huge areas of downtown Stockholm. You'll pay 86SEK ($9.10) for a whiskey with soda. It is open Monday through Friday from 11:30am to 1am, Saturday from 1pm to 1am. Stadtsgården 6. © 08/641-70-90. T-bana: Slussen.

Icebar *(Finds* Located in the Nordic Sea Hotel, this is known as Stockholm's "coolest" bar. The world's first permanent ice bar opened in 2001 in the heart of Stockholm. Amazingly, the interior is kept at temperatures of 27°F (–5°C) all year. The decor and all the interior fittings, right down to the cocktail glasses themselves, are made of pure, clear ice shipped down from the Torne River in Sweden's Arctic north. If you own one of those fabulous Swedish fur coats, the Icebar would be the place to wear it. Dress as you would for a dog-sled ride in Alaska. In the bar you can order any drink from a Bahama Mama to an Alabama Slammer, although you may have to order liquor-laced coffee such as Jim Beam Kentucky Coffee to keep warm. 4-7 Vasaplan. © 08/21-71-77. T-bana: Centralen.

Sturehof   Since 1897, this pub and restaurant has been one of Stockholm's major drinking and dining venues. In the exact center of the city, it is now surrounded by urban sprawl and is attached to an arcade with other restaurants and shops. It remains a pleasant refuge from the city's congestion, and is popular as both an after-work bar and a restaurant. It's open daily from 11am to 1am. Beer costs 53SEK ($5.60). Stureplan 2. © 08/440-57-30. T-bana: Östermalmstorg.

T.G.I. Friday's   This popular chain has invaded Stockholm and is today one of the most popular places for drinks or casual dining. Drawing homesick Americans as well as a fun-loving crowd of young Stockholmers, T.G.I. Friday's lies near the Stureplan at the heart of the city. On weekends, the place is a favorite with local families, drawing more of a singles crowd during the week. A big place with large windows, the restaurant decorates its walls with maps of various U.S. states. All the familiar T.G.I. food items are here, including smoked chicken quesadillas, potato skins, and Buffalo chicken strips, along with pastas, sandwiches, steaks, and ribs. It's open Monday through Thursday from 11:30am to midnight. From Friday at 11:30am, they stay open all weekend until Sunday midnight. Birger Jarlsgatan 16. © 08/611-31-31. T-bana: Östermalmstorg.

Tiger Bar/Avec Bar   This is one of the most talked-about bars in Stockholm, and it attracts a bevy of supermodels and TV actors. The street-level Tiger Bar has black leather upholstery and an atmosphere of postmodern cool. The clean, modern decor of the basement-level Avec Bar draws an equally chic crowd. On both levels, everybody's favorite drink seems to be the Russian-inspired *caprinoshka,* concocted from vodka and limes. You might hear anything from recorded dance hits (every Fri and Sat beginning at midnight) to live salsa and merengue (every Wed 9pm–5am). The place is open Thursday from 7pm to 3am, Friday and Saturday from 7pm to 4am. Incidentally, no one will object if you light up a cigar. 18 Kungsgatan. © **08/24-47-00.** Cover 60SEK ($6.35) Wed, 70SEK ($7.40) Thurs, 125SEK ($13) Fri–Sat. T-bana: Östermalmstorg.

16 Side Trips from Stockholm

Some of Sweden's best-known attractions are clustered around Lake Mälaren. Centuries-old villages and castles revive the pomp and glory of the 16th-century Vasa dynasty.

You can spend a very busy day exploring Sigtuna, Skokloster Castle, Uppsala, and Gamla (Old) Uppsala, and stay overnight in Sigtuna or Uppsala. Other easy day trips are to Gripsholm Castle in Mariefred, or Tullgarn Palace.

A popular boat excursion leaves from Klara Mälarstrand Pier, near Stockholm's Town Hall and the T-Bana Centralen station, at 9:45am. It goes along the beautiful waterway Mälaren and the Fyris River to Sigtuna, where it makes a 2-hour stop. The boat arrives in Uppsala at 5pm. Visit the cathedral and other interesting sights, dine, and take the 45-minute train trip back to Stockholm. Trains run every hour until 11pm. The one-way boat fare from the pier to Sigtuna is around 80SEK ($8.50), and the one-way overland fare (which combines train and bus transfer) costs 50SEK ($5.30).

SIGTUNA ⍟
45km (28 miles) NW of Stockholm

Founded at the beginning of the 11th century, Sigtuna, on the shores of Lake Mälaren, is Sweden's oldest town. **High Street (Stora Gatan),** with its low-timbered buildings, is thought to be the oldest street in Sweden that follows its original route. Traces of Sigtuna's Viking and early Christian heritage can be seen throughout the town.

ESSENTIALS
GETTING THERE   From Stockholm's train station, take a 45-minute train ride to Märsta. Trains depart at 30-minute intervals throughout the day and evening. In Märsta, transfer to a bus (it will be marked either SIGTUNA NO. 575 or SIGTUNA NO. 570) for an additional 20-minute ride on to Sigtuna. In the summer, boats run to Sigtuna from Klara Mälarstrand Pier in Stockholm and from Uppsala.

VISITOR INFORMATION   For information contact the Sigtuna Tourist Info office at © **08/592-500-20.**

SEEING THE SIGHTS
Sigtuna has many church ruins, mostly from the 12th century. Chief among them is **St. Per's,** Sweden's first cathedral. The 13th-century **Monastery of St. Maria** is open to the public daily. The well-preserved **Town Hall** dates from the 18th century.

Wander the narrow streets and, if you have time, visit the **Sigtuna Museum,** Storogatan (© **08/597-838-70**), an archaeological museum that features early-medieval artifacts found in the surrounding area. You'll see gold rings, runic inscriptions, and coins, as well as exclusive objects from Russia and Byzantium. Admission is 30SEK ($3.20); admission is free for children 16 and under. Hours are June through August daily from noon to 4pm; September through May, Tuesday through Sunday from noon to 4pm.

One reason for the town's resurgence is the **Sigtuna Foundation,** a Lutheran retreat and cultural center founded near the turn of the 20th century and often frequented by writers. Although there are no exhibits here, the foundation is intellectually alluring, and its two chapels and rose garden are a source of pride and tranquillity. The superb library is composed of mostly Swedish- and, to a lesser extent, German-language texts, plus a clipping file that chronicles the course of Sweden and the world's theological history. It's open to the public daily free from 1 to 3pm.

WHERE TO STAY & DINE

Sigtuna Foundation *Finds* A stay at this massive building might provide one of your most memorable stopovers in Sweden. Intended as a center where sociological and philosophical viewpoints can be exchanged, the 1917 structure is more a way of life than a hotel. Over the years, guest lecturers have included the Dalai Lama, various Indian gurus, and many of postwar Europe's leading theologians. The establishment functions as both a conference center and a guesthouse. There's no proselytizing, although there might be opportunities to share experiences. There are secluded courtyards, lush rose and herb gardens, and fountains. Recently all the guest rooms were refurbished in bland modern style, and modern bathrooms with shower-tub combinations were added. To guarantee a room, be sure to make arrangements in advance. The foundation is less than 1.5km (1 mile) from the town center.

Manfred Björkquists Allé 2–4, S-193 31 Sigtuna. © **08/592-589-00.** Fax 08/592-589-99. www.sigtuna stistilsen.se. 62 units. 600SEK–680SEK ($64–$72) double. Rates include breakfast. MC, V. Free parking. Bus: 570 or 575. **Amenities:** Restaurant; lounge. *In room:* No phone.

EN ROUTE FROM SIGTUNA TO UPPSALA
Skokloster Castle

From Stockholm, take the train to Bålsta, then bus no. 894.

The splendid 17th-century castle **Skokloster,** S-746 96 Skokloster (© **018/ 38-60-77**), is one of the most interesting baroque museums in Europe. It's next to Lake Mälaren, 64km (40 miles) from Stockholm and 50km (30 miles) from Uppsala. With original interiors, the castle is noted for its extensive collections of paintings, furniture, applied art, tapestries, arms, and books.

Admission is 65SEK ($6.90) for adults, 50SEK ($5.30) for seniors, 20SEK ($2.10) for students and children. Guided tours in English are offered from May to August, daily on the hour from 11am to 4pm; in September, Monday through Friday at 1pm and Saturday and Sunday at 1, 2, and 3pm. It's closed from October to April.

Skokloster Motor Museum (© **018/38-61-06**), on the palace grounds, houses the largest collection of vintage automobiles and motorcycles in the country. One of the most notable cars is a 1905 8-horsepower De Dion Bouton. The museum is open year-round. Admission is 40SEK ($4.25) for adults, 10SEK ($1.05) for children 7 to 14, and free for children under 7. It's open from May to September, daily from noon to 4pm; from October to April, Saturday and Sunday from 11am to 5pm.

UPPSALA ✭✭✭
68km (42 miles) NW of Stockholm

Sweden's major university city, Uppsala is the most popular destination of day-trippers from Stockholm—and for good reason. It has a great university and a celebrated 15th-century cathedral. Even in the Viking period, Uppsala was a religious center, and the scene of animal and human sacrifices in honor of the Norse gods. It's a former center of royalty as well. Queen Christina occasionally held court here. The church is still the seat of the archbishop, and the first Swedish university was founded here in 1477.

The best time to visit Uppsala is on April 30, Walpurgis Eve, when the academic community celebrates the rebirth of spring with a torchlight parade. The rollicking festivities last until dawn throughout the 13 student "nations" (residential halls).

ESSENTIALS

GETTING THERE   The **train** from Stockholm's Central Station takes about 45 minutes. Trains leave about every hour during peak daylight hours. Some visitors spend the day in Uppsala and return to Stockholm on the commuter train in the late afternoon. Eurailpass holders ride free. **Boats** between Uppsala and Skokloster depart Uppsala Tuesday through Sunday at 11:45am, returning to Uppsala at 5:30pm. Round-trip passage costs 120SEK ($13). For details, check with the tourist office in any of the towns.

VISITOR INFORMATION   The **Tourist Information Office** is at Fyris Torg 8 (② **018/27-48-00**). It's open Monday through Friday from 10am to 6pm, Saturday from 10am to 3pm.

GETTING AROUND   Buses come in from the surrounding suburbs to the center of Uppsala and arrive at the Central Station, where the trains also arrive. Once you reach the center of Uppsala, all the major attractions are within easy walking distance. However, if you're going to explore Gamla Uppsala (see the box below) you need to take bus no. 2 or 24, departing from the Central Station.

SEEING THE SIGHTS

Carolina Rediviva (University Library)   At the end of Drottninggatan is the Carolina Rediviva, with more than five million volumes and 40,000 manuscripts, including many rare works from the Middle Ages. The most interesting manuscript is the *Codex Argenteus* (Silver Bible). Displayed in the exhibit room, it was translated into Gothic in the middle of the 3rd century and copied in about A.D. 525. It's the only book extant in old Gothic script. Also worth seeing is *Carta Marina*, the earliest map (1539) of Sweden and its neighboring countries.

Drottninggatan. ② **018/471-39-00.** Admission 20SEK ($2.10) adults, free for children under 12. Exhibit room, June 18–Aug 17 Mon–Fri 9am–5pm, Sat 10am–4pm, Sun 11am–4pm; June 2–17 and Aug 18–Sept 15 Sun 1–3:30pm. Closed Sept 16–June 1. Bus: 6, 7, or 22.

Linnaeus Garden & Museum ⚐   Swedish botanist Carl von Linné, known as Carolus Linnaeus, developed a classification system for the world's plants and flowers. His garden and former home are on the spot where Uppsala University's botanical garden was restored by Linnaeus in the style of a miniature baroque garden. Linnaeus, who arranged the plants according to his "sexual classification system," left detailed sketches and descriptions of the garden, which have been faithfully followed.

Linnaeus was a professor of theoretical medicine, including botany, pharmacology, and zoology, at Uppsala University. You can visit his house, which has been restored to its original design, and an art gallery that exhibits the works of contemporary local artists.

Svartbäcksgatan 27. ② **018/13-65-40** for the museum, or 018/10-94-90 for the garden. Museum 25SEK ($2.65) adults, free for children. For gardens, donation suggested, free for children. Museum, June–Aug Tues–Sun noon–4pm; closed Sept–May. Gardens, May–Aug daily 9am–9pm; Sept daily 9am–7pm; closed Oct–Apr. Walk straight from the train station to Kungsgatan, turn right, and walk about 10 min.

Uppsala Domkyrka ⚐⚐   The largest cathedral in Scandinavia, this twin-spired Gothic structure stands nearly 120m (400 ft.) tall. Founded in the 13th century, it was severely damaged in 1702 in a disastrous fire, then was restored near the turn of the 20th century. Among the regal figures buried in the crypt is Gustavus Vasa. The remains of St. Erik, patron saint of Sweden, are entombed in a silver shrine. The botanist Linnaeus and the philosopher-theologian Swedenborg are also buried here. A small museum displays ecclesiastical relics.

Gamla Uppsala

About 15 centuries ago, "Old Uppsala" was the capital of the Svea kingdom. In its midst was a grove set aside for human and animal sacrifices. Viking burial mounds dating from the 6th century are believed to contain the pyres of three kings.

Nearby, on the site of the old pagan temple, is a 12th-century **parish church,** once badly damaged by fire and never properly restored. Indeed, some people describe it as a stave church that turned to stone. Before Uppsala Cathedral was built, Swedish kings were crowned here.

Across from the church is the **Stiftelsen Upplandsmuseet,** Sankt Eriksgränd 6 (© **018/16-91-00**). The open-air museum with reassembled buildings depicts peasant life in Uppland. It's open from mid-May to August, Tuesday through Sunday from noon to 5pm. Admission is 30SEK ($3.20) adults, 15SEK ($1.60) seniors, free for children under 18.

Gamla Uppsala, about 5km (3 miles) north of the commercial heart of Uppsala, is easily accessible by bus no. 2 or 24, which leaves frequently from the Central Station.

Domkyrkoplan 2. © **018/18-72-01.** Free admission to cathedral; museum, 30SEK ($3.20) adults, 15SEK ($1.60) seniors and students, 10SEK ($1.05) children 7–15, free for children under 7. Cathedral, daily 8am–6pm. Museum, Apr–Aug daily 10am–5pm; Sept–Mar Tues–Sat 11am–3pm, Sun 12:30–3pm. Bus: 1.

Museum Gustavianum *(Finds* Gustavianum is Uppsala University's oldest preserved building. Here you can see a number of attractions, including an Anatomical Theatre, the Augsburg Art Cabinet, and an exhibition about the history of the university itself. The museum also includes archaeological exhibitions, from Swedish prehistory to the Middle Ages. Some of the rarer pieces are from the Mediterranean and the Nile Valley, including the sarcophagus of a priest, Khonsumes, from the 21st dynasty. In the historical exhibition on the ground floor you can see everything from student lecture notes from the first term in 1477—the year the university was founded—to the development of the institution over the years as a seat of learning.

Akademigatan 3. © **018/471-75-71.** Admission 40SEK ($4.25) adults, 30SEK ($3.20) students and seniors, free for children under 12. Mid–May to mid-Sept Tues–Sun 11am–5pm (until 9pm Thurs); off season Wed–Sun 11am–4pm (until 9pm Thurs). Bus: 1, 2, 51, or 53.

WHERE TO STAY
Diakonistiftelsen Samariterhemmet *(Value* One of the best bargains in town, this large guesthouse, run by a Christian charity, has spotlessly maintained rooms with comfortable beds. Some units have neatly kept bathrooms with shower units. You can use a kitchenette with a refrigerator, and there's a TV lounge. Most of the units evoke an Ivy League dormitory. Smoking is not permitted.

Samaritegränd 2, S-753 19 Uppsala. © **018/10-34-00.** Fax 018/10-83-75. 25 units, 12 with bathroom. 670SEK ($71) double without bathroom; 770SEK ($82) double with bathroom. Rates include breakfast. MC, V. **Amenities:** Lounge. *In room:* No phone.

First Hotel Linné *(★* At the edge of Linnaeus Garden, this is one of the best-managed hotels in town. You'll probably be able to see Linnaeus's lovely garden from your window. The rooms feature modern furniture and plumbing, and each unit has a neatly kept bathroom with a shower-tub combination. One drawback is that the less expensive doubles are a bit cramped. One floor, with 36 rooms, is reserved for nonsmokers.

Skolgatan 45, S-753 32 Uppsala. ✆ 018/10-20-00. Fax 018/13-75-97. www.firsthotels.se. 119 units. Sun–Thurs 1,462SEK–1,549SEK ($155–$164) double, from 1,600SEK ($170) suite; Fri–Sat 852SEK ($90) double, from 999SEK ($106) suite. Rates include breakfast. AE, DC, MC, V. Parking 30SEK ($3.20). **Amenities:** 2 restaurants; bar; fitness center; sauna; room service; laundry/dry cleaning. *In room:* TV, minibar, hair dryer, safe.

Radisson SAS Hotel Gillet ⚜ This attractively designed first-class hotel, built in 1972, offers medium-sized rooms with good beds, modern furnishings, and beautifully kept bathrooms with shower-tub combinations. With its two restaurants, the hotel is also one of Uppsala's major dining venues. The East West Bistro serves dinner Monday through Saturday; the more upscale Gillet Restaurant offers lunch and dinner Monday through Saturday.

Dragarbrunnsgatan 23, S-753 20 Uppsala. ✆ 018/15-53-60. Fax 018/68-18-18. www.radissonsas.com. 160 units. 990SEK–1,740SEK ($105–$184) double; 1,500SEK–3,500SEK ($159–$371) suite. Rates include breakfast. AE, DC, MC, V. Parking 170SEK ($18). Bus: 801. **Amenities:** 2 restaurants; bar; pool; sauna; room service; laundry/dry cleaning. *In room:* A/C, TV, minibar, hair dryer.

Scandic Hotel Uplandia ⚜⚜ Located next to the bus terminal, this is the best hotel in town. It was constructed in two stages, in the 1960s and early 1980s, in two connected buildings of three and six floors each. During the final enlargement, all rooms in the older section were brought up to modern standards. The hotel offers comfortably furnished rooms with newly renovated bathrooms equipped with shower-tub combinations.

Dragarbrunnsgatan 32, S-751 40 Uppsala. ✆ 800/528-1234 in the U.S., or 018/495-26-00. Fax 018/495-26-11. www.scandic-hotels.com. 133 units. 960SEK–1,780SEK ($102–$189) double. Rates include breakfast. AE, DC, MC, V. **Amenities:** Restaurant; bar; sauna; room service; laundry/dry cleaning. *In room:* TV, hair dryer.

WHERE TO DINE

Domtrappkällaren ⚜⚜ SWEDISH No other restaurant in Uppsala can compete with this one for charm and atmosphere. It was built in the town center on the ruins of 12th-century cathedral buildings. The vaulted ceilings and copies of Jacobean paintings in the main dining room complement the low-ceilinged, sun-flooded intimacy of the upper floors. On request, you can dine in a narrow room where unruly students were imprisoned in the Middle Ages or in one that served as a classroom in the 17th century. The restaurant serves delectable salmon and reindeer and specializes in game. Salads are often exotic—one includes breast of pigeon with roasted nuts.

Sankt Eriksgränd 15. ✆ 018/13-09-55. Reservations recommended. Main courses 170SEK–250SEK ($18–$27). AE, DC, MC, V. Mon–Sat 11:30am–11pm. Closed Dec 24–26. Bus: 1.

Restaurant Flustret FRENCH In a riverside setting near the castle, this pavilion is an exact replica of its predecessor, a demolished Victorian building. Its spacious ground-floor dining room serves tasty meals, which might include lobster soup, salmon "boathouse style," veal steak Oscar, pheasant Véronique, or bananas flambé. A dance club on the second floor is open Saturday from 9pm to 4am. Admission is free before 9pm, 80SEK ($8.50) after 9pm.

Svandammen. ✆ 018/13-01-14. Reservations recommended. Main courses 60SEK–200SEK ($6.35–$21). AE, DC, MC, V. Mon–Fri 11am–2pm and 4–9pm; Sat–Sun 11am–10pm. Bus: 24.

Restaurant Odinsborg ✦ *(Value* SWEDISH In a century-old former private house, this restaurant serves strictly old-fashioned Swedish food. The culinary highlight in the Viking-theme dining room is the Sunday smörgåsbord. A traditional roster of foods you might expect at a Swedish family celebration is laboriously prepared and laid out. The rest of the week, menu items include traditional preparations of fried herring, marinated salmon, smoked eel, and whitefish with a dill-flavored butter sauce. You might also try roasted lamb, chicken filets, or steak. Street addresses aren't used in Gamla Uppsala, but the restaurant is easy to spot.

Near the burial grounds, Gamla Uppsala. ℂ 018/32-35-25. Main courses 150SEK–400SEK ($16–$42); Sun smörgåsbord 150SEK ($16). AE, DC, MC, V. Daily noon–6pm.

GRIPSHOLM CASTLE ✦✦
On an island in Lake Mälaren, **Gripsholm Castle** (ℂ **0159/101-94**) is one of the best-preserved castles in Sweden. The fortress, built by Gustavus Vasa in the late 1530s, is near Mariefred, an idyllic small town known for its vintage narrow-gauge railroad.

During the reign of the 18th-century actor-king Gustavus III, a theater was built at Gripsholm, but the castle's outstanding feature is its large collection of portrait paintings.

Gripsholm Castle is 68km (42 miles) southwest of Stockholm. By **car,** follow E20 south; you can drive right to the castle parking lot. The Eskilstuna **bus** runs to the center of Mariefred, as do the boats. **Boats** leave from mid-May to September at 10am from Klara Mälarstrand Pier. The castle is a 10-minute walk from the center of Mariefred.

Even though Gripsholm was last occupied by royalty (Charles XV) in 1864, it's still a royal castle. It's open from May to August, daily from 10am to 4pm; September, Tuesday through Sunday from 10am to 3pm; and from October to April, Saturday and Sunday from noon to 3pm. Admission is 60SEK ($6.35) for adults, 30SEK ($3.20) ages 7 to 15. Ages 6 and under free.

WHERE TO STAY
Gripsholms Värdshus & Hotel ✦✦ Built as an inn in 1609 (it's one of the oldest in Sweden), this building was restored and reopened in 1989. It's now the most stylish and charming hotel in the region. It's a few steps from the village church, in the center of Mariefred, a 10-minute walk from the castle. Each guest room is individually decorated and furnished with a mixture of antiques and contemporary pieces. Bathrooms come equipped with shower-tub combinations, heated floors, and towel racks.

The hotel has the best restaurant in the region (see "Where to Dine," below).

Kyrkogatan 1, S-647 23 Mariefred. ℂ 0159/347-50. Fax 0159/347-77. www.gripsholms-vardshus.se. 45 units. 1,760SEK–2,190SEK ($187–$232) double; 500SEK–2,500SEK ($53–$265) supplement for suite, depending on the unit and the season. Rates include breakfast. AE, DC, MC, V. **Amenities:** 2 restaurants; bar; fitness center; sauna; room service; laundry/dry cleaning. *In room:* A/C, TV, minibar, hair dryer, safe.

WHERE TO DINE
Gripsholms Värdshus Restaurant ✦ SWEDISH/INTERNATIONAL This elegantly appointed restaurant serves traditional Swedish food, local game dishes, and international cuisine. The main dining room has a veranda that opens onto Gripsholm Bay. The menu changes every season, but is likely to include baked saddle of venison with herbs and mushroom pastry, grilled halibut accompanied by red paprika cream and basil ratatouille, or lamb cutlets

smothered in Dijon mustard and shallots. For dessert, try the raspberry mousse parfait. Tastings in the wine cellar can be arranged.

Kyrkogatan 1. ℭ **0159/347-50.** Reservations recommended. Main courses 115SEK–245SEK ($12–$26). AE, DC, MC, V. Midsummer daily noon–10pm. Rest of year Mon–Fri noon–2pm, Sat noon–4pm; Mon–Sat 6–10pm.

TULLGARN PALACE ☼

Tullgarn Palace is 60km (37 miles) south of Stockholm. By **car,** take E4 south about 60km (37 miles) and turn right at the sign that directs you to Tullgarns Slott, near Vagnhärad. It's another .5km (¼ mile) to the palace. Getting here by public transportation is extremely inconvenient and not worth the trouble. You first have to take a train to Södertälje Södra (about 20 min.), and then wait for a bus to Trosa, which lies 7km (4½ miles) south of the castle. From Trosa, you have to take a taxi the rest of the way. You could spend all morning just trying to get to the castle, so we recommend skipping it unless you have private transportation or endless amounts of time.

The royal palace of Tullgarn, in Vagnhärad (ℭ **08/551-720-11**), occupies a panoramic setting on a bay of the Baltic Sea. It was the favorite of Gustavus V (1858–1950), the great-grandfather of Sweden's present king. Construction began in 1719, and the well-kept interiors date from the late 18th century.

Admission is 50SEK ($5.30) for adults, 25SEK ($2.65) for students and children. The palace is open to the public on weekends from early May to early September. Guided tours leave the main entrance every hour from 11am to 4pm.

WHERE TO DINE

Tullgarns Värdshus SWEDISH/FRENCH   This inn, in a wing of Tullgarn Palace, offers three-course lunches or dinners. You can sample such dishes as salted salmon with creamed potatoes (an old Swedish specialty), or perhaps paté of wild boar. You can also order breast of wild duck with chicken liver mousse, or poached filet of salmon with chive-flavored butter sauce.

Or you can order a picnic lunch and eat in the royal park. Picnics of cold chicken, roast beef, or sandwiches, with beer or coffee (in takeout containers), can be ordered at the inn daily from 11am to 5pm.

In Tullgarn Palace, Vagnhärad. ℭ **08/551-720-26.** Main courses 105SEK–255SEK ($11–$27). MC, V. May 15–Sept 8 Mon–Fri noon–2:30pm and 5–7pm, Sat–Sun noon–7pm. Closed Sept 9–May 14.

SANDHAMN, VAXHOLM & THE ARCHIPELAGO OF STOCKHOLM

Stockholm is in what the Swedes call a "garden of skerries," an **archipelago** ☼☼☼ of more than 24,000 islands, islets, and mere rocks jutting out of the water. The islands nearest the city have become part of the suburbs, thickly populated and connected to the mainland by car ferries or bridges. Many others are wild and largely deserted, attracting boaters for picnics and swimming. Summer homes dot some of the islands. July is the peak vacation month, when yachts crowd the waters.

You can see the islands by taking a boat trip from Stockholm harbor. If you'd like to stop at a resort island, consider **Sandhamn,** where you'll find shops and restaurants. It takes about an hour to explore the entire island on foot. The beaches at the eastern tip are the best in the archipelago. **Vaxholm,** a bathing resort known as "the gateway to the northern archipelago," also makes a pleasant stop. Artists and writers have traditionally been drawn to Vaxholm, and some hold exhibits during the summer, when the tourist influx quadruples the population. The west harbor and the main sea route north are filled with pleasure craft.

ESSENTIALS
GETTING THERE   Throughout the year (but more often in the summer), boats operated by several companies depart from in front of the Grand Hotel at Södra Blasieholmshamnen. Most of them are marked VAXHOLM, and usually continue to Sandhamn after a stop in Vaxholm. Be sure to ask before boarding.

The trip from Stockholm through the archipelago to Sandhamn takes 3½ hours each way and costs 110SEK ($12) one-way. The ferry trip to Vaxholm from Stockholm takes less than 40 minutes and costs 65SEK ($6.90) one-way. There are no car ferries. If you plan lots of travel around the archipelago, consider buying an **Inter-Skerries Card** for 385SEK ($41). The card allows 16 days of unlimited travel anywhere within the Stockholm archipelago for much less than the cost of individual tickets.

Vaxholm-bound boats depart every hour during the summer (about five times a day in winter) from the Strömkagen, the piers outside the Grand Hotel. For information, call the steamship company **Vaxholmes Belaget** (© **08/679-58-30**).

Buses to Vaxholm (nos. 670, 671, 672, and 673) often—but not always—go on to Sandhamn. They depart from the Central Station daily (unless inclement weather prevents it) every 30 minutes beginning at 6am. The last bus from Vaxholm leaves at 1am. A round-trip fare is 100SEK ($11).

ORGANIZED TOURS
Strömma Kanal Steamship (© **08/541-314-80**) offers a guided cruise in English to Sandhamn. Ships sail through canals and bays. Tours depart from June to August at 10am and last 8 hours. The "Canal Cruise to Sandhamn" begins at 185SEK ($20); it's free for children under 12. The company also offers the "Thousand Island Cruise" through the Stockholm archipelago. The 11-hour guided tour includes lunch, dinner, and stopovers on four islands. Tours are available in July and August.

WHERE TO STAY
Vaxholm Hotel   Built in 1902, this stone hotel, painted bright yellow, is at the pier where the ferries from Stockholm dock. It offers modern but rather bland guest rooms. Each unit has a well-kept bathroom with a shower unit. Its dance club is open in the summer, Friday and Saturday from 9pm to 2am. The cover charge is 90SEK ($9.55). An informal pub, Kabyssen, is at street level. One floor above is the Vaxholm Hotel Restaurant (see "Where to Dine," below).

Hamngatan 2, S-185 21 Vaxholm. © 08/541-301-50. Fax 08/541-313-76. www.vaxholmhotel.se. 42 units. 1,015SEK–1,500SEK ($108–$159) double. Rates include breakfast. AE, DC, MC, V. Free parking. Closed Dec 24–Jan 1. **Amenities:** 2 restaurants; bar; sauna; babysitting; laundry/dry cleaning. *In room:* TV, hair dryer.

WHERE TO DINE
In Vaxholm
Vaxholm Hotel Restaurant ★ (Finds) SEAFOOD   This is the best place to dine in Vaxholm. It overlooks the water from the second floor of the hotel. The chef says his specialties are "fish, fish, fish." The uncompromising house specialty—and the best buy—is a platter of pan-fried Swedish herring served with mashed potatoes. You can also order a number of other dishes, notably smoked reindeer with horseradish, tender tournedos stuffed with herbs and served with a mustard sauce, or poached filet of sole with white wine sauce. Summer desserts, including rhubarb pie, elderberry sorbet, and lingonberries (often with almond flan), are prepared from locally grown berries and fruits.

Hamngatan 2. © 08/541-301-50. Reservations required in summer. Main courses 108SEK–298SEK ($11–$32). AE, DC, MC, V. Summer daily noon–11pm; off season daily noon–10pm. Closed Dec 24–Jan 1.

In Sandhamn

Sandhamns Värdshus SWEDISH   The islanders' favorite restaurant was established in 1672. It offers a view of the moored boats at the harbor. You can always get a good and reasonably priced meal here by selecting a fish dish or the local choice—steak with red onions.

Harbourfront. ⓒ **08/571-530-51.** Reservations required Sat–Sun. Main courses 145SEK–260SEK ($15–$28); 3-course fixed-price menu 299SEK ($32). AE, DC, MC, V. Sun–Thurs noon–9pm; Fri–Sat noon–10:30pm.

Gothenburg

Called the gateway to northern Europe, Gothenburg (Göteborg in Swedish) is the country's chief port and second-largest city. Swedes often say that Gothenburg is a friendlier town than Stockholm. Canals, parks, and flower gardens enhance its appeal.

The city has many museums, and the largest amusement park in northern Europe. It's a convenient center for excursions to the fishing villages and holiday resorts to the north of the city.

A walk down "The Avenue" is a Gothenburg tradition. This is Kungsportsavenyn, called *Avenyn* (Avenue), with its many outdoor cafes where you can watch the passing parade of people. Start at Parkgatan, at the foot of The Avenue. Gothenburg's pedestrian street is heated by underground pipes in the winter so that the snow melts quickly.

Gustavus Adolphus II granted Gothenburg's charter in 1621. The port contains a shipyard—Cityvarvet—and a manufacturer of platforms for oil rigs (Götaverken/Arendal). The city is also the home of Volvo, the car manufacturer (whose plant is about a 15-min. drive from the city center), and of the Hasselblad space camera. Spanning the Göta River, Älvsborg Bridge (the longest suspension bridge in Sweden) is almost 900m (3,000 ft.) long and built high enough to allow ocean liners to pass underneath.

1 Orientation

ARRIVING

BY PLANE   Many residents of Sweden's west coast consider Copenhagen's airport more convenient than Stockholm's. **SAS** (© **800/221-2350** in the U.S.; www.flysas.com) operates 8 to 10 daily flights from Copenhagen to Gothenburg between 7:30am and 11:05pm. (Most of them are nonstop.) SAS also operates 10 to 20 daily flights between Stockholm and Gothenburg, beginning about 7am and continuing until early evening.

Planes arrive at **Landvetter Airport** (© **031/94-10-00**), 26km (16 miles) east of Gothenburg. An airport bus (Flygbuss) departs every 30 minutes for the half-hour ride to the city's central bus terminal, just behind Gothenburg's main railway station. Buses run daily between 5am and 11:30pm. A one-way trip costs 50SEK ($5.30).

BY TRAIN   The **Oslo–Copenhagen express train** runs via Gothenburg and Helsingborg, connecting two Scandinavian capitals. North-south trains run frequently between Gothenburg and Helsingborg and Malmö in the south. The most traveled rail route is between Gothenburg and Stockholm, with trains leaving hourly in both directions; the trip takes 4 hours, 40 minutes.

Trains arrive at the Central Station, on one side of Drottningtorget. The station has a currency-exchange bureau and an office of the Swedish National Railroad Authority (SJ), which sells rail and bus tickets for connections to nearby areas.

BY BUS   There are several buses from Gothenburg to Helsingborg and Malmö (and vice versa) daily. Trip time from Gothenburg to Helsingborg is 3½ hours; Gothenburg to Malmö, 4½ hours. Several daily buses connect Stockholm and Gothenburg. The trip takes 7 to 8 hours. If you plan to travel by public land transportation, we recommend taking the train—it's cheaper and faster. Gothenburg's bus station is behind the railway station, at Nils Ericson Gate. For information in Gothenburg, call **Swebus,** Sweden's largest bus company (✆ **031/10-38-00**).

BY FERRY   The **Stena Line** (✆ **031/704-00-00;** www.stenaline.se) has six crossings a day in summer from northern Jutland (a 3-hr. trip); call for information on departure times, which vary seasonally. The vessels have excellent dining rooms.

Stena offers twice-weekly ferry service between Harwich (England) and Gothenburg. The trip generally takes 24 hours. From June to mid-August, there's also service from Newcastle-upon-Tyne (England) to Gothenburg once a week, also taking 24 hours. This service is operated by **Scandinavian Seaways** (✆ **031/65-06-50** for information; www.dfdsseaways.se). There's no rail-pass discount on the England–Sweden crossings.

BY CAR   From either Malmö or Helsingborg, the two major west coast "gateways" to Sweden, take E6 north. Gothenburg is 279km (173 miles) north of Malmö and 227km (141 miles) north of Helsingborg. From Stockholm, take E4 west to Jönköping and continue on Route 40 the rest of the way via Bors to Gothenburg, a total distance of 470km (292 miles).

VISITOR INFORMATION

The **Gothenburg Tourist Office** is located at Kungsportsplatsen 2 (✆ **031/61-25-00;** www.goteborg.com). It's open from June to August, daily from 9am to 6pm; from September to May, Monday through Friday from 9am to 6pm, Saturday from 10am to 2pm.

CITY LAYOUT

Gothenburg's design, with its network of streets separated by canals, is reminiscent of Amsterdam's—not surprisingly, because it was laid out by Dutch architects in the 17th century. Its wealth of parks and open spaces has given it a reputation as Sweden's greenest city.

Some of the old canals have now been filled in, but you can explore the major remaining waterway and the busy harbor—the most important in Sweden—by taking one of the city's famous Paddan sightseeing boats. *Paddan* is the Swedish word for "toad," and the allusion is to the boats' squat shape, which enables them to navigate under the many low bridges. A Paddan service takes you from the point of embarkation, Drottningtorget (near the Central Station), to the Liseberg amusement park. The amusement park is the most popular visitor attraction in the area, with some three million visitors annually.

The best place to start sightseeing on foot is Kungsportsavenyn (The Avenyn, or The Avenue), a wide, tree-lined boulevard with many sidewalk cafes. The Avenyn leads to Götaplatsen, a square that's the city's artistic and historic center. Its centerpiece is a huge bronze fountain with a statue of the sea god Poseidon sculpted by Carl Milles.

Gothenburg's old and commercial section lies on either side of the central canal. At the central canal is Gustav Adolfs Torg, dominated by a statue of Gustav himself. Facing the canal is the **Börshuset (Stock Exchange building).** On the western side is the **Rådhuset (Town Hall),** originally constructed in 1672. Around the corner, as you move toward the river, is the **Kronhuset** (off Kronhusgatan). The 17th-century Dutch-designed building is the oldest in Gothenburg.

Gothenburg is dominated by its harbor, which is best viewed from one of the Paddan boats. The major attraction here is the **Maritime Center** (see "Seeing the Sights," later in this chapter). The shipyards, whose spidery forms look as though they were constructed from an Erector set, are dominated by the IBM building and other industries. An overhead walkway connects part of the harbor to the shopping mall of Nordstan.

2 Getting Around

Visitors usually find that the cheapest way to explore Gothenburg (except on foot) is to buy a **Göteborgskortet (Gothenburg Card).** Available at hotels, newspaper kiosks, and the city's tourist office, it entitles you to unlimited travel on local trams, buses, and ferries. The card also covers certain sightseeing tours; either free or discounted admission to the city's major museums and sightseeing attractions; discounts at some shops; free parking in some centrally located parking lots; and several other extras, which usually make the card worthwhile. A ticket valid for 24 hours costs 175SEK ($19) for adults, 95SEK ($10) for children; a 48-hour ticket is 295SEK ($31) for adults and 190SEK ($20) for children.

BY PUBLIC TRANSPORTATION (TRAM)   A single tram ticket costs 16SEK ($1.70); a 24-hour travel pass is 50SEK ($5.30). If you don't have an advance ticket, board the first car of the tram—the driver will sell you a ticket, and stamp one-way tickets. Previously purchased tickets must be stamped in the automatic machine as soon as you board the tram.

BY TAXI   Taxis are not as plentiful as you might like. However, you can always find one by going to the Central Station. To call a taxi, dial ✆ **031/27-27-27.** A taxi ride within the city limits now costs 155SEK to 275SEK ($16–$29). With the Gothenburg Card, you get a 10% reduction.

BY CAR   Because of parking problems, a car is not a practical vehicle for touring Gothenburg. However, the city has good public transportation. You might need a car to tour the surrounding area, but public transportation is available to many sights. **Avis** (✆ **031/80-57-80**) has a rental office at the Central Station and another at the airport (✆ **031/94-60-30**). **Hertz** also has an office in the center of town at the Central Station (✆ **031/80-37-30**) and one at the airport (✆ **031/94-60-20**). Compare rates and make sure you understand the insurance coverage before you sign a contract.

 FAST FACTS: Gothenburg

Area Code   The international country code for Sweden is **46**; the city code for Gothenburg is **031** (if you're calling Gothenburg from abroad, drop the zero).

Bookstores   The biggest and most central is **Akademi Bokhandeln,** Norra Hamngatan 32 (✆ **031/61-70-31**).

Business Hours   Generally, shops are open Monday through Friday from 9am to 6pm, and Saturday from 9am to 2pm; banks, Monday through Friday from 9:30am to 3pm; and offices, Monday through Friday from 9am to 5pm.

Currency Exchange Currency can be exchanged at **Forex,** in the Central Station ((*C* 031/15-65-16). There's also a currency-exchange desk at Landvetter Airport, open daily from 8am to 9pm.

Dentists Call the referral agency **Akuttandkliniken** ((*C* 031/80-78-00) Monday through Friday from 7am to 8pm, Saturday and Sunday from 9am to 8pm.

Doctors If it's not an emergency, your hotel can call a local doctor and arrange an appointment. In an emergency, go to **City Akuten,** Drottninggatan 45 ((*C* 031/10-10-10).

Drugstores A good pharmacy is **Apoteket Vasen,** Götgatan 12, Nordstan ((*C* 031/80-44-10), open daily from 8am to 10pm.

Embassies & Consulates There is no U.S. consulate in Gothenburg. Citizens of the U.S., Australia, Ireland, and New Zealand must contact their embassy in Stockholm. The **British Consulate,** at Götgatan 15 ((*C* 031/339-22-00), is open Monday through Friday from 9am to 1pm and 2 to 5pm.

Emergencies For nearly all emergencies (fire, police, medical), call (*C* **112.**

Eyeglasses Go to **Wasa Optik,** Vasaplatsen 7 ((*C* 031/711-05-35). It's open Monday through Friday from 9am to 6pm.

Hairdressers & Barbers A good one is **Salong Noblesse,** Södra Larmgatan 6 ((*C* 031/711-71-30). It's open Monday through Friday from 9am to 7pm, Saturday from 9am to 3pm.

Internet Access The city library, **Stadsbibliotek,** Götaplatsen ((*C* 031/61-65-00), has free Internet access. It's open Monday through Thursday from 10am to 8pm, Friday from 10am to 8pm, and Saturday and Sunday from 11am to 5pm. There's also an Internet cafe, with at least a dozen Internet terminals, at **Game Station,** Kungstorget 1 ((*C* 031/13-19-10).

Laundry & Dry Cleaning Laundries are hard to find. There's one at **Käärralund Camping,** Olbersgatan ((*C* 031/25-27-61). For dry cleaning, go to **Express Kem,** Sriggattan ((*C* 031/15-84-83).

Liquor Laws You must be 18 to consume alcohol in a restaurant, but 20 to purchase alcohol in liquor stores. No alcohol can be served before noon. Most pubs stop serving liquor at 3am, except some nightclubs with licenses to stay open later. State-owned liquor shops known as **Systembolag** sell liquor, but only Monday through Friday from 9am to 6pm.

Lost Property Go to the police station (see "Police," below).

Luggage Storage & Lockers You can store luggage and rent lockers at the **Central Station** ((*C* 031/10-44-64). It's open Monday through Saturday from 8am to 8pm.

Photographic Needs An excellent store is **Arkadens Fotoexpert,** Arkaden 9 ((*C* 031/80-20-70). It's open Monday through Friday from 10am to 6pm, Saturday from 10am to 2pm.

Police The main police station is **Polismyndigheten,** Skånegatan 5 ((*C* 031/739-20-00).

Post Office The main post office is at **Drottningtorget 10** ((*C* 031/62-39-63), next to the Central Station. It's open Monday through Saturday from 10am to 3am.

Radio & TV Gothenburg has Swedish-language TV broadcasts on TV1, TV2, TV3, and TV4, and receives British channels such as Super Sky and BBC. National radio stations include P1, P2, P3, and P4; Radio Gothenburg broadcasts on 101.9 MHz (FM).

Shoe Repair Try **Norrdvan's Klackbar,** Nyagatan (✆ **031/215-91-02**). Repairs are made while you wait.

Taxes Gothenburg imposes no special city taxes other than the value-added tax *(moms),* which applies nationwide.

Telegrams, Telex & Fax To send such communications, go to the post office recommended above.

Transit Information For tram and bus information, call ✆ **0771/41-43-00.**

3 Where to Stay

Reservations are important, but if you need a place to stay on the spur of the moment, try the **Gothenburg Tourist Office,** at Kungsportsplatsen 2 (✆ **031/ 61-25-00;** www.goteborg.com). It lists the city's hotels and boardinghouses, and reserves rooms in private homes. Reservations can also be made in advance, by letter or phone. The tourist office charges a booking fee of 60SEK ($6.35). Double rooms in private homes start at around 200SEK ($21) per person. Breakfast is always extra.

The hotels listed below as "Expensive" actually become "Moderate" in price on Friday and Saturday and during the middle of the summer.

EXPENSIVE

Elite Plaza 🏨🏨   Equaled in Gothenburg only by the Radisson SAS Scandinavia, this late-19th-century insurance office was stunningly converted into a superior first-class hotel. All the major architectural features of the palatial 1889 structure were preserved, including the stucco ceilings and mosaic floors. The public lounges are adorned with modern art, and all the rooms and plumbing have been updated to give the building a new lease on life. Lying in the center of town, the hotel is within a short walk of the Central Station and the Opera House. Guest rooms are midsize to spacious, each with a new private bathroom with tub and shower. The hotel's drinking and dining facilities—with friendly bartenders and smooth service—are another reason to stay here.

Vastra Hamngatan 3, S-404 22 Gothenburg. ✆ 031/720-40-00. Fax 031/720-40-10. www.2scandinavia. com/goth/plaza/html. 144 units. Sun–Thurs 2,125SEK–2,360SEK ($225–$250) double, 3,100SEK ($329) suite. Fri–Sat 1,200SEK–1,300SEK ($127–$138) double, 2,700SEK ($286) suite. Rates include breakfast. AE, DC, MC, V. Tram: 1, 2, 7, 9, or 11. **Amenities:** Restaurant; bar; room service; babysitting; laundry/dry cleaning. *In room:* A/C, TV, minibar, hair dryer, safe, trouser press.

Hotel Gothia Towers 🏨🏨   This well-respected government-rated four-star hotel, which rises 18 mirror-plated stories above Sweden's largest convention center, was the tallest building in Gothenburg until it was surpassed in the late 1990s by a competitor. It opened in 1985 and was renovated in the mid-1990s. The brisk, friendly format places it among Scandinavia's best business-oriented hotels. Rooms are comfortable, contemporary, and tasteful. Touches of wood, particularly the hardwood floors, take the edge off any sense of cookie-cutter standardization. Bathrooms are spacious, with shower-tub combinations.

Rooms on the top three floors are plusher, and feature enhanced amenities and services. A covered passageway runs directly to the convention center.

Mässans Gata 24, S-402 26 Göteborg. ©️ **031/750-88-00.** Fax 031/750-88-82. www.hotel-gothia.se. 704 units. Mon–Thurs 1,690SEK–1,795SEK ($179–$190) double; Fri–Sun 940SEK–1,320SEK ($100–$140) double. All week long 3,500SEK–7,000SEK ($371–$742) suite. AE, DC, MC, V. Tram: 4 or 5. **Amenities:** 2 restaurants; 2 bars; fitness center; sauna; room service; laundry/dry cleaning. *In room:* A/C, TV, minibar, hair dryer, safe.

Radisson SAS Park Avenue Hotel ⭐⭐ Constructed in 1950 and renovated in 1992, this Radisson property stands on Gothenburg's major boulevard. Everyone from Henry Kissinger to the Beatles, and from David Rockefeller to the Rolling Stones, has stayed here. The hotel has 10 floors, with attractively designed bedrooms. Upper-floor units enjoy excellent views of the city. Bathrooms are a bit tiny but equipped with shower-tub combinations, and overall the rooms are well maintained.

The hotel's gourmet dining room, Belle Avenue, is one of the best known in Gothenburg. It specializes in game and fresh fish from the Atlantic. The hotel's famous nightclub, Park Lane, is recommended separately (see "Gothenburg After Dark," later in this chapter).

Kungsportsavenyn 36–38, S-400 16 Göteborg. ©️ **800/333-3333** in the U.S., or 031/758-40-00. Fax 031/758-40-01. www.radissonsas.com. 318 units. June 19–Aug 16 1,090SEK ($116) double, 2,500SEK ($265) suite; Aug 17–June 18 1,435SEK–2,225SEK ($152–$236) double, 3,800SEK ($403) suite. Rates include breakfast. AE, DC, MC, V. Parking 200SEK ($21). Tram: 1, 4, 5, or 6. Bus: 40. **Amenities:** Restaurant; bar; fitness center; sauna; room service; babysitting; laundry/dry cleaning. *In room:* TV, minibar, hair dryer, safe.

Radisson SAS Scandinavia Hotel ⭐⭐⭐ This unusual deluxe hotel surrounds a large atrium, which seems like a tree-lined city square indoors. It stands opposite the railroad station, and it's one of the best-run and best-equipped hotels in Sweden. Opened in 1986, the hotel offers the finest rooms in town; they're large, have good beds, and are luxuriously appointed. Some are suitable for people with disabilities. Bathrooms are small but have shower-tub combinations. The fifth floor of the hotel contains the exclusive concierge rooms with extended service and speedier check-ins. These upgraded accommodations are most often booked by the business community.

Södra Hamngatan 59–65, S-401 24 Göteborg. ©️ **800/333-3333** in the U.S., or 031/758-50-50. Fax 031/758-50-01. www.radissonsas.com. 349 units. 1,190SEK–2,350SEK ($126–$249) double; 2,050SEK–4,800SEK ($217–$509) suite. Rates include breakfast. AE, DC, MC, V. Parking 245SEK ($26). Tram: 1, 2, 3, 4, 5, or 7. Bus: 40. **Amenities:** Restaurant; bar; pool; fitness center; sauna; room service; babysitting; laundry/dry cleaning. *In room:* A/C, TV, minibar, hair dryer, safe.

MODERATE

Hotel Best Western Eggers ⭐ *Finds* The second-oldest hotel in Gothenburg was built in 1859, predating the Swedish use of the word to describe a building with rooms for travelers. Many emigrants to the New World spent their last night in the old country at the Hotel Eggers, and during World War II, the Germans and the Allies met here for secret negotiations. Today it's just as good as or better than ever, with stained-glass windows, ornate staircases, and wood paneling. Rooms vary in size, but they are all individually furnished and beautifully appointed, with large bathrooms equipped with shower-tub combinations. In the hotel dining room, gilt leather tapestries and polished mahogany evoke the 19th century.

Drottningtorget, S-401 25 Göteborg. ©️ **800/528-1234** in the U.S. and Canada, or 031/80-60-70. Fax 031/15-42-43. hotel.eggers@mailbox.swipnet.se. 67 units. June 29–Aug 6 and Fri–Sat year-round 950SEK–1,295SEK ($101–$137) double; rest of year 1,690SEK–1,950SEK ($179–$207) double. Rates include breakfast. AE, DC, MC, V. Parking 80SEK ($8.50). Tram: 1, 2, 3, 4, 5, 6, 7, 8, or 9. Bus: 40. **Amenities:** Restaurant; bar; laundry/dry cleaning. *In room:* TV, hair dryer.

Hotel Onyxen *Value*   Clean, well run, and family-managed, this hotel was originally built around 1900 as a many-balconied apartment house. In the 1980s, the hotel was extensively reconfigured and given a streamlined and efficiently decorated interior. Guest rooms have high ceilings, comfortable beds and, in most cases, a color scheme of white and pale blue. Bathrooms come with shower units and are small but well maintained. There's a residents' pub and cocktail lounge near the lobby, but the only meal served is breakfast.

Sten Sturegatan 23, S-412 52 Göteborg. *(C)* **031/81-08-45.** Fax 031/16-56-72. www.hotelonyxen.com. 34 units. July–Aug and Fri–Sat year-round 950SEK ($101) double; rest of year 1,350SEK ($143) double. Extra bed 200SEK ($21). Rates include breakfast. AE, DC, MC, V. Tram: 4 or 5. **Amenities:** Bar; room service; laundry/dry cleaning. *In room:* TV, hair dryer.

Hotel Opera   In 1994, the Hotel Ekoxen joined forces (and facilities) with another hotel to become the Hotel Opera. It's an up-to-date, well-run hotel that often attracts business travelers, although summer visitors gravitate to it as well. Both buildings date from the late 19th century but were upgraded in the 1990s. All rooms are individually designed and tastefully furnished, with neatly kept bathrooms equipped with shower-tub combinations.

Norra Hamngatan 38, S-411 06 Göteborg. *(C)* **031/80-50-80.** Fax 031/80-58-17. www.hotelopera.se. 145 units. June 26–Aug 17 and Fri–Sat year-round 695SEK–895SEK ($74–$95) double; rest of year 1,195SEK–1,450SEK ($127–$154) double. Rates include breakfast. AE, DC, MC, V. Parking 100SEK ($11). Tram: 1, 4, 5, 6, 7, 8, or 9. **Amenities:** Restaurant; bar; Jacuzzi; sauna; room service; laundry/dry cleaning. *In room:* TV, hair dryer.

Novotel Göteborg *(★)*   This converted harbor-front brewery 4km (2½ miles) west of the center is a stylish hotel run by the French hotel conglomerate Accor. Each plush-carpeted room offers panoramic views of the industrial landscape. The room style is Swedish modern, with many built-in pieces, good-sized closets, and firm sofa beds. Bathrooms tend to be small but they do have shower-tub combinations. When it was completed in the 1980s, it was one of the most unusual restorations of a 19th-century building in Sweden. There's a well-accessorized sauna, and laundry facilities are available.

Klippan 1, S-414 51 Göteborg. *(C)* **800/221-4542** in the U.S., or 031/14-90-00. Fax 031/42-22-32. www. novotel.se. 148 units. June 26–Aug 10 and Fri–Sat year-round 830SEK ($88) double, 1,490SEK ($158) suite. Rest of year 1,320SEK ($140) double, 1,790SEK ($190) suite. Rates include breakfast. AE, DC, MC, V. Free parking. From Gothenburg, follow the signs on E20 to Frederikshavn, then the signs to Kiel; exit at Klippan, where signs direct you to the hotel. Tram: 3 or 9. Bus: 91 or 92. **Amenities:** Restaurant; bar; room service; laundry/dry cleaning. *In room:* TV, minibar (in some), hair dryer, safe.

Panorama Hotel *(★)* *(Finds)*   Spacious and dramatic, this 13-story hotel is a 10-minute walk west of the center of town. One of the tallest buildings in Gothenburg, the Panorama is a major hotel that gets surprisingly little publicity. The plant-filled lobby has a skylight, piano bar, and balcony-level restaurant. The guest rooms have stylish furnishings and soft lighting. Extras include wood floors and double-glazed windows. Bathrooms tend to be small, mostly without showers and tubs. The finest accommodations are found on floors 7 through 13.

Eklandagatan 5153, S-400 22 Göteborg. *(C)* **031/767-70-00.** Fax 031/767-70-70. www.panorama.se. 338 units, some with shower only. June 20–Aug 10 and Fri–Sat year-round 990SEK ($105) double, 1,330SEK ($141) suite. Rest of year 1,650SEK ($175) double, 2,100SEK ($223) suite. Rates include breakfast. AE, DC, MC, V. Free parking. Closed Dec 21–Jan 7. Tram: 4 or 5. Bus: 40 or 51. **Amenities:** Restaurant; bar; sauna; room service; laundry/dry cleaning. *In room:* TV, minibar.

INEXPENSIVE

Hotel Örgryte   Named after the leafy residential district of Örgryte, this hotel lies 1.5km (1 mile) east of the commercial core of Gothenburg. It was originally built around 1960, and renovated many times since, most recently in the mid-1990s. Rooms were upgraded and outfitted with pastel-colored upholstery and streamlined, uncomplicated furniture that makes use of birch-veneer woods. Rooms are medium-sized, often big enough to contain a sitting area; bathrooms are rather cramped but do contain shower-tub combinations. Both the exterior and the public areas are clean but not particularly inspired in their design. Overall, the place provides decent, safe accommodations at a relatively reasonable price.

Danska Vägen 68–70, S-416 59 Göteborg. (€ 031/707-89-00. Fax 031/707-89-99. www.hotelorgryte.se. 70 units. Sun–Thurs 1,375SEK ($146) double; Fri–Sat 850SEK ($90) double. All week long 1,550SEK–1,930SEK ($164–$205) suite. Rates include breakfast. AE, DC, MC, V. Parking 95SEK ($10). Bus: 60 or 62. **Amenities:** Restaurant; bar; sauna; laundry/dry cleaning. *In room:* TV, hair dryer.

Hotell Royal   Founded in 1852, the oldest hotel in Gothenburg still in use is about .5km (¼ mile) from the railroad station. All major bus and tram lines pass close by. It's decorated in a typical 19th-century style, with wrought-iron banisters and heavy cast-bronze lamps at the stairs. In the reception area is a unique hand-painted glass ceiling. The rooms are individually designed and modernized, with ample bathrooms equipped with shower units.

Drottninggatan 67, S-411 07 Göteborg. (€ 031/700-11-70. Fax 031/700-11-79. www.hotel-royal.com. 82 units. June 22–Aug 14 and Fri–Sat year-round 790SEK–910SEK ($84–$96) double. Rest of year 1,295SEK–1,395SEK ($137–$148) double. Rates include buffet breakfast. AE, DC, MC, V. Parking 120SEK ($13) depending on the size of the car. Tram: 1, 2, 3, 4, 5, or 6. Bus: 60. **Amenities:** Lounge. *In room:* TV, hair dryer.

Hotel Winn   This no-nonsense but comfortable and affordable four-story hotel is about 3km (2 miles) north of Gothenburg's ferryboat terminal. Functional and modern, its bedrooms are more comfortable than you might imagine from the uninspired exterior. Each is outfitted in pastel shades, with well-kept bathrooms equipped with shower-tub combinations.

Gamla Tingstadsgatan 1, S-402 76 Göteborg. (€ 031/750-19-00. Fax 031/750-15-50. www.winnhotel.com. 121 units. June 15–Aug 15 and Fri–Sat year-round 900SEK ($95) double; rest of year 1,345SEK ($143) double. Rates include breakfast. AE, DC, MC, V. Free parking. Bus: 40. **Amenities:** Restaurant; bar; pool; sauna; room service; laundry/dry cleaning. *In room:* TV, minibar, hair dryer.

Tidbloms Hotel ⚐ *(Finds*   Set about 3km (2 miles) east of Gothenburg's center, in a residential neighborhood filled with other Victorian buildings, this hotel was built in 1897 as a dormitory for Scottish craftsmen imported to work at the nearby lumber mill. Despite its functional purpose, its builders graced it with a conical tower, fancy brickwork, and other architectural adornments that remain in place today. After stints as a warehouse, a delicatessen, and a low-rent hotel, the building was upgraded in 1987 into a cozy, charming, and well-accessorized hotel. Guest rooms have good firm beds, ample bathrooms with shower-tub combinations, and wooden floors—and have more flair and character than you'll find at many larger, more anonymous hotels in Gothenburg's center. On the premises is a restaurant, which is recommended separately in "Where to Dine," below.

Olskroksgatan 23, S-416 66 Göteborg. (€ 031/707-50-00. Fax 031/707-50-99. www.tidbloms.com. 42 units. Sun–Thurs 1,200SEK–1,500SEK ($127–$159) double; Fri–Sat 890SEK ($94) double. Rates include breakfast. AE, DC, MC, V. Free parking. Tram: 1, 3, or 6. **Amenities:** Restaurant; bar; sauna; room service; laundry/dry cleaning. *In room:* TV, minibar, hair dryer, safe.

4 Where to Dine

EXPENSIVE

Bistro Mannerström *Finds* SWEDISH   This place is appealing because of the way it combines old-fashioned Swedish wholesomeness and *husmanskost* (home cooking) with a sophisticated and often upscale flair. Despite the high standards it attains, it modestly defines itself as a simple neighborhood restaurant. You'll be seated within one of two white-walled dining rooms whose only color is the varnished light-grained wood floor. Menu items are considerably more elegant than the decor, and include poached halibut with a turbot and scallop mousseline; breast of wild Swedish duck served with a confit of bacon-flavored purée of potatoes served in a cabbage shell; and broiled cutlets of turbot with glazed carrots, salsify, and a sauce concocted from red wine, butter, lemon, and rosemary. You might also try filet of veal with truffle-flavored potatoes and Jerusalem artichokes, or grilled and cured brisket of beef with chanterelles, bacon, and spring onions. Expect a clientele of entrepreneurs and corporate leaders who tend to conduct business while eating.

Archivgatan 7. © 031/16-03-33. Reservations recommended. Main courses 250SEK–400SEK ($27–$42); fixed-price menus 245SEK–300SEK ($26–$32). AE, DC, MC, V. Mon–Sat 5–11pm. Closed July. Tram: 4 or 5.

Fiskekrogen SEAFOOD   One of the most appealing seafood restaurants in Gothenburg occupies a building across the canal from the Stadtsmuseum, in a handsome, internationally modern setting whose sea-green and dark-blue color scheme reflects the shades of the ocean. Fiskekrogen prides itself on a medley of fresh seafood that's artfully displayed and prepared with a zest that earns many loyal customers throughout the city. One of the most appealing aspects of the place is a display of seafood on ice—succulent oysters, fresh lobster, fat crayfish, clams, and mussels. After viewing this spread, you can tell the waiter what you prefer for dinner. More conventional seafood dishes include poached tournedos of cod with beet-root marmalade and a horseradish-butter sauce; and grilled halibut with a ragout of baby scallops, bacon, onions, mushrooms, and Zinfandel.

Lilla Torget 1. © 031/10-10-05. Reservations recommended. Main courses 245SEK–325SEK ($26–$34); vegetarian menu 295SEK ($31); small menu 595SEK ($63); big menu 795SEK ($84). AE, DC, MC, V. Mon–Fri 11:30am–2pm and 5:30–11pm; Sat 1–11pm. Tram: 2 or 5.

Restaurang Räkan/Yellow Submarine SEAFOOD   This is one of Gothenburg's best seafood restaurants. Not surprisingly, it has a nautical decor with buoy lamps, wooden-plank tables typical of the Swedish west coast, and a shallow-bottomed re-creation of a Swedish lake. Your seafood platter arrives on a battery-powered boat with you directing the controls. You can order various combinations of crayfish (in season), along with prawns, poached sole, mussels, lobster, filet of gray sole, and fresh crabs. If you don't want fish, chicken and beef dishes are available. Attached to the restaurant is a popular pub, Yellow Submarine, named for the Beatles song.

Lorensbergsgatan 16. © 031/16-98-39. Reservations recommended. Main courses 135SEK–265SEK ($14–$28). AE, DC, MC, V. Mon–Sat 5–11pm; Sun 3–10pm. Tram: 1, 4, 5, or 6. Bus: 40.

Restaurant 28+ INTERNATIONAL   Cozy, intimate, and reeking of old-world charm, this is a chic and stylish restaurant whose trio of dining rooms are lit with flickering candles and capped with soaring masonry ceiling vaults. It's the city's hippest culinary venue, featuring main courses that include cooked crayfish with a fennel-flavored *nage* (an aromatic broth); smoked filet of char in a red wine and butter sauce; grilled breast of pigeon, or saddle of reindeer with Jerusalem artichokes and blackberry vinaigrette. We have consistently found that the finest—and most imaginative—cuisine in Gothenburg is served here. The items taste fabulously fresh, and the food is handled faultlessly and is delicately seasoned by the kitchen. The service is the city's best, and the sommelier will offer expert guidance—although you might think the tax on wine is so high that you're putting someone's kid through college. The most demanding palates in Gothenburg leave here satisfied.

Götabergsgatan 28. © 031/20-21-61. Reservations recommended. Main courses 275SEK–395SEK ($29–$42); fixed-price menus 725SEK–845SEK ($77–$90). AE, DC, MC, V. Mon–Sat 6–11pm. Bus: 40. Tram: 1, 4, 5, or 6.

Sjömagasinet ★★★ *Finds* SEAFOOD By far the most elegant and atmospheric restaurant in town, Sjömagasinet is located near the Novotel in the western suburb of Klippan, about 4km (2½ miles) from the center. The building, erected in 1775, was originally a warehouse. It contains a bar in cozy English colonial style, and another bar in the eyrie.

Very fresh seafood is served here, evidenced in the shrimp-stuffed crepes with dill, shellfish with curry sauce, baked filet of beef and lobster, poached filet of sole with crayfish, and turbot béarnaise. Two very special dishes are the pot-au-feu of fish and shellfish, served with a chive-flavored crème fraîche; and the poached filet of halibut with warm cabbage salad and potato salad.

Klippans Kulturreservat. © 031/775-59-20. Reservations recommended. Main courses 300SEK–450SEK ($32–$48); 1-course fixed-price lunch 135SEK ($14). AE, DC, MC, V. Mon–Fri 11:30am–11pm; Sat 5–11pm; Sun 2–8pm. From the town center, head west on E3, following the signs to Frederikshavn, and then to Kiel; exit at Klippan and then follow the signs for the Novotel. Tram: 3 or 9.

MODERATE

A Hereford Beefstouw ★ *Value* STEAK This is the best and most appealing steakhouse in Gothenburg, with a reputation for expertly prepared Australian beef, and a salad bar that's the most varied and copious in town. One of the three separate dining rooms is smoke-free, and all have thick-topped wooden tables, lots of varnished pine, and touches of African oak. The only sauces available to accompany your beef are béarnaise butter sauce, parsley butter sauce, and garlic butter sauce: The management believes in allowing the flavor of the meat to come through, unmasked by more elaborate seasonings. The largest platter is a 500-gram (17½-oz.) T-bone steak, a portion so large that we advise you to finish it at your own risk. Other platters, such as filet steaks, veal sirloins, or tenderloins, are more reasonably sized. A full list of wines and beers is available.

Linnégatan. © 031/775-04-41. Reservations recommended. Main courses 120SEK–315SEK ($13–$33); salad bar as a main course 85SEK ($9). AE, DC, MC, V. Mon–Fri 11:30am–2pm and 5–10pm; Sat 4–11pm; Sun 3–9pm. Tram: 1, 3, 4, or 9.

Brasserie Lipp SWEDISH/FRENCH Located on Gothenburg's busiest avenue, this brasserie was established in 1987, inspired by the legendary Left Bank bistro in Paris, with palate adjustments for Swedish tastes. Its good food is a combination of French and Swedish—for example, escargots in garlic-butter sauce, Lipp's Skagen toast (piled high with shrimp), Swedish entrecôte of beef with Dijon mustard sauce, grilled halibut with garlic-tomato sauce, carpaccio of beef, and Thai chicken. There's also *choucroute garnie* (sauerkraut with sausage and pork, the most famous dish served at its Paris namesake) and many different kinds of fish, most caught in the waters near Gothenburg.

Kungsportsavenyn 8. © 031/711-50-58. Reservations required. Main courses 155SEK–250SEK ($16–$27); daily platters 65SEK ($6.90). AE, DC, MC, V. Daily 11:30am–2am. Tram: 1, 4, 5, or 6. Bus: 40.

La Gondola ITALIAN   This lively restaurant, with its striped poles, sidewalk awnings, and summer outdoor cafe, evokes Venice. It makes the best pizzas in town, but there's also an elaborate menu with many classic Italian dishes. The spaghetti Gondola is very good, and the saltimbocca ("jump in your mouth") alla romana, a veal-and-ham dish, is tasty. You might also try one of the grilled specialties including a tender, juicy steak. The minestrone is freshly made and filling, and a velvet-smooth ice cream is served. Every day there's a different lunch special and an a la carte dinner.

Kungsportsavenyn 4. ✆ 031/711-68-28. Reservations recommended. Main courses 85SEK–400SEK ($9–$42); *dagens* (daily) lunch 65SEK–150SEK ($6.90–$16). AE, DC, MC, V. Daily 11:30am–11pm. Tram: 1, 4, 5, or 6. Bus: 38 or 75.

Lilla London SWEDISH/FRENCH   The quiet, pub-like atmosphere is a local favorite. The restaurant, down a flight of steps, is dark and attractively designed, with illuminated paintings of clipper ships and nautical accents. Full meals might include grilled chicken with morels, beef and lamb filet in a mustard-flavored cream sauce, filet mignon, or broiled salmon with fresh asparagus. This is merely good, standard fare, prepared with fresh ingredients and sold for a fair price. Less expensive light meals are also available. The pub sells about 10 different kinds of beer.

Avenyn/Vasagatan 41. ✆ 031/18-40-62. Reservations recommended. Main courses 79SEK–210SEK ($8.35–$22). AE, DC, MC, V. Daily 5pm–midnight. Tram: 1, 4, 5, or 6. Bus: 40.

Restaurang Gillestugan SWEDISH/INTERNATIONAL   In the mid-1990s, local entrepreneurs put a new spin on one of Gothenburg's most nostalgic restaurants. They transformed the antique-looking establishment, which dates from 1918, into the city's busiest and most creative cabaret and supper club—though the street-level bar, the Tullen Pub, remains.

During the day the only entertainment is the good-natured, hardworking staff. But every evening from 9 to 11pm, musical, theatrical, or poetic events take over a small stage. Recent examples include folk singers whose repertoire is in both Swedish and English, and an Elvis impersonator who is, local residents insist, better than the real thing. Some of the entertainment involves Swedish-language satire, so phone in advance to avoid any production that's too cryptic for foreigners.

The food is well prepared and served in generous portions, and there's no cover charge for the entertainment. Menu items include salmon tartare with horseradish sauce and fried onions, a mushroom and apple terrine with air-dried ham and spicy oil, filet of lamb with tomato and feta-cheese sauce, and baked, sliced, and fried potatoes.

Järntorget 6. ✆ 031/24-00-50. Reservations recommended. Main courses 79SEK–178SEK ($8.35–$19); fixed-price menus 250SEK–275SEK ($27–$29). AE, DC, MC, V. Daily 11:30am–2pm and 5–11:30pm; bar Sun–Thurs 11am–1am, Fri–Sat 11am–3am. Entertainment 9pm–midnight. Tram: 1, 3, 4, or 9.

INEXPENSIVE

Froken Olssons Café SWEDISH   Less than 2 blocks from The Avenyn, this is a traditional favorite with Gothenburgers. It tends to be crowded and noisy at lunchtime. Even though there's a large interior, the crowd overflows onto an outdoor terrace in summer. At night, hot pies with a salad are featured, and you can also order baguette sandwiches filled with such ingredients as shrimp or ham and cheese. Light beer is served, but no wine or liquor. Basically, it's light cafe dining, with homemade soups and such main courses as entrecôte.

Östra Larmgatan 14. ✆ 031/13-81-93. Coffee 22SEK ($2.35); *dagens* (daily) menu 60SEK–69SEK ($6.35–$7.30); hot pies with salad 55SEK ($5.85); sandwiches 25SEK–65SEK ($2.65–$6.90). MC, V. Mon–Fri 9am–10pm. Tram: 1, 4, 5, or 6. Bus: 40.

Perfect Picnics

Go to Saluhallen, Kungstorget, for the makings of an elegant picnic. Built in 1888, this is the city's colorful indoor market. Shops sell meat, fruit, vegetables, and delicatessen products. You can buy, for example, quail and all sorts of game, including moose and reindeer, and even lamb from Iceland. The produce (including exotic fruit) comes from all over the world. Bread, coffee, olives, and patés are also sold. There are, in addition, four restaurants and one coffee bar in the building. Much of the food is already cooked and can be packaged for you to take out. The hall is open Monday through Thursday from 9am to 6pm, Friday from 8am to 6pm, and Saturday from 8am to 1pm. Take tram no. 1, 4, 5, or 6 to Kungsportsplatsen.

Take your picnic basket to any of Gothenburg's major parks (see "Parks & Gardens," in "Seeing the Sights," below). Trädgårdsföreningen, across from the Central Station, is especially pleasant, although there's a 15SEK ($1.60) entrance fee.

Solrosen (Sunflower) _Finds_ VEGETARIAN   In the Haga district, a low-rise neighborhood of 18th- and early-19th-century buildings, this is the best vegetarian restaurant in Gothenburg. You serve yourself at the counter, with an all-you-can-eat salad bar that accompanies the main dishes. There's unlimited coffee and second helpings. Beer and wine are available.

Kaponjärgatan 4. ℂ **031/711-66-97.** Main courses 90SEK–180SEK ($9.55–$19). AE, DC, MC, V. Mon–Fri 11:30am–1am; Sat 2pm–1am. Tram: 1, 3, or 4.

Tidbloms Restaurang INTERNATIONAL   Set near the lobby of the recommended Tidbloms Hotel, this restaurant is particularly charming, thanks to the staff that works hard to keep things personalized. In the wood-paneled dining room, you can order well-seasoned dishes that include cream of chanterelle soup, seafood medley on toast, African-style beef in a piquant peanut sauce, salmon in a saffron-flavored cream sauce, and a combination of pork and beef prepared Provençal style with red wine and Lyonnaise potatoes.

Olskroksgatan 23. ℂ **031/707-50-00.** Main courses 169SEK–279SEK ($18–$30); fixed-price menus 99SEK–200SEK ($10–$21). AE, DC, MC, V. Mon–Fri 11:30am–1:30pm and 6–10pm; Sat 4–10pm; Sun 1–8pm. Tram: 1, 3, or 6.

5 Seeing the Sights

SUGGESTED ITINERARIES
If You Have 1 Day
Enjoy a cup of coffee at one of the cafes along The Avenyn in the center of Gothenburg; then take the classical Paddan boat ride, traveling through the moat and canal out to the harbor and the giant docks. Return for a stroll along The Avenyn, and then take one of the summertime vintage trams to see part of the city ashore. Go to Liseberg amusement park in the evening. Winter visitors can explore some of Gothenburg's numerous museums, including the Röhsska Museum of Arts and Crafts, the Göteborg Maritime Center, and the East India House.

Gothenburg Attractions

Botaniska Trädgården
(Botanical Garden) **10**

Drottning Kristinas Jaktslott
(Queen Christina's
Hunting Lodge) **5**

East India House
(Museum of Gothenburg) **3**

Feskekörka (Fish Church) **8**

Göteborg Martima Centrum **2**

Göteborgs Konstmuseum **12**

Göteborgsoperan
(Gothenburg Opera House) **1**

Guldhedens Våttentorn **11**

Konserthuset **13**

Liseberg Park **6**

Röhsska Konstslöjdmuseet **7**

Slottsskogen **9**

Stadsbibliotek (Library) **15**

Stadsteatern (Theater) **14**

Trägårdsföreningen **4**

If You Have 2 Days

On the first day, follow the suggestions above. On Day 2, take a boat trip to Elfsborg Fortress, leaving from Stenpiren in the Gothenburg harbor and continuing under the Älvsborg Bridge to Elfsborg. In the afternoon, visit the Göteborgs Konstmuseum and the Botanical Garden.

If You Have 3 Days

For the first 2 days, follow the itinerary suggested above. On Day 3, get up early to visit the fish auction at the harbor (it begins at 7am), then go to the nearby Feskekörka (Fish Church). Take tram no. 6 to Guldhedens Våttentorn (water tower) for a panoramic view of Gothenburg. Go to Götaplatsen to see the famed Poseidon fountain by Carl Milles. In the afternoon, visit the Röhsska Museum of Arts and Crafts and stroll through the rose-filled Trädgårdsföreningen, across from the Central Station.

If You Have 4 or 5 Days

For Days 1 to 3, follow the itinerary suggested above. On Day 4, take an excursion to Marstrand, north of the city. On Day 5, visit Nordstan, the biggest shopping center in Scandinavia. Spend the rest of the day exploring the southern archipelago, which you can do free with your Gothenburg Card (see "Getting Around," earlier in this chapter). The MS *Styrsö* and the steamboat *Bohuslän* depart from Skeppsbron/Stenpiren for trips around the archipelago.

THE TOP ATTRACTIONS

For a quick orientation to Gothenburg, visit the 120m (400-ft.) tall **Guldhedens Våttentorn (water tower),** Syster Estrids Gata (℗ **031/82-00-09**); take tram no. 6 or 7 from the center of the city, about a 10-minute ride. The elevator ride up the tower is free, and there's a cafeteria/snack bar on top. The tower is open from May to September daily from noon to 10pm.

Early risers can visit the daily fish auction at the harbor, the largest fishing port in Scandinavia. The entertaining sale begins at 7am sharp. You can also visit the Feskekörka (Fish Church), on Rosenlundsgatan, which is in the fish market. The Feskekörka is not a church at all—rather, its architectural outline evokes one. It's open Tuesday through Friday from 9am to 5pm, Saturday from 9am to 1pm.

The traditional starting point for seeing Gothenburg is the cultural center, Götaplatsen. Its Poseidon fountain is the work of Carl Milles, one of Sweden's most important sculptors. The big trio of buildings here is the Concert Hall, the municipally owned theater, and the Göteborgs Konstmuseum.

Göteborgs Konstmuseum 🖈🖈🖈 Göteborgs Konstmuseum is the leading art museum of Gothenburg, with a good collection of modern art, especially French Impressionist. Bonnard, Cézanne, van Gogh, and Picasso are represented, along with sculptures by Milles and Rodin. The gallery is noted for its collection of the works of 19th- and 20th-century Scandinavian artists (Zorn and Larsson of Dalarna, Edvard Munch and Christian Krohg of Norway). Old masters, including Rembrandt and Rubens, are also represented. The modern section includes works by Francis Bacon and Henry Moore.

Götaplatsen. ℗ 031/61-29-80. Admission 40SEK ($4.25) adults, 10SEK ($1.05) children 7–16, free for children under 7. May–Aug Mon–Fri 11am–4pm, Sat–Sun 11am–5pm; Sept–Apr Tues and Thurs–Fri 11am–6pm, Wed 11am–9pm, Sat–Sun 11am–5pm. Tram: 4 or 5. Bus: 40.

Liseberg Park 🖈🖈 With three million visitors a year, Liseberg Park is the number-one tourist attraction in Sweden. Since 1923 it has been the largest amusement park in Scandinavia. For dining, nightlife, and entertainment in general, Gothenburgers head for this pleasure garden of fountains, pavilions, and flowers. The festively lit park comes alive with music, artists, dances, dozens of rides, and open-air vaudeville shows on seven stages. The park's complicated daily schedule is announced yearly. It's generally open on some days in April, daily May through August, and weekends in September.

Korsvägen. ✆ **031/40-01-00**, or 031/40-02-20 for daily programs and times. Admission 50SEK ($5.30), free for children under 7. June–Aug Mon–Fri 3–11pm, Sat 11am–midnight, Sun 11am–10pm; Sept–Nov Fri 5–11pm, Sat 11am–midnight, Sun 11am–10pm. Tram: 4 or 5 from the city.

Röhsska Konstslöjdmuseet ★★ This museum houses a large collection of European furnishings, china, glass, and pottery, and Asian artifacts. It mounts permanent and temporary exhibits of modern handicrafts and industrial design. Among the exhibits are books, silver, and Chinese and Japanese art. The museum presents lecture series and guided tours.

Vasagatan 37–39. ✆ **031/61-38-50.** Admission 40SEK ($4.25) adults, 10SEK ($1.05) children 7–16, free for children under 7. May–Aug Mon–Fri noon–4pm, Sat–Sun noon–5pm; Sept–Apr Tues noon–9pm, Wed–Sun noon–5pm. Closed Aug 15–Sept 21. Tram: 1, 4, 5, 6, or 8. Bus: 40.

Göteborg Maritima Centrum Located on the harbor, this museum is partly aboard the destroyer *Småland*, which is equipped with guns and torpedoes. In authentic settings, you can see lightships, steamships, and tugboats, among other watercraft. There are cafes at the center and on the quay.

Packhujkajem 8. ✆ **031/10-59-50.** Admission 70SEK ($7.40) adults, 30SEK ($3.20) children 7–15, free for children under 7. July daily 10am–9pm; May–June and Aug daily 10am–6pm; Mar–Apr and Sept–Nov daily 10am–4pm. Closed Dec–Feb. Tram: 5 to Lilla Bommen.

East India House (Museum of Gothenburg) ★★ This museum focuses on the history of Gothenburg and its environs—archaeological, cultural, technical, and medical. It has an array of interesting permanent exhibits, including displays from the Viking era and unique artifacts found in the area.

Norra Hamngatan 12. ✆ **031/61-27-70.** Admission 40SEK ($4.25) adults, 10SEK ($1.05) children 7–14, free for children under 7. June–Aug daily 10am–5pm; Sept–May Tues–Sun 10am–5pm. Tram: 1 or 9. Bus: 40, 58, or 60 to Brunnsparken.

Stadsbibliotek Toward the end of The Avenyn is the public library, on the left at Götaplatsen. This is the city's main library, the home of some 450,000 volumes in 50 languages, a listening room with recorded music, and a reading room with more than 100 foreign daily newspapers. One hall features continuously changing exhibits. The library also has a cafe.

Götaplatsen. ✆ **031/61-65-00.** Free admission. Mon–Fri 10am–8pm; Sat–Sun 11am–5pm. Tram: 1, 4, 5, or 6. Bus: 40.

PARKS & GARDENS

Botaniska Trädgården (Botanical Garden) The Botanical Garden lies opposite Slottsskogen Park in southern Gothenburg. It features trees and shrubs from Asia, rock gardens, orchids, and greenhouses. The rhododendrons bloom in May and June.

Carl Skottsbergsgata 22. ✆ **031/741-11-00.** Free admission to garden; greenhouses, 20SEK ($2.10) adults, free for children under 17. Garden, daily 9am–sunset. Greenhouses, May–Aug daily 10am–4pm; Sept–Apr daily 10am–4pm. Tram: 1, 2, or 7.

Slottsskogen ★★ At 110 hectares (274 acres), this is the largest park in Gothenburg. Laid out in 1874 in a naturally wooded area, today it has beautiful walks, animal enclosures, a saltwater pool, bird ponds, and an aviary. The children's zoo is open from May to August. A variety of events and entertainment takes place here in the summer. There's an outdoor cafe at the zoo, and restaurants at Villa Bel Park and Björngårdsvillan.

Near Linnéplatsen. ℂ 031/61-18-90. Free admission. Daily 24 hr. Tram: 1 or 2 to Linnéplatsen.

Trädgårdsföreningen 𝒢𝒢   Across the canal from the Central Station, this park boasts a large *rosarium* that flourishes with about 10,000 rose bushes of 4,000 different species. The park's centerpiece is the Palm House, a greenhouse maintained at subtropical temperatures even in the depths of winter. The Butterfly House contains beautiful butterflies that flutter through a simulation of a natural habitat. The city of Gothenburg sometimes hosts exhibits, concerts (occasionally during the lunch hour), and children's theater pieces in the park.

Entrances on Slussgatan (across from the Central Station) and Södra Vägen. ℂ 031/611-12-78. Park 15SEK ($1.60) adults, free for children under 17, free for everyone Sept–Apr; Palm House 20SEK ($2.10) adults and children; Butterfly House 35SEK ($3.70) adults, 10SEK ($1.05) children. Daily 10am–5pm.

ARCHITECTURAL HIGHLIGHTS

Drottning Kristinas Jaktslott (Queen Christina's Hunting Lodge)   The oldest dwelling in Gothenburg, this hunting lodge was saved from demolition in 1971 by the Ötterhallen Historical Preservation Society and the Historical Museum. Today you can visit this 17th-century lodge and enjoy coffee and waffles in its old-world atmosphere. Waffles cost 30SEK ($3.20) and up.

Ötterhallegatan 16. ℂ 031/13-34-26. Free admission. Daily 11am–4pm. Tram: 2, 3, 4, or 7 to Lilla Torget.

ORGANIZED TOURS

A sightseeing boat trip along the canals and out into the harbor will show you the old parts of central Gothenburg and take you under 20 bridges. **Paddan Sightseeing Boats** (ℂ 031/60-96-70) offers 55-minute tours from May to September 15, daily from 10am to 5pm; from September 12 to October 6, daily from noon to 3pm. They leave from the terminal at Kungsportsplatsen in the city center. The fare is 80SEK ($8.50) for adults, 50SEK ($5.30) for children 4 to 15, and free for kids under 4. A family ticket (for two adults and two children) costs 205SEK ($22).

Nya Elfsborg (ℂ 031/10-07-40) is docked in the 17th-century fortress at the harbor's mouth. This boat takes you from Lilla Bommen on a 90-minute tour through the harbor to and around Elfsborg Fortress, built in the 17th century to protect the Göta Älv estuary and the western entrance to Sweden. It still bears traces of hard-fought sea battles against the Danes. Carvings on the prison walls tell the tales of 19th-century lifetime prisoners. A guide will be waiting for you at the cafeteria, museum, and souvenir shop. There are five departures a day from mid-May to the end of August. The fare is 85SEK ($9) for adults, 55SEK ($5.85) for children.

MS *Poseidon* is available for an evening cruise of the archipelago. For information about available tours, check with the tourist office (see "Visitor Information," earlier in this chapter), or **Bohus Line** (ℂ 031/13-30-37), which provides excursion packages, brochures, tickets, and timetables. The tour costs 345SEK ($37) for adults and 170SEK ($18) for children 6 to 12. The 4-hour trip departs at 7pm.

For a guided 1-hour **bus tour** of Gothenburg, go to the tourist office (see "Visitor Information," earlier in this chapter) or call ℂ **031/60-96-70** for details. City tours are offered daily from May to September. The fare is 75SEK ($7.95) for adults, 50SEK ($5.30) for children. Tours last 1½ hours.

6 Especially for Kids

At **Liseberg Park** (see "The Top Attractions," above), every day is children's day. The Liseberg Cirkus is a fun fair, and there are always actors in animal costumes to play with children. The pony merry-go-round, children's boats, and a fun-on-wheels ride are all free for tots.

Your children might want to stay at the amusement park's hotel, in the city center, a short walk from the park. **Hotel Liseberg Heden,** Sten Sturegatan S-411 38 Göteborg (© **031/750-69-109;** fax 031/750-69-30; www.liseberg.se), offers discounted summer rates. They include breakfast and coupons for free admission to the amusement park and many of its rides and shows. Between May and September, the discounted rate for double rooms is 850SEK ($90). From October to April, doubles cost 895SEK ($95) Friday through Sunday, and 1,495SEK ($158) Monday through Thursday. The hotel accepts major credit cards (American Express, Diners Club, MasterCard, Visa). It was built in the 1930s as an army barracks and later functioned as a youth hostel. Today, after numerous improvements, it's a first-class, very comfortable hotel. To reach the 172-room hotel, take tram no. 4 or 5 to Berzeliegaten.

Naturhistoriska Museet I Göteborg, Slottsskogen (© **031/775-24-00**), displays stuffed and mounted animals from all over the world, including Sweden's only stuffed blue whale. It's open Tuesday through Friday from 9am to 6pm, and Saturday and Sunday from 11am to 5pm. Admission is 40SEK ($4.25) for adults, 10SEK ($1.05) for ages 7 to 20, and free for children under 7. To reach the museum, you can use trams no. 1, 2, or 6, or buses no. 51 or 54 to Linnéplatsen.

There's also a children's zoo at Slottsskogen from May to August (see "Parks & Gardens," above).

7 Shopping

THE SHOPPING SCENE

Many residents of Copenhagen and Helsingør come to Gothenburg just for the day to buy Swedish merchandise. You can, too, but you should shop at the stores bearing the yellow-and-blue tax-free shopping sign. These stores are scattered throughout Gothenburg. If your purchases in one of these stores total more than 200SEK ($21), you're entitled to a tax refund. You must pay the tax along with the purchase price, but then ask for a tax-refund voucher before leaving the store. You'll get a tax refund, minus a small service charge, when you clear Customs as you leave Sweden. You're not permitted to use your purchase in Sweden, and you must take it out of the country within 1 month of purchase.

MAJOR SHOPPING DISTRICTS   Nordstan, with its 150 shops and stores, restaurants, hotels, patisseries, coffee shops, banks, travel agencies, and post office, is the largest shopping mall in Scandinavia (call the main tourist office for more information). You can find almost anything, ranging from exclusive clothing boutiques to outlets of the major confectionery chains to bookshops. There's also a tourist information center. Most shops here are open Monday through Friday from 9:30am to 7pm, and Saturday from 9:30am to 4pm.

Kungsgatan and **Fredsgatan** make up Sweden's longest pedestrian mall (3km/2 miles in length). The selection of shops is enormous. Near these two streets, you'll also find some smaller shopping centers, including Arkaden, City-passagen, and Kompassen.

At **Grönsakstorget** and **Kungstorget,** you'll see flowers, fruits, handicrafts, and jewelry, among other items, arranged on little trolleys. They're right in the city center, a throwback perhaps to the Middle Ages.

The oft-mentioned **Avenyn,** with its many restaurants and cafes, also has a number of stores selling merchandise of interest to visitors.

Kronhusbodarna, Kronhusgatan 1D (✆ 031/711-08-32), one of the city's architectural showpieces, was originally built in the 1650s; it's the oldest non-ecclesiastical building in town. In the 1660s, it was pressed into service as the meeting place for the Swedish Parliament, which convened hastily to welcome a visit from Charles X Gustav during his wars with Denmark. For many years, the building functioned as a military warehouse and repair center, stockpiling sail-cloth and armaments. Today its echoing interior accommodates a number of small-scale and rather sleepy studios for glass blowers, watchmakers, potters, and coppersmiths. Some sell their goods to passersby. You can visit the various studios, if the artisans happen to show up. Take tram no. 1 or 7 to Brunnsparken.

SHOPPING A TO Z
DEPARTMENT STORES
Bohusslöjds   This store has one of the best collections of Swedish handicrafts in Gothenburg. Amid a light-grained birch decor, you'll find wrought-iron chandeliers, unusual wallpaper, and fabric by the yard. Other items, ideal as gifts or souvenirs, include hand-woven rugs, pine and birch bowls, and assorted knickknacks. Kungsportsavenyn 25. ✆ 031/16-00-72. Bus: 40.

C. J. Josephssons Glas & Porslin   This store has been selling Swedish glass since 1866 and has established an enviable reputation. The selection of Orrefors crystal and porcelain is stunning. It carries signed original pieces by such well-known designers as Bertil Vallien and Goran Warff. There's a tourist tax-free shopping service, plus full shipping service. Korsgatan 12. ✆ 031/17-56-15. Tram: 1, 2, 3, 4, 5, or 7. Bus: 60.

Nordiska Kompaniet (NK)   Since this is a leading department store, shoppers are likely to come here first. The store stocks typical Swedish and Scandinavian articles. It carries more than 200,000 items, ranging from Kosta Boda "sculpture" crystal, Orrefors crystal in all types and shapes, Rorstrand high-fired earthenware and fine porcelain, stainless steel, pewter items, dolls in national costume, leather purses, Dalarna horses, Finnish carpeting, books about Sweden, Swedish recordings, and much, much more. The store's packing specialists will ship your purchases home. There's another NK in Stockholm (see "Shopping" in chapter 14, "Exploring Stockholm"). Östra Hamngatan 42. ✆ 031/710-10-00. Bus: 40.

FASHION
Gillblad's   This fashion outlet is known for its high-quality, well-made clothing for men and women. It's especially noted for men's and women's business suits. The inventory is tasteful, and not too flashy, which is just the way many of its long-standing clients like it. Krykøgatan 19. ✆ 031/10-88-46. Tram: 1, 2, or 3.

Hennes & Mauritz   Established in the 1940s, this is an established clothing store for women that keeps an eye on what's happening in cutting-edge fashion around the world. The spirit here is trendy, with an emphasis on what makes a woman look chic and youthful for nights out on the town. Despite its undeniable sense of flair, garments are less expensive than you might suppose, with lots of low-markup bargains for cost-conscious shoppers. The same outfit maintains a menswear store a few storefronts away at no. 61 Kungsgatan (© **031/711-00-32**). Kungsgatan 55–57. © 031/711-00-11. Tram: 1, 2, or 3.

Ströms   This is the most visible men's clothing emporium in Gothenburg, with a history that stretches back to 1886. Scattered over two floors of retail space, you'll find garments that range from the very formal to the very casual, and boutique-inspired subdivisions with ready-to-wear garments from Europe's leading fashion houses. It also sells women's and children's clothing, but most of its fame and reputation derives from its appeal to men. Kungsgatan 27–29. © 031/17-71-00. Tram: 1, 2, or 3.

HANDICRAFTS

Aside from some of the markets and streets already mentioned, the following establishment also specializes in handicrafts.

Lerverk   This is a permanent exhibit center for 30 potters and glassmakers. Västra Hamngatan 24 26. © 031/13-13-49. Tram: 1, 2, 3, 4, or 7 to Grönsakstorget.

8 Gothenburg After Dark

If Swedish dinner theater interests you, see **Restaurang Gillestugan** under "Where to Dine," earlier in this chapter.

To the Gothenburgers, there's nothing more exciting than sitting outdoors at a cafe along The Avenyn enjoying the short-lived summer. Residents also like to take the whole family to the **Liseberg Park** (see "The Top Attractions," earlier in this chapter). Although clubs are open in the summer, they're not well patronized until the cool weather sets in.

For a listing of entertainment events scheduled at the time of your visit, check the newspapers or inquire at the tourist office.

THE PERFORMING ARTS

THEATER

The Gothenburg Card (see "Getting Around," earlier in this chapter) allows you to buy two tickets for the price of one. Call the particular theater or the tourist office for program information. Performances are also announced in the newspapers.

Folkteatern   This theater stages productions of Swedish plays or foreign plays translated into Swedish. The season is from September to May, and performances are Tuesday through Friday at 7pm and Saturday at 6pm. Olof Palmes Plats (byat Järntorget). © 031/60-75-75. Tickets 80SEK–110SEK ($8.50–$12). Tram: 1, 3, 4, or 9.

Stadsteatern   This is one of Gothenburg's major theaters, but the plays are performed in Swedish only. Ibsen translated into Swedish can be a bit hard to take, but a musical might still be enjoyable. The season runs from September to May. Performances are usually Tuesday through Friday at 7pm, Saturday at 6pm, and Sunday at 3pm. Götaplatsen. © 031/61-50-50. Tickets 120SEK–160SEK ($13–$17). Bus: 40.

OPERA & BALLET

Göteborgsoperan (Gothenburg Opera House)   The Swedish king opened this elegant new opera house in 1994. It features theater, opera, operettas, musicals, and ballet performances. It's situated right on a dock (a short walk from the Central Station), with views overlooking the water, and there are five bars and a cafe in the lobby. The main entrance (on Östra Hamngatan) leads to a foyer with a view of the harbor; here you'll find the box office and cloakroom. Big productions can be staged on a full scale. You'll have to check to see what performances are scheduled at the time of your visit. Packhuskajen. ℂ **031/10-80-00**, or 031/13-13-00 for ticket information. Ticket prices depend on the event.

CLASSICAL MUSIC

Konserthuset   In the very center of Gothenburg, this is the major performance hall for classical music. In season (Sept–June), world-class performers appear. Götaplatsen. ℂ **031/61-53-10**. Tickets usually 150SEK–450SEK ($16–$48), but can range lower or higher depending on the performance. Bus: 40.

THE CLUB & MUSIC SCENE
NIGHTCLUBS

Bubbles   In stark contrast to the sprawling size of the Trädgoårn (see below), this nightclub and cocktail lounge is small-scale and intimate. Outfitted in pale colors, and attracting a clientele over 30, it's the most popular late-night venue in Gothenburg, sometimes attracting workers from restaurants around town, who relax and chitchat here after a hard night's work in the restaurant trade. There's a small dance floor, but most visitors ignore it in favor of mingling at the bar instead. Open daily from 8pm to 5am. Avenyn 8. ℂ **031/10-58-20**. Tram: 1, 4, 5, or 6.

Oakley's Country Club   This restaurant with the eye-catching scarlet facade opened in a former fire station in 1998. It's a tongue-in-cheek parody of what you might expect in the Nevada deserts. At midday, it looks something like an upscale luncheonette in a state west of the Rocky Mountains, with service by female students from a nearby ballet academy dressed as Gold Rush–era cancan ingenues.

   Beginning at 9pm, things get lively, with singers reminiscent of Dale Evans, cancan dancers who belt out excerpts from *Annie Get Your Gun,* and a scantily clad trapeze artist who advises men in the audience how to lasso a bedmate or a bride. Expect a sense of camp and an interpretation of the American vernacular style that you might never, ever have expected east of the Atlantic. Menu items include sophisticated interpretations of New American cuisine, including chile-roasted crayfish, Mississippi alligator ribs, Caesar salads studded with crayfish, "Annie's Blackened Salmon," "Buffalo Bill's Rib-eye Steak," and the restaurant's own version of spare ribs. A particularly elegant room offers cigars and brandies. Main courses cost 140SEK to 210SEK ($15–$22). The club is open daily from 11am to 2pm and 6 to 11pm. Tredje Långgatan 16. ℂ **031/42-60-80**. Reservations recommended. Tram: 1, 3, 4, or 9.

Park Lane Nightclub   The leading nightclub on Sweden's west coast, this dinner-dance room sometimes features international stars. Past performers have included Marlene Dietrich, Eartha Kitt, and Prince. The dance floor is usually packed. Light suppers, such as crab salad or toasted sandwiches, are served. Beer begins at 50SEK ($5.30). It's open Wednesday through Sunday from 11pm to 3am. In the Radisson SAS Park Avenue Hotel, Kungsportsavenyn 36–38. ℂ **031/20-60-58**. Cover 80SEK ($8.50); no cover for hotel guests. Tram: 1, 4, 5, or 6. Bus: 40.

Trädgoårn   This is the largest and most comprehensive nightspot in Gothenburg, with a cavernous two-story interior that echoes on weekends with the simultaneous sounds of a restaurant, a cabaret, and a dance club. This cosmopolitan and urbane venue has at one time or another welcomed virtually every night-clubber in town. No one under 25 is admitted. Restaurant hours are Monday through Friday from 11:30am to 3:30pm and Wednesday through Saturday from 6 to 10:30pm. Cabaret hours are Wednesday through Saturday beginning at 8pm.

Dance club hours are Friday through Saturday from 11pm to 5am. Allegaten 8. © 031/10-20-80. Cover charge for dance club 100SEK ($11); 2-course dinner and access to cabaret show 530SEK ($56); main courses in restaurant 175SEK–250SEK ($19–$27). Tram: 1, 3, or 5.

A DANCE CLUB
Valand   This combination restaurant and dance club, one floor above street level in the center of town, is the biggest and most famous in Gothenburg. As you enter, there's a restaurant on your left and a large bar and dance floor on your right. There's also a small-stakes casino with blackjack and roulette. You must be 23 to enter. The club is open Thursday through Saturday from 8pm to 3am. For more memorable food, head for Lilla London, one floor below (see "Where to Dine," earlier in this chapter). Vasagatan 41. © 031/18-30-93. Cover 83SEK–103SEK ($8.80–$11) for dance club. Tram: 1, 4, 5, or 6. Bus: 40.

GAY GOTHENBURG
Greta   Named in honor of Greta Garbo, whose memorabilia adorns the walls here, this is the leading gay bar and restaurant in Gothenburg, with a clientele that includes all ages and types of gay men and lesbians. Two animated bars, completely independent from the on-site restaurant, know how to "rock and roll." Decor is a mixture of old-fashioned kitsch and new wave, juxtaposed in ways that are almost as interesting as the clientele. Menu items change at least every season, but might include fish and lime soup; lamb filet with mushrooms in a red wine sauce; breast of duck with potato croquettes; or a creamy chicken stew baked in phyllo pastry. Main courses run 85SEK to 169SEK ($9–$18). American Express, MasterCard, and Visa are accepted. It's open Monday through Saturday from 4pm to 3am. Every Friday and Saturday night, the place is transformed into a dance club, from 10pm till 3am. Drottningsgatan 35. © 031/13-69-49. Reservations recommended Fri–Sat. Cover 50SEK ($5.30). Tram: 1, 2, or 3.

Leche   It's tiny and it's open only 1 night a week, but during that brief interlude, it reigns as the premier women's bar of Gothenburg, attracting lesbians of all ages from kilometers around the city limits. Other nights of the week, gay women tend to congregate at Greta (see above). Leche is open only on Saturday from 8pm to 3am. Vallgaten 30. No phone. Cover 60SEK ($6.35). Tram: 1, 3, or 4.

Skåne (Including Helsingborg & Malmö)

In Sweden's southernmost corner, the province of Skåne offers varied scenery, large forests, and many waterways. The sea and the ample, uncrowded beaches are always within reach. Many of the larger towns have a Continental aura, because of the nearness of Denmark and the rest of Europe.

Denmark and the rest of Europe are now easier to reach than ever before. In 2000, the Øresund Fixed Link between Denmark and Sweden was completed and opened to the public. A new artificial island was constructed halfway across the Øresund Sound to connect approximately 3km (2 miles) of immersed railway and motorway tunnels and an 8km (5-mile) bridge. This link between Copenhagen and Malmö benefits culture, education, and research between the two countries, as well as business and transportation. With three million people living within a 50km (31-mile) radius of the link, the region has the largest population concentration in Scandinavia.

Skåne's major urban cities are Malmö, Helsingborg, and the university and cathedral city of Lund. Many summer visitors also seek out the little villages and undiscovered coastal towns.

The topography of the area includes almost every type of Nordic scenery, except fjords and snowcapped Lapp mountains. For decades, poets, authors, and painters have found it inspirational. The tip of the Scandinavian peninsula was where Selma Lagerlöf's *The Wonderful Adventures of Nils* began. The story of the hero, a boy who travels on the back of a wild goose, has been translated into all major languages.

The first settlers were deer hunters and fishers who moved here from southern Europe as the Ice Age ended and the glaciers melted. Over thousands of years, their ancestors—from the Stone Age right to the Viking Age and the early beginnings of Christianity—left many traces. There are no fewer than 300 small medieval parish churches in the province, and all are still in use. Castles and mansions, many constructed 400 or 500 years ago, dot the landscape.

Skåne once belonged to Denmark, but since 1658, it has firmly been part of the Swedish kingdom. The famous Swedish smörgåsbords are served in the province. Skåne is known as the "Swedish Riviera." There are many beaches along its coast for swimming and sunbathing.

Skåne is associated with young Nils's wild goose, but the web-footed, flat-billed, large-bodied bird is actually tame, never traveling far from home—until November 10, that is. On that date Scanians celebrate their (almost) sacred bird with a gargantuan dinner, enjoyed by all but the bird.

Skåne is easy to reach. You have a wide choice of conventional flights, either to Malmö's Sturup Airport, or to the Copenhagen airport, from which there are frequent hovercraft connections directly to the center of Malmö. Hovercraft also run between the

Skåne

Copenhagen airport and downtown Copenhagen and Malmö. Every 15 or 20 minutes, day or night, connections are possible by car ferry from Helsingør, Denmark, to Helsingborg, Sweden.

If you're traveling by car, there are ferry routes from Denmark, Germany, and Poland.

Our driving tour of Skåne begins at Båstad. If you're coming south from Gothenburg, our last stopover, you can take the E6. If you're motoring from Malmö, follow the E6 north to the Båstad turnoff. The resort lies 6.5km (4 miles) off this main road.

1 Båstad ✶

179km (111 miles) SW of Gothenburg, 105km (65 miles) N of Malmö

Jutting out on a peninsula, surrounded by hills and a beautiful landscape, Båstad is the most fashionable international seaside resort in Sweden.

All the famous international tennis stars have played on the courts at Båstad, which hosts the annual Swedish Open. Swedish players, inspired by the playing of Björn Borg, do much of their training here. There are more than 50 courts in the district, in addition to the renowned Drivan Sports Centre. Tennis was played here as early as the 1880s and became firmly established in the 1920s. King Gustaf V took part in these championships from 1930 to 1945, under the pseudonym of "Mr. G.," and Ludvig Nobel guaranteed financial backing for international tournaments.

Golf has established itself as much as tennis, and the Bjäre peninsula offers a choice of five courses. In 1929 Nobel purchased land at Boarp for Båstad's first golf course. The bay provides opportunities for regattas and different kinds of boating. Windsurfing is popular, as is skin diving. In summer, sea bathing is also popular along the coast.

The Bjäre peninsula, a traditional farming area, is known for its early potatoes, which are in demand all over Sweden. They appear on the midsummer table with a selection of pickled herring.

ESSENTIALS

GETTING THERE   From Gothenburg by car, continue southwest along the E6 until you see the turnoff for Båstad. If you're not driving, you'll find speedy trains running frequently throughout the day between Gothenburg and Malmö, with a stopover at Båstad. Six buses a day also make the 1-hour trip from Helsingborg.

VISITOR INFORMATION   For tourist information, **Båstad Turism,** Köpmangatan 1, Stortorget (© **0431/750-45;** www.bastad.se), is open from June 20 to August 7, Sunday through Friday from 10am to 6pm, Saturday from 10am to 4pm; off season, Monday through Saturday from 10am to 2pm. You can book private rooms here—rates start at 150SEK ($17) per person—or rent bikes for 60SEK ($6.60) per day. The staff can also provide information about booking tennis courts, renting sports equipment, or reserving a round of golf.

GETTING AROUND   You don't need to rely on buses once you're in Båstad, as you can walk around the center of town in about 30 minutes. To reach the harbor and the beach, follow Tennisvägen off Köpmansgatan through a residential district until you come to Strandpromenaden. To your immediate west, you'll see a number of old bathhouses now converted to restaurants and bars. If you don't have a car, you'll need a bus to reach the Bjäre peninsula. From Båstad, bus no. 525 leaves every other hour Monday through Saturday only, and runs through the center of the peninsula. If it's a Sunday, you'll have to rely on a taxi. Call © **0431/696-66** for service.

EXPLORING THE AREA

The most interesting sights are not in Båstad itself but on the Bjäre peninsula (see below). However, before leaving the resort, you may want to call on **Mariakyrkan,** Köpmansgatan (© **0431/750-45**). One of Skåne's landmark churches, Saint Mary's was built between 1450 and 1500. Its tower was restored in 1986, and the entire interior renewed in 1967. It holds many treasures, including a sculpture of Saint Mary and Christ from about 1460 (found in the sanctuary). The altarpiece is from 1775, but the crucifix is medieval. The trumpet-angel above the altar is from about the same time as the altarpiece. The pulpit is from 1836, its hourglass from 1791. In the northern nave is a church clock from 1802 and fresco paintings. The church is open daily from 9am to 4pm.

Båstad is noted for one of southern Sweden's principal attractions, the **Norrvikens Trädgårdar (Norrviken Gardens)** ⭐⭐, Kattvik (© **0431/36-90-40**), 2.5km (1½ miles) west of the resort's center. Founded in 1906 by Rudolf Abelin, these gardens have been expanded and maintained according to his plans, and they embrace a number of styles. One garden is in Italian baroque style, with a pond framed by pyramid-shaped boxwood hedges and tall cypresses. The Renaissance Garden, with its boxwood patterns, is reminiscent of the tapestry art of 15th-century Italy, and there is a flower garden with bulb flowers competing with annuals. There are also a Japanese Garden, an Oriental Terrace, a Rhododendron Dell, a Romantic Garden, and a Water Garden.

At Villa Abelin, designed by the garden's founder, wisteria climbs the wall and is in bloom twice a year. The villa houses shops, exhibits, and information facilities. There are also a restaurant and cafeteria on the grounds.

The gardens may be viewed from May 1 to September 6, daily from 10am to 5pm. Admission is 60SEK ($6.35) for adults, free for children under 12.

THE BJÅRE PENINSULA 🕱🕱

After exploring the gardens, you may want to turn your attention to the **Bjåre Peninsula.** It's the highlight of the entire region because of its widely varied scenery, ranging from farm fields to cliff formations. Before exploring it in depth, it's best to pick up a detailed map from the Båstad tourist office (see "Visitor Information," above).

The peninsula is devoted to sports, including windsurfing, tennis, golf, hiking, and mountain biking. It has white sandy beaches along the sea, riding paths, and cycle roads set aside for these activities. Starting in early spring you can play golf at five different 18-hole courses; the Båstad tourist office can supply information.

If you don't have a car, you can take bus. no. 525, which leaves Båstad every hour Monday through Saturday. It traverses the center of the peninsula.

The **Skaneleden walking trail** runs the entire perimeter of the peninsula and is also great for cycling. However, the terrain is quite hilly in places, so you need to be in fabulous shape.

On the peninsula's western coast is the sleepy village of **Torekov,** a short drive from Kattvik. Here you'll find a beach and pier where early-morning swimmers can be seen walking down to the sea in bathing gowns and sandals.

From Torekov, you can set out to explore **Hallands Väderö,** an island off Sweden's west coast. Old wooden fishing boats make the 15-minute crossing on the hour from June to August. From September to May, departures are every 2 hours. The cost is 70SEK ($7.40) round-trip. The last departure is at 4:30pm daily. For more information, call **Bokningstelefon Halmstead** (© **035/10-50-70**).

The Bjåre peninsula has one of Sweden's few remaining **seal colonies.** "Seal safaris" come here to view (but not disturb) these animals. In addition to seals, the island is noted for its rich bird life, including guillemots, cormorants, eiders, and gulls.

OUTDOOR ACTIVITIES

GOLF   The region around Båstad is home to five separate golf courses. Two of them allow nonmembers to use the course during short-term visits to the region. To reach the **Båstad Golf Club,** Boarp, S-269 21 Båstad (© **0431/731-36**), follow the signs to Boarp and drive 4km (2½ miles) south of town. To reach the **Bjåre Golf Club,** Solomonhög 3086, S-269 93 Båstad (© **0431/36-10-53**), follow the signs to Förslöv, about 10km (6 miles) east of Båstad. Both charge greens fees of 350SEK to 400SEK ($37–$42) for 18 holes, depending on the season, and both have pro shops that rent clubs. Advance reservations for tee-off times are essential.

TENNIS   Båstad is inextricably linked to the game of tennis, which it celebrates with fervor thanks to its role as the longtime home of the Swedish Open tennis tournament. There are 14 outdoor courts (available only Apr–Sept) and six indoor courts (available year-round) at the **Drivan Tennis Center,** Drivangårdens Vandrarhem (© **0431/685-00**). About 1km (½ mile) north of Båstad's town center, it employs a corps of tennis professionals and teachers, who give lessons for 250SEK ($27) per hour. Indoor and outdoor courts rent for 80SEK to 110SEK ($8.50–$12) per hour, depending on the time of day or night you arrive, and whether the courts need to be illuminated.

To immerse yourself in the spirit of the game, consider renting a bunk bed in the establishment's youth hostel, priced at 110SEK to 130SEK ($12–$14) per person. The functional, barracks-style rooms hold two to four occupants, and are often the temporary home of members of tennis teams from throughout Scandinavia. Originally established in 1929, this club built most of the tennis courts you see today around 1980.

WHERE TO STAY

Hotel Buena Vista ✶✶   The most historic and glamorous hotel in town is a venerable white-walled mansion perched on a hilltop, a 3-minute walk uphill from the center of town. It was built in 1906 by John Francis Andersson, a late-19th-century emigrant from Småland who moved to Britain and then to the United States. In the process, he made a respectable income as the general contractor for the construction of bridges spanning the Thames and many of the streams and rivers of the New World. Later, he invested $5,000 with a then-unknown automaker named Henry Ford. When that investment evolved into a massive fortune, he opted to retire in Sweden, and built this elegant Italianate mansion with some of the profits.

Today, it's a site for small-scale conventions, wedding parties (there's a chapel with a vaulted ceiling on the premises), honeymooners, and regular tourists as well as sightseers. Public areas have been restored to some of their original Edwardian-era opulence, with dark colors and lots of varnished hardwoods. Guest rooms, however, are relatively contemporary, and in many cases, are a bit cramped. Bathrooms equipped with shower units are tiled, relatively small, and in many ways equivalent to what you'd expect in a modern roadside hotel.

Tarravägen 5, S-269 35 Båstad. ✆ 0431/760-00. Fax 0431/791-00. 24 units. Mon–Thurs 975SEK ($103) double; Fri–Sun 895SEK ($95) double; 1,600SEK ($170) suite. Rates include breakfast. AE, DC, MC, V. Free parking. Bus: 226. **Amenities:** Restaurant; bar. *In room:* TV, hair dryer.

Hotel-Pension Enehall *Value*   On the slope of a Hallandsåsen mountain, only a few minutes' walk from the sea, this cozy, intimate place caters mainly to Swedish families and some occasional Danes and Germans. There are many personal touches, and the rooms, although small, are adequately equipped with good beds and small bathrooms. The food is tasty, and the service polite and efficient.

Stationsterrassen 10, S-269 36 Båstad. ✆ **0431/750-15.** Fax 0431/750-14. www.enehall.se. 55 units. 750SEK–800SEK ($80–$85) double. Half board 480SEK ($51) per person. Rates include breakfast. AE, DC, MC, V. Free parking. Bus: 513. **Amenities:** Restaurant; bar; laundry/dry cleaning. *In room:* TV.

Hotel Riviera ✶   A favorite venue for conferences, this is one of the better hotels in the area. It takes on a somewhat festive air in summer. By the sea, less than 1km (½ mile) from the railroad station and about 3km (2 miles) east of the town center, it offers views from many of its modern rooms and its 300-seat restaurant. Guest rooms and bathrooms with shower stalls are small but comfortably furnished, with good beds and excellent housekeeping. Everything is functionally furnished, but in good taste. Many guests sit out in the gardens or on the terrace. The excellent kitchen serves a combination of Scandinavian and international food. Dinners with dancing to a live band are often scheduled in season.

Rivieravägen, S-269 39 Båstad. ✆ **0431/36-90-50.** Fax 0431/761-00. www.hotelriviera.nu. 50 units. 740SEK ($78) double. Rates include breakfast. MC, V. Closed Sept–Apr. Free parking. Bus: 513. **Amenities:** Restaurant; bar; 2 tennis courts. *In room:* TV.

Hotel Skansen 🏰🏰 Although it isn't as expensive as some of the other hotels within the chain that controls it, the Hotel Skansen *is* associated with some of Sweden's most opulent and prestigious lodgings, including the Grand Hotel in Stockholm. It's also the most visible tennis venue in Sweden—its eight tennis courts are the home every year to the annual Swedish Open. As such, it has housed, usually more than once, the most famous tennis stars in Sweden, including Björn Borg, Anders Järryd, and Henrik Holm. Built as a grain warehouse in 1877, it's a few minutes' walk from the marina and 45m (150 ft.) from the beach. The hotel incorporates its original building (which is today listed as a Swedish national monument) along with four more recent structures that surround eight tennis courts, some of which are equipped with stadiums for tennis competitions. The interior has a beamed roof, pillars, and views over the sea. Renovated in 1997, guest rooms are airy, elegant, and traditionally outfitted with conservative furniture, including good beds, and ample private bathrooms with shower units.

Kyrkogatan 2, S-269 21 Båstad. ⓒ 0431/55-81-00. Fax 0431/55-81-10. www.hotelskansen.se. 112 units. 910SEK–1,560SEK ($96–$165) double; 3,450SEK–4,100SEK ($366–$435) suite. Rates include breakfast. AE, DC, MC, V. Free parking. Bus: 513; 5-min. walk. **Amenities:** Restaurant; cafe; bar; pool; 4 tennis courts; fitness center; sauna. *In room:* TV, minibar, hair dryer, safe.

WHERE TO DINE

The hotels listed above all have good restaurants, although you should call in advance for a reservation. If you're just passing through, consider dropping in at the **Solbackens Café & Wåffelbruk,** Italienska vägen (ⓒ **0431/702-00**). If the weather is fair, opt for a table on the terrace overlooking the water. This cafe is locally famous, and has been known for serving Swedish waffles and other delights since 1907.

Centrecourten SWEDISH/INTERNATIONAL In a town as obsessed with tennis as Båstad, you'd expect at least one restaurant to be outfitted in a tennis-lovers' theme. In this case, it consists of a cozy and small-scale dining room with photos of such stars as Björn Borg, a scattering of trophies, and old-fashioned tennis memorabilia. Menu items include fresh fish such as mussels, lemon sole, and cod; breast of duck with bacon-flavored purée of potatoes; and brisket of beef with chanterelles and shallots. The ingredients are fresh and the flavors are often enticing, especially in the seafood selections.

Köpmansgatan 70b. ⓒ 0431/752-75. Reservations recommended. Main courses 65SEK–145SEK ($6.90–$15); pizzas 55SEK–70SEK ($5.85–$7.40); .AE, M, V. Mon–Thurs 4–10pm; Fri 4–11:30pm; Sat noon–10:30pm; Sun noon–10pm.

Swenson's Krog 🏰 *(Finds* SWEDISH One of the most consistently popular restaurants in Båstad lies in the satellite village of Torekov (pop. 300), about 3km (2 miles) west of the center of Båstad. Its core is an ocher-colored, wooden fisherman's cottage built at least a century ago; it features a blue interior with a dignified and formal—but unpretentious—ambience. A newer section—a high-ceilinged, big-windowed affair whose design was inspired by a greenhouse—sprawls to one side, offering a setting in a high-ceilinged room that is a bit less formal. The menu focuses on traditional Swedish food whose recipes are remembered with fondness by many older residents of the town, and include a creamy tomato-based version of fish soup made entirely with local sea fish; cod cooked in a salt crust and served with buttered vegetables; well-prepared *frikadeller* (meatballs), and various cuts of duck, veal, and fish. There's a big bar area set midway between the old and new sections of this place which sometimes draws a crowd that has no intention of doing anything but drinking. Katarina and Jarl Toremalm are the hardworking owners of this place.

Pål Romares Gata 2. ℡ **0431/36-45-90.** Reservations recommended. Main courses 129SEK–250SEK ($14–$27); set menus 380SEK–495SEK ($40–$52). AE, DC, MC, V. May–Oct daily noon–9pm; Nov–Apr Fri–Sat dinner only, 6–9pm.

BÅSTAD AFTER DARK

The best choice is **Pepe's Bodega,** Warmbadhuset Hamnen (℡ **0431/36-91-69**), where there's spicy food, colorful cocktails, and a spirited atmosphere. It's open Wednesday through Sunday, from 5 till 11pm for food, and till 1am for drinks.

2 Helsingborg ⟨★⟩

230km (143 miles) S of Gothenburg, 559km (347 miles) SW of Stockholm, 63km (39 miles) N of Malmö

This industrial city and major port is situated at the narrowest point of the Øresund (Öresund in Swedish) Sound, about 5km (3 miles) across the water that separates Sweden and Denmark. Many people who travel from Copenhagen to visit Kronborg Castle (in Helsingør, Denmark) take a 25-minute ferry ride across the sound (leaving every 20 min.) for a look at Sweden.

What they see isn't "Sweden," but a modern city with an ancient history. Helsingborg and Helsingør jointly controlled shipping along the sound in the Middle Ages. Helsingborg is mentioned in the 10th-century *Nial-Saga,* and documents show that there was a town here in 1085. The city now has more than 100,000 inhabitants and the second-busiest harbor in the country. This is the home of Sweden's first pedestrian streets, and it has long promenades along the shore of the sound.

Helsingborg (Hålsingborg) recently rebuilt large, vacant-looking sections of its inner city into one of the most innovative urban centers in Sweden. The centerpiece of these restorations lies beside the harbor, and includes an all-glass building, the Knutpunkten, on Järnvägsgatan. It contains the railroad, bus, and ferryboat terminals; an array of shops similar to those in a North American mall; and a heliport. Many visitors say that the railroad station, which is flooded with sunlight, is the cleanest, brightest, and most memorable they've ever seen. In addition, many dozens of trees and shrubs have transformed the center into something like a verdant park, with trees between the lanes of traffic.

ESSENTIALS

GETTING THERE   From Malmö, drive north on the E6. The trip takes 1 hour. From Gothenburg, drive south on the E6 for 2½ hours. From Stockholm, take the E4 south for 7½ hours until you reach Helsingborg. If you're not driving, there are many other ways to reach Helsingborg.

Ferries from Helsingør, Denmark, leave the Danish harbor every 20 minutes day or night (trip time 25 min.). For information about ferryboats in Helsingborg, call ℡ **042/18-61-00;** for information on the Danish side, call ℡ **33-15-15-15.** Pedestrians pay 23SEK ($2.45) each way or 40SEK ($4.25) round-trip. The regular round-trip cost of the ferryboat price for a car with up to five passengers is 510SEK ($54) Sunday through Wednesday, 445SEK ($47) Thursday through Saturday. A round-trip journey commencing and ending on the same day costs 295SEK ($31).

Ångelholm–Helsingborg airport lies 30 minutes from the center of the city, with regular connections to Stockholm's Arlanda airport. There are between seven and nine SAS flights per day from Stockholm's Arlanda airport (trip time 1 hr.). For SAS reservations, call ☎ **0431/55-80-10.**

Trains run hourly during the day between Helsingborg and Malmö. The trip takes 50 minutes. Trains arrive from and return to Stockholm twice a day; it's a 7-hour trip. Trains between Gothenburg and Helsingborg depart and arrive twice a day (trip time 2½ hr.). Call ☎ **042/10-43-50** for information.

Three buses a day link Malmö and Helsingborg. Two leave in the morning, and one in the afternoon. The trip takes 1 hour, 10 minutes. Buses leave twice a day for the 3¼-hour trip from Gothenburg. Buses to and from Stockholm leave once a day (trip time 10 hr.).

VISITOR INFORMATION   The tourist office, **Helsingborg Turistbyrå,** Knutpunkten (☎ **042/10-43-50;** www.helsingborg.se), is open from May to September 15, Monday through Friday from 9am to 8pm, and Saturday and Sunday from 9am to 5pm; from September 16 to April, Monday through Friday from 9am to 6pm, and Saturday from 10am to 2pm.

GETTING AROUND   Most of Helsingborg's sights are within walking distance. But if your legs are tired or the weather is less than perfect, you can always take a city bus, numbered 1 to 7. Most buses on their way north pass the Town Hall. Those heading south go by Knutpunkten. Tickets are valid for transfer to another city bus line as long as you transfer within 3 hours from the time the ticket was stamped. Tickets bought on board cost 14SEK ($1.50). For information, call ☎ **042/10-43-50.**

SEEING THE SIGHTS

Built in 1897, the **Town Hall (Rådhuset),** Drottninggatan 7 (☎ **042/10-50-00**), has handsome stained-glass windows depicting scenes from the town's history. Two memorial stones, presented by the Danes and the Norwegians to the Swedes for their assistance during the World War II, stand outside. There is also a sculpture relief representing the arrival of Danish refugees.

In the main town square, the Stortorget, is a monument commemorating General Stenbock's victory at the Battle of Helsingborg (1710) between Sweden and Denmark.

Fredriksdal Open-Air Museum and Botanical Garden 𝄢𝄢   This is among the largest and most complete open-air museums in Sweden, covering some 28 hectares (70 acres) of rolling land. (Skansen, in Stockholm, is larger, but few others are.) The park, a 20-minute walk east of the town center, was built around a manor house constructed in 1787. The rose garden contains about 450 different varieties, all part of one of Sweden's most remarkable botanical gardens. An open-air theater was established in 1927. You can also wander through the French Park and the English Park.

Hävertgatan (at Fredriksdal). ☎ **042/10-45-40.** Admission 40SEK ($4.25) adults, free for children 9 and under. Park, June–Aug daily 10am–8pm; Sept–May daily 11am–4pm. Manor, Oct–May daily 10am–3pm. Bus: 2, 3, or 250.

Kärnan (The Keep) 𝄢   One of the most important medieval monuments in Sweden, and the symbol of Helsingborg, this monument rises from the crest of a rocky ridge in the town center. The origins of this 30m (100-ft.) tall square tower—built in the 11th century—are mysterious; it adopted its present form in the 1300s. Its name translates as "the core," and it was so labeled because it was originally conceived as the most central tower (and prison) of the once-mighty Helsingborg Castle. The thickness of its walls (about 4m/14 ft.) makes it the most solidly constructed building in the region. An object of bloody fighting between the Swedes and the Danes for generations, the castle and its fortifications were demolished in 1679. Of the once-mighty fortress, only Kärnan (which was restored and rebuilt in 1894) remains.

The easiest way to reach Kärnan is to board the elevator, which departs from the *terrasen* (terrace) of the town's main street, the Stortorget. For 10SEK ($1.05) per person, you'll be carried up the rocky hillside to the base of the tower. Many visitors, however, avoid the elevator, preferring instead to climb a winding set of flower-flanked steps as part of their exploration of the city. Once inside the tower, an additional 147 steps lie between you and one of the most sweeping views in the district.

Kärngränden (off the Stortorget). ℂ 042/10-59-91. Admission 15SEK ($1.60) adults, 5SEK (55¢) children. Apr–May Tues–Sun 9am–4pm; June–Aug Tues–Sun 11am–7pm; Sept daily 9am–3pm; Oct–Mar Tues–Sun 11am–3pm. Bus: 1 or 6.

Mariakyrkan (Church of St. Mary)   A short walk from the harbor, this 13th-century church was substantially rebuilt in the 15th century in a Danish Gothic style, evoking a basilica. The facade is plain, but the interior is striking, especially the medieval altarpiece and its intricately carved pulpit. If the sun is shining, the modern stained-glass windows are jewel-like.

Södra Storgaten. ℂ 042/37-28-30. Free admission. June–Aug Mon–Sat 8am–6pm, Sun 9am–6pm; Sept–May Mon–Sat 8am–4pm, Sun 9am–4pm. Bus: 1 or 6.

Sofiero Slott 🏰🏰   One of the most famous buildings in southern Sweden, lying about 5km (3 miles) north of Helsingborg, this was constructed in 1864 and 1865 as the summer residence of King Oscar II and his wife, Sofia. In 1905 it was bequeathed to their grandson, Gustav Adolph, and his wife, Margareta, who enlarged the site and created some of the most memorable gardens in the country. Their interests supposedly sparked a nationwide interest in landscape architecture that's stronger than ever throughout Sweden today. After his coronation, King Gustav Adolph spent his last days here, eventually bequeathing Sofiero as a gift to the city of Helsingborg in 1973. In 1993 many of the original gardens were re-created in memory of their designer, Queen Margareta. Today the most-visited sites include the 1865 castle, which contains a cafe and restaurant; the rose garden; and the Rhododendron Ravine, which holds an estimated 10,000 rhododendrons that reach their full glory in early June.

Sofierovägen. ℂ 042/13-74-00. Admission 60SEK ($6.35) adults, free for children. Daily 10am–6pm. Closed Oct to mid-Apr. Bus: 219 or 221.

SHOPPING

Northwest Scania (English for Skåne) is known as the pottery district of Sweden. The region's first pottery factory was founded in 1748 in Bosarp, 15km (9¼ miles) east of Helsingborg. The city of **Helsingborg** got its first factory in 1768 and another began manufacturing in 1832. Since then, the traditional pottery industry has been developed and revitalized, making the area famous far beyond the borders of Sweden.

At a point about 7km (4½ miles) south of Helsingborg, you can visit **Raus Stenkarlsfabrik,** less than 1km (½ mile) east of Råå (look for signs along Landskronavagen). One of the leading potteries of the area, it is open from May to December, Monday through Friday from 10am to 6pm, Saturday from 10am to 4pm; off season, from January to April, Saturday from 10am to 6pm. Call ℂ 042/ 26-01-30 for more information.

In Gantofta, about 10km (6¼ miles) southeast of Helsingborg, lies **Jie-Keramik** (℗ **042/990-31**). It's one of Scandinavia's leading manufacturers of hand-painted decorative ceramics, wall reliefs, wall clocks, figures, and other such items. You can visit the factory shop or patronize a cafe on-site. From Helsingborg, drive south to Råå, and then follow the signs to Gantofta. You can also take bus no. 209 from Knutpunkten in the center of Helsingborg. From June to August, the outlet is open Monday through Friday from 8am to 6pm, Saturday from 10am to 4pm, and Sunday from 11am to 5pm. Off-season hours are Monday through Friday from 10am to 5pm, Saturday from 10am to 4pm, and Sunday from noon to 4pm.

Höganäs, 20km (13 miles) north of Helsingborg, is home to two famous stoneware factories. **Höganäs Saltglaserat** (℗ **042/33-83-33**) has been manufacturing salt-glazed stoneware since 1835. Salt-glazed Höganäs jars with an anchor symbol are considered their classic pieces. Everything is made by hand and fired in coal-burning circular kilns that date from around the beginning of the 20th century. The shop here is within the factory, so you can see the throwers in action and go inside the old kilns. Hours are Monday through Friday from 9am to 4pm; from June to August and during December, it's also open Saturday from 10am to 1pm.

The other outlet, **Höganäs Keramik** (℗ **042/33-20-75**), is Scandinavia's largest stoneware manufacturer. In the Factory Shop, inaugurated in 1994, flawed goods from both Höganäs Keramik and Boda Nova are on sale at bargain prices. This outlet is open from May to August, Monday through Friday from 9am to 6pm, Saturday and Sunday from 10am to 5pm. Off-season hours are Monday through Friday from 10am to 6pm, Saturday from 10am to 4pm, and Sunday from 11am to 4pm.

Motorists can also visit **Gröna Gården,** Välluvsvågen 34, in Påarp (℗ **042/22-71-70**), southeast of Helsingborg. Head toward Malmö, but exit at Barslov toward Påarp-Välluv. The outlet offers many beautiful handicrafts in ceramic, glass, birch bark, forged metal, and wood. Hand-woven fabrics, baskets, candles, wooden toys, and handmade jewelry are just some of the merchandise also on sale. Hours are Tuesday through Friday from 1 to 6pm, Saturday from 10am to 1pm. In November and December, it's also open Sunday from 1 to 4pm.

In the center of Helsingborg, you'll find a number of shopping possibilities, including **Väla Centrum,** which is one of the largest shopping centers in Scandinavia. To reach it, follow Hälsovågen and Ångelholmsvägen north about 6km (3½ miles)—it's signposted—or else take bus no. 202 from Knutpunkten. Seemingly everything is here under one roof, including two large department stores and some 42 specialty shops, selling everything from shoes and clothing to tropical fish.

The best bookstore in town is **Bokman,** Järnvägsgatan 3 (℗ **042/13-75-75**), with many English-language editions. The best center for quality glass is **Duka Carl Anders,** Södergatan 22 (℗ **042/24-27-00**), which carries the works of such prestigious manufacturers as Kosta Boda and Orrefors.

WHERE TO STAY
EXPENSIVE
Radisson SAS Grand Hotel Helsingborg ★★★   Helsingborg's grandest hotel, an imposing brick monument built in 1926, underwent a radical upgrade in 1996. It's now one of the most visible Swedish hotels in the Radisson SAS chain, and one of the most appealing hotels in southern Sweden. It combines

high-ceilinged, richly paneled public areas and spacious, well-accessorized guest rooms with elaborate ceiling moldings, old-world decorative touches, and lots of modern comforts and conveniences. The newly renovated rooms have ample bathrooms, with shower-tub combinations. Some rooms are equipped with facilities for people with disabilities; there are also nonsmoking rooms.

Stortorget 8–12, Box 1104, S-251 11 Helsingborg. © **800/333-3333** in the U.S., or 042/38-04-00. Fax 042/ 38-04-04. www.radissonsas.com. 117 units. Mid-June to Aug and Fri–Sun year-round 850SEK–975SEK ($90–$103) double, 1,160SEK–2,200SEK ($123–$233) suite. Rest of year 1,595SEK ($169) double, 1,800SEK–2,700SEK ($191–$286) suite. Rates include breakfast. AE, DC, MC, V. Parking 150SEK ($16). Bus: 7B or 1A. **Amenities:** Restaurant; bar; sauna; room service; laundry/dry cleaning. *In room:* TV, minibar, hair dryer.

MODERATE

Hotel Helsingborg ⭐ Of the three hotels that lie along a grand avenue, this one is closest to the city's medieval tourist attraction, the Kärnan. Dating from 1901, it has a heroic neoclassical frieze and three copper-sheathed towers, and occupies four floors of what used to be a bank headquarters. The high-ceilinged rooms are pleasantly modernized and flooded with sunlight. They retain a certain *Jugendstil* (Art Nouveau) look, with strong colors and many decorative touches. All rooms were upgraded and renovated in the early 1990s, and feature good beds and functional bathrooms equipped with shower-tub combinations.

Stortorget 20, S-252 23 Helsingborg. © 042/37-18-00. Fax 042/37-18-50. www.hkchotels.se. 56 units. 845SEK–1,495SEK ($90–$158) double; 1,100SEK–1,800SEK ($117–$191) suite. Rates include breakfast. AE, DC, MC, V. Parking 90SEK ($9.55). Bus: 7A, 7B, 1A, or 1B. **Amenities:** Bar; sauna; laundry/dry cleaning. *In room:* TV, hair dryer.

Hotel Mollberg Hotel Mollberg is arguably Sweden's oldest continuously operated hotel and restaurant. Although a tavern has stood on this site since the 14th century, most of the building was constructed in 1802 by the establishment's namesake, Peter Mollberg. Its elaborate wedding-cake exterior and high-ceilinged interior are its hallmarks. A major renovation was carried out in 1986, with several minor restorations throughout the 1990s. Its first-class rooms are equipped with beautifully maintained bathrooms with shower-tub combinations.

Stortorget 18, S-251 10 Helsingborg. © **800/528-1234** in the U.S., or 042/12-02-70. Fax 042/14-96-18. www.hotelmollberg.se. 100 units. 790SEK–1,150SEK ($84–$122) double; 1,300SEK–2,200SEK ($138–$233) suite. Rates include breakfast. AE, DC, MC, V. Parking 85SEK ($9). Bus: 7A, 7B, 1A, or 1B. **Amenities:** Restaurant; bar; sauna; room service; laundry/dry cleaning. *In room:* TV, minibar, hair dryer.

Hotel Nouveau ⭐ *(Finds)* Once a somewhat nondescript and outmoded hotel from the 1960s, the Hotel Nouveau was radically reconfigured and upgraded in 1996. The result is a tastefully decorated building built of ocher brick and touches of marble. The decor throughout draws on upscale models from England and France, and includes chintz curtains, varnished mahogany—often with wood inlays—and warm colors inspired by autumn. Rooms are nice and cozy—not particularly large, but well maintained—with tasteful fabrics, frequently renewed linen, and small but adequate bathrooms equipped with shower units. As a thoughtful touch, a fresh flower is often placed on your pillow at night.

Gasverksgatan 11, S-250 02 Helsingborg. © 042/18-53-90. Fax 042/14-08-85. www.nouveauhotel.se. 79 units. Mid-June to mid-Aug and Fri–Sat year-round 845SEK ($90) double; rest of year 1,345SEK ($143) double; 1,145SEK–1,995SEK ($121–$211) suite year-round. AE, DC, MC, V. Free parking. Bus: 7A or 1A. **Amenities:** Restaurant; bar; pool; sauna; room service; laundry/dry cleaning. *In room:* TV, minibar, hair dryer.

Marina Plaza ⭐⭐ This is Helsingborg's most innovative and most talked-about hotel. It's adjacent to the city's transportation hub, the Knutpunkten. The atrium-style lobby overflows with trees, flowers, rock gardens, and fountains.

Guest rooms line the inner walls of the hotel's atrium and have, as you might expect from the hotel's name, a marine-blue color scheme and nautical accessories. The adequate bathrooms are equipped with shower-tub combinations.

Kungstorget 6, S-251 10 Helsingborg. © **800/528-1234** in the U.S., or 042/19-21-00. Fax 042/14-96-16. www.marinaplaza.elite.se. 190 units. 790SEK–1,450SEK ($84–$154) double; 1,995SEK–2,700SEK ($211–$286) suite. Midsummer discounts available. AE, DC, MC, V. Parking 120SEK ($13). Bus: 41, 42, 43, or 44. **Amenities:** Restaurant; bar; sauna; room service; laundry/dry cleaning. *In room:* TV, minibar, hair dryer, safe.

Scandic Partner Hotel Horisont   Near a park at the edge of the town's commercial center, this hotel with the futuristic facade was erected in 1985. The guest rooms are comfortably conservative, with plush upholstery, soundproof windows, and comfortable mattresses. The bathrooms are well maintained and contain shower-tub combinations. The hotel is about 1km (½ mile) south of the ferryboat terminal.

Gustav Adolfs Gate 47, S-250 02 Helsingborg. © **042/495-21-00.** Fax 042/495-21-11. www.scandic-hotels. com. 164 units. 850SEK–1,524SEK ($90–$162) double; 2,195SEK ($233) suite. Rates include breakfast. AE, DC, MC, V. Free parking. Bus: 7B or 1B. **Amenities:** Restaurant; bar; Jacuzzi; sauna; laundry/dry cleaning. *In room:* TV, hair dryer.

INEXPENSIVE

Hotel Högvakten ★ *(Value*   A 5-minute walk from the terminal for ferryboats headed across the straits to Denmark, this hotel was built as a private town house in 1914. Its well-designed interior underwent a radical renovation in 1996. The recently refurbished rooms are bright and fresh, and generally quite spacious. State-of-the-art bathrooms come with shower-tub combinations and are extremely well maintained. Only breakfast is served, but a member of the polite, attentive staff can direct you to restaurants within easy walking distance from the hotel.

Stortorget 14, P.O. Box 1074, SE-251 10 Helsingborg. © **042/12-03-99.** Fax 042/12-03-99. www.hotel hogvakten.com. 41 units. Mid-June to mid-Aug and Fri–Sun year-round 750SEK ($80) double; rest of year 1,150SEK ($122) double. Rates include breakfast. AE, DC, MC, V. Parking 95SEK ($10). Bus: 7A, 7B, 1A, or 1B. **Amenities:** Lounge; sauna; laundry/dry cleaning. *In room:* TV, hair dryer.

Hotell Linnéa ★ *(Finds*   Conveniently located a few yards from where ferries from Denmark pull in, this is a pleasant, small-scale hotel that occupies a pink Italianate house (ca. 1897). The scale and detailing might remind you of something in a historic neighborhood of New Orleans. Guest rooms are appealingly outfitted, with comfortable beds and high-quality furnishings that include tasteful reproductions of 19th-century antiques. Bathrooms are small but adequate and most come with shower-tub combinations. Only breakfast is served, but many reliable dining choices are close by.

Prästgatan 4, S-252 24 Helsingborg. © **042/21-46-60.** Fax 042/14-16-55. www.hotel-linnea.se. 30 units. July–Aug and Fri–Sat year-round 565SEK–720SEK ($60–$76) double; rest of year 895SEK ($95) double; year-round 1,025SEK–1,350SEK ($109–$143) suite. Rates include breakfast. AE, DC, MC, V. Parking 110SEK ($12). Bus: 7A or 7B. **Amenities:** Bar; laundry/dry cleaning. *In room:* TV.

Hotell Viking   In the center of town, less than 2 blocks north of the Drottninggatan, this hotel looks more historic, more cozy, and a bit more artfully cluttered, than many of its more formal and streamlined competitors. It was built during the late 19th century as a row of shops, in which the owners usually lived upstairs from their businesses. Today, after a radical remodeling in the mid-1990s, you'll find a carefully preserved sense of history; a pale color scheme of grays, beiges, and ochers; and a hands-on management style by the resident owners. Guest rooms are cozy, neat, and functional. Bathrooms are a bit small, but adequately supplied with shower-tub combinations.

Fågelsångsgatan 1, S-252 20 Helsingborg. ② **042/14-44-20.** Fax 042/18-43-20. www.hotellviking.se. 42 units. Mid-June to July and Fri–Sun year-round 845SEK ($90) double; rest of year 1,245SEK ($132) double. Rates include breakfast. AE, DC, MC, V. Free parking. Bus: 7A, 7B, 1A, or 1B. **Amenities:** Bar; laundry/dry cleaning. *In room:* TV, minibar, hair dryer.

WHERE TO DINE
Anna Kock ⭐⭐ SWEDISH   Decorated with modern Swedish watercolors and the kind of antique knickknacks you might find in a Swedish farmstead, this cozy restaurant contains only 11 tidy tables. Opened in 1989, it was named after "Anna the Cook," a locally famous chef to the region's early-20th-century bourgeoisie and aunt of the present owners, Claes and Sussan Andren. Menu items reflect the best of both modern and old-fashioned culinary techniques. Your meal might include Anna's pickled herring served with a Dutch bleu cheese sauce, filet of reindeer on a bed of morels and lingonberry sauce, breast of wild duck with kumquat sauce and rhubarb chutney, fried filet of lemon sole with vermouth sauce and whitebait roe, or sautéed eggplant on a bed of mushrooms with pasta and tomato sauce. Lunches are simpler and less expensive than the carefully executed dinners that are the norm here.

Järnvägsgatan 23. ② **042/18-13-00.** Reservations recommended at lunch, required at dinner. Main courses 125SEK–195SEK ($13–$21); lunch platters 65SEK ($6.90); 2-course fixed-price dinner 185SEK ($20). AE, DC, MC, V. Tues–Fri 11am–2pm and 5:30–10pm; Sat noon–10:30pm. Bus: 3, 5, 7, 9, or 12.

Elinor ⭐ SWEDISH/CONTINENTAL   One of the best restaurants in town, Elinor is in a modest 1920s house on a pleasant walkway in the town center. There's a small bar for aperitifs and a well-upholstered dining room outfitted in soft pastels. The menu depends on seasonal changes. Though less influenced by nouvelle cuisine than it was in the past years, the restaurant offers well-prepared and often tantalizing dishes such as marinated herring with Swedish caviar and an onion and sour-cream sauce; filet of reindeer with fresh morels; a ragout of shrimp with chanterelles; and unusual preparations of crayfish, lobster, turbot, salmon, trout, pheasant, duck, and partridge. Desserts often showcase such semi-wild fruits as lingonberries, cloudberries, and blueberries. Plans are in the works for a less expensive wine bar annex.

Kullagatan 53. ② **042/12-23-30.** Reservations required. Main courses 205SEK–280SEK ($22–$30); fixed-price lunch 240SEK ($25); fixed-price dinner 300SEK–400SEK ($32–$42). AE, DC, MC, V. Mon–Sat 11:30am–2:30pm and 6–10:30pm. Closed July and lunch in early Aug. Bus: 1 or 6.

Gastro ⭐⭐ CONTINENTAL   Set within a modern, big-windowed building of yellow brick overlooking the city's historic core, this is one of the best restaurants in Helsingborg. Within a room decorated with birch veneer, pale tones of monochromatic gray, and a medley of riveting modern paintings, you can enjoy specialties based on all-Swedish ingredients, prepared using culinary techniques inspired by the Mediterranean. Menu items vary with the season, but some of our favorite dishes are pan-fried scallops with sun-dried and marinated tomatoes, served with a terrine of green peas; or a superb fried breast of duckling with onions, carrots, and prosciutto. Expect lots of fresh fish from the straits of Helsingborg and the Baltic, and lots of savoir-faire from the well-versed and attentive staff.

Södra Storg 11–13. ② **042/24-34-70.** Reservations recommended. Main courses 200SEK–275SEK ($21–$29). AE, DC, MC, V. Mon–Sat 7–10pm. Closed July. Bus: 11.

Pälsjö Krog SWEDISH   Set within a 10-minute drive north of the center of Helsingborg, this brightly painted yellow wood-sided building was originally constructed around 1900 as a bathhouse beside the beach. As such, it was filled at the time with cubicles in which sea bathers changed clothes. In the late 1990s, it was transformed into a cozy Swedish restaurant, the kind of place where local families—often with grandmothers in tow—come to enjoy recipes that haven't changed very much since the end of World War II. Within a large dining room painted in tones of pale yellow and decorated with hints of Art Deco, you'll get food items that include grilled pepper-steak, sirloin with béarnaise sauce, poached Swedish salmon with dill sauce, and aromatic local mussels steamed with herbs in white wine. Drinkers and smokers appreciate the cozy aperitif bar near the entrance, where cigars are welcome and the staff can propose a wide assortment of after-dinner cognacs.

Drottinggatan 151. (℃ **042/14-97-30.** Reservations not necessary. Main courses 129SEK–225SEK ($14–$24). AE, DC, MC, V. Daily 11:30am–2:30pm and 6–10pm.

Restaurant Oscar 𝕽𝕽 SEAFOOD/GAME   In the center of town, overlooking a large parking lot near the ferryboat piers, this is Helsingborg's best-known and most frequently recommended seafood restaurant. Decorated like an upscale tavern, it contains nautical antiques that many diners find very appealing. Seafood is impeccably fresh, with a wide array of choices that range from the savory but unpretentious (filet of cod fried in butter with capers, garlic, and boiled potatoes) to the rather grand (butterflied filet of sole flambéed tableside with brandy and served with a ragout of shrimp in lobster sauce). Other options include a worthwhile version of Marseilles bouillabaisse, which must be ordered a full day in advance, and a succulent version of Baltic-style fish stew, which is usually available anytime. Also look for poached filet of sole with a Chablis sauce and whitebait roe, and in the autumn and winter, a roster of well-prepared venison dishes. Before or after your meal, check out the proudly displayed stuffed and mounted 11-pound lobster—a zoological oddity that might remind you of a prop from a grade-B horror flick—that was caught long ago in offshore waters.

Sundstorget 7. (℃ **042/21-25-21.** Reservations recommended. Main courses 78SEK–269SEK ($8.25–$29); fixed-price lunch 64SEK–129SEK ($6.80–$14); fixed-price dinner 300SEK ($32). AE, DC, MC, V. Mon–Fri 11:30am–2pm; Mon–Sat 7:30–10pm. Bus: 7A, 7B, 1, or 6.

HELSINGBORG AFTER DARK

Helsingborg has had its own symphony orchestra since 1912. In 1932, its **Concert Hall (Konserthuset)** opened at Drottinggatan 19 (℃ **042/17-65-00**). One of the finest examples of 1930s Swedish functionalism, the hall is today the venue for performances by the 50-member orchestra. The season opens in the middle of August with a 10-day **Festspel,** a festival with a different theme every year. Tickets are available at the 1817 **Helsingborg Stadsteater (City Theater),** Karl Johans Gata (℃ **042/10-68-10**). The theater is one of the most modern in Europe. Performances, of course, are in Swedish.

Somewhat more attuned to hipsters, with a decor that includes crystal chandeliers and lots of original paintings (which are often rotated with works by other artists), is **Marina Nightclub,** Kungstorget 6, in the Marina Plaza hotel (℃ **042/19-21-00**). It only admits patrons over 23. It's open only Friday and Saturday from 11pm till around 5am.

A cozy, English-inspired pub that draws a busy and sometimes convivial crowd is **Telegrafen,** Norra Storgatan 14 (℃ **042/18-14-50**). Live music is sometimes presented on either of the two levels devoted to drinking, chatting, and flirting.

Jazz enthusiasts might enjoy an evening at one of the largest jazz venues in Sweden, **Jazzklubben,** Nedre Långvinkelsgatan 22 (© **042/18-49-00**). Keynote nights are Wednesday, Friday, and Saturday, when live Dixieland, blues, Celtic ballads, and progressive jazz are featured beginning at around 8:30pm. Most other nights, based on a schedule that varies with the season and the whims of the staff, the place functions as a conventional bar.

3 Malmö ★★

285km (177 miles) S of Gothenburg, 620km (384 miles) SW of Stockholm

The capital of Skåne and Sweden's third-largest city, Malmö is a busy port across the Øresund Sound from Copenhagen. A good base for exploring the ancient castles and manors nearby, Malmö is an old city, dating from the 13th century.

From early days, Malmö (pronounced Mahl-*mer*) has prospered because of its location on a sheltered bay. In the 16th century, when it was the second-largest city in Denmark, it vied with Copenhagen for economic and cultural leadership. Reminders of that age are Malmöhus Castle (see below), the Town Hall, and the Stortorget, plus several homes of rich burghers. Malmö has been a Swedish city since the end of a bloody war in 1658, when the Treaty of Roskilde awarded Sweden the province of Skåne.

ESSENTIALS

GETTING THERE   Motorists coming from Copenhagen can take the new Øresund Bridge. From Helsingborg, motorists can drive southeast along Route 110, directly into the center of Malmö. Malmö's airport (© **040/613-11-00**) is at Sturup, 30km (19 miles) southeast of the city; it receives flights from London and cities within Sweden, including Gothenburg (50 min.) and Stockholm (1 hr.). Two airlines that serve the airport are **Malmö Aviation** (© **040/ 660-29-00**) and **SAS** (© **040/635-72-00**). The airport's major international link to the world is Denmark's Kastrup Airport, near Copenhagen, to which Malmö is connected by hovercraft service.

The **Stockholm–Copenhagen express train** (© **040/20-20-00**) has a branch that serves Malmö. Service is frequent between Gothenburg and Malmö (trip time 3½ hr.). From Helsingborg to Malmö (trip time 45 min.), trains leave hourly. From Stockholm, travel takes 4½ hours aboard the high-speed X-2000 train, and 6 to 7 hours aboard slower trains. Two buses daily make the 4½-hour run from Gothenburg to Malmö. For bus information, call **Swebus** (© **040/34-12-00**).

Malmö and Copenhagen are linked by the Flygbåtana (hydrofoil), with hourly service year-round from 5am to midnight. The ride takes 45 minutes. Call © **040/10-39-30** for information. The one-way fare is 120SEK ($13).

VISITOR INFORMATION   The **Malmö Tourist Office,** Central Station, Skeppsbron 2 (© **0411/53-60-58;** www.malmo.se), is open Monday through Friday from 9am to 5pm, Saturday from 10am to 2pm.

GETTING AROUND   It's easy to walk around the city center, although you may need to rely on public transport if you're branching out to sights on the periphery. An individual bus ticket costs 12SEK ($1.25) and is valid for 1 hour. You can also purchase a 100SEK ($11) magnetic card, which offers a slight reduction on the fare discount and can be used by several passengers at the same time. Both types of tickets are sold on the bus.

SEEING THE SIGHTS

The **Malmö Card,** which is available from the Malmö Tourist Office (see "Visitor Information," above), entitles visitors to free admission to most of the city's museums. It also includes free parking, free bus travel within the city limits, and discounts in selected shops and restaurants. A card that's valid for 1 day costs 125SEK ($13); for 2 days, 150SEK ($16); for 3 days, 180SEK ($19).

In the center of the square stands an equestrian statue of Carl X Gustav, commemorating the return of Skåne to Sweden from Denmark in 1658. There are occasional tours of the interior; check with the tourist office (see "Visitor Information," above).

Nearby lies **Lilla Torg** 𝒜𝒜, Malmö's most charming square, with many fine half-timbered buildings dating from the 16th century to the 18th century. It looks like a film set. In addition to its fountains and cafes, many handicraft shops are also here in what used to be marshland. For many centuries, this was Malmö's bustling open-air marketplace. However, in the 20th century a covered market replaced the open-air booths and stalls. Today, a modern market building also houses a number of restaurants. In summer, there are a lot of jewelry stalls.

Four major attractions are under the direction of **Malmö Museer** (© 040/34-10-00). Heading the list is **Malmöhus Castle,** on Malmöhusvägen. It was founded in the 15th century by Eric of Pomerania, and rebuilt by Christian III in the 16th century. It was also a prison—the Earl of Bothwell, third husband of Mary, Queen of Scots, was incarcerated here from 1568 to 1573. The castle now houses the City Museum, the Natural History Museum, the Aquarium and Tropicarium, and the **Konstmuseet** 𝒜𝒜. The latter's collection of old Scandinavian masters is especially noted for its works by artists from southern Sweden, such as Carl Fredrik Hill (1849–1911), one of Sweden's best landscape painters and a forerunner of European modernism. Most interesting is the large collection of Russian oil paintings from around 1900—the largest collection outside Russia. It also houses some modern art and good samples of Swedish furniture and textiles. The lyrical sketches in the foyer are by Carl Larsson, one of Sweden's best-known artists. West of Stortorget, the castle can be easily reached on foot.

Also in the group, across the street from the castle on Malmöhusvägen, is **Kommendanthuset,** a military museum and a piece of history in its own right. **Teknik-Och Sjöfartsmuseet (Museum of Technology and Shipping),** on Malmöhusvägen, is near the Kommendanthuset. You can see exhibits of ancient means of communication, as well as the submarine U-3. Technical history can be followed from the steam engine to the jet. The children's department even has a pirate ship, and in summer an old-fashioned tramway is in operation. The **Vagnmusset (Carriage Museum),** housed in the former military horse stable at Drottningtorget, displays carriages dating back to the 18th century, coaches, and cycles.

A 1-day ticket good for all the Malmö Museer properties costs 40SEK ($4.25) for adults, 10SEK ($1.05) for children 7 to 16, if visited on the same day. The museums are open daily from noon to 4pm.

Malmö's **St. Petri (St. Peter's Church)** 𝒜, on Göran Olsgatan (© 040/35-90-40), lies a block east of the Rådhus. Dark and a bit foreboding on the outside, it is light and airy within. This Gothic church originated in the 14th century, when Malmö was under the control of the Hanseatic League. It was modeled on Marienkirche, a famous church in Lübeck, Germany. Other than the slender pillars and supporting ogive (diagonal) vaulting, the church's most stunning feature is its 15th-century Krämarkapellet (tradesmen's chapel).

Amazingly, the original artwork remains. During the Reformation, the decoration was viewed as "redundant," and the chapel was sealed off—in effect protecting its paintings from the reformers' overzealous "restoration." Look for the New Testament figures on the vaulted ceiling; they are quite impressive, and surrounded by decorative foliage. Look also for a tall retable from 1611 and an exquisitely carved black limestone and sandstone pulpit from 1599. The pulpit and the octagonal baptismal font from 1601 were the work of master craftsman Daniel Tommisen. The church is open Monday through Friday from 8am to 6pm, Saturday from 9am to 6pm, and Sunday from 10am to 6pm. Admission is free.

A final attraction, **Rooseum** ஃஃ, Gasverksgatan 22 (© **040/12-17-16**), is one of the country's outstanding art museums. It's installed in a former electricity generating station built around the start of the 20th century. In 1988 it was converted into this elegant museum, the brainchild of art collector Fredrik Ross (1951–91). He set out to showcase modern art movements through a series of thematic exhibitions and shows. Although strongest in Nordic art, the exhibitions are international. Hours are Tuesday through Sunday from 11am to 5pm (until 8pm Thurs), and admission is 40SEK ($4.25).

A NEARBY ATTRACTION

Svaneholm, between Malmö and Ystad, was established in 1530 as a fortress, and later partially converted into an Italian-style palace. Today it houses a museum of paintings, furnishings, and tools dating primarily from the 18th and 19th centuries.

Admission to the castle is 40SEK ($4.25) for adults, 20SEK ($2.10) for children. It's open from April to June and from September to December, Wednesday through Sunday from 11am to 4pm. In July and August, it's open Tuesday through Sunday from 11am to 5pm. The castle is completely closed from January to March. There is a restaurant on-site (© **0411/450-40**) serving regional specialties. For more information about the castle, write to Svaneholm Museum, S-274 00 Skurup (© **0411/400-12**).

Reaching Svaneholm by public transportation is difficult; a train from Malmö stops at Skurup, but it's about a 3km (2-mile) walk from there. Many visitors opt to go by taxi the rest of the way.

SHOPPING

Malmö's main pedestrian shopping street is **Södergatan,** which runs south of Stortorget toward the canal. Nearby, at the 16th-century Lilla Torg, a charming 16th-century antique square, you can visit the **Form Design Centre** (© **040/ 10-36-10**). It combines a museum-like exhibition space with boutiques selling upscale handicrafts, including Swedish textiles-by-the-yard, woodcarvings, and all manner of other crafts.

At **Röda Tråden,** Adelgatan 5 (© **040/23-70-46**), you'll find clothes by the well-known designer Maria Haid, plus handicrafts and souvenirs. You'll also see unique ceramics, studio-designed glass, bronze and silver jewelry, and decorative tiles. On the top floor is an art gallery.

A well-respected name in glassware and crystal is **Silverbergs i Malmö,** Baltzarsgatan 31 (© **040/740-80**). This famous store reliably ships its stunning collection of glassware, crystal, furniture, and gifts all over the world. Established in 1927, **Juvelerare Hugo Nilsson,** Södra Tullgatan 2 (© **040/12-65-92**), features some of the most famous names in Danish jewelry making,

including Georg Jensen, Rauff, and Ole Lynggaard. Jewelry by Finnish designers such as Lapponia is also sold.

You'll find an unusual collection of Nordic arts and crafts at **Älgamark,** Ö.
Rönneholmsvägen 4 (© **040/97-49-60**). It carries Viking jewelry (replicas in
pewter, bronze, silver, and gold), along with handicrafts from Swedish Lapland.
Traditional pendants, bracelets, and knives are also for sale.

One of Sweden's leading furriers is **Mattssons Päls,** Norra Vallgatan 98
(© **040/12-55-33**). Saga mink coats and jackets are the most luxurious buys,
but Mattssons has a full range of fine furs at prices lower than you'll see in the
United States. In the boutique are fur-lined poplins and accessories, all tax-free
for tourists. The store is 5 minutes on foot from the Central Station and the
Copenhagen boats.

Finally, if you haven't found what you're looking for in the specialty shops, try
Hansa Companiet, Stora Nygatan 50 (© **040/770-00**). It's a shopping complex with more than 40 shops, cafes, and restaurants. The latest fashions and
items for the home are among the many specialties featured here. However, most
foreign visitors come by to check out its selection of Swedish souvenirs and
handicrafts.

WHERE TO STAY
EXPENSIVE
Hotel Noble House ★★ One of the most modern and up-to-date hotels in
town—and certainly the most glamorous—is named after the best-selling novel
by James Clavell (the former owner was a great devotee of the writings of
Clavell). The comfortable pastel-colored rooms are decorated with copies of
early-20th-century Swedish paintings. Because of the four-story hotel's convenient location in the town center, its quietest rooms face the interior courtyard.
Each room has standard hotel-size bathrooms with shower-tub combinations.

Gustav Adolfs Torg 47, S-211 39 Malmö. © **040/664-30-00.** Fax 040/664-30-50. www.hkchotels.se. 130
units. June 24–Aug 15 and Fri–Sat year-round 895SEK ($95) double; rest of year 1,575SEK ($167) double. Year-
round 1,775SEK ($188) suite. Rates include breakfast. AE, DC, MC, V. Closed Dec 22–26. Parking 145SEK ($15).
Bus: 10, 11, 17, or 20. **Amenities:** Bar; sauna; laundry/dry cleaning. *In room:* TV, minibar, hair dryer, safe.

Radisson SAS Hotel ★ The Radisson SAS contains tastefully decorated
rooms with elegant bathrooms equipped with shower-tub combinations. Built
in 1988, the seven-story hotel was designed to accommodate people with disabilities. Although it's affiliated with Scandinavia's most visible airline, SAS,
some visitors consider this hotel bland, anonymous, and somewhat sterile.

Östergatan 10, S-211 25 Malmö. © **800/333-3333** in the U.S., or 040/698-40-00. Fax 040/698-40-01.
www.radissonsas.com. 229 units. June 5–Aug 5 Mon–Thurs 1,940SEK ($206) double; Aug 6–June 4 Mon–Thurs
2,390SEK ($253) double; year-round Fri–Sun 1,100SEK ($117) double. Year-round from 3,000SEK ($318) suite.
Rates include breakfast. AE, DC, MC, V. Parking 160SEK ($17). Bus: 14 or 17. **Amenities:** Restaurant; bar; fit-
ness center; sauna; room service; babysitting; laundry/dry cleaning. *In room:* TV, minibar, hair dryer.

Scandic Hotel Triangeln ★★ Malmö's most visible international luxury
hotel, in the commercial heart of town, rises 20 stories. Built in 1989, it boasts
sweeping views from almost all its guest rooms. The top three floors contain only
suites and a well-engineered health club. Many of the guests are business travelers, often attending one of the dozens of conventions that attract participants
from throughout Europe. The rooms are tastefully and comfortably appointed,
with light colors, many electronic amenities, and firm mattresses. The bathrooms
are more than adequate and equipped with shower-tub combinations.

Triangeln 2, S-200 10 Malmö. ⓒ 040/693-47-00. Fax 040/693-47-11. www.scandic-hotels.com. 214 units. June 24–Aug 7 and Fri–Sat year-round 950SEK ($101) double; rest of year 1,150SEK–1,983SEK ($122–$210) double. Year-round 3,900SEK ($413) suite. Rates include breakfast. AE, DC, MC, V. Parking 90SEK ($9.55). Bus: 14 or 17. **Amenities:** 2 restaurants; bar; fitness center; sauna; room service; babysitting; laundry/dry cleaning. *In room:* TV, minibar, hair dryer.

MODERATE

Elite Hotel Savoy ⓡ   This hotel has figured prominently in Malmö's history; famous guests have included Dag Hammarskjöld, Liv Ullmann, Alan Alda, and Johnny ("Tarzan") Weissmuller. It boasts some of the plushest accommodations in Sweden. Rooms contain champagne-colored upholstery, cabriole-legged or Chippendale-style furniture, excellent beds, and all the extras of a deluxe hotel. Well-maintained bathrooms come in a wide variety of sizes, with shower-tub combinations. In the hotel restaurant, you can order from an international menu, perhaps stopping for a before-dinner beer in the British-style pub, the Bishop's Arms.

Norra Vallgatan 62, S-201 80 Malmö. ⓒ 040/664-48-00. Fax 040/664-48-50. www.savoy.elite.se. 109 units. June 19–Aug 9 and Fri–Sat year-round 900SEK ($95) double; rest of year 1,690SEK ($179) double. Year-round 2,490SEK ($264) suite. Rates include breakfast. AE, DC, MC, V. Parking 125SEK ($13). Bus: 14 or 17. **Amenities:** Restaurant; bar; fitness center; sauna; room service; laundry/dry cleaning. *In room:* TV, minibar, hair dryer, safe.

Hotell Baltzar ⓡⓡ *(Finds* Around 1900, an entrepreneur who had made a fortune selling chocolate moved into a private home whose turrets, towers, and fanciful ornamentation resembled a stone-carved confection. Several decades later, when it became an elegant and prestigious hotel, it expanded into one of the neighboring buildings. Today, you'll find a hotel with many charming corners and cubbyholes. Grace notes include frescoed ceilings, substantial-looking antiques, and elaborate draperies in some of the public areas. The comfortable, high-ceilinged guest rooms have been upgraded, with furnishings (including good beds) and parquet floors that would suit a prosperous private home. The medium-sized bathrooms are impeccably maintained and equipped with shower-tub combinations. The location on an all-pedestrian street keeps things relatively quiet inside. Breakfast is the only meal served.

Södergatan 20, S-211 24 Malmö. ⓒ 040/665-57-00. Fax 040/665-57-10. www.baltzarhotel.se. 41 units. Mon–Thurs 1,080SEK–1,600SEK ($114–$170) double; Fri–Sun 850SEK–1,350SEK ($90–$143) double. Rates include breakfast. AE, DC, MC, V. Parking 120SEK ($13) per night. Bus: 10. **Amenities:** Lounge; room service; laundry/dry cleaning. *In room:* TV, minibar, hair dryer, safe.

Rica City Hotel Built in 1912, the hotel lies on Malmö's main square, facing the Town Hall, a short walk from the railway station and the ferryboat terminals for Copenhagen-bound ships. In 1992 the guest rooms were rebuilt in a tasteful modern format. The hotel is owned by the Salvation Army, which strictly forbids the consumption of alcohol on the premises. It's also part of a hotel chain (City Hotels) that operates four other Swedish hotels. The rooms are larger than you might expect, and have good mattresses. Bathrooms tend to be cramped, but are well maintained with shower-tub combinations.

Stortorget 15, S-211 22 Malmö. ⓒ 040/660-95-50. Fax 040/660-95-59. www.rica.se. 80 units. Mon–Thurs 1,555SEK ($165) double; Fri–Sun 990SEK ($105) double. Rates include breakfast. AE, DC, MC, V. Parking 60SEK ($6.35). Bus: 14 or 17. **Amenities:** Lounge; sauna; laundry/dry cleaning. *In room:* TV, minibar, hair dryer, safe.

Scandic Hotel Kramer ⓡ   At the side of the town's main square, this chateau-like twin-towered building is one of Malmö's landmark hotels. Built in

1875, it was renovated at the height of the Art Deco era. Between 1992 and 1994 the rooms were redecorated again with an old-fashioned sense of nostalgia, vaguely reminiscent of staterooms on a pre–World War II ocean liner. Each has a firm mattress, a marble bathroom with shower-tub combinations, dark paneling, curved walls, and kitschy, 1930s-style accessories.

Stortorget 7, S-201 21 Malmö. ⓒ 040/693-54-00. Fax 040/693-54-11. www.scandic-hotels.com. 113 units. 900SEK–1,695SEK ($95–$180) double; 3,795SEK ($402) suite. Rates include breakfast. AE, DC, MC, V. Parking 175SEK ($19). Bus: 14, 17, or 20. **Amenities:** Restaurant; bar; sauna; room service; laundry/dry cleaning. *In room:* TV, minibar, hair dryer.

Teaterhotellet   The only negative aspect to this hotel is its banal-looking 1960s-era facade; it's no uglier than hundreds of other contemporaneous Scandinavian buildings, but isn't particularly inviting or pleasing. Inside, however, you'll find a cozy, tasteful, and colorful establishment that attracts many repeat clients. Appealing touches include tawny-colored marble floors, lots of elegant hardwood paneling, lacquered walls in tones of amber and beige, and spots of vibrant colors in the guest rooms (especially jewel tones of red and green) that perk up even the grayest of Swedish winter days. Rooms were renovated in 1996 with new furniture and mattresses, plus new bathrooms with showers and tubs. Less than 1km (½ mile) south of the railway station, the hotel is near a verdant park and the Stadtstheater. Only breakfast is served, but you can usually get someone to bring you a sandwich and coffee.

Rönngatan 3, S-211 47 Malmö. ⓒ 040/665-58-00. Fax 040/665-58-10. www.teaterhotellet.se. 44 units. Mon–Thurs 1,400SEK ($148) double; Fri–Sun 750SEK ($80) double; 1,550SEK–1,750SEK ($164–$186) suite. Rates include breakfast. AE, DC, MC, V. Parking 125SEK ($13). Bus: 11. **Amenities:** Bar; room service; laundry/dry cleaning. *In room:* TV, minibar (in some), hair dryer.

INEXPENSIVE

Elite Hotel Residens 🎖 *Value*   In 1987, a team of local investors enlarged the white-sided premises of a historic 1517 inn with the addition of a new brick-and-stone structure. The interconnected structures provide solid, comfortable, and upscale lodgings near the railroad station. Except for certain corners where an effort was made to duplicate a woodsy-looking men's club in London, many of the public areas are outfitted in a glossy, modern setup with lots of mirrors, touches of chrome, and polished marble floors. Guest rooms are more traditionally outfitted and larger than you might expect. They have hardwood floors or wall-to-wall carpeting, good beds, well-upholstered furnishings and, in some cases, Oriental carpets. The medium-size bathrooms are equipped with shower-tub combinations. Windows are large and double-insulated against noise from the urban landscape outside.

Adelgatan 7, S-211 22 Malmö. ⓒ 040/611-25-30. Fax 040/30-09-60. www.elite.se. 70 units. June to mid-Aug and Fri–Sat year-round 800SEK ($85) double; rest of year 1,450SEK ($154) double. Rates include breakfast. AE, DC, MC, V. Free parking. Bus: 14 or 17. **Amenities:** Lounge; laundry/dry cleaning. *In room:* TV, hair dryer.

Hotell Royal   This hotel, adjacent to a canal in the historic core of Malmö, is composed of three antique buildings. The most visible is a stately early-20th-century neoclassical town house; the oldest dates from the 1500s. Guest rooms are rather small but inviting. Bathrooms are a bit cramped but do contain shower-tub combinations. The owners, the hardworking Kilström brothers, maintain a small conference center, and work hard to keep their hotel ship-shape.

Norra Vallgatan 94, S-211 22 Malmö. ⓒ 040/664-25-00. Fax 040/12-77-12. www.hotellroyal.com. 38 units. July and Fri–Sat year-round 795SEK–895SEK ($84–$95) double; rest of year 995SEK–1,250SEK ($105–$133) double. AE, DC, MC, V. Free parking on street 6pm–9am; otherwise, 15SEK ($1.60) per hour 9am–6pm. Bus: 14 or 17. **Amenities:** Bar; laundry/dry cleaning. *In room:* TV, minibar, hair dryer.

WHERE TO DINE
EXPENSIVE

Årstiderna I Kockska Huset ★★ SWEDISH/INTERNATIONAL   One of the most prestigious restaurants in Malmö lies on a "perpetually shadowed" medieval street. It was built in the 1480s as the home and political headquarters of the Danish-appointed governor of Malmö, Jürgen Kock. In its richly Gothic way, it's the most unusual restaurant setting in town, with vaulted brick ceilings, severe-looking medieval detailing, and a deliberate lack of other kinds of adornment. Owners Marie and Wilhelm Pieplow have created an environment where the prime ministers of Sweden and Finland, as well as dozens of politicians, artists, and actors, have dined exceedingly well. Menu items change with the seasons; the establishment's name, *Årstiderna*, translates from the Swedish as "The Four Seasons." Likely to be featured are fried monkfish with parsley butter, salmon roe, and Norwegian lobster; orange-glazed wild duck with flap mushrooms and honey-rosemary sauce; filet of venison in an herb crust with chanterelle mushrooms and juniper-berry sauce; Swedish beefsteak with red wine and potato gratin; and a chocolate terrine with cloudberry sorbet and a compote of blackberries.

Frans Suellsgatan 3. ℂ **040/23-09-10.** Reservations recommended. Main courses 190SEK–325SEK ($20–$34); fixed-price lunch 150SEK–280SEK ($16–$30); fixed-price dinner 320SEK–450SEK ($34–$48). AE, DC, MC, V. Mon–Fri 11:30am–midnight; Sat 5pm–1am. Bus: 14 or 17.

Hipp ★★ SWEDISH/FRENCH   Set beneath one of the most ornate and stately looking gilded ceilings in Malmö, this restaurant—noted for its superb and often very complex food—has welcomed some of the town's most prestigious visitors. These have included prime ministers, ambassadors, and the Hollywood actor who played the role of Freddy Kruger in the blood-fest *Nightmare on Elm Street*. This spot began life in 1897 as a cabaret theater; and many of its original Belle Epoque embellishments and soaring crystal chandeliers are still in place. Menu items are lavish, French-inspired, and served with panache; they might include a superb breast of duckling with chanterelles, garlic puree, sweetbreads, and Szechuan-style pepper sauce; or roasted lamb with sauerkraut, braised salsify, and truffles. Every Friday and Saturday, the place is transformed into a dance club of the same name.

Kalendegatan 12. ℂ **040/94-70-30.** Reservations recommended. Main courses 165SEK–195SEK ($17–$21); set menu 595SEK ($63). AE, MC, V. Tues–Sat 5–10pm. Closed 2 weeks in July. Bus: 14 or 17.

Johan P ★ *Finds* FISH/SEAFOOD   Some of the most appealing seafood in Malmö is prepared and served in this artfully simple, mostly white dining room. The result is an almost pristine setting where the freshness of the seafood is the main draw. Menu items are prepared fresh every day, based on whatever is available at the nearby *Saluhallen* (marketplace). Examples include an award-winning fish soup that's inspired by the traditions of Provence; a leek and potato vichyssoise served with fresh mussels and a timbale of pike; baked monkfish with mustard-flavored spaetzle, served with dried ham and braised cabbage in a tomato-flavored broth; and an old-fashioned version of chicken dumplings with mushroom risotto and sweet-and-sour tomato sauce. Dessert might include a mousse made with bitter white chocolate, served with dark-chocolate madeleines and coffee sauce.

Saluhallen, Landbygatan. ℂ **040/97-18-18.** Reservations recommended. Main courses 180SEK–270SEK ($19–$29); 2-course fixed-price menu 275SEK ($29); 3-course fixed-price menu 285SEK ($30). AE, MC, V. Mon–Thurs 11:30am–10:30pm; Fri 11:30am–11pm; Sat 11:30am–11pm. Bus: 14 or 17.

Restaurant Kramer Gastronomie ☆ CONTINENTAL   Accessed through the lobby of the also-recommended hotel, this restaurant serves the best food of any hotel dining room in Malmö. There's an upscale, woodsy-looking bar that's separated from the brown and off-white dining room by a leaded glass divider, and an attention to cuisine that brings a conservative, not particularly flashy clientele back again and again. The composition of the fixed-price menu changes every week, and it's relatively common for a group of business partners to spend 3 hours at table sampling the seven-course *menu dégustation*. The food is faultlessly fresh and handled beautifully by a kitchen staff that believes in delicate seasonings and perfectly cooked dishes. The chef is dedicated to his job, personally shopping for market-fresh ingredients to inspire his imagination. Menu items include shots of shellfish bouillon served with Parmesan chips and coriander salsa; scallops with grilled tuna and bacon; blackened filet of beef with pecorino cheese, lemon wedges, arugula, and a sauce made with a reduction of *court bouillon* and red wine; and char-grilled halibut with glazed turnips, truffle butter, and dill oil. Pastas here are upscale and esoteric, including a version with spinach, crayfish, fried filet of sole, and dill sauce.

In the Scandic Hotel Kramer, Stortorget 7. ✆ 040/693-54-00. Reservations recommended. Main courses 95SEK–175SEK ($10–$19); 3-course fixed-price menu 285SEK ($30). AE, DC, MC, V. Mon–Fri 5–11pm; Sat 6–11pm. Bar open till 1am. Bus: 10.

MODERATE

Centiliter & Gram ☆ CONTINENTAL   This is one of Malmö's hottest restaurants, with a hipster clientele that includes lots of well-known painters and football (soccer) stars, as well as dozens of media and PR people. It occupies an artfully minimalist gray-and-mauve space whose focal point is a centrally placed bar. Guests often stay to flirt long after their dishes have been cleared away. Menu items change with the seasons, and with whatever food fad happens to be in vogue in London, Stockholm, or Paris at the time. Stellar examples include a parcel of Italian goat cheese baked in phyllo pastry with a tomato and basil sauce; black mussels with white wine and cream sauce served with a tomato bruschetta; deliberately undercooked ("pink") duck breast with teriyaki sauce and an orange and mango flavored chutney; and grilled halibut and scallops with a spicy Thai red curry, coconut milk, and jasmine-flavored rice. The establishment's name, incidentally, derives from wine (which is measured in centiliters) and food (which is measured in grams).

Stortorget 17. ✆ 040/12-18-12. Reservations recommended. Main courses 96SEK–209SEK ($10–$22). AE, DC, MC, V. Wed–Thurs 4:30pm–1am; Fri–Sat 4:30pm–3am. Bus: 10.

Lemongrass ASIAN   Lemongrass is set in one large, spartan room that's devoid of the artsy clutter of many Asian restaurants. Instead, on pale gray walls, you'll find clusters of exotic-looking orchids, as well as tufted bunches of the lemon grass for which it was named. There's a bar where you can wait for your table, if you have to. The menu contains food items from Japan (including sushi), China, and Thailand. A staff member will help you coordinate a meal from disparate culinary styles in ways that you might have expected only in Los Angeles, London, or New York.

Grunbodgatan 9. ✆ 40/30-69-79. Reservations recommended. Main courses 105SEK–220SEK ($11–$23); 7-course fixed-price menu 400SEK ($42). AE, MC, V. Mon–Thurs 6pm–midnight; Fri–Sat 6pm–1am. Bus: 6 or 10.

Rådhuskällern *Value* SWEDISH   This is the most atmospheric place in Malmö, located in the cellar of the Town Hall. Even if you don't eat here, at least drop in for a drink in the pub or lounge. The severe exterior and labyrinth of underground vaults were built in 1546; the dark-vaulted dining room was used for centuries to store gold, wine, furniture, and food. Menu staples include halibut with lobster sauce, plank steak, filet of veal, pepper steak, and roast duck; and there's always an array of daily specials. Although the fare is first-rate here, it never overexcites the palate.

Kyrkogatan 5. ℂ **040/790-20.** Reservations recommended. Main courses 160SEK–210SEK ($17–$22); single-course lunch 75SEK ($7.95). AE, DC, MC, V. Mon–Fri 11:30am–2pm and 6–11pm; Sat 5–11pm. Bus: 14 or 17.

Wallman's Salonger CONTINENTAL   Large enough for 400 diners at a time, and painted a heady shade of Bordeaux red, this is the most entertaining restaurant in Malmö—with a most entertaining staff. At one end of the restaurant is a stage upon which members of the staff—each a candidate for a job in the theater—will sing, dance, and wonderfully amuse you. Meals consist of an assortment of steaks, soups, salads, seafood, veal, or pork dishes; they are flavorful, although not particularly spectacular, but since most clients are gyrating on the dance floor before 11pm anyway, no one especially cares.

Generalsgatan 1. ℂ **040/749-45.** Reservations recommended. 3-course fixed-price menus 395SEK–488SEK ($42–$52). AE, DC, MC, V. Wed–Sat 7pm–2am. Closed May to mid-Aug.

INEXPENSIVE

Anno 1900 🏕 *Finds* SWEDISH   The name of this place gives a hint about its decor, which includes lots of antique woodwork and accessories from the heyday of the Industrial Revolution. A garden in back is open during warm weather, if you want a break from turn-of-the-20th-century fussiness. Menu items derive from tried-and-true classics: old-fashioned versions of cauliflower soup, halibut with horseradish sauce, chicken dumplings with noodles, roasted beef, steaks, *frikadeller* (meatballs), and fried herring. If you have a Swedish grandmother, bring her here—she'll feel right at home.

Norra Bultoftavagen 7. ℂ **040/18-47-47.** Reservations recommended. Main courses 100SEK–225SEK ($11–$24); fixed-price lunch 100SEK ($11). AE, DC, MC, V. Mon–Fri 11:15am–2pm; Tues–Thurs 6–11pm. Bus: 14 or 17.

Casa Mia ITALIAN   Venetian gondola moorings ornament the front terrace of this Nordic version of a neighborhood trattoria. Troubadours stroll from table to crowded table singing Neapolitan ballads, and your waiter is likely to address you in Italian. You might begin with a steaming bowl of *stracciatella alla romana* (egg-and-chicken soup) or the fish soup of the house, then move on to penne with shrimp, basil, cream, and tomatoes, or spaghetti with seafood. Later you can dig into *saltimbocca alla romana* (veal with ham), a portion of grilled scampi, escalope of veal stuffed with goose liver, or an array of grilled meats with aromatic herbs. There are more than 15 types of pizza on the menu, and pastries are offered for dessert. Okay, it's not as good as the food served in a typical trattoria in northern Italy, but the cuisine is a refreshing change of pace.

Södergatan 12. ℂ **040/23-05-00.** Reservations recommended. Pastas and pizzas 75SEK–100SEK ($7.95–$11); single-course *dagens* (daily) menu 75SEK ($7.95). AE, DC, MC, V. Mon–Sat 11am–11pm; Sun noon–10pm. Bus: 14 or 17.

Restaurant B & B (Butik och Bar) SWEDISH/INTERNATIONAL   This well-managed, relatively inexpensive bistro is in a corner of the *Saluhallen* (food market), which provides the fresh ingredients that go into each menu item. In a simple, old-fashioned setting, with glowing hardwood floors, pristine white walls, and a scattering of antiques that evoke the Sweden of long ago, you'll find flavorful, unpretentious food. It's international cuisine, with occasional emphasis on

Swedish staples known to every grandmother, including creamy fish soup in the Swedish style. Most of the other dishes are more exotic, including New Orleans versions of jambalaya, Cajun-inspired tagliatelle with blackened chicken and fiery sauces, teriyaki pork, roasted chicken with tiger prawns, and pasta with a salmon-flavored vodka sauce.

Saluhallen, Landbygatan 52. © 040/12-71-20. Reservations recommended. Main courses 60SEK–125SEK ($6.35–$13); fixed-price lunch 58SEK ($6.15). AE, DC, MC, V. Mon–Sat noon–10:30pm. Bus: 14 or 17.

MALMÖ AFTER DARK

For serious nighttime pursuits, many locals—especially young people—head for easily reached Copenhagen. However, there are several local amusements, the best of which is previewed below. See "Copenhagen After Dark" in chapter 4, "Exploring Copenhagen."

From May to September, locals head for **Folkets Park (People's Park),** Amiralsgatan 35 (© **040/709-90**). It consists of sprawling amusement grounds and pleasure gardens. The dancing pavilions, vaudeville performances, and open-air concerts also draw big crowds. There's even a reptile center. Children will find a playhouse, plus a small zoo and a puppet theater. Restaurants dot the grounds. The park is open daily from 3pm to midnight in summer, daily from noon to 6pm in winter. Admission is usually free; however, for some performances it's 50SEK to 110SEK ($5.30–$12). Take bus no. 11, 13, or 17 from Gustav Adolfs Torg.

Dancing is the rage at the creatively designed **Nightclub Etage,** Stortorget 6 (© **040/23-20-60**). Initially conceived in the late 1980s as an upscale bar and restaurant, this nightspot lowered its prices and began marketing to a mass audience a few years later—and it hasn't seemed to suffer as a result of the change. To get there, climb a circular staircase from an enclosed courtyard in the town's main square. Bars open and close regularly on other floors. The complex is open Monday and Thursday through Saturday from 9pm to at least 4am, depending on the crowd. Cover for the dance club is 60SEK to 90SEK ($6.35–$9.55).

Hipp, Kalendegatan 12 (© **040/94-70-30**), set beneath the elaborate gilt-and-frescoed ceiling of the also-recommended restaurant, is an animated dance club that at its best can be stylish and fun. Expect nothing till 11pm on Friday and Saturday nights only, after which it explodes with rhythm, lights, music, and flirtations. A cover charge of 80SEK ($8.50) per person is imposed.

Love often blooms at **Restaurang Stadt,** Hamburgsgatan 3 (© **040/12-22-21**). Romantic dancing, sometimes cheek to cheek, is the norm here. Patrons tend to be over 35, and they enjoy recorded music of the style that might remind you of a 1960s variety show—Martin, Como, and Damone. A restaurant on the premises serves platters of traditional Swedish food Tuesday through Saturday between 8 and 11:30pm. Main courses cost 100SEK to 165SEK ($11–$17). The bar is open for music and dancing Monday through Wednesday from 7pm to 1am, Thursday from 8pm to 2am, and Friday and Saturday from 8pm to 3am. The cover charge is 70SEK ($7.40).

The largest nightclub in Malmö, five-floor **Club Privée,** Malmborgsgatan 7 (© **040/97-46-66**), attracts a devoted clientele whose calendars seem to revolve around the limited number of nights the place is open. Near the Gustav Adolfs Torg in the center of town, it has a decor that replicates an English pub—there are, for example, lots of Chesterfield sofas—and a clientele of mostly 20-somethings. There's a bar, and different musical ambiences on each of the establishment's five floors. You'll pay 42SEK ($4.45) for a large beer. The club is open only on Friday and Saturday nights from 11pm to 5am. The cover charge is 60SEK to 70SEK ($6.35–$7.40).

Nostalgic for Britain? The best replica of a British pub is the **Bishop's Arms,** Norra Vallgatan 62 (© **040/702-30**), in the Savoy Hotel. Some of the best and coldest beer in town is served here, and there's always a congenial crowd.

The **Malmö Symphony Orchestra,** which performs at the Konserthus, Föreningsgatan 35 (© **040/34-35-00**), is renowned across Europe. The tourist office distributes programs for such cultural events.

4 Lund (★(★

18km (11 miles) NE of Malmö, 301km (187 miles) S of Gothenburg, 602km (374 miles) SW of Stockholm

The city was probably founded in 1020 by Canute the Great, ruler of the United Kingdom of England and Denmark, when this part of Sweden was a Danish possession. The city really made its mark when its cathedral was consecrated in 1145. The city's 1,000-year anniversary was celebrated in 1990, since archaeological excavations show that a stave church was built here in 990. Lund quickly became a center of religion, politics, culture, and commerce for all of Scandinavia.

Lund has winding passageways, centuries-old buildings, and the richness of a university town—Lund University, founded in 1666, plays an active role in town municipal life.

The most exciting time to be in Lund, as in Uppsala, is on Walpurgis Eve, April 30, when student revelries signal the advent of spring. A visit to Lund at any time is a pleasure.

ESSENTIALS

GETTING THERE   From Gothenburg, drive south along the E6; Malmö and Lund are 20 minutes apart on an express highway. If you're not driving, trains run hourly from Malmö, a 15-minute ride. Buses leave Malmö hourly for the 30-minute trip.

VISITOR INFORMATION   The tourist information office, **Lunds Turistbyrå,** is at Kyrkogatan 11 (© **046/35-50-40;** www.lund.se). It's open from June to August, Monday through Friday from 10am to 6pm and Saturday and Sunday from 10am to 2pm; from September to May, Monday through Friday from 10am to 5pm and Saturday from 10am to 2pm.

GETTING AROUND   All the major sights are within a 10-minute walk of each other, so exploring Lund on foot is the only way to go.

SEEING THE SIGHTS

Botaniska Trädgården (Botanical Gardens)   A block east of the cathedral, these gardens contain some 7,500 specimens of plants gathered from all over the world. On a hot summer day, this is the city's most pleasant place to be. Clusters of students congregate here, stretching out beneath the trees, and families often picnic on the grounds. Serious horticulturists will want to visit when the greenhouses are open.

Östra Vallgatan 20. © 046/222-73-20. Free admission. Gardens, daily 6am–8pm; greenhouses, daily noon–3pm. Bus: 1, 2, 3, 4, 5, 6, or 7.

Domkyrkan (Cathedral of Lund) (★(★(★   With this ancient cathedral, Romanesque architecture in Scandinavia reached its height. The church's **eastern exterior** (★(★ is one of the finest expressions of Romanesque architecture in northern Europe. The sandstone interior has sculptural details similar in quality and character to those in Lombardy and other parts of Italy. There is also a **crypt** (★(★(★

with a high altar dedicated in 1123, and intricately carved **choir stalls** ✿✿✿ from about 1375.

A partly reconstructed 14th-century **astronomical clock** not only tells the time and the date, but is the stage for a splashy Middle Ages–style tournament—complete with clashing knights and the blare of trumpets. That's not all: The Three Wise Men come out to pay homage to the Virgin and Child. To see all this, time your visit so you're in the cathedral when the clock strikes noon (1pm on Sun) or 3pm.

Kyrkogatan. ✆ **046/35-87-00**. Free admission. Mon–Sat 8am–6pm; Sun 9am–6pm. Bus: 1, 2, 3, 4, 5, 6, or 7.

Drottens Museum (Medieval Museum)
During the excavations for an inner-city office building, workers discovered the remnants of one of Sweden's earliest churches—a now-ruined Romanesque building that was built about 1,000 years ago. Recognizing the remnants as historically and aesthetically valuable, civic leaders ordered the construction of a series of large windows in the new building, allowing pedestrians on the sidewalk outside to see the ruins from above. Visitors can walk among the ruins, viewing an exhibition of mannequins dressed in medieval garb, in scenes of everyday life. Also on display are some of the skeletons unearthed at the excavation site.

Kattesund 6. ✆ **046/14-13-28**. Admission 10SEK ($1.05) adults, free for children. Tues–Fri 9am–4pm; Sat–Sun noon–4pm. Bus: 1, 2, 3, 4, 5, 6, or 7.

Historiska Museet
Founded in 1805, this is the second-largest museum of archaeology in Sweden. Collections trace the development of the people of Skåne from antiquity to the Middle Ages. One of the skeletons on display is that of a young man, one of the oldest finds of a human body in northern Europe, dating from around 7000 B.C. Most collections from the Bronze Age came from tombs. During excavations in eastern Skåne, a large grave field turned up jewelry and weapons, which are on display. Church art dominates the medieval exhibition.

Kraftstorg 1. ✆ **046/222-79-44**. Admission 30SEK ($3.20) adults, 15SEK ($1.60) children 7–18, free for children under 7. Tues–Fri 11am–4pm. Bus: 1, 2, 3, 4, 5, 6, or 7.

Kulturen (Museum of Cultural History) ✿✿
After leaving Domkyrkan (the Cathedral of Lund), walk across the university grounds to Adelgatan, which the local citizens consider their most charming street. Here you'll find Kulturen, another open-air museum. It contains reassembled, sod-roofed farms and manor houses, a carriage museum, ceramics, peasant costumes, Viking artifacts, and old handicrafts. A wooden church was moved to this site from the glassworks district.

Tegnérsplatsen. ✆ **046/35-04-00**. Admission 50SEK ($5.30) adults, free for children. Apr 15–Sept daily 11am–5pm; Oct–Apr 14 Tues–Sun noon–4pm. Bus: 1, 2, 3, 4, 5, 6, or 7.

WHERE TO STAY
The tourist office (see "Visitor Information," above) can help you find housing in private homes for as little as 175SEK ($19) per person per night.

EXPENSIVE
Grand Hotel ✿✿ This château-style hotel, the most prestigious in town, overlooks the fountains and flowers of a city park. The marble lobby is grand. Rooms in the hotel's conical corner tower are the most desirable. All the guest rooms are decorated in an old-fashioned style. The bathrooms are moderate in size, with shower-tub combinations.

Bantorget 1, S-221 04 Lund. © 046/280-61-00. Fax 046/280-61-50. www.grandilund.se. 84 units. June 7–Aug 8 and Fri–Sat year-round 850SEK–1,790SEK ($90–$190) double; 2,700SEK ($286) suite. Aug 9–June 6 1,995SEK–2,200SEK ($211–$233) double; 3,900SEK ($413) suite. Rates include breakfast. AE, DC, V. Parking 100SEK ($11). Bus: 1, 2, 3, 4, 5, 6, or 7. **Amenities:** Restaurant; bar; fitness center; sauna; room service; laundry/dry cleaning. *In room:* TV, minibar.

Hotel Concordia ✿   Next door to the brick house where August Strindberg lived in 1897, this charming, ornate building was constructed in 1882 as a private home. It served as a student hotel for some time and was then upgraded to a pleasant hotel. The modernized rooms are sedate and moderate in size, with good beds; a few are reserved for nonsmokers. The bathrooms are a bit small, but are equipped with neatly kept shower units. Housekeeping here is among the finest in town. The hotel is a 5-minute walk south of the railroad station.

Stålbrogatan 1, S-222 24 Lund. © 046/13-50-50. Fax 046/13-74-22. www.concordia.se. 65 units. Sun–Thurs 1,520SEK ($161) double; Fri–Sat 950SEK ($101) double. All week long 1,800SEK ($191) suite. Rates include breakfast. AE, DC, MC, V. Parking 50SEK ($5.30). Bus: 1, 2, 3, 4, 5, 6, or 7. **Amenities:** Lounge; fitness center; sauna; laundry/dry cleaning. *In room:* TV, minibar (in some), hair dryer.

MODERATE

Hotel Djingis Khan ✿ *Finds*   Within a 15-minute walk north of the town center, this hotel was originally built in the 1970s as employee housing for a local hospital. It became a pleasant, well-managed hotel in the early 1990s. Two of its wings still contain private apartments, but it's mostly made up of attractively modern guest rooms outfitted in a conservatively comfortable style. They have good beds and small but adequate bathrooms with shower stalls. Public areas contain lots of English-inspired dark paneling, Chesterfield sofas, and an ambience that might remind you of a private men's club in London.

The hotel's name, incidentally, comes from the most famous satirical comedy *(Ghenghis Khan)* ever produced in Lund. It was written in the 1950s by Hasse Alfredsson, and this hotel was named in its honor.

Margarethevägen 7, S—222 40 Lund. © **800/528-1234** in the U.S., or 046/33-36-00. Fax 046/46-33-36-10. www.djingiskhan.se. 55 units. Sun–Thurs 1,500SEK ($159) double; Fri–Sat 800SEK ($85) double. Rates include breakfast. AE, DC, MC, V. Closed July. Free parking. Bus: 3 or 93. **Amenities:** Restaurant; bar; pool; fitness center; sauna; room service; laundry/dry cleaning. *In room:* TV, minibar, hair dryer.

Hotel Lundia   Under the same management as the Grand Hotel (see above), this is the most pleasantly situated and one of the most modern hotels in town. The interior has winding staircases, white marble sheathing, and big windows. Guest rooms have adequately sized tile bathrooms with shower-tub combinations, and are designed with Scandinavian fabrics and unusual lithographs. Most units are moderate in size; singles are a bit cramped.

Knut den Stores Gata 2, S-221 04. © **046/280-65-00.** Fax 046/280-65-10. www.lundia.se. 97 units. Late June to early Aug and Fri–Sat year-round 995SEK ($105) double; rest of year 1,375SEK–1,890SEK ($146–$200) double. Year-round 2,100SEK–3,750SEK ($223–$398) suite. Rates include breakfast. AE, DC, MC, V. Closed Dec 22–26. Parking 100SEK ($11). Bus: 1, 2, 3, 4, 5, 6, or 7. **Amenities:** Restaurant; bar; casino; sauna; room service; laundry/dry cleaning. *In room:* TV, minibar, hair dryer.

Scandic Hotel Star ✿   This hotel, a 20-minute walk from the town center, is the most comfortable in Lund. Built in 1991, it attracts lots of business conventions, as well as rock stars and movie actors known throughout Sweden. Each of the hotel's double rooms is configured as a mini-suite, with a separate sitting area and traditional, conservative furnishings that would fit into a well-appointed upper-middle-class Swedish home. Guest rooms have lots of potted or hanging plants, wicker furnishing, and well-maintained bathrooms with shower-tub combinations. The public areas are more international and contemporary than the guest rooms.

Glimmervägen 5, P.O. Box 11026, SE-220 11 Lund. © **046/285-25-00.** Fax 046/285-25-11. www.scandic-hotels.com. 196 units. Mid-June to mid-Aug and Fri–Sat year-round 880SEK ($93) double; rest of year 1,180SEK ($125) double. Year-round 2,500SEK–3,500SEK ($265–$371) suite. AE, DC, MC, V. Free parking. Bus: 3 or 7. **Amenities:** Restaurant; bar; pool; fitness center; sauna; room service; laundry/dry cleaning. *In room:* TV, minibar, hair dryer, safe.

WHERE TO DINE
MODERATE

Barntorget 9 ⋆ SWEDISH/CONTINENTAL   Charming and traditional, this restaurant occupies a white-painted, wood-sided structure that, at the time of its construction in the 1860s, contained three separate residences, and which later functioned as a bakery, a motorcycle repair shop, and a clothing store. Today, in a much-gentrified form, amid frescoed ceilings, flowerpots, and holders for the candles (up to 120 per night) that illuminate this place, you'll enjoy a sophisticated medley of Swedish ingredients cooked in Swedish, and sometimes vaguely French, ways. The best examples include marinated mussels and snails in garlic sauce; traditional Swedish meatballs and duck breast with orange sauce; and a dish of minced veal with cream-based gravy and mashed potatoes. Other excellent choices include roast lamb, tournedos of veal, braised pike-perch, and pan-fried filets of lemon sole. It lies within a very short walk of Lund's railway station.

Barntorget 7–9. © **046/32-02-00.** Reservations recommended. Main courses 150SEK–210SEK ($16–$22). AE, DC, MC, V. Mon–Thurs 6–10pm; Fri–Sat 6–11pm. Bus: 2 or 4.

Brasserie Lundia SWEDISH   This brasserie is the only restaurant in Lund with its own in-house bakery. At lunch, when it's one of the most popular cafeterias in town, it serves crisp salads, open-faced sandwiches, and hot dishes as part of the full cafeteria meals. At night, it's an a la carte restaurant with waitstaff service, serving steak tartare, fettuccine with salmon, tagliatelle bolognese, grilled filet mignon, grilled pork cutlet with pepper sauce, deep-fried Camembert, and seven kinds of alcohol-rich after-dinner coffees. Although no one ever accused the kitchen staff of being overly experimental here, what you get isn't bad. Everything is well prepared, and there's good, relaxed service. It has an inviting decor with wood and russet-colored marble tables.

In the Hotel Lundia, Knut den Stores Gata 2. © **046/12-41-40.** Reservations required Fri–Sat. Main courses 115SEK–175SEK ($12–$19). AE, DC, MC, V. Mon–Fri 11am–midnight; Sat noon–10pm; Sun 1–11pm. Bus: 1, 2, 3, 4, 5, 6, or 7.

Ø Bar ⋆ *(Finds* INTERNATIONAL   One of the most interesting restaurants in Lund defines itself as a "laboratory for chefs" because of the experimental nature of a menu that changes virtually every week. The venue looks like it might have been designed by a Milanese post-modernist, with blue and ash-white walls and a strictly minimalist kind of angularity. It's usually mobbed every night both with diners and with clients of the convivial bar area. Here, you're likely to meet students from the university *and* their professors, all animated in dialogue. Menu items include filet of elk with thyme sauce, served with apple and potato muffins; grilled halibut served with lemon oil, horseradish, and house-made pasta; and lime-flavored clam chowder with Vietnamese spring rolls.

Mårtenstorget 9. © **046/211-22-88.** Reservations recommended. Main courses 125SEK–285SEK ($13–$30). AE, DC, MC, V. Daily 11:30am–midnight; bar until 1 or 2am.

Staket *(Value* SWEDISH/CONTINENTAL   An old tavern that serves good food in an unspoiled atmosphere, this establishment occupies the cellar and street level of a 15th-century building. The step-gabled brick facade is a historic landmark. Menu items include crabmeat cocktail, lobster or goulash soup, white filet of pork, tournedos of beef, a mixed grill, marinated salmon, pickled herring, baked potatoes with black curry, and whitefish toast. Although both dining rooms are equally appealing, fondues (a ritual in which skewers of meat are cooked at your table in pots of heated oil) are served only in the cellar.

Stora Södergatan 6. (*C*) **046/211-93-67.** Reservations recommended. Main courses 145SEK–180SEK ($15–$19). AE, DC, MC, V. Mon–Thurs noon–10:30pm; Fri–Sat noon–11:30pm; Sun noon–10pm. Bus: 1, 2, 3, 4, 5, 6, or 7.

INEXPENSIVE

Dalby Gästgifveri *(Finds* SWEDISH   If you really want to flatter the pride of the local residents of this hamlet (pop. 2,000), you'll acknowledge that the village inn, Dalby Gästgifveri, is the oldest of its kind in Skåne. That isn't completely true, however, as the house that contains it has burned to the ground (and been rebuilt) at least twice since it was built around 1870. But during excavations conducted on the village church next door, evidence was unearthed that supports the belief that a tavern and inn associated with the church was serving food and drink to passersby in the 12th century. So come to this tavern knowing that there has been a tradition of inn-keeping here for a long, long time. The wood-sided structure is painted in the colors of the Skanish flag (ocher and oxblood red). Within a pair of street-level dining rooms loaded with rustic antiques, from a church-side location in the heart of the village, you'll enjoy menu items that local homes have served in Skåne for many decades. Fine examples include smoked eel with lemon sauce, yellow-tomato soup, a Skanish omelet laced with pork and served with lingonberries, roasted lamb with rosemary, entrecôte with garlic butter sauce, and an all-vegetarian main course of corn schnitzels (a form of fritter). The restaurant is a 15-minute drive east of Lund.

Tengsgatan 6, in Lund's suburban hamlet of Dalby. (*C*) **046/20-00-06.** Reservations recommended. Main courses 90SEK–180SEK ($9.55–$19); set-price lunch (available Mon–Fri only) 68SEK ($7.20). AE, DC, MC, V. Mon–Fri 11:30am–8pm; Sat 1–8pm; Sun 1–5pm. Bus: 160 from Lund.

Gloria's Bar and Restaurant AMERICAN   The success of this American-inspired sports and Western bar would gladden the heart of any U.S.-born ideologue. On two floors of an old-fashioned building in the historic center of town, it has a crowded and likable bar in the cellar and an even larger bar upstairs. Scattered throughout the premises are photographs and posters of American sports heroes, baseball and football memorabilia, and Wild West artifacts. Draft beer costs 45SEK ($4.75) for a foamy mug. The restaurant serves copious portions of such rib-stickers as hamburgers, steaks, and an array of Cajun-inspired dishes. The staff wears jeans, cowboy boots, and shirts emblazoned with Gloria's logo. Various kinds of live music are performed between 9:30pm and 1am each Wednesday. Thursday features a DJ spinning rock.

S:t Petri Kyrkogata 9. (*C*) **046/15-19-85.** Reservations recommended. Main courses 89SEK–219SEK ($9.45–$23). AE, MC, V. Mon–Fri 11:30am–10:30pm; Sat 12:30–11pm; Sun 1–11pm. Bus: 1, 2, 3, 4, 5, 6, or 7.

LUND AFTER DARK

Most dance clubs in Lund operate only on weekends, when the clientele mostly includes university students. Examples include **Tetner's Restaurant,** Sandgatan 2 (*C* **046/13-13-33**), which opens a dance floor in the cellar every Saturday from 9pm till 2am. There's also a dance floor in the basement of the also-recommended **Gloria's Restaurant,** every Friday and Saturday beginning at 10:30pm. Entrance is free. A final dance choice, also open only Friday and Saturday, is the **Palladium,** Stora Södergatan 13 (© **046/211-66-60**), a beer pub with a college-age clientele. Admission is free.

Lundia Nightcafé   In the cellar of the Hotel Lundia (see "Where to Stay," above) is a small-stakes casino (blackjack and roulette), two bars, a dance floor, and a modern club popular with students. Residents of the Hotel Lundia and guests and clients of diners from the Brasserie Lundia enter free, but everyone else pays the cover. Draft beer costs 45SEK ($4.75). It's open from 11pm to 3am. Knut den Stores Gata 2. © **046/280-65-22.** Cover 100SEK ($11). Bus: 1, 2, 3, 4, 5, 6, or 7.

EASY EXCURSIONS

You may want to make a side trip to **Dalby Church,** 5-240 12 Dalby (© **046/ 20-00-65**), 13km (8 miles) east of Lund. The starkly beautiful, well-preserved 11th-century former bishop's church built of stone is the oldest church in Scandinavia. Be sure to visit its crypt. The church is open daily from 9am to 4pm. Several buses (nos. 158 and 161) run each day between Lund center and Dalby.

About a 30-minute drive northeast of Lund (off Rte. 23) is the **Castle of Bosjökloster,** Höör by Ringsjön (© **0413/250-48**). Once a Benedictine convent founded around 1080, it was closed during the Reformation in the 16th century. The spectacular Great Courtyard contains thousands of flowers and exotic shrubs, terraces, and a park with animals and birds. In the park stands a 1,000-year-old oak tree. In the vaulted refectory and the Stone Hall, native arts and crafts, jewelry, and other Swedish goods are displayed. You can picnic on the grounds or enjoy a lunch at a simple restaurant in the garden, for around 100SEK ($11).

The entire complex is open daily from May 1 to September 30 from 8am to 8pm; the museum and exhibition hall inside the castle, daily from 10am to 6pm. Admission is 45SEK ($4.75) for adults; 40SEK ($4.25) for seniors, students, and children 6 to 16; and free for children under 6. The castle lies 46km (28 miles) from Malmö and 29km (18 miles) from Lund. From Lund, there's a train link to Höör; after that, take bus no. R02 to Bösjokloster on Route 23, about 5km (3 miles) south to Höör.

5 Ystad (★

55km (34 miles) E of Malmö, 46km (28 miles) W of Simrishamn

Ystad makes a good base for exploring the castles and manors of Skåne. An important port during the Middle Ages, Ystad retains its ancient look, with about 300 half-timbered houses, mazes of narrow lanes, and even a watchman who sounds the hours of the night in the tower of St. Mary's Church.

ESSENTIALS

GETTING THERE   From Malmö, drive east on Route 65. If you're not driving, there are good rail connections. Monday through Friday, trains run roughly on the hour between Malmö and Ystad. The trip takes 1 hour. On Saturday there are four daily trains from Malmö, and on Sunday six trains. Three daily buses make the 1-hour trip Monday through Saturday from Malmö to Ystad. On Sunday, there's only one bus.

VISITOR INFORMATION   The tourist bureau, **Ystads Turistbyrå,** St. Knuts Torg (© **0411/57-76-81;** www.ystad.se), is at the bus station in the same building as the art museum (Konstmuseum). It's open from mid-June to mid-August, Monday through Saturday from 11am to 6pm and Sunday from 10am to 7pm; off season, Monday through Friday from 9am to 5pm and Saturday from 10am to 2pm.

SEEING THE SIGHTS

The focal point of the town is **St. Maria Kyrka,** Stortorget (© **0411/692-00**), which dates to the early 1200s. Each successive century brought new additions and changes. Regrettably, many of its richest decorative features were deemed unfashionable and removed in the 1880s because of changing tastes. (However, some of the more interesting ones were brought back in a restoration program 4 decades later.) The chancel with the ambulatory is late Gothic, and the church spire dates from 1688. Inside, look for the baptismal chapel, with a richly carved German altar from the 15th century. The font came from Lübeck, Germany, in 1617, and the iron candelabra is a very early one, from the 1300s. The early-17th-century baroque pulpit is also worth a look. The church is open from June to mid-September only, daily from 10am to 6pm. There is no admission fee.

The **Museum of Modern Art (Ystads Konstmuseum),** St. Knuts Torg (© **0411/57-72-85**) in central Ystad, includes a small military museum. Permanent exhibits feature mainly art from Denmark and Skåne from the past 100 years. Admission is 20SEK ($2.10). The Ystad Tourist Office is in the same building as the museum. The museum is open Tuesday through Friday from noon to 5pm, Saturday and Sunday from noon to 4pm.

The only museum in Sweden in a medieval monastic house is the **City Museum in the Grey Friars Monastery (Stadsmuséet i Gråbrödraklostret),** St. Petri Kykoplan (© **0411/57-72-86**). Constructed in 1267, the building is a monument from the Danish era of Ystad. Various antiquities in the museum trace the area's history. The museum is open year-round Monday through Friday from 10am to 5pm, and Saturday through Sunday from noon to 4pm. The admission fee is 20SEK ($2.10).

WHERE TO STAY

Hotel Continental 🅐🅐   Although it has modern appointments, this may be Skåne's oldest hotel, dating from 1829. The rooms are furnished in tasteful Italian-inspired decor and have a number of modern extras. The bathrooms are well proportioned and equipped with shower-tub combinations. A restoration added marble sheathing to the lobby and gleaming crystal chandeliers. The hotel owners take a personal interest in the welfare of their guests. It's opposite the train station and close to the ferry terminal.

Hamngatan 13 S-271 00 Ystad. © **0411/137-00.** Fax 0411/125-70. www.hotelcontinental-ystad.se. 52 units. June 21–Aug 4 and Fri–Sat year-round 950SEK ($101) double; rest of year 1,090SEK–1,200SEK ($116–$127) double. AE, DC, MC, V. Parking 20SEK ($2.10). **Amenities:** Restaurant; bar; room service; babysitting; laundry/dry cleaning. In room: TV, hair dryer.

Hotel Tornväktaren *(Value*   Much of the charm of this simple bed-and-breakfast hotel derives from its hardworking owner, Ms. Inger Larsson. Her home is a turn-of-the-20th-century stone-built, red-trimmed structure with a garden, 10 minutes on foot from the railway station. Rooms are outfitted in pale pastels with lots of homey touches that include frilly curtains, wall-to-wall carpeting, and lace doilies covering painted wooden furniture. Units with bathrooms have neatly kept showers. Other than a filling morning breakfast, no meals are served.

St. Östergatan 33, S-271 34 Ystad. ℂ **0411/784-80.** Fax 0411/729-27. 9 units, 5 with bathroom. 695SEK ($74) double with bathroom; 595SEK ($63) double without bathroom. Rates include breakfast. AE, MC, V. Free parking. **Amenities:** Lounge. *In room:* TV.

Ystads Saltsjöbad ✿ *(Finds)*   Beautifully situated on 4 hectares (10 acres) of forested land beside the sea, this hotel is close to Sweden's southernmost tip. It was built in 1897 by one of the most famous opera stars of his day, Swedish-born Solomon Smith. Designed as a haven for the Gilded Age aristocracy of northern Europe, it consists of three connected four-story buildings with big-windowed corridors, set close to the sands of an expansive beach. The guest rooms are comfortably furnished in turn-of-the-20th-century style. Each unit has a neatly kept bathroom with a shower-tub combination. About half of them were refurbished in the mid-1990s.

The clientele changes throughout the year. In the summer, the hotel caters to beachgoers; in the winter, it's often filled with corporate conventions. The neighborhood provides good opportunities for healthy pastimes such as tennis and golf.

Saltsjöbadsgatan 6, S-271 39 Ystad. ℂ **0411/136-30.** Fax 0411/55-58-35. www.ystadssaltsjöbad.se. 108 units. June 19–Aug 31 990SEK–1,090SEK ($105–$116) double; Sept–June 18 1,230SEK–1,710SEK ($130–$181) double. Year-round Mon–Thurs 2,070SEK–2,300SEK ($219–$244) suite; Fri–Sun 1,500SEK–1,790SEK ($159–$190) suite. AE, DC, MC, V. Closed Dec 23–Jan 6. Free parking. **Amenities:** Restaurant; cafe; bar; pool; sauna; room service; laundry/dry cleaning. *In room:* A/C, TV, hair dryer.

WHERE TO DINE

Lottas Restaurang SWEDISH   Fans praise it as one of the most popular and bustling restaurants in town; its detractors avoid it because of slow service by a small staff that sometimes seems impossibly overworked. Everyone awards high marks, however, for the well-prepared cuisine. Meals are served in a brick dining room within a century-old building that once functioned as a private home. The menu runs to conservative, old-timey Swedish cuisine, which might include fried and creamed filet of cod with dill-flavored boiled potatoes, pork schnitzel with asparagus and béarnaise sauce, tenderloin of pork with mushrooms in cream sauce, and marinated breast of chicken with roasted potatoes. For dessert, try warm chocolate cake with ice cream.

Stortorget 11. ℂ **0411/788-00.** Reservations recommended. Main courses 87SEK–164SEK ($9.20–$17). AE, DC, MC, V. Mon–Sat 5–10.30pm.

Rådhuskällaren Ystad SWEDISH   One of the most reliable lunchtime restaurants in Ystad occupies a series of vaulted cellars that were built as part of a monastery in the 1500s. Several hundred years later, the Rådhus (Town Hall) was reconstructed after a disastrous fire above the monastery's cellars. Today, amid small tables and romantic candlelight, you can enjoy such tasty dishes as shellfish soup with saffron, beef filet stuffed with lobster, marinated and grilled tenderloin steak, grilled angler-fish with basil-cream sauce, saddle of lamb with fresh herbs, and roast reindeer with mushrooms and game sauce.

Stortorget. ℂ **0411/185-10.** Main courses 98SEK–189SEK ($10–$20). AE, DC, MC, V. Mon–Sat 11:30am–2:30pm; Sun 4–9pm.

Restaurant Bruggeriet ✿ SWEDISH/INTERNATIONAL   This novel restaurant was originally built in 1749 as a warehouse for malt. In 1996, a team of local entrepreneurs installed a series of large copper vats and transformed the site into a pleasant, cozy restaurant and brewery. Today, they specialize in two "tastes" of beer—a lager and a dark—that are marketed under the brand name *Ysta Färskö*. Depending on their size, they sell for 25SEK to 50SEK ($2.65–$5.30) per mug. Food items served here seem carefully calibrated to taste best when consumed with either of the two beers. Examples include fried herring marinated in mustard and sour cream and served with mashed potatoes; grilled salmon with red wine sauce; marinated and baked Swedish lamb with garlic and herbs; tenderloin steak with brandy sauce; and a succulent version of barbecued ribs you might have expected in New Orleans.

Långgatan 20. ℂ **0411/69-99-99.** Reservations recommended. Main courses 95SEK–192SEK ($10–$20). AE, DC, MC, V. Mon–Sat 11:30am–10:30pm; Sun 12:30–10pm.

Sandskogens Vardshus SWEDISH   Set about 1.5km (1 mile) east of Ystad's center, this structure was originally built in 1899 as a summer home for the town's mayor. It was converted to a restaurant in the 1930s, and ever since then it has provided local diners with well-prepared Swedish specialties that include marinated mussels; toast with whitebait roe, sour cream, and onions; fried brill with caramelized butter sauce; turbot with shrimp and Swedish caviar; gratin of lobster with lemon sole; and lingonberry or cloudberry parfait (in season).

Saltsjøvagen, Sandskogen. ℂ **0411/147-60.** Reservations recommended. Main courses 169SEK–220SEK ($18–$23); fixed-price lunch 98SEK ($10); fixed-price dinner 210SEK ($22). AE, DC, MC, V. Tues–Sun 11:30am–10pm. Closed Jan–Feb.

6 Simrishamn 🖈

630km (391 miles) S of Stockholm, 95km (59 miles) E of Malmö, 40km (25 miles) E of Ystad

One of the most idyllic towns along the Skåne coastline, Simrishamn features old half-timbered buildings, courtyards, and gardens. This seaport is the jumping-off point for the Danish island of Bornholm.

ESSENTIALS

GETTING THERE   From Ystad, our last stopover, continue east along Route 10. If you're not driving, four trains a day (three on weekends) make the 45-minute trip between Malmö and Simrishamn. Nine buses a day arrive from Kristianstad (four on weekends), and 10 buses a day from Ystad (three on weekends). From Lund, there are eight daily buses. Tickets can be purchased on board the bus.

VISITOR INFORMATION   For information about hotels, boardinghouses, summer cottages, and apartments, check with the tourist bureau. **Simrishamns Kommun Turistbyrå,** Tullhusgatan 2 (ℂ **0414/160-60;** www.turistbyra. simrishamn.se), is open from June to August, Monday through Friday from 9am to 8pm, Saturday from 10am to 8pm, and Sunday from 11am to 8pm; from September to May, Monday through Friday from 9am to 5pm.

SEEING THE SIGHTS

Other than the charming little town itself, there isn't much to see after you've walked through the historic core. (The major attractions are nearby; see below.) The old town is a maze of tiny fondant-colored cottages that in some ways evoke a movie set. The chief attraction here is **St. Nicolai Kirke,** Storgatan (ℂ **0414/ 41-24-80**). It's open daily from noon to 5pm, charging no admission.

Originally constructed as a fisherman's chapel in the 12th century, the church literally dominates the town. It's built of chunky sandstone blocks, with a brick porch and step gables. Over the years, there have been many additions. A nave was added in the 1300s, and the vault dates from the 1400s. Inside, look for the flamboyantly painted pulpit from the 1620s. The pews and votive ships on display were installed much later, in the 1800s. Outside you'll see two sculptures, both by Carl Milles, called *The Sisters* and *Angel with Trumpet*.

NEARBY ATTRACTIONS

Backakra 𝔊 Located off the coastal road between Ystad and Simrishamn is the farm that Dag Hammarskjöld, the late United Nations secretary-general, purchased in 1957 and intended to make his home. Although he died in a plane crash before he could live there, the old farm has been restored according to his instructions. The rooms are filled with gifts to Mr. Hammarskjöld—everything from a Nepalese dagger to a lithograph by Picasso.

The site is 31km (19 miles) southwest of Simrishamn, and can be reached by the bus from Simrishamn marked YSTAD. Likewise, a bus from Ystad, marked SIMRISHAMN, also goes by the site. Scheduling your return might be difficult because of infrequent service—check in advance.

Other than the caretakers, the site is unoccupied most of the year, with the occasional exception of some of the 18 members of the Swedish Academy, who are allowed to use the house for meditation and writing whenever they want.

S-270 20 Loderup. 𝒞 **0411/52-66-11.** Admission 40SEK ($4.25) adults, free for children. June 8–Aug 16 daily noon–5pm; May 16–June 7 and Aug 17–Sept 20 Sat–Sun noon–5pm. Closed Sept 21–May 15.

Glimmingehus 𝔊 Located about 10km (6 miles) southwest of Simrishamn, this bleak castle was built between 1499 and 1505. It's the best-preserved medieval keep in Scandinavia, but the somewhat Gothic, step-gabled building is unfurnished. Visitors can order snacks or afternoon tea at a cafe on the premises. June through August, a guided tour in English leaves at 2pm every day. Lots of events take place in summer, including theatrical presentations, lectures, medieval meals with entertainment, even a medieval festival in August.

Hammenhög. 𝒞 **0414/186-20.** Admission 50SEK ($5.30) adults, 30SEK ($3.20) children. Daily 10am–4pm. Closed Nov–Mar.

Kivik Tomb 𝔊 Discovered in 1748, Sweden's most notable Bronze Age relic is north of Simrishamn along the coast of Kivik. In a 1931 excavation, tomb furniture, bronze fragments, and some grave carvings were uncovered. A total of eight floodlit runic slabs depict pictures of horses, a sleigh, and what appears to be a fun-loving troupe of dancing seals. Kivik has long been recognized as one of the most amazing monuments of the Bronze Age. You can reach the site by car.

Bredaror. No phone. Admission 15SEK ($1.60). Daily 10am–6pm. Closed Sept–Apr.

WHERE TO STAY

Hotel Kockska Gården (Value) An unspoiled black-and-white half-timbered coaching inn, this hotel is built around a large medieval courtyard in the town center. Its lounge combines the old and new, with a stone fireplace contrasted with balloon lamps. The guest rooms have been modernized, and the furnishings are up-to-date with tastefully coordinated colors and good beds. Bathrooms tend to be small but do contain neatly kept shower units. The only meal served is breakfast.

Storgatan 25, S-272 31 Simrishamn. 𝒞 **0414/41-17-55.** Fax 0414/117-55. 18 units. 630SEK–890SEK ($67–$94) double. Rates include breakfast. AE, MC, V. Free parking. **Amenities:** Lounge. *In room:* TV.

Hotel Svea 𝔊 Painted pale yellow, with a red tile roof like those of older buildings nearby, this is the most-recommended hotel in town, and the site of a fine restaurant (Restaurant Svea, see below). Although much of what you'll see today was rebuilt and radically renovated in 1986, the origins of this waterfront hotel in the town center date from around 1900. Many of its well-appointed, conservatively comfortable rooms overlook the harbor; all rooms have good beds and medium-size bathrooms equipped with shower-tub combinations. The hotel's only suite, the Prince Eugen, is named after a member of the royal family of Sweden who stayed here shortly after the hotel was built.

Strandvägen 3, S-272 31 Simrishamn. © **0414/41-17-20.** Fax 0414/143-41. www.hotelsvea-simrishamn. com. 59 units. Mid-June to mid-Aug and Fri–Sun year-round 1,090SEK ($116) double, 1,290SEK ($137) suite. Rest of year 1,190SEK ($126) double, 1,290SEK ($137) suite. AE, DC, MC, V. Free parking. **Amenities:** Restaurant; bar; sauna; laundry/dry cleaning. *In room:* TV, hair dryer, safe.

WHERE TO DINE

Restaurant Svea ⚑ SWEDISH/INTERNATIONAL   The best restaurant in town lies within the pale yellow walls of the recommended Hotel Svea. Within a modern, mostly beige room whose windows overlook the harbor, the kitchen focuses on very fresh fish pulled from local waters. However, the kitchen also turns out beef, pork, chicken, and some exotic meats, such as grilled filet of ostrich (the chef added it to the menu mainly as a conversational oddity). Other menu items include strips of smoked duck breast in lemon sauce; a platter of artfully arranged herring that can be prepared at least three different ways; filet of fried sole with white wine or tartar sauce; fish of the day prepared au gratin with shrimp and lobster sauce; medallions of pork with béarnaise sauce; and a succulent filet of beef with salsa-style tomato sauce.

In the Hotel Svea. Strandvägen 3. © **0414/41-17-20.** Reservations recommended. Main courses 95SEK–210SEK ($10–$22). AE, DC, MC, V. Daily 6–9:30pm. Closed Dec 21–Jan 8.

Exploring the Swedish Countryside

After seeing Stockholm, visitors often face a difficult decision about what else to do. Sweden is a large country, and most travelers have limited time. In this chapter we'll focus on several interesting possibilities, including an excursion on the **Göta Canal,** one of Scandinavia's major attractions. Another trip is to **Dalarna.** More than any other, this folkloric province is quintessential Sweden. Besides the traditional customs, handicrafts, and festive costumes, the region is important artistically. Two of Sweden's most famous painters came from Dalarna: Anders Zorn and Carl Larsson.

We'll also take a ferry to **Gotland,** Sweden's holiday island, which is known for its cliff formations and wide, sandy beaches. Inhabited since 5000 B.C., Gotland is Scandinavia's

most intriguing island. Visby is the capital.

For the more adventurous, **Swedish Lapland** is an alluring destination. Home of the once-nomadic Lapps (or Sami, as they prefer to be known), it is one of Europe's last great open spaces. As golden eagles soar above snow-capped crags, you can "listen to the silence." Skiers flock to the area, but the summer miracle of the midnight sun shining above the Arctic Circle attracts the most visitors. This area is so vast (some 1,000km/620 miles from north to south) that we've highlighted only a few destinations. Swedish Lapland is also a great place for summer sports—canoeing, river rafting, salmon fishing, hiking, and climbing. Local tourist offices can put you in touch with outfitters who arrange offbeat adventures.

1 The Göta Canal ★★★

The 4-day Göta Canal cruise, one of Sweden's major attractions, is a fascinating summer boat trip. It covers about 560km (350 miles) from Gothenburg (Göteborg) in the west to Stockholm in the east (or vice versa); the cruise includes four or five stops, and you sleep onboard. The Göta Canal consists of a series of man-made canals, lakes, and rivers connected by 58 locks. The highest is more than 90m (300 ft.) above sea level.

The canal, begun in the early 19th century, was designed to transport goods across Sweden, avoiding the expensive tolls levied by Denmark on ships entering and leaving the Baltic Sea. Soon after the canal opened, however, Denmark waived the tolls, and the railway between Stockholm and Gothenburg was completed. Both options allowed cheaper and faster shipment of goods across Sweden, so the canal became more of a tourist attraction than a means of transportation.

Boats from Gothenburg head east along the Göta Älv River. About 30 minutes outside Gothenburg, passengers can view the 14th-century **Bohus Fortress.**

It played a leading role in the battles waged by Sweden, Norway, and Denmark. Bohus Castle and Fortress (Bohus Fästning) was built by order of Norway's Haakon V on Norwegian territory. After the territory was ceded to Sweden in 1658, Bohus Fortress was used as a prison. Most of the boats (but not necessarily all) will stop here so you can climb the tower known as *Fars Hatt* ("Father's Hat") for a panoramic view. Farther down the river, the boat passes the town of **Kungälv** (known to the Vikings as Konghälla). Its traditions date back 1,000 years.

As the boat proceeds east on the Göta's clear water, the landscape becomes wilder. About 5 hours into the journey, you reach the town of **Trollhättan,** home of one of Europe's largest power stations. The once-renowned Trollhättan Falls can be seen at their full capacity only in July. The rest of the year, they're almost dry. Today a series of underground channels diverts most of the water to the power station.

After passing through a series of locks, boats enter **Lake Vänern,** Sweden's largest lake, with a surface area of more than 3,380 sq. km (2,100 sq. miles). The trip across takes about 8 hours. Along the way, you'll pass **Lidköping,** home of the famous Rörstrand porcelain. Lidköping received its charter in 1446. North of Lidköping, on the island of Kållandsö, stands **Läckö Slott,** a castle dating from 1298. Originally home of the bishops of Skara, the castle was given to King Gustavus Vasa in 1528, and later presented to Sweden's great military hero Gen. Jacob de la Gardie.

Once across Lake Vänern, boats return to the canal. A series of locks, including the canal's oldest (at Forsvik), carries the steamers to Sweden's second-largest lake, **Lake Vättern.** It's famous for its beauty and translucent water. At some points, visibility reaches a depth of 15m (50 ft.).

On the eastern shore of Lake Vättern sits the medieval town of **Vadstena,** the most important stop on the Göta Canal trip. It has old, narrow streets and frame buildings. The town is known throughout Sweden for its delicate handmade lace, which you can see by walking along Stora Gatan, the main street. Also of interest is the **Klosterkyrkan (Abbey Church).** Built between the mid–14th century and the 15th century to specifications outlined by its founder, St. Birgitta (Bridget) of Sweden, the Gothic church is rich in medieval art. Parts of the abbey date from 1250; the building sheltered the nuns of St. Birgitta's order until they were expelled in 1595.

Another important sight is **Vadstena Castle.** Construction began in 1545 under Gustavus Vasa, king of Sweden, but was not completed until 1620. This splendid Renaissance castle, erected during a period of national expansion, dominates the town from its position on the lake, just behind the old courthouse in the southern part of town.

Boats bound for Stockholm leave Lake Vättern and pass through two small lakes, Boren and Roxen. South of Lake Roxen is the university town of **Linköping,** site of a battle between Roman Catholic King Sigismund of Poland and Duke Charles of Södermanland (later Charles IX). Charles won the battle and made Linköping part of Sweden, rather than a province of Rome. In the town's main square stands the Folkung Fountain, one of sculptor Carl Milles's most popular works. Northwest of the main square is the cathedral, a not-always-harmonious blend of Romanesque and Gothic architecture.

From Linköping, boats enter Lake Roxen and continue northeast by canal to **Slätbaken,** a fjord that stretches to the sea. The route continues along the coast to Stockholm.

The **Göta Canal Steamship Company** offers turn-of-the-20th-century steamers, including its 1874 *Juno,* which claims to be the world's oldest passenger vessel that offered overnight accommodations. The line also operates the 1912 *Wilhelm Tham* and the newer—that is, 1931—*Diana.* Passengers walk, jog, or bike along the canal path, and there are organized shore excursions at many stops along the way.

For bookings, contact **Scantours** (© **800/223-7226;** www.scantours.com). The 4-day cruises range from 6,600 to 11,250SEK ($775–$1,325) per person double occupancy; 6-day cruises from 10,400 to 14,000SEK ($1,225–$1,650). Discounts are given for early reservations.

2 Dalarna ✶✶✶

This province offers everything from maypole dancing and fiddle music to folk costumes and handicrafts (including the Dala horse). Dalarna means "valleys," and you'll sometimes see it referred to as "Dalecarlia," the Anglicized form of the name.

Lake Siljan, arguably the most beautiful lake in Europe, is ringed with resort villages and towns. Leksand, Rättvik, and Mora attract summer visitors with sports, folklore, and a week of music. In the winter, people come here to ski.

From June 23 to June 26, the Dalecarlians celebrate midsummer with maypole dancing. They go through the forest gathering birch boughs and nosegays of wildflowers to cover the maypole. Then the pole is raised and they dance around it until dawn, a good old respectable pagan custom.

FALUN ⚓

488km (303 miles) NE of Gothenburg, 229km (142 miles) NW of Stockholm

Our driving tour of the region begins in Falun, the old capital of Dalarna; it lies on both sides of the Falu River. The town is noted for its copper mines; copper revenue has supported many Swedish kings. Just 10km (6½ miles) northeast, you can visit the home of the famed Swedish painter Carl Larsson.

ESSENTIALS

GETTING THERE From Stockholm, take the E18 expressway northwest to the junction with Route 70. Take Route 70 to the junction with Route 60, where you head northwest. The train takes 3 hours from Stockholm, 6 hours from Gothenburg.

Swebus (© **0200/21-82-18** in Sweden only) express buses run between Stockholm and Falun once or twice daily, depending on the season. From Gothenburg, local buses arrive twice every day. A second bus company that services Falun is **Masexpressen** (© **08/10-77-66**), which operates additional buses into Falun from Stockholm and other points within Sweden.

VISITOR INFORMATION The **Falun Tourist Office,** Trotzgatan 10–12 (© **023/830-50;** www.welcome.falun.se), is open from mid-August to mid-June, Monday through Friday from 9am to 6pm and Saturday from 10am to 2pm. During summer, from mid-June to mid-August, it's open Monday through Friday from 9am to 7pm, Saturday from 10am to 5pm, and Sunday from 10am to 5pm.

A SPECIAL EVENT The 4-day **Falun Folkmusik Festival,** celebrated annually in July, attracts hundreds of folk musicians from around the world in one of Scandinavia's major musical events. In addition to concerts, there are films, lectures, and seminars. For information, contact the Falun Tourist Office (see address and phone above).

SEEING THE SIGHTS

You might go first to the market square, Stora Torget, to see the **Kristine Church** (℃ 023/545-70). The copper-roofed structure dates from the mid–17th century, the tower from 1865. From June to August, it's open daily from 10am to 6pm. The rest of the year, it's open daily from 10am to 4pm. Admission is free.

Falun is the site of **Lugnet** (℃ 023/835-00), one of Sweden's largest sports complexes. The Bjursberget ski resort is 20km (13 miles) away.

Carl Larsson-gården *(Finds)*   The small village of Sundborn is the site of Lilla Hyttnas, Carl Larsson's home (now known as Carl Larsson-gården). Larsson became Sweden's most admired artist during his lifetime (1853–1919). However, when his erstwhile friend August Strindberg published a vicious attack on Larsson, the artist took a knife and stalked the playwright through the streets of Stockholm. Larsson's watercolor paintings have made his house known throughout Sweden. In the United States, reproductions of Larsson's watercolors, mainly of his wife, Karin, and their children, appear frequently on prints, calendars, and greeting cards. There are guided tours throughout the day, and English-language tours are sometimes available.

Bus no. 64 leaves from the Falun bus station several times a day. It's a 20-minute trip to Sundborn, 5 minutes from Carl Larsson-gården. Sundborn is a 2½-hour train ride from Stockholm.

Carl Larssons Väg 12, Sundborn. ℃ **023/600-53,** or 023/600-69 for off-season reservations. Admission 70SEK ($7.40) adults, 30SEK ($3.20) children 7–15, free for children under 7. May–Sept daily 10am–5pm; Oct–Apr by appointment only. Bus: 64 from Falun.

Falun Copper Mine (Falu Koppargruva) *(★★★)*   This mine in the town center was the world's largest producer of copper during the 17th century. It supplied the raw material for the roof of Versailles. The mine tour begins with an elevator trip 54m (180 ft.) below the surface. Guides take you through old chambers and winding passages dating from the Middle Ages. In one section of the mine, you'll see a shaft divided by a timber wall that's more than 195m (650 ft.) high; it may be the world's tallest wooden structure.

Gruvplatsen. ℃ **023/71-14-75.** Guided tour 80SEK ($8.50) adults, 30SEK ($3.20) children under 18. May–Aug daily 10am–4:30pm; Mar–Apr and Sept–Nov 15 Sat–Sun 12:30–4:30pm. Closed Nov 16–Feb.

WHERE TO STAY

First Hotel Grand *(★)*   This buff-colored hotel 90m (300 ft.) south of the landmark Falun Church was built in the late 19th century, with a modern addition constructed in 1974. The complex was renovated in 2000 and the tastefully modern guest rooms are among the best decorated in town. All have good beds and ample-size bathrooms equipped with shower units.

Trotzgatan 9–11, S-791 71 Falun. ℃ **023/79-48-80.** Fax 023/141-43. www.firsthotels.se. 152 units. Sun–Thurs 1,302SEK ($138) double; Fri–Sat 750SEK ($80) double. All week long 2,495SEK ($264) suite. Rates include breakfast. AE, DC, MC, V. Parking 80SEK ($8.50). Bus: 701 or 704. **Amenities:** Restaurant; bar; pool; fitness center; sauna; room service; laundry/dry cleaning. *In room:* TV.

LEKSAND *(★★)*

48km (30 miles) W of Falun, 267km (166 miles) NW of Stockholm

Leksands Noret is a doorway to Lake Siljan. No less an authority than Hans Christian Andersen found the setting idyllic. In its present form, Leksand dates to the turn of the 20th century, when it was reconstructed following a fire that had razed the community. A settlement has existed on this site since pagan times.

Many of the province's old traditions flourish here. Women don traditional dress for church on Sunday, and in June and July the long "church boats" from Viking times may cross the lake carrying parishioners to services. These boats compete in a race on the first Sunday in July. Since World War II, a miracle play, *The Road to Heaven,* has been presented in open-air performances. It provides insight into Dalarna's customs and folklore. The play runs for 10 days at the end of July.

ESSENTIALS

GETTING THERE   From Falun, head north on Route 80 to Bjursås, and then go west on a secondary road toward Sågmyra. Follow the signs to Leksand.

You can fly from Stockholm on **Skyways** (© 0250/301-75). From **Dala-Airport** (© 0243/645-00) in Borlänge, 50km (31 miles) south, there is frequent bus and train service to Leksand. Car rentals are available at the airport.

The train from Stockholm to Mora stops in Leksand. Travel time is 3½ hours. For reservations and information, call © 0771/75-75-75.

Another way to reach Leksand is by boat. The *Gustaf Wasa* (© 010/252-32-92) leaves Mora for Leksand (via Rättvik) every Monday at 3pm, and takes about 2 hours. The round-trip fare is 120SEK ($13), free for children 12 and under. All trips depart Leksand during the day, and tickets are sold on board.

VISITOR INFORMATION   The **Leksands Turistbyrå** is at Norsgatan 23 (© 0247/79-61-30; www.stab.se). It's open from June 15 to August 10, Monday through Friday from 9am to 7pm, Saturday from 10am to 5pm, and

---

Moments Happy Trails

The Orsa "outback" is an almost unpopulated area of wild beauty. From May to October you can rent a horse and covered wagon (with space for up to five people) and tour the region's beautiful summer pastures, small forest lakes, and panoramic views. Contact **Häst och Vagn** (Torsmo 1646, S-794 91 Orsa; ℭ **2505/530-14**) to arrange your 3- or 6-day trek across Dalarna forest and tundra. Each tour is self-guided, but a brief course in care and feeding of horses is conducted first. Each wagon sleeps four adults plus an indeterminate number of children, and contains bedding and kitchen equipment. No more than 15km (10 miles)—often less—are scheduled per day, and overnights are scheduled beside lakes and streams. A 6-day trek for all participants (without food) costs 4,900SEK ($519); a 3-day trek costs 3,100SEK ($329). Year-round, the same organization will rent individual horses for use on the tundra, on a per-day basis.

Sunday from 11am to 8pm; from August 11 to 18, Monday through Friday from 9am to 6pm, Saturday from 10am to 6pm, and Sunday from 11am to 4pm; from August 19 to June 14, Monday through Friday from 9am to 5pm and Saturday from 10am to 4pm.

A SPECIAL EVENT   Sweden's biggest music festival, **Music at Lake Siljan,** takes place during the first week of July. Some 100 concerts feature a wide range of music at venues in Leksand and Rättvik. Fiddle music predominates. For information, contact Music at Lake Siljan, Box 28, S-795 21 Rättvik (ℭ **0248/ 102-90**).

SEEING THE SIGHTS

Leksand's **parish church** ℛ (Leksands Kyrka) is in the town center, on Norsgatan, near the lake (ℭ **0247/807-60**). Founded in the 13th century, it assumed its present form in 1715 and is one of the largest rural churches in Sweden. During renovations in 1971, a burial site was found that dates to the period when the Vikings were being converted to Christianity. The church is open for worship throughout the year, but guided tours (in Swedish and English) are offered only from mid-June to early August. Tours are scheduled Monday through Saturday from 9:30am to 1pm and 2 to 8pm, Sunday from 1 to 5pm. Admission to the church is free; the tour costs 50SEK ($5.30) per person.

Nearby, also on Norsgatan, is an open-air museum, **Hembygdsgårdar** (ℭ **0247/802-45**). The cluster of 18th- and 19th-century buildings (which are part of the museum's collections) features depictions by that period's peasants of Christ and his Apostles in Dalarna dress. The museum is open only from mid-June to mid-August, Tuesday through Friday from 10am to 4pm, Saturday and Sunday from noon to 5pm. Admission is 20SEK ($2.10) for adults, free for children.

An athletic and health-conscious town, Leksand has ample opportunity for **outdoor sports.** There are downhill skiing facilities at the popular resort **Granberget,** about 20km (13 miles) to the southwest. The town's tourist office can provide information on swimming, cross-country skiing, curling, ice-skating, tennis, and boat rides on Lake Siljan. All are available in or near the town center, depending on the season and weather.

WHERE TO STAY

During the summer, you might find it fun to rent a *stuga* (log cabin) with four beds for 1,900SEK to 4,500SEK ($201–$477) a week. The **Leksands Turist-byrå**, Box 52, S-793 22 Leksand (*©* **0247/79-61-30**), can book you into one. You can also inquire about renting a room in a private home.

Masesgården ★★ *(Finds)*   This is one of the most sports-and-fitness-conscious hotels in Sweden. It has a reputation for educating guests about new eating and exercise habits, and a philosophy of preventing disease and depression through proper diet and exercise. Most people spend a week, participating in supervised aerobic and sports regimes, not indulging in conventional spa-style pampering. Beside a sea inlet, with a view of Leksand across the fjord, it's a sprawling compound of low-slung buildings. Guest rooms are soothing and more plush than you might have imagined. Each comes with a well-maintained bathroom equipped with a shower unit.

The daily program includes lectures that stress the link between a healthy body and a healthy soul ("astrological reincarnation and modern lifestyles" is a favorite), and physical disciplines such as tai chi. Theme weeks concentrate on individual subjects, such as meditation and modern yoga, and Reiki healing through applied massage. Other activities include aerobics, sometimes in a swimming pool, and weight training. Classes are conducted in Swedish, but most staff members speak English. This is not a holiday for the faint-hearted. Be prepared to sweat and re-evaluate your lifestyle, in ways that might not always be completely comfortable.

Grytnäs 61, S-793 92 Leksand. *©* **0247/122-31.** Fax 0247/122-51. www.masesgarden.se. 34 units, 23 with bathroom. 4,850SEK ($514) per person per week double without bathroom; 5,450SEK ($578) per person per week double with bathroom. Rates include all meals and 30 hr. of supervised sports activities. AE, DC, MC, V. Free parking. **Amenities:** Restaurant; lounge; pool; sauna; wellness programs. *In room:* No phone.

Moskogen Motel   The motel and red wooden huts at this "self-service holiday village" make a good base for excursions around the Lake Siljan area. The rooms are well furnished and comfortable, with good beds. Each unit has a tiny kitchen and a neatly kept bathroom with shower unit. A restaurant on the premises serves light lunches and dinners. The Moskogen is about 1.5km (1 mile) west of the railway station.

Insjövägen 50, S-793 00 Leksand. *©* **0247/146-00.** Fax 0247/144-30. 52 units. 830SEK ($88) double; 1,130SEK ($120) suite. Rates include breakfast. DC, MC, V. Free parking. Bus: 58. **Amenities:** Restaurant; bar; pool; exercise room; Jacuzzi; sauna; laundry/dry cleaning. *In room:* TV, safe.

WHERE TO DINE

Bosporen SWEDISH/TURKISH   This restaurant, 360m (1,200 ft.) west of the railroad station, maintains longer, more reliable hours than any other place in town. Its Istanbul-derived name comes from the Turkish-born owners. The chefs are equally at home in the Swedish and Turkish kitchens. Shish kabobs and Turkish salads are featured, but you can also order fried Baltic herring, sautéed trout, fresh salmon, or plank steak. The cooking is fair and even a bit exotic in a town not renowned for its restaurants.

Torget 1. *©* **0247/132-80.** Main courses 45SEK–185SEK ($4.75–$20). AE, DC, MC, V. Daily 11am–11pm.

RÄTTVIK ★★

20km (13 miles) NE of Leksand, 275km (171 miles) NW of Stockholm

Rättvik is one of the most popular resorts on Lake Siljan and has some of the best hotels in the district. Summer tours of the lake begin here. Culture and tradition are associated with Rättvik—you might find peasant costumes, folk dancing, Dalarna paintings, arts and crafts, "church boats," and fiddle music. There's an expression: "If you meet two men from Rättvik, three of them will be fiddlers." The old style of architecture is still prevalent, and there are many timber houses. Carpenters and painters from Rättvik are known for their craftsmanship.

ESSENTIALS

GETTING THERE   From Leksand, head north on Route 70. The train from Stockholm to Mora stops in Leksand, where you can catch another train for the short trip to Rättvik. Train information in Stockholm is available at the **Central Station** (© 0771/75-75-75). Buses to Rättvik from outlying areas operate Friday through Sunday, but once in town you shouldn't need bus transportation. For information, call **Swebus** (© 0200/218-18 in Sweden only).

VISITOR INFORMATION   The **Rättvik Tourist Office** is in the train station (© 0248/702-00). It's open from June 15 to August 10, Monday through Friday from 9am to 7pm, Saturday from 10am to 4pm, and Sunday from 11am to 4pm; from August 11 to 18, Monday through Friday from 9am to 6pm, Saturday from 10am to 4pm, and Sunday from 11am to 4pm; from August 18 to June 14, Monday through Friday from 9am to 5pm and Saturday from 10am to 1pm.

SEEING THE SIGHTS

In central Sweden, it's sometimes hard to get an overview of the forests. For an antidote—a sweeping view that stretches for many kilometers—drive about 5km (3 miles) east of town along the road leading to Falun. Here, soaring more than 24m (80 ft.) skyward, is a red wooden tower, the **Vidablick,** in Hantverksbyn (© 0248/302-50). There's no elevator, and the stairs are steep. Admission is 20SEK ($2.10) for adults, 5SEK (55¢) for children. On the premises are a coffee shop and a souvenir stand. The complex is open only from June to August 15, daily from 10am to 9pm.

One mile from the village is **Gammelgården** ★★ (© 0248/514-45), an antique farmstead whose pastures and architecture evoke the 19th century. Phone ahead, because hours are erratic; it's open when a farm resident is able to conduct a tour. With enough notice, visits can be arranged throughout the year. The likely schedule between mid-June and mid-August is daily from noon to 5pm. Admission is 20SEK ($2.10).

You can also visit an artists' village established by the Swedish artist Sören Erikson. It's at **Rättviks Hantverksby,** Gårdebyn (© 0248/302-50).

WHERE TO STAY
Expensive
Hotel Lerdalshöjden ★ *Finds*   Near the top of a hill overlooking Rättvik, a 10-minute walk north of the lake, this building is a stylish renovation of a turn-of-the-20th-century hotel. The only remaining part of the original is the Lerdalshöjden restaurant (see "Where to Dine," below). The guest rooms are well furnished and maintained. They have modern accessories and good-sized bathrooms equipped with shower units.

S-795 22 Rättvik. © 0248/511-50. Fax 0248/511-77. 95 units. 853SEK ($90) double; 1,400SEK ($148) suite. Rates include breakfast. DC, MC, V. Free parking. Bus: 58 or 70. **Amenities:** Restaurant; bar; fitness center; sauna; room service; laundry/dry cleaning. *In room:* TV, minibar (in some).

Inexpensive
Hotel Gärdebygården *Value*   This hotel, off Storgaten in the town center, is a very good value. It opened in 1906 and was renovated in 1995. It lies within

a short walk of the lake, and the hotel has expanded to include a trio of outlying buildings. The comfortable rooms are sedately outfitted, with conservative furniture and good firm beds, but the bathrooms with shower units are very small. Some units have a view of the lake. The big breakfast is almost like a Swedish smörgåsbord. Some nights are devoted to communal sing-alongs. Cross-country ski trails and jogging paths are a short distance away.

S-795 36 Rättvik. (℃) 0248/302-50. Fax 0248/306-60. vidablick@hantverksbyn.se. 87 units. 795SEK–995SEK ($84–$105) double. Rates include breakfast. MC, V. Free parking. Bus: 58 or 70. **Amenities:** Restaurant; bar; laundry/dry cleaning. *In room:* TV, minibar, hair dryer.

WHERE TO DINE
Lerdalshöjden SWEDISH This summer-only restaurant is the only original section remaining in the turn-of-the-20th-century hotel. It has long been a favorite with lake-district locals. They like its traditional, tasty Swedish home-style cooking, including fresh fish and beef dishes. Try steak tartare with bleak (a freshwater fish) roe, or fried ptarmigan with red-currant sauce.

If a hungry visitor arrives off season, he or she is often referred to the **Green Hotel** (℃ **0248/247-502-50**), signposted from the center of town and lying less than 1km (about ½ mile) away. This traditional hotel dates from the 1600s when it first opened as an inn. Additional rooms were added in the 1960s. With breakfast and dinner included, charges year-round range from 750SEK to 1,690SEK ($80–$179).

In the Lerdalshöjden Hotel. (℃) 0248/511-50. Reservations recommended. Fixed-price menu 295SEK ($31). DC, MC, V. Daily noon–2pm and 6–9pm. Closed Aug 16–June 14.

MORA ✿
45km (28 miles) W of Rättvik, 328km (204 miles) NW of Stockholm

In Upper Dalarna, between Lake Orsa and Lake Siljan, the provincial town of Mora is our final major stop in the province. Summer travelers find this business and residential center a good base for exploring the district.

Mora was the village where Gustavus Vasa finally rallied the peasants in Sweden's 16th-century war against Danish rule. Every year in March the 80km (50-mile) Vasa Race, a major ski event, commemorates the uprising.

ESSENTIALS
GETTING THERE From Rättvik, continue around Lake Siljan on Route 70.

You can fly from Stockholm on **Skyways Air** (℃ **08/595-135-00**) Sunday through Friday. Flight time is 40 minutes. The airport (℃ **0250/301-75**) is about 6.5km (4 miles) from the town center; taxis meet arriving flights.

There's also direct daily rail service from Stockholm, which takes 4 hours. On weekends, buses leave from Stockholm's Central Station for the 4-hour, 15-minute trip. Contact **Swebus Vasatrafik** (℃ **020/65-65-65**).

The *Gustaf Wasa* (℃ **010/252-32-92;** see "Essentials" under "Leksand," above) travels between Mora and Leksand. The boat departs from Leksand in the afternoon and leaves Mora at 3pm on Monday. The round-trip cost is 120SEK ($13) for adults and 60SEK ($6.35) for children.

VISITOR INFORMATION Contact the **Mora Turistbyrå,** Angbåtskajen (℃ **0250/265-50**). It's open from June 15 to August 10, Monday through Friday from 9am to 8pm, Saturday from 10am to 8pm, and Sunday from 11am to 8pm; from August 11 to August 18, Monday through Friday from 9am to 6pm, Saturday from 10am to 6pm, and Sunday from 11am to 6pm; from August 19 to June 14, Monday through Friday from 9am to 5pm and Saturday from 10am to 1pm.

SEEING THE SIGHTS

Mora is home to a **Santa complex** (© 0250/212-00), with a house and a factory. Visitors can meet Santa and see his favorite helpers making and gift-wrapping presents for children all over the world. Children can enroll in "Santa School" and participate in troll and treasure hunts.

Mora was the hometown of **Anders Zorn** (1860–1920), Sweden's most famous painter. The town's top sights are all associated with him. The first, **Lisselby,** is an area near the Zorn Museum made up of old houses now used as arts and crafts studios and boutiques. At **Balder-Lisselby,** a crafts center, you can watch handicrafts being made Monday through Saturday between 9am and 6pm, except at lunchtime.

Zornmuseet (Zorn Museum) ⭐⭐ This museum displays a wide array of the artist's works, including *Midnight.* You'll also see paintings from his private collection by Prince Eugen and by Carl Larsson, also of Dalarna. Works by major foreign artists (sculptures by Kai Nielsen of Denmark and etchings by Rembrandt) are also exhibited, as well as rural art and handicrafts from Dalarna.

Vasagatan 36. © **0250/165-60.** Admission 35SEK ($3.70) adults, 10SEK ($1.05) children. Mid-May to Aug Mon–Sat 9am–5pm, Sun 11am–5pm; Sept to mid-May Mon–Sat noon–5pm, Sun 1–5pm.

Zorngården The artist's former home, adjoining the museum, has been left just as it was when Mrs. Anders Zorn died in 1942. Its chief attraction, aside from the paintings on display, is the Great Hall on the top floor, that Zorn designed himself.

Vasagatan 36. © **0250/165-60.** Admission 45SEK ($4.95) adults, 15SEK ($1.65) children. Mid-May to mid-Sept Mon–Sat 10am–4pm, Sun 11am–4pm; mid-Sept to mid-May Mon–Sat noon–3pm, Sun 1–4pm. Full guided tours of the house at noon, 1pm, 2pm, 3pm.

SHOPPING IN NEARBY NUSNÄS

In Nusnäs, about 9.5km (6 miles) southeast of Mora, you can watch the famous wooden **Dalarna horse** *(dalahäst),* one of Sweden's most popular souvenirs, being made at **Nils Olsson Hemslöjd** (© 0250/372-00). You're free to walk around the workshops and watch the craftspeople at work, and the finished products can be purchased at a shop on the premises. It also sells wooden shoes and other craft items.

The crafts store is open from June to mid-August, Monday through Friday from 8am to 6pm, Saturday and Sunday from 9am to 5pm; from mid-August to May, Monday through Friday from 8am to 5pm, Saturday from 10am to 2pm. To find Nusnäs, take the signposted main road east from Mora, turning off to the right at Farnas. From Mora, bus no. 108 also runs to Nusnäs.

WHERE TO STAY

First Resort Mora ⭐ The Mora is in the center of town across from the lakefront, a minute's walk from the tourist bureau. Renovations over the years have added sun terraces and glassed-in verandas. The interior is tastefully decorated with bright colors. All accommodations have comfortable furniture, including good beds and ample bathrooms equipped with shower units. On Friday and Saturday, the hotel's dance club charges 70SEK ($7.40) admission for visitors, but is free for hotel guests.

Strandgatan 12, S-792 00 Mora. © **800/528-1234** in the U.S. and Canada, or 0250/59-26-50. Fax 0250/189-81. www.firsthotels.com. 141 units. 952SEK–1,402SEK ($101–$149) double. Rates include breakfast. AE, DC, MC, V. Parking 90SEK ($9.55) in garage, free outdoors. **Amenities:** Restaurant; bar; nightclub; pool; sauna; room service; laundry/dry cleaning. *In room:* TV, safe.

WHERE TO DINE

Terrassen ✦ SWEDISH   One of the finest dining rooms in the area, this is a good bet for a meal even if you aren't staying at the hotel. Fresh produce is used whenever possible, and fresh fish and Swedish beef dishes are featured. You might begin with herring or a freshly made salad. Service is polite and efficient.

In the First Resort Mora, Strandgatan 12. ℭ **0250/59-26-50.** Reservations recommended. Main courses 175SEK–265SEK ($19–$28). AE, DC, MC, V. Mon–Sat 11:30am–11pm; Sun 6–9pm.

FROM MORA BACK TO STOCKHOLM

From Mora, take Route 70. In Enköping, pick up E18, which takes you to Stockholm.

3 Gotland ✦✦ (Visby)

219km (136 miles) S of Stockholm, 150km (93 miles) S of Nynäshamn, 89km (55 miles) E of the Swedish mainland

In the middle of the Baltic Sea sits the ancient home of the Goths, the island of Gotland. Swedes go to the country's most popular tourist island for sunny holidays by the sea; North Americans tend to be more interested in the old walled city of Visby. With its cliffs, rock formations, bathing beaches, and rolling countryside, Gotland is rich territory. Buses cover the island, which is about 120km (75 miles) long and 56km (35 miles) wide, as do organized tours from Visby, the capital.

In the 12th and 13th centuries, the walled city of Visby rose to the zenith of its power. It was the seat of the powerful Hanseatic merchants and the trade center of northern Europe. Seventeen churches were built during its heyday. Step-gabled stone houses were erected, and the townspeople lived in relative luxury. Visby was eventually ransacked by the Danes, however, and the city declined. After Visby was recognized as a treasure house of medieval art and became the number-one spot in Scandinavia for experiencing the charm of the Middle Ages, it became a major tourist attraction.

ESSENTIALS

GETTING THERE   SAS (ℭ **800/221-2350** in the U.S., or 08/595-135-00; www.flysas.com) flies to Gotland from Stockholm three times a day. Flights take about 30 minutes. There is bus service between Visby and the airport.

The boat to Gotland leaves from Nynäshamn; by bus from Stockholm, it's about a 1-hour ride. The car ferry to Visby leaves at midnight and takes about 5 hours. In summer there are also daytime trips. You can make reservations through your travel agent or directly with the ferry service, **Destination Gotland** (ℭ **0498/20-10-20** in Stockholm), for a cabin, car space, or both. Book deck space if you plan to travel on a weekend.

VISITOR INFORMATION   More than one agency is available within Visby to help you get the most out of your visit to Gotland. The official government-sponsored **Gotland Tourist Office** is at Hamngatan 4 (ℭ **0498/20-17-00**). It's open daily, year-round, from 8am to noon and from 12:30 to 7pm. Also useful is a privately owned travel agency, **Gotlands Turist Service,** located at Östervåg 1 (ℭ **0498/24-70-65**). This group can arrange organized tours for groups, and can in many instances be helpful at providing tourist-related information about the island. From May to August, it's open Monday through Friday from 7am to 7pm; Saturday and Sunday from 7am to 6pm; the rest of the year, it's open Monday through Friday from 8am to 5pm, Saturday and Sunday from 10am to 4pm.

A SPECIAL EVENT   During the annual **Medieval Week** in August, for 8 days Visby becomes a Hanseatic town again. At the harbor, Strandgatan swarms with people in medieval dress, many of them tending market stalls. You meet the blacksmith, barber, cobbler, and trader. Musicians play the hurdy-gurdy, the fiddle, and the flute, and jesters play the fool. Toward nightfall, a kingly procession comes into the square. More than 100 such events take place during the festival, along with medieval mystery plays, masses, choral and instrumental music, jousting tournaments, and displays of horses. There are archery competitions, fire-eaters, belly dancers, and walking tours of the medieval town.

SEEING THE SIGHTS
IN VISBY 🏰🏰
This town is meant for walking. It can easily be explored on foot, and you may want to take one of the organized tours that are offered in season. Because so many sights, particularly the ruins of the 13th- and 14th-century churches, are better appreciated with some background, we recommend the tour. Ask at the tourist office (see "Visitor Information," above).

In town, you can walk about, observing houses from the Middle Ages, ruined fortifications, and churches. Notable among these is the **Burmeisterska Huset,** the home of the leading German merchant *(burmeister),* at Strandgatan 9.

You can walk down to the old **Hanseatic harbor** (not the harbor in use today) and stroll through the **Botanical Gardens,** which have earned Visby the title "City of Roses." You'll pass two of the most famous towers in the old wall. In the **Maiden's Tower,** a peasant girl was buried alive for helping a Danish king. The **Powder Tower** is the oldest fortification in Visby. Later you'll see **Gallow Hill,** a medieval hanging station in use until the mid-1800s.

At the height of its power and glory, little Visby boasted 16 churches. Only one, **Domkyrkan** 🏰🏰 (Cathedral of St. Mary), at Kyrkberget, is in use today. It was dedicated in 1225 and built with funds collected by German merchant ships. Pope Clement VI (in Avignon) gave his permission to build the "Swertingska chapel" in 1349. The church was damaged in serious fires in 1400, 1586, 1610, and 1744. It became a cathedral in 1572. The only original fixture left is a sandstone font from the 1200s. Visby's primary landmarks are the church's towers. The tower at the western front is square; two slimmer ones appear on the east. In the interior, one of the curiosities is the frieze of grotesque angels' faces beneath the pulpit. Hours are Monday through Friday and Sunday from 8am to 8pm, Saturday from 8am to 6:30pm. Admission is free. For more information, call ℭ **0498/20-68-00** daily from 10am to noon.

Also of interest are the ruins of the **Dominican Monastery of St. Nicholas,** just down the road from Domkyrkan (same phone for information). The church's rose window, cut from a single big stone, is more than 3m (10 ft.) in diameter. Work began on the monastery in 1230, but it was destroyed by Lübeck forces in 1525.

Another sightseeing sojourn you can do on your own is to **Gotlands Fornsal,** the Historical Museum of Gotland, Strandgatan 14 (ℭ **0498/29-27-00**). It's on a medieval street noted for its step-gabled houses. The museum contains some of the most interesting artifacts discovered on Gotland, including carved stones dating to A.D. 400, art from medieval and later periods, and furniture and household items. It's open from May 15 to August, daily from 10am to 5pm; from September to May 14, Tuesday through Sunday from noon to 4pm. Admission is 60SEK ($6.35) for adults, free for children under 17.

EXPLORING THE ISLAND

Tours of the island leave from the tourist office. They're different every day, but always include the **Lummelunda Grottan,** Lummelunds Bruk (℃ **0498/ 27-30-50**). It's a cave with stalactite and stalagmite formations, fossil remains, and subterranean waters. Visits on your own cost 60SEK ($6.35) for adults, 35SEK ($3.70) for children 5 to 15, free for children under 5.

Lummelunda is a karst cave—formed of limestone bedrock by a subterranean stream. The explored part of the stream cave stretches for about 4km (2½ miles), and there's more that has not yet been investigated. Part of the cave with some of the biggest and most beautiful chambers is open to visitors. It's 13km (8 miles) north of Visby along Route 149. A bus departs from Österport Visby (the port in town) from June 19 to August 14, daily at 2pm. The cave is open from May to June 25, daily from 9am to 4pm; from June 26 to August 14, daily from 9am to 6pm; from August 15 to September 14, daily from 9am to 4pm.

ISLAND TOURS   Ask at the **Turistbyrå** (see above) about what island tours are scheduled during your visit (summer only). These tours, if offered, are the best way to get a quick overview of Gotland. The price may be as low as 50SEK ($5.30) or as high as 360SEK ($38), but the lower end of the scale tends to be more likely.

An 11-hour bus tour of **northern Gotland** and **Fårö** takes you to the port of Fårösund for the 10-minute ferry ride over the strait. On the excursion around Fårö (Sheep Island), you can see dwarf forests and moors.

Returning to Gotland, the bus takes you to the open-air history museum at **Bunge,** which documents the old peasant culture. That's followed by a tour of the **Blase limestone museum** in Fleringe, which has two restored 19th-century lime kilns.

Another tour takes you to the southern tip of the island to see the legendary "old man of **Hoburgen**," a rock formation known as a chalk stack. The tour includes the Iron Age village of **Gervide** as well as two 17th-century farms. The bus travels along the windswept shoreline of the west coast.

A DRIVING TOUR   From Visby, head north on Route 149 until you reach the little fishing port of Lickershamn. Here narrow trails are cut into the *klint* (high rocky coastline). At the finishing harbor, you can see the "Maiden," the largest stone stack on Gotland. These limestone stacks—called *Raukar* in Swedish—were shaped by the wind and the sea and are unique to Gotland. The promontory here offers panoramic views of the sea and of the Gotland coast.

From Lickershamn, continue along Route 149, passing through the towns of **Ire** and **Kappelshamn.** From Kappelshamn, follow Route 149 south to the junction with Route 148 in **Lärbro,** and then go north on Route 148 to **Fårösund.** The village sits on the shores of the Fårösund, the kilometer-wide channel separating the small island of **Fårö (Sheep Island)** from Gotland. You can take a ferry to Fårö, which has superb beaches.

From Fårösund, take Route 148 back to Lärbro. A few kilometers past Lärbro, take Route 146 southwest toward **Slite.** Follow it down the coast to **Aurungs,** and then go west on a secondary road heading toward **Siggur.** In Siggur, follow signs south to the village of **Dalhem.** The most remarkable sight in Dalhem is the village church, just outside town. Its wall paintings and stained glass are the finest on Gotland. Train buffs might enjoy visiting the Railway Museum in the old train station.

From Dalhem, continue south on the road that brought you to town. Head toward **Roma.** Look for the ruins of Roma Abbey, a Cistercian monastery destroyed during the Protestant Reformation.

Head west from Roma on a secondary road toward Route 140, which runs along Gotland's west coast. You'll pass through the villages of **Bander** and **Sojvide** before you reach Route 140. Follow it south to Burgsvik, a popular port and resort town. Just east of **Burgsvik,** visit the small hamlet of **Öja.** Its church boasts a triumphal cross dating from the 13th century.

After visiting Öja, return to Burgsvik and head south, passing through the villages of **Bottarvegården** and **Vamlingbo.** At the southern tip of Gotland you'll find **Hoburgen,** with its towering lighthouse. Along with the lighthouse, you'll see cliffs, many with strange rock formations, and a series of caves.

Return to Burgsvik and get back on Route 140. Turn off after **Fidenäs,** following Route 142 toward **Hemse.** Outside Hemse, take Route 144 to **Ljugarn,** a small port and resort town on Gotland's east coast. You can visit the small Customs museum. Just south of Ljugarn, on a secondary road, is a series of Bronze Age stone sculptures. The seven rock formations, depicting ancient ships, are the largest group of stone-settings on the island.

Follow Route 143 northwest from Ljugarn and return to Visby. Moving rather quickly, you could do this tour in 2 hours or so, or you could spend all day, depending on where you want to stop and how long you want to spend at a particular place. The best place for a rest or a snack is the little summer resort of Ljugarn, which is filled with bars and snack shops that are open only from June to September. These places sell beer, ice cream, sandwiches, pizzas, and the like.

SHOPPING

The most memorable goods are produced on the island, usually by individual craftspeople working on highly detailed, small-scale productions. You can find the fruits of their labor at any of the following shops.

Yllet, St. Hansgatan 19 (✆ **0498/21-40-44**), carries clothing made from wool produced by local sheep. It comes in the form of sweaters, scarves, hats, gloves, coats, and winter-wear for men, women, and children. Colors tend to be natural and soft, usually deriving from the untinted, unbleached fibers produced by the sheep.

Don't overlook the gift shop at the island's historical museum, **Gotlands Fornsal,** Strandgatan 14 (✆ **0498/29-27-00**). Reproductions of some of the museum's art are for sale, as well as handicrafts and textiles made on the island.

Most of Gotland's dozens of independent artists work out of their houses or have studios. They produce ceramics, textiles, woodcarvings, and metalwork. The high-quality merchandise is usually marketed by cooperatives. These loosely organized networks publicize and display articles by artists whose work was approved by a panel. Objects are displayed and can be purchased at two places: **Galerie & Butik Gotland Konsthantverkare,** Hästgatan (✆ **0498/21-03-49**), and **Galerie Kvinnfolki,** Donnersplats 4 (✆ **0498/21-00-51**). Kvinnfolki limits its merchandise to items crafted by women—jars of marmalade made from local berries, textiles, children's clothing, and a line of cosmetics made from all-natural oils, emollients, and pigments.

WHERE TO STAY

For all its attractions, Visby doesn't have enough hotels. Because accommodations are packed in summer, you need to reserve in advance. If at all possible, try to telephone for reservations from Stockholm. If you arrive without reservations, contact the **Gotland Resort** (© **0498/20-12-60**). The English-speaking staff will try to arrange rooms in a hotel or private home in or near Visby. The average rate for an accommodation in a private home is 250SEK ($27) per person per night.

Hotell St Clemens ★ (Finds)

This 18th-century building in the town center has been transformed into a well-run little hotel. A comfortable, cozy atmosphere permeates these five antique buildings connected by two pleasant gardens. The place is decorated tastefully in modern style. It's open all year, and the staff is helpful and efficient. In spite of the hotel's age, all of its rooms have modern shower/toilet facilities with adequate shelf space. No two rooms are identical—the smallest single is in the shoemaker's old house, with a view over church ruins, and there's a four-bed unit with a sloping ceiling that overlooks the Botanical Gardens. Even the old stable has rooms especially for guests with allergies. In these rooms the toilets are wheelchair accessible.

Smedjegatan 3, S-621 55 Visby. © **0498/21-90-00.** Fax 0498/27-94-43. www.clemenshotell.se. 32 units. 763SEK–1,340SEK ($81–$142) double. Extra bed 200SEK ($21). Rates include breakfast. DC, MC, V. Free parking. **Amenities:** Lounge; sauna. *In room:* TV, hair dryer.

Hotell Solhem

One of the most recently renovated hotels in Visby overlooks the harbor from a hilly slope a few blocks south of the center. It was built in 1987 and doubled in size in 1998, when an addition opened. Guest rooms are comfortable, cozy, and warm, with simple but tasteful furniture and small bathrooms equipped with shower units.

Solhemsgatan 3, S-621 46 Visby. © **0498/27-90-70.** Fax 0498/25-90-11. www.strandhotel.net/solhem. 94 units. 800SEK–1,320SEK ($85–$140) double. Rates include breakfast. Closed Sat–Sun Jan–Feb. AE, DC, MC, V. Free parking. **Amenities:** Lounge; sauna; babysitting; laundry/dry cleaning. *In room:* TV, hair dryer.

Strand Hotel

This popular four-story hotel, a Best Western, was built in 1982 on the waterfront a short walk from the harbor. Groups of people are always congregating in the lobby, and the comfortable rooms are decorated in a tasteful modern style. Mattresses are renewed as the need arises, and the bathrooms are well maintained, with up-to-date plumbing.

Strandgatan 34, S-621 56 Visby. © **800/528-1234** in the U.S., or 0498/25-88-00. Fax 0498/27-81-11. www.strandhotel.net. 112 units. 800SEK–1,580SEK ($85–$167) double; 2,600SEK ($276) suite. Rates include breakfast. AE, MC, V. Free parking. **Amenities:** Bar; pool; sauna; babysitting; laundry/dry cleaning. *In room:* TV, minibar, hair dryer.

Wisby Hotell ★★

This 1855 hotel (yes, it's spelled with a *w*) was radically restored and upgraded in the early 1990s. It's now the best and most glamorous hotel on the island, with a conscientious staff. Set close to the harbor in the town center, its historic core includes medieval foundations. Radiating outward from the core are newer additions that span several centuries. Guest rooms are conservatively elegant, and some have reproductions of 18th-century furniture. Housekeeping is excellent, and bathrooms, although small, are equipped with shower-tub combinations. The feature that makes it the finest place to stay in the off season is a Winter Garden—a bold combination of steel, glass, and Gotland sandstone. You can relax in a leather armchair with a drink and admire the greenery and the changing Nordic light.

Strandgatan 6, S-621 21 Visby. © **0498/25-75-00.** Fax 0498/25-75-50. www.wisbyhotell.se. 133 units. 1,240SEK–1,870SEK ($131–$198) double; 1,525SEK–2,555SEK ($162–$271) suite. Rates include breakfast. AE, DC, MC, V. Free parking. **Amenities:** 2 restaurants; bar; lounge; pool; sauna; room service; babysitting; laundry/dry cleaning. *In room:* TV, minibar, hair dryer.

WHERE TO DINE

Burmeister ITALIAN/INTERNATIONAL   This large, summer-only restaurant in the town center offers dining indoors or under shady fruit trees in the garden of a 16th-century house. Diners can look out on the surrounding medieval buildings from many tables. The cuisine is rather standard, never achieving any glory, but not disappointing either. The place is often incredibly crowded in summer, and long lines form, so they must be doing something right. Pizza is the most popular menu choice. After 10pm on certain nights the restaurant becomes a dance club; the cover charge ranges from 60SEK to 100SEK ($6.35–$11).

Strandgatan 6, Visby. © 0498/21-03-73. Reservations required. Main courses 135SEK–215SEK ($14–$23); pizzas 95SEK–117SEK ($10–$12). AE, DC, MC, V. Daily noon–4pm and 6–10:30pm. Dance club mid-June to mid-Aug Tues–Wed 10pm–2am; year-round Fri–Sat 10pm–2am.

Gutekällaren SWEDISH   This restaurant and bar, in the town center, was built as a tavern in the early 1600s, probably on older foundations. It was enlarged in 1789 and today is one of the oldest buildings (if not *the* oldest) in Visby. It offers fresh fish and meat dishes and some vegetarian specialties. You might begin with fish soup with lobster and shrimp, and follow with filet of sole Waleska or roast lamb chops. The dessert specialty in summer is a parfait of local berries. This is solid, reliable fare, prepared with fresh ingredients. The aura is sober—a contrast to the fun-loving island—but once the dining is out of the way, the place livens up considerably.

Stortorget 3, Visby. © 0498/21-00-43. Main courses 160SEK–195SEK ($17–$21). AE, DC, MC, V. Daily 6–11pm.

Munkkällaren *(Finds* SWEDISH/INTERNATIONAL   You'll recognize this restaurant in the center of Visby by its brown wooden facade. The dining room, which is only a few steps from the street, is sheathed in white stone, and parts of it date from 1100. The restaurant is one of the best in town. In summer, the management opens the doors to two more pubs in the compound. Glasses of beer cost 45SEK ($4.75). The main pub, Munken, offers platters of *husmanskost* (Swedish home cooking), including *frikadeller* (meatballs). In the restaurant you might begin with escargots in creamy garlic sauce or toast with Swedish caviar. Specialties include shellfish stew, salmon-stuffed sole with spinach and saffron sauce, and venison in port wine sauce. Live music is often performed in the courtyard, beginning around 8pm. After the live music stops on Saturday and Sunday, a dance club opens every night from 11pm to 2am. Admission to the club is 80SEK ($8.50).

Lilla Torggränd 2, Visby. © 0498/27-14-00. Reservations required in summer. Main courses 105SEK–170SEK ($11–$18). AE, DC, MC, V. Daily 6–11pm; pubs daily 6pm–2am.

VISBY AFTER DARK

There's less emphasis on bar-hopping and nocturnal flirting on Gotland than you might want. A lot more energy is expended on stargazing, wave watching, and ecology. But there is some nightlife.

The island's premier draw for people over 40 who enjoy dancing ballroom-style is the **Borgen Bar** on Saturday nights, Hästgatan 24 (© 0498/24-79-55). The recorded music ranges from the Big Band era to more modern supper-club selections. There's also a restaurant.

A trendier alternative, where dancers are less inclined to wrap themselves in each other's arms, is the **Munkkällaren** (see "Where to Dine," above). **Gutekällaren** (see "Where to Dine," above) attracts high-energy dancers ages 35 and under. If you happen to be a bit older, you can still hang out at the bar, soaking up aquavit and local color.

4 Swedish Lapland ⟨★⟨★⟨★

Swedish Lapland—*Norrland,* to the Swedes—is the last wilderness of Europe. The vast northern land of the midnight sun has crystal-blue lakes, majestic mountains, glaciers, waterfalls, rushing rivers, and forests. Norrland covers roughly half the area of Sweden (one-quarter of which lies north of the Arctic Circle).

The sun doesn't set for 6 weeks in June and July, and brilliant colors illuminate the sky. In spring and autumn, many visitors come here to see the northern lights.

Swedish Lapland is a paradise for hikers and campers (if you don't mind the mosquitoes in the summer). Before you go, get in touch with the **Svenska Turistförening (Swedish Touring Club),** P.O. Box 25, Amiralitetshuset 1, Flagmansvägen 8, S101 20 Stockholm (**℗ 08/463-21-00**). It maintains mountain hotels, and has built bridges and marked hiking routes. The touring club has a number of boats in Lapland that visitors can use for tours of lakes. There are hundreds of kilometers of marked hiking and skiing tracks. March, April, and even May are recommended for skiing. Some 90 mountain hotels or Lapp-type huts (called *fjällstugor* and *kåtor*) are available, with beds and bedding, cooking utensils, and firewood. Huts can be used for only 1 or 2 nights. The club also sponsors mountain stations (*fjällstationer*).

You must be in good physical condition and have suitable equipment before you set out because most of the area is uninhabited. Neophytes are advised to join one of the hiking or conducted tours offered by the Swedish Touring Club. Contact the club for more details.

Contact the outdoors outfitter **Borton Overseas** (**℗ 800/843-0602; www.bortonoverseas.com**) to arrange a safari tour of the Swedish Lapland from March to October. Highlights include visits to old churches and village settlements (usually along a lake), and seeing reindeer.

LULEÅ
931km (578 miles) N of Stockholm

Our driving tour begins in Luleå, a port city on Sweden's east coast at the northern end of the Gulf of Bothnia, about 115km (70 miles) south of the Arctic Circle. It's often called the "gateway to Lapland." Founded by Gustavus Adolphus in 1621, it's the largest town in Norrbotten, and from its piers boats depart for some 300 offshore islets and skerries (rocky islets) known for their flora and fauna.

Luleå has a surprisingly mild climate—its average annual temperature is only 3° to 5° lower than that of Malmö, on Sweden's southern tip. Still, the harbor is frozen over until May. In the summer it's a port for shipping iron ore.

The settlement, which was once ravaged by Russian Cossacks, has an interesting history. Fires have destroyed most of the Old Town. Establishing a city this far north was laden with difficulties; development didn't really take hold until after 1940. The state-owned ironworks has led to a dramatic growth in population. Today, the population is 70,000, and the city is livelier when the students from the University of Luleå are there in winter. Most foreigners (except businesspeople) see it only in summer.

ESSENTIALS
GETTING THERE   From Stockholm, **SAS** (© **800/221-2350** in the U.S., or 020/72-70-00; www.flysas.com) runs 12 flights each weekday and 10 on Saturday and Sunday. The trip takes 1¼ hours. From Gothenburg, there are 11 flights each weekday, 7 on Saturday and Sunday. Trip time is 2¼ hours.

Six trains daily make the 15-hour trip from Stockholm, and six trains daily make the 19-hour trip from Gothenburg. Trains from Stockholm to Kiruna usually deposit passengers at the railway junction at Boden, about 9.5km (6 miles) northwest of Luleå. Three connecting trains a day go between Boden and Luleå. Passengers from Gothenburg to Luleå also transfer in Boden.

A bus runs between Stockholm and Luleå on Friday and Sunday. The trip takes 14 hours. For more information, call **Swebus** (© **020/64-06-40** in Sweden only).

VISITOR INFORMATION   The **Luleå Tourist Office** is at Storgatan 43B, S-972 31 Luleå (© **0920/29-35-00**). It's open in summer, Monday through Friday from 9am to 7pm, Saturday and Sunday from 10am to 4pm; off season, Monday through Friday from 10am to 6pm, Saturday from 10am to 2pm.

SEEING THE SIGHTS
Gammelstad 𝕲𝕲𝕲 is about 9.5km (6 miles) north of the city center. Gathered around its 15th-century church, the largest of its kind in Norrland, are 30 old houses and the largest "church village" in Sweden. It consists of more than 450 small church cottages. These cottages are used today as they were in the past—as overnight lodgings for parishioners during important religious festivals.

Gammelstad Bay was part of a navigable channel into Luleå, but sailing stopped when the city moved in 1649. (The city actually transferred its locale to be more accessible to harbor traffic). The bay has become shallow and is now a wetland area. In this region, just about 5km (3 miles) north of the city center, ornithologists have counted 285 species of birds during the spring migration. The area is classified as a nature reserve, but the public has access to it. Signposted tracks lead to the bird-watching tower and barbecue fireplaces.

Norrbottens Museum, Storgatan 2 (© **0920/24-35-00**), close to the city center at Hermelin Park, offers a comprehensive look at Norrbotten's history. Exhibits show how people lived in the northern regions over the centuries. The museum has perhaps the world's most complete collection of Lapp artifacts. Admission is free. It's open Monday through Friday from 10am to 4pm, Saturday and Sunday from noon to 4pm. Take bus no. 1, 2, 4, 5, 8, or 9.

WHERE TO STAY & DINE
Best Western Stadshotellet Luleå 𝕲   The stately, ornate brick-and-stone building is the oldest (1900), grandest, and most traditional hotel in town. It's in the center of the city, next to the waterfront. The modernized public area has kept a few old-fashioned details from the original building. Guest rooms are comfortable and well furnished. Each unit has a well-maintained bathroom with a shower-tub combination.

Storgatan 15, S-971 81 Luleå. © **0920/670-00.** Fax 0920/670-92. www.bestwestern.com. 135 units. Mon–Thurs 1,650SEK–1,820SEK ($175–$193) double, 2,500SEK ($265) suite; Fri–Sun 1,020SEK ($108) double, 2,500SEK ($265) suite. Rates include breakfast. AE, DC, MC, V. Parking 100SEK ($11). Bus: 1, 2, 4, 5, 8, or 9. **Amenities:** Restaurant; bar; lounge; sauna; room service; laundry/dry cleaning. *In room:* TV, minibar, hair dryer.

Quality Hotel Luleå 𝕲   Built in 1979 and most recently renovated in 1990, this hotel has six stories, two of which are underground. It lies on Luleå's main street in the town center. Guest rooms are comfortable but blandly international

Lapland

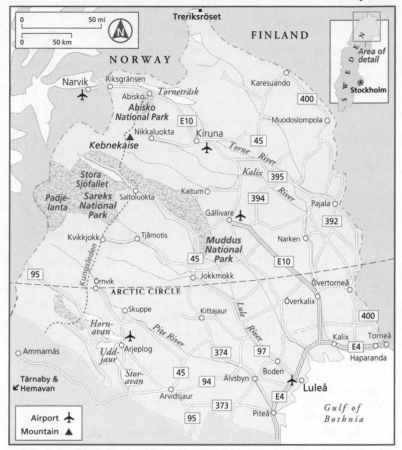

in style and decor. Each unit has a neatly kept bathroom with a shower-tub combination.

Hotel Luleå's restaurant specializes in charcoal-grilled meats. There is a nightclub in the cellar open Thursday through Saturday from 9pm to 3am, year-round. The admission fee is 80SEK ($8.50).

Storgatan 17, S-971 28 Luleå. ℂ **800/221-2350** in the U.S., or 0920/940-00. Fax 0920/20-10-12. www. radissonsas.com. 210 units. Mon–Thurs 1,395SEK–1,595SEK ($148–$169) double; Fri–Sun 890SEK ($94) double. All week 2,995SEK ($317) suite. Rates include breakfast. AE, DC, MC, V. Parking 125SEK ($13). Bus: 1, 2, 4, 5, 8, or 9. **Amenities:** Restaurant; bar; nightclub; pool; sauna; room service; laundry/dry cleaning. *In room:* TV, minibar, hair dryer.

FROM LULEÅ TO JOKKMOKK

From Luleå, take Route 97 northwest. Thirty minutes into the trip, you can stop at **Boden.** Founded in 1809, this is Sweden's oldest garrison town. After losing Finland to Russia, Sweden built this fortress to protect its interior from a Russian invasion. Visit the **Garnisonsmuseet (Garrison Museum),** which has exhibits on military history, as well as many uniforms and weapons used throughout Sweden's history. It is open from June to September daily from

Holiday on Ice

Since the late 1980s, the most unusual, and least permanent, hotel in Sweden has returned early every winter to the frozen steppes near the iron mines of Jukkasjärvi, 200km (125 miles) north of the Arctic Circle. The architect Yngve Bergqvist, financed by a group of friends who developed the concept over bottles of vodka in an overheated sauna, uses jackhammers, bulldozers, and chain saws to fashion a 14-room hotel out of 4,000 tons of densely packed snow and ice.

The basic design is that of an igloo, but with endless whimsical sculptural detail. Like Conrad Hilton's worst nightmare, the resulting "hotel" buckles, collapses, and finally vanishes during the spring thaw. During the long, frigid darkness of north Sweden's midwinter, it attracts a steady stream of engineers, theatrical designers, sociologists, and the merely curious. They avail themselves of dog-sled and snowmobile rides, cross-country skiing, and shimmering views of the aurora borealis. On the premises are an enormous reception hall, a multimedia theater, two saunas, and an ice chapel that's used for simple meditation, weddings, and baptisms.

Available for occupancy (temperatures permitting) between mid-December and sometime in March, the hotel resembles a cross between an Arabian casbah and a medieval cathedral. Minarets are formed by dribbling water (for about a week) onto what eventually becomes a slender, soaring pillar of ice. Domes are formed igloo-style out of ice blocks arranged in a circle. Reception halls boast rambling vaults supported by futuristic-looking columns of translucent ice. Fanciful sculptures heighten the surreal atmosphere. Some are angled to amplify the weak midwinter daylight, which filters through panes of (what else?) chain-sawed ice.

Purists quickly embrace the structure as the perfect marriage of architecture and environment; sensualists usually admire it hastily before heading off to warmer climes and more conventional hotels.

11am to 4pm, charging 10SEK ($1.05) for admission. Not on a street plan, it lies at the southwest edge of town.

After visiting Boden, continue along Route 97 to Jokkmokk.

JOKKMOKK 🐾
198km (123 miles) NW of Luleå, 1,191km (740 miles) N of Stockholm

This community on the Luleå River, just north of the Arctic Circle, has been a Lapp (Sami) trading and cultural center since the 17th century. With a population of 3,400 hearty souls, Jokkmokk (which means "bend in the river") is the largest settlement in the *kommun* (community). Bus routes link Jokkmokk with other villages in the area.

ESSENTIALS
GETTING THERE   If you're not driving, you can reach Luleå, 198km (123 miles) away, by plane; from there you must take a bus. The one scheduled bus a day to Jokkmokk is timed to meet the plane's arrival. There is one train a day

Almost everyone who shows up asks the same question: "Is it comfortable?" Not particularly, but a stay will probably enhance your appreciation for the comforts of conventional housing. Upon arrival, guests are issued thermal jumpsuits of "beaver nylon." The air-lock cuffs are designed to help the wearer survive temperatures as low as –8°F (–22°C). Beds are fashioned from blocks of chiseled ice, lavishly draped, Inuit-style, with reindeer skins. Guests keep warm with insulated body bags developed for use during walks on the moon. Other than a temporary escape into the sauna, be prepared for big chills—room temperatures remain cold enough to keep the walls from melting. Some claim the exposure bolsters your immune system when you return to your usual environment.

The interior decor is what you'd expect. Most rooms resemble a setting from a scary 1950s sci-fi flick, sometimes with an icy version of a pair of skin-draped Adirondack chairs pulled up to the surreal glow of an electric fireplace that emits light but—rather distressingly—no heat. Throughout, there's an endearing decorative reliance on bas-reliefs and curios the artisans have chiseled into the ice.

There's lots of standing up at the long countertop crafted from ice that doubles as a bar. What should you drink? Swedish vodka, of course, dyed a frigid shade of blue and served in cups crafted from ice. Vodka never gets any colder than this.

For information and reservations, contact **The Ice Hotel,** Jukkas AB, Marknadsvägen 63, S-981 91 Jukkasjärvi, Sweden (© **980/668-00;** fax 980/668-90). Doubles cost 2,490SEK ($264) per day, including breakfast. Heated cabins near the ice palace are available for 1,050SEK to 1,700SEK ($111–$180) a night for a double.

from Stockholm to Jokkmokk, with a change of trains in Östersund. The train ride from Stockholm could be 8 or 9 hours, but everything depends on your connection when you change trains. There are seasonal variations here, and it's a pretty complicated schedule. Trains heading to Kiruna do not stop here.

VISITOR INFORMATION   The **Jokkmokk Turistbyrå** is at Stortorget 4 (© **0971/121-40**). It's open from mid-June to mid-August, daily from 8am to 5pm; from mid-August to mid-June, Monday through Friday from 8:30am to 4pm.

SEEING THE SIGHTS
The Lapps (Sami) have an **annual market** ✿✿✿ here in early February, when they sell their handicrafts. The "Great Winter Market" is a tradition that dates back 400 years. Held on the first Thursday, Friday, Saturday, and Sunday of February, it attracts some 30,000 buyers. People come to the market not so much

for buying and selling, but for the special experience of the place. If you're planning a subzero visit during this time of the year, you need to make hotel reservations a year in advance.

There's **salmon fishing** in the town's central lake, and in the summer locals sometimes take a dip in the river, but we suggest that you watch from the sidelines because of the water temperature. Jokkmokk is one of the coldest places in Sweden in winter, with temperatures plunging below –30°F (–34°C) for days at a time.

Karl IX decreed that the winter meeting place of the Jokkmokk Sami would be the site of a market and church. The first church, built in 1607, was known as the **Lapp Church.** Because of the cold weather, the church had to inter corpses in wall vaults until the spring thaw permitted burial in the ground.

A nearby hill, known as **Storknabben,** has a cafe. From there, if the weather is clear, you can see the midnight sun for about 20 days in midsummer.

Jokkmokk is the center of Sami culture in this area, and thus the logical home of the national Swedish Mountain and Sami Museum, **Ájtte** 🐾🐾🐾, Kyrkogatan (© **0971/170-70**); you'll find it in the center of town. Its exhibits reflect nature and life in the Swedish mountain region, especially the Sami culture. The museum is one of the largest of its kind, integrating nature and culture. There's also a restaurant and a gift shop. Museum admission is 50SEK ($5.30) for adults, free for children under 17. The museum is open year-round. In the summer, hours are Monday through Friday from 9am to 7pm, Saturday and Sunday from 11am to 6pm; in the off season, it closes at 4pm.

WHERE TO STAY & DINE

Hotell Gästis 🐾🐾   Dating from 1932, this landmark hotel is in the exact center of town, about 360m (600 ft.) from the railroad station. In some respects, it has the qualities of a frontier-country hotel. Run by the Åkerlund family, the hotel offers well-maintained guest rooms with modern furnishings, good beds, and small bathrooms equipped with shower units. The sauna is free for hotel guests. The restaurant has won many awards and offers well-prepared dishes, including what the Swedes call *husmanskost* (good home cooking) and Continental dishes. There's also entertainment and dancing once a week.

Harrevägen 1, S-962 31 Jokkmokk. © **0971/100-12.** Fax 0971/100-44. 26 units. 700SEK–900SEK ($74–$95) double. Rates include breakfast. AE, DC, MC, V. Free parking. **Amenities:** Restaurant; bar; lounge; sauna. *In room:* TV, hair dryer.

A SIDE TRIP TO KVIKKJOKK

One of the most beautiful resorts in Lapland, this mountain village is the gateway to **Sarek National Park** 🐾🐾🐾, the largest wilderness area in Europe. Kvikkjokk is 130km (80 miles) west of Jokkmokk and 1,110km (689 miles) north of Stockholm. The park is virtually inaccessible, almost entirely without tracks, huts, or bridges. Nevertheless, the most adventurous visitors go to see the fascinating flora and fauna.

The national park, between the Stora and Lilla Luleälv rivers, covers an area of 1,200 sq. km (750 sq. miles), with about 100 glaciers and 87 mountains rising more than 1,770m (5,900 ft.)—eight are over 1,950m (6,500 ft.). The most visited valley, **Rapadel** 🐾, opens onto Lake Laidaure. In the winter, sled dogs pull people through this valley.

The park includes remains of 17th-century silver mines. Kvikkjokk was a silver-ore center in the 17th century, and many historical relics from that period can be seen in the area today. In 1909 Sweden established this nature reserve in the

The Lapps (Sami) in Sweden

The Lapps (Sami) have inhabited this area since ancient times, and 15,000 to 17,000 live in Sweden today. Some 2,500 still lead the nomadic life of their ancestors, herding reindeer and wearing multi-colored costumes. The area of Lapp settlement (known as Sapmi) extends over the entire Scandinavian Arctic region. It stretches along the mountain districts on both sides of the Swedish-Norwegian border, down to the northernmost part of Dalarna.

Many Lapps maintain links to their ancient culture, but others have completely assimilated. Their language belongs to the Finno-Ugric group. As with all Arctic people, oral—not written—literature has played the most prominent role. Among Lapps, the oral tradition takes the form of *yoiking,* a type of singing. Governments once tried to suppress this, but now yoiking is enjoying a renaissance. Much Lapp literature has been published in northern Sami, which is spoken by approximately 75% of Lapps. One classic work is Johan Turi's *Tale of the Lapps,* first published in 1910.

Handicrafts are important in the Lapp economy. Several designers have developed new forms of decorative art, producing a revival of the handicraft tradition.

Many members of the community feel that the term "Lapp" has negative connotations; it's gradually being replaced by the indigenous minority's name for itself, *sábme,* or other dialect variations. *Sami* seems to be the most favored English translation of Lapp, and the word is becoming more common.

wilderness to preserve it for future generations. To walk through the entire park would take at least a week; most visitors stay only a day or two. Explore only with an experienced guide. Hotels in the area can put you in touch with a guide.

Kvikkjokk, at the end of Route 805, is the starting or finishing point for many hikers using the **Kungsleden (King's Trail).** One- or 2-day outings can be made in various directions. A local guide can also lead you on an interesting boat trip; inquire at Kvikkjokk Fjällstation (see "Where to Stay," below). The boat will take you to a fascinating delta where the Tarra and Karnajokk rivers meet. The area is also good for canoeing.

From Jokkmokk, drive north on Route 45. After passing the town of Vaikijaur, turn west on a secondary road, following the signs to Klubbudden. Continue west on this road, passing through the towns of Tjåmotis, Njavve, and Arrenjarka until you reach Kvikkjokk.

If you're not driving, you can reach Kvikkjokk by taking a train to Jokkmokk (see "Getting There," above), then a bus. Two buses a day run between Jokkmokk and Kvikkjokk, but they don't always connect with train arrivals from Stockholm.

WHERE TO STAY
Kvikkjokk Fjällstation   Established by the Swedish Touring Club in 1907, this mountain chalet gained an annex in the 1960s. It offers no-frills accommodations for hikers, hill-walkers, and rock climbers. It's also the headquarters for

a network of guides who operate canoeing and hiking trips into the vast wilderness areas that fan out on all sides. Accommodations are functional and woodsy. There are eight double rooms, eight four-bed rooms, and two cabins with four beds each. There's a simple restaurant, and access to canoe rentals and a variety of guided tours that depart at frequent intervals. The chalet is open only in summer. For information about the Kvikkmokk Fjällstation out of season, call the tourist information office in Jokkmokk (130km/80 miles away) at © **0971/ 121-40.**

S-962 02 Kvikkjokk. © **0971/210-22.** 18 units, none with bathroom. 235SEK–335SEK ($25–$36) per person. AE, MC, V. Closed Sept 15–Mar 15. Free parking. **Amenities:** Restaurant; lounge; sauna. *In room:* No phone.

FROM JOKKMOKK TO KIRUNA

After visiting Kvikkjokk, return to Jokkmokk and then head north on Route 45 toward Gällivare. Along the way, you'll pass **Muddus National Park** 🏕🏕. You can enter from the town of **Saite.** Although not as dramatic as Sarek (see "A Side Trip to Kvikkjokk," above), this park, established in 1942, is worth a visit. Its 50,417 hectares (121,000 acres) are home to bears, moose, otters, wolverines, and many bird species. The Muddusjokk River flows through the park and over a panoramic 42m (140-ft.) waterfall. Trails cross the park; they're well marked and lead visitors to the most interesting sights.

Continue along Route 45 through Gällivare, toward Svappavaara. In Svappavaara, take E10 northwest to Kiruna.

KIRUNA

193km (120 miles) N of Jokkmokk, 1,317km (818 miles) N of Stockholm

Covering more than 4,830 sq. km (3,000 sq. miles), Kiruna is the largest (in terms of geography) city in the world. Its extensive boundaries incorporate both Kebnekaise Mountain and Lake Torneträsk.

The northernmost town in Sweden, Kiruna lies at about the same latitude as Greenland. The midnight sun can be seen here from mid-May to mid-July.

ESSENTIALS

GETTING THERE   You can fly to Kiruna on **SAS** (© **800/221-2350** in the U.S., or 020/72-70-00; www.flysas.com); there are three daily flights from Stockholm. Travel time is 1 hour, 35 minutes. Two or three trains a day make the 16-hour trip from Stockholm to Gällivare (a major rail junction). Three trains a day run between Gällivare and Kiruna; the trip takes 1½ hours. There's also daily bus service between Gällivare and Kiruna. Contact **Länstrafiken** (© **0926/756-80**).

VISITOR INFORMATION   The **Kiruna Turistbyrå** is at Lars Janssons Vagen 17 (© **0980/188-80**). It's open from June 15 to August 20, daily from 9am to 6pm; from August 21 to June 14, Monday through Saturday from 9am to 4pm.

SEEING THE SIGHTS

Eighty kilometers (50 miles) from the commercial center of town, **Kebnekaise Mountain** 🏕🏕 rises 2,090m (6,965 ft.) above sea level. It's the highest mountain in Sweden. Take a bus to **Aroksjokk** village, where a motorboat will take you to the Lapp village of **Nikkaluokta.** From there, it's 21km (13 miles) on foot, including a short boat trip, to Kebnekaise. Lapp families can put you up overnight and arrange hikes or boating trips. The Swedish Touring Club has a mountain station at Kebnekaise, and the station guide can arrange group hikes to the summit. The ascent takes about 4 hours.

The town of Kiruna, which emerged at the turn of the 20th century, owes its location to nearby deposits of iron ore. Guided tours of the mines are offered year-round, but only to people over 9 years old. Visitors are taken through an underground network of tunnels and chambers. For details on the tours, contact **LKAB Mining Company,** LKAB, S-981 86 Kiruna (✆ **0980/710-16**).

Southeast of the railroad station, the tower of the **Stadshus** (✆ **0980/704-96**) dominates Kiruna. Inside there's an art collection and some Sami handicraft exhibits. It's open from June to August, Monday through Friday from 9am to 6pm, Saturday and Sunday from 10am to 6pm; from September to May, Monday through Friday from 10am to 5pm.

A short walk up the road takes you to the **Kiruna Kyrka** ★★ (✆ **0980/101-40**). This church was constructed in 1912 to resemble a stylized Sami hut—it's an origami-like design of rafters and wood beams. The church is open in July daily from 9am to 5pm, and the rest of the summer daily from 8am to 10pm.

You can also visit **Hjalmar Lundbohmsgården** (✆ **0980/701-10**), the official city museum. It's in a manor house built in 1899 by the city's founder, Hjalmar Lundbohm, the owner of most of the region's iron mines. Many of the museum's exhibits deal with the city's origins in the late 19th century, the economic conditions that made its growth possible, and the personality of the entrepreneur who persuaded thousands of Swedes to move north to work in the mines. It's open from June to August, daily from 8am to 6pm; in the off season, phone ahead for hours, which could be any day in the afternoon. Admission is 20SEK ($2.10) for adults, free for children.

About 4km (2½ miles) north of Kiruna along the E10 highway is a showcase of Lapp artifacts, **Mattarahkka** (✆ **0980/191-91**). It's a log house capped proudly with the red, blue, yellow, and green Sami flag. The site includes workshops where visitors can watch traditional Sami products (knives, leather knapsacks, hats, gloves, and tunics) being made. Many of the items are for sale. The center has a simple cafe. The site is open in summer, daily from 10am to 6pm; off season, Monday through Friday from noon to 6pm.

WHERE TO STAY & DINE
Moderate
Scandic Hotel Ferrum ★   Run by the Scandic chain, this hotel is named after the iron ore *(ferrum)* for which Kiruna is famous. The six-story hotel, built in 1967, is one of the tallest buildings in town—functional and standard in design, it's one of your best bets for lodging and food. It has two well-run restaurants, Reenstiern and Mommas (a steakhouse), as well as a cocktail bar and a small casino. The modern guest rooms are comfortably furnished, with excellent beds and neatly kept bathrooms with shower-tub combinations. Rooms for people with disabilities and for guests with allergies are available.

Lars Janssongatan 15, S-981 31 Kiruna. ✆ **0980/39-86-00.** Fax 0980/39-86-11. ferrum@scandic-hotels. com. 171 units. 1,733SEK–1,840SEK ($184–$195) double; 2,306SEK ($244) suite. Rates include breakfast. AE, DC, MC, V. Closed Dec 23–26. Parking 75SEK ($7.95). **Amenities:** 2 restaurants; bar; lounge; casino; sauna; laundry/dry cleaning. *In room:* TV, hair dryer.

Inexpensive
Hotel Kebne   Next to the police station on the main road through Kiruna, this hotel consists of two separate buildings. They were constructed around 1911 but radically renovated in the 1980s. The modern, comfortable guest

---

Finds **Tee Off at Midnight**

Because of their Lapland locale, the following two golf courses are a player's dream: exquisite scenery coupled with the possibility of playing any time the mood hits—day or night.

About 100km (60 miles) west of Kiruna, near the hamlet of Björkliden, is the world's northernmost golf course (and one of the most panoramic), the Björkliden Arctic Golf Course. Set on the tundra against a backdrop of snowcapped peaks, green valleys, and crystal lakes, the nine-hole, par-35 course offers many challenges because of its narrow fairways, small greens, and tricky winds. For details between late June and mid-August (the only time the course is open), contact the Björkliden Arctic Golf Club at ℰ **0980/641-00.** The rest of the year, contact its affiliate, the Stockholm-based Bromma Golf Course, Kvarnbacksvägen 28, 16874 Bromma, Stockholm. For information call ℰ **08/26-29-55.**

The unique **Tornio Golf Club** (popularly called "Green Zone") allows you to play nine holes in one country (Finland) and the remaining nine in Sweden. Located 140km (87 miles) north of Oulu on the Finnish/Swedish border, the par-73 course is named for the Torino River, which runs through the course. For information, contact the tourist office at ℰ **0980/ 188-80.** Believe it or not, dedicated Finnish and Swedish golfers play in the snow, and also in the darkness (with the aid of artificial lighting), during the colder months. This course closes only in January.

---

rooms are decorated in bland international style. Each unit has a well-maintained bathroom with a shower-tub combination. The airport buses stop at the door.

The hotel also operates one of the best restaurants in Kiruna. Open only for breakfast and dinner, it offers a two-course fixed-price menu for 99SEK ($10), which some visitors tout as the best evening bargain in town. Dinner is served Monday through Thursday from 5 to 11pm.

Konduktogrsatan 7, S-981 34 Kiruna. ℰ **0980/123-80.** Fax 0980/681-81. 54 units. June 15–Aug 15 595SEK ($63) double. Aug 16–June 14 Sun–Thurs 1,125SEK ($119) double, Fri–Sat 595SEK ($63) double. Rates include breakfast. AE, DC, MC, V. Free parking. **Amenities:** Restaurant; bar; sauna; room service; laundry/dry cleaning. *In room:* TV, safe.

ABISKO

89km (55 miles) NW of Kiruna, 1,467km (911 miles) N of Stockholm

A resort north of the Arctic Circle is a curiosity. Abisko, a resort on the southern shore of Lake Torneträsk, has a scenic valley, a lake, and an island. An elevator takes passengers to Mount Nuolja (Njulla). Nearby is Abisko National Park, which contains remarkable flora, including orchids.

ESSENTIALS

GETTING THERE   From Kiruna, continue northwest on E10. You can take the train to Kiruna (see above), then a train or bus. Several buses a day run from Kiruna to Abisko, with continuing service to Narvik, Norway. Contact **Länstrafiken** (ℰ **0926/756-80**).

VISITOR INFORMATION   Contact the tourist office in Kiruna (see "Visitor Information" under "Kiruna," above).

EXPLORING THE AREA

Abisko National Park 🐾🐾🐾 (© **0980/402-00**), established in 1903, is around the Abiskojokk River, which flows into Lake Tornetråsk. This is a typical alpine valley with a rich variety of flora and fauna. The highest mountain is Slåttatjåkka, 1,170m (3,900 ft.) above sea level. Njulla Mountain (1,140m/3,800 ft.) has a cable car. *Abisko* is a Lapp word meaning "ocean forest." The park's proximity to the Atlantic gives it a maritime character, with milder winters and cooler summers than the continentally influenced areas east of the Scandes, or Caledonian Mountains.

In the area is the smaller **Vadvetjåkka National Park** 🐾. Established in 1920, it lies northwest of Lake Tornetråsk, extending to the Norwegian border. It's made up of mountain precipices and large tracts of bog and delta. It also has rich flora and impressive brook ravines. The highest mountain is Vadvetjåkka, with a southern peak at 1,095m (3,650 ft.) above sea level.

Abisko is more easily accessible than Vadvetjåkka. Three sides of Vadvetjåkka Park are bounded by water (which is difficult to wade through), and the fourth side is rough terrain with treacherously slippery bogs and steep precipices that are susceptible to rock slides. This park was once inhabited, and then abandoned.

Abisko is one of the best centers for watching the **midnight sun** 🐾🐾🐾, which you can see from June 13 to July 4. It's also the start of the longest marked trail in Sweden, the Kungsleden. You'll also see a reconstruction of a Lapp encampment at the resort.

The **Kungsleden (King's Trail)** 🐾🐾🐾 runs about 340km (210 miles) from Abisko to Hemavan. It's marked, and mountain huts are spaced a day's hike apart. Most of the stops are at what Swedes call *kåtors* (Lapp cottages). You can hike the trail on your own, and no special permits are needed. Lodgings are available on a first-come, first-served basis. Call the **Swedish Touring Club** (© **08/463-21-00**) for more information and a trail map. *Note:* Since you'll cook your own food, be sure to clean up before leaving. At certain points the trail crosses lakes and rivers, where boats can be found for that purpose. The trail follows the Lapps' old nomadic paths. Travelers with less time or energy can explore a smaller segment of the trail.

WHERE TO STAY & DINE

Abisko Touriststation   Owned by the Swedish Touring Club since 1910, this big, modern hotel stands about 450m (1,500 ft.) from the bus station. It offers accommodations in the main building and the annex, and 28 cabins with two apartments each. Each cabin unit has a kitchen and a private bathroom with a shower unit. From the hotel you can see the lake and the mountains. The helpful staff can provide information about excursions. The rooms are basic but reasonably comfortable, and some offer exceptional views. Abisko Touriststation has a plain restaurant serving standard Swedish cuisine.

S-981 07 Abisko. © **0980/402-00.** Fax 0980/401-40. www.abisko.nu. 77 units, 43 with bathroom; 56 cabin apts. 650SEK ($69) double without bathroom; 910SEK–1,280SEK ($96–$136) double with bathroom. Room rates include breakfast. Cabin apt (without meals) 975SEK ($103) per night or 5,425SEK ($575) per week for up to 6 occupants. AE, MC, V. Free parking. **Amenities:** Restaurant; bar. *In room:* No phone.

ENDING YOUR DRIVING TOUR

Abisko is close to the Norwegian border. To cross into Norway, take E10 west across the border toward Narvik. To return to Stockholm, follow E10 east toward the coast, and then head south on E4 to the capital.

18

The Best of Finland

Finland offers visitors a tremendous variety of sights and experiences, everything from sophisticated Helsinki to magnificent islands and lakes, wilderness adventures, reindeer safaris, dog-sledding, and more. To help you decide how best to spend your time in Finland, we've compiled a list of our favorite experiences and discoveries. In the following pages, you'll find the kind of candid advice we'd give our close friends.

1 The Best Travel Experiences

- **Taking a Finnish Sauna:** With some 1.6 million saunas in Finland—roughly one for every three citizens—there's a sauna waiting for you here in the country that virtually invented this steamy bath. Ideally, your sauna experience should be in a log cabin with windows and a view of the lake. Naturally, you'd be joined by friends with whom you'd share beer cooled in a frigid lake and sausages roasted on heat-retaining stones. After a sauna, the best way to cool off is to go for a swim in a cold lake. In winter, when the lakes are frozen over, a hole is sometimes cut through the ice so that the really keen can take a dip. Visitors can enjoy saunas at most hotels, motels, holiday villages, and camping sites.

- **Exploring Europe's Last Frontier:** Located in Scandinavia's far north—its northern tier traversed by the Arctic Circle—Finnish Lapland seems like a forgotten corner of the world. Its indigenous peoples, the Sami, have managed to preserve their distinctive identity and are an integral part of Lapland and its culture. One of the greatest travel experiences in Europe is to explore this land and enjoy a reindeer-sled ride. Lapland is both a summer and a winter destination. In the winter darkness, you can experience the northern lights in all their glory, go dog-sledding behind a team of huskies, float in a frozen fjord in a space-age survival suit, take a snowmobile safari (with an overnight stay in a log cabin), go skiing, or even celebrate Christmas in Lapland. Dozens of such tours are available through **Nordique Tours/Norvista,** a subdivision of Picasso Travel, 11099 S. La Cienega Blvd., Suite 210, Los Angeles, CA 90045 (© **800/ 995-7997** or 310/645-7527; www. nordiquetours.com).

- **Traversing the Finnish Waterworld:** From the coastal islands to the Saimaa lake district, from the tens of thousands of other lakes to the sleepy rivers of the west coast, Finland is one vast world of water. Adventures range from daring the giddy, frothing rapids of the midlands to paddling the deserted streams or swift currents and cascades of Lapland. You can explore Finland's vast bodies of water in many types of boats; there are even wooden boat cruises on both rivers and lakes that end with a sauna in the wilds. Every major town in Finland has canoe-rental outfitters, and local tourist offices can offer advice on touring the local waters.

- **Wandering Finnish Forests:** Finland has been called one huge forest with five million people hiding in it. In fact, nearly four-fifths of the country's total land area is forested, which is remarkable in a world where so many trees have been cut down elsewhere. The Finnish people enjoy a strong and ongoing relationship with their forests and have preserved vast tracts of precious natural areas with rare flora and fauna. To walk in these woods and to pick wild berries and mushrooms (nonpoisonous only, please) is one of their favorite pastimes— and can quickly be enjoyed by the foreign visitor as well.

- **Discovering Finnish Design & Architecture:** Finnish buildings are among the world's newest—more than 90% have been erected since 1920—but their avant-garde design has stunned the world and spread the fame of such architects as Alvar Aalto. In Helsinki you can see the neoclassical Senate Square, Eliel Saarinen's controversial railway station (dating from 1914), and the Temppeliaukio Church, which has been hollowed out from rock with only its dome showing. The Gallen-Kallela Museum, built on a rocky peninsula, was designed by the artist to display his works, ranging from paintings to sculpture and furniture. While in Helsinki, you can also visit the University of Industrial Arts—the largest of its kind in Scandinavia—to learn about current exhibits of Finnish design.

2 The Best Scenic Towns & Villages

- **Turku:** Finland's most charming, evocative, and atmospheric town developed around an ancient trading post. Its castle played a prominent role in Finnish (as well as Scandinavian) history. The national capital until 1812, Turku today is an important cultural center, with two universities. It's also a good base for short cruises of the Turku Archipelago. See chapter 19.

- **Savonlinna:** The commercial and cultural center of the eastern Savo region, one of Finland's most ancient provinces, this town is the center of Lake Saimaa traffic. It's also a spa. Home to the fabled Savonlinna Opera Festival, it has a history dating back to 1475 when Olavinlinna Castle was founded as a fortress on the eastern border of Sweden and Finland. Filled with attractions, including museums and art galleries, it's also a good center for exploring—often by

boat—one of the most scenic parts of Finland. See chapter 19.

- **Lappeenranta:** Founded in 1649 by Queen Christina of Sweden, this town lies at the southernmost edge of Lake Saimaa. It covers a large area stretching from the lake to the Russian border. The commercial and cultural center of South Karelia, it's a spa town and the gateway to the Saimaa Canal. It's filled with attractions, including Finland's oldest Orthodox church and several museums, plus fortified walls dating from the 18th century. It's also a good base for lots of excursions, including visa-free day tours to Vyborg in Russia. See chapter 19.

- **Rauma:** Founded in 1442, and known for its old wooden buildings (dating mostly from the 18th and 19th centuries) and lace making, Rauma contains the best-preserved area of historic structures in Scandinavia. UNESCO has declared its Old Town a World Heritage Site. You can visit museums, churches, and the houses of craftspeople, including lace shops.

- **Porvoo:** Situated about 50km (30 miles) northeast of Helsinki (at the mouth of the River Porvoo), this was an important trading center in the Middle Ages. Porvoo has been especially loved by poets and artists, including some of Finland's greatest. Old Porvoo, with its lanes and wooden houses—the oldest of which date from the 16th century—is well worth exploring. You can visit the home of the painter Albert Edelfelt, south of town, as well as the home of the Finnish national poet, Johan Ludwig Runeberg, which has been restored to its original condition. See chapter 20.

3 The Best Active Vacations

For additional sporting and adventure travel information, please see "The Active Vacation Planner" in chapter 19.

- **Bicycling:** Thousands of miles of narrow paths and captivating gravel tracks lead to towns where broad highways are flanked by well-maintained bicycle routes. Wherever you ride in Finland, you'll find many opportunities to enjoy the great outdoors to the fullest; local tourist offices can provide maps of the best trails. The town of Kuopio, for example, has a network of well-signposted paths, and the local bicycling association has created special off-road routes outside the town proper, ranging from about 10km to 30km (6–19 miles).
- **Canoeing:** Choose from among a large variety of waterscapes: coastal waters dotted with thousands of islands, rivers flowing to the sea, or lakes in the Greater Saimaa region. The best coastal areas are the archipelago along the southwest coast, the coast of Uusimaa province, and the Åland Islands. A popular region for canoeing is the lake district; here the lakes are linked in long chains by short channels with strong currents. Together the lakes form a network of routes extending for thousands of kilometers.
- **Fishing:** For those who are skilled, Finland offers the chance to fish year-round. Fishermen here divide their calendar not into months, but according to the fish in season. Sea trout become plentiful as the rivers rise in March and April. May and June are the golden months for pike, which become ravenous, especially after spawning. Midsummer, when the rapids are at their best, marks the season for Lapland grayling and pike-perch. Also in midsummer, salmon fishermen prepare for the high point of their year when the shiny, silver-flanged rangers of the deep, the salmon, arrive at their home rivers to spawn. Autumn brings sea trout inshore, along with the "Flying Dutchmen of the Deep"—pike—that stalk the shoals of herring. Even in winter, Finnish fishermen drill through the ice to catch perch, pike, and trout. Ice fishermen angle for burbot during the dark winter nights, since its roe is regarded as the choicest of caviars.
- **Hiking:** Hiking is a popular form of recreation in heavily forested Finland, which is full of places to wander. Lapland holds its own special appeal, but you can ramble for a day or more even in southern Finland. Outside Helsinki, for example, there are numerous trails in Nuuksio National Park. The provinces of middle Finland have

a network of hiking trails that total some 300km (185 miles).

- **Skiing:** The ski season in Finland is longest in Lapland, from October until mid-May. However, the days are quite dark in early winter; and in the period preceding and following the winter solstice, the sun doesn't rise above the horizon north of the Arctic Circle. In northern Finland, south of Lapland, there's good skiing for more than 5 hours a day in natural light even when the days are short. Numerous ski trails are lit artificially when winter is at its darkest. The peak holiday ski season is just before spring, when there's lots of daylight and sunshine. In southern Finland, skiing conditions are ideal in January and February, in central Finland the best months are December through March, and in northern Finland the best months are December through April. Finland's ski trails are varied, with beautiful forest scenery and ample climbs and descents. Lakes and fields are ideal for beginners.

4 The Best Festivals & Special Events

- **Savonlinna Opera Festival** (Savonlinna): Dating back to 1912, this annual event takes place in July; there are usually classic operas, supplemented by Finnish works. Every year from early July to early August the festival stages three or four of its own productions and hosts visiting opera companies from abroad. See chapter 19.

- **Helsinki Festival:** Beginning in mid-August, international artists come to Helsinki to perform chamber music and recitals, or to present visual arts exhibits, dance programs, film screenings, and theatrical performances in the theater, as well as opera, jazz, pop, and rock concerts—and lots more. See chapter 19.

- **Tar Skiing Race** (Oulu): This cross-country ski race was established more than a century ago, and has been held almost every year since then. In March hundreds of participants from around the world show up to compete on the 76km (47-mile) racecourse. See chapter 19.

- **Midnight Sun Film Festival** (Sodankylä): Held each June, this is the world's northernmost film festival, featuring works by well-known directors as well as new names in the industry. See chapter 19.

- **Kuopio Dance and Music Festival** (Kuopio): This is Scandinavia's oldest drama festival, held in late June and the first week of July; distinguished performers and troupes from all over the world come to participate. There's a different theme each year. See chapter 19.

5 The Best Museums

- **Finnish National Gallery** (Helsinki): The nation's major repository of modern art includes graphics, sculpture, paintings—the widest possible range in the country. Naturally, native-born sons and daughters are emphasized, with the work of Finnish artists dating back to the mid–18th century. See chapter 20.

- **National Museum of Finland** (Helsinki): No other museum in the country documents the history of the Finnish people like this one. The tools that shaped ordinary life in the country since the Stone Age are documented here, with exhibits ranging from folk costumes to church art. See chapter 20.

- **Ainola** (Järvenpää, outside Helsinki): This was the home of Finland's famous composer, Jean Sibelius, who lived here for more than half a century until his death in 1957. Along with his wife, Aino (for whom the house is named), he's buried on the property. Situated about 40km (24 miles) from Helsinki, Ainola is filled with Sibelius memorabilia. See chapter 20.

- **Seurasaari Open-Air Museum** (Seurasaari): This museum is on an island off the coast of Helsinki (now a national park). Here some 100 authentically furnished and decorated houses have been reassembled—everything from a 1600s church to an "aboriginal" sauna. If you don't have the opportunity to explore Finland in depth, these buildings will help you understand something of Finnish life past and present. On

summer evenings, folk dances are presented here to the tunes of a fiddler. See chapter 20.

- **Mannerheim Museum** (Helsinki): This was the home of Baron Carl Gustaf Mannerheim, marshal of Finland and president of the republic from 1944 to 1946. It has been turned into a museum filled with memorabilia, including his swords, medals, and uniforms, along with his collection of antiques and furnishings. The house remains as it was when he died in 1951. See chapter 20.

- **Gallen-Kallela Museum** (Espoo): On a wooded peninsula, this museum honors the Finnish artist Akseli Gallen-Kallela (1865–1931), who is known mainly for his paintings, especially those from the *Kalevala* ("Land of Heroes"), the Finnish national epic. Often compared to Homer's *Iliad* and *Odyssey,* the *Kalevala* was first published in 1835, and a later edition was illustrated by Gallen-Kallela. See chapter 20.

6 The Best Offbeat Experiences

- **Camping Outdoors:** Join the Finns as they enjoy the great outdoors in the summer. There are about 350 campsites with some 6,300 camp cabins and holiday cottages. Most have washing and cooking facilities, as well as canteens (where you can buy food and miscellaneous supplies). If you have an international camping card (FICC), you don't need a Finnish camping card. Campers can buy a family camping card at the first site at which they intend to stay; it costs 5€ for the whole year. Regional tourist offices can provide information about campsites, or write to the **Finnish Campingsite Association,** Mäntytie 7, FIN-00270 Helsinki (© **09/477-407-40**). In North America, the card is

available from **Family Campers and RVers Association,** 4804 Transit Rd., Building 2, Depew, NY 14043; www.fcrv.org. Finnish Camping Cards are available from the Finnish Campsite Association above.

- **Experiencing a Finnish Farm:** Despite its role as an industrialized nation, Finland's roots extend deep into the soil, with a hardy group of farmers who are adept at coaxing crops out of the often-frozen earth. Several hundred English-speaking farmers have opened their homes to temporary guests, offering a firsthand view of how the country grows such flavorful produce and vegetables.

   A well-respected travel expert, **Lomarengas Finnish Country**

Holidays, Hämeentie 105D, FIN-00550 Helsinki (© **09/576-633-50**), compiles an annual booklet with descriptions, map locations, and photographs of scenic farms, antique and modern cottages, and log cabins. Prices for rooms within farms vary from place to place, depending on the level of accommodation, but even the most expensive generally fall in the budget category, costing no more than 50€ per person per night, including breakfast. It's also possible to arrange rentals of cabins and cottages suitable for two to eight occupants. Again, prices depend on the individual listings, but are invariably affordable on a weekly basis.

• **Panning for Gold:** In the Lemmenjoki region (near Inari), in Finnish Lapland, there are all-day gold-panning trips along the River Lemmenjoki between mid-June and mid-September. A motorboat will take you a distance of 25km (16 miles), and then you'll disembark and walk about 4km (2¼ miles) to the gold-panning site. Participants are shown how to wash gold by sluicing and panning. On the return trip you'll stop at Ravadas waterfall, one of the most spectacular sights in northern Finland. For more information, contact **Lemmenjoki Cabins,** Ahkun Tupa, FIN-99885 (© **016/67-34-35**). Lemmenjoki Cabins is 45km (28 miles) southwest of the village of Inari. Its dozen cabins, each with kitchens, lie on both sides of the Lemmenjoki River, and you must use a rowboat to cross over to the other side to reach them. It's very rustic. The cabins rent for 31€ per day, double occupancy. Technically, they can be used in winter, but no one does, as it's simply too cold.

• **Lighthouse-watching in the Gulf of Bothnia:** The waters separating Finland from Sweden are dotted with thousands of islands, some of them forested, some of them wind-scoured and rocky, and most of them uninhabited. Between May and August, when the waters are ice-free and the northern lights shimmer down upon waters where human contact is extremely limited, you might opt for lighthouse-watching cruises that last between 1 and 3 days. The most famous of the lighthouses in the archipelago near Vaasa is the **Valasaaret Lighthouse,** designed by an associate of Gustave Eiffel (Henri Lipart) in the 1890s. Others lighthouses date from the early 1960s. Your exposure to the bird life, marine life, and botany of the Gulf of Bothnia will be unparalleled. For more information and more creative options, contact **Botnia Tourist,** Vaasanpuistikko 22, FIN-65100 Vaasa (© **06/325-11-25;** www.botniatourist.com).

• **Seeing Lapland on a Safari: Borton Overseas** (© **800/843-0602**) will take you on a tour of Finnish Lapland. You get to experience close encounters with the Sami people and their culture and to see one of the last great wildernesses of Europe. You're taken to old village settlements and along lakes, where you can watch herds of reindeer. Summer tours of the tundra are held between May and early September, and in winter it's also possible to traverse the snow-covered tundra on tours between January and April.

• **Taking a Snowmobile Safari:** From the first week of January until mid-April, you can take a 6-day/5-night snowmobile safari; you fly from Helsinki to Ivalo in the north of Finland and back again. At the Saarisellkä Skiing Resort, you first get snowmobile driving lessons and then have the opportunity to go snowmobile trekking through varying winter landscapes. Overnights are sometimes arranged in wilderness huts; safari outfits and all meals are provided. For more information, contac **Nordique Tours/Norvista,** 11099 S. La Cienega Blvd., Suite 210, Los Angeles, CA 90045 (© **800/995-7997** or 310/645-7527; www.nordiquetours.com).

7 The Best Buys

- **Clothing & Textiles:** There's everything from cottons and linens (often in stunning modern fashions such as those by Marimekko) to warm stoles and shawls. Collectors also seek out *ryijy* rugs and *raanu* wall hangings. Many of these goods are displayed and sold at shops along the Esplanade in Helsinki.
- **Glass & Ceramics:** Finland offers a wide variety in stunning designs, ranging from practical everyday items at moderate prices to one-of-a-kind objects designed by well-known Finnish artisans. The best-known factory names (and the best quality) to look for are Arabia for china, or Nuutajärvi, Iittala, and Riihimäki for glass. Their products are displayed in shops throughout the country. Showrooms for both Arabia and Iittala are on the Esplanade in Helsinki.

Many Finnish glassworks can be visited; contact local tourist offices for further information.
- **Jewelry:** Although Finland is not often associated with jewelry making, it has some rare items for sale—especially from the *Kalevala* series based on centuries-old Finnish ornaments. Modern designers working in gold or silver produce many bold and innovative pieces of jewelry as well, sometimes as settings for Finnish semiprecious stones, or combined wood and silver. Lapponia jewelry—sold all over the country—is one example of modern Finnish design.
- **Wines & Spirits:** Vodka and liqueurs made from local berries are popular, especially the rare cloudberry, the Arctic bramble, and the cranberry. Alcohol is sold at retail through the outlets of Alko, the State Alcohol Company.

8 The Best Hotels

- **Hotel Kämp** (Helsinki; © 09/ 57-61-11): One of the most luxurious hotels in the north of Europe, the Kämp brings five-star comforts to the Finnish capital. It was constructed in 1887 but has been dramatically and beautifully restored. A great deal of Finnish history took place under its roof, and the politics of the country, a blend of east and west, continue to thrive on its dramatic premises. See p. 521.
- **Palace Hotel** (Helsinki; © 09/ 13-45-61): On the south harbor, this glamorous hotel—known for

its scenic 10th-floor dining room— is the city's finest. The accommodations are spacious, with sleek Finnish styling such as dark-wood paneling and built-in furniture. The Palace offers the highest level of personal service, and amenities include three saunas on the 11th floor. See p. 521.
- **Scandic Hotel Kalastajatorppa** (Helsinki; © 09/458-11): Set in a bucolic park on the sea, this is a tranquil and luxurious choice. Comprising three buildings with two restaurants, plus two modern

glass wings linked by tunnels, it's a cozy, snug retreat—ideal on a cold winter's day but also enjoyable in summer, when its sports amenities, including a beach with watersports equipment, are put to full use. See p. 527.

- **Radisson SAS Hesperia Hotel Helsinki** (Helsinki; ✆ 800/333-3333 or 09/431-01): One of the leading hotels of Scandinavia, this bastion of the good life was constructed of Carrara marble and set behind landscaped grounds. A favorite of the business community, the large hotel is also ideal for

the visitor, each housed in comfort and style in the well-designed and spotlessly maintained guest rooms. See p. 526.

- **Scandic Hotel Continental** (Helsinki; ✆ 800/327-0200 or 09/393-51): Opening onto a bay of water, this deluxe chain member boasts the most dramatic atrium in Helsinki. Some of Finland's top designers were called in to create some of the capital's most tasteful and comfortable guest rooms, often using deluxe construction materials such as marble from Lapland. See p. 527.

9 The Best Restaurants

- **Chez Dominique** (Helsinki; ✆ 09/612-73-93): One of only two Michelin-starred restaurants in all of Finland, this is a gourmet citadel reigning as Helsinki's "restaurant of the year" with most of the city's newspaper and magazine food critics. Near Esplanadi Park, the first-class restaurant offers French-inspired cuisine using fresh Scandinavian products whenever available. See p. 528.
- **G. W. Sundmans** (Helsinki; ✆ 09/622-64-10): The only restaurant in Helsinki to equal—but not surpass—Chez Dominique is housed in a former mansion. It, too, is Michelin starred. A deluxe French and Scandinavian cuisine is served in these elegant surroundings, including many succulent dishes native to Finland, featuring, for example, grilled sirloin of elk with a rowanberry *sabayon* sauce. See p. 528.
- **Havis Amanda** (Helsinki; ✆ 09/66-68-82): Known for its fine seafood, this upscale tavern was established in 1973. Most of its saltwater fish comes from Finnish coastal waters, while its freshwater

fish—everything from Baltic crayfish to brook trout—is from Finnish lakes. The restaurant has a beautiful atmosphere and some of the finest service in Helsinki. See p. 532.

- **Olivo** (in the Scandic Hotel Continental; Helsinki; ✆ 09/405-51): Finland's most sumptuous Mediterranean cuisine is served in a relaxed atmosphere in this modern hotel. The menu is diverse and includes dishes from Italy, Morocco, Turkey, and the Middle East, and it also features a well-chosen assortment of wines. The fresh quality of the produce astonishes and delights the palate. See p. 537.
- **Palace Gourmet** (Helsinki; ✆ 09/13-45-61): In one of the city's best hotels, this restaurant provides Helsinki's most scenic dining—a panoramic view of the harbor. A refined Finnish-French cuisine is served. Dishes are delectable, prepared only with the highest quality ingredients. Finnish salmon is the perennial favorite. The chef's filet and tongue of reindeer are the best in town. See p. 529.

19

Planning Your Trip to Finland

This chapter provides many of the details you need to know for planning your trip to Finland. See also chapter 2, "Planning Your Trip to Denmark," since much information about Scandinavia as a whole is discussed there.

1 The Regions in Brief

HELSINKI & THE SOUTHERN COAST The capital city and its environs comprise the most industrialized area of the country, and have the densest population. More than 25% of Finland's people live here. **Helsinki** is the capital of the country and the center of entertainment and culture; it's also a crossroads between western and eastern Europe. The eastern and central areas of the south are characterized by fertile farmland, crisscrossed by many rivers. This is the agriculture belt. The western land in the south has many shallow lakes and ridges. **Porvoo,** 48km (30 miles) northeast of Helsinki, was founded by the Swedes in 1346. It was the site of the first Finnish Diet, when the country became a Grand Duchy. **Kotka** is home to the Langinkoski Imperial Fishing Lodge, used by Tsar Alexander III, and later a favorite play spot for his granddaughter Anastasia.

TURKU & THE ÅLAND ISLANDS The city of **Turku,** Finland's oldest city and former capital, is on the west coast. Its location on the Gulf of Bothnia, combined with a mild climate (its port remains ice-free year-round), have made this city an important center for trade and commerce. **Naantali,** 19km (12 miles) northwest of Turku, is one of the finest examples of a medieval Finnish town. It developed around the convent and monastery of St. Birgitta

and was a favorite spa for Russians tired of St. Petersburg. At the entrance to the Gulf of Bothnia, only 120km (75 miles) from Stockholm, lie the **Åland Islands** (about 6,500 in number). Only about 80 of the islands are inhabited, and all of their residents speak Swedish. The only significant town in the Ålands is **Mariehamn,** a fishing and tourist community founded in 1861.

THE LAKE REGION Central Finland is home to thousands of lakes created millions of years ago by glaciers. This region is an important tourist area, with many resorts along the shores of the lakes. In this region you'll find **Tampere,** Finland's second-largest city. Although an industrial city, Tampere's location on an isthmus nestled between two lakes provides an enchanting backdrop for this young, vibrant city. **Lahti,** Finland's most "American" city, lies on the shores of Lake Vesijärvi, the gateway to Finland's most scenic lake systems. The resort of **Lappeenranta,** founded in 1649 just 16km (10 miles) from the Russian border, has been one of Finland's most popular spa resorts. Here you'll find Linnoitus, a fortress that was used by the Swedes and the Russians to stave off hostile attacks along this contested border. **Imatra,** in the southeast near the Russian border, is as close to St. Petersburg as it is to

Finland

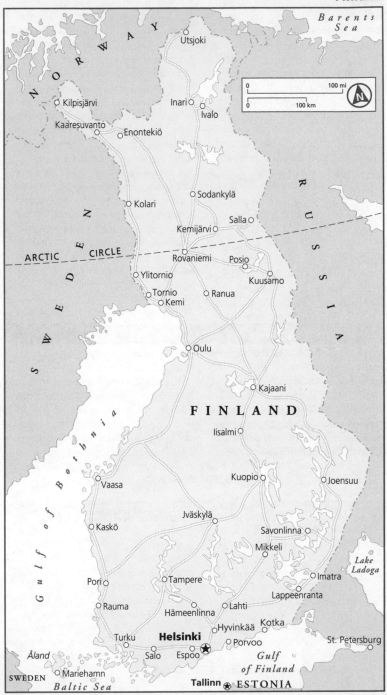

Barents Sea

NORWAY

Utsjoki

Kilpisjärvi

Inari
Ivalo

Kaaresuvanto
Enontekiö

0   100 mi
0   100 km

Kolari   Sodankylä

Salla
Kemijärvi

S W E D E N

ARCTIC   CIRCLE
Rovaniemi   Posio
Ylitornio   Kuusamo
Tornio   Ranua
Kemi

R U S S I A

Oulu

Kajaani

FINLAND

Iisalmi

Vaasa   Kuopio   Joensuu

Jväskylä

Kaskö   Savonlinna

Mikkeli

Gulf of Bothnia

Lake Ladoga

Pori   Tampere   Imatra

Lappeenranta

Rauma   Lahti

Hämeenlinna   Kotka
Hyvinkää
Turku   **Helsinki**   Porvoo   St. Petersburg

Åland   Salo   Espoo   *Gulf of Finland*

SWEDEN   Mariehamn   Tallinn ⊛ ESTONIA
Baltic Sea

Helsinki. This border town, with its distinctly Russian flavor, has enjoyed a wave of prosperity since the dissolution of the Soviet Union. Outside town is the Imatra Rapids, one of Europe's most powerful waterfalls. The most visited town in the Lake Region is **Savonlinna.** Because of its strategic location on the Saimaa waterway, many battles have been waged for control of its 15th-century castle, Olavinlinna. This spa town was also a favorite resort of the Russian tsars.

FINNISH LAPLAND Lapland makes up more than one-third of Finland. Known throughout the world, this is the land of the midnight sun, reindeer, and the Lapps with their traditional garb. Lapland is largely forested and untamed; bears and wolves still rule the land. Fishing and logging are the mainstays of the economy. Eight kilometers (5 miles) south of the Arctic Circle, the capital city, **Rovaniemi,** is a modern new town, rebuilt after the Nazis destroyed it during their retreat from Finland. The port of **Kemi,** which is situated at the mouth of the Kemikoji river, is the transit point for the many thousands of logs that are felled in Lapland, floated downriver, and either loaded onto seagoing barges or transformed into lumber and paper products on-site. The village of **Tankavaara** is a major destination for those hunting for gold. Its rivers are ripe for gold panning. The Lapp village of **Inari,** on the shores of Lake Inari, is a thriving community that depends on reindeer farming and tourism. Not far from here is Finland's largest ski resort, **Saariselk.** Lapland is also home to Finland's largest national park, **Lemmenjoki,** and countless panoramic waterfalls and swift rivers.

2 Visitor Information

In the United States, contact the **Scandinavian Tourist Board,** 655 Third Ave., 18th Floor, New York, NY 10017 (© **212/885-9700;** www.finland-tourism.com), at least 3 months in advance for maps, sightseeing information, ferry schedules, and so forth.

In the United Kingdom, contact the Finnish Tourist Board at P.O. Box 33213 London, W6 8JX (© **020/** 7365-2512; www.finlandtourism.com).

If you use a **travel agent,** make sure he or she is a member of the **American Society of Travel Agents (ASTA),** so that—in case a problem arises—you can complain to the consumer affairs department of the society at 1101 King St., Alexandria, VA 22314 (© **703/706-0387;** www.astanet.com).

3 Entry Requirements & Customs

ENTRY REQUIREMENTS

DOCUMENTS American, Canadian, Australian, and New Zealand citizens need only a valid **passport** to enter Finland. Members of EU countries (except Greece), Liechtenstein, San Marino, and Switzerland are allowed entry with a valid **identity card** issued by those countries. You need to apply for a visa only if you want to stay more than 3 months. For UK subjects, a **visitor's passport** is also valid for a holiday or even for some business trips of less than 3 months. The passport can include both a husband and wife, and it's valid for 1 year. You can apply in person at a main post office in the British Isles and the passport will be issued that same day.

Your current domestic **driver's license** is acceptable in Finland. An international driver's license is not required.

CUSTOMS

All personal effects, including cameras and a reasonable amount of film (or other items intended for your own use) can be brought in duty-free. Gifts costing up to 230€ for adults and 115€ for children may also be brought in duty-free. You can bring in 200 cigarettes or 250 grams of other manufactured tobacco. You can also bring in 15 liters of beer, 2 liters of wine, and 1 liter of spirits *or* 2 liters of beer and 2 liters of wine. You must be over the age of 20 to bring in alcohol and over 18 to bring in beer and wine. There are no restrictions on the amount of euros that can be taken in or out of the country.

4 Money

See "Money" in chapter 2 for a general discussion of changing currency, using credit and charge cards, and other matters.

CURRENCY The **euro,** the new single European currency, became the official currency of Finland and 11 other participating countries on January 1, 1999.

However, the euro didn't go into general circulation until early in 2002. The old currency, the Finnish mark, disappeared into history on March 1, 2002, replaced by the euro, whose official abbreviation is "EUR." The symbol of the euro is a stylized *E:* €. Exchange rates of participating countries are locked into a common currency fluctuating against the dollar.

For more details on the euro, check out **www.europa.eu.int/euro**.

The relative value of the euro fluctuates against the U.S. dollar, the pound sterling, and most of the world's other currencies, and its value might not be the same by the time you actually travel to Helsinki. A last-minute check is also advised before you begin your trip.

Exchange rates are more favorable at the point of arrival. Nevertheless, it's often helpful to exchange at least some money before going abroad (standing in line at the *cambio* exchange bureau in the Helsinki airport isn't fun after a long overseas flight). Check with any of your local American Express or Thomas Cook offices or major banks. Or order in advance from the following: **American Express** (© 800/721-9768; cardholders only), **Thomas Cook** (© 800/223-7373; www.thomas cook.com), or **Capital for Foreign Exchange** (© 888/842-0880; www. afex.com).

It's best to exchange currency or traveler's checks at a bank, and not at an exchange bureau, hotel, or shop. Currency and traveler's checks (for which you'll receive a better rate than cash) can be changed at all principal airports and at some travel agencies, such as American Express and Thomas Cook. Note the rates and ask about commission fees; it can sometimes pay to shop around.

5 When to Go

CLIMATE

Spring arrives in May and the summers are short. A standing joke is that in Helsinki, summer lasts from Tuesday through Thursday. July is the warmest month, with temperatures averaging around 59°F (15°C). The coldest months are January and February, when the Finnish climate has been compared to that of New England. Snow arrives in southern Finland in December; it arrives in northern Finland in October. In Lapland, snow generally lasts until late April.

The Euro, the U.S. Dollar & the British Pound

Regarding the Euro   At the time of this writing, the U.S. dollar and the euro traded almost on par ($1 approximately equals 1€). But that relationship can and probably will change during the lifetime of this edition. For more exact ratios between these and other currencies, check an up-to-date source at the time of your arrival in Europe.

For British Readers   At this writing, £1 = approximately US$1.56, and at approximately the same rate vis-à-vis the euro. These were the rates of exchange used to calculate the values in the table below.

Euro	US$	UK£	Euro	US$	UK£
1	1	0.64	75	75	48.23
2	2	1.29	100	100	64.30
3	3	1.93	125	125	80.38
4	4	2.57	150	150	96.45
5	5	3.22	175	175	112.53
6	6	3.86	200	200	128.60
7	7	4.50	225	225	144.68
8	8	5.14	250	250	160.75
9	9	5.79	275	275	176.83
10	10	6.43	300	300	192.90
15	15	9.65	350	350	225.05
20	20	12.86	400	400	257.20
25	25	16.08	500	500	321.50
50	50	32.15	1,000	1,000	643.00

Finland's Average Daytime Temperatures

		Jan	Feb	Mar	Apr	May	June	July	Aug	Sept	Oct	Nov	Dec
Helsinki	°F	26	27	33	44	57	66	69	66	57	48	39	31
	°C	–3	–3	1	7	14	19	21	19	14	9	4	–1
Tampere	°F	24	24	32	44	57	66	72	68	58	45	36	29
	°C	–4	–4	0	7	14	19	22	20	14	7	2	–2
Jyväskylä	°F	20	22	32	42	58	67	69	65	54	43	32	24
	°C	–7	–6	0	6	14	37	21	18	12	6	0	–4
Ivalo	°F	17	17	26	27	47	60	67	62	50	37	28	21
	°C	–8	–8	–3	–3	8	16	37	17	10	3	–2	–6

THE MIDNIGHT SUN   In Lapland the midnight sun offers the visitor an unforgettable experience.

The following places and dates are the best for seeing the midnight sun in Finland: **Utsjoki,** from May 17 to July 28; **Ivalo,** from May 23 to July 22; **Sodankyl,** from May 30 to July 5; on the **Arctic Circle** and **Rovaniemi,** from June 6 to July 7; **Kuusamo,** from June 13 to July 1; and **Kemi,** from June 19 to June 25. Helsinki has almost 20 hours of daylight during the summer months.

HOLIDAYS

The following holidays are observed in Finland: New Year's Day (Jan 1);

What Things Cost in Helsinki	US$/€
Taxi from the airport to the city center	$20.00
Single ticket on a tram or bus	$1.50
Local telephone call	$.40
Double room at the Ramada Presidentti Hotel (expensive)	$190.00
Double room at the Martta Hotelli (moderate)	$132.00
Double room at the Hotel Arthur (inexpensive)	$106.00
Lunch for one, without wine, at Kellarikrouvi (moderate)	$25.00
Lunch for one, without wine, at Manala (inexpensive)	$16.00
Dinner for one, without wine, at Havis Amanda (expensive)	$58.00
Dinner for one, without wine, at Bellevue (moderate)	$32.00
Dinner for one, without wine, at Kynsilaukka Garlic Restaurant (inexpensive)	$20.00
Pint of beer (draft Pilsner) in a pub	$4.00
Coca-Cola at a cafe	$3.00
Cup of coffee at a cafe	$3.00
Admission to Mannerheim Museum	$7.00
Movie ticket	$10.00
Opera ticket	$12.00–80.00

Epiphany (Jan 6); Good Friday; Easter Monday; Labor Day (May 1); Ascension Day (mid-May); Whitmonday (late May); Midsummer Eve and Midsummer Day (Fri and Sat of weekend closest to June 24); All Saints' Day (Nov 6); Independence Day (Dec 6); and Christmas and Boxing Days (Dec 25 and 26).

FINLAND CALENDAR OF EVENTS

The dates given in this calendar can vary from year to year. Check with the Scandinavian Tourist Board for the exact dates and contact information (see "Visitor Information," above).

February

Finlandia Ski Race, Hämeenlinna-Lahti. With almost 80km (50 miles) of cross-country skiing, this mass event is part of the Euroloppet and Worldloppet competitions. Late February.

March

Tar Skiing Race, Oulu. This cross-country ski race has taken place each year, without interruption, since it was first established more than a century ago. Following a course that stretches more than 76km (47 miles)—and with hundreds of participants—it's the oldest long-distance cross-country ski race in the world. Early to mid-March.

April

Walpurgis Eve Celebration. After a long, cold winter, most Helsinki residents turn out to celebrate the arrival of spring. Celebrations are held at Market Square, followed by May Day parades and other activities the next morning. April 30.

May

May Day. Parades and other celebrations herald the arrival of spring. May 1.

Women's 10km. This is a 10km (6-mile) foot race for women. For more detailed information on this event, contact any office of the Scandinavian Tourist Board (②212/885-9700 in the U.S.). Late May.

June

Kuopio Dance and Music Festival. This international dance event has a different theme every year, such as dances in Japan, the Middle East, and North Africa. Last week in June to first week in July.

Midnight Sun Film Festival, Sodankylä. The world's northernmost film festival features nostalgic releases from the great film masters—mainly European—but also new names in the film world. For more information, call ℭ **016/ 61-45-24.** Dates vary.

July

Savonlinna Opera Festival. One of Europe's most important and best-known music festivals, this is part of a cultural tradition established in 1912. Traditionally, dozens of performances are held in the island fortress of Olavinlinna Castle in July. Internationally renowned artists perform a variety of works, including at least one Finnish opera. For details and complete information, contact the Savonlinna Opera Festival, Olavinkatu 27, FIN-57130 Savonlinna (ℭ **015/47-67-50**). Early July to early August.

Kaustinen Folk Music Festival. This is the biggest international folk festival in Scandinavia. July 17 to July 25.

August

Turku Music Festival. A wide range of music is presented from the Renaissance and the baroque periods (played on the original instruments) to modern, light music. Second week of August.

Helsinki Marathon. This event attracts both Finnish and foreign runners of varying abilities. Mid-August.

Helsinki Festival. A major Scandinavian musical event, the Helsinki Festival presents orchestral concerts by outstanding soloists and ensembles; chamber music and recitals; exhibitions; ballet, theater, and opera performances; and jazz, pop, and rock concerts. For complete information about the program, contact the Helsinki Festival, Lasipalatsi Mannerheimintie 22–24 FIN-00100 Helsinki (ℭ **09/612-651-00;** www.helsinkifestival.fi). Mid-August to early September.

October

The Baltic Herring Market. Since the 1700s, there has been an annual herring market along the quays of Market Square in early October. Prizes and blue ribbons go to the tastiest herring. Fishers continue the centuries-old tradition of bringing their catch into the city and selling it from their boats. First week in October.

6 The Active Vacation Planner

ADVENTURE TOURS Summer and winter are both great periods for a holiday in Finland. Apart from the midnight sun and the northern lights, Finland has much to offer the adventurer. For information about adventure vacation packages in Lapland, we recommend **Lapland Travel,** Koskikatu 1, PL-8156 Rovaniemi (ℭ **016/332-34-00**). It might be more convenient to contact one of the U.S. tour operators: **Nordique**

Tours at ℭ **800/995-7997; Passage Tours** at ℭ **800/548-5960;** and **Scantours** at ℭ **800/223-7226.**

BICYCLING In Finland, you can either rent a bike and cycle on your own or join one of dozens of cycling tours. One 6-day/5-night tour in the Åland Islands, for example, takes you along an excellent road network, past low hills and shimmering water. For bookings, contact **Alandsresor,** P.O.

Box 62, FIN-22101 Mariehamn (℡ **018/283-00;** www.alandsresor.fi). Some hotels, holiday villages, camping sites—even tourist information offices—rent bicycles. More information is available from the **Cycling Union of Finland,** Radiokatu 20, FIN-00093 Helsinki (fax **09/278-65-85**).

CANOEING The Finnish Canoe Federation arranges guided canoe tours along the country's most scenic waterscapes. One- and two-seat kayaks or canoes are available for rent, and charts of the coastal waters are provided. For more information, contact the **Finnish Canoe Federation,** Olympiastadion, Etelääkaarre, FIN-00250 Helsinki (℡ **09/49-49-65**).

FISHING Finland has more than 6,000 professional fishers and about 1.5 million people fishing for recreation. For foreign visitors who'd like to fish for recreation, the usual methods permitted are summer and winter angling, and fishing with lure and fly.

In Finland most fishing waters are privately owned; cities and private companies also own fishing waters. The National Board of Forestry administers state fishing waters, mainly in northern and eastern Finland.

Foreign visitors must buy a general fishing license if you intend to do recreational fishing in Finland (a separate license is needed for the Åland Islands). You can get a general fishing license from post offices; it costs 5€ per person and is valid for 1 week; a year's license costs 15€. More information is available from the **Federation of Finnish Fisheries Association,** Köydenpunojankatu 7B, FIN-00180 Helsinki (℡ **09/684-45-90**).

GOLFING There are 98 golf courses in Finland, and 66,000 members of the **Finnish Golf Union,** the organization that keeps tabs on the locations and attributes of every golf course in Finland. The best courses are in Helsinki and include Tali Manor, 6.5km (4 miles) from the center, and the Espoo Golf Course. Information about golf courses and their pars, entry requirements, and greens fees is available from the Finnish Golf Union at Radiokatu 20, FIN-00240 Helsinki (℡ **09/348-122-44**). **ITC Golf Tours** (℡ **800/257-4981**) offers golf tour packages to Finland, including golf tournaments under the midnight sun.

HIKING Finland is an ideal country for hiking. The northern wilderness boasts the highest *fells* (rolling and barren hills), clear streams, and lots of open country. Eastern Finland's forested hills and vast woodlands conceal many lakes and deep gullies. Western Finland's low, cultivated plain is cut by fertile river valleys leading to the Gulf of Bothnia. Central Finland is known for its thousands of lakes and rolling woodlands, and the south of Finland, even though densely populated, has many forests suitable for hiking. Hiking maps can be ordered from **Karttakeskkus (Map Centre),** P.O. Box 85, FIN-00521 Helsinki (℡ **020/44-51-44**). A special brochure on hiking is available from the Scandinavian Tourist Board abroad.

SKIING Skiing conditions in Finland are among the best in the world. The season is long and the trails are good. The best skiing season in northern Finland is March through April, when there may be up to 16 hours of sunshine daily. But the early winter— *kaamos,* the season when the sun doesn't appear at all—has its own attractions for visitors who want to experience something different.

Finland is about 1,125km (700 miles) long, with distinct differences at each end. The south consists of gently rolling hills, with no elevations exceeding .9m (3 ft.), but the farther north you go, the more deeply forested and mountainous the country becomes. The highest hills are in Lapland.

The slopes of Finnish ski resorts are maintained in excellent condition. Skiing instruction—both cross-country and downhill—is available at most resorts, and equipment can be rented on the spot.

Long-distance ski races are becoming increasingly popular, and the long trails, ranging from 40km to 90km (25–55 miles), attract more and more participants from all over the world every year. As many as 15,000 skiers take part in the biggest event—the Finlandia Ski Race. A fair number of resorts organize guided ski treks. They last a few days, and overnight accommodations are arranged along the trail in farmhouses or, in Lapland, in wilderness huts or shelters.

7 Health & Insurance

For a general discussion of health and insurance concerns, see chapter 2, "Planning Your Trip to Denmark."

Finland's national health plan does not cover U.S. or Canadian visitors. Any medical expenses that arise must be paid in cash. (Medical costs in Finland, however, are generally more reasonable than elsewhere in western Europe.) British and other EU citizens can ask their insurer for an E111 form, which will cover emergencies in Finland and all other EU countries.

8 Tips for Travelers with Special Needs

There are a number of resources and organizations in both North America and Britain to assist travelers with special needs in planning their trip to Finland. For details, see "Tips for Travelers with Special Needs" in chapter 2.

FOR TRAVELERS WITH DIS-ABILITIES Like its Scandinavian neighbors, Finland has been in the vanguard of providing services for people with disabilities. In general, trains, airlines, ferries, department stores, and malls are accessible. For information about wheelchair access, ferry and air travel, parking, and other matters, your best bet is to contact the Scandinavian Tourist Board (see "Visitor Information," above).

In Finland, you may obtain general information from **Rullaten ry,** Hile Meckelborg, Pajutie 7, FIN-02770 Espoo, Finland (© **09/805-73-93;** www.rullaten.fi).

FOR GAY & LESBIAN TRAVELERS Helsinging seudun SETA ry, Hietalahdenkatu 2B, FIN-00180 Helsinki (© **09/681-258-80**), is a good source of information about gay life in the capital and Finland as a whole. The office is open Monday, Tuesday, and Thursday from 10am to 6pm; Wednesday from noon to 6pm; and Friday from 10am to 2pm.

FOR SENIORS In Finland, passengers age 65 and over are entitled to a 50% reduction on many Finnair flights. The domestic route system is divided into blue, black, and red flights; seniors cannot get reductions on blue flights since they are in the greatest demand. For the others, any generally accepted document of identification suffices for this purpose. The passenger's date of birth must be inserted in the "Fare Basis" column.

By showing your passport as proof of age, visitors over age 65 may buy regular railway tickets (either one-way or round-trip) at a 50% reduction.

FOR FAMILIES On Finnair flights, one parent pays the full one-way or round-trip adult fare, the spouse pays 75% of the fare, children 12 to 23 are charged 50%, and children 2 to 11 are charged 25%. One child under 2 may be carried free.

On the Finnish national rail system, a maximum of four children ages 6 and under can travel free with one adult. A 50% reduction is granted for children 6 to 16.

9 Getting There

BY PLANE

With more flights to Helsinki from more parts of the world (including Europe, Asia, and North America) than any other airline, **Finnair** (© **800/950-5000** in the U.S.; www.finnair.com) is the only airline flying nonstop from North America to Finland (an 8-hr. trip). From New York, Finnair flies to Helsinki every day. The airline also maintains twice-weekly nonstop service to Helsinki throughout the year from Miami.

Midsummer round-trip fares from New York to Helsinki range from $810 to $1,666 (plus about $66 tax) for those who book your passage 21 days in advance and agree to remain abroad for 7 to 60 days. These prices are substantially lower in winter, and also lower during Finnair's frequent promotional sales. **Finnair** (© **020/ 7408-1222** in London; www.finnair. com) also offers more frequent service to Helsinki from several airports in Britain; there are three or four daily nonstop flights from either Heathrow or Stanstead Airport, and one or two daily flights from Manchester. Flight time from London to Helsinki is 2 hours, 50 minutes; from Manchester, it's 3 hours, 40 minutes.

Several other airlines fly from all parts of the world to gateway European cities and then connect to Helsinki. Foremost among these is **British Airways (BA)** (© **800/247-9297** in the U.S., or 08457/733-377 in London; www.ba.com), which offers hundreds of daily flights into the U.K. from all over the world. From London's Heathrow, BA offers one or two daily nonstop flights to Helsinki, depending on the day of the week.

BY CAR

FROM WESTERN SCANDINAVIA The quickest routes to Finland are the E3 or E4 to Stockholm and the year-round 14- to 16-hour ferry from there to Helsinki.

FROM GERMANY From Travemünde there's a year-round high-speed car ferry that takes 22 hours to reach Helsinki.

FROM DENMARK Take the car ferry from Helsingør to Helsingborg in Sweden or the Øresund Bridge from Copenhagen to Malmö, and then drive to Stockholm and catch the car ferry to Helsinki or Turku.

BY TRAIN

A rail and ferryboat link between London and Helsinki goes via Ostende (Belgium), Cologne, Hamburg, and Stockholm. If you've taken the ferry from Stockholm and are arriving at Turku, on the west coast of Finland, you can catch one of the seven daily trains (including the high-speed Pendolino) that take you across southern Finland to Helsinki. The trip takes 2¼ hours. Rail connections are also possible from London to Hook of Holland (the Netherlands), Bremen, Hamburg, and Stockholm. However, each of these itineraries takes about 50 hours, plus a 2-hour stopover in Stockholm. It's possible to reserve sleepers and couchettes, but do so as far in advance as possible. Helsinki is also linked by rail to the major cities of Finland.

RAIL PASSES

Refer to chapter 2, "Planning Your Trip to Denmark."

BY BUS

Although there are international bus links to Finland, this is the least convenient mode of transportation. One of the most popular is a bus connection from Stockholm—it includes a sea crossing to Turku, with continuing land service to Helsinki.

It's also possible to take coaches from Gothenburg going cross-country to Stockholm and to the ferry dock beyond, with land travel resuming after Turku on the same bus all the way to Helsinki.

For information about international bus connections and reservations, contact **Oy Matkahuolto Ab,** Simonkatu 3, FIN-00101 Helsinki (© **09/9800-32582**).

BY SHIP/FERRY

FROM SWEDEN   Frequent ferries run between Sweden and Finland, especially between Stockholm and Helsinki. Service is on either the Viking or Silja Line. Each company also operates a twice-daily service from Stockholm to Turku on Finland's west coast.

FROM GERMANY   The Silja Line also maintains regular passenger service from June 5 to September 15 between Travemünde (Germany) and Helsinki. You can get information about the **Silja Line** at Mannerheimintie 2, FIN-00101 Helsinki (© **09/180-41**; www.silja.fi). Information on the **Viking Line** is available at Mastokatu 1, FIN-00160 (© **09/123-51**; www.vikingline.fi).

PACKAGE TOURS

The best tours of Finland are offered by **Finnair** (© **800/950-5000** in the U.S.; www.finnair.com), including its most popular, the **Midnight Sun Flight** (Helsinki–Rovaniemi–Helsinki). This tour is offered daily in June and July. Any Finnair office around the world can provide information about tours for exploring Finland.

If you'd like to see as much as possible of Finland's highlights in the shortest possible time, consider one of the **Friendly Finland Tours,** lasting 3 to 6 days. They're offered at various times between June and August. This tour is operated by the **Finland Travel Bureau,** Kaivokatu 10A, PB 319, FIN-00101 Helsinki (© **09/182-61**; www.smt.fi). Bookings can be made through any travel agent.

10 Getting Around

BY PLANE

Finnair (© **800/950-5000** in the U.S.), along with its domestic subsidiaries, Karair and Finnaviation, offers reasonably priced air transportation to virtually every settlement of any size in Finland, including some that are not accessible by any other means. Its routes cover the length and breadth of the country with at least 100 flights a day.

If you plan to travel extensively throughout Scandinavia or into the Baltic countries, then consider the **Finnair Nordic Air Pass.** It is available only from May 1 to September 30, and you must have a transatlantic plane ticket to be eligible. A maximum of 12 passes and a minimum of three entitle you to huge discounts on flights within Finland, Denmark, Sweden, and the Baltic countries. Prices range from $92 to $145 for one-way flights. Call **Finnair** (© **800/950-5000**) or **Norvista** (© **0870/744-7315** in the U.K.; www.norvista.co.uk) for more information.

BY TRAIN

Finland has its own **Finnrailpass** for use on the country's elaborate network of railroads. It's a "flexipass," entitling the holder to unlimited travel for any 3, 5, or 10 days within a 1-month period on all passenger trains of the

VR Ltd. Finnish Railways. Travel days may be used either consecutively or non-consecutively. Prices are as follows: any 3 days in 1 month, $108 in second class, $162 in first class; any 5 days in 1 month, $144 in second class, $216 in first class; and any 10 days in 1 month, $194 in second class, $291 in first class. Travelers over 65 and children 6 to 16 are charged half the full fare (it may be necessary to show proof of age); children 5 and under ride free.

Second-class trains in Finland are comparable to first-class trains in many other countries. The Finnrailpass should be purchased before you enter Finland; sometimes it's available at border stations at the frontier.

Because Finnish trains tend to be crowded, you should reserve a seat in advance—in fact, seat reservations are obligatory on all express trains marked "IC" or "EP" on the timetable. The charge for seat reservations, which depends on the class and the length of the journey, ranges from 3€ to 61€.

For more information, contact **VR Ltd. Finnish Railways,** P.O. Box 488, Vilhonkatu 13, FIN-00101 Helsinki (✆ **09/307-209-02**). In the United States, contact **RailEurope, Inc.** (✆ **800/848-7245** or 800/4EURAIL; www.raileurope.com).

BY BUS

Finland has an extensive bus network operated by private companies. Information on bus travel is available at the **Helsinki Bus Station,** just west of the post office between Salomonkatu and Simonkatu (✆ **09/613-684-33**). Tickets can be purchased on board or at the bus station. Ask about a "Coach Holiday Ticket," allowing travel up to 186km (621 miles) during any 2-week period. These discount tickets can be purchased in Finland at a cost of $70.

BY TAXI IN FINNISH CITIES

Service on most forms of public transportation ends around midnight throughout Finland, forcing night owls to drive themselves or to rely on the battalions of *taksi* (taxis) that line up at taxi stands in every Finnish town. In Helsinki, taxi stands are strategically situated throughout the downtown area, and it's usually less expensive to wait in line at a stand until one arrives. If you decide to call a taxi—they can be found under *Taksiasemat* in the local Yellow Pages—you have to pay the charges that accumulate on the meter from the moment the driver first receives the call, not from when he or she picks you up.

BY CAR

Because of the far-flung scattering of Finland's attractions and the relative infrequency of its trains and long-distance buses, touring the country by car is the best way to savor its sights and charms, especially during the summer months. Bear in mind that driving conditions can be very bad during the long winter months. Snow tires are compulsory in winter. Studded tires are not required, but they are allowed from November 1 until the first Sunday after Easter, and at other times if justified by weather conditions. All car-rental companies supply winter tires during the appropriate seasons as part of their standard equipment.

If you plan to rent a car, you get the best rates if you reserve one through a car-rental company before you leave North America.

Foreigners bringing a motor vehicle into Finland must have a driver's license and a clearly visible sign attached to the vehicle showing its nation of origin. This rule is enforced at the border. Your home driver's license will be honored; an international driver's license is not required.

RENTALS Avis (✆ **800/331-1084** in the U.S. and Canada), **Budget** (✆ **800/472-3325** in the U.S. and Canada), and **Hertz** (✆ **800/654-3001** in the U.S. and Canada) are represented in Finland. Each company maintains 22 to 24 locations in Finland, usually in town centers or at airports, and sometimes in surprisingly obscure settings. For those who want to begin and end your tour of Finland in different cities, a drop-off within Finland can be arranged for a modest surcharge. A drop-off outside Finland, however—if allowed at all—is much more expensive; the surcharge could range from 340€ to 680€, plus additional charges for each kilometer driven. Because of the horrendous costs of one-way international car rentals originating in Finland, most visitors rent cars separately in each country you visit.

Most companies provide child seats, rooftop racks, and ski racks, usually for a nominal one-time fee of between $20 and $25 per item. The charge to rent a luxury car begins at around $519 a week, plus the 22% Finnish tax.

If you plan to do a lot of touring, you'll find that a weekly rental with unlimited mileage is your best bet. All three companies offer a prepaid plan that requires you to complete the paperwork and make an advance payment within a reasonable time before you leave home. The main advantage of prepayment is that it "locks in" a specified net rental price in dollars before you actually use the car; this could save you about $100 a week over what you'd have to pay if you wait until you arrive in Finland.

All three companies offer small, cost-efficient cars that might be able to seat four passengers. However, we recommend these subcompact cars for no more than two passengers plus luggage. Rentals range from $389 at Avis to $442 at Budget per week, with unlimited mileage; Hertz's cheapest car, quoted at $463 per week, makes a comparison difficult since it includes the whopping 22% government tax in its rates. Both Budget and Avis consider the 22% government tax a supplemental charge that's added to your bill.

INSURANCE   Collision-damage waiver insurance (CDW) is available at each of the three companies usually for $9 to $15 a day, depending on the value of your car. This coverage eliminates your financial responsibility in case of an accident. If you don't have a CDW and you have an accident, you'll probably have to pay for some or all of the damage to the car, even if it's not your fault. Some credit- and charge-card companies (including American Express, MasterCard, Visa, and Diners Club) reimburse their cardholders for the deductible in the event of an accident, but only after your private car insurance has paid the damages (your future premiums at home might be raised if you submit a substantial claim for damage to a rental car abroad). Although the card issuers reimburse the renter for the cost of some or all of the damages (usually several weeks after the accident), payments have occasionally been delayed pending completion of all the paperwork. Unless you have a large line of credit on your card, you might be obliged to pay a large sum of cash on the spot if you have an accident. To avoid any misunderstanding, some car-rental companies offer their clients the choice of automatically including the CDW as part of the total rental price. In any event, it's always a good idea to ask your insurance and credit-card companies about the extent of your coverage beforehand, and check with the rental companies about your liabilities when you reserve your car.

DRIVING RULES   Finns drive on the right side of the road, as in the U.S. and Europe. Speed limits are strictly enforced. It's illegal to drive a motor vehicle under the influence of alcohol (blood alcohol may not exceed 0.5%), and the penalties for doing so are severe.

FLY & DRIVE Government taxes, insurance coverage, and the high cost of gasoline (petrol) can make the use of a rented vehicle in Finland more expensive than you might have assumed. One way to reduce these costs is to arrange for your fly-drive trip through **Finnair** (☎ 800/950-5000). When you book your flight, the airline may be able to arrange a lower car-rental price through Budget, Hertz, or Avis than you could have gotten on your own.

BY FERRY & LAKE STEAMER

Finland's nearly 188,000 lakes form Europe's largest inland waterway. Although railroads and highways now link most Finnish towns and villages, the romantic old steamers (and their modern counterparts) give both Finns and visitors a relaxing way to enjoy the inland archipelago areas of Finland in summer.

The excursion trips of most vessels last from just a couple of hours to a full day. In some cases you can travel from one lakeside town to another. There are even a couple of car ferries that cross some of the biggest lakes, significantly reducing the time required to drive around the lake. Unlike highway ferries, which are few in number today but can be used at no charge, the car ferries charge a fare for both cars and passengers. Information on all lake traffic schedules and fares is available from local tourist offices.

11 Organized Tours

Given its vastness and often-difficult driving conditions during the long winter months, Finland is the one Scandinavian country where an organized tour makes sense. Even for those who enjoy the outdoors, it may be best to enter Finland's true wilderness areas with a guide.

There's no better way to discover the natural beauty of Finland's lake region than by cruising its waters. **Norvista** offers an excursion trip on Finland's largest lake, Lake Saimaa. Beginning in Helsinki, the tour's first stop is the medieval town of Porvoo. Other stops include the fishing lodge in Langinlipslo and a brief visit to the monastery of Valamo. Lunch and dinner are served on board, and nights are spent in a hotel in town. The excursion lasts 3 days and begins at $540. For information, call ☎ 0870/744-7315; or go to www.norvistatravel.co.uk. This tour is available only during the summer months.

Norvista also has a "Sample Icebreaker," which includes an icebreaker cruise, a reindeer drive, a 2-day ski and snowmobile safari, and even a visit to Santa. These tours cost $1,535 and include all transfers, accommodations, full board, and equipment. One of the more popular tours is the "Northern Lights"—2 days of husky-sledding, a half day of ice fishing, and a full-day reindeer safari. These tours, which cost $1,065, include the flight from Helsinki to Kittilla, all accommodations, full board, and equipment.

Intourist (☎ 800/556-5305) offers a "Snowmobile Adventure to the Arctic Ocean." From February 15 to April 20, guides escort participants through Finland's snowfields. The tours include 2 nights in a hotel and 2 nights in a cabin in the wilderness, full board, equipment, and sauna.

Intourist also offers a "Dogsled Safari to the Lapp Fells." Guides take participants through northwestern Lapland. The 7-day tour covers approximately 19km to 31km (12–21 miles) per day. Prices include all equipment and full board. Another great adventure trip is Intourist's canoeing tour of northern Karelia. Canoers paddle through the Lieksa region in eastern Finland. The 7-day tours are available from June to September. Call to determine rates for specific itineraries.

If you yearn for relaxation rather than action, consider a Finnish spa. **Great Spas of the World** (© 800/ SPA-TIME or 212/889-8170; www. greatspas.com) sponsors a 7-day jaunt to the Levitunturi Hotel and Spa in Lapland. Its "Arctic Spa Holiday" includes 1 night in Helsinki and 5 at the spa. Activities vary according to the season. This excursion is offered year-round. Great Spas of the World also sponsors trips to the Katinkulta Holiday Resort and Spa. "Winter Holiday" includes 1 night in Helsinki and 5 nights at the resort. The cost includes all spa and fitness programs. Among the available activities are snowmobile safaris, skiing, and dog-sled excursions. Call for rates.

SUGGESTED ITINERARIES
If You Have 1 Week

Although traveling by car is the best way to see sights and charms, most people rely on trains and airplanes more often in Finland than they might elsewhere in Europe. Nevertheless, we've outlined a weeklong, 510km (317-mile) driving tour through the country's "southern triangle."

Days 1–3 Spend your first day in Helsinki recovering from your flight. On Day 2, see the major sights, including the Finnish National Gallery, the National Museum of Finland, and the Mannerheim Museum. On Day 3, explore the nearby islands of the Baltic, such as Suomenlinna, or take a steamer to Porvoo, Finland's second-oldest town.

Day 4 Drive from Helsinki to Hämeenlinna, a distance of 98km (61 miles). Take E79 past forest-covered hills and meadows, which eventually give way to open country dotted with lakes. About 32km (20 miles) south of Hämeenlinna you can visit Riihimaki, which has a Glass Museum (Suomen Lasimuseo) and a glass shop. By afternoon you'll be in Hämeenlinna, Finland's oldest inland town, founded in 1639, and the birthplace of composer Jean Sibelius. You can also explore a castle on the shores of Lake Vanajavesi. Hämeenlinna is the starting point for many Silja Line cruise boats that go to Tampere. However, if you're pressed for time, you may want to just stay overnight in Hämeenlinna and then continue the tour.

Day 5 Leave Hämeenlinna and drive along E79 for 80km (50 miles) to Tampere. Folk dances and open-air concerts are performed in Hämeenpuisto Park in summer, and the city boasts one of the most famous summer theaters in the world. Many lake tours start from here. Spend the night in Tampere.

Day 6 Head for Turku on the west coast. Leaving Tampere, it's only 16km (10 miles) to Nokia, famous for its rapids in the Nokia River. Continue southwest on Route 41 for 53km (33 miles) until you reach Vammala. The road continues to Huittinen, only 90km (56 miles) from Turku. Plan to spend the night in Turku, Finland's oldest city, visiting its many attractions.

Day 7 From Turku, you could return directly to Helsinki on E3. This 166km (103-mile) drive can be broken by a stop at Salo, a lively town 53km (33 miles) from Turku. About 10km (6 miles) past Salo, you might want to stop at the Muurla Glass Factory. Spend the night in Helsinki.

If You Have 2 Weeks

Days 1–7 Spend the first week as suggested above.

Day 8 Spend a full day in Helsinki getting to know the city better.

Day 9 From Helsinki, head northeast to Lappeenranta, one of Finland's most charming provincial towns, 221km (137 miles) from Helsinki and only 16km (10 miles) from the Russian border, for a full day of sightseeing in Finland's glorious lake district.

Day 10 From Lappeenranta, continue northeast to the historic city of Imatra, favored by the tsars and site of the famous Imatra Rapids.

Days 11–12 From Lappeenranta, go to Savonlinna for 2 nights.

During the first day, explore the land attractions, such as Olavinlinna Castle, the marketplace, and the art center of Retretti; the next day, take the lake steamer.

Day 13 Go to Kuopio, in the northern lake district, for a day of sightseeing.

Day 14 Drive to Joensuu, the major town in northern Karelia, for a day's sightseeing in this richly folkloric province. Finland was obliged to cede half of this province to the Soviet Union during World War II.

 ## FAST FACTS: Finland

American Express The Helsinki branch is at Kanavaranta 9 (℃ 09/ 613-204-00). It's open Monday through Friday from 9am to 5pm. Whenever it's closed, you can call an active 24-hour-a-day toll-free information line about lost or stolen credit cards or traveler's checks by dialing ℃ 0800/11-46-46. That number is valid only within Finland.

Area Code The international country code for Finland is **358**. The local city (area) codes are given for all phone numbers in the Finland chapters of this book.

Business Hours Most **banks** are open Monday through Friday from 9:15am to 4:15pm. You can also exchange money at the railway station in Helsinki daily from 8am to 9pm, and at the airport daily from 6:30am to 11pm.

The hours for **stores and shops** vary. Most are open Monday through Friday from 9am to 6pm and Saturday from 9am to 3pm. Nearly everything is closed on Sunday. There are **R-kiosks**—which sell candy, tobacco, toiletries, cosmetics, and souvenirs—all over Helsinki and elsewhere; they're open Monday through Saturday from 8am to 9pm and Sunday from 9 or 10am to 9pm.

Customs See "Entry Requirements," above.

Drug Laws Drug offenses are divided into two categories: normal drug offenses and aggravated drug offenses. Normal drug offenses include the possession of a small amount of marijuana (which carries a maximum penalty of 2 years in prison and a minimum penalty of a fine for Finns and possible deportation for non-Finns). Aggravated drug offenses entail the ownership, sale, or dealing of dangerous drugs, including cocaine and heroin. This offense always carries a prison term of 1 to 10 years. Penalties for smuggling drugs across the Finnish border are even more severe.

Drugstores Medicines are sold at pharmacies (*apteekki* in Finnish). Chemists (*kemikaalipauppa*) sell cosmetics only. Some pharmacies are open 24 hours, and all of them display notices giving the address of the nearest one on night duty.

Electricity Finland operates on 220 volts AC. Plugs are usually the continental size with rounded pins. Always ask at your hotel desk before plugging in any electrical appliance. Without an appropriate transformer or adapter, you'll probably destroy the internal mechanism of your appliance or blow out one of the hotel's fuses.

Embassies & Consulates The embassy of the **United States** is at Itäinen Puistotie 14A, FIN-00140 Helsinki (✆ **09/17-19-31**); the embassy of the **United Kingdom** is at Itäinen Puistotie 17, FIN-00140 Helsinki (✆ **09/228-651-00**); and the embassy of **Canada** is at Pohjoisesplanadi 25B, FIN-00100 Helsinki (✆ **09/22-85-30**). Travelers from Australia and New Zealand should contact the British embassy.

If you're planning to visit Russia after Finland and need information about visas, the **Russian embassy** is at Tehtaankatu 1B, FIN-00140 Helsinki (✆ **09/66-18-77**). However, it's better to make all your travel arrangements to Russia before you leave home.

Emergencies In Helsinki, dial ✆ **112**; for the police, call ✆ **100-22**.

Language The Finns speak a language that, from the perspective of grammar and linguistics, is radically different from Swedish and Danish. Finnish is as difficult to learn as Chinese, and a source of endless frustration to newcomers. More than 90% of Finns speak Finnish, and the remaining population speaks mostly Swedish. Officially, Finland is a bilingual country, as you'll quickly see from maps and street signs in Helsinki (the street names are usually given in both languages).

The use of English, however, is amazingly common throughout Finland, especially among young people. In all major hotels, restaurants, and nightclubs, English is spoken almost without exception. The best phrase book is *Berlitz Finnish for Travellers,* with 1,200 phrases and 2,000 useful words, as well as the corresponding pronunciations.

Liquor Laws Alcohol can be bought at retail from **Alko,** the state liquor-monopoly shops. They're open Monday through Thursday from 10am to 5pm, Friday from 10am to 6pm, and Saturday from 9am to 3pm; they're closed on Sunday and on May 1 and September 30. Alcoholic drinks can also be purchased at hotels, restaurants, and nightclubs. Some establishments, incidentally, are licensed only for beer (or beer and wine). Only beer can be served from 9 to 11am. In Helsinki most licensed establishments stay open until midnight or 1am (until 11pm in some cities).

You must be at least 20 years of age to buy hard liquor at the Alko shops; 18- and 19-year-olds can buy beer, wine, or other beverages that contain less than 22% alcohol.

Mail Airmail letters take about 7 to 10 days to reach North America; surface mail—sent by boat—takes 1 to 2 months. Parcels are weighed and registered at the post office, which may ask you to declare the value and contents of the package on a pre-printed form. Stamps are sold at post offices in all towns and cities, at most hotels, sometimes at news kiosks, and often by shopkeepers who offer the service for customers' convenience. In Finland, mailboxes are bright yellow with a trumpet embossed on them. Airmail letters cost .60€ for up to 20 grams. For postal information, call © **09/980-071-00.**

Maps The National Board of Survey publishes *Road Map of Finland* (GT 1:200,000), an accurate, detailed road and touring map; and *Motoring Road Map* (1:800,000), a new edition of the *Motoring Road Map of Finland,* appearing annually, and the only map with complete information on road surfaces. These maps are the most important ones, although the board also publishes numerous touring maps. They're for sale at major bookstores in Helsinki (see "Fast Facts: Helsinki," in chapter 20).

Newspapers & Magazines English-language newspapers, including the *International Herald Tribune* and *USA Today,* are available at the larger bookstores, the railway station, and many kiosks in central Helsinki and other cities.

Police Dial © **112** in Helsinki. In smaller towns, ask the operator to connect you with the nearest police station.

Radio & TV "Northern Report," a program in English, is broadcast at 558 kHz on the AM dial in Helsinki daily at 9:30am, 9:35pm, and midnight. There's also a special Saturday-morning program from 10:30 to 11:30am. A news summary in English is given on the domestic FM networks 1 and 4 daily at 10:55pm. Radio Finland international programs at 100.8 MHz (FM) in Helsinki are presented daily at 5:30, 7:35, 9:30, 11, and 11:30am; at 1:30, 2, 3, 4, 5:05, and 9:35pm; and at midnight, as well as on 94.0 MHz (FM) in Helsinki at 10:30pm. For information and a free publication, *Radio Finland,* about radio programs in foreign languages, call © **09/148-01** in Helsinki.

Restrooms Most public restrooms are in terminals (air, bus, and rail). Hotels usually have very clean toilets, as do the better restaurants and clubs. Most toilets have symbols to designate men or women. Otherwise, *naisille* is for women and *miehille* is for men.

Safety Finland is one of the safest countries in Europe, although with the arrival of desperately poor immigrants from former Communist lands to the south, the situation is not as tranquil or as safe as before.

Taxes An 18% sales tax is added to most retail purchases in Finland. However, anyone residing outside the EU, Norway, or Finland can shop tax-free in Finland, saving 12% to 16% on purchases costing more than 40€. Look for the TAX-FREE FOR TOURISTS sticker that indicates which shops participate in this program. These shops give you a voucher covering the tax, which you can cash when you leave the country—even if you bought the items with a credit or charge card. The voucher and your purchases must be presented at your point of departure from the country, and you are then reimbursed for the amount of the tax. You're not permitted to use these tax-free purchases within Finland. Your refund can be collected at an airport, ferry port, or highway border point.

Telephone, Telex & Fax To make **international calls** from Finland by direct dialing, first dial the international prefix of 990, 994, or 999, then the country code, then the area code (without the general prefix 0), and finally the local number. For information on long-distance calls and tariffs, call © **0800/909-99.**

To place calls to Finland, dial whatever code is needed in your country to reach the international lines (for example, in the United States, dial **011** for international long distance), then the country code for Finland (**358**), then the area code (without the Finnish long-distance prefix 0), and finally the local number.

To make long-distance calls within Finland, dial 0 to reach the long-distance lines (the choice of carrier is at random), the area code, and the local number. (Note that all area codes in this guide are given with the prefix 0.) For phone number information, dial ✆ **02-02-02.** Besides phone booths and hotels, calls can be made from local post and telephone offices.

You can send faxes and telex messages from your hotel (at an additional charge).

Time Finnish Standard Time is 2 hours ahead of Greenwich Mean Time (GMT) and 7 hours ahead of U.S. Eastern Standard Time (when it's midnight in New York, it's 7am in Finland). While Finland is on "summer time" (Mar 28–Sept 26), it is 3 hours ahead of GMT.

Tipping It's standard for **hotels and restaurants** to add a service charge of 15%, and usually no further tipping is necessary. In restaurants, it's customary to leave just small change. **Taxi drivers** don't expect a tip. However, it's appropriate to tip **doormen** at least 1€, and **bellhops** usually get 1€ per bag (in most Finnish provincial hotels, guests normally carry your own luggage to your room). At railway stations, **porters** are usually tipped 1€ per bag. Hairdressers and barbers don't expect tips. **Coat check charges** are usually posted; there's no need for additional tipping unless you want to.

Helsinki

Helsinki may stand at the doorway to Russia, but its cultural links are firmly in Scandinavia. It was originally founded in 1550, halfway between Stockholm and St. Petersburg, on orders of the Swedish king Gustavus Vasa, and is still known to the Swedes as "Helsingfors."

Surrounded by water on three sides and fringed by islands, Helsinki grew up around a natural harbor overlooking the Gulf of Finland. A city of wide streets, squares, and parks, adorned with sculpture, Helsinki was one of the world's first planned municipalities and is noted for its 19th-century neoclassical architecture. Because the city is relatively compact, most of it can be explored on foot.

From the capital of an autonomous Grand Duchy of Russia, Helsinki was transformed in 1917 (the year of the Russian Revolution) into the capital of the newly independent Finland. Today it's not only a center of government but the nation's intellectual capital, with a major university and many cultural and scientific institutions. Although Helsinki is also a business and industrial center (most major Finnish firms have their headquarters here), and the hub of Finland's transportation networks, the city is relatively free of pollution.

With a population of about half a million, Helsinki enjoys a certain urban sophistication—although the locals still refer to it as "a big village." Helsinki's residents are some of the best educated, best clothed, best fed, and best housed on earth.

1 Orientation

ARRIVING

BY PLANE   The **Helsinki-Vantaa Airport** (© **09/827-71**) is 19km (12 miles) north of the center of town, about a 30-minute bus ride. Special buses to the airport leave from the City Terminal at Asemaukio 3, and stop at the Air Terminal at Töölönkatu 21 (near the Scandic Hotel Continental) at 15- to 30-minute intervals every day between 5am and midnight. Tickets cost 4.90€ each way. A slightly less expensive, but also less comfortable, option is taking public bus no. 615, which departs from Railway Square (Platform 12) two or three times an hour between 5:30am and 10:20pm. The price is 3€ each way.

A conventional taxi ride from the airport to the center of Helsinki costs about 20€ to 25€ each way; you'll be assured of a private car shared only by members of your immediate party. A slightly cheaper alternative is to hire a special yellow taxi (© **09/220-025-00**) at the airport terminal, which might be shared by up to four separate travelers; the cost is 18€ per person.

On your departure, note that the airport requires passengers on domestic flights within Finland to check in 30 minutes before flight time. Passengers on flights to other points in Europe usually must check in between 45 and 60 minutes before takeoff, and passengers bound for any of the former regions of the

Soviet Union or anywhere in North America usually need to check in between 1 and 2 hours in advance.

BY TRAIN   The **Helsinki Railway Station** is on Kaivokatu (© **0358/ 307-209-02** for train information). See "Getting Around" in chapter 19, "Planning Your Trip to Finland," for more information. The station has luggage-storage lockers costing 2€. The lost-luggage department is open daily from 5:30am to midnight.

BY BUS   The **Helsinki Bus Station** does not have a street address, but it's located between Salomonkatu and Simonkatu in the city center (© **09/61-36-81**). See "Getting Around" in chapter 19 for more information. If you're arriving from Stockholm, you can take the ferry to Turku on the west coast. At Turku, you can board one of about 20 daily buses that make the 2½-hour run to Helsinki.

BY CAR   Helsinki is connected by road to all Finnish cities. If you arrive at the port of Turku on a car ferry from Sweden, you can take the E18 express highway east to Helsinki. See "Getting Around" below and in chapter 19 for information about car rentals.

BY FERRY   Ferries from Germany and Sweden operated by the **Viking Line** and **Silja Line** arrive at and depart from terminals on the island of Katajanokka, which is just east of Market Square (Kauppatori). The ferry terminals are within easy walking distance of downtown; you can also take tram no. 2 or 4 or a taxi. For tickets and information, contact **Silja Line,** Mannerheimintie 2 (© **09/ 180-41**), or **Viking Line,** Mastokatu 1 (© **09/123-51**).

VISITOR INFORMATION

Helsinki City Tourist Office, Pohjoisesplanadi 19, FIN-00100 Helsinki (© **09/169-37-57**), is open from May 2 to September 30, Monday through Friday from 9am to 7pm and Saturday and Sunday from 9am to 6pm; off season, Monday through Friday from 9am to 5pm and Saturday from 9am to 4pm. **TourExpert,** a service at the Helsinki tourist office, is your best bet for booking tours once you reach Helsinki. The tourist office also sells tickets to events; air, bus, and cruise tickets; and the money-saving **Helsinki Card.** Hotel packages and guide bookings are also available through this office.

CITY LAYOUT

MAIN ARTERIES & STREETS   Helsinki is a peninsula city, skirted by islands and skerries. The main artery is the wide and handsome **Mannerheimintie,** named in honor of the former field marshal. East of Mannerheimintie, opening onto Kaivokatu, is the Helsinki Railway Station. Toward the harbor is **Senaatintori,** crowned by the landmark cathedral. Designed by Carl Ludwig Engel, this "Senate Square" also includes the government and university buildings.

Continuing east is a bridge crossing over a tiny island—**Katajanokka**—dominated by the Eastern Orthodox cathedral. Back across the bridge, sticking close to the harbor, past the President's Palace, is the most colorful square in Helsinki, the **Kauppatori (Market Square)**—see it early in the morning when it's most lively. From the pier here, it's possible to catch boats for **Suomenlinna,** fortified islands that guard the sea lanes to Helsinki. The sea fortress celebrated its 250th anniversary in 1998.

The great promenade street of Helsinki—**Esplanadi (Esplanade)**—begins west of Market Square. Directly north of the Esplanade and running parallel to it is **Aleksanterinkatu,** the principal shopping street.

FINDING AN ADDRESS   Street numbers always begin at the south end of north-south streets and at the eastern end of streets running east-west. All odd numbers are on one side of the street and all even numbers on the opposite side. In some cases, where a large building houses several establishments, there might be an A or B attached to the number.

MAPS   The best city map of Helsinki is called **Falk Plan.** Containing a highly detailed and alphabetized street index, it can easily be carried in your pocket. Falk Plan maps are sold at nearly all bookstores and many news kiosks in the central city, including Helsinki's major bookstore, **Academic,** Keskuskapu 1 (✆ 09/121-41).

NEIGHBORHOODS IN BRIEF
Helsinki is divided roughly into districts.

The Center The historic core stretches from Senaatintori (Senate Square) to Esplanadi. Senate Square is dominated by the Lutheran cathedral at its center, and Esplanadi itself is an avenue lined with trees. At one end of Esplanadi, the wide Mannerheimintie, extending for about 5km (3 miles), is the main road from the city center to the expanding suburbs. The section south of Esplanadi is one of the wealthiest in the capital, lined with embassies and elegant houses, rising into Kaivopuisto Park.

North of Center If you'd like to escape the congestion in the center of town, especially around the rail terminus, you can follow the main artery, Mannerheimintie, north. This section of Helsinki lies between Sibelius Park in the west and a lake, Töölönlahti, in the east. It has a more residential feel than does the area in the center, and several fine restaurants are located here. Those driving cars into Helsinki prefer this section.

Kruununhaka & Hakaniemi The district of Kruununhaka is one of the oldest. Helsinki was founded in 1550 at the mouth of the Vantaa River, but was relocated in 1640 on the peninsula of Vironniemi in what's known as Kruununhaka today. This section, along with neighboring Hakaniemi,

encompasses the remaining buildings from 17th-century Helsinki. The waters of Kaisaniemenlahti divide the districts of Hakaniemi and Kruununhaka.

The Islands Helsinki also includes several islands, some of which are known as "tourist islands," including **Korkeasaari,** site of the Helsinki Zoo. The main islands are linked by convenient ferries and water taxis.

Called the "fortress of Finland" and the "Gibraltar of the North," **Suomenlinna** consists of five main islands, all interconnected, and is the site of many museums. You can spend a day here exploring the old fortifications. **Seurasaari,** another island, has a bathing beach and recreation area, as well as a national park and the largest open-air museum in Finland. One of the islands, tiny Kustaanmiekka, is the site of a longtime favorite restaurant (Walhalla) where you might want to enjoy lunch while exploring the Suomenlinna fortress and museums.

Espoo Many workers in Helsinki treat Espoo as a bedroom suburb. Actually, since 1972, when it received its charter, it has been the second-largest city of Finland, with a population of nearly 200,000.

Tapiola Another "suburb city," Tapiola was founded in 1951, providing homes for some 16,000 residents. This "model city" greatly influenced housing developments around the world with its varied housing, which ranges from multistory condo units to more luxurious one-family villas. The great Finnish architect, Alvar Aalto, was one of its planners.

2 Getting Around

Helsinki has an efficient transportation network, which includes buses, trams, a subway (metro), ferries, and taxis.

BY PUBLIC TRANSPORTATION

DISCOUNT PASSES   Visitors to Helsinki can purchase the **Helsinki Card,** which offers unlimited travel on the city's public buses, trams, subway, and ferries, and a free guided sightseeing tour by bus (in summer daily, off season on Sun), as well as free entry to about 50 museums and other sights in Helsinki. The Helsinki Card is available for 1-, 2-, or 3-day periods. The price of the card for adults is 24€ for 1 day, 32€ for 2 days, and 38€ for 3 days. A card for children costs 2€ for 1 day, 14€ for 2 days, and 17€ for 3 days. The cards can be bought at 50 sales points in the Helsinki area, including the Helsinki City Tourist Office, the Hotel Booking Center (see "Where to Stay," later in this chapter), travel agencies, and hotels. For further information, check with any Finnish Tourist Board worldwide or the **Helsinki City Tourist Office,** Pohjoisesplanadi 19 (℃ **09/169-37-57**).

You can also buy a **Tourist Ticket** for travel over a 1-, 3-, or 5-day period. This ticket lets you travel as much as you like within the city limits on all forms of public transportation except regional buses. A 1-day ticket costs 4€ for adults, 2€ for children 7 to 16; a 2-day ticket, 8€ for adults, 4€ for children 7 to 16; and a 5-day ticket, 13€ for adults, 6.40€ for children 7 to 16. Children under 7 travel free. Tickets can be purchased at many places throughout Helsinki, including the Helsinki City Tourist Office and transportation service depots, such as the Railway Square Metro Station, open Monday through Thursday from 7:30am to 6pm and Friday from 7:30am to 4pm.

BY METRO/BUS/TRAIN   The **City Transport Office** is at the Rautatientori metro station (℃ **09/472-24-54**), open Monday through Thursday from 7:30am to 6pm and Friday from 7:30am to 4pm. The transportation system operates daily from 5:30am to 1:35am. A single ticket with transfer costs 2€ for adults, 1€ for children; a tram ticket is 1.50€, with no right of transfer. It's cheaper to buy a multitrip ticket, allowing 10 individual trips for 12€ for adults, 6.40€ for children. Transfers are allowed for single and multitrip tickets within 1 hour of the time stamped on the ticket.

BY FERRY   Ferries depart from the end of Eteläesplanadi (no terminal) heading for the offshore islands of Suomenlinna and Korkeasaari (Zoo).

BY TAXI

You can order taxis by telephone (℃ **09/70-07-00**), find them at taxi ranks, or hail them on the street. All taxis have an illuminated yellow sign: *taksi*/TAXI. The basic fare costs 5€ and rises on a per-kilometer basis, as indicated on the meter. Surcharges are imposed in the evening (6–10pm) and on Saturday after 2pm. There's also a surcharge at night from 10pm to 6am and on Sunday.

A taxi from the Helsinki–Vantaa Airport to the center of Helsinki costs 20€ to 25€, and the ride generally takes 30 to 40 minutes. Call ℃ **09/70-08-00.** An airport taxi shuttle service is available for individual travelers to any point in the greater Helsinki area, costing anywhere from 40€ to 50€. The van is shared by a maximum of eight passengers. Call ℂ **09/220-025-00** at any time.

BY CAR

Driving around Helsinki by car is not recommended because parking is limited. Either walk or take public transportation. However, touring the environs by car is ideal.

CAR RENTALS   The major car-rental companies maintain offices at the Helsinki airport (where airport surcharges apply to car pickups) and in the center of town. Most new visitors prefer to take a taxi to their hotel, and then rent a car after becoming oriented to the city. (This system also avoids parking fees.) **Avis Rent-a-Car** is at Pohjoinen Rautatiekatu 17 (ℂ **09/44-11-55**), **Budget Rent-a-Car** is at Malminkatu 24 (ℂ **09/686-65-00**), and **Hertz** is at Mannerheimintie 44 (ℂ **0800/11-22-33**).

PARKING   Helsinki has several multistory parking garages, including two centrally located facilities that almost always have an available space: **City-Paikoitus,** Keskuskatu (no numbered address; ℂ **09/686-968-51**), and **Parking Eliel,** adjacent to the railway station (ℂ **09/686-968-50**).

BY BICYCLE

You can rent a bicycle from **Kimmo Suontakanen,** Mannerheimintie 13 (ℂ **09/850-228-50**), at rates that range from 10€ to 15€ per day, depending on the type of bicycle you rent. A deposit of 16€ is required, or presentation of your passport. Otherwise, ask at your hotel for addresses within your immediate neighborhood.

 ## FAST FACTS: Helsinki

American Express   The Helsinki branch is at Kanavaranta 9 (ℂ **09/613-204-00**), and is open Monday through Friday from 9am to 5pm. Whenever it's closed, you can call an active 24-hour-a-day toll-free information line about lost or stolen credit cards or traveler's checks at ℂ **0800/11-46-46**. That number is valid only within Finland.

Area Code   The country code for Finland is **358**; the city code for Helsinki is **9**.

Babysitters   Every hotel in Finland has a list of employees, such as maids, who, with advance notice, can babysit your child. Most speak English. The rate in Helsinki is about 6€ per hour, per child, perhaps less in certain provincial towns. Although hotels are the main procurers of babysitters throughout Helsinki, there are alternatives. During daytime hours, if you're a devoted shopper, the well-respected **Stockmann Department Store,** Aleksanterinkatu 52 (ℂ **09/1211**), offers a free child-minding service every Monday through Friday from 10am to 7pm and Saturday from 9am to 6pm.

Bookstores   The most famous bookstore in Finland—and the best stocked, with thousands of English titles—is Helsinki's **Academic Bookstore,** Kekuskapv 1 (ℂ **09/121-41**).

Business Hours Most **banks** are open Monday through Friday from 9:15am to 4:15pm. Most **businesses and shops** are open Monday through Friday from 9am to 5pm and Saturday from 9am to 2pm. Larger stores are usually open until 7pm Monday through Friday and as late as 6pm on Saturdays. With a few exceptions (noted below), nearly everyplace is closed on Sunday. Many shops in the center of Helsinki are open until 8pm on certain nights, especially Monday and Friday. Shops in the Station Tunnel are generally open Monday through Saturday from 10am to 10pm and Sunday from noon to 10pm.

R-kiosks, which sell candy, tobacco, toiletries, cosmetics, and souvenirs all over Helsinki and elsewhere, are open Monday through Saturday from 8am to 9pm and Sunday from 9 or 10am to 9pm.

Currency Exchange You can exchange dollars for euros at most banks and (if the amount is large enough) often in your hotel; however, you're likely to get less euros at hotels than at banks. You can also exchange money at the railway station Monday through Friday from 9am to 6pm; and at the airport daily from 6am to 11pm.

Dentists Go to the **Ympyrätalo Dental Clinic,** Siltasaarenkatu 18A (✆ 09/709-66-11), open Monday through Friday from 8am to 8pm and Saturday from 9am to 1pm.

Doctors To summon a physician in an emergency, dial ✆ 112. For private medical advice, dial ✆ 09/4711.

Drugstores Pharmacies dispensing medicines are known as *apteekki.* The **Yliopiston Apteekki,** Mannerheimintie 96 (✆ 09/41-57-78), is open 24 hours daily.

Embassies & Consulates The embassy of the **United States** is at Itäinen Puistotie 14B (✆ 09/17-19-31); the embassy of **Canada,** at Pohjoisesplanadi 25B (✆ 09/17-11-41); and the embassy of the **United Kingdom,** at Itäinen Puistotie 17 (✆ 09/228-651-00). Citizens of Australia and New Zealand should go to the British embassy.

Emergencies Dial ✆ 112 for medical help, an ambulance, or police, or in case of fire.

Eyeglasses One of the best and most conveniently situated opticians—where you can get new glasses or contact lenses in about a day—is the optical department at **Stockmann Department Store,** Aleksanterinkatu 52 (✆ 09/1211; Tram: 3b). One floor above street level, it's open Monday through Friday from 9am to 8pm and Saturday from 9am to 6pm.

Hairdressers & Barbers **Salon Alex/Salon Alexandra,** Urgönkatu 23A (✆ 09/612-24-70), is a well-managed association of semi-independent hairdressers who specialize in cutting and styling men's (at Salon Alex) and women's (at Salon Alexandra) hair. Your fellow clients are likely to include some of Finland's most visible fashion models. Unless you prefer a specific hairdresser, an advance appointment is usually not necessary.

Hospitals An emergency hospital for foreigners is the **Helsinki University Central Hospital,** Meilahti Hospital (for both medical and surgical care), at Haartmaninkatu 4 (✆ 09/4711).

Internet Access Opposite the train station, **Sonero,** Kaivokatu 2, gives you the first 15 minutes of access to the Internet free. It's open Monday through Friday from 9am to 7pm, Saturday from10am to 4pm.

Laundry At the laundry **Exprès Pikapesula,** Laivurinrinne 2 (© **09/63-95-24**), clothes brought in early in the morning can be ready by the 5:30pm closing time.

Liquor Laws The legal age for drinking beer and hard liquor throughout Finland is 18. Many nightclubs and dance clubs, however, admit only "well-dressed" (and non-rowdy) patrons, and sometimes insist that they appear to be 24 or older. Age limits (or even the appearance of age limits), however, usually don't apply to pubs. Laws against drunken driving are rigidly enforced in Helsinki.

Lost Property The **Lost Property Office** is at Päijänteentie 12A (© **030/72-12-16**), open year-round, Monday through Friday from 9am to 5pm.

Luggage Storage & Lockers These facilities are at the Central Station on Kaivokatu. The staff offers both lockers with keys and an employee-staffed area where you get a ticket for your luggage. The charge is 2€ per bag. The service operates daily from 5:30am to midnight.

Mail For post office information, call © **0800/171-00.** The main post office in Helsinki is at Mannerheimintie 1A, open Monday through Friday from 9am to 5pm. If you don't know your address in Helsinki, have your mail sent to you at FIN-00100 Poste Restante (general delivery) in care of the main post office. At this Poste Restante, you can pick up mail (after presenting your passport) Monday through Saturday from 8am to 10pm and Sunday from 11am to 10pm. You can buy stamps at the railway station post office Monday through Friday from 7am to 9pm, Saturday from 9am to 6pm, and Sunday from 11am to 9pm. Yellow stamp machines outside post offices take 1€ coins.

Photographic Needs One of the most reliable chains in Helsinki, with three centrally located branches, is **Helios,** open Monday through Friday from 9am to 6pm and Saturday from 10am to 2pm. It takes only an hour to develop prints. Look for its outlets in the Central Station (© **09/65-76-27**), at Mannerheimintie 69 (© **09/241-96-82**), or at Mannerheimintie 14 (© **09/680-14-00**).

Police In an emergency, dial © **112.** Otherwise, dial © **100-22** for information about the precinct nearest you. One central precinct is at the Helsinki Central Station (© **09/189-41-60**).

Radio & TV **Radio Finland** (© **09/148-01**) broadcasts news in English every day on the national YLE-3 network at 9:55pm. The external service of the Finnish Broadcasting Company has daily programs in English which can be heard on 103.7 MHz (FM) Monday through Friday at 7:30, 9:30, 11, and 11:30am, and at 1:30, 3, 4, 5, and 9:30pm, midnight, and 2am. **Radio One** features the BBC World Service News daily at noon (in winter, broadcasts are at 11am). Helsinki has two TV channels. Programs from abroad, such as those from the United States and Britain, are broadcast in their original languages, with Finnish subtitles.

Restrooms There's a centrally located public toilet at Sofiankatu 2. Otherwise, many locals use cafe toilets (where you should at least order a cup of coffee or a soft drink), or they make use of the facilities at transit terminals.

Taxes Throughout Finland there's a value-added tax of between 6% and 22% on all goods and services. Most hotels carry a surcharge of 6%, but nearly everything else a foreign visitor is likely to buy in Finland is taxed at 22%.

Telephones, Telegrams, Telex & Fax For **information** and number inquiries, dial 🕾 **118** in Helsinki. If you're thinking about calling home (providing you're not calling collect) and want to know the cost, dial 🕾 **0800/909-99.**

Direct-dialed **long-distance calls** (intercity calls) can be made from public pay phones located throughout the city that take 25€ coins; the routing numbers and rates are listed in the phone directory. Direct-dialed calls to other countries can also be made from these pay phones, or from the **Tele-Service** office, Mannerheimintie 11B. The Tele-Service office also handles other long-distance calls, telegrams, and telex; it's open daily from 9am to 9pm, but it offers 24-hour service by phone (🕾 **020/211**). If you call from your hotel, your phone charge might be doubled or tripled.

For local calls within the city of Helsinki, you don't need to dial the area code **(09)**.

You can send faxes from most hotels. If your hotel does not have a fax machine, go to one of the larger hotels and ask someone on the staff to send your fax. You'll be billed for the transmission, and probably a surcharge, too.

Transit Information See "Orientation," earlier in this chapter.

Weather Summers in Helsinki are often sunny, but the weather is rarely uncomfortably hot. The best weather is in July, when the highest temperature is usually about 69°F (20°C). Midsummer nights in Helsinki are greatly extended (at this time Lapland is bathed in the midnight sun). In winter, temperatures hover between 21°F and 27°F (–6°C to –3°C), but it's not true that polar bears roam the streets.

3 Where to Stay

There's a big choice of accommodations in Helsinki. The trick is to find something that suits your budget. As elsewhere in Scandinavia, Finland isn't cheap. Your best bet with hotels is to plan as far in advance as possible and to take advantage of any discounts that might be offered. Even an expensive hotel sometimes offers a few moderately priced rooms, but they are usually booked quickly and are difficult for the average visitor to get. In Helsinki, peak rates are charged in the winter because most of the major hotels depend on business travelers to fill their rooms.

Note: Taxes are included in the rates given here, and many hotels also include breakfast. Unless otherwise indicated, all our recommended accommodations below come with a private bathroom.

A ROOM IN A HURRY Hotellikeskus (Hotel Booking Center), Rautatieasema (🕾 **09/228-814-00**), in the heart of the city at the railway station (beside Platform 4), is open year-round, Monday through Friday from 9am to 5pm. You tell them the price you're willing to pay, and an English-speaking employee will make a reservation for you and give you a map and instructions for reaching your lodgings. Hotellikeskus charges a booking fee of 3€.

IN THE CITY CENTER
VERY EXPENSIVE

Hotel Kämp 🌟🌟🌟   Finland's most opulent hotel resulted from a recent renovation of what many Finns remembered as the most luxurious Belle Epoque palace in the days before World War II. It reopened with fanfare, immediately attracting a bevy of politicians (including the president of Finland), writers, and rock stars, each lending their cachet to what is already a household name within Helsinki. Originally built in 1887, with a newer wing added in the 1960s, and a radical upgrade shortly before its "rebirth" in 1999, it is adjacent to the city's most prestigious boulevard. Public areas are appropriately opulent, a combination of turn-of-the-20th-century grandeur and conservatively traditional decors, with lots of glistening hardwoods and polished stone. The large guest rooms are lavishly outfitted with elaborate curtains and reproductions of furniture from the early 19th century. Each bathroom is beautifully kept, with shower-tub combinations. Service, as you'd expect, is superb.

Pohjoisesplanadi 29, FIN-00100 Helsinki. © **800/325-3859** or 09/57-61-11. Fax 09/576-11-22. www.hotelkamp.fi. 179 units. 330€–365€ double; 690€–2,624€ suite. Weekend packages available. AE, DC, MC, V. Parking 32€. Tram: 1 or 7. **Amenities:** 2 restaurants; bar; fitness center; sauna; room service; babysitting; laundry/dry cleaning. *In room:* A/C, TV, minibar, hair dryer, safe.

Palace Hotel 🌟🌟   Overlooking the Presidential Palace, just a few steps from Market Square, this gem of a hotel was built in 1952 and subsequently renovated to high standards of glamour (most recently in 1996). The hotel offers guest rooms overlooking the harbor. All rooms are decorated with elegant but restrained taste, and the most expensive ones have balconies. Most units have sitting areas; all have good-sized tiled bathrooms, with shower-tub combinations. The best units also come with double basins, robes, and bidets.

The specialty dining room, Restaurant Palace, is one of the best in Finland, offering a panoramic view from the 10th floor.

Eteläranta 10, FIN-00130 Helsinki. © **09/13-45-61.** Fax 09/65-47-86. www.palacehotel.fi. 44 units. 220€–270€ double; 270€–590€ suite. Rates include breakfast. AE, DC, MC, V. Parking 15€. Tram: 3B or 3T. **Amenities:** 2 restaurants; bar; sauna; room service; babysitting; laundry/dry cleaning. *In room:* A/C, TV, minibar, hair dryer, safe.

EXPENSIVE

Ramada Presidentti Hotel 🌟   Built in 1980 and renovated in 1997, this hotel stands in the commercial center of Helsinki, close to Finlandia Hall, Parliament House, and the railway station. It's a granite-and-copper structure with lots of drinking and dining facilities. The guest rooms are warm, comfortable, modern, and filled with nice conveniences. The windows are triple-glazed. The bathrooms tend to be small but come equipped with shower-tub combinations, adequate shelf space, and heated towel racks. Airport taxis depart from here directly for the airport.

The hotel's largest, and most visible, restaurant is the Brasserie President, which offers a two-tiered price scale, one focusing on simple bistro-style platters, another emphasizing upscale gourmet food in the Continental tradition. There's also a separate restaurant adjacent to the hotel's Casino Ray.

Eteläinen Rautatiekatu 4, FIN-00100 Helsinki. © **800/272-6232** in the U.S., or 09/6911. Fax 09/694-78-86. www.ramadahotels.com. 495 units. Mon–Thurs 190€ double, 664€–832€ suite; Fri–Sun 108€–128€ double, 338€ suite. Rates include buffet breakfast. AE, DC, MC, V. Parking 22€. Tram: 3B or 3T. **Amenities:** 2 restaurants; bar; pool; sauna; room service; babysitting; laundry/dry cleaning. *In room:* A/C, TV, minibar, hair dryer.

Helsinki Accommodations

Cumulus Seurahuone **9**

Hotel Arthur **16**

Hotel Finn **10**

Hotel Kämp **15**

Lord Hotel **6**

Martta Hotelli **7**

Palace Hotel **14**

Radisson SAS
  Hesperia Hotel Helsinki **3**

Radisson SAS Hotel Espoo **2**

Ramada Presidentti Hotel **5**

Rivoli Jardin **13**

Scandic Hotel
  Kalastajatorppa **1**

Scandic Hotel Marski **11**

Sokos Hotel Klaus Kurki **12**

Sokos Hotel Vaakuna **4**

Sokos Torni Hotel **8**

Strand Inter-Continental **17**

- - - - Ferry
———— Railway

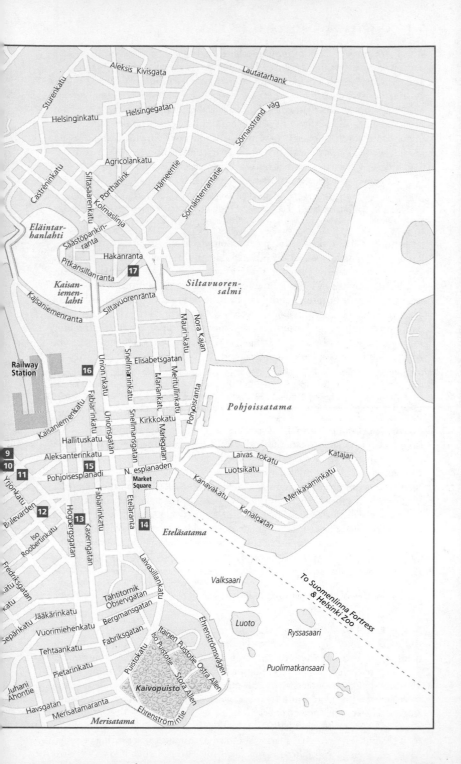

Aleksis Kivisgata

Lautatarhank

Sturenkatu

Helsinginkatu

Helsingegatan

Sörnässtrand väg

Agricolankatu

Cästreninkatu

Siltasaarenkatu

Porthanink

Kolmaslinja

Hämeentie

Sörnäistenrantatie

*Eläintar-
hanlahti*

Säästöpankin-
ranta

Hakanranta

Pitkansillanranta

17

*Kaisan-
iemen-
lahti*

Kaisaniemenranta

Siltavuorenränta

*Siltavuoren-
salmi*

Maurinkatu

Nora Kajan

Pohjoisranta

**Railway
Station**

Union nkatu

Snellmaninkatu

Elisabetsgatan

Mariankatu

Meritullinkatu

16

Fabianinkatu

Unionsgatan

Snellmansgatan

Kirkkokatu

Mariegatan

Pohjoissatama

Kaisaniemenkatu

Hallituskatu

9

Aleksanterinkatu

10

11

15

Pohjoisesplanadi

N. esplanaden

**Market
Square**

Laivas tokatu

Katajan

Luotsikatu

Kanavakatu

Merikasaminkatu

Yrjönkatu

Fabianinkatu

Eteläranta

Kanalgatan

Bulevarden

12

Hogbergsgatan

Kaserngatan

13

Iso
Roobertinkatu

14

Eteläsatama

Fredriksgatan

Laivasillankatu

Valksaari

*To Suomenlinna Fortress
& Helsinki Zoo*

Sepänkatu

katu

Jääkärinkatu

Tähtitornik
Observgatan

Bergmansgatan

Luoto

Ryssasaari

Vuorimiehenkatu

Fabriksgatan

Itäinen Puistotie Ostra Allen

Ehrenströmsvägen

Tehtaankatu

Puistokatu

Iso Puistotie

Stora Allen

Puolimatkansaari

Pietarinkatu

Juhani
Ahontie

Kaivopuisto

Havsgatan

Merisatamaranta

Ehrenströmintie

Merisatama

523

Rivoli Jardin ♠ Custom-built as a hotel in 1984, in a neighborhood that's convenient to everything in central Helsinki, this is a small-scale, well-managed, and stylish address that lodges lots of business travelers. You'll register in a stone-and-marble–sheathed lobby that's accented with tapestries. Guest rooms, although a bit smaller than you might have thought, are comfortable; they are monochromatically outfitted in pale colors and have either wall-to-wall carpeting or hand-woven Oriental rugs scattered over hardwood floors. Bathrooms are attractively tiled, usually with tub and shower combinations.

A hideaway bar serves sandwiches and drinks. Breakfast, the only meal served, is available in a greenhouse-inspired winter garden.

Kasarmikatu 40, FIN-00130 Helsinki. © **09/68-15-00.** Fax 09/65-69-88. www.rivoli.fi. 55 units. 225€ double; 325€ suite. Rate includes breakfast. AE, DC, MV, V. Free parking. Tram: 10. **Amenities:** Bar; sauna; room service; babysitting; laundry/dry cleaning. *In room:* A/C, TV, minibar, hair dryer.

Scandic Hotel Marski ♠ Despite its somewhat stern appearance (resembling a bulky and anonymous-looking office building), this hotel is one of the best in Helsinki, conveniently located in the city's commercial core. Originally built in 1962 and renovated in 1996, it offers comfortable rooms outfitted with unusual textures, modern furniture, and good beds. If possible, opt for one of the 67 guest rooms in the hotel's extension; they are roomier and better decorated with dark wood furnishings, adequate work space, and print fabrics. Bathrooms throughout tend to be small but have neatly kept shower-tub combinations. About 10 rooms boast a private sauna.

Mannerheimintie 10, FIN-00100 Helsinki. © **09/680-61.** Fax 09/64-23-77. www.scandic-hotels.com. 289 units. Sun–Thurs 199€–252€ double; Fri–Sat 93€–120€ double. All week long 437€ suite. Rates include breakfast. AE, DC, MC, V. Parking 17€. Tram: 3B, 3T, or 6. **Amenities:** Restaurant; cafe; bar; fitness center; sauna; room service; laundry/dry cleaning. *In room:* A/C, TV, minibar, hair dryer, safe.

Sokos Hotel Klaus Kurki ♠ Opposite the Swedish Theater and a short walk from Stockmann Department Store, this 1912 brick building, constructed in the Romantic Jugend style, was originally a lodging for hardware buyers. The hotel was named after a near-mythical Finnish hero who fought both the Swedes and the Russians. All the guest rooms were renovated in 2000 and most of them are handsomely decorated, often with Finnish rugs, French poster art, and Tiffany-style lamps. Tiled bathrooms are a bit small but contain shower-tub combinations with heated towel racks. Although the hotel is a suitable choice, our major complaint is that it appears understaffed and service needs a vast improvement.

Bulevardi 2, FIN-00120 Helsinki. © **09/61-89-11.** Fax 09/433-471-00. www.sokoshotels.fi. 136 units. June 15–Aug 15 and selected weekends (Fri–Sat only) 100€ double, from 216€ suite; rest of year 185€ double, from 270€ suite. Rates include breakfast. AE, DC, MC, V. Free parking on street. Tram: 3B, 3T, 6, or 10. **Amenities:** 2 restaurants; bar; sauna; room service; babysitting; laundry/dry cleaning. *In room:* TV, minibar, hair dryer.

Sokos Hotel Vaakuna *Kids* Built for the Helsinki Olympics in 1952, and still going strong, this most central Helsinki hotel lies atop the Sokos department store. Balconies overlook the main rail terminal and its bustling square. The interior design remains a period piece of what Finland looked like in the 1950s, although maintenance is still good here. The buffet breakfast is still served on the 10th floor rooftop terrace, where you might collide with a darting seagull. The restored guest rooms are midsize to spacious, with a minimalist decor and well-maintained bathrooms with tub or shower. There is no charge for a child under 5 years old sharing a room with parents using existing bedding. Many residents of Helsinki visit this hotel for its restaurants, known for their regional and international cuisine. We recently were introduced to several members of the Finnish Parliament dining here.

Asema-Aukio 2, FIN-00100 Helsinki. ℂ 09/433-70. Fax 09/433-771-00. www.allfinlandhotels.com/finland,helsinki,sokosvaakuna.html. 266 units. Sun–Thurs 209€ double; Fri–Sat 110€ double. Extra bed 27€. Rates include buffet breakfast. AE, DC, MC, V. Tram: All trams to rail station. **Amenities:** 3 restaurants; bar; business center; room service; babysitting; laundry/dry cleaning. *In room:* TV, hair dryer, minibar.

Sokos Torni Hotel ℱ   The Torni was the first "skyscraper" built in Helsinki (1931) and many irate locals demanded that it be torn down. Nevertheless, it prospered and has become the number-one choice for visiting celebrities. During the Winter War the hotel had to use paper sheets, and during the postwar era, it became the headquarters of the Soviet Control Commission. Once a meeting place of diplomats and spies during World War II, the refurbished hotel has an entrance lobby and paneled dining room that retain their old look. The recently renovated rooms are comfortably contemporary, with big windows and carpeting. The finest units are those in the tower, but all the rooms are average in size, with double-glazed windows; bathrooms are fully tiled shower-tub combinations.

Yrjönkatu 26, FIN-00100 Helsinki. ℂ **09/13-11-31.** Fax 09/433-671-00. www.sokos.hotel.fi. 160 units. Sun–Thurs 205€ double; Fri–Sat 112€ double. All week long 255€–337€ suite. Rates include breakfast. AE, DC, MC, V. Parking 16€. Tram: 3, 4, or 8. **Amenities:** Restaurant; 2 bars; sauna; room service; laundry/dry cleaning. *In room:* TV, minibar, hair dryer.

MODERATE

Cumulus Seurahuone ℱ *Finds*   The origins of this hotel began in 1833, when it opened in cramped and not particularly grand premises that it quickly outgrew. In 1913, it moved into a five-story Art Nouveau town house that was custom-built to house it across the street from Helsinki's railway station. Since then, it has been expanded and enlarged as part of a series of comprehensive upgrades, one of which included a new wing. Despite frequent improvements, the most recent in 1994, it has retained a battered sense of pride in once having been known as the *grande dame* of Helsinki hotels. About half the rooms are outfitted in a warm, earth-toned contemporary style; the other half are more consciously old-fashioned, sometimes with their original turn-of-the-20th-century architectural details and brass headboards. Rooms are moderate in size, mostly with twin beds, along with combination bathrooms (both showers and bathtubs). The public rooms are often crowded, thanks to this hotel's role as host of the meetings of many public organizations, and because of its position in the commercial heart of town.

Kaivokatu 12. FIN-00100. Helsinki. ℂ **09/691-41.** Fax 09/691-40-10. 118 units. Sun–Thurs 199€ double; Fri–Sat 140€ double. Rates include breakfast. AE, DC, MC, V. Parking 20€ per night. Tram: 3B, 3T, or 4. **Amenities:** Restaurant; bar; sauna; room service; laundry/dry cleaning. *In room:* A/C, TV, minibar, hair dryer, safe.

Lord Hotel ℱ   This hotel consists of two interconnected buildings. The older and more interesting was built in 1903 as a student center and dormitory for the local university. Guest rooms are in the annex, an angular but comfortable building erected around 1990. Many aspects of the older building evoke a mock-medieval fortress, thanks to heavy ceiling beams, crenellations, and Art Nouveau touches. The staff is polite and hardworking, maintaining stylish rooms that boast hardwood floors, pastel-colored upholsteries, lots of storage space, and either queen-size or twin beds. All have blackout curtains, generous work-space, and easy chairs. Bathrooms are small but tiled, mostly without tubs, but all have showers. Eighteen have whirlpool tubs, and are the most desirable.

Lonnrotinkatu 29. FIN-00180 Helsinki. ℂ **09/61-58-15.** Fax 09/680-13-15. www.lordhotel.fi. 48 units. Sun–Thurs 164€ double; Fri–Sat 90€ double. All week long 260€ suite. Rates include breakfast. AE, DC, MC,

V. Parking 16€ per night. Tram: 3B or 3T. **Amenities:** 2 restaurants; 2 bars; 2 saunas; room service; babysitting; laundry/dry cleaning. *In room:* A/C, TV, minibar, hair dryer.

Martta Hotelli *(Finds)*   Less than 1km (½ mile) north of the main train station, in a quiet residential area, this cozy little hotel is owned by a women's organization (formerly a radical feminist group that supported Finland's educational advancement and was opposed by the tsarist government). Since the group has now achieved all its goals, it runs a home economics educational program. The hotel was built in the late 1950s on land bequeathed by a wealthy donor, and it was most recently renovated in 1995. It's strictly functional but comfortable. Both men and women are accepted. The small guest rooms have a no-nonsense Finnish design, but the bathrooms are adequate and contain shower-tub combinations. The restaurant on the upper floor serves breakfast and lunch. There is a free covered parking area.

Uudenmaankatu 24, FIN-00120 Helsinki. © **09/618-74-00.** Fax 09/618-74-01. www.marttahotelli.fi. 44 units. Mid-June to mid-Aug and Fri–Sat year-round 80€ double; rest of year 132€ double. Year-round 150€ suite. Rates include breakfast. AE, DC, MC, V. Closed Christmas. Free parking. Tram: 3T. **Amenities:** Restaurant; lounge; sauna; room service; laundry/dry cleaning. *In room:* TV, hair dryer, safe.

INEXPENSIVE

Hotel Arthur *(Value)*   A large and well-maintained establishment, the Arthur is owned and operated by the YMCA. It was built around the beginning of the 20th century and a newer wing was added in 1950. The neighborhood is quiet, even though it's only a 4-minute walk from the main train station. The rooms are decorated in a functional, modern style, offering cleanliness and comfort instead of soul and character. Thirty of the rooms have a minibar. Both bedrooms and bathrooms (which have shower-tub combinations) are a bit cramped but well maintained—stay here for reasons of economy. An inexpensive restaurant on the premises serves a lunch buffet.

Vuorikatu 19, FIN-00100 Helsinki. © **09/17-34-41.** Fax 09/62-68-80. www.hotelarthur.fi. 143 units. June 15–Aug 18 and some weekends (Fri–Sun) in winter 88€ double; rest of year 106€ double. Year-round 148€–166€ suite. Rates include breakfast. Additional bed 10€. AE, DC, MC, V. Parking 11€. Tram: 1, 2, 3, 6, or 7. **Amenities:** Restaurant; bar; sauna; room service; laundry/dry cleaning. *In room:* A/C, TV, minibar (in some), hair dryer, safe.

Hotel Finn   This is a clean and functional government-rated one-star hotel, built shortly after World War II and partially renovated in 1996. It occupies the top two floors (5th and 6th) of a centrally located office building. It prides itself on being the cheapest hotel in Helsinki, and accommodates a scattering of summer tourists, dockworkers from northern and western Finland, and a handful of businesspeople from the Baltics. Rooms are small and just slightly better than the average college dorm lodgings, but the price is right. Units with private bathrooms have neatly kept shower units.

Kalevankatu 3B, FIN-00100 Helsinki. © **09/684-43-60.** Fax 09/684-436-10. www.hotellifinn.fi. 37 units, 18 with bathroom. 58€ double without bathroom; 70€ double with bathroom. AE, DC, MC, V. Free parking overnight; 2€ per hour 8am–5pm. Tram: 3, 4, 7, or 10. **Amenities:** Lounge. *In room:* TV.

NORTH OF CENTER

Radisson SAS Hesperia Hotel Helsinki *(ℛℛ)*   Partially constructed of Carrara marble, and set behind a landscaped garden beside one of the city's most prominent boulevards, this establishment is one of the leading hotels of Finland. Built in 1972 and renovated 20 years later, it's favored by business travelers who appreciate its uncluttered contemporary design. The guest rooms are comfortably furnished with conservatively upscale furniture and are well maintained.

Textured wallpaper and fine carpeting add to the allure of the place, although many of the rooms are a bit small. Bathrooms, either in tile or marble, are first rate, and have shower-tub combinations. Two floors are nonsmoking.

Mannerheimintie 50, FIN-00260 Helsinki. © **800/333-3333** in the U.S., or 09/431-01. Fax 09/431-09-95. www.radissonsas.com. 383 units. Summer and Fri–Sun year-round 185€ double; rest of year 244€ double. Year-round 380€–720€ suite. Rates include breakfast. AE, DC, MC, V. Parking 15€. Tram: 3B or 3T. **Amenities:** Restaurant; bar; nightclub; pool; fitness center; sauna; room service; babysitting; laundry/dry cleaning. *In room:* A/C, TV, minibar, hair dryer, safe.

Scandic Hotel Continental 🐾🐾🐾 The Scandic Hotel is one of our preferred modern hotels here. Set at the edge of the water behind a bay-windowed facade of beige and brown brick, it has the most dramatic atrium in the capital, festooned with plants and featuring glass elevators rising to the top of the building. An octagonal shape is repeated throughout the hotel's design. The rooms were conceived by some of Finland's best talent and decorated with local designs, including weaving and Finnish parquet floors. Marble from Lapland was used extensively. Half the well-furnished guest rooms provide views of the harbor. Some rooms are equipped for people with disabilities and others are reserved for nonsmokers. The good-sized units have medium-sized bathrooms, robes, toiletries, and shower-tub combinations.

John Stenbergin Ranta 4, FIN-00530 Helsinki. © **800/327-0200** in the U.S., or 09/393-51. Fax 09/393-532-55. www.interconti.com. 200 units. June 17–Sept 2 140€ double; rest of year (winter) 225€ double. Year-round 550€–1,130€ suite. Rates include breakfast. AE, DC, MC, V. Parking 16€. Tram: 3T, 6, or 7. **Amenities:** 2 restaurants; bar; pool; sauna; room service; babysitting; laundry/dry cleaning. *In room:* A/C, TV, minibar, hair dryer, safe.

WEST OF THE CENTER

Scandic Hotel Kalastajatorppa 🐾🐾 Translated from the Finnish, the tongue-twisting name of this hotel means "cottage of the fisherman." It's certainly no cottage, but it is close to the water, and just 5km (3 miles) northwest of the city center. Located on a ridge of land between two arms of the sea, this pair of marble- and granite-faced buildings was designed to blend in as closely as possible with the surrounding landscape of birch and pines. The core of the hotel dates from 1937, and the newer sections contain some of the most modern convention facilities in Finland. The guest rooms are in either the main building or a seashore annex that provides panoramic views of the water. The medium-sized rooms were renovated and upgraded after the hotel's acquisition by the Scandic chain in 1998. Outfitted with wood paneling and hardwood floors, units are tasteful, understated, and comfortable, with adequate bathrooms with shower-tub combinations. On the premises is the state guesthouse where Pres. Ronald Reagan rested en route to a summit meeting in Moscow. President George Bush and former German prime minister Helmut Kohl have also stayed here. In March 1997, Pres. Bill Clinton conducted a well-publicized meeting here with Russian Pres. Boris Yeltsin.

Kalastajatorpantie 1, FIN-00330 Helsinki. © **09/458-11.** Fax 09/458-16-68. www.scandic-hotels.com. 235 units. 187€–210€ double; 242€–605€ suite. Rates include breakfast. AE, DC, MC, V. Free parking outside, 12€ inside. Tram: 4. **Amenities:** 2 restaurants; bar; nightclub; pool; sauna; room service; babysitting; laundry/dry cleaning. *In room:* A/C, TV, minibar, hair dryer.

ESPOO

Radisson SAS Hotel Espoo 🐾 About 10km (6 miles) west of the center of Helsinki, this four-story hotel offers a soothing, somewhat isolated setting at the edge of the water surrounded by pine forests. The area is the "Silicon Valley" of

Finland, with the Helsinki University of Technology, research institutes, and technological enterprises nearby. With views over the water, guest rooms are moderate in size, with attractive built-in furniture, double-glazed windows, and adequate and well-lit work space. Most of the bathrooms lack tubs (there are shower stalls instead), but have spotless maintenance. Some accommodations are suitable for those who have allergies, and others are nonsmoking.

Otaranta 2, FIN-02150 Espoo. ⓒ 09/435-80. Fax 09/46-66-93. www.radissonsas.com. 208 units. 170€–212€ double; from 215€ suite. Rates include breakfast and morning sauna. AE, DC, MC, V. Free parking. Bus: 102 (from Platform 51 at the Helsinki Bus Station). **Amenities:** Restaurant; bar; pool; sauna; room service; babysitting; laundry/dry cleaning. *In room:* TV, minibar, hair dryer.

4 Where to Dine

Many restaurants bring variety to their menus with typically Finnish dishes, particularly those offering a Scandinavian smörgåsbord. There are restaurants to suit every purse and taste in Helsinki, as well as an increasing number of ethnic restaurants.

IN THE CITY CENTER
VERY EXPENSIVE

Chez Dominique 🅐🅐🅐 FRENCH/SCANDINAVIAN One of only two Michelin-starred restaurants in Finland, this gourmet citadel wins our nomination as Helsinki restaurant of the year. Near Esplanadi Park, this is the gourmet restaurant with the town's most visually appealing and tasty dishes. The restaurant is the culinary showcase for Hans Välimäki, one of Scandinavia's most outstanding chefs. From first-class, market-fresh ingredients, to the elegant decor, Chez Dominique represents dining at its finest in Helsinki. The only restaurant that rivals (but does not top it) is the also-recommended G. W. Sundmans (see below).

The most discerning food and wine lovers in Finland flock to this modern, intimate, 36-seat restaurant founded by Frenchman Dominique Rubaud. He has since moved back to France, but the restaurant still honors his name.

Each appetizer is inspired, be it the terrine of foie gras with a duck confit and a side of shallot ice cream (a first for many diners), or slightly smoked tuna with a "Granny Smith" gratin granite. But the real successes are the main dishes, especially the roasted turbot with a potato risotto with garlic sauce, and the lamb medallions with fried chanterelles. The repertoire continues to glow with such wonders as a lobster tortellini with vanilla and anise sauce.

Ludviginkatu 3. ⓒ 09/612-73-93. Reservations required. Main courses 29€–39€; fixed-price menus 49€–89€. AE, DC, MC, V. Tues–Fri 11:30am–2pm; Tues–Sat 6–11pm. Tram: 10.

G. W. Sundmans 🅐🅐🅐 SCANDINAVIAN/FRENCH The only other Michelin-starred restaurant in Finland, this is a bastion of gourmet cuisine. The award from a publication that tends to view restaurants outside of France with a certain skepticism is all the more remarkable in that Helsinki over the decades has existed virtually "starless" in the Michelin galaxy. The elegant setting is a restored Empire-styled mansion on the waterfront, next to the Market Square, with windows opening onto panoramic vistas. The mansion was the former residence of Capt. G. W. Sundman, who hired the famous Finnish architect, C. I. Engel, to build it for him; Engel was the architect for Tsar Alexander I. Tiled stoves and paintings on the ceiling evoke the Finland of the 19th century. The main restaurant, which is divided into five rooms, lies on the second floor. At street level is the cozy Sundman Krog. Chef Jarmo Vähä-Savo and his staff prepare light, contemporary fare, using the best raw materials available in Helsinki. There's also a celebratory feeling to the cuisine, as you launch your repast with such delightful appetizers as Jerusalem artichoke crème with a white fish roe, or foie gras with a fig compote. Cooking times are unerringly accurate, as reflected by the poached veal or the fried pike-perch with sautéed boletus mushrooms and a white tomato sauce. One of the fixed-price offerings, the Menu Skandinavia, recently featured such showcase dishes as salted salmon with scallops and langoustines, a light escargot soup, grilled sirloin of elk with a rowanberry sabayon sauce, and apple pie with cardamom ice cream.

Eteläranta 16. ℂ **09/622-64-10.** Reservations required. Main courses 33€–39€; fixed-price menus 45€–79€. AE, DC, MC, V. Mon–Fri 11am–2:30pm; Sat 6pm–midnight. Tram: 1, 2, 3T, or 4.

Palace Gourmet ★★ FINNISH/FRENCH   With a panoramic view of the harbor from the 10th floor of the Palace Hotel, this is one of the most acclaimed restaurants in Helsinki, and has been offering exquisite cuisine combined with excellent service and a unique ambience since 1952. The design hasn't been changed since it was created by Viljo Rewell a half-century ago. (Rewell was Finland's second most famous architect at that time, competing with Aalto.) It has wood paneling, large windows, and—to a trained eye—an excellent postwar Finnish design; a live pianist is featured. Its wine cellar is one of the best in the country, having won many awards. Fixed-price menus at lunch supplant a la carte meals. You might begin with poached asparagus with smoked ham or celery-and-Parmesan soup. Fish dishes include grilled rolls of perch filet with parsley sauce and warm smoked salmon with creamed morels. Other specialties include filet and tongue of reindeer with rowanberry mousse, and duck flavored with honey and a raspberry-vinegar sauce.

In the Palace Hotel, Eteläranta 10. ℂ 09/13-45-61. Reservations required. 3-course fixed-price menu 53€; 4-course fixed-price menu 68€. AE, DC, MC, V. July Mon–Fri 6pm–1am; Aug–June Mon–Fri 11am–2:30am. Tram: 3B. Bus: 16.

Restaurant Kämp ★★★ CONTINENTAL/INTERNATIONAL   One of Helsinki's newest and most opulent restaurants occupies a Belle Epoque dining room whose soaring columns and glittering accessories evoke the grandest moments of the late 19th century. With room for only 56 diners at a time, it features a menu that changes every month or so, emphasizing a mix of upscale Finnish dishes and the best aspects of pan-European, postmodern cuisine. Stellar examples include hot blinis with seasonal fish roe and garnish; a consommé of forest mushrooms with a profiterole of veal kidneys; and an old-fashioned version of traditional Finnish *vorschmack* (savory hash) with pickled vegetables and sour cream. Baked salmon a la Kämp manages to stuff a salmon with mashed potatoes and onions and accompany it with a roe-enhanced sour cream sauce. A delectable marinated rack of lamb with herb-dried tomatoes and spiced polenta is appropriate for cold days along the Baltic. Dessert might be an old-fashioned *tarte tatin* with Calvados-flavored ice cream and vanilla sauce.

Note that within the same hotel, adjacent to the lobby, is a well-managed brasserie, C.K.'s, whose prices are about 40% less than those at this gastronomic citadel. C.K.'s specializes in fresh meats, fish, and vegetarian dishes, serving them every day of the week from 7am to 11pm.

In the Hotel Kämp, Pohjoisesplanadi 29. ℂ 09/57-61-11. Reservations recommended. Main courses 13€–63€; fixed-price lunch 35€–45€; fixed-price dinner 83€. AE, DC, MC, V. Tues–Sat 7–10:30pm. Tram: 1 or 7.

Helsinki Dining

Alexander Nevski **18**
Bellevue **25**
Chez Dominique **11**
Chica's **1**
G.W. Sundmans **14**
Havis Amanda **23**
Kartano Ravintola **8**
Kellarikrouvi **15**
König **21**
Kosmos Restaurant **9**
Kynsilaukka
  Restaurant Garlic **12**
Manala **16**
Mother's **5**
Olivo **2**
Palace Gormet **3**
Ravintola Perho **4**
Ravintola Rivoli **6**
Ravintola Sipuli **24**
Restaurant Kämp **22**
Restaurant Kappeli **19**
Restaurant Savoy **17**
Restaurant Torni **7**
Restaurant Walhalla **13**
Strindberg Café **20**
Teatteri Ravintola **10**
Wellamo **26**

- - - - Ferry
········· Railway

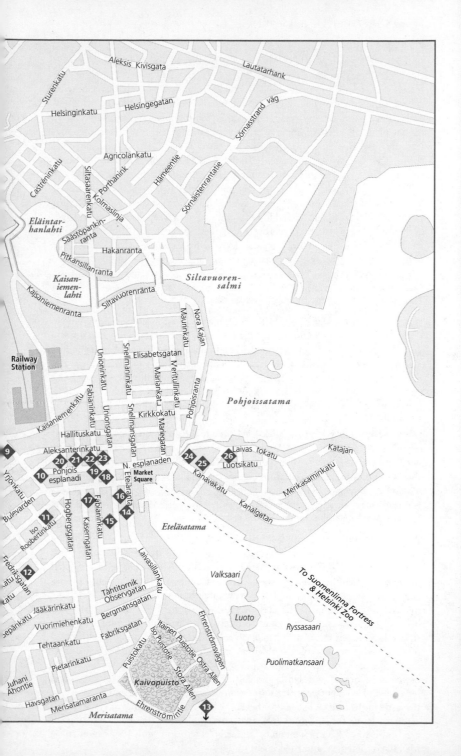

Aleksis Kivisgata
Lautatarhank
Sturenkatu
Helsinginkatu
Helsingegatan
Sörnasstrand väg
Agricolankatu
Castreninkatu
Siltasaarenkatu
Porthanink
Kolmaslinja
Hämeentie
Sörnäistenrantatie
Eläintar-
hanlahti
Säästöpankin-
ranta
Hakanranta
Pitkansillanranta
Kaisan-
iemen-
lahti
Kaisaniemenranta
Siltavuorenränta
Siltavuoren-
salmi
Maunnkatu
Nora Kajan
Snellmaninkatu
Elisabetsgatan
Unioninkatu
Merltullinkatu
Mariankatu
Railway
Station
Fabianinkatu
Unionsgatan
Snellmansgatan
Kirkkokatu
Kaisaniemenkatu
Pohjoisranta
Pohjoissatama
Hallituskatu
Mariegatan
Aleksanterinkatu
Laivas tokatu
Katajan
9
20 **21** **22** **23**
24 **25** **26**
Luotsikatu
Yrjönkatu
Pohjois
esplanadi
19 **18**
N. esplanaden
Market
Square
Kanavakatu
Merikasaminkatu
10
Eteläranta
Kanalgatan
Bulevarden
17
Fabianinkatu
16
11
Höbergsgatan
Kaserngatan
15
14
Iso
Roobertinkatu
Eteläsatama
Fredriksgatan
12
Laivasillankatu
katu
Jääkärinkatu
Tähtitornik
Observgatan
Bergmansgatan
Valksaari
To Suomenlinna Fortress
& Helsinki Zoo
epänkatu
Vuorimiehenkatu
Fabriksgatan
Luoto
Ryssasaari
Tehtaankatu
Puistokatu
Itainen Puistotie Ostra Allén
Iso Puistotie Stora Allén
Pietarinkatu
Puolimatkansaari
Juhani
Ahontie
Ehrenströmsvägen
Kaivopuisto
Havsgatan
Merisatamaranta
13
Ehrenströmintie
Merisatama

EXPENSIVE

Alexander Nevski ✿ RUSSIAN   At the southern corner of Market Square, this is the finest Russian restaurant in Finland. Set in a 200-year-old building, the restaurant is named for a 12th-century Russian military hero. It has large beveled mirror panels in pastel frames, Lapland marble floors, stained-glass windows emblazoned with Romanov double-headed eagles, and *faux-marbre* columns. The cuisine blends the best of imperial tsarist cooking with the best Russian regional (peasant) dishes. While you dine, you're treated to live Russian musicians performing at the piano or perhaps the violin, and Gypsy songs fill the air. Begin with borscht, one of several kinds of blinis, Russian-style crayfish soup with caviar and sour cream, or a julienne of forest mushrooms marinated in sour cream. There's also smoked salmon with parsley-studded risotto, roasted pike-perch with champagne sauce, rabbit braised in a clay pot with cream sauce and sour cabbage, and fried wild duck with cranberries and fennel. Sturgeon and salmon prepared in the traditional Russian way, grilled filet of lamb Caucasian-style, or breast of willow grouse in a goose-liver sauce are equally and deservedly popular.

Pohjoisesplanadi 17. © **09/686-95-60.** Reservations required. Main courses 25€–66€; 3-course fixed-price lunch 21€–26€; menu Romanov 55€. AE, DC, MC, V. July daily 6pm–midnight; Aug–June Mon–Fri 11am–midnight, Sat noon–midnight, Sun 6pm–midnight. Tram: 1, 2, 3T, or 4.

Havis Amanda ✿✿ FINNISH/SEAFOOD   Named after the heroic female statue (the *Havis Amanda*) that stands a few steps from its entrance, this upscale tavern is the finest seafood restaurant in Helsinki. Located in a cellar, its booths and banquettes are tucked away between pillars, columns, and walls for maximum dining privacy. Established in 1973, the restaurant prides itself on serving seafood primarily from Finland (don't expect North Atlantic lobster, Alaskan crabmeat, or tropical grouper). Depending on the season, menu choices might include a starter-sized platter of Finnish fish roe, Baltic crayfish, ceviche of whitefish and king crab, whitefish "glow-fried" beside the gentle coals of a log fire and served with Lapp cheese and Madeira sauce, poached filet of perch with white wine and crayfish sauce, grilled perch with chanterelle sauce, or charcoal-grilled slices of salmon with morel-flavored cream sauce. The service is impeccable.

Unioninkatu 23. © **09/66-68-82.** Reservations required. Main courses 16€–35€; 2-course fixed-price lunch 18€–28€; 4-course fixed-price dinner 58€. AE, DC, MC, V. May 15–Sept 15 daily noon–midnight; Sept 16–May 14 Mon–Sat noon–midnight. Tram: 1, 2, 3T, or 4. Bus: 16.

Restaurant Savoy ✿✿ FINNISH/INTERNATIONAL   In an office building near the harbor, this restaurant's decor exemplifies the quintessence of Finnish modernism. In 1937 Finland's greatest architect, Alvar Aalto, designed every detail of the place, even the lighting fixtures. The restaurant, a national monument, has largely adhered to the original design. Few other restaurants in Finland celebrate the memory and tastes of the nation's greatest national hero, Marshal Mannerheim, as devotedly as this one does. It proudly serves his favorite drink—a *Marskin Ryyppy* (a schnapps made with vodka, aquavit, dry vermouth, and dry gin, stirred together and served icy cold)—which he consumed in large quantities here during the ravages of World War II. And it justifiably declares its *vorschmack* (a stew concocted from minced beef, lamb, and Baltic herring that's simmered for 2 days and served with baked potatoes and sour cream) as the best in town, and authentic to the tastes of the general himself. Other specialties include a terrine of venison with cranberry sauce, fish-and-seafood soup flavored with saffron, poached filet of pike-perch with crayfish and caviar sauce, sautéed filet of turbot with a red-onion sauce, fried filet of reindeer, and fried breast of duck.

Eteläesplanadi. ℂ **09/684-402-10**. Reservations required. Main courses 30€–37€; 3-course fixed-price menu 57€. AE, DC, DISC, MC, V. June–Aug Mon–Fri 11am–10:30pm; Sept–May Mon–Fri 11am–3pm and 6–10:30pm. Tram: 3B.

MODERATE

Bellevue RUSSIAN   In the heart of Helsinki, next to the Uspenski Orthodox cathedral, the Bellevue has been an enduring favorite since 1917 because of its good cooking and moderate prices. Actually, the restaurant has operated since 1913, but in a different location. You can dine in a long, corridor-like main room or in one of the smaller, cozier side rooms. Herring, still served Russian style, is always a good appetizer, or perhaps blinis and caviar. The chicken Kiev is a recommended main dish, as is the tantalizing roasted snow grouse, as well as cabbage rolls with wild mushrooms served in a stoneware crock. For dessert, a flaming baba cake is carried through the main dining room; one longtime patron likened its presentation to "a wake for Tsar Nicholas II." Russian wine is served.

Rahapajankatu 3. ℂ **09/17-95-60**. Reservations required. Main courses 16€–33€; fixed-price lunch 22€. AE, DC, MC, V. Mon–Fri 11am–midnight; Sat–Sun 5pm–midnight. Tram: 4.

Kartano Ravintola 𝕂 *Finds* FINNISH   This restaurant takes the preparation of its Finnish menu so seriously that some of its fans consider it almost a symbol of national pride. You'll dine within one of two birch-paneled dining rooms that are accessorized with tones of red and blue, and feast on menu items whose ingredients mostly derive from nearby lakes and forests. The cookery doesn't rate rave reviews, but it is substantial and satisfying. Examples include roasted filet of reindeer with forest mushrooms and red-wine sauce, grilled pike-perch with garlic-flavored mayonnaise and horseradish-enhanced potatoes, filet of veal with Finnish mushrooms and red-wine sauce, carpaccio of venison, and a "cappuccino" of Finnish chanterelles. Thanks to its location in the heart of Helsinki's commercial center, the place bustles at lunchtime, but is somewhat calmer and more sedate at dinner.

Simonkatu 6. ℂ **09/586-07-10**. Reservations recommended. Main courses 12€–25€. AE, DC, MC, V. Mon–Fri 11am–midnight; Sat 1pm–midnight; Sun 4–10pm. Tram: 4, 7, or 10.

Kellarikrouvi FINNISH/INTERNATIONAL   This restaurant, built in 1901, was originally a storage cellar for potatoes and firewood for the apartment house above it. Fuel was winched upstairs to send off the brutal winter cold. Since 1965 it has been a cozy restaurant, the first in Finland to serve beer from a keg. Enjoy it at the street-level bar (where you can also dine if you like) before descending a steep staircase to the vaulted labyrinth of the cellar. Here, depending on which room within the vast place you opt for, the ambience can be noisy and animated—especially on weekends—or relatively subdued. Your dinner might begin with a terrine of perch followed by pork cutlets with a potato-and-cheese gratin, grilled kidneys in a mustard-cream sauce, reindeer steak with game sauce and roasted potatoes, or fried cubed salmon with root vegetables and whiskey sauce. Dessert might consist of a Bavarian-style cream puff stuffed with cloudberries. The cuisine is inspired and adroit, combining local Finnish culinary techniques with innovative touches from the international schools of cooking.

Pohjoinen Makasiinikatu 6. ℂ **09/686-07-30**. Reservations recommended for dinner. Main courses 12€–26€; fixed-price lunch (11am–2pm) 12€–30€. AE, DC, MC, V. Mon–Fri 11am–midnight; Sat 4pm–midnight; Sun (upstairs section only) 2pm–midnight. Tram: 3B.

König 𝕂 SCANDINAVIAN   Established in 1892, this restaurant is Helsinki's most traditional, situated in the cellar of what was once one of Finland's four largest banks. The great architect Eliel Saarinen redesigned the restaurant along the lines of the internationally modern style that would later sweep the world. In 1996 the restaurant was renovated, taking care to preserve Saarinen's aesthetic vision. Here, in what was at the time a private dining room, Marshal Mannerheim and his generals gathered for food and strategy talks during the darkest days of World War II. The restaurant has hosted all of Finland's presidents and many of its greatest artists and composers, including Jean Sibelius. Dishes might include pike-perch Waleska, smoked whitefish a la König, filet of reindeer with Madeira sauce, filet steak with mushrooms and red-wine sauce, *filet de boeuf a la patronne,* and a seasonal variety of fish. The fare has varied little over the years, and if the greats of yesterday were to miraculously return, they wouldn't be surprised by the offerings on the menu. "If we've always done it right," a waiter confided, "why change it?"

Mikonkatu 4. ℂ **09/684-407-13.** Reservations required. Main courses 13€–22€. AE, DC, MC, V. Mon–Sat noon–midnight. Tram: 3B or 3T.

Kosmos Restaurant 𝒜 FINNISH   Near the center of Helsinki's main street, Mannerheimintie, this restaurant is known throughout Finland as a gathering place for artists, writers, and television personalities. The decor is 1930s and simple, and the menu specialties include grilled whitefish, smoked eel, fried Baltic herring, mutton chops with a creamy herb sauce, and chicken in cherry sauce. Light meals, such as open tartar sandwiches, *vorschmack* with duchesse potatoes, and borscht, are also available. (*Vorschmack,* made with chopped mutton, herring, and anchovies, is served with salted cucumbers and beets.) If you want traditional Finnish cuisine without a lot of innovative Continental touches, this is your place. We liked the comments of one habitué: "I come here at least once or twice a week. The kitchen staff never causes me grief." In the summertime, you can order "deep-fried" strawberries for dessert; pears drenched with a chocolate-cream sauce are also delicious. The special lunch is served until 3pm.

Kalevankatu 3. ℂ **09/64-72-55.** Reservations recommended. Main courses 13€–22€; fixed-price lunch 20€. AE, DC, MC, V. Mon–Fri 11:30am–midnight; Sat 4pm–midnight. Tram: 3B, 3T, or 4. Bus: 17 or 18.

Ravintola Rivoli FRENCH/FINNISH   The dining room is an Art Nouveau fantasy set in a labyrinthine dining room with upholstered banquettes. One of its subdivisions is named "Fish Rivoli," and from its separate menu you can order some of the finest seafood dishes in the city. In both dining rooms, you can enjoy such fare as filet of perch with herb butter, and grilled salmon with mustard sauce. At lunchtime, special *humanskost* cookery is offered, a reference to "grandmother's style," featuring such old-fashioned, good-tasting dishes as onion soup and grilled rainbow trout. The management also operates an adjoining pizzeria.

Albertinkatu 38. ℂ **09/64-34-55.** Reservations recommended. Main courses 15€–38€. AE, DC, MC, V. Mon–Fri 11am–midnight; Sat 5pm–midnight. Closed Sat June–July and bank holidays. Tram: 6. Bus: 14.

Ravintola Sipuli 𝒜𝒜 FINNISH/CONTINENTAL   Set within five rooms of what was originally built in the 19th century as a warehouse, this restaurant takes its name from the gilded onion-shaped domes of the Russian Orthodox Uspenski Cathedral, which rises majestically a short distance away (*Sipuli* translates as "onion"). While renovating the premises for its new role as a restaurant, a team of architects thoughtfully added a skylight that allows views of the cathedral. This, coupled with red brick walls, intricate paneling, and thick beams, creates coziness and charm. Upon every visit we fall under the bewitching spell of the chef, who is an expert at creating robust flavors. He always uses the finest of ingredients from stream and field, and Finnish products when available. Cooked with precision and a certain enthusiasm are such dishes as snails flavored with sherry and served with a Gorgonzola sauce. This is surprisingly good, but filled with flavors not for the faint-hearted. He can really do something special with such main courses as smoked filet of pike-perch served with a salmon mousse. From Lapland he imports reindeer meat in season that has been carefully butchered and shaped as noisettes; it comes with a richly flavored game sauce.

Kanavaranta 3. © **09/17-99-00.** Reservations recommended. Main courses 23€–35€. AE, DC, MC, V. Mon–Fri noon–2pm and 6–11pm. Tram: 2 or 4.

Restaurant Torni FINNISH   The Sokos Torni Hotel (see "Where to Stay," earlier in this chapter) throws all its culinary energies into this showcase of Finnish cuisine. In a pastel-colored Art Nouveau dining room on the hotel's street level, a crew of formally dressed waiters serves specialties from the forests and streams of Finland. Examples include baked snow grouse with game sauce, breast of wild duck with port wine and ginger sauce, and "glow-fried" (that is, gently heated) trout served with honey-flavored fennel sauce. The refined cuisine is prepared with admirable products from all over the country. Here you are served a true "taste of Finland."

In the Sokos Torni Hotel, Kalevankatu 5. © **0433/663-20.** Reservations recommended. Main courses 19€–26€; 4-course fixed-price menu 59€. AE, DC, MC, V. Mon–Fri 11:30am–midnight; Sat 5pm–1am. Tram: 3, 4, or 10.

Teatteri Ravintola INTERNATIONAL   The management of this very popular, sprawling complex of bars, nightclubs, and restaurants compares it to "a Caribbean cruise ship, in that we've got almost everything, and we're almost never closed." There's a deli and takeout service near the entrance (open daily from 9am) and a well-managed restaurant whose menu includes the cuisines of Cuba, Asia, India, and Italy, with frequent changes and reinventions. Also on the premises are two bars. The Teatteri Bar attracts deal-making business folk relaxing after work. The more animated of the two, the Clock Bar, sports a blazing fireplace and plays recorded rhythm and blues. One flight above street level, there's a nightclub, Clubbi Teatteri, where a crowd ages 35 to 50 dances the night away. It's open nightly from 10:30pm. Entrance is usually free, except on Friday and Saturday nights, when there's a cover charge of 7.50€.

In the Svenska Teather, Pohjoisesplandi 2. © **09/681-11-36.** Main courses 10€–20€; 3-course fixed-price menus 35€–40€. AE, DC, MC, V. Food service Mon–Thurs 11am–11pm; Fri–Sat 11am–midnight; Sun 1–10pm. Bar service Mon–Sat 11am–4am; Sun 2pm–1am. Tram: 1, 7.

Wellamo FINNISH/FRENCH/RUSSIAN   Established near Finland's foreign ministry, on a quiet residential island (Katajanokka Island) central to the rest of town, this is a charming, well-managed restaurant with a loyal clientele that sometimes travels from other neighborhoods of Helsinki to reach it. Paneled and outfitted in warmly textured shades of dark brown, it features flickering candles and a revolving series of for-sale paintings by local artists. Menu items include selections from Russia, Finland, and France, and are thus more exotic than those offered at many of Wellamo's competitors. Examples include lamb soup; snails a la Bourguignonne; goat-cheese salad; mussels Provençale with aioli and chips; whitefish a la Russe; *pelmens* (Siberian ravioli) stuffed with minced lamb, herbs, mushrooms, and sour cream; and a sauté of rabbit, elk, and mutton "in the style of the Finnish hunters." Sweetbreads with Gorgonzola sauce is another popular choice, as is Georgian-style chicken served with fried cheese, rice pilaf, and *smetana* (sour cream) sauce. During the evening hours, you're likely to hear the sounds of a live pianist.

Vyäkatu 9. ⓒ **09/66-31-39.** Reservations recommended. Main courses 12€–18€. AE, MC, V. Tues–Fri 11am–2pm and 5–11pm; Sat 5–11pm; Sun 1–8pm. Tram: 4.

INEXPENSIVE

Kynsilaukka Restaurant Garlic ⚜ *Finds* INTERNATIONAL   Its name translates from medieval Finnish as "garlic," and that's exactly what you'll get at this restaurant that prides itself on its use of more than 20 pounds of Spanish garlic every day. It's used in every imaginable foodstuff, a fact that's deeply appreciated by a clientele that tends to believe that garlic fights disease and might possibly even ward off vampires. You'll dine within a pair of cozy and consciously rustic dining rooms, perhaps preceding your meal with a garlic martini (chilled gin, shaken not stirred, and served with a clove of vermouth-marinated garlic), or a pint of garlic-flavored beer (the staff claims they add the garlic secretly). The cuisine is not for the fainthearted, but garlic aficionados flock here. Menu items are influenced by the cuisine of Russia more than anywhere else, as in the example of grilled gratin of vegetables with garlic and *smetana* (sour cream). Other examples include pike balls in garlic-flavored cream sauce, a fish stew modeled on a Provençale bouillabaisse, cream of garlic soup, chicken casseroles, filet steak with garlic and red-wine sauce, and brochettes of seafood. Desserts include cloudberry crepes with ice cream, which can be rendered more or less garlicky depending on the degree to which you add the omnipresent condiment: garlic marmalade.

Frederikkatu 22. ⓒ **09/65-19-39.** Reservations recommended. Main courses 10€–21€; fixed-price lunch 10€. AE, DC, MC, V. Mon–Fri 11am–11pm; Sat–Sun 1–11pm. Tram: 3B or 3T.

Manala FINNISH/INTERNATIONAL   In a residential neighborhood several blocks west of the Scandic Hotel Continental and the Finnair Bus Terminal, this restaurant prides itself on both its cuisine and the collection of 19th-century Finnish paintings that line its walls. There's a popular and interesting bar with an outdoor terrace, which you'll see as you enter. You can enjoy such specialties as fresh fish, sautéed reindeer, grilled chicken with garlic potatoes on a hot iron grill, and fried Baltic herring. There's also a wide range of pizzas. The chef is well known for his homemade Finnish bread, served with a homemade cheese paté. Virtually every night of the week the late-night bar attracts lots of actors and musicians, and on Friday and Sunday between 11pm and 4am, there's live "Finnish style" dance music, including the tango, a dance that's all the rage in Finland today.

Dagmarinkatu 2. ⓒ **09/58-07-07.** Reservations recommended. Main courses 8.50€–15€; pizzas 6.90€–9.40€; fixed-price menu 24€. AE, DC, MC, V. Mon–Fri 11am–4am; Sat–Sun 2pm–4am. Tram: 4, 7, or 10.

Mother's ⚜ INTERNATIONAL   Its owners and staff define this place as Helsinki's "Trend Bar of the Minute," and newspapers throughout town have praised (or vilified) the avant-garde design by Finland's "Bad Boy" architectural designer, Stefan Lindfors. It incorporates a restaurant with a long and action-packed bar, both of them with soaringly high ceilings and color schemes of orange and blue. At the top of a low flight of stairs, there's a black-and-white dance club (Club Cube) that's open only on Friday and Saturday, whose movable furniture helps encourage spontaneous conversation among the young, beautiful, and educated professionals who have made this artsy-looking hangout their darling. Although the cuisine at this place might be reconfigured during the lifetime of this edition into something more tapas-oriented and more posh, the venue as we experienced it included only an array of meal-sized salads, such as Caesar, goat cheese, and Cobb, and a long list of Thai and Chinese-inspired noodle dishes. These include versions studded with chicken, vegetables, beef, or shrimp; versions with or without curry; and versions with degrees of spiciness that include "mildly hot," "piquant," and "hot-hot-hot." The bar lists at least 50 different kinds of cocktails, but its smooth, well-trained bartenders are well versed in making many others that aren't necessarily listed on the menu. There's no cover charge for any of the components of this place.

2 Eerikinkatu. ℭ **09/612-39-90.** Reservations recommended for the restaurant, not for the nightclub. Main courses in restaurant 7.50€–9€. Cocktails in bar 5.50€–7.50€. Restaurant Mon–Fri 4–10pm; Sat 7–10pm. Bar Mon 4pm–midnight; Tues–Thurs 4pm–2am; Fri 4pm–4am; Sat 7pm–4am. Dance club Fri–Sat 11pm–4am. Tram: 3B or 10.

Restaurant Kappeli INTERNATIONAL   This famous restaurant and drinking complex is a Victorian Gothic fantasy, situated like an oversize gazebo in the middle of Esplanade Park, near the harbor. Originally built in 1837 as a rendezvous for artists and "high-society gentlemen" (Sibelius had a favorite table), it was closed for many years until its restoration in 1976. There are five different dining areas, one of them a summertime-only outdoor terrace. Long lines sometimes form here in the evening, and the place goes through wild mood swings throughout the day and night, everything from sedate to rowdy. Doormen and bouncers keep the crowd in order later in the evening. In the oldest section—the cafe—most patrons order sandwiches, pastries, or coffee. The middle section is the main restaurant, Runeberg, where white-linen tablecloths, lots of elbow room, and formal service are the hallmarks. Well-prepared main dishes, inexpensive by Finnish standards, include chateaubriand, pepper steak, entrecôte, fried salmon with red-wine and pepper sauce, and whitefish.

Eteläesplanadi 1. ℭ **09/687-24-40.** Reservations recommended. Main courses 14€–24€. AE, DC, MC, V. Daily 9am–1am. Closed Dec 24–25. Tram: 3B. Bus: 16.

Strindberg Café CONTINENTAL   Named after one of Sweden's greatest playwrights, a short walk from the Swedish Theater, this is a warm and convivial rendezvous point with a street-level cafe and an upstairs "Library Bar" whose shelves are lined with books. The heart and soul of the place, however, is the upstairs dining room, where a conservatively modern setting acts as a foil for dishes that include a savory version of Finnish *vorschmack* (hash), grilled Baltic herring in herb sauce, grilled filet of salmon with hollandaise, and a sumptuous pike-perch with dill sauce.

Pohjoisesplanadi 33. ℭ **09/681-20-30.** Main courses in upstairs restaurant 10€–22€; sandwiches and pastries in street-level cafe 4€–11€. AE, DC, MC, V. Mon–Sat 11am–1am. Tram: 1, 7, or 10.

NORTH OF CENTER
EXPENSIVE
Olivo 🏵🏵 MEDITERRANEAN   In 1998, the culinary experts at one of Helsinki's most sophisticated modern hotels threw out their longtime roster of prestigious but dull restaurants and focused all their attention, and their enormous resources, on this well-appointed charmer. Set on the hotel's lobby level, it specializes in cuisine from around the edges of the Mediterranean, and does so within a cutting-edge, sand-colored decor that includes lots of exposed wood and a cheerful emphasis on southern climes. You'll find some succulent salads and pastas (black tagliatelle with squid ink, tomatoes, garlic, and shellfish) inspired by the traditions of Italy. There's also *saltimbocca* (veal with ham). But

aficionados of the Mediterranean world usually opt for a medley of Moroccan, Middle Eastern, and North African dishes that, as a whole, contribute to one of the most exotic and sophisticated menus in Helsinki. Examples include *mezze,* a platter of Turkish delicacies that features stuffed grape leaves and hummus; lemon-marinated salmon with tabouleh salad; grilled jumbo prawns wrapped in bacon and served with shellfish and tomato sauce; Moroccan-style braised lamb served in a *tagine* (clay pot) with *harissa* (very spicy) sauce; and crispy Moorish duck breast with olives, dates, almonds, and couscous, served with a spinach salad. A vague hint of Finland appears in such dishes as warm carpaccio of reindeer with Parmesan cheese, but otherwise, the venue is based purely on olive oil and Mediterranean traditions.

In the Scandic Hotel Continental, Mannerheimintie 46. © **09/405-51**. Reservations recommended. Main courses 10€–19€. AE, DC, MC, V. Mon–Fri 11:30am–11:30pm; Sat noon–11:30pm. Tram: 4, 7, or 10.

INEXPENSIVE

Chica's TEX-MEX   This is the least expensive and most popular of the limited number of Mexican restaurants in Helsinki. We'll be frank: The food served here is not the equal of even a middling good Mexican place in the American Southwest, but it comes as a welcome respite when you've had too many herring balls in cream sauce. The decor evokes the colors of the Mexican desert, accented with fiesta shades of green, yellow, and blue, and there's lots of exposed wood and a bar with comfortable sofas, which is worth visiting for a margarita even if you don't plan to have dinner afterward. Menu choices include seven kinds of fajitas, enchiladas, stuffed chiles, and a barbecue platter that everyone seems to like. The place was founded by an entrepreneurial Finn after visiting New Mexico and Arizona, so it has a distinctive American touch. The beer of choice is Coors, something of a novelty here.

Mannerheimintie 68. © **09/49-35-91**. Reservations recommended for dinner. Main courses 10€–18€. AE, DC, MC, V. Mon–Tues 11am–11pm; Wed–Fri 11am–1am; Sat noon–1am; Sun 1–11pm. Tram: 3B or 3T.

Ravintola Perho FINNISH/CONTINENTAL   Owned and managed by the Helsinki Culinary School, this is the only restaurant of its kind in Finland. Completely staffed by students and trainees, it offers a comfortable modern setting and a cuisine that's professionally supervised (though not necessarily prepared) by the teaching staff. Diners can choose either large or small portions of virtually any dish, so it's possible to sample combinations not available elsewhere. Menu items include tuna salads; "Finnish pasta," served with salmon, cream, and herbs; and filet of reindeer with black currant sauce. Many diners find the youthful enthusiasm of the staff charming. However, the cuisine depends on the culinary lesson of the day. On any number of occasions, we've found it excellent and always a pleasant surprise.

Mechelininkatu 7. © **09/580-78-66**. Reservations not accepted. Main courses 9€–20€. AE, DC, MC, V. Sept–June Mon–Fri 11am–midnight, Sat–Sun noon–midnight; July–Aug Mon–Sat 11am–5pm. Tram: 8.

THE ISLANDS

Restaurant Walhalla *Finds* FINNISH   On the fortified island many historians view as the cradle of modern Finland, this restaurant provides a sunny, cheerful, and historic insight into Finnish cuisine and culture. Open only in summertime, it requires access by ferryboats, which depart from Helsinki's harbor adjacent to the *Havis Amanda* statue at intervals of every 30 and 60 minutes, depending on the time of day, daily from 9am to 11pm. The return trip to the center of Helsinki occurs at equivalent intervals daily between 9:30am and

Perfect Picnics

To buy all the foods you want for a picnic, head for the delicatessen on the street level of **Stockmann Department Store,** Aleksanterinkatu 52 (© **09/1211**). (See "Shopping," later in this chapter, for more information.) At this deli, display cases are filled with gourmet food worthy of the great capitals of Europe—albeit with an East-Nordic twist. You'll find several types of smoked or marinated carp, whitefish, perch, or salmon along with marinated terrines of reindeer, and perhaps cloudberry or lingonberry preserves (sold in small jars), which can be thickly spread on fresh-baked herb bread. You'll also find little bottles of wine and Arctic liqueurs to enliven your picnic. The deli is open Monday through Friday from 9am to 9pm and Saturday from 9am to 6pm. Tram: 3B, 3T, 4, 6, or 10.

With your picnic basket, you can head for the **national park** on the island of Seurasaari, the best spot in Helsinki for a family outing.

11:30pm. Round-trip fares are 5€ per person. Once you land on Kustaanmiekka Island, walk for about 5 minutes to a series of brick-and-granite vaults in the center of the Viapori fortress. There's a simple cafeteria on the premises, but the preferred spot is a panoramic terrace with waiter service and water views. The menu focuses on traditional Finnish specialties such as salmon soup, filet of reindeer, fried snow grouse, and different preparations of salmon, lamb, pikeperch, and duck. The cooking is competent in every way and the ingredients first-rate, although the setting might outshine the food offerings.

Kustaanmiekka Island, Suomenlinna. © **09/66-85-52.** Reservations not required. Main courses 26€–36€. AE, DC, MC, V. Daily noon–midnight. Closed Sept 11–Apr 30. Bus: Water bus to Kustaanmiekka.

5 Seeing the Sights

Helsinki is filled with many interesting activities, from exploring museums to enjoying a Finnish sauna, to taking a summer cruise through the archipelago, or even sampling a Finnish *seisovapöytä* (smörgåsbord). If your time is limited, though, be sure to visit the Mannerheim Museum, the home of Sibelius, the Seurasaari Open-Air Museum, and the Suomenlinna Fortress. For those with more time and money, Helsinki offers a number of specialty shops. For an overview of Finnish products, stop in at Stockmann, Helsinki's largest department store (see "Shopping," later in this chapter).

SUGGESTED ITINERARIES
If You Have 1 Day

Start your morning by visiting Market Square and, following in the footsteps of the late president, Lyndon B. Johnson, have coffee and a Karelian meat pie. The market opens at 7am. See the Presidential Palace and Uspenski Cathedral, and visit Senate Square and Eliel Saarinen's Central Railway Station. Before it's too late, stop by Stockmann Department Store or walk along Pohjoisesplanadi for a look at modern Finnish design in the store windows.

Helsinki Attractions

Botanical Gardens **2**

"Church in the Rock" **9**

Eduskuntatalo
(Finnish Parliament) **10**

Finlandia Hall **13**

Finnish National Gallery **5**

Finnish National Opera **16**

Helsinki City Museum **12**

Helsinki Zoo **7**

Linnanmäki
Amusement Park **18**

Lutheran Cathedral
(Tuomiokirkko) **4**

Mannerheim Museum **8**

Military Museum
of Finland **1**

National Museum
of Finland **11**

Olympic Stadium **17**

Seurasaari
Open-Air Museum **15**

Sibelius Park
& Monument **14**

Suomen Kansallisteatteri **3**

Svenska Teatern **6**

Urho Kekkonen
Museum Tamminiemi **15**

- - - - Ferry
——— Railway

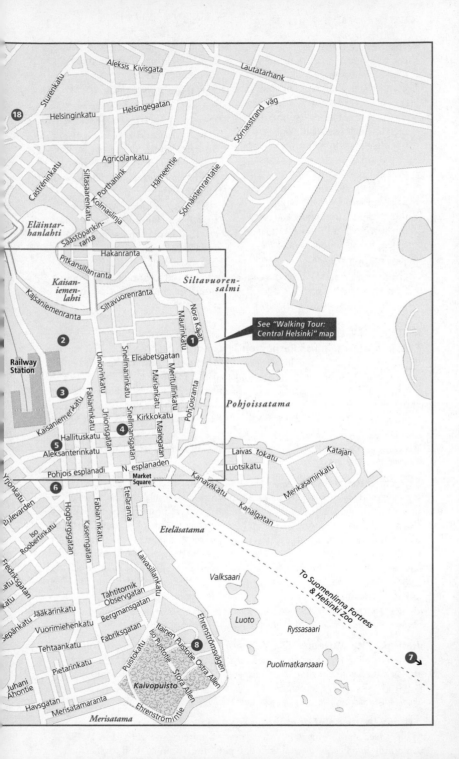

Aleksis Kivisgata
Lautatarhank
Sturenkatu
18
Helsinginkatu
Helsingegatan
Sörnästränd väg
Agricolankatu
Castréninkatu
Siltasaarenkatu
Kolmaslinja
Porthaninkatu
Hämeentie
Sörnäistenrantatie
Eläintar-
hanlahti
Säästöpankin-
ranta
Pitkänsillanranta
Hakanranta
Siltavuoren-
salmi
Kaisan-
iemenlahti
Siltavuorenränta
Kaisaniemenranta
Nora Kaan
Maurinkatu
See "Walking Tour:
Central Helsinki" map
1
2
Railway
Station
Elisabetsgatan
Snellmaninkatu
Meritullinkatu
Pohjoisranta
Unioninkatu
3
Fabianinkatu
Mariankatu
Pohjoissatama
Kaisaniemenkatu
Jhionsgatan
Snellmansgatan
Kirkkokatu
4
Mariegatan
Katajan
Hallituskatu
Laivas tokatu
5
Aleksanterinkatu
Luotsikatu
Merkasaminkatu
Pohjois esplanadi
N. esplanaden
6
Market
Square
Kanavakatu
Yrjonkatu
Bulevarden
Hogbergsgatan
Fabian nkatu
Eteläranta
Kanalgatan
Iso
Roobertinkatu
Kaserngatan
Eteläsatama
Fredriksgatan
Laivasillankatu
Valksaari
To Suomenlinna Fortress
& Helsinki Zoo
Jääkärinkatu
Tähtitornik
Observgatan
Luoto
Ryssasaari
sepänkatu
Vuorimiehenkatu
Bergmansgatan
Itainen Puistotie Ostra Allen
8
Tehtaankatu
Fabriksgatan
Puistokatu
Iso Puistotie
Stora Allen
Ehrenströmsvägen
Puolimatkansaari
7
Pietarinkatu
Juhani
Ahontie
Kaivopuisto
Havsgatan
Merisatamaranta
Ehrenströmintie
Merisatama

If You Have 2 Days

For your first day, follow the suggestions above. On Day 2, visit the Mannerheim Museum, housed in the home of Baron Carl Gustaf Mannerheim, Finland's former field marshal and president. Go to the Olympic Stadium to see the controversial nude statue of the famous runner Paavo Nurmi, and visit Finlandia Hall, Helsinki's main concert hall, designed by Alvar Aalto. Go to the National Museum and stroll through Sibelius Park, with its monument to the famous composer.

If You Have 3 Days

On the first 2 days, follow the itinerary suggested above. On Day 3, visit some of the attractions in the archipelago, including the Seurasaari Open-Air Museum and Suomenlinna Fortress.

If You Have 4 or 5 Days

For your first 3 days, follow the recommendations given above. On Day 4, head north on an excursion to visit Ainola, the home of Jean Sibelius, in Järvenpää. Explore the nearby town of Hämeenlinna and see his birthplace.

On Day 5, take a 1-day excursion to Porvoo, Finland's second-oldest town, 48km (30 miles) northeast of Helsinki. Dating back to 1346, the old town features cobblestone streets and charming red wooden buildings along the Porvoo River.

IN THE CITY CENTER

Eduskuntatalo (Finnish Parliament)   Near the post office, this 1931 building of pink Finnish granite houses the 200 members of the one-chamber parliament (40% of whose members are women). The building looks austere on the outside, but it's much warmer inside. Members meet in the domed interior of Parliament Hall, which is decorated with sculpture by Wäinö Aaltonen. The architect, J. S. Sirén, chose a modernized neoclassic style in celebration of the new republic.

Mannerheimintie 30. (℃) 09/4321. Free admission. Tours Sat 11am and noon, Sun noon and 1pm; July–Aug, also Mon–Fri at 2pm. Tram: 3B or 3T.

Finnish National Gallery 𝆣𝆣   Finland's largest selection of sculpture, painting, and graphic art is displayed at this museum. The Finnish National Gallery is host to three independent museums: the **Museum of Finnish Art,** the **Kiasma (Museum of Contemporary Art),** and the **Sinebrychoff Art Museum (Museum of Foreign Art).** The first museum is housed in the Ateneum building across from the railway station. More than a century old, it was designed by Theodore Höijer. The Museum of Finnish Art has the largest collection of Finnish artists, from the mid-1700s to 1960, as well as the works of some 19th- and 20th-century foreign artists. For visiting times to the other museums, see below.

Kaivokatu 2. (℃) 09/17-33-61. Admission 5.50€ adults, 4€ students and seniors, free for children under 18. Special exhibits, 6€–10€. Tues and Fri 9am–6pm; Wed–Thurs 9am–8pm; Sat–Sun 11am–5pm. Tram: 3 or 6.

Helsinki City Museum   The history of Helsinki from its founding up to modern times is presented from various viewpoints. Exhibits trace the growth of the city, the people moving in or out, and different aspects of Helsinki life.

Sofiankatu 4 (by Senate Sq.). (℃) 09/1691. Admission 3€, free for children under 18, free for everyone on Thurs. Mon–Fri 9am–5pm; Sat–Sun 11am–5pm. Tram: 1, 2, 3B, 3T, 4, 7A, or 7B.

Kiasma (Museum of Contemporary Art) 𝆣   Part of the Finnish National Gallery (see above), this is Helsinki's newest museum—it opened in 1998. An American architect, Steven Hall, designed the stunning building, which is ideally lit for displaying modern art. The collection exhibits post-1960 Finnish and international art. Look for changing exhibitions here. The name of this museum, based on the word *chiasma,* suggests Finland's special ability to achieve crossovers between the worlds of fine art and high technology. The 4,300-sq.-m (14,400-sq.-ft.) structure houses Finland's finest collection of contemporary art. A "mediatheque" concentrates on displaying the museum's media collections. Kiosks also function as Internet stations.

Mannerheiminaukio 2. ℂ **09/173-365-01**. Admission 5.50€ adults, 4€ students and seniors, free for those under 18. Tues 9am–5pm; Wed–Sun 10am–10pm. Tram: 3B or 3T.

Lutheran Cathedral (Tuomiokirkko) ℛ
Dominating the city's skyline is one of the city's most visible symbols, a green-domed cathedral erected between 1830 and 1852. Built during the Russian administration of Helsinki in a severe, almost stark interpretation that reflected the glory of ancient Greece and Rome, the Lutheran Cathedral was designed by German-born architect Carl Ludvig Engel. It was inaugurated as part of the 19th-century reconstruction of Helsinki, which primarily emphasized a neoclassical style. (A fire had destroyed most of the city after it was forcibly annexed by the Russians.) Today, the rites celebrated inside conform to the Evangelical Lutheran denomination. Extensive renovations, both to the cathedral and to its crypt, brought it back to its original beauty in 1998.

Senaatintori. ℂ **09/709-24-55**. Free admission. June–Aug Mon–Sat 9am–6pm, Sun noon–8pm; Sept–May Mon–Fri 10am–4pm, Sat 10am–6pm, Sun noon–6pm. Tram: 1, 2, 3B, or 3T.

Mannerheim Museum ℛℛ
This was the home of Baron Carl Gustaf Mannerheim, marshal of Finland and president of the republic from 1944 to 1946—a sort of George Washington to his country and one of the most effective military strategists of his era. Now a museum, the residence houses his collection of European furniture, Asian art, and personal items, such as uniforms, swords, decorations, and gifts from admirers. The house remains as it was when he died in 1951.

Kallionlinnantie 14. ℂ **09/63-54-43**. Admission (including guided tour) 7€ adults, 5€ children 12–16, free for children under 12. Fri–Sun 11am–4pm. Tram: 3B or 3T.

Military Museum of Finland
Founded in 1929, this museum records, preserves, and displays material and traditions associated with Finland's defense forces and with general military history. The museum has more than 200,000 items, but only relatively few can be displayed at any one time. Highlights include objects from the days of Swedish rule and from the period between the two world wars. Of special interest is an exhibit of gripping photographs from World War II.

Maurinkatu 1. ℂ **09/1812-63-81**. Admission 3.50€ adults, 1€ children. Tues–Thurs 11am–6pm; Fri–Sun 11am–6pm. Bus: 16 or 18.

National Museum of Finland ℛℛ
Designed in the National Romantic style, this museum opened in 1916 and has three major sections—prehistoric, historic, and ethnographic. Archaeological finds on display reveal that people have inhabited Finland since the Stone Age. Other exhibits include church art from the medieval and Lutheran periods, folk-culture artifacts, folk costumes and textiles, furniture, foreign ethnographic collections, an important coin collection, and the Finno-Ugric collections.

Mannerheimintie 34. ℂ **09/405-01**. Admission 4€ adults, 3€ students, free for children under 18. Tues–Wed 11am–8pm; Thurs–Sun 11am–6pm. Tram: 4, 7A, 7B, or 10.

Olympic Stadium (Olympiastadion)   Helsinki was host to the Olympic Games in 1952; a tower remains from its impressive sports stadium, and an elevator whisks passengers up to the top for a panoramic view of the city and the archipelago. The stadium, 2km (1¼ miles) from the city center, was originally built in 1940, but the Olympic Games scheduled for that year were cancelled when World War II broke out. The seating capacity of the stadium is 40,000, larger than any other arena in the country. The stadium was closed and rebuilt between 1992 and 1994, and today it conforms to the highest standards of a venue for mass-market sports. Outside the stadium is a statue by Wäinö Aaltonen of the great athlete Paavo Nurmi, "The Flying Finn." The runner is depicted in full stride and is completely nude, which caused considerable controversy when it was unveiled in 1952.

Paavo Nurmi tie 1. (C) **09/44-03-63.** Admission 2€ adults, 1€ children under 16. Mon–Fri 9am–8pm; Sat–Sun 9am–6pm. Closed during athletic competitions. Tram: 3B, 3T, 4, or 10.

Sinebrychoff Art Museum (Museum of Foreign Art) 🛧 *Finds*   Part of the Finnish National Gallery (see above), this museum was built in 1842 and still displays its original furnishings. It houses an extensive collection of foreign paintings from the 14th century to the 19th century and has a stunning collection of foreign miniatures. The collection originated from the wealthy Sinebrychoff dynasty, a family of Russians who owned a local brewery and occupied this yellow-and-white neo-Renaissance mansion built in 1840. They were great collectors of antiques, their taste leaning toward the opulent in furnishings. Their art collection was wide ranging, especially noted for its Dutch and Swedish portraits of the 17th and 18th centuries. There is also a stunning collection of porcelain. Outdoor concerts in summer are often staged in the formerly private park surrounding the estate.

Sinebrychoff, Bulevardi 40. (C) **09/17-33-61.** Admission 2.50€ adults, 1.50€ children under 18. Special exhibits 4€–8€. Mon and Thurs–Fri 9am–6pm; Wed 9am–8pm; Sat–Sun 11am–5pm. Tram: 6.

"Church in the Rock" 🛧🛧   Built into solid rock and consecrated in 1969, this church is about 2 blocks west of the National Museum in the Töölö residential district west of Mannerheimintie. Only the roof is visible from outside. It was designed by two architect brothers, Tuomo and Timo Suomalainen. They chose a rocky outcrop rising some 12m (40 ft.) above street level. The interior walls were blasted from bedrock. Because of its superb acoustics, the church is often used as a concert hall. English-language services are conducted every Sunday at 2pm. Before its change to an English name, this church was known for most of its life as the Temppeliaukio Church.

Lutherinkatu 3. (C) **09/49-86-98.** Free admission. Mon–Tues and Thurs–Fri 10am–8pm; Wed 10am–7pm; Sat 10am–6pm; Sun noon–1:45pm and 3:15–5:45pm. Closed during special events and Tues Sept–May. Tram: 3B or 3T.

Urho Kekkonen Museum Tamminiemi   This site celebrates the accomplishments of Urho Kekkonen (1900–86), who served as president of Finland longer (1956–82—some of the trickiest days of the Cold War) than anyone else. Built in 1904 in the Jugendstil (Art Nouveau) style, it's a not particularly large house whose official functions were transferred to a larger structure in another part of Helsinki in 1995. As a sign of respect for their president, who was the eldest son of a foreman in the logging industry in an isolated region of northeast Finland, the Finnish parliament allowed the then-ailing Kekkonen to remain a resident here until his death in 1986. Today, the site is a testimonial to the survival of Finland against the Soviet menace, and a testimonial to the man who helped make that happen. Of particular interest is a view of the most famous sauna in Finland. A log-sided, old-fashioned building with a wood-fired stove, it hosted several pivotal diplomatic meetings, including some with Nikita Khrushchev. (As the Finns say, who can possibly remain hostile in the blazing heat of a sauna?) The sauna can be visited only between June and August. Finnish-language tours depart at 30-minute intervals throughout opening hours; an English-language tour is conducted every day at 1:30pm. Otherwise, you can borrow an English-language cassette and player for a self-guided tour.

Seurasarrentie 15. ✆ 09/48-06-84. Admission 3.50€ adults, free for children under 18. June–Aug daily 11am–5pm; Sept–May Tues–Sun 11am–5pm. Bus: 24 from Erottaja bus stop, adjacent to the Swedish Theater and Stockmann Department Store.

NEAR HELSINKI

Ainola 👁👁   Few countries seem as proud of a native composer as Finns are of Jean Sibelius, who lived here for more than half a century. He named the house after his wife, Aino (sister of the artist Eero Järnefelt), and lived here from 1904 until his death in 1957; he and his wife are buried on the property. Avant-garde at the time of its construction, the house was designed by Lars Sonck, who also designed the summer residence of the president of Finland. The wooden interior of Ainola is lined with books and some surprisingly modern-looking furniture. Järvenpää is 39km (24 miles) from Helsinki.

Ainolantie, in Järvenpää. ✆ 09/28-73-22. Admission 5€ adults, 1€ children. June–Aug Tues–Sun 10am–5pm; May and Sept Wed–Sun 10am–5pm. Closed Oct–Apr. Bus: From Platform 1 of the Helsinki Bus Station, follow the Helsinki–Hyryla–Järvenpää route, to where the road forks at a sign saying AINOLA; from there, it's a 4-mln. walk to the home. Train: Järvenpää station.

Gallen-Kallela Museum 👁👁   On a wooded peninsula in a suburb of Helsinki, this museum is dedicated to the great Finnish artist Akseli Gallen-Kallela (1865–1931), who built the studio between 1911 and 1913, calling it his "castle in the air." A restless, fanciful personality, Gallen-Kallela's reputation is based mainly on his paintings, especially those from the *Kalevala (Land of Heroes)*. This Finnish national epic, first published in 1835, and often compared to Homer's *Iliad* and *Odyssey*, was in later editions illustrated by the artist. He wanted to illustrate all the cantos, but managed only a small part, which rank among the masterpieces of Finnish art. The museum houses a large collection of his paintings, graphics, posters, and industrial design products. Beside the museum is a cafe in a wooden villa dating from the 1850s.

Tarvaspää, Gallen-Kallelantie 27, Espoo. ✆ 09/541-33-88. Admission 8€ adults, 4€ children 7–16, free for children under 7. May 15–Aug Mon–Thurs 10am–8pm, Fri–Sun 10am–5pm; Sept–May 14 Tues–Sat 10am–4pm, Sun 10am–5pm. Tram: 4 to Munkkiniemi; then take bus no. 33 to Tarvo or walk about 2.4km (1½ miles) along the seaside (bus no. 33 runs Mon–Sat 9:20–11am and 1–3pm).

ON NEARBY ISLANDS
ON SEURASAARI

Seurasaari Open-Air Museum 👁👁   One of the largest collections of historic buildings in Finland, each moved here from somewhere else, lies on the island of Seurassari, a national park. Representing the tastes and evolution of Finnish architecture through the centuries, the collection includes a 17th-century church, an 18th-century gentleman's manor house, and dozens of oddly diverse farm buildings, each erected with a specific function in mind. There's also an old-fashioned "aboriginal" sauna, a kind of smokehouse that takes hours to heat.

The verve associated with this collection of historic, free-standing buildings is most visible during the summer months, when you can visit the interiors, and

Frommer's Favorite Helsinki Experiences

Enjoying a Finnish Sauna   Regardless of where you've bathed before, you haven't been cleansed to the core until you've experienced a Finnish sauna. Whether used for giving birth to babies or entertaining Russian ambassadors, the sauna is often looked upon with almost religious awe.

Hearing a Sibelius Concert   To listen to the work of Finland's greatest composer, Jean Sibelius, is a moving experience. This sensitive, vulnerable artist achieved a universal melodic language. In his lifetime Sibelius and his music became the symbol of Finland, a nation striving for independence and recognition.

Partaking of a Finnish Smörgåsbord   Feast on the harvest of the sea: Baltic herring in a tangy marinade, followed by lightly salted fish and roe, and smoked- and other cold-fish dishes. Then try smoked reindeer meat for a touch of Lapland (flavored with lingonberries) and, for a finale, a selection of Finnish desserts, including fresh Arctic berries.

Cruising the Archipelago   Since Helsinki is the capital of a country of 188,000 lakes, it, too, is best seen from the water. On a warm summer day, take a cruise through the archipelago; you'll pass innumerable little islands and navigate around many peninsulas.

when an unpretentious restaurant serves coffee, drinks, and platters of food. Although the buildings are locked during the winter months, you can still view the exteriors and explore on foot the park that surrounds them. A stroll through this place in the wintertime is not as far-fetched an idea as you might think; the park is favored by strollers and joggers even during snowfalls.

Seurasaari Island. © **09/405-096-60.** Admission 4.50€, free for children under 18. May 15–31 and Sept 1–15 Mon–Fri 9am–3pm and Sat–Sun 11am–5pm; June 1–Aug 30 Thurs–Tues 11am–5pm, Wed 11am–7pm. Closed Sept 16–May 14. Bus: 24 from the Erottaja bus stop, near Stockmann Department Store, to the island. The 5km (3-mile) ride takes about 15 min., and costs 2€ each way.

ON SUSISAARI & KUSTAANMIEKKA

Suomenlinna Fortress 🎯🎯 is known as the "Gibraltar of the North." This 18th-century fortress (© **09/684-18-80**) lies in the Baltic's archipelago on five interconnected islands that guard the maritime approaches to Helsinki. With their walks and gardens, cafes, restaurants, and old frame buildings, the islands are one of the most interesting outings from Helsinki. Originally built in the mid–18th century when Finland was a part of Sweden, the fortress was named "Sveaborg" by the Swedes, and later became known by the Finns and Russians (who assumed control in 1808) as Viapori. After Finland became an independent country in 1917, the fortress acquired its present name, Suomenlinna, which means "the fortress of Finland." It served as a working part of the nation's defenses until 1973.

Today the main attraction is that part of the fortress on Susisaari and Kustaanmiekka islands, which are now joined together as one land body. Specifically, the sights include a small, well-preserved fort on Kustaanmiekka, with defense walls and tunnels, and another, larger fortress on Susisaari, which includes a number of parks, squares, and gardens.

You can take a **ferry** from Market Square to Suomenlinna year-round beginning at 6:20am daily. The boats run about once an hour, and the last one returns from the island at 1:45am. The round-trip ferry ride costs 2€ for adults and 1€ for children.

The island has no "streets," but individual attractions are signposted. During the peak summer months (June–Sept), Suomenlinna maintains two information kiosks, one at Market Square (by the departure point for the Suomenlinna ferryboat) and a second on the island itself (near Tykistolahti Bay). The latter kiosk serves as the starting point for **guided tours**—offered in English—of the fortress with a focus on its military history. Tours are scheduled between June and September, daily at 10:30 and 1pm, and cost 5€ for adults and 2.50€ for children. The rest of the year, the guided tours, which must be reserved in advance, are offered on an as-needed basis and priced at 125€ for up to 16 participants.

The Museums of Suomenlinna

A number of minor museums on either Susisaari or the connected island of Kustaanmiekka can be explored if you have the time.

Coastal Artillery Museum   Set within the thick walls and vaulted ceilings of an area of the Suomenlinna fortress originally built to store gunpowder, this museum contains exhibits that show how Finland defended itself from foreign aggression during World Wars I and II. Opened in 1948, the museum traces the stages in the defense of Finnish shores from prehistoric times to the present. The weapons for defending the coastline now include missiles, motorized artillery, and turret guns. Also on display are equipment for directing fire, range finders, and a marine surveillance camera. Newer technology is represented by close-range missiles and a laser range finder.

Kustaanmiekka. ✆ **09/181-452-95.** Admission 2€ adults, 1€ children. May 11–Aug daily 10am–5pm; Sept daily 11am–4pm; Apr 4–May 10 and Oct 1–23 Sat–Sun 11am–3pm. Closed Oct 24–Apr 3.

Ehrensvärd Museum   This historical museum includes a model ship collection and officers' quarters from the 18th century, as well as displays based on Suomenlinna's military history. The museum bears the name of Augustin Ehrensvärd, who supervised construction of the fortress and whose tomb is on Susisaari.

Susisaari. ✆ **09/684-18-50.** Admission 3€ adults, 1.50€ children 7–16, free for children under 7. Mar 1–May 3 Sat–Sun 11am–4:30pm; May 4–Aug 30 daily 10am–6pm; Sept daily 10am–4:30pm; Oct Sat–Sun 11am–4:30pm. Closed Nov–Feb.

Submarine Vesikko   The submarine *Vesikko* was built in Turku and launched in 1933. Germany had ordered the submarine built for experimental purposes, but Finland bought it in 1936. The submarine, which was used during World War II, torpedoed the 4,100-ton Russian ship *Vyborg*. The Paris Peace Treaty of 1947 forbade Finland to have submarines, so all except the *Vesikko* were scrapped. The *Vesikko* was opened as a museum in 1973.

Susisaari. ✆ **09/181-452-95.** Admission 2€ adults, 1€ children. May 9–Aug 30 daily 10am–4:45pm; Aug 31–Sept 27 daily 11am–3pm. Closed Sept 28–May 8.

ON KORKEASAARI

Helsinki Zoo   An interesting collection of northern European animals, including a herd of wild forest reindeer, wolverines, northern owl species, and many other mammals and birds from Europe and Asia, can be found here.

Korkeasaari Island. ✆ **09/16-95-91.** Admission by water bus, 8€ adults, 4€ children; by bridge, 5€ adults, 3€ children. The Helsinki Card (see "Getting Around," earlier in this chapter) covers admission to the zoo as well as free rides on the ferry and water bus. Mar–Apr daily 10am–6pm; May–Sept daily 10am–8pm; Oct–Feb

> **Fun Fact** **Did You Know?**
> - Helsinki is famed for its architects, but it was a German, Carl Ludvig Engel, who laid out the present inner city.
> - Two brothers designed Temppeliaukio Church from solid rock; it occupies nearly a whole block, but from the street only the dome is visible.
> - The Havis Amanda fountain scandalized the city when it was placed in Market Square in 1908, but now it's Helsinki's symbol.
> - The major boulevard, Esplanadi, was once a political dividing line— Finns walked on the south side and Swedes on the north.
> - Wäinö Aaltonen caused an uproar in 1952 when his statue of Paavo Nurmi, the champion runner of the 1920s, was unveiled—he had depicted Nurmi fully nude.

daily 10am–4pm. Water bus: From Market Square and Hakaniemenranta in front of the Merihotelli. Bus: 16 (year-round) to Kulosaari, then walk less than 1.5km (1 mile) via Mustikkamaa Island to the zoo; or take no. 11 (summer only) from the Herttoniemi subway station.

PARKS & GARDENS
Botanical Gardens   These gardens, a 5-minute walk from the Central Station, feature shrubs and flowers, herbs, ornamentals, Finnish wildflowers, and indigenous trees and bushes. The greenhouses here reopened in 1998 after extensive renovations, making them better than ever. However, unlike the rest of the gardens, they are closed on Monday.

University of Helsinki, Unioninkatu 44. ℂ **09/708-19-11.** Admission 4€ adults, 2€ children, free for children under 7. May–Sept daily 7am–8pm; Oct–Apr daily 7am–6pm.

Pihlajasaari Recreational Park   A popular attraction favored by bird-watchers and joggers, this park is made up of two small neighboring islands filled with sandy beaches—it's a summer playground for the city. A restaurant and a cafe are in the park.

ℂ **09/63-00-65.** Admission 4€ adults, 2€ seniors and children. Daily 24 hr. Motorboat leaves from the end of Laivurinkatu May to mid-Oct daily at 9am, 9:30am, and then at hourly intervals until 8:30pm, depending on weather.

Sibelius Park & Monument   Called *Sibeliuksen puisto* in Finnish, this park was planned to honor Jean Sibelius, Finland's most famous composer. The grounds are not manicured, but are maintained in a somewhat natural state. Old birch trees shade park benches, and rocky outcrops divide the landscape. The park was meant to reflect the rugged natural beauty of Finland itself, as inspired by Sibelius's work *Finlandia*. At one side of the park is the monumental sculpture, Eila Hiltunen's tribute to Sibelius, the genius whose music is believed to embody the soul of Finland. The monument was unveiled in 1967, a decade after the composer's death; Sibelius is depicted at the peak of his powers and his career.

Mechelininkatu. Free admission. Daily 24 hr. Bus: 24.

ARCHITECTURAL HIGHLIGHTS
Hvittrask 𝄇𝄇, in Luoma, Kirrkkonummi (ℂ **09/405-096-30**), the studio home of architects Eliel Saarinen, Armas Lindgren, and Herman Gesellius, was

Impressions

I became aware at once of the translucent, transparent, pure, elusive, clean, and clinical quality of Helsinki. I began to hate the almost paralyzing perfection of modern buildings, equipment, accommodation, accessories, service.

—James Kirkup, *One Man's Russia,* 1968

built of logs and natural stone and ranks among the most remarkable architectural creations of its time. The artistic unity of the house with its forest surroundings was a remarkable achievement. Today it's used as a center for exhibits of Finnish art and handicrafts. A first-rate restaurant, **Hvittrask** (**℃ 09/297-60-33**), is open Tuesday through Thursday from noon to 8pm and Friday through Monday from noon to 6pm.

Admission to the center is 4€ for adults, 2.50€ for children. It's open daily from 10am to 7pm. To get there, take bus no. 166 from the Central Bus Station, Platform 62, then walk about 2km (1¼ miles). Or take the train to Luoma, and then walk about 2km (1¼ miles). By car, follow the Jorvas motorway about 20km (12 miles), turn off at the Kivenlahti exit, drive about 5km (3 miles) toward Kauklahti, and then follow the Hvittrask signs.

Tapiola, a notable model community, is in Espoo, 10km (6 miles) west of Helsinki. This garden city, from the pre–World War II era, is filled with parks, splashing fountains, handsomely designed homes and apartments, shopping centers, playgrounds, schools, and churches. In the center of Tapiola is a large office building with a self-service cafeteria on top (a good choice for lunch). To reach Tapiola, go to stop no. 52 or no. 53 near the Central Station. From either stop, take any bus marked TAPIOLA.

ESPECIALLY FOR KIDS

Helsinki has many interesting activities for children, beginning with the opportunity to travel around on the **ferryboats** and **water buses** that link the city's islands and attractions. The Helsinki Card (see "Getting Around," earlier in this chapter) entitles them to free admission or reduced rates at a number of attractions. We've noticed that children like the "Traditional Helsinki by Sea" **boat tours** (see "Organized Tours," below), the **Helsinki Zoo,** the **Pihlajasaari Recreational Park, Suomenlinna Fortress,** the model-ship collection in the **Ehrensvärd Museum,** the submarine *Vesikko* on **Susisaari Island,** the outdoor **Olympic Stadium,** and many other sights and excursions.

Linnanmäki Amusement Park Linnanmäki, 3km (2 miles) north of Helsinki, is a fun fair of splashing fountains, merry-go-rounds, Ferris wheels, restaurants, cafes, and theaters. Founded in 1950 by the Children's Foundation to raise money to care for the thousands of children orphaned by World War II, Linnanmäki is still raising money for a new generation of children. The amusement park has 34 different rides.

Linnanmäki. ℃ 09/77-39-91. Admission 2.50€ adults, 1.50€ children 6–16, free for children 5 and under. Mon–Fri 4–10pm; Sat–Sun 1–9 or 10pm. Closed Sept–Apr. Tram: 3B or 3T.

The Building of Finland

Finland's architectural heritage before the 20th century incorporates Swedish, Russian, and Viking motifs into buildings that often seem to arise from the human subconscious as interpreted by Scandinavian mythology. More than in any other nation, Finland's identity is intimately associated with its postwar architecture.

The architectural landscape of Finland is relatively young—more than 90% of the country's structures were built after 1920. Part of this is because of Finland's ongoing struggle to survive during the many years it swung back and forth between the orbits of the often-violent regimes of Sweden and Russia. Much of the destruction during the 20th century was initiated by Nazi Germany, to a somewhat lesser degree by the Soviet Union. In some cases, however (as occurred in such "lost" provinces as Karelia, which was painfully ceded to the Soviets after World War II), it was the Finns themselves who burned their buildings.

At least some of the impetus for postwar rebuilding came from the government's passage of the "Arava System," which, in an attempt to honor the sacrifices of Finns during the war, offered state-subsidized loans to construct houses. So many utilitarian objects were created and so many homes built between 1940 and 1958 that Finns refer to this period as "The Age of Heroic Materialism." Everything from armaments to medicine to construction materials were marshaled into programs designed for the good (and the survival) of the Finnish nation.

In many cases the signature of the individual architect could rarely be discerned in the typical private home. Throughout Finland, many dwellings were designed as a simple cube, warmed with a centrally located stove (often wood-burning) and capped with a steeply pitched roof that sheltered a high attic suitable for conversion into additional bedrooms.

Alvar Aalto (1898–1976), an architect whose comfortably minimalist and sometimes eccentric designs are now intertwined with the Finnish

---

WALKING TOUR CENTRAL HELSINKI

Start:	Senate Square.
Finish:	Helsinki Railway Station.
Time:	Allow 3 hours, not including museum and shopping stops.
Best Times:	Any day it's not raining.
Worst Times:	Rush hours (Mon–Fri between 8 and 9:30am and 5 and 6:30pm), because of the heavy traffic.

The tour begins at:

❶ Senate Square

You'll find the square in front of the monument to the Russian tsar Alexander II, erected in his honor shortly after the annexation of Finland.

Helsinki's most historic and beautiful square was designed in the early 1800s at the height of the Russian Empire's fascination with the architectural glories of ancient Greece and Rome. The aesthetic, became an important visionary in the postwar rebuilding of Finland. His work was already well known to connoisseurs, thanks to his designs for the Finnish Pavilions at the Paris World's Fair of 1937 and the New York World's Fair of 1939.

A noteworthy (and pragmatic) moment in Aalto's career included designing a series of standardized wood-sided homes partially prefabricated in a Finnish lumberyard. By 1943, during an unexpected lull in the hostilities of World War II, 14 two-family homes designed by Aalto were completed, launching him into a postwar career that shifted his focus from classicism to functionalism and that continued at a fast pace throughout the 1950s and 1960s.

Since then, Aalto has been referred to as "a vitalist to whom nothing human was alien." Bold but tasteful, he developed the Finnish preference for exposed wood and free forms into undemonstrative, functional, and nurturing buildings that are noteworthy for their cost-effectiveness, comfort, and sense of style. Important commissions often incorporated fieldstone and red brick, poured concrete and, later, large expanses of white stone, marble, or plaster. Noteworthy buildings include such monuments as the Säynätsalo Town Hall (completed in 1952); the Sunila pulp mill, which included a new town (Kotka) to house its workers; some of the buildings on the campus of the University of Jväskylä (completed in 1966); the main building of Helsinki University in Otaniemi (built between 1955 and 1964); and Finlandia Hall, Helsinki's main symphonic concert hall, completed in 1971. Other commissions included hospitals, libraries (such as the one at Viipuri), and private homes, some filled with the distinctive laminated wood furniture for which he and his wife, Aino (who died in 1949), eventually became world-famous.

designer was Berlin-born Carl Ludvig Engel, who created other public buildings in St. Petersburg.

On the north side of the square is the:

❷ Lutheran Cathedral

Featuring triplicate statues of saints, it has four small cupolas ringing its central dome.

As you face the cathedral, the Senate, capped by a low dome and graced by six Corinthian columns, is on your right. Opposite the cathedral, on the south side of the square, stand the ocher facade and Ionic columns of a house from 1762 that was redesigned by Engel.

Leaving the square, ascend the steeply inclined Unioninkatu, skirting the right-hand (western) edge of the square. The street was dedicated to the tsar in 1819 and, because of its difficult terrain, was considered extremely expensive at the time of its construction. The elegantly graceful building opposite the western facade of the cathedral is the:

❸ Library of the University of Helsinki

Some critics consider this the most beautiful of the many buildings created by Engel. Admire its rhythmically repetitive Corinthian pilasters and columns.

Continue uphill. At the northwestern corner of the cathedral's rear side rises the spire of the:

④ Russian Orthodox Church of the Holy Trinity

Designed by Engel in 1827, it has an ocher-colored facade and an artfully skewed Orthodox double cross placed above its doorway.

After passing Kirkkokatu, turn right (east) onto Rauhankatu, where you'll see the statue called:

⑤ *Dawn*

This statue of a young girl is set onto a porphyry base near the corner. The gray-fronted modern building serving as the statue's backdrop contains the printing presses and engravers' shops for banknotes issued by the Bank of Finland.

Continue east on the same street, passing an ornately neoclassical building with a trio of wise women set on its pediment. This is the storage space for the:

⑥ Finnish State Archives

Originally designed in 1890, over the course of time the archives were greatly expanded with annexes and underground vaults.

At the corner of Snellmaninkatu, turn right. The russet-fronted temple with four Corinthian columns and a single acanthus leaf at the pinnacle of its pediment is the:

⑦ House of Scientific Studies

Just below its heraldic plaques is a heroic frieze cast in solid bronze, paying homage to the generosity of Alexander II, who promised to retain the internal laws and religion of Finland after its 1809 annexation. For many years the frieze was the largest bronze casting in Finland. The building was erected in 1891.

Across Snellmaninkatu is a somber gray building set above a steep embankment—the central headquarters of the:

⑧ Bank of Finland

The bank was designed in 1892 by Bohnsted, a Russian-German architect. In front of the bank stands a statue of the Finnish statesman J. V. Snellman, the patriot whose life was devoted to raising the Finnish language to the same legal status as Swedish. Snellman was also responsible for making the Finnish *markka* the official currency of the country, thereby replacing the Russian ruble.

Continue to walk downhill along Snellmaninkatu, skirting the eastern edge of the cathedral's outbuildings. Shortly you'll re-enter Senate Square. Proceed to the bottom of the square and turn left onto Aleksanterinkatu. At no. 14 on that street, behind a russet-colored 1823 facade, is the:

⑨ Official Residence of the Lord Mayor of Helsinki

This structure stands next door to the Theater Museum at Aleksanterinkatu 12.

Continue walking east along Aleksanterinkatu. In a short time, you'll enter a small gate dotted with a handful of birch trees. Behind the trees rises the neo-Venetian facade of the:

⑩ House of the Nobility

Originally a private club and the reunion hall of the Finnish and Russian aristocracy, the House of Nobility was completed in 1861.

Walk along Aleksanterinkatu, crossing Mariankatu, and continue toward the harbor. Some of the buildings along the harbor date from the 1760s and are among the oldest in Helsinki.

At the waterfront, turn left onto Merit-ullintori, skirting the edge of the harbor. A sweeping vista of the Russian Orthodox Uspenski Kathedralen (cathedral) comes into view. At this point the street changes its name to Pohjoisranta and continues to follow the harbor. Continue along this street to the third intersection, Maneeskikatu, where the quay will widen into a formal park ringed with Art Nouveau buildings, some of the finest in Helsinki. Facing the park, notice on your left the redbrick neo-Victorian building, the:

⑪ Finnish War College and Military Museum

The college was originally constructed as a barracks in the 1880s.

Walking Tour: Central Helsinki

1 Senate Square
2 Lutheran Cathedral
3 Library of the University of Helsinki
4 Russian Orthodox Church of the Holy Trinity
5 Dawn
6 Finnish State Archives
7 House of Scientific Studies
8 Bank of Finland
9 Official residence of the Lord Mayor of Helsinki
10 House of Nobility
11 Finnish War College and Military Museum
12 Burger's House
13 Kaisaniemi Park
14 National Theater
15 The Ateneum
16 Helsinki Railway Station

† Church
▬ Railway

HELSINKI

Map Area

553

Turn left onto Liisankatu. Completed in 1813, the street honored the Russian tsarina Elisabeth (*Liisa* is the Finnish version of *Elisabeth*).

Take the second right, turning uphill onto Meritullinkatu. Cross (but don't turn onto) Kulmakatu. At this point, Meritullinkatu becomes a pedestrians-only walkway for residents of the surrounding apartment buildings. At the dead end, turn left and negotiate a narrow, elevated sidewalk high above the street running below (Kristianinkatu). One block later, cross (but don't turn onto) Kulmakatu. A few paces later, at Kristianinkatu 12, you'll see the simple stone foundation and ocher-colored clapboards of the:

⑫ Burger's House

Helsinki's oldest remaining wooden house, dating from the early 1800s, now accommodates a small museum.

A few steps later, Kristianinkatu dead-ends at a pedestrians-only sidewalk, Oikokatu. Go right (downhill), descending two narrow flights of concrete stairs heading toward the lake. At the bottom you emerge onto a busy avenue, Siltavuorenranta; turn left and notice the stylish bulk of the Scandic Hotel Continental rising across the water. Walk along the curving embankment for a while, coming to the tramway and car traffic hub of Unioninkatu, which you should cross. You'll then enter:

⑬ Kaisaniemi Park ("The Company Keeping Park")

This tract of waterfront land, beloved by residents of Helsinki, was only a marshy bogland until the 1830s, when it was drained and opened as Helsinki's first park. The park contains the Botanical Gardens of the University of Helsinki, which date from 1833.

Walk through the park, flanking the water on your right, and then follow the natural left-bending southward curve of the park's main path. (Don't cross any of the railroad tracks.) After exiting from the park, your path becomes Lantinen Teatterikuja, in a neighborhood of Art Nouveau apartment buildings. Follow the street for a block through the theatrical headquarters of Finland. On your left stands the:

⑭ National Theater

Vaguely reminiscent of the opera house in Vienna, the National Theater features decorative sculptures on its facade—note especially the representation of bears. The theater was designed by the architect Tarjanne in 1902.

Across the square, immediately opposite the National Theater, is:

⑮ The Ateneum

The Finnish National Gallery, designed by Hoijer and completed in 1887, is the best art museum in Finland.

On the western side of the square (to your right as you face the Ateneum) is one of the most famous public buildings in Europe, the:

⑯ Helsinki Railway Station

Designed by Eliel Saarinen in 1916, the station includes sculptures evocative of the monumental works of Pharaonaic Egypt. It has been copied endlessly ever since by avant-garde set designers of plays and films such as "Batman."

After such an exhausting tour, you'll want to:

TAKE A BREAK From the railway station, head directly south until you reach Pohjoisesplanadi, site of a number of cafes. Our favorite is **Pariisin Viloe**, Pohjoisesplanadi 21 (ⓒ **09/62-43-27**), which is by the pulsating shopping street near the Market Place. In addition to ordering food and drink here, you'll find it great for people-watching.

6 Organized Tours

CITY TOURS   A city tour lasting 1½ hours, offered by **Helsinki Expert** (ⓒ **09/228-812-22**), costs 19€ for adults, 10€ for children under 13. The tour covers all the main sights of Helsinki, including the Sibelius Monument.

Tickets can be purchased from TourExpert at the Helsinki City Tourist Office or at either of the departure points: the Olympia Terminal and Market Square. The Olympia Terminal tour departs at 10am daily year-round; the Market Square tour departs daily July through September at 2pm.

For an **orientation sightseeing trip** without a guide, catch tram no. 3T, which takes you past 35 major city buildings and monuments. The 45-minute trip is available only in summer. You can board tram no. 3T in front of the railway station or at Market Square Monday through Saturday from 6am to 1am and Sunday from 7:30am to 1am. The tram departs regularly at intervals ranging from 5 to 15 minutes. During rush hours, you might have difficulty finding a seat. A ticket costs 2€, 1€ for children under 13.

HARBOR TOURS   For a waterside view of Helsinki and its nearby islands, contact the **Royal Line,** Meritullintori 6 (© **09/65-20-88**). It has two big-windowed ships (each accommodating up to 250 passengers): the MS *Katarina* and the MS *Natalia*. The most popular tours are "Traditional Helsinki by Sea" and "Helsinki Under the Bridges," which explore the central and western views of the city, respectively, and offer distant views of some of the more accessible islands of the archipelago. Both depart four times a day from mid-May to August, last 90 minutes, and cost 10€ per person. The tour with lunch sells for 21€.

There's also a 7-hour excursion that includes a visit to the historic town of Porvoo. It departs between mid-May and mid-September on Monday, Wednesday, Friday, and Saturday at 10am; returns at 6pm; and costs 29€ per person.

7 Spectator Sports & Outdoor Activities

Major sports events take place at the **Olympic Stadium,** Paavo Nurmi tie 1 (© **09/44-03-63**), described under "Seeing the Sights," above. In summer, soccer games between Finland and other European countries are scheduled. Check *Helsinki This Week,* which lists the events taking place at the stadium at the time of your visit. Take tram no. 3B, 3T, 4, or 10.

JOGGING   Finns are just as fond of jogging as Americans or Canadians. The best paths are close to **Olympic Stadium** (see above) and in **Kaivopuisto Park** (the southern part of Helsinki). There are also some good jogging trails around **Hesperia Park,** which is convenient if you're staying at a hotel in the city center.

SAUNAS & BEACHES   Most hotels (at least the better ones) have a sauna. If you want to sample a Finnish sauna and your hotel doesn't have one, the reception desk can direct you to the nearest sauna that's open to the general public.

Traditionally every Finnish city had a wood-heated public sauna. The only one wood-heated public sauna remaining in Helsinki is the **Kothiharjun Sauna,** Harjutorinkatu, near the Sörnäien metro station (© **09/753-15-35**). Visitors are welcome to experience a real Finnish sauna in newly renovated premises, open Tuesday through Friday from 2 to 8pm and Saturday from 1 to 6pm.

If you're in Helsinki in the summer, you'll find the best beaches at **Mustikkamaa, Uunisaari, Pihlajasaari, Hietaniemi,** and **Sevrasaari.** There's also a popular beach on Suomenlinna; you might combine a trip to the beach with a visit to Suomenlinna fortress. However, if you're from a warmer climate, you may find the waters of the Baltic, even in July, too chilly for your tastes.

TENNIS   The best bet for playing tennis in Helsinki is to travel 5.5km (3½ miles) northwest of the railway station to the Pitäjämäki district. Here the **Tali**

Tennis Center, Kutonokuja 3, Pitäjämäki (© **09/55-62-71**), welcomes foreign visitors. Built in 1967, this is the largest, most modern, and most popular tennis complex in Helsinki. The center maintains 10 indoor tennis courts and six outdoor courts. In winter, five of the six outdoor courts are covered with a plastic "bubble." Depending on the time of day and season, indoor courts cost 11€ to 19€ per hour; outdoor courts range from 11€ to 16€ per hour. Use of outdoor courts is severely limited by the weather and the seasons. You can rent a tennis racquet for 2€ and buy tennis balls once you're there. Take bus no. 14 or 39 from the center of the city. The center is open daily from 6am to 10:30pm, but call first to see if the courts are available.

8 Shopping

Finland has taken a bold, creative lead in the highly competitive world of interior design. Search out ceramics and glassware (Arabia is famous), hand-woven articles, hand-carved wood, jaunty fashions, and rugs.

Textiles and jewelry also bear the distinctive stamp of Finland, and toy stores brim with educational toys for each stage of a child's development. Souvenir possibilities include decorations made from reindeer skin, costumed dolls, baskets, and pungent berry liqueurs made from yellow cloudberries, cranberries, and Arctic brambleberries. Of course, you'll find all your sauna needs here as well.

THE SHOPPING SCENE

Most stores are open Monday through Friday from 9am to 5pm and Saturday from 9am to 2pm. Sometimes stores stay open until 4pm on Saturday, especially in the summer.

SHOPPING AREAS   The most important shopping neighborhoods are in the center of the city. They include **Esplanadi,** which offers the finest of Finnish design—but at high prices. Even if you don't buy anything, it's a delightful street for promenading in summer. Airline offices, banks, and travel agencies share the street with shops filled with the best of Finnish crafts, as well as a number of art galleries.

Esplanadi leads from the commercial heart of town all the way to the waterfront. Bordering the water is **Market Square (Kauppatori),** a fresh open-air market open Monday through Saturday. In summer, peddlers set up trolleys and tables to display their wares. Most of the goods for sale are produce (some of them ideal for picnic food), but there are souvenir and gift items as well.

The other main shopping section is called simply **Central,** beginning at Esplanadi and extending to the famous Helsinki Railway Station. Many of the big names in Finnish shopping are here, none more notable than the Stockmann Department Store. Many shopping complexes are also situated in this district, including the Forum. One of the main shopping streets here is **Aleksanterinkatu,** which runs parallel to Esplanadi, stretching from the harbor to Mannerheimintie.

Other shopping streets, all in the center, include **Iso Roobertinkatu** and **Bulevardi,** lying off Esplanadi. Bulevardi, starting at the Klaus Kurki Hotel, winds its way to the water.

TAX REFUNDS   Tax-free shopping is available at stores that display EUROPE TAX-FREE SHOPPING signs in their windows. It's available to all visitors who reside outside the European Union. The value-added tax (usually 22%) on articles bought in these shops is refunded to you when you leave Finland. The minimum tax-free purchase is 40€.

Most of the large department stores and shops can ship your purchases directly to your home address. That way you avoid having to file a claim at Customs. If you take the merchandise with you, ask for a check for the tax amount. This check can be cashed at the airport or harbor where you depart. The savings, which come to about 12% to 16%, apply to both cash and credit- and charge-card purchases. However, if you use your purchased goods before leaving Finland, you won't get a tax refund. Most international cards, such as American Express and Visa, are accepted at major shops, but always ask beforehand.

If you have any questions about tax-free shopping, contact **Europe Tax-Free Shopping (Finland) Ltd.,** Salomonkatu 17A (✆ **09/613-296-00**).

SHOPPING HOURS   Most stores are open Monday through Friday from 9am to 6pm and Saturday from 9am to 1pm. A new government regulation allows shopping on Sunday in June, July, August, and December. As a result, Forum and Stockmann are open during those months on Sunday from noon to 4pm.

A PREVIEW OF FINNISH DESIGN   Before you begin to shop, you might want to survey modern Finnish design. Go to the **Museum of Art and Design,** Korkeavuorenkatu 23 (✆ **09/622-05-40**), which is open Monday through Friday from 11am to 7pm, Saturday and Sunday from 10am to 6pm. Admission is 6€ for adults, 5€ for seniors, and free for children. In what used to be a schoolhouse, the museum has on permanent display the best of Finnish design in wood, textiles, ceramics, glass, and other materials. Other examples of Finnish design can be found at **Design Forum Finland,** Fabianinkatu 10 (✆ **09/62-92-90**), which is open Monday through Friday from 10am to 6pm and Saturday and Sunday from 11am to 4pm. Design Forum specializes in industrial design, applied arts, graphic arts, and interior architecture. A shop and a business gift service are available.

SHOPPING A TO Z
BOOKS
Academic Bookstore   Sprawling over two floors crammed with books in many languages, this store (judging from the number of titles in stock) could be the largest bookstore in Europe. It offers many English-language books, along with a number of travel aids. It also has the finest stationery department in Finland and sells greeting cards as well as high-quality gift and hobby articles. If you're here on a Friday, you can attend a literary get-together in the store, which brings together writers and members of the reading public. All of Finland's major authors and leading politicians, and many foreign writers (including Kurt Vonnegut and Norwegian actress Liv Ullmann), have attended these meetings. The building, with large sky-lit windows and Carrara marble slabs, was designed by Aalto. Pohjoisesplanadi 39. ✆ 09/121-41. Tram: 3B.

DEPARTMENT STORES
Stockmann   Helsinki's largest department store is also Finland's finest and oldest. Its main entrance is on Aleksanterinkatu, with other entrances on Keskuskatu, Pohjoisesplanadi, and Mannerheimintie. Stockmann has the most diversified sampling of Finnish and imported merchandise of any store: glassware, stoneware, ceramics, lamps, furniture, furs, contemporary jewelry, clothes and textiles, handmade candles, reindeer hides—a little bit of everything. Purchases made through the store's Export Service entitle you to a full and

immediate 18% deduction, and you don't have to carry your purchases home with you. Aleksanterinkatu 52. © 09/1211. Tram: 3B.

FASHION

Annikki Karvinen   Ms. Karvinen became famous for elevating *poppana* (Finnish cotton) into the stellar peaks of fashion. All *poppana* fabrics are hand-woven, and Ms. Karvinen has adapted the same style to velvet, silk, and viscose for more formal and more expensive fashions. She designs jackets for both indoors and outdoors. In addition, her outlet offers tablecloths, bedspreads, and other household items for sale. Pohjoisesplanadi 23. © 09/681-17-50. Tram: 3B.

Marimekko   Ever since the early 1960s when Jacqueline Kennedy was photographed wearing Marimekko outfits, the name has been familiar to Americans. Meaning "Mary's frock," Marimekko offers a large variety of prints in vivid colors that stand in sharp contrast to the gray landscape of the Finnish winter. The company, founded in 1951 by Armi Ratia, now includes a collection of unusually textured fabrics sold by the yard for decorating homes and offices. Equally important are the dresses, suits, coats, bags, interior accessories, and many other goods that are sold here, including Marimekko's famous striped T-shirts and dresses. The inventory of shirts and colors changes with the season. Pohjoisesplanadi 31. © 09/686-02-40. Tram: 3B.

Ril's Concept Store   This women's boutique highlights the designs of Kuopio (Ritva Lisa Pohjolainen), who is currently enjoying international attention from the fashion industry—and giving Marimekko some serious competition in the process. The designer creates innovative, daring styles for business and social engagements; Kuopio designs are favored by various female members of the Finnish government and the media. Pohjoisesplanadi 25. © 09/17-45-00. Tram: 3B, 3T, or 4. Bus: 18.

Tarja Niskanen   This is the most famous milliner in Finland, known for designing attractive headgear that protects women from the rigors of the Finnish winter. Don't expect delicate designs here—the emphasis is on warmth. Heavy-duty designs made from fur, leather, or velvet range in price from about 75€ for a velvet hat to about 470€ for something made from sable. Korkovuorenkatu 4. © 09/62-40-22. Tram: 3B or 3T.

FURNITURE

Artek   The roots of this shop go back to 1935, when it was established by Alvar Alto (the greatest design luminary ever to come out of Finland) and three of his colleagues. Inside, you'll find meticulously crafted reproductions of Alto's distinctive bentwood and laminated chairs, tables, wall units, and lamps, the originals of which changed forever the use of industrial materials for home furnishings. Each of the designs is ferociously patented, and although they're distributed at other furniture stores in Finland, they each bear the Artek label. Because in some ways the shop is a showcase for the Finnish national aesthetic, and because its floor space is so large, it's also the venue for exhibitions of arts, crafts, and designs from other countries. 18 Eteläesplandi. © 09/61-32-50. Tram: 4 or 10.

Skanno   This family enterprise, dating from 1946, has long been a big name in home furnishings and textiles; it continues to offer the best designs of the past along with innovative 21st-century ones. One of its most famous designs is the novel sofa, the *Kameleleonitti*, or chameleon, which can be stripped of its cover and given a new one. A visit to Skanno will help explain why Finland is one of the world leaders in modern design. Kluuvikatu 4. Tram: 3 or 4.

GIFTS

Anne's Shop   Opposite the Temppeliaukio Church, this shop offers tax-free shopping. It also has some of the finest gifts in town, including Finnish knives, wood and ceramic products, dolls and hats from Lapland, wool sweaters, reindeer skin, and jewelry. Fredrikinkatu 68. © 09/44-58-23. Tram: 3B or 3T.

Kiseleff Bazaar Hall   This shopping quarter in the old center of Helsinki, between the cathedral and Market Square, contains a group of small, specialized shops that sell lots of unique gifts. Here you can find handicrafts, souvenirs, old-fashioned toys, antiques, sauna accessories, knives, and Christmas decorations. Aleksanterinkatu 28. Tram: 3B, 3T, or 4.

GLASS, PORCELAIN & CERAMICS

Hackman Shop Arabia *(Finds)*   This shop assembles under one roof the products of some of the world's most prestigious manufacturers of household porcelain and art ceramics. Most of the goods are made by Arabia, although some Finnish-made glass and art glass by Nuutajarvi Ittala are also offered. Located in the center of Helsinki's most prestigious shopping district, it inventories first-rate household goods by Finland's leading designers. The multilingual staff can arrange for any of your purchases to be mailed home.

Arabia was established in a suburb of Helsinki in 1873. Today its ceramic factories are among the most modern in the world. Arabia's artists create their own works, sometimes in highly collectible limited editions.

Although most visitors buy their goods at the company's main store, Hackman Shop Arabia maintains a small museum and a spacious discount sales area at its factory 5km (3 miles) east of the center at Hämeentie 135 (© 0204/39-35-00). Here, discontinued styles and slightly imperfect seconds are available at significant reductions off the regular prices. To reach the suburban factory, take tram no. 6 to the end of the line or, between June and mid-September, take Arabia's special bus (it's hard to miss, since it's covered with Arabia signs) from a point near the main store. The free bus runs hourly Monday through Saturday from 10am to 4pm. Pohjoisesplanadi 25. © 0204/39-35-01. Tram: 3B.

HANDICRAFTS

Aarikka   This shop carries one of Finland's best selections of gifts, wooden and silver jewelry, and wooden toys. Unusual household utensils, fashioned from wood, are also available. Pohjoisesplanadi 25–27. © 09/65-22-77. Tram: 3B.

Artisaani   Near Market Square, Artisaani is a cooperative of about 20 artisans who sell their own arts and crafts direct from their country workshops. Ceramic sculptures; pottery; glassware; gold, silver, and bronze jewelry; leather goods; printed fabrics, and other textiles are displayed. Unioninkatu 28. © 09/66-52-25. Tram: 3B.

Kalevala Koru   Although this store is best known for its collection of jewelry, it also offers a fine collection of handicrafts and gifts. Its extensive knitwear, in both traditional and modern designs, includes pullovers, caps, and mittens for both men and women. Unioninkatu 25. © 09/17-15-20. Tram: 3B.

Ryijypalavelu   A well-stocked second-floor shop specializing in *ryas* (Finnish woven goods) is operated by the Women's Organization of the Disabled War Veterans' Association, to raise money for Finland's disabled veterans. You can also buy kits for producing the same rugs at home for about one-third the price. Abrahamink 7. © 09/66-06-15. Tram: 6.

Suomen Käsityön Ystävät (Friends of Finnish Handicrafts) *Finds*
Suomen Käsityön Ystävät was founded in 1879 to develop and preserve the traditions of Finnish handicrafts. Some of the designs are more than a century old,
and others, introduced by well-known Finnish artists, are fresh and contemporary. If you want to save money and produce something with your own hands,
you can purchase complete rug and embroidery kits. Here you can see a permanent exhibit of museum-quality *ryijy* tapestries. Textiles, table linens, towels, and
gift items, such as shawls and embroidered work—including early-20th-century
Jugendstil patterns—can be purchased here. Shipping service is available.
Runeberginkatu 40. ✆ **09/612-60-50.** Tram: 3B or 3T.

JEWELRY
Galerie Björn Weckström   Specializing in Lapponia jewelry, as well as sculpture and glass, this store has won the Grand Prix in international jewelry competitions. Björn Weckström has earned a reputation for nature-inspired shapes,
and the jewelry here has been called "miniature sculptures." The glass collection
of bowls, vases, and sculptures sometimes comes in lovely, mysterious colors
whose exact ingredients remain a secret of the manufacturer. Kluuvikatu 4. ✆ **09/
65-65-29.** Tram: 3T.

Kalevala Koru   Founded in 1937, this store is owned by the Association of
Kalevala Women in Finland, whose aim is to preserve the best cultural traditions
of a long-ago Finland. They accomplish this through educational programs and
through sales of the most authentic reproductions of traditional designs and styles
they can find. (See "Handicrafts," above, for some of their offerings.) The name
of their organization is derived from the *Kalevala,* the Finnish national epic.
   The store sells both traditional and modern jewelry in bronze, silver, and
gold. Many of these pieces are based on originals uncovered in archaeological
excavations that date from the 10th and 11th centuries. Each is produced by
some of Finland's foremost artisans. Copies of Lapp jewelry are also sold. The
store cooperates with the Finnish National Museum. Unioninkatu 25. ✆ **09/686-
04-00.** Tram: 3B.

MUSIC
Digelius Music   This store has the best selection of Finnish folk music and
jazz in the country, as well as one of the largest offerings of folk music in Europe
(about 10,000 titles). The store provides mail-order service to customers worldwide. Laivurinrinne 2. ✆ **09/66-63-75.** Tram: 3B or 3T.

Fuga   This is one of the best music stores in Helsinki, with classical recordings
from all over Europe, as well as folk and a smattering of jazz. One of the two
Nuotio brothers can offer advice. Kaisaniemenkatu 7. ✆ **09/700-182-51.** Tram: 2, 3B, or 6.

SAUNA
Sauna Soppi-Shop   Two Finnish women established this shop in 1974
because they believe in the therapeutic and emotional benefits of sauna rituals.
Everything sold here is functionally important to the sauna. They offer buckets,
ladles, thermometers, linen seat covers, washing mitts, loincloths, and even a
sauna "visitors' book." This may be the most complete selection of sauna-related
articles in the world. Eteläranta 14. ✆ **09/668-99-70.** Tram: 3B.

SCULPTURE
Galleria Sculptor   The organization that maintains this store, the Association of Finnish Sculptors, was originally established in 1910. Today it's the

oldest artists' association in Finland, comprising 230 carefully screened members and 200 somewhat less active members. Works exhibited here must be by Finnish members who are living (or deceased within the past 2 years). Sculptures—crafted from wood, bronze, stone, plastic, aluminum, steel, or ceramics—range from small medallions to monumental pieces. Eteläranta 12. ℂ 09/621-63-37. Tram: 3B.

SHOPPING COMPLEXES

Forum Shopping Center   Covering an entire block, the Forum includes 120 shops, restaurants, service enterprises, and a seven-story atrium—making it the number-one shopping center in Finland. You'll find a wide array of merchandise here, including art, gold, jewelry, food, decorating items, clothing, yarns, leather, records, glasses, rugs, watches, and sporting goods. Mannerheimintie 20. Tram: 3B, 3T, 7A, or 7B.

Itäkeskus Shopping Complex   This complex of shops and restaurants opened in 1992 in a residential suburb a 15-minute subway ride east of Helsinki's center. It has some resemblance to an American shopping mall, but the emphasis is on Scandinavian and Finnish merchandise. You'll find at least 180 shops, including about 20 kiosks and food stalls. Itäkeskus. ℂ 09/343-10-05. Metro: Itäkeskus.

Kämp Galleria   This is Helsinki's most desirable shopping arcade, with a cluster of about 50 mostly upscale shops, set close to the newly developed Hotel Kämp. Pohjoisesplanadi 33. Tram: 3B or 3T.

9 Helsinki After Dark

In recent years Helsinki has seen an explosion of nighttime possibilities. Friday and Saturday nights are impossibly overcrowded, so if you plan to go out, you need to show up early at a club, or you may not get in. The older crowd sticks mainly to bars in popular hotels, such as the Scandic Hotel Continental.

Nearly all theatrical performances are presented in Finnish or Swedish. However, music is universal, and the Helsinki cultural landscape is always rich in music whatever the season. The major orchestral and concert performances take place in Finlandia Hall (see "Classical Music & Concerts," below). Operas at the Finnish National Opera are sung in their original languages.

The main agency for theater, concert, and opera tickets is **Ticket Service Finland (Lippupalvelu),** Mannerheimintie 5 (ℂ **0961/38611**), in the center.

Your best source of information—virtually your only source, other than Finnish newspapers—is a little magazine called *Helsinki Guide,* distributed free at most hotels and at the tourist office. It has complete listings, not only of cultural events, but of practically anything that's happening in the Finnish capital—from the Baltic herring market to body-building contests.

THE PERFORMING ARTS
THEATER
Suomen Kansallisteatteri (Finnish National Theater)   The Finnish National Theater enjoys international fame because of its presentations of the classics of Finland and many other countries; each play, however, is performed in Finnish. The theater itself, one of the architectural gems of 19th-century Helsinki, was established in 1872 and stages about 10 premieres a year. Läntinen Teatterikuja 1B. ℂ 09/173-313-31. Tickets 10€–18€. Tram: 3B.

Svenska Teatern (Swedish Theater) If you speak Swedish, you might want to attend a performance at the horseshoe-shaped Swedish Theater, which has been presenting plays since 1866. The theater is in the absolute center of Helsinki, opposite Stockmann Department Store. The theatrical season begins in early September and runs through May. The box office is open Monday from 10am to 6pm, Tuesday through Friday from 10am to 7pm, and Saturday from noon to 7pm. The theater is closed on Sunday. Norra Esplanaden 2. ℭ 09/616-214-11. Tickets 14€–25€. Tram: 3B.

OPERA & BALLET

Finnish National Opera The ballet and opera performances of the Finnish National Opera enjoy international fame. Operas are sung in their original languages. The original Finnish National Opera was built in the 1870s as a Russian garrison theater, but in 1993 the opera house moved to its new home. The ticket office is open Monday through Friday from 9am to 6pm and Saturday from 3 to 6pm. On performance nights, the ticket office stays open until the performance begins. The opera and ballet season runs from September to June. Helsinginkatu 58. ℭ 09/403-022-11. Tickets 10€–77€. Tram: 3B.

CLASSICAL MUSIC & CONCERTS

Helsingin Kaupunginorkesteri (Helsinki Philharmonic Orchestra) The oldest symphony orchestra in Scandinavia performs from September to May in the gracefully modern Finlandia Hall, designed by Alvar Aalto of white Carrara marble. Just a short distance from the town center, it's the musical nerve center of Finland. The box office opens at 6pm, and all concerts begin at 7pm. For information and reservations, call ℭ **09/613-862-46.** Finlandia Hall, Karamzininkatu 4. ℭ **09/402-41.** Tickets 14€–19€. Tram: 3B.

THE CLUB & MUSIC SCENE
NIGHTCLUBS/CABARET

Baker's Family Although it has been reconfigured, redecorated, and reincarnated many times since it was established in 1915, Baker's Family is the most deeply entrenched, long-lived drinking and dining complex in Helsinki. It sprawls across three floors, and on busy nights is crammed with nightclubbers—many of them single. The place sometimes gives the effect of an upscale railway station, where food and drink are dispensed with gusto, dance music plays, and the roulette wheel of a small-stakes casino whirs. Most people come for the cafe, open daily from 7am to 4am, or for one of the bars, open Monday through Saturday from 11am to 2am. If you're hungry, a restaurant (which can be reached through the rest of the complex or from a separate entrance on Kalevankatu 2) serves fish dishes, such as salmon, and meat dishes, such as grilled steaks, Monday through Saturday from 11am to 1am. Fixed-price menus cost 28€. If you want to dance, a club supplies hot music, sometimes Latin-derived, Friday and Saturday from 9pm to 4am. Mannerheimintie 12. ℭ 09/612-63-30. Cover Sept–May only, 2€. Tram: 3B.

Club Cream One of the newest dance clubs in Helsinki, Cream offers two floors of space, two animated bars, lots of night owls under 35 from all Finnish subcultures, and powerful references to whatever's happening in nightlife circles of London and Los Angeles. Thursday night is Latin night; Friday and Saturday, house and garage music reign supreme. The club is open Wednesday through Saturday from 9pm to 4am. Erottajan 7. ℭ 09/680-26-65. Cover 5€. Tram: 3B or 3T.

Hesperia Hotel Nightclub   The largest nightclub in Helsinki fills most of the cellar of a well-known hotel along one of the city's showcase boulevards. Renovated and upgraded in 1998, and outfitted in pale grays with touches of red, it hosts live bands (jazz, rock, soul, blues, or whatever) every Tuesday, Wednesday, and Thursday, and a well-trained DJ every Friday and Saturday, when the focus is on high-energy dancing. No one under 24 is admitted inside, and the revelers range from 24 to around 38 years old. It's open Wednesday through Sunday from 9pm to 2am. In the Radisson SAS Hesperia Hotel Helsinki, Mannerheimintie 50. ℰ 09/431-01. Cover 6€–8€. Tram: 4, 7, or 10.

Storyville   One of the busiest and most active live music venues in Helsinki was named after the fabled red-light district of New Orleans, and as such, focuses on a menu of Creole and Cajun specialties. It occupies the street level and cellar of a building in the heart of town, and has an open-minded policy that offers full restaurant service to anyone who wants it, but doesn't pressure anyone into dining. Full meals average 20€ to 25€ each. More important, live music—blues, jazz, Dixieland, soul, or funk—is heard nightly from 8pm to 3:30am. Museokatu 8. ℰ 09/40-80-07. Cover 6€–8€. Tram: 4, 7, or 10.

Tenth Floor   Set on the uppermost floor of a well-known Helsinki hotel, with an unobtrusive decor and views that stretch over the city, this is one of the capital's most popular and animated dance clubs. Open Monday through Saturday 9pm to 4am, it plays the kind of dance music you might expect in London or Los Angeles. No one under 24 is admitted. Although most of the clients are 24 to 35-ish, some clients in their fifties seem to enjoy the spectacle of the animated dancing from their bar-stool perches. Hotel Vaakuna, Asemaaukio 2. ℰ 09/13-11-81. Cover 6€ Fri–Sat. Tram: 3, 4, 6, 7, or 10.

ROCK

Tavastia Club   The most visible emporium for rock 'n' roll is Tavastia, a battered, all-purpose room whose venue changes with every rock group that performs. Don't expect any semblance of a regularly maintained schedule, as everything is very iffy, depending only on the ability of management to book acts from Finland and abroad, and then on that group's ability to show up on time. It includes everything from heavy metal to blues and soul, and is likely to attract many Finnish students in their early twenties—some of them into punk rock. Local newspapers, plus flyers distributed in counterculture sites throughout the city, publicize this place's upcoming events. Urho Kekkosenk 4–6. ℰ 09/694-30-66. Cover 6€–18€. Tram: 4 or 7.

DANCE CLUBS

Club König   In the restaurant's cellar is a smoky, cramped, and convivial nightclub, the Club König, open Tuesday through Saturday from 9pm to 4am. Clubgoers range in age from 25 to 55, and many of the regular barflies here seem to have known one another forever. Mikonkatu 4. ℰ 09/684-407-13. Tram: 3B or 3T.

Kaarle XII   This is a tried-and-true, much-visited, much-battered nightclub where a congenial crew of locals gets together, gets rowdy, sometimes drinks too much, and often tries to flirt with newcomers. Some of them, according to management, even met their future partners here thanks to chance encounters on otherwise cold Helsinki nights. The most crowded nights, when lines form outside, are Thursday, Saturday and, to a lesser degree, Friday. Named in honor of a long-deceased Swedish king, the club contains a street-level pub, an upstairs dance club, and a total of six bars. The decor is plush, albeit a bit battered, and nostalgic. It's open Tuesday and Wednesday from 4 to 11pm, Thursday through Saturday from 4pm to 3am. Beer costs 4€ per mug. The only food service here is sandwiches dispensed at the bars. Kasarmikatu 40. ℂ 09/612-99-90. Tram: 3B.

THE BAR SCENE
PUBS

Corona Bar for Billiards   Although it has one of the largest collections of pool tables in Helsinki (nine of them, each positioned into a high-energy cluster at the back of the premises), most of the hip young people who gravitate here don't really bother with them. Gathered at the bar near the entrance are lots of actors and writers, most of them under 35, enjoying the raffish and sometimes raucous ambience that might remind you of an urban scene in Los Angeles or New York—except all the characters happen to be Finnish. Pints of beer cost from 4.30€ each; sandwiches are available if you're hungry. If you are interested in actually playing pool, a table rents for 6.50€ to 8.40€ per hour, depending on the time of day. (*Caution:* Some Finns are avid gamblers, so be alert to the possibility that your friendly billiards game with a local might be riskier than you imagined.) The place is open daily from 11am to 2am. Eerikinkatu 11. ℂ 09/ 64-20-02. Tram: 1.

O'Malley's Pub   This cramped, convivial, and gregarious pub—one of the most popular in Helsinki—evokes the spirit, legend, and lore of Ireland, despite the Finnish doorman and clientele. Bar snacks are available, although they appear to be an afterthought to an evening devoted to drinking, more drinking, and animated conversation. Beer costs from 4.70€. O'Malley's is open Monday through Saturday from noon to about 1 or 2am, depending on the night. Live music, usually from an Irish-derived rock band, is presented 2 nights a week, often Monday and Tuesday. In the Sokos Torni Hotel, Yrjönkatu 26. ℂ 09/13-11-31. Tram: 3B.

BARS

Atelier Bar *Finds*   On the top floor of the famous old Sokos Torni Hotel (see "Where to Stay," earlier in this chapter), site of many well-documented episodes of espionage during World War II, this is one of Helsinki's most famous bars, yet many foreign visitors never find it. It welcomes many local artists and writers, who don't seem to mind the cramped space. The walls are decorated with original paintings, some of them by regular patrons. Take the elevator up as far as it will go, but then you must navigate a narrow iron staircase. Drinks cost 8€, and beer prices begin at 4.70€. It's open Monday through Saturday from 3:30pm to 1am and Sunday from 3pm to midnight. In the Sokos Torni Hotel, Yrjönkatu 26. ℂ 09/13-11-31. Tram: 3, 4, or 10.

König Restaurant Bar   Visiting diplomats and the haute bourgeoisie like this landmark restaurant and bar (see "Where to Dine," above). Established in 1892, the bar was designed by Eliel Saarinen, one of Finland's greatest architects. The bar is paneled with wood and sheathed in carefully restored leather wallpaper. Portraits of the most famous patrons of the 1930s hang on the walls (something of a historical gallery of Finland's famous), and the food is relatively inexpensive, considering the poshness of the place. You can come here just to drink, although a bar menu lists such items as club sandwiches and salads priced at 10€ to 15€. It's open Monday through Wednesday from 11:30am to midnight, Thursday and Friday from 11:30am to 1am, and Saturday from 1pm to 1am. Mikonkatu 4. ℂ 09/684-407-13. Tram: 3B or 3T.

The Lobby Bar   On the street level of the Hotel Klaus Kurki, this fashionable bar is vividly scarlet, with formal architectural details and a hanging collection of 19th-century engravings. Find yourself a cubbyhole in the labyrinth of seating arrangements and perhaps order the bartender's special, a "Finnish Marguerita" (Finnish vodka, Cointreau, and lemon juice). The bar is open Monday through Saturday from 4pm to 2am. In the Hotel Klaus Kurki, Bulevardi 2. ℂ 09/61-89-11. Tram: 3B, 3T, or 6.

Palace Bar   It has been suggested that if Betty Grable and Marilyn Monroe were trying to figure out *How to Marry a Millionaire* today, they'd come to this lofty retreat. Now a fashionable bar in a fashionable hotel, this 11th-floor room actually dates from the 1960s when it was originally designed as a men's restroom! Those memories are all but forgotten today in this charming little bar with glowing paneling and nautical accessories. In summer, tables are placed on an outdoor terrace that overlooks the harbor. Special cocktails include Singapore Slings. Drinks cost 8€. The bar is open Monday through Friday from 11am to 1am, and Saturday from 3pm to midnight. In the Palace Hotel, Eteläranta 10. ℂ 09/13-45-61. Tram: 3B. Bus: 16.

GAMBLING CASINOS

Several Helsinki nightclubs have small-stakes casinos—usually just a roulette wheel with an attractive croupier and a deliberately low maximum bet. For more serious action, head directly for Casino Ray (see below).

Casino Ray   This is Finland's only large-stakes casino (although a handful of betting parlors operate on cruise ships in offshore waters). Here, on the second floor of one of the city's largest hotels, maximum bets can range from 2€ to 3,100€ in blackjack, *Punto Banco*, Red Dog, Money Wheel, and roulette; smaller sums can be used in nearly 120 slot machines on the premises. Non-Finns must show their passport at the door and pay a first-time registration fee of 2€ for a weekly casino card. Roulette and blackjack are played daily from noon to 4am; the slot machines are open daily from 2pm to 4am. In the Ramada Presidentti Hotel, Eteläinen Rautatiekatu 4. ℂ 09/68-08-00. Tram: 3B or 3T.

GAY & LESBIAN NIGHTLIFE

Con Hombres   Most of the clientele at this dark but accommodating bar are gay men, and although the energy level might be a bit lower than you might prefer, it's viewed as an important link in the small-scale world of Finnish gay life. You'll almost certainly be able to strike up a dialogue with someone here, at least after the second drink. The place has two bars on a single ground-floor setting: one blue, one green. Literally translated from Spanish, *con hombres* means "with guys" or "among guys." It's open daily from 4pm to 2am. Eerikinkatu 14. ℂ 09/60-88-26. Tram: 3B, 4, 7, or 10.

Don't Tell Mama   This is the largest and most visible gay bar in Finland, with a central location and a two-story format that's painted a Nordic shade of blue. About 80% of the clientele is gay and male; the remaining 20% is for the most part lesbian. Look for two very active and busy bar areas, recorded music, Finns and other Europeans from every walk of life, and a particular emphasis on dance clubbing every Friday and Saturday, the only nights a cover charge is imposed. The bar is open every night from 10pm to 4am. In some ways, this place is the envy of many straight folk who like to dance, as the energy on the dance floor, and the cutting-edge music, is said by insiders to be the best in Helsinki. Annankatu 32. ℂ 09/694-11-22. Cover Fri–Sat 5€. Tram: 1 or 4.

Lost & Found   This is Helsinki's "other" gay bar, although with a higher percentage of straight people than at Don't Tell Mama. You'll find a larger-than-expected dance club that sprawls over two floors, each with a busy bar area and lots of Europeans from outside Finland. It's open nightly from 6pm till around 4am. There's no cover charge, but the coat check will cost you around 1.30€. Annankatu 6. © **09/680-10-10**. Tram: 1 or 4.

Nalle Pub   This was the premier lesbian bar in Helsinki, with a devoted following and a reputation as a rendezvous site for the country's tightly knit network of gay women. Many gay men also like to patronize the place. Set about a half mile north of the city's commercial core, it's open daily from 3pm to 2am, and has an active billiard table, a large bar area, recorded music, and a strong sense of community. Kaarlenkatu 3–5. © **09/701-55-43**. Tram 3, 3B, or 3T.

10 Side Trips from Helsinki

PORVOO (BORGÅ)
48km (30 miles) NE of Helsinki

This colorful hamlet gives visitors a look at what a small town in this area was like a century or so ago—it's the second-oldest town in Finland. Simply strolling the Old Quarter with its narrow, winding streets is a fun way to spend an afternoon.

Founded as a Swedish town in 1346 at the mouth of a river, Porvoo was already an important trading center in the Middle Ages. Even before the town was given its charter, the Swedes had a wooden fortress on a hill that helped control river and sea trade for several centuries. After Sweden finally relinquished Finland to Russia, Porvoo was the site of the first Finnish Diet in the early 19th century, when Tsar Alexander I made the little country a Grand Duchy.

ESSENTIALS
GETTING THERE   The most interesting way to go to Porvoo is on the MS *J. L. Runeberg*, which sails from May 19 to September 1 from Market Square in Helsinki Wednesday through Tuesday only. A round-trip ticket costs 29€ for adults, 13€ for children. For bookings and inquiries, contact **J. L. Runeberg** (© **019/524-33-31**).

VISITOR INFORMATION   The **Porvoo Tourist Office** is at Rihkamakatu 20, SF-06100 Porvoo (© **019/520-23-16**). In summer only, it's open Monday through Friday from 9am to 6pm, and Saturday and Sunday from 10am to 4pm. Otherwise, hours are Monday through Friday from 10am to 4:30pm and Saturday from 10am to 2pm.

SEEING THE SIGHTS
If you arrive in Porvoo by boat, you'll get a good view of the old merchants' houses and warehouses along the waterfront—most dating from the 18th century.

Cathedral of Porvoo   The oldest part of the present granite building dates from the late 13th century or early 14th century. The church has since been plundered and even burned down several times. It became a cathedral in 1723 when the Episcopal see was moved from Viipuri to Porvoo. The church was once attended by Alexander I of Russia.

Kirkkotori. © **019/661-12-50**. Free admission. May–Sept Mon–Fri 10am–6pm, Sat 10am–2pm, Sun 10am–5pm; Oct–Apr Tues–Sat 10am–2pm, Sun 10am–4pm.

Porvoo Museum   This museum's collections are housed in two buildings, the **Historical Museum** in the Old Town Hall and the art collection in the **Edelfelt-Vallgren Museum,** originally a merchant's house. The stone buildings stand on Museum Square (also known as Old Town Hall Square) in the Old Town, and both buildings display artifacts from the 1700s that survived the big fires in 1760 and the 1800s. The art museum also has collections of Finnish Art Nouveau furniture and ceramics.

Valikatu 11. (℡ 019/574-75-89. Admission 5€ adults, 1€ children under 16. May–Aug daily 11am–4pm; Sept–Apr Wed–Sun noon–4pm.

WHERE TO DINE
Wanha Laamanni *(Finds* FINNISH   Originally constructed as a private house near the medieval cathedral, this late Gustavian–style restaurant (whose name translates as "The Old Judge's Chambers") has an 18th-century decor. The chef turns out many excellent Finnish specialties. Begin with such appetizers as Russian blini with roe, or perhaps wild mushrooms in sour cream marinated in cloves of garlic, or even soup (possibly black salsify with sweet pepper). Main dishes include Baltic herring stewed in sour cream, a delectable grilled salmon with wild-mushroom sauce, and filet of beef in a green-pepper and beet-root sauce.

Vuorikatu 17. (℡ 019/523-04-55. Reservations recommended. Main courses 15€–22€. AE, DC, MC, V. Summer daily 11am–11pm; off season Mon–Fri 11am–10pm, Sat–Sun noon–8pm.

HYVINKÄÄ
56km (35 miles) N of Helsinki

This young town, chartered in 1960, is visited chiefly because of its Finnish Railway Museum (see below). Only 56km (35 miles) north of Helsinki, Hyvinkää can be reached by "H train," which leaves twice an hour from Helsinki's Central Station, and by car, which takes an hour on Route 3. Buses bearing the sign HYVINKÄÄ also arrive here from the Helsinki bus station.

This rapidly growing industrial and commercial center is in a very scenic part of Finland. Visitors can walk through **Hyvinkää Sveitsi,** the "Switzerland of Hyvinkää," a park within walking distance of the center of town, which has marked and lit walking paths and skiing tracks of various lengths. It also has a jogging track and ski slopes and jumps.

Hyvinkää's connection with the railway dates from 1862, when the link was added between Hämeenlinna and Helsinki. This railway culture is preserved in the **Finnish Railway Museum,** in the center of town at Hyvinkäänkatu 9 (℡ 03/072-52-41). The museum is housed in the original railway buildings dating from the 1870s. Exhibits include the oldest steam engine preserved in Finland, *Passi,* from 1868; Finland's oldest rail car, a Fiat from 1914; and a model railway, the largest of its kind in the country. But our favorite exhibit is a three-coach imperial train dating from the 1870s. Built for the Russian tsar, the imperial coach train originally consisted of five coaches: two for the tsar and tsarina, a saloon, a dining room, and a kitchen. It's open from June to August 15 daily from 11am to 5pm; otherwise, Tuesday through Saturday from noon to 3pm and Sunday from noon to 5pm. Admission is 6€ for ages 16 and over, 2€ for ages 7 to 15, and free for children 6 and under.

HÄMEENLINNA ⚓
98km (61 miles) N of Helsinki

Finland's oldest town (founded in 1639), Hämeenlinna (Tavastehus in Swedish) is one of the starting points for **cruises** on the Silja Line vessels (Suomen

Hopealinja), which run to Tampere or along the scenic route to the ridge of Kangasala. Hämeenlinna is also the starting point for a series of 1-day cruises, the most popular of which goes to the Aulanko Tourist Center and to sculptor Emil Wikström's studio museum, Visavuori. If you go on one of these cruises, your car can be driven by the car-pilot service to await your arrival.

The **Hämeenlinna City Tourist Information Office,** Sibeliuksenkatu 5A (© **03/621-33-73**), is open from June to August, Monday through Friday from 9am to 5pm and Saturday from 9am to 2pm; from September to May, Monday through Friday from 9am to 5pm.

SEEING THE SIGHTS

The large park at **Aulanko,** about 4km (2½ miles) from the center of town, is one of the best-known tourist centers in Finland. Here you'll find a hotel (see "Where to Stay," below), a panoramic tower, tennis courts, a golf course, and a bathing beach.

Häme Castle   Häme Castle dominates the town. Construction has been going on here for 700 years. The oldest sections date from the 1260s and are known as the fortified camp, including a square gray-stone wall with defensive towers at three corners. Once the residence of mighty nobles, the castle later became a strictly supervised outpost of the Swedish Crown. As the years went by, it served as both a granary and a prison. The main castle is now a historic monument. It houses exhibits and rents out its facilities for meetings and celebrations. There's also a summer cafe and a restaurant that can be booked for events in advance.

Kustaa III Katu 6. © **03/675-68-20.** Admission 4€ adults, 2.50€ children 7–17, free for children under 7. May to mid-Aug daily 10am–6pm; mid-Aug to Apr daily 10am–4pm. Bus: 5 or 12 from the marketplace.

Sibelius Birthplace   The great composer Jean Sibelius was born at Hämeen-linna on December 8, 1865, in this wooden house. It stands in the center of town, about 45m (150 ft.) from the marketplace. The museum is also the setting for small chamber concerts and sells recordings of Sibelius's music.

Hallituskatu 11. © **03/621-27-55.** Admission 3€ adults, 1€ students and children 7 and over, free for children under 7. May–Aug daily 10am–4pm; Sept–Apr daily noon–4pm.

WHERE TO STAY

Hotel Cumulus   Next to the main commercial street of the town, within walking distance of Kauppatori (Market Square), this early 1970s concrete-and-glass hotel has comfortable rooms with good beds and small bathrooms (mostly with showers and tubs), plus an attractive Finnish restaurant, Hubiretky. You can book a nonsmoking room, but you must specifically request it when making your reservations.

Raatihuoneenkatu 16–18, FIN-13100 Hämeenlinna (Aulanko). © **03/648-81.** Fax 03/648-82-99. 100 units. June 16–Aug 2 and Fri–Sun year-round 79€ double; rest of year 119€ double. Rates include breakfast and evening use of sauna. Children 13 and under stay free in parent's room with existing bedding. Additional bed 21€ extra. AE, DC, MC, V. Free parking. Bus: 2 or 13. **Amenities:** Restaurant; bar; nightclub; pool; 2 saunas; room service; babysitting; laundry/dry cleaning. *In room:* A/C, TV, minibar, hair dryer.

Rantasipi Aulanko ★ *Finds*   This name is instantly recognizable throughout Finland because of the hotel's location in one of the country's best-known nature preserves. The hotel has been enlarged many times since it was originally built in the 1930s. It sits at the edge of Vanajavesi Lake near a sweep of open grassland surrounded by forested hillsides. Each room has an open-air balcony. Rooms for the most part are medium in size and functionally furnished. Bathrooms, though small, are beautifully maintained and equipped with shower-tub combinations. On weekends year-round the dining room is likely to be over-flowing. On the premises are a labyrinth of walking paths, a lakeside bathing beach, and riding stables. In winter, cross-country skiing is popular. The hotel, a venue for important conferences, lies at the end of a series of prominent signs in Aulanko Park, about 5km (3 miles) north of the train station at Hämeenlinna.

FIN-13210 Hämmenlinna (Aulanko). ℰ 03/65-88-01. Fax 03/219-22. www.rantasipi.fi. 50 units. June 15–Aug 15 and selected weekends (Fri–Sun) 89€ double; rest of year 144€ double. Year-round 200€–420€ suite. Rates include breakfast and morning use of sauna. AE, DC, MC, V. Free parking. Bus: 2 or 13. **Amenities:** Restaurant; bar; pool; 18-hole golf course; 4 tennis courts; fitness center; 4 saunas; room service; babysitting; laundry/dry cleaning. *In room:* TV, minibar, hair dryer.

WHERE TO DINE

Restaurant Piparkakkutalo ✧ INTERNATIONAL   The town's most charming restaurant, adjacent to the village church, occupies a historic manor house built during the 19th century. The building's name (Piparkakkutalo) translates from the Finnish as "the gingerbread cookie" because of its lavish ornamentation. The same menu is offered on both floors of the restaurant, but somehow the upstairs dining room has the distinction of being called "The Bistro." You can come here for flank steak with onions, chateaubriand, or pepper steak, but when in this part of the world, you should try something more exotic like Lappish reindeer with juniper-berry sauce. A recent pasta dish of tagliatelle with a cream and herb sauce was succulent. We followed the advice of some of the habitués and opted for a main course of sautéed pike-perch—and were glad we did. For a more raucous and sudsy time, consider dropping into O'Maggie's pub, an ode to Irish nationalism in the building's cellar. Here, foamy mugs of beer are priced according to their alcohol content, and a limited pub menu is available.

In the Piparkakkutalo "Gingerbread" House, Kirkkorinne 2. ℰ 03/64-80-40. Reservations recommended. Main courses 8€–21€. AE, MC, V. Mon–Fri 11am–midnight; Sat noon–10pm; Sun noon–11pm. Basement-level pub Sun–Thurs 3pm–midnight, Fri–Sat 3pm–2am.

KOTKA
134km (83 miles) E of Helsinki

The **Langinkoski Imperial Fishing Lodge** ✧✧✧, Langinkoski (ℰ 05/228-33-00), about 5km (3 miles) north of Kotka, was the imperial fishing lodge of the Russian tsar's family, the summer retreat for Alexander III from 1889 to 1894. This log house on the River Kymi offers an insight into how the last of the Romanovs lived their summers before they met violent deaths during the Russian Revolution. Near the Langinkoski Rapids (for which it was named), the lodge is open from May to September only, daily from 10am to 7pm; admission is 4€.

The tsar chose a spot in Finland's premier salmon-fishing area to build the lodge (in 1889) on property consisting of half a dozen small islands connected by bridges. Its deliberately unpretentious architecture was in the Finnish style of hand-hewn pine logs, far removed from the grandeur of the family's 900-room palace outside St. Petersburg.

Information is available from the **Kotka Tourist Office,** Kyrkokatu 8 (ℰ 05/234-44-24), open from June to August, Tuesday through Friday from 9am to 7pm and Saturday from 10am to 7pm; from September to May, Monday through Friday from 9am to 5pm. If you drive, Kotka is a 2-hour trip from Helsinki. Five buses leave Helsinki daily, traveling to Kotka in 2 hours. Once at the bus station at Kotka, you can take bus no. 12, 13, or 14 to the lodge at Langinkoski.

Appendix A:
Denmark in Depth

The Danes live in a small country, but they extend a big welcome to visitors. Americans and Canadians, as well as their longtime friends, the British, are enthusiastically greeted—in English. Denmark is an important stopover for any travelers who want to say you've seen the best of Europe.

Made up mostly of islands, Denmark is a heavily industrialized nation, known for its manufactured products as well as its arts and crafts. It also boasts a quarter of a million farmers.

The British novelist Evelyn Waugh (author of *Brideshead Revisited*) called the Danes "the most exhilarating people of Europe." Few Danes would dispute that—and neither would we.

1 Denmark Today

Denmark has been called a bridge because it links northern Europe with the Scandinavian peninsula. In 2000 that became truer than ever when the Øresund Bridge was completed, connecting the island of Zealand, on which Copenhagen sits, with southern Sweden and the city of Malmö, for the first time in history.

The smallest of the Scandinavian countries, Denmark has a total landmass of about 26,700 sq. km (16,600 sq. miles), most of which is on the peninsula of Jutland (bordering Germany). The major islands are Zealand, Funen, and Bornholm. Denmark has adequate space for its 5.5 million or so residents, but its population density is much greater than that of the other Scandinavian countries. About 1.4 million Danes live in the capital city, Copenhagen, on the island of Zealand.

Only about 4.5% of Denmark's inhabitants are immigrants, primarily from other Nordic or European nations. About 98% of all Danes belong to the state church (Danish Lutheran), although church attendance is low. The second-largest group is Catholics (30,000), and there are about 6,500 Jews.

Technically, Denmark is a parliamentary democracy and constitutional monarchy. Its territories include the Faeroe Islands (an autonomous area) and Greenland (which was granted regional autonomy in 1985). The sovereign is Queen Margrethe II, who ascended to the throne in 1972; her husband is a Frenchman, Prince Henrik. Margrethe is the first female sovereign in Denmark in 6 centuries. Real power is vested in the unicameral parliament (the Folketing), which is elected every 4 years by all citizens over the age of 23. The royal family functions primarily in a ceremonial capacity.

Although it has been a NATO member since 1949, Denmark does not permit nuclear weapons to be deployed on its soil. Denmark became the first NATO country to grant women the right to serve in front-line units. Denmark enjoys harmonious relations with its Scandinavian neighbors and other European countries. It's also an active member of the European Union, but not part of the "euro blanket," having voted in September 2000 to retain the Danish kroner.

Denmark enjoys one of the world's highest standards of living and has a comprehensive social welfare system, which is funded through extremely high taxes.

> (*Fun Fact* **Did You Know?**
>
> • Denmark is a nation of nearly 500 islands.
> • The reigning queen, Margrethe II, designs postage stamps and opera and ballet sets.
> • The writings of Hans Christian Andersen are the second most widely translated literary works in the world (after the Bible).
> • Some historians argue that the fairy-tale writer Andersen wasn't the son of a poor cobbler, but the child of Christian VIII.
> • Denmark has the largest proportion of female clerics per population.
> • The country has a celebration honoring America's Fourth of July.

Danes enjoy 7½-hour work days, cradle-to-grave security, state-funded hospitals and schools, and even a month-long annual vacation. During vacations, they tend to travel extensively. The Danes tend to be extremely well educated; they pioneered the establishment of adult education centers (for those ages 18–35), a movement that has spread to other European countries.

Although a progressive, modern, and liberal state (it was the first country to recognize same-sex marriage), Denmark has its share of problems, including high unemployment. The institution of marriage is increasingly rejected by the young, so common-law relationships are becoming the norm. The divorce rate is rising, too.

The "melancholy Dane" aspect of their character (if there is one) is reflected in a relatively high suicide rate. Otherwise, their general state of health is excellent—a Danish girl born today has a life expectancy of 78 years; a Danish boy, 72 years.

Culturally, Denmark is a world leader; its citizens are eager media consumers and avid readers. Even though it's a small country, Denmark publishes some 12,000 books a year. There are 42 newspapers; and the theater and film industries are thriving in spite of cutbacks in government funding.

On June 14, 1998, Queen Margrethe II cut a ribbon before driving across the Great Belt Bridge, a span that links the island of Zealand (on which Copenhagen sits) with the island of Funen. Because Funen is linked by bridge to Jutland (part of mainland Europe), Copenhageners can now drive to Germany without having to rely on ferries. Traveling time across the "Belt" has been cut by more than 1 hour compared to traveling time by ferry.

2 The Natural Environment

Denmark has more than 7,240km (4,500 miles) of irregular coastline and is linked geologically with northern Europe. It's a low-lying country—its highest elevation is only 170m (565 ft.) above sea level. But that doesn't mean the country is flat. Most of its terrain consists of folds; undulations; small and often steep hills; and long, low rises. There are also forests, small rivers, lakes, and even beaches. Many are excellent for swimming, although the water may be too cold for some people.

The west coast of Jutland is on the North Sea, but it's not suitable for exploration by ship because it's obstructed by sand dunes and small sand banks. "Island hills" that rise from sandy plains represent the oldest glacial terrain in Denmark. Much of this landscape was formed during the last Ice Age, when icebergs carved the country into its present shape. The east coast of Jutland has fjords (such as Lim and Mariager), but they lack the drama of those on Norway's west coast. Denmark's longest river is the 130km (80-mile) Gudenå, which rises in north-central Jutland and feeds into Lake Lanso on the eastern side of the peninsula.

Winters in Denmark tend to be mild along the North Sea coast and harsh in the interior of Jutland. In general, eastern Denmark receives more precipitation than the west; in the winter, that situation is reversed.

In the east, Denmark opens toward the Baltic Sea, which surrounds its small offshore island of Bornholm. Bornholm's flora differs from that found elsewhere in the country.

Denmark's vegetation resembles that of the Continent. The woods in southern Denmark are largely deciduous, with oak and birch forests. Major reforestation is underway, especially with coniferous forests, mostly pine and spruce. The most beautiful beech forests are on the island of Møn.

Humans and agriculture have reduced the living space for Denmark's native fauna, but roe, red deer, badgers, and foxes are still found. Fallow deer are widely scattered throughout the country. Birders can spot woodpeckers, robins, tits, chaffinches, and song thrushes in the Danish wetlands, which survive more or less in their natural state. The best place for bird-watching is near the Limfjord in northern Jutland.

Denmark, a leader among environmentally conscious nations, has set aside 3.5% of its landmass as a protected nature reserve. That includes Rebild National Park in northern Jutland, the chalk cliffs of Møn, and the tidal sands off the west coast of Jutland—one of the world's most valued wetlands.

3 History 101

The first recorded Danish king was Godfred, who died in 810. Little is known about him except that he played a significant role in halting the Frankish conquests of the Holy Roman Emperor Charlemagne. Godfred's successor, Hemming, made a treaty marking the Eider River as Denmark's southern border. It remained the border until 1864.

Two famous kings emerged in the 10th century: Gorm (883–940) and his son, Harald Bluetooth (940–85). They united Denmark, establishing its center at Jelling. Harald also introduced Christianity, which became the predominant religion.

Harald conquered Norway and attempted to conquer England. Harald's son, Sweyn I, took over England in 1013. Under Sweyn's son, Canute II (994–1035), England, Denmark, and part of Sweden came under the rule of one crown. After Canute's

Dateline

- 810 The reign of the first Danish king ends.
- 940–85 Harald Bluetooth brings Christianity to Denmark.
- 1013–42 The crowns of Denmark and England are united.
- 1397 The Union of Kalmar unites Denmark, Norway, and Sweden.
- 1471 Sweden bows out; Denmark and Norway are ruled by Christian I (1426–81).
- 1530 Lutheran preachers bring the Reformation to Denmark.
- 1577–1648 The long reign of Christian IV brings prosperity but ends in a losing war with Sweden.
- 1814 Denmark cedes Norway to Sweden.
- 1866 Denmark loses Schleswig-Holstein to Prussia.
- 1915 A new constitution gives Denmark universal suffrage.
- 1933 Denmark gains all of Greenland.
- 1940–45 Denmark is invaded and occupied by Nazi Germany.

death, however, the kingdom was reduced to just Denmark. Canute's nephew, Sweyn II, ruled the Danish kingdom, and upon his death his five sons governed Denmark successively.

The Holy Roman Empire was the "overlord" of Denmark until the Danes established independent leadership under Archbishop Eskil (1100–82) and King Waldemar I (1131–82). The monarchy was strong. During a celebration at Ringsted in 1190, church and state were united. Bishop Absalon (1128–1201), a soldier and statesman, is credited with restoring Danish political and ecclesiastical independence from German influences.

Waldemar II (1170–1241) helped strengthen the Danish government. His son, Eric IV (1216–50), succeeded him as king, but argued with his brothers and the church. Eric's brother, Duke Abel of Schleswig, proclaimed himself king and assassinated Eric in 1250. Civil wars ensued, and three of the four successive kings were killed in battle. Eric VI (1274–1319) also waged war with Norway and Sweden, which led to Denmark's debilitation. Between 1332 and 1340, Denmark had no king and was ruled by nobles. Waldemar IV Atterdag (1320–75) became king by signing the peace treaty of Stralsund in 1370.

- **1949** Over some protests, Denmark joins NATO.
- **1953** A new constitution provides for a single-chamber parliament.
- **1972** Denmark joins the European Economic Community; Margrethe, daughter of Frederik IX, becomes queen of Denmark.
- **1982** Paul Schluter becomes the first Conservative prime minister since 1894.
- **1989** Denmark becomes the first NATO country to allow women in front-line military units, and the first country to recognize same-sex marriages.
- **1992** Denmark votes against the Maastricht Treaty, which established the framework for the European Economic Union.
- **1993** Denmark resists the European Union for the first half of the year, then reverses its position and votes to support the Maastricht Treaty.
- **1996** Copenhagen is designated the "Cultural Capital of Europe." The "Copenhagen 96" festival attracts artists and performers from all over the world, with more than 25,000 performances staged.
- **1998** By a narrow margin, Denmark votes to enlarge its ties with the European Union.
- **2000** Danes vote against the euro; Øresund Bridge links the island of Zealand (Copenhagen) with Sweden.

UNITED SCANDINAVIA   After Waldemar IV died in 1375, the dynasty was left without a male heir. Olaf, his grandson, succeeded him as king. Olaf helped unite the crowns of Denmark and Norway and inherited the Swedish throne. He was the son of Margaret (1353–1412), daughter of Waldemar and wife of Haakon VI Magnusson (1339–80), king of Norway. Margaret actually ruled the country as regent. When both Haakon and Olaf died, she was acknowledged as queen of Norway and Denmark. An ambitious woman, she wanted to rule Sweden as well.

The Union of Kalmar came about in 1397. Margaret arranged for her nephew, Eric of Pomerania (1382–1459), to be crowned king of all three countries as Eric VII. Margaret, however, continued to rule until her death.

Eric VII had no heirs, so he tried to pass the kingdom on to one of his relatives in Pomerania. That didn't please the nobility, and he was dethroned in 1439. The Danish Privy Council chose Christopher of Bavaria (Eric's nephew) to become king in 1440.

Upon Christopher III's death, Sweden pressed for autonomy. It elected Charles VIII as king in 1471, and Denmark and Norway took a joint king, Christian I (1426–81).

THE 16TH CENTURY   The unpopular Christian II (1481–1559) ascended the throne in 1513. Having no faith in democracy, he turned over control of the kingdom's finances to his mistress's mother. He recaptured Sweden in 1520 but was defeated a year later by Gustavus Vasa. Christian was deposed in 1522 and fled to the Netherlands.

His successor, Frederik I (1471–1533), signed a charter granting the nobility many privileges. Upon Frederik's death, the Reformation took hold in Denmark. Conflicts between Lutherans and Catholics erupted in a civil war, which ended in 1536 with the surrender of Copenhagen. The Danish Lutheran Church was founded in 1536 during the reign of Christian III (1534–59), who tried—but failed—to make the crown hereditary. Frederik II, Christian's son, was elected in 1559. Frederik launched a war against Eric XIV of Sweden, during a territorial dispute over Baltic provinces. This became the Seven Years' War of the North (1563–70), in which the Danes were overwhelmed.

WARS WITH SWEDEN   Hostilities with Sweden continued, but the reign of Christian IV (1577–1648) was one of relative prosperity. Christiania (now Oslo) was named after him. However, in the closing years of his reign, Sweden invaded Jutland, defeating the Danes. Under the Treaty of Christianople, Denmark was forced to cede many of its possessions to Sweden.

Frederik III (1609–70) tried to regain the lost territories when Sweden went to war with Poland, but Charles X defeated him. Frederik ended up giving Sweden additional territory. Charles X attacked Denmark in an attempt to control the whole country, but this time Denmark won, regaining its lost territories. Sweden ended the war upon the death of Charles X in 1660.

Christian V (1646–99) started the Skaane War (1675–79), in which Denmark attempted to acquire additional territory, but it lost. Frederik IV (1671–1730), his successor, resumed the war with Sweden in 1699. Named the "Great Northern War," it raged from 1699 to 1730.

During the 18th century Denmark achieved many reforms; it also gained control of colonies in the West Indies (now the U.S. Virgin Islands) and Greenland. Agriculture and trade prospered.

THE 19TH CENTURY   At the start of the Napoleonic wars, Denmark was neutral. In 1801 England destroyed the Danish fleet in Copenhagen, forcing Denmark to choose Napoleon's side. It was a disaster for Denmark. Napoleon lost the war in 1814, and peace was made at Kiel. Denmark was forced to yield Norway to Sweden and Heligoland, an island in the North Sea, to England. Denmark sank into poverty.

Following the Napoleonic wars, the rulers Frederik VI and Christian VIII formed conservative governments. In 1848 the Danes demanded a more liberal constitution. Absolute rule was abolished, and Frederik VII established a government based on representation. The Danish constitution was signed on June 5, 1849.

In March 1848 the Schleswig-Holstein revolution began, leading to conflict with Prussia. It lasted 2 years. The Danes initially triumphed over Prussia, but in the 1866 Treaty of Prague, Denmark lost Schleswig-Holstein to Prussia.

On July 28, 1866, a new constitution was adopted, but it was more conservative than the 1849 document. The Conservatives quickly gained power, instituting reforms and improving the economy.

THE 20TH CENTURY   When World War I broke out, Denmark remained neutral. However, the Danes mined their waters for Germany. Denmark joined the other Scandinavian countries and adopted a uniform trade policy in November 1914. Unemployment and higher taxes marked the war years. A new constitution was signed on June 5, 1915, establishing a two-chamber parliament and granting equal voting rights to men and women. Because Germany lost the war, many people felt that all of Schleswig should be returned to Denmark, but ultimately it got only North Schleswig.

Iceland and Denmark agreed to a new treaty in 1918. Although separate sovereign states, the two countries were united under one king. The Danish armed forces represented Iceland.

Denmark participated in the creation of the League of Nations and officially joined it in 1920. A crisis arose in 1921 when Norway claimed jurisdiction over the territory of Greenland. On April 5, 1933, the Permanent Court of International Justice granted Denmark sovereignty over Greenland.

In May 1939, Hitler asked Denmark to sign a nonaggression pact. Denmark accepted; Norway and Sweden did not. The pact specified that Denmark and Germany would not go to war with each other for 10 years. When war broke out in 1939, Denmark declared its neutrality. Denmark's ties with Iceland were severed, and the United States and Great Britain occupied Greenland and the Faeroe Islands, respectively.

Despite the pact, Nazi forces invaded and occupied Denmark in 1940. In 1943 Hitler sent Gen. Hermann von Hanneken to impose martial law on Denmark. The heroic Danish resistance opposed the German occupying forces. When Germany surrendered in 1945, British troops occupied Denmark. Denmark joined the United Nations.

After the war, the Liberal Party, under Knud Kristensen, assumed control. In 1947 Kristensen resigned. The Social Democratic Party, under Hans Hedtoft, headed the new government under Frederik IX. The economy remained sluggish until 1948.

In 1949 Denmark joined NATO. In 1953 Denmark, Norway, Sweden, and Iceland formed the Scandinavian Council; it lasted until 1961. Also in 1953, Denmark adopted a new constitution, which provided for a single-chamber parliament.

In 1972 Denmark became the sole Nordic member of the European Economic Community. That year, Queen Margrethe, born in 1940 (the year of the Nazi invasion), became queen of Denmark upon the death of her father, Frederik IX.

In 1982 Denmark seemed to abandon its long-cherished liberalism when it elected Paul Schuler its first Conservative prime minister since 1894. However, by 1989 Denmark was leading the world in the development of a liberal social agenda. It became the first NATO country to allow women to join front-line military units. Later, it became the first country to recognize marriages between partners of the same sex.

The early 1990s were dominated by Denmark's continuing debate over its role (or lack of it) in the European Union. In 1992 Denmark rejected the Maastricht Treaty, which had established a framework for the European Economic Union. However, in a 1993 referendum Denmark reversed its position, voting to support the Maastricht Treaty and the country's limited involvement in it. Denmark presided over the European Union for the first part of that year.

Also in 1993, Denmark observed the 50th anniversary of the rescue of 8,000 of its Jewish citizens, who were smuggled out of the country into neutral Sweden virtually overnight. That year the Tivoli Gardens celebrated its 150th year, and *The Little Mermaid* turned 80.

In 1996 Copenhagen was named the "Cultural Capital of Europe." Following in the footsteps of Athens, Florence, Paris, and Madrid, Copenhagen celebrated with a year-long festival; exhibitions, performances, community events, and environmental programs attracted artists from around the world. The city staged more than 25,000 performances. A massive campaign of restoration and new construction revitalized the city.

In May 1998, Denmark conducted a referendum on extending its ties and connections with the European Union (EU). In a tight race, Denmark, including the North Atlantic territories of Greenland and the Faeroe Islands, voted for enlargement of its position within the EU. But the margin was so narrow that it indicated how divided Danes remain on this important issue.

THE 21ST CENTURY   Two major events occurred in the Danish republic in 2000, each expected to have far-reaching implications for the tiny nation.

It made headlines across Europe in the summer of 2000 when the Øresund Bridge officially opened, linking Sweden and Denmark. The 16km (10-mile) motor and railway link, on which construction began in the summer of 1995, gives the island of Zealand (the eastern part of Denmark) and Skåne (the southern part of Sweden) a shared bridge, serving some 3½ million inhabitants in the area.

The Øresund region, which encompasses parts of both Sweden and Denmark, is the largest domestic market in northern Europe—larger than Stockholm and equal in size to Berlin, Hamburg, and Amsterdam combined. Built at a cost of $3 billion, it is the largest combined rail/road tunnel in the world. The price of a one-way fare in a passenger car is $30.

In theory, a vehicle can now travel in roughly a straight line from the Arctic coast of Norway to the Mediterranean shores of Spain. For centuries, it has been a dream to link the continent from its northern tip to its southern toe. The "Øresund Fixed Link" spans Øresund Sound between the cities of Copenhagen and Malmö.

Already the Danes, who like nicknames, have called the new span "The Beer Bridge." Denmark has cheaper prices and lower taxes than Sweden for alcoholic beverages, which sends many a Swedish motorist across the bridge to avail themselves of the lower tariffs.

The double-decker bridge, with a four-lane highway on top, plus a train link underneath, arches like a ribbon for about 8km (5 miles) over the water before descending to a nearly 3km (2-mile) long artificial island. From that point it drops beneath the sound into a tunnel at the Danish side.

In September 2000, a majority of Danes voted "no" on adopting the euro, the single currency of the European Union of which Denmark is a member. That "no" vote is expected to deter Britain and Sweden (two other EU countries) from participating. In Sweden, officials predicted that the Danish "no" could postpone their own entry into the euro zone indefinitely. Prime Minister Tony Blair predicted in London that the Danish vote would have no impact on Britain, but polls show public opinion hardening against the euro.

Supporters of the euro in Denmark claimed that their participation would help maintain Denmark's influence in Europe and perhaps gain the country a seat at the European Central Bank, which sets monetary police for the euro zone. Already Denmark pegs its kroner to the euro.

Opponents of the euro maintained successfully that Danish participation would end the country's independence, hasten the developing of an all-encompassing "superstate" of Europe, and eventually consume the identity of the little Danish nation.

Danes have been re-examining their political system as well, which some suggest is no longer workable or tenable. Currently, many small political parties join themselves into a series of politically expedient coalitions as the need arises. Some propose a merging of several small splinter groups into a smaller number of more powerful parties.

Denmark also bears the unusual problems of an economy that's one of the most affluent in the world. Despite an awesomely high standard of living, life in Denmark does not come without fiscal fears and neuroses. Families are burdened under a national debt that's equivalent to around 69,000DKK per person; as a result, living standards are beginning to decline, subtly but inexorably.

Under pressure from growing foreign competition, Danish industry increasingly faces the need to streamline. Welfare payments, health services, and the quality of education have felt the strain of government cutbacks and austerity programs. As a result, racist condemnations of newly arrived immigrants from Asia and Africa have flared up, causing insiders to question the degree to which Denmark is really the ultra-liberal, ultra-secure nation everyone always assumed it was.

4 Dining with the Danes

Danish food is the best in Scandinavia—in fact, it's among the best in Europe.

Breakfast is usually big and hearty, just right before a day of sightseeing. It usually consists of homemade breads, Danish cheeses, and often a boiled egg or salami. In most establishments you can order bacon and eggs. However, you may prefer simply a continental breakfast of Danish *wienerbrød* (pastry) and coffee. The "Danish" is moist, airy, and rich.

The favorite dish at midday, the ubiquitous *smørrebrød* (open-faced sandwiches), is a national institution. It means "bread and butter," but the Danes stack it as though it were the Leaning Tower of Pisa. Then they throw in a slice of curled cucumber and bits of parsley, or perhaps sliced peaches or a mushroom for color.

Two of these sandwiches can make a more-than-filling lunch. They're seen everywhere, from the grandest dining rooms to the lowliest pushcart. In restaurants, guests look over a checklist and mark the ones they want. Some are made with sliced pork (perhaps with a prune on top), roast beef with béarnaise sauce and crispy fried bits of onion, or liver paste adorned with an olive or cucumber slice and gelatin made from strong beef stock.

Smørrebrød is often served as an hors d'oeuvre. The most popular, most tempting, and usually most expensive of these delicacies is prepared with a mound of tiny Danish shrimp, on which a lemon slice and caviar often perch, perhaps with fresh dill. The "ugly duckling" of the smørrebrød family is anything with a cold sunny-side-up egg on top.

At dinner, the Danes tend to keep farmers' hours. Eating at 6:30pm is common, although restaurants remain open much later. Many main dishes are familiar to North Americans, but they're prepared with a distinct Danish flourish—for example, *lever med løg* (liver and fried onions), *bøf* (beef in a thousand different ways), *lammesteg* (roast lamb), or that old reliable, *flaeskesteg med rødkål* (roast pork with red cabbage).

Danish chefs are especially noted for fresh fish dishes. Tiny Danish shrimp, *rejer*, are splendid; herring and kippers are also greeted with enthusiasm.

Favorites include *rodspaette* (plaice), *laks* (salmon), *makrel* (mackerel), and *kogt torsk* (boiled cod).

Danish cheese may be consumed at any meal, then eaten again on a late-night smørrebrød at the Tivoli. Danish blue is already familiar to most people. For something softer and milder, try havarti.

Danish specialties that are worth sampling include *frikadeller* (meatballs or rissoles prepared in various ways); an omelet with a rasher of bacon covered with chopped chives and served in a skillet; and hamburger patties topped with fried onions and coated with rich brown gravy.

Two great desserts are apple Charlotte, best when decorated with whipped cream, dried bread crumbs, and chopped almonds; and *rødgrød med fløde*—basically a jellied fruit-studded juice, served with thick cream.

Carlsberg or Tuborg beer is Denmark's national beverage. A bottle of Pilsner costs about half the price of the stronger export beer with the fancy label. Value-conscious Danes rely on the low-priced *fadøl* (draft beer); visitors on a modest budget might want to do the same.

You may gravitate more toward aquavit (schnapps), which comes from the city of Aalborg in northern Jutland. The Danes, who usually drink it at mealtime, follow it with a beer chaser. It should only be served icy cold.

For those with daintier tastes, the world-famous Danish liqueur, Cherry Heering, is a delightful drink; it can be consumed anytime except with meals.

Appendix B:
Norway in Depth

The "Land of the Midnight Sun" is a special experience. Norwegians view their scrub-covered islands, snow-crested peaks, and glacier-born fjords as symbols of a wilderness culture. The majestic scenery inspired the symphonies of Grieg, the plays of Ibsen, and the paintings of Munch. The landscape has also shaped the Norwegians' view of themselves as pastoral dwellers in one of the world's most splendid countrysides.

The name Norway (in Norwegian, *Norge* or *Noreg*) is derived from *Norvegr,* meaning "the way to the north." The Vikings used the term more than 1,000 years ago to describe the shipping route along the west coast of Norway. Norwegians have been seafarers since the dawn of history, so it seems natural for the country to have a nautical name.

To the ancients, Norway was a mythical land. A journey there held unspeakable perils. Writers called the mythical land "Ultima Thule," and feared that it was inhabited by strange, barbaric, even fabulous creatures. In the 4th century B.C., the Greek writer Pytheas thought the laws of nature did not apply there, and said that everything—water and earth included—floated in midair. In what may have been an attempt to describe a snowstorm, Herodotus claimed that in Norway feathers covered everything and constantly blew into one's face.

Norway is a land of tradition, exemplified by its rustic stave churches and its folk dances. But Norway is also modern. It's a technologically advanced nation, rich in petroleum and hydroelectric energy. Norwegians also enjoy a well-developed national social insurance system that provides pensions, health insurance, unemployment insurance, and rehabilitation assistance. The system is financed by contributions from the insured, which makes Norway one of the most heavily taxed nations on earth.

One of the last great natural frontiers of the world, Norway invites exploration, with its steep and jagged fjords, salmon-filled rivers, glaciers, mountains, and meadows. In the winter, the shimmering aurora borealis (northern lights) are the lure, before giving way to the midnight sun of summer.

1 Norway Today

The long, narrow country stretches some 1,770km (1,100 miles) north to south, but rarely more than 95km (60 miles) east to west. Norway is a land of raw nature. It occupies the western and extreme northern portions of the Scandinavia peninsula, bordering Finland, Sweden, and Russia. In the west, its 20,900km (13,000 miles) of coastline confront the often-turbulent North Atlantic Ocean.

There's plenty of breathing room for everybody. When you factor in the Arctic desolation of the north, Norway averages about 20 people per square mile.

Most of the four million inhabitants are concentrated in the south, where the weather is less severe. Even so, the population of Oslo, the capital, is less than half a million. Aside from Oslo, there are no really big cities; the populations of Bergen and Trondheim are 208,000 and 134,000, respectively.

Norway does not want to be a melting pot, and immigration is strictly controlled. The largest minority group is the Lapps (or Sami), who live in the far north; they have broad powers of self-government, including their own parliament. Although many people have emigrated from Norway—about one million to America alone—immigration to Norway from other countries has been limited. About 3.2% of the population originally came from Great Britain, Denmark, and Sweden.

Norway is a constitutional monarchy. Although without political power, Norway's royal family enjoys the subjects' unwavering support. The real power is in the Storting, or parliament. Women play a major role in government. Some 40% of all elected officials are women, and women head several government ministries. Many industries—especially energy—are fully or partially state controlled. Oil from the North Sea is a vital resource; the government has a Ministry of Oil and Energy. The government grants large subsidies to agriculture and fisheries.

As a result of their natural surroundings, Norwegians are among the most athletic people in Europe. Nearly every Norwegian child learns to ski as well as walk. They are also among the best-educated people in the world. Norway's educational standard has risen considerably since World War II, and some 90% of Norwegian young people take a 3-year course in academic or vocational school after completing their compulsory education.

About 90% of the population belongs to the national Lutheran church, of which the king is the titular head. Freedom of worship is guaranteed to all.

Because the economy depends significantly on foreign trade, most business is conducted in English. Norway has two official languages, Riksmal and Landsmal, both of Danish origin. The Lapps, the indigenous people of the north, have their own language.

Cultural activities are important in Norway. The government subsidizes book publishing, guaranteeing sales of 1,000 copies of each book published for distribution to public libraries. Encouraging Norwegian writers helps preserve the language. Movie production, limited by population and language, fares poorly, however. Opera is fairly new to the country, and Norway acquired its first professional ballet ensemble in 1948. Folk music, however, has roots going back to Norse times, and is still very much alive. Norway encourages the arts by providing a guaranteed income to active artists whose work has achieved and maintained a high standard over a period of years.

2 The Natural Environment

Norway is one of nature's last great frontiers in Europe—mountains, glaciers, and lakes cover 70% of its land. Less than 4% of its territory, mostly in the south-central area, is arable. Within Norway's Jotunheimen range are the highest mountain peaks in Europe north of the Alps. Norway has about 17,000 glaciers. Along the western coast, some 50,000 islands protect the mainland from some of the worst storms in the North Atlantic.

Norway has a varied and changing climate. The coastal zones in the west and east normally experience cool summers and temperate winters. Inland, summers are warm, and winters cold and dry. In the extreme north, 100 days of annual snowfall each year isn't uncommon.

> *Fun Fact* **Did You Know?**
>
> - Norwegians have one of the highest per-capita incomes in the world.
> - While medieval alchemists were trying to make gold, they discovered *akevitt* (aquavit, or schnapps), the national "firewater" of Norway.
> - Norway has the world's largest foreign trade per capita.
> - The average population density is only 13 inhabitants per square kilometer, compared with 96 for Europe as a whole.
> - Norway and Russia share a short land border and have disputed control of a sea area the size of Belgium, Switzerland, and Austria combined.
> - Hammerfest is the world's northernmost town.
> - More people of Norwegian descent (five million) live in the United States than in Norway (4.3 million in 1994).

The fjords are not only a distinguishing feature of Norway's landscape, but a special attraction to visitors. The fjords were created thousands of years ago when the ocean flowed into glacial valleys. These "fingers" of water cut deep into the landscape. The most intriguing of the fjords, the Sognefjord, is more than 160km (100 miles) long and extremely deep.

Norway's rivers tend to be short and volatile. A smooth flow of water is often "agitated" by waterfalls and patches of white water. Because they're not suited for transportation, rivers are primarily sources of food, principally salmon. The longest river in Scandinavia, the Glomma, runs through southwestern Norway.

Norway's position on the globe has earned it the nickname "Land of the Midnight Sun." In summer, towns in northern Norway such as Tromsø experience 24 hours of sunshine, followed by 24 hours of darkness in winter. Even in southern Norway, the summer days are long, and the winter nights may last more than 17 hours.

Thick birch and pine forests cover the mountains; in the lowlands, oak forests abound. Spruce forests cover the southeast and middle regions. The steep mountains in the east are among the tallest in Europe and the site of some of the world's most challenging alpine ski runs. There is excellent hiking in the Vassafaret district around Flåm, where the mountains are rounded, gentle, and dotted with alpine lakes and rivers.

The mountains are also home to ravens, eagles, grouse, and gyrfalcons. They serve as a migratory home to the pure-white snowy owl. Norway's countryside and forests teem with Arctic animals such as reindeer, Arctic fox, wolves, bears, lynx, elk, beavers, and otters. Along the coast are nesting grounds for puffins and cormorants; whales, salmon, and cod frolic in the icy seas offshore. Through Norway's conservation efforts and strict regulations regarding the environment, these animals and fish flourish much as they have in the past.

3 History 101

Norway has been inhabited since the end of the Ice Age. The earliest Scandinavian settlers hunted reindeer and other game in these northern lands. Some 5,000 to 6,000 years ago, the inhabitants turned to agriculture,

Dateline

- 800–1050 The age of the Vikings, when Norsemen terrorized the coasts of Europe.

continues

especially around the Oslofjord. Artifacts show that in the Roman era, Norway had associations with areas to the south.

THE AGE OF THE VIKINGS

Prehistory ended during the Viking era, roughly A.D. 800 to 1050. Much of what is known about this era wasn't written down, but has been conveyed through sagas passed by word of mouth or revealed by archaeological finds. Some scholars consider the looting of the Lindisfarne monastery in northern England in 793 the beginning of the "age of the Vikings."

"The Vikings are coming!" became a dreadful cry along the coasts of Europe. The victims expected fire and sword. Scandinavian historians are usually kinder to the Vikings, citing the fact they often went abroad to trade and colonize. From Norway, the Vikings branched out to settle in the Orkney and Shetland Islands (now part of Scotland). They also settled in the Scottish Hebrides and on the Isle of Man. Viking settlements were established on Greenland and Iceland, which had previously been uninhabited. The Norse communities on Greenland eventually died out. The sagas claim that in 1001, Leif Eriksson discovered "wineland of the good," a reference to the American continent. Many scholars, however, claim that the Vikings' long ships reached America long before Leif Eriksson.

The road to unification of Norway was rough. In 872 Harald Fairhair, after winning a battle near Stavanger, conquered many of the provinces, but other battles for unification took decades. Harald was followed by his son, Eric I—"Bloody Axe," to his enemies. Eric began his reign by assassinating two of his eight brothers, and later killed five other brothers. His one

- **872** Harald Fairhair conquers many small provinces and reigns as first king.
- **1001** Leif Eriksson discovers America (or so the sagas claim).
- **1030** Christianity is firmly established; Olaf II is declared a saint.
- **1066** The Viking Age ends with the defeat of Harald III in England.
- **1350** The Black Death wipes out much of the population.
- **1397** Margaret becomes queen of Norway, Denmark, and Sweden at the Union of Kalmar.
- **1439** Danish rule is imposed on Norway.
- **1814** Norway breaks from Denmark and adopts a constitution, but comes under Swedish rule.
- **1905** The Norwegian parliament breaks from Sweden and declares independence.
- **1914** Norway declares its neutrality in World War I.
- **1920** Norway joins the League of Nations, ending its isolation.
- **1940** Nazi troops invade Norway; the king and government flee.
- **1945** Norway regains independence and executes its Nazi puppet ruler, Quisling.
- **1960s** Oil boom hits Norway.
- **1986** Labour Party installs first female prime minister, Gro Harlem Brundtland.
- **1989** Center-right coalition regains power.
- **1990** Brundtland becomes prime minister again.
- **1991** Harald V becomes king.
- **1994** Lillehammer plays host to XVII Olympic Winter Games.
- **1995** Norway wins Eurovision Song Contest, an annual cultural event observed by 600 million viewers.
- **1996** Eurovision Song Contest is held in Oslo; Norway takes second place.
- **1998** Oil prices fall, but Norway plunges ahead with costly engineering projects.
- **2001** UN group votes Norway most desirable place to live in the world.

surviving brother, Haakon, succeeded him as king in 954. Haakon tried unsuccessfully to convert Norway to Christianity. After he died in the Battle of Fitjar (960), Harald II Graafell, one of Eric's sons, became king of Norway. Cruel and oppressive, he died in battle in 970.

Haakon, son of Sigurd of Lade, became the next king of Norway. He resisted Danish attacks and ruled for about 25 years, but died in a peasant riot in 995. After the Battle of Swold in 1000, Norway was divided between Denmark and the Jarl of Lade.

Olaf II Haraldsson was a Viking until 1015, when he became king of Norway. Although oppressive and often cruel, he continued to spread Christianity. Canute of Denmark invaded Norway in 1028, sending Olaf fleeing to England. Canute's son, Sweyn, ruled Norway from 1028 to 1035. Sweyn was forced out when Olaf II was proclaimed a saint and his son, Magnus I, was made king. Magnus was also king of Denmark, a position he lost when Canute's nephew led a revolt against him and he was killed. Olaf's sainthood firmly established Christianity in Norway.

Harald Sigurdsson (known as Harald III) ruled Norway from 1046 until his death in 1066. His death marks the end of the Viking Age.

THE MIDDLE AGES Wars with Denmark continued, and civil wars raged from 1130 to 1227. Norwegian towns and the church continued to grow. Under Haakon V in the 13th century, Oslo became the capital of Norway. The Black Death reached Norway in 1350 and wiped out much of the population.

From 1362 to 1364 Norway and Sweden had a joint monarch, Haakon VI (1340–80), son of the Swedish king, Magnus Eriksson. Haakon married Margaret, daughter of the Danish king Valdemar Atterdag. Their son, Olaf, was chosen to be the Danish king upon Valdemar's death in 1375. He inherited the throne of Norway after his father died in 1380, bringing Norway into a union with Denmark. The union lasted until 1814.

UNION WITH DENMARK When Olaf died at the age of 17, Margaret became regent of Norway, Denmark, and Sweden. She ruled through her nephew, Eric of Pomerania, who had become king of Norway in 1389. He was recognized as a joint ruler at Kalmar. Margaret was actually the power behind the throne until her death in 1412. Eric of Pomerania tried to rule the three countries, but Sweden and Norway rebelled. Eric fled in 1439 and Christopher III of Bavaria became the ruler, imposing Danish rule.

Denmark led Norway into the Seven Years' War of the North in 1563, and took unfair advantage of its position in trade, in the military, and even in surrendering Norwegian land to Sweden.

During the Napoleonic Wars (1807–14), Denmark and Norway were allied with France, although the alliance created much economic hardship. Famine was widespread. In 1814 Frederik VI of Denmark surrendered to Napoleon's opponents and handed Norway over to Sweden. That officially ended 434 years of Danish rule over Norway.

SECESSION FROM SWEDEN On May 17, 1814, an assembly adopted a constitution and chose Christian Frederik as the Norwegian king. May 17 is celebrated as Norwegian National Day. The Swedes objected and launched a military campaign, eventually subduing Norway. The Swedes accepted the Norwegian constitution, but only within a union of the two kingdoms. Christian Frederik fled.

Soon thereafter, Norway suffered through one of its greatest economic depressions. Norway's parliamentary assembly, the Storting (Stortinget), engaged in repeated conflicts with the Swedish monarchs. Bernadotte ruled over both Norway and Sweden as Charles XIV from 1818 to 1844.

By the 1830s the economy of Norway had improved. The first railway line was laid in 1854. Its merchant fleet grew significantly between 1850 and 1880.

From the 1880s on, the Liberals in the Storting brought much-needed reform to the country. But by the end of the century, the conflict with Sweden was growing as more and more Norwegians demanded independence.

In August 1905 the Storting decided to dissolve the union with Sweden. Sweden agreed to let Norway rule itself. In October 1905 Norway held an election, and the son of Denmark's king was proclaimed king of Norway. He chose the name Haakon VII.

AN INDEPENDENT NORWAY   Free at last, Norway enjoyed peace and prosperity until the beginning of World War I. Even though the economy was satisfactory, thousands of Norwegians emigrated to the United States around the turn of the 20th century. In 1914 Norway joined Sweden and Denmark in declaring a policy of neutrality. Despite the declaration, around 2,000 Norwegian seamen lost their lives in the war because of submarine attacks and underwater mines.

In 1920 Norway joined the League of Nations, ending its policy of isolation. At the outbreak of World War II, Norway again declared its neutrality. Nonetheless, Allied forces mined Norway's waters in 1940, and the Nazis attacked on April 9, 1940. Great Britain and France provided some military assistance, but Norway fell after a 2-month struggle. The government and the royal family fled into exile in England, taking 1,000 ships of the Norwegian merchant fleet. In spite of the resistance movement, Norway was occupied by the Nazis until the end of the war in 1945. Vidkun Quisling, the Norwegian minister of defense in the 1930s, served the Nazis as leader of the puppet government.

Quisling was executed following the Nazi retreat from Norway. On June 7, 1945, the government-in-exile returned from Britain. The retreating Nazis had followed a scorched-earth policy in Finnmark, destroying almost everything of value. In the late 1940s, Norway began to rebuild its shattered economy.

After an abortive attempt to form a Nordic defense alliance, Norway and Denmark joined NATO in 1949. The Communist Party tried to secure recognition in Norway, but failed.

By the 1960s oil prospecting in the North Sea had yielded rich finds, which led to a profound restructuring of Norwegian trade and industry. In 1972 Norway voted not to enter the Common Market, following a bitter political dispute.

Norway had a nonsocialist government from 1981 to 1986. In 1986, Labour Party leader Gro Harlem Brundtland headed a minority government as Norway's first female prime minister. She introduced seven women into her 18-member cabinet. Soon, however, tumbling oil prices and subsequent unemployment led to a recession. The Labour government lost the 1989 elections. A center-right coalition assumed control of government. In November 1990, Brundtland returned to office as prime minister, this time with nine women in her 19-member cabinet. In 1991 Olav V died and was succeeded by his son, Harald V.

Today the Norwegian government faces many of the same problems that confront other nations: violent crime, drugs, immigration control, unemployment, acid rain, and pollution. Concern about acid rain and pollution, much of which comes from Great Britain, was so great that riots erupted when Margaret Thatcher visited Norway in 1987.

Although some Conservatives objected, Norway applied for membership in the European Union (EU) in 1993. The country also began to assert itself more on the international scene. Thorvald Stoltenberg, the minister of foreign affairs, was named peace negotiator for ravaged Bosnia-Herzegovina, and in clandestine meetings held outside Oslo he helped effect a rapprochement between the PLO and Israel. All these history-making events were eclipsed by the XVII Olympic Winter Games, held in Lillehammer in February 1994. In November 1994, Norwegians rejected a nonbinding referendum on EU membership. Following that, everyone waited for the Norwegian parliament to vote on whether the country would join. The parliament deliberately avoided the issue and did not vote on the matter. The referendum, though non-binding, remains in force, and Norway is not a member of the EU. But that does not mean the country has no economic links with the rest of Europe. In 1994 Norway reinforced its commitments to membership in the EEAA (European Economic Area Agreement), an association initiated in 1992 to ensure its access to the EU's single market. It includes cooperation in a variety of cultural and economic areas.

In 1995 Norway won the Eurovision Song Contest for best songs evocative of a country, repeating its sweep of a decade earlier and ensuring that the event would be held there in 1996. As the host country, Norway captured second place.

By 1998 Norway was having its share of troubles, as oil prices plunged to their lowest levels in a decade. Turmoil in financial markets knocked the krone lower and prompted the central bank to double interest rates to 10%. The popular prime minister, Kjell Magne Bondevik, who took over the office in 1997, stunned the country by taking a temporary leave from office. His doctors said he was having a "depressive reaction" to too much work and stress. In late 1998, Bondevik came back to his job—and is now running the country.

Today, Norway continues pushing forward with major engineering projects. The country is connecting its sparsely inhabited outcroppings and linking its interior fjordside villages in an effort to stem the flow of people to larger towns and villages. At Hitra, a largely barren island off the west coast, a new 5.6km (3½-mile) tunnel (the world's deepest) has been built at a cost of $41 million. It links mainland Norway to a hamlet with some 4,100 residents. On the North Cape at Norway's Arctic tip, a $140-million bridge and tunnel was constructed to Mager Island, home to only 3,600 people (and more than that many reindeer). An additional $135 million went into the earth in the mountains east of Bergen to link the towns of Aurland (pop. 1,900) and Laerdal (pop. 2,250). Its 24km (15-mile) length casts the previous world record-holder, the 16km (10-mile) St. Gotthard tunnel in Switzerland, into a distant second place.

A more artistic bridge opened in December of 2001. The designer? None other than Leonardo da Vinci in 1502. The 530km (329-mile) laminated timber bridge links Norway and Sweden over a highway at the town of Aas, 26km (16 miles) south of Oslo.

In 2001, Norway ranked first (with the U.S. in 6th place) as the best country in the world in which to live, according to the United Nations Human Development Report. Australia followed Norway in second place, with both countries moving narrowly ahead of Canada. The annual survey is based on statistical profiles of what people can expect in life beyond economic growth.

The year 2001 also was witness to the marriage of Crown Prince Haakon and Mette-Mari Tjessem Hoiby, a single mom who lived with the royal before marrying him. The couple's marriage has raised some astonishment among Norway's more conservative factions, since the father of Hoiby's child is a convicted cocaine supplier, and she has been well known on Oslo's "dance and drugs house party scene," as one newspaper commentator put it. Some Norwegians wonder if the modern-minded heir to the throne, a direct descendant of Queen Victoria, even plans to maintain the monarchy.

4 Dining with the Norwegians

Norwegians are proud—and rightly so—of their many tempting specialties, ranging from boiled cod (considered a delicacy) to reindeer steak smothered in brown gravy and accompanied by tart little lingonberries, which resemble wild cranberries.

Fish, both fresh and saltwater, is at the center of Norwegian cuisine. Prepared in countless ways, dishes are always fresh and usually well prepared. Besides the aforementioned cod, in early summer, *kokt laks* (boiled salmon) is a wonderful treat. *Kreps* (crayfish) and *ørret* (mountain trout) are also popular. For those willing to splurge, we recommend the delicately seasoned *fiskegratin* (fish soufflé). Norwegians love their *rølet al* (smoked fatty eel), although most visitors tend to bypass this one at the smörgåsbord table. The national appetizer is brine-cured herring with raw onions.

You may want to try reindeer steak or *faar-i-kaal,* the national dish, a heavily creamed cabbage-and-mutton stew with boiled potatoes. The *kjøttkaker,* Norwegian hamburger—often pork patties—served with sautéed onions, brown gravy, and boiled potatoes, is a great way to introduce the children to Norwegian cuisine.

The boiled potato is ubiquitous. The Norwegians prefer it without butter—just a bit of parsley. Nowadays, fresh vegetables and crisp salads are a regular feature of the Norwegian diet as well.

Rømmergrøt is a sour-cream porridge covered with melted butter, brown sugar, and cinnamon. If they're in season, try the tasty, amber-colored *muiter* (cloudberries). An additional treat is a pancake accompanied by lingonberries.

Frokost (breakfast) is often a whopping *koldtbord,* the famous cold board, consisting of herring and goat's milk cheese, and often salmon and soft-boiled eggs, plus *wienerbrød* (Danish pastry). Many visitors may not want to spend the extra kroner for this big spread, but those going on glacier expeditions need this early-morning fortification.

Incidentally, the multi-dish smörgåsbord and smørrebrød (*smørbrød* in Norway), an open-faced sandwich, are very popular in Norway, although they seem to be served here without the elaborate rituals associated with such events in Denmark and Sweden. Customarily, smörgåsbord in Norway is only a prelude to the main meal.

The chief criticism leveled against Norwegian cooking is that it's too bland. The food is always abundant (the Norwegians are known for their second helpings), substantial, and well prepared—but no threat to the French for a *cordon bleu* award.

Appendix C:
Sweden in Depth

Sweden is one of the most paradoxical nations on earth. An essentially conservative country, it is nonetheless a leader in social welfare, prison reform, and equal opportunity for women.

Swedes have long enjoyed a very high standard of living in Europe and wages that are among the highest. During the worldwide recession in the 1990s, the country had trouble maintaining the value of its currency. It has also faced its highest unemployment rate since World War II. There's definitely trouble in paradise, but compared with the rest of the world, Sweden is better off than most nations.

The past and the future exist side by side in Sweden. Stockholm and some west coast cities have stunning modern shopping complexes and up-to-date hotels. But a journey to Dalarna and Värmland, or the historic walled city of Visby on the island of Gotland, transports you to a more distant time.

Many visitors come to explore the "Kingdom of Crystal" in Småland province, where dozens of so-called glass huts, such as Orrefors and Kosta Boda, are tucked away among lakes and forests.

The Swedes are responsible for many inventions that have changed modern life. They include the safety match, alternating current, the milk separator, the refrigerator, the vacuum cleaner, and the ball bearing.

1 Sweden Today

Sweden's 280,000 sq. km (174,000 sq. miles) of lush forests and more than 100,000 lakes make up a land where the urbane and the untamed are said to live harmoniously. There's ample space for the 8.3 million residents—it has a density of only 48 people per square mile. About 85% of the citizens live in the southern half of the country. The north is populated by the two chief minority groups: the Lapps (Sami), and the Finnish-speaking people of the northeast. Stockholm is the political capital, with a population of 1,435,000; Gothenburg, a major automobile manufacturing town, is home to 704,000; and Malmö, the port city, home to 458,000.

Once an ethnically homogeneous society, Sweden has experienced a vast wave of immigration in the past several years. Today more than 10% of its residents are immigrants or the children of immigrants. Most of the influx has come from other Scandinavian countries. Because of Sweden's strong stance on human rights, it has also become a major destination for political and social refugees from Africa and the Middle East. Many immigrants seeking asylum come from the former Yugoslavia.

Sweden's government is a constitutional monarchy supported by a parliamentary government. The royal family functions primarily in a ceremonial

(Fun Fact Did You Know?

- Sweden, today a symbol of neutrality, once pursued war. It has invaded Russia, conquered Britain, and grabbed Normandy.
- A survey showed that a large percentage of Americans confuse Sweden and Switzerland.
- Half the couples living together in Sweden are unmarried.
- Sweden has added two words to international gastronomy: smörgåsbord and Absolut.
- The world's longest smörgåsbord was prepared in Sweden. It stretched 720m (2,395 ft.).
- James Joyce, F. Scott Fitzgerald, George Orwell, Marcel Proust, and Aldous Huxley did *not* win Sweden's Nobel Prize for literature.
- Sweden is one of five nations that established colonies in North America.

capacity. The ruling body is a one-chamber parliament, whose members are popularly elected for 3-year terms. A Social Democrat, Goeran Persson, heads the present government. Because of Sweden's location, it has been active in promoting peace among its warring Baltic neighbors. The country is an active member of the United Nations and was admitted to the European Union as a full member in 1995.

Like other European countries, Sweden has seen its policy of cradle-to-grave welfare threatened in recent years. The main topic of debate in the Social Democrat–dominated parliament is how to sustain the generous welfare system while putting a curb on ever-increasing taxes. The state provides health insurance and many generous family benefits, including an allowance for care providers, 15 months of paid parental leave after the birth of a child (divided between both parents), tax-free child allowances, and education stipends for children. When they reach retirement (age 65), Swedes are entitled to a hefty pension that rises with inflation.

Education plays an important role in Sweden. Schools, run by municipalities, provide free tuition, books, and lunches. Although attendance is mandatory for only 9 years, 90% of Swedes pursue some form of higher education. Adult education and the university are funded by the state.

Sweden's high level of education complements its high-tech industrial economy. Although in years past the economy was based on agriculture, in the latter half of the 20th century industry became predominant, employing nearly 80% of all workers. More than 50% of exports are heavy machinery, including cars, trucks, and telecommunications equipment. Companies such as Saab and Volvo produce vehicles familiar throughout the world. Despite Sweden's industrial predominance, the country still produces some 80% of its own food.

Although such a highly industrialized nation depends on its factories, Sweden has enacted stringent environmental policies. Monitoring the environment is the responsibility of local governments. Each of Sweden's 286 municipalities has the right to limit pollutant emissions in its sector.

The environment has always played an integral role in Swedish life. There are 20 national parks. Although not regulated by law, Sweden has a policy that entitles citizens to unlimited free access to the nation's wilderness areas.

Another important element is Sweden's strong focus on culture. Over the past 25 years Swedes have turned their attention to music. Today young people are purchasing more recorded music and attending more live concerts than they were even a decade ago. Reading is on the rise (more than 9,000 book titles are published in Sweden every year), museum attendance has increased, and there's greater interest in the media. The average Swede spends 6 hours a day immersed in some form of mass media (newspapers, magazines, television, radio, and so forth).

Many Swedes claim that their country—once the "world's conscience"—is drifting. "We are no longer exceptional," says Lars Sahlin, a bartender in a popular Stockholm nightclub and a self-styled philosopher. "Our unemployment remains. There have been social-spending scandals, a decline in competitiveness."

Sweden's per capita income standing has fallen from 4th to 15th in the world, behind its three Scandinavian neighbors. Once Sweden preached racial tolerance and was particularly critical of the United States. Now Stockholm suburbs have segregated communities for their 800,000 immigrants.

A certain nostalgia is sweeping the nation today, a desire to return to the way life was when Sweden was one of the three or four richest countries in the world.

The country is under increasing pressure to drop its neutrality and join an expanding NATO. It is firmly resisting that, but has taken part in Bosnia peacekeeping. Although Sweden has been a member of the European Union since 1995, polls indicate that the people would reject membership if a new election were held.

As Sweden moves into the 21st century, its problems continue. For example, businesses can't grow because it's too expensive to hire people. Observers have noted that young Swedes are starting to think internationally, and some of them are leaving Sweden to take positions elsewhere in the global economy. "The people leaving are the very people that Sweden needs the most," one Swedish businessman lamented to the press.

2 The Natural Environment

Sweden is the fourth-largest nation in Europe. It's roughly the size of California, but sparsely populated. It stretches about 1,595km (990 miles) from north to south, with a disproportionate amount of territory above the Arctic Circle. From north to south, Sweden lies at roughly the same latitude as Alaska. While forests cover more than half the land, it's a heavily industrialized nation, and less than 10% of its land is used for agriculture. Sweden can be divided into three main regions: the mountainous northern zone, Norrland; the lake-filled, hilly central region, Svealand; and the broad southern plateau, Götaland, home of most of the country's agricultural enterprises.

Sweden has more than 100,000 lakes, including Vänern, the largest in western Europe. Lakes cover about 9% of the countryside, and play an important role in transporting goods from the Baltic ports to cities throughout Sweden and the rest of Scandinavia. Canals link many lakes to the sea. The most important is the 595km (370-mile) Göta Canal. Constructed in the 19th century, it links Gothenburg in the west to Stockholm in the east. Some 195km (121 miles) of canals were built to connect the lakes and rivers that make up the waterway.

Sweden's rivers tend to be short, and usually empty into one of the numerous lakes. They're used for short-haul transportation and especially for providing hydroelectric power to fuel the many factories scattered throughout the country. The most important rivers are the Pite, the Lule, and the Indal.

Impressions

Sweden appeared to me the country in the world most proper to form the botanist and natural historian; every object seemed to remind me of the creation of things, of the first efforts of sportive nature.

—Mary Wollstonecraft, letters written during a short residence in Sweden, 1796

Sweden's expansive seacoast is more than 2,495km (1,550 miles) long. The west is bounded by the Kattegat and the Skagerrak seas, and the east by the Gulf of Bothnia and the Baltic Sea. Numerous small islands and reefs dot the east and southwest coasts. If all the inlets and islands were included, the coastline of Sweden would measure 7,485km (4,650 miles). Öland and Gotland, Sweden's largest, most populated islands, are in the Baltic Sea, off the eastern coast.

Sweden is a center for alpine activities (including skiing, hiking, and glacier walking), most of which take place in the mountainous regions of Norrland. The far northern area is home to many of the country's highest peaks, including its highest mountain, 2,084m (6,946-ft.) Kebnekaise.

There are five climate zones, each supporting a distinct array of plant life: the tundra in the north, coniferous forests below the timberline, central Sweden's birch forests, deciduous forests in the south, and the beech and oak zones in the southernmost regions. The countryside teems with bears, elk, reindeer, foxes, wolves, and otters. Numerous game birds also make their home in Sweden's expansive forests.

3 History 101

The first mention of Swedish people is found in *Germania,* by the Roman historian Tacitus (A.D. 56–120). He called the tribe "Svear" and described them as a "militant Germanic race." Later historians would describe them as "skiing hunters." The word *Sverige* (or "the domain of the Svear") eventually became *Sweden.*

The early Swedes were Vikings who pursued a thriving slave trade. St. Anskar, a Frankish missionary, introduced Christianity in 829, hoping it would tame the Viking spirit. It took at least 2 centuries for paganism to die out, but by the second half of the 11th century, Christianity had gained a foothold. It finally became accepted under Eric IX, who ruled until 1160. He led a crusade to Finland and later became the patron saint of Sweden.

Sweden's greatest medieval statesman was Birger Jarl, who ruled from

Dateline

- **98** Sweden is first mentioned in a book, *Germania,* by Tacitus.
- **829** St. Anskar introduces Christianity.
- **1248** Birger Jarl abolishes serfdom and founds Stockholm.
- **1319** Magnus VII of Norway unites Sweden with Norway.
- **1350s** The Black Death decimates the population.
- **1397** Margaret rules Sweden, Norway, and Denmark after the Union of Kalmar.
- **1521** Gustavus Vasa founds the Vasa dynasty.
- **1648** Treaty of Westphalia grants Sweden the possessions of Stettin, Bremen, and West Pomerania.
- **1809** Napoleon names Jean Bernadotte heir to the throne of Sweden.
- **1889** The Social Democratic Party is formed.
- **1905** Sweden grants independence to Norway.

1248 to 1266; during his reign, serfdom was abolished and Stockholm was founded. When his son, Magnus Ladulås, became king in 1275, he granted extensive power to the Catholic Church and founded a hereditary aristocracy.

A NORDIC UNION Magnus VII of Norway (1316–74) was only 3 when he was elected to the Swedish throne, but his election signaled a recognition of the benefits of increased cooperation within the Nordic world. During his reign, distinct social classes emerged. They included the aristocracy; the Catholic clergy (who owned more than 20% of the land); peasant farmers and laborers; and a commercial class of landowners, foresters, mine owners, and merchants. The merchants' fortunes and power were based on trade links with the Hanseatic League. The association consisted of a well-organized handful of trading cities scattered in Germany and along the Baltic coastline. As commerce increased, the league's trading partners (especially Visby, on the island of Gotland) and their residents flourished, and the league's power grew.

In 1389 the Swedish aristocracy, fearing the growing power of the

- **1909** Suffrage for men is achieved.
- **1921** Suffrage for women and an 8-hour workday are established.
- **1940** Sweden declares its neutrality in World War II.
- **1946** Sweden joins the United Nations.
- **1953** Dag Hammarskjöld becomes secretary-general of the United Nations.
- **1973** Carl XVI Gustaf ascends the throne.
- **1986** Olof Palme, prime minister and leader of the Social Democrats, is assassinated.
- **1992** Sweden faces currency crisis.
- **1994** Refugees and the welfare system strain Sweden's budget.
- **1995** Sweden, Finland, and Austria gain full membership in the European Union.
- **1996** Social Democrat Goeran Persson, Sweden's finance minister, is elected prime minister.
- **1997** World headlines link Sweden to past sterilization programs and to Nazi gold.
- **1998** Social Democrats remain in power on a pledge to continue huge welfare programs.
- **2000** The $3 billion Øresund bridge links Denmark and Sweden for the first time.

Germans in the Hanseatic League, negotiated an intra-Nordic union with Denmark and the remaining medieval fiefdoms in Norway and Finland. The experimental process began in 1397 in Kalmar, Sweden, which gave its name to the brief but farsighted Union of Kalmar. A leading figure in its development was the Danish queen Margaret, who was also queen of Norway when the Swedish aristocracy offered her the throne in 1389. Despite its ideals, the union collapsed after about 40 years. Merchants, miners, and peasants staged a revolt in defense of Sweden's trade links with the Hanseatic League, and power struggles between Danish and Swedish nobles took a toll.

Although the union was a failure, one of its legacies was the establishment of a Riksdag (parliament). Created partly as a compromise among different political factions, it consisted of representatives from various towns and regions; the peasant classes also had limited representation.

Queen Margaret's heir, her nephew, Eric of Pomerania (1382–1459), became the crowned head of Norway, Denmark, and Sweden. He spent most of his reign fighting with the Hanseatic League. Deposed in 1439, he was replaced by Christopher of Bavaria, whose early death in 1448 led to a major conflict and the eventual dissolution of the Kalmar Union. King Christian II of Denmark invaded Stockholm in 1520, massacred the leaders who opposed him, and established an unpopular reign; there was much civil disobedience until the emergence of the Vasa dynasty, which expelled the Danes.

THE VASA DYNASTY In May 1520 a Swedish nobleman, Gustavus Vasa, returned from captivity in Denmark and immediately began planning the military expulsion of the Danes from Sweden. In 1523 he captured Stockholm, won official recognition of Swedish independence, and was elected king.

In a power struggle with the Catholic Church, Gustavus confiscated most church-held lands (increasing the power of the state overnight) and established Lutheranism as the national religion. He commissioned a complete translation of the Bible and other religious works into Swedish, and forcefully put down uprisings in the provinces. He established the right of succession for his offspring and decreed that his son, Eric XIV, would follow him as king (which he did, in 1543).

Although at first Eric was a wise ruler, his eventual downfall came in part from his growing conflicts with noblemen and his marriage to his unpopular mistress, Karin Mansdotter. (He had previously tried to negotiate marriage with Queen Elizabeth I of England.) Eric eventually went insane.

> **Impressions**
>
> Sweden seems to me to be the most comfortable country in Europe—and the least cozy.
> —Kathleen Nott, *A Clean, Well-Lighted Place*, 1961

The next 50 years were marked by Danish plots to regain control of Sweden and Swedish plots to conquer Poland, Estonia, and the Baltic trade routes leading to Russia. A dynastic link to the Polish royal families led to the ascension of Sigismund (son of the Swedish king Johan III) in Warsaw. When his father died, Sigismund became king of Sweden and Poland simultaneously. But Sweden opposed his Catholicism and expelled him; he was followed by Karl (Charles) IX, who led Sweden into a dangerous and expensive series of wars with Denmark, Russia, and Poland.

By 1611, as Sweden was fighting simply to survive, Gustavus II Adolphus (1594–1632) ascended the throne. Viewed today as a brilliant politician and military leader, he was one of the century's most stalwart Protestants at a time when political alliances often formed along religious lines. After organizing an army composed mainly of farmers and field hands (financed by money from the Falun copper mines), he secured Sweden's safety.

He died fighting the Hapsburg emperor's Catholic army near the city of Luützen in 1632. His heir and only child, Christina (1626–89), was 6 years old. Christina, who did not want to pursue war and had converted to Catholicism (against the advice of her counselors), abdicated the throne in 1654 in favor of her cousin, Charles X Gustav (1622–60).

Ten years after his rise to power, Charles X expelled the Danes from many of Sweden's southern provinces, establishing the country's borders approximately where they are today. The endless wars with Denmark (and other kingdoms in northern Germany) continued in the years that followed. An even greater problem was the growing power of the nobles, who had amassed (usually through outright purchase from the cash-poor monarchy) an estimated 72% of Sweden's land. In an acrimonious process, Charles XI (1655–97) redistributed the land into approximately equal shares held by the monarchy, the nobles, and the independent farmers. The position of small landowners has remained secure in

Sweden ever since, although the absolute monarchy gained increased power. With Charles's newfound wealth, he greatly strengthened the country's military power.

Charles XII (1682–1718) came to the throne at the age of 4, with his mother, the queen, as regent. His war-torn reign may have signaled the collapse of the Swedish empire.

Under Frederick I (1676–1751), Sweden regained some of its former prestige and waged war against Russia. Gustavus III (1746–92) initiated many reforms, encouraged the arts, and transformed the architectural landscape of Stockholm, but he also revived the absolute power of the monarchy, perhaps as a reaction against the changes effected by the French Revolution. He was assassinated by a group of fanatical noblemen while attending a ball at the opera.

THE 19TH CENTURY   The next king, Gustavus IV (1778–1837), hated Napoleon. He led Sweden into the Third Coalition against France (1805–07). For his efforts, he lost Stralsund and Swedish Pomerania; in the wars against Russia and Denmark, Sweden lost Finland in 1808. The next year, Gustavus IV was overthrown. He died in exile.

A new constitution was written in 1808, granting the Riksdag (parliament) equal power with the king. Charles XIII (1748–1818), the uncle of the deposed king, became the new monarch.

Napoleon arranged for his aide, Jean Bernadotte (1763–1844), to become heir to the Swedish throne. Bernadotte won a war with Denmark, forcing that country to cede Norway to Sweden (1814). Upon the death of Charles XIII, Bernadotte became king of Sweden and Norway, ruling as Charles XIV. During his reign Sweden adopted a policy of neutrality, and the royal line that he established is still on the throne. Charles XIV was succeeded by his son, Oscar I (1799–1859), who introduced many reforms, including freedom of worship and of the press.

The Industrial Revolution changed the face of Sweden. The Social Democratic Party was launched in 1889, leading to a universal suffrage movement. All males gained the right to vote in 1909.

THE 20TH CENTURY   Norway declared its independence in 1905, and Sweden accepted the secession. Sweden adhered to a policy of neutrality during World War I, although many Swedes were sympathetic to the German cause. Many Swedish volunteers enlisted in the White Army during the Russian Revolution of 1917.

In 1921 women gained the right to vote, and an 8-hour workday was established. The Social Democratic Party continued to grow in power, and after 1932, a welfare state was instituted.

Although Sweden offered weapons and volunteers to Finland during its Winter War against the Soviet Union in 1939, it declared its neutrality during World War II. Sweden provoked long-lived resentment from Norway, whose cities were leveled by Nazi troops that had been granted free passage across Swedish territory. Under heavy Allied threats against Sweden in 1943 and 1944, Nazi troop transports through the country were halted. Throughout the war Sweden accepted many refugees.

Sweden joined the United Nations in 1946 but refused to join NATO in 1949. More disturbing was Sweden's decision to return to the Soviet Union many German and Baltic refugees who had opposed Russia during the war. They were presumably killed on Stalin's orders.

Native son Dag Hammarskjöld became secretary-general of the United Nations in 1953, and he did much to help Sweden regain the international respect it had lost because of its wartime policies.

Sweden continued to institute social reforms in the 1950s and 1960s, including the establishment of a national health service.

Carl XVI Gustaf, who was just 27, became king in 1973, following the death of his grandfather, Gustaf VI Adolf. In 1976 he married Silvia Sommerlath, who was born in Germany. King Carl XVI Gustaf and Queen Silvia have three children.

The leader of the Social Democrats, Olof Palme, was prime minister from 1969 to 1976 and again from 1982 until his assassination outside a movie theater in Stockholm in 1986. A pacifist, he was a staunch critic of the United States, especially during the Vietnam War.

In 1995 Sweden was granted full membership in the European Union, providing the setting for much-needed economic growth. Prime Minister Ingvar Carlsson retired in 1996, and in an effort to control rapidly increasing taxes and cut government spending, Finance Minister Goeran Persson was elected prime minister of the ruling Social Democratic Party.

Just as Sweden's image of itself as one of the most progressive nations on earth was being questioned, a chilling chapter from the past was revealed in 1997. Sweden had as many as 60,000 of its citizens sterilized from 1935 to 1976. The ideas behind the program resembled Nazi ideas of racial superiority. Singled out were those judged to be inferior, flawed by bad eyesight, mental retardation, and otherwise "undesirable" racial characteristics. Some citizens were sterilized involuntarily. The respected newspaper *Dagens Nyheter* stirred national debate and worldwide headlines when it ran a series of articles about the program.

Sweden's reputation received more battering in 1997. There were revelations of wartime iron exports—which fed Hitler's military machine—and of postwar Swedish hoarding of the German gold received in payment, much of it looted from victims of the Nazis.

In the September 1998 elections, Social Democrats remained in power on a pledge to increase spending on the country's huge welfare program. The Social Democrats have been in power for 57 of the past 66 years. The government spends 46% of the gross national product on welfare, more than any other industrialized country. Income taxes take 59% of people's pay. Employers pay up to 41% of employee remuneration into social security and pension plans.

In May of 2000, Sweden for the first time in its history became physically linked with the Continent via the Øresund Bridge. Both Queen Margrethe of Denmark and King Carl Gustaf of Sweden inaugurated the span that links the Scandinavian peninsula with Europe. Construction on the 16km (10-mile) motor and railway link began in 1995.

The bridge gives the island of Zealand (the eastern part of Denmark) and Scania (the southern part of Sweden) a shared bridge, serving some 3½ million inhabitants in the area. The price of a one-way fare in a passenger car is $30.

In theory, a vehicle can now travel in roughly a straight line from the Arctic coast of Norway to the Mediterranean shores of Spain. For centuries, it has been a dream to link the Continent from its northern tip to its southern toe. The "Øresund Fixed Link" spans the icy Øresund Sound between the cities of Copenhagen and Malmö.

4 Dining with the Swedes

The fame of the smörgåsbord is justly deserved. Incorporating a vast array of dishes—everything from Baltic herring to smoked reindeer—selections from the smörgåsbord may be eaten either as hors d'oeuvres or as a meal in itself.

One cardinal rule of the smörgåsbord: Don't mix fish and meat dishes. It is customary to begin with *sill* (herring), prepared in many ways. Herring is usually followed by other treats from the sea, such as jellied eel, smoked fish, or raw pickled salmon. Then diners proceed to the cold meat dishes, where baked ham, liver paste, and the like are accompanied by vegetable salads. Hot dishes, often Swedish meatballs, come next, backed up by cheese and crackers, and perhaps a fresh fruit salad.

The smörgåsbord is not served as often in Sweden as many visitors seem to expect, as it requires time-consuming preparation. Many Swedish families reserve it for special occasions. In lieu of the 40-dish smörgåsbord, some restaurants have taken to serving a plate of *assietter* (hors d'oeuvres). One of the tricks for enjoying smörgåsbord is timing. It's best to go early, when fish dishes are fresh. Late arrivals may be more fashionable, but the food is often stale.

Typical mealtimes in Sweden are 8 to 11am for the standard continental breakfast, noon to 2:30pm for lunch, and as early as 5:30pm to around 8 or 8:30pm for dinner. Many restaurants in Stockholm are open until midnight, but don't count on this in the small villages.

A Swedish breakfast at your hotel may consist of cheese, ham, sausage, egg, bread, and perhaps *filmjölk,* a kind of sour-milk yogurt. *Smörgas,* the famous Swedish open-faced sandwich, like the Danish smørrebrød and Norwegian smørbrød, is a slice of buttered bread with something on top. It is eaten at any time of day, and you'll find it varying in price, depending on what you order and where you order it.

Unless you decide to have smörgåsbord at lunch (it's never served in the evenings), you'll find that the Swedes do not go for lavish spreads in the middle of the day. The usual luncheon order consists of one course, as you'll observe on menus, especially in the larger towns. Dinner menus are for complete meals, with appetizer, main course and side dishes, and dessert.

Swedish chefs generally tend to be far more expert with fish dishes (freshwater pike and salmon are star choices) than meat courses. The Swedes go mad at the sight of *kraftor* (crayfish), in season from mid-August to mid-September. This succulent, dill-flavored delicacy is eaten with the fingers, and much of the fun is the elaborate ritual surrounding its consumption. A platter of thin pancakes, served with lingonberries (comparable to cranberries), is the traditional Thursday-night dinner in Sweden. It's good on any other night of the week—but somehow better on Thursday.

Swedish cuisine used to be deficient in fresh vegetables and fruits, relying heavily on canned foods, but this is no longer true. Potatoes are the staff of life, but fresh salad bars long ago peppered the landscape, especially in the big cities.

The calorie-laden Swedish pastry—the mainstay of the *konditori* (confectionary)—is tempting and fatal to weight watchers. *Kaffe* (coffee) is the universal drink in Sweden, although tea (taken straight) and milk are also popular. The water is perfectly safe to drink all over Sweden. Those who want a reprieve from alcohol might enjoy the fruit-flavored Pommac soft drink, and Coca-Cola is ubiquitous. The state monopoly, or *Systembolaget,* controls the sale of alcoholic beverages. Licensed restaurants may sell alcohol after noon only (1pm on Sun). Schnapps or aquavit—served icy cold—is a superb Swedish drink, often used to accompany smörgåsbord. The run-of-the-mill Swedish beer (Pilsner) has only a small amount of alcohol. All restaurants serve *lättol* (light beer) and *folköl,* a somewhat stronger brew. Swedish vodka, or *brännvin,* is made from corn and potatoes and flavored with different spices. All *brännvin* is served ice cold in schnapps glasses. Keep in mind that aquavit is much stronger than it looks, and Sweden has strictly enforced rules about drinking and driving. Most Swedes seem to drink their liquor straight; mixed drinks are uncommon. Either way, the drink prices are sky-high.

Appendix D:
Finland in Depth

One of the world's northernmost countries, Finland is the last frontier of western Europe. Lapland, which makes up nearly one-third of Finland, is north of the Arctic Circle.

Technically, Finland is not part of Scandinavia, but it is in spirit, as reflected in its modern architecture; its high standard of living; its avant-garde designs in textiles, furniture, and ceramics; and its advances in education.

Geographically remote (although easily accessible), Finland does not attract the number of visitors that go to Denmark, Norway, and Sweden—and that's a shame, as Finland has much to offer the visitor in both summer and winter.

1 Finland Today

Covering an area of 209,300 sq. km (130,000 sq. miles) and home to five million people, Finland has a relatively low population density—about 38 people per square mile. More than one-third of its territory lies above the Arctic Circle, home to one of its large minority groups—the Lapps, or Sami. Helsinki, the capital, has a population of about half a million.

Finland is a republic; a president governs with a 200-member unicameral parliament. The president serves a 6-year term, and members of parliament are popularly elected for 4-year terms. Finland was the first nation to grant suffrage to women, so women have played an active role in government since the early 1900s. Women members compose about 40% of the parliament. In 1995, along with Sweden and Austria, Finland joined the European Union.

Finland's welfare system is among the best in the world. Universal health care is offered, supplemented by extensive preventive health education. Maternal health is stressed through free medical care and a "maternity package" consisting of either money for the infant's basic needs or the actual products, such as clothes, diapers, bottles, and bibs (only 15% of families choose the cash). Families with children under 17 also receive allowances from the state. Children get free medical and dental care through the age of 19.

Finland's literacy rate is nearly 100%. This has been achieved through an emphasis on bilingualism (Finnish and Swedish) as well as free schooling. All primary education and university courses are conducted in Finnish and Swedish—the two official languages. Because of the obscurity of the Finnish language, Finns have had to master other languages, primarily English, French, and German. Students are required to attend 10 years of primary school, after which they can pursue vocational training or university studies. Finland is the best-educated nation in Europe.

Finland's economy relies primarily on exporting high-tech industrial goods. Metal and engineering products account for more than 40% of the country's

exports. Many of these are computer-controlled mechanical goods and specialized vehicles, used mainly in the mining industry. Finland also exports a large
amount of paper products from its birch forests. In fact, Finland is the primary
supplier of paper products for all of western Europe.

Finland's location in the Baltic, as well as its shared border with Russia, has
opened the gates to a strong eastern trade. Many goods pass through Finland on
their way to Russia and the rest of Asia. Since the demise of the Soviet Union
and the rise of capitalism, Russian exports have also begun to move through Finland.

The Finnish government has taken steps to ensure Finland's role in northern
European commerce. Through membership in the European Union and close
ties to the recently liberated Baltic states (such as Estonia), Helsinki is rapidly
expanding as the hub for commerce between the established nations in the West
and the emerging Baltic states and central and eastern Europe.

The Finns are generally a homogenous group, having one of the most genetically pure gene pools in the world (see "Those Mysterious Genes" box, above).
Most Finns live in the southern region, many in the Helsinki area. Finland's two
principal minority groups—the Lapps in the north and the Roma (gypsies) in
the south—constitute less than 1% of the entire population. Immigration is dis-
couraged; most of the country's present immigrant population—about
20,000—are refugees who have been assigned to Finland by the United Nations.

2 The Natural Environment

Suomi (its Finnish name) is one of the largest countries in Europe, about
1,100km (700 miles) long, with a maximum breadth of 540km (335 miles).
Finland's coastline is approximately 1,095km (680 miles) long.

Finland shares its border with Sweden, Norway, and Russia. Its geography can
be divided into three distinct areas—the coastal plain, the lake district, and the
highland in the north—each characterized by a slightly different climate and
topography.

Most of the country is lowland, with the highest point at Halti, 1,300m
(4,344 ft.) above sea level. More than 65% of the land is forested; arable farmland makes up about 8% of the landmass.

Finland has more lakes than any other country—a total of 187,888 that cover
some 10% of the country. Although abundant in number, most of the lakes are
relatively shallow (around 7m/25 ft.), and none is more than 90m (300 ft.)
deep. The lakes are narrow, and many are dotted with islands; most of them are
frozen in winter. The largest is Lake Saimaa, near the Russian border.

Finland's rivers tend to be short. The major rivers are the Kemi, Torne, Muo-
nio, Oulu, and Vuoksi. The Kemi, Finland's longest river, is its primary source
of hydroelectric power; it's also Finland's major salmon producer. The Vuoksi,
which originates from Lake Saimaa, has Finland's most striking waterfall. All of
Finland's waterways play a vital role in the logging industry.

Finland has a gentle coastline, with many bays and inlets. There is little tidal
action, so the seashore resembles the shores of the country's many lakes. Off the
coast are thousands of small islands, the most important of which are the Åland
Islands, a chain of more than 6,500 islands located in the Gulf of Bothnia off
Finland's southern coast.

As in Norway and Sweden, Finland's flora varies tremendously by region. The
coastal zones are much milder than the interior and can sustain such species as
oaks, elms, and maples. The central region is home to conifers, and the north,

...Know?

...3,000 lakes and 180,000 islands.

...as the first country to grant women the right

...he highest per-capita Internet connection rates in

...hold the world's record for sitting on an anthill.

...of fairy tale and mythology—the whooper swan,
...been saved from extinction and once again nests

...most film festival is held under the midnight sun
...xyl.

...ersion of the tango, a far cry from Argentina's.

...news broadcasts in Latin.

...most heavily forested regions on earth, Finland
...out of fiberglass.

...is the leading book-publishing country in the
...published per year for every 10,000 inhabitants.

...can sustain little vegetation. Throughout Finland,
...ies of flowering plants.

...irds of Finland covered with forest, the countryside
...are home to wolves, bears, lynx, and various species
...ll roam the extreme north, although their numbers
...luced for the usual reasons: unrestricted killing for
...the encroachment of human population, pollutants,
...l breeding grounds. Finland's thousands of lakes are
...to hundreds of species of birds; most come to dine
...und in the chilly streams and lakes.

...s to protect their natural resources. The government
...national parks. Wildlife areas have generally been left
...rail markings and rustic campsites. National parks in
...o be smaller and less rugged than their larger, wilder

...k in Finland is Lemmenjoki, north of the Arctic Cir-
...home to the magnificent Lemmenjoki River Valley,
...Cliffs rise dramatically on each side of the river.

3 History 101

As the Ice Age receded throughout Scandinavia, widely scattered Stone Age settlements emerged among the lakes and forests of what is now Finland. The tribes that established these communities were probably nomadic Lapps of Mongolian origin, although the mists of time have greatly obscured the exact nature of the communities.

Dateline

- **A.D. 100** Finland is inhabited by people from the southern Gulf of Finland and by Finno-Ugrians.
- **1155** Eric IX, king of Sweden, brings the Crusades to Finland.
- **1581** Johan III of Sweden makes Finland a Grand Duchy.

continues

With the arrival of new tribes of Finno-Ugric origin (starting in the 1st century A.D.) and other unrelated Germanic tribes from the southern edge of the Gulf of Finland, the original Lapps retreated farther and farther north. Recent genetic research into the distribution of blood groups points to evidence that about two-thirds of the Finnish population today is of Western (that is, European) origin (see "Those Mysterious Genes" box, above). Nonetheless, philologists stress the uniqueness of the Finnish language, Suomia, whose only close relative is Hungarian. Both languages belong to the Finno-Ugric subdivision of the Uralic subfamily of the Ural-Altaic family, unrelated to the Indo-European family to which almost all western European languages belong.

The arrival of the Vikings, mentioned in written records as beginning about A.D. 800, led to the establishment of cultural and trade routes as far east as Constantinople. Early in their recorded history, inhabitants of the region now known as Finland probably had many contacts with the Russian empire as well as the kingdoms of Estonia and Latvia. More important, they also established trade links with the shores of the southern Baltic—the area that's now Poland and part of Germany. Many different cultures and bloodlines met and mingled in Finland, leading to bloody wars among the Finnish tribes, until Sweden—fearing for the stability of its eastern neighbor—launched a series of attacks into the area.

SWEDISH INTRUSIONS   In A.D. 1155, Eric IX, assisted by St. Henry, the English-born bishop of Uppsala, launched a crusade for the political and religious conversion of the Finnish tribes. Their major opposition was from the Novgorodians (a powerful Russian kingdom) in eastern Finland (Karelia), who were seizing land

- **1713–21** Russia invades and occupies Finland.
- **1721** Sweden regains control of western Finland, but loses much Finnish territory in the east to Russia.
- **1809** Finland becomes a Grand Duchy of Russia under Tsar Alexander I.
- **1821** The capital is moved from Turku to Helsinki.
- **1878** Under Tsar Alexander II, Finland gains its own conscript army; Finnish replaces Swedish as the official language.
- **1905** Finns launch a national strike to oppose the oppressive policies of Tsar Nicholas II, who had revoked Finnish autonomy in 1899.
- **1906** Finland is allowed a single-chamber Diet with 200 elected deputies.
- **1917** Russia restores Finnish autonomy, as Finland declares its independence.
- **1918** Mannerheim succeeds in driving Russian forces out of Finland.
- **1919** Finland adopts a constitution.
- **1920** Finland joins the League of Nations.
- **1939–40** The first Russo-Finnish War begins.
- **1941–44** Russo-Finnish Continuation War rages, with Finland allied with Germany.
- **1955** Helsinki hosts the Olympic Games, as Finland pursues a policy of neutrality.
- **1956** Urho Kekkonen becomes president of Finland and presides over the long and tense Cold War era.
- **1982** Kekkonen resigns; Mauno Koivisto is elected president.
- **1988** Koivisto is reelected to a second 6-year term, as Communists decline in power.
- **1992** Finland celebrates the 75th anniversary of its independence.
- **1994** Koivisto steps down; Martti Ahtisaari assumes the presidency.
- **1995** Finland, along with Sweden and Austria, joins the European Union.
- **1998** It's announced that Finland will chair the EU for last half of 1999; a "Northern Dimension" policy is planned.

continues

and spreading the Russian Orthodox faith from the East. A famous battle occurred in 1240 at the River Neva, when Alexander Nevski, a noted hero of Russian literature, defeated Sweden. Later, in 1323, a treaty between Sweden and the Novgorodians divided Finland's easternmost province of Karelia between Novgorod and Sweden. Eastern Finland, from that moment on, became part of the Russian-Byzantine world; although it shared a common language with the western sector, that region would not be reunited with the rest of Finland again except for a brief period early in the 20th century.

2000 Tarja Halonen is elected Finland's first female president. Finland grants rights to same-sex couples to register their unions like heterosexual couples.

Meanwhile, with the largest portion of Finland under Swedish rule, most of the population enjoyed considerable autonomy and mercantile prosperity. The Swedish language became dominant. Under Sweden's king, Gustavus Vasa, Helsinki became one of the Swedish Empire's most important trading bases in the Baltic. Lutheranism was introduced into Finland by Michael Agricola (1506–57) who, because of his translation of the New Testament into Finnish and his compilation of a Finnish grammar, is called "the father of Finnish literature."

Sweden's King Johan III (1537–92) granted Finland the status of Grand Duchy in 1581. Unfortunately, Finland became a battleground in the continuing wars among Russia, Sweden, Denmark, and Poland. New boundaries were established in 1671, when Russia was forced to yield certain lands in Karelia.

Finland entered the Thirty Years' War on Sweden's side, to which it was subjugated, its own language and culture suppressed in favor of Sweden's. The great famine of 1676 killed one-third of the population.

During the reign of Sweden's King Charles XII (1682–1718), Russia invaded and occupied Finland from 1713 to 1721. At the end of the war Sweden still ruled Finland, although some eastern territories, including southern Karelia, passed back to Russia. Russia gained new territories in another Swedish-Russian war, which raged from 1741 to 1743.

In 1808, at the peak of the Napoleonic wars, Russia finally seized all of Finland. Under Tsar Alexander I (1777–1825), Finland was granted the status of Grand Duchy, and throughout the 19th century it enjoyed broad autonomy, developing a democratic system without interference from St. Petersburg.

LIFE UNDER THE RUSSIANS   Turku was the capital of Finland until 1821 when the tsar moved it to Helsinki. In 1878, under Tsar Alexander II (1818–81), Finland gained its own independent conscript army, and the Finnish language became the official language, replacing Swedish.

Although Tsar Alexander III (1845–94) tried to follow a liberal policy toward Finland, most of his advisers were opposed, preferring to keep Finland as a buffer zone between the Russian capital (then St. Petersburg) and the rest of Europe. Alexander's conservative and reactionary son, Nicholas II (1868–1918), revoked Finnish autonomy in 1899 and began an intensive campaign of Russification. Russian became the official language in 1900, and the following year the separate Finnish army was abolished. Mass arrests followed. In 1905 Finland called a national strike to protest these conditions, forcing Nicholas II to ease some of his edicts. In 1906 Finland was permitted to have a unicameral parliament (the Diet) composed of 200 elected deputies, but it had little real power.

At the outbreak of World War I, Russia totally dominated Finland, and Finnish autonomy became just a memory. Finland lost its status as a Grand Duchy and became just a dominion of its more powerful neighbor to the east.

AN INDEPENDENT FINLAND   Finland was saved by the outbreak of the Russian Revolution and the collapse of tsarist rule. The Russian provisional government restored Finnish autonomy on March 20, 1917. Nevertheless, the Finns called a general strike, seeking total independence. A civil war followed, in which the leftist, pro-Russian Red Guard, supporting Russian troops in Finland, was opposed by the conservative-nationalist civil guard, the Whites.

On November 15, 1917, a proclamation placed control of the country's affairs in the hands of a Finnish government, and on December 6, President Svinhufvrud (1861–1944) declared the independence of Finland. Russia recognized Finnish independence on January 5, 1918, although 40,000 Russian troops were still stationed in Finland supporting the Red Guard.

Baron Carl Gustaf Emil von Mannerheim (1867–1951) assumed control of the Whites with the intention of driving Russia out of Finland. With the help of a German expeditionary force, he managed to win the civil war, which ended on May 16, 1918. At the end of the war, Finland was in dire economic circumstances and faced starvation.

On December 12, 1918, Mannerheim was named regent of Finland, and a constitution was adopted in June 1919, making Finland a republic. The new document called for the election of a president every 6 years. In his position, Mannerheim wielded supreme executive power, as did K. J. Stahlberg (1865–1952), the first president.

Russia and Finland signed a peace treaty at Tartu in October 1920. Russia got East Karelia. Finland joined the League of Nations on December 16, 1920, and the following year the League ruled that Finland—not Sweden—was entitled to the Åland Islands.

The 1920s saw continuing struggles between the government and Finnish communists. In 1923 the Communist Party was outlawed, but it returned under the title of the Democratic League. During the 1930s, many social and economic reforms were carried out.

WARS WITH RUSSIA   A Soviet-Finnish nonaggression pact was signed on January 12, 1932, but Russia continued to make demands on Finland, including the annexation of the Hanko peninsula for use as a Soviet naval base. When Finland refused, Russian troops invaded on November 30, 1939.

The Winter War of 1939–40 was one of the harshest ever in Finland, but the Finns, greatly outnumbered, resisted with bravery and courage. In March 1940 they accepted Russian terms, ceding territories in the north, the province of Viipuri, and the naval base at Hanko. The inhabitants of those districts left their homeland and moved within Finland's new borders.

Resentment against Russia led to a treaty with Germany. Hitler's request for transit rights across Finland was granted. Finland tried to remain neutral when the Nazis invaded Russia on June 22, 1941, but Russia bombed towns in southern Finland and Mannerheim launched the Russo-Finnish Continuation War. Territories that had been lost to Russia were retaken. But in 1944 Russia launched a large-scale attack, forcing Finland to ask for peace. Russia retook the territory it had ceded to Finland and imposed severe war reparations. The situation was complicated since German troops stationed in northern Finland refused to withdraw. Therefore, Finland had to launch a war against the Nazis in Lapland in 1945.

Mannerheim became president in 1944 but was obliged to step down in 1946 because of ill health. In Paris in 1947 Finland and Russia signed an armistice.

MODERN FINLAND   J. K. Paasikivi assumed the presidency of Finland in 1946, and concluded a mutual assistance treaty with the Soviet Union in 1948. In 1952 Helsinki became the site of the Olympic Games, focusing world attention on Finland, which in 1955 joined the United Nations.

In 1956 Urho Kekkonen became president of Finland; he continued in office during the long Cold War era, resigning in 1982 because of ill health. During his 25 years in office, Kekkonen successfully pursued a precarious policy of neutrality, earning a reputation for skillful diplomacy. At the end of his tenure, he saw the decline of the Communist Party in Finland. In 1975 he hosted the Conference on Security and Cooperation in Europe, where he received the heads of state and the heads of government of 35 countries who signed the Helsinki Agreement on international human rights.

Upon Kekkonen's resignation in 1982, Mauno Koivisto was elected president. Nearing the end of the long Cold War, Koivisto was re-elected to a second 6-year term in 1988. The country celebrated its 75th year of independence in 1992. After 12 years in office, the two-term Finnish president, Koivisto, stepped down in 1994. In his place, Martti Ahtisaari was elected president. In 1995 Finland, together with Austria and Sweden, joined the European Union.

The early 1990s witnessed epochal changes in Finland's neighbors to the east and south. Contacts, both commercial and social, with its formerly communist southern neighbor Estonia dramatically increased, and there was a modest increase in contacts with the other two Baltic countries, Latvia and Lithuania. As a result, there are now several daily flights, car ferries, and other ship connections between Helsinki and Tallinn (capital of Estonia), and direct air service to both Riga (Latvia) and Vilnius (Lithuania). Relations with Russia have also been improving since the fall of communism.

In 1998 Finland began plans to develop a "coherent strategy" toward Moscow on the part of the EU. This "coordinated" Russian policy was in place when Finland assumed the presidency of the EU in the last 6 months of 1999. This developing policy is known as the "Northern Dimension" to European policy, and it was the cornerstone of the EU summit meeting in Helsinki in December 1999, the last such major EU summit before the arrival of the millennium.

Finnish leaders continue to define the "common interests" of all 15 EU members vis-à-vis Moscow. These are not just lofty words, but practical, too—for example, in less than 20 years EU countries will depend on deposits in Russia's Barents and Kara Sea areas for up to 70% of their natural gas.

While Sweden and Denmark have chosen to remain outside the Economic and Monetary Union, Finland continues to support a European single currency (Norway and Iceland aren't members of the EU). Although not a member of NATO, Finland has contributed troops to peacekeeping operations in Bosnia. Russia, according to one high-ranking Russian military official, would view Finland in NATO "as an extremely serious threat."

In step with the other advanced Scandinavian countries, Johannes Koskinen, the Finnish minister, backed a proposal in 2000 to allow same-sex couples to register their unions the same way as married straight couples. Finland has long been known as a gay-friendly nation—in fact, Tarja Halonen, the president of Finland, was a former chairman of the Finnish National Organization for Sexual Equality and has been speaking out on gay rights for years.

4 Dining with the Finns

Breakfast in Finland is usually served between 7 and 10am, lunch between 11am and 2pm, and dinner any time after 4pm. Some restaurants stay open as late as 1am; nightclubs and discos—some of which serve food—are often open until 3am.

In Finland, full-fledged restaurants are called *ravintola*. Inexpensive lunches are available at places called *kahvila* and *baari*. A *baari* serves light food and perhaps a mild beer, although coffee is more common. All well-known alcoholic beverages are available throughout Finland in fully licensed restaurants and bars.

Potatoes, meat, fish, milk, butter, and rye bread are the mainstays of the Finnish diet. Soups are popular, especially pea soup and rich meat soups, in which potatoes and vegetables are cooked with chunks of beef.

Every Finn looks forward to the crayfish season between July 20 and September, when some 225,000 pounds of this delicacy are caught in inland waters. Finns take special care in eating crayfish, sucking out every morsel of flavor. After devouring half a dozen, they down a glass of schnapps. Called *rapu,* the crayfish is usually boiled in salted water and seasoned with dill. Of course, with all this slurping and shelling, you'll need a bib.

The icy-cold waters of Finland produce very fine fish, some of which are unknown elsewhere in the world. A cousin to the salmon, the 2-inch-long *muikku fritti* is found in Finland's inland waters. This fish is highly praised by gastronomes, and its roe is a delicacy. The most common fish, however, is *silakka* (Baltic herring), which is consumed in vast quantities. Rarely larger than sardines, the herring is not only pickled, but fried or grilled. Sometimes it's baked between layers of potatoes in a sauce made with milk, cheese, and egg. The fish is usually spiced with dill; in fact, dill is the most popular herb in the country.

Finland's version of the Swedish smörgåsbord is called *voileipäpöytä* (which means "bread and butter table"). That definition is too literal. Expect not only bread and butter, but an array of dishes, including many varieties of fish (for example, pickled salted herring and fresh salted salmon) and several cold meat dishes, including smoked reindeer—all at a fixed price.

Along with elk, bear, and reindeer tongue, Finns like the sharp taste of *puolukka,* a lingonberry. The Arctic cloudberry is a rare delicacy.

The two most popular salads in Finland are beet and cucumber. Bread is invariably served, including whole wheat, white, black, and varieties of rye. The most typical is a dark, sour rye called *ruislëipa.* Those open-faced sandwiches, so familiar in all Scandinavian countries, are called *voileivat* here.

Fresh vegetables are plentiful in the summer, but they appear less often during the long winter months. Boiled new potatoes, the most common vegetable, are typically served with sprays of fresh dill. In elegant restaurants and homes, you may be served a convoluted morel known as "the black truffle of the north." It's the prize of all the mushrooms that grow in the vast forests of Finland.

The national beverage of Finland is milk (sometimes curdled), which is safe to drink (as is water) throughout the country. Two famous Finnish liqueurs should be tasted: *lakka,* made from the saffron-colored wild cloudberry; and *mesimarja,* made from the Arctic brambleberry.

Schnapps is a Finn's favorite, an all-around tipple. Hard liquor, often imported, is expensive—and anyone on a budget had better stick to a domestic beer (Koff and Lapinkulta are good local brands).

Index

FROMMER'S® COMPLETE TRAVEL GUIDES

Alaska
Alaska Cruises & Ports of Call
Amsterdam
Argentina & Chile
Arizona
Atlanta
Australia
Austria
Bahamas
Barcelona, Madrid & Seville
Beijing
Belgium, Holland & Luxembourg
Bermuda
Boston
Brazil
British Columbia & the Canadian
  Rockies
Budapest & the Best of Hungary
California
Canada
Cancún, Cozumel & the Yucatán
Cape Cod, Nantucket & Martha's
  Vineyard
Caribbean
Caribbean Cruises & Ports of Call
Caribbean Ports of Call
Carolinas & Georgia
Chicago
China
Colorado
Costa Rica
Denmark
Denver, Boulder & Colorado
  Springs
England
Europe
European Cruises & Ports of Call
Florida

France
Germany
Great Britain
Greece
Greek Islands
Hawaii
Hong Kong
Honolulu, Waikiki & Oahu
Ireland
Israel
Italy
Jamaica
Japan
Las Vegas
London
Los Angeles
Maryland & Delaware
Maui
Mexico
Montana & Wyoming
Montréal & Québec City
Munich & the Bavarian Alps
Nashville & Memphis
Nepal
New England
New Mexico
New Orleans
New York City
New Zealand
Northern Italy
Nova Scotia, New Brunswick &
  Prince Edward Island
Oregon
Paris
Philadelphia & the Amish Country
Portugal
Prague & the Best of the Czech
  Republic

Provence & the Riviera
Puerto Rico
Rome
San Antonio & Austin
San Diego
San Francisco
Santa Fe, Taos & Albuquerque
Scandinavia
Scotland
Seattle & Portland
Shanghai
Singapore & Malaysia
South Africa
South America
South Florida
South Pacific
Southeast Asia
Spain
Sweden
Switzerland
Texas
Thailand
Tokyo
Toronto
Tuscany & Umbria
USA
Utah
Vancouver & Victoria
Vermont, New Hampshire &
  Maine
Vienna & the Danube Valley
Virgin Islands
Virginia
Walt Disney World® & Orlando
Washington, D.C.
Washington State

FROMMER'S® DOLLAR-A-DAY GUIDES

Australia from $50 a Day
California from $70 a Day
Caribbean from $70 a Day
England from $75 a Day
Europe from $70 a Day

Florida from $70 a Day
Hawaii from $80 a Day
Ireland from $60 a Day
Italy from $70 a Day
London from $85 a Day

New York from $90 a Day
Paris from $80 a Day
San Francisco from $70 a Day
Washington, D.C. from $80 a Day

FROMMER'S® PORTABLE GUIDES

Acapulco, Ixtapa & Zihuatanejo
Amsterdam
Aruba
Australia's Great Barrier Reef
Bahamas
Berlin
Big Island of Hawaii
Boston
California Wine Country
Cancún
Charleston & Savannah
Chicago
Disneyland®
Dublin
Florence

Frankfurt
Hong Kong
Houston
Las Vegas
London
Los Angeles
Los Cabos & Baja
Maine Coast
Maui
Miami
New Orleans
New York City
Paris
Phoenix & Scottsdale

Portland
Puerto Rico
Puerto Vallarta, Manzanillo &
  Guadalajara
Rio de Janeiro
San Diego
San Francisco
Seattle
Sydney
Tampa & St. Petersburg
Vancouver
Venice
Virgin Islands
Washington, D.C.

FROMMER'S® NATIONAL PARK GUIDES

Banff & Jasper
Family Vacations in the National
  Parks
Grand Canyon

National Parks of the American
  West
Rocky Mountain

Yellowstone & Grand Teton
Yosemite & Sequoia/ Kings Canyon
Zion & Bryce Canyon

Frommer's® Memorable Walks

Chicago
London

New York
Paris

San Francisco
Washington, D.C.

Frommer's® Great Outdoor Guides

Arizona & New Mexico
New England

Northern California
Southern New England

Vermont & New Hampshire

Suzy Gershman's Born to Shop Guides

Born to Shop: France
Born to Shop: Hong Kong,
  Shanghai & Beijing

Born to Shop: Italy
Born to Shop: London

Born to Shop: New York
Born to Shop: Paris

Frommer's® Irreverent Guides

Amsterdam
Boston
Chicago
Las Vegas
London

Los Angeles
Manhattan
New Orleans
Paris
Rome

San Francisco
Seattle & Portland
Vancouver
Walt Disney World®
Washington, D.C.

Frommer's® Best-Loved Driving Tours

Britain
California
Florida
France

Germany
Ireland
Italy
New England

Northern Italy
Scotland
Spain
Tuscany & Umbria

Hanging Out™ Guides

Hanging Out in England
Hanging Out in Europe

Hanging Out in France
Hanging Out in Ireland

Hanging Out in Italy
Hanging Out in Spain

The Unofficial Guides®

Bed & Breakfasts and Country
  Inns in:
  California
  Great Lakes States
  Mid-Atlantic
  New England
  Northwest
  Rockies
  Southeast
  Southwest
Best RV & Tent Campgrounds in:
  California & the West
  Florida & the Southeast
  Great Lakes States
  Mid-Atlantic
  Northeast
  Northwest & Central Plains

Southwest & South Central
  Plains
  U.S.A.
Beyond Disney
Branson, Missouri
California with Kids
Chicago
Cruises
Disneyland®
Florida with Kids
Golf Vacations in the Eastern U.S.
Great Smoky & Blue Ridge Region
Inside Disney
Hawaii
Las Vegas
London

Mid-Atlantic with Kids
Mini Las Vegas
Mini-Mickey
New England and New York with
  Kids
New Orleans
New York City
Paris
San Francisco
Skiing in the West
Southeast with Kids
Walt Disney World®
Walt Disney World® for Grown-ups
Walt Disney World® with Kids
Washington, D.C.
World's Best Diving Vacations

Special-Interest Titles

Frommer's Adventure Guide to Australia &
  New Zealand
Frommer's Adventure Guide to Central America
Frommer's Adventure Guide to India & Pakistan
Frommer's Adventure Guide to South America
Frommer's Adventure Guide to Southeast Asia
Frommer's Adventure Guide to Southern Africa
Frommer's Britain's Best Bed & Breakfasts and
  Country Inns
Frommer's Caribbean Hideaways
Frommer's Exploring America by RV
Frommer's Fly Safe, Fly Smart
Frommer's France's Best Bed & Breakfasts and
  Country Inns
Frommer's Gay & Lesbian Europe

Frommer's Italy's Best Bed & Breakfasts and
  Country Inns
Frommer's New York City with Kids
Frommer's Ottawa with Kids
Frommer's Road Atlas Britain
Frommer's Road Atlas Europe
Frommer's Road Atlas France
Frommer's Toronto with Kids
Frommer's Vancouver with Kids
Frommer's Washington, D.C., with Kids
Israel Past & Present
The New York Times' Guide to Unforgettable
  Weekends
Places Rated Almanac
Retirement Places Rated

Booked seat 6A, open return.

Rented red 4-wheel drive.

Reserved cabin, no running water.

Discovered space.

With over 700 airlines, 50,000 hotels, 50 rental car companies and 5,000 cruise and vacation packages, you can create the perfect get-away for you. Choose the car, the room, even the ground you walk on.

Travelocity.com
A Sabre Company
Go Virtually Anywhere.

You Need
A Vacation.

700 Airlines, 50,000 Hotels, 50 Rental Car
Companies, And A Million Ways To Save Money.

Travelocity.com
A Sabre Company
Go Virtually Anywhere.